PROFESSIONAL
VISUAL BASIC® 2010 AND .NET 4

PROFESSIONAL

Visual Basic® 2010 and .NET 4

PROFESSIONAL

Visual Basic® 2010 and .NET 4

Bill Sheldon
Billy Hollis
Kent Sharkey
Jonathan Marbutt
Rob Windsor
Gastón C. Hillar

WILEY

Wiley Publishing, Inc.

Professional Visual Basic® 2010 and .NET 4

Published by
Wiley Publishing, Inc.
10475 Crosspoint Boulevard
Indianapolis, IN 46256
www.wiley.com

Copyright © 2010 by Wiley Publishing, Inc., Indianapolis, Indiana

Published by Wiley Publishing, Inc., Indianapolis, Indiana

Published simultaneously in Canada

ISBN: 978-0-470-50224-2

Manufactured in the United States of America

10 9 8 7 6 5 4 3 2 1

For general information on our other products and services please contact our Customer Care Department within the United States at (877) 762-2974, outside the United States at (317) 572-3993 or fax (317) 572-4002.

Wiley also publishes its books in a variety of electronic formats. Some content that appears in print may not be available in electronic books.

Library of Congress Control Number: 2010921246

ABOUT THE AUTHORS

 BILL SHELDON is a software architect and engineer, originally from Baltimore, Maryland. Holding a degree in computer science from the Illinois Institute of Technology (IIT), Bill has been actively employed as a software engineer since resigning his commission with the United States Navy. He is a Microsoft MVP for Visual Basic employed in Carlsbad, California. Bill also works as an instructor for .NET courses at the University of California San Diego Extension. In addition to writing books, Bill has published dozens of articles, including the Developer Update Newsletter, SQL Server Magazine feature articles, and other Penton publications. He is an established online presenter for MSDN and speaks at live events such as VSLive, DevConnections, Office Developers Conference, and community events such as user groups and code camp. Bill is an avid cyclist and is active in the fight against diabetes. Bill can be tracked down through his blog: www.nerdnotes.net/blog or via Twitter: NerdNotes.

 BILLY HOLLIS is an author and software consultant based in Nashville, Tennessee. Billy was co-author of the first book ever published on Visual Basic .NET, as well as many other books on software development. He is a member of the Microsoft Regional Director program and a Microsoft MVP. In 2002, Billy was selected as one of the original .NET "Software Legends." He is heavily involved with consulting, training, and development on the .NET platform, focusing on architecture, smart-client development, commercial packages, and user-interface technologies. He regularly speaks on software development at major conferences all over the world, including Microsoft's PDC and TechEd events, DevConnections, VSLive, and architecture events such as the Patterns and Practices Architect Summit.

 KENT SHARKEY is an independent consultant who lives and codes in Comox, British Columbia. Before going solo, Kent worked at Microsoft as a technical evangelist and content strategist, promoting the use of .NET technologies. He lives with his wife, Margaret, and three "children" — Squirrel, Cica, and Toffee.

 JONATHAN MARBUTT is Vice President of Development for WayCool Software, Inc., based in Birmingham, AL. He has been working professionally in software development since 1996, where he has covered various Microsoft technologies from VB6 to .NET. Over the recent years, Jonathan has been developing with Silverlight to build Rich Internet Line of Business applications for the non-profit sector. Through this development, he is beginning to focus on User Experience (UX) by utilizing Microsoft products like Expression Blend and technologies like Silverlight. For more information, contact Jonathan at www.jmtechware.com.

 ROB WINDSOR is a developer, trainer, writer and Senior Consultant with ObjectSharp Consulting — a Microsoft Gold Partner based in Toronto, Canada. He has over fifteen years experience developing rich-client and web applications with Delphi, VB, C# and VB.NET and is currently spending a majority of his time working with SharePoint. Rob is a member of both the INETA Speakers Bureau and the MSDN Canada Speakers Bureau and is a regular speaker at conferences, code camps, and user groups across North America and Europe. He is President of the Toronto Visual Basic User Group and has been recognized as a Microsoft Most Valuable Professional for his involvement in the developer community.

GASTÓN C. HILLAR has been working with computers since he was eight. He began programming with the legendary Texas TI-99/4A and Commodore 64 home computers in the early 80s. He has worked as developer, architect, and project manager for many companies in Buenos Aires, Argentina. Now, he is an independent IT consultant working for several Spanish, German, and Latin American companies, and a freelance author. He is always looking for new adventures around the world.

Gastón is the author of more than forty books in Spanish and has written two books in English. He contributes to Dr. Dobb's Go Parallel programming portal at www.ddj.com/go-parallel/, Dr. Dobb's at http://drdobbs.com, and is a guest blogger at Intel Software Network at http://software.intel.com.

He lives with his wife, Vanesa, and his son, Kevin. When not tinkering with computers, he enjoys developing and playing with wireless virtual reality devices and electronics toys with his father, his son, and his nephew Nico.

You can reach him at: gastonhillar@hotmail.com

You can follow him on Twitter at: http://twitter.com/gastonhillar

Gastón's blog is at: http://csharpmulticore.blogspot.com

ABOUT THE TECHNICAL EDITORS

DIANNE SIEBOLD is a software developer and writer specializing in VB, C#, .NET Framework, WCF, ADO, and SQL Server. She has worked for a number of Microsoft partners writing enterprise applications with an emphasis on services and data access. Currently, she works for Microsoft writing developer documentation in the Dynamics product group. Reach her by e-mail at dsiebold@earthlink.net.

DOUG PARSONS is a .NET Software Architect and professional Technical Editor who specializes in C#, SQL Server, and numerous architectural paradigms. Over the course of his career, he has worked on a myriad of projects; most notably, however, was the United States 2008 Presidential Campaign website of John McCain. He is currently employed by NJI New Media, writing software for clients of a predominantly political nature. He can be reached by email at douglas.c.parsons@gmail.com.

DOUG WATERFIELD is a software architect and engineer who lives with his family in Avon, Indiana. Since earning a degree in computer science from Rose-Hulman Institute of Technology, Doug has been designing and developing commercial and enterprise applications in a wide variety of technologies. Doug led development teams and departments for several firms before becoming an independent consultant with a focus on .NET technologies. He is a retired officer in the US Army Reserve and serves as a volunteer leader in Cub Scouts and Boy Scouts.

CREDITS

ACQUISITIONS EDITOR
Paul Reese

SENIOR PROJECT EDITOR
Adaobi Obi Tulton

TECHNICAL EDITORS
Dianne Siebold
Doug Parsons
Doug Waterfield

SENIOR PRODUCTION EDITOR
Debra Banninger

COPY EDITOR
Luann Rouff

EDITORIAL DIRECTOR
Robyn B. Siesky

EDITORIAL MANAGER
Mary Beth Wakefield

ASSOCIATE DIRECTOR OF MARKETING
David Mayhew

PRODUCTION MANAGER
Tim Tate

VICE PRESIDENT AND EXECUTIVE GROUP PUBLISHER
Richard Swadley

VICE PRESIDENT AND EXECUTIVE PUBLISHER
Barry Pruett

ASSOCIATE PUBLISHER
Jim Minatel

PROJECT COORDINATOR, COVER
Lynsey Stanford

PROOFREADERS
Nancy Carrasco
Beth Prouty, Word One

INDEXER
Robert Swanson

COVER DESIGNER
Michael E. Trent

COVER IMAGE
© Dan Barnes/istockphoto

ACKNOWLEDGMENTS

AS WITH ANY MAJOR PROJECT PUTTING A BOOK OF this size and scope together is a team effort and we as authors were really lucky to have such a great support team helping to keep us on track and focused. I'd like to publicly call out and thank our editor, Adaobi, who managed to turn around several of the late chapters (those would be mine) in an incredibly short time, and our technical editors, in particular Dianne, who did an outstanding job. They found hundreds of issues so that our readers wouldn't need to, and helped ensure that everything worked and flowed in a logical fashion.

—BILL SHELDON

WHILE WRITING can be a solitary activity, writing for a book definitely is not, and I have many people to thank for getting me here.

Thank you to all my coworkers who picked up the slack while I worked on this (Oh, wait — I work alone — never mind). Thank you to my co-authors, and my fine editors: Adaobi Obi Tulton, Paul Reese, and Dianne Siebold. If there is any quality here, it is likely due to their hard work.

I am definitely grateful to all the people who regularly put up with my negativity, and help me to become better: Eileen, Chris, Tharun, Kraig and Duncan. Thank you, thank you, thank you.

And finally, thanks to all of you that have selected this book. I hope it helps.

—KENT SHARKEY

THANKS TO BETH MASSI for being too busy to work on this project and thanks to the people at Wrox for accepting Beth's suggestion that I would be a suitable replacement.

As a first time author, I have to give special thanks to Adaobi Obi Tulton, Dianne Siebold, Doug Parsons, Doug Waterfield, and Luann Rouff for helping me make my work appear as if it was written by a professional author. I'm sure it wasn't easy.

Finally, I'd like to thank those who helped me advance professionally to the point that this opportunity was even possible: Craig Flanagan, Sasha Krsmanovic, Jean-Rene Roy, Mark Dunn, Carl Franklin, Richard Campbell, all the Canadian RDs, and everyone at ObjectSharp.

—ROB WINDSOR

I WISH TO ACKNOWLEDGE Paul Reese and Adaobi Obi Tulton; they had a lot of patience and they allowed me to make the necessary changes to my chapter in order to include the most appropriate information about the new parallel programming features introduced in .NET Framework 4 and Visual Basic 2010.

Special thanks go to my wife, Vanesa S. Olsen, because she understood that I needed to work with many computers at the same time to test each code snippet.

—GASTÓN C. HILLAR

CONTENTS

INTRODUCTION

IN 2002, VISUAL BASIC EXPERIENCED the biggest leap in innovation since it was released, with the introduction of Visual Basic .NET (as it was then named). After more than a decade, Visual Basic was overdue for a major overhaul. Nevertheless, .NET went beyond an overhaul. The changes affected almost every aspect of development with Visual Basic. The entire runtime model shifted to a new common language runtime (CLR) environment and the language went from object-based to object-oriented. From integrating Internet functionality to creating object-oriented frameworks, Visual Basic .NET challenged traditional VB developers to learn dramatic new concepts and techniques.

The various releases since then have continued to provide even more enhancements to the Visual Basic language. New features have been added that both cement this language's position as a true object-oriented language and provide access to new and better technologies. Visual Basic 2010 continues this evolution; and while it remains a challenge for VB6 developers to learn, it's an easy road for those with any familiarity with previous versions, and this book is here to help you on your way.

Visual Studio 2010 ships with version 4 of the .NET Framework. This book provides details about not only the latest version of Visual Basic — version 10 — but also the new .NET Framework 4. Combined, these products give Visual Basic developers the capability to build applications using Windows Presentation Foundation (WPF), Windows Forms, Visual Studio Tools for Office, and applications and libraries based upon the Windows Communication Foundation (WCF), the Windows Workflow Foundation (WF), and SharePoint.

The .NET Framework 4 is the most significant change to the core framework since .NET Framework 2.0. Fortunately, as with Visual Studio 2008, Visual Studio 2010 enables developers to continue to build and deploy applications that target both the newly released version of .NET, and previously released versions of the .NET Framework.

For those who may only now be transitioning from the VB6 development model, you'll find that this version of Visual Basic Professional is targeted less than ever at traditional VB6 code differences. With each of the four .NET versions, the core language has continued to progress and differentiate itself from where it was 10+ years ago. In some cases, the same functionality is implemented in a different way. This was not done arbitrarily — there are good reasons for the changes. However, you must be prepared to unlearn old habits and form new ones.

Next, you must be open to the new concepts. Full object orientation, new component techniques, new visual tools for both local and Internet interfaces — all of these and more must become part of your skill set to effectively develop applications in Visual Basic.

This book covers Visual Basic from start to finish. It starts by introducing Visual Studio 2010. As the tool you'll use to work with Visual Basic, understanding Visual Studio's core capabilities is key to your success and enjoyment with building .NET applications. In these pages, you have the opportunity to learn everything from database access, Language Integrated Queries (LINQ), and the Entity Framework, to integration with other technologies such as WPF, WCF, and service-based solutions. Along with investigating new features in detail, you'll see that Visual Basic 10 has emerged as a powerful yet easy-to-use language that enables you to target the Internet just as easily as the desktop. This book covers the .NET Framework 4.

THE FUTURE OF VISUAL BASIC

Early in the adoption cycle of .NET, Microsoft's new language, C#, got the lion's share of attention. However, as .NET adoption has increased, Visual Basic's continuing importance has also been apparent. Microsoft has publicly stated that it considers Visual Basic to be the language of choice for applications for which developer productivity is one of the highest priorities.

Future development of Visual Basic will emphasize capabilities that enable access to the whole expanse of the .NET Framework in the most productive way. In the past, it was common for Microsoft and others to "target" different development styles; with Visual Studio 2010, Microsoft announced that VB and C# will follow a process of coevolution. As new language features are developed, they will be introduced to both Visual Basic and C# at the same time. This release is the first step in that process, although it's not complete at this time.

Coevolution does *not* mean that the languages will look the same, but rather that they will support the same capabilities. For example, Visual Basic has XML literals, but that doesn't mean C# will get exactly the same functionality, as C# has the capability to work with XML through the existing framework classes. The old process of first introducing a feature in Visual Basic and then in the next release having C# catch up, and vice versa, is over. As new capabilities and features are introduced, they will be introduced to both Visual Basic and C# at the same time.

As mentioned earlier, although the changes aren't complete, the next version of Visual Basic will be coordinated with a new release of Visual Studio, and the capabilities of C# and Visual Basic should fully mirror each other, as both will be first-class .NET development languages. That fits the traditional role of Visual Basic as the language developers use in the real world to create business applications as quickly as possible.

One of the most important advantages of the .NET Framework is that it enables applications to be written with dramatically less code. In the world of business applications, the goal is to concentrate on writing business logic and to eliminate routine coding tasks as much as possible. In other words, of greatest value in this new paradigm is writing robust, useful applications without churning out a lot of code.

Visual Basic is an excellent fit for this type of development, which makes up the bulk of software development in today's economy. Moreover, it will grow to be an even better fit as it is refined and evolves for exactly that purpose.

WHO THIS BOOK IS FOR

This book was written to help experienced developers learn Visual Basic 2010. For those who are just starting the transition from earlier versions to those who have used Visual Basic for a while and need to gain a deeper understanding, this book provides information on the most common programming tasks and concepts you need.

Professional Visual Basic 2010 offers a wide-ranging presentation of Visual Basic concepts, but the .NET Framework is so large and comprehensive that no single book can cover it all. The focus in this book is providing a working knowledge of key technologies that are important to Visual Basic developers. It provides adequate knowledge for a developer to work in any of these areas, although developers may choose to add to their knowledge by leveraging a book dedicated entirely to a single technology area.

WHAT YOU NEED TO USE THIS BOOK

Although it is possible to create Visual Basic applications using the command-line tools contained in the .NET Framework, you'll want Visual Studio 2010 (Standard Edition or higher), which includes the .NET Framework 4, to get the most out of this book. You may use Visual Basic Express Edition instead, but in some cases the exercises won't work because functionalities and capabilities are not available in this limited version. In addition, note the following:

➤ You'll need .NET Framework 4, which is installed with whatever version of Visual Studio 2010 you select.

➤ Some chapters make use of SQL Server 2008. You can run the example code using Microsoft's SQL Express, which ships with Visual Studio 2010.

➤ Chapter 7 makes reference to the Unit Test tools, which are included with Visual Studio Professional Edition or higher.

➤ Several chapters make use of Internet Information Services (IIS). IIS is part of every operating system released by Microsoft since Windows XP, but on newer operating systems you'll need to run as administrator to develop against it. Alternatively, you can leverage the development server that ships with Visual Studio 2010.

➤ Chapter 18 makes use of Expression Blend 3.0. Blend is available with upper-tier MSDN subscriptions, but you should be able to leverage a trial version to explore the capabilities described in that chapter.

➤ Chapter 24 looks at SharePoint development. SharePoint services ship with Windows Server versions. The full Microsoft Office SharePoint Server is a product that requires a license, although MSDN owners can get access to a development server.

➤ Chapter 25 looks at Visual Studio Tools for Office, so in order to leverage products built against the Office suite, you'll need a copy of the specified product(s).

➤ Appendix D makes use of MSMQ to work with queued transactions. MSMQ also ships with Windows, but it is not installed by default.

➤ Appendix E looks at the online services that are accessible to Microsoft developers. Azure has a trial period so that you can work with the examples in that chapter.

WHAT THIS BOOK COVERS

Part I, "Language Constructs and Environment" — The first seven chapters of the book focus on core language elements and development tools used by Visual Basic developers. This section introduces Visual Studio 2010, objects, syntax, and debugging.

Chapter 1, "Visual Studio 2010" — Start with the environment where you will work with Visual Basic 10. This chapter looks at the newly redesigned WPF-based Visual Studio development environment. Introducing a simple Windows forms project and reviewing key capabilities like the debugger, this chapter will help you to prepare for and become comfortable with this powerful environment.

Chapter 2, "Objects and Visual Basic" — This is the first of three chapters that explore object-oriented programming and the role of the .NET Framework in Visual Basic. This chapter introduces the basics of objects, types, type conversion, reference types, and the key syntax which make up the core of Visual Basic.

Chapter 3, "Custom Objects" — This chapter examines creating objects, and describes how they fit within Visual Basic. Starting with inheritance, you create simple and abstract classes and learn how to create base classes from which other classes can be derived. This chapter puts the theory of object-oriented development into practice. The four defining object-oriented concepts (abstraction, encapsulation, polymorphism, inheritance) are described, and you will learn how these concepts can be applied in design and development to create effective object-oriented applications.

Chapter 4, "The Common Language Runtime" — This chapter examines the core of the .NET platform: the common language runtime (CLR). The CLR is responsible for managing the execution of code compiled for the .NET platform. You learn about versioning and deployment, memory management, cross-language integration, metadata, and the IL Disassembler. The chapter also introduces namespaces and their hierarchical structure. An explanation of namespaces and some common examples are provided. In addition, you learn about custom namespaces, and how to import and alias existing namespaces within projects. This chapter also looks at the My namespace available in Visual Basic.

Chapter 5, "Declarative Programming with Visual Basic" — The introduction of Windows Presentation Foundation, Windows Workflow (WF), and Silverlight brought a new syntax to .NET: XAML. XML for Application Markup Language, commonly pronounced "zamel," is the core of a new declarative programming model. Using this model, developers describe what they want — e.g., a window. The code that implements the creation of that window is abstracted from the request. As noted, XAML is an enabling syntax for several new technology feature sets. This chapter introduces the core common elements of the XAML syntax so that the other chapters that leverage this syntax have a common baseline.

Chapter 6, "Exception Handling and Debugging" — This chapter covers how error handling and debugging work in Visual Basic 2010 by discussing the CLR exception handler and the `Try...Catch...Finally` structure. Also covered are error and trace logging, and how you can use these methods to obtain feedback about how your program is working.

Chapter 7, "Test-Driven Development" — This chapter introduces the concepts of test-driven development (TDD) with Visual Studio 2010 and the unit test tools.

Part II, "Business Objects and Data Access" — The next seven chapters, Chapter 8 through Chapter 14, look at common structures used to contain and access data. This includes framework elements such as arrays and collections, XML, database access, and Windows Communication Foundation (WCF) services. These chapters focus on gathering data for use within your applications.

Chapter 8, "Arrays, Collections, Generics" — This chapter focuses on introducing arrays and collections as a baseline for having a sets of related items. It then expands on these basic structures by exploring generics. Introduced with version 2.0 of the .NET Framework, generics enable strongly typed collections. One of the important new features associated with .NET Framework 4 is the extension of generic support to include covariance.

Chapter 9, "Using XML with Visual Basic" — This chapter presents the features of the .NET Framework that facilitate the generation and manipulation of XML. We describe the .NET Framework's XML-related namespaces, and a subset of the classes exposed by these namespaces is examined in detail. This chapter also touches on a set of technologies that utilize XML — specifically, ADO.NET and SQL Server — and then describes in detail how to work with LINQ for XML.

Chapter 10, "ADO.NET and LINQ" — This chapter focuses on what you need to know about the ADO.NET object model in order to build flexible, fast, and scalable data-access objects and applications. The evolution of ADO into ADO.NET is explored, and the main objects in ADO.NET that you need to understand in order to build data access into your .NET applications are explained. Additionally, this chapter delves into LINQ to SQL. LINQ offers the capability to easily access underlying data — basically a layer on top of ADO.NET. Microsoft has provided LINQ as a lightweight façade that provides a strongly typed interface to the underlying data stores.

Chapter 11, "Data Access with the Entity Framework" — One of the major enhancements being released with Visual Studio 2010 is the Entity Framework (EF). The EF represents Microsoft's implementation of an Entity Relationship Modeling (ERM) tool. Using EF, developers can generate classes to represent the data structures that are defined within SQL Server, and leverage these objects within their applications.

Chapter 12, "Working with SQL Server" — This chapter describes how to work with SQL Server 2008 along with your .NET applications. SQL Server provides a strong connection to your applications, and this chapter explains how to effectively utilize this powerful database.

Chapter 13, "Services (XML/WCF)" — This chapter looks at the newest way to build service-oriented components that allow for standards-based communications over a number of protocols. WCF is Microsoft's latest answer for component communications within and outside of the enterprise. Additionally, this chapter reviews the creation and consumption of XML Web services. The abstract classes provided by the CLR to set up and work with Web services are discussed, as well as some of the technologies that support Web services. Also examined are some of the disadvantages to using any distributed architecture.

Part III, "Smart Client Applications" — The next six chapters, Chapter 15 through Chapter 20, focus on creating client applications. Starting with the Windows Forms application model, which was introduced with .NET 1.0, these chapters move through the migration to Windows Presentation Foundation and the introduction of the Blend design engine and Silverlight.

Chapter 14, "Windows Forms" — This chapter looks at Windows Forms, concentrating primarily on forms and built-in controls. What is new and what has been changed from previous versions of Visual Basic are discussed, along with the System.Windows.Forms namespace.

Chapter 15, "Advanced Windows Forms" — This chapter explores some of the more advanced features that are available to you in building your Windows Forms applications.

Chapter 16, "User Controls Combining WPF and Windows Forms" — One of the best practices for creating Windows client applications is the use of user controls. User controls allow for the encapsulation of related user interface elements. In addition, these controls become key for the migration from Windows Forms to WPF. Because many organizations have made significant investments in Windows Forms and are not ready to fully switch their applications to this new technology, Microsoft has provided significant support to integrate WPF into your Windows Forms applications, as well as the capability to bring your Windows Forms components to a WPF application.

Chapter 17, "WPF Desktop Applications" — A technology that was introduced in .NET 3.0, Windows Presentation Foundation offers an alternate mechanism for building desktop applications. This chapter describes how WPF provides a presentation layer that you should find rather fluid and enriching.

Chapter 18, "Expression Blend 3" — In conjunction with the release of WPF, Microsoft introduced a new suite of tools called "Expression Studio." These tools target building rich user interfaces based on XAML. The Blend tool (included in Expression Studio) in particular has proven valuable for designing WPF user interfaces. This chapter introduces you to Expression Blend, which provides a powerful set of tools for designing applications and working with XAML.

Chapter 19, "Silverlight" — This chapter looks at the latest use of XAML for building user interfaces: Silverlight. Silverlight provides a platform-independent solution for .NET-based client application development. Silverlight enables developers to use XAML markup, and brings a more fluid experience to the end user in the browser or on the desktop.

Part IV, "Internet Applications" — The next five chapters, Chapter 20 through Chapter 24, focus on creating applications for the Web. Leveraging Silverlight, which has a client-like feel, these chapters introduce ASP.NET and capabilities such as AJAX and MVC, including fully cloud-hosted solutions, and introduce SharePoint.

Chapter 20, "Silverlight and Services" — Once you've been introduced to Silverlight and what it can do for client applications, this chapter looks at both hosting Silverlight within your website and hooking it to Web services to provide business data.

Chapter 21, "Working with ASP.NET" — This chapter explores the basics of ASP.NET in detail. It looks at building Web applications using Visual Studio and includes discussions on the overall application and page frameworks.

Chapter 22, "ASP.NET Advanced Features" — This chapter looks at several of ASP.NET's advanced features, in particular focusing on AJAX. Examples of items covered include cross-page posting, master pages, site navigation, personalization, and more.

Chapter 23, "ASP.NET MVC" — Visual Studio 2010 introduces the MVC (Model-View-Controller) pattern for ASP.NET to mainstream development. This pattern provides a more structured framework for developing Web applications. This chapter outlines the advantages of using this pattern for new ASP.NET projects.

Chapter 24, "SharePoint 2010 Development" — SharePoint, which includes a number of technologies and services, is Microsoft's fastest-growing product. This chapter looks at how Visual Basic developers can customize and leverage this versatile tool for hosting custom solutions.

Part V, "Libraries and Specialized Topics" — The final 10 chapters, Chapter 25 through Chapter 34, focus on a disparate collection of specialized topics. These topics reference specific .NET libraries that you will probably be interested in working with as you create new solutions and modify existing ones.

Chapter 25, "Visual Studio Tools for Office" — This chapter looks at using Visual Basic to work with your Microsoft Office–focused applications.

Chapter 26, "Windows Workflow Foundation" — This chapter covers the newly updated Workflow implementation. The new capabilities introduced with Visual Studio 2010 make it easy to integrate workflow into your applications. Windows Workflow was introduced in the .NET Framework 3.0, but the new release is a significant departure from the original logic (coverage of the original workflow has been moved to Appendix D).

Chapter 27, "Localization" — This chapter looks at some of the important items to consider when building your applications for worldwide use. It looks closely at the `System.Globalization` namespace and everything it offers your applications.

Chapter 28, "COM-Interop" — This chapter discusses COM and .NET component interoperability, and what tools are provided to help link the two technologies.

Chapter 29, "Network Programming" — This chapter covers working with some of the networking protocols that are available to you in your development and how to incorporate a wider network into the functionality of your applications.

Chapter 30, "Application Services" — This chapter examines how Visual Basic is used in the production of Windows Services. The creation, installation, running, and debugging of Windows Services are covered.

Chapter 31, "Assemblies and Reflection" — This chapter examines assemblies and their use within the CLR. The structure of an assembly, what it contains, and the information it contains are described. In addition, you will look at the manifest of the assembly and its role in deployment, and how to use remoting. You examine the basic architecture of remoting and build a basic server and client that uses a singleton object for answering client requests in the business tier. You will also learn how to use serialization to return more complex objects from the server to the client, and how to use the call context for passing extra data from the client to the server along with each call, without having to change the object model.

Chapter 32, "Security in the .NET Framework" — This chapter examines additional tools and functionality with regard to the security provided by .NET. `Caspol.exe` and `Permview.exe`, which assist in establishing and maintaining security policies, are discussed. The `System.Security.Permissions` namespace is also covered, including how it relates to managing permissions. Finally, you look at the `System.Security` `.Cryptography` namespace and run through some code that demonstrates its capabilities.

Chapter 33, "Parallel Programming Using Tasks and Threads" — This chapter explores threading and explains how the various objects in the .NET Framework enable any of its consumers to develop multithreaded applications. You will learn how threads can be created, how they relate to processes, and the differences between multitasking and multithreading. Additionally, Visual Studio 2010 introduces an entirely new parallel processing framework, which is addressed in this chapter.

Chapter 34, "Deployment" — This chapter takes a close look at the available deployment options for Windows Forms and Web Forms, including the ClickOnce deployment feature and creating `.msi` files.

Appendix A, "The Visual Basic Compiler" — This appendix covers the Visual Basic compiler `vbc.exe` and the functionality it provides.

Appendix B, "Visual Basic Power Packs Tools" — This appendix looks at the Visual Basic Power Packs Tools, originally released as off-cycle packages to aid developers who are maintaining traditional Visual Basic 6.0 applications or are looking for capabilities similar to those in Visual Basic 6. These tools were integrated with Visual Studio and help begin the process of transitioning to the current version of Visual Basic.

Appendix C, "Workflow 2008 Specifics" — The Windows Workflow Foundation introduced with .NET 3.0 and supported by Visual Studio 2008 has been completely redone for Visual Studio 2010. However, we moved coverage of the original Workflow services to this appendix so that you will continue to be able to reference this material for existing solutions.

Appendix D, "Enterprise Services" — Over time, with new transaction support and related capabilities, the material in this appendix, which was previously its own chapter, has become less applicable. It has been migrated to this appendix to support those with existing implementations that reference Enterprise Services. This chapter explores the .NET component services — in particular, transaction processing and queued components.

Appendix E, "Programming for the Cloud" — This chapter looks at several new cloud-based environments that Microsoft has introduced and how they affect you as a Visual Basic developer. Whether you are keeping data in the cloud or developing applications that will live in the cloud, this chapter will help you understand this new application paradigm.

CONVENTIONS

To help you get the most from the text and keep track of what's happening, we've used a number of conventions throughout the book.

Boxes like this one hold important, not-to-be forgotten information that is directly relevant to the surrounding text.

Tips, hints, tricks, and asides to the current discussion are offset and placed in italics like this.

As for styles in the text:

➤   We *italicize* new terms and important words when we introduce them.

➤   We show keyboard strokes like this: Ctrl+A.

➤   We show filenames, URLs, and code within the text like so: `persistence.properties`.

➤   We present code in two different ways:

```
We use a monofont type with no highlighting for most code examples.
```

```
We use bold to emphasize code that is particularly important in the present context or to show
changes from a previous code snippet.
```

SOURCE CODE

As you work through the examples in this book, you may choose either to type in all the code manually or to use the source code files that accompany the book. All the source code used in this book is available for download at `http://www.wrox.com`. When at the site, simply locate the book's title (use the Search box or one of the title lists) and click the Download Code link on the book's detail page to obtain all the source code for the book. Code that is included on the Web site is highlighted by the following icon:

Available for
download on
Wrox.com

Listings include the filename in the title. If it is just a code snippet, you'll find the filename in a code note such as this:

Code snippet filename

Because many books have similar titles, you may find it easiest to search by ISBN; this book's ISBN is 978-0-470-50224-2.

Once you download the code, just decompress it with your favorite compression tool. Alternately, you can go to the main Wrox code download page at `www.wrox.com/dynamic/books/download.aspx` to see the code available for this book and all other Wrox books.

ERRATA

We make every effort to ensure that there are no errors in the text or in the code. However, no one is perfect, and mistakes do occur. If you find an error in one of our books, such as a spelling mistake or a faulty piece of code, we would be very grateful for your feedback. By sending in errata, you may save another reader hours of frustration, and at the same time you will be helping us provide even higher-quality information.

To find the errata page for this book, go to `www.wrox.com` and locate the title using the Search box or one of the title lists. Then, on the book details page, click the Book Errata link. On this page, you can view all errata that has been submitted for this book and posted by Wrox editors. A complete book list, including links to each book's errata, is also available at `www.wrox.com/misc-pages/booklist.shtml`.

If you don't spot "your" error on the Book Errata page, go to `www.wrox.com/contact/techsupport.shtml` and complete the form there to send us the error you have found. We'll check the information and, if appropriate, post a message to the book's errata page and fix the problem in subsequent editions of the book.

P2P.WROX.COM

For author and peer discussion, join the P2P forums at `p2p.wrox.com`. The forums are a Web-based system for you to post messages relating to Wrox books and related technologies, and interact with other readers and technology users. The forums offer a subscription feature to e-mail you topics of interest of your choosing when new posts are made to the forums. Wrox authors, editors, other industry experts, and your fellow readers are present on these forums.

At `http://p2p.wrox.com`, you will find a number of different forums that will help you not only as you read this book, but also as you develop your own applications. To join the forums, just follow these steps:

1. Go to `p2p.wrox.com` and click the Register link.
2. Read the terms of use and click Agree.
3. Complete the required information to join, as well as any optional information you wish to provide, and click Submit.
4. You will receive an e-mail with information describing how to verify your account and complete the joining process.

You can read messages in the forums without joining P2P, but in order to post your own messages you must join.

Once you join, you can post new messages and respond to messages other users post. You can read messages at any time on the Web. If you would like to have new messages from a particular forum e-mailed to you, click the Subscribe to this Forum icon by the forum name in the forum listing.

For more information about how to use the Wrox P2P, be sure to read the P2P FAQs for answers to questions about how the forum software works, as well as many common questions specific to P2P and Wrox books. To read the FAQs, click the FAQ link on any P2P page.

PART I
Language Constructs and Environment

1

Visual Studio 2010

WHAT YOU WILL LEARN IN THIS CHAPTER

- ➤ Versions of Visual Studio
- ➤ An introduction to key Visual Basic terms
- ➤ Targeting a runtime environment
- ➤ Creating a baseline Visual Basic Windows Form
- ➤ Project templates
- ➤ Project properties — application, compilation, debug
- ➤ Setting properties
- ➤ IntelliSense, code expansion, and code snippets
- ➤ Debugging
- ➤ Recording and using macros
- ➤ The Class Designer
- ➤ Team Foundation Server — Team Explorer

You can work with Visual Basic without Visual Studio. In fact, Appendix A focuses on using the Visual Basic compiler from the command line. In practice, however, most Visual Basic developers treat the two as almost inseparable; without a version of Visual Studio, you're forced to work from the command line to create project files by hand, to make calls to the associated compilers, and to manually address the tools necessary to build your application. While Visual Basic supports this at the same level as C#, F#, C++ and other .NET languages, this isn't the typical focus of a Visual Basic professional.

Visual Basic's success rose from its increased productivity in comparison to other languages when building business applications. Visual Studio 2010 increases your productivity and provides assistance in debugging your applications and is the natural tool for Visual Basic developers.

Accordingly, the current edition of this book is going to start off by introducing you to Visual Studio 2010 and how to build and manage Visual Basic applications. The focus of this chapter is on ensuring that everyone has a core set of knowledge related to tasks like creating and debugging applications in Visual Studio 2010. Visual Studio 2010 will be used throughout the book for building solutions. Note while this is the start, don't think of it as an 'intro' chapter. This chapter will intro key elements of working with Visual Studio, but will also go beyond that. You may find yourself referencing back to it later for advanced topics that you glossed over your first time through. Visual Studio is a powerful and, at times, complex tool and you aren't expected to master it on your first read through this chapter.

When Visual Studio 2005 was released, Microsoft expanded on the different versions of Visual Studio available for use. At the low-cost end, and currently free, is Visual Basic Express Edition. This tool enables you to build desktop applications with Visual Basic only. Its companion for Web development is Visual Web Developer Express, which enables you to build ASP.NET applications. At the high end, Microsoft offers Visual Studio Ultimate. Each of the high-end, Professional, Premium, and Ultimate editions is available as part of an MSDN subscription and each of these editions further extends the core Visual Studio 2010 capabilities beyond the core Integrated Development Environment (IDE) to help improve design, testing, and collaboration between developers.

Of course, the focus of this chapter is how Visual Studio enables you to use Visual Basic to build applications geared toward "better, faster, cheaper" business goals. To this end, we'll be examining features of Visual Studio starting with those in the core Visual Basic 2010 Express Edition and building up to the full Visual Studio Team Suite.

This chapter provides an overview of many of the capabilities of Visual Studio 2010. It also provides a brief introduction to the features available by using one of the more feature-rich versions of Visual Studio. Experienced developers will probably gloss over much of this information although I encourage them to review the new historical debugging features available in Visual Studio 2010 Ultimate covered in this chapter. The goal is to demonstrate how Visual Studio makes you, as a developer, more productive and successful.

VISUAL STUDIO 2010: EXPRESS THROUGH ULTIMATE

For those who aren't familiar with the main elements of .NET development there is the common language runtime (CLR), the .NET Framework, the various language compilers and Visual Studio. Each of these plays a role, for example the CLR — covered in Chapter 4 — manages the execution of code on the .NET platform. Thus code can be targeted to run on a specific version of this runtime environment.

The .NET Framework provides a series of classes that developers leverage across implementation languages. This framework or Class Library is versioned and targeted to run on a specific minimum version of the CLR. It is this library along with the language compilers that are referenced by Visual Studio. Visual Studio allows you to build applications that target one or more of the versions of what is generically called .NET.

In some cases the CLR and the .NET Framework will be the same; for example, .NET Framework version 1.0 ran on CLR version 1.0. In other cases just as Visual Basic's compiler is on version 10, the .NET Framework might have a newer version targeting an older version of the CLR.

The same concepts carry into Visual Studio. Visual Studio 2003 was focused on .NET 1.1, while the earlier Visual Studio .NET (2002) was focused on .NET 1.0. Originally, each version of Visual Studio was optimized for a particular version of .NET. Similarly, Visual Studio 2005 was optimized for .NET 2.0, but then along came the exception of the .NET Framework version 3.0. This introduced a new Framework, which was supported by the same version 2.0 of the CLR, but which didn't ship with a new version of Visual Studio.

Fortunately, Microsoft chose to keep Visual Basic and ASP.NET unchanged for the .NET 3.0 Framework release. However, when you looked at the.NET 3.0 Framework elements, such as Windows Presentation Foundation, Windows Communication Foundation, and Windows Workflow Foundation, you found that those items needed to be addressed outside of Visual Studio. Thus, while Visual Studio is separate from Visual Basic, the CLR and .NET development, in practical terms Visual Studio was tightly coupled to each of these items.

With Visual Studio 2008, Microsoft loosened this coupling by providing robust support that allowed the developer to target any of three different versions of the .NET Framework. Visual Studio 2010 continues this, enabling you to target an application to run on .NET 2.0, .NET 3.0,.NET 3.5, or .NET 4.

However, as you'll discover, this support doesn't mean that Visual Studio 2010 isn't tightly coupled to a specific version of each compiler. In fact, the new support for targeting frameworks is designed to support a runtime environment, not a compile-time environment. This is important because when projects from previous versions of Visual Studio are converted to the Visual Studio 2010 format, they cannot be reopened by a previous version.

The reason for this is that the underlying build engine used by Visual Studio 2010 accepts syntax changes and even language feature changes, but previous versions of Visual Studio do not recognize these new elements of the language. Thus, if you move source code written in Visual Studio 2010 to a previous version of Visual Studio, you face a strong possibility that it would fail to compile. There are ways to manually work with a project across versions of Visual Studio on the same team, but they are not supported. Bill Sheldon, one of the authors of this book, has a blog post from August 2007 that deals with his experience doing this in Visual Studio 2008. The post titled "Working with Both VS 2005 and VS 2008 B2 on the Same Project" is still applicable for those working with Visual Studio 2010: `http://nerdnotes` `.net/blog/default,date,2007-08-29.aspx`.

Multi-targeting support by Visual Studio 2010 ensures that your application will run on a specific version of the framework. Thus, if your organization is not supporting .NET 3.0, .NET 3.5, or .NET 4, you can still use Visual Studio 2010. The compiler generates byte code based on the language syntax, and at its core that byte code is version agnostic. Where you can get in trouble is if you reference one or more classes that aren't part of a given version of the CLR. Visual Studio therefore manages your references when targeting an older version of .NET allowing you to be reasonably certain that your application will not reference files from one of those other framework versions. Multi-targeting is what enables you to safely deploy without requiring your customers to download additional framework components they don't need.

With those ground rules in place, what versions of Visual Studio 2010 are available, and what are the primary differences between them? As already mentioned, Visual Basic 2010 Express is at the bottom tier in terms of price and features. It is accompanied there by Visual Web Developer 2010 Express Edition, for those developers who are developing Web applications, rather than desktop applications. These two tools are separate, but both support developing different types of Visual Basic applications, and both are free. Note, however, that neither is extensible; these tools are meant to be introductory, and Microsoft's license prevents vendors from extending these tools with productivity enhancements.

However, each of the Express Edition development tools also ships with two additional components covered briefly here: MSDN Express Edition and SQL Server 2008 Express Edition. MSDN is, of course, the Microsoft Developer Network, which has placed most of its content online. It's the source for not only the core language documentation for Visual Basic, but also articles on almost every product oriented to developers using Microsoft technology. Full versions of Visual Studio ship with the full MSDN library so that you can access its content locally. However, the Express Edition tools actually ship with a pared-down set of documentation files.

Similar to the language and Web-based tools, Microsoft has a SQL Server Express Edition package. This package has a history, in that it replaces the MSDE database engine that was available with SQL Server 2000. The SQL Server Express engine provides the core SQL Server 2008 database engine. For more information on SQL Server Express go to `www.microsoft.com/express/database`. Note that a free database management application is available via a separate download from Microsoft.

When you install Visual Studio 2010, including the Express Editions, you also have the opportunity to install this core database engine. The elements of this engine are freely redistributable, so if you are looking for a set of core database features based on ADO.NET, you can create your application and deploy your SQL Server 2008 Express Edition database without being concerned about licensing.

Getting back to the differences in versions, the Express Edition tools provide the core components necessary to create Visual Basic applications (Windows or Web) based on the core IDE. Table 1-1 provides a quick summary of what versions are available, including a description of how each extends Visual Studio.

TABLE 1-1: Visual Studio Editions

VISUAL STUDIO EDITION	DESCRIPTION
Visual Basic 2008 Express Edition	This is the core set of functionality required for creating Windows-based applications. It includes the IDE with full local debugging support and support for five project types: Windows Forms Application, Dynamic Link Library, WPF Application, WPF Browser Application, and Console Application.
Visual Web Developer 2008 Express Edition	The core set of functionality required for building Web applications. It supports both Visual Basic and C# and allows for local debugging of your Web application.
Visual Studio 2010 Standard Edition	Provides a combined development language for the core Visual Studio languages (J#, VB, C# and C++). It adds the Object Modeling tool, and provides combined support for both Windows and Web applications. It also provides additional support for application deployment, and support for Mobile Application Development, integration with a source control tool, and macros within Visual Studio; it is also extensible.
Visual Studio 2010 Professional Edition	Expands on Visual Studio Standard Edition with additional integration to SQL Server and support for XSLTs. It also includes support for Visual Studio Tools for Office (VSTO), which enables you to create custom client (Word, Excel, Outlook, etc.) and SharePoint Workflow applications. This version also allows for remote debugging of Web applications, and unit testing of all projects. (This edition supports VSTO but the associated MSDN subscription does not include a license for Office.)
Visual Studio 2010 Premium Edition	This version begins to pull in many of the extensions that were originally introduced with what was known as Team Suite. This version has expanded test features like Code Coverage and coded UI test support. It includes tools to support database development, change management, testing, and so on, as well as tools for static code analysis and code metrics.
Visual Studio 2010 Ultimate Edition	This version includes all of the core features of Visual Studio 2010 Premium Edition. It then adds historical debugging, Web and load-testing tools, and a variety of related tools to enhance development. This tool, like the Premium version of Visual Studio, is focused on enabling developers to be productive in a shared collaborative environment.

The Express Edition tools are best described as targeting students and hobbyists, not because you can't create serious applications but because they provide only limited support for team development, have limited extensibility, and offer a standalone environment. The Express Tools are oriented toward developers who work independently, while still providing full access to features of the Visual Basic language. This chapter begins working in the IDE using features available in this version, which is essentially the lowest common denominator, and then goes beyond the capabilities of this free tool.

Eventually, however, a developer needs additional tools and projects. This is where the full versions of Visual Studio 2010 (Standard, Professional, Premium and Ultimate) come in. With an increasing level of support for team development, these feature-rich versions add macro support, and, more important, an Object Modeling tool. As discussed in the section titled "Class Diagrams," later in this chapter, Visual Studio enables you to create a visual representation of the classes in your solution and then convert that representation into code. Moreover, the tool supports what is known as *round-trip engineering*. This means that not only can you use the graphical model to generate code, you can also take a project's source files and regenerate an updated version of the graphical model — that is, edit that model in its graphical format and then update the associated source files.

For those choosing Visual Studio 2008 Professional or above, Visual Studio Tools for Office (VSTO) is targeted primarily at enterprise developers, those who work in corporate organizations (either as employees or consultant/contractors). This tool provides a way for users of the enterprise editions of Microsoft Office 2007 and Microsoft Office 2010 to extend these office productivity tools with application-like features. Many organizations use Microsoft Office for tasks that border on custom applications. This is especially true for Microsoft Excel. VSTO provides project templates based on these Microsoft Office products that enable, for example, a spreadsheet to retrieve its contents from an SQL Server database instead of the local file system. These tools provide the capability not only to manipulate data retrieval and saving, but also to customize the user interface, including direct access to the task pane and custom toolbar options within Microsoft Office products; they are covered in more detail in Chapter 25.

Visual Studio 2010 Premium and Ultimate focus on extending a developer's reach beyond just writing code. These tools are used to examine code for flaws, manage the deployment environment, and define relationships between applications. The high-end versions are focused on tools that support repeatable software processes and best practices. They are geared toward examining source code for hidden flaws that might not cause the code to fail, but might hide a hidden security flaw or make it difficult to maintain or deploy the application. More important, the suite includes tools for creating unit test tools that attempt to cause the code to fail, whether through bad input data or heavy load.

Complete coverage of all of Visual Studio Ultimate's features warrants a book of its own, especially when you take into account all of the collaborative features introduced by Team Foundation Server and its tight integration with both Team Build and SharePoint Server. Team Foundation Server goes beyond just being a replacement for Visual Source Safe. It is the basis for true process-driven development, and it even includes documentation to help train your organization on two process models supported by Microsoft.

VISUAL BASIC KEYWORDS AND SYNTAX

Those with previous experience with Visual Basic are already familiar with many of the language keywords and syntax. However, not all readers will fall into this category so this introductory section is for those new to Visual Basic. A glossary of keywords is provided after which this section will use many of these keywords in context.

Although they're not the focus of the chapter, with so many keywords, a glossary follows. Table 1-2 briefly summarizes most of the keywords discussed in the preceding section, and provides a short description of their meaning in Visual Basic. Keep in mind there are two commonly used terms that aren't Visual Basic keywords that you will read repeatedly including in the glossary:

➤ **Method** — A generic name for a named set of commands. In Visual Basic, both subs and functions are types of methods.

➤ **Instance** — When a class is created, the resulting object is an instance of the class's definition.

TABLE 1-2: Commonly Used Keywords in Visual Basic

KEYWORD	DESCRIPTION
Namespace	A collection of classes that provide related capabilities. For example, the System.Drawing namespace contains classes associated with graphics.
Class	A definition of an object. Includes properties (variables) and methods, which can be Subs or Functions.
Sub	A method that contains a set of commands, allows data to be transferred as parameters, and provides scope around local variables and commands, but does not return a value
Function	A method that contains a set of commands, returns a value, allows data to be transferred as parameters, and provides scope around local variables and commands
Return	Ends the currently executing Sub or Function. Combined with a return value for functions.
Dim	Declares and defines a new variable
New	Creates an instance of an object

continues

TABLE 1-2 (*continued*)

KEYWORD	DESCRIPTION
Nothing	Used to indicate that a variable has no value. Equivalent to null in other languages and databases.
Me	A reference to the instance of the object within which a method is executing
Console	A type of application that relies on a command-line interface. Console applications are commonly used for simple test frames. Also refers to a .NET Framework Class that manages access of the command window to and from which applications can read and write text data.
Module	A code block that isn't a class but which can contain Sub and Function methods. Used when only a single copy of code or data is needed in memory.

Even though the focus of this chapter is on Visual Studio, during this introduction a few basic elements of Visual Basic will be referenced and need to be spelled out. This way as you read, you can understand the examples. Chapter 4, for instance, covers working with namespaces, but some examples and other code are introduced in this chapter that will mention the term, so it is defined here.

Let's begin with namespace. When .NET was being created, the developers realized that attempting to organize all of these classes required a system. A namespace is an arbitrary system that the .NET developers used to group classes containing common functionality. A namespace can have multiple levels of grouping, each separated by a period (.). Thus, the System namespace is the basis for classes that are used throughout .NET, while the Microsoft.VisualBasic namespace is used for classes in the underlying .NET Framework but specific to Visual Basic. At its most basic level, a namespace does not imply or indicate anything regarding the relationships between the class implementations in that namespace; it is just a way of managing the complexity of both your custom application's classes, whether it be a small or large collection, and that of the .NET Framework's thousands of classes. As noted earlier, namespaces are covered in detail in Chapter 4.

Next is the keyword Class. Chapters 2 and 3 provide details on object-oriented syntax and the related keywords for objects and types, but a basic definition of this keyword is needed here. The Class keyword designates a common set of data and behavior within your application. The class is the definition of an object, in the same way that your source code, when compiled, is the definition of an application. When someone runs your code, it is considered to be an instance of your application. Similarly, when your code creates or instantiates an object from your class definition, it is considered to be an instance of that class, or an instance of that object.

Creating an instance of an object has two parts. The first part is the New command, which tells the compiler to create an instance of that class. This command instructs code to call your object definition and instantiate it. In some cases you might need to run a method and get a return value, but in most cases you use the New command to assign that instance of an object to a variable. A variable is quite literally something which can hold a reference to that class's instance.

To declare a variable in Visual Basic, you use the Dim statement. Dim is short for "dimension" and comes from the ancient past of Basic, which preceded Visual Basic as a language. The idea is that you are telling the system to allocate or dimension a section of memory to hold data. As discussed in subsequent chapters on objects, the Dim statement may be replaced by another keyword such as Public or Private that not only dimensions the new value, but also limits the accessibility of that value. Each variable declaration uses a Dim statement similar to the example that follows, which declares a new variable, winForm:

```
Dim winForm As System.Windows.Forms.Form = New System.Windows.Forms.Form()
```

In the preceding example, the code declares a new variable (winForm) of the type Form. This variable is then set to an instance of a Form object. It might also be assigned to an existing instance of a Form object or alternatively to Nothing. The Nothing keyword is a way of telling the system that the variable does not currently have any value, and as such is not actually using any memory on the heap. Later in this chapter, in the discussion of value and reference types, keep in mind that only reference types can be set to Nothing.

A class consists of both state and behavior. State is a fancy way of referring to the fact that the class has one or more values also known as properties associated with it. Embedded in the class definition are zero or more `Dim` statements that create variables used to store the properties of the class. When you create an instance of this class, you create these variables; and in most cases the class contains logic to populate them. The logic used for this, and to carry out other actions, is the *behavior*. This behavior is encapsulated in what, in the object-oriented world, are known as *methods*.

However, Visual Basic doesn't have a "method" keyword. Instead, it has two other keywords that are brought forward from Visual Basic's days as a procedural language. The first is `Sub`. `Sub`, short for "subroutine," and it defines a block of code that carries out some action. When this block of code completes, it returns control to the code that called it without returning a value. The following snippet shows the declaration of a `Sub`:

```
Private Sub Load(ByVal object As System.Object)

End Sub
```

The preceding example shows the start of a `Sub` called `Load`. For now you can ignore the word `Private` at the start of this declaration; this is related to the object and is further explained in the next chapter. This method is implemented as a `Sub` because it doesn't return a value and accepts one parameter when it is called. Thus, in other languages this might be considered and written explicitly as a function that returns `Nothing`.

The preceding method declaration for `Sub Load` also includes a single parameter, `object`, which is declared as being of type `System.Object`. The meaning of the `ByVal` qualifier is explained in chapter 2, but is related to how that value is passed to this method. The code that actually loads the object would be written between the line declaring this method and the `End Sub` line.

Alternatively, a method can return a value; Visual Basic uses the keyword `Function` to describe this behavior. In Visual Basic, the only difference between a `Sub` and the method type `Function` is the return type.

The `Function` declaration shown in the following sample code specifies the return type of the function as a `Long` value. A `Function` works just like a `Sub` with the exception that a `Function` returns a value, which can be `Nothing`. This is an important distinction, because when you declare a function the compiler expects it to include a `Return` statement. The `Return` statement is used to indicate that even though additional lines of code may remain within a `Function` or `Sub`, those lines of code should not be executed. Instead, the `Function` or `Sub` should end processing at the current line, and if it is in a function, the return value should be returned. To declare a `Function`, you write code similar to the following:

```
Public Function Add(ByVal ParamArray values() As Integer) As Long
    Dim result As Long = 0
    'TODO: Implement this function
    Return result
    'What if there is more code
    Return result
End Function
```

In the preceding example, note that after the function initializes the second line of code, there is a `Return` statement. There are *two* `Return` statements in the code. However, as soon as the first `Return` statement is reached, none of the remaining code in this function is executed. The `Return` statement immediately halts execution of a method, even from within a loop.

As shown in the preceding example, the function's return value is assigned to a local variable until returned as part of the `Return` statement. For a `Sub`, there would be no value on the line with the `Return` statement, as a `Sub` does not return a value when it completes. When returned, the return value is usually assigned to something else. This is shown in the next example line of code, which calls a function to retrieve the currently active control on the executing Windows Form:

```
Dim ctrl = Me.Add(1, 2)
```

The preceding example demonstrates a call to a function. The value returned by the function `Add` is a `Long`, and the code assigns this to the variable `ctrl`. It also demonstrates another keyword that you should be aware of: `Me`. The `Me` keyword is how, within an object, that you can reference the current instance of that object.

You may have noticed that in all the sample code presented thus far, each line is a complete command. If you're familiar with another programming language, then you may be used to seeing a specific character that indicates the end of a complete set of commands. Several popular languages use a semicolon to indicate the end of a command line.

Visual Basic doesn't use visible punctuation to end each line. Traditionally, the BASIC family of languages viewed source files more like a list, whereby each item on the list is placed on its own line. At one point the term was *source listing*. By default, Visual Basic ends each source list item with the carriage-return linefeed, and treats it as a command line. In some languages, a command such as X = Y can span several lines in the source file until a semicolon or other terminating character is reached. Thus previously, in Visual Basic, that entire statement would be found on a single line unless the user explicitly indicates that it is to continue onto another line.

To explicitly indicate that a command line spans more than one physical line, you'll see the use of the underscore at the end of the line to be continued. However, one of the new features of Visual Basic 10, which ships with Visual Studio 2010, is support for an implicit underscore when extending a line past the carriage-return linefeed. However, this new feature is limited as there are still places where underscores are needed.

When a line ends with the underscore character, this explicitly tells Visual Basic that the code on that line does not constitute a completed set of commands. The compiler will then continue to the next line to find the continuation of the command, and will end when a carriage-return linefeed is found without an accompanying underscore.

In other words, Visual Basic enables you to use exceptionally long lines and indicate that the code has been spread across multiple lines to improve readability. The following line demonstrates the use of the underscore to extend a line of code:

```
MessageBox.Show("Hello World", "A Message Box Title", _
    MessageBoxButtons.OK, MessageBoxIcon.Information)
```

Prior to Visual Basic 10 the preceding example illustrated the only way to extend a single command line beyond one physical line in your source code. The preceding line of code can now be written as follows:

```
MessageBox.Show("Hello World", "A Message Box Title",
    MessageBoxButtons.OK, MessageBoxIcon.Information)
```

The compiler now recognizes certain key characters like the "," or the "=" as the type of statement where a line isn't going to end. The compiler doesn't account for every situation and won't just look for a line extension anytime a line doesn't compile. That would be a performance nightmare; however, there are several logical places where you, as a developer, can choose to break a command across lines and do so without needing to insert an underscore to give the compiler a hint about the extended line.

Finally, note that in Visual Basic it is also possible to place multiple different statements on a single line, by separating the statements with colons. However, this is generally considered a poor coding practice because it reduces readability.

Console Applications

The simplest type of application is a *console application*. This application doesn't have much of a user interface; in fact, for those old enough to remember the MS-DOS operating system, a console application looks just like an MS-DOS application. It works in a command window without support for graphics or input devices such as a mouse. A console application is a text-based user interface that displays text characters and reads input from the keyboard.

The easiest way to create a console application is to use Visual Studio. For the current discussion let's just look at a sample source file for a Console application, as shown in the following example. Notice that the console application contains a single method, a Sub called Main. By default if you create a console application in Visual Studio, the code located in the Sub Main is the code which is by default started. However, the Sub Main isn't contained in a class, instead the Sub Main that follows is contained in a Module:

```
Module Module1
    Sub Main()
        Console.WriteLine("Hello World")
```

```
        Dim line = Console.ReadLine()
    End Sub
End Module
```

A `Module` isn't truly a class, but rather a block of code that can contain methods, which are then referenced by code in classes or other modules — or, as in this case, it can represent the execution start for a program. A `Module` is similar to having a `Shared` class. The `Shared` keyword indicates that only a single instance of a given item exists.

For example in C# the `Static` keyword is used for this purpose, and can be used to indicate that only a single instance of a given class exists. Visual Basic doesn't support the use of the `Shared` keyword with a `Class` declaration; instead Visual Basic developers create modules that provide the same capability. The `Module` represents a valid construct to group methods that don't have state-related or instance-specific data.

Note a console application focuses on the `Console Class`. The `Console Class` encapsulates Visual Basic's interface with the text-based window that hosts a command prompt from which a command-line program is run. The console window is best thought of as a window encapsulating the older non-graphical style user interface, whereby literally everything was driven from the command prompt. A `Shared` instance of the `Console` class is automatically created when you start your application, and it supports a variety of `Read` and `Write` methods. In the preceding example, if you were to run the code from within Visual Studio's debugger, then the console window would open and close immediately. To prevent that, you include a final line in the `Main Sub`, which executes a `Read` statement so that the program continues to run while waiting for user input.

Creating a Project from a Project Template

While it is possible to create a Visual Basic application working entirely outside of Visual Studio 2010, it is much easier to start from Visual Studio 2010. After you install Visual Studio you are presented with a screen similar to the one shown in Figure 1-1. Different versions of Visual Studio may have a different overall look, but typically the start page lists your most recent projects on the left, some tips for getting started, and a headline section for topics on MSDN that might be of interest. You may or may not immediately recognize that this content is HTML text; more important, the content is based on an RSS feed that retrieves and caches articles appropriate for your version of Visual Studio.

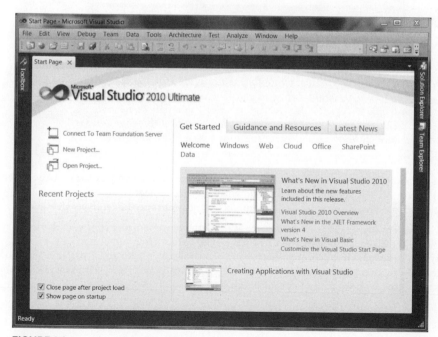

FIGURE 1-1

The start page looks similar regardless of which version of Visual Studio 2010 you are running. Conceptually, it provides a generic starting point either to select the application you intend to work on, to quickly receive vital news related to offers, as shown in the figure, or to connect with external resources via the community links.

Once here, the next step is to create your first project. Selecting File ⇨ New Project opens the New Project dialog, shown in Figure 1-2. This dialog provides a selection of templates customized by application type. One option is to create a Class Library project. Such a project doesn't include a user interface; and instead of creating an assembly with an .exe file, it creates an assembly with a .dll file. The difference, of course, is that an .exe file indicates an executable that can be started by the operating system, whereas a .dll file represents a library referenced by an application.

FIGURE 1-2

One of the ongoing challenges with describing the menu options for Visual Studio is that the various versions have slight differences in look and feel too numerous to mention. For example File ⇨ New Project in Visual Basic Express becomes File ⇨ New ⇨ Project in Visual Studio. Thus, your display may vary slightly from what is shown or described here, although we attempt to showcase significant differences.

Figure 1-2 includes the capability to target a specific .NET version in the drop-down box located above the list of project types. In Figure 1-2 this shows .NET 2.0, and with only six project types below the selection listed. With .NET 4 selected, as shown in Figure 1-3, the number of project types has increased.

Targeting keeps you from attempting to create a project for WPF without recognizing that you also need at least .NET 3.0 available on the client. Although you can change your target after you create your project, be very careful when trying to reduce the version number, as the controls to prevent you from selecting dependencies don't check your existing code base for violations. Changing your targeted framework version for an existing project is covered in more detail later in this chapter.

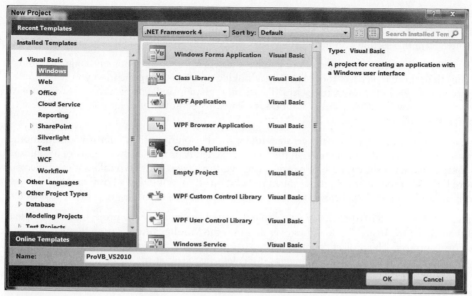

FIGURE 1-3

Not only can you choose to target a specific version of the framework when creating a new project, but this window has a new feature that you'll find all over the place in Visual Studio 2010. In the upper-right corner, there is a control that enables you to search for a specific template. As you work through more of the windows associated with Visual Studio, you'll find that a context-specific search capability has often been added to the new user interface.

Expanding the top level of the Visual Basic tree in Figure 1-3 shows that a project type can be further separated into a series of categories:

➤ **Windows** — These are projects used to create applications that run on the local computer within the CLR. Because such projects can run on any operating system (OS) hosting the framework, the category "Windows" is something of a misnomer when compared to, for example, "Desktop."

➤ **Web** — You can create these projects, including Web services, from this section of the New Project dialog.

➤ **Office** — Visual Studio Tools for Office (VSTO). These are .NET applications that are hosted under Office. Visual Studio 2010 includes a set of templates you can use to target Office 2010, as well as a separate section for templates that target Office 2007.

➤ **Cloud Services:** — These are projects that target the Azure online environment model. These projects are deployed to the cloud and as such have special implementation and deployment considerations.

➤ **Reporting** — This project type enables you to create a Reports application.

➤ **SharePoint** — This category provides a selection of SharePoint projects, including Web Part projects, SharePoint Workflow projects, Business Data Catalog projects, as well as things like site definitions and content type projects. Visual Studio 2010 includes significant new support for SharePoint.

➤ **Silverlight** — With Visual Studio 2010, Microsoft has finally provided full support for working with Silverlight projects. Whereas in the past you've had to add the Silverlight SDK and tools to your existing development environment, with Visual Studio 2010 you get support for both Silverlight projects and user interface design within Visual Studio.

➤ **Test** — This section is available only to those using Visual Studio Team Suite. It contains the template for a Visual Basic Unit Test project.

➤ **WCF** — This is the section where you can create Windows Communication Foundation projects.

➤ **Workflow** — This is the section where you can create Windows Workflow Foundation (WF) projects. The templates in this section also include templates for connecting with the SharePoint workflow engine.

Visual Studio has other categories for projects, and you have access to other development languages and far more project types than this chapter has room for. When looking to create an application you will choose from one or more of the available project templates. To use more than a single project to create an application you'll leverage what is known as a solution. A solution is created by default whenever you create a new project and contains one or more projects.

When you save your project you will typically create a folder for the solution, then later if you add another project to the same solution, it will be contained in the solution folder. A project is always part of a solution, and a solution can contain multiple projects, each of which creates a different assembly. Typically for example you will have one or more Class Libraries that are part of the same solution as your Windows Form or ASP.NET project. For now, you can select a Windows Application project template to use as an example project for this chapter.

For this example, use ProVB_VS2010 as the project name to match the name of the project in the sample code download and then click OK. Visual Studio takes over and uses the Windows Application template to create a new Windows Forms project. The project contains a blank form that can be customized, and a variety of other elements that you can explore. Before customizing any code, let's first look at the elements of this new project.

The Solution Explorer

The Solution Explorer is a window that is by default located on the right-hand side of your display when you create a project. It is there to display the contents of your solution and includes the actual source file(s) for each of the projects in your solution. While the Solution Explorer window is available and applicable for Express Edition users, it will never contain more than a single project. Those with a version of Visual Studio above the Express Edition level have the capability to leverage multiple projects in a single solution. A .NET solution can contain projects of any .NET language and can include the database, testing, and installation projects as part of the overall solution. The advantage of combining these projects is that it is easier to debug projects that reside in a common solution.

Before discussing these files in depth, let's take a look at the next step, which is to reveal a few additional details about your project. Click the second button on the left in the Solution Explorer to display all of the project files, as shown in Figure 1-4. As this image shows, many other files make up your project. Some of these, such as those under the My Project grouping, don't require you to edit them directly. Instead, you can double-click the My Project entry in the Solution Explorer and open the pages to edit your project settings. You do not need to change any of the default settings for this project, but the next section of this chapter walks you through the various property screens.

FIGURE 1-4

The bin and obj directories shown are used when building your project. The obj directory contains the first-pass object files used by the compiler to create your final executable file. The "binary" or compiled version of your application is then placed in the bin directory by default. Of course, referring to the Microsoft intermediate language (MSIL) code as binary is something of a misnomer, as the actual translation to binary does not occur until runtime when your application is compiled by the just-in-time (JIT) compiler. However, Microsoft continues to use the bin directory as the default output directory for your project's compilation.

Figure 1-4 also shows that the project does not contain an app.config file by default. Most experienced ASP .NET developers are familiar with using web.config files. app.config files work on the same principle in that they contain XML, which is used to store project-specific settings such as database connection strings and other application-specific settings. Using a .config file instead of having your settings in the Windows registry enables your applications to run side-by-side with another version of the application without the settings from either version affecting the other. Because each version of your application resides in its own directory, its settings are contained in the directory with it, which enables the different versions to run with unique settings. Before we are done going through the project properties, we will add an app.config file to this project.

For now however, you have a new project and an initial Windows Form, Form1, available in the Solution Explorer. In this case, the Form1.vb file is the primary file associated with the default Windows form Form1. You'll be customizing this form shortly, but before looking at that, it would be useful to look at some of the settings available by opening your project properties. An easy way to do this is to right-click on the My Project heading shown in Figure 1-4.

Project Properties

Visual Studio uses a vertically tabbed display for editing your project settings. The project properties display shown in Figure 1-5 provides access to the newly created ProVB_VS2010 project settings. The project properties window gives you access to several different aspects of your project. Some, such as Signing, Security, and Publish, are covered in later chapters. For now, just note that this display makes it easier to carry out several tasks that once required engineers to work outside the Visual Studio environment.

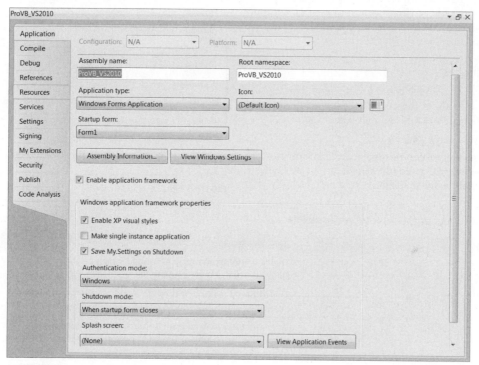

FIGURE 1-5

You can customize your assembly name from this screen, as well as reset the type of application and object to be referenced when starting your application. However, resetting the type of your application is not recommended. If you start with the wrong application type, it is better to create a new application, due to all the embedded settings in the application template. In the next section you will look at a button for changing your assembly information, as well as the capability to define a root namespace for your application classes. Namespaces are covered in detail in Chapter 4.

You can also associate a given default icon with your form (refer to Figure 1-5), and select a screen other than the default Form1 as the startup screen.

Near the middle of the dialog are two buttons. Assembly Information is covered in the next section. The other button, labeled View Windows Settings refers to User Access Control settings, which enable you to specify that only certain users can successfully start your application. In short, you have the option to limit your application access to a specific set of users.

Finally, there is a section associated with enabling an application framework. The application framework is a set of optional components that enable you to extend your application with custom events and items, such as a splash screen, with minimal effort. Enabling the framework is the default, but unless you want to change the default settings, the behavior is the same — as if the framework weren't enabled. The third button, View Application Events, adds a new source file, `ApplicationEvents.vb`, to your project, which includes documentation about which application events are available.

Assembly Information Screen

Selecting the Assembly Information button from within your My Project window opens the Assembly Information dialog. Within this dialog, shown in Figure 1-6, you can define file properties, such as your company's name and versioning information, which will be embedded in the operating system's file attributes for your project's output. Note these values are stored as assembly attributes in `AssemblyInfo.vb`.

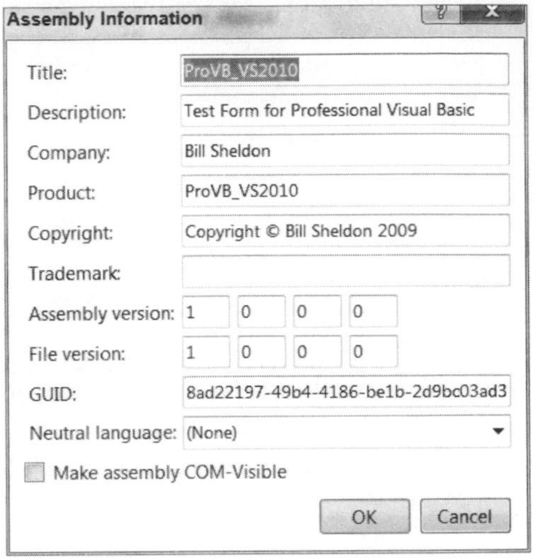

Assembly Attributes

The `AssemblyInfo.vb` file contains attributes, that are used to set information about the assembly. Each attribute has an *assembly modifier*, shown in the following example:

```
<Assembly: AssemblyTitle("")>
```

All the attributes set within this file provide information that is contained within the assembly metadata. The attributes contained within the file are summarized in Table 1-3:

FIGURE 1-6

TABLE 1-3: Attributes of the AssemblyInfo.vb File

ATTRIBUTE	DESCRIPTION
Assembly Title	This sets the name of the assembly, which appears within the file properties of the compiled file as the description.
Assembly Description	This attribute is used to provide a textual description of the assembly, which is added to the `Comments` property for the file.
Assembly Company	This sets the name of the company that produced the assembly. The name set here appears within the Version tab of the file properties.
Assembly Product	This attribute sets the product name of the resulting assembly. The product name appears within the Version tab of the file properties.
Assembly Copyright	The copyright information for the assembly. This value appears on the Version tab of the file properties.
Assembly Trademark	Used to assign any trademark information to the assembly. This information appears on the Version tab of the file properties.
Assembly Version	This attribute is used to set the version number of the assembly. Assembly version numbers can be generated, which is the default setting for .NET applications. This is covered in more detail in Chapter 31.

ATTRIBUTE	DESCRIPTION
Assembly File Version	This attribute is used to set the version number of the executable files. This and other deployment-related settings are covered in more detail in Chapter 34.
COM Visible	This attribute is used to indicate whether this assembly should be registered and made available to COM applications.
Guid	If the assembly is to be exposed as a traditional COM object, then the value of this attribute becomes the ID of the resulting type library.
NeutralResourcesLanguageAttribute	If specified, provides the default culture to use when the current user's culture settings aren't explicitly matched in a localized application. Localization is covered further in Chapter 27.

Compiler Settings

When you select the Compile tab of the project properties, you should see a window similar to the one shown in Figure 1-7. One update to Visual Studio 2010 is the return of the Build Configuration settings. In Visual Studio 2008, the Visual Basic Settings for Visual Studio removed these items from the display; and instead, when developers asked to debug their code, a debug version was built and executed, and only if the developer did an explicit build. (Note that if you are using Beta 2, you won't see these settings restored by default.)

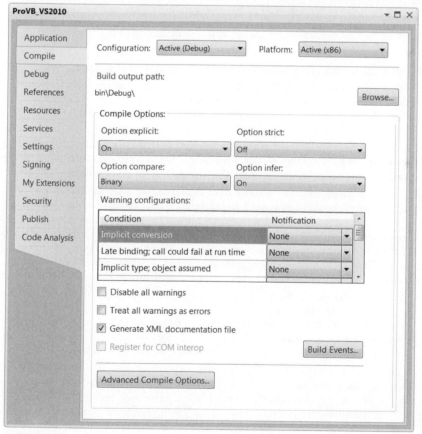

FIGURE 1-7

This presented a challenge because this wasn't the situation for any other set of Visual Studio settings; and Visual Basic developers were sometimes caught-out when sending what they thought was the latest build of their source code. If on their last "build" they were testing a fix and starting the debugger, then they hadn't rebuilt the release version. Thus, instead of sending a copy of the released version of their application with that last tested fix, they were really sending the last release build made before the fix. The return of these settings means that you, as the developer, have explicit control over the type of executable (release or debug, x64 or x86) that Visual Studio produces.

If you don't see these drop-downs in your display, you can restore them by selecting Tools ➪ Options, and then turning on the Advanced compile options. The main reason to restore these options has to do with two key features that are dependent on this setting. The first is Edit and Continue, which provides the capability to make a change in executing code and without restarting, having that change available in your running code while you continue to debug. This is a great tool for simple mistakes that are found during a debug session, and it is only supported for x86 (32-bit) targeted assemblies. This means you must explicitly target x86, as shown in Figure 1-7.

In Visual Studio 2008, the default was to target AnyCPU, but this meant that on a 64-bit developer workstation, Visual Studio was targeting a 64-bit assembly for your debug environment. When working on a 64-bit workstation, you must explicitly target an x86 environment in order to enable both Edit and Continue as well as the other dependency, COM-Interop. The second key feature related to x86 is COM. COM is a 32-bit protocol (as you'll see in Chapter 28 on COM-Interop, so you are required to target a 32-bit/x86 environment to support COM-Interop.

Aside from your default project file output directory, this page contains several compiler options. The Option Explicit, Option Infer, and Option Strict settings directly affect your variable usage. Each of the following settings can be edited by adding an `Option` declaration to the top of your source code file. When placed within a source file each of the following settings applies to all of the code entered in that source file, but only to the code in that file:

- ➤ **Option Explicit** — This option has not changed from previous versions of Visual Basic. When enabled, it ensures that every variable is explicitly declared. Of course, if you are using Option Strict, then this setting doesn't matter because the compiler won't recognize the type of an undeclared variable. To my knowledge, there's no good reason to ever turn this option off unless you are developing pure dynamic solutions, for which compile time typing is unavailable.

- ➤ **Option Strict** — When this option is enabled, the compiler must be able to determine the type of each variable, and if an assignment between two variables requires a type conversion — for example, from `Integer` to `Boolean` — then the conversion between the two types must be expressed explicitly.

- ➤ **Option Compare** — This option determines whether strings should be compared as binary strings or whether the array of characters should be compared as text. In most cases, leaving this as binary is appropriate. Doing a text comparison requires the system to convert the binary values that are stored internally prior to comparison. However, the advantage of a text-based comparison is that the character "A" is equal to "a" because the comparison is case-insensitive. This enables you to perform comparisons that don't require an explicit case conversion of the compared strings. In most cases, however, this conversion still occurs, so it's better to use binary comparison and explicitly convert the case as required.

- ➤ **Option Infer** — This option was new in Visual Studio 2008 and, was added due to the requirements of LINQ. When you execute a LINQ statement, you can have returned a data table that may or may not be completely typed in advance. As a result, the types need to be inferred when the command is executed. Thus, instead of a variable that is declared without an explicit type being defined as an object, the compiler and runtime attempt to infer the correct type for this object.

  Existing code developed with Visual Studio 2005 is unaware of this concept, so this option will be off by default for any project that is migrated to Visual Studio 2008 or Visual Studio 2010. New projects will have this option turned on, which means that if you cut and paste code from a Visual Studio 2005 project into a Visual Studio 2010 project, or vice versa, you'll need to be prepared for an error in the pasted code because of changes in how types are inferred.

From the properties page Option Explicit, Option Strict, Option Compare, and Option Infer can be set to either On or Off for your project. Visual Studio 2010 makes it easy for you to customize specific compiler conditions for your entire project. However, as noted, you can also make changes to the individual compiler checks that are set using something like Option Strict.

Notice that as you change your Option Strict settings in particular, the notifications with the top few conditions are automatically updated to reflect the specific requirements of this new setting. Therefore, you can literally create a custom version of the Option Strict settings by turning on and off individual compiler settings for your project. In general, this table lists a set of conditions that relate to programming practices you might want to avoid or prevent, and which you should definitely be aware of. The use of warnings for the majority of these conditions is appropriate, as there are valid reasons why you might want to use or avoid each but might also want to be able to do each.

Basically, these conditions represent possible runtime error conditions that the compiler can't detect in advance, except to identify that a possibility for that runtime error exists. Selecting a Warning for a setting bypasses that behavior, as the compiler will warn you but allow the code to remain. Conversely, setting a behavior to Error prevents compilation; thus, even if your code might be written to never have a problem, the compiler will prevent it from being used.

An example of why these conditions are noteworthy is the warning of an Instance variable accessing a `Shared` property. A `Shared` property is the same across all instances of a class. Thus, if a specific instance of a class is updating a `Shared` property, then it is appropriate to get a warning to that effect. This action is one that can lead to errors, as new developers sometimes fail to realize that a `Shared` property value is common across all instances of a class, so if one instance updates the value, then the new value is seen by all other instances. Thus, you can block this dangerous but certainly valid code to prevent errors related to using a `Shared` property.

As noted earlier, option settings can be specific to each source file. This involves adding a line to the top of the source file to indicate to the compiler the status of that `Option`. The following lines will override your project's default setting for the specified options. However, while this can be done on a per-source listing basis, this is not the recommended way to manage these options. For starters, consistently adding this line to each of your source files is time-consuming and potentially open to error:

```
Option Explicit On
Option Compare Text
Option Strict On
Option Infer On
```

Most experienced developers agree that using Option Strict and being forced to recognize when type conversions are occurring is a good thing. Certainly, when developing software that will be deployed in a production environment, anything that can be done to help prevent runtime errors is desirable. However, Option Strict can slow the development of a program because you are forced to explicitly define each conversion that needs to occur. If you are developing a prototype or demo component that has a limited life, you might find this option limiting.

If that were the end of the argument, then many developers would simply turn the option off and forget about it, but Option Strict has a runtime benefit. When type conversions are explicitly identified, the system performs them faster. Implicit conversions require the runtime system to first identify the types involved in a conversion and then obtain the correct handler.

Another advantage of Option Strict is that during implementation, developers are forced to consider every place a conversion might occur. Perhaps the development team didn't realize that some of the assignment operations resulted in a type conversion. Setting up projects that require explicit conversions means that the resulting code tends to have type consistency to avoid conversions, thus reducing the number of conversions in the final code. The result is not only conversions that run faster, but also, it is hoped, a smaller number of conversions.

Option Infer is a powerful feature. It is used as part of LINQ and the features that support LINQ, but it affects all code. In the past, you needed to write the `AS <type>` portion of every variable definition in order to have a variable defined with an explicit type. However, now you can dimension a variable and assign it an integer or set it equal to another object, and the `AS Integer` portion of your declaration isn't required, it is inferred as part of the assignment operation. Be careful with Option Infer; if abused it can make your code obscure, since it reduces readability by potentially hiding the true type associated with a variable. Some developers prefer to limit Option Infer to per file declarations to limit its use to when it is needed, for example with LINQ.

 How to use Option Infer in LINQ is covered in Chapter 10.

In addition, note that Option Infer is directly affected by Option Strict. In an ideal world, Option Strict Off would require that Option Infer also be turned off or disabled in the user interface. That isn't the case, although it is the behavior that is seen; once Option Strict is off, Option Infer is essentially ignored.

Below the grid of individual settings in Figure 1-7 is a series of check boxes. Two of these are self-explanatory and; the third is the option to generate XML comments for your assembly. These comments are generated based on the XML comments that you enter for each of the classes, methods, and properties in your source file.

Visual Basic Express has fewer check boxes, but users do have access to the Advanced Compile Options button. This button opens the Advanced Compiler Settings dialog shown in Figure 1-8. Note a couple of key elements on this screen, the first being the "Remove integer overflow checks" check box. When these options are enabled, the result is a performance hit on Visual Basic applications in comparison to C#. The compilation constants are values you shouldn't need to touch normally. Similarly, the generation of serialization assemblies is something that is probably best left in auto mode.

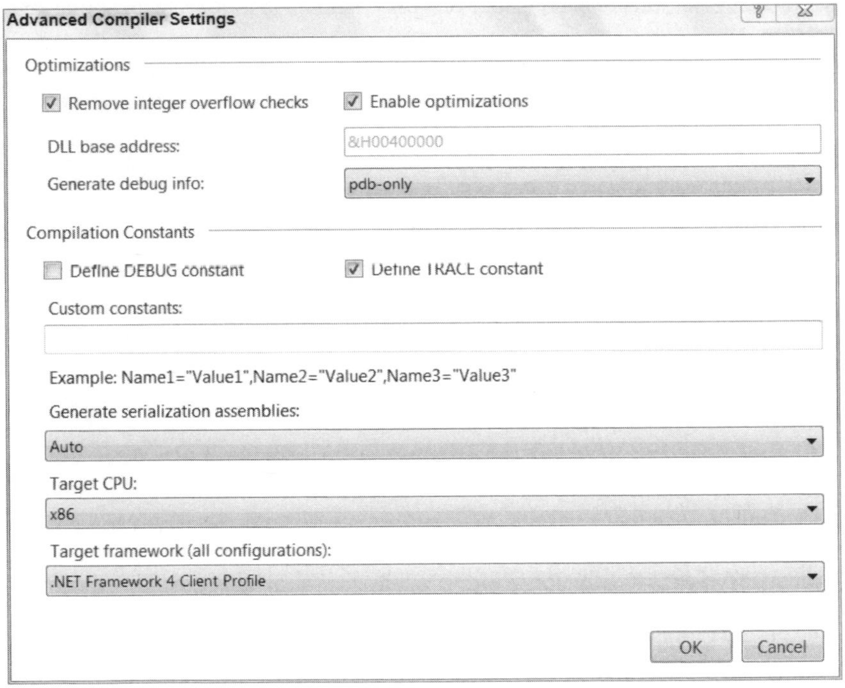

Advanced Compiler Settings

Optimizations

☑ Remove integer overflow checks   ☑ Enable optimizations

DLL base address: &H00400000

Generate debug info: pdb-only

Compilation Constants

☐ Define DEBUG constant   ☑ Define TRACE constant

Custom constants:

Example: Name1="Value1",Name2="Value2",Name3="Value3"

Generate serialization assemblies:

Auto

Target CPU:

x86

Target framework (all configurations):

.NET Framework 4 Client Profile

OK   Cancel

FIGURE 1-8

However, the last item on the screen enables you to target different environments. If you select a version prior to version 4, then, when you begin to add references, the Add References tab recognizes which version of .NET you are targeting and adjusts the list of available references to exclude those that are part of version 4 — similarly excluding 4, 3.5, and 3.0 if you are targeting .NET 2.0.

Note that this check occurs when adding references; there is no check when you change this value to see whether your updated value conflicts with any existing references. Therefore, if you change this value, then make sure you update any of your existing references to remove any that are part of .NET 4. You are bound to have at least one because when the template creates your project it automatically adds a series of references determined in part by the target framework specified when you created your application.

Debug Properties

The Express Edition of Visual Basic 2010 supports local debugging. This means it supports not only the .NET-related `Debug` and `Trace` classes discussed in Chapter 6, but also actual breakpoints and the associated interactive debugging available in all versions of Visual Studio. However, as noted, the full versions of Visual Studio provide enhanced debugging options not available in Visual Basic 2010 Express Edition. Figure 1-9 shows the project debugger startup options from Visual Studio 2010.

The default action shown is actually the only option available to Express users — which is to start the current project. However, Visual Studio 2010 developers have two additional options. The first is to start an external program. In other words, if you are working on a DLL or a user control, then you might want to have that application start, which can then execute your assembly. Doing this is essentially a shortcut, eliminating the need to bind to a running process.

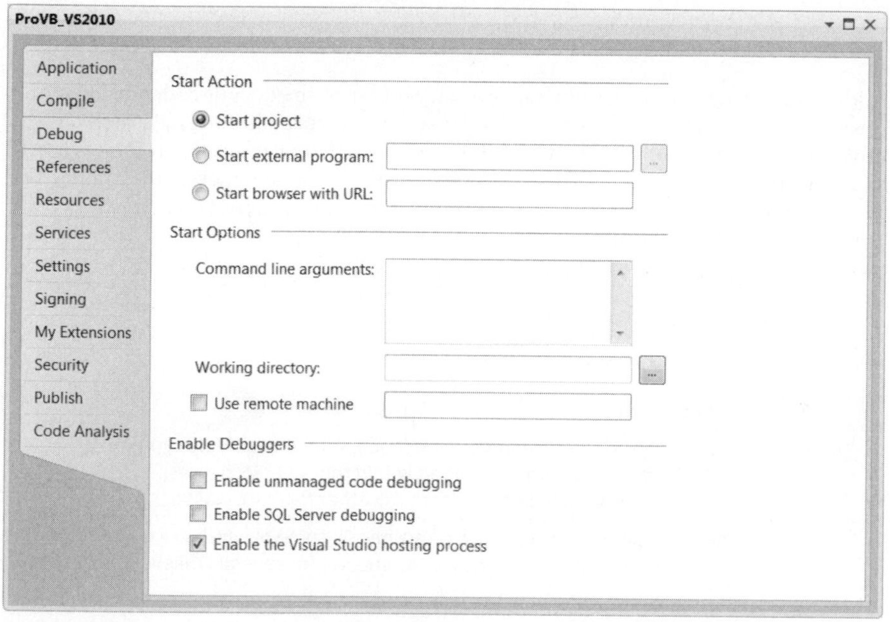

FIGURE 1-9

Similarly for Web development, you can reference a specific URL to start that Web application. This is often a mixed blessing, as with ASP.NET 2.0, Visual Studio automatically attempts to start an ASP.NET application based on the page you are currently editing. This is a change from ASP.NET 1.x, which allowed you to define a start page. Because ASP.NET 2.0 does not use project files, the new behavior was introduced. In most cases it works just fine, but if you have a Web application requiring authentication, then in most cases it makes more sense to actually place that URL into the debug settings for your application.

However, developers have three options related to starting the debugger. The first is to apply command-line arguments to the startup of a given application. This, of course, is most useful for console applications, but in some cases developers add command-line parameters to GUI applications. The second option is to select a different directory, a working directory, to be used to run the application. Generally, this isn't necessary; but it's desirable in some cases because of path or permission requirements or having an isolated runtime area.

As noted, Visual Studio 2010 provides support for remote debugging, although such debugging is involved and not configured for simple scenarios. Remote Debugging can be a useful tool when working with an integration test environment where developers are prevented from installing Visual Studio but need to be able to debug issues. However, you shouldn't be limited by just using the debugger for understanding what is occurring in your application at runtime.

Another alternative for determining what is occurring within a remote application is using the `Debug` and `Trace` classes. As noted in Chapter 6, the Debug and Trace classes combined with effective error handling, often make it faster and easier to determine remote errors then setting up the remote debugger. However, for those environments where an application runs only on a central server, and for which developers have the necessary permissions to run the debugger but not install a copy of Visual Studio, it is possible to leverage remote debugging.

Finally, as might be expected, users of Visual Studio 2010 who work with multiple languages, and who use tools that are tightly integrated with SQL Server, have additional debuggers. The first of these is support for debugging outside of the CLR — what is known as *unmanaged code*. As a Visual Basic developer, the only time you should be using unmanaged code is when you are referencing legacy COM components. The developers most likely to use this debugger work in C++.

The next option turns on support for SQL Server debugging, a potentially useful feature. In short, it's possible, although the steps are not trivial, to have the Visual Studio debugging engine step directly into T-SQL stored procedures so that you can see the interim results as they occur within a complex stored procedure.

References

It's possible to add additional references as part of your project. Similar to the default code files that are created with a new project, each project template has a default set of referenced libraries. Actually, it has a set of imported namespaces and a subset of the imported namespaces also referenced across the project. This means that while you can easily reference the classes in the referenced namespaces, you still need to fully qualify a reference to something less common. For example, to use a `StringBuilder` you'll need to specify the fully qualified name of `System.Text.StringBuilder`. Even though the `System.Text` namespace is referenced it hasn't been imported by default. For Windows Forms applications targeting .NET 4, the list of default referenced namespaces is fairly short, as shown in Table 1-4.

TABLE 1-4: Default References in a New Project

REFERENCE	DESCRIPTION
System	Often referred to as the root namespace. All the base data types (`String`, `Object`, and so on) are contained within the `System` namespace. This namespace also acts as the root for all other `System` classes.
System.Core	This dll contains a collection of namespaces, some of which are required to support LINQ to in-memory objects, as well as support for several OS-level interfaces.
System.Data	Classes associated with ADO.NET and database access. This namespace is the root for SQL Server, Oracle, and other data access classes.
System.Data .DataSetExtensions	Defines a collection of extension methods used by the core `DataSet` class. These are used when working with LINQ to DataSets.
System.Deployment	Classes used for ClickOnce Deployment. This namespace is covered in more detail in Chapter 34.
System.Drawing	Provides access to the GDI+ graphics functionality
System.Windows.Forms	Classes used to create traditional Windows-based applications. This namespace is covered in more detail in Chapters 14 and 15.
System.XML	Root namespace for all of the XML classes
System.XML.Linq	Root namespace to support the Language Integrated Query (LINQ) native language queries for XML data sources.

The preceding list of referenced libraries is for .NET 4, so if you instead create a project that targets .NET 2.0, this list will be shorter. Keep in mind that changing your target framework does not update any existing references. If you are going to attempt to target the .NET 2.0 Framework, then you'll want to remove references that have a version higher than 2.0.0.0. References such as System.Core enable new features in the System namespace that are associated with .NET 3.5.

To review details about the imported and referenced namespaces, select the References tab in your project properties display, as shown in Figure 1-10. This tab enables you to check for unused references and even define reference paths. More important, it is from this tab that you select other .NET Class Libraries and applications, as well as COM components. Selecting the Add drop-down button gives you the option to add a reference to a local DLL or a Web service.

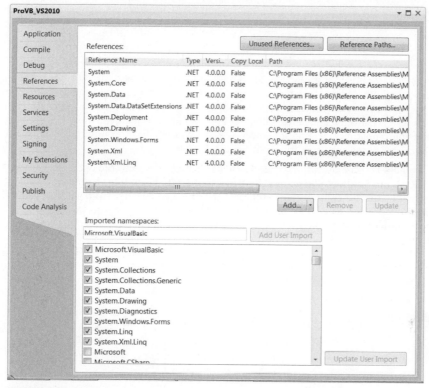

FIGURE 1-10

When referencing DLLs you have three options: Reference an assembly from the GAC, reference an assembly based on a file path, or reference another assembly from within your current solution. Each of these options has advantages and disadvantages. The only challenge for assemblies that are in the GAC is that your application is dependent on what is potentially a shared resource. In general, however, for assemblies that are already in the GAC, referencing them is a straightforward, easily maintainable process.

In addition to referencing libraries, you can reference other assemblies that are part of your solution. If your solution consists of more than a single project, then it is straightforward and highly recommended to use project references in order to enable those projects to reference each other. While you should avoid circular references — Project A references Project B which references Project A — using project references is preferred over file references. With project references, Visual Studio can map updates to these assemblies as they occur during a build of the solution. It's possible for Visual Studio to automatically update the referenced assemblies in your executable project to be the latest build of the referenced DLLs that are part of the same solution. Note that the target needs to be an executable. Visual Studio will automatically update references between DLL projects in a common solution.

This is different from adding a reference to a DLL that is located within a specified directory. When you create a reference via a path specification, Visual Studio can check that path for an updated copy of the reference, but your code is no longer as portable as it would be with a project reference. More important, unless there is a major revision, Visual Studio usually fails to detect the types of changes you are likely to make to that file during the development process. As a result, you'll need to manually update the referenced file in the local directory of the assembly that's referencing it. For your own code often it's best to leverage project references, rather than path-based references. However, for third party controls where you'll often only have an installed location, one which isn't likely to change as you move between machines, a path based reference can work.

On the other hand an alternative solution which is commonly used, is to ensure that instead of referencing third party controls based on their location, that instead 'copy local' references are used so that the version specific copy of the control deploys with the code that depends on it. This means that different versions of the controls can exist on the same server in different applications. Additionally because a local copy of the control is with the application, the application can be XCopy deployed without needing to register the controls.

Resources

In addition to referencing other assemblies, it is quite common for a .NET application to need to reference things such as images, icons, audio, and other files. These files aren't used to provide application logic but are used at runtime to provide support for the look, feel, and even text used to communicate with the application's user. In theory, you can reference a series of images associated with your application by looking for those images based on the installed file path of your application. Doing so, however, places your application's runtime behavior at risk, because a user might choose to replace, copy for profit, or just delete your files.

This is where project references become useful. Instead of placing the raw files onto the operating system alongside your executable, Visual Studio will package these files into your executable so that they are less likely to be lost or damaged. Figure 1-11 shows the Resources tab, which enables you to review and edit all the existing resources within a project, as well as import files for use as resources in your project. It even allows you to create new resources from scratch.

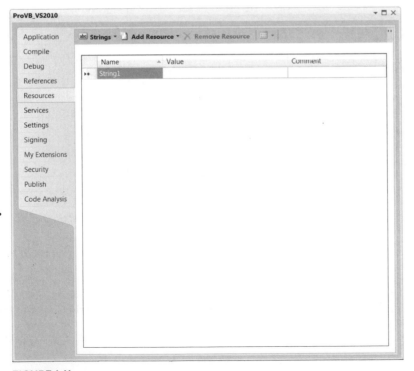

FIGURE 1-11

Note one little-known feature of this tab: Using the Add Resource drop-down button and selecting an image (not an existing image but one based on one of the available image types) will create a new image file and automatically open Microsoft Paint (for Express Edition developers); this enables you to actually create the image that will be in the image file.

Users of Visual Studio 2010 have additional capabilities not supported by Visual Basic's Express Edition. For one thing, instead of using Paint, Visual Studio provides a basic image-editing tool, so when Visual Studio developers add a new image (not from a file), this editor opens within Visual Studio.

Additionally, within the list of Add Resource items, Visual Studio users can select or create a new icon. Choosing to create a new icon opens Visual Studio's icon editor, which provides a basic set of tools for creating custom icons to use as part of your application. This makes working with `.ico` files easier because you don't have to hunt for or purchase such files online; instead, you can create your own icons.

However, images aren't the only resources that you can embed with your executable. Resources also apply to the fixed text strings that your application uses. By default, people tend to embed this text directly into the source code so that it is easily accessible to the developer. Unfortunately, this leaves the application difficult to localize for use with a second language. The solution is to group all of those text strings together, thereby creating a resource file containing all of the text strings, which is still part of and easily accessible to the application source code. When the application is converted for use in another language, this list of strings can be converted, making the process of localization easier. Localization is covered in detail in Chapter 27.

 The next tab is the Services tab. This tab is discussed in more detail in Chapter 13, which addresses services.

Settings

As noted earlier in the discussion of the Solution Explorer, the default project template does not create any application settings; accordingly, an `app.config` file is neither needed nor created. `app.config` files are XML files that define any custom application settings that a developer wants to be able to change without needing to recompile the application. Because these settings live in an XML file, they can be modified in between or even during application execution.

One original goal of .NET was to reduce the version conflict that can occur when a component has registered with global settings. A conflict would occur if two different applications were attempting to reference two different versions of that component. Because the settings were global and stored in the central system registry, only one could be registered correctly. Since the different applications each wanted its specific version of the component and related settings, one of the applications worked while the other application broke.

.NET provided the capability to place version-specific project references in a local directory with the application, enabling two different applications to reference the appropriate version of that component. However, the second part of the problem was the central application settings. The `app.config` file provides the same capability, but its goal is to allow for local storage of application settings. Under .NET 1.x, support for application settings was still minimal, as most developers were still looking to the central system registry for this purpose. At the same time, the developer tools associated with settings were also minimal.

Fortunately, under .NET 2.0 this changed dramatically. Visual Studio 2010 provides significant support for application settings, including the Settings tab, shown in Figure 1-12. This tab enables Visual Basic developers to identify application settings and automatically create these settings within the `app.config` file.

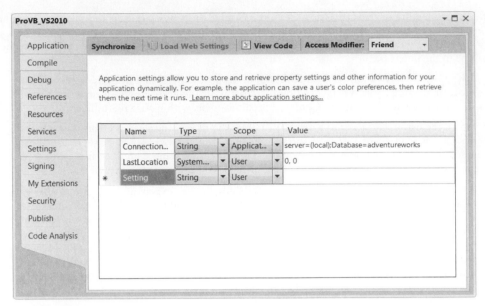

FIGURE 1-12

Figure 1-12 illustrates several elements related to the application settings capabilities of Visual Basic. The first setting is of type String. Under .NET 1.x, all application settings were seen as strings, and this was considered a weakness. Accordingly, the second setting, LastLocation, exposes the Type drop-down, illustrating that under Visual Studio 2010 you can create a setting that has a well-defined type.

However, strongly typed settings are not the most significant set of changes related to application settings. The very next column defines the scope of a setting. There are two possible options: application wide or user specific. The settings defined with application scope are available to all users of the application. As shown in Figure 1-12, this example creates a sample connection string to store for the application.

The alternative is a user-specific setting. Such settings have a default value; in this case, the last location defaults to 0,0. However, once a user has read that default setting, the application generally updates and saves the user-specific value for that setting. As indicated by the LastLocation setting, each user of the application might close it after having moved it to a new location on the screen; and the goal of such a setting would be to reopen the application where it was last located. Thus, the application would update this setting value, and Visual Basic makes it easy to do this, as shown in the following code:

```
My.Settings.LastLocation = Me.Location
My.Settings.Save()
```

That's right — Visual Basic requires only two lines of code that leverage the My namespace in order for you to update a user's application setting and save the new value. Meanwhile, let's take a look at what is occurring within the newly generated app.config file. The following XML settings demonstrate how the app.config file defines the setting values that you manipulate from within Visual Studio:

```
<?xml version="1.0" encoding="utf-8" ?>
<configuration>
    <configSections>
        <sectionGroup name="userSettings" type="System.Configuration.
UserSettingsGroup, System, Version=4.0.0.0, Culture=neutral,
PublicKeyToken=b77a5c561934e089" >
```

```xml
                    <section name="ProVB_VS2010.My.MySettings" type="System.
Configuration.ClientSettingsSection, System, Version=4.0.0.0, Culture=neutral,
PublicKeyToken=b77a5c561934e089" allowExeDefinition="MachineToLocalUser"
requirePermission="false" />
            </sectionGroup>
            <sectionGroup name="applicationSettings" type="System.Configuration.
ApplicationSettingsGroup, System, Version=4.0.0.0, Culture=neutral,
PublicKeyToken=b77a5c561934e089" >
                    <section name="ProVB_VS2010.My.MySettings" type="System.Configuration.
ClientSettingsSection, System, Version=4.0.0.0, Culture=neutral,
PublicKeyToken=b77a5c561934e089" requirePermission="false" />
            </sectionGroup>
        </configSections>
        <system.diagnostics>
            <sources>
                <!-- This section defines the logging configuration for My.Application.Log -->
                <source name="DefaultSource" switchName="DefaultSwitch">
                    <listeners>
                        <add name="FileLog"/>
                        <!-- Uncomment the below section to write to the Application Event Log -->
                        <!--<add name="EventLog"/>-->
                    </listeners>
                </source>
            </sources>
            <switches>
                <add name="DefaultSwitch" value="Information" />
            </switches>
            <sharedListeners>
                <add name="FileLog"
                    type="Microsoft.VisualBasic.Logging.FileLogTraceListener, Microsoft.
VisualBasic, Version=8.0.0.0, Culture=neutral, PublicKeyToken=b03f5f7f11d50a3a,
processorArchitecture=MSIL"
                    initializeData="FileLogWriter"/>
                <!-- Uncomment the below section and replace APPLICATION_NAME with the
name of your application to write to the Application Event Log -->
                <!--<add name="EventLog"
type="System.Diagnostics.EventLogTraceListener" initializeData="APPLICATION_NAME"/>-->
            </sharedListeners>
        </system.diagnostics>
        <userSettings>
            <ProVB_VS2010.My.MySettings>
                <setting name="LastLocation" serializeAs="String">
                    <value>0, 0</value>
                </setting>
            </ProVB_VS2010.My.MySettings>
        </userSettings>
        <applicationSettings>
            <ProVB_VS2010.My.MySettings>
                <setting name="ConnectionString" serializeAs="String">
                    <value>server=(local);Database=adventureworks</value>
                </setting>
            </ProVB_VS2010.My.MySettings>
        </applicationSettings>
</configuration>
```

Code snippet from app.config

As shown here, Visual Studio automatically generated all the XML needed to define these settings and save the default values. Note that individual user settings are not saved back into the config file, but rather to a user-specific working directory. In fact, it is possible not only to update application settings with Visual Basic, but also to arrange to encrypt those settings, although this behavior is outside the scope of what you can do from Visual Studio.

Other Project Property Tabs

In addition to the tabs that have been examined in detail, there are other tabs which are more specific. In most cases these tabs are used only in specific situations that do not apply to all projects.

Signing

This tab is typically used in conjunction with deployment. If you are interested in creating a commercial application that needs to be installed on client systems, you'll want to sign your application. There are several advantages to signing your application, including the capability to publish it via ClickOnce deployment. Therefore, it is possible to sign an application with a developer key if you want to deploy an application internally.

My Extensions

The My Extensions tab enables you to create and leverage extensions to Visual Basic's My namespace. By default, Visual Studio 2010 ships with extensions to provide My namespace shortcuts for key WPF and Web applications.

Security

This tab enables you to define the security requirements of your application. You'll need these as part of the ClickOnce publishing process, which is covered as part of deployment in Chapter 34.

Publish

This tab is used to configure and initiate the publishing of an application. From this tab you can update the published version of the application and determine where to publish it. This tab is also covered in more detail in Chapter 34.

Code Analysis

This tab is only available for Visual Studio 2010 Premium or Ultimate. The tab enables the developer to turn on and configure the static code analysis settings. These settings are used after compilation to perform automated checks against your code. Because these checks can take significant time, especially for a large project, they must be manually turned on.

PROJECT PROVB_VS2010

The Form Designer opens by default when a new project is created. If you have closed it, then you can easily reopen it by right-clicking Form1.vb in the Solution Explorer and selecting View Designer from the pop-up menu. From this window, you can also bring up the Code view for this form. However, Figure 1-13 illustrates the default view you see when your project template completes. On the screen is the design surface upon which you can drag controls from the Toolbox to build your user interface and update properties associated with your form.

The Properties pane, shown in more detail in Figure 1-14, is by default placed in the lower-right corner of the Visual Studio window. Like many of the other windows in the IDE, if you close it, it can be accessed through the View menu. Alternatively, you can use the F4 key to reopen this window. The Properties pane is used to set the properties of the currently selected control, or for the Form as a whole.

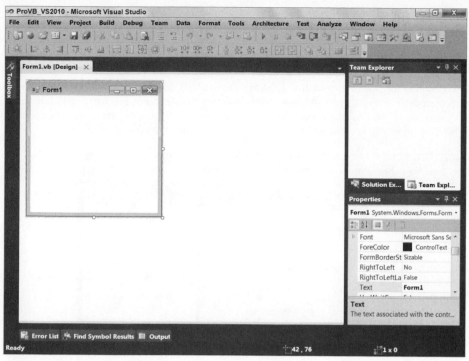

FIGURE 1-13

Each control you place on your form has its own distinct set of properties. For example, in the Design view, select your form. You'll see the Properties window adjust to display the properties of Form1 (refer to Figure 1-14). This is the list of properties associated with your form. If you want to limit how small a user can reduce the display area of your form, then you can now define this as a property.

For your sample, go to the Text property and change the default of Form1 to "Professional VB.NET." Once you have accepted the property change, the new value is displayed as the caption of your form. Later in this section, you'll set form properties in code. You'll see that .NET properties are defined within your source file, unlike other environments where properties you edit through the user interface are hidden in some binary or proprietary portion of the project.

Now that you've looked at the form's properties, open the code associated with this file by either right-clicking Form1.vb in the Solution Explorer and selecting Code view, or right-clicking the form in the Design view and selecting View Code from the pop-up menu.

The initial display of the form looks very simple. There is no code in the `Form1.vb` file. Visual Basic 2005 introduced a capability called *partial classes*. Partial classes are covered briefly in Chapter 2, and Visual Studio leverages them for the code, which is generated as part of the user interface designer.

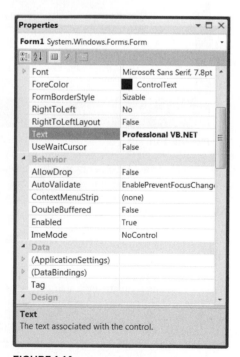

FIGURE 1-14

Visual Studio places all the generated source code for your form in the file `Form1.Designer.vb`. Because the "Designer" portion of this name is a convention that Visual Studio recognizes, it hides these files by default when you review your project in the Solution Explorer. As noted earlier, by asking Visual Studio to "show all files," you can find these generated files. If you open a "Designer.vb" file, you'll see that quite a bit of custom code is generated by Visual Studio and already in your project.

To do this, go to the toolbar located in the Solution Explorer window and select the Show All Files button. This will change your project display and a small plus sign will appear next to the `Form1.vb` file. Expanding this entry displays the `Form1.Designer.vb` file, which you can open within the IDE. Doing this for `Form1.Designer.vb` for the ProVB_VS2010 project you created will result in a window similar to the one shown in Figure 1-15.

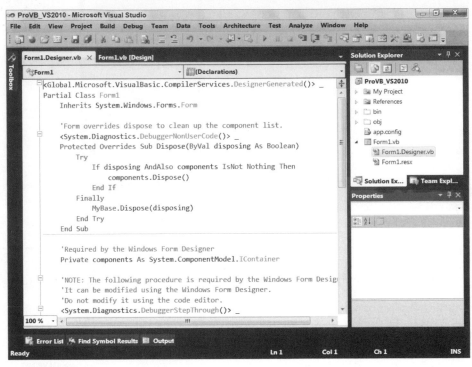

FIGURE 1-15

Note that the contents of this file are generated. For now, don't try to make any changes. Visual Studio automatically regenerates the entire file when a property is changed, so any changes you make will be lost. The following lines start the declaration for your form in the file `Form1.Designer.vb`:

Available for download on Wrox.com

```
<Global.Microsoft.VisualBasic.CompilerServices.DesignerGenerated()> _
Partial Class Form1
    Inherits System.Windows.Forms.Form
```

Code snippet from Form1.Designer

The first line is an attribute that can be ignored. Next is the line that actually declares a new class called `Form1`. Note that in spite of the naming convention used by Visual Studio to hide the generated UI class implementation, the name of your class and the file in which it exists are not tightly coupled. Thus, your form will be referenced in the code as Form1 unless you modify the name used in the class declaration. Similarly, you can rename the file that contains the class without changing the actual name of the class.

One powerful result of forms being implemented as classes is that you can now derive one form from another form. This technique is called *visual inheritance*, although the elements that are actually inherited may not be displayed.

Form Properties Set in Code

As noted earlier, Visual Studio keeps every object's custom property values in the source code. To do this, it adds a method to your form class called `InitializeComponent`. As the name suggests, this method handles the initialization of the components contained on the form. A comment before the procedure warns you that the Form Designer modifies the code contained in the procedure, and that you should not modify the code directly. This module is part of the `Form1.Designer.vb` source file, and Visual Studio updates this section as changes are made through the IDE.

```
'NOTE: The following procedure is required by the Windows Form Designer
'It can be modified using the Windows Form Designer.
'Do not modify it using the code editor.
<System.Diagnostics.DebuggerStepThrough()> _
Private Sub InitializeComponent()
    Me.SuspendLayout()
    '
    'Form1
    '
    Me.AutoScaleDimensions = New System.Drawing.SizeF(8.0!, 16.0!)
    Me.AutoScaleMode = System.Windows.Forms.AutoScaleMode.Font
    Me.ClientSize = New System.Drawing.Size(328, 258)
    Me.Name = "Form1"
    Me.Text = "Professional VB.NET"
    Me.ResumeLayout(False)

End Sub
```

Code snippet from Form1.Designer

The seven lines of the `InitializeComponent` procedure assign values to the properties of your `Form1` class. All the properties of the form and controls are now set directly in code. When you change the value of a property of the form or a control through the Properties window, an entry is added to `InitializeComponent` that assigns that value to the property. Previously, while examining the Properties window, you set the `Text` property of the form to Professional VB.NET, which caused the following line of code to be added automatically:

```
Me.Text = "Professional VB.NET"
```

The properties of the form class that are set in `InitializeComponent` are shown in Table 1-5.

TABLE 1-5: Properties Set by InitializeComponent

PROPERTY	DESCRIPTION
SuspendLayout	Specifies that the form should not make updates to what is displayed to the user. It is called so that as each change is made, the form doesn't seem to appear in pieces.
AutoScaleDimensions	Initializes the size of the font used to lay out the form at design time. At runtime, the font that is actually rendered is compared with this property, and the form is scaled accordingly.
AutoScaleMode	Indicates that the form will use fonts that are automatically scaled based on the display characteristics of the runtime environment.
ClientSize	Sets the area in which controls can be placed (the client area). It is the size of the form minus the size of the title bar and form borders.
Name	This property is used to set the textual name of the form.
ResumeLayout	This tells the form that it should resume the normal layout and displaying of its contents.

Code Regions

Source files in Visual Studio allow you to collapse blocks of code. The idea is that in most cases you can reduce the amount of onscreen code, which seems to separate other modules within a given class, by collapsing the code so it isn't visible; this feature is known as *outlining*. For example, if you are comparing the load and save methods and in between you have several other blocks of code, then you can effectively "hide" this code, which isn't part of your current focus.

By default, there is a minus sign next to every method (sub or function). This makes it easy to hide or show code on a per-method basis. If the code for a method is hidden, the method declaration is still shown and has a plus sign next to it indicating that the body code is hidden. This feature is very useful when you are working on a few key methods in a module and you want to avoid scrolling through many screens of code that are not relevant to the current task.

It is also possible to create custom regions of code so you can hide and show portions of your source files. For example, it is common to see code where all of the properties are placed in one region, and all of the public methods are placed in another. The `#Region` directive is used for this within the IDE, though it has no effect on the actual application. A region of code is demarcated by the `#Region` directive at the top and the `#End Region` directive at the end. The `#Region` directive that is used to begin a region should include a description, which appears next to the plus sign shown when the code is minimized.

The outlining enhancement was in part inspired by the fact that the original Visual Studio designers generated a lot of code and placed all of this code in the main vb file for that form. It wasn't until Visual Studio 2005 and partial classes that this generated code was placed in a separate file. Thus the region allowed the generated code section to be hidden when a source file was opened. Being able to see the underpinnings of your generated UI does make it is easier to understand what is happening, and possibly to manipulate the process in special cases. However, as you can imagine, it can become problematic; hence the `#Region` directive, which can be used to organize groups of common code and then visually minimize them.

Visual Studio 2010 developers, but not Express Edition developers, can also control outlining throughout a source file. Outlining can be turned off by selecting Edit ➪ Outlining ➪ Stop Outlining from the Visual Studio menu. This menu also contains some other useful functions. A section of code can be temporarily hidden by highlighting it and selecting Edit ➪ Outlining ➪ Hide Selection. The selected code will be replaced by ellipses with a plus sign next to it, as if you had dynamically identified a region within the source code. Clicking the plus sign displays the code again.

Tear-Away Tabs

You may have noticed in Figure 1-15 that the Code View and Form Designer windows open in a tabbed environment. This environment is the default for working with the code windows inside Visual Studio, but you can change this. As with any other window in Visual Studio 2010, you can mouse down on the tab and drag it to another location.

What makes this especially useful in Visual Studio 2010 is that you can drag a tab completely off of the main window and have it open as a standalone window elsewhere. Thus, you can take the current source file you are editing and drag it to a separate monitor from the remainder of Visual Studio — examples of this are the screens earlier in this chapter showing the project properties. If you review those images you'll see that they are not embedded within the larger Visual Studio 2010 frame but have been pulled out into their own window.

Running ProVB_VS2010

Now that you've reviewed the elements of your generated project, let's test the code before continuing. To run an application from within Visual Studio, you have several options; the first is to click the Start button, which looks like the Play button on a tape recorder. Alternatively, you can go to the Debug menu and select Start. Finally, the most common way of launching applications is to press F5.

Once the application starts, an empty form is displayed with the standard control buttons (in the upper-right corner) from which you can control the application. The form name should be Professional VB.NET, which you applied earlier. At this point, the sample doesn't have any custom code to examine, so the next step is to add some simple elements to this application.

Customizing the Text Editor

In addition to being able to customize the overall environment provided by Visual Studio, you can customize several specific elements related to your development environment. More so than in any previous version, the capability to modify the environment has been enhanced. With Visual Studio 2010, the user interface components have been rewritten using WPF so that the entire display provides a much more graphical environment and better designer support.

Both Visual Studio 2010 and Visual Basic 2010 Express Edition have a rich set of customizations related to a variety of different environment and developer settings. Admittedly, Visual Studio 2010's feature set offers a larger number of options for editing, but rest assured that the Express Edition contains many more options for editing than most people expect. For example, common to both IDEs is a text editor that allows for customization. If you've ever had to show code to an audience — for example, in a group code review — the capability to adjust things such as font size and other similar options is great.

To leverage Visual Studio's settings, select Tools ➪ Options to open the Options dialog, shown in Figure 1-16. Within the dialog, make sure the Show all settings check box is selected. Next, select the Text Editor folder, and then the All Languages folder. This section enables you to make changes to the text editor that are applied across every supported development language. Additionally, you can select the Basic folder to make changes that are specific to how the text editor behaves when you edit VB source code.

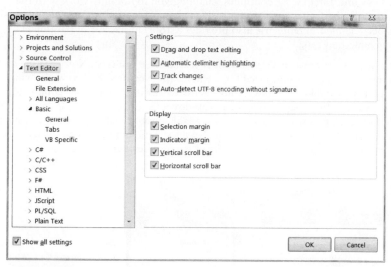

FIGURE 1-16

From this dialog, it is possible to modify the number of spaces that each tab will insert into your source code and to manage several other elements of your editing environment. Within this dialog you see settings that are common for all text editing environments, as well as the ability to customize specific settings for specific languages. For example the section specific to Visual Basic includes settings that allow for word wrapping and line numbers. One little-known but useful capability of the text editor is line numbering. Checking the Line numbers check box will cause the editor to number all lines, which provides an easy way to unambiguously reference lines of code.

Visual Studio also provides a visual indicator so you can track your changes as you edit. Enabling the Track changes setting under the Text Editor options causes Visual Studio to provide a colored indicator in places where you have modified a file. This indicator appears as a colored bar at the left margin of your display. It shows which portions of a source file have been recently edited and whether those changes have been saved to disk.

IntelliSense, Code Expansion, and Code Snippets

One of the reasons why Microsoft Visual Studio is such a popular development environment is because it was designed to support developer productivity. That sounds really good, but let's back it up. People who are unfamiliar with Visual Studio might just assume that "productivity" refers to organizing and starting projects. Certainly, as shown by the project templates and project settings discussed so far, this is true, but those features don't speed your development after you've created the project.

This section covers three features that target your productivity while writing code. They are of differing value and are specific to Visual Studio. The first, IntelliSense, has always been a popular feature of Microsoft tools and applications. The second feature, code expansion, is another popular feature available since Visual Studio 2005: It enables you to type a keyword, such as "select," and then press the Tab key to automatically insert a generic select-case code block, which you can then customize. Finally, going beyond this, you can use the right mouse button and insert a code snippet at the location of your mouse click. As you can tell, each of these builds on the developer productivity capabilities of Visual Studio.

IntelliSense

IntelliSense has been enhanced in Visual Studio 2010. Early versions of IntelliSense required you to first identify a class or property in order to make uses of the IntelliSense feature. Beginning with Visual Studio 2008, IntelliSense is activated with the first letter you type, so you can quickly identify classes, commands, and keywords that you need. This capability continues with Visual Studio 2010, but the IDE team worked hard to enhance IntelliSense performance so that it won't sometimes feel like the IDE is trying to keep up with your typing.

Once you've selected a class or keyword, IntelliSense continues, enabling you to not only work with the methods of a class, but also automatically display the list of possible values associated with an enumerated list of properties when one has been defined. IntelliSense also provides a ToolTip-like list of parameter definitions when you are making a method call.

Figure 1-17 illustrates how IntelliSense becomes available with the first character you type. Note that the drop-down window has two tabs on the bottom; one is optimized for the items that you are likely to want, while the other shows you everything that is available. In addition, IntelliSense works with multiword commands. For example, if you type **Exit** and a space, IntelliSense displays a drop-down list of keywords that could follow Exit. Other keywords that offer drop-down lists to present available options include Goto, Implements, Option, and Declare. In most cases, IntelliSense displays more ToolTip information in the environment than in past versions of Visual Studio, and helps developers match up pairs of parentheses, braces, and brackets.

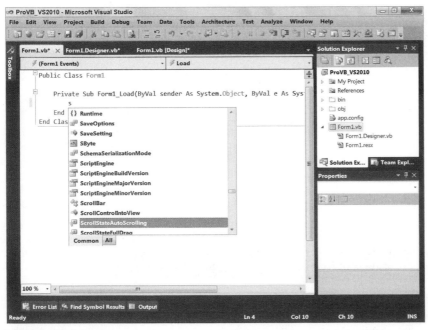

FIGURE 1-17

Finally, note that IntelliSense is based on your editing context. While editing a file, you may reach a point where you are looking for a specific item to show up in IntelliSense but when you repeatedly type slightly different versions, nothing appears. IntelliSense recognizes that you aren't in a method or you are outside of the scope of a class, so it removes items that are inappropriate for the current location in your source code from the list of items available from IntelliSense.

Code Expansion

Going beyond IntelliSense is code expansion. Code expansion recognizes that certain keywords are consistently associated with other lines of code. At the most basic level, this occurs when you declare a new `Function` or `Sub`: Visual Studio automatically inserts the `End Sub` or `End Function` line once you press Enter. Essentially, Visual Studio is expanding the declaration line to include its matching endpoint.

However, true code expansion goes further than this. With true code expansion, you can type a keyword such as `For`, `ForEach`, `Select`, or any of a number of Visual Basic keywords. If you then use the Tab key, Visual Studio will attempt to recognize that keyword and insert the block of code that you would otherwise need to remember and type yourself. For example, instead of needing to remember how to format the control values of a `Select` statement, you can just type this first part of the command and then press Tab to get the following code block:

```
Select Case VariableName
    Case 1
    Case 2
    Case Else
End Select
```

Unfortunately, this is a case where just showing you the code isn't enough. That's because the code that is inserted has active regions within it that represent key items you will customize. Thus, Figure 1-18 provides a better representation of what is inserted when you expand the `Select` keyword into a full `Select Case` statement.

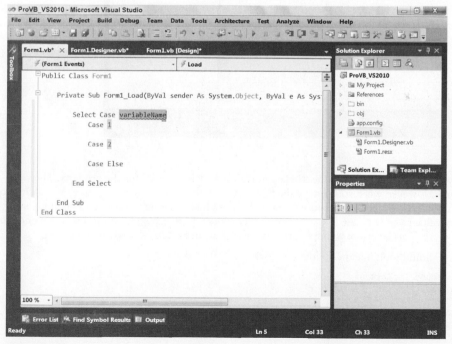

FIGURE 1-18

When the block is inserted, the editor automatically positions your cursor in the first highlighted block — `VariableName`. When you start typing the name of the variable that applies, the editor automatically clears that static `VariableName` string, which is acting as a placeholder. Once you have entered the variable name you want, you can just press Tab. At that point the editor automatically jumps to the next highlighted item. This capability to insert a block of boilerplate code and have it automatically respond to your customization is extremely useful.

Code expansion enables you to quickly shift between the values that need to be customized, but these values are also linked where appropriate, as in the next example. Another code expansion shortcut creates a new property in a class. If at the class level you type the letters "prop" and then press the Tab key twice, after the first tab you'll find that your letters become the word "Property"; and after the second tab the code shown in Figure 1-19 will be added to your existing code. On the surface this code is similar to what you see when you expand the `Select` statement. Note that although you type **prop**, even the internal value is part of this code expansion. Furthermore, although Visual Basic implemented a property syntax that is no longer dependent on an explicit backing field, this expansion provides the more robust syntax that uses an explicit backing field.

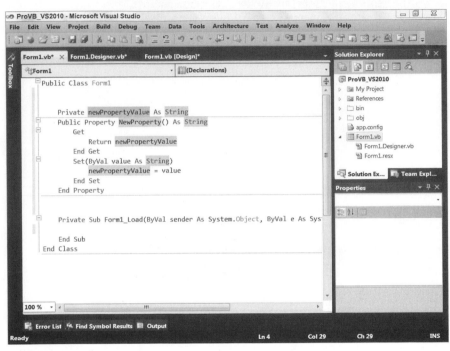

FIGURE 1-19

The difference, however, is that the same value `String` in Figure 1-19 is repeated for the property. The value you see is the default. However, when you change the first such entry from `String` to `Integer`, Visual Studio automatically updates all three locations because it knows they are linked. Using the code shown in Figure 1-19, update the property value to be `m_Count`. Press Tab and change the type to `Integer`; press Tab again and label the new property `Count`. This gives you a simple property on this form for use later when debugging.

The completed code should look like the following block:

Available for download on Wrox.com

```
Private m_Count As Integer
Public Property Count() As Integer
    Get
        Return m_Count
    End Get
    Set(ByVal value As Integer)
        m_Count = value
    End Set
End Property
```

Code snippet from Form1

This capability to fully integrate the template supporting the expanded code with the highlighted elements, helping you navigate to the items you need to edit, makes code expansion such a valuable tool.

Code Snippets

You can, with a click of your mouse, browse a library of code blocks, which, as with code expansion, you can insert into your source file. However, unlike code expansion, these snippets aren't triggered by a keyword. Instead, you right-click and (as shown in Figure 1-20) select Insert Snippet from the context menu. This starts the selection process for whatever code you want to insert.

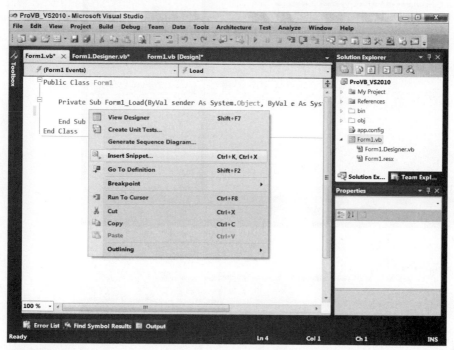

FIGURE 1-20

The snippet library, which is installed with Visual Studio, is fully expandable, as discussed later in this chapter. Snippets are categorized by the function on which each is focused. For example, all the code you can reach via code expansion is also available as snippets, but snippets go well beyond that list. There are snippet blocks for XML-related actions, for operating system interface code, for items related to Windows Forms, and, of course, a lot of data-access-related blocks. Unlike code expansion, which enhances the language in a way similar to IntelliSense, code snippets are blocks of code focused on functions developers often write from scratch.

As shown in Figure 1-21, the insertion of a snippet triggers the creation of a placeholder tag and a context window showing the categories of snippets. Each of the folders can contain a combination of snippet files or subdirectories containing still more snippet files. Visual Basic 2010 Express contains a subset of the folders provided with Visual Studio 2010. In addition, Visual Studio includes the folder My Code Snippets, to which you can add your own custom snippet files.

Selecting a folder enables you to select from one of its subfolders or a snippet file. Once you select the snippet of interest, Visual Studio inserts the associated code into your source file. Figure 1-22 shows the result of adding an operating system snippet to some sample code. The selected snippet was Windows ⇨ Event Logs ⇨ Read Entries Created by a Particular Application from the Event Log, which isn't included with Visual Basic 2010 Express, although the code is still valid.

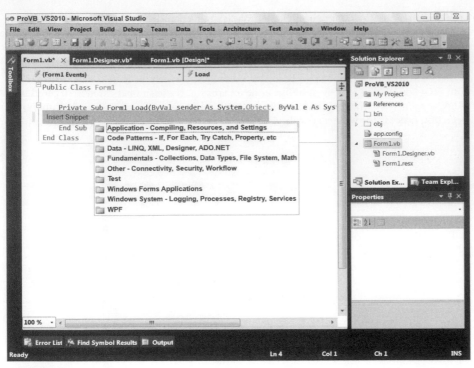

FIGURE 1-21

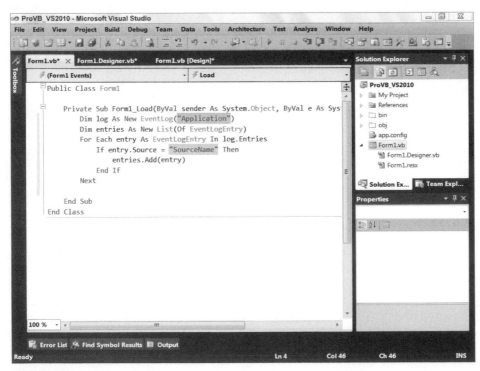

FIGURE 1-22

As you can see, this code snippet is specific to reading the Application Log. This snippet is useful because many applications log their errors to the Event Log so that they can be reviewed either locally or from another machine in the local domain. The key, however, is that the snippet has pulled in the necessary class references, many of which might not be familiar to you, and has placed them in context. This reduces not only the time spent typing this code, but also the time spent recalling exactly which classes need to be referenced and which methods need to be called and customized.

Finally, it is also possible to shortcut the menu tree. Specifically, if you know the shortcut for a snippet, you can type that and then press Tab to have Visual Studio insert the snippet. For example, typing **evReadApp** followed by pressing Tab will insert the same snippet shown in Figure 1-22.

Tools such as code snippets and especially code expansion are even more valuable when you work in multiple languages. Keep in mind, however, that Visual Studio isn't limited to the features that come in the box. It's possible to extend Visual Studio not only with additional controls and project templates, but also with additional editing features.

Additional Components for Visual Studio

You might be interested in two additional tools that work with Visual Studio. Even better, both are free. The first is a tool for creating your own Visual Basic snippets. As discussed, snippets can be powerful tools when you need to replicate relatively small but commonly used blocks of code that will be customized. While Visual Studio ships with several such snippets, Microsoft probably hasn't included the snippet you want the most.

This is where the first tool comes in: a Snippet Editor for Visual Basic code snippets. This editor doesn't actually live within Visual Studio; it just updates the snippet files you want to use from Visual Studio. Behind the scenes, snippets are actually XML files with embedded text that represents the code used in the snippet. What the Snippet Editor does is read that XML and interpret all of the embedded logic related to things such as replacement blocks. This tool makes it possible for Visual Basic developers to create custom snippets without worrying about the XML formatting details. It is available from MSDN at `http://msdn2` `.microsoft.com/en-us/vbasic/ms789085.aspx`.

The second tool is a true add-in to Visual Basic. When Microsoft was announcing features for .NET 2.0, it was apparent that Visual Basic and C# had different feature lists. Over time, the developers in each community started to better understand what these features represented, and in many cases demanded their inclusion. One such feature was native support in C# for refactoring, the capability to modify a variable name — for example, to take "i" and call it "loopControl" so that it's more readable. Modifying code to improve structure, performance, and maintainability is referred to generically as *refactoring*.

Traditionally, such changes might make the code more maintainable but it often entailed more risk than reward; as a result they seldom were made. The problem, of course, is that a human tends to miss that one remaining reference to the old version of that method or variable name. More important, it was a time-consuming task to find all of the correct references. Fortunately, the compiler knows where these are, and that's the idea behind automated refactoring: You tell Visual Studio what you want to change and it goes through your code and makes all the necessary changes, using the same rules the compiler uses to compile your code.

This is a great maintenance tool; unfortunately, by the time most Visual Basic developers understood what it implied, it was too late for the Visual Basic team to implement a solution in Visual Studio 2005. However, the team did do better than just say, "So sad, too bad." They found a commercial product that actually had more features than what the C# team was developing from scratch. Then they bought a license for every Visual Studio developer, allowing free download of the tool. This solution worked so well for everyone involved that they chose to continue it in Visual Studio 2008 and Visual Studio 2010. With refactoring, you can quickly clean up gnarly, hard-to-read code and turn it into well-structured logic that's much more maintainable. The free version of the refactoring tool is available at `www.devexpress` `.com/Products/NET/IDETools/VBRefactor/`.

ENHANCING A SAMPLE APPLICATION

To start enhancing the application, you are going to use the control Toolbox. Close the `Form1.designer.vb` file and switch your display to the Form1.vb [Design] tab. The Toolbox window is available whenever a form is in Design view. By default, the Toolbox, shown in Figure 1-23, is docked to the left side of Visual Studio as a tab. When you click this tab, the control window expands, and you can drag controls onto your form. Alternatively, if you have closed the Toolbox tab, you can go to the View menu and select Toolbox.

If you haven't set up the Toolbox to be permanently visible, it will slide out of the way and disappear whenever focus is moved away from it. This helps maximize the available screen real estate. If you don't like this feature and want the Toolbox to be permanently visible, just click the pushpin icon on the Toolbox's title bar.

The Toolbox contains literally dozens of standard controls, which are categorized so it's easier to find them. Figure 1-23 shows the result of dragging a `Button` control from the Toolbox and depositing it on the form: a new button displaying the text "Button1." Adding another button would trigger the default naming and text of "Button2."

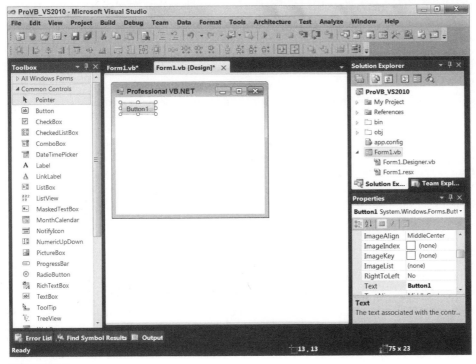

FIGURE 1-23

Before customizing the first control added to this form, take a closer look at the Visual Studio Toolbox. The tools are broken out by category, but this list of categories isn't static. Visual Studio 2010 Standard and above editions enable you to create your own custom controls. When you create such controls, the IDE will — after they have been compiled — automatically add them to the display when you are working in the same solution as the controls. These would be local references to controls that become available within the current solution.

Additionally, depending on whether you are working on a Web or a Windows Forms application, your list of controls in the Toolbox will vary. Windows Forms has a set of controls that leverages the power of the Windows operating system. Web applications, conversely, tend to have controls oriented to working in a disconnected environment.

It's also possible to have third-party controls in your environment. Such controls can be registered with Visual Studio and are then displayed within every project you work on. When controls are added to the Toolbox they typically appear in their own custom categories so that they are grouped together and therefore easy to find.

Return to the button you've dragged onto the form; it's ready to go in all respects. However, Visual Studio has no way of knowing how you want to customize it. Start by going to the Properties window and changing the `Text` property to **Run Code**. You can then change the button's (*Name*) property to **ButtonTest**. Having made these changes, double-click the button in the display view. Double-clicking tells Visual Studio that you want to add an event handler to this control, and by default Visual Studio adds an `On_Click` event handler for buttons. The IDE then shifts the display to the Code view so that you can customize this handler (Figure 1-24 shows the code for this event handler being edited).

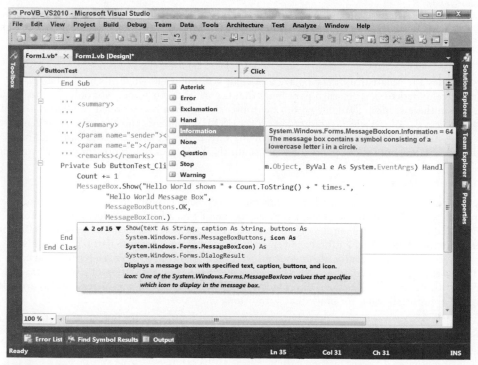

FIGURE 1-24

Although the event handler can be added through the designer, it's also possible to add event handlers from Code view. After you double-click the button, Visual Studio will transfer you to Code view and display your new event handler. Notice that in Code view there are drop-down lists on the top of the edit window. The boxes indicate the current object on the left — in this case, your new button — and the current method on the right — in this case, the click event handler. You can add new handlers for other events on your button or form using these drop-down lists.

The drop-down list on the left side contains the objects for which event handlers can be added. The drop-down list on the right side contains all the events for the selected object. For now, you have created a new handler for your button's click event, so let's look at customizing the code associated with this event.

Customizing the Code

With the code window open to the newly added event handler for the `ButtonTest` control, you can start to customize this handler. Note that adding a control and event handler involves elements of generated code.

Visual Studio adds code to the `Form1.Designer.vb` file. These changes occur in addition to the default method implementation shown in the editable portion of your source code.

Adding XML Comments

One of Visual Studio's features is the capability to generate an XML comments template for Visual Basic. XML comments are a much more powerful feature than you might realize, because they are also recognized by Visual Studio for use in IntelliSense. To add a new XML comment to your handler, go to the line before the handler and type three single quotation marks: '''. This triggers Visual Studio to replace your single quotation marks with the following block of comments. You can trigger these comments in front of any method, class, or property in your code:

```
'''  <summary>
'''
'''  </summary>
'''  <param name="sender"></param>
'''  <param name="e"></param>
'''  <remarks></remarks>
```

Visual Studio provides a template that offers a place to include a summary of what this method does. It also provides placeholders to describe each parameter that is part of this method. Not only are the comments entered in these sections available within the source code, when it's compiled you'll also find an XML file in the project directory, which summarizes all your XML comments and can be used to generate documentation and help files for the said source code. By the way, if you refactor a method and add new parameters, the XML comments also support IntelliSense for the XML tags that represent your parameters.

Customizing the Event Handler

Now customize the code for the button handler, as this method doesn't actually do anything by default. Start by adding a new line of code to increment the property `Count` you added to the form earlier. Next, use the `System.Windows.Forms.MessageBox` class to open a message box and show the message indicating the number of times the Hello World button has been pressed. Fortunately, because that namespace is automatically imported into every source file in your project, thanks to your project references, you can reference the `MessageBox.Show` method directly. The `Show` method has several different parameters; and as shown in Figure 1-24, not only does the IDE provide a ToolTip for the list of parameters, it also provides help regarding the appropriate value for individual parameters.

The completed call to `MessageBox.Show` should look similar to the following code block. Note that the underscore character is used to continue the command across multiple lines. In addition, unlike previous versions of Visual Basic, for which parentheses were sometimes unnecessary, in .NET the syntax best practice is to use parentheses for every method call:

Available for download on Wrox.com

```
Private Sub ButtonTest_Click(ByVal sender As System.Object,
                             ByVal e As System.EventArgs) Handles ButtonTest.Click
    Count += 1
    MessageBox.Show("Hello World shown " + Count.ToString() + " times.",
            "Hello World Message Box",
            MessageBoxButtons.OK,
            MessageBoxIcon.Information)

End Sub
```

Code snippet from Form1

Once you have entered this line of code, you may notice a squiggly line underneath some portions of your text. This occurs when there is an error in the line you have typed. The Visual Studio IDE works more like the latest version of Word. It highlights compiler issues while allowing you to continue working on your code. Visual Basic is constantly reviewing your code to ensure that it will compile; and when it encounters a problem it immediately notifies you of the location without interrupting your work.

Reviewing the Code

Now that you have created a simple Windows application, let's review the elements of the code that have been added by the IDE. Following is the entire `Form1.Designer.vb` source listing. Highlighted in this listing are the lines of code that have changed since the original template was used to generate this project:

```vb
<Global.Microsoft.VisualBasic.CompilerServices.DesignerGenerated()> _
Partial Class Form1
    Inherits System.Windows.Forms.Form

    'Form overrides dispose to clean up the component list.
    <System.Diagnostics.DebuggerNonUserCode()> _
    Protected Overrides Sub Dispose(ByVal disposing As Boolean)
        Try
            If disposing AndAlso components IsNot Nothing Then
                components.Dispose()
            End If
        Finally
            MyBase.Dispose(disposing)
        End Try
    End Sub

    'Required by the Windows Form Designer
    Private components As System.ComponentModel.IContainer

    'NOTE: The following procedure is required by the Windows Form Designer
    'It can be modified using the Windows Form Designer.
    'Do not modify it using the code editor.
    <System.Diagnostics.DebuggerStepThrough()> _
    Private Sub InitializeComponent()
        Me.ButtonTest = New System.Windows.Forms.Button()
        Me.SuspendLayout()
        '
        'ButtonTest
        '
        Me.ButtonTest.Location = New System.Drawing.Point(13, 13)
        Me.ButtonTest.Name = "ButtonTest"
        Me.ButtonTest.Size = New System.Drawing.Size(104, 23)
        Me.ButtonTest.TabIndex = 0
        Me.ButtonTest.Text = "Run Code"
        Me.ButtonTest.UseVisualStyleBackColor = True
        '
        'Form1
        '
        Me.AutoScaleDimensions = New System.Drawing.SizeF(8.0!, 16.0!)
        Me.AutoScaleMode = System.Windows.Forms.AutoScaleMode.Font
        Me.ClientSize = New System.Drawing.Size(328, 258)
        Me.Controls.Add(Me.ButtonTest)
        Me.Name = "Form1"
        Me.Text = "Professional VB.NET"
        Me.ResumeLayout(False)

    End Sub
    Friend WithEvents ButtonTest As System.Windows.Forms.Button

End Class
```

Code snippet from Form1.Designer

After the class declaration in the generated file, the first change made to the code is the addition of a new variable to represent the new button:

```vb
Friend WithEvents ButtonTest As System.Windows.Forms.Button
```

When any type of control is added to the form, a new variable is added to the form class. Controls are represented by variables; and, just as form properties are set in code, form controls are added in code. The `Button` class in the `System.Windows.Forms` namespace implements the `Button` control on the Toolbox. Each control added to a form has a class that implements the functionality of the control. For the standard controls, these classes are usually found in the `System.Windows.Forms` namespace. The `WithEvents` keyword has been used in the declaration of the new variable so that it can respond to events raised by the button.

The bulk of the code changes are in the `InitializeComponent` procedure. Nine lines of code have been added to help set up and display the `Button` control. The first addition to the procedure is a line that creates a new instance of the `Button` class and assigns it to the button variable:

```
Me. ButtonTest = New System.Windows.Forms.Button()
```

Before a button is added to the form, the form's layout engine must be paused. This is done using the next line of code:

```
Me.SuspendLayout()
```

The next four lines of code set the properties of the button. The `Location` property of the `Button` class sets the location of the top-left corner of the button within the form:

```
Me. ButtonTest.Location = New System.Drawing.Point(13, 13)
```

The location of a control is expressed in terms of a `Point` structure. Next, the `Name` property of the button is set:

```
Me. ButtonTest.Name = "ButtonTest"
```

The `Name` property acts exactly as it did for the form, setting the textual name of the button. The `Name` property has no effect on how the button is displayed on the form; it is used to recognize the button's context within the source code. The next four lines of code assign values to the `Size`, `TabIndex`, `Text`, and `UseVisualStyleBackColor` properties of the button:

```
Me.ButtonTest.Size = New System.Drawing.Size(104, 23)
Me. ButtonTest.TabIndex = 0
Me. ButtonTest.Text = "Run Code"
Me. ButtonTest.UseVisualStyleBackColor = True
```

Code snippet from Form1.Designer

The `Size` property defines the height and width of the control; it is being set because the default button size didn't display the full label, and so the button's size was increased. The `TabIndex` property of the button is used to set the order in which the control is selected when a user cycles through the controls on the form using the Tab key. The higher the number, the later the control gains focus. Each control should have a unique number for its `TabIndex` property. The `Text` property of a button sets the text that appears on the button. Finally, the `UseVisualStyleBackColor` property indicates that when this button is drawn, it uses the current visual style. This is a Boolean value and typically you can accept this default, but you can customize the background so that a given button doesn't default to the current visual style.

Once the properties of the button have been set, it needs to be added to the form. This is accomplished with the next line of code:

```
Me.Controls.Add(Me.ButtonTest)
```

The `System.Windows.Forms.Form` class (from which your `Form1` class is derived) has a property called `Controls` that keeps track of all of the child controls of the form. Whenever you add a control to a form in the designer, a line similar to the preceding one is added automatically to the form's initialization process.

Finally, near the bottom of the initialization logic is the final code change. The form is given permission to resume the layout logic:

```
Me.ResumeLayout(False)
```

In addition to the code that has been generated in the `Form1.Designer.vb` source file, you have created code that lives in the `Form1.vb` source file:

```vbnet
Public Class Form1

    Private m_count As Integer
    Public Property Count() As Integer
        Get
            Return m_count
        End Get
        Set(ByVal value As Integer)
            m_count = value
        End Set
    End Property

    ''' <summary>
    '''
    ''' </summary>
    ''' <param name="sender"></param>
    ''' <param name="e"></param>
    ''' <remarks></remarks>
    Private Sub ButtonTest_Click(ByVal sender As System.Object,
                            ByVal e As System.EventArgs) Handles ButtonTest.Click
        Count += 1
        MessageBox.Show("Hello World shown " + Count.ToString() + " times.",
                "Hello World Message Box",
                MessageBoxButtons.OK,
                MessageBoxIcon.Information)

    End Sub
End Class
```

Code snippet from Form1

This code reflects the event handler added for the button. The code contained in the handler was already covered, with the exception of the naming convention for event handlers. Event handlers have a naming convention similar to that in previous versions of Visual Basic: The control name is followed by an underscore and then the event name. The event itself may also have a standard set of parameters. At this point, you can test the application, but to do so let's first look at your build options.

Building Applications

For this example, it is best to build your sample application using the Debug build configuration. The first step is to ensure that Debug is selected as the active configuration. As noted earlier in this chapter around Figure 1-7 you'll find the setting available on your project properties. It's also available from the main Visual Studio display in the Solution Configurations drop-down list box that's part of the Standard Toolbar. Visual Studio provides an entire Build menu with the various options available for building an application. There are essentially two options for building applications:

➤ **Build** — This option uses the currently active build configuration to build the project or solution, depending upon what is available.

➤ **Publish** — For Visual Basic developers, this option starts the process of creating a release build, but note that it also ties in with the deployment of your application, in that you are asked to provide an URL where the application will be published.

The Build menu supports building for either the current project or the entire solution. Thus, you can choose to build only a single project in your solution or all of the projects that have been defined as part of the current configuration. Of course, anytime you choose to test-run your application, the compiler will automatically perform a compilation check to ensure that you run the most recent version of your code.

You can either select Build from the menu or use the Ctrl+Shift+B keyboard combination to initiate a build. When you build your application, the Output window along the bottom edge of the development environment will open. As shown in Figure 1-25, it displays status messages associated with the build process. This window should indicate your success in building the application.

If problems are encountered while building your application, Visual Studio provides a separate window to help track them. If an error occurs, the Task List window will open as a tabbed window in the same region occupied by the Output window (refer to Figure 1-25). Each error triggers a separate item in the Task List; if you double-click an error, Visual Studio automatically repositions you on the line with the error. Once your application has been built successfully, you can run it.

Once your application has been built successfully, you will find the executable file located in the targeted directory. By default, for .NET applications this is the \bin subdirectory of your project directory.

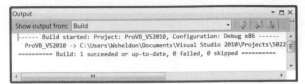

FIGURE 1-25

Running an Application in the Debugger

As discussed earlier, there are several ways to start your application. Starting the application launches a series of events. First, Visual Studio looks for any modified files and saves those files automatically. It then verifies the build status of your solution and rebuilds any project that does not have an updated binary, including dependencies. Finally, it initiates a separate process space and starts your application with the Visual Studio debugger attached to that process.

When your application is running, the look and feel of Visual Studio's IDE changes, with different windows and button bars becoming visible (see Figure 1-26). While your code remains visible, the IDE displays additional windows — by default, the Immediate Window appears in the same location as the Output Window as a new tabbed window. Others, such as the Call Stack, Locals, and Watch windows, may also be displayed over time as you work with the debugger. (Not all of these windows are available to users of Visual Studio Express Edition.) These windows are used by the debugger for reviewing the current value of variables within your code.

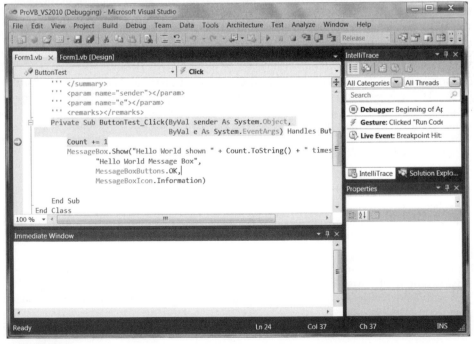

FIGURE 1-26

The true power of the Visual Studio debugger is its interactive debugging. To demonstrate this, with your application running, select Visual Studio as the active window. Change your display to the Form1.vb Code view (not Design view) and click in the border alongside the line of code you added to increment the count when the button is clicked. Doing this creates a breakpoint on the selected line (refer to Figure 1-26). Return to your application and then click the "Hello World" button. Visual Studio takes the active focus, returning you to the code window, and the line with your breakpoint is now selected.

Visual Studio 2010 introduces a new window that is located in the same set of tabs as the Solution Explorer. As shown in Figure 1-26, the IntelliTrace window tracks your actions as you work with the application in Debug mode. Figure 1-27 focuses on this new feature available to the Ultimate edition of Visual Studio. Sometimes referred to as *historical debugging*, the IntelliTrace window provides a history of how you got to a given state.

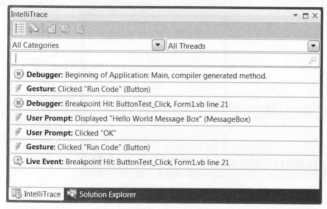

FIGURE 1-27

When an error occurs during debugging, your first thought is likely to be "What just happened?" But how do you reproduce that error? As indicated in Figure 1-27, the IntelliTrace window tracks the steps you have taken — in this case showing that I had used the Run Code button a second time since the steps shown in Figure 1-26. By providing a historical trail, IntelliTrace enables you to reproduce a given set of steps through your application. You can also filter the various messages either by message type or by thread.

The ability to select these past break points and review the state of variables and classes in your running application can be a powerful tool for tracking down runtime issues. The historical debugging capabilities are unfortunately only available in Visual Studio 2010 Ultimate, but they take the power of the Visual Studio debugger to a new level.

However, even if you don't have the power of historical debugging, the Visual Studio debugger is a powerful development ally. It is, arguably, more important than any of the other developer productivity features of Visual Studio. With the execution sitting on this breakpoint, it is possible to control every aspect of your running code. Hovering over the property Count, as shown in Figure 1-28, Visual Studio provides a debug ToolTip showing you the current value of this property. This "hover over" feature works on any variable in your local environment and is a great way to get a feel for the different values without needing to go to another window.

Windows such as Locals and Autos display similar information about your variables, and you can use these to update those properties while the application is running. However, you'll note that the image in Figure 1-28 includes a small pin symbol. Using this you can keep the status window for this variable open in your Code view. This was done in Figure 1-29, and now as I step past the line where my breakpoint was set, the information in the window is updated to show the new value of Count. Visual Studio has just allowed you to create a custom watch window to reflect the value of Count.

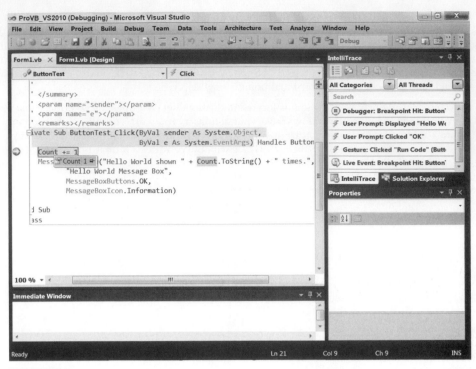

FIGURE 1-28

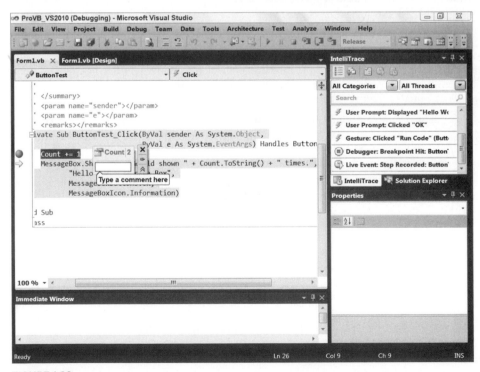

FIGURE 1-29

This isn't the end of it. As you'll note in Figure 1-29, by clicking on the down arrows you see on the right hand side of your new custom watch window, just below the pin, you can add one or more comments to your custom watch window for this value. You also have the option to unpin the initial placement of this window and move it off of your Code view display. Not only that but, the custom watch window is persistent in Debug mode. If you stop debugging and restart, the window is automatically restored and remains available until you choose to close it using the close button.

Next, move your mouse and hover over the parameter sender. This will open a window similar to the one for Count as you review the reference to this object. More important, note the small plus sign on the right-hand side, which if clicked expands the pop-up to show details about the properties of this object. As shown in Figure 1-30, this capability is available even for parameters like sender, which you didn't define. Figure 1-30 also illustrates a key point about looking at variable data. Notice that by expanding the top-level objects you can eventually get to the properties inside those objects. Next to some of those properties, on the right-hand side, is a little magnifying glass icon. That icon tells you that Visual Studio will open the potentially lengthy string value in any one of three visualization windows. When working with complex XML or other complex data, these visualizers offer significant productivity benefits by enabling you to review data.

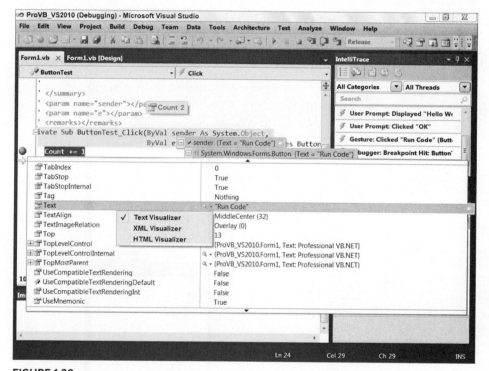

FIGURE 1-30

Once you are at a breakpoint, you can control your application by leveraging the Debug buttons on the Standard toolbar. These buttons, shown in Figure 1-31, provide several options for managing the flow of your application. From the left are the following buttons: Start Debugging, Break All, Stop Debugging, and three buttons that look like a carriage return next to a set of lines. The first of these, which is the fourth button overall represents stepping into code. The last two buttons represent stepping over and stepping out, respectively. In this case you should use the Step Into or Step Over buttons to move to the next line of code as shown in Figure 1-29.

FIGURE 1-31

Step-In tells the debugger to jump to whatever line of code is first within the next method or property you call. Keep in mind that if you pass a property value as a parameter to a method, then the first such line of code is in the Get method of the parameter. Once there, you may want to step out. Stepping out of a method tells the debugger to execute the code in the current method and return you to the line that called the method. Thus, you could step out of the property and then step in again to get into the method you are actually interested in debugging.

Of course, sometimes you don't want to step into a method; this is where the Step-Over button comes in. It enables you to call whatever method(s) are on the current line and step to the next sequential line of code in the method you are currently debugging. The final button, Step-Out, is useful if you know what the code in a method is going to do, but you want to determine which code called the current method. Stepping out takes you directly to the calling code block.

Each of the buttons shown on the debugging toolbar in Figure 1-31 has an accompanying shortcut key for experienced developers who want to move quickly through a series of breakpoints.

Of course, the ability to leverage breakpoints goes beyond what you can do with them at runtime. You can also disable breakpoints that you don't currently want to stop your application flow, and you can move a breakpoint, although it's usually easier to just click and delete the current location, and then click and create a new breakpoint at the new location.

Keeping in mind that Visual Basic 2010 Express Edition does not support the advanced properties of breakpoints, Visual Studio provides additional properties for managing and customizing breakpoints. As shown in Figure 1-32, it's also possible to add specific properties to your breakpoints. The context menu shows several possible options.

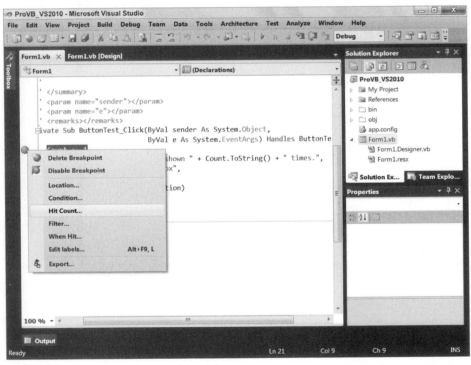

FIGURE 1-32

More important, it's possible to specify that a given breakpoint should execute only if a certain value is defined (or undefined). In other words, you can make a given breakpoint conditional, and a pop-up window enables you to define this condition. Similarly, if you've ever wanted to stop, for example, on the thirty-seventh iteration of a loop, then you know the pain of repeatedly stopping at a breakpoint inside a loop. Visual Studio enables you to specify that a given breakpoint should only stop your application after a specified number of hits.

The next option is one of the more interesting options if you need to carry out a debug session in a live environment. You can create a breakpoint on the debug version of code and then add a filter that ensures you are the only user to stop on that breakpoint. For example, if you are in an environment where multiple people are working against the same executable, then you can add a breakpoint that won't affect the other users of the application.

Similarly, instead of just stopping at a breakpoint, you can also have the breakpoint execute some other code, possibly even a Visual Studio macro, when the given breakpoint is reached. These actions are rather limited and are not frequently used, but in some situations this capability can be used to your advantage.

Note that breakpoints are saved when a solution is saved by the IDE. There is also a Breakpoints window, which provides a common location for managing breakpoints that you may have set across several different source files.

Finally, at some point you are going to want to debug a process that isn't being started from Visual Studio — for example, if you have an existing website that is hosting a DLL you are interested in debugging. In this case, you can leverage Visual Studio's capability to attach to a running process and debug that DLL. At or near the top (depending on your settings) of the Tools menu in Visual Studio is the Attach to Process option. This menu option opens a dialog showing all of your processes. You could then select the process and have the DLL project you want to debug loaded in Visual Studio. The next time your DLL is called by that process, Visual Studio will recognize the call and hit a breakpoint set in your code.

Other Debug-Related Windows

As noted earlier, when you run an application in Debug mode, Visual Studio .NET 2010 can open a series of windows related to debugging. Each of these windows provides a view of a limited set of the overall environment in which your application is running. From these windows, it is possible to find things such as the list of calls (stack) used to get to the current line of code or the present value of all the variables currently available. Visual Studio has a powerful debugger that is fully supported with IntelliSense, and these windows extend the debugger.

Output

Recall that the build process puts progress messages in this window. Similarly, your program can also place messages in it. Several options for accessing this window are discussed in later chapters, but at the simplest level the `Console` object echoes its output to this window during a debug session. For example, the following line of code can be added to your sample application:

```
Console.WriteLine("This is printed in the Output Window")
```

This line of code will cause the string "This is printed in the Output Window" to appear in the Output window when your application is running. You can verify this by adding this line in front of the command to open the message box. Then, run your application and have the debugger stop on the line where the message box is opened. If you check the contents of the Output window, you will find that your string is displayed.

Anything written to the Output window is shown only while running a program from the environment. During execution of the compiled module, no Output window is present, so nothing can be written to it. This is the basic concept behind other objects such as `Debug` and `Trace`, which are covered in more detail in Chapter 6.

Call Stack

The Call Stack window lists the procedures that are currently calling other procedures and waiting for their return. The call stack represents the path through your code that leads to the currently executing command. This can be a valuable tool when you are trying to determine what code is executing a line of code that you didn't expect to execute.

Locals

The Locals window is used to monitor the value of all variables currently in scope. This is a fairly self-explanatory window that shows a list of the current local variables, with the value next to each item. As in previous versions of Visual Studio, this display enables you to examine the contents of objects and arrays via a tree-control interface. It also supports the editing of those values, so if you want to change a string from empty to what you thought it would be, just to see what else might be broken, then feel free to do so from here.

Watch Windows

There are four Watch windows, numbered Watch 1 to Watch 4. Each window can hold a set of variables or expressions for which you want to monitor the values. It is also possible to modify the value of a variable from within a Watch window. The display can be set to show variable values in decimal or hexadecimal format. To add a variable to a Watch window, you can either right-click the variable in the Code Editor and then select Add Watch from the pop-up menu, or drag and drop the variable into the watch window.

Immediate Window

The Immediate window, as its name implies, enables you to evaluate expressions. It becomes available while you are in Debug mode. This is a powerful window, one that can save or ruin a debug session. For example, using the sample from earlier in this chapter, you can start the application and press the button to stop on the breakpoint. Go to the Immediate window and enter **?Button1.Text = "Click Me"** and press Enter. You should get a response of false as the Immediate window evaluates this statement.

Notice the preceding **?**, which tells the debugger to evaluate your statement, rather than execute it. Repeat the preceding text but omit the question mark: **Button1.Text = "Click Me"**. Press F5 or click the Run button to return control to your application, and notice the caption on your button. From the Immediate window you have updated this value. This window can be very useful if you are working in Debug mode and need to modify a value that is part of a running application.

Autos

Finally, as the chapter prepares to transition to features that are only available in Visual Studio and not Visual Basic 2010 Express, there is the Autos window. The Autos window displays variables used in the statement currently being executed and the statement just before it. These variables are identified and listed for you automatically, hence the window's name. This window shows more than just your local variables. For example, if you are in Debug mode on the line to open the MessageBox in the ProVB_VS2010 sample, then the MessageBox constants referenced on this line are shown in this window. This window enables you to see the content of every variable involved in the currently executing command. As with the Locals window, you can edit the value of a variable during a debug session. However, this window is in fact specific to Visual Studio and not available to users of Visual Basic 2010 Express.

Reusing Your First Windows Form

As you proceed through the book and delve further into the features of Visual Basic you'll want a way to test sample code. Chapter 2 in particular has snippets of code which you'll want to test. One way to do this is to enhance the ProVB_VS2010 application. Its current use of a MessageBox isn't exactly the most useful method of testing code snippets. So let's update this application so it can be reused in other chapters and at random by you when you are interested in testing a snippet.

At the core you'll continue to access code to test where it can be executed from the ButtonTest Click event. However, instead of using a message box, you can use a text box to hold the output from the code being tested.

The first step in this process as shown in Figure 1-33 is to drag a TextBox control onto the display and then click on the small arrow in the upper-right corner of the control's display. This will open the TextBox tasks menu, which contains some of the most common customizations for this control. This small arrow appears on all Windows Forms controls, although what is listed will vary between controls. In this case you should select the MultiLine property.

Once you have selected that property it is possible to expand the TextBox to allow you to fill the entire bottom portion of the window. As shown in Figure 1-34, you can then move to the properties for the TextBox control and update the Anchor property to anchor the current control's size based on the window containing it. Having tied this control to all four sides of the window, when the window is resized, this control will automatically resize with the window. You'll find if you review the properties of ButtonTest that it is anchored only to the top and left sides of the window, so it remains unchanged while the window changes size.

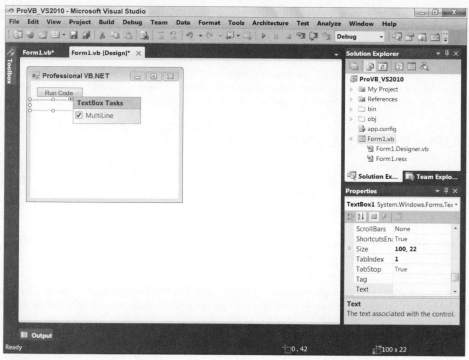

FIGURE 1-33

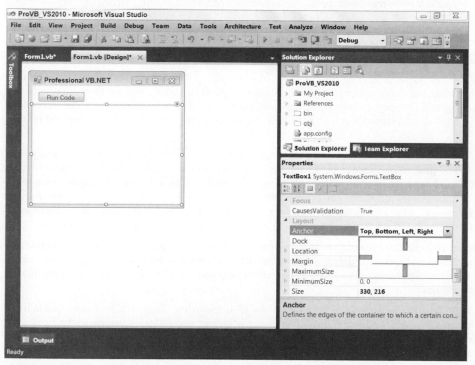

FIGURE 1-34

Additionally, you can follow the example shown here, which is to access the font property for the textbox and increase the size of the font from the default to 14pt. This was done only to make the sample results more readable within the screenshots used for the book. It has no other impact on the application.

At this point you have a display that will allow you to show the results from various code snippets simply by updating the Text property on the TextBox1 control of your window. Keep in mind that you'll want to remove (or as some of the chapters will show) comment out code that you are done working with, for example, the Count property and the related message box code used during the debugging demonstration in this chapter.

USEFUL FEATURES OF VISUAL STUDIO 2010

The focus of most of this chapter has been on creating a simple application, working in either Visual Basic 2010 Express Edition or Visual Studio 2010. It's now time to completely leave the set of features supported by the Express Edition and move on to some features that are available only to Visual Studio developers. These features include, but are not limited to, the following items, beginning with features available to all Visual Studio 2010 developers.

When Visual Studio 2010 is first started, you configure your custom IDE profile. Visual Studio enables you to select either a language-specific or task-specific profile and then change that profile whenever you desire.

Configuration settings are managed through the Tools ⇨ Import and Export Settings menu option. This menu option opens a simple wizard, which first saves your current settings and then allows you to select an alternate set of settings. By default, Visual Studio ships with settings for Visual Basic, Web development, and C#, to name a few, but by exporting your settings you can create and share your own custom settings files.

The Visual Studio settings file is an XML file that enables you to capture all your Visual Studio configuration settings. This might sound trivial, but it is not. This feature enables the standardization of Visual Studio across different team members. The advantages of a team sharing settings go beyond just a common look and feel.

Build Configurations

Prior to .NET, a Visual Basic project had only one set of properties. There was no way to have one set of properties for a debug build and a separate set for a release build. As a result, you had to manually change any environment-specific properties before you built the application. This has changed with the introduction of *build configurations*, which enable you to have different sets of project properties for debug and release builds.

Visual Studio does not limit you to only two build configurations. It's possible to create additional custom configurations. The properties that can be set for a project have been split into two groups: those that are independent of build configuration and therefore apply to all build configurations, and those that apply only to the active build configuration. For example, the Project Name and Project Location properties are the same irrespective of what build configuration is active, whereas the code optimization options vary according to the active build configuration.

The advantage of multiple configurations is that it's possible to turn off optimization while an application is in development and add symbolic debug information that helps locate and identify errors. When you are ready to ship the application, you can switch to the release configuration and create an executable that is optimized for production.

At the top of Figure 1-35 is a drop-down list box labeled Configuration. Typically, four options are listed in this box: the currently selected configuration, Active; the Debug and Release options; and a final option, All Configurations. When changes are made on this screen, they are applied only to the selected configuration(s). Thus, when Release is selected, any changes are applied only to the settings for the Release build. If, conversely, All Configurations is selected, then any changes made are applied to all of the configurations, Debug, and Release. Similarly, if Active is selected, then in the background the changes are made to the underlying configuration that is currently active.

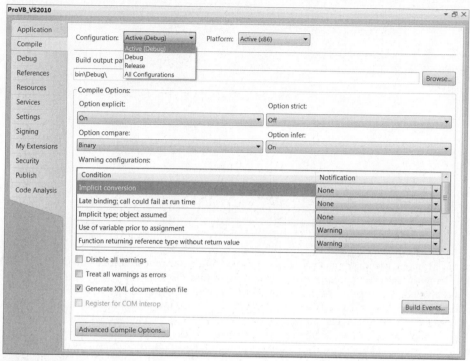

FIGURE 1-35

Alongside this is a Platform drop-down. In the past it was recommended that you not change this, as it was set to Any CPU, which was an acceptable setting. However, with Visual Studio 2010 you'll want to consider this value, since in most cases it will default to x86. x86 represents 32-bit operating system environments and as a result, so if you are targeting a 64-bit environment you would want to change this value to be 64-bit. As mentioned earlier in this chapter, keep in mind that certain capabilities such as COM-Interop and Edit and Continue debugging are dependent on an x86 environment.

All of your compile settings are project-specific, but when you are working with a solution it is possible to have more than one project in the same solution. Although you are forced to manage these settings independently for each project, there is another form of project configuration related to multiple projects. You are most likely to use this when working with integrated Setup projects, where you might want to build only the Setup project when you are working on a release build.

To customize which projects are included in each build configuration, you need the Configuration Manager for the solution. Projects are assigned to build configurations through the Configuration Manager. You can access the Configuration Manager from the Build menu. Alternatively, the Configuration Manager can be opened using the drop-down list box to the right of the Run button on the Visual Studio toolbar. The Active Configuration drop-down box contains the following options: Debug, Release, and Configuration Manager. The first two default options are the currently available configurations. Selecting the bottom option, Configuration Manager, opens the dialog shown in Figure 1-36.

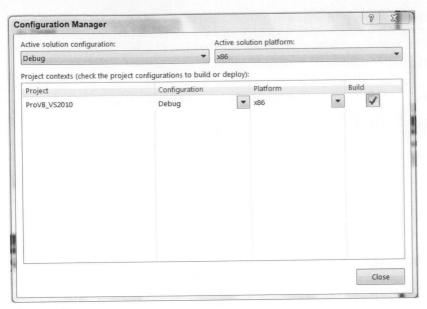

FIGURE 1-36

The Configuration Manager contains an entry for each project in the current solution. You can include or exclude a project from the selected configuration by enabling or disabling the check box in the Build column of the grid. This is a valuable capability when a solution has multiple projects, as time isn't wasted waiting while a project that isn't being worked on is recompiled. The build configuration is commonly used when a Setup project is added to a solution. The normal plan is to rebuild only the Setup package when a release version of the actual application project is created. Note that regardless of the build configuration, you can build any assembly by right-clicking that project and selecting the Build option from the pop-up menu.

The Task List

The Task List is a great productivity tool that tracks not only errors, but also pending changes and additions. It's also a good way for the Visual Studio environment to communicate information that the developer needs to know, such as any current errors. The Task List is displayed by selecting Task List from the View menu. It offers two views, Comments and User Tasks, and it displays either group of tasks based on the selection in the drop-down box that is part of this window.

The Comment option is used for tasks embedded in code comments. This is done by creating a standard comment with the apostrophe and then starting the comment with the Visual Studio keyword TODO. The keyword can be followed with any text that describes what needs to be done. Once entered, the text of these comments shows up in the Task List. Note that users can create their own comment tokens in the options for Visual Studio via Tools ➪ Options ➪ Environment ➪ Task List. Other predefined keywords include HACK and UNDONE.

Besides helping developers track these pending coding issues as tasks, leveraging comments embedded in code results in another benefit. Just as with errors, clicking a task in the Task List causes the Code Editor to jump to the location of the task without hunting through the code for it. Also of note, though we are not going to delve into it, the Task List is integrated with Team Foundation Server if you are using this for your collaboration and source control.

The second type of tasks is user tasks. These may not be related to a specific item within a single file. Examples are tasks associated with resolving a bug, or a new feature. It is possible to enter tasks into the Task List manually. Within the Task List is an image button showing a red check mark. Pressing this button creates a new task in the Task List, where you can edit the description of your new task.

In early versions of Visual Studio, the Task List window was used to display compilation errors, but starting with Visual Studio 2005 the Error List became a separate window.

The Command Window

The Command window can be opened from the Other Windows section of the View menu. When opened, the window displays a > prompt. This is a command prompt at which you can execute commands — specifically, Visual Studio commands. While Visual Studio is designed to be a GUI environment with limited shortcuts, the Command window enables you to type — with the assistance of IntelliSense — the specific command you want.

You can use the Command window to access Visual Studio menu options and commands by typing them instead of selecting them in the menu structure. For example, type **File.AddNewProject** and press Enter — the dialog box to add a new project will appear. Similarly, if you type **Debug.Start**, you initiate the same build and start actions that you would from the Visual Studio UI.

Server Explorer

As development has become more server-centric, developers have a greater need to discover and manipulate services on the network. Visual InterDev, used for building classic ASP web sites, and which was available around the same time as Visual Basic 6, started in this direction with a Server Object section in the InterDev Toolbox. The Server Explorer feature in Visual Studio takes this concept and makes working with servers easier. The Server Explorer is more sophisticated in that it enables you to explore and alter your application's database or your local registry values. With the assistance of an SQL Database project template (part of the Other Project types), it's possible to fully explore and alter an SQL Server database. You can define the tables, stored procedures, and other database objects as you might have previously done with the SQL Server Enterprise Manager.

If the Server Explorer hasn't been opened, it can be opened from the View menu. Alternatively it should be located near the control Toolbox. It has behavior similar to the Toolbox in that if you hover over or click the Server Explorer's tab, the window expands from the left-hand side of the IDE. Once it is open, you will see a display similar to the one shown in Figure 1-37. Note that this display has three top-level entries. The first, Data Connections, is the starting point for setting up and configuring the database connection. You can right-click on the top-level Data Connections node and define new SQL Server connection settings that will be used in your application to connect to the database. The Server Explorer window provides a way to manage and view project-specific database connections such as those used in data binding.

FIGURE 1-37

The second top-level entry, Servers, focuses on other server data that may be of interest to you and your application. When you expand the list of available servers, you have access to several server resources. The Server Explorer even provides the capability to stop and restart services on the server. Note the wide variety of server resources that are available for inspection or use in the project. Having the Server Explorer available means you don't have to go to an outside resource to find, for example, what message queues are available.

By default, you have access to the resources on your local machine; but if you are in a domain, it is possible to add other machines, such as your Web server, to your display. Use the Add Server option to select and inspect a new server. To explore the Event Logs and registry of a server, you need to add this server to your display. Use the Add Server button in the button bar to open the dialog and identify the server to which you would like to connect. Once the connection is made, you can explore the properties of that server.

The third top-level node, SharePoint Connections, enables you to define and reference elements associated with one or more SharePoint servers for which you might be creating solutions.

Recording and Using Macros in Visual Studio 2010

Visual Studio macros are part of the environment and are available to any language. Macro options are accessible from the Tools ⇨ Macros menu, as shown in Figure 1-38. The concept of macros is simple: Record a series of keystrokes and/or menu actions, and then play them back by pressing a certain keystroke combination.

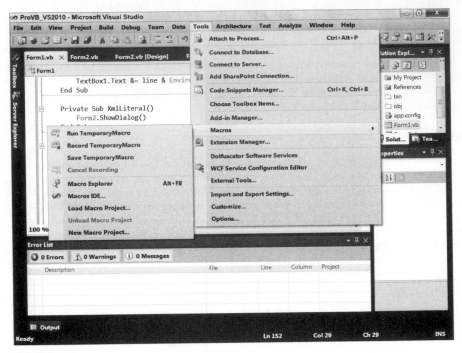

FIGURE 1-38

For example, suppose that one particular function call with a complex set of arguments is constantly being called on in code, and the function call usually looks the same except for minor variations in the arguments. The keystrokes to code the function call could be recorded and played back as necessary, which would insert code to call the function, which could then be modified as necessary.

Macros can be far more complex than this, containing logic as well as keystrokes. The macro capabilities of Visual Studio are so comprehensive that macros have their own IDE (accessed via Tools ⇨ Macros ⇨ Macros IDE).

Macros can also be developed from scratch in this environment, but more commonly they are recorded using the Record Temporary Macro option on the Macros menu and then renamed and modified in the development environment. Here is an example of recording and modifying a macro:

1. Start a new Windows Application project.

2. In the new project, add a button to Form1, which was created with the project.

3. Double-click the button to get to its Click event routine.

4. Select Tools ⇨ Macros ⇨ Record Temporary Macro. A small toolbar (see Figure 1-39) will appear on top of the IDE with buttons to control the recording of a macro (Pause, Stop, and Cancel).

FIGURE 1-39

5. Press Enter and then type the following line of code:

```
TextBox1.Text = "Macro Test"
```

6. Press Enter again.

7. In the small toolbar, press the Stop button.

8. Select Tools ⇨ Macros ⇨ Macro Explorer. The Macro Explorer will appear (in the location normally occupied by the Solution Explorer), with the new macro in it (see Figure 1-40). You can name the macro anything you like. Note that the Macro Explorer ships with several sample macros that you can "explore."

FIGURE 1-40

9. Right-click the macro and select Edit to get to the Macro Editor. You will see the following code, as shown in Figure 1-41, in your macro:

```
DTE.ActiveDocument.Selection.NewLine()
DTE.ActiveDocument.Selection.Text = TextBox1.Text = "Macro Test"
DTE.ActiveDocument.Selection.NewLine()
```

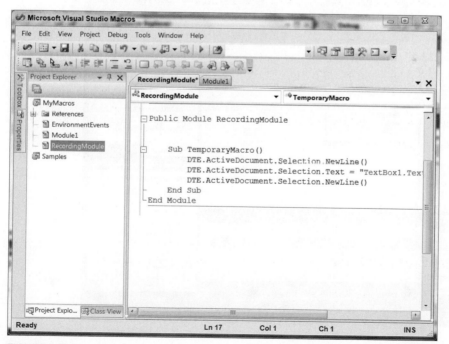

FIGURE 1-41

The code that appears in step 9 may vary depending on how you typed in the line. For example, if you made a mistake and backspaced, those actions will have their own corresponding lines of code. As a result, after you record a macro, it is worthwhile to examine the code and remove any unnecessary lines.

The code in a macro recorded this way is just standard VB code, and it can be modified as desired. However, there are some restrictions regarding what you can do inside the macro IDE. For example, you cannot refer to the namespace for setting up database connections, because this might constitute a security violation.

To run a macro, you can just double-click it in the Macro Explorer or select Tools ➪ Macros ➪ Run Macro. You can also assign a keystroke to a macro in the Keyboard dialog in the Tools ➪ Options ➪ Environment folder.

One final note on macros is that they essentially enable you to generate code that can then be transferred to a Visual Studio Add-In project. An Add-In project is a project designed to extend the properties of Visual Studio. To create a new Add-In project, open the New Project dialog and select Other Project Types — Extensibility. You can then create a Visual Studio Add-In project. Such a project enables you to essentially share your macro as a new feature of Visual Studio. For example, if Visual Studio 2010 didn't provide a standard way to get formatted comments, you might create an add-in that enables you to automatically generate your comment template so you wouldn't need to retype it repeatedly.

Class Diagrams

One of the features introduced with Visual Studio 2005 was the capability to generate class diagrams. A *class diagram* is a graphical representation of your application's objects. By right-clicking on your project in the Solution Explorer, you can select View Class Diagram from the context menu. Alternatively, you can choose to Add a New Item to your project. In the same window where you can add a new class, you have the option to add a new class diagram. The class diagram uses a `.cd` file extension for its source files. It is a graphical display, as shown in Figure 1-42.

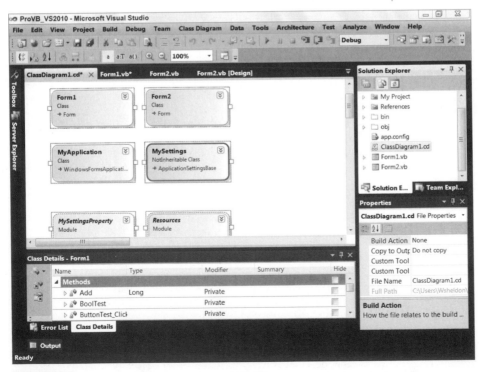

FIGURE 1-42

Adding such a file to your project creates a dynamically updated representation of your project's classes. As shown in Figure 1-42, the current class structures for even a simple project are immediately represented when you create the diagram. It is possible to add multiple class diagrams to your project. The class diagram graphically displays the relationships between objects — for example, when one object contains another object or even object inheritance. When you change your source code the diagram is also updated. In other words, the diagram isn't something static that you create once at the start of your project and then becomes out-of-date as your actual implementation changes the class relationships.

More important, you can at any time open the class diagram, make changes to one or more of your existing objects, or create new objects and define their relationship to your existing objects, and when done, Visual Studio will automatically update your existing source files and create new source files as necessary for the newly defined objects.

As shown in Figure 1-42, the class diagram files (*.cd) open in the same main display area used for the Visual Studio UI designer and viewing code. They are, however, a graphical design surface that behaves more like Visio than the User Interface designer. You can compress individual objects or expose their property and method details. Additionally, items such as the relationships between classes can be shown graphically instead of being represented as properties.

In addition to the editing surface, when working with the Class Designer a second window is displayed. As shown at the bottom of Figure 1-42, the Class Details window is generally located in the same space as your Output, Tasks, and other windows. The Class Details window provides detailed information about each of the properties and methods of the classes you are working with in the Class Designer. You can add and edit methods, properties, fields, and even events associated with your classes. While you can't write code from this window, you can update parameter lists and property types. The Class Diagram tool is an excellent tool for reviewing your application structure.

Application Lifecycle Management

The focus of this chapter has been on how you, as a Visual Basic developer, can leverage Visual Studio 2010. At the top end of the Visual Studio 2010 product line is the full Ultimate edition, and just below that is the Premium Edition. These two versions of Visual Studio have replaced the umbrella of products referred to as *Application Lifecycle Management (ALM)*. In order to reduce confusion, this section takes a brief look at some of the tools from ALM that are part of Visual Studio 2010 These tools are focused less on languages and developing code than on managing development and the development of applications.

Architecturally, ALM had two main elements: the server-side components, which operate under Team Foundation Server (TFS); and the client components, which are part of Visual Studio. TFS is the replacement for Visual Source Safe (VSS), although thinking of it only in those terms is a bit like thinking of the modern automobile as the replacement for the horse and carriage. TFS was updated with Visual Studio 2010, and includes a client installation package: Team Explorer. Team Explorer is installed as an add-in to Visual Studio and provides access to TFS. However, the Team Explorer client package, isn't just a Visual Studio add-in, it also includes add-ins to Office, implemented using Visual Studio Tools for Office that you need in order to work with the TFS features like task and bug lists.

Team Foundation Server (TFS)

The server components of Visual Studio Application Lifecycle Management (ALM) are not automatically integrated into Visual Studio, but it is appropriate to mention a couple of key attributes of TFS that extend it beyond VSS. Similar to VSS, the primary role most developers see for TFS is that of source control. This is the capability to ensure that if multiple people are working on the same project and with the same set of source files, then no two of them can make changes to the same file at the same time.

Actually, that's a bit of an oversimplification. The default mode for TFS allows two people to work on the same file, and then the second person attempting to save changes merges them with the previously saved changes. The point of this is to ensure that developers check files in and out of source control so that they don't overwrite or lose each other's changes. In terms of its features and usability compared with VSS, TFS is much more capable of supporting remote team members. A project that literally takes hours to download remotely from VSS can download in a few minutes from TFS.

However, that covers just the source control features; and as mentioned previously, TFS goes well beyond source control. In particular, TFS approaches project development from the role of the project manager. It doesn't consider a Visual Studio project file to represent the definition of a project. Instead, it recognizes that a project is based on a customer or contract relationship, and may consist of several seemingly unrelated projects in Visual Studio. Thus, when you define a project you create an area where all of the projects and solutions and their associated source files can be stored.

As part of the creation process you select a process template — and third-party templates are available — and create a SharePoint website based on that template. The SharePoint website becomes the central point of collaboration for the project's team. In addition to hosting the documentation associated with your selected software development process, this site acts as a central location for task lists, requirements, Microsoft project files, and other materials related to your project. In essence, TFS leverages SharePoint to add a group collaboration element to your projects.

As important as this is, an even more important capability TFS supports is that of a build lab. TFS provides another optional product called *Team Foundation Build*, which leverages the Visual Studio build engine to enable you to schedule automated builds. This isn't just a simple scheduling service; the Team Foundation Build engine not only retrieves and compiles your application files, but also sends update notices regarding the status of the build, and can be instructed to automatically leverage some of the ALM tools such as Code Analysis and Unit Testing. The capability to automate your builds and deploy them on a daily basis to a test environment encourages processes that both focus on product quality and mirror industry best practices.

Team Explorer is a Visual Studio add-in on steroids. It includes not only new menu items for Visual Studio, but also a new window similar in concept to the Solution Explorer but that instead provides access to your TFS projects. It also provides a series of windows in Visual Studio, some of which are related to source control, and others related to tasks. TFS is in many ways the single most important tool in the ALM product line.

Team Foundation Server also includes new features for 2010. One of these, Team Project Collections, provides a means of better organizing your TFS server. In the past all of your TFS projects were in one giant collection and any form of hierarchy was entirely voluntary. With TFS 2010 and Team Project Collections it is possible to create divisions within your projects. Thus, you can create different groups for different departments and can group access control, storage, and backup operations as appropriate for each division.

 Be aware that there are two versions of TFS 2010. One is designed to provide a rich collaborative environment for a large organization. The other is a simpler version which omits some of the high-end integration with things like Project Server but which enables a small organization to replace any legacy VSS installations. The details of TFS are beyond the scope of this book.

Code Analysis

Code analysis, or static code analysis, is a tool for reviewing your source code — although that's not quite how it works. The basic paradigm reflects the fact that there are certain common best practices when writing code; and that once these best practices have been documented, a tool can be written that examines source code and determines whether these practices have been followed. Visual Studio's static code analysis is incorporated into your project settings for Windows Forms-based projects, as shown in Figure 1-43. For Web applications, there isn't a project file to hold the project settings, so it is possible to configure and run static code analysis from the website menu in Visual Studio.

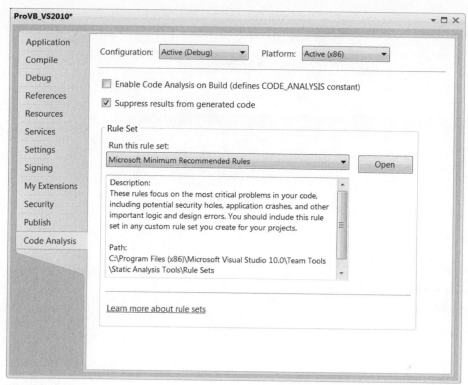

FIGURE 1-43

In fact, the tool doesn't actually look at your source code. Instead, it uses reflection; and once your project has been compiled, it queries the MSIL code your project generates. While this may seem surprising, remember that this tool is looking for several best practices, which may be implemented in different ways in your source code but will always compile in a standard manner.

Figure 1-43 shows the optional Code Analysis screen. Note that even when you have the code analysis tools available, by default, they are not enabled for your project. This is because enabling code analysis significantly extends your compile time. In most cases you'll want to enable these settings for a build or two, and then disable the checks for most of your debug builds. As you can see, to enable analysis you merely check the Enable Code Analysis on Build check box.

Below this check box is a check box to suppress results from generated code. One of the code analysis issues for which Microsoft was criticized after the Visual Studio 2005 release was that if you used the standard project template to create your project and then ran Code Analysis, you would get warnings related to the generated code. Microsoft's solution was to enable you to automatically bypass checking their generated code, which at least enables you to avoid having to manually mark all of the issues related to the generated code as being suppressed.

Once you have enabled the code analysis checks, you also have the option to define exactly which rules you want to apply. The checks are divided into different rule sets. Selecting a rule set such as the Microsoft Minimum Recommended Rules, you can use the Open button to access the display shown in Figure 1-44.

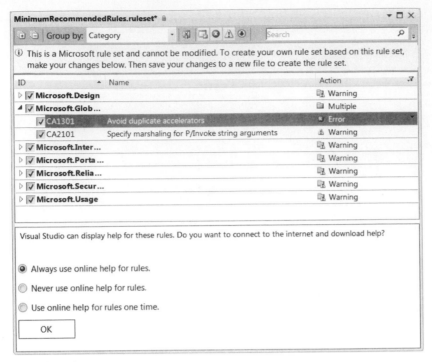

FIGURE 1-44

Within the rule set you see that there is a set of categories, each of which contains one or more rules. When expanded, next to each category and rule is a check box to indicate if that particular rule will be checked. By default, Visual Studio issue warnings if your code fails to meet the requirements associated with a rule. However, you can change the default — for example, by selecting an error status if a given rule fails. This enables you to have some rule violations act as compilation errors instead of warnings. Outside the scope of this chapter is the capability to actually identify within your source code those items that may be flagged by the code analyzer but that are valid exceptions to the rule being checked.

Performance Tools

Every developer wants performance checks. Visual Studio provides *dynamic code analysis*, or *performance*, tools for your application. These tools are available from the Analyze menu, shown in Figure 1-45. Selecting the Performance Explorer from the menu shown in Figure 1-45 opens the window shown on the left side of the display in Figure 1-45. This window has a small bar and provides access to details and results of your performance testing.

A good way to get started with the performance tools is to select the first item from the Analyze menu, the Performance Wizard, shown in Figure 1-46. The performance tools provide four runtime environments to measure the performance of your application: CPU Sampling, Instrumentation, .NET Memory Allocation (Sampling), and Concurrency.

Sampling for performance testing is a non-intrusive method of checking your application performance. Essentially, Visual Studio starts your application normally, but behind the scenes it is interfaced into the system performance counters. As your application runs, the performance monitoring engine captures system performance, and when your application completes it provides reports describing that performance. Details about what your application was actually doing to cause a behavior isn't available, but you can get a realistic idea of the impact on the system.

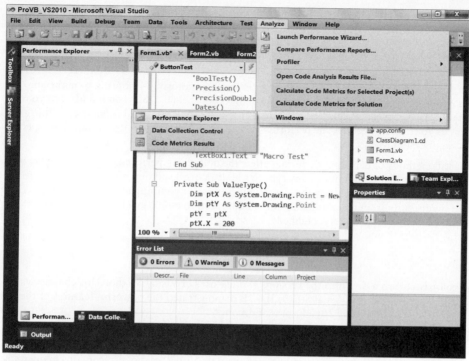

FIGURE 1-45

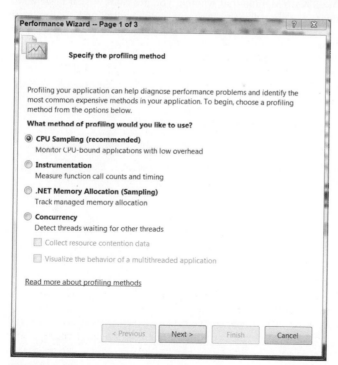

FIGURE 1-46

Concurrency checks are designed to detect issues with multi-threaded applications. The concurrency checks support two modes. The first checks for resource contention issues. This occurs when two threads are, for example, attempting to write output to the same data file or data table, thus forcing your parallel processing to behave in a serial manner. The second mode enables you to better track how threaded events are behaving.

Instrumentation, conversely, is an intrusive form of performance monitoring. Choosing to make an instrumentation run the performance tools triggers the addition of special MSIL commands into your compiled executable. These calls are placed at the start and finish of methods and properties within your executable. Then, as your code executes, the performance engine can gauge how long it takes for specific calls within your application to execute.

Keep in mind that all methods of performance testing affect the underlying performance of the application. It is true that running a performance monitor of any type has built-in overhead that affects your application, but the goal of performance testing isn't to know the exact timing marks of your application, but rather to identify areas that deviate significantly from the norm, and, more important, to establish a baseline from which you can track any significant changes as code is modified.

SUMMARY

In this chapter, you have taken a dive into the versions and features of Visual Studio. This chapter was intended to help you explore the new Visual Studio IDE. It demonstrated the powerful features of the IDE, even in the freely available Visual Basic 2010 Express Edition.

You've seen that Visual Studio 2010 is highly customizable and comes in a variety of flavors. As you worked within Visual Studio 2010, you've seen how numerous windows can be hidden, docked, or undocked. They can be layered in tabs and moved both within and beyond the IDE. Visual Studio also contains many tools, including some that extend its core capabilities. Keep in mind that whether you are using Visual Basic 2010 Express Edition or Visual Studio 2010 Ultimate, the core elements associated with compiling your application are the same.

2

Objects and Visual Basic

WHAT YOU WILL LEARN IN THIS CHAPTER

➤ Object Oriented Terminology

➤ Composition of an Object

➤ Characteristics of Value Types versus Reference Types

➤ Primitive Types

➤ Commands: If Then, Else, Select Case

➤ Common Value Types (Structures)

➤ Common Reference Types (Classes)

➤ XML literals

➤ Parameter passing ByVal and ByRef

➤ Variable scope

➤ Working with Objects

➤ Understanding Binding

➤ Data type conversions

➤ Creating Classes

➤ Event Handling

➤ Advanced Object Oriented Programming

➤ Using Lambdas

Visual Basic supports the four major defining concepts required for a language to be fully object-oriented:

➤ **Abstraction** — Abstraction is merely the ability of a language to create "black box" code, to take a concept and create an abstract representation of that concept within a program. A `Customer` object, for instance, is an abstract representation of a real-world customer. A `DataTable` object is an abstract representation of a set of data.

➤ **Encapsulation** — Encapsulation is the concept of a separation between interface and implementation. The idea is that you can create an interface (public methods, properties, fields, and events in a class), and, as long as that interface remains consistent, the application can interact with your objects. This remains true even when you entirely rewrite the code within a given method — thus, the interface is independent of the implementation. The publicly exposed interface becomes what is known as a contract. It is this contract that you will look to limit changes to for those who consume your objects. For example, the algorithm you use to compute pi might be proprietary. You can expose a simple API to the end user, but hide all the logic used by the algorithm by encapsulating it within your class. Later if you change that algorithm, as long as the consumers of your object get the same results from your public interface, they won't need to make changes to support your updates. Encapsulation enables you to hide the internal implementation details of a class.

➤ **Polymorphism** — Polymorphism is reflected in the ability to write one routine that can operate on objects from more than one class — treating different objects from different classes in exactly the same way. For instance, if both the `Customer` and the `Vendor` objects have a `Name` property and you can write a routine that calls the `Name` property regardless of whether you are using a `Customer` or `Vendor` object, then you have polymorphism.

Visual Basic supports polymorphism in two ways — through late binding (much like Smalltalk, a classic example of a true object-oriented language) and through the implementation of multiple interfaces. This flexibility is very powerful and is preserved within Visual Basic.

➤ **Inheritance** — Inheritance is the concept that a new class can be based on an existing class gaining the interface and behaviors of that base class. The child or sub-class of that base or parent class is said to inherit the existing behaviors and properties. The new class can also customize or override existing methods and properties, as well as extending the class with new methods and properties. When inheriting from an existing class, the developer is implementing a process known as *subclassing*.

Chapter 3 discusses these four concepts in detail; this chapter focuses on the syntax that enables you to utilize classes which already implement these concepts. The concepts are then illustrated through a review of the core types which make up Visual Basic, as well as through the creation of a custom class that leverages these core concepts.

Visual Basic is also a component-based language. Component-based design is often viewed as a successor to object-oriented design, so component-based languages have some other capabilities. These are closely related to the traditional concepts of object orientation:

➤ **Multiple interfaces** — Each class in Visual Basic defines a *primary interface* (also called the *default* or *native interface*) through its public methods, properties, and events. Classes can also implement other, secondary interfaces in addition to this primary interface. An object based on this class has multiple interfaces, and a client application can choose with which interface it will interact with the object.

➤ **Assembly (component) level scoping** — Not only can you define your classes and methods as `Public` (available to anyone), `Protected` (available through inheritance), and `Private` (available only locally), you can also define them as `Friend` — meaning they are available only within the current assembly or component. This is not a traditional object-oriented concept, but is very powerful when used with component-based applications.

This chapter explains how to create and use classes and objects in Visual Basic. We won't get too deeply into code, but it is important that you spend a little time familiarizing yourself with basic object-oriented terms and concepts.

OBJECT-ORIENTED TERMINOLOGY

To begin, let's take a look at the word *object* itself, along with the related *class* and *instance* terms. Then we will move on to discuss the four terms that define the major functionality in the object-oriented world: abstraction, encapsulation, polymorphism, and inheritance.

Objects, Classes, and Instances

An *object* is a code-based abstraction of a real-world entity or relationship. For instance, you might have a `Customer` object that represents a real-world customer, such as customer number 123, or you might have a `File` object that represents `C:\config.sys` on your computer's hard drive.

A closely related term is *class*. A class is the code that defines an object, and all objects are created based on a class. A class is an abstraction of a real-world concept, and it provides the basis from which you create instances of specific objects. For example, in order to have a `Customer` object representing customer number 123, you must first have a `Customer` class that contains all of the code (methods, properties, events, variables, and so on) necessary to create `Customer` objects. Based on that class, you can create any number of objects, each one an instance of the class. Each object is identical to the others, except that it may contain different data.

You can create many instances of `Customer` objects based on the same `Customer` class. All of the `Customer` objects are identical in terms of what they can do and the code they contain, but each one contains its own unique data. This means that each object represents a different physical customer.

Composition of an Object

You use an *interface* to get access to an object's data and behaviors. This defines a contract for the object to follow. This is much like a real world legal contract that binds the object to a standard definition of data and behaviors, where in your interface you can define a what is needed to fulfill a contract. The object's data and behaviors are contained within the object, so a client application can treat the object like a black box, accessible only through its interface. This is a key object-oriented concept called *encapsulation*. The idea is that any program that makes use of this object will not have direct access to the behaviors or data; rather, those programs must make use of your object's interface.

Interface

The interface is defined as a set of methods (Sub and Function methods), properties (property methods), events, and fields (also known as variables) that are declared public in scope.

You can also have private methods and properties in your code. While these methods can be called by code within your object, they are not part of the interface and cannot be called by programs written to use your object. Another option is to use the `Friend` keyword, which defines the scope to be your current project, meaning that any code within your project can call the method, but no code outside your project (that is, from a different .NET assembly) can call the method. To complicate things a bit, you can also declare methods and properties as `Protected`, and these are available to classes that inherit from your class. You will look at `Protected` in Chapter 3, along with inheritance.

For example, you might have the following code in a class:

```
Public Function CalculateValue() As Integer

End Function
```

Because this method is declared with the `Public` keyword, it is part of the interface and can be called by client applications that are using the object. You might also have a method such as this:

```
Private Sub DoSomething()

End Sub
```

This method is declared as being `Private`, so it is not part of the interface. This method can only be called by code within the class — not by any code outside the class, such as code in a program that's using one of the objects.

Conversely, you can do something like this:

```
Public Sub CalculateValue()
   DoSomething()
End Sub
```

In this case, you're calling the `Private` method from within a `Public` method. While code using your objects can't directly call a `Private` method, you will frequently use `Private` methods to help structure the code in a class to make it more maintainable and easier to read.

Finally, you can use the `Friend` keyword:

```
Friend Sub DoSomething()

End Sub
```

In this case, the `DoSomething` method can be called by code within the class, or from other classes or modules within the current Visual Basic project. Code from outside the project will not have access to the method.

The `Friend` scope is very similar to the `Public` scope in that it makes methods available for use by code outside the object itself. Unlike `Public`, however, the `Friend` keyword restricts access to code within the current Visual Basic project, preventing code in other .NET assemblies from calling the method. One of the more common uses of `Protected` is with the `Friend` modifier as will be discussed in Chapter 3.

Implementation or Behavior

The code inside a method is called the *implementation*. Sometimes it is also called *behavior*, as it is this code that actually makes the object do useful work. For instance, you might have an `Age` property as part of the object's interface. Within that method, you might have code similar to the following:

```
Public ReadOnly Property Age() As Integer
```

In this case, the code is returning a value directly out of a variable, rather than doing something better, such as calculate the value based on a birth date. However, this kind of code is often written in applications, and it seems to work fine for a while.

The key point is to understand that client applications can use the object even if you change the implementation, as long as you do not change the public interface. If the method name and its parameter list and return data type remain unchanged, then you can change the implementation any way you want.

The code necessary to call the `Age` property would look something like this:

```
theAge = myObject.Age
```

The result of running this code is that you get the `Age` value returned. While the client application will work fine, you will soon discover that hard-coding the age into the application is a problem, so at some point you'll want to improve this code. Fortunately, you can change the implementation without changing the client code:

```
Private _BirthDate As Date

Public ReadOnly Property Age() As Integer
  Get
      Return CInt(DateDiff(DateInterval.Year, _BirthDate, Now))
  End Get
End Property
```

You have changed the implementation behind the public interface, effectively changing how it behaves without changing the interface itself. Now, when you run the client application, the `Age` value returned is accurate over time, whereas in the previous implementation it was not.

Additionally, to implement this change you've moved from one of the new features of Visual Basic 2010 — auto-implemented properties, to a traditional property with a backing field implementation. Much of the existing .NET code you'll see in Visual Basic will use a backing field for properties because up until this release that was the only way to implement a property.

Keep in mind that encapsulation is a *syntactic* tool — it enables the code to continue to run without change. However, it is not *semantic*, meaning that just because the code continues to run, that does not mean it continues to do what you actually want it to do.

In this example, the client code may have been written to overcome the initial limitations of the implementation in some way, and thus the client code might both rely on being able to retrieve the Age value, and count on the result of that call being a fixed value over time.

The update to the implementation won't stop the client program from running, but it may very well prevent it from running correctly.

Fields or Instance Variables

The third key part of an object is its data, or state. In fact, it might be argued that the only important part of an object is its data. After all, every instance of a class is absolutely identical in terms of its interface and its implementation; the only thing that can vary at all is the data contained within that particular object.

Fields are variables that are declared so that they are available to all code within the class. Typically, fields that are declared Private in scope are available only to the code in the class itself. They are also sometimes referred to as *instance variables* or *member variables*.

Don't confuse fields with properties. In Visual Basic, a property is a type of method geared to retrieving and setting values, whereas a field is a variable within the class that may hold the value exposed by a property. For instance, you might have a class that has these fields:

```
Public Class TheClass

    Private _Name As String
    Private _BirthDate As Date
End Class
```

Each instance of the class — each object — will have its own set of these fields in which to store data. Because these fields are declared with the Private keyword, they are only available to code within each specific object.

While fields can be declared as Public in scope, this makes them available to any code using the objects in a manner you cannot control. This directly breaks the concept of encapsulation, as code outside your object can directly change data values without following any rules that might otherwise be set in the object's code.

Consider the Age property shown in the previous section. You'll notice that by using a property, the underlying implementation, even though initially generated, was hidden to the outside world. When you decided to change the implementation to use a dynamically generated age you could change that implementation without changing your interface.

If you want to make the value of a field available to code outside of the object, you should instead use a property:

```
Public Class TheClass
    Private _Name As String
    Private _BirthDate As Date

    Public ReadOnly Property Name() As String
        Get
            Return _Name
        End Get
    End Property

End Class
```

Because the Name property is a method, you are not directly exposing the internal variables to client code, so you preserve encapsulation of the data. At the same time, through this mechanism, you are able to safely provide access to your data as needed. Fields can also be declared with the Friend scope, meaning they are available to all code in your project.

Now that you have a grasp of some of the basic object-oriented terminology, you are ready to explore the creation of classes and objects. First you will see how Visual Basic enables you to interact with objects and provides core types (all of which are objects), and then you will dive into the actual process of authoring those objects.

System.Object

For now, the one key to remember is that all classes in Visual Basic, all classes in .NET for that matter, inherit from the base class `System.Object`. `System.Object` is the parent class for everything from `Strings` and `Integers` to `Windows` and custom classes developed by you. When a `Class` doesn't explicitly state its parent, .NET will automatically have the class inherit from `System.Object`. This also means that even if a `Class` does explicitly inherit from another `Class`, that `Parent Class` or its parent or base `Class`, or at some point some class in the inheritance chain, will inherit from `System.Object`. There was an old saying about how all roads lead to Rome. Well, in .NET all object hierarchies lead to `System.Object`. `System.Object` is the base `Class` for all `Classes`.

This is where the term polymorphism becomes important. Since you can cast any object to a type from which it inherits, any type of object can be cast to the base class of `System.Object`. Casting is the name for code which takes an object of, for example, type `Integer` and assigns it to a variable of type `System.Object`. As you'll see as you work with Visual Basic or another object oriented language, this means that you'll see many methods that are written to handle a parameter of type `Object`. This has several advantages for code reuse, but you'll learn that reuse can come at a cost.

The thing you'll want to keep in mind is that when an object is cast to its parent class it only makes the methods of that parent class available. While the underlying object can be cast back to its original type, because it knows what that type is, it doesn't make all of its data and behavior available until it is cast back to its original type. Note you can cast to any type in an object's inheritance hierarchy, but that will be covered in more detail in Chapter 3.

`System.Object` provides a member in which you will be interested. The method `ToString` provides a way to get a string representation of any object. The default implementation of this method will return the type of that `object`; however, many types provide a custom implementation of this method, and doing so is considered best practice.

WORKING WITH VISUAL BASIC TYPES

Having introduced a combination of keywords and concepts for objects in Visual Basic, it is time to start exploring specific types. In order to ensure this is hands on, you need a project in Visual Studio 2010. The previous chapter focused on Visual Studio 2010 and many of its features as your primary development tool. This chapter is much more focused on the Visual Basic language, and to limit its size you are going to reference the project created in the last chapter in this chapter. As this chapter introduces some of the core types of Visual Basic, classes provided by the .NET Framework which are at the core of Visual Basic, you test code snippets in that project.

To host the example snippets in the project based on the ProVB_VS2010 project built in Chapter 1, there are very few changes. The code download for this chapter includes the final version of the samples. This means that as you progress through the chapter, you can either look in the sample download for the same code, or step by step build up your own copy of the sample, using the sample when something doesn't seem quite right in your own code. The one change from the previous chapter's code is that the custom property and message box used in that chapter have already been removed from this project.

At this point, you have a display that allows you to show the results from various code snippets simply by updating the `Text` property on the `TextBox1` control of your window. The display for the baseline Windows Form application is shown in Figure 2-1.

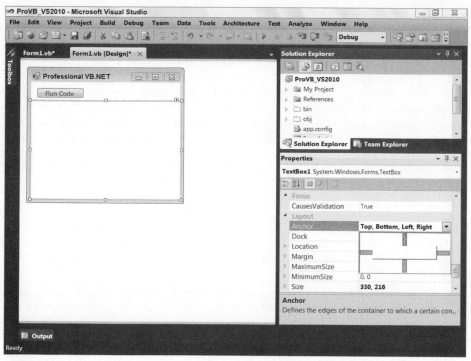

FIGURE 2-1

As you can see, the baseline is simply a button to initiate the custom code combined with a text box. As you want to test a snippet, you will add a new method to Form1, and then call this method from the Click event handler for the button. The sample download shows how these methods can be added, and then when you are ready to add the next method, use the single quote line to comment out the method call for the previous test. In this way, you'll be able to comment out a single line call to your method and within the method the code to demonstrate that feature of Visual Basic will remain available. The following section on the difference between value and reference types will create two such methods, and if you look at the sample download code you'll find the calls to the methods shown in the snippet are in the event handler commented out already.

Value and Reference Types

Experienced developers generally consider integers, characters, Booleans, and strings to be the basic building blocks of any language. As noted above in .NET, all objects share a logical inheritance from the base `Object` class. One of the advantages of this common heritage is the capability to rely on certain common methods of every variable. Another is that this enables all of .NET to build on a common type system. Visual Basic builds on the common type system shared across .NET languages.

Because all data types are based on the core `Object` class, every variable you dimension can be assured of having a set of common characteristics. However, this logical inheritance does not require a common physical implementation for all variables. This is important because while everything in .NET is based on the `Object` class, under the covers .NET has two major implementations of types: value and reference.

For example, what most programmers consider to be some of the basic underlying types, such as `Integer`, `Long`, `Character`, and even `Byte`, are not implemented as classes. This is important, as you'll see when we look at boxing and the cost of transitioning between value types and reference types. The difference between value types and reference types is an underlying implementation difference:

➤ Value types represent simple data storage located on the stack. The stack is used for items of a known size, so items on the stack can be retrieved faster than those on the managed heap.

➤ Reference types are based on complex classes with implementation inheritance from their parent classes, and custom storage on the managed heap. The managed heap is optimized to support dynamic allocation of differently sized objects.

Note that the two implementations are stored in different portions of memory. As a result, value types and reference types are treated differently within assignment statements, and their memory management is handled differently. It is important to understand how these differences affect the software you will write in Visual Basic. Understanding the foundations of how data is manipulated in the .NET Framework will enable you to build more reliable and better-performing applications.

Consider the difference between the stack and the heap. The stack is a comparatively small memory area in which processes and threads store data of fixed size. An integer or decimal value needs the same number of bytes to store data, regardless of the actual value. This means that the location of such variables on the stack can be efficiently determined. (When a process needs to retrieve a variable, it has to search the stack. If the stack contained variables that had dynamic memory sizes, then such a search could take a long time.)

Reference types do not have a fixed size — a string can vary in size from two bytes to nearly all the memory available on a system. The dynamic size of reference types means that the data they contain is stored on the heap, rather than the stack. However, the address of the reference type (that is, the location of the data on the heap) does have a fixed size, and thus can be (and, in fact, is) stored on the stack. By storing a reference only to a custom allocation on the stack, the program as a whole runs much more quickly, as the process can rapidly locate the data associated with a variable.

Storing the data contained in fixed and dynamically sized variables in different places results in differences in the way variables behave. Rather than limit this discussion to the most basic of types in .NET, this difference can be illustrated by comparing the behavior of the `System.Drawing.Point` structure (a value type) and the `System.Text.StringBuilder` class (a reference type).

The `Point` structure is used as part of the .NET graphics library, which is part of the `System.Drawing` namespace. The `StringBuilder` class is part of the `System.Text` namespace and is used to improve performance when you're editing strings.

First, let's examine how the `System.Drawing.Point` structure is used. To do this, you'll create a new method called `ValueType()` within your ProVB_VS2010 application. This new private `Sub` will be called from the `ButtonTest` click event handler. The new method will have the following format:

Available for download on Wrox.com

```
Private Sub ValueType()
    Dim ptX As System.Drawing.Point = New System.Drawing.Point(10, 20)
    Dim ptY As System.Drawing.Point
    ptY = ptX
    ptX.X = 200
    TextBox1.Text = "Pt Y = " & ptY.ToString()
End Sub
```

Code snippet from Form1

The output from this operation will be {{X = 10, Y = 20}}, is shown in Figure 2-2. When the code copies `ptX` into `ptY`, the data contained in `ptX` is copied into the location on the stack associated with `ptY`. Later, when the value of `ptX` changes, only the memory on the stack associated with `ptX` is altered. Altering the value of `ptX` has no effect on `ptY`. This is not the case with reference types. Consider the following code, a new method called `RefType` which uses the `System.Text.StringBuilder` class:

```
Private Sub RefType()
    Dim objX As System.Text.StringBuilder = New System.Text.StringBuilder("Hello World")
    Dim objY As System.Text.StringBuilder
    objY = objX
    objX.Replace("World", "Test")
    TextBox1.Text = "objY = " & objY.ToString()
End Sub
```

Code snippet from Form1

The output from this operation will be "Hello Test," as shown in Figure 2-3, not "Hello World". The previous example using points demonstrated that when one value type is assigned to another, the data stored on the stack is copied. Similarly, this example demonstrates that when objY is assigned to objX, the data associated with objX on the stack is copied to the data associated with objY on the stack. However, what is copied in this case isn't the actual data, but rather the address on the managed heap where the data is actually located. This means that objY and objX now reference the same data. When the data on the heap is changed, the data associated with every variable that holds a reference to that memory is changed. This is the default behavior of reference types, and is known as a *shallow copy*. Later in this chapter, you'll see how this behavior has been overridden for strings (which perform a *deep copy*).

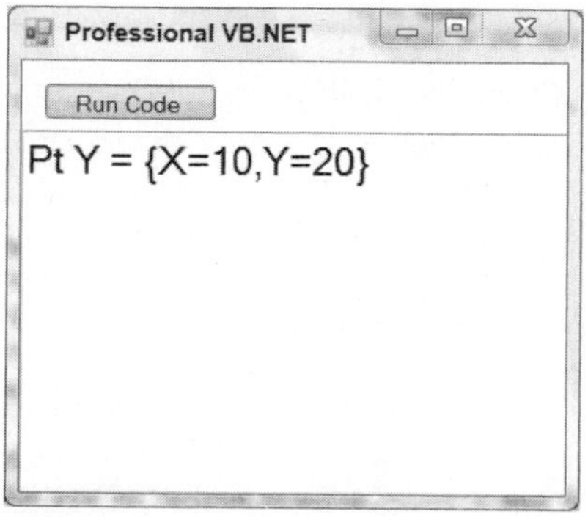

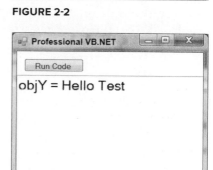

FIGURE 2-2

FIGURE 2-3

The differences between value types and reference types go beyond how they behave when copied, and later in this chapter you'll encounter some of the other features provided by objects. First, though, let's take a closer look at some of the most commonly used value types and learn how .NET works with them.

Primitive Types

Visual Basic, in common with other development languages, has a group of elements such as integers and strings that are termed *primitive types*. These primitive types are identified by keywords such as String, Long, and Integer, which are aliases for types defined by the .NET class library. This means that the line

```
Dim i As Long
```

is equivalent to the line

```
Dim i As System.Int64
```

The reason why these two different declarations are available has to do with long-term planning for your application. In most cases (such as when Visual Basic transitioned to .NET), you want to use the Short, Integer, and Long designations. When Visual Basic moved to .NET, the Integer type went from 16 bits to 32 bits. Code written with this Integer type would automatically use the larger value if you rewrote the code in .NET. Interestingly enough, however, the Visual Basic Migration Wizard actually recast Visual Basic 6 Integer values to Visual Basic .NET Short values.

This is the same reason why Int16, Int32, and Int64 exist. These types specify a physical implementation; therefore, if your code is someday migrated to a version of .NET that maps the Integer value to Int64, then those values defined as Integer will reflect the new larger capacity, while those declared as Int32 will not. This could be important if your code were manipulating part of an interface where changing the physical size of the value could break the interface.

Table 2-1 lists the primitive types that Visual Basic 2008 defines, and the structures or classes to which they map:

TABLE 2-1: Primitive Types in .NET

PRIMITIVE TYPE	.NET CLASS OR STRUCTURE
Byte	System.Byte (structure)
Short	System.Int16 (structure)
Integer	System.Int32 (structure)
Long	System.Int64 (structure)
Single	System.Single (structure)
Double	System.Double (structure)
Decimal	System.Decimal (structure)
Boolean	System.Boolean (structure)
Date	System.DateTime (structure)
Char	System.Char (structure)
String	System.String (class)

> *The* String *primitive type stands out from the other primitives. Strings are implemented as a class, not a structure. More important, strings are the one primitive type that is a reference type.*

You can perform certain operations on primitive types that you can't on other types. For example, you can assign a value to a primitive type using a literal:

```
Dim i As Integer = 32
Dim str As String = "Hello"
```

It's also possible to declare a primitive type as a constant using the Const keyword, as shown here:

```
Dim Const str As String = "Hello"
```

The value of the variable str in the preceding line of code cannot be changed elsewhere in the application containing this code at runtime. These two simple examples illustrate the key properties of primitive types. As noted, most primitive types are, in fact, value types. The next step is to take a look at core language commands that enable you to operate on these variables.

COMMANDS: CONDITIONAL

Unlike many programming languages, Visual Basic has been designed to focus on readability and clarity. Many languages are willing to sacrifice these attributes to enable developers to type as little as possible. Visual Basic, conversely, is designed under the paradigm that the readability of code matters more than saving a few keystrokes, so commands in Visual Basic tend to spell out the exact context of what is being done.

Literally dozens of commands make up the Visual Basic language, so there isn't nearly enough space here to address all of them. Moreover, many of the more specialized commands are covered later in this book. However, if you are not familiar with Visual Basic or are relatively new to programming, a few would be helpful to look at here. These fall into two basic areas: *conditional statements* and *looping statements*. This chapter addresses two statements within each of these categories, starting with the conditional statements; later, after collections and arrays have been introduced, looping statements are covered.

Each of these statements has the ability not only to call another method, the preferred way to manage blocks of code, but also to literally encapsulate a block of code. Note that the variables declared within the context of a conditional statement (between the `If` and `End If` lines) are only visible up until the `End If` statement. After that, these variables go out of scope. The concept of scoping is discussed in more detail later in this chapter.

If Then

The conditional is one of two primary programming constructs (the other being the loop) that is present in almost every programming language. After all, even in those rare cases where the computer is just repeatedly adding values or doing some other repetitive activity, at some point a decision is needed and a condition evaluated, even if the question is only "is it time to stop?" Visual Basic supports the `If-Then` statement as well as the `Else` statement; — and unlike some languages, the concept of an `ElseIf` statement. The `ElseIf` and `Else` statements are totally optional, and it is not only acceptable but common to use conditionals that do not utilize either of these code blocks. The following example illustrates a simple pair of conditions that have been set up serially:

```
If i > 1 Then
    'Code A1
ElseIf i < 1 Then
    'Code B2
Else
    'Code C3
End If
```

If the first condition is true, then code placed at marker `A1` is executed. The flow would then proceed to the `End If`, and the program would not evaluate any of the other conditions. Note that for best performance, it makes the most sense to have your most common condition first in this structure, because if it is successful, none of the other conditions need to be tested.

If the initial comparison in the preceding example code were false, then control would move to the first `Else` statement, which in this case happens to be an `ElseIf` statement. The code would therefore test the next conditional to determine whether the value of `i` were less than 1. If so, then the code associated with block `B2` would be executed.

However, if the second condition were also false, then the code would proceed to the `Else` statement, which isn't concerned with any remaining condition and just executes the code in block `C3`. Not only is the `Else` optional, but even if an `ElseIf` is used, the `Else` condition is still optional. It is acceptable for the `Else` and `C3` block to be omitted from the preceding example.

Comparison Operators

There are several ways to discuss what is evaluated in an `If` statement. Essentially, the code between the `If` and `Then` portions of the statement must eventually evaluate out to a `Boolean`. At the most basic level, this means you can write `If True Then`, which results in a valid statement, although the code would always execute the associated block of code with that `If` statement. The idea, however, is that for a basic comparison, you take two values and place between them a comparison operator. Comparison operators include the following symbols: =, >, <, >=, <=.

Additionally, certain keywords can be used with a comparison operator. For example, the keyword `Not` can be used to indicate that the statement should consider the failure of a given comparison as a reason to execute the code encapsulated by its condition. An example of this is shown in the next example:

```
If Not i = 1 Then
    'Code A1
End If
```

It is therefore possible to compare two values and then take the resulting Boolean from this comparison and reevaluate the result. In this case, the result is only reversed, but the `If` statement supports more complex comparisons using statements such as And and Or. These statements enable you to create a complex condition based on several comparisons, as shown here:

```
If Not i = 1 Or i < 0 And str = "Hello" Then
    'Code A1
Else
    'Code B2
End If
```

The And and Or conditions are applied to determine whether the first comparison's results are true or false along with the second value's results. The And conditional means that both comparisons must evaluate to true in order for the If statement to execute the code in block A1, and the Or statement means that if the condition on either side is true, then the If statement can evaluate code block A1. However, in looking at this statement, your first reaction should be to pause and attempt to determine in exactly what order all of the associated comparisons occur.

There is a precedence. First, any numeric style comparisons are applied, followed by any unary operators such as Not. Finally, proceeding from left to right, each Boolean comparison of And and Or is applied. However, a much better way to write the preceding statement is to use parentheses to identify in what order you want these comparisons to occur. The first If statement in the following example illustrates the default order, while the second and third use parentheses to force a different priority on the evaluation of the conditions:

```
If ((Not i = 1) Or i < 0) And (str = "Hello") Then
If (Not i = 1) Or (i < 0 And str = "Hello") Then
If Not ((i = 1 Or i < 0) And str = "Hello") Then
```

All three of the preceding If statements are evaluating the same set of criteria, yet their results are potentially very different. It is always best practice to enclose complex conditionals within parentheses to indicate the desired order of evaluation. Of course, these comparisons have been rather simple; you could replace the variable value in the preceding examples with a function call that might include a call to a database. In such a situation, if the desired behavior were to execute this expensive call only when necessary, then you might want to use one of the shortcut comparison operators.

Since you know that for an And statement both sides of the If statement must be true, there are times when knowing that the first condition is false could save processing time; you would not bother executing the second condition. Similarly, if the comparison involves an Or statement, then once the first part of the condition is true, there is no reason to evaluate the second condition because you know that the net result is success. In this case, the AndAlso and OrElse statements allow for performance optimization:

```
If ((Not i = 1) Or i < 0) AndAlso (MyFunction() = "Success") Then
If Not i = 1 OrElse (i < 0 And MyFunction() = "Success") Then
```

The preceding code illustrates that instead of using a variable like str as used in the preceding samples, your condition might call a function you've written that returns a value. In this case, MyFunction would return a string that would then be used in the comparison. In the statements above, each conditional statement has been optimized so that there are situations where the code associated with MyFunction won't be executed.

This is potentially important, not only from a performance standpoint, but also in a scenario where, given the first condition, your code might throw an error. For example, it's not uncommon to first determine whether a variable has been assigned a value and then to test that value. This introduces yet another pair of conditional elements: the Is and IsNot conditionals.

Using If enables you to determine whether a variable has been given a value, or to determine its type. In the past it was common to see nested If statements, with the first determining whether the value was null, followed by a separate If statement to determine whether the value was valid. Starting with .NET 2.0, the short-circuit conditionals enable you to check for a value and then check whether that value meets the desired criteria. The short-circuit operator prevents the check for a value from occurring and causing an error if the variable is undefined, so both checks can be done with a single If statement:

```
Dim mystring as string = Nothing
If mystring IsNot Nothing AndAlso mystring.Length > 100 Then
    'Code A1
ElseIf mystring.GetType Is GetType(Integer) Then
    'Code B2
End If
```

The preceding code would fail on the first comparison because `mystring` has only been initialized to `Nothing`, meaning that by definition it doesn't have a length. Note also that the second condition will fail because you know that `myString` isn't of type `Integer`.

Select Case

The preceding section makes it clear that the `If` statement is the king of conditionals. However, in another scenario you may have a simple condition that needs to be tested repeatedly. For example, suppose a user selects a value from a drop-down list and different code executes depending on that value. This is a relatively simple comparison, but if you have 20 values, then you would potentially need to string together 20 different `If Then` and `ElseIf` statements to account for all of the possibilities.

A cleaner way of evaluating such a condition is to leverage a `Select Case` statement. This statement was designed to test a condition, but instead of returning a `Boolean` value, it returns a value that is then used to determine which block of code, each defined by a `Case` statement, should be executed:

```
Select Case i
    Case 1
        'Code A1
    Case 2
        'Code B2
    Case Else
        'Code C3
End Select
```

The preceding sample code shows how the `Select` portion of the statement determines the value represented by the variable `i`. Depending on the value of this variable, the `Case` statement executes the appropriate code block. For a value of 1, the code in block `A1` is executed; similarly, a 2 results in code block `B2` executing. For any other value, because this `Case` statement includes an `Else` block, the `Case` statement executes the code represented by `C3`. Note that while in this example each item has its own block, it is also possible to have more than a single match on the same `Case`. Thus `Case 2, 3` would match if the value of `i` were either a 2 or a 3. Finally, the next example illustrates that the cases do not need to be integer values, and can, in fact, even be strings:

```
Dim mystring As String = "Intro"
Select Case mystring
    Case "Intro"
        'Code A1
    Case "Exit"
        'Code A2
    Case Else
        'Code A3
End Select
```

Now that you have been introduced to these two control elements that enable you to specify what happens in your code, your next step is to review details of the different variable types that are available within Visual Basic 2010, starting with the value types.

VALUE TYPES (STRUCTURES)

Value types aren't as versatile as reference types, but they can provide better performance in many circumstances. The core value types (which include the majority of primitive types) are `Boolean`, `Byte`, `Char`, `DateTime`, `Decimal`, `Double`, `Guid`, `Int16`, `Int32`, `Int64`, `SByte`, `Single`, and `TimeSpan`. These are not the only value types, but rather the subset with which most Visual Basic developers consistently work. As you've seen, value types by definition store data on the stack.

Value types can also be referred to by their proper name: structures. The underlying principles and syntax of creating custom structures mirrors that of creating classes, covered in the next chapter. This section focuses on some of the built-in types provided by the .NET Framework — in particular, the built-in types known as *primitives*.

Boolean

The .NET `Boolean` type represents true or false. Variables of this type work well with the conditional statements that were just discussed. When you declare a variable of type `Boolean`, you can use it within a conditional statement directly. Test the following sample by creating a `Sub` called `BoolTest` within ProVB_VS2010:

Available for
download on
Wrox.com

```
Private Sub BoolTest()
    Dim blnTrue As Boolean = True
    Dim blnFalse As Boolean = False
    If (blnTrue) Then
        TextBox1.Text = blnTrue & Environment.NewLine
        TextBox1.Text &= blnFalse.ToString
    End If
End Sub
```

Code snippet from Form1

The results of this code are shown in Figure 2-4. There are a couple things outside of the Boolean logic to review within the preceding code sample. These are related to the update of `Textbox1.Text`. In this case, because you want two lines of text, you need to embed a new line character into the text. There are two ways of doing this in Visual Basic. The first is to use the `Environment.Newline` constant, which is part of the core .NET Framework. Alternatively, you may find a Visual Basic developer leveraging the Visual Basic–specific constant `vbCRLF`, which does the same thing.

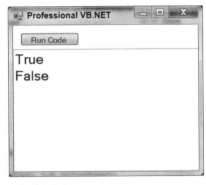

FIGURE 2-4

The second issue related to that line is that I am concatenating the implicit value of the variable `blnTrue` with the value of the `Environment.Newline` constant. Note the use of an ampersand (`&`) for this action. This is a best practice in Visual Basic because while Visual Basic does overload the plus (+) sign to support string concatenation, in this case the items being concatenated aren't necessarily strings. This is related to not setting `Option Strict` to `On`. In that scenario, the system will look at the actual types of the variables and if there were two integers side by side in your string concatenation you would get unexpected results. This is because the code would first process the "+" and would add the values as numeric values.

Thus, since neither you nor the sample download code has set `Option String` to `On` for this project, if you replace the preceding `&` with a `+`, you'll find a runtime conversion error in your application. Therefore, in production code it is best practice to always use the `&` to concatenate strings in Visual Basic unless you are certain that both sides of the concatenation will always be a string. However, neither of these issues directly affect the use of the `Boolean` values, which when interpreted this way provide their `ToString()` output, not a numeric value.

 Always use the `True` *and* `False` *constants when working with* `Boolean` *variables.*

Unfortunately, in the past developers had a tendency to tell the system to interpret a variable created as a `Boolean` as an `Integer`. This is referred to as *implicit conversion* and is related to `Option Strict`. It is not the best practice, and when .NET was introduced, it caused issues for Visual Basic because the underlying representation of `True` in other languages wasn't going to match those of Visual Basic. The result was that Visual Basic represents `True` differently for implicit conversions than other .NET languages.

`True` has been implemented in such a way that when converted to an integer, Visual Basic converts a value of `True` to -1 (negative one). This is one of the few (but not the only) legacy carryovers from older versions of Visual Basic, and is different from other languages, which typically use the integer value 1. Generically, all languages tend to implicitly convert `False` to 0, and `True` to a nonzero value.

However, Visual Basic works as part of a multilanguage environment, with metadata-defining interfaces, so the external value of `True` is as important as its internal value. Fortunately, Microsoft implemented Visual Basic in such a way that while -1 is supported, the .NET standard of 1 is exposed from Visual Basic methods to other languages.

To create reusable code, it is always better to avoid implicit conversions. In the case of Booleans, if the code needs to check for an integer value, then you should explicitly evaluate the Boolean and create an appropriate integer. The code will be far more maintainable and prone to fewer unexpected results.

Integer Types

Now that Booleans have been covered in depth, the next step is to examine the `Integer` types that are part of Visual Basic. Visual Basic 6.0 included two types of integer values: The `Integer` type was limited to a maximum value of 32767, and the `Long` type supported a maximum value of 2147483647.

The .NET Framework added a new integer type, the `Short`. The `Short` is the equivalent of the `Integer` value from Visual Basic 6.0; the `Integer` has been promoted to support the range previously supported by the Visual Basic 6.0 `Long` type, and the Visual Basic .NET `Long` type is an eight-byte value. The new `Long` type provides support for 64-bit values, such as those used by current 64-bit processors. In addition, each of these types also has two alternative types. In all, Visual Basic supports the nine `Integer` types described in Table 2-2.

TABLE 2-2: Visual Basic Integer Types

TYPE	ALLOCATED MEMORY	MINIMUM VALUE	MAXIMUM VALUE
Short	2 bytes	-32768	32767
Int16	2 bytes	-32768	32767
UInt16	2 bytes	0	65535
Integer	4 bytes	-2147483648	2147483647
Int32	4 bytes	-2147483648	2147483647
UInt32	4 bytes	0	4294967295
Long	8 bytes	-9223372036854775808	9223372036854775807
Int64	8 bytes	-9223372036854775808	9223372036854775807
UInt64	8 bytes	0	18446744073709551615

Short

A `Short` value is limited to the maximum value that can be stored in two bytes. This means there are 16 bits and the value can range between -32768 and 32767. This limitation may or may not be based on the amount of memory physically associated with the value; it is a definition of what must occur in the .NET Framework. This is important, because there is no guarantee that the implementation will actually use less memory than when using an `Integer` value. It is possible that in order to optimize memory or processing, the operating system will allocate the same amount of physical memory used for an `Integer` type and then just limit the possible values.

The `Short` (or `Int16`) value type can be used to map SQL `smallint` values.

Integer

An `Integer` is defined as a value that can be safely stored and transported in four bytes (not as a four-byte implementation). This gives the `Integer` and `Int32` value types a range from –2147483648 to 2147483647. This range is more than adequate to handle most tasks.

The main reason to use an `Int32` in place of an `Integer` value is to ensure future portability with interfaces. For example, the `Integer` value in Visual Basic 6.0 was limited to a two-byte value, but is now a four-byte value. In future 64-bit platforms, the `Integer` value might be an eight-byte value. Problems could occur if an interface used a 64-bit `Integer` with an interface that expected a 32-bit `Integer` value, or, conversely, if code using the `Integer` type is suddenly passed to a variable explicitly declared as `Int32`.

The solution is to be consistent. Use `Int32`, which would remain a 32-bit value, even on a 64-bit platform, if that is what you need. In addition, as a best practice, use `Integer` so your code is not constrained by the underlying implementation.

The Visual Basic .NET `Integer` value type matches the size of an `Integer` value in SQL Server, which means that you can easily align the column type of a table with the variable type in your programs.

Long

The `Long` type is aligned with the `Int64` value. The `Long` has an eight-byte range, which means that its value can range from –9223372036854775808 to 9223372036854775807. This is a big range, but if you need to add or multiply `Integer` values, then you need a large value to contain the result. It's common while doing math operations on one type of integer to use a larger type to capture the result if there's a chance that the result could exceed the limit of the types being manipulated.

The `Long` value type matches the `bigint` type in SQL.

Unsigned Types

Another way to gain additional range on the positive side of an `Integer` type is to use one of the unsigned types. The unsigned types provide a useful buffer for holding a result that might exceed an operation by a small amount, but this isn't the main reason they exist. The `UInt16` type happens to have the same characteristics as the `Character` type, while the `UInt32` type has the same characteristics as a system memory pointer on a 32-byte system.

However, never write code that attempts to leverage this relationship. Such code isn't portable, as on a 64-bit system the system memory pointer changes and uses the `UInt64` type. However, when larger integers are needed and all values are known to be positive, these values are of use. As for the low-level uses of these types, certain low-level drivers use this type of knowledge to interface with software that expects these values, and they are the underlying implementation for other value types. This is why, when you move from a 32-bit system to a 64-bit system, you need new drivers for your devices, and why applications shouldn't leverage this same type of logic.

Decimal Types

Just as there are several types to store integer values, there are three implementations of value types to store real number values, shown in Table 2-3. The `Single` and `Double` types work the same way in Visual Basic .NET as they did in Visual Basic 6.0. The difference is the Visual Basic 6.0 `Currency` type (which was a specialized version of a `Double` type), is now obsolete; it was replaced by the `Decimal` value type for very large real numbers.

TABLE 2-3: Memory Allocation for Real Number Types

TYPE	ALLOCATED MEMORY	NEGATIVE RANGE	POSITIVE RANGE
Single	4 bytes	–3.402823E38 to –1.401298E-45	1.401298E-45 to 3.402823E38
Double	8 bytes	–1.79769313486231E308 to –4.94065645841247E-324	4.94065645841247E-324 to 1.79769313486232E308
Currency	Obsolete	—	—
Decimal	16 bytes	–79228162514264 337593543950335 to 0.00000000000000 00000000000001	0.00000000000000 00000000000001 to 792281625142643 37593543950335

Single

The Single type contains four bytes of data, and its precision can range anywhere from 1.401298E-45 to 3.402823E38 for positive values and from –3.402823E38 to –1.401298E-45 for negative values.

It can seem strange that a value stored using four bytes (like the Integer type) can store a number that is larger than even the Long type. This is possible because of the way in which numbers are stored; a real number can be stored with different levels of precision. Note that there are six digits after the decimal point in the definition of the Single type. When a real number gets very large or very small, the stored value is limited by its significant places.

Because real values contain fewer significant places than their maximum value, when working near the extremes it is possible to lose precision. For example, while it is possible to represent a Long with the value of 9223372036854775805, the Single type rounds this value to 9.223372E18. This seems like a reasonable action to take, but it isn't a reversible action. The following code demonstrates how this loss of precision and data can result in errors. To run it, a Sub called Precision is added to the ProVB_VS2010 project and called from the Click event handler for the ButtonTest control:

Available for download on Wrox.com

```
Private Sub Precision()
    Dim l As Long = Long.MaxValue
    Dim s As Single = Convert.ToSingle(l)
    TextBox1.Text = l & Environment.NewLine
    TextBox1.Text &= s & Environment.NewLine
    s -= 1000000000000
    l = Convert.ToInt64(s)
    TextBox1.Text &= l & Environment.NewLine
End Sub
```

Code snippet from Form1

The code creates a Long that has the maximum value possible, and outputs this value. Then it converts this value to a Single and outputs it in that format. Next, the value 1000000000000 is subtracted from the Single using the -= syntax, which is similar to writing s = s - 1000000000000. Finally, the code assigns the Single value back into the Long and then outputs both the Long and the difference between the original value and the new value. The results, shown in Figure 2-5, probably aren't consistent with what you might expect.

The first thing to notice is how the values are represented in the output based on type. The Single value actually uses an exponential display instead of displaying all of the significant digits. More important, as you can see, the result of what is stored in the

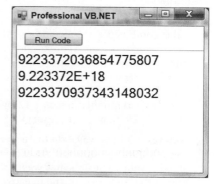

FIGURE 2-5

Single after the math operation actually occurs is not accurate in relation to what is computed using the Long value. Therefore, both the Single and Double types have limitations in accuracy when you are doing math operations. These accuracy issues result from storage limitations and how binary numbers represent decimal numbers. To better address these issues for large numbers, .NET provides the Decimal type.

Double

The behavior of the previous example changes if you replace the value type of Single with Double. A Double uses eight bytes to store values, and as a result has greater precision and range. The range for a Double is from 4.94065645841247E-324 to 1.79769313486232E308 for positive values and from −1.79769313486231E308 to −4.94065645841247E-324 for negative values. The precision has increased such that a number can contain 15 digits before the rounding begins. This greater level of precision makes the Double value type a much more reliable variable for use in math operations. It's possible to represent most operations with complete accuracy with this value. To test this, change the sample code from the previous section so that instead of declaring the variable s as a Single you declare it as a Double and rerun the code. Don't forget to also change the conversion line from ToSingle to ToDouble. The resulting code is shown here with the Sub called PrecisionDouble:

```
Private Sub PrecisionDouble()
    Dim l As Long = Long.MaxValue
    Dim s As Double = Convert.ToDouble(l)
    TextBox1.Text = l & Environment.NewLine
    TextBox1.Text &= s & Environment.NewLine
    s -= 1000000000000
    l = Convert.ToInt64(s)
    TextBox1.Text &= l & Environment.NewLine
    TextBox1.Text &= Long.MaxValue - l
End Sub
```

Code snippet from Form1

The results shown in Figure 2-6 look very similar to those from Single precision except they almost look correct. The result as you can see is off by just 1. On the other hand, this method closes by demonstrating how a 64-bit value can be modified by just one and the results are accurate. The problem isn't specific to .NET; it can be replicated in all major development languages. Whenever you choose to represent very large or very small numbers by eliminating the precision of the least significant digits, you have lost that precision. To resolve this, .NET introduced the Decimal, which avoids this issue.

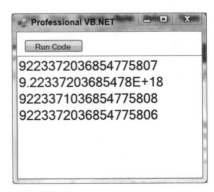

FIGURE 2-6

Decimal

The Decimal type is a hybrid that consists of a 12-byte integer value combined with two additional 16-bit values that control the location of the decimal point and the sign of the overall value. A Decimal value consumes 16 bytes in total and can store a maximum value of 79228162514264337593543950335. This value can then be manipulated by adjusting where the decimal place is located. For example, the maximum value while accounting for four decimal places is 7922816251426433759354395.0335. This is because a Decimal isn't stored as a traditional number, but as a 12-byte integer value, with the location of the decimal in relation to the available 28 digits. This means that a Decimal does not inherently round numbers the way a Double does.

As a result of the way values are stored, the closest precision to zero that a Decimal supports is 0.000000 0000000000000000000001. The location of the decimal point is stored separately; and the Decimal type stores a value that indicates whether its value is positive or negative separately from the actual value. This means that the positive and negative ranges are exactly the same, regardless of the number of decimal places.

Thus, the system makes a trade-off whereby the need to store a larger number of decimal places reduces the maximum value that can be kept at that level of precision. This trade-off makes a lot of sense. After all, it's not often that you need to store a number with 15 digits on both sides of the decimal point, and for those cases you can create a custom class that manages the logic and leverages one or more decimal values as its properties. You'll find that if you again modify and rerun the sample code you've been using in the last couple of sections that converts to and from `Long` values by using `Decimals` for the interim value and conversion, now your results are completely accurate.

Char and Byte

The default character set under Visual Basic is Unicode. Therefore, when a variable is declared as type `Char`, Visual Basic creates a two-byte value, since, by default, all characters in the Unicode character set require two bytes. Visual Basic supports the declaration of a character value in three ways. Placing a `$c$` following a literal string informs the compiler that the value should be treated as a character, or the `Chr` and `ChrW` methods can be used. The following code snippet shows that all three of these options work similarly, with the difference between the `Chr` and `ChrW` methods being the range of available valid input values. The `ChrW` method allows for a broader range of values based on wide character input.

```
Dim chrLtr_a As Char = "a"c
Dim chrAsc_a As Char = Chr(97)
Dim chrAsc_b as Char = ChrW(98)
```

To convert characters into a string suitable for an ASCII interface, the runtime library needs to validate each character's value to ensure that it is within a valid range. This could have a performance impact for certain serial arrays. Fortunately, Visual Basic supports the `Byte` value type. This type contains a value between 0 and 255 that exactly matches the range of the ASCII character set. When interfacing with a system that uses ASCII, it is best to use a `Byte` array. The runtime knows there is no need to perform a Unicode-to-ASCII conversion for a `Byte` array, so the interface between the systems operates significantly faster.

In Visual Basic, the `Byte` value type expects a numeric value. Thus, to assign the letter "a" to a `Byte`, you must use the appropriate character code. One option to get the numeric value of a letter is to use the `Asc` method, as shown here:

```
Dim bytLtrA as Byte = Asc("a")
```

DateTime

The Visual Basic `Date` keyword has always supported a structure of both date and time. You can, in fact, declare date values using both the `DateTime` and `Date` types. Note that internally Visual Basic no longer stores a date value as a `Double`; however, it provides key methods for converting the current internal date representation to the legacy `Double` type. The `ToOADate` and `FromOADate` methods support backward compatibility during migration from previous versions of Visual Basic.

Visual Basic also provides a set of shared methods that provides some common dates. The concept of shared methods is described in more detail in the next chapter, which covers object syntax, but, in short, shared methods are available even when you don't create an instance of a class. For the `DateTime` structure, the `Now` method returns a `Date` value with the local date and time. This method has not been changed from Visual Basic 6.0, but the `Today` and `UtcNow` methods have been added. These methods can be used to initialize a `Date` object with the current local date, or the date and time based on Universal Coordinated Time (also known as Greenwich Mean Time), respectively. You can use these shared methods to initialize your classes, as shown in the following code sample:

```
Private Sub Dates()
    Dim dtNow = Now()
    Dim dtToday = Today()
    TextBox1.Text = dtNow & Environment.NewLine
    TextBox1.Text &= dtToday.ToShortDateString & Environment.NewLine
```

```
        TextBox1.Text &= DateTime.UtcNow() & Environment.NewLine
        Dim dtString = #12/13/2009#
        TextBox1.Text &= dtString.ToLongDateString()
    End Sub
```

Code snippet from Form1

Running this code results in the output shown in Figure 2-7. As noted earlier, primitive values can be assigned directly within your code, but many developers seem unaware of the format for doing this with dates. Another key feature of the Date type is the capability to subtract dates in order to determine a difference between them. The subtract method is demonstrated later in this chapter, with the resulting Timespan object used to output the number of milliseconds between the start and end time of a set of commands.

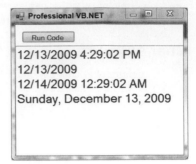

FIGURE 2-7

REFERENCE TYPES (CLASSES)

A lot of the power of Visual Basic is harnessed in objects. An object is defined by its class, which describes what data, methods, and other attributes an instance of that class supports. Thousands of classes are provided in the .NET Framework class library.

When code instantiates an object from a class, the object created is a reference type. Recall that the data contained in value and reference types is stored in different locations, but this is not the only difference between them. A class (which is the typical way to refer to a reference type) has additional capabilities, such as support for protected methods and properties, enhanced event-handling capabilities, constructors, and finalizers; and it can be extended with a custom base class via inheritance. Classes can also be used to define how operators such as "=" and "+" work on an instance of the class.

The intention of this section is to introduce you to some commonly used classes, and to complement your knowledge of the common value types already covered. This section examines the features of the Object, String, DBNull, and Array classes, as well as the Collection classes found in the System.Collections namespace.

The Object Class

As noted earlier, the Object class is the base class for every type in .NET, both value and reference types. At its core, every variable is an object and can be treated as such.

Because the Object class is the basis of all types, you can cast any variable to an object. Reference types maintain their current reference and implementation but are generically handled, whereas value types are taken from their current location on the stack and placed into the heap with a memory location associated with the Object. This process is called 'boxing' because you are taking the value and shipping it from one location to another. Boxing is discussed in more detail in Chapter 8.

The key addition to your understanding of Object is that if you create an implementation of ToString in your class definition, then even when an instance of your object is cast to the type Object, your custom method will still be called. The following snippet shows how to create a generic object.

```
    Dim objVar as Object

    objVar = Me

    CType(objVar, Form).Text = "New Dialog Title Text"
```

That Object is then assigned a copy of the current instance of a Visual Basic form. In order to access the Text property of the original Form class, the Object must be cast from its declared type of Object to its actual type (Form), which supports the Text property. The CType command (covered later) accepts the object as its first parameter, and the class name (without quotes) as its second parameter. In this case, the current instance variable is of type Form; and by casting this variable, the code can reference the Text property of the current form.

The String Class

Another class that plays a large role in most development projects is the String class. The String class is a special class within .NET because it is the one primitive type that is not a value type. To make String objects compatible with some of the underlying behavior in .NET, they have some interesting characteristics.

These methods are shared, which means that the methods are not specific to any instance of a String. The String class also contains several other methods that are called based on an instance of a specific String object. The methods on the String class replace the functions that Visual Basic 6.0 had as part of the language for string manipulation, and they perform operations such as inserting strings, splitting strings, and searching strings.

String()

The String class has several different constructors for those situations in which you aren't simply assigning an existing value to a new string. The term *constructor* is expanded upon in Chapter 3. Constructors are methods that are used to construct an instance of a class. String() would be the default constructor for the String class, but the String class does not expose this constructor publicly. The following example shows some of the most common methods for creating a String. This example method does not show the end of this Sub because it will be used for all of the string-related examples, with the output from these methods shown together. The following code snippet is the start of a method; the End Sub is not shown. The full Sub in the code download is the concatenation of this snippet with the next five snippets. You can build and test these parts sequentially.

Available for download on Wrox.com

```
Private Sub StringSamples()
    Dim strSample As String = "ABC"
    Dim strSample2 = "DEF"
    Dim strSample3 = New String("A"c, 20)
    Dim line = New String("-", 80)
```

Code snippet from Form1

A variable is declared of type String and as a primitive is assigned the value "ABC." The second declaration uses one of the parameterized versions of the String constructor. This constructor accepts two parameters: The first is a character and the second specifies how many times that character should be repeated in the string.

In addition to creating an instance of a string and then calling methods on your variable, the String class has several shared methods. A shared method refers to a method on a class that does not require an instance of that class. Shared methods are covered in more detail in relation to objects in Chapter 3; for the purpose of this chapter, the point is that you can reference the class String followed by a "." and see a list of shared methods for that class. For strings, this list includes the methods described in Table 2-4.

TABLE 2-4: Methods Available on the Class String

SHARED METHOD	DESCRIPTION
Empty	This is actually a property. It can be used when an empty String is required. It can be used for comparison or initialization of a String.
Compare	Compares two objects of type String
CompareOrdinal	Compares two Strings, without considering the local national language or culture

continues

TABLE 2-4 *(continued)*

SHARED METHOD	DESCRIPTION
Concat	Concatenates one or more Strings
Copy	Creates a new String with the same value as an instance provided
Equals	Determines whether two Strings have the same value
IsNullorEmpty	This shared method is a very efficient way of determining whether a given variable has been set to the empty string or Nothing.

Not only have creation methods been encapsulated, but other string-specific methods, such as character and substring searching, and case changes, are now available from String object instances.

The SubString Method

The .NET String class has a method called SubString. This is a powerful method when you want to break out a portion of a string. For example, if you have a string "Hello World" and only want the first word, you would take the substring of the first five characters. There are ways to call this method. The first accepts a starting position and the number of characters to retrieve, while the second accepts the starting location. The following code shows examples of using both of these methods on an instance of a String, and the resulting output is the first pair of strings shown in Figure 2-8:

```
' Sub String
Dim subString = "Hello World"
TextBox1.Text = subString.Substring(0, 5) & Environment.NewLine
TextBox1.Text &= subString.Substring(6) & Environment.NewLine
TextBox1.Text &= line & Environment.NewLine
```

Code snippet from Form1

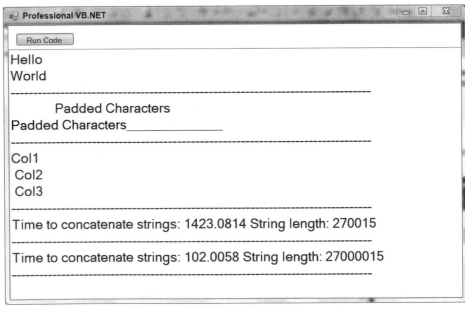

FIGURE 2-8

The PadLeft and PadRight Methods

These methods enable you to justify a String so that it is left- or right-justified. As with SubString, the PadLeft and PadRight methods are overloaded. The first version of these methods requires only a maximum length of the String, and then uses spaces to pad the String. The other version requires two parameters: the length of the returned String and the character that should be used to pad the original String:

```
' Pad Left & Pad Right
Dim padString = "Padded Characters"
TextBox1.Text &= padString.PadLeft("30") & Environment.NewLine
TextBox1.Text &= padString.PadRight("30", "_") &
    Environment.NewLine
TextBox1.Text &= line & Environment.NewLine
```

Code snippet from Form1

Figure 2-8 shows the same string first with the left padded with spaces, then with the right padded with underscores. Note that because the default font on this screen isn't fixed size, the spaces are compacted and the two strings do not appear as the same length.

The String.Split Method

This instance method on a string enables you to separate it into an array of components. For example, if you want to quickly find each of the different elements in a comma-delimited string, you could use the Split method to turn the string into an array of smaller strings, each of which contains one field of data. As shown in Figure 2-8, the csvString is converted to an array of three elements:

```
' String Split
Dim csvString = "Col1, Col2, Col3"
Dim stringArray As String() = csvString.Split(",")
TextBox1.Text &= stringArray(0) & Environment.NewLine
TextBox1.Text &= stringArray(1) & Environment.NewLine
TextBox1.Text &= stringArray(2) & Environment.NewLine
TextBox1.Text &= line & Environment.NewLine
```

Code snippet from Form1

The String Class Is Immutable

The Visual Basic String class isn't entirely different from the String type that programmers have used for years. The majority of string behaviors remain unchanged, and the majority of methods are now available as classes. However, to support the default behavior that people associate with the String primitive type, the String class isn't declared in the same way as several other classes. Strings in .NET do not allow editing of their data. When a portion of a string is changed or copied, the operating system allocates a new memory location and copies the resulting string to this new location. This ensures that when a string is copied to a second variable, the new variable references its own copy.

To support this behavior in .NET, the String class is defined as an *immutable class*. This means that each time a change is made to the data associated with a string, a new instance is created, and the original referenced memory is released for garbage collection. Note that garbage collection is the automated process of cleaning memory of data that is no longer needed. It is covered in more detail in Chapter 4. However, for now you should be aware that this is a comparatively expensive operation. However, having strings be immutable is important to ensure that the String class behaves as people expect a primitive type to behave. Additionally, when a copy of a string is made, the String class forces a new version of the data into the referenced memory. This ensures that each instance of a string references only its own memory. Consider the following code:

```
' String Concatenation vs String Builder
Dim start = Now()
Dim strRedo = "A simple string"
For index = 1 To 10000 'Only 10000 times for concatenation
    strRedo &= "Making a much larger string"
Next
' The date processing below uses the built in capability
' to subtract one datetime from another to get the difference
' between the dates as a timespan. This is then output as a
' number of milliseconds.
```

```
TextBox1.Text &= "Time to concatenate strings: " &
    (Now().Subtract(start)).TotalMilliseconds().ToString() &
    " String length: " & strRedo.Length.ToString()
TextBox1.Text &= line & Environment.NewLine
```

Code snippet from Form1

This code does not perform well. For each assignment operation on the strMyString variable, the system allocates a new memory buffer based on the size of the new string, and copies both the current value of strMyString and the new text that is to be appended. The system then frees the previous memory that must be reclaimed by the garbage collector. As this loop continues, the new memory allocation requires a larger chunk of memory. Therefore, operations such as this can take a long time.

To illustrate this, you'll note that the code captures the start time before doing the 10,000 concatenations, and then within the print statement uses the DateTime.Subtract method to get the difference. That difference is returned as an object of type Timespan, between the start time and the print time. This difference is then expressed in milliseconds (refer to Figure 2-8).

However, .NET offers an alternative in the System.Text.StringBuilder object, shown in the following snippet:

```
start = Now()
Dim strBuilder = New System.Text.StringBuilder("A simple string")
For index = 1 To 1000000 '1 million times....
    strBuilder.Append("Making a much larger string")
Next
TextBox1.Text &= "Time to concatenate strings: " &
    (Now().Subtract(start)).TotalMilliseconds().ToString() &
    " String length: " & strBuilder.ToString().Length.ToString()
TextBox1.Text &= line & Environment.NewLine
End Sub
```

Code snippet from Form1

The preceding code works with strings but does not use the String class. The .NET class library contains the System.Text.StringBuilder class, which performs better when strings will be edited repeatedly. This class does not store strings in the conventional manner; it stores them as individual characters, with code in place to manage the ordering of those characters. Thus, editing or appending more characters does not involve allocating new memory for the entire string. Because the preceding code snippet does not need to reallocate the memory used for the entire string, each time another set of characters is appended it performs significantly faster.

Note that the same timing code is used in this snippet. However, for the StringBuilder, the loop executes one million times (versus ten thousand). Note the increase in the number of iterations was made in order to cause enough of a delay to actually show it requiring more than just one or two milliseconds to complete. Even with 100 times the number of iterations, Figure 2-8 still illustrates that this is a much more efficient use of system resources.

Ultimately, an instance of the String class is never explicitly needed, because the StringBuilder class implements the ToString method to roll up all of the characters into a string. While the concept of the StringBuilder class isn't new, because it is available as part of the Visual Basic implementation, developers no longer need to create their own string memory managers.

String Constants

If you ever have to produce output based on a string you'll quickly find yourself needing to embed certain constant values. For example, it's always useful to be able to add a carriage-return linefeed combination to trigger a new line in a message box. One way to do this is to learn the underlying ASCII codes and then embed these control characters directly into your String or StringBuilder object.

Visual Basic provides an easier solution for working with these: the Microsoft.VisualBasic.Constants class. The Constants class, which you can tell by its namespace is specific to Visual Basic, contains definitions for several standard string values that you might want to embed. The most common, of course, is `Constants.VbCrLf`, which represents the carriage-return linefeed combination. Feel free to explore this class for additional constants that you might need to manipulate string output.

XML Literals

One of the main new features in Visual Basic 2008 was the introduction of XML literals. It is possible within Visual Basic to create a new variable and assign a block of well-formatted XML code to that string. This is being introduced here because it demonstrates a great example of a declaration that leverages `Option Infer`. Start by adding a new form to the VBPro_VS2010 project, accepting the default name of Form2. This new form will be called from the click event for the ButtonTest on Form1 using the code shown in the `Sub XmlLiteral` that follows.

Available for download on Wrox.com

```
Private Sub XmlLiteral()
    Form2.ShowDialog()
End Sub
```

Code snippet from Form1

Within the designer for Form2, drag a `RichTextBox` control onto the display area and set the control to dock within the parent container. This can be done from the Properties display or by using the Tasks context menu in the upper-right corner of the control. Next, double-click on the form to create an event handler for the window `Load` event. Within this event you will place the code to demonstrate XML literals. A separate window is being used in order to demonstrate the string formatting capabilities of XML literals, which do not work within a `TextBox` control.

This code starts by declaring a string variable called `myString` and setting this to a value such as `"Hello World"`. In the code block that follows, notice that the first `Dim` statement used does not include the "As" clause that is typically used in such declarations. The declaration of the `myString` variable relies on type inference:

Available for download on Wrox.com

```
Private Sub Form2_Load(ByVal sender As System.Object,
                       ByVal e As System.EventArgs) _
                   Handles MyBase.Load
    Dim myString = "Embedded string variable data."
    Dim myXmlElement = <AnXmlNode attribute="1">This is formatted text.
Embedded carriage returns will be kept.
        These lines will print separately.
    Whitespace will also be maintained.
<%= myString %>
                  </AnXmlNode>
    RichTextBox1.Text = myXmlElement.ToString() &
        Environment.NewLine & Environment.NewLine
    RichTextBox1.Text &= myXmlElement.Value.ToString()
End Sub
```

Code snippet from Form2

Running this `XmlLiteral Sub` results in the output shown in Figure 2-9. Within this code, the compiler recognizes that this newly declared variable is being assigned a string, so the variable is automatically defined as a string. After the first variable is declared on the first line of the code block, the second line of code makes up the remainder of the code block, which you may notice spans multiple lines without any line-continuation characters.

The second `Dim` statement declares another new variable, but in this case the variable is set equal to raw XML. Note that the "<" is not preceded by any quotes in the code. Instead, that angle bracket indicates that what follows will be a well-formed XML statement. At this point the Visual Basic compiler stops treating what you have typed as Visual Basic code and instead reads this text as XML. Thus, the top-level node can be named, attributes associated with that node can be defined, and text can be assigned to the value of the node. The only

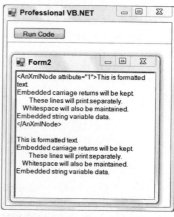

FIGURE 2-9

requirement is that the XML be well formed, which means you need to have a closing declaration, the last line in the preceding code block, to end that XML statement.

By default, because this is just an XML node and not a full document, Visual Basic infers that you are defining an XMLElement and will define the mXMLElement variable as an instance of that class. Beyond this, however, there is the behavior of your static XML. Note that the text itself contains comments about being formatted. That's because within your static XML, Visual Basic automatically recognizes and embeds literally everything.

Thus, the name *XML literal*. The text is captured as is, with any embedded white space or carriage returns/ linefeeds captured. The other interesting capability is shown on the line that reads as follows:

```
<%= myString %>
```

This is a shorthand declaration that enables you to insert the value of the variable myString into your literal XML. In this case, myString is set on the preceding line, but it could easily be an input parameter to a method that returns an XML element. When you run this code, the current value of myString will be inserted into your XML declaration.

Two statements display the output shown in Figure 2-9 from your XML element. Two different statements displaying the contents of the XML element as a string appear, because each results in slightly different output.

The first statement on the second line instructs the XML element object to return a string representing itself. As such, the XML element will return all of the content of that object, including the raw XML itself. The second output has output the XML element to a string that only reflects the value of the data defined for that element. Note that if the basic XML element you defined in the previous code block had any nested XML elements, then these would be considered part of the contents of your XML element, and their definitions and attributes would be output as part of this statement.

As shown in Figure 2-9, the result of this output is that the first block of text includes your custom XML node and its attribute. Not only do you see the text that identifies the value of the XML, you also see that actual XML structure. However, when you instead print only the value from the XML block, what you see is in fact just that text. Note that XML has embedded the carriage returns and left-hand white space that was part of your XML literal so that your text appears formatted. With the use of XML literals, you "literally" have the capability to replace the somewhat cryptic String.Format method call with a very explicit means of formatting an output string.

The DBNull Class and IsDBNull Function

When working with a database, a value for a given column may not be defined. For a reference type this isn't a problem, as it is possible to set reference types to Nothing. However, for value types, it is necessary to determine whether a given column from the database or other source has an actual value prior to attempting to assign a potentially null value. The first way to manage this task is to leverage the DBNull class and the IsDBNull function. This class is part of the System namespace, and you reference it as part of a comparison. The IsDBNull function accepts an object as its parameter and returns a Boolean that indicates whether the variable has been initialized. The following snippet shows two values, one a string being initialized to Nothing and the other being initialized as DBNull.Value:

```
Private Sub NullValues()
    Dim strNothing As String = Nothing
    Dim objectNull As Object = DBNull.Value
    TextBox1.Text = ""
    If IsDBNull(strNothing) Then
        TextBox1.Text = "But strNothing is not the same as Null."
    End If
    If System.DBNull.Value.Equals(objectNull) Then
        TextBox1.Text &= "objectNull is null." & Environment.NewLine
    End If
End Sub
```

Code snippet from Form1

The output of this code is shown in Figure 2-10. In this code, the `strNothing` variable is declared and initialized to `Nothing`. The first conditional is evaluated to `False`, which may seem counterintuitive, but in fact VB differentiates between a local value, which might not be assigned, and the actual `DBNull` value. This can be a bit misleading, because it means that you need to separately check for values which are `Nothing`. The second conditional references the second variable, `objectNull`. This value has been explicitly defined as being a `DBNull.Value` as part of its initialization. This is similar to how a null value would be returned from the database. The second condition evaluates to `True`. While `DBNull` is available, in most cases, developers now leverage the generic `Nullable` class described in Chapter 8, rather than working with `DBNull` comparisons.

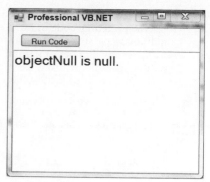

FIGURE 2-10

PARAMETER PASSING

When an object's methods or an assembly's procedures and methods are called, it's often appropriate to provide input for the data to be operated on by the code. The values are referred to as *parameters*, and any object can be passed as a parameter to a `Function` or `Sub`.

When passing parameters, be aware of whether the parameter is being passed "by value" (`ByVal`) or "by reference" (`ByRef`). Passing a parameter by value means that if the value of that variable is changed, then when the `Function`/`Sub` returns, the system automatically restores that variable to the value it had before the call. Passing a parameter by reference means that if changes are made to the value of a variable, then these changes affect the actual variable and, therefore, are still present when the variable returns.

This is where it gets a little challenging for new Visual Basic developers.. Under .NET, passing a parameter by value indicates only how the top-level reference (the portion of the variable on the stack) for that object is passed. Sometimes referred to as a *shallow copy operation*, the system copies only the top-level reference value for an object passed by value. This is important to remember because it means that referenced memory is not protected.

When you pass an integer by value, if the program changes the value of the integer, then your original value is restored. Conversely, if you pass a reference type, then only the location of your referenced memory is protected, not the data located within that memory location. Thus, while the reference passed as part of the parameter remains unchanged for the calling method, the actual values stored in referenced objects can be updated even when an object is passed by value.

In addition to mandatory parameters, which must be passed with a call to a given function, it is possible to declare optional parameters. Optional parameters can be omitted by the calling code. This way, it is possible to call a method such as `PadRight`, passing either a single parameter defining the length of the string and using a default of space for the padding character, or with two parameters, the first still defining the length of the string but the second now replacing the default of space with a dash:

```
Public Sub PadRight(ByVal intSize as Integer, _
                    Optional ByVal chrPad as Char = " "c)
End Function
```

Code snippet from Form1

To use optional parameters, it is necessary to make them the last parameters in the function declaration. Visual Basic also requires that every optional parameter have a default value. It is not acceptable to merely declare a parameter and assign it the `Optional` keyword. In Visual Basic, the `Optional` keyword must be accompanied by a value that is assigned if the parameter is not passed in.

ParamArray

In addition to passing explicit parameters, it is also possible to tell .NET that you would like to allow a user to pass any number of parameters of the same type. This is called a *parameter array*, and it enables a user to pass as many instances of a given parameter as are appropriate. For example, the following code creates a function Add, which allows a user to pass an array of integers and get the sum of these integers:

```
Public Function Add(ByVal ParamArray values() As Integer) As Long
    Dim result As Long
    For Each value As Integer In values
        result += value
    Next
    Return result
End Function
```

Code snippet from Form1

The preceding code illustrates a function (first shown at the beginning of this chapter without its implementation) that accepts an array of integers. Notice that the ParamArray qualifier is preceded by a ByVal qualifier for this parameter. The ParamArray requires that the associated parameters be passed by value; they cannot be optional parameters.

You might think this looks like a standard parameter passed by value except that it's an array, but there is more to it than that. In fact, the power of the ParamArray derives from how it can be called, which also explains many of its limitations. The following code shows two ways this method can be called:

```
Private Sub CallAdd()
    Dim int1 As Integer = 2
    Dim int2 = 3
    TextBox1.Text = "Adding 3 integers: " & Add(1, int1, int2) &
        Environment.NewLine
    Dim intArray() = {1, 2, 3, 4}
    TextBox1.Text &= "Adding an array of 4 integers: " & Add(intArray)
End Sub
```

Code snippet from Form1

The output from running this CallAdd method is shown in Figure 2-11. Notice that the first call, to the Add function, doesn't pass an array of integers; instead, it passes three distinct integer values. The ParamArray keyword tells Visual Basic to automatically join these three distinct values into an array for use within this method. The second call, to the Add method, actually leverages using an actual array of integers to populate the parameter array. Either of these methods works equally well. Arrays are covered in more detail in Chapter 8.

Finally, note one last limitation of the ParamArray keyword: It can only be used on the last parameter defined for a given method. Because Visual Basic is grabbing an unlimited number of input values to create the array, there is no way to indicate the end of this array, so it must be the final parameter.

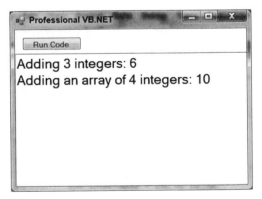

FIGURE 2-11

VARIABLE SCOPE

The concept of variable scope encapsulates two key elements. In all the discussion so far of variables, we have not focused on the allocation and deallocation of those variables from memory. The first allocation challenge is related to what happens when you declare two variables with the same name but at different locations in the code. For example, suppose a class declares a variable called `myObj` that holds a property for that class. Then, within one of that class's methods, you declare a different variable also named `myObj`. What will happen in that method? *Scope* defines the lifetime and precedence of every variable you declare, and it handles this question.

Similarly, there is the question of the removal of variables that you are no longer using, so you can free up memory. Chapter 4 covers the collection of variables and memory once it is no longer needed by an application, so this discussion focuses on priority, with the understanding that when a variable is no longer "in scope," it is available to the garbage collector for cleanup.

.NET essentially defines four levels of variable scope. The outermost scope is *global*. Essentially, just as your source code defines classes, it can also declare variables that exist the entire time that your application runs. These variables have the longest lifetime because they exist as long as your application is executing. Conversely, these variables have the lowest precedence. Thus, if within a class or method you declare another variable with the same name, then the variable with the smaller, more local scope is used before the global version.

After global scope, the next scope is at the *class* or *module* level. When you add properties to a class, you are creating variables that will be created with each instance of that class. The methods of that class will then reference those member variables from the class, before looking for any global variables. Note that because these variables are defined within a class, they are only visible to methods within that class. The scope and lifetime of these variables is limited by the lifetime of that class, and when the class is removed from the system, so are those variables. More important, those variables declared in one instance of a class are not visible in other classes or in other instances of the same class (unless you actively expose them, in which case the object instance is used to fully qualify a reference to them).

The next shorter lifetime and smaller scope is that of method variables. When you declare a new variable within a method, such variables, as well as those declared as parameters, are only visible to code that exists within that module. Thus, the method `Add` wouldn't see or use variables declared in the method `Subtract` in the same class.

Finally, within a given method are various commands that can encapsulate a block of code (mentioned earlier in this chapter). Commands such as `If Then` and `For Each` create blocks of code within a method, and it is possible within this block of code to declare new variables. These variables then have a scope of only that block of code. Thus, variables declared within an `If Then` block or a `For` loop only exist within the constraints of the `If` block or execution of the loop. Creating variables in a `For` loop is a poor coding practice and performance mistake and should be avoided.

WORKING WITH OBJECTS

In the .NET environment in general and within Visual Basic in particular, you use objects all the time without even thinking about it. As noted earlier, every variable, every control on a form — in fact, every form — inherits from `System.Object`. When you open a file or interact with a database, you are using objects to do that work.

Objects Declaration and Instantiation

Objects are created using the `New` keyword, indicating that you want a new instance of a particular class. There are numerous variations on how or where you can use the `New` keyword in your code. Each one provides different advantages in terms of code readability or flexibility.

The most obvious way to create an object is to declare an object variable and then create an instance of the object:

```
Dim obj As TheClass
obj = New TheClass()
```

The result of this code is that you have a new instance of `TheClass` ready for use. To interact with this new object, you use the `obj` variable that you declared. The `obj` variable contains a reference to the object, a concept explored later.

You can shorten the preceding code by combining the declaration of the variable with the creation of the instance, as illustrated here:

```
Dim obj As New TheClass()
```

 At runtime there is no difference between the first example and this one, other than code length.

The preceding code both declares the variable `obj` as data type `TheClass` and creates an instance of the class, immediately creating an object that you can use. Another variation on this theme is as follows:

```
Dim obj As TheClass = New TheClass()
```

Again, this both declares a variable of data type `TheClass` and creates an instance of the class. It is up to you how you create these instances, as it is really a matter of style. This third syntax example provides a great deal of flexibility while remaining compact. Though it is a single line of code, it separates the declaration of the variable's data type from the creation of the object.

Such flexibility is very useful when working with inheritance or multiple interfaces. You might declare the variable to be of one type — say, an interface — and instantiate the object based on a class that implements that interface. You will revisit this syntax when interfaces are covered in detail in Chapter 3.

So far, you've been declaring a variable for new objects, but sometimes you simply need to pass an object as a parameter to a method, in which case you can create an instance of the object right in the call to that method:

```
DoSomething(New TheClass())
```

This calls the `DoSomething` method, passing a new instance of `TheClass` as a parameter. This can be even more complex. Perhaps, instead of needing an object reference, your method needs an `Integer`. You can provide that `Integer` value from a method on the object:

```
Public Class TheClass
  Public Function GetValue() As Integer
    Return 42
  End Function
End Class
```

You can then instantiate the object and call the method all in one shot, thus passing the value returned from the method as a parameter:

```
DoSomething(New TheClass().GetValue())
```

Obviously, you need to carefully weigh the readability of such code against its compactness. At some point, having code that is more compact can detract from readability, rather than enhance it.

Object References

Typically, when you work with an object, you are using a reference to that object. Conversely, when you are working with simple data types, such as `Integer`, you are working with the actual value, rather than a reference. Let's explore these concepts and see how they work and interact.

When you create a new object using the `New` keyword, you store a reference to that object in a variable, as shown here:

```
Dim obj As New TheClass()
```

This code creates a new instance of `TheClass`. You gain access to this new object via the `obj` variable. This variable holds a reference to the object. You might then do something like this:

```
Dim another As TheClass
another = obj
```

Now, you have a second variable, `another`, which also has a reference to the same object. You can use either variable interchangeably, as they both reference the exact same object. Remember that the variable you have is not the object itself but just a reference, or pointer, to the object.

Dereferencing Objects

When you are done working with an object, you can indicate that you are through with it by *dereferencing* the object. To dereference an object, simply set the object reference to `Nothing`:

```
Dim obj As TheClass

obj = New TheClass()
obj = Nothing
```

After any or all variables that reference an object are set to `Nothing`, the .NET runtime knows that you no longer need that object. At some point, the runtime destroys the object and reclaims the memory and resources it consumed. You can find more information on the garbage collector in Chapter 4.

Between the time when you dereference the object and the time when the .NET Framework gets around to actually destroying it, the object simply sits in the memory, unaware that it has been dereferenced. Right before .NET destroys the object, the `Finalize` method is called on the object (if it has one).

Early Binding versus Late Binding

One of the strengths of Visual Basic has long been that it provides access to both early and late binding when interacting with objects. *Early binding* means that code directly interacts with an object by directly calling its methods. Because the Visual Basic compiler knows the object's data type ahead of time, it can directly compile code to invoke the methods on the object. Early binding also enables the IDE to use IntelliSense to aid development efforts by enabling the compiler to ensure that you are referencing methods that exist and are providing the proper parameter values.

Late binding means that your code interacts with an object dynamically at runtime. This provides a great deal of flexibility because the code doesn't care what type of object it is interacting with as long as the object supports the methods you want to call. Because the type of the object is not known by the IDE or compiler, neither IntelliSense nor compile-time syntax checking is possible, but in exchange you get unprecedented flexibility.

If you enable strict type checking by using `Option Strict On` in the project's Properties dialog or at the top of the code modules, then the IDE and compiler enforce early binding behavior. By default, `Option Strict` is turned off, so you have easy access to the use of late binding within the code. Chapter 1 discusses `Option Strict`. You can change this default directly in Visual Studio 2010 by selecting Tools ➪ Options from the VS menu. The Options dialog is shown in Figure 2-12. Expanding the Projects and Solutions node reveals the VB defaults. Feel free to change any of these default settings.

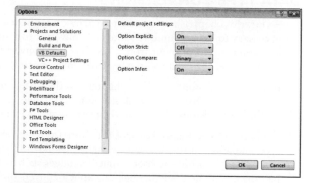

FIGURE 2-12

Implementing Late Binding

Late binding occurs when the compiler cannot determine the type of object that you'll be calling. This level of ambiguity is achieved using the `Object` data type. A variable of data type `Object` can hold virtually any value, including a reference to any type of object. Thus, code such as the following could be run against any object that implements a DoSomething method that accepts no parameters:

```
Option Strict Off

Module LateBind
  Public Sub DoWork(ByVal obj As Object)
   obj.DoSomething()
  End Sub
End Module
```

If the object passed into this routine does not have a DoSomething method that accepts no parameters, then an exception will be thrown. Thus, it is recommended that any code that uses late binding always provide exception handling:

```
Option Strict Off

Module LateBind
  Public Sub DoWork(ByVal obj As Object)
    Try
       obj.DoSomething()
    Catch ex As MissingMemberException
     ' do something appropriate given failure
     ' to call this method
    End Try
  End Sub
End Module
```

Here, the call to the DoSomething method has been put in a Try block. If it works, then the code in the Catch block is ignored; but in the case of a failure, the code in the Catch block is run. You need to write code in the Catch block to handle the case in which the object does not support the DoSomething method call. This Catch block only catches the MissingMemberException, which indicates that the method does not exist on the object.

While late binding is flexible, it can be error prone and is slower than early-bound code. To make a late-bound method call, the .NET runtime must dynamically determine whether the target object actually has a method that matches the one you are calling. It must then invoke that method on your behalf. This takes more time and effort than an early-bound call, whereby the compiler knows ahead of time that the method exists and can compile the code to make the call directly. With a late-bound call, the compiler has to generate code to make the call dynamically at runtime.

DATA TYPE CONVERSIONS

So far, this chapter has focused primarily on individual variables; but when developing software, it is often necessary to take a numeric value and convert it to a string to display in a text box. Similarly, it is often necessary to accept input from a text box and convert this input to a numeric value. These conversions, unlike some, can be done in one of two fashions: *implicitly* or *explicitly*.

Implicit conversions are those that rely on the system to adjust the data at runtime to the new type without any guidance. Often, Visual Basic's default settings enable developers to write code containing many implicit conversions that the developer may not even notice.

Explicit conversions, conversely, are those for which the developer recognizes the need to change a variable's type and assign it to a different variable. Unlike implicit conversions, explicit conversions are easily recognizable within the code. Some languages such as C# require that essentially all conversions that might be type unsafe be done through an explicit conversion; otherwise, an error is thrown.

It is therefore important to understand what a type-safe implicit conversion is. In short, it's a conversion that cannot fail because of the nature of the data involved. For example, if you assign the value of a smaller type, Short, into a larger type, Long, then there is no way this conversion can fail. As both values are integer-style numbers, and the maximum and minimum values of a `Short` variable are well within the range of a `Long`, this conversion will always succeed and can safely be handled as an implicit conversion:

```
Dim shortNumber As Short = 32767
Dim longNumber As Long = shortNumber
```

However, the reverse of this is not a type-safe conversion. In a system that demands explicit conversions, the assignment of a `Long` value to a `Short` variable results in a compilation error, as the compiler doesn't have any safe way to handle the assignment when the larger value is outside the range of the smaller value. It is still possible to explicitly cast a value from a larger type to a smaller type, but this is an explicit conversion. By default, Visual Basic supports certain unsafe implicit conversions. Thus, adding the following line will not, by default, cause an error under Visual Basic:

```
shortNumber = longNumber
```

This is possible for two reasons. One is based on Visual Basic's legacy support. Previous versions of Visual Basic supported the capability to implicitly cast across types that don't fit the traditional implicit casting boundaries. It has been maintained in the language because one of the goals of Visual Basic is to support rapid prototyping. In a rapid prototyping model, a developer is writing code that "works" for demonstration purposes but may not be ready for deployment. This distinction is important because in the discussion of implicit conversions, you should always keep in mind that they are not a best practice for production software.

Performing Explicit Conversions

Keep in mind that even when you choose to allow implicit conversions, these are only allowed for a relatively small number of data types. At some point you'll need to carry out explicit conversions. The following code is an example of some typical conversions between different integer types when `Option Strict` is enabled:

```
Dim myShort As Short
Dim myUInt16 As UInt16
Dim myInt16 As Int16
Dim myInteger As Integer
Dim myUInt32 As UInt32
Dim myInt32 As Int32
Dim myLong As Long
Dim myInt64 As Int64

myShort = 0
myUInt16 = Convert.ToUInt16(myShort)
myInt16 = myShort
myInteger = myShort
myUInt32 = Convert.ToUInt32(myShort)
myInt32 = myShort
myInt64 = myShort
myLong = Long.MaxValue

If myLong < Short.MaxValue Then
    myShort = Convert.ToInt16(myLong)
End If
myInteger = CInt(myLong)
```

The preceding snippet provides some excellent examples of what might not be intuitive behavior. The first thing to note is that you can't implicitly cast from `Short` to `UInt16`, or any of the other unsigned types for that matter. That's because with `Option Strict` the compiler won't allow an implicit conversion that might result in a value out of range or lead to loss of data. You may be thinking that an unsigned `Short` has a maximum that is twice the maximum of a signed `Short`, but in this case, if the variable `myShort` contained a `-1`, then the value wouldn't be in the allowable range for an unsigned type.

Just for clarity, even with the explicit conversion, if `myShort` were a negative number, then the `Convert.ToUInt32` method would throw a runtime exception. Managing failed conversions requires either an understanding of exceptions and exception handling, as covered in Chapter 6, or the use of a conversion utility such as `TryParse`, covered in the next section.

The second item illustrated in this code is the shared method `MaxValue`. All of the integer and decimal types have this property. As the name indicates, it returns the maximum value for the specified type. There is a matching `MinValue` method for getting the minimum value. As shared properties, these properties can be referenced from the class (`Long.MaxValue`) without requiring an instance.

Finally, although this code will compile, it won't always execute correctly. It illustrates a classic error, which in the real world is often intermittent. The error occurs because the final conversion statement does not check to ensure that the value being assigned to `myInteger` is within the maximum range for an integer type. On those occasions when `myLong` is larger than the maximum allowed, this code will throw an exception.

Visual Basic provides many ways to convert values. Some of them are updated versions of techniques that are supported from previous versions of Visual Basic. Others, such as the `ToString` method, are an inherent part of every class (although the .NET specification does not define how a `ToString` class is implemented for each type).

The set of conversion methods shown in Table 2-5 is based on the conversions supported by Visual Basic. They coincide with the primitive data types described earlier; however, continued use of these methods is not considered a best practice. That bears repeating: While you may find the following methods in existing code, you should strive to avoid and replace these calls.

TABLE 2-5: Traditional Visual Basic Specific Conversion Methods

CBool()	CByte()
CChar()	CDate()
CDbl()	CDec()
CInt()	CLng()
CObj()	CShort()
CSng()	CStr()

Each of these methods has been designed to accept the input of the other primitive data types (as appropriate) and to convert such items to the type indicated by the method name. Thus, the `CStr` class is used to convert a primitive type to a `String`. The disadvantage of these methods is that they only support a limited number of types and are specific to Visual Basic. If you are working in an environment with C# developers, they will find these methods distracting. Additionally, you may find that you have trouble quickly recalling how to leverage `CType` and the `Convert` class when you are working with types that aren't supported by these Visual Basic functions. A more generic way to handle conversions is to leverage the `System.Convert` class shown in the following code snippet:

```
Dim intMyShort As Integer = 200
Convert.ToInt32(intMyShort)
Convert.ToDateTime("9/9/2001")
```

The class `System.Convert` implements not only the conversion methods listed earlier, but also other common conversions. These additional methods include standard conversions for things such as unsigned integers and pointers.

All the preceding type conversions are great for value types and the limited number of classes to which they apply, but these implementations are oriented toward a limited set of known types. It is not possible to convert a custom class to an `Integer` using these classes. More important, there should be no reason to have such a conversion. Instead, a particular class should provide a method that returns the appropriate type. That way, no type conversion is required. However, when `Option Strict` is enabled, the compiler requires you to cast an object to an appropriate type before triggering an implicit conversion. Note, however, that the `Convert` method isn't the only way to indicate that a given variable can be treated as another type.

Parse and TryParse

Most value types, at least those which are part of the .NET Framework, provide a pair of shared methods called `Parse` and `TryParse`. These methods accept a value of your choosing and then attempt to convert this variable into the selected value type. The `Parse` and `TryParse` methods are only available on value types. Reference types have related methods called `DirectCast` and `Cast`, which are optimized for reference variables.

The `Parse` method has a single parameter. This input parameter accepts a value that is the target for the object you want to create of a given type. This method then attempts to create a value based on the data passed in. However, be aware that if the data passed into the `Parse` method cannot be converted, then this method will throw an exception that your code needs to catch. The following line illustrates how the `Parse` function works:

```
result = Long.Parse("100")
```

Unfortunately, when you embed this call within a `Try-Catch` statement for exception handling, you create a more complex block of code. Note that exception handling and its use is covered in Chapter 6, for now just be aware that exceptions require additional system resources for your running code that impacts performance. Because you always need to encapsulate such code within a `Try-Catch` block, the .NET development team decided that it would make more sense to provide a version of this method that encapsulated that exception-handling logic.

This is the origin of the `TryParse` method. The `TryParse` method works similarly to the `Parse` method except that it has two parameters and returns a `Boolean`, rather than a value. Instead of assigning the value of the `TryParse` method, you test it as part of an `If-Then` statement to determine whether the conversion of your data to the selected type was successful. If the conversion was successful, then the new value is stored in the second parameter passed to this method, which you can then assign to the variable you want to hold that value:

```
Dim converted As Long
If Long.TryParse("100", converted) Then
    result = converted
End If
```

Using the CType Function

Whether you are using late binding or not, it can be useful to pass object references around using the `Object` data type, converting them to an appropriate type when you need to interact with them. This is particularly useful when working with objects that use inheritance or implement multiple interfaces, concepts discussed in Chapter 3.

If `Option Strict` is turned off, which is the default, then you can write code using a variable of type `Object` to make an early-bound method call:

```
Public Sub objCType(ByVal obj As Object)
    Dim local As String
    local = obj
    local.ToCharArray()
End Sub
```

Code snippet from Form1

This code uses a strongly typed variable, `local`, to reference what was a generic object value. Behind the scenes, Visual Basic converts the generic type to a specific type so that it can be assigned to the strongly typed variable. If the conversion cannot be done, then you get a trappable runtime error.

The same thing can be done using the `CType` function. If `Option Strict` is enabled, then the previous approach will not compile, and the `CType` function must be used. Here is the same code making use of `CType`:

```
Public Sub CType1(ByVal obj As Object)
    Dim local As String
    local = CType(obj, String)
    local.ToLower()
End Sub
```

Code snippet from Form1

This code declares a variable of type TheClass, which is an early-bound data type that you want to use. The parameter you're accepting is of the generic Object data type, though, so you use the CType method to gain an early-bound reference to the object. If the object isn't of type TheClass, then the call to CType fails with a trappable error.

Once you have a reference to the object, you can call methods by using the early-bound variable local. This code can be shortened to avoid the use of the intermediate variable. Instead, you can simply call methods directly from the data type:

Available for download on Wrox.com

```
Public Sub CType2(obj As Object)
    CType(obj, String).ToUpper()
End Sub
```

Code snippet from Form1

Even though the variable you are working with is of type Object and therefore any calls to it will be late bound, you use the CType method to temporarily convert the variable into a specific type — in this case, the type TheClass.

> *If the object passed as a parameter is not of type* TheClass, *then you get a trappable error, so it is always wise to wrap this code in a* Try...Catch *block.*

As shown in Chapter 3, the CType function can also be very useful when working with objects that implement multiple interfaces. When an object has multiple interfaces, you can reference a single object variable through the appropriate interface as needed by using CType.

Using DirectCast

Another function that is very similar to CType is the method DirectCast. The DirectCast call also converts values of one type into another type. It works in a more restrictive fashion than CType, but the trade-off is that it can be somewhat faster than CType:

```
Dim obj As TheClass

obj = New TheClass
DirectCast(obj, ITheInterface).DoSomething()
```

This is similar to the last example with CType, illustrating the parity between the two functions. There are differences, however. First, DirectCast works only with reference types, whereas CType accepts both reference and value types. For instance, CType can be used in the following code:

```
Dim int As Integer = CType(123.45, Integer)
```

Trying to do the same thing with DirectCast would result in a compiler error, as the value 123.45 is a value type, not a reference type.

Second, DirectCast is not as aggressive about converting types as CType. CType can be viewed as an intelligent combination of all the other conversion functions (such as CInt, CStr, and so on). DirectCast, conversely, assumes that the source data is directly convertible, and it won't take extra steps to convert it.

As an example, consider the following code:

```
Dim obj As Object = 123.45

Dim int As Integer = DirectCast(obj, Integer)
```

If you were using CType this would work, as CType uses CInt-like behavior to convert the value to an Integer. DirectCast, however, will throw an exception because the value is not directly convertible to Integer.

Using TryCast

A method similar to `DirectCast` is `TryCast`. `TryCast` converts values of one type into another type, but unlike `DirectCast`, if it can't do the conversion, then `TryCast` doesn't throw an exception. Instead, `TryCast` simply returns `Nothing` if the cast can't be performed. `TryCast` only works with reference values; it cannot be used with value types such as `Integer` or `Boolean`.

Using `TryCast`, you can write code like this:

Available for download on Wrox.com

```
Public Sub TryCast1 (ByVal obj As Object)
    Dim temp = TryCast(obj, Object)      If temp Is Nothing Then
      ' the cast couldn't be accomplished
      ' so do no work
    Else
      temp.DoSomething()
    End If
End Sub
```

Code snippet from Form1

If you are not sure whether a type conversion is possible, then it is often best to use `TryCast`. This function avoids the overhead and complexity of catching possible exceptions from `CType` or `DirectCast` and still provides you with an easy way to convert an object to another type.

CREATING CLASSES

Using objects is fairly straightforward and intuitive. It is the kind of thing that even the most novice programmers pick up and accept rapidly. Creating classes and objects is a bit more complex and interesting.

Basic Classes

As discussed earlier, objects are merely instances of a specific template (a class). The class contains the code that defines the behavior of its objects, and defines the instance variables that will contain the object's individual data.

Classes are created using the `Class` keyword, and include definitions (declaration) and implementations (code) for the variables, methods, properties, and events that make up the class. Each object created based on this class will have the same methods, properties, and events, and its own set of data defined by the fields in the class.

The Class Keyword

If you want to create a class that represents a person — a `Person` class — you could use the `Class` keyword:

```
Public Class Person

    ' Implementation code goes here

End Class
```

As you know, Visual Basic projects are composed of a set of files with the `.vb` extension. It is possible for each file to contain multiple classes, which means that within a single file you could have something like this:

```
Public Class Adult
  ' Implementation code goes here.
End Class

Public Class Senior
  ' Implementation code goes here.
End Class
```

```
Public Class Child
    ' Implementation code goes here.
End Class
```

The most common and preferred approach is to have a single class per file. This is because the Visual Studio 2010 Solution Explorer and the code-editing environment are tailored to make it easy to navigate from file to file to find code. For instance, if you create a single class file with all these classes, the Solution Explorer simply displays a single entry, as shown in Figure 2-13.

FIGURE 2-13

However, the Visual Studio IDE does provide the Class View window. If you do decide to put multiple classes in each physical .vb file, you can make use of the Class View window, shown in Figure 2-14, to quickly and efficiently navigate through the code, jumping from class to class without having to manually locate those classes in specific code files. To show the Class View, select View from the menu then Class Window.

FIGURE 2-14

The Class View window is extremely useful even if you stick with one class per file, because it still provides you with a class-based view of the entire application.

This chapter uses one class per file in the examples, as this is the most common approach. To begin, open the Visual Studio IDE and create a new Windows Forms Application project named "ObjectIntro." Choose the Project ⇨ Add Class menu option to add a new class module to the project. You'll be presented with the standard Add New Item dialog. Change the name to `Person.vb` and click Add. The result will be the following code, which defines the `Person` class:

```
Public Class Person

End Class
```

With the `Person` class created, you are ready to start adding code to declare the interface, implement the behaviors, and declare the instance variables.

Fields

Fields are variables declared in the class. They will be available to each individual object when the application is run. Each object gets its own set of data — basically, each object gets its own copy of the fields.

Earlier, you learned that a class is simply a template from which you create specific objects. Variables that you define within the class are also simply templates — and each object gets its own copy of those variables in which to store its data.

Declaring member variables is as easy as declaring variables within the `Class` block structure. Add the following code to the `Person` class:

```
Public Class Person

    Private mName As String
    Private mBirthDate As Date
End Class
```

You can control the scope of the fields with the following keywords:

➤ `Private` — Available only to code within the class

➤ `Friend` — Available only to code within the project/component

➤ `Protected` — Available only to classes that inherit from the class (discussed in detail in Chapter 3)

➤ `Protected Friend` — Available to code within your project/component and classes that inherit from the class whether in the project or not (discussed in detail in Chapter 3)

➤ `Public` — Available to code outside the class and to any projects that reference the assembly

Typically, fields are declared using the `Private` keyword, making them available only to code within each instance of the class. Choosing any other option should be done with great care, because all the other options allow code outside the class to directly interact with the variable, meaning that the value could be changed and your code would never know that a change took place.

 One common exception to making fields `Private` is to use the `Protected` keyword, discussed in Chapter 3.

Methods

Objects typically need to provide services (or functions) that can be called when working with the object. Using their own data or data passed as parameters to the method, they manipulate information to yield a result or perform an action.

Methods declared as `Public`, `Friend`, or `Protected` in scope define the interface of the class. Methods that are `Private` in scope are available to the code only within the class itself, and can be used to provide structure and organization to code. As discussed earlier, the actual code within each method is called an *implementation*, while the declaration of the method itself is what defines the interface.

Methods are simply routines that are coded within the class to implement the services you want to provide to the users of an object. Some methods return values or provide information to the calling code. These are called *interrogative methods*. Others, called *imperative methods*, just perform an action and return nothing to the calling code.

In Visual Basic, methods are implemented using Sub (for imperative methods) or Function (for interrogative methods) routines within the class module that defines the object. Sub routines may accept parameters, but they do not return any result value when they are complete. Function routines can also accept parameters, and they always generate a result value that can be used by the calling code.

A method declared with the Sub keyword is merely one that returns no value. Add the following code to the Person class:

```
Public Sub Walk()

    ' implementation code goes here

End Sub
```

The Walk method presumably contains some code that performs some useful work when called but has no result value to return when it is complete. To make use of this method, you might write code such as this:

```
Dim myPerson As New Person()
myPerson.Walk()
```

Once you've created an instance of the Person class, you can simply invoke the Walk method.

Methods That Return Values

If you have a method that does generate some value that should be returned, you need to use the Function keyword:

```
Public Function Age() As Integer
    Return CInt(DateDiff(DateInterval.Year, mBirthDate, Now()))
End Function
```

Note that you must indicate the data type of the return value when you declare a function. This example returns the calculated age as a result of the method. You can return any value of the appropriate data type by using the Return keyword.

You can also return the value without using the Return keyword by setting the value of the function name itself:

```
Public Function Age() As Integer
    Age = CInt(DateDiff(DateInterval.Year, mBirthDate, Now()))
End Function
```

This is functionally equivalent to the previous code. Either way, you can use this method with code similar to the following:

```
Dim myPerson As New Person()
Dim age As Integer

age = myPerson.Age()
```

The Age method returns an Integer data value that you can use in the program as required; in this case, you're just storing it in a variable.

Indicating Method Scope

Adding the appropriate keyword in front of the method declaration indicates the scope:

```
Public Sub Walk()
```

This indicates that Walk is a public method and thus is available to code outside the class and even outside the current project. Any application that references the assembly can use this method. Being public, this method becomes part of the object's interface.

Alternately, you might restrict access to the method somewhat:

```
Friend Sub Walk()
```

By declaring the method with the Friend keyword, you are indicating that it should be part of the object's interface only for code inside the project; any other applications or projects that make use of the assembly will not be able to call the Walk method.

The Private keyword indicates that a method is only available to the code within your particular class:

```
Private Function Age() As Integer
```

Private methods are very useful to help organize complex code within each class. Sometimes the methods contain very lengthy and complex code. In order to make this code more understandable, you may choose to break it up into several smaller routines, having the main method call these routines in the proper order. Moreover, you can use these routines from several places within the class, so by making them separate methods, you enable reuse of the code. These subroutines should never be called by code outside the object, so you make them Private.

Method Parameters

You will often want to pass information into a method as you call it. This information is provided via parameters to the method. For instance, in the Person class, you may want the Walk method to track the distance the person walks over time. In such a case, the Walk method would need to know how far the person is to walk each time the method is called. The following code is the full version Person class:

```
Public Class Person
  Private mName As String
  Private mBirthDate As Date
  Private mTotalDistance As Integer
  Public Sub Walk(ByVal distance As Integer)
    mTotalDistance += distance
  End Sub
  Public Function Age() As Integer
    Return CInt(DateDiff(DateInterval.Year, mBirthDate, Now()))
  End Function
End Class
```

Code snippet from Person

With this implementation, a Person object sums all of the distances walked over time. Each time the Walk method is called, the calling code must pass an Integer value, indicating the distance to be walked. The code to call this method would be similar to the following:

```
Dim myPerson As New Person()
myPerson.Walk(12)
```

The parameter is accepted using the ByVal keyword, which indicates that the parameter value is a copy of the original value, whereas the ByRef creates a reference to the object. This is the default way in which Visual Basic accepts all parameters. Typically, this is desirable because it means that you can work with the parameter inside the code, changing its value with no risk of accidentally changing the original value in the calling code.

If you do want to be able to change the value in the calling code, you can change the declaration to pass the parameter by reference by using the ByRef qualifier:

```
Public Sub Walk(ByRef distance As Integer)
```

In this case, you get a reference (or pointer) back to the original value, rather than a copy. This means that any change you make to the distance parameter is reflected back in the calling code, very similar to the way object references work, as discussed earlier in this chapter.

Properties

The .NET environment provides for a specialized type of method called a *property*. A property is a method specifically designed for setting and retrieving data values. For instance, you declared a variable in the `Person` class to contain a name, so the `Person` class may include code to allow that name to be set and retrieved. This can be done using regular methods:

```
Public Sub SetName(ByVal name As String)
    mName = name
End Sub

Public Function GetName() As String
    Return mName
End Function
```

Code snippet from Person

Using methods like these, you write code to interact with the object:

```
Dim myPerson As New Person()

myPerson.SetName("Jones")
Messagebox.Show(myPerson.GetName())
```

While this is perfectly acceptable, it is not as nice as it could be with the use of a property. A `Property` style method consolidates the setting and retrieving of a value into a single structure, and makes the code within the class smoother overall. You can rewrite these two methods into a single property. Add the following code to the `Person` class:

```
Public Property Name() As String
    Get
        Return _Name
    End Get
    Set(ByVal Value As String)
        _Name = Value
    End Set
End Property
```

Code snippet from Person

With the introduction of Visual Studio 2010, the code above can be represented in a much simplier manner:

```
Public Property Name() As String
```

This method of defining a property actually creates a field called `_Name` which is not defined in the code, but by compiler. For most properties where you are not calculating a value during the get or set, this is the easiest way to define it.

By using a property method instead, you can make the client code much more readable:

```
Dim myPerson As New Person()

myPerson.Name = "Jones"
Messagebox.Show(myPerson.Name)
```

The `Property` method is declared with both a scope and a data type:

```
Public Property Name() As String
```

In this example, you've declared the property as `Public` in scope, but it can be declared using the same scope options as any other method — `Public`, `Friend`, `Private`, or `Protected`.

The return data type of this property is `String`. A property can return virtually any data type appropriate for the nature of the value. In this regard, a property is very similar to a method declared using the `Function` keyword.

Though a `Property` method is a single structure, it is divided into two parts: a getter and a setter. The getter is contained within a `Get...End Get` block and is responsible for returning the value of the property on demand:

```
Get
    Return mName
End Get
```

Though the code in this example is very simple, it could be more complex, perhaps calculating the value to be returned, or applying other business logic to change the value as it is returned. Likewise, the code to change the value is contained within a `Set...End Set` block:

```
Set(ByVal Value As String)
    mName = Value
End Set
```

The `Set` statement accepts a single parameter value that stores the new value. The code in the block can then use this value to set the property's value as appropriate. The data type of this parameter must match the data type of the property itself. Declaring the parameter in this manner enables you to change the name of the variable used for the parameter value if needed.

By default, the parameter is named `Value`, but you can change the parameter name to something else, as shown here:

```
Set(ByVal NewName As String)
    mName = NewName
End Set
```

In many cases, you can apply business rules or other logic within this routine to ensure that the new value is appropriate before you actually update the data within the object. It is also possible to restrict the `Get` or `Set` block to be narrower in scope than the scope of the property itself. For instance, you may want to allow any code to retrieve the property value, but only allow other code in your project to alter the value. In this case, you can restrict the scope of the `Set` block to `Friend`, while the `Property` itself is scoped as `Public`:

```
Public Property Name() As String
    Get
        Return mName
    End Get
    Friend Set(ByVal Value As String)
        mName = Value
    End Set
End Property
```

Code snippet from Person

The new scope must be more restrictive than the scope of the property itself, and either the `Get` or `Set` block can be restricted, but not both. The one you do not restrict uses the scope of the `Property` method.

Parameterized Properties

The `Name` property you created is an example of a single-value property. You can also create property arrays or parameterized properties. These properties reflect a range, or array, of values. For example, people often have several phone numbers. You might implement a `PhoneNumber` property as a parameterized property, storing not only phone numbers, but also a description of each number. To retrieve a specific phone number you would write code such as the following:

```
Dim myPerson As New Person()

Dim homePhone As String
homePhone = myPerson.Phone("home")
```

Code snippet from Person

Or, to add or change a specific phone number, you'd write the following code:

```
myPerson.Phone("work") = "555-9876"
```

Not only are you retrieving and updating a phone number property, you are also updating a specific phone number. This implies a couple of things. First, you can no longer use a simple variable to hold the phone number, as you are now storing a list of numbers and their associated names. Second, you have effectively added a parameter to your property. You are actually passing the name of the phone number as a parameter on each property call.

To store the list of phone numbers, you can use the `Hashtable` class. The `Hashtable` is very similar to the standard VB Collection object, but it is more powerful — allowing you to test for the existence of a specific element. Add the following declaration to the `Person` class:

```
Public Class Person
    Public Property Name As String
    Public Property BirthDate As Date
    Public Property TotalDistance As Integer
    Public Property Phones As New Hashtable
```

Code snippet from Person

You can implement the `Phone` property by adding the following code to the `Person` class:

```
Public Property Phone(ByVal location As String) As String
    Get
        Return CStr(Phones.Item(Location))
    End Get
    Set(ByVal Value As String)
        If Phones.ContainsKey(location) Then
            Phones.Item(location) = Value
        Else
            Phones.Add(location, Value)
        End If
    End Set
End Property
```

Code snippet from Person

The declaration of the `Property` method itself is a bit different from what you have seen:

```
Public Property Phone(ByVal location As String) As String
```

In particular, you have added a parameter, `location`, to the property itself. This parameter will act as the index into the list of phone numbers, and must be provided when either setting or retrieving phone number values.

Because the `location` parameter is declared at the `Property` level, it is available to all code within the property, including both the `Get` and `Set` blocks. Within your `Get` block, you use the `location` parameter to select the appropriate phone number to return from the `Hashtable`:

```
Get
    Return Phones.Item(location)
End Get
```

With this code, if no value is stored matching the location, then you get a trappable runtime error.

Similarly, in the `Set` block, you use the location to update or add the appropriate element in the `Hashtable`. In this case, you are using the `ContainsKey` method of `Hashtable` to determine whether the phone number already exists in the list. If it does, then you simply update the value in the list; otherwise, you add a new element to the list for the value:

```
Set(ByVal Value As String)
    If Phones.ContainsKey(location) Then
        Phones.Item(location) = Value
    Else
```

```
        Phones.Add(location, Value)
      End If
    End Set
```

This way, you are able to add or update a specific phone number entry based on the parameter passed by the calling code.

Read-Only Properties

Sometimes you may want a property to be read-only, so that it cannot be changed. In the `Person` class, for instance, you may have a read-write property, `BirthDate`, and a read-only property, `Age`. If so, the `BirthDate` property is a normal property, as follows:

```
Public Property BirthDate() As Date
```

The `Age` value, conversely, is a derived value based on `BirthDate`. This is not a value that should ever be directly altered, so it is a perfect candidate for read-only status.

You already have an `Age` method implemented as a function. Remove that code from the `Person` class because you will replace it with a Property routine instead. The difference between a function routine and a ReadOnly property is quite subtle. Both return a value to the calling code, and either way the object is running a subroutine defined by the class module to return the value.

The difference is less a programmatic one than a design choice. You could create all your objects without any Property routines at all, just using methods for all interactions with the objects. However, Property routines are obviously attributes of an object, whereas a Function might be an attribute or a method. By carefully implementing all attributes as ReadOnly Property routines, and any interrogative methods as Function routines, you create more readable and understandable code.

To make a property read-only, use the `ReadOnly` keyword and only implement the `Get` block:

```
Public ReadOnly Property Age() As Integer
  Get
    Return CInt(DateDiff(DateInterval.Year, mBirthDate, Now()))
  End Get
End Property
```

Because the property is read-only, you will get a syntax error if you attempt to implement a `Set` block.

Write-Only Properties

As with read-only properties, sometimes a property should be write-only, whereby the value can be changed but not retrieved.

Many people have allergies, so perhaps the `Person` object should have some understanding of the ambient allergens in the area. This is not a property that should be read from the `Person` object, as allergens come from the environment, rather than from the person, but it is data that the `Person` object needs in order to function properly. Add the following variable declaration to the class:

```
Public Class Person
  Public Property Name As String
  Public Property BirthDate As Date
  Public Property TotalDistance As Integer
  Public Property Phones As New Hashtable
  Public WriteOnly Property Allergens As Integer
```

You can implement an `AmbientAllergens` property as follows:

```
Public WriteOnly Property AmbientAllergens() As Integer
  Set(ByVal Value As Integer)
    mAllergens = Value
  End Set
End Property
```

Code snippet from Person

To create a write-only property, use the `WriteOnly` keyword and only implement a `Set` block in the code. Because the property is write-only, you will get a syntax error if you try to implement a `Get` block.

The Default Property

Objects can implement a default property, which can be used to simplify the use of an object at times by making it appear as if the object has a native value. A good example of this behavior is the `Collection` object, which has a default property called `Item` that returns the value of a specific item, allowing you to write the following:

```
Dim mData As New HashTable()

Return mData(index)
```

Default properties must be parameterized properties. A property without a parameter cannot be marked as the default. This is a change from previous versions of Visual Basic, in which any property could be marked as the default.

Our `Person` class has a parameterized property — the `Phone` property you built earlier. You can make this the default property by using the `Default` keyword:

```
Default Public Property Phone(ByVal location As String) As String
  Get
    Return CStr(mPhones.Item(location))
  End Get
  Set(ByVal Value As String)
    If mPhones.ContainsKey(location) Then
      mPhones.Item(location) = Value
    Else
      mPhones.Add(location, Value)
    End If
  End Set
End Property
```

Code snippet from Person

Prior to this change, you would have needed code such as the following to use the `Phone` property:

```
Dim myPerson As New Person()

MyPerson.Phone("home") = "555-1234"

Now, with the property marked as Default, you can simplify the code:

myPerson("home") = "555-1234"
```

As you can see, the reference to the property name `Phone` is not needed. By picking appropriate default properties, you can potentially make the use of objects more intuitive.

Events

Both methods and properties enable you to write code that interacts with your objects by invoking specific functionality as needed. It is often useful for objects to provide notification as certain activities occur during processing. You see examples of this all the time with controls, where a button indicates that it was clicked via a `Click` event, or a text box indicates that its contents have been changed via the `TextChanged` event.

Objects can raise events of their own, providing a powerful and easily implemented mechanism by which objects can notify client code of important activities or events. In Visual Basic, events are provided using the standard .NET mechanism of delegates; but before discussing delegates, let's explore how to work with events in Visual Basic.

Handling Events

We are all used to seeing code in a form to handle the `Click` event of a button, such as the following code:

```
Private Sub Button1_Click(ByVal sender As System.Object, _
    ByVal e As System.EventArgs) Handles Button1.Click

End Sub
```

Typically, we write our code in this type of routine without paying a lot of attention to the code created by the Visual Studio IDE. However, let's take a second look at that code, which contains some important things to note.

First, notice the use of the `Handles` keyword. This keyword specifically indicates that this method will be handling the `Click` event from the `Button1` control. Of course, a control is just an object, so what is indicated here is that this method will be handling the `Click` event from the `Button1` object.

Second, notice that the method accepts two parameters. The `Button` control class defines these parameters. It turns out that any method that accepts two parameters with these data types can be used to handle the `Click` event. For instance, you could create a new method to handle the event:

Available for download on Wrox.com

```
Private Sub MyClickMethod(ByVal s As System.Object, _
    ByVal args As System.EventArgs) Handles Button1.Click
End Sub
```

Code snippet from Form1

Even though you have changed the method name and the names of the parameters, you are still accepting parameters of the same data types, and you still have the `Handles` clause to indicate that this method handles the event.

Handling Multiple Events

The `Handles` keyword offers even more flexibility. Not only can the method name be anything you choose, a single method can handle multiple events if you desire. Again, the only requirement is that the method and all the events being raised must have the same parameter list.

> *This explains why all the standard events raised by the .NET system class library have exactly two parameters — the sender and an* `EventArgs` *object. Being so generic makes it possible to write very generic and powerful event handlers that can accept virtually any event raised by the class library.*

One common scenario where this is useful is when you have multiple instances of an object that raises events, such as two buttons on a form:

Available for download on Wrox.com

```
Private Sub MyClickMethod(ByVal sender As System.Object, _
    ByVal e As System.EventArgs) _
    Handles Button1.Click, Button2.Click

End Sub
```

Code snippet from Form1

Notice that the `Handles` clause has been modified so that it has a comma-separated list of events to handle. Either event will cause the method to run, providing a central location for handling these events.

The WithEvents Keyword

The `WithEvents` keyword tells Visual Basic that you want to handle any events raised by the object within the code:

```
Friend WithEvents Button1 As System.Windows.Forms.Button
```

The `WithEvents` keyword makes any event from an object available for use, whereas the `Handles` keyword is used to link specific events to the methods so that you can receive and handle them. This is true not only for controls on forms, but also for any objects that you create.

The `WithEvents` keyword cannot be used to declare a variable of a type that does not raise events. In other words, if the `Button` class did not contain code to raise events, you would get a syntax error when you attempted to declare the variable using the `WithEvents` keyword.

The compiler can tell which classes will and will not raise events by examining their interface. Any class that will be raising an event has that event declared as part of its interface. In Visual Basic, this means that you will have used the `Event` keyword to declare at least one event as part of the interface for the class.

Raising Events

Your objects can raise events just like a control, and the code using the object can receive these events by using the `WithEvents` and `Handles` keywords. Before you can raise an event from your object, however, you need to declare the event within the class by using the `Event` keyword.

In the `Person` class, for instance, you may want to raise an event anytime the `Walk` method is called. If you call this event `Walked`, you can add the following declaration to the `Person` class:

Available for download on Wrox.com

```
Public Class Person
    Private msName As String
    Private mBirthDate As Date
    Private mTotalDistance As Integer
    Private mPhones As New Hashtable()
    Private mAllergens As Integer
    Public Event Walked()
```

Code snippet from Person

Events can also have parameters, values that are provided to the code receiving the event. A typical button's `Click` event receives two parameters, for instance. In the `Walked` method, perhaps you want to also indicate the distance that was walked. You can do this by changing the event declaration:

```
Public Event Walked(ByVal distance As Integer)
```

Now that the event is declared, you can raise that event within the code where appropriate. In this case, you'll raise it within the `Walk` method, so anytime a `Person` object is instructed to walk, it fires an event indicating the distance walked. Make the following change to the `Walk` method:

Available for download on Wrox.com

```
Public Sub Walk(ByVal distance As Integer)
    mTotalDistance += distance
    RaiseEvent Walked(distance)
End Sub
```

Code snippet from Person

The `RaiseEvent` keyword is used to raise the actual event. Because the event requires a parameter, that value is passed within parentheses and is delivered to any recipient that handles the event.

In fact, the `RaiseEvent` statement causes the event to be delivered to all code that has the object declared using the `WithEvents` keyword with a `Handles` clause for this event, or any code that has used the `AddHandler` method. The `AddHandler` method is discussed shortly.

If more than one method will be receiving the event, then the event is delivered to each recipient one at a time. By default, the order of delivery is not defined — meaning you can't predict the order in which the recipients receive the event — but the event is delivered to all handlers. Note that this is a serial, synchronous process. The event is delivered to one handler at a time, and it is not delivered to the next handler until the current handler is complete. Once you call the `RaiseEvent` method, the event is delivered to all listeners one after another until it is complete; there is no way for you to intervene and stop the process in the middle.

Declaring and Raising Custom Events

As just noted, by default you have no control over how events are raised. You can overcome this limitation by using a more explicit form of declaration for the event itself. Rather than use the simple `Event` keyword, you can declare a custom event. This is for more advanced scenarios, as it requires you to provide the implementation for the event itself.

The concept of delegates is covered in detail later in this chapter, but it is necessary to look at them briefly here in order to declare a custom event. A delegate is a definition of a method signature. When you declare an event, Visual Basic defines a delegate for the event behind the scenes based on the signature of the event. The `Walked` event, for instance, has a delegate like the following:

```
Public Delegate Sub WalkedEventHandler(ByVal distance As Integer)
```

Notice how this code declares a "method" that accepts an `Integer` and has no return value. This is exactly what you defined for the event. Normally, you do not write this bit of code, because Visual Basic does it automatically; but if you want to declare a custom event, then you need to manually declare the event delegate.

You also need to declare within the class a variable where you can keep track of any code that is listening for, or handling, the event. It turns out that you can tap into the prebuilt functionality of delegates for this purpose. By declaring the `WalkedEventHandler` delegate, you have defined a data type that automatically tracks event handlers, so you can declare the variable like this:

```
Private mWalkedHandlers As WalkedEventHandler
```

You can use the preceding variable to store and raise the event within the custom event declaration:

Available for download on Wrox.com

```
Public Custom Event Walked As WalkedEventHandler
  AddHandler(ByVal value As WalkedEventHandler)
    mWalkedHandlers = _
      CType([Delegate].Combine(mWalkedHandlers, value), WalkedEventHandler)
  End AddHandler

  RemoveHandler(ByVal value As WalkedEventHandler)
    mWalkedHandlers = _
      CType([Delegate].Remove(mWalkedHandlers, value), WalkedEventHandler)
  End RemoveHandler

  RaiseEvent(ByVal distance As Integer)
    If mWalkedHandlers IsNot Nothing Then
      mWalkedHandlers.Invoke(distance)
    End If
  End RaiseEvent
End Event
```

Code snippet from Person

In this case, you have used the `Custom Event` key phrase, rather than just `Event` to declare the event. A `Custom Event` declaration is a block structure with three sub-blocks: `AddHandler`, `RemoveHandler`, and `RaiseEvent`.

The `AddHandler` block is called anytime a new handler wants to receive the event. The parameter passed to this block is a reference to the method that will be handling the event. It is up to you to store the reference to that method, which you can do however you choose. In this implementation, you are storing it within the delegate variable, just like the default implementation provided by Visual Basic.

The `RemoveHandler` block is called anytime a handler wants to stop receiving your event. The parameter passed to this block is a reference to the method that was handling the event. It is up to you to remove the reference to the method, which you can do however you choose. In this implementation, you are replicating the default behavior by having the delegate variable remove the element.

Finally, the `RaiseEvent` block is called anytime the event is raised. Typically, it is invoked when code within the class uses the `RaiseEvent` statement. The parameters passed to this block must match the parameters declared by the delegate for the event. It is up to you to go through the list of methods that are handling the event and call each of those methods. In the example shown here, you are allowing the delegate variable to do that for you, which is the same behavior you get by default with a normal event.

The value of this syntax is that you could opt to store the list of handler methods in a different type of data structure, such as a `Hashtable` or `collection`. You could then invoke them asynchronously, or in a specific order based on some other behavior required by the application.

Receiving Events with WithEvents

Now that you have implemented an event within the `Person` class, you can write client code to declare an object using the `WithEvents` keyword. For instance, in the project's Form1 code module, you can write the following code:

```
Public Class Form1
    Private WithEvents mPerson As Person
```

By declaring the variable `WithEvents`, you are indicating that you want to receive any events raised by this object. You can also choose to declare the variable without the `WithEvents` keyword, although in that case you would not receive events from the object as described here. Instead, you would use the `AddHandler` method, which is discussed after `WithEvents`.

You can then create an instance of the object, as the form is created, by adding the following code:

Available for download on Wrox.com

```
Private Sub Form1_Load(ByVal sender As System.Object, _
    ByVal e As System.EventArgs) Handles MyBase.Load

    mPerson = New Person()

End Sub
```

Code snippet from Form1

At this point, you have declared the object variable using `WithEvents` and have created an instance of the `Person` class, so you actually have an object with which to work. You can now proceed to write a method to handle the `Walked` event from the object by adding the following code to the form. You can name this method anything you like; it is the `Handles` clause that is important because it links the event from the object directly to this method, so it is invoked when the event is raised:

```
Private Sub OnWalk(ByVal distance As Integer) Handles mPerson.Walked
    MsgBox("Person walked " & distance)
End Sub
```

You are using the `Handles` keyword to indicate which event should be handled by this method. You are also receiving an `Integer` parameter. If the parameter list of the method doesn't match the list for the event, then you'll get a compiler error indicating the mismatch.

Finally, you need to call the `Walk` method on the `Person` object. Add a button to the form and write the following code for its `Click` event:

```
Private Sub Button1_Click(ByVal sender As System.Object, _
    ByVal e As System.EventArgs) Handles button1.Click

  mPerson.Walk(42)

End Sub
```

Code snippet from Form1

When the button is clicked, you simply call the `Walk` method, passing an `Integer` value. This causes the code in your class to be run, including the `RaiseEvent` statement. The result is an event firing back into the form, because you declared the `mPerson` variable using the `WithEvents` keyword. The `OnWalk` method will be run to handle the event, as it has the `Handles` clause linking it to the event.

Figure 2-15 illustrates the flow of control, showing how the code in the button's `Click` event calls the `Walk` method, causing it to add to the total distance walked and then raise its event. The `RaiseEvent` causes the form's `OnWalk` method to be invoked; and once it is done, control returns to the `Walk` method in the object. Because you have no code in the `Walk` method after you call `RaiseEvent`, the control returns to the `Click` event back in the form, and then you are done.

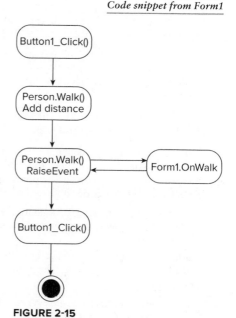

FIGURE 2-15

 Many people assume that events use multiple threads to do their work. This is not the case. Only one thread is involved in the process. Raising an event is like making a method call, as the existing thread is used to run the code in the event handler. Therefore, the application's processing is suspended until the event processing is complete.

Receiving Events with AddHandler

Now that you have seen how to receive and handle events using the `WithEvents` and `Handles` keywords, consider an alternative approach. You can use the `AddHandler` method to dynamically add event handlers through your code, and `RemoveHandler` to dynamically remove them.

`WithEvents` and the `Handles` clause require that you declare both the object variable and event handler as you build the code, effectively creating a linkage that is compiled right into the code. `AddHandler`, conversely, creates this linkage at runtime, which can provide you with more flexibility. However, before getting too deeply into that, let's see how `AddHandler` works.

In `Form1`, you can change the way the code interacts with the `Person` object, first by eliminating the `WithEvents` keyword:

```
Private mPerson As Person
```

And then by also eliminating the `Handles` clause:

```
Private Sub OnWalk(ByVal distance As Integer)
  MsgBox("Person walked " & distance)
End Sub
```

With these changes, you've eliminated all event handling for the object, and the form will no longer receive the event, even though the `Person` object raises it.

Now you can change the code to dynamically add an event handler at runtime by using the `AddHandler` method. This method simply links an object's event to a method that should be called to handle that event. Anytime after you have created the object, you can call `AddHandler` to set up the linkage:

Available for download on Wrox.com

```
Private Sub Form1_Load(ByVal sender As System.Object, _
    ByVal e As System.EventArgs) Handles MyBase.Load

    mPerson = New Person()
    AddHandler mPerson.Walked, AddressOf OnWalk
End Sub
```

Code snippet from Form1

This single line of code does the same thing as the earlier use of `WithEvents` and the `Handles` clause, causing the `OnWalk` method to be invoked when the `Walked` event is raised from the `Person` object.

However, this linkage is performed at runtime, so you have more control over the process than you would have otherwise. For instance, you could have extra code to determine which event handler to link up. Suppose that you have another possible method to handle the event for cases when a message box is not desirable. Add this code to `Form1`:

```
Private Sub LogOnWalk(ByVal distance As Integer)
    System.Diagnostics.Debug.WriteLine("Person walked " & distance)
End Sub
```

Rather than pop up a message box, this version of the handler logs the event to the output window in the IDE. Now you can enhance the `AddHandler` code to determine which handler should be used dynamically at runtime:

Available for download on Wrox.com

```
Private Sub Form1_Load(ByVal sender As System.Object, _
    ByVal e As System.EventArgs) Handles MyBase.Load
    mPerson = New Person()
    If Microsoft.VisualBasic.Command = "nodisplay" Then
        AddHandler mPerson.Walked, AddressOf LogOnWalk
    Else
        AddHandler mPerson.Walked, AddressOf OnWalk
    End If
End Sub
```

Code snippet from Form1

If the word `"nodisplay"` is on the command line when the application is run, then the new version of the event handler is used; otherwise, you continue to use the message-box handler.

The counterpart to `AddHandler` is `RemoveHandler`. `RemoveHandler` is used to detach an event handler from an event. One example of when this is useful is if you ever want to set the `mPerson` variable to `Nothing` or to a new `Person` object. The existing `Person` object has its events attached to handlers, and before you get rid of the reference to the object, you must release those references:

Available for download on Wrox.com

```
If Microsoft.VisualBasic.Command = "nodisplay" Then
    RemoveHandler mPerson.Walked, AddressOf LogOnWalk
Else
    RemoveHandler mPerson.Walked, AddressOf OnWalk
End If
mPerson = New Person
```

Code snippet from Form1

If you do not detach the event handlers, the old `Person` object remains in memory because each event handler still maintains a reference to the object even after `mPerson` no longer points to the object.

This illustrates one key reason why the `WithEvents` keyword and `Handles` clause are preferable in most cases. `AddHandler` and `RemoveHandler` must be used in pairs; failure to do so can cause memory leaks in the application, whereas the `WithEvents` keyword handles these details for you automatically.

Constructor Methods

In Visual Basic, classes can implement a special method that is always invoked as an object is being created. This method is called the *constructor*, and it is always named `New`.

The constructor method is an ideal location for such initialization code, as it is always run before any other methods are ever invoked, and it is only run once for an object. Of course, you can create many objects based on a class, and the constructor method will be run for each object that is created.

You can implement a constructor in your classes as well, using it to initialize objects as needed. This is as easy as implementing a Public method named `New`. Add the following code to the `Person` class:

Available for download on Wrox.com

```
Public Sub New()
  Phone("home") = "555-1234"
  Phone("work") = "555-5678"
End Sub
```

Code snippet from Person

In this example, you are simply using the constructor method to initialize the home and work phone numbers for any new `Person` object that is created.

Parameterized Constructors

You can also use constructors to enable parameters to be passed to the object as it is being created. This is done by simply adding parameters to the `New` method. For example, you can change the `Person` class as follows:

Available for download on Wrox.com

```
Public Sub New(ByVal name As String, ByVal birthDate As Date)
  mName = name
  mBirthDate = birthDate
  Phone("home") = "555-1234"
  Phone("work") = "555-5678"
End Sub
```

Code snippet from Person

With this change, anytime a `Person` object is created, you will be provided with values for both the name and birth date. However, this changes how you can create a new `Person` object. Whereas you used to have code such as

```
Dim myPerson As New Person()
```

now you will have code such as

```
Dim myPerson As New Person("Bill", "1/1/1970")
```

In fact, because the constructor expects these values, they are mandatory — any code that needs to create an instance of the `Person` class must provide these values. Fortunately, there are alternatives in the form of optional parameters and method overloading (which enables you to create multiple versions of the same method, each accepting a different parameter list). These topics are discussed later in the chapter.

Termination and Cleanup

In the .NET environment, an object is destroyed and the memory and resources it consumes are reclaimed when there are no references remaining for the object. As discussed earlier in the chapter, when you are using objects, the variables actually hold a reference or pointer to the object itself. If you have code such as

```
Dim myPerson As New Person()
```

you know that the `myPerson` variable is just a reference to the `Person` object you created. If you also have code like

```
Dim anotherPerson As Person
anotherPerson = myPerson
```

you know that the `anotherPerson` variable is also a reference to the same object. This means that this specific `Person` object is being referenced by two variables.

When there are no variables left to reference an object, it can be terminated by the .NET runtime environment. In particular, it is terminated and reclaimed by a mechanism called *garbage collection*, or the *garbage collector*, covered in detail in Chapter 4.

 Unlike other runtime environments, the .NET runtime does not use reference counting to determine when an object should be terminated. Instead, it uses garbage collection to terminate objects. This means that in Visual Basic you do not have deterministic finalization, so it is not possible to predict exactly when an object will be destroyed.

Let's review how you can eliminate references to an object. You can explicitly remove a reference by setting the variable equal to `Nothing`, with the following code:

```
myPerson = Nothing
```

You can also remove a reference to an object by changing the variable to reference a different object. Because a variable can only point to one object at a time, it follows naturally that changing a variable to point at another object must cause it to no longer point to the first one. This means that you can have code such as the following:

```
myPerson = New Person()
```

This causes the variable to point to a brand-new object, thus releasing this reference to the prior object. These are examples of *explicit dereferencing*.

Visual Basic also provides facilities for implicit dereferencing of objects when a variable goes out of scope. For instance, if you have a variable declared within a method, then when that method completes, the variable is automatically destroyed, thus dereferencing any object to which it may have pointed. In fact, anytime a variable referencing an object goes out of scope, the reference to that object is automatically eliminated. This is illustrated by the following code:

Available for download on Wrox.com

```
Private Sub DoSomething()
   Dim myPerson As Person

   myPerson = New Person()
End Sub
```

Code snippet from Form1

Even though the preceding code does not explicitly set the value of `myPerson` to `Nothing`, you know that the `myPerson` variable will be destroyed when the method is complete because it will fall out of scope. This process implicitly removes the reference to the `Person` object created within the routine.

Of course, another scenario in which objects become dereferenced is when the application itself completes and is terminated. At that point, all variables are destroyed, so, by definition, all object references go away as well.

ADVANCED CONCEPTS

So far, you have learned how to work with objects, how to create classes with methods, properties, and events, and how to use constructors. You have also learned how objects are destroyed within the .NET environment and how you can hook into that process to do any cleanup required by the objects.

Now you can move on to some more complex topics and variations on what has been discussed so far. First you'll look at some advanced variations of the methods you can implement in classes, including an exploration of the underlying technology behind events.

Overloading Methods

Methods often accept parameter values. The `Person` object's `Walk` method, for instance, accepts an `Integer` parameter:

```
Public Sub Walk(ByVal distance As Integer)
  mTotalDistance += distance
    RaiseEvent Walked(distance)
End Sub
```

Code snippet from Person

Sometimes there is no need for the parameter. To address this, you can use the `Optional` keyword to make the parameter optional:

```
Public Sub Walk(Optional ByVal distance As Integer = 0)
  mTotalDistance += distance
    RaiseEvent Walked(distance)
End Sub
```

Code snippet from Person

This does not provide you with a lot of flexibility, however, as the optional parameter or parameters must always be the last ones in the list. In addition, this merely enables you to pass or not pass the parameter. Suppose that you want to do something fancier, such as allow different data types or even entirely different lists of parameters.

Method overloading provides exactly those capabilities. By overloading methods, you can create several methods of the same name, with each one accepting a different set of parameters, or parameters of different data types.

As a simple example, instead of using the `Optional` keyword in the `Walk` method, you could use overloading. You keep the original `Walk` method, but you also add another `Walk` method that accepts a different parameter list. Change the code in the `Person` class back to the following:

```
Public Sub Walk(ByVal distance As Integer)
  mTotalDistance += distance
    RaiseEvent Walked(distance)
End Sub
```

Code snippet from Person

Now create another method with the same name but with a different parameter list (in this case, no parameters). Add this code to the class, without removing or changing the existing `Walk` method:

```
Public Sub Walk()
  RaiseEvent Walked(0)
End Sub
```

Code snippet from Person

At this point, you have two `Walk` methods. The only way to tell them apart is by the list of parameters each accepts: the first requiring a single `Integer` parameter, the second having no parameter.

There is an `Overloads` keyword as well. This keyword is not needed for the simple overloading of methods described here, but it is required when combining overloading and inheritance, which is discussed in Chapter 3.

You can call the `Walk` method either with or without a parameter, as shown in the following examples:

```
objPerson.Walk(42)
objPerson.Walk()
```

You can have any number of `Walk` methods in the class as long as each individual `Walk` method has a different method signature.

Method Signatures

All methods have a signature, which is defined by the method name and the data types of its parameters:

```
Public Function CalculateValue() As Integer

End Sub
```

In this example, the signature is `f()`. The letter *f* is often used to indicate a method or function. It is appropriate here because you do not care about the name of the function; only its parameter list is important.

If you add a parameter to the method, then the signature is considered changed. For instance, you could change the method to accept a `Double`:

```
Public Function CalculateValue(ByVal value As Double) As Integer
```

In that case, the signature of the method is `f(Double)`.

Notice that in Visual Basic the return value is not part of the signature. You cannot overload a function routine by just having its return value's data type vary. It is the data types in the parameter list that must vary to utilize overloading.

Also note that the name of the parameter is totally immaterial; only the data type is important. This means that the following methods have identical signatures:

```
Public Sub DoWork(ByVal x As Integer, ByVal y As Integer)

Public Sub DoWork(ByVal value1 As Integer, ByVal value2 As Integer)
```

In both cases, the signature is `f(Integer, Integer)`.

The data types of the parameters define the method signature, but whether the parameters are passed `ByVal` or `ByRef` does not. Changing a parameter from `ByVal` to `ByRef` will not change the method signature.

Combining Overloading and Optional Parameters

Overloading is more flexible than using optional parameters, but optional parameters have the advantage that they can be used to provide default values, as well as make a parameter optional.

You can combine the two concepts: overloading a method and having one or more of those methods utilize optional parameters. Obviously, this sort of thing can become very confusing if overused, as you are employing two types of method "overloading" at the same time.

The `Optional` keyword causes a single method to effectively have two signatures. This means that a method declared as

```
Public Sub DoWork(ByVal x As Integer, Optional ByVal y As Integer = 0)
```

has two signatures at once: `f(Integer, Integer)` and `f(Integer)`.

Because of this, when you use overloading along with optional parameters, the other overloaded methods cannot match either of these two signatures. However, as long as other methods do not match either signature, you can use overloading, as discussed earlier. For instance, you could implement methods with the signatures

```
Public Sub DoWork(ByVal x As Integer, Optional ByVal y As Integer = 0)
```

and

```
Public Sub DoWork(ByVal data As String)
```

because there are no conflicting method signatures. In fact, with these two methods, you have actually created three signatures:

➤ f(Integer, Integer)

➤ f(Integer)

➤ f(String)

The IntelliSense built into the Visual Studio IDE will indicate that you have two overloaded methods, one of which has an optional parameter. This is different from creating three different overloaded methods to match these three signatures, in which case the IntelliSense would list three variations on the method, from which you could choose.

Overloading Constructor Methods

In many cases, you may want the constructor to accept parameter values for initializing new objects, but also want to have the capability to create objects without providing those values. This is possible through method overloading, which is discussed later, or by using optional parameters.

Optional parameters on a constructor method follow the same rules as optional parameters for any other Sub routine: They must be the last parameters in the parameter list, and you must provide default values for the optional parameters.

For instance, you can change the Person class as shown here:

```
Public Sub New(Optional ByVal name As String = "", _
    Optional ByVal birthDate As Date = #1/1/1900#)
  mName = name
  mBirthDate = birthDate

  Phone("home") = "555-1234"
  Phone("work") = "555-5678"
End Sub
```

Code snippet from Person

The preceding example changes both the Name and BirthDate parameters to be optional, and provides default values for both of them. Now you have the option to create a new Person object with or without the parameter values:

```
Dim myPerson As New Person("Bill", "1/1/1970")
```

or

```
Dim myPerson As New Person()
```

If you do not provide the parameter values, then the default values of an empty String and 1/1/1900 will be used and the code will work just fine.

Overloading the Constructor Method

You can combine the concept of a constructor method with method overloading to allow for different ways of creating instances of the class. This can be a very powerful combination because it allows a great deal of flexibility in object creation.

You have already explored how to use optional parameters in the constructor. Now let's change the implementation in the Person class to make use of overloading instead. Change the existing New method as follows:

```
Public Sub New(ByVal name As String, ByVal birthDate As Date)
  mName = name
  mBirthDate = birthDate
  Phone("home") = "555-1234"
  Phone("work") = "555-5678"
End Sub
```

Code snippet from Person

With this change, you require the two parameter values to be supplied. Now add that second implementation, as shown here:

```
Public Sub New()
   Phone("home") = "555-1234"
   Phone("work") = "555-5678"
End Sub
```

This second implementation accepts no parameters, meaning you can now create `Person` objects in two different ways — either with no parameters or by passing the name and birth date:

```
Dim myPerson As New Person()
```

or

```
Dim myPerson As New Person("Fred", "1/11/60")
```

This type of capability is very powerful because it enables you to define the various ways in which applications can create objects. In fact, the Visual Studio IDE considers this, so when you are typing the code to create an object, the IntelliSense tooltip displays the overloaded variations on the method, providing a level of automatic documentation for the class.

Shared Methods, Variables, and Events

So far, all of the methods you have built or used have been instance methods, methods that require you to have an actual instance of the class before they can be called. These methods have used instance variables or member variables to do their work, which means that they have been working with a set of data that is unique to each individual object.

With Visual Basic, you can create variables and methods that belong to the class, rather than to any specific object. In other words, these variables and methods belong to all objects of a given class and are shared across all the instances of the class.

You can use the `Shared` keyword to indicate which variables and methods belong to the class, rather than to specific objects. For instance, you may be interested in knowing the total number of `Person` objects created as the application is running — kind of a statistical counter.

Shared Variables

Because regular variables are unique to each individual `Person` object, they do not enable you to easily track the total number of `Person` objects ever created. However, if you had a variable that had a common value across all instances of the `Person` class, you could use that as a counter. Add the following variable declaration to the `Person` class:

```
Public Class Person
   Implements IDisposable
      Private Shared mCounter As Integer
```

By using the `Shared` keyword, you are indicating that this variable's value should be shared across all `Person` objects within your application. This means that if one `Person` object makes the value 42, then all other `Person` objects will see the value as 42: It is a shared piece of data.

You can now use this variable within the code. For instance, you can add code to the constructor method, `New`, to increment the variable so that it acts as a counter — adding 1 each time a new `Person` object is created. Change the `New` methods as shown here:

Available for
download on
Wrox.com

```
Public Sub New()
   Phone("home") = "555-1234"
   Phone("work") = "555-5678"
   mCounter += 1
End Sub

Public Sub New(ByVal name As String, ByVal birthDate As Date)
```

```
        mName = name
        mBirthDate = birthDate

        Phone("home") = "555-1234"
        Phone("work") = "555-5678"
        mCounter += 1
    End Sub
```

Code snippet from Person

The `mCounter` variable will now maintain a value indicating the total number of `Person` objects created during the life of the application. You may want to add a property routine to allow access to this value by writing the following code:

```
Public ReadOnly Property PersonCount() As Integer
    Get
        Return mCounter
    End Get
End Property
```

Code snippet from Form1

Note that you are creating a regular property that returns the value of a shared variable, which is perfectly acceptable. As shown shortly, you could also create a shared property to return the value.

Now you could write code to use the class as follows:

```
Dim myPerson As Person
myPerson = New Person()
myPerson = New Person()
myPerson = New Person()

Messagebox.Show(myPerson.PersonCount)
```

Code snippet from Form1

The resulting display would show 3, because you've created three instances of the `Person` class. You would also need to decrement the counter after the objects are destroyed.

Shared Methods

You can share not only variables across all instances of a class, but also methods. Whereas a regular method or property belongs to each specific object, a shared method or property is common across all instances of the class. There are a couple of ramifications to this approach.

First, because shared methods do not belong to any specific object, they can't access any instance variables from any objects. The only variables available for use within a shared method are shared variables, parameters passed into the method, or variables declared locally within the method itself. If you attempt to access an instance variable within a shared method, you'll get a compiler error.

In addition, because shared methods are actually part of the class, rather than any object, you can write code to call them directly from the class without having to create an instance of the class first.

For instance, a regular instance method is invoked from an object:

```
Dim myPerson As New Person()

myPerson.Walk(42)
```

However, a shared method can be invoked directly from the class itself without having to declare an instance of the class first:

```
Person.SharedMethod()
```

This saves the effort of creating an object just to invoke a method, and can be very appropriate for methods that act on shared variables, or methods that act only on values passed in via parameters. You can also invoke a shared method from an object, just like a regular method. Shared methods are flexible in that they can be called with or without creating an instance of the class first.

To create a shared method, you again use the `Shared` keyword. For instance, the `PersonCount` property created earlier could easily be changed to become a shared method instead:

```
Public Shared ReadOnly Property PersonCount() As Integer
   Get
      Return mCounter
   End Get
End Property
```

Code snippet from Form1

Because this property returns the value of a shared variable, it is perfectly acceptable for it to be implemented as a shared method. With this change, you can now determine how many `Person` objects have ever been created without having to actually create a `Person` object first:

```
Messagebox.Show(CStr(Person.PersonCount))
```

As another example, in the `Person` class you could create a method that compares the ages of two people. Add a shared method with the following code:

```
Public Shared Function CompareAge(ByVal person1 As Person, _
    ByVal person2 As Person) As Boolean

   Return person1.Age > person2.Age
End Function
```

Code snippet from Form1

This method simply accepts two parameters — each a `Person` — and returns true if the first is older than the second. Use of the `Shared` keyword indicates that this method doesn't require a specific instance of the `Person` class in order for you to use it.

Within this code, you are invoking the `Age` property on two separate objects, the objects passed as parameters to the method. It is important to recognize that you're not directly using any instance variables within the method; rather, you are accepting two objects as parameters, and invoking methods on those objects. To use this method, you can call it directly from the class:

```
If Person.CompareAge(myPerson1, myPerson2) Then
```

Alternately, you can also invoke it from any `Person` object:

```
Dim myPerson As New Person()

If myPerson.CompareAge(myPerson, myPerson2) Then
```

Either way, you're invoking the same shared method, and you'll get the same behavior, whether you call it from the class or a specific instance of the class.

Shared Properties

As with other types of methods, you can also have shared property methods. Properties follow the same rules as regular methods. They can interact with shared variables but not member variables. They can also invoke other shared methods or properties, but cannot invoke instance methods without first creating an instance of the class. You can add a shared property to the `Person` class with the following code:

```
Public Shared ReadOnly Property RetirementAge() As Integer
   Get
      Return 62
   End Get
End Property
```

Code snippet from Person

This simply adds a property to the class that indicates the global retirement age for all people. To use this value, you can simply access it directly from the class:

```
Messagebox.Show(Person.RetirementAge)
```

Alternately, you can access it from any `Person` object:

```
Dim myPerson As New Person()

Messagebox.Show(myPerson.RetirementAge)
```

Either way, you are invoking the same shared property.

Shared Events

As with other interface elements, events can also be marked as `Shared`. For instance, you could declare a shared event in the `Person` class:

```
Public Shared Event NewPerson()
```

Shared events can be raised from both instance methods and shared methods. Regular events cannot be raised by shared methods. Because shared events can be raised by regular methods, you can raise this one from the constructors in the `Person` class:

Available for download on Wrox.com

```
Public Sub New()
  Phone("home") = "555-1234"
  Phone("work") = "555-5678"
  mCounter += 1
  RaiseEvent NewPerson()
End Sub

Public Sub New(ByVal name As String, ByVal birthDate As Date)
  mName = Name
  mBirthDate - BirthDate

  Phone("home") = "555-1234"
  Phone("work") = "555-5678"
  mCounter += 1
  RaiseEvent NewPerson()
End Sub
```

Code snippet from Person

The interesting thing about receiving shared events is that you can get them from either an object, such as a normal event, or from the class itself. For instance, you can use the `AddHandler` method in the form's code to catch this event directly from the `Person` class.

First, add a method to the form to handle the event:

```
Private Sub OnNewPerson()
  Messagebox.Show("new person " & Person.PersonCount)
End Sub
```

Then, in the form's `Load` event, add a statement to link the event to this method:

Available for download on Wrox.com

```
Private Sub Form1_Load(ByVal sender As System.Object, _
  ByVal e As System.EventArgs) Handles MyBase.Load

  AddHandler Person.NewPerson, AddressOf OnNewPerson

  mPerson = New Person()
  If Microsoft.VisualBasic.Command = "nodisplay" Then
    AddHandler mPerson.Walked, AddressOf LogOnWalk
  Else
```

```
        AddHandler mPerson.Walked, AddressOf OnWalk
      End If
End Sub
```

Code snippet from Form1

Notice that you are using the class, rather than any specific object in the AddHandler statement. You could use an object as well, treating this like a normal event, but this illustrates how a class itself can raise an event. When you run the application now, anytime a Person object is created you will see this event raised.

Shared Constructor

A class can also have a Shared constructor:

```
Shared Sub New()

End Sub
```

Normal constructors are called when an instance of the class is created. The Shared constructor is called only once during the lifetime of an application, immediately before any use of the class.

This means that the Shared constructor is called before any other Shared methods, and before any instances of the class are created. The first time any code attempts to interact with any method on the class, or attempts to create an instance of the class, the Shared constructor is invoked.

Because you never directly call the Shared constructor, it cannot accept any parameters. Moreover, because it is a Shared method, it can only interact with Shared variables or other Shared methods in the class.

Typically, a Shared constructor is used to initialize Shared fields within an object. In the Person class, for instance, you can use it to initialize the mCount variable:

```
Shared Sub New()
  mCount = 0
End Sub
```

Because this method is called only once during the lifetime of the application, it is safe to do one-time initializations of values in this constructor.

Operator Overloading

Many basic data types, such as Integer and String, support the use of operators, including +, –, =, <>, and so forth. When you create a class, you are defining a new type, and sometimes it is appropriate for types to also support the use of operators.

In your class, you can write code to define how each of these operators works when applied to objects. What does it mean when two objects are added together? Or multiplied? Or compared? If you can define what these operations mean, you can write code to implement appropriate behaviors. This is called *operator overloading*, as you are overloading the meaning of specific operators.

Operator overloading is performed by using the Operator keyword, in much the same way that you create a Sub, Function, or Property method.

Most objects at least provide for some type of comparison, and so will often overload the comparison operators (=, <>, and maybe <, >, <=, and >=). You can do this in the Person class, for example, by adding the following code:

```
Public Shared Operator =(ByVal person1 As Person, _
  ByVal person2 As Person) As Boolean

  Return person1.Name = person2.Name
End Operator

Public Shared Operator <>(ByVal person1 As Person, _
```

```
            ByVal person2 As Person) As Boolean

        Return person1.Name <> person2.Name
    End Operator
```

Code snippet from Form1

Note that you overload both the = and <> operators. Many operators come in pairs, including the equality operator. If you overload =, then you must overload <> or a compiler error will result. Now that you have overloaded these operators, you can write code in Form1 such as the following:

Available for
download on
Wrox.com

```
Dim p1 As New Person("Fred", #1/1/1960#)
Dim p2 As New Person("Mary", #1/1/1980#)
Dim p3 As Person = p1

Debug.WriteLine(CStr(p1 = p2))
Debug.WriteLine(CStr(p1 = p3))
```

Code snippet from Form1

Normally, it would be impossible to compare two objects using a simple comparison operator, but because you overloaded the operator, this becomes valid code. The result will display False and True.

Both the = and <> operators accept two parameters, so these are called *binary operators*. There are also *unary operators* that accept a single parameter. For instance, you might define the capability to convert a String value into a Person object by overloading the CType operator:

Available for
download on
Wrox.com

```
Public Shared Narrowing Operator CType(ByVal name As String) As Person
    Dim obj As New Person
    obj.Name = name
    Return obj
End Operator
```

Code snippet from Form1

To convert a String value to a Person, you assume that the value should be the Name property. You create a new object, set the Name property, and return the result. Because String is a broader, or less specific, type than Person, this is a *narrowing conversion*. Were you to do the reverse, convert a Person to a String, that would be a *widening conversion*:

```
Public Shared Widening Operator CType(ByVal person As Person) As String
    Return person.Name
End Operator
```

Few non-numeric objects will overload most operators. It is difficult to imagine the result of adding, subtracting, or dividing two Customer objects against each other. Likewise, it is difficult to imagine performing bitwise comparisons between two Invoice objects. Table 2-6 lists the various operators that can be overloaded.

TABLE 2-6: Visual Basic Operators

OPERATORS	DESCRIPTION
=, <>	Equality and inequality. These are binary operators to support the a = b and a <> b syntax. If you implement one, then you must implement both.
>, <	Greater than and less than. These are binary operators to support the a > b and a < b syntax. If you implement one, then you must implement both.
>=, <=	Greater than or equal to and less than or equal to. These are binary operators to support the a >= b and a <= b syntax. If you implement one, then you must implement both.

continues

TABLE 2-6 *(continued)*

OPERATORS	DESCRIPTION
IsFalse, IsTrue	Boolean conversion. These are unary operators to support the AndAlso and OrElse statements. The IsFalse operator accepts a single object and returns False if the object can be resolved to a False value. The IsTrue operator accepts a single value and returns True if the object can be resolved to a True value. If you implement one, then you must implement both.
CType	Type conversion. This is a unary operator to support the CType(a) statement. The CType operator accepts a single object of another type and converts that object to the type of your class. This operator must be marked as either Narrowing, to indicate that the type is more specific than the original type, or Widening, to indicate that the type is broader than the original type.
+, –	Addition and subtraction. These operators can be unary or binary. The unary form exists to support the a += b and a –= b syntax, while the binary form exists to support a + b and a – b.
*, /, \, ^, Mod	Multiplication, division, exponent, and Mod. These are binary operators to support the a * b, a / b, a \ b, a ^ b, and a Mod b syntax.
&	Concatenation. This binary operator supports the a & b syntax. While this operator is typically associated with String manipulation, the & operator is not required to accept or return String values, so it can be used for any concatenation operation that is meaningful for your object type.
<<, >>	Bit shifting. These binary operators support the a << b and a >> b syntax. The second parameter of these operators must be a value of type Integer, which will be the integer value to be bit-shifted based on your object value.
And, Or, Xor	Logical comparison or bitwise operation. These binary operators support the a And b, a Or b, and a Xor b syntax. If the operators return Boolean results, then they are performing logical comparisons. If they return results of other data types, then they are performing bitwise operations.
Like	Pattern comparison. This binary operator supports the a Like b syntax.

If an operator is meaningful for your data type, then you are strongly encouraged to overload that operator.

Defining AndAlso and OrElse

Notice that neither the AndAlso nor the OrElse operators can be directly overloaded. This is because these operators use other operators behind the scenes to do their work. To overload AndAlso and OrElse, you need to overload a set of other operators, as shown in the following table:

ANDALSO	ORELSE
Overload the And operator to accept two parameters of your object's type and to return a result of your object's type.	Overload the Or operator to accept two parameters of your object's type and to return a result of your object's type.
Overload IsFalse for your object's type (meaning that you can return True or False by evaluating a single instance of your object).	Overload IsTrue for your object's type (meaning that you can return True or False by evaluating a single instance of your object).

If these operators are overloaded in your class, then you can use AndAlso and OrElse to evaluate statements that involve instances of your class.

Delegates

Sometimes it would be nice to be able to pass a procedure as a parameter to a method. The classic scenario is when building a generic sort routine, for which you need to provide not only the data to be sorted, but also a comparison routine appropriate for the specific data.

It is easy enough to write a sort routine that sorts `Person` objects by name, or to write a sort routine that sorts `SalesOrder` objects by sales date. However, if you want to write a sort routine that can sort any type of object based on arbitrary sort criteria, that gets pretty difficult. At the same time, because some sort routines can get very complex, it would be nice to reuse that code without having to copy and paste it for each different sort scenario.

By using *delegates*, you can create such a generic routine for sorting; and in so doing, you can see how delegates work and can be used to create many other types of generic routines. The concept of a delegate formalizes the process of declaring a routine to be called and calling that routine.

The underlying mechanism used by the .NET environment for callback methods is the delegate. Visual Basic uses delegates behind the scenes as it implements the `Event`, `RaiseEvent`, `WithEvents`, *and* `Handles` *keywords.*

Declaring a Delegate

In your code, you can declare what a delegate procedure must look like from an interface standpoint. This is done using the `Delegate` keyword. To see how this works, let's create a routine to sort any kind of data.

To do this, you will declare a delegate that defines a method signature for a method that compares the value of two objects and returns a Boolean indicating whether the first object has a larger value than the second object. You will then create a sort algorithm that uses this generic comparison method to sort data. Finally, you create an actual method that implements the comparison, and then you pass the method's address to the sort routine.

Add a new module to the project by choosing Project ➪ Add Module. Name the module `Sort.vb`, click Add, and then add the following code:

Available for
download on
Wrox.com

```
Module Sort
    Public Delegate Function Compare(ByVal v1 As Object, ByVal v2 As Object) _
        As Boolean
End Module
```

Code snippet from Sort

This line of code does something interesting. It actually defines a method signature as a data type. This new data type is named `Compare`, and it can be used within the code to declare variables or parameters that are accepted by your methods. A variable or parameter declared using this data type could actually hold the address of a method that matches the defined method signature, and you can then invoke that method by using the variable.

Any method with the following signature can be viewed as being of type `Compare`:

```
f(Object, Object)
```

Using the Delegate Data Type

You can write a routine that accepts the delegate data type as a parameter, meaning that anyone calling your routine must pass the address of a method that conforms to this interface. Add the following sort routine to the code module `Sort`:

Available for
download on
Wrox.com

```
Public Sub DoSort(ByVal theData() As Object, ByVal greaterThan As Compare)
    Dim outer As Integer
    Dim inner As Integer
    Dim temp As Object

    For outer = 0 To UBound(theData)
    For inner = outer + 1 To UBound(theData)
      If greaterThan.Invoke(theData(outer), theData(inner)) Then
        temp = theData(outer)
        theData(outer) = theData(inner)
```

```
        theData(inner) = temp
      End If
    Next
  Next
End Sub
```

The `GreaterThan` parameter is a variable that holds the address of a method matching the method signature defined by the `Compare` delegate. The address of any method with a matching signature can be passed as a parameter to your Sort routine.

Note the use of the `Invoke` method, which is how a delegate is called from the code. In addition, note that the routine deals entirely with the generic `System.Object` data type, rather than with any specific type of data. The specific comparison of one object to another is left to the delegate routine that is passed in as a parameter.

Implementing a Delegate Method

Now create the implementation of the delegate routine and call the sort method. On a very basic level, all you need to do is create a method that has a matching method signature, add the following code to your Sort module:

```
Public Function PersonCompare(ByVal person1 As Object, _
  ByVal person2 As Object) As Boolean

End Function
```

The method signature of this method exactly matches what you defined by your delegate earlier:

```
Compare(Object, Object)
```

In both cases, you are defining two parameters of type `Object`.

Of course, there is more to it than simply creating the stub of a method. The method needs to return a value of `True` if its first parameter is greater than the second parameter. Otherwise, it should be written to deal with some specific type of data.

The `Delegate` statement defines a data type based on a specific method interface. To call a routine that expects a parameter of this new data type, it must pass the address of a method that conforms to the defined interface.

To conform to the interface, a method must have the same number of parameters with the same data types defined in your `Delegate` statement. In addition, the method must provide the same return type as defined. The actual name of the method does not matter; it is the number, order, and data type of the parameters and the return value that count.

To find the address of a specific method, you can use the `AddressOf` operator. This operator returns the address of any procedure or method, enabling you to pass that value as a parameter to any routine that expects a delegate as a parameter.

The `Person` class already has a shared method named `CompareAge` that generally does what you want. Unfortunately, it accepts parameters of type `Person`, rather than of type `Object` as required by the `Compare` delegate. You can use method overloading to solve this problem.

Create a second implementation of `CompareAge` that accepts parameters of type `Object` as required by the delegate, rather than of type `Person` as shown in the existing implementation:

Available for
download on
Wrox.com

```
Public Shared Function CompareAge(ByVal person1 As Object, _
    ByVal person2 As Object) As Boolean

  Return CType(person1, Person).Age > CType(person2, Person).Age

End Function
```

This method simply returns `True` if the first `Person` object's age is greater than the second. The routine accepts two `Object` parameters, rather than specific `Person` type parameters, so you have to use the `CType` method to access those objects as type `Person`. You accept the parameters as type `Object` because that is what is defined by the `Delegate` statement. You are matching its method signature:

```
f(Object, Object)
```

Because this method's parameter data types and return value match the delegate, you can use it when calling the `Sort` routine. Place a button on the `Form1` form and write the following code behind that button:

```
Private Sub Button2_Click(ByVal sender As System.Object, _
    ByVal e As System.EventArgs) Handles button2.Click

    Dim myPeople(4) As Person

    myPeople(0) = New Person("Fred", #7/9/1960#)
    myPeople(1) = New Person("Mary", #1/21/1955#)
    myPeople(2) = New Person("Sarah", #2/1/1960#)
    myPeople(3) = New Person("George", #5/13/1970#)
    myPeople(4) = New Person("Andre", #10/1/1965#)

    DoSort(myPeople, AddressOf Person.CompareAge)
End Sub
```

Code snippet from Form1

This code creates an array of `Person` objects and populates them. It then calls the `DoSort` routine from the module, passing the array as the first parameter, and the address of the shared `CompareAge` method as the second parameter. To display the contents of the sorted array in the IDE's output window, you can add the following code:

```
Private Sub button2_Click(ByVal sender As System.Object, _
    ByVal e As System.EventArgs) Handles button2.Click

    Dim myPeople(4) As Person

    myPeople(0) = New Person("Fred", #7/9/1960#)
    myPeople(1) = New Person("Mary", #1/21/1955#)
    myPeople(2) = New Person("Sarah", #2/1/1960#)
    myPeople(3) = New Person("George", #5/13/1970#)
    myPeople(4) = New Person("Andre", #10/1/1965#)

    DoSort(myPeople, AddressOf Person.CompareAge)
    Dim myPerson As Person
    For Each myPerson In myPeople
        System.Diagnostics.Debug.WriteLine(myPerson.Name & " " & myPerson.Age)
    Next
End Sub
```

Code snippet from Form1

When you run the application and click the button, the output window displays a list of the people sorted by age, as shown in Figure 2-16.

What makes this so powerful is that you can change the comparison routine without changing the sort mechanism. Simply add another comparison routine to the `Person` class:

```
Public Shared Function CompareName(ByVal person1 As Object, _
    ByVal person2 As Object) As Boolean

    Return CType(person1, Person).Name > CType(person2, Person).Name

End Function
```

FIGURE 2-16

Code snippet from Sort

Then, change the code behind the button on the form to use that alternate comparison routine:

```
Private Sub Button2_Click(ByVal sender As System.Object, _
    ByVal e As System.EventArgs) Handles Button2.Click

Dim myPeople(4) As Person

myPeople(0) = New Person("Fred", #7/9/1960#)
myPeople(1) = New Person("Mary", #1/21/1955#)
myPeople(2) = New Person("Sarah", #2/1/1960#)
myPeople(3) = New Person("George", #5/13/1970#)
myPeople(4) = New Person("Andre", #10/1/1965#)

DoSort(myPeople, AddressOf Person.CompareName)

Dim myPerson As Person

For Each myPerson In myPeople
    System.Diagnostics.Debug.WriteLine(myPerson.Name & " " & myPerson.Age)
Next
End Sub
```

Code snippet from Form1

When you run this updated code, you will find that the array contains a set of data sorted by name, rather than age, as shown in Figure 2-17.

Simply by creating a new compare routine and passing it as a parameter, you can entirely change the way that the data is sorted. Better still, this sort routine can operate on any type of object, as long as you provide an appropriate delegate method that knows how to compare that type of object.

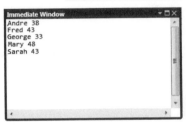

FIGURE 2-17

Classes versus Components

Visual Basic has another concept that is very similar to a class: the *component*. In fact, you can pretty much use a component and a class interchangeably, though there are some differences.

A component is little more than a regular class, but one that supports a graphical designer within the Visual Studio IDE. This means you can use drag-and-drop to provide the code in the component with access to items from the Server Explorer or the Toolbox.

To add a component to a project, select Project ➪ Add Component, give the component a name such as Component1, and click Add in the Add New Item dialog.

When you add a class to the project, you are presented with the code window. When you add a component, you are presented with a graphical designer surface, much like what you would see when adding a Web Form to the project.

If you switch to the Code view (by right-clicking in the Design view and choosing View Code), you will see the code that is created automatically, just as it is with a Windows Form, Web Form, or regular class:

```
Public Class Component1

End Class
```

This is not a lot more code than you see with a regular class, though there are differences behind the scenes. A component uses the same partial class technology as Windows Forms or Web Forms. This means that the code here is only part of the total code in the class. The rest of the code is hidden behind the designer's surface and is automatically created and managed by Visual Studio.

In the designer code (in this case, found in the Solution Explorer in `Component1.Designer.vb`) is an `Inherits` statement that makes every component inherit from `System.ComponentModel.Component`. Chapter 3 discusses the concept of inheritance, but note here that this `Inherits` line is what brings in all the support for the graphical designer in Visual Studio.

The designer also manages any controls or components that are dropped on it. Those controls or components are automatically made available to your code. For instance, if you drag and drop a `Timer` control from the Windows Forms tab of the Toolbox onto the component, it will be displayed in the designer.

From here, you can set the component properties using the standard Properties window in the IDE, just as you would for a control on a form. Using the Properties window, set the `Name` property to `theTimer`. You now automatically have access to a `Timer` object named `theTimer`, simply by dragging and dropping and setting some properties.

This means that you can write code within the component, just as you might in a class, to use this object:

Available for download on Wrox.com

```vb
Public Sub Start()
    theTimer.Enabled = True
End Sub

Public Sub StopIt()
    theTimer.Enabled = False
End Sub

Private Sub theTimer_Tick(ByVal sender As System.Object, _
    ByVal e As System.EventArgs) Handles theTimer.Tick

    ' do work
End Sub
```

Code snippet from ObjectIntro\Component.vb

For the most part, you can use a component interchangeably with a basic class, but using a component also provides some of the designer benefits of working with Windows Forms or Web Forms.

Lambdas

The introduction of VB.NET 9.0 introduced a new feature, lambda expressions, which combine several concepts from this chapter. Using a lambda, you can create simple anonymous methods and their delegate in one line. The main driving force of lambdas is LINQ, which is discussed in much greater detail in Chapter 10.

The following example demonstrates how you might write a function to add 10 to an integer:

```vb
Function   AddToInteger(ByVal i as integer) as Integer
     Return i + 10
End Function
```

Now let's make this into a simple lambda expression:

```vb
Dim myLambda = Function (i as Integer) i += 10
```

From this one line of code you have created a delegate that can be called easily throughout the scope of the delegate. To call this delegate, simply use the following:

```vb
myLambda(10)
```

By combining what you know about delegates, you can simplify declaration by using a lambda. One item to note is that prior to Visual Basic 2010, Visual Basic was limited to single line lambda statements that returned a value. It wasn't possible to create a lambda that defined a `Sub` or have a lambda span more than a single line. With Visual Studio 2010, it is now possible for Visual Basic developers to write this code.

SUMMARY

Visual Basic offers a fully object-oriented language with all the capabilities you would expect. This chapter described the basic concepts behind classes and objects, as well as the separation of interface from implementation and data.

The chapter introduced the `System.Object` class and explained how this class is the base class for all classes in .NET. You were then introduced to concepts such as `Value` and `Reference` types as well as the implementation for primitive types. The chapter looked at most of the core primitive types available in Visual Basic and how to convert between types.

You have learned how to use the `Class` keyword to create classes, and how those classes can be instantiated into specific objects, each one an instance of the class. These objects have methods and properties that can be invoked by the client code, and can act on data within the object stored in member or instance variables.

You also explored some more advanced concepts, including method overloading, shared or static variables and methods, and the use of delegates and lambda expressions.

The next chapter continues the discussion of object syntax as you explore the concept of inheritance and all the syntax that enables inheritance within Visual Basic. You will also walk through the creation, implementation, and use of multiple interfaces — a powerful concept that enables objects to be used in different ways, depending on the interface chosen by the client application.

Also covered in the next chapter is a discussion of objects and object-oriented programming, applying all of this syntax. It explains the key object-oriented concepts of abstraction, encapsulation, polymorphism, and inheritance, and shows how they work together to provide a powerful way to design and implement applications.

Chapter 4 explores the .NET common language runtime (CLR). Because the .NET platform and runtime are object-oriented at their very core, this chapter examines how objects interact with the runtime environment and covers topics such as using and disposing of objects and memory management.

3

Custom Objects

WHAT YOU WILL LEARN IN THIS CHAPTER

➤ Inheritance

➤ The MyBase keyword

➤ Event Handling in Sub Classes

➤ Creating Abstract Base Class

➤ Interfaces

➤ Abstraction

➤ Encapsulation

➤ Polymorphism

Visual Basic is a fully object-oriented language. Chapter 2 covered the basics of creating classes and objects, including the creation of methods, properties, events, operators, and instance variables. You have seen the basic building blocks for abstraction, encapsulation, and polymorphism — concepts discussed in more detail at the end of this chapter. The final major techniques you need to understand are inheritance and the use of multiple interfaces.

Inheritance is the idea that you can create a class that reuses methods, properties, events, and variables from another class. You can create a class with some basic functionality, and then use that class as a base from which to create other, more detailed, classes. All these derived classes will have the same common functionality as that base class, along with new, enhanced, or even completely changed functionality.

This chapter covers the syntax that supports inheritance within Visual Basic. This includes creating the base classes from which other classes can be derived, as well as creating those derived classes.

Visual Basic also supports a related concept: multiple interfaces. As shown in Chapter 2, all objects have a native or default interface, which is defined by the public methods, properties, and events declared in the class. In the .NET environment, an object can have other interfaces in addition to this native interface — in other words, .NET objects can have multiple interfaces.

These secondary interfaces define alternative ways in which your object can be accessed by providing clearly defined sets of methods, properties, and events. Like the native interface, these secondary interfaces define how the client code can interact with your object, essentially providing a "contract" that enables the client to know exactly what methods, properties, and events the object will provide.

When you write code to interact with an object, you can choose which of the interfaces you want to use; basically, you are choosing how you want to view or interact with that object.

This chapter uses relatively basic code examples so that you can focus on the technical and syntactic issues surrounding inheritance and multiple interfaces. The last part of this chapter revisits these concepts using a more sophisticated set of code as you continue to explore object-oriented programming and how to apply inheritance and multiple interfaces in a practical manner.

Of course, just knowing the syntax and learning the tools is not enough to be successful. Successfully applying Visual Basic's object-oriented capabilities requires an understanding of object-oriented programming. This chapter also applies Visual Basic's object-oriented syntax, showing how it enables you to build object-oriented applications. It also describes in detail the four major object-oriented concepts: abstraction, encapsulation, polymorphism, and inheritance. By the end of this chapter, you will understand how to apply these concepts in your design and development efforts to create effective object-oriented applications.

INHERITANCE

Inheritance is the concept that a new class can be based on an existing class, inheriting the interface and functionality from the original class. In Chapter 2, you explored the relationship between a class and an object, and saw that the class is essentially a template from which objects can be created.

While this is very powerful, it does not provide all the capabilities you might like. In particular, in many cases a class only partially describes what you need for your object. You may have a class called Person, for instance, which has all the properties and methods that apply to all types of people, such as first name, last name, and birth date. While useful, this class probably does not have everything you need to describe a specific type of person, such as an employee or a customer. An employee would have a hire date and a salary, which are not included in Person, while a customer would have a credit rating, something neither the Person nor the Employee classes would need.

Without inheritance, you would probably end up replicating the code from the Person class in both the Employee and Customer classes so that they would have that same functionality as well as the ability to add new functionality of their own.

Inheritance makes it very easy to create classes for Employee, Customer, and so forth. You do not have to recreate that code for an employee to be a person; it automatically inherits any properties, methods, and events from the original Person class.

You can think of it this way: When you create an Employee class, which inherits from a Person class, you are effectively merging these two classes. If you then create an object based on the Employee class, then it has not only the interface (properties, methods, and events) and implementation from the Employee class, but also those from the Person class.

While an Employee object represents the merger between the Employee and Person classes, understand that the variables and code contained in each of those classes remain independent. Two perspectives are involved.

From the outside, the client code that interacts with the Employee object sees a single, unified object that represents the inheritance of the Employee and Person classes.

From the inside, the code in the Employee class and the code in the Person class are not totally intermixed. Variables and methods that are Private are only available within the class they were written. Variables and methods that are Public in one class can be called from the other class. Variables and methods that are declared as Friend are only available between classes if both classes are in the same Visual Basic project. As discussed later in the chapter, there is also a Protected scope that is designed to work with inheritance, but, again, this provides a controlled way for one class to interact with the variables and methods in the other class.

Visual Studio 2010 includes a Class Designer tool that enables you to easily create diagrams of your classes and their relationships. The Class Designer diagrams are a derivative of a standard notation called the Unified Modeling Language (UML) that is typically used to diagram the relationships between classes, objects, and other object-oriented concepts. The Class Designer diagrams more accurately and completely model .NET classes, so that is the notation used in this chapter. The relationship between the `Person`, `Employee`, and `Customer` classes is illustrated in Figure 3-1.

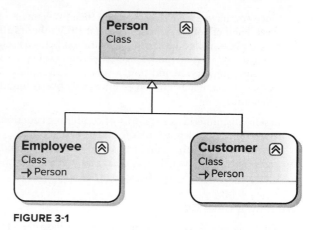

FIGURE 3-1

Each box in this diagram represents a class; in this case, you have `Person`, `Employee`, and `Customer` classes. The line from `Employee` back up to `Person`, terminating in a triangle, indicates that `Employee` is derived from, or inherits from, `Person`. The same is true for the `Customer` class.

Later in this chapter, you will learn when and how inheritance should be used in software design. The beginning part of this chapter covers the syntax and programming concepts necessary to implement inheritance. First, you will create a base `Person` class. Then, you will use that class to create both `Employee` and `Customer` classes that inherit behavior from `Person`.

Before getting into the implementation, however, it's necessary to understand some basic terms associated with inheritance — and there are a lot of terms, partly because there are often several ways to say the same thing. The various terms are all used quite frequently and interchangeably.

 Though we attempt to use consistent terminology in this book, be aware that in other books and articles, and online, all these terms are used in various permutations.

Inheritance, for instance, is also sometimes referred to as *generalization* because the class from which you are inheriting your behavior is virtually always a more general form of your new class. A person is more general than an employee, for instance.

The inheritance relationship is also referred to as an *is-a* relationship. When you create a `Customer` class that inherits from a `Person` class, that customer is a person. The employee is a person as well. Thus, you have the is-a relationship. As shown later in the chapter, multiple interfaces can be used to implement something similar to the is-a relationship, the act-as relationship.

When you create a class using inheritance, it inherits behaviors and data from an existing class. That existing class is called the *base class*. It is also often referred to as a *superclass* or a *parent class*.

The class you create using inheritance is based on the parent class. It is called a *subclass*. Sometimes it is also called a *child class* or a *derived class*. In fact, the process of inheriting from a base class by a subclass is referred to as *deriving*. You are deriving a new class from the base class. This process is also called *subclassing*.

Implementing Inheritance

When you set out to implement a class using inheritance, you must first start with an existing class from which you will derive your new subclass. This existing class, or base class, may be part of the .NET system class library framework, it may be part of some other application or .NET assembly, or you may create it as part of your existing application.

Once you have a base class, you can then implement one or more subclasses based on that base class. Each of your subclasses automatically inherits all of the methods, properties, and events of that base class — including the implementation behind each method, property, and event. Your subclass can also add new methods, properties, and events of its own, extending the original interface with new functionality. In addition, a subclass can replace the methods and properties of the base class with its own new implementation — effectively overriding the original behavior and replacing it with new behaviors.

Essentially, inheritance is a way of combining functionality from an existing class into your new subclass. Inheritance also defines rules for how these methods, properties, and events can be merged, including control over how they can be changed or replaced, and how the subclass can add new methods, properties, and events of its own. This is what you will learn in the following sections — what these rules are and what syntax you use in Visual Basic to make it all work.

Creating a Base Class

Virtually any class you create can act as a base class from which other classes can be derived. In fact, unless you specifically indicate in the code that your class cannot be a base class, you can derive from it (you will come back to this later).

Create a new Windows Forms Application project in Visual Basic by selecting File ⇨ New Project and selecting Windows Forms Application. Then add a class to the project using the Project ⇨ Add Class menu option and name it `Person.vb`. Begin with the following code:

```
Public Class Person

End Class
```

At this point, you technically have a base class, as it is possible to inherit from this class even though it doesn't do or contain anything. You can now add methods, properties, and events to this class as you normally would. All of those interface elements would be inherited by any class you might create based on `Person`. For instance, add the following code:

```
Public Class Person


    Public Property Name() As String
    Public Property BirthDate() As Date
End Class
```

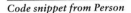
Code snippet from Person

This provides a simple method that can be used to illustrate how basic inheritance works. This class can be represented by the class diagram in Visual Studio, as shown in Figure 3-2.

In this representation of the class as it is presented from Visual Studio, the overall box represents the `Person` class. In the top section of this box is the name of the class and a specification that it is a class. The section below it contains a list of the instance variables, or fields, of the class, with their scope marked as Private (note the lock icon). The bottom section lists the properties exposed by the class, both marked as Public. If the class had methods or events, then they would be displayed in their own sections in the diagram.

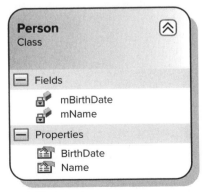

FIGURE 3-2

Creating a Subclass

To implement inheritance, you need to add a new class to your project. Use the Project ⇨ Add Class menu option and add a new class named `Employee.vb`. Begin with the following code:

```
Public Class Employee

    Public Property HireDate() As Date

    Public Property Salary() As Double
End Class
```

Code snippet from Person

This is a regular standalone class with no explicit inheritance. It can be represented by the class diagram shown in Figure 3-3.

Again, you can see the class name, its list of instance variables, and the properties it includes as part of its interface. It turns out that, behind the scenes, this class inherits some capabilities from `System .Object`. In fact, every class in the entire .NET platform ultimately inherits from `System.Object` either implicitly or explicitly. This is why all .NET objects have a basic set of common functionality, including, most notably, the `GetType` method, which is discussed in detail later in the chapter.

While having an `Employee` object with a hire date and salary is useful, it should also have `Name` and `BirthDate` properties, just as you implemented in the `Person` class. Without inheritance, you would probably just copy and paste the code from `Person` directly into the new `Employee` class, but with inheritance, you can directly reuse the code from the `Person` class. Let's make the new class inherit from `Person`.

FIGURE 3-3

The Inherits Keyword

To make `Employee` a subclass of `Person`, add a single line of code:

```
Public Class Employee
    Inherits Person
```

The `Inherits` keyword indicates that a class should derive from an existing class, inheriting the interface and behavior from that class. You can inherit from almost any class in your project, from the .NET system class library, or from other assemblies. It is also possible to prevent inheritance, which is covered later in the chapter. When using the `Inherits` keyword to inherit from classes outside the current project, you need to either specify the namespace that contains that class or place an `Imports` statement at the top of the class to import that namespace for your use.

The diagram in Figure 3-4 illustrates the fact that the `Employee` class is now a subclass of `Person`.

The line running from `Employee` back up to `Person` ends in an open triangle, which is the symbol for inheritance when using the Class Designer in Visual Studio. It is this line that indicates that the `Employee` class includes all the functionality, as well as the interface, of `Person`.

This means that an object created based on the `Employee` class has not only the methods `HireDate` and `Salary`, but also `Name` and `BirthDate`. To test this, bring up the designer for `Form1`

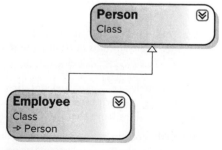

FIGURE 3-4

(which is automatically part of your project because you created a Windows Forms Application project) and add the following `TextBox` controls, along with a button, to the form:

CONTROL TYPE	NAME	TEXT PROPERTY VALUE
TextBox	txtName	<blank>
TextBox	txtBirthDate	<blank>
TextBox	txtHireDate	<blank>
TextBox	txtSalary	<blank>
button	btnOK	OK

You can also add some labels to make the form more readable. The Form Designer should now look something like Figure 3-5.

FIGURE 3-5

Double-click the button to bring up the code window and enter the following code:

```
Private Sub btnOK_Click(ByVal sender As System.Object, _
                   ByVal e As System.EventArgs) Handles btnOK.Click
    Dim emp As New Employee()

    With emp
      .Name = "Fred"
      .BirthDate = #1/1/1960#
      .HireDate = #1/1/1980#
      .Salary = 30000

      txtName.Text = .Name
      txtBirthDate.Text = Format(.BirthDate, "Short date")
      txtHireDate.Text = Format(.HireDate, "Short date")
      txtSalary.Text = Format(.Salary, "$0.00")
    End With
```

Code snippet from Person

 The best Visual Basic practice is to use the With *keyword, but be aware that this might cause issues with portability and converting code to other languages.*

Even though `Employee` does not directly implement the `Name` or `BirthDate` methods, they are available for use through inheritance. When you run this application and click the button, your controls are populated with the values from the `Employee` object.

When the code in `Form1` invokes the `Name` property on the `Employee` object, the code from the `Person` class is executed, as the `Employee` class has no such method built in. However, when the `HireDate` property is invoked on the `Employee` object, the code from the `Employee` class is executed, as it does have that method as part of its code.

From the form's perspective, it doesn't matter whether a method is implemented in the `Employee` class or the `Person` class; they are all simply methods of the `Employee` object. In addition, because the code in these classes is merged to create the `Employee` object, there is no performance difference between calling a method implemented by the `Employee` class or calling a method implemented by the `Person` class.

Overloading Methods

Although your `Employee` class automatically gains the `Name` and `BirthDate` methods through inheritance, it also has methods of its own — `HireDate` and `Salary`. This shows how you have extended the base `Person` interface by adding methods and properties to the `Employee` subclass.

You can add new properties, methods, and events to the `Employee` class, and they will be part of any object created based on `Employee`. This has no impact on the `Person` class whatsoever, only on the `Employee` class and `Employee` objects.

You can even extend the functionality of the base class by adding methods to the subclass that have the same name as methods or properties in the base class, as long as those methods or properties have different parameter lists. You are effectively overloading the existing methods from the base class. It is essentially the same thing as overloading regular methods, as discussed in Chapter 2.

For example, your `Person` class is currently providing your implementation for the `Name` property. Employees may have other names you also want to store, perhaps an informal name and a formal name in addition to their regular name. One way to accommodate this requirement is to change the `Person` class itself to include an overloaded `Name` property that supports this new functionality. However, you are really only trying to enhance the `Employee` class, not the more general `Person` class, so what you want is a way to add an overloaded method to the `Employee` class itself, even though you are overloading a method from its base class.

You can overload a method from a base class by using the `Overloads` keyword. The concept is the same as described in Chapter 2, but in this case an extra keyword is involved. To overload the `Name` property, for instance, you can add a new property to the `Employee` class. First, though, define an enumerated type using the `Enum` keyword. This `Enum` will list the different types of name you want to store. Add this `Enum` to the `Employee.vb` file, before the declaration of the class itself:

```
Public Enum NameTypes
  Informal = 1
  Formal = 2
End Enum


Public Class Employee
```

You can then add an overloaded `Name` property to the `Employee` class itself:

Available for download on Wrox.com

```
Public Class Employee
  Inherits Person

  Public Property HireDate As Date
  Public Property Salary As Double
  Private mNames As New Generic.Dictionary(Of NameTypes, String)
  Public Overloads Property Name(ByVal type As NameTypes) As String
    Get
      Return mNames(type)
    End Get
    Set(ByVal value As String)
      If mNames.ContainsKey(type) Then
        mNames.Item(type) = value
      Else
        mNames.Add(type, value)
      End If
    End Set
  End Property
```

Code snippet from Person

This Name property is actually a property array, which enables you to store multiple values via the same property. In this case, you are storing the values in a Generic.Dictionary(Of K, V) object, which is indexed by using the Enum value you just defined. Chapter 6 discusses generics in detail. For now, you can view this generic Dictionary just like any collection object that stores key/value data.

If you omit the Overloads *keyword here, your new implementation of the* Name *method will shadow the original implementation. Shadowing is very different from overloading, and is covered later in the chapter.*

Though this method has the same name as the method in the base class, the fact that it accepts a different parameter list enables you to use overloading to implement it here. The original Name property, as implemented in the Person class, remains intact and valid, but now you have added a new variation with this second Name property, as shown in Figure 3-6.

The diagram clearly indicates that the Name method in the Person class and the Name method in the Employee class both exist. If you hover over each Name property, you will see a tooltip showing the method signatures, making it clear that each one has a different signature.

You can now change Form1 to make use of this new version of the Name property. First, add a couple of new TextBox controls and associated labels. The TextBox controls should be named txtFormal and txtInformal, and the form should now look like the one shown in Figure 3-7. Double-click the form's button to bring up the code window and overwrite the code to work with the overloaded version of the Name property:

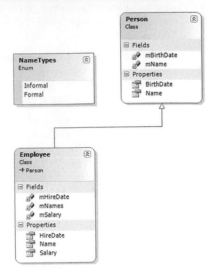

FIGURE 3-6

Available for
download on
Wrox.com

```
Private Sub btnOK_Click(ByVal sender As System.Object, _
    ByVal e As System.EventArgs) Handles btnOK.Click

Dim emp As New Employee()

With emp
  .Name = "Fred"
  .Name(NameTypes.Formal) = "Mr. Frederick R. Jones, Sr."
  .Name(NameTypes.Informal) = "Freddy"
  .BirthDate = #1/1/1960#
  .HireDate = #1/1/1980#
  .Salary = 30000

  txtName.Text = .Name
  txtFormal.Text = .Name(NameTypes.Formal)
  txtInformal.Text = .Name(NameTypes.Informal)
  txtBirthDate.Text = Format(.BirthDate, "Short date")
  txtHireDate.Text = Format(.HireDate, "Short date")
  txtSalary.Text = Format(.Salary, "$0.00")
End With
End Sub
```

Code snippet from Form1

The code still interacts with the original `Name` property as implemented in the `Person` class, but you are now also invoking the overloaded version of the property implemented in the `Employee` class.

FIGURE 3-7

Overriding Methods

So far, you have seen how to implement a base class and then use it to create a subclass. You also extended the interface by adding methods, and you explored how to use overloading to add methods that have the same name as methods in the base class but with different parameters.

However, sometimes you may want to not only extend the original functionality, but also actually change or entirely replace the functionality of the base class. Instead of leaving the existing functionality and just adding new methods or overloaded versions of those methods, you might want to entirely override the existing functionality with your own.

You can do exactly that. If the base class allows it, then you can substitute your own implementation of a base class method — meaning your new implementation will be used instead of the original.

The Overridable Keyword

By default, you can't override the behavior of methods on a base class. The base class must be coded specifically to allow this to occur, by using the `Overridable` keyword. This is important, as you may not always want to allow a subclass to entirely change the behavior of the methods in your base class. However, if you do wish to allow the author of a subclass to replace your implementation, you can do so by adding the `Overridable` keyword to your method declaration.

Returning to the employee example, you may not like the implementation of the `BirthDate` method as it stands in the `Person` class. Suppose, for instance, that you can't employ anyone younger than 16 years of age, so any birth-date value more recent than 16 years ago is invalid for an employee.

To implement this business rule, you need to change the way the `BirthDate` property is implemented. While you could make this change directly in the `Person` class, that would not be ideal. It is perfectly acceptable to have a person under age 16, just not an employee.

Open the code window for the `Person` class and change the `BirthDate` property to include the `Overridable` keyword:

Available for download on Wrox.com

```
Public Overridable Property BirthDate() As Date
  Get
    Return mBirthDate
  End Get
  Set(ByVal value As Date)
    mBirthDate = value
  End Set
End Property
```

Code snippet from Person

This change allows any class that inherits from `Person` to entirely replace the implementation of the `BirthDate` property with a new implementation.

By adding the `Overridable` keyword to your method declaration, you are indicating that you allow any subclass to override the behavior provided by this method. This means you are permitting a subclass to totally ignore your prior implementation, or to extend your implementation by doing other work before or after your implementation is run.

If the subclass does not override this method, the method works just like a regular method and is automatically included as part of the subclass's interface. Putting the `Overridable` keyword on a method simply allows a subclass to override the method if you choose to let it do so.

The Overrides Keyword

In a subclass, you override a method by implementing a method with the same name and parameter list as the base class, and then you use the `Overrides` keyword to indicate that you are overriding that method.

This is different from overloading, because when you overload a method you are adding a new method with the same name but a different parameter list. When you override a method, you are actually replacing the original method with a new implementation.

Without the `Overrides` keyword, you will receive a compilation error when you implement a method with the same name as one from the base class. Open the code window for the `Employee` class and add a new `BirthDate` property:

```
Public Class Employee
   Inherits Person

   Public Property HireDate As Date
   Public Property Salary As Double
   Public Property BirthDate As Date

   Private mNames As New Generic.Dictionary(Of NameTypes, String)

   Public Overrides Property BirthDate() As Date
     Get
       Return mBirthDate
     End Get
     Set(ByVal value As Date)
       If DateDiff(DateInterval.Year, Value, Now) >= 16 Then
         mBirthDate = value
       Else
         Throw New ArgumentException( _
           "An employee must be at least 16 years old.")
       End If
     End Set
   End Property
```

Code snippet from Person

Because you are implementing your own version of the property, you have to declare a variable to store that value within the `Employee` class. This is not ideal, and there are a couple of ways around it, including the `MyBase` keyword and the `Protected` scope.

Notice also that you have enhanced the functionality in the `Set` block, so it now raises an error if the new birth-date value would cause the employee to be less than 16 years of age. With this code, you have now entirely replaced the original `BirthDate` implementation with a new one that enforces your business rule (see Figure 3-8).

The diagram now includes a `BirthDate` method in the `Employee` class. While perhaps not entirely intuitive, this is how the class diagram indicates that you have overridden the method. If you hover the mouse over the `BirthDate` property in the `Employee` class, the tooltip will show the method signature, including the `Overrides` keyword.

If you run your application and click the button on the form, then everything should work as it did before, because the birth

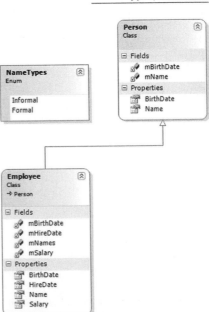

FIGURE 3-8

date you are supplying conforms to your new business rule. Now change the code in your form to use an invalid birth date:

```
With emp
  .Name = "Fred"
  .Name(NameTypes.Formal) = "Mr. Frederick R. Jones, Sr."
  .Name(NameTypes.Informal) = "Freddy"
  .BirthDate = #1/1/2000#
```

When you run the application (from within Visual Studio) and click the button, you receive an error indicating that the birth date is invalid. This proves that you are now using the implementation of the `BirthDate` method from the `Employee` class, rather than the one from the `Person` class. Change the date value in the form back to a valid value so that your application runs properly.

The MyBase Keyword

You have just seen how you can entirely replace the functionality of a method in the base class by overriding it in your subclass. However, this can be somewhat extreme; sometimes it's preferable to override methods so that you extend the base functionality, rather than replace it.

To do this, you need to override the method using the `Overrides` keyword as you just did, but within your new implementation you can still invoke the original implementation of the method. This enables you to add your own code before or after the original implementation is invoked — meaning you can extend the behavior while still leveraging the code in the base class.

To invoke methods directly from the base class, you can use the `MyBase` keyword. This keyword is available within any class, and it exposes all the methods of the base class for your use.

> *Even a base class such as* `Person` *is an implicit subclass of* `System.Object`, *so it can use* `MyBase` *to interact with its base class as well.*

This means that within the `BirthDate` implementation in `Employee`, you can invoke the `BirthDate` implementation in the base `Person` class. This is ideal, as it means that you can leverage any existing functionality provided by `Person` while still enforcing your Employee-specific business rules.

To take advantage of this, you can enhance the code in the Employee implementation of `BirthDate`. First, remove the declaration of `mBirthDate` from the `Employee` class. You won't need this variable any longer because the `Person` implementation will keep track of the value on your behalf. Then, change the `BirthDate` implementation in the `Employee` class as follows:

Available for download on Wrox.com

```
Public Overrides Property BirthDate() As Date
  Get
    Return MyBase.BirthDate
  End Get

  Set(ByVal value As Date)
    If DateDiff(DateInterval.Year, Value, Now) >= 16 Then
      MyBase.BirthDate = value
    Else
      Throw New ArgumentException( _
        "An employee must be at least 16 years old.")
    End If
  End Set
End Property
```

Code snippet from Person

Run your application and you will see that it works just fine and returns the error, even though the `Employee` class no longer contains any code to actually keep track of the birth-date value. You have effectively merged the `BirthDate` implementation from `Person` right into your enhanced implementation in `Employee`, creating a hybrid version of the property.

The `MyBase` keyword is covered in more detail later in the chapter. Here, you can see how it enables you to enhance or extend the functionality of the base class by adding your own code in the subclass but still invoking the base-class method when appropriate.

Virtual Methods

The `BirthDate` method is an example of a virtual method. *Virtual methods* are methods in a base class that can be overridden and replaced by subclasses.

Virtual methods are more complex to understand than regular nonvirtual methods. With a nonvirtual method, only one implementation matches any given method signature, so there's no ambiguity about which specific method implementation will be invoked. With virtual methods, however, there may be several implementations of the same method, with the same method signature, so you need to understand the rules that govern which specific implementation of that method will be called.

When working with virtual methods, keep in mind that the data type of the object is used to determine the implementation of the method to call, rather than the type of the variable that refers to the object.

Looking at the code in your form, you can see that you are declaring an object variable of type `Employee`, and then creating an `Employee` object that you can reference via that object:

```
Dim emp As New Employee()
```

It is not surprising, then, that you are able to invoke any of the methods that are implemented as part of the `Employee` class, and through inheritance, any of the methods implemented as part of the `Person` class:

```
With emp
  .Name = "Fred"
  .Name(NameTypes.Formal) = "Mr. Frederick R. Jones, Sr."
  .Name(NameTypes.Informal) = "Freddy"
  .BirthDate = #1/1/1960#
  .HireDate = #1/1/1980#
  .Salary = 30000
```

When you call the `BirthDate` property, you know that you are invoking the implementation contained in the `Employee` class, which makes sense because you know that you are using a variable of type `Employee` to refer to an object of type `Employee`.

Because your methods are virtual methods, you can experiment with some much more interesting scenarios. For instance, suppose that you change the code in your form to interact directly with an object of type `Person` instead of one of type `Employee`:

```
Private Sub btnOK_Click(ByVal sender As System.Object, _
    ByVal e As System.EventArgs) Handles btnOK.Click

  Dim person As New Person()

  With person
    .Name = "Fred"
    .BirthDate = #1/1/1960#

    txtName.Text = .Name
    txtBirthDate.Text = Format(.BirthDate, "Short date")
  End With

End Sub
```

Code snippet from Form1

You can no longer call the methods implemented by the `Employee` class, because they do not exist as part of a `Person` object, but only as part of an `Employee` object. However, you can see that both the `Name` and `BirthDate` properties continue to function as you would expect. When you run the application now, it will work just fine. You can even change the birth-date value to something that would be invalid for `Employee`:

```
.BirthDate = #1/1/2000#
```

The application will now accept it and work just fine, because the `BirthDate` method you are invoking is the original version from the `Person` class.

These are the two simple scenarios, when you have a variable and object of type `Employee` or a variable and object of type `Person`. However, because `Employee` is derived from `Person`, you can do something a bit more interesting. You can use a variable of type `Person` to hold a reference to an `Employee` object. For example, you can change the code in `Form1` as follows:

Available for download on Wrox.com

```
Private Sub btnOK_Click(ByVal sender As System.Object, _
    ByVal e As System.EventArgs) Handles btnOK.Click

    Dim person As Person
    person = New Employee()
    With person
        .Name = "Fred"
        .BirthDate = #1/1/1960#

        txtName.Text = .Name
        txtBirthDate.Text = Format(.BirthDate, "Short date")
    End With
End Sub
```

Code snippet from Form1

What you are doing now is declaring your variable to be of type `Person`, but the object itself is an instance of the `Employee` class. You have done something a bit complex here, as the data type of the variable is not the same as the data type of the object itself. Remember that a variable of a base-class type can always hold a reference to an object of any subclass.

This is why a variable of type `System.Object` *can hold a reference to literally anything in the .NET Framework, because all classes are ultimately derived from* `System.Object`.

This technique is very useful when creating generic routines. It makes use of an object-oriented concept called *polymorphism*, which is discussed more thoroughly later in this chapter. This technique enables you to create a more general routine that populates your form for any object of type `Person`. Add the following code to the form (but not in the button `Click` event):

Available for download on Wrox.com

```
Private Sub DisplayPerson(ByVal thePerson As Person)
    With thePerson
        txtName.Text = .Name
        txtBirthDate.Text = Format(.BirthDate, "Short date")
    End With
End Sub
```

Code snippet from Form1

Now you can change the code behind the button to make use of this generic routine:

Available for download on Wrox.com

```
Private Sub btnOK_Click(ByVal sender As System.Object, _
    ByVal e As System.EventArgs) Handles btnOK.Click

    Dim person As Person
```

```
    person = New Employee()

    With person
      .Name = "Fred"
      .BirthDate = #1/1/2000#
    End With

    DisplayPerson(person)
  End Sub
```

Code snippet from Form1

The benefit here is that you can pass a `Person` object or an `Employee` object to `DisplayPerson` and the routine will work the same either way.

When you run the application now, things get interesting. You will get an error when you attempt to set the `BirthDate` property because it breaks your 16-year-old business rule, which is implemented in the `Employee` class. How can this be when your person variable is of type `Person`?

This clearly demonstrates the concept of a virtual method. It is the data type of the object, in this case `Employee`, that is important. The data type of the variable is not the deciding factor when choosing which implementation of an overridden method is invoked.

The following table shows which method is actually invoked based on the variable and object data types when working with virtual methods:

VARIABLE TYPE	OBJECT TYPE	METHOD INVOKED
Base	Base	Base
Base	Subclass	Subclass
Subclass	Subclass	Subclass

Virtual methods are very powerful and useful when you implement polymorphism using inheritance. A base-class data type can hold a reference to any subclass object, but it is the type of that specific object which determines the implementation of the method. Therefore, you can write generic routines that operate on many types of objects as long as they derive from the same base class. You will learn how to make use of polymorphism and virtual methods in more detail later in this chapter.

Overriding Overloaded Methods

Earlier, you wrote code in your `Employee` class to overload the `Name` method in the base `Person` class. This enabled you to keep the original `Name` functionality, but also extend it by adding another `Name` method that accepts a different parameter list.

You have also overridden the `BirthDate` method. The implementation in the `Employee` class replaced the implementation in the `Person` class. Overriding is a related but different concept from overloading. It is also possible to both overload and override a method at the same time.

In the earlier overloading example, you added a new `Name` property to the `Employee` class, while retaining the functionality present in the base `Person` class. You may decide that you not only want to have your second overloaded implementation of the `Name` method in the `Employee` class, but also want to replace the existing one by overriding the existing method provided by the `Person` class.

In particular, you may want to do this so that you can store the `Name` value in the `Hashtable` object along with your Formal and Informal names. Before you can override the `Name` method, you need to add the `Overridable` keyword to the base implementation in the `Person` class:

```
Public Overridable Property Name() As String
  Get
    Return mName
  End Get
```

```
      Set(ByVal value As String)
        mName = value
      End Set
   End Property
```

With that done, the `Name` method can now be overridden by any derived class. In the `Employee` class, you can now override the `Name` method, replacing the functionality provided by the `Person` class. First, add a `Normal` option to the `Enum` that controls the types of `Name` value you can store:

```
   Public Enum NameTypes
      Informal = 1
      Formal = 2
      Normal = 3
   End Enum
```

Now you can add code to the `Employee` class to implement a new `Name` property. This is in addition to the existing `Name` property already implemented in the `Employee` class:

Available for
download on
Wrox.com

```
   Public Overloads Overrides Property Name() As String
      Get
         Return mNames(NameTypes.Normal)
      End Get
      Set(ByVal value As String)
         mNames(NameTypes.Normal) = value
      End Set
   End Property
```

Note that you are using both the `Overrides` keyword (to indicate that you are overriding the `Name` method from the base class) and the `Overloads` keyword (to indicate that you are overloading this method in the subclass).

This new `Name` property merely delegates the call to the existing version of the `Name` property that handles the parameter-based names. To complete the linkage between this implementation of the `Name` property and the parameter-based version, you need to make one more change to that original overloaded version:

Available for
download on
Wrox.com

```
   Public Overloads Property Name(ByVal type As NameTypes) As String
      Get
         Return mNames(Type)
      End Get
      Set(ByVal value As String)
         If mNames.ContainsKey(type) Then
            mNames.Item(type) = value
         Else
            mNames.Add(type, value)
         End If

         If type = NameTypes.Normal Then
            MyBase.Name = value
         End If
      End Set
   End Property
```

This way, if the client code sets the `Name` property by providing the `Normal` index, you are still updating the name in the base class as well as in the `Dictionary` object maintained by the `Employee` class.

Shadowing

Overloading enables you to add new versions of existing methods as long as their parameter lists are different. *Overriding* enables your subclass to entirely replace the implementation of a base-class method with a new method that has the same method signature. As you just saw, you can even combine these concepts not only to replace the implementation of a method from the base class, but also to simultaneously overload that method with other implementations that have different method signatures.

However, anytime you override a method using the Overrides keyword, you are subject to the rules governing virtual methods — meaning that the base class must give you permission to override the method. If the base class does not use the Overridable keyword, then you can't override the method. Sometimes, however, you may need to override a method that is not marked as Overridable, and shadowing enables you to do just that.

The Shadows keyword can also be used to entirely change the nature of a method or other interface element from the base class, although that is something which should be done with great care, as it can seriously reduce the maintainability of your code. Normally, when you create an Employee object, you expect that it can act not only as an Employee, but also as a Person because Employee is a subclass of Person. However, with the Shadows keyword, you can radically alter the behavior of an Employee class so that it does not act like a Person. This sort of radical deviation from what is normally expected invites bugs and makes code hard to understand and maintain.

Shadowing methods is very dangerous and should be used as a last resort. It is primarily useful in cases for which you have a preexisting component, such as a Windows Forms control that was not designed for inheritance. If you absolutely *must* inherit from such a component, you may need to use shadowing to "override" methods or properties. Despite the serious limits and dangers, it may be your only option. You will explore this in more detail later. First, let's see how Shadows can be used to override nonvirtual methods.

Overriding Nonvirtual Methods

Earlier in the chapter, you learned about virtual methods and how they are automatically created in Visual Basic when the Overrides keyword is employed. You can also implement nonvirtual methods in Visual Basic. Nonvirtual methods are methods that cannot be overridden and replaced by subclasses, so most methods you implement are nonvirtual.

 If you do not use the Overridable *keyword when declaring a method, then it is nonvirtual.*

In the typical case, nonvirtual methods are easy to understand. They can't be overridden and replaced, so you know that there's only one method by that name, with that method signature. Therefore, when you invoke it, there is no ambiguity about which specific implementation will be called. The reverse is true with virtual methods, where there may be more than one method of the same name, and with the same method signature, so you should understand the rules governing which implementation will be invoked.

Of course, you knew it couldn't be that simple, and it turns out that you can override nonvirtual methods by using the Shadows keyword. In fact, you can use the Shadows keyword to override methods regardless of whether or not they have the Overridable keyword in the declaration.

 The Shadows *keyword enables you to replace methods on the base class that the base-class designer didn't intend to be replaced.*

Obviously, this can be very dangerous. The designer of a base class must be careful when marking a method as Overridable, ensuring that the base class continues to operate properly even when that method is replaced by another code in a subclass. Designers of base classes typically just assume that if they do not mark a method as Overridable, it will be called and not overridden. Thus, overriding a nonvirtual method by using the Shadows keyword can have unexpected and potentially dangerous side effects, as you are doing something that the base-class designer assumed would never happen.

If that isn't enough complexity, it turns out that shadowed methods follow different rules than virtual methods when they are invoked. That is, they do not act like regular overridden methods; instead, they follow a different set of rules to determine which specific implementation of the method will be invoked. In particular, when you call a nonvirtual method, the data type of the variable refers to the object that indicates which implementation of the method is called, not the data type of the object, as with virtual methods.

To override a nonvirtual method, you can use the `Shadows` keyword instead of the `Overrides` keyword. To see how this works, add a new property to the base `Person` class:

```
Public ReadOnly Property Age() As Integer
   Get
      Return CInt(DateDiff(DateInterval.Year, Now, BirthDate))
   End Get
End Property
```

Here you have added a new method called `Age` to the base class, and thus automatically to the subclass. This code has a bug, introduced intentionally for illustration. The `DateDiff` parameters are in the wrong order, so you will get negative age values from this routine. The bug was introduced to highlight the fact that sometimes you will find bugs in base classes that you didn't write (and which you can't fix because you don't have the source code).

The following example walks you through the use of the `Shadows` keyword to address a bug in your base class, acting under the assumption that for some reason you can't actually fix the code in the `Person` class.

Note that you are not using the `Overridable` keyword on this method, so any subclass is prevented from overriding the method by using the `Overrides` keyword. The obvious intent and expectation of this code is that all subclasses will use this implementation and not override it with their own.

However, the base class cannot prevent a subclass from shadowing a method, so it does not matter whether you use `Overridable` or not; either way works fine for shadowing.

Before you shadow the method, let's see how it works as a regular nonvirtual method. First, you need to change your form to use this new value. Add a text box named `txtAge` and a related label to the form. Next, change the code behind the button to use the `Age` property. You will include the code to display the data on the form right here to keep things simple and clear:

```
Private Sub btnOK_Click(ByVal sender As System.Object, _
   ByVal e As System.EventArgs) Handles btnOK.Click

   Dim person As Employee = New Employee()

   With person
      .Name = "Fred"
      .BirthDate = #1/1/1960#

      txtName.Text = .Name
      txtBirthDate.Text = Format(.BirthDate, "Short date")
      txtAge.Text = CStr(.Age)
   End With

End Sub
```

Code snippet from Form1

Remember to change the `Employee` birth-date value to something valid. At this point, you can run the application. The age field should appear in your display as expected, though with a negative value due to the bug we introduced. There's no magic or complexity here. This is basic programming with objects, and basic use of inheritance as described earlier in this chapter.

Of course, you don't want a bug in your code, but nor do you have access to the `Person` class, and the `Person` class does not allow you to override the `Age` method, so what can you do? The answer lies in the `Shadows` keyword, which allows you to override the method anyway.

Let's shadow the `Age` method within the `Employee` class, overriding and replacing the implementation in the `Person` class, even though it is not marked as `Overridable`. Add the following code to the `Employee` class:

```
Public Shadows ReadOnly Property Age() As Integer
   Get
      Return CInt(DateDiff(DateInterval.Year, BirthDate, Now))
   End Get
End Property
```

Code snippet from Person

In many ways, this looks very similar to what you have seen with the `Overrides` keyword, in that you are implementing a method in your subclass with the same name and parameter list as a method in the base class. In this case, however, you will see some different behavior when you interact with the object in different ways.

Technically, the `Shadows` keyword is not required here. Shadowing is the default behavior when a subclass implements a method that matches the name and method signature of a method in the base class. However, if you omit the `Shadows` keyword, the compiler will issue a warning indicating that the method is being shadowed, so it is always better to include the keyword, both to avoid the warning and to make it perfectly clear that you chose to shadow the method intentionally.

Remember that your form's code is currently declaring a variable of type `Employee` and is creating an instance of an `Employee` object:

```
Dim person As Employee = New Employee()
```

This is a simple case, and, unsurprisingly, when you run the application now you will see that the value of the age field is correct, indicating that you just ran the implementation of the `Age` property from the `Employee` class. At this point, you are seeing the same behavior that you saw when overriding with the `Overrides` keyword.

Let's take a look at the other simple case, when you are working with a variable and object that are both of data type `Person`. Change the code in `Form1` as follows:

```
Private Sub btnOK_Click(ByVal sender As System.Object, _
    ByVal e As System.EventArgs) Handles btnOK.Click

  Dim person As Person = New Person()

  With person
    .Name = "Fred"
    .BirthDate = #1/1/1960#

    txtName.Text = .Name
    txtBirthDate.Text = Format(.BirthDate, "Short date")
    txtAge.Text = CStr(.Age)
  End With
End Sub
```

Now you have a variable of type `Person` and an object of that same type. You would expect that the implementation in the `Person` class would be invoked in this case, and that is exactly what happens: The age field displays the original negative value, indicating that you are invoking the buggy implementation of the method directly from the `Person` class. Again, this is exactly the behavior you would expect from a method overridden via the `Overrides` keyword.

This next example is where things get truly interesting. Change the code in `Form1` as follows:

```
Private Sub btnOK_Click(ByVal sender As System.Object, _
    ByVal e As System.EventArgs) Handles btnOK.Click

  Dim person As Person = New Employee()
  With person
    .Name = "Fred"
```

```
        .BirthDate = #1/1/1960#

        txtName.Text = .Name
        txtBirthDate.Text = Format(.BirthDate, "Short date")
        txtAge.Text = CStr(.Age)
    End With
End Sub
```

Now you are declaring the variable to be of type `Person`, but you are creating an object that is of data type `Employee`. You did this earlier in the chapter when exploring the `Overrides` keyword as well, and in that case you discovered that the version of the method that was invoked was based on the data type of the object. The `BirthDate` implementation in the `Employee` class was invoked.

If you run the application now, you will see that the rules are different when the `Shadows` keyword is used. In this case, the implementation in the `Person` class is invoked, giving you the buggy negative value. When the implementation in the `Employee` class is ignored, you get the exact opposite behavior of what you got with `Overrides`.

The following table summarizes which method implementation is invoked based on the variable and object data types when using shadowing:

VARIABLE TYPE	OBJECT TYPE	METHOD INVOKED
Base	Base	Base
Base	Subclass	Base
Subclass	Subclass	Subclass

In most cases, the behavior you will want for your methods is accomplished by the `Overrides` keyword and virtual methods. However, in cases where the base-class designer does not allow you to override a method and you want to do it anyway, the `Shadows` keyword provides you with the needed functionality.

Shadowing Arbitrary Elements

The `Shadows` keyword can be used not only to override nonvirtual methods, but also to totally replace and change the nature of a base-class interface element. When you override a method, you are providing a replacement implementation of that method with the same name and method signature. Using the `Shadows` keyword, you can do more extreme things, such as change a method into an instance variable or change a property into a function.

However, this can be very dangerous, as any code written to use your objects will naturally assume that you implement all the same interface elements and behaviors as your base class, because that is the nature of inheritance. Any documentation or knowledge of the original interface is effectively invalidated because the original implementation is arbitrarily replaced.

By totally changing the nature of an interface element, you can cause a great deal of confusion for programmers who might interact with your class in the future.

To see how you can replace an interface element from the base class, let's entirely change the nature of the `Age` property. In fact, let's change it from a read-only property to a read-write property. You could get even more extreme — change it to a Function or a Sub.

Remove the `Age` property from the `Employee` class and add the following code:

```
Public Shadows Property Age() As Integer
  Get
    Return CInt(DateDiff(DateInterval.Year, BirthDate, Now))
  End Get
  Set(ByVal value As Integer)
```

```
        BirthDate = DateAdd(DateInterval.Year, -value, Now)
      End Set
  End Property
```

Code snippet from Person

With this change, the very nature of the Age method has changed. It is no longer a simple read-only property; now it is a read-write property that includes code to calculate an approximate birth date based on the age value supplied.

As it stands, your application will continue to run just fine because you are only using the read-only functionality of the property in your form. You can change the form to make use of the new read-write functionality:

```
Private Sub btnOK_Click(ByVal sender As System.Object, _
    ByVal e As System.EventArgs) Handles btnOK.Click

  Dim person As Person = New Employee()

  With person
    .Name = "Fred"
    .BirthDate = #1/1/1960#
    .Age = 20

    txtName.Text = .Name
    txtBirthDate.Text = Format(.BirthDate, "Short date")
    txtAge.Text = CStr(.Age)
  End With
End Sub
```

However, this results in a syntax error. The variable you are working with, person, is of data type Person, and that data type doesn't provide a writeable version of the Age property. In order to use your enhanced functionality, you must use a variable and object of type Employee:

```
  Dim person As Employee = New Employee()
```

If you now run the application and click the button, the Age is displayed as 20, and the birth date is now a value calculated based on that age value, indicating that you are now running the shadowed version of the Age method as implemented in the Employee class.

As if that weren't odd enough, you can do some even stranger and more dangerous things. You can change Age into a variable, and you can even change its scope. For instance, you can comment out the Age property code in the Employee class and replace it with the following code:

```
  Private Shadows Age As String
```

Private Shadows Age As String

At this point, you have changed everything. Age is now a String instead of an Integer. It is a variable instead of a property or function. It has Private scope instead of Public scope. Your Employee object is now totally incompatible with the Person data type, something that shouldn't occur normally when using inheritance.

This means that the code you wrote in Form1 will no longer work. The Age property is no longer accessible and can no longer be used, so your project will no longer compile. This directly illustrates the danger in shadowing a base-class element such that its very nature or scope is changed by the subclass.

Because this change prevents your application from compiling, remove the line in the Employee class that shadows Age as a String variable, and uncomment the shadowed Property routine:

Available for
download on
Wrox.com

```
Public Shadows Property Age() As Integer
  Get
    Return CInt(DateDiff(DateInterval.Year, BirthDate, Now))
  End Get
```

```
    Set(ByVal value As Integer)
       BirthDate = DateAdd(DateInterval.Year, -value, Now)
    End Set
End Property
```

Code snippet from Person

This restores your application to a working state.

Levels of Inheritance

So far, you have created a single base class and a single subclass, thus demonstrating that you can implement inheritance that is a single level deep. You can also create inheritance relationships that are several levels deep. These are sometimes referred to as *chains of inheritance*.

Multiple Inheritance

Don't confuse multilevel inheritance with multiple inheritance, which is an entirely different concept that is not supported by either Visual Basic or the .NET platform itself. The idea behind multiple inheritance is that you can have a single subclass that inherits from two base classes at the same time.

For instance, an application might have a class for Customer and another class for Vendor. It is quite possible that some customers are also vendors, so you might want to combine the functionality of these two classes into a CustomerVendor class. This new class would be a combination of both Customer and Vendor, so it would be nice to inherit from both of them at once.

While this is a useful concept, multiple inheritance is complex and somewhat dangerous. Numerous problems are associated with multiple inheritance, but the most obvious is the possibility of collisions of properties or methods from the base classes. Suppose that both Customer and Vendor have a Name property. CustomerVendor would need two Name properties, one for each base class. Yet it only makes sense to have one Name property on CustomerVendor, so to which base class does it link, and how will the system operate if it does not link to the other one?

These are complex issues with no easy answers. Within the object-oriented community, there is ongoing debate as to whether the advantages of code reuse outweigh the complexity that comes along for the ride.

Multiple inheritance isn't supported by the .NET Framework, so it is likewise not supported by Visual Basic, but you can use multiple interfaces to achieve an effect similar to multiple inheritance, a topic discussed later in the chapter when we talk about implementing multiple interfaces.

Multilevel Inheritance

You have seen how a subclass derives from a base class with the Person and Employee classes, but nothing prevents the Employee subclass from being the base class for yet another class, a sub-subclass, so to speak. This is not at all uncommon. In the working example, you may have different kinds of employees, some who work in the office and others who travel.

To accommodate this, you may want OfficeEmployee and TravelingEmployee classes. Of course, these are both examples of an employee and should share the functionality already present in the Employee class. The Employee class already reuses the functionality from the Person class. Figure 3-9 illustrates how these classes are interrelated.

The Employee is a subclass of Person, and your two new classes are both subclasses of Employee. While both OfficeEmployee and TravelingEmployee are employees, and thus also people, they are each unique. An OfficeEmployee almost certainly has a cube or office number, while a TravelingEmployee will keep track of the number of miles traveled.

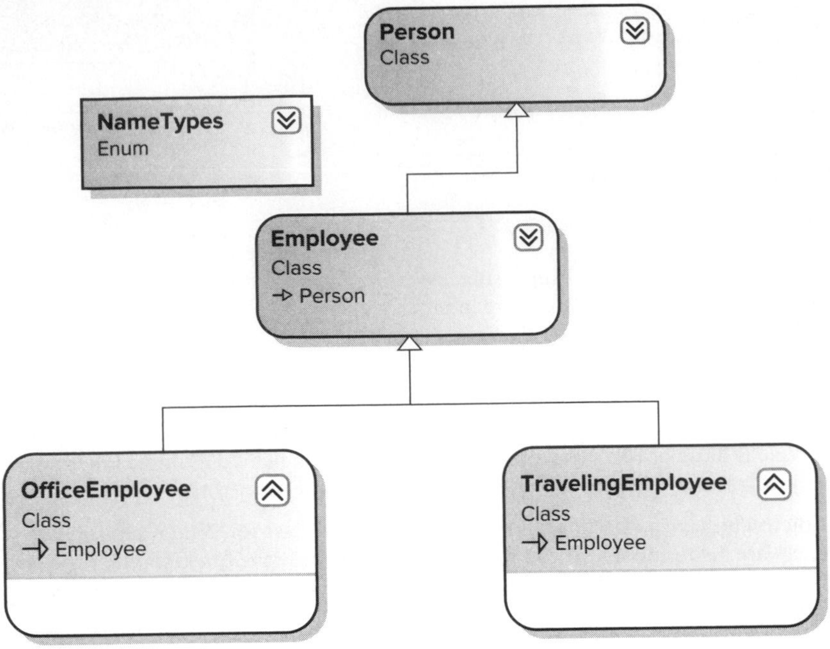

FIGURE 3-9

Add a new class to your project and name it OfficeEmployee. To make this class inherit from your existing Employee class, add the following code to the class:

```
Public Class OfficeEmployee

    Inherits Employee
End Class
```

With this change, the new class now has Name, BirthDate, Age, HireDate, and Salary methods. Notice that methods from both Employee and Person are inherited. A subclass always gains all the methods, properties, and events of its base class.

You can now extend the interface and behavior of OfficeEmployee by adding a property to indicate which cube or office number the employee occupies:

Available for download on Wrox.com

```
Public Class OfficeEmployee
    Inherits Employee

    Private mOffice As String

    Public Property OfficeNumber() As String
        Get
            Return mOffice
        End Get
        Set(ByVal value As String)
            mOffice = value
        End Set
    End Property
End Class
```

Code snippet from OfficeEmployee

To see how this works, let's enhance the form to display this value. Add a new `TextBox` control named `txtOffice` and an associated label so that your form looks like the one shown in Figure 3-10.

Now change the code behind the button to use the new property:

```
Private Sub btnOK_Click(ByVal sender As System.Object, _
    ByVal e As System.EventArgs) Handles btnOK.Click

  Dim person As OfficeEmployee = New OfficeEmployee()

  With person
    .Name = "Fred"
    .BirthDate = #1/1/1960#
    .Age = 20

    .OfficeNumber = "A42"

    txtName.Text = .Name
    txtBirthDate.Text = Format(.BirthDate, "Short date")
    txtAge.Text = CStr(.Age)

    txtOffice.Text = .OfficeNumber
  End With
End Sub
```

FIGURE 3-10

Code snippet from Form1

You have changed the routine to declare and create an object of type `OfficeEmployee` — thus enabling you to make use of the new property, as well as all existing properties and methods from `Employee` and `Person`, as they've been "merged" into the `OfficeEmployee` class via inheritance. If you now run the application, the name, birth date, age, and office values are displayed in the form.

Inheritance like this can go many levels deep, with each level extending and changing the behaviors of the previous levels. In fact, there is no specific technical limit to the number of levels of inheritance you can implement in Visual Basic, although very deep inheritance chains are typically not recommended and are often viewed as a design flaw, something discussed in more detail later in this chapter.

Interacting with the Base Class, Your Class, and Your Object

You have already seen how you can use the `MyBase` keyword to call methods on the base class from within a subclass. The `MyBase` keyword is one of three special keywords that enable you to interact with important object and class representations:

➤   Me

➤   MyBase

➤   MyClass

The Me Keyword

The `Me` keyword provides you with a reference to your current object instance. Typically, you do not need to use the `Me` keyword, because whenever you want to invoke a method within your current object, you can just call that method directly.

To see clearly how this works, let's add a new method to the `Person` class that returns the data of the `Person` class in the form of a `String`. This is interesting in and of itself, as the base `System.Object` class defines the `ToString` method for this exact purpose. Remember that all classes in the .NET Framework ultimately derive from `System.Object`, even if you do not explicitly indicate it with an `Inherits` statement.

This means that you can simply override the `ToString` method from the `Object` class within your `Person` class by adding the following code:

```
Public Overrides Function ToString() As String
    Return Name
End Function
```

This implementation returns the person's `Name` property as a result when `ToString` is called.

> *By default,* `ToString` *returns the class name of the class. Until now, if you called the* `ToString` *method on a* `Person` *object, you would get a result of* `InheritanceAnd Interfaces.Person.` `InheritanceAndInterfaces` *represents your assembly name when you create your project.*

Notice that the `ToString` method is calling another method within your same class — in this case, the `Name` method.

You could also write this routine using the `Me` keyword:

```
Public Overrides Function ToString() As String
    Return Me.Name
End Function
```

This is redundant because `Me` is the default for all method calls in a class. These two implementations are identical, so typically the `Me` keyword is simply omitted to avoid the extra typing.

To see how the `ToString` method now works, you can change your code in `Form1` to use this value instead of the `Name` property:

```
Private Sub btnOK_Click(ByVal sender As System.Object, _
    ByVal e As System.EventArgs) Handles btnOK.Click
Dim objPerson As OfficeEmployee = New OfficeEmployee()

With objPerson
    .Name = "Fred"
    .BirthDate = #1/1/1960#
    .Age = 20
    .OfficeNumber = "A42"

    txtName.Text = .ToString()
    txtBirthDate.Text = Format(.BirthDate, "Short date")
    txtAge.Text = CStr(.Age)
    txtOffice.Text = .OfficeNumber
End With
End Sub
```

Code snippet from Form1

When you run the application, the person's name is displayed appropriately, which makes sense, as the `ToString` method is simply returning the result from the `Name` property.

Earlier, you looked at virtual methods and how they work. Because either calling a method directly or calling it using the `Me` keyword invokes the method on the current object, the method calls conform to the same rules as an external method call. In other words, your `ToString` method may not actually end up calling the `Name` method in the `Person` class if that method was overridden by a class farther down the inheritance chain, such as the `Employee` or `OfficeEmployee` classes.

For example, you could override the `Name` property in your `OfficeEmployee` class such that it always returns the informal version of the person's name, rather than the regular name. You can override the `Name` property by adding this method to the `OfficeEmployee` class:

Available for download on Wrox.com

```
Public Overloads Overrides Property Name() As String
  Get
    Return MyBase.Name(NameTypes.Informal)
  End Get
  Set(ByVal value As String)
    MyBase.Name = value
  End Set
End Property
```

Code snippet from OfficeEmployee

This new version of the `Name` method relies on the base class to actually store the value, but instead of returning the regular name on request, now you are always returning the informal name:

```
Return MyBase.Name(NameTypes.Informal)
```

Before you can test this, you need to enhance the code in your form to actually provide a value for the informal name. Make the following change to the code:

```
Private Sub btnOK_Click(ByVal sender As System.Object,
    ByVal e As System.EventArgs) Handles btnOK.Click

  Dim objPerson As OfficeEmployee = New OfficeEmployee()

  With objPerson
    .Name = "Fred"
    .Name(NameTypes.Informal) = "Freddy"
    .BirthDate = #1/1/1960#
    .Age = 20
    .OfficeNumber = "A42"

    txtName.Text = .ToString()
    txtBirthDate.Text = Format(.BirthDate, "Short date")
    txtAge.Text = CStr(.Age)
    txtOffice.Text = .OfficeNumber
  End With
End Sub
```

Code snippet from Form1

When you run the application, the `Name` field displays the informal name. Even though the `ToString` method is implemented in the `Person` class, it is invoking the implementation of `Name` from the `OfficeEmployee` class. This is because method calls within a class follow the same rules for calling virtual methods as code outside a class, such as your code in the form. You will see this behavior with or without the `Me` keyword, as the default behavior for method calls is to implicitly call them via the current object.

While methods called from within a class follow the same rules for virtual methods, this is not the case for shadowed methods. Here, the rules for calling a shadowed method from within your class are different from those outside your class.

To see how this works, make the `Name` property in `OfficeEmployee` a shadowed method instead of an overridden method:

```
Public Shadows Property Name() As String
  Get
    Return MyBase.Name(NameTypes.Informal)
  End Get
  Set(ByVal value As String)
    MyBase.Name = value
  End Set
End Property
```

Before you can run your application, you must adjust some code in the form. Because you have shadowed the `Name` property in `OfficeEmployee`, the version of `Name` from `Employee` that acts as a property array is now invalid.

> *Shadowing a method replaces all implementations from higher in the inheritance chain, regardless of their method signature.*

To make your application operate, you need to change the variable declaration and object creation to declare a variable of type `Employee` so that you can access the property array while still creating an instance of `OfficeEmployee`:

```
Dim person As Employee = New OfficeEmployee()
```

Because your variable is now of type `Employee`, you also need to comment out the lines that refer to the `OfficeNumber` property, as it is no longer available:

```
With person
  .Name = "Fred"
  .Name(NameTypes.Informal) = "Freddy"
  .BirthDate = #1/1/1960#
  .Age = 20

  '.OfficeNumber = "A42"

  txtName.Text = .ToString()
  txtBirthDate.Text = Format(.BirthDate, "Short date")
  txtAge.Text = CStr(.Age)

  'txtOffice.Text = .OfficeNumber
End With
```

Code snippet from Form1

When you run the application now, it displays the name Fred, rather than Freddy, meaning it is not calling the `Name` method from `OfficeEmployee`; instead, it is calling the implementation provided by the `Employee` class. Remember that the code to make this call still resides in the `Person` class, but it now ignores the shadowed version of the `Name` method.

Shadowed implementations in subclasses are ignored when calling the method from within a class higher in the inheritance chain. You will get this same behavior with or without the `Me` keyword. The `Me` keyword, or calling methods directly, follows the same rules for overridden methods as any other method call. For shadowed methods, however, any shadowed implementations in subclasses are ignored, and the method is called from the current level in the inheritance chain.

The `Me` keyword exists primarily to enable you to pass a reference to the current object as a parameter to other objects or methods. As shown when you look at the `MyBase` and `MyClass` keywords, things can get very confusing, and there may be value in using the `Me` keyword when working with `MyBase` and `MyClass` to ensure that it is always clear which particular implementation of a method you intended to invoke.

The MyBase Keyword

While the `Me` keyword allows you to call methods on the current object instance, at times you might want to explicitly call into methods in your parent class. Earlier, you saw an example of this when you called back into the base class from an overridden method in the subclass.

The `MyBase` keyword references only the immediate parent class, and it works like an object reference. This means that you can call methods on `MyBase` knowing that they are being called just as if you had a reference to an object of your parent class's data type.

There is no way to directly navigate up the inheritance chain beyond the immediate parent, so you can't directly access the implementation of a method in a base class if you are in a sub-subclass. Such behavior isn't a good idea anyway, which is why it isn't allowed.

The `MyBase` keyword can be used to invoke or use any Public, Friend, or Protected element from the parent class. This includes all elements directly on the base class, and any elements the base class inherited from other classes higher in the inheritance chain.

You already used `MyBase` to call back into the base `Person` class as you implemented the overridden `Name` property in the `Employee` class.

 Any code within a subclass can call any method on the base class by using the `MyBase` keyword.

You can also use `MyBase` to call back into the base class implementation even if you have shadowed a method. Though it wasn't noted at the time, you have already done this in your shadowed implementation of the `Name` property in the `OfficeEmployee` class. The bold lines indicate where you are calling into the base class from within a shadowed method:

```
Public Shadows Property Name() As String
  Get
    Return MyBase.Name(NameTypes.Informal)
  End Get
  Set(ByVal value As String)
    MyBase.Name = value
  End Set
End Property
```

Code snippet from OfficeEmployee

The `MyBase` keyword enables you to merge the functionality of the base class into your subclass code as you deem fit.

The MyClass Keyword

As you have seen, when you use the `Me` keyword or call a method directly, your method call follows the rules for calling both virtual and nonvirtual methods. In other words, as shown earlier with the `Name` property, a call to `Name` from your code in the `Person` class actually invoked the overridden version of `Name` located in the `OfficeEmployee` class.

While this behavior is often useful, sometimes you will want to ensure that you truly are running the specific implementation from your class; even if a subclass overrode your method, you still want to ensure that you are calling the version of the method that is directly in your class.

Maybe you decide that your `ToString` implementation in `Person` should always call the `Name` implementation that you write in the `Person` class, totally ignoring any overridden versions of `Name` in any subclasses.

This is where the `MyClass` keyword shines. This keyword is much like `MyBase`, in that it provides you with access to methods as though it were an object reference — in this case, a reference to an instance of the class that contains the code you are writing when using the `MyClass` keyword. This is true even when the instantiated object is an instance of a class derived from your class.

You have seen that a call to `ToString` from within `Person` actually invokes the implementation in `Employee` or `OfficeEmployee` if your object is an instance of either of those types. Let's restore the `Name` property in `OfficeEmployee` so that it is an overridden method, rather than a shadowed method, to demonstrate how this works:

Available for
download on
Wrox.com

```
Public Overloads Overrides Property Name() As String
  Get
    Return MyBase.Name(NameTypes.Informal)
  End Get
  Set(ByVal value As String)
    MyBase.Name = value
  End Set
End Property
```

Code snippet from OfficeEmployee

With this change, and based on your earlier testing, you know that the `ToString` implementation in `Person` will automatically call this overridden version of the `Name` property, as the call to the `Name` method follows the normal rules for virtual methods. In fact, if you run the application now, the Name field on the form displays Freddy, the informal name of the person.

You can force the use of the implementation in the current class through the use of `MyClass`. Change the `ToString` method in `Person` as follows:

```
Public Overrides Function ToString() As String
  Return MyClass.Name
End Function
```

You are now calling the `Name` method, but you are doing it using the `MyClass` keyword. When you run the application and click the button, the Name field in the form displays Fred rather than Freddy, proving that the implementation from `Person` was invoked even though the data type of the object itself is `OfficeEmployee`.

The `ToString` method is invoked from `Person`, as neither `Employee` nor `OfficeEmployee` provides an overridden implementation. Then, because you are using the `MyClass` keyword, the `Name` method is invoked directly from `Person`, explicitly defeating the default behavior you would normally expect.

Constructors

As discussed in Chapter 2, you can provide a special constructor method, named `New`, on a class and it will be the first code run when an object is instantiated. You can also receive parameters via the constructor method, enabling the code that creates your object to pass data into the object during the creation process.

Constructor methods are affected by inheritance differently than regular methods. A normal Public method, such as `BirthDate` on your `Person` class, is automatically inherited by any subclass. From there you can overload, override, or shadow that method, as discussed already.

Simple Constructors

Constructors do not quite follow the same rules. To explore the differences, let's implement a simple constructor method in the `Person` class:

```
Public Sub New()
  Debug.WriteLine("Person constructor")
End Sub
```

If you now run the application, you will see the text displayed in the output window in the IDE. This occurs even though the code in your form is creating an object of type `OfficeEmployee`:

```
Dim person As Employee = New OfficeEmployee()
```

As you might expect, the `New` method from your base `Person` class is invoked as part of the construction process of the `OfficeEmployee` object — simple inheritance at work. However, interesting things occur if you implement a `New` method in the `OfficeEmployee` class itself:

```
Public Sub New()
  Debug.WriteLine("OfficeEmployee constructor")
End Sub
```

Notice that you are not using the `Overrides` keyword, nor did you mark the method in `Person` as `Overridable`. These keywords have no use in this context, and in fact will cause syntax errors if you attempt to use them on constructor methods.

When you run the application now, you would probably expect that only the implementation of `New` in `OfficeEmployee` would be invoked. Certainly, that is what would occur with a normal overridden method. Of course, `New` isn't overridden, so when you run the application, both implementations are run, and both strings are output to the output window in the IDE.

Note that the implementation in the `Person` class ran first, followed by the implementation in the `OfficeEmployee` class. This occurs because when an object is created, all the constructors for the classes in the inheritance chain are invoked, starting with the base class and including all the subclasses one by one. In fact, if you implement a `New` method in the `Employee` class, you can see that it too is invoked:

```
Public Sub New()
  Debug.WriteLine("Employee constructor")
End Sub
```

When the application is run and the button is clicked, three strings appear in the output window. All three constructor methods were invoked, from the `Person` class to the `OfficeEmployee` class.

Constructors in More Depth

The rules governing constructors without parameters are pretty straightforward, but things get a bit more complex if you start requiring parameters on your constructors.

To understand why, you need to consider how even your simple constructors are invoked. While you may see them as being invoked from the base class down through all subclasses to your final subclass, what is really happening is a bit different.

In particular, it is the subclass `New` method that is invoked first. However, Visual Basic automatically inserts a line of code into your routine at compile time. For instance, in your `OfficeEmployee` class you have a constructor:

```
Public Sub New()
  Debug.WriteLine("OfficeEmployee constructor")
End Sub
```

Behind the scenes, Visual Basic inserts what is effectively a call to the constructor of your parent class on your behalf. You could do this manually by using the `MyBase` keyword with the following change:

```
Public Sub New()
  MyBase.New()
  Debug.WriteLine("OfficeEmployee constructor")
End Sub
```

This call must be the first line in your constructor. If you put any other code before this line, you will get a syntax error indicating that your code is invalid. Because the call is always required, and because it always must be the first line in any constructor, Visual Basic simply inserts it for you automatically.

Note that if you don't explicitly provide a constructor on a class by implementing a `New` method, Visual Basic creates one for you behind the scenes. The automatically created method simply has one line of code:

```
MyBase.New()
```

All classes have constructor methods, either created explicitly by you as you write a `New` method or created implicitly by Visual Basic as the class is compiled.

A constructor method is sometimes called a ctor, short for constructor. This term is often used by tools such as ILDASM or .NET Reflector.

By always calling `MyBase.New` as the first line in every constructor, you are guaranteed that it is the implementation of `New` in your top-level base class that actually runs first. Every subclass invokes the parent class implementation all the way up the inheritance chain until only the base class remains. Then its code runs, followed by each individual subclass, as shown earlier.

Constructors with Parameters

This works great when your constructors don't require parameters, but if your constructor does require a parameter, then it becomes impossible for Visual Basic to automatically make that call on your behalf. After all, how would Visual Basic know what values you want to pass as parameters?

To see how this works, change the `New` method in the `Person` class to require a `Name` parameter. You can use that parameter to initialize the object's `Name` property:

```
Public Sub New(ByVal name As String)
  Me.Name = name
  Debug.WriteLine("Person constructor")
End Sub
```

Now your constructor requires a `String` parameter and uses it to initialize the `Name` property. You are using the `Me` keyword to make your code easier to read. Interestingly enough, the compiler actually understands and correctly compiles the following code:

```
Name = name
```

However, that is not at all clear to a developer reading the code. By prefixing the property name with the `Me` keyword, you make it clear that you are invoking a property on the object and providing it with the parameter value.

At this point, your application won't compile because there is an error in the `New` method of the `Employee` class. In particular, Visual Basic's attempt to automatically invoke the constructor on the `Person` class fails because it has no idea what data value to pass for this new name parameter. There are three ways you can address this error:

➤ Make the name parameter `Optional`.

➤ Overload the `New` method with another implementation that requires no parameter.

➤ Manually provide the `Name` parameter value from within the `Employee` class.

If you make the `Name` parameter `Optional`, then you are indicating that the `New` method can be called with or without a parameter. Therefore, one viable option is to call the method with no parameters, so Visual Basic's default of calling it with no parameters works just fine.

If you overload the `New` method, then you can implement a second `New` method that doesn't accept any parameters, again allowing Visual Basic's default behavior to work as you have seen. Keep in mind that this solution only invokes the overloaded version of `New` with no parameter; the version that requires a parameter would not be invoked.

The final way you can fix the error is by simply providing a parameter value yourself from within the `New` method of the `Employee` class. To do this, change the `Employee` class as shown:

```
Public Sub New()
  MyBase.New("George")
  Debug.WriteLine("Employee constructor")
End Sub
```

By explicitly calling the New method of the parent class, you are able to provide it with the required parameter value. At this point, your application will compile, but it won't run.

Constructors, Overloading, and Variable Initialization

What isn't clear from this code is that you have now introduced a very insidious bug. The constructor in the Person class is using the Name property to set the value:

```
Public Sub New(ByVal name As String)
  Me.Name = name
  Debug.WriteLine("Person constructor")
End Sub
```

However, the Name property is overridden by the Employee class, so it is that implementation that will be run. Unfortunately, that implementation makes use of a Dictionary object, which isn't available yet! It turns out that any member variables declared in a class with the New statement, such as the Dictionary object in Employee, won't be initialized until after the constructor for that class has completed:

```
Private mNames As New Generic.Dictionary(Of NameTypes, String)
```

Because you are still in the constructor for Person, there's no way the constructor for Employee can be complete. To resolve this, you need to change the Employee class a bit so that it does not rely on the Dictionary being created in this manner. Instead, you will add code to create it when needed.

First, change the declaration of the variable in the Employee class:

```
Private mNames As Generic.Dictionary(Of NameTypes, String)
```

Then, update the Name property so that it creates the Hashtable object if needed:

```
Public Overloads Property Name(ByVal type As NameTypes) As String
  Get
    If mNames Is Nothing Then mNames = New Generic.Dictionary(Of NameTypes, String)
    Return mNames(type)
  End Get
  Set(ByVal value As String)
    If mNames Is Nothing Then mNames = New Generic.Dictionary(Of NameTypes, String)
    If mNames.ContainsKey(type) Then
      mNames.Item(type) = value
    Else
      mNames.Add(type, value)
    End If
    If type = NameTypes.Normal Then
      MyBase.Name = value
    End If
  End Set
End Property
```

Code snippet from OfficeEmployee

This ensures that a Dictionary object is created in the Employee class code, even though its constructor hasn't yet completed.

More Constructors with Parameters

Obviously, you probably do not want to hard-code a value in a constructor as you did in the Employee class, so you may choose instead to change this constructor to also accept a name parameter. Change the Employee class constructor as shown:

```
Public Sub New(ByVal name As String)
MyBase.New(name)
  Debug.WriteLine("Employee constructor")
End Sub
```

Of course, this just pushed the issue deeper, and now the OfficeEmployee class has a compile error in its New method. Again, you can fix the problem by having that method accept a parameter so that it can provide it up the chain as required. Make the following change to OfficeEmployee:

```
Public Sub New(ByVal name As String)
MyBase.New(name)
  Debug.WriteLine("OfficeEmployee constructor")
End Sub
```

Finally, the code in the form is no longer valid. You are attempting to create an instance of OfficeEmployee without passing a parameter value. Update that code as shown and then you can run the application:

```
Private Sub btnOK_Click(ByVal sender As System.Object, _
    ByVal e As System.EventArgs) Handles btnOK.Click

    Dim person As Employee = New OfficeEmployee("Mary")

    With person
     '.Name = "Fred"
```

Here, you are passing a name value to the constructor of OfficeEmployee. In addition, you have commented out the line of code that sets the Name property directly — meaning the value passed in the constructor will be displayed in the form.

Protected Scope

You have seen how a subclass automatically gains all the Public methods and properties that compose the interface of the base class. This is also true of Friend methods and properties; they are inherited as well and are available only to other code in the same project as the subclass.

Private methods and properties are not exposed as part of the interface of the subclass, meaning that the code in the subclass cannot call those methods, nor can any code using your objects. These methods are only available to the code within the base class itself. This can get confusing, as the implementations contained in the Private methods are inherited and used by any code in the base class; it is just that they are not available to be called by any other code, including code in the subclass.

Sometimes you will want to create methods in your base class that can be called by a subclass, as well as the base class, but not by code outside of those classes. Basically, you want a hybrid between Public and Private access modifiers — methods that are private to the classes in the inheritance chain but usable by any subclasses that might be created within the chain. This functionality is provided by the Protected scope.

Protected methods are very similar to Private methods in that they are not available to any code that calls your objects. Instead, these methods are available to code within the base class and to code within any subclass. The following table lists all the available scope options:

SCOPE	DESCRIPTION
Private	Available only to code within your class
Protected	Available only to classes that inherit from your class
Friend	Available only to code within your project/component
Protected Friend	Available to classes that inherit from your class (in any project) and to code within your project/component. This is a combination of Protected and Friend.
Public	Available to code outside your class

The Protected scope can be applied to Sub, Function, and Property methods. To see how the Protected scope works, let's add an Identity field to the Person class:

```
Public Class Person
    Private mName As String
    Private mBirthDate As String
    Private mID As String

    Protected Property Identity() As String
      Get
         Return mID
      End Get
      Set(ByVal value As String)
         mID = value
      End Set
    End Property
```

Code snippet from Person

This data field represents some arbitrary identification number or value assigned to a person. This might be a social security number, an employee number, or whatever is appropriate.

The interesting thing about this value is that it is not currently accessible outside your inheritance chain. For instance, if you try to use it from your code in the form, you will discover that there is no Identity property on your Person, Employee, or OfficeEmployee objects.

However, there is an Identity property now available inside your inheritance chain. The Identity property is available to the code in the Person class, just like any other method. Interestingly, even though Identity is not available to the code in your form, it is available to the code in the Employee and OfficeEmployee classes, because they are both subclasses of Person. Employee is directly a subclass, and OfficeEmployee is indirectly a subclass of Person because it is a subclass of Employee.

Thus, you can enhance your Employee class to implement an EmployeeNumber property by using the Identity property. To do this, add the following code to the Employee class:

```
Public Property EmployeeNumber() As Integer
    Get
       Return CInt(Identity)
    End Get
    Set(ByVal value As Integer)
       Identity = CStr(value)
    End Set
End Property
```

Code snippet from Employee

This new property exposes a numeric identity value for the employee, but it uses the internal Identity property to manage that value. You can override and shadow Protected elements just as you do with elements of any other scope.

Protected Variables

Up to this point, we've focused on methods and properties and how they interact through inheritance. Inheritance, and, in particular, the Protected scope, also affects instance variables and how you work with them.

Though it is not recommended, you can declare variables in a class using Public scope. This makes the variable directly available to code both within and outside of your class, allowing any code that interacts with your objects to directly read or alter the value of that variable.

Variables can also have Friend scope, which likewise allows any code in your class or anywhere within your project to read or alter the value directly. This is also generally not recommended because it breaks encapsulation.

> *Rather than declare variables with Public or Friend scope, it is better to expose the value using a Property so that you can apply any of your business rules to control how the value is altered as appropriate.*

Of course, you know that variables can be of Private scope, and this is typically the case. This makes the variables accessible only to the code within your class, and it is the most restrictive scope.

As with methods, however, you can also use the Protected scope when declaring variables. This makes the variable accessible to the code in your class and to the code in any class that derives from your class — all the way down the hierarchy chain.

Sometimes this is useful, because it enables you to provide and accept data to and from subclasses, but to act on that data from code in the base class. At the same time, exposing variables to subclasses is typically not ideal, and you should use Property methods with Protected scope for this instead, as they allow your base class to enforce any business rules that are appropriate for the value, rather than just hope that the author of the subclass provides only good values.

Events and Inheritance

So far, we've discussed methods, properties, and variables in terms of inheritance — how they can be added, overridden, overloaded, and shadowed. In Visual Basic, events are also part of the interface of an object, and they are affected by inheritance as well.

Inheriting Events

Chapter 2 discusses how to declare, raise, and receive events from objects. You can add such an event to the Person class by declaring it at the top of the class:

Available for download on Wrox.com

```
Public Class Person
    Private mName As String
    Private mBirthDate As String
    Private mID As String

    Public Event NameChanged(ByVal newName As String)
```

Code snippet from Person

Then, you can raise this event within the class anytime the person's name is changed:

Available for download on Wrox.com

```
Public Overridable Property Name() As String
    Get
        Return mName
    End Get
    Set(ByVal value As String)
        mName = value
        RaiseEvent NameChanged(mName)
    End Set
End Property
```

Code snippet from Person

At this point, you can receive and handle this event within your form anytime you are working with a Person object. The nice thing about this is that your events are inherited automatically by subclasses — meaning your Employee and OfficeEmployee objects will also raise this event. Thus, you can change the code in your form to handle the event, even though you are working with an object of type OfficeEmployee.

First, you can add a method to handle the event to Form1:

```
Private Sub OnNameChanged(ByVal newName As String)
  MsgBox("New name: " & newName)
End Sub
```

Note that you are not using the `Handles` clause here. In this case, for simplicity, you use the `AddHandler` method to dynamically link the event to this method. However, you could have also chosen to use the `WithEvents` and `Handles` keywords, as described in Chapter 2 — either way works.

With the handler built, you can use the `AddHandler` method to link this method to the event on the object:

```
Private Sub btnOK_Click(ByVal sender As System.Object, _
    ByVal e As System.EventArgs) Handles btnOK.Click

  Dim person As Employee = New OfficeEmployee("Mary")

  AddHandler person.NameChanged, AddressOf OnNameChanged
  With person
    .Name = "Fred"
```

Code snippet from Form1

Also note that you are uncommenting the line that changes the `Name` property. With this change, you know that the event should fire when the name is changed.

When you run the application now, you will see a message box, indicating that the name has changed and proving that the `NameChanged` event really is exposed and available, even though your object is of type `OfficeEmployee`, rather than `Person`.

Raising Events from Subclasses

One caveat you should keep in mind is that while a subclass exposes the events of its base class, the code in the subclass cannot raise the event. In other words, you cannot use the `RaiseEvent` method in `Employee` or `OfficeEmployee` to raise the `NameChanged` event. Only code directly in the `Person` class can raise the event.

To see this in action, let's add another event to the `Person` class, an event that can indicate the change of other arbitrary data values:

```
Public Class Person
  Private mName As String
  Private mBirthDate As String
  Private mID As String

  Public Event NameChanged(ByVal newName As String)
  Public Event DataChanged(ByVal field As String, ByVal newValue As Object)
```

You can then raise this event when the BirthDate is changed:

```
Public Overridable Property BirthDate() As Date
  Get
    Return mBirthDate
  End Get
  Set(ByVal value As Date)
    mBirthDate = value
    RaiseEvent DataChanged("BirthDate", value)
  End Set
End Property
```

Code snippet from Person

It would also be nice to raise this event from the `Employee` class when the `Salary` value is changed. Unfortunately, you can't use the `RaiseEvent` method to raise the event from a base class, so the following code won't work (do not enter this code):

```
Public Property Salary() As Double
  Get
    Return mSalary
  End Get
  Set(ByVal value As Double)
    mSalary = value
    RaiseEvent DataChanged("Salary", value)
  End Set
End Property
```

Code snippet from Employee

Fortunately, there is a relatively easy way to get around this limitation. You can simply implement a `Protected` method in your base class that allows any derived class to raise the method. In the `Person` class, you can add such a method:

```
Protected Sub OnDataChanged(ByVal field As String, _
    ByVal newValue As Object)

  RaiseEvent DataChanged(field, newValue)
End Sub
```

Code snippet from Person

You can use this method from within the `Employee` class to indicate that `Salary` has changed:

```
Public Property Salary() As Double
  Get
    Return mSalary
  End Get
  Set(ByVal value As Double)
    mSalary = value
    OnDataChanged("Salary", value)
  End Set
End Property
```

Code snippet from Employee

Note that the code in `Employee` is not raising the event, it is simply calling a Protected method in `Person`. The code in the `Person` class is actually raising the event, meaning everything will work as desired.

You can enhance the code in `Form1` to receive the event. First, create a method to handle the event:

```
Private Sub OnDataChanged(ByVal field As String, ByVal newValue As Object)
  MsgBox("New " & field & ": " & CStr(newValue))
End Sub
```

Then, link this handler to the event using the AddHandler method:

```
Private Sub btnOK_Click(ByVal sender As System.Object, _
    ByVal e As System.EventArgs) Handles btnOK.Click

  Dim person As Employee = New OfficeEmployee("Mary")

  AddHandler person.NameChanged, AddressOf OnNameChanged
  AddHandler person.DataChanged, AddressOf OnDataChanged
```

Code snippet from Form1

Finally, ensure that you are changing and displaying the Salary property:

Available for
download on
Wrox.com

```
With person
  .Name = "Fred"
  .Name(NameTypes.Informal) = "Freddy"
  .BirthDate = #1/1/1960#
  .Age = 20
  .Salary = 30000


  txtName.Text = .ToString()
  txtBirthDate.Text = Format(.BirthDate, "Short date")
  txtAge.Text = CStr(.Age)

  txtSalary.Text = Format(.Salary, "0.00")
End With
```

Code snippet from Form1

When you run the application and click the button now, you will get message boxes displaying the changes to the `Name` property, the `BirthDate` property (twice, once for the `BirthDate` property and once for the `Age` property, which changes the birth date), and the `Salary` property.

Shared Methods

Chapter 2 explored shared methods and how they work: providing a set of methods that can be invoked directly from the class, rather than requiring that you create an actual object.

Shared methods are inherited just like instance methods and so are automatically available as methods on subclasses, just as they are on the base class. If you implement a shared method in `base class`, you can call that method using any class derived from `base class`.

Like regular methods, shared methods can be overloaded and shadowed. They cannot, however, be overridden. If you attempt to use the `Overridable` keyword when declaring a shared method, you will get a syntax error. For instance, you can implement a method in your `Person` class to compare two `Person` objects:

Available for
download on
Wrox.com

```
Public Shared Function Compare(ByVal person1 As Person, _
    ByVal person2 As Person) As Boolean

    Return (person1.Name = person2.Name)

End Function
```

Code snippet from Sort

To test this method, add another button to the form, name it `btnCompare`, and set its `Text` value to `Compare`. Double-click the button to bring up the code window and enter the following:

Available for
download on
Wrox.com

```
Private Sub btnCompare_Click(ByVal sender As System.Object, _
    ByVal e As System.EventArgs) Handles btnCompare.Click

  Dim emp1 As New Employee("Fred")
  Dim emp2 As New Employee("Mary")

  MsgBox(Employee.Compare(emp1, emp2))

End Sub
```

Code snippet from Form1

This code simply creates two `Employee` objects and compares them. Note, though, that the code uses the `Employee` class to invoke the `Compare` method, displaying the result in a message box. This establishes that the `Compare` method implemented in the `Person` class is inherited by the `Employee` class, as expected.

Overloading Shared Methods

Shared methods can be overloaded using the `Overloads` keyword in the same manner as you overload an instance method. This means that your subclass can add new implementations of the shared method as long as the parameter list differs from the original implementation.

For example, you can add a new implementation of the `Compare` method to `Employee`:

Available for download on Wrox.com

```
Public Overloads Shared Function Compare(ByVal employee1 As Employee, _
    ByVal employee2 As Employee) As Boolean

  Return (employee1.EmployeeNumber = employee2.EmployeeNumber)

End Function
```

Code snippet from Sort

This new implementation compares two `Employee` objects, rather than two `Person` objects, and in fact compares them by employee number, rather than name. You can enhance the code behind `btnCompare` in the form to set the `EmployeeNumber` properties:

Available for download on Wrox.com

```
Private Sub btnCompare_Click(ByVal sender As System.Object, _
    ByVal e As System.EventArgs) Handles btnCompare.Click

  Dim emp1 As New Employee("Fred")
  Dim emp2 As New Employee("Mary")

  emp1.EmployeeNumber = 1
  emp2.EmployeeNumber = 1

  MsgBox(Employee.Compare(emp1, emp2))
End Sub
```

Code snippet from Form1

While it might make little sense for these two objects to have the same `EmployeeNumber` value, it does prove a point. When you run the application now, even though the `Name` values of the objects are different, your `Compare` routine will return `True`, proving that you are invoking the overloaded version of the method that expects two `Employee` objects as parameters.

The overloaded implementation is available on the `Employee` class or any classes derived from `Employee`, such as `OfficeEmployee`. The overloaded implementation is not available if called directly from `Person`, as that class contains only the original implementation.

Shadowing Shared Methods

Shared methods can also be shadowed by a subclass. This allows you to do some very interesting things, including converting a shared method into an instance method or vice versa. You can even leave the method as shared but change the entire way it works and is declared. In short, just as with instance methods, you can use the `Shadows` keyword to entirely replace and change a shared method in a subclass.

To see how this works, use the `Shadows` keyword to change the nature of the `Compare` method in `OfficeEmployee`:

Available for download on Wrox.com

```
Public Shared Shadows Function Compare(ByVal person1 As Person, _
    ByVal person2 As Person) As Boolean

  Return (person1.Age = person2.Age)

End Function
```

Code snippet from Sort

Notice that this method has the same signature as the original Compare method you implemented in the Person class; but instead of comparing by name, here you are comparing by age. With a normal method you could have done this by overriding, but Shared methods can't be overridden, so the only thing you can do is shadow it.

Of course, the shadowed implementation is only available via the OfficeEmployee class. Neither the Person nor Employee classes, which are higher up the inheritance chain, are aware that this shadowed version of the method exists.

To use this from your Form1 code, you can change the code for btnCompare as follows:

```
Private Sub btnCompare_Click(ByVal sender As System.Object, _
    ByVal e As System.EventArgs) Handles btnCompare.Click

    Dim emp1 As New Employee("Fred")
    Dim emp2 As New Employee("Mary")

    emp1.Age = 20
    emp2.Age = 25

    MsgBox(OfficeEmployee.Compare(emp1, emp2))
End Sub
```

Code snippet from Form1

Instead of setting the EmployeeNumber values, you are now setting the Age values on your objects. More important, notice that you are now calling the Compare method via the OfficeEmployee class, rather than via Employee or Person. This causes the invocation of the new version of the method, and the ages of the objects are compared which returns False.

Shared Events

As discussed in Chapter 2, you can create shared events, events that can be raised by shared or instance methods in a class, whereas regular events can only be raised from within instance methods.

When you inherit from a class that defines a shared event, your new subclass automatically gains that event, just as it does with regular events. As with instance events, a shared event cannot be raised by code within the subclass; it can only be raised using the RaiseEvent keyword from code in the class where the event is declared. If you want to be able to raise the event from methods in your subclass, you need to implement a Protected method on the base class that actually makes the call to RaiseEvent.

This is no different from what you saw earlier in the chapter, other than that with a shared event you can use a method with Protected scope that is marked as shared to raise the event, rather than use an instance method.

Creating an Abstract Base Class

So far, you have seen how to inherit from a class, how to overload and override methods, and how virtual methods work. In all of the examples so far, the parent classes have been useful in their own right and could be instantiated and do some meaningful work. Sometimes, however, you want to create a class such that it can only be used as a base class for inheritance.

MustInherit Keyword

The current Person class is being used as a base class, but it can also be instantiated directly to create an object of type Person. Likewise, the Employee class is also being used as a base class for the OfficeEmployee class you created that derives from it.

If you want to make a class act only as a base class, you can use the MustInherit keyword, thereby preventing anyone from creating objects based directly on the class, and requiring them instead to create a subclass and then create objects based on that subclass.

This can be very useful when you are creating object models of real-world concepts and entities. You will look at ways to leverage this capability later in this chapter. Change `Person` to use the `MustInherit` keyword:

```
Public MustInherit Class Person
```

This has no effect on the code within `Person` or any of the classes that inherit from it, but it does mean that no code can instantiate objects directly from the `Person` class; instead, you can only create objects based on `Employee` or `OfficeEmployee`.

This does not prevent you from declaring variables of type `Person`; it merely prevents you from creating an object by using `New Person`. You can also continue to make use of Shared methods from the `Person` class without any difficulty.

MustOverride Keyword

Another option you have is to create a method (Sub, Function, or Property) that must be overridden by a subclass. You might want to do this when you are creating a base class that provides some behaviors but relies on subclasses to also provide other behaviors in order to function properly. This is accomplished by using the `MustOverride` keyword on a method declaration.

If a class contains any methods marked with `MustOverride`, the class itself must also be declared with the `MustInherit` keyword or you will get a syntax error.

Public MustInherit Class Person

This makes sense. If you are requiring that a method be overridden in a subclass, it stands to reason that your class can't be directly instantiated; it must be subclassed to be useful.

Let's see how this works by adding a `LifeExpectancy` method in `Person` that has no implementation and must be overridden by a subclass:

```
Public MustOverride Function LifeExpectancy() As Integer
```

Notice that there is no `End Function` or any other code associated with the method. When using `MustOverride`, you cannot provide any implementation for the method in your class. Such a method is called an *abstract method* or *pure virtual function*, as it only defines the interface, and no implementation.

Methods declared in this manner must be overridden in any subclass that inherits from your base class. If you do not override one of these methods, you will generate a syntax error in the subclass and it won't compile. You need to alter the `Employee` class to provide an implementation for this method:

```
Public Overrides Function LifeExpectancy() As Integer
   Return 90
End Function
```

Your application will compile and run at this point because you are now overriding the `LifeExpectancy` method in `Employee`, so the required condition is met.

Abstract Base Classes

You can combine these two concepts, using both `MustInherit` and `MustOverride`, to create something called an *abstract base class*, sometimes referred to as a *virtual class*. This is a class that provides no implementation, only the interface definitions from which a subclass can be created, as shown in the following example:

```
Public MustInherit Class AbstractBaseClass
   Public MustOverride Sub DoSomething()
   Public MustOverride Sub DoOtherStuff()
End Class
```

This technique can be very useful when creating frameworks or the high-level conceptual elements of a system. Any class that inherits `AbstractBaseClass` must implement both `DoSomething` and `DoOtherStuff`; otherwise, a syntax error will result.

In some ways, an abstract base class is comparable to defining an interface using the `Interface` keyword. The `Interface` keyword is discussed in detail later in this chapter. You could define the same interface shown in this example with the following code:

```
Public Interface IAbstractBaseClass
   Sub DoSomething()
   Sub DoOtherStuff()
End Interface
```

Any class that implements the `IAbstractBaseClass` interface must implement both `DoSomething` and `DoOtherStuff` or a syntax error will result, and in that regard this technique is similar to an abstract base class.

Preventing Inheritance

If you want to prevent a class from being used as a base class, you can use the `NotInheritable` keyword. For instance, you can change your `OfficeEmployee` as follows:

```
Public NotInheritable Class OfficeEmployee
```

At this point, it is no longer possible to inherit from this class to create a new class. Your `OfficeEmployee` class is now sealed, meaning it cannot be used as a base from which to create other classes.

If you attempt to inherit from `OfficeEmployee`, you will get a compile error indicating that it cannot be used as a base class. This has no effect on `Person` or `Employee`; you can continue to derive other classes from them.

Typically, you want to design your classes so that they can be subclassed, because that provides the greatest long-term flexibility in the overall design. Sometimes, however, you want to ensure that your class cannot be used as a base class, and the `NotInheritable` keyword addresses that issue.

MULTIPLE INTERFACES

In Visual Basic, objects can have one or more interfaces. All objects have a primary, or native, interface, which is composed of any methods, properties, events, or member variables declared using the Public keyword. You can also have objects implement secondary interfaces in addition to their native interface by using the `Implements` keyword.

Object Interfaces

The native interface on any class is composed of all the methods, properties, events, and even variables that are declared as anything other than Private. Though this is nothing new, let's quickly review what is included in the native interface to set the stage for discussing secondary interfaces. To include a method as part of your interface, you can simply declare a Public routine:

```
Public Sub AMethod()

End Sub
```

Notice that there is no code in this routine. Any code would be implementation and is not part of the interface. Only the declaration of the method is important when discussing interfaces. This can seem confusing at first, but it is an important distinction, as the separation of the interface from its implementation is at the very core of object-oriented programming and design.

Because this method is declared as Public, it is available to any code outside the class, including other applications that may make use of the assembly. If the method has a property, then you can declare it as part of the interface by using the `Property` keyword:

```
Public Property AProperty() As String

End Property
```

You can also declare events as part of the interface by using the Event keyword:

```
Public Event AnEvent()
```

Finally, you can include actual variables, or attributes, as part of the interface:

```
Public AnInteger As Integer
```

This is strongly discouraged, because it directly exposes the internal variables for use by code outside the class. Because the variable is directly accessible from other code, you give up any and all control over the way the value may be changed or the code may be accessed.

Rather than make any variable Public, it is far preferable to make use of a Property method to expose the value. That way, you can implement code to ensure that your internal variable is set only to valid values and that only the appropriate code has access to the value based on your application's logic.

Using the Native Interface

Ultimately, the native (or primary) interface for any class is defined by looking at all the methods, properties, events, and variables that are declared as anything other than Private in scope. This includes any methods, properties, events, or variables that are inherited from a base class.

You are used to interacting with the default interface on most objects, so this should seem pretty straightforward. Consider this simple class:

Available for
download on
Wrox.com

```
Public Class TheClass
    Public Sub DoSomething()

    End Sub

    Public Sub DoSomethingElse()

    End Sub
End Class
```

Code snippet from TheClass

This defines a class and, by extension, defines the native interface that is exposed by any objects you instantiate based on this class. The native interface defines two methods: DoSomething and DoSomethingElse. To make use of these methods, you simply call them:

Available for
download on
Wrox.com

```
Dim myObject As New TheClass()

myObject.DoSomething()

myObject.DoSomethingElse()
```

Code snippet from Form1

This is the same thing you did in Chapter 2 and so far in this chapter. However, let's take a look at creating and using secondary interfaces, because they are a bit different.

Secondary Interfaces

Sometimes it's helpful for an object to have more than one interface, thereby enabling you to interact with the object in different ways. Inheritance enables you to create subclasses that are specialized cases of the base class. For example, your Employee is a Person. Throughout this section we will be referencing the InheritanceAndInterfaces project we created earlier in this chapter.

However, sometimes you have a group of objects that are not the same thing, but you want to be able to treat them as though they were the same. You want all these objects to act as the same thing, even though they are all different.

For instance, you may have a series of different objects in an application: product, customer, invoice, and so forth. Each of these would have default interfaces appropriate to each individual object — and each of them is a different class — so there's no natural inheritance relationship implied between these classes. At the same time, you may need to be able to generate a printed document for each type of object, so you would like to make them all act as a printable object.

This chapter discusses the is-a and act-as relationships in more detail later.

To accomplish this, you can define a generic interface that enables generating such a printed document. You can call it `IPrintableObject`.

By convention, this type of interface is typically prefixed with a capital "I" to indicate that it is a formal interface.

Each of your application objects can choose to implement the `IPrintableObject` interface. Every object that implements this interface must include code to provide actual implementation of the interface, which is unlike inheritance, whereby the code from a base class is automatically reused.

By implementing this common interface, you can write a routine that accepts any object that implements the `IPrintableObject` interface and then print it — while remaining totally oblivious to the "real" data type of the object or methods its native interface might expose. Before you learn how to use an interface in this manner, let's walk through the process of actually defining an interface.

Defining the Interface

You define a formal interface using the `Interface` keyword. This can be done in any code module in your project, but a good place to put this type of definition is in a standard module. An interface defines a set of methods (Sub, Function, or Property) and events that must be exposed by any class that chooses to implement the interface.

Add a module to the project using Project ➪ Add Module and name it `Interfaces.vb`. Then, add the following code to the module, outside the Module code block itself:

Available for download on Wrox.com

```
Public Interface IPrintableObject

End Interface

Module Interfaces

End Module
```

Code snippet from Interfaces

A code module can contain a number of interface definitions, and these definitions must exist outside of any other code block. Thus, they do not go within a Class or Module block; they are at a peer level to those constructs.

Interfaces must be declared using either Public or Friend scope. Declaring a Private or Protected interface results in a syntax error. Within the Interface block of code, you can define the methods, properties, and events that make up your particular interface. Because the scope of the interface is defined by the `Interface` declaration itself, you can't specify scopes for individual methods and events; they are all scoped like the interface itself.

For instance, add the following code:

```
Public Interface IPrintableObject
    Function Label(ByVal index As Integer) As String
    Function Value(ByVal index As Integer) As String
    ReadOnly Property Count() As Integer
End Interface
```

Code snippet from Interfaces

This defines a new data type, somewhat like creating a class or structure, which you can use when declaring variables. For instance, you can now declare a variable of type `IPrintableObject`:

```
Private printable As IPrintableObject
```

You can also have your classes implement this interface, which requires each class to provide implementation code for each of the three methods defined on the interface.

Before you implement the interface in a class, let's see how you can use the interface to write a generic routine that can print any object that implements `IPrintableObject`.

Using the Interface

Interfaces define the methods and events (including parameters and data types) that an object is required to implement if you choose to support the interface. This means that, given just the interface definition, you can easily write code that can interact with any object that implements the interface, even though you do not know what the native data types of those objects will be.

To see how you can write such code, let's create a simple routine in your form that can display data to the output window in the IDE from any object that implements `IPrintableObject`. Bring up the code window for your form and add the following routine:

```
Public Sub PrintObject(obj As IPrintableObject)
    Dim index As Integer

    For index = 0 To obj.Count
        Debug.Write(obj.Label(index) & ": ")
        Debug.WriteLine(obj.Value(index))
    Next
End Sub
```

Code snippet from Form1

Notice that you are accepting a parameter of type `IPrintableObject`. This is how secondary interfaces are used, by treating an object of one type as though it were actually of the interface type. As long as the object passed to this routine implements the `IPrintableObject` interface, your code will work fine.

Within the `PrintObject` routine, you are assuming that the object will implement three elements — `Count`, `Label`, and `Value` — as part of the `IPrintableObject` interface. Secondary interfaces can include methods, properties, and events, much like a default interface, but the interface itself is defined and implemented using some special syntax.

Now that you have a generic printing routine, you need a way to call it. Bring up the designer for Form1, add a button, and name it `btnPrint`. Double-click the button and put this code behind it:

```
Private Sub btnPrint_Click(ByVal sender As System.Object, _
    ByVal e As System.EventArgs) Handles btnPrint.Click

    Dim obj As New Employee("Andy")

    obj.EmployeeNumber = 123
```

```
    obj.BirthDate = #1/1/1980#
    obj.HireDate = #1/1/1996#

    PrintObject(obj)
End Sub
```

This code simply initializes an `Employee` object and calls the `PrintObject` routine. Of course, this code produces runtime exceptions, because `PrintObject` is expecting a parameter that implements `IPrintableObject`, and `Employee` implements no such interface. Let's move on and implement that interface in `Employee` so that you can see how it works.

Implementing the Interface

Any class (other than an abstract base class) can implement an interface by using the `Implements` keyword. For instance, you can implement the `IPrintableObject` interface in `Employee` by adding the following line:

```
Public Class Employee
   Inherits Person
   Implements IPrintableObject
```

This causes the interface to be exposed by any object created as an instance of `Employee`. Adding this line of code and pressing Enter triggers the IDE to add skeleton methods for the interface to your class. All you need to do is provide implementations (write code) for the methods.

> *To implement an interface, you must implement all the methods and properties defined by that interface.*

Before actually implementing the interface, however, let's create an array to contain the labels for the data fields so that you can return them via the `IPrintableObject` interface. Add the following code to the `Employee` class:

```
Public Class Employee
   Inherits Person
   Implements IPrintableObject
   Private mLabels() As String = {"ID", "Age", "HireDate"}
   Private mHireDate As Date
   Private mSalary As Double
```

To implement the interface, you need to create methods and properties with the same parameter and return data types as those defined in the interface. The actual name of each method or property does not matter because you are using the `Implements` keyword to link your internal method names to the external method names defined by the interface. As long as the method signatures match, you are all set.

This applies to scope as well. Although the interface and its methods and properties are publicly available, you do not have to declare your actual methods and properties as Public. In many cases, you can implement them as Private, so they do not become part of the native interface and are only exposed via the secondary interface.

However, if you do have a Public method with a method signature, you can use it to implement a method from the interface. This has the interesting side effect that this method provides implementation for both a method on the object's native interface and one on the secondary interface.

In this case, you will use a Private method, so it is only providing implementation for the
`IPrintableObject` interface. Implement the `Label` method by adding the following code to `Employee`:

**Available for
download on
Wrox.com**

```
Private Function Label(ByVal index As Integer) As String _
     Implements IPrintableObject.Label

     Return mLabels(index)
End Function
```

Code snippet from Employee

This is just a regular Private method that returns a `String` value from the pre-initialized array. The interesting
part is the `Implements` clause on the method declaration:

```
Private Function Label(ByVal index As Integer) As String _
     Implements IPrintableObject.Label
```

By using the `Implements` keyword in this fashion, you are indicating that this particular method is
the implementation for the `Label` method on the `IPrintableObject` interface. The actual name of the
private method could be anything. It is the use of the `Implements` clause that makes this work. The only
requirement is that the parameter data types and the return value data type must match those defined
by the `IPrintableObject` interface method.

This is very similar to using the `Handles` clause to indicate which method should handle an event. In fact,
like the `Handles` clause, the `Implements` clause allows you to have a comma-separated list of interface
methods that should be implemented by this one function.

You can then move on to implement the other two elements defined by the `IPrintableObject` interface by
adding this code to `Employee`:

**Available for
download on
Wrox.com**

```
Private Function Value(ByVal index As Integer) As String _
     Implements IPrintableObject.Value

   Select Case index
     Case 0
       Return CStr(EmployeeNumber)
     Case 1
       Return CStr(Age)
     Case Else
       Return Format(HireDate, "Short date")
   End Select
End Function

Private ReadOnly Property Count() As Integer _
     Implements IPrintableObject.Count
   Get
     Return UBound(mLabels)
   End Get
End Property
```

Code snippet from Employee

You can now run this application and click the button. The output window in the IDE will display your
results, showing the ID, age, and hire-date values as appropriate.

Any object could create a similar implementation behind the `IPrintableObject` interface, and the `PrintObject`
routine in your form would continue to work, regardless of the native data type of the object itself.

Reusing a Common Implementation

Secondary interfaces provide a guarantee that all objects implementing a given interface have exactly the
same methods and events, including the same parameters.

The `Implements` clause links your actual implementation to a specific method on an interface. For instance, your `Value` method is linked to `IPrintableObject.Value` using the following clause:

```
Private Function Value(ByVal index As Integer) As String _
    Implements IPrintableObject.Value
```

Sometimes, your method might be able to serve as the implementation for more than one method, either on the same interface or on different interfaces.

Add the following interface definition to `Interfaces.vb`:

```
Public Interface IValues
   Function GetValue(ByVal index As Integer) As String
End Interface
```

This interface defines just one method, `GetValue`. Notice that it defines a single `Integer` parameter and a return type of `String`, the same as the `Value` method from `IPrintableObject`. Even though the method name and parameter variable name do not match, what counts here is that the parameter and return value data types do match.

Now bring up the code window for `Employee`. You will have it implement this new interface in addition to the `IPrintableObject` interface:

```
Public Class Employee
    Inherits Person
    Implements IPrintableObject
    Implements IValues
```

Code snippet from Employee

You already have a method that returns values. Rather than reimplement that method, it would be nice to just link this new `GetValues` method to your existing method. You can easily do this because the `Implements` clause allows you to provide a comma-separated list of method names:

```
Private Function Value(ByVal index As Integer) As String _
    Implements IPrintableObject.Value, IValues.GetValue

    Select Case Index
      Case 0
        Return CStr(EmployeeNumber)
      Case 1
        Return CStr(Age)
      Case Else
        Return Format(HireDate, "Short date")
    End Select

End Function
```

Code snippet from Employee

This is very similar to the use of the `Handles` keyword, covered in Chapter 2. A single method within the class, regardless of scope or name, can be used to implement any number of methods as defined by other interfaces, as long as the data types of the parameters and return values all match.

Combining Interfaces and Inheritance

You can combine implementation of secondary interfaces and inheritance at the same time. When you inherit from a class that implements an interface, your new subclass automatically gains the interface and implementation from the base class. If you specify that your base-class methods are overridable, then the subclass can override those methods. This not only overrides the base-class implementation for your native interface, but also overrides the implementation for the interface. For instance, you could declare the `Value` method in the interface as follows:

```
Public Overridable Function Value(ByVal index As Integer) As String _
    Implements IPrintableObject.Value, IValues.GetValue
```

Now it is Public, so it is available on your native interface, and it is part of both the `IPrintableObject` and `IValues` interfaces. This means that you can access the property three ways in client code:

```
Dim emp As New Employee()
Dim printable As IPrintableObject = emp
Dim values As IValues = emp

Debug.WriteLine(emp.Value(0))
Debug.WriteLine(printable.Value(0))
Debug.WriteLine(values.GetValue(0))
```

Code snippet from Form1

Note that you are also now using the `Overrides` keyword in the declaration. This means that a subclass of `Employee`, such as `OfficeEmployee`, can override the `Value` method. The overridden method will be the one invoked, regardless of whether you call the object directly or via an interface.

Combining the implementation of an interface in a base class with overridable methods can provide a very flexible object design.

ABSTRACTION

Abstraction is the process by which you can think about specific properties or behaviors without thinking about a particular object that has those properties or behaviors. Abstraction is merely the ability of a language to create "black box" code, to take a concept and create an abstract representation of that concept within a program.

A `Customer` object, for example, is an abstract representation of a real-world customer. A `DataSet` object is an abstract representation of a set of data.

Abstraction enables you to recognize how things are similar and to ignore differences, to think in general terms and not in specifics. A `TextBox` control is an abstraction because you can place it on a form and then tailor it to your needs by setting properties. Visual Basic enables you to define abstractions using classes.

Any language that enables a developer to create a class from which objects can be instantiated meets this criterion, and Visual Basic is no exception. You can easily create a class to represent a customer, essentially providing an abstraction. You can then create instances of that class, whereby each object can have its own attributes, representing a specific customer.

In Visual Basic, you implement abstraction by creating a class using the `Class` keyword. To see this in action, bring up Visual Studio and create a new Visual Basic Windows Forms Application project named "OOExample." Once the project is open, add a new class to the project using the Project ⇨ Add Class menu option. Name the new class `Customer.vb`, and add some code to make this class represent a real-world customer in an abstract sense:

```
Public Class Customer
    Private mID As Guid = Guid.NewGuid
    Private mName As String
    Private mPhone As String

    Public Property ID() As Guid
      Get
        Return mID
      End Get
```

```
      Set(ByVal value As Guid)
        mID = value
      End Set
    End Property

    Public Property Name() As String
      Get
        Return mName
      End Get
      Set(ByVal value As String)
        mName = value
      End Set
    End Property

    Public Property Phone() As String
      Get
        Return mPhone
      End Get
      Set(ByVal value As String)
        mPhone = value
      End Set
    End Property
  End Class
```

Code snippet from Customer

You know that a real customer is a lot more complex than an ID, name, and phone number; but at the same time, you know that in an abstract sense, your customers really do have names and phone numbers, and that you assign them unique ID numbers to keep track of them. In this case, you are using a globally unique identifier (GUID) as a unique ID. Thus, given an ID, name, and phone number, you know which customer you are dealing with, and so you have a perfectly valid abstraction of a customer within your application.

You can then use this abstract representation of a customer from within your code by using data binding to link the object to a form. First, build the project by selecting Build ➪ OOExample. Then click the Data ➪ Show Data Sources menu option to open the Data Sources window. Select the Add New Data Source link in the window to bring up the Data Source Configuration Wizard. Within the wizard, choose to add a new Object data source, click Next, and then select your Customer class, as shown in Figure 3-11.

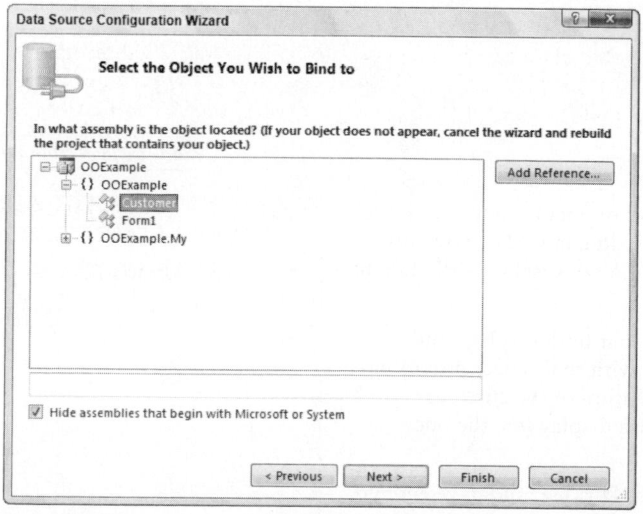

FIGURE 3-11

Finish the wizard. The `Customer` class will be displayed as an available data source, as shown in Figure 3-12, if you are working in Design view.

Click on Customer in the window. Customer should change its display to a combo box. Open the combo box and change the selection from DataGridView to Details. This way, you get a details view of the object on your form. Open the designer for `Form1` and drag the Customer class from the Data Sources window onto the form. The result should look something like the dialog shown in Figure 3-13.

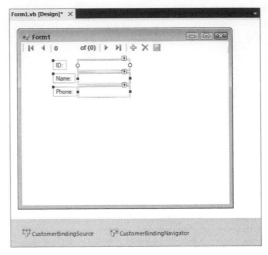

FIGURE 3-12

FIGURE 3-13

All you need to do now is add code to create an instance of the `Customer` class to act as a data source for the form. Double-click on the form to bring up its code window and add the following code:

Available for download on Wrox.com

```vb
Public Class Form1

    Private Sub Form1_Load(ByVal sender As System.Object, _
      ByVal e As System.EventArgs) Handles MyBase.Load

        Me.CustomerBindingSource.DataSource = New Customer()

    End Sub

End Class
```

Code snippet from Form1

You are using the ability of Windows Forms to data bind to a property on an object. You learn more about data binding later. For now, it is enough to know that the controls on the form are automatically tied to the properties on your object.

Now you have a simple user interface (UI) that both displays and updates the data in your `Customer` object, with that object providing the UI developer with an abstract representation of the customer. When you run the application, you will see a display like the one shown in Figure 3-14.

Here, you have displayed the pre-generated ID value, and have entered values for Name and Phone directly into the form.

FIGURE 3-14

ENCAPSULATION

Perhaps the most important of the object-oriented concepts is that of encapsulation. Encapsulation is the idea that an object should totally separate its interface from its implementation. All the data and implementation code for an object should be entirely hidden behind its interface. This is the concept of an object as a black box.

The idea is that you can create an interface (by creating public methods in a class) and, as long as that interface remains consistent, the application can interact with your objects. This remains true even if you entirely rewrite the code within a given method. The interface is independent of the implementation.

Encapsulation enables you to hide the internal implementation details of a class. For example, the algorithm you use to find prime numbers might be proprietary. You can expose a simple API to the end user but hide all of the logic used in your algorithm by encapsulating it within your class.

This means that an object should completely contain any data it requires and should contain all the code required to manipulate that data. Programs should interact with an object through an interface, using the properties and methods of the object. Client code should never work directly with the data owned by the object.

> *Programs interact with objects by sending messages to the object indicating which method or property they want to have invoked. These messages are generated by other objects or external sources such as the user. The object reacts to these messages through methods or properties.*

Visual Basic classes entirely hide their internal data and code, providing a well-established interface of properties and methods with the outside world. Let's look at an example. Add the following class to your project by selecting Project ⇨ Add Class; the code defines its native interface:

Available for download on Wrox.com

```vb
Public Class Encapsulation

    Public Function DistanceTo(ByVal x As Single, ByVal y As Single) As Single

    End Function

    Public Property CurrentX() As Single
      Get

      End Get
      Set(ByVal value As Single)

      End Set
    End Property

    Public Property CurrentY() As Single
      Get

      End Get
      Set(ByVal value As Single)

      End Set
    End Property

End Class
```

Code snippet from Encapsulation

This creates an interface for the class. At this point, you can write client code to interact with the class, because from a client perspective, all you care about is the interface. Bring up the designer for Form1 and add a button to the form, and then write the following code behind the button:

```
Private Sub btnEncapsulation_Click(ByVal sender As System.Object, _
   ByVal e As System.EventArgs) Handles btnEncapsulation.Click

  Dim obj As New Encapsulation
  MsgBox(obj.DistanceTo(10, 10))

End Sub
```

Code snippet from Form1

Even though you have no actual code in the Encapsulation class, you can still write code to use that class because the interface is defined.

This is a powerful idea. It means you can rapidly create class interfaces against which other developers can create the UI or other parts of the application while you are still creating the implementation behind the interface.

From here, you could do virtually anything you like in terms of implementing the class. For example, to use the values to calculate a direct distance, overwrite the previous code with:

```
Imports System.Math

Public Class Encapsulation
    Private mX As Single
    Private mY As Single

    Public Function DistanceTo(ByVal x As Single, ByVal y As Single) As Single
      Return CSng(Sqrt((x - mX)^ 2 ^ (y - mY) ? 2))
    End Function

    Public Property CurrentX() As Single
    Get
        Return mX
    End Get
    Set(ByVal value As Single)
       mX = value
    End Set
  End Property

  Public Property CurrentY() As Single
    Get
        Return mY
    End Get
    Set(ByVal value As Single)
       mY = value

    End Set
  End Property
End Class
```

Code snippet from Encapsulation

Now when you run the application and click the button, you get a meaningful value as a result. Even better, encapsulation enables you to change the implementation without changing the interface. For example, you can change the distance calculation to find the distance between the points (assuming that no diagonal travel is allowed):

```
Public Function DistanceTo(ByVal x As Single, ByVal y As Single) As Single
    Return Abs(x - mX) + Abs(y - mY)
End Function
```

This results in a different value being displayed when the program is run. You have not changed the interface of the class, so your working client program has no idea that you have switched from one implementation to the other. You have achieved a total change of behavior without any change to the client code. This is the essence of encapsulation.

Of course, a user might have a problem if you make such a change to your object. If applications were developed expecting the first set of behaviors, and then you changed to the second, there could be some interesting side effects. The key point is that the client programs would continue to function, even if the results are quite different from when you began.

POLYMORPHISM

Polymorphism is often considered to be directly tied to inheritance (discussed next). In reality, it is largely independent. Polymorphism means that you can have two classes with different implementations or code, but with a common set of methods, properties, or events. You can then write a program that operates upon that interface and does not care about which type of object it operates at runtime.

Method Signatures

To properly understand polymorphism, you need to explore the concept of a *method signature*, sometimes also called a *prototype*. All methods have a signature, which is defined by the method's name and the data types of its parameters. You might have code such as this:

```
Public Function CalculateValue() As Integer

End Sub
```

In this example, the signature is as follows:

```
f()
```

If you add a parameter to the method, the signature will change. For example, you could change the method to accept a `Double`:

```
Public Function CalculateValue(ByVal value As Double) As Integer
```

Then, the signature of the method is as follows:

```
f(Double)
```

Polymorphism merely says that you should be able to write client code that calls methods on an object, and as long as the object provides your methods with the method signatures you expect, it doesn't matter from which class the object was created. The following sections look at some examples of polymorphism within Visual Basic.

Implementing Polymorphism

You can use several techniques to achieve polymorphic behavior:

➤ Late binding
➤ Multiple interfaces
➤ Reflection
➤ Inheritance

Late binding actually enables you to implement "pure" polymorphism, although at the cost of performance and ease of programming. Through multiple interfaces and inheritance, you can also achieve polymorphism with much better performance and ease of programming. Reflection enables you to use either late binding or multiple interfaces, but against objects created in a very dynamic way, even going so far as to dynamically load a DLL into your application at runtime so that you can use its classes. The following sections walk through each of these options to see how they are implemented and to explore their pros and cons.

Polymorphism through Late Binding

Typically, when you interact with objects in Visual Basic, you are interacting with them through strongly typed variables. For example, in `Form1` you interacted with the `Encapsulation` object with the following code:

```
Private Sub btnEncapsulation_Click(ByVal sender As System.Object, _
  ByVal e As System.EventArgs) Handles btnEncapsulation.Click

  Dim obj As New Encapsulation
  MsgBox(obj.DistanceTo(10, 10))

End Sub
```

Code snippet from Form1

The `obj` variable is declared using a specific type (`Encapsulation`) — meaning that it is strongly typed or early bound.

You can also interact with objects that are late bound. Late binding means that your object variable has no specific data type, but rather is of type `Object`. To use late binding, you need to use the `Option Strict Off` directive at the top of your code file (or in the project's properties). This tells the Visual Basic compiler that you want to use late binding, so it will allow you to do this type of polymorphism. Add the following to the top of the Form1 code:

```
Option Strict Off
```

With Option Strict turned off, Visual Basic treats the `Object` data type in a special way, enabling you to attempt arbitrary method calls against the object, even though the `Object` data type does not implement those methods. For example, you could change the code in `Form1` to be late bound as follows:

```
Private Sub btnEncapsulation_Click(ByVal sender As System.Object, _
  ByVal e As System.EventArgs) Handles btnEncapsulation.Click

  Dim obj As Object = New Encapsulation
  MsgBox(obj.DistanceTo(10, 10))

End Sub
```

Code snippet from Form1

When this code is run, you get the same result as you did before, even though the `Object` data type has no `DistanceTo` method as part of its interface. The late-binding mechanism, behind the scenes, dynamically determines the real type of your object and invokes the appropriate method.

When you work with objects through late binding, neither the Visual Basic IDE nor the compiler can tell whether you are calling a valid method. Here, there is no way for the compiler to know that the object referenced by your `obj` variable actually has a `DistanceTo` method. It just assumes that you know what you are talking about and compiles the code.

At runtime, when the code is actually invoked, it attempts to dynamically call the `DistanceTo` method. If that is a valid method, then your code will work; otherwise, you will get an error.

Obviously, there is a level of danger when using late binding, as a simple typo can introduce errors that can only be discovered when the application is actually run. However, it also offers a lot of flexibility, as code that makes use of late binding can talk to any object from any class as long as those objects implement the methods you require.

There is a substantial performance penalty for using late binding. The existence of each method is discovered dynamically at runtime, and that discovery takes time. Moreover, the mechanism used to invoke a method through late binding is not nearly as efficient as the mechanism used to call a method that is known at compile time.

To make this more obvious, change the code in `Form1` by adding a generic routine that displays the distance:

Available for download on Wrox.com

```
Private Sub btnEncapsulation_Click(ByVal sender As System.Object, _
    ByVal e As System.EventArgs) Handles btnEncapsulation.Click

    Dim obj As New Encapsulation
    ShowDistance(obj)
End Sub

Private Sub ShowDistance(ByVal obj As Object)
    MsgBox(obj.DistanceTo(10, 10))
End Sub
```

Code snippet from Form1

Notice that the new `ShowDistance` routine accepts a parameter using the generic `Object` data type — so you can pass it literally any value — `String`, `Integer`, or one of your own custom objects. It will throw an exception at runtime, however, unless the object you pass into the routine has a `DistanceTo` method that matches the required method signature.

You know that your `Encapsulation` object has a method matching that signature, so your code works fine. Now let's add another simple class to demonstrate polymorphism. Add a new class to the project by selecting Project ➪ Add Class and name it `Poly.vb`:

Available for download on Wrox.com

```
Public Class Poly
    Public Function DistanceTo(ByVal x As Single, ByVal y As Single) As Single
        Return x + y
    End Function
End Class
```

Code snippet from Poly

This class is about as simple as you can get. It exposes a `DistanceTo` method as part of its interface and provides a very basic implementation of that interface.

You can use this new class in place of the `Encapsulation` class without changing the `ShowDistance` method by using polymorphism. Return to the code in `Form1` and make the following change:

Available for download on Wrox.com

```
Private Sub btnEncapsulation_Click(ByVal sender As System.Object, _
    ByVal e As System.EventArgs) Handles btnEncapsulation.Click

    Dim obj As New Poly
    ShowDistance(obj)
End Sub
```

Code snippet from Form1

Even though you changed the class of object you are passing to `ShowDistance` to one with a different overall interface and different implementation, the method called within `ShowDistance` remains consistent, so your code will run.

Polymorphism with Multiple Interfaces

Late binding is flexible and easy, but it is not ideal because it defeats the IDE and compiler type checking that enables you to fix bugs due to typos during the development process. It also has a negative impact on performance.

Another way to implement polymorphism is to use multiple interfaces. This approach avoids late binding, meaning the IDE and compiler can check your code as you enter and compile it. Moreover, because the compiler has access to all the information about each method you call, your code runs much faster.

Remove the `Option Strict` directive from the code in Form1 in the OOExample project. This will cause some syntax errors to be highlighted in the code, but don't worry — you will fix those soon enough.

Visual Basic not only supports polymorphism through late binding, it also implements a stricter form of polymorphism through its support of multiple interfaces. (Earlier you learned about multiple interfaces, including the use of the `Implements` keyword and how to define interfaces.)

With late binding, you have learned how to treat all objects as equals by making them all appear using the `Object` data type. With multiple interfaces, you can treat all objects as equals by making them all implement a common data type or interface.

This approach has the benefit that it is strongly typed, meaning the IDE and compiler can help you find errors due to typos, because the names and data types of all methods and parameters are known at design time. It is also fast in terms of performance: Because the compiler knows about the methods, it can use optimized mechanisms for calling them, especially compared to the dynamic mechanisms used in late binding.

Return to the project to implement polymorphism with multiple interfaces. First, add a module to the project using the Project ➪ Add Module menu option and name it `Interfaces.vb`. Replace the Module code block with an `Interface` declaration:

```
Public Interface IShared
    Function CalculateDistance(ByVal x As Single, ByVal y As Single) As Single
End Interface
```

Code snippet from Interfaces

Now you can make both the `Encapsulation` and the `Poly` classes implement this interface. First, in the `Encapsulation` class, add the following code:

```
Public Class Encapsulation
    Implements IShared

    Private mX As Single
    Private mY As Single
    Public Function DistanceTo(ByVal x As Single, ByVal y As Single) _
        As Single Implements IShared.CalculateDistance
      Return CSng(Sqrt((x - mX) ^ 2 + (y - mY) ^ 2))
    End Function
```

Code snippet from Encapsulation

Here you are implementing the `IShared` interface, and because the `CalculateDistance` method's signature matches that of your existing `DistanceTo` method, you are simply indicating that it should act as the implementation for `CalculateDistance`.

You can make a similar change in the `Poly` class:

```
Public Class Poly
    Implements IShared
    Public Function DistanceTo(ByVal x As Single, ByVal y As Single) As Single _
        Implements IShared.CalculateDistance
        Return x + y
    End Function
End Class
```

Code snippet from Poly

Now this class also implements the `IShared` interface, and you are ready to see polymorphism implemented in your code. Bring up the code window for `Form1` and change your `ShowDistance` method as follows:

```
Private Sub ShowDistance(ByVal obj As IShared)
  MsgBox(obj.CalculateDistance(10, 10))
End Sub
```

Note that this eliminates the compiler error you saw after removing the `Option Strict` directive from `Form1`.

Instead of accepting the parameter using the generic `Object` data type, you are now accepting an `IShared` parameter — a strong data type known by both the IDE and the compiler. Within the code itself, you are calling the `CalculateDistance` method as defined by that interface.

This routine can now accept any object that implements `IShared`, regardless of what class that object was created from or what other interfaces that object may implement. All you care about here is that the object implements `IShared`.

Polymorphism through Reflection

You have learned how to use late binding to invoke a method on any arbitrary object as long as that object has a method matching the method signature you are trying to call. You have also walked through the use of multiple interfaces, which enables you to achieve polymorphism through a faster, early-bound technique. The challenge with these techniques is that late binding can be slow and hard to debug, and multiple interfaces can be somewhat rigid and inflexible.

Enter reflection. Reflection is a technology built into the .NET Framework that enables you to write code that interrogates an assembly to dynamically determine the classes and data types it contains. Using reflection, you can load the assembly into your process, create instances of those classes, and invoke their methods.

When you use late binding, Visual Basic makes use of the `System.Reflection` namespace behind the scenes on your behalf. The `System.Reflection` namespace can give you insight into classes by enabling to traverse information about an assembly or class. You can choose to manually use reflection as well. This gives you even more flexibility in terms of how you interact with objects.

For example, suppose that the class you want to call is located in some other assembly on disk — an assembly you did not specifically reference from within your project when you compiled it. How can you dynamically find, load, and invoke such an assembly? Reflection enables you to do this, assuming that the assembly is polymorphic. In other words, it has either an interface you expect or a set of methods you can invoke via late binding.

To see how reflection works with late binding, we'll create a new class in a separate assembly (project) and use it from within the existing application. Choose File ➪ Add ➪ New Project to add a new Class Library project to your solution. Name it "Objects." It begins with a single class module that you can use as a starting point. Change the code in that class to the following:

Available for
download on
Wrox.com

```
Public Class External
  Public Function DistanceTo(ByVal x As Single, ByVal y As Single) As Single
    Return x * y
  End Function
End Class
```

Code snippet from External

Now compile the assembly by choosing Build ➪ Build Objects. Next, bring up the code window for `Form1`. Add an `Imports` statement at the top, and add back the `Option Strict Off` statement:

```
Option Strict Off
Imports System.Reflection
```

Remember that because you are using late binding, `Form1` also must use `Option Strict Off`. Otherwise, late binding isn't available.

Add a button with the following code (you have to import the `System.Reflections` namespace for this to work):

```
Private Sub Button1_Click(ByVal sender As System.Object, _
        ByVal e As System.EventArgs) Handles button1.Click
    Dim obj As Object
    Dim dll As Assembly
    dll = Assembly.LoadFrom("..\..\..\Objects\bin\Release\Objects.dll")
    obj = dll.CreateInstance("Objects.External")
    MsgBox(obj.DistanceTo(10, 10))
End Sub
```

Code snippet from Form1

There is a lot going on here, so let's walk through it. First, notice that you are reverting to late binding; your `obj` variable is declared as type `Object`. You will look at using reflection and multiple interfaces in a moment, but for now you will use late binding.

Next, you have declared a `dll` variable as type `Reflection.Assembly`. This variable will contain a reference to the `Objects` assembly that you will be dynamically loading through your code. Note that you are not adding a reference to this assembly via Project ⇨ Add Reference. You will dynamically access the assembly at runtime.

You then load the external assembly dynamically by using the `Assembly.LoadFrom` method:

```
dll = Assembly.LoadFrom("..\..\Objects\bin\Objects.dll")
```

This causes the reflection library to load your assembly from a file on disk at the location you specify. Once the assembly is loaded into your process, you can use the `dll` variable to interact with it, including interrogating it to get a list of the classes it contains or to create instances of those classes.

 You can also use the `AssemblyLoad` method, which scans the directory containing your application's `.exe` file (and the global assembly cache) for any EXE or DLL containing the `Objects` assembly. When it finds the assembly, it loads it into memory, making it available for your use.

You can then use the `CreateInstance` method on the assembly itself to create objects based on any class in that assembly. In this case, you are creating an object based on the `External` class:

```
obj = dll.CreateInstance("Objects.External")
```

Now you have an actual object to work with, so you can use late binding to invoke its `DistanceTo` method. At this point, your code is really no different from that in the earlier late-binding example, except that the assembly and object were created dynamically at runtime, rather than being referenced directly by your project.

Now you should be able to run the application and have it dynamically invoke the assembly at runtime.

Polymorphism via Reflection and Multiple Interfaces

You can also use both reflection and multiple interfaces together. You have seen how multiple interfaces enable you to have objects from different classes implement the same interface and thus be treated identically. You have also seen how reflection enables you to load an assembly and class dynamically at runtime.

You can combine these concepts by using an interface shared in common between your main application and your external assembly, using reflection to load that external assembly dynamically at runtime.

First, create the interface that will be shared across both application and assembly. To do so, add a new Class Library project to your solution named "Interfaces" by selecting File ⇨ Add ⇨ New Project. Once it is created, drag and drop the `Interfaces.vb` module from your original application into the new project (hold down the Shift key as you move it). This makes the `IShared` interface part of that project and no longer part of your base application.

Of course, your base application still uses `IShared`, so you want to reference the Interfaces project from your application to gain access to the interface. Do this by right-clicking your OOExample project in the Solution Explorer window and selecting Add Reference. Then add the reference, as shown in Figure 3-15.

Because the `IShared` interface is now part of a separate assembly, add an `Imports` statement to Form1, Encapsulation, and `Poly` so that they are able to locate the `IShared` interface:

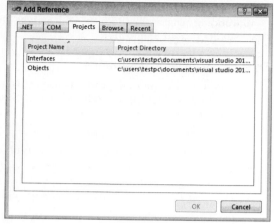

FIGURE 3-15

```
Imports Interfaces
```

Be sure to add this to the top of all three code modules. You also need to have the Objects project reference Interfaces, so right-click Objects in the Solution Explorer and choose Add Reference there as well. Add the reference to Interfaces and click OK. At this point, both the original application and the external assembly have access to the `IShared` interface. You can now enhance the code in Objects by changing the `External` class:

Available for
download on
Wrox.com

```
Imports Interfaces
Public Class External
  Implements IShared
  Public Function DistanceTo(ByVal x As Single, ByVal y As Single) _
      As Single Implements IShared.CalculateDistance
    Return x * y
  End Function
End Class
```

Code snippet from Interfaces

With both the main application and the external assembly using the same data type, you are ready to implement the polymorphic behavior using reflection.

Remove the `Option Strict Off` code from Form1. Bring up the code window for Form1 and change the code behind the button to take advantage of the `IShared` interface:

Available for
download on
Wrox.com

```
Private Sub btnReflection_Click(ByVal sender As System.Object, _
  ByVal e As System.EventArgs) Handles Button1.Click
  Dim obj As IShared
  Dim dll As Assembly
  dll = Assembly.LoadFrom("..\..\..\Objects\bin\Release\Objects.dll")
  obj = CType(dll.CreateInstance("Objects.External"), IShared)
  ShowDistance(obj)
End Sub
```

Code snippet from Form1

All you have done here is change the code so that you can pass your dynamically created object to the `ShowDistance` method, which you know requires a parameter of type `IShared`. Because your class implements the same `IShared` interface (from Interfaces) used by the main application, this will work perfectly. Rebuild and run the solution to see this in action.

This technique is very nice, as the code in ShowDistance is strongly typed, providing all the performance and coding benefits; but both the DLL and the object itself are loaded dynamically, providing a great deal of flexibility to your application.

Polymorphism with Inheritance

Inheritance, discussed earlier in this chapter, can also be used to enable polymorphism. The idea here is very similar to that of multiple interfaces, as a subclass can always be treated as though it were the data type of the parent class.

> *Many people consider the concepts of inheritance and polymorphism to be tightly intertwined. As you have seen, however, it is perfectly possible to use polymorphism without inheritance.*

At the moment, both your Encapsulation and Poly classes are implementing a common interface named IShared. You can use polymorphism to interact with objects of either class via that common interface. The same is true if these are child classes based on the same base class through inheritance. To see how this works, in the OOExample project, add a new class named Parent by selecting Add ➪ Class and insert the following code:

```
Public MustInherit Class Parent
    Public MustOverride Function DistanceTo(ByVal x As Single, _
        ByVal y As Single) As Single
End Class
```

As described earlier, this is an abstract base class, a class with no implementation of its own. The purpose of an abstract base class is to provide a common base from which other classes can be derived.

To implement polymorphism using inheritance, you do not need to use an abstract base class. Any base class that provides overridable methods (using either the MustOverride or Overridable keywords) will work fine, as all its subclasses are guaranteed to have that same set of methods as part of their interface, and yet the subclasses can provide custom implementation for those methods.

In this example, you are simply defining the DistanceTo method as being a method that must be overridden and implemented by any subclass of Parent. Now you can bring up the Encapsulation class and change it to be a subclass of Parent:

```
Public Class Encapsulation
    Inherits Parent
    Implements IShared
```

You do not need to stop implementing the IShared interface just because you are inheriting from Parent; inheritance and multiple interfaces coexist nicely. You do, however, have to override the DistanceTo method from the Parent class.

The Encapsulation class already has a DistanceTo method with the proper method signature, so you can simply add the Overrides keyword to indicate that this method will override the declaration in the Parent class:

```
Public Overrides Function DistanceTo(ByVal x As Single, _ByVal y As Single) _
    As Single Implements IShared.CalculateDistance
```

At this point, the Encapsulation class not only implements the common IShared interface and its own native interface, but also can be treated as though it were of type Parent, as it is a subclass of Parent. You can do the same thing to the Poly class:

```
Public Class Poly
    Inherits Parent
    Implements IShared
    Public Overrides Function DistanceTo( _
```

```
      ByVal x As Single, ByVal y As Single) _
      As Single Implements IShared.CalculateDistance
    Return x + y
  End Function
End Class
```

Finally, you can see how polymorphism works by altering the code in `Form1` to take advantage of the fact that both classes can be treated as though they were of type `Parent`. First, you can change the `ShowDistance` method to accept its parameter as type `Parent` and to call the `DistanceTo` method:

```
Private Sub ShowDistance(ByVal obj As Parent)
  MsgBox(obj.DistanceTo(10, 10))
End Sub
```

Then, you can add a new button to create an object of either type `Encapsulation` or `Poly` and pass it as a parameter to the method:

```
Private Sub btnInheritance_Click(ByVal sender As System.Object, _
  ByVal e As System.EventArgs) Handles btnInheritance.Click
  ShowDistance(New Poly)
  ShowDistance(New Encapsulation)
End Sub
```

Polymorphism Summary

Polymorphism is a very important concept in object-oriented design and programming, and Visual Basic provides you with ample techniques through which it can be implemented.

The following table summarizes the different techniques and their pros and cons, and provides some high-level guidelines about when to use each:

TECHNIQUE	PROS	CONS	GUIDELINES
Late binding	Flexible, "pure" polymorphism	Slow, hard to debug, no IntelliSense	Use to call arbitrary methods on literally any object, regardless of data type or interfaces
Multiple interfaces	Fast, easy to debug, full IntelliSense	Not totally dynamic or flexible, requires class author to implement formal interface	Use when you are creating code that interacts with clearly defined methods that can be grouped together into a formal interface
Reflection and late binding	Flexible, "pure" polymorphism, dynamically loads arbitrary assemblies from disk	Slow, hard to debug, no IntelliSense	Use to call arbitrary methods on objects when you do not know at design time which assemblies you will be using
Reflection and multiple interfaces	Fast, easy to debug, full IntelliSense, dynamically loads arbitrary assemblies from disk	Not totally dynamic or flexible, requires class author to implement formal interface	Use when you are creating code that interacts with clearly defined methods that can be grouped together into a formal interface, but when you do not know at design time which assemblies you will be using

continues

(continued)

TECHNIQUE	PROS	CONS	GUIDELINES
Inheritance	Fast, easy to debug, full IntelliSense, inherits behaviors from base class	Not totally dynamic or flexible, requires class author to inherit from common base class	Use when you are creating objects that have an *is-a* relationship, i.e., when you have subclasses that are naturally of the same data type as a base class. Polymorphism through inheritance should occur because inheritance makes sense, not because you are attempting to merely achieve polymorphism.

INHERITANCE

Inheritance is the concept that a new class can be based on an existing class, inheriting its interface and functionality. The mechanics and syntax of inheritance are described earlier in this chapter, so we won't rehash them here. However, you have not yet looked at inheritance from a practical perspective, and that is the focus of this section.

When to Use Inheritance

Inheritance is one of the most powerful object-oriented features a language can support. At the same time, inheritance is one of the most dangerous and misused object-oriented features.

Properly used, inheritance enables you to increase the maintainability, readability, and reusability of your application by offering you a clear and concise way to reuse code, via both interface and implementation. Improperly used, inheritance creates applications that are very fragile, whereby a change to a class can cause the entire application to break or require changes.

Inheritance enables you to implement an is-a relationship. In other words, it enables you to implement a new class that "is a" more specific type of its base class. Properly used, inheritance enables you to create child classes that are actually the same as the base class.

For example, you know that a duck is a bird. However, a duck can also be food, though that is not its primary identity. Proper use of inheritance enables you to create a `Bird` base class from which you can derive a `Duck` class. You would not create a `Food` class and subclass `Duck` from `Food`, as a duck isn't primarily food — it merely acts as food sometimes.

This is the challenge. Inheritance is not just a mechanism for code reuse, but a mechanism to create classes that flow naturally from another class. If you use it anywhere you want code reuse, you will end up with a real mess on your hands. If you use it anywhere you just want a common interface but where the child class is not really the same as the base class, then you should use multiple interfaces — something we'll discuss shortly.

 The question you must ask when using inheritance is whether the child class is a more specific version of the base class.

For example, you might have different types of products in your organization. All of these products have some common data and behaviors — e.g., they all have a product number, a description, and a price. However, if you have an agricultural application, you might have chemical products, seed products, fertilizer products, and retail products. These are all different — each having its own data and behaviors — and yet each one of them really is a product. You can use inheritance to create this set of products, as illustrated by the class diagram in Figure 3-16.

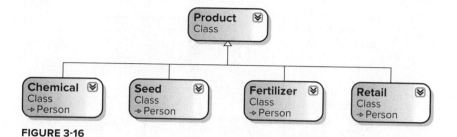

FIGURE 3-16

This diagram shows that you have an abstract base `Product` class, from which you derive the various types of product your system actually uses. This is an appropriate use of inheritance because each child class is obviously a more specific form of the general `Product` class.

Alternately, you might try to use inheritance just as a code-sharing mechanism. For example, you may look at your application, which has `Customer`, `Product`, and `SalesOrder` classes, and decide that all of them need to be designed so that they can be printed to a printer. The code to handle the printing will all be somewhat similar, so to reuse that printing code, you create a base `PrintableObject` class. This would result in the diagram shown in Figure 3-17.

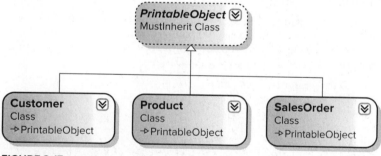

FIGURE 3-17

Intuitively, you know that this does not represent an is-a relationship. A Customer can be printed, and you are getting code reuse, but a customer is not a specific case of a printable object. Implementing a system such as this results in a fragile design and application. This is a case where multiple interfaces are a far more appropriate technology.

To illustrate this point, you might later discover that you have other entities in your organization that are similar to a customer but not quite the same. Upon further analysis, you may determine that Employee and Customer are related because they are specific cases of a `Contact` class. The `Contact` class provides commonality in terms of data and behavior across all these other classes (see Figure 3-18).

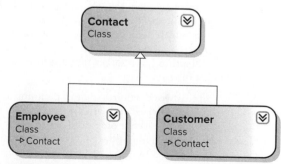

FIGURE 3-18

However, now your `Customer` is in trouble; you have said it is a `PrintableObject`, and you are now saying it is a Contact. You might be able to just derive Contact from `PrintableObject` (see Figure 3-19).

The problem with this is that now `Employee` is also of type `PrintableObject`, even if it shouldn't be, but you are stuck because, unfortunately, you decided early on to go against intuition and say that a `Customer` is a `PrintableObject`.

This problem could be solved by multiple inheritance, which would enable `Customer` to be a subclass of more than one base class — in this case, of both `Contact` and `PrintableObject`. However, the .NET platform and Visual Basic do not support multiple inheritance in this way. An alternative is to use inheritance for the is-a relationship with Contact, and use multiple interfaces to enable the `Customer` object to act as a `PrintableObject` by implementing an `IPrintableObject` interface.

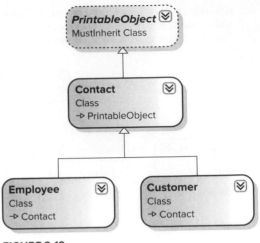

FIGURE 3-19

Application versus Framework Inheritance

What you have just seen is how inheritance can accidentally cause reuse of code where no reuse was desired, but you can take a different view of this model by separating the concept of a framework from your actual application. The way you use inheritance in the design of a framework is somewhat different from how you use inheritance in the design of an actual application.

In this context, the word framework is being used to refer to a set of classes that provide base functionality that isn't specific to an application, but rather may be used across a number of applications within the organization, or perhaps even beyond the organization. The .NET Framework base class library is an example of a very broad framework you use when building your applications.

The `PrintableObject` class discussed earlier, for example, may have little to do with your specific application, but may be the type of thing that is used across many applications. If so, it is a natural candidate for use as part of a framework, rather than being considered part of your actual application.

Framework classes exist at a lower level than application classes. For example, the .NET base-class library is a framework on which all .NET applications are built. You can layer your own framework on top of the .NET Framework as well (see Figure 3-20).

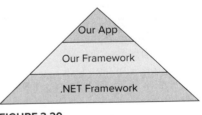

FIGURE 3-20

If you take this view, then the `PrintableObject` class wouldn't be part of your application at all, but part of a framework on which your application is built. If so, then the fact that `Customer` is not a specific case of `PrintableObject` does not matter as much, as you are not saying that it is such a thing, but rather that it is leveraging that portion of the framework's functionality.

To make all this work requires a lot of planning and forethought in the design of the framework itself. To see the dangers you face, consider that you might want to not only print objects, but also store them in a file. In that case, you might have not only `PrintableObject`, but also `SavableObject` as a base class.

The question is, what do you do if `Customer` should be both printable and savable? If all printable objects are savable, you might have the result shown in Figure 3-21.

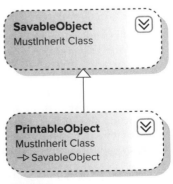

FIGURE 3-21

Alternately, if all savable objects are printable, you might have the result shown in Figure 3-22. However, neither of these truly provides a decent solution, as it is likely that the concept of being printable and the concept of being savable are different and not interrelated in either of these ways.

When faced with this sort of issue, it is best to avoid using inheritance and instead rely on multiple interfaces.

Inheritance and Multiple Interfaces

While inheritance is powerful, it is really geared for implementing the is-a relationship. Sometimes you will have objects that need a common interface, even though they are not really a specific case of some base class that provides that interface. We've just explored that issue in the discussion of the `PrintableObject`, `SavableObject`, and `Customer` classes.

Sometimes multiple interfaces are a better alternative than inheritance. The syntax for creating and using secondary and multiple interfaces was discussed.

Multiple interfaces can be viewed as another way to implement the is-a relationship, although it is often better to view inheritance as an is-a relationship and to view multiple interfaces as a way of implementing an act-as relationship.

Considering this further, we can say that the `PrintableObject` concept could perhaps be better expressed as an interface — `IPrintableObject`.

When the class implements a secondary interface such as `IPrintableObject`, you are not really saying that your class is a printable object, you are saying that it can "act as" a printable object. A Customer is a Contact, but at the same time it can act as a printable object. This is illustrated in Figure 3-23.

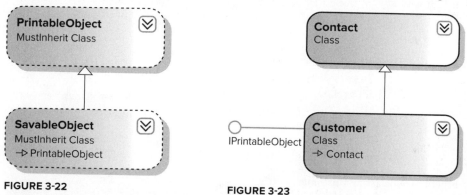

FIGURE 3-22   **FIGURE 3-23**

The drawback to this approach is that you have no inherited implementation when you implement `IPrintable Object`. Earlier you saw how to reuse common code as you implement an interface across multiple classes. While not as automatic or easy as inheritance, it is possible to reuse implementation code with a bit of extra work.

Applying Inheritance and Multiple Interfaces

Perhaps the best way to see how inheritance and multiple interfaces interact is to look at an example. Returning to the original OOExample project, the following example combines inheritance and multiple interfaces to create an object that has both an is-a and act-as relationship at the same time. As an additional benefit, you will be using the .NET Framework's capability to print to a printer, or the Print Preview dialog.

Creating the Contact Base Class

You already have a simple `Customer` class in the project, so now add a `Contact` base class. Choose Project ➪ Add Class and add a class named Contact:

```
Public MustInherit Class Contact
   Private mID As Guid = Guid.NewGuid
   Private mName As String
```

```
Public Property ID() As Guid
  Get
    Return mID
  End Get
  Set(ByVal value As Guid)
    mID = value
  End Set
End Property
Public Property Name() As String
  Get
    Return mName
  End Get
  Set(ByVal value As String)
    mName = value
  End Set
End Property
End Class
```

Code snippet from Contact

Subclassing Contact

Now you can make the `Customer` class inherit from this base class because it is a Contact. In addition, because your base class now implements both the `ID` and `Name` properties, you can simplify the code in `Customer` by removing those properties and their related variables:

Available for download on Wrox.com

```
Public Class Customer
  Inherits Contact
  Private mPhone As String
  Public Property Phone() As String
    Get
      Return mPhone
    End Get
    Set(ByVal value As String)
      mPhone = value
    End Set
  End Property
End Class
```

Code snippet from Customer

This shows the benefit of subclassing Customer from Contact, as you are now sharing the ID and Name code across all other types of Contact as well.

Implementing IPrintableObject

You also know that a Customer should be able to act as a printable object. To do this in such a way that the implementation is reusable requires a bit of thought. First, though, you need to define the `IPrintableObject` interface.

You will use the standard printing mechanism provided by .NET from the `System.Drawing` namespace. As shown in Figure 3-24, add a reference to `System.Drawing.dll` to the Interfaces project by selecting Project ➪ Add reference.

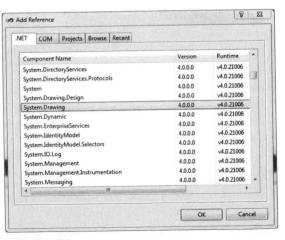

FIGURE 3-24

With that done, bring up the code window for `Interfaces.vb` in the Interfaces project and add the following code:

```
Imports System.Drawing
Public Interface IPrintableObject
    Sub Print()
    Sub PrintPreview()
    Sub RenderPage(ByVal sender As Object, _
        ByVal ev As System.Drawing.Printing.PrintPageEventArgs)
End Interface
```

Code snippet from Interfaces

This interface ensures that any object implementing `IPrintableObject` will have `Print` and `PrintPreview` methods so you can invoke the appropriate type of printing. It also ensures that the object has a `RenderPage` method, which can be implemented by that object to render the object's data on the printed page.

At this point, you could simply implement all the code needed to handle printing directly within the `Customer` object. This isn't ideal, however, as some of the code will be common across any objects that want to implement `IPrintableObject`, and it would be nice to find a way to share that code.

To do this, you can create a new class, `ObjectPrinter`. This is a framework-style class, in that it has nothing to do with any particular application, but can be used across any application in which `IPrintableObject` will be used.

Add a new class named `ObjectPrinter` to the ObjectAndComponents project by selecting Project ➪ Add class. This class will contain all the code common to printing any object. It makes use of the built-in printing support provided by the .NET Framework class library. To use this, you need to import a couple of namespaces, so add the following code to the new class:

```
Imports System.Drawing
Imports System.Drawing.Printing
Imports Interfaces
```

You can then define a `PrintDocument` variable, which will hold the reference to your printer output. You will also declare a variable to hold a reference to the actual object you will be printing. Notice that you are using the `IPrintableObject` interface data type for this variable:

```
Public Class ObjectPrinter
    Private WithEvents document As PrintDocument
    Private printObject As IPrintableObject
```

Now you can create a routine to kick off the printing process for any object implementing `IPrintableObject`. This code is totally generic; you will write it in the `ObjectPrinter` class so it can be reused across other classes:

```
Public Sub Print(ByVal obj As IPrintableObject)
    printObject = obj
    document = New PrintDocument()
    document.Print()
End Sub
```

Code snippet from Form1

Likewise, you can implement a method to show a print preview of your object. This code is also totally generic, so add it here for reuse:

```
Public Sub PrintPreview(ByVal obj As IPrintableObject)
    Dim PPdlg As PrintPreviewDialog = New PrintPreviewDialog()
    printObject = obj
    document = New PrintDocument()
    PPdlg.Document = document
    PPdlg.ShowDialog()
End Sub
```

Code snippet from Form1

Finally, you need to catch the `PrintPage` event that is automatically raised by the .NET printing mechanism. This event is raised by the `PrintDocument` object whenever the document determines that it needs data rendered onto a page. Typically, it is in this routine that you would put the code to draw text or graphics onto the page surface. However, because this is a generic framework class, you won't do that here; instead, delegate the call back into the actual application object that you want to print:

```
Private Sub PrintPage(ByVal sender As Object, _
    ByVal ev As System.Drawing.Printing.PrintPageEventArgs) _
    Handles document.PrintPage
  printObject.RenderPage(sender, ev)
End Sub
```

Code snippet from Form1

This enables the application object itself to determine how its data should be rendered onto the output page. You can see how to do that by implementing the `IPrintableObject` interface on the `Customer` class:

```
Imports Interfaces
Public Class Customer
  Inherits Contact
  Implements IPrintableObject
```

Code snippet from Interfaces

By adding this code, you require that your `Customer` class implement the `Print`, `PrintPreview`, and `RenderPage` methods. To avoid wasting paper as you test the code, make both the `Print` and `PrintPreview` methods the same and have them just do a print preview display, add this code to the `Customer` class:

```
Public Sub Print() _
    Implements Interfaces.IPrintableObject.Print
  Dim printer As New ObjectPrinter()
  printer.PrintPreview(Me)
End Sub
```

Code snippet from Customer

Notice that you are using an `ObjectPrinter` object to handle the common details of doing a print preview. In fact, any class you ever create that implements `IPrintableObject` will have this exact same code to implement a print-preview function, relying on your common `ObjectPrinter` to take care of the details.

You also need to implement the `RenderPage` method, which is where you actually put your object's data onto the printed page:

```
Private Sub RenderPage(ByVal sender As Object, _
    ByVal ev As System.Drawing.Printing.PrintPageEventArgs) _
    Implements IPrintableObject.RenderPage
  Dim printFont As New Font("Arial", 10)
  Dim lineHeight As Single = printFont.GetHeight(ev.Graphics)
  Dim leftMargin As Single = ev.MarginBounds.Left
  Dim yPos As Single = ev.MarginBounds.Top
  ev.Graphics.DrawString("ID: " & ID.ToString, printFont, Brushes.Black, _
    leftMargin, yPos, New StringFormat())
  yPos += lineHeight
  ev.Graphics.DrawString("Name: " & Name, printFont, Brushes.Black, _
    leftMargin, yPos, New StringFormat())
  ev.HasMorePages = False
End Sub
```

Code snippet from Customer

All of this code is unique to your object, which makes sense because you are rendering your specific data to be printed. However, you don't need to worry about the details of whether you are printing to paper or print preview; that is handled by your `ObjectPrinter` class, which in turn uses the .NET Framework. This enables you to focus on generating the output to the page within your application class.

By generalizing the printing code in `ObjectPrinter`, you have achieved a level of reuse that you can tap into via the `IPrintableObject` interface. Anytime you want to print a `Customer` object's data, you can have it act as an `IPrintableObject` and call its `Print` or `PrintPreview` method. To see this work, add a new button control to `Form1` with the following code:

Available for download on Wrox.com

```
Private Sub btnPrint_Click(ByVal sender As System.Object, _
    ByVal e As System.EventArgs) Handles btnPrint.Click
    Dim obj As New Customer
    obj.Name = "Douglas Adams"
    CType(obj, IPrintableObject).PrintPreview()
End Sub
```

Code snippet from Form1

This code creates a new `Customer` object and sets its `Name` property. You then use the `CType` method to access the object via its `IPrintableObject` interface to invoke the `PrintPreview` method.

When you run the application and click the button, you will get a print preview display showing the object's data (see Figure 3-25).

ID: bcb4dcbe-9760-42f6-88c2-c52f210c4a0c
Name: Douglas Adams

FIGURE 3-25

How Deep to Go?

Most of the examples discussed so far have illustrated how you can create a child class based on a single parent class. That is called *single-level inheritance*. In fact, inheritance can be many levels deep. For example, you might have a deep hierarchy such as the one shown in Figure 3-26.

From the root of `System.Object` down to `NAFTACustomer` you have four levels of inheritance. This can be described as a four-level inheritance chain.

There is no hard-and-fast rule about how deep inheritance chains should go, but conventional wisdom and general experience with inheritance in other languages such as Smalltalk and C++ indicate that the deeper an inheritance chain becomes, the harder it is to maintain an application.

This happens for two reasons. First is the fragile base class or fragile superclass issue, discussed shortly. The second reason is that a deep inheritance hierarchy tends to seriously reduce the readability of your code by scattering the code for an object across many different classes, all of which are combined by the compiler to create your object.

One of the reasons for adopting object-oriented design and programming is to avoid so-called *spaghetti code*, whereby any bit of code you might look at does almost nothing useful but instead calls various other procedures and routines in other

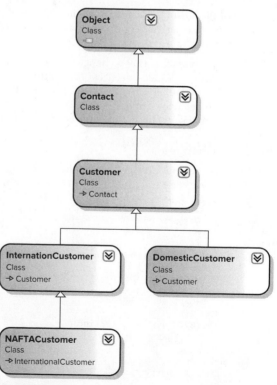

FIGURE 3-26

parts of your application. To determine what is going on with spaghetti code, you must trace through many routines and mentally piece together what it all means.

Object-oriented programming can help you avoid this problem, but it is most definitely not a magic bullet. In fact, when you create deep inheritance hierarchies, you are often creating spaghetti code because each level in the hierarchy not only extends the previous level's interface, but almost always also adds functionality. Thus, when you look at the final NAFTACustomer class, it may have very little code. To figure out what it does or how it behaves, you have to trace through the code in the previous four levels of classes, and you might not even have the code for some of those classes, as they might come from other applications or class libraries you have purchased.

On the one hand, you have the benefit of reusing code; but on the other hand, you have the drawback that the code for one object is actually scattered through five different classes. Keep this in mind when designing systems with inheritance — use as few levels in the hierarchy as possible to provide the required functionality.

The Fragile-Base-Class Problem

You have explored where it is appropriate to use inheritance and where it is not. You have also explored how you can use inheritance and multiple interfaces in conjunction to implement both is-a and act-as relationships simultaneously within your classes.

Earlier, we noted that while inheritance is an incredibly powerful and useful concept, it can also be very dangerous if used improperly. You have seen some of this danger in the discussion of the misapplication of the is-a relationship, and how you can use multiple interfaces to avoid those issues.

One of the most classic and common problems with inheritance is the fragile base-class problem. This problem is exacerbated when you have very deep inheritance hierarchies, but it exists even in a single-level inheritance chain.

The issue you face is that a change in the base class always affects all child classes derived from that base class. This is a double-edged sword. On the one hand, you get the benefit of being able to change code in one location and have that change automatically cascade through all derived classes. On the other hand, a change in behavior can have unintended or unexpected consequences farther down the inheritance chain, which can make your application very fragile and hard to change or maintain.

Interface Changes

There are obvious changes you might make, which require immediate attention. For example, you might change your Contact class to have FirstName and LastName instead of simply Name as a property. In the Contact class, replace the mName variable declaration with the following code:

```
Private mFirstName As String
Private mLastName As String
```

Now replace the Name property with the following code:

```
Public Property FirstName() As String
  Get
    Return mFirstName
  End Get
  Set(ByVal value As String)
    mFirstName = value
  End Set
End Property
Public Property LastName() As String
  Get
    Return mLastName
  End Get
  Set(ByVal value As String)
```

```
        mLastName = value
      End Set
  End Property
```

At this point, the Errors window in the IDE will display a list of locations where you need to alter your code to compensate for the change. This is a graphic illustration of a base-class change that causes cascading changes throughout your application. In this case, you have changed the base-class interface, thus changing the interface of all subclasses in the inheritance chain.

To avoid having to fix code throughout your application, always strive to keep as much consistency in your base class interface as possible. In this case, you can implement a read-only Name property that returns the full name of the Contact:

```
Public ReadOnly Property Name() As String
  Get
     Return mFirstName & " " & mLastName
  End Get
End Property
```

This resolves most of the items in the Errors window. You can fix any remaining issues by using the FirstName and LastName properties. For example, in Form1 you can change the code behind your button to the following:

```
Private Sub Button1_Click(ByVal sender As System.Object, _
    ByVal e As System.EventArgs) Handles button1.Click
  Dim obj As New Customer
  obj.FirstName = "Douglas"
  obj.LastName = "Adams"
  CType(obj, Interfaces.IPrintableObject).Print()
End Sub
```

Any change to a base class interface is likely to cause problems, so think carefully before making such a change.

Implementation Changes

Unfortunately, there is another, more subtle type of change that can wreak more havoc on your application: an implementation change. This is the core of the fragile-base-class problem.

Encapsulation provides you with a separation of interface from implementation. However, keeping your interface consistent is merely a syntactic concept. If you change the implementation, you are making a semantic change, a change that does not alter any of your syntax but can have serious ramifications on the real behavior of the application.

In theory, you can change the implementation of a class, and as long as you do not change its interface, any client applications using objects based on that class will continue to operate without change. Of course, reality is never as nice as theory, and more often than not a change to the implementation will have some consequences on the behavior of a client application.

For example, you might use a SortedList to sort and display some Customer objects. To do this, add a new button to Form1 with the following code:

```
Private Sub btnSort_Click(ByVal sender As System.Object, _
  ByVal e As System.EventArgs) Handles btnSort.Click
  Dim col As New Generic.SortedDictionary(Of String, Customer)
  Dim obj As Customer
```

```
    obj = New Customer()
    obj.FirstName = "Douglas"
    obj.LastName = "Adams"
    col.Add(obj.Name, obj)
    obj = New Customer()
    obj.FirstName = "Andre"
    obj.LastName = "Norton"
    col.Add(obj.Name, obj)
    Dim item As Generic.KeyValuePair(Of String, Customer)
    Dim sb As New System.Text.StringBuilder
    For Each item In col
      sb.AppendLine(item.Value.Name)
    Next
    MsgBox(sb.ToString)
End Sub
```

Code snippet from Form1

This code simply creates a couple of `Customer` objects, sets their `FirstName` and `LastName` properties, and inserts them into a generic `SortedDictionary` object from the `System.Collections.Generic` namespace.

Items in a `SortedDictionary` are sorted based on their key value, and you are using the `Name` property to provide that key, meaning that your entries will be sorted by name. Because your `Name` property is implemented to return first name first and last name second, your entries will be sorted by first name.

If you run the application, the dialog will display the following:

```
Andre Norton
Douglas Adams
```

However, you can change the implementation of your `Contact` class — not directly changing or affecting either the `Customer` class or your code in `Form1` — to return last name first and first name second, as shown here:

Available for download on Wrox.com

```
Public ReadOnly Property Name() As String
   Get
      Return mLastName & ", " & mFirstName
   End Get
End Property
```

Code snippet from Customer

While no other code requires changing, and no syntax errors are flagged, the behavior of the application is changed. When you run it, the output will now be as follows:

```
Adams, Douglas
Norton, Andre
```

Maybe this change is inconsequential. Maybe it totally breaks the required behavior of your form. The developer making the change in the `Contact` class might not even know that someone was using that property for sort criteria.

This illustrates how dangerous inheritance can be. Changes to implementation in a base class can cascade to countless other classes in countless applications, having unforeseen side effects and consequences of which the base-class developer is totally unaware.

SUMMARY

This chapter demonstrated how Visual Basic enables you to create and work with classes and objects. Visual Basic provides the building blocks for abstraction, encapsulation, polymorphism, and inheritance.

You have learned how to create both simple base classes as well as abstract base classes. You have also explored how you can define formal interfaces, a concept quite similar to an abstract base class in many ways.

You also walked through the process of subclassing, creating a new class that derives both interface and implementation from a base class. The subclass can be extended by adding new methods or altering the behavior of existing methods on the base class.

By the end of this chapter, you have seen how object-oriented programming flows from the four basic concepts of abstraction, encapsulation, polymorphism, and inheritance. The chapter provided basic information about each concept and demonstrated how to implement them using Visual Basic.

By properly applying object-oriented design and programming, you can create very large and complex applications that remain maintainable and readable over time. Nonetheless, these technologies are not a magic bullet. Improperly applied, they can create the same hard-to-maintain code that you might create using procedural or modular design techniques.

It is not possible to fully cover all aspects of object-oriented programming in a single chapter. Before launching into a full-blown object-oriented project, we highly recommend looking at other books specifically geared toward object-oriented design and programming.

The Common Language Runtime

WHAT YOU WILL LEARN IN THIS CHAPTER

➤ Elements of a .NET Application

➤ Versioning and Deployment

➤ Understanding the Common Language Runtime

➤ IL Disassembler

➤ Memory Management

➤ Namespaces

➤ The My Keyword

You've learned how to create simple applications and looked at how to create classes. Now it's time not only to start tying these elements together, but also to learn how to dispose of some of the classes that you have created. The architects of .NET realized that all procedural languages require certain base functionality. For example, many languages ship with their own runtime that provides features such as memory management, but what if, instead of each language shipping with its own runtime implementation, all languages used a common runtime? This would provide languages with a standard environment and access to all of the same features. This is exactly what the common language runtime (CLR) provides.

The CLR manages the execution of code on the .NET platform. .NET provided Visual Basic developers with better support for many advanced features, including operator overloading, implementation inheritance, threading, and the ability to marshal objects. Building such features into a language is not trivial. The CLR enabled Microsoft to concentrate on building this plumbing one time and then reuse it across different programming languages. Because the CLR supports these features and because Visual Basic is built on top of the CLR, Visual Basic can use these features. As a result, going forward, Visual Basic is the equal of every other .NET language, with the CLR eliminating many of the shortcomings of the previous versions of Visual Basic.

Visual Basic developers can view the CLR as a better Visual Basic runtime. However, this runtime, unlike the old standalone Visual Basic runtime, is common across all of .NET regardless of the underlying operating system. Thus, the functionality exposed by the CLR is available to all .NET languages; more important, all of the features available to other .NET languages via the CLR are available to Visual Basic developers. Additionally, as long as you develop using managed code — code that runs in the CLR — you'll find that it doesn't matter whether your application is installed on a Windows XP client, a Vista client, or a Windows 7 client; your application will run. The CLR provides an abstraction layer separate from the details of the operating system.

This chapter gets down into the belly of the application runtime environment — not to examine how .NET enables this abstraction from the operating system, but instead to look at some specific features related to how you build applications that run against the CLR. This includes an introduction to several basic elements of working with applications that run in the CLR, including the following:

➤ Elements of a .NET application

➤ Versioning and deployment

➤ Integration across .NET languages

➤ Microsoft intermediate language (MSIL)

➤ Memory management and the garbage collector (GC)

ELEMENTS OF A .NET APPLICATION

A .NET application is composed of four primary entities:

➤ **Classes** — The basic units that encapsulate data and behavior

➤ **Modules** — The individual files that contain the intermediate language (IL) for an assembly

➤ **Assemblies** — The primary unit of deployment of a .NET application

➤ **Types** — The common unit of transmitting data between modules

Classes, covered in the preceding two chapters, are defined in the source files for your application or class library. Upon compilation of your source files, you produce a module. The code that makes up an assembly's modules may exist in a single executable (.exe) file or as a dynamic link library (.dll). A module, is in fact, a Microsoft intermediate language (MSIL) file, which is then used by the CLR when your application is run. However, compiling a .NET application doesn't produce only an MSIL file; it also produces a collection of files that make up a deployable application or assembly. Within an assembly are several different types of files, including not only the actual executable files, but also configuration files, signature keys, and, most important of all, the actual code modules.

Modules

A module contains Microsoft intermediate language (MSIL, often abbreviated to IL) code, associated metadata, and the assembly's manifest. By default, the Visual Basic compiler creates an assembly that is composed of a single module containing both the assembly code and the manifest.

IL is a platform-independent way of representing managed code within a module. Before IL can be executed, the CLR must compile it into the native machine code. The default method is for the CLR to use the JIT (just-in-time) compiler to compile the IL on a method-by-method basis. At runtime, as each method is called by an application for the first time, it is passed through the JIT compiler for compilation to machine code. Similarly, for an ASP.NET application, each page is passed through the JIT compiler the first time it is requested, to create an in-memory representation of the machine code that represents that page.

Additional information about the types declared in the IL is provided by the associated metadata. The metadata contained within the module is used extensively by the CLR. For example, if a client and an object reside within two different processes, then the CLR uses the type's metadata to marshal data between the client and the object. MSIL is important because every .NET language compiles down to IL. The CLR doesn't care about or even need to know what the implementation language was; it knows only what the IL contains. Thus, any differences in .NET languages exist at the level where the IL is generated; but once generated, all .NET languages have the same runtime characteristics. Similarly, because the CLR doesn't care in which language a given module was originally written, it can leverage modules implemented in entirely different .NET languages.

A question that always arises when discussing the JIT compiler and the use of a runtime environment is "Wouldn't it be faster to compile the IL language down to native code before the user asks to run it?" Although the answer is not always yes, Microsoft has provided a utility to handle this compilation: the Native Image Generator, or `Ngen.exe`. This tool enables you to essentially run the JIT compiler on a specific assembly, which is then installed into the user's application cache in its native format. The obvious advantage is that now when the user asks to execute something in that assembly, the JIT compiler is not invoked, saving a small amount of time. However, unlike the JIT compiler, which compiles only those portions of an assembly that are actually referenced, `Ngen.exe` needs to compile the entire code base, so the time required for compilation is not the same as what a user actually experiences.

`Ngen.exe` is executed from the command line. The utility was updated as part of .NET 2.0 and now automatically detects and includes most of the dependent assemblies as part of the image-generation process. To use `Ngen.exe`, you simply reference this utility followed by an action; for example, `install` followed by your assembly reference. Several options are available as part of the generation process, but that subject is beyond the scope of this chapter, given that `Ngen.exe` itself is a topic that generates heated debate regarding its use and value.

Where does the debate begin about when to use `Ngen.exe`? Keep in mind that in a server application, where the same assembly will be referenced by multiple users between machine restarts, the difference in performance on the first request is essentially lost. This means that compilation to native code is more valuable to client-side applications. Unfortunately, using `Ngen.exe` requires running it on each client machine, which can become cost prohibitive in certain installation scenarios, particularly if you use any form of self-updating application logic.

Another issue relates to using reflection, which enables you to reference other assemblies at runtime. Of course, if you don't know what assemblies you will reference until runtime, then the Native Image Generator has a problem, as it won't know what to reference either. You may have occasion to use `Ngen.exe` for an application you've created, but you should fully investigate this utility and its advantages and disadvantages beforehand, keeping in mind that even native images execute within the CLR. Native image generation only changes the compilation model, not the runtime environment.

Assemblies

An assembly is the primary unit of deployment for .NET applications. It is either a dynamic link library (`.dll`) or an executable (`.exe`). An assembly is composed of a manifest, one or more modules, and (optionally) other files, such as `.config`, `.ASPX`, `.ASMX`, images, and so on.

The manifest of an assembly contains the following:

➤ Information about the identity of the assembly, including its textual name and version number.

➤ If the assembly is public, then the manifest contains the assembly's public key. The public key is used to help ensure that types exposed by the assembly reside within a unique namespace. It may also be used to uniquely identify the source of an assembly.

➤ A declarative security request that describes the assembly's security requirements (the assembly is responsible for declaring the security it requires). Requests for permissions fall into three categories: required, optional, and denied. The identity information may be used as evidence by the CLR in determining whether or not to approve security requests.

➤ A list of other assemblies on which the assembly depends. The CLR uses this information to locate an appropriate version of the required assemblies at runtime. The list of dependencies also includes the exact version number of each assembly at the time the assembly was created.

➤ A list of all types and resources exposed by the assembly. If any of the resources exposed by the assembly are localized, the manifest will also contain the default culture (language, currency, date/time format, and so on) that the application will target. The CLR uses this information to locate specific resources and types within the assembly.

The manifest can be stored in a separate file or in one of the modules. By default, for most applications, it is part of the .dll or .exe file, which is compiled by Visual Studio. For Web applications, you will find that although there is a collection of ASPX pages, the actual assembly information is located in a DLL referenced by those ASPX pages.

Types

The type system provides a template that is used to describe the encapsulation of data and an associated set of behaviors. It is this common template for describing data that provides the basis for the metadata that .NET uses when applications interoperate. There are two kinds of types: reference and value. The differences between these two types are discussed in Chapter 1.

Unlike COM, which is scoped at the machine level, types are scoped at either the global level or the assembly level. All types are based on a common system that is used across all .NET languages. Similar to the MSIL code, which is interpreted by the CLR based upon the current runtime environment, the CLR uses a common metadata system to recognize the details of each type. The result is that all .NET languages are built around a common type system, unlike the different implementations of COM, which require special notation to enable translation of different data types between different .exe and .dll files.

A type has fields, properties, and methods:

> **Fields** — Variables that are scoped to the type. For example, a Pet class could declare a field called Name that holds the pet's name. In a well-engineered class, fields are often kept private and exposed only as properties or methods.

> **Properties** — Properties look like fields to clients of the type but can have code behind them (which usually performs some sort of data validation). For example, a Dog data type could expose a property to set its gender. Code could then be placed behind the property so that it could be set only to "male" or "female," and then this property could be saved internally to one of the fields in the Dog class.

> **Methods** — Methods define behaviors exhibited by the type. For example, the Dog data type could expose a method called Sleep, which would suspend the activity of the Dog.

The preceding elements make up each application. Note that some types are defined at the application level, and others are defined globally. Under COM, all components are registered globally; and certainly if you want to expose a .NET component to COM, you must register it globally. However, with .NET it is not only possible but often encouraged that the classes and types defined in your modules be visible only at the application level. The advantage of this is that you can run several different versions of an application side by side. Of course, once you have an application that can be versioned, the next challenge is knowing which version of that application you have.

VERSIONING AND DEPLOYMENT

Components and their clients are often installed at different times by different vendors. For example, a Visual Basic application might rely on a third-party grid control to display data. Runtime support for versioning is crucial for ensuring that an incompatible version of the grid control does not cause problems for the Visual Basic application.

In addition to this issue of compatibility, deploying applications written in previous versions of Visual Basic was problematic. Fortunately, .NET provides major improvements over the versioning and deployment offered by COM and the previous versions of Visual Basic before .NET.

Better Support for Versioning

Managing component versions was challenging in previous versions of Visual Basic. The version number of the component could be set, but this version number was not used by the runtime. COM components are often referenced by their ProgID, but Visual Basic does not provide any support for appending the version number on the end of the ProgID.

For those of you who are unfamiliar with the term *ProgID*, it's enough to understand that ProgIDs are developer-friendly strings used to identify a component. For example, `Word.Application` describes Microsoft Word. ProgIDs can be fully qualified with the targeted version of the component — for example, `Word.Application.10` — but this is a limited capability and relies on both the application and whether the person using it chooses this optional addendum. As you'll see in Chapter 7, a namespace is built on the basic elements of a ProgID, but provides a more robust naming system.

For many applications, .NET has removed the need to identify the version of each assembly in a central registry on a machine. However, some assemblies are installed once and used by multiple applications. .NET provides a global assembly cache (GAC), which is used to store assemblies that are intended for use by multiple applications. The CLR provides versioning support for all components loaded in the GAC.

The CLR provides two features for assemblies installed within the GAC:

➤ **Side-by-side versioning** — Multiple versions of the same component can be simultaneously stored in the GAC.

➤ **Automatic Quick Fix Engineering (QFE)** — Also known as hotfix support, if a new version of a component, which is still compatible with the old version, is available in the GAC, the CLR loads the updated component. The version number, which is maintained by the developer who created the referenced assembly, drives this behavior.

The assembly's manifest contains the version numbers of referenced assemblies. The CLR uses the assembly's manifest at runtime to locate a compatible version of each referenced assembly. The version number of an assembly takes the following form:

```
Major.Minor.Build.Revision
```

Major.Minor.Build.Revision

Changes to the major and minor version numbers of the assembly indicate that the assembly is no longer compatible with the previous versions. The CLR will not use versions of the assembly that have a different major or minor number unless it is explicitly told to do so. For example, if an assembly was originally compiled against a referenced assembly with a version number of 3.4.1.9, then the CLR will not load an assembly stored in the GAC unless it has major and minor numbers of 3 and 4, respectively.

Incrementing the revision and build numbers indicates that the new version is still compatible with the previous version. If a new assembly that has an incremented revision or build number is loaded into the GAC, then the CLR can still load this assembly for applications that were compiled referencing a previous version.

Better Deployment

Applications written using previous versions of Visual Basic and COM were often complicated to deploy. Components referenced by the application needed to be installed and registered (this information was stored in the registry); and for Visual Basic components, the correct version of the Visual Basic runtime needed to be available. The Component Deployment tool helped in the creation of complex installation packages, but applications could be easily broken if the dependent components were inadvertently replaced by incompatible versions on the client's computer during the installation of an unrelated product.

In .NET, most components do not need to be registered. When an external assembly is referenced, the application decides between using a global copy (which must be in the GAC on the developer's system) or copying a component locally. For most references, the external assemblies are referenced locally, which means they are carried in the application's local directory structure. Using local copies of external assemblies enables the CLR to support the side-by-side execution of different versions of the same component. As noted earlier, to reference a globally registered assembly, that assembly must be located in the GAC. The GAC provides a versioning system that is robust enough to allow different versions of the same external assembly to exist side by side. For example, an application could use a newer version of ADO.NET without adversely affecting another application that relies on a previous version.

As long as the client has the .NET runtime installed (which only has to be done once), a .NET application can be distributed using a simple command like this:

```
xcopy \\server\appDirectory "C:\Program Files\appDirectory" /E /O /I
```

The preceding command would copy all of the files and subdirectories from `\\server\appDirectory` to `C:\Program Files\appDirectory` and would transfer the file's access control lists (ACLs).

Besides the capability to copy applications, Visual Studio provides a built-in tool for constructing simple `.msi` installations. The deployment settings can be customized for your project solution, enabling you to integrate the deployment project with your application output. Additionally, Visual Studio 2005 introduced the capability to create a "ClickOnce" deployment.

ClickOnce deployment provided an entirely new method of deployment, referred to as *smart-client deployment*. In the smart-client model, your application is placed on a central server from which the clients access the application files. Smart-client deployment builds on the XML Web Services architecture about which you are learning. It has the advantages of central application maintenance combined with a richer client interface and fewer server communication requirements, all of which you have become familiar with in Windows Forms applications.

CROSS-LANGUAGE INTEGRATION

Prior to .NET, interoperating with code written in other languages was challenging. There were pretty much two options for reusing functionality developed in other languages: COM interfaces or DLLs with exported C functions. As for exposing functionality written in Visual Basic, the only option was to create COM interfaces.

Because Visual Basic is now built on top of the CLR, it's able to interoperate with the code written in other .NET languages. It's even able to derive from a class written in another language. To support this type of functionality, the CLR relies on a common way of representing types, as well as rich metadata that can describe these types.

The Common Type System

Each programming language seems to bring its own island of data types with it. For example, previous versions of Visual Basic represent strings using the basic, or binary, string (BSTR) structure, C++ offers the char and wchar data types, and MFC offers the CString class. Moreover, because the C++ int data type is a 32-bit value, whereas the Visual Basic 6 Integer data type is a 16-bit value, that makes it difficult to pass parameters between applications written using different languages.

To help resolve this problem, C has become the lowest common denominator for interfacing between programs written in multiple languages. An exported function written in C that exposes simple C data types can be consumed by Visual Basic, Java, Delphi, and a variety of other programming languages. In fact, the Windows API is exposed as a set of C functions.

Unfortunately, to access a C interface, you must explicitly map C data types to a language's native data types. For example, a Visual Basic 6 developer would use the following statement to map the GetUserNameA Win32 function (GetUserNameA is the ANSI version of the GetUserName function):

```
' Map GetUserName to the GetUserNameA exported function
' exported by advapi32.dll.
'    BOOL GetUserName(
'        LPTSTR lpBuffer, // name buffer
'        LPDWORD nSize // size of name buffer
' );
Public Declare Function GetUserName Lib "advapi32.dll" _
Alias "GetUserNameA" (ByVal strBuffer As String, nSize As Long) As Long
```

This code explicitly maps the `lpBuffer` C character array data type `LPSTR` to the Visual Basic 6 `String` parameter `strBuffer`. This is not only cumbersome, but also error prone. Accidentally mapping a variable declared as `Long` to `lpBuffer` wouldn't generate any compilation errors, but calling the function would more than likely result in difficult-to-diagnose, intermittent access violations at runtime.

COM provides a more refined method of interoperation between languages. Visual Basic 6 introduced a common type system (CTS) for all applications that supported COM — that is, variant-compatible data types. However, variant data types are as cumbersome to work with for non-Visual Basic 6 developers as the underlying C data structures that make up the variant data types (such as `BSTR` and `SAFEARRAY`) were for Visual Basic developers. The result is that interfacing between unmanaged languages is still more complicated than it needs to be.

The CTS provides a set of common data types for use across all programming languages. It provides every language running on top of the .NET platform with a base set of types, as well as mechanisms for extending those types. These types may be implemented as classes or as structs, but in either case they are derived from a common `System.Object` class definition.

Because every type supported by the CTS is derived from `System.Object`, every type supports a common set of methods, as shown in Table 4-1.

TABLE 4-1: Common Type Methods

METHOD	DESCRIPTION
`Boolean Equals(Object)`	Used to test equality with another object. Reference types should return `True` if the `Object` parameter references the same object. Value types should return `True` if the `Object` parameter has the same value.
`Int32 GetHashCode()`	Generates a number corresponding to the value of an object. If two objects of the same type are equal, then they must return the same hash code.
`Type GetType()`	Gets a `Type` object that can be used to access metadata associated with the type. It also serves as a starting point for navigating the object hierarchy exposed by the Reflection API (discussed shortly).
`String ToString()`	The default implementation returns the fully qualified name of the object's class. This method is often overridden to output data that is more meaningful to the type. For example, all base types return their value as a string.

Metadata

Metadata is the information that enables components to be self-describing. It is used to describe many aspects of a .NET component, including classes, methods, and fields, and the assembly itself. Metadata is used by the CLR to facilitate all sorts of behavior, such as validating an assembly before it is executed or performing garbage collection while managed code is being executed. Visual Basic developers have used metadata for years when developing and using components within their applications:

➤ Visual Basic developers use metadata to instruct the Visual Basic runtime how to behave. For example, you can set the `Unattended Execution` property to determine whether unhandled exceptions are shown on the screen in a message box or are written to the Event Log.

➤ COM components referenced within Visual Basic applications have accompanying type libraries that contain metadata about the components, their methods, and their properties. You can use the Object Browser to view this information. (The information contained within the type library is what is used to drive IntelliSense.)

➤ Additional metadata can be associated with a component by installing it within COM+. Metadata stored in COM+ is used to declare the support a component needs at runtime, including transactional support, serialization support, and object pooling.

Better Support for Metadata

Metadata associated with a Visual Basic 6 component was scattered in multiple locations and stored using multiple formats:

➤ Metadata instructing the Visual Basic runtime how to behave (such as the `Unattended Execution` property) is compiled into the Visual Basic–generated executable.

➤ Basic COM attributes (such as the required threading model) are stored in the registry.

➤ COM+ attributes (such as the transactional support required) are stored in the COM+ catalog.

.NET refines the use of metadata within applications in three significant ways:

➤ .NET consolidates the metadata associated with a component.

➤ Because a .NET component does not have to be registered, installing and upgrading the component is easier and less problematic.

➤ .NET makes a much clearer distinction between attributes that should only be set at compile time and those that can be modified at runtime.

 All attributes associated with Visual Basic components are represented in a common format and consolidated within the files that make up the assembly.

Because much of a COM/COM+ component's metadata is stored separately from the executable, installing and upgrading components can be problematic. COM/COM+ components must be registered to update the registry/COM+ catalog before they can be used, and the COM/COM+ component executable can be upgraded without upgrading its associated metadata.

The process of installing and upgrading a .NET component is greatly simplified. Because all metadata associated with a .NET component must reside within the file that contains the component, no registration is required. After a new component is copied into an application's directory, it can be used immediately. Because the component and its associated metadata cannot become out of sync, upgrading the component becomes much less of an issue.

Another problem with COM+ is that attributes that should only be set at compile time may be reconfigured at runtime. For example, COM+ can provide serialization support for neutral components. A component that does not require serialization must be designed to accommodate multiple requests from multiple clients simultaneously. You should know at compile time whether or not a component requires support for serialization from the runtime. However, under COM+, the attribute describing whether or not client requests should be serialized can be altered at runtime.

.NET makes a much better distinction between attributes that should be set at compile time and those that should be set at runtime. For example, whether a .NET component is serializable is determined at compile time. This setting cannot be overridden at runtime.

Attributes

Attributes are used to decorate entities such as assemblies, classes, methods, and properties with additional information. Attributes can be used for a variety of purposes. They can provide information, request a certain behavior at runtime, or even invoke a particular behavior from another application. An example of this can be demonstrated by using the `Demo` class defined in the following code block:

```
Module Module1
  <Serializable()> Public Class Demo
    <Obsolete("Use Method2 instead.")> Public Sub Method1()
      ' Old implementation …
    End Sub
    Public Sub Method2()
```

```
        ' New implementation …
      End Sub
    End Class
    Public Sub Main()
      Dim d As Demo = New Demo()
      d.Method1()
    End Sub
  End Module
```

Code snippet from ProVB_Attributes\Module1.vb

Create a new console application for Visual Basic by selecting File ⇨ New Project and selecting Windows Forms Application and then add a new class into the sample file by copying the above code into `Module1`. A best practice is to place each class in its own source file, but in order to simplify this demonstration, the class `Demo` has been defined within the main module.

The first attribute on the `Demo` class marks the class with the `Serializable` attribute. The base class library will provide serialization support for instances of the `Demo` type. For example, the `ResourceWriter` type can be used to stream an instance of the `Demo` type to disk. The second attribute is associated with `Method1`. `Method1` has been marked as obsolete, but it is still available. When a method is marked as obsolete, there are two options, one being that Visual Studio should prevent applications from compiling. However, a better strategy for large applications is to first mark a method or class as obsolete and then prevent its use in the next release. The preceding code causes Visual Studio to display an IntelliSense warning if `Method1` is referenced within the application, as shown in Figure 4-1. Not only does the line with Method1 have a visual hint of the issue, but a task has also been automatically added to the task window.

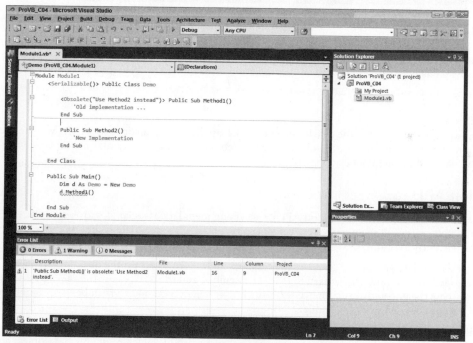

FIGURE 4-1

If the developer leaves this code unchanged and then compiles it, the application will compile correctly. As shown in Figure 4-2, the compilation is complete, but the developer receives a warning with a meaningful message that the code should be changed to use the correct method.

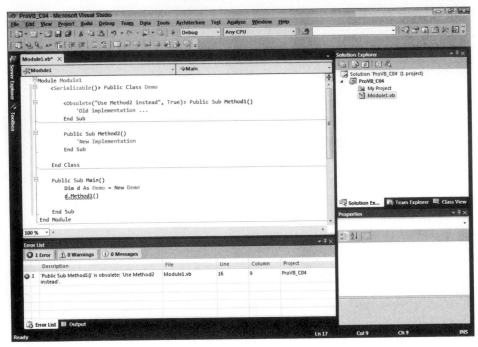

FIGURE 4-2

Sometimes you might need to associate multiple attributes with an entity. The following code shows an example of using both of the attributes from the previous code at the class level. Note that in this case the `Obsolete` attribute has been modified to cause a compilation error by setting its second parameter to `True`:

```
<Serializable(), Obsolete("No longer used.", True)> Public Class Demo
    ' Implementation …
End Class
```

Attributes play an important role in the development of .NET applications, particularly XML Web Services. As you'll see in Chapter 13, the declaration of a class as a Web service and of particular methods as Web methods are all handled through the use of attributes.

The Reflection API

The .NET Framework provides the Reflection API for accessing metadata associated with managed code. You can use the Reflection API to examine the metadata associated with an assembly and its types, and even to examine the currently executing assembly.

The `Assembly` class in the `System.Reflection` namespace can be used to access the metadata in an assembly. The `LoadFrom` method can be used to load an assembly, and the `GetExecutingAssembly` method can be used to access the currently executing assembly. The `GetTypes` method can then be used to obtain the collection of types defined in the assembly.

It's also possible to access the metadata of a type directly from an instance of that type. Because every object derives from `System.Object`, every object supports the `GetType` method, which returns a `Type` object that can be used to access the metadata associated with the type.

The `Type` object exposes many methods and properties for obtaining the metadata associated with a type. For example, you can obtain a collection of properties, methods, fields, and events exposed by the type by calling the `GetMembers` method. The `Type` object for the object's base type can also be obtained by calling the `DeclaringType` property.

A good tool that demonstrates the power of reflection is Lutz Roeder's Reflector for .NET (see www.red-gate.com/products/reflector). In addition to the core tool, you can find several add-ins related to the tool at www.codeplex.com/reflectoraddins.

IL DISASSEMBLER

One of the many handy tools that ships with Visual Studio is the IL Disassembler (ildasm.exe). It can be used to navigate the metadata within a module, including the types the module exposes, as well as their properties and methods. The IL Disassembler can also be used to display the IL contained within a module.

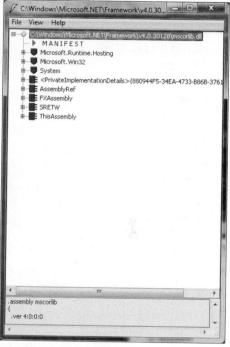

You can find the IL Disassembler under your installation directory for Visual Studio 2010; the default path is C:\ Program Files\Microsoft SDKs\Windows\v7.0A\Bin\ ILDasm.exe. Once the IL Disassembler has been started, select File ➪ Open. Open mscorlib.dll, which is located in your system directory with a default path of C:\Windows\ Microsoft.NET\Framework\V4.0.21006\mscorlib.dll. Once mscorlib.dll has been loaded, ILDasm will display a set of folders for each namespace in this assembly. Expand the System namespace, then the ValueType namespace, and finally double-click the Equals method. A window similar to the one shown in Figure 4-3 will be displayed.

Figure 4-3 shows the IL for the Equals method. Notice how the Reflection API is used to navigate through the instance of the value type's fields in order to determine whether the values of the two objects being compared are equal.

The IL Disassembler is a useful tool for learning how a particular module is implemented, but it could jeopardize your company's proprietary logic. After all, what's to prevent

FIGURE 4-3

someone from using it to reverse engineer your code? Fortunately, Visual Studio 2010, like previous versions of Visual Studio, ships with a third-party tool called an *obfuscator*. The role of the obfuscator is to ensure that the IL Disassembler cannot build a meaningful representation of your application logic.

A complete discussion of the obfuscator that ships with Visual Studio 2010 is beyond the scope of this chapter, but to access this tool, select the Tools menu and choose Dotfuscator Community Edition. The obfuscator runs against your compiled application, taking your IL file and stripping out many of the items that are embedded by default during the compilation process.

MEMORY MANAGEMENT

This section looks at one of the larger underlying elements of managed code. One of the reasons why .NET applications are referred to as "managed" is that memory deallocation is handled automatically by the system. The CLR's memory management fixes the shortcomings of COM's memory management. Developers are accustomed to worrying about memory management only in an abstract sense. The basic rule has been that every object created and every section of memory allocated needs to be released (destroyed). The CLR introduces a garbage collector (GC), which simplifies this paradigm. Gone are the days when a misbehaving component — for example, one that fails to properly dispose of its object references or allocates and never releases memory — could crash a Web server.

However, the use of a GC introduces new questions about when and if objects need to be explicitly cleaned up. There are two elements in manually writing code to allocate and deallocate memory and system resources. The first is the release of any shared resources, such as file handles and database connections. This type of activity needs to be managed explicitly and is discussed shortly. The second element of manual memory management involves letting the system know when memory is no longer in use by your application. Visual Basic COM developers, in particular, are accustomed to explicitly disposing of object references by setting variables to Nothing. While you can explicitly show your intent to destroy the object by setting it to Nothing manually, this doesn't actually free resources under .NET.

.NET uses a GC to automatically manage the cleanup of allocated memory, which means that you don't need to carry out memory management as an explicit action. Because the system is automatic, it's not up to you when resources are actually cleaned up; thus, a resource you previously used might sit in memory beyond the end of the method where you used it. Perhaps more important is the fact that the GC will at times reclaim objects in the middle of executing the code in a method. Fortunately, the system ensures that collection only happens as long as your code doesn't reference the object later in the method.

For example, you could actually end up extending the amount of time an object is kept in memory just by setting that object to Nothing. Thus, setting a variable to Nothing at the end of the method prevents the garbage collection mechanism from proactively reclaiming objects, and therefore is generally discouraged.

Given this change in paradigms, the next few sections look at the challenges of traditional memory management and peek under the covers to reveal how the garbage collector works, the basics of some of the challenges with COM-based memory management, and then a quick look at how the GC eliminates these challenges from your list of concerns. In particular, you should understand how you can interact with the garbage collector and why the Using command, for example, is recommended over a finalization method in .NET.

Traditional Garbage Collection

The unmanaged (COM/Visual Basic 6) runtime environment provides limited memory management by automatically releasing objects when they are no longer referenced by any application. Once all the references are released on an object, the runtime automatically releases the object from memory. For example, consider the following Visual Basic 6 code, which uses the Scripting.FileSystem object to write an entry to a log file:

```
' Requires a reference to Microsoft Scripting Runtime (scrrun.dll)
Sub WriteToLog(strLogEntry As String)
Dim objFSO As Scripting.FileSystemObject
Dim objTS As Scripting.TextStream
objTS = objFSO.OpenTextFile("C:\temp\AppLog.log", ForAppending)
Call objTS.WriteLine(Date & vbTab & strLogEntry)
End Sub
```

WriteToLog creates two objects, a FileSystemObject and a TextStream, which are used to create an entry in the log file. Because these are COM objects, they may live either within the current application process or in their own process. Once the routine exits, the Visual Basic runtime recognizes that they are no longer referenced by an active application and dereferences them. This results in both objects being deactivated. However, in some situations objects that are no longer referenced by an application are not properly cleaned up by the Visual Basic 6 runtime. One cause of this is the *circular reference*.

Circular References

One of the most common situations in which the unmanaged runtime is unable to ensure that objects are no longer referenced by the application is when these objects contain a circular reference. An example of a circular reference is when object A holds a reference to object B and object B holds a reference to object A.

Circular references are problematic because the unmanaged environment relies on the reference counting mechanism of COM to determine whether an object can be deactivated. Each COM object is responsible for maintaining its own reference count and for destroying itself once the reference count reaches zero. Clients of the object are responsible for updating the reference count appropriately, by calling the AddRef and

Release methods on the object's IUnknown interface. However, in this scenario, object A continues to hold a reference to object B, and vice versa, so the internal cleanup logic of these components is not triggered.

In addition, problems can occur if the clients do not properly maintain the COM object's reference count. For example, an object will never be deactivated if a client forgets to call Release when the object is no longer referenced. To avoid this, the unmanaged environment may attempt to take care of updating the reference count for you, but the object's reference count can be an invalid indicator of whether or not the object is still being used by the application. For example, consider the references that objects A and B hold.

The application can invalidate its references to A and B by setting the associated variables equal to Nothing. However, even though objects A and B are no longer referenced by the application, the Visual Basic runtime cannot ensure that the objects are deactivated because A and B still reference each other. Consider the following (Visual Basic 6) code:

```
' Class:  CCircularRef
' Reference to another object.
Dim m_objRef As Object
Public Sub Initialize(objRef As Object)
  Set m_objRef = objRef
End Sub
Private Sub Class_Terminate()
  Call MsgBox("Terminating.")
  Set m_objRef = Nothing
End Sub
```

The CCircularRef class implements an Initialize method that accepts a reference to another object and saves it as a member variable. Notice that the class does not release any existing reference in the m_objRef variable before assigning a new value. The following code demonstrates how to use this CCircularRef class to create a circular reference:

```
Dim objA As New CCircularRef
Dim objB As New CCircularRef
Call objA.Initialize(objB)
Call objB.Initialize(objA)
Set objA = Nothing
Set objB = Nothing
```

After creating two instances (objA and objB) of CCircularRef, both of which have a reference count of one, the code then calls the Initialize method on each object by passing it a reference to the other. Now each of the object's reference counts is equal to two: one held by the application and one held by the other object. Next, explicitly setting objA and objB to Nothing decrements each object's reference count by one. However, because the reference count for both instances of CCircularRef is still greater than zero, the objects are not released from memory until the application is terminated. The CLR garbage collector solves the problem of circular references because it looks for a reference from the root application or thread to every class, and all classes that do not have such a reference are marked for deletion, regardless of any other references they might still maintain.

The CLR's Garbage Collector

The .NET garbage collection mechanism is complex, and the details of its inner workings are beyond the scope of this book, but it is important to understand the principles behind its operation. The GC is responsible for collecting objects that are no longer referenced. It takes a completely different approach from that of the Visual Basic runtime to accomplish this. At certain times, and based on internal rules, a task will run through all the objects looking for those that no longer have any references from the root application thread or one of the worker threads. Those objects may then be terminated; thus, the garbage is collected.

As long as all references to an object are either implicitly or explicitly released by the application, the GC will take care of freeing the memory allocated to it. Unlike COM objects, managed objects in .NET are not responsible for maintaining their reference count, and they are not responsible for destroying themselves. Instead, the GC is responsible for cleaning up objects that are no longer referenced by the application. The

GC periodically determines which objects need to be cleaned up by leveraging the information the CLR maintains about the running application. The GC obtains a list of objects that are directly referenced by the application. Then, the GC discovers all the objects that are referenced (both directly and indirectly) by the "root" objects of the application. Once the GC has identified all the referenced objects, it is free to clean up any remaining objects.

The GC relies on references from an application to objects; thus, when it locates an object that is unreachable from any of the root objects, it can clean up that object. Any other references to that object will be from other objects that are also unreachable. Thus, the GC automatically cleans up objects that contain circular references.

In some environments, such as COM, objects are destroyed in a deterministic fashion. Once the reference count reaches zero, the object destroys itself, which means that you can tell exactly when the object will be terminated. However, with garbage collection, you can't tell exactly when an object will be destroyed. Just because you eliminate all references to an object doesn't mean that it will be terminated immediately. It just remains in memory until the garbage collection process gets around to locating and destroying it, a process called *nondeterministic finalization.*

This nondeterministic nature of CLR garbage collection provides a performance benefit. Rather than expend the effort to destroy objects as they are dereferenced, the destruction process can occur when the application is otherwise idle, often decreasing the impact on the user. Of course, if garbage collection must occur when the application is active, then the system may see a slight performance fluctuation as the collection is accomplished.

It is possible to explicitly invoke the GC by calling the `System.GC.Collect` method, but this process takes time, so it is not the sort of behavior to invoke in a typical application. For example, you could call this method each time you set an object variable to `Nothing`, so that the object would be destroyed almost immediately, but this forces the GC to scan all the objects in your application — a very expensive operation in terms of performance.

It's far better to design applications such that it is acceptable for unused objects to sit in memory for some time before they are terminated. That way, the garbage collector can also run based on its optimal rules, collecting many dereferenced objects at the same time. This means you need to design objects that don't maintain expensive resources in instance variables. For example, database connections, open files on disk, and large chunks of memory (such as an image) are all examples of expensive resources. If you rely on the destruction of the object to release this type of resource, then the system might be keeping the resource tied up for a lot longer than you expect; in fact, on a lightly utilized Web server, it could literally be days.

The first principle is working with object patterns that incorporate cleaning up such pending references before the object is released. Examples of this include calling the `close` method on an open database connection or file handle. In most cases, it's possible for applications to create classes that do not risk keeping these handles open. However, certain requirements, even with the best object design, can create a risk that a key resource will not be cleaned up correctly. In such an event, there are two occasions when the object could attempt to perform this cleanup: when the final reference to the object is released and immediately before the GC destroys the object.

One option is to implement the `IDisposable` interface. When implemented, this interface ensures that persistent resources are released. This is the preferred method for releasing resources. The second option is to add a method to your class that the system runs immediately before an object is destroyed. This option is not recommended for several reasons, including the fact that many developers fail to remember that the garbage collector is nondeterministic, meaning that you can't, for example, reference an `SQLConnection` object from your custom object's finalizer.

Finally, as part of .NET 2.0, Visual Basic introduced the `Using` command. The `Using` command is designed to change the way that you think about object cleanup. Instead of encapsulating your cleanup logic within your object, the `Using` command creates a window around the code that is referencing an instance of your object. When your application's execution reaches the end of this window, the system automatically calls the `IDIsposable` interface for your object to ensure that it is cleaned up correctly.

The Finalize Method

Conceptually, the GC calls an object's `Finalize` method immediately before it collects an object that is no longer referenced by the application. Classes can override the `Finalize` method to perform any necessary cleanup. The basic concept is to create a method that fills the same need as what in other object-oriented languages is referred to as a destructor. Similarly, the `Class_Terminate` event available in previous versions of Visual Basic does not have a functional equivalent in .NET. Instead, it is possible to create a `Finalize` method that is recognized by the GC and that prevents a class from being cleaned up until after the finalization method is completed, as shown in the following example:

```
Protected Overrides Sub Finalize()
   ' clean up code goes here
   MyBase.Finalize()
End Sub
```

Code snippet from ProVB_Finalization\Form1.vb

This code uses both `Protected` scope and the `Overrides` keyword. Notice that not only does custom cleanup code go here (as indicated by the comment), but this method also calls `MyBase.Finalize`, which causes any finalization logic in the base class to be executed as well. Any class implementing a custom `Finalize` method should always call the base finalization class.

Be careful, however, not to treat the `Finalize` method as if it were a destructor. A destructor is based on a deterministic system, whereby the method is called when the object's last reference is removed. In the GC system, there are key differences in how a finalizer works:

➤ Because the GC is optimized to clean up memory only when necessary, there is a delay between the time when the object is no longer referenced by the application and when the GC collects it. Therefore, the same expensive resources that are released in the `Finalize` method may stay open longer than they need to be.

➤ The GC doesn't actually run `Finalize` methods. When the GC finds a `Finalize` method, it queues the object up for the finalizer to execute the object's method. This means that an object is not cleaned up during the current GC pass. Because of how the GC is optimized, this can result in the object remaining in memory for a much longer period.

➤ The GC is usually triggered when available memory is running low. As a result, execution of the object's `Finalize` method is likely to incur performance penalties. Therefore, the code in the `Finalize` method should be as short and quick as possible.

➤ There's no guarantee that a service you require is still available. For example, if the system is closing and you have a file open, then .NET may have already unloaded the object required to close the file, and thus a `Finalize` method can't reference an instance of any other .NET object.

All cleanup activities should be placed in the `Finalize` method, but objects that require timely cleanup should implement a `Dispose` method that can then be called by the client application just before setting the reference to `Nothing`:

```
Class DemoDispose
   Private m_disposed As Boolean = False
   Public Sub Dispose()
      If (Not m_disposed) Then
         ' Call cleanup code in Finalize.
         Finalize()
         ' Record that object has been disposed.
         m_disposed = True
         ' Finalize does not need to be called.
         GC.SuppressFinalize(Me)
      End If
   End Sub
   Protected Overrides Sub Finalize()
```

```
        ' Perform cleanup here
      End Sub
   End Class
```

Code snippet from ProVB_Finalization\DemoDispose.vb

The DemoDispose class overrides the Finalize method and implements the code to perform any necessary cleanup. This class places the actual cleanup code within the Finalize method. To ensure that the Dispose method only calls Finalize once, the value of the private m_disposed field is checked. Once Finalize has been run, this value is set to True. The class then calls GC.SuppressFinalize to ensure that the GC does not call the Finalize method on this object when the object is collected. If you need to implement a Finalize method, this is the preferred implementation pattern.

This example implements all of the object's cleanup code in the Finalize method to ensure that the object is cleaned up properly before the GC collects it. The Finalize method still serves as a safety net in case the Dispose or Close methods were not called before the GC collects the object.

The IDisposable Interface

In some cases, the Finalize behavior is not acceptable. For an object that is using an expensive or limited resource, such as a database connection, a file handle, or a system lock, it is best to ensure that the resource is freed as soon as the object is no longer needed.

One way to accomplish this is to implement a method to be called by the client code to force the object to clean up and release its resources. This is not a perfect solution, but it is workable. This cleanup method must be called directly by the code using the object or via the use of the Using statement. The Using statement enables you to encapsulate an object's life span within a limited range, and automate the calling of the IDisposable interface.

The .NET Framework provides the IDisposable interface to formalize the declaration of cleanup logic. Be aware that implementing the IDisposable interface also implies that the object has overridden the Finalize method. Because there is no guarantee that the Dispose method will be called, it is critical that Finalize triggers your cleanup code if it was not already executed.

Having a custom finalizer ensures that, once released, the garbage collection mechanism will eventually find and terminate the object by running its Finalize method. However, when handled correctly, the IDisposable interface ensures that any cleanup is executed immediately, so resources are not consumed beyond the time they are needed.

Note that any class that derives from System.ComponentModel.Component automatically inherits the IDisposable interface. This includes all of the forms and controls used in a Windows Forms UI, as well as various other classes within the .NET Framework. Because this interface is inherited, let's review a custom implementation of the IDisposable interface based on the Person class defined in the preceding chapters. The first step involves adding a reference to the interface to the top of the class:

```
Public Class Person
   Implements IDisposable
```

This interface defines two methods, Dispose and Finalize, that need to be implemented in the class. Visual Studio automatically inserts both these methods into your code:

```
#Region " IDisposable Support "
   Private disposedValue As Boolean ' To detect redundant calls

   ' IDisposable
   Protected Overridable Sub Dispose(ByVal disposing As Boolean)
      If Not Me.disposedValue Then
         If disposing Then
            ' TODO: dispose managed state (managed objects).
         End If
         ' TODO: free unmanaged resources (unmanaged objects)
```

```
                          '    and override Finalize() below.
                          ' TODO: set large fields to null.
                  End If
                  Me.disposedValue = True
          End Sub


          ' TODO: override Finalize() only if Dispose(ByVal disposing As Boolean) above
          '          has code to free unmanaged resources.
          Protected Overrides Sub Finalize()
              ' Do not change this code.  Put cleanup code in
              '         Dispose(ByVal disposing As Boolean) above.
              Dispose(False)
              MyBase.Finalize()
          End Sub


          ' This code added by Visual Basic to correctly implement the disposable pattern.
          Public Sub Dispose() Implements IDisposable.Dispose
              ' Do not change this code.  Put cleanup code in
              '         Dispose(ByVal disposing As Boolean) above.
              Dispose(True)
              GC.SuppressFinalize(Me)
          End Sub
      #End Region
```

Code snippet from ProVB_Finalization\Person.vb

Notice the use of the `Overridable` and `Overrides` keywords. The automatically inserted code is following a best-practice design pattern for implementation of the `IDisposable` interface and the `Finalize` method. The idea is to centralize all cleanup code into a single method that is called by either the `Dispose` method or the `Finalize` method as appropriate.

Accordingly, you can add the cleanup code as noted by the `TODO:` comments in the inserted code. As mentioned in Chapter 1, the `TODO:` keyword is recognized by Visual Studio's text parser, which triggers an entry in the task list to remind you to complete this code before the project is complete. Because this code frees a managed object (the `Hashtable`), it appears as shown here:

```
      Protected Overridable Sub Dispose(ByVal disposing As Boolean)
          If Not Me.disposedValue Then
              If disposing Then
                  ' TODO: dispose managed state (managed objects).
              End If
              ' TODO: free unmanaged resources (unmanaged objects)
              '    and override Finalize() below.
              ' TODO: set large fields to null.
          End If
          Me.disposedValue = True
      End Sub
```

Code snippet from ProVB_Finalization\Person.vb

In this case, we're using this method to release a reference to the object to which the `mPhones` variable points. While not strictly necessary, this illustrates how code can release other objects when the `Dispose` method is called. Generally, it is up to your client code to call this method at the appropriate time to ensure that cleanup occurs. Typically, this should be done as soon as the code is done using the object.

This is not always as easy as it might sound. In particular, an object may be referenced by more than one variable, and just because code in one class is dereferencing the object from one variable doesn't mean that it has been dereferenced by all the other variables. If the `Dispose` method is called while other references remain, then the object may become unusable and cause errors when invoked via those other references. There is no easy solution to this problem, so careful design is required if you choose to use the `IDisposable` interface.

Using IDisposable

One way to work with the IDisposable interface is to manually insert the calls to the interface implementation everywhere you reference the class. For example, in an application's Form1 code, you can override the OnLoad event for the form. You can use the custom implementation of this method to create an instance of the Person object. Then you create a custom handler for the form's OnClosed event, and ensure cleanup by disposing of the Person object. To do this, add the following code to the form:

```
Private Sub Form1_Closed(ByVal sender As Object,
                         ByVal e As System.EventArgs) Handles MyBase.Closed
    CType(mPerson, IDisposable).Dispose()
End Sub
```

Code snippet from ProVB_Finalization\Form1.vb

The OnClosed method runs as the form is being closed, so it is an appropriate place to do cleanup work. Note that because the Dispose method is part of a secondary interface, use of the CType method to access that specific interface is needed in order to call the method.

This solution works fine for patterns where the object implementing IDisposable is used within a form, but it is less useful for other patterns, such as when the object is used as part of a Web service. In fact, even for forms, this pattern is somewhat limited in that it requires the form to define the object when the form is created, as opposed to either having the object created prior to the creation of the form or some other scenario that occurs only on other events within the form.

For these situations, .NET 2.0 introduced a new command keyword: Using. The Using keyword is a way to quickly encapsulate the life cycle of an object that implements IDisposable, and ensure that the Dispose method is called correctly:

```
Dim mPerson As New Person()

Private Sub Form1_Load(ByVal sender As System.Object,
                       ByVal e As System.EventArgs) Handles MyBase.Load
    Using (mPerson)
       'insert custom method calls
    End Using
End Sub
End Using
```

Code snippet from ProVB_Finalization\Form1.vb

The preceding statements allocate a new instance of the mPerson object. The Using command then instructs the compiler to automatically clean up this object's instance when the End Using command is executed. The result is a much cleaner way to ensure that the IDisposable interface is called.

Faster Memory Allocation for Objects

The CLR introduces the concept of a *managed heap*. Objects are allocated on the managed heap, and the CLR is responsible for controlling access to these objects in a type-safe manner. One of the advantages of the managed heap is that memory allocations on it are very efficient. When unmanaged code (such as Visual Basic 6 or C++) allocates memory on the unmanaged heap, it typically scans through some sort of data structure in search of a free chunk of memory that is large enough to accommodate the allocation. The managed heap maintains a reference to the end of the most recent heap allocation. When a new object needs to be created on the heap, the CLR allocates memory on top of memory that has previously been allocated, and then increments the reference to the end of heap allocations accordingly. Figure 4-4 illustrates a simplification of what takes place in the managed heap for .NET:

➤ State 1 — A compressed memory heap with a reference to the endpoint on the heap.

➤ State 2 — Object B, although no longer referenced, remains in its current memory location. The memory has not been freed and does not alter the allocation of memory or other objects on the heap.

➤ **State 3** — Even though there is now a gap between the memory allocated for object A and object C, the memory allocation for object D still occurs on the top of the heap. The unused fragment of memory on the managed heap is ignored at allocation time.

➤ **State 4** — After one or more allocations, before there is an allocation failure, the garbage collector runs. It reclaims the memory that was allocated to object B and repositions the remaining valid objects. This compresses the active objects to the bottom of the heap, creating more space for additional object allocations (refer to Figure 4-4).

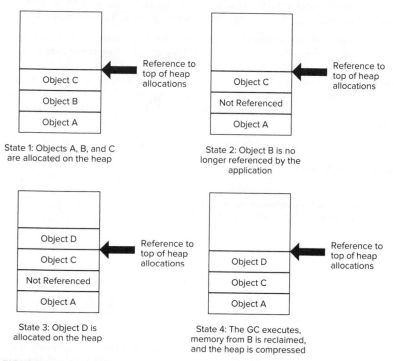

FIGURE 4-4

This is where the power of the GC really shines. Before the CLR is unable to allocate memory on the managed heap, the GC is invoked. The GC not only collects objects that are no longer referenced by the application, but also has a second task: compacting the heap. This is important because if the GC only cleaned up objects, then the heap would become progressively more fragmented. When heap memory becomes fragmented, you can wind up with the common problem of having a memory allocation fail — not because there isn't enough free memory, but because there isn't enough free memory in a contiguous section of memory. Thus, not only does the GC reclaim the memory associated with objects that are no longer referenced, it also compacts the remaining objects. The GC effectively squeezes out all of the spaces between the remaining objects, freeing up a large section of managed heap for new object allocations.

Garbage Collector Optimizations

The GC uses a concept known as *generations*, the primary purpose of which is to improve its performance. The theory behind generations is that objects that have been recently created tend to have a higher probability of being garbage-collected than objects that have existed on the system for a longer time.

To understand generations, consider the analogy of a mall parking lot where cars represent objects created by the CLR. People have different shopping patterns when they visit the mall. Some people spend a good portion of their day in the mall, and others stop only long enough to pick up an item or two. Applying the theory of generations to trying to find an empty parking space for a car yields a scenario in which the highest probability of finding a parking space is a function of where other cars have recently parked. In other words, a space that was occupied recently is more likely to be held by someone who just needed to quickly pick up an item or two. The longer a car has been parked, the higher the probability that its owner is an all-day shopper and the lower the probability that the parking space will be freed up anytime soon.

Generations provide a means for the GC to identify recently created objects versus long-lived objects. An object's generation is basically a counter that indicates how many times it has successfully avoided garbage collection. An object's generation counter starts at zero and can have a maximum value of two, after which the object's generation remains at this value regardless of how many times it is checked for collection.

You can put this to the test with a simple Visual Basic application. From the File menu, select either File ➪ New ➪ Project, or, if you have an open solution, File ➪ Add ➪ New Project. This opens the Add New Project dialog. Select a console application, provide a name and directory for your new project, and click OK. After you create your new project, you will have a code module that looks similar to the code that follows. Within the Main module, add the highlighted code. In Solution Explorer, right-click your second project (if the new project was added to an existing project) and select the Set as StartUp Project option so that when you run your solution, your new project is automatically started.

```vb
Module Module1
  Sub Main()
    Dim myObject As Object = New Object()
    Dim i As Integer
     For i = 0 To 3
       Console.WriteLine(String.Format("Generation = {0}", _
                         GC.GetGeneration(myObject)))
       GC.Collect()
       GC.WaitForPendingFinalizers()
     Next i
     Console.Read()
  End Sub
End Module
```

Code snippet from ProVB_C04_Memory\Module1.vb

Regardless of the project you use, this code sends its output to the .NET console. For a Windows application, this console defaults to the Visual Studio Output window. When you run this code, it creates an instance of an object and then iterates through a loop four times. For each loop, it displays the current generation count of myObject and then calls the GC. The GC.WaitForPendingFinalizers method blocks execution until the garbage collection has been completed.

As shown in Figure 4-5, each time the GC was run, the generation counter was incremented for myObject, up to a maximum of 2.

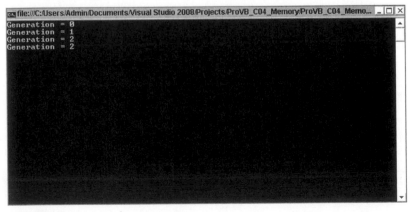

FIGURE 4-5

Each time the GC is run, the managed heap is compacted, and the reference to the end of the most recent memory allocation is updated. After compaction, objects of the same generation are grouped together. Generation-2 objects are grouped at the bottom of the managed heap, and generation-1 objects are grouped next. New generation-0 objects are placed on top of the existing allocations, so they are grouped together as well.

This is significant because recently allocated objects have a higher probability of having shorter lives. Because objects on the managed heap are ordered according to generations, the GC can opt to collect newer objects. Running the GC over a limited portion of the heap is quicker than running it over the entire managed heap.

It's also possible to invoke the GC with an overloaded version of the `Collect` method that accepts a generation number. The GC will then collect all objects no longer referenced by the application that belong to the specified (or younger) generation. The version of the `Collect` method that accepts no parameters collects objects that belong to all generations.

Another hidden GC optimization results from the fact that a reference to an object may implicitly go out of scope; therefore, it can be collected by the GC. It is difficult to illustrate how the optimization occurs only if there are no additional references to the object and the object does not have a finalizer. However, if an object is declared and used at the top of a module and not referenced again in a method, then in the release mode, the metadata will indicate that the variable is not referenced in the later portion of the code. Once the last reference to the object is made, its logical scope ends; and if the garbage collector runs, the memory for that object, which will no longer be referenced, can be reclaimed before it has gone out of its physical scope.

NAMESPACES

Even if you did not realize it, you have been using namespaces since the beginning of this book. For example, `System`, `System.Diagnostics`, and `System.Windows.Forms` are all namespaces contained within the .NET Framework. Namespaces are an easy concept to understand, but this chapter puts the ideas behind them on a firm footing — and clears up any misconceptions you might have about how they are used and organized.

If you are familiar with COM, you will find that the concept of namespaces is the logical extension of programmatic identifier (ProgID) values. For example, the functionality of Visual Basic 6's `FileSystemObject` is now mostly encompassed in .NET's `System.IO` namespace, though this is not a one-to-one mapping. However, namespaces reflect more than a change in name; they represent the logical extension of the COM naming structure, expanding its ease of use and extensibility.

In addition to the traditional `System` and `Microsoft` namespaces (for example, used in things such as Microsoft's Web Services Enhancements), the .NET Framework 3.5 included a way to access some tough-to-find namespaces using the `My` namespace. The `My` namespace is a powerful way of "speed-dialing" specific functionalities in the base.

What Is a Namespace?

Namespaces are a way of organizing the vast number of classes, structures, enumerations, delegates, and interfaces that the .NET Framework class library provides. They are a hierarchically structured index into a class library, which is available to all of the .NET languages, not only the Visual Basic 2010 language (with the exception of the `My` namespace). The namespaces, or object references, are typically organized by function. For example, the `System.IO` namespace contains classes, structures, and interfaces for working with input/output streams and files. The classes in this namespace do not necessarily inherit from the same base classes (apart from `Object`, of course).

A namespace is a combination of a naming convention and an assembly, which organizes collections of objects and prevents ambiguity about object references. A namespace can be, and often is, implemented across several physical assemblies, but from the reference side, it is the namespace that ties these assemblies together. A namespace consists of not only classes, but also other (child) namespaces. For example, `IO` is a child namespace of the `System` namespace.

Namespaces provide identification beyond the component name. With a namespace, it is possible to use a more meaningful title (for example, System) followed by a grouping (for example, Text) to group together a collection of classes that contain similar functions. For example, the System.Text namespace contains a powerful class called StringBuilder. To reference this class, you can use the fully qualified namespace reference of System.Text.StringBuilder, as shown here:

```
Dim sb As New System.Text.StringBuilder()
```

The structure of a namespace is not a reflection of the physical inheritance of classes that make up the namespace. For example, the System.Text namespace contains another child namespace called RegularExpressions. This namespace contains several classes, but they do not inherit or otherwise reference the classes that make up the System.Text namespace.

Figure 4-6 shows how the System namespace contains the Text child namespace, which also has a child namespace, called RegularExpressions. Both of these child namespaces, Text and RegularExpressions, contain a number of objects in the inheritance model for these classes, as shown in the figure.

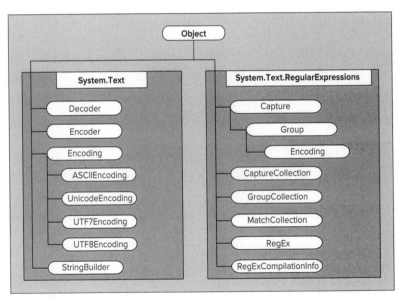

FIGURE 4-6

As shown in Figure 4-6, while some of the classes in each namespace do inherit from each other, and while all of the classes eventually inherit from the generic Object, the classes in System.Text.RegularExpressions do not inherit from the classes in System.Text.

To emphasize the usefulness of namespaces, we can draw another good example from Figure 4-6. If you make a reference to System.Drawing.Imaging.Encoder in your application, then you are making a reference to a completely different Encoder class than the namespace shown in Figure 4-6 — System.Text.Encoder. Being able to clearly identify classes that have the same name but very different functions, and disambiguate them, is yet another advantage of namespaces.

If you are an experienced COM developer, you may note that unlike a ProgID, which reflects a one-level relationship between the project assembly and the class, a single namespace can use child namespaces to extend the meaningful description of a class. The System namespace, imported by default as part of every project created with Visual Studio, contains not only the default Object class, but also many other classes that are used as the basis for every .NET language.

What if a class you need isn't available in your project? The problem may be with the references in your project. For example, by default, the System.DirectoryServices namespace, used to get programmatic access to the Active Directory objects, is not part of your project's assembly. Using it requires adding a reference to the project assembly. The concept of referencing a namespace is very similar to the capability to reference a COM object in VB6.

In fact, with all this talk about referencing, it is probably a good idea to look at an example of adding an additional namespace to a project. Before doing that, though, you should know a little bit about how a namespace is actually implemented.

Namespaces are implemented within .NET assemblies. The `System` namespace is implemented in an assembly called `System.dll` provided with Visual Studio. By referencing this assembly, the project is capable of referencing all the child namespaces of `System` that happen to be implemented in this assembly. Using the preceding table, the project can import and use the `System.Text` namespace because its implementation is in the `System.dll` assembly. However, although it is listed, the project cannot import or use the `System.Data` namespace unless it references the assembly that implements this child of the `System` namespace, `System.Data.dll`.

Let's create a sample project so you can examine the role that namespaces play within it. Using Visual Studio 2010, create a new Visual Basic Windows Forms Application project called Namespace_Sampler.

The `Microsoft.VisualBasic.Compatibility.VB6` library is not part of Visual Basic 2010 projects by default. To gain access to the classes that this namespace provides, you need to add it to your project. You can do this by using the Add Reference dialog (available by right-clicking the Project Name node within the Visual Studio Solution Explorer). The Add Reference dialog has five tabs, each containing elements that can be referenced from your project:

> **.NET** — This tab contains .NET assemblies that can be found in the GAC. In addition to providing the name of the assembly, you can also get the version of the assembly and the version of the framework to which the assembly is compiled. The final data point found in this tab is the location of the assembly on the machine.

> **COM** — This tab contains all the available COM components. It provides the name of the component, the TypeLib version, and the path of the component.

> **Projects** — This tab contains any custom .NET assemblies from any of the various projects contained within your solution.

> **Browse** — This tab enables you to look for any component files (`.dll`, `.tlb`, `.olb`, `.ocx`, `.exe`, or `.manifest`) on the network.

> **Recent** — This tab lists the most recently made references for quick referencing capabilities.

The Add Reference dialog is shown in Figure 4-7.

The available .NET namespaces are listed by component name. This is the same as the namespace name. Within the dialog, you can see a few columns that supply the namespace of the component, the version number of the component, the version of the .NET Framework for which the particular component is targeted, and the path location of the file. You can select a single namespace to make a reference to by clicking your mouse on the component that you are interested in. Holding down the Ctrl key and pressing the mouse button enables you to select multiple namespaces to reference.

To select a range of namespaces, first click on either the first or the last component in the dialog that is contained in the range, and then complete the range selection by holding down the Shift key and using the mouse to select the other components in the range. Once you have selected all the components that you are interested in referencing, click OK.

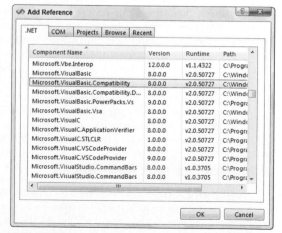

FIGURE 4-7

The example in Figure 4-7 is importing some namespaces from the `Microsoft.VisualBasic` namespace, even though only one selection has been made. This implementation, while a bit surprising at first, is very powerful. First, it shows the extensibility of namespaces. This is because the single `Microsoft.VisualBasic` `.Compatibility.VB6` namespace is actually implemented in two separate assemblies. If you also make a reference to the `Microsoft.VisualBasic.Compatibility` namespace, as well as the `Microsoft` `.VisualBasic.Compatibility.Data` namespace, you will see (through the Object Browser found in Visual Studio) that the `Microsoft.VisualBasic.Compatibility.VB6` namespace is actually found in both locations, as shown in Figure 4-8.

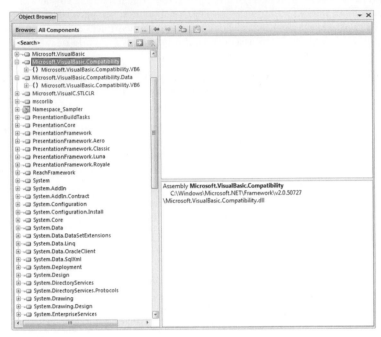

FIGURE 4-8

Second, this implementation enables you to include only the classes that you need — in this case, those related to the VB6 (Visual Basic 6) environment or to database tools, or both types.

Note some interesting points about the `Microsoft.VisualBasic` namespace. First, this namespace gives you access to all the functions that VB6 developers have had for years. Microsoft has implemented these in the .NET Framework and made them available for use within your .NET projects. Because these functions have been implemented in the .NET Framework, there is absolutely no performance hit for using them, but you will most likely find the functionality that they provide available in newer .NET namespaces. Second, contrary to what the name of the namespace suggests, this namespace is available for use by all of the .NET languages, which means that even a C# developer could use the `Microsoft.VisualBasic` namespace if desired.

Namespaces and References

Highlighting their importance to every project, references (including namespaces) are no longer hidden from view, available only after opening a dialog as they were in VB6. As shown in the Solution Explorer window in Figure 4-9, every new project includes a set of

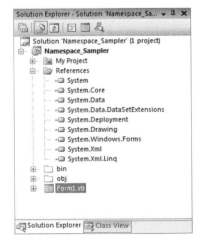

FIGURE 4-9

referenced namespaces. (If you do not see the references listed in the Solution Explorer, click the Show All Files button from the Solution Explorer menu.)

The list of default references varies depending on the type of project. The example in Figure 4-9 shows the default references for a Windows Forms project in Visual Studio 2010. If the project type were an ASP.NET Web Application, the list of references would change accordingly — the reference to the `System.Windows` `.Forms` namespace assembly would be replaced by a reference to `System.Web`. If the project type were an ASP.NET Web service (not shown), then the `System.Windows.Forms` namespace would be replaced by references to the `System.Web` and `System.Web.Services` namespaces.

In addition to making the namespaces available, references play a second important role in your project. One of the advantages of .NET is using services and components built on the common language runtime (CLR), which enables you to avoid DLL conflicts. The various problems that can occur related to DLL versioning, commonly referred to as *DLL hell*, involve two types of conflict.

The first situation occurs when you have a component that requires a minimum DLL version, and an older version of the same DLL causes your product to break. The alternative situation is when you require an older version of a DLL, and a new version is incompatible. In either case, the result is that a shared file, outside of your control, creates a systemwide dependency that affects your software. With .NET, it is possible, but not required, to indicate that a DLL should be shipped as part of your project to avoid an external dependency.

To indicate that a referenced component should be included locally, you can select the reference in the Solution Explorer and then examine the properties associated with that reference. One editable property is called `Copy Local`. You will see this property and its value in the Properties window within Visual Studio 2010. For those assemblies that are part of a Visual Studio 2010 installation, this value defaults to `False`, as shown in Figure 4-10. However, for custom references, this property defaults to `True` to indicate that the referenced DLL should be included as part of the assembly. Changing this property to `True` changes the path associated with the assembly. Instead of using the path to the referenced file's location on the system, the project creates a subdirectory based on the reference name and places the files required for the implementation of the reference in this subdirectory.

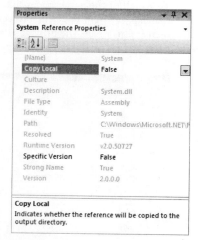

FIGURE 4-10

The benefit of this is that even when another version of the DLL is later placed on the system, your project's assembly will continue to function. However, this protection from a conflicting version comes at a price: Future updates to the namespace assembly to fix flaws will be in the system version, but not in the private version that is part of your project's assembly.

To resolve this, Microsoft's solution is to place new versions in directories based on their version information. If you examine the path information for all of the Visual Studio 2010 references, you will see that it includes a version number. As new versions of these DLLs are released, they are installed in a separate directory. This method allows for an escape from DLL hell, by keeping new versions from overwriting old versions, and it enables old versions to be easily located for maintenance updates. Therefore, it is often better to leave alone the default behavior of Visual Studio 2010, which is set to copy only locally custom components, until your organization implements a directory structure with version information similar to that of Microsoft.

The Visual Basic 2010 compiler will not allow you to add a reference to your assembly if the targeted implementation includes a reference that is not also referenced in your assembly. The good news is that the compiler will help. If, after adding a reference, that reference does not appear in the IntelliSense list generated by Visual Studio 2010, then go ahead and type the reference to a class from that reference. The compiler will flag it with underlining, similar to the Microsoft Word spelling or grammar error underlines. When you click the underlined text, the compiler will tell you which other assemblies need to be referenced in the project in order to use the class in question.

Common Namespaces

The generated list of references shown in the Solution Explorer for the newly created Namespace_ Sampler project includes most, but not all, of the namespaces that are part of your Windows Forms Application project. For example, one namespace not displayed as a reference is `Microsoft.VisualBasic`, and the accompanying `Microsoft.VisualBasic.dll`. Every Visual Basic 2010 project includes the namespace `Microsoft.VisualBasic`. This namespace is part of the Visual Studio project templates for Visual Basic 2010 and is, in short, what makes Visual Basic 2010 different from C# or any other .NET language. The implicit inclusion of this namespace is the reason why you can call `IsDBNull` and other methods of Visual Basic 2010 directly. The only difference in the default namespaces included with Visual Basic 2010 and C# Windows Forms Application projects is that the former use `Microsoft.VisualBasic` and the latter use `Microsoft.CSharp`.

To see all of the namespaces that are imported automatically, such as the `Microsoft.VisualBasic` namespace, right-click the project name in the Solution Explorer and select Properties from the context menu. This opens the project's Properties window in Visual Studio. Select the References tab from the left pane and you will see the reference `Microsoft.VisualBasic` at the top of the list (see Figure 4-11).

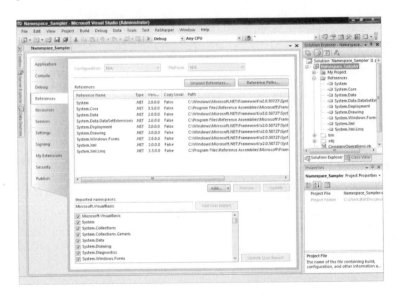

FIGURE 4-11

When looking at the project's global list of imports in the text area at the bottom of the page, you can see that in addition to the `Microsoft.VisualBasic` namespace, the `System.Collections` and `System .Diagnostics` namespaces are also imported into the project. This is signified by the check marks next to the namespace. Unlike the other namespaces in the list, these namespaces are not listed as references in the text area directly above this. That's because implementation of the `System.Collections` and `System. Diagnostics` namespaces is part of the referenced `System.dll`. Similarly to `Microsoft.VisualBasic`, importing these namespaces allows references to the associated classes, such that a fully qualified path is not required. Because these namespaces contain commonly used classes, it is worthwhile to always include them at the project level.

The following list briefly summarizes some of the namespaces commonly used in Visual Basic 2010 projects:

➤ **System.Collections** — Contains the classes that support various feature-rich object collections. Included automatically, it has classes for arrays, lists, dictionaries, queues, hash tables, and so on.

➤ **System.Collections.Generic** — Ever since .NET 2.0, this namespace has enabled working with the generics capabilities of the framework — a way to build type-safe collections as well as provide generic methods and classes.

➤ **System.Data** — This namespace contains the classes needed to support the core features of ADO.NET.

➤ **System.Diagnostics** — Included in all Visual Basic 2010 projects, this namespace includes the debugging classes. The `Trace` and `Debug` classes provide the primary capabilities, but the namespace contains dozens of classes to support debugging.

➤ **System.Drawing** — This namespace contains simple drawing classes to support Windows Application projects.

➤ **System.EnterpriseServices** — Not included automatically, the `System.EnterpriseServices` implementation must be referenced to make it available. This namespace contains the classes that interface .NET assemblies with COM+.

➤ **System.IO** — This namespace contains important classes that enable you to read and write to files as well as data streams.

➤ **System.Linq** — This namespace contains an object interface to work with disparate data sources in a new and easy manner.

➤ **System.Text** — This commonly used namespace enables you to work with text in a number of different ways, usually in regard to string manipulation. One of the more popular objects that this namespace offers is the `StringBuilder` object.

➤ **System.Threading** — This namespace contains the objects needed to work with and manipulate threads within your application.

➤ **System.Web** — This is the namespace that deals with one of the more exciting features of the .NET Framework: ASP.NET. This namespace provides the objects that deal with browser-server communications. Two main objects include `HttpRequest`, which deals with the request from the client to the server, and `HttpResponse`, which deals with the response from the server to the client.

➤ **System.Web.Services** — This is the main namespace you use when creating Web Services, one of the more powerful capabilities provided with the .NET Framework. This namespace offers the classes that deal with SOAP messages and the manipulation of these messages.

➤ **System.Windows.Forms** — This namespace provides classes to create Windows Forms in Windows Forms Application projects. It contains the form elements.

Of course, to really make use of the classes and other objects in this list, you need more detailed information. In addition to resources such as Visual Studio 2010's help files, the best source of information is the Object Browser, available directly in the Visual Studio 2010 IDE. You can find it by selecting View ➪ Object Browser if you are using Visual Studio 2010, 2005, or 2003, or View ➪ Other Windows ➪ Object Browser if you are using Visual Studio 2002. The Visual Studio 2010 Object Browser is shown in Figure 4-12.

The Object Browser displays each of the referenced assemblies and enables you to drill down into the various namespaces. Figure 4-12 illustrates how the `System.dll` implements a number of namespaces, including some that are part of the `System` namespace. By drilling down into a namespace, you can see some of the classes available. By further selecting a class, the browser shows not only the methods and properties associated with the selected class, but also a brief outline of what that class does.

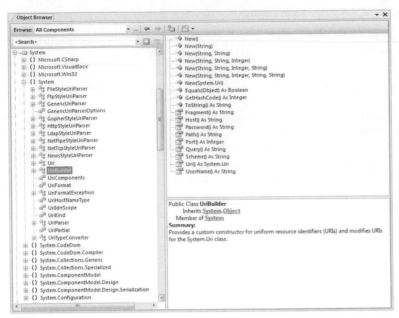

FIGURE 4-12

Using the Object Browser is an excellent way to gain insight into which classes and interfaces are available via the different assemblies included in your project, and how they work. Clearly, the ability to actually see which classes are available and know how to use them is fundamental to being able to work efficiently. Working effectively in the .NET CLR environment requires finding the right class for the task.

Importing and Aliasing Namespaces

Not all namespaces should be imported at the global level. Although you have looked at the namespaces included at this level, it is much better to import namespaces only in the module where they will be used. As with variables used in a project, it is possible to define a namespace at the module level. The advantage of this is similar to using local variables in that it helps to prevent different namespaces from interfering with each other. As this section shows, it is possible for two different namespaces to contain classes or even child namespaces with the same name.

Importing Namespaces

The development environment and compiler need a way to prioritize the order in which namespaces should be checked when a class is referenced. It is always possible to unequivocally specify a class by stating its complete namespace path. This is referred to as fully qualifying your declaration. The following example fully qualifies a `StringBuilder` object:

```
Dim sb As New System.Text.StringBuilder
```

However, if every reference to every class needed its full namespace declaration, then Visual Basic 2010 and every other .NET language would be very difficult to program in. After all, who wants to type `System`
`.Collections.ArrayList` each time an instance of the `ArrayList` class is wanted? If you review the global references, you will see the `System.Collections` namespace. Thus, you can just type **ArrayList** whenever you need an instance of this class, as the reference to the larger `System.Collections` namespace has already been made by the application.

In theory, another way to reference the `StringBuilder` class is to use `Text.StringBuilder`, but with all namespaces imported globally, there is a problem with this, caused by what is known as *namespace crowding*.

Because there is a second namespace, `System.Drawing`, that has a child called `Text`, the compiler does not have a clear location for the `Text` namespace and, therefore, cannot resolve the `StringBuilder` class. The solution to this problem is to ensure that only a single version of the `Text` child namespace is found locally. That way, the compiler will use this namespace regardless of the global availability of the `System.Drawing.Text` namespace.

`Imports` statements specify to the compiler those namespaces that the code will use:

```
Imports Microsoft.Win32
Imports System
Imports SysDraw = System.Drawing
```

Once they are imported into the file, you are not required to fully qualify your object declarations in your code. For instance, if you imported the `System.Data.SqlClient` namespace into your file, then you would be able to create a `SqlConnection` object in the following manner:

```
Dim conn As New SqlConnection
```

Each of the preceding `Imports` statements illustrates a different facet of importing namespaces. The first namespace, `Microsoft.Win32`, is not imported at the global level. Looking at the reference list, you may not see the Microsoft assembly referenced directly. However, opening the Object Browser reveals that this namespace is actually included as part of the `System.dll`.

As noted earlier, the `StringBuilder` references become ambiguous because both `System.Text` and `System.Drawing.Text` are valid namespaces at the global level. As a result, the compiler has no way to determine which `Text` child namespace is being referenced. Without any clear indication, the compiler flags `Text.StringBuilder` declarations in the command handler. However, using the `Imports System` declaration in the module tells the compiler that before checking namespaces imported at the global level, it should attempt to match incomplete references at the module level. Because the `System` namespace is declared at this level, if `System.Drawing` is not, then there is no ambiguity regarding to which child namespace `Text.StringBuilder` belongs.

This sequence demonstrates how the compiler looks at each possible declaration:

➤   It first determines whether the item is a complete reference, such as `System.Text.StringBuilder`.

➤   If the declaration does not match a complete reference, then the compiler tries to determine whether the declaration is from a child namespace of one of the module-level imports.

➤   Finally, if a match is not found, then the compiler looks at the global-level imports to determine whether the declaration can be associated with a namespace imported for the entire assembly.

While the preceding logical progression of moving from a full declaration through module-level to global-level imports resolves the majority of issues, it does not handle all possibilities. Specifically, if you import `System.Drawing` at the module level, the namespace collision would return. This is where the third `Imports` statement becomes important — this `Imports` statement uses an alias.

Aliasing Namespaces

Aliasing has two benefits in .NET. First, aliasing enables a long namespace such as `System.EnterpriseServices` to be replaced with a shorthand name such as `COMPlus`. Second, it adds a way to prevent ambiguity among child namespaces at the module level.

As noted earlier, the `System` and `System.Drawing` namespaces both contain a child namespace of `Text`. Because you will be using a number of classes from the `System.Drawing` namespace, it follows that this namespace should be imported into the form's module. However, were this namespace imported along with the `System` namespace, the compiler would again find references to the `Text` child namespace ambiguous. By aliasing the `System.Drawing` namespace to `SysDraw`, the compiler knows that it should only check the `System.Drawing` namespace when a declaration begins with that alias. The result is that although multiple namespaces with the same child namespace are now available at the module level, the compiler knows that one (or more) of them should only be checked at this level when they are explicitly referenced.

Aliasing as defined here is done in the following fashion:

```
Imports SysDraw = System.Drawing
```

Referencing Namespaces in ASP.NET

Making a reference to a namespace in ASP.NET is quite similar to working with Windows Forms, but you have to take some simple, additional steps. From your ASP.NET solution, first make a reference to the assemblies from the References folder, just as you do with Windows Forms. Once there, import these namespaces at the top of the page file in order to avoid having to fully qualify the reference every time on that particular page.

For example, instead of using `System.Collections.Generic` for each instance, use the `< %# Import % >` page directive at the top of the ASP.NET page (if the page is constructed using the inline coding style) or use the `Imports` keyword at the top of the ASP.NET page's code-behind file (just as you would with Windows Forms applications). The following example shows how to perform this task when using inline coding for ASP.NET pages:

```
<%# Import Namespace="System.Collections.Generic" %>
```

Now that this reference is in place on the page, you can access everything this namespace contains without having to fully qualify the object you are accessing. Note that the `Import` keyword in the inline example is not missing an "s" at the end. When importing in this manner, it is `Import` (without the "s") instead of `Imports` — as it is in the ASP.NET code-behind model and Windows Forms.

In ASP.NET 1.0/1.1, if you used a particular namespace on each page of your application, you needed the `Import` statement on each and every page where that namespace was needed. ASP.NET 3.5 introduced the ability to use the `web.config` file to make a global reference so that you don't need to make further references on the pages themselves, as shown in the following example:

```
<pages>
    <namespaces>
        <add namespace="System.Drawing" />
        <add namespace="Wrox.Books" />
    </namespaces>
</pages>
```

In this example, using the `<namespaces>` element in the `web.config` file, references are made to the `System.Drawing` namespace and the `Wrox.Books` namespace. Because these references are now contained within the `web.config` file, there is no need to again reference them on any of the ASP.NET pages contained within this solution.

CREATING YOUR OWN NAMESPACES

Every assembly created in .NET is part of some root namespace. By default, this logic actually mirrors COM, in that assemblies are assigned a namespace that matches the project name. However, unlike COM, in .NET it is possible to change this default behavior. Just as Microsoft has packaged the system-level and CLR classes using well-defined names, you can create your own namespaces. Of course, it is also possible to create projects that match existing namespaces and extend those namespaces, but that is very poor programming practice.

Creating an assembly by default creates a custom namespace. Namespaces can be created at one of two levels in Visual Basic. Similar to C# it is possible to explicitly assign a namespace within a source file using the `Namespace` keyword. However, Visual Basic provides a second way of defining your custom namespace. By default one of your project properties is the root namespace for your application in Visual Basic. This root namespace will be applied to all classes which don't explicitly define a namespace. You can review your projects default namespace by accessing the project properties. This is done through the assembly's project pages, reached by right-clicking the solution name in the Solution Explorer window and working off the first tab (Application) within the Properties page that opens in the document window, as shown in Figure 4-13.

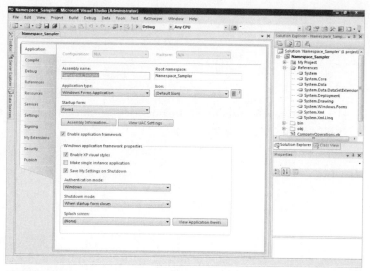

FIGURE 4-13

The next step is optional, but, depending on whether you want to create a class at the top level or at a child level, you can add a Namespace command to your code. There is a trick to being able to create top-level namespaces or multiple namespaces within the modules that make up an assembly. Instead of replacing the default namespace with another name, you can delete the default namespace and define the namespaces only in the modules, using the Namespace command.

The Namespace command is accompanied by an End Namespace command. This End Namespace command must be placed after the End Class tag for any classes that will be part of the namespace. The following code demonstrates the structure used to create a MyMetaNamespace namespace, which contains a single class:

```
Namespace MyMetaNamespace
    Class MyClass1
        ' Code
    End Class
End Namespace
```

You can then utilize the MyClass1 object simply by referencing its namespace, MyMetaNamespace.MyClass1. It is also possible to have multiple namespaces in a single file, as shown here:

```
Namespace MyMetaNamespace1
    Class MyClass1
        ' Code
    End Class
 End Namespace
Namespace MyMetaNamespace2
    Class MyClass2
        ' Code
    End Class
 End Namespace
```

Using this kind of structure, if you want to utilize MyClass1, then you access it through the namespace MyMetaNamespace.MyClass1. This does not give you access to MyMetaNamespace2 and the objects that it offers; instead, you have to make a separate reference to MyMetaNamespace2.MyClass2.

The Namespace command can also be nested. Using nested Namespace commands is how child namespaces are defined. The same rules apply — each Namespace must be paired with an End Namespace and must fully encompass all of the classes that are part of that namespace. In the following example, the MyMetaNamespace has a child namespace called MyMetaNamespace.MyChildNamespace:

```
Namespace MyMetaNamespace
    Class MyClass1
```

```
        ' Code
     End Class
   Namespace MyChildNamespace
        Class MyClass2
           ' Code
        End Class
     End Namespace
  End Namespace
```

This is another point to be aware of when you make references to other namespaces within your own custom namespaces. Consider the following example:

```
Imports System
Imports System.Data
Imports System.Data.SqlClient
Imports System.IO
Namespace MyMetaNamespace1
    Class MyClass1
       ' Code
    End Class
End Namespace
Namespace MyMetaNamespace2
    Class MyClass2
       ' Code
    End Class
End Namespace
```

In this example, a number of different namespaces are referenced in the file. The four namespaces referenced at the top of the code listing — the `System`, `System.Data`, and `System.Data.SqlClient` namespace references — are available to every namespace developed in the file. This is because these three references are sitting outside of any particular namespace declarations. However, the same is not true for the `System.IO` namespace reference. Because this reference is made within the `MyMetaNamespace2` namespace, it is unavailable to any other namespace in the file.

> When you create your own namespaces, Microsoft recommends that you use a convention of `CompanyName.TechnologyName` — for example, `Wrox.Books`. This helps to ensure that all libraries are organized in a consistent way.

Sometimes when you are working with custom namespaces, you might find that you have locked yourself out of accessing a particular branch of a namespace, purely due to naming conflicts. Visual Basic includes the `Global` keyword, which can be used as the outermost root class available in the .NET Framework class library. Figure 4-14 shows a diagram of how the class structure looks with the `Global` keyword.

This means that you can make specifications such as

```
Global.System.String
```

or

```
Global.Wrox.System.Titles
```

THE MY KEYWORD

The `My` keyword is a novel concept that was introduced in the .NET Framework 2.0 to quickly give you access to your application, your users, your resources, the

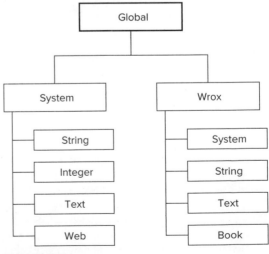

FIGURE 4-14

computer, or the network on which the application resides. The My keyword has been referred to as a way of speed-dialing common but complicated resources to which you need access. Using the My keyword, you can quickly access a wide variety of items, such as user details or specific settings of the requester browser.

Though not really considered a true namespace, the My object declarations that you make work in the same way as the .NET namespace structure you are used to working with. To give you an example, let's first look at how you get the user's machine name using the traditional namespace structure:

```
Environment.MachineName.ToString()
```

For this example, you simply need to use the Environment class and use this namespace to get at the MachineName property. The following shows how you would accomplish this same task using the My keyword:

```
My.Computer.Info.MachineName.ToString()
```

Looking at this example, you may be wondering what the point is if the example that uses My is lengthier than the first example that just works off of the Environment namespace. Remember that the point is not the length of what you type to access specific classes, but a logical way to find frequently accessed resources without spending a lot of time hunting for them. Would you have known to look in the Environment class to get the machine name of the user's computer? Maybe, but maybe not. Using My.Computer.Info .MachineName.ToString is a tremendously more logical approach; and once compiled, this namespace declaration will be set to work with the same class as shown previously without a performance hit.

If you type the My keyword in your Windows Forms application, IntelliSense provides you with seven items to work with: Application, Computer, Forms, Resources, Settings, User, and WebServices. Though this keyword works best in the Windows Forms environment, there are still things that you can use in the Web Forms world. If you are working with a Web application, then you will have three items off the My keyword: Application, Computer, and User. Each of these is described further in the following sections.

My.Application

The My.Application namespace gives you quick access to specific settings and points that deal with your overall application. Table 4-2 details the properties and methods of the My.Application namespace.

TABLE 4-2: My.Application Properties and Methods

PROPERTY/METHOD	DESCRIPTION
ApplicationContext	Returns contextual information about the thread of the Windows Forms application
ChangeCulture	A method that enables you to change the culture of the current application thread
ChangeUICulture	A method that enables you to change the culture that is being used by the Resource Manager
Culture	Returns the current culture being used by the current thread
Deployment	Returns an instance of the ApplicationDeployment object, which allows for programmatic access to the application's ClickOnce features
GetEnvironmentVariable	A method that enables you to access the value of an environment variable
Info	Provides quick access to the assembly of Windows Forms. You can retrieve assembly information such as version number, name, title, copyright information, and more.
IsNetworkDeployed	Returns a Boolean value that indicates whether the application was distributed via the network using the ClickOnce feature. If True, then the application was deployed using ClickOnce — otherwise False.

continues

TABLE 4.2 *(continued)*

PROPERTY/METHOD	DESCRIPTION
Log	Enables you to write to your application's Event Log listeners
MinimumSplashScreenDisplayTime	Enables you to set the time for the splash screen
OpenForms	Returns a `FormCollection` object, which allows access to the properties of the forms currently open
SaveMySettingsOnExit	Provides the capability to save the user's settings upon exiting the application. This method works only for Windows Forms and console applications.
SplashScreen	Enables you to programmatically assign the splash screen for the application
UICulture	Returns the current culture being used by the Resource Manager

Much can be accomplished using the `My.Application` namespace. For an example of its use, let's focus on the `Info` property. This property provides access to the information stored in the application's `AssemblyInfo.vb` file, as well as other details about the class file. In one of your applications, you can create a message box that is displayed using the following code:

```
MessageBox.Show("Company Name: " & My.Application.Info.CompanyName &
    vbCrLf &
    "Description: " & My.Application.Info.Description & vbCrLf &
    "Directory Path: " & My.Application.Info.DirectoryPath & vbCrLf &
    "Copyright: " & My.Application.Info.Copyright & vbCrLf &
    "Trademark: " & My.Application.Info.Trademark & vbCrLf &
    "Name: " & My.Application.Info.AssemblyName & vbCrLf &
    "Product Name: " & My.Application.Info.ProductName & vbCrLf &
    "Title: " & My.Application.Info.Title & vbCrLf &
    "Version: " & My.Application.Info.Version.ToString())
```

Code snippet from Message Box - Assembly.txt

From this example, it is clear that you can get at quite a bit of information concerning the assembly of the running application. Running this code produces a message box similar to the one shown in Figure 4-15.

Another interesting property to look at from the `My.Application` namespace is the `Log` property. This property enables you to work with the log files for your application. For instance, you can easily write to the system's Application Event Log by first changing the application's `app.config` file to include the following:

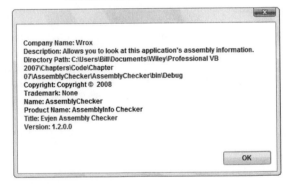

Company Name: Wrox
Description: Allows you to look at this application's assembly information.
Directory Path: C:\Users\Bill\Documents\Wiley\Professional VB 2007\Chapters\Code\Chapter 07\AssemblyChecker\AssemblyChecker\bin\Debug
Copyright: Copyright © 2008
Trademark: None
Name: AssemblyChecker
Product Name: AssemblyInfo Checker
Title: Evjen Assembly Checker
Version: 1.2.0.0

FIGURE 4-15

```
<?xml version="1.0" encoding="utf-8" ?>
<configuration>
    <system.diagnostics>
        <sources>
            <source name="DefaultSource" switchName="DefaultSwitch">
                <listeners>
                    <add name="EventLog"/>
                </listeners>
            </source>
        </sources>
        <switches>
            <add name="DefaultSwitch" value="Information" />
```

```
            </switches>
            <sharedListeners>
                <add name="EventLog"
                  type="System.Diagnostics.EventLogTraceListener"
                  initializeData="EvjenEventWriter" />
            </sharedListeners>
        </system.diagnostics>
    </configuration>
```

Code snippet from app.config.txt

Once the configuration file is in place, you can record entries to the Application Event Log, as shown in the following simple example:

Available for
download on
Wrox.com

```
Private Sub Form1_Load(ByVal sender As System.Object, _
    ByVal e As System.EventArgs) Handles MyBase.Load
    My.Application.Log.WriteEntry("Entered Form1_Load", _
        TraceEventType.Information, 1)
End Sub
```

Code snippet from Form1.vb

You could also just as easily use the WriteExceptionEntry method in addition to the WriteEntry method. After running this application and looking in the Event Viewer, you will see the event shown in Figure 4-16.

The previous example shows how to write to the Application Event Log when working with the objects that write to the event logs. In addition to the Application Event Log, there is also a Security Event Log and a System Event Log. Note that when using these objects, it is impossible to write to the Security Event Log, and it is only possible to write to the System Event Log if the application does it under either the Local System or the Administrator accounts.

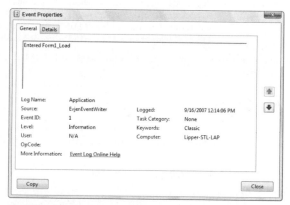

FIGURE 4-16

In addition to writing to the Application Event Log, you can just as easily write to a text file. As with writing to the Application Event Log, writing to a text file also means that you need to make changes to the app.config file:

Available for
download on
Wrox.com

```
<?xml version="1.0" encoding="utf-8" ?>
<configuration>
    <system.diagnostics>
        <sources>
            <source name="DefaultSource" switchName="DefaultSwitch">
                <listeners>
                    <add name="EventLog"/>
                    <add name="FileLog" />
                </listeners>
            </source>
        </sources>
        <switches>
            <add name="DefaultSwitch" value="Information" />
        </switches>
        <sharedListeners>
            <add name="EventLog"
              type="System.Diagnostics.EventLogTraceListener"
              initializeData="EvjenEventWriter" />
            <add name="FileLog"
              type="Microsoft.VisualBasic.Logging.FileLogTraceListener,
              Microsoft.VisualBasic, Version=8.0.0.0, Culture=neutral,
```

```
                    PublicKeyToken=b03f5f7f11d50a3a, processorArchitecture=MSIL"
                    initializeData="FileLogWriter"/>
            </sharedListeners>
        </system.diagnostics>
    </configuration>
```

Code snippet from app.config writing to file.txt

Now with this `app.config` file in place, you simply need to run the same `WriteEntry` method as before. This time, however, in addition to writing to the Application Event Log, the information is also written to a new text file. You can find the text file at `C:\Documents and Settings\[username]\Application Data\ [AssemblyCompany]\[AssemblyProduct]\[Version]`. For instance, in my example, the log file was found at `C:\Documents and Settings\Administrator\Application Data\Wrox\Log Writer\1.2.0.0\`. In the `.log` file found, you will see a line such as the following:

```
DefaultSource    Information    1        Entered Form1_Load
```

By default, it is separated by tabs, but you can change the delimiter yourself by adding a delimiter attribute to the FileLog section in the `app.config` file:

```
<add name="FileLog"
        type="Microsoft.VisualBasic.Logging.FileLogTraceListener,
        Microsoft.VisualBasic, Version=8.0.0.0, Culture=neutral,
        PublicKeyToken=b03f5f7f11d50a3a, processorArchitecture=MSIL"
        initializeData="FileLogWriter" delimiter=";" />
```

In addition to writing to Event Logs and text files, you can also write to XML files, console applications, and more.

My.Computer

The `My.Computer` namespace can be used to work with the parameters and details of the computer in which the application is running. Table 4-3 details the objects contained in this namespace.

TABLE 4-3: My.Computer Objects

PROPERTY	DESCRIPTION
Audio	This object enables you to work with audio files from your application. This includes starting, stopping, and looping audio files.
Clipboard	This object enables you to read and write to the clipboard.
Clock	This enables access to the system clock to get at GMT and the local time of the computer running the application. You can also get at the tick count, which is the number of milliseconds that have elapsed since the computer was started.
FileSystem	This object provides a large collection of properties and methods that enable programmatic access to drives, folders, and files. This includes the ability to read, write, and delete items in the file system.
Info	This provides access to the computer's details, such as amount of memory, the operating system type, which assemblies are loaded, and the name of the computer itself.
Keyboard	This object provides information about which keyboard keys are pressed by the end user. Also included is a single method, SendKeys, which enables you to send the pressed keys to the active form.
Mouse	This provides a handful of properties that enable detection of the type of mouse installed, including details such as whether the left and right mouse buttons have been swapped, whether a mouse wheel exists, and how much to scroll when the user uses the wheel.
Name	This is a read-only property that provides access to the name of the computer.

PROPERTY	DESCRIPTION
Network	This object provides a single property and some methods that enable you to interact with the network to which the computer running the application is connected. With this object, you can use the IsAvailable property to first verify that the computer is connected to a network. If so, then the Network object enables you to upload or download files, and ping the network.
Ports	This object can provide notification when ports are available, as well as allow access to the ports.
Registry	This object provides programmatic access to the registry and the registry settings. Using the Registry object, you can determine whether keys exist, determine values, change values, and delete keys.
Screen	This provides the capability to work with one or more screens that may be attached to the computer.

There is a lot to the My.Computer namespace, and it is impossible to cover all or even most of it. For an example that uses this namespace, we'll take a look at the FileSystem property. The FileSystem property enables you to easily and logically access drives, directories, and files on the computer.

To illustrate the use of this property, first create a Windows Form with a DataGridView with a single column and a Button control. It should appear as shown in Figure 4-17.

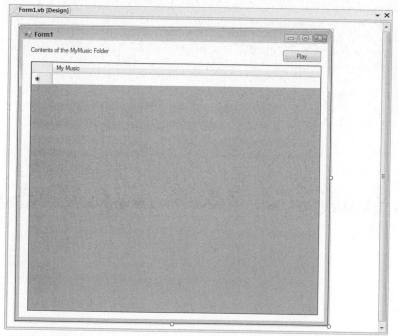

FIGURE 4-17

This little application will look in the user's My Music folder and list all of the .wma files found therein. Once listed, the user of the application will be able to select one of the listed files; and after pressing the Play button, the file will be launched and played inside Microsoft's Windows Media Player.

The first step after getting the controls on the form in place is to make a reference to the Windows Media Player DLL. You can find this on the COM tab, and the location of the DLL is C:\WINDOWS\System32\wmp.dll. This provides you with an object called WMPLib in the References folder of your solution.

You might be wondering why you would make a reference to a COM object in order to play a .wma file from your application, instead of using the My.Computer.Audio namespace that is provided to you. The Audio property only allows for the playing of .wav files, because to play .wma, .mp3, and similar files, users must have the proper codecs on their machine. These codecs are not part of the Windows OS, but are part of Windows Media Player.

Now that the reference to the wmp.dll is in place, let's put some code in the Form1_Load event:

Available for download on Wrox.com

```vb
Private Sub Form1_Load(ByVal sender As System.Object,
                        ByVal e As System.EventArgs) Handles MyBase.Load
    For Each MusicFile As String In
        My.Computer.FileSystem.GetFiles(
            My.Computer.FileSystem.SpecialDirectories.MyMusic,
            FileIO.SearchOption.SearchAllSubDirectories, "*.wma*")
        Dim MusicFileInfo As System.IO.FileInfo =
            My.Computer.FileSystem.GetFileInfo(MusicFile.ToString())
        Me.DataGridView1.Rows.Add(MusicFileInfo.Directory.Parent.Name &
            "\" & MusicFileInfo.Directory.Name & "\" & MusicFileInfo.Name)
    Next
End Sub
```

Code snippet from MusicPlayer\Form1.vb

In this example, the My.Computer.FileSystem.GetFiles method points to the My Music folder through the use of the SpecialDirectories property. This property enables logical and easy access to folders such as Desktop, My Documents, My Pictures, Programs, and more. Though it is possible to use just this first parameter with the GetFiles method, this example makes further definitions. The second parameter defines the recurse value — which specifies whether the subfolders should be perused as well. In this case, the SearchOption enumeration is set to SearchAllSubDirectories. The last parameter defines the wildcard that should be used in searching for elements. In this case, the value of the wildcard is *.wma, which instructs the GetFile method to get only the files that are of type .wma. You could just as easily set it to *.mp3 or even just *.* to get anything contained within the folders. After it is retrieved with the GetFile method, the file is then placed inside the DataGridView control, again using the My.Computer.FileSystem namespace to define the value of the item placed within the row.

After the Form1_Load event is in place, the last event to construct is the Button1_Click event:

Available for download on Wrox.com

```vb
Private Sub Button1_Click(ByVal sender As System.Object,
                          ByVal e As System.EventArgs) Handles Button1.Click
    Dim MediaPlayer As New WMPLib.WindowsMediaPlayer
    MediaPlayer.openPlayer(My.Computer.FileSystem.SpecialDirectories.MyMusic &
            "\" & DataGridView1.SelectedCells.Item(0).Value)
End Sub
```

Code snippet from MusicPlayer\Form1.vb

From this example, you can see that it is pretty simple to play one of the provided .wma files. It is as simple as creating an instance of the WMPLib.WindowsMediaPlayer object and using the openPlayer method, which takes as a parameter the location of the file to play. In this case, you are again using the SpecialDirectories property. The nice thing about using this property is that whereas it could be more difficult to find the user's My Music folder due to the username changing the actual location of the files that the application is looking for, using the My namespace enables it to figure out the exact location of the items. When built and run, the application provides a list of available music files, enabling you to easily select one for playing in the Media Player. This is illustrated in Figure 4-18.

Though it would be really cool if it were possible to play these types of files using the Audio property from the My.Computer namespace, it is still possible to use the My.Computer.Audio namespace for playing .wav files and system sounds.

FIGURE 4-18

To play a system sound, use the following construct:

```
My.Computer.Audio.PlaySystemSound(SystemSounds.Beep)
```

The system sounds in the `SystemSounds` enumeration include Asterisk, Beep, Exclamation, Hand, and Question.

My.Forms Namespace

The `My.Forms` namespace provides a quick and logical way to access the properties and methods of the forms contained within your solution. For instance, to access the first form in your solution (assuming that it's named `Form1`), use the following namespace construct:

```
My.Form.Form1
```

To get at other forms, you simply change the namespace so that the name of the form you are trying to access follows the `Form` keyword in the namespace construction.

My.Resources

The `My.Resources` namespace is a very easy way to get at the resources stored in your application. If you open the `MyResources.resx` file from the My Project folder in your solution, you can easily create as many resources as you wish. For example, you could create a single `String` resource titled `MyResourceString` and give it a value of St. Louis Rams.

To access the resources that you create, use the simple reference shown here:

```
My.Resources.MyResourceString.ToString()
```

Using IntelliSense, all of your created resources will appear after you type the period after the `MyResources` string.

My.User

The `My.User` namespace enables you to work with the `IPrincipal` interface. You can use the `My.User` namespace to determine whether the user is authenticated or not, the user's name, and more. For instance, if you have a login form in your application, you could allow access to a particular form with code similar to the following:

```
If (Not My.User.IsInRole("Administrators")) Then
    ' Code here
End If
You can also just as easily get the user's name with the following:

My.User.Name
In addition, you can check whether the user is authenticated:

If My.User.IsAuthenticated Then
    ' Code here
End If
```

My.WebServices

When not using the `My.WebServices` namespace, you access your Web services references in a lengthier manner. The first step in either case is to make a Web reference to some remote XML Web Service in your solution. These references will then appear in the Web References folder in the Solution Explorer in Visual Studio 2010. Before the introduction of the `My` namespace, you would have accessed the values that the Web reference exposed in the following manner:

```
Dim ws As New ReutersStocks.GetStockDetails
Label1.Text = ws.GetLatestPrice.ToString()
```

This works, but now with the My namespace, you can use the following construct:

```
Label1.Text = My.WebServices.GetStockDetails.GetLatestPrice.ToString()
```

EXTENDING THE MY NAMESPACE

You are not limited to only what the `My` namespace provides. Just as you can with other namespaces, you can extend this namespace until your heart is content. To show an example of extending the `My` namespace so that it includes your own functions and properties, in your Windows Forms application, create a new module called `CompanyExtensions.vb`.

The code for the entire module and the associated class is presented here:

Available for
download on
Wrox.com

```
Namespace My
    <HideModuleName()> _
    Module CompanyOperations
        Private _CompanyExtensions As New CompanyExtensions
        Friend Property CompanyExtensions() As CompanyExtensions
            Get
                Return _CompanyExtensions
            End Get
            Set(ByVal value As CompanyExtensions)
                _CompanyExtensions = value
            End Set
        End Property
    End Module
End Namespace
Public Class CompanyExtensions
    Public ReadOnly Property CompanyDateTime() As DateTime
        Get
            Return DateTime.Now()
```

```
        End Get
    End Property
End Class
```

Code snippet from MusicPlayer\CompanyExtensions.vb

From this example, you can see that the module `CompanyOperations` is wrapped inside the `My` namespace. From there, a single property is exposed — `CompanyExtensions`. The class, `CompanyExtensions`, is a reference to the class found directly below in the same file. This class, `CompanyExtensions`, exposes a single `ReadOnly` Property called `CompanyDateTime`.

With this in place, build your application, and you are now ready to see the new expanded `My` namespace in action. From your Windows Forms application's `Page_Load` event, add the following code snippet:

```
MessageBox.Show(My.CompanyExtensions.CompanyDateTime)
```

From the `My` namespace, you will now find the `CompanyExtensions` class directly in the IntelliSense, as presented in Figure 4-19.

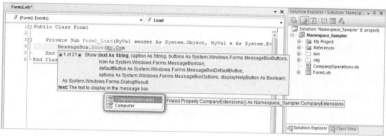

FIGURE 4-19

The name of the module `CompanyOperations` doesn't also appear in the list off `My` because the `<HideModuleName() >` attribute precedes the opening module statement. This attribute signifies that you don't want the module name exposed to the `My` namespace.

The preceding example shows how to create your own sections within the `My` namespace, but you can also extend the sections that are already present (for example, Computer, User, etc.). Extending the `My` namespace is simply a matter of creating a partial class and extending it with the feature sets that you want to appear in the overall `My` namespace. An example of such an extension is presented in the following code sample:

```
Namespace My
    Partial Class MyComputer
        Public ReadOnly Property Hostname() As String
            Get
                Dim iphostentry As System.Net.IPHostEntry = _
                    System.Net.Dns.GetHostEntry(String.Empty)
                Return iphostentry.HostName.ToString()
            End Get
        End Property
    End Class
End Namespace
```

Code snippet from MusicPlayer\CompanyExtensions.vb

From this, you can see that this code is simply extending the already present `MyComputer` class:

```
Partial Class MyComputer
End Class
```

This extension exposes a single `ReadOnly` property called `Hostname` that returns the local user's hostname. After compiling or utilizing this class in your project, you will find the `Hostname` property available to you within the `My.Computer` namespace, as shown in Figure 4-20.

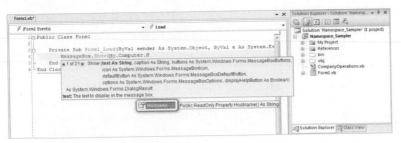

FIGURE 4-20

SUMMARY

This chapter introduced the CLR. You first looked at its memory management features, including how the CLR eliminates the circular reference problem that has plagued COM developers. Next, the chapter examined the `Finalize` method and explained why it should not be treated like the `Class_Terminate` method. Chapter highlights include the following:

➤ Whenever possible, do not implement the `Finalize` method in a class.

➤ If the `Finalize` method is implemented, then also implement the `IDisposable` interface, which can be called by the client when the object is no longer needed.

➤ Code for the `Finalize` method should be as short and quick as possible.

➤ There is no way to accurately predict when the GC will collect an object that is no longer referenced by the application (unless the GC is invoked explicitly).

➤ The order in which the GC collects objects on the managed heap is nondeterministic. This means that the `Finalize` method cannot call methods on other objects referenced by the object being collected.

➤ Leverage the `Using` keyword to automatically trigger the execution of the `IDisposable` interface.

This chapter also examined the value of a common runtime and type system that can be targeted by multiple languages. You saw how the CLR offers better support for metadata. Metadata is used to make types self-describing and is used for language elements such as attributes. Included were examples of how metadata is used by the CLR and the .NET class library, and you learned how to extend metadata by creating your own properties. The chapter also presented a brief overview of the Reflection API and the IL Disassembler utility (ildasm.exe), which can display the IL contained within a module.

While there are differences in the syntax of referencing objects from a namespace and referencing the same object from a COM-style component implementation, there are several similarities. After demonstrating the hierarchical structure of namespaces, this chapter covered the following:

➤ Why namespace hierarchies are not related to class hierarchies

➤ How to review and add references to a project

➤ How to import and alias namespaces at the module level

➤ How to create custom namespaces

➤ How to use the `My` namespace

Namespaces play an important role in enterprise software development. They enable you to separate the implementation of related functional objects while retaining the ability to group these objects, which improves the overall maintainability of your code. Anyone who has ever worked on a large project has experienced situations in which a fix to a component was delayed because of the potential impact on other components in the same project. Regardless of the logical separation of components in the same project, developers who take part in the development process worry about testing. With separate implementations for related components, it is not only possible to alleviate this concern, but also easier than ever before for a team of developers to work on different parts of the same project.

5

Declarative Programming with Visual Basic

WHAT YOU WILL LEARN IN THIS CHAPTER

- ➤ Declarative programming in VB
- ➤ Using XAML to create a window
- ➤ XAML syntax
- ➤ Using XAML to declare a workflow

Declarative programming is the new buzzword for creating applications with .NET. It revolves around the concept that developers should define "what" is needed versus "how" to do it. The borders in many areas are a little unclear, however, and given that declarative programming is at the core of things like Windows Presentation Foundation (WPF), Silverlight, and Workflow Foundation (WF), it is worth discussing in some detail here.

This chapter focuses on using a more declarative way of defining applications. The idea is that you can use a declaration to describe, for example, an element in your user interface, and then compile or include that definition with either a desktop, the Web, or even a version for another operating system.

Visual Basic has some declarative elements, such as the Handles clause and portions of LINQ, but Microsoft introduced a new language format called XAML that specifically targets declarative application development. It is designed around a standard known as the *Extensible Application Markup Language (XAML)*. This standard is pronounced "zamel" (rhymes with camel). It enables you to layer elements, and include elements such as colors and 3-D shapes.

With the introduction of XAML and the integration of XAML with Visual Basic for things like WPF, Silverlight, WF, and over time other technologies, you—as a Visual Basic developer—will be doing more and more declarative programming. In most cases, once you understand how XAML differs from and works with imperative languages like Visual Basic, you'll find it easier to master XAML; and this chapter will help provide that common baseline for the XAML language.

Rather than just drop you into a topic such as WPF and hope you'll pick up on XAML, this chapter will illustrate some simple examples of declarative programming. Many developers are introduced to XAML as part of working to master another technology such as Silverlight or WPF. However, this chapter will illustrate that XAML and thinking about declarative custom programming isn't limited to a single technology. At the same time, the format should feel somewhat familiar to those who know HTML and/or XML and XSLT. The implementation code to interpret and act on XAML declarations, becomes plumbing that a declarative programmer leaves to Microsoft (or some component implementation vendor).

DECLARATIVE PROGRAMMING AND VISUAL BASIC

In any discussion of "declarative" programming, it is probably best to first consider to what it is being compared. Visual Basic, like most modern OOP languages (C#, C/C++, F#, etc.), is not primarily a declarative language. It is what is known as a *procedural* or *imperative language*. This reflects that developers in these languages focus on "how" to get the computer to complete a task.

These languages are powerful, and declarative programming isn't going to completely replace them. However, they work at the level where the developer is defining algorithms, and are concerned with things like loops, conditionals, and method calls. These languages define the way the majority of us have learned to create applications.

On the other hand most of us have been exposed to T-SQL which is more of a declarative language. While it supports imperative contructs and as such isn't a pure declarative language, when we consider a Select statement or an insert statement we are thinking about a declarative statement. The T-SQL query indicates what you want; it doesn't dictate the implementation used to get it. When you tell the database to select data where column 1 is "Wrox" you aren't telling it how to find that data. This query is thus declarative in that you specify what you want and don't focus on the steps taken by the database engine to find and return those items.

However, as noted, T-SQL isn't a pure declarative language; it has support for imperative constructs. Similarly, as will be explored further in this chapter, Visual Basic, a language considered to be imperative, includes some declarative constructs.

XAML however is much closer to a pure declarative language. It focuses only on the result or current state and not on how to achieve or implement changes to that state. This is important to understand because it ties to one of the primary hurdles that most developers new to declarative programming face. This is the reality that two of our most common development paradigms are less important in declarative programming. The first is the concept of *state*; the second is the *ordering of events*, or the *execution path*.

When working in an imperative language programmers tend to focus on evaluating statements such as "If X equals Y, then Z is True." This statement, which could easily be translated into Visual Basic (If X = Y Then Z = True) is imperative in that we need to evaluate it whenever X or Y changes. The developer must ensure that when state changes, this code is evaluated, and the appropriate updates are shown as a result. Order of execution can be important because if the statement is executed before the state of X or Y is modified, in the overall execution the end state of Z could be wrong given the end state of X and Y. The preceding should be easily recognizable as the issues we address every day as Visual Basic developers.

With a declarative model, the value of Z is bound to the relationship of X and Y. The end result should be the same—that is, when X equals Y, then the value of Z will be True; however, unlike the Visual Basic code, when defined declaratively, the decisions regarding when to evaluate this statement, how often to evaluate this statement, or any dependencies on the evaluation of this statement leave the hands of the developer.

The declarative developer doesn't care when X equals Y, only that the end result will be reflected. This doesn't mean there isn't code somewhere behind the scenes carrying out the necessary evaluation(s); it means that code is now plumbing. In other words, the "how" of this evaluation isn't handled by the application developer, only the "what."

This paradigm isn't as new as it might seem. Consider the event model. When you define an event you indicate that when the state of object X changes, you will send a message to everyone who has registered for that message. The object generating the event doesn't know what will be done with that message. For the objects receiving the message, they only know that when it is received they should react in response to the information relayed by the message.

With Visual Basic you can declare that a given object instance is defined "with events." At that point you might not know or care about all of the events the object may trigger, only that you are interested in one or more of those events. You can then take the next step and indicate that certain methods "handle" a specific event. Visual Basic's inclusion of the `Handles` clause is a declarative construct. While you define what is being handled you are not concerned with the state of the event owner, you have no flow of execution concern for when the event will be handled.

New XAML developers often get hung up on this concept of "how." In general, the basic idea is that you just need to accept that the plumbing to handle these declarative statements is in place. When it comes to the `Handles` clause, very few VB developers have an issue. However, as we move to a much larger footprint, an entire language syntax, the "how" question can become distracting if we don't address it.

While it's not important to know the exact implementation, having a general idea of how it might work tends to resolve these concerns. The same concept that is applied within Visual Basic for the `WithEvents` and `Handles` clauses, whereby your object defines an event and another object subscribes to that event, offers an interesting paradigm for declarative programming.

Consider how a declarative language might handle the situation where changes to the values X and Y trigger an update to the value of Z. You might imagine an event model that could be defined when creating bindings between the various elements X and Y, with a handler that sets Z appropriately. I'm not claiming this is the underlying implementation, but by considering declarative programming under this model, it is hoped that you can recognize "how it might work" and instead of focusing on the magic of declarations, focus on declaring your desired functionality.

As you'll see when we consider applying styles or mapping values, the concept of "binding" has an all new importance. If you remember that a 'binding' is similar to mapping event handlers for known plumbing within framework objects, you quickly see that binding becomes a focus of declarative programming. Instead of assigning values, you are binding the item which holds that value.

The good news is that XAML isn't going to fully replace imperative languages anytime soon, despite supporters such as Chris Anderson (architect of WPF in .NET 3.0), who was famously quoted as wanting to register a Tech Ed session titled "XAML As a Better C#." While some simple interfaces may be defined only in XAML, there will typically still be the need for an implementation layer made up of an imperative language. The combination of XAML with Visual Basic provides a much more productive and effective combination for getting things done than either one does in isolation.

When you create a new WPF or other XAML application project, you'll find that you do so in the context of an imperative language (Visual Basic or C#). Your customer application logic, which often doesn't have generic implementation plumbing, will still need an imperative implementation. However, you now have the option of binding these imperative code blocks with a declarative interface. These two aspects of your application logic are typically referred to as *code* (Visual Basic) and *markup* (XAML).

USING XAML TO CREATE A WINDOW

Since the most common way to interact with XAML is as a Windows definition language, let's create a simple window definition to put some of what we'll discuss in context. Most early WPF applications were built by hand or with tools such as XAMLpad that could output graphics as well as XAML. With the release of Visual Studio 2008, WPF, like the other .NET 3.0 technologies, gained a true IDE; and with the availability of Blend, a powerful design tool. The focus for WPF is now on creating applications with Visual Studio 2010 and potentially having a designer customize the design surface with Blend.

Because of the value of having generated XAML we'll use Visual Studio to generate a baseline WPF application titled ProVB_XAML. Begin by using the File menu in Visual Studio 2010 and select the option to create a new project. Navigate to the new Visual Basic Window section of the New Project dialog, as shown in Figure 5-1.

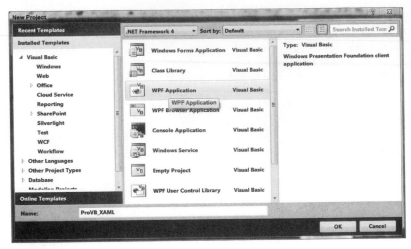

FIGURE 5-1

For the purpose of this chapter you can create a .NET 4 application called ProVB_XAML. This application could also be created as a .NET 3.0 or .NET 3.5 application. However, changing the compatability level also impacts the availability of other .NET libraries which the application can reference. For example you wouldn't be able to reference the Entity Framework or LINQ libraries if you were maintaining .NET 3.0 compatibility. Additionally, note that the list of available templates for WPF disappears if you choose to target a .NET 2.0 baseline.

Similar to other project templates, Visual Studio opens in the main window you've just declared; but unlike Windows Forms, this isn't just a design surface. The first thing to notice is that there isn't a line of VB code in this project, just a few XAML snippets. As shown in Figure 5-2, the default application does not look entirely different from that of a Windows Form, except when it comes to the design surface. In Windows Forms, the design surface generates code that is placed in the `*.designer.vb` file. The generated file `*.designer.vb` is a partial class definition that Visual Studio uses to hold the definition of each control you place onto the form, as well as the form itself.

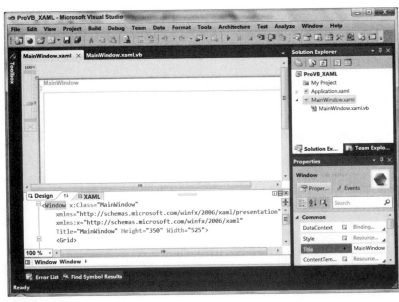

FIGURE 5-2

However, with WPF and XAML, that partial class definition is instead a collection of XML declarations that define your window and its behavior. More important, although parts may be generated, that XAML file isn't considered generated code; instead, it is an editable source file, definining your window and as such is displayed in parallel with the window it defines. You'll find that as you work with your design surface, Visual Studio 2010 automatically updates the XAML file; similarly, when you edit the XAML file, Visual Studio 2010 automatically updates the design surface.

The design surface shown in Figure 5-2 has several features specific to WPF. The first you'll find in the upper left-hand corner. That scrollbar enables you to zoom in on a specific portion of your interface. For example, you can choose to limit your view to just a portion of the overall window by zooming in for a closer look at how elements are aligned. Alternatively, you can zoom out to view the entire window, even when the window is larger then the design area available on your screen.

The second item to note about the display relates to the relationship between the currently top design surface in the display and the XAML tab located below it. Between these two tabs, in the middle of the screen, is a pair of up and down arrows. These arrows aren't there to indicate that these two surfaces are related, but rather to swap the location of each of these two surfaces so that the code is on the top and the window is below it. Thus, if you are working with the XAML and directly making changes to it, you can shift that to the top of the display and reduce the graphical display.

However, having the code located above or below your design surface may not be your preferred display. That's where the three little icons located on the tab bar come in. The first two are a vertical line and a horizontal line, respectively. These buttons indicate that you can choose to place the XAML code and the design surface in a side-by-side display mode or in a top-bottom design mode, respectively. The third button, which shows double down arrows, enables you to collapse the combined display so that the tabs are along the bottom or the right side of the design display. Thus, if you prefer to maximize the available display surface, you can create a display similar to what you have when editing ASP.NET Web pages.

Of course, you are probably wondering about the XAML that is shown in Figure 5-2 and that defines your main window. This is one of two XAML files that are generated with your project. This XAML file has a top-level node named "Window" that tells the compiler that it defines a window. The top-level node ties this window to the class `MainWindow`, which matches the default filename, as shown in the following code:

```
<Window x:Class="ProVB_XAML.MainWindow"
        xmlns="http://schemas.microsoft.com/winfx/2006/xaml/presentation"
        xmlns:x="http://schemas.microsoft.com/winfx/2006/xaml"
        Title="MainWindow" Height="350" Width="525">
    <Grid>

    </Grid>
</Window>
```

Code snippet from MainWindow

Because the XML namespace declarations are shared between this file and the second XAML file, let's jump to the remaining attributes of the window. By default, the window is given a title that matches the class same, as in Windows Forms, and the default size is a height of 350 and a width of 525. In addition to these attributes, the Window node that declares the actual main window contains a single control, a grid. The grid is the default control in the window because it provides developers with the most consistent design experience from Windows Forms.

Next, let's review the second XAML file, `application.xaml`. This file contains the application definition. Like your Visual Basic Windows Forms code, the `Application` object represents the application to the CLR. It is this object that represents the base reference for things such as garbage collection, and it is registered as the primary process. Because the `Application` object is implemented as an object in the `System.Windows` namespace, it supports properties, methods, and events just like any other class. The contents of `Application.xaml` are shown in the following example:

```
<Application x:Class="Application"
            xmlns="http://schemas.microsoft.com/winfx/2006/xaml/presentation"
            xmlns:x="http://schemas.microsoft.com/winfx/2006/xaml"
            StartupUri="MainWindow.xaml">
    <Application.Resources>
    </Application.Resources>
</Application>
```

Code snippet from Application

This file is a good place to take a moment to discuss the basics of XAML. As you can see, this file starts with a reference to an `x:Class` declaration as an attribute of the `Application` node. The `x:` represents an alias similar to what you find in Visual Basic, where the `x:` indicates that `Class` is defined in the schema `http://schemas.microsoft.com/winfx/2006/xaml`, the XAML schema. You'll notice there is a second declaration for `http://schemas.microsoft.com/winfx/2006/xaml/presentation`. This second declaration is the one that references the actual WPF libraries. The last item in the attributes of the `Application` node is a `StartupUri`. This property tells the compiler that when this application is started, the next step is to open the file `MainWindow.xaml` in order to find the definition of the window to be displayed.

Similar to a traditional Windows Forms application, the application doesn't actually define a window; instead, it defines the application context, and then it calls another class to create the window. However, this file is a great place to add XAML resources that will apply across your application. The term `Resources` refers to how with XAML it is possible to declare the attributes of an object with XAML. For example the color, shape, and behavior (in terms of hover over, mouse down, etc.) of a control.

Placing these XAML declarations in the `Application.Resources` section of the application definition is a natural way to share them across all controls of that type in your application; but the details of shared resources are covered in Chapter 18.

XAML SYNTAX

The ProVB_XAML example doesn't have much purpose yet, but it makes it easier to keep the discussion of XAML in context. The next step is to take a more detailed look at just what XAML is and how it relates to WPF. XAML is a markup-based protocol. Similar to SOAP and several other XML-based formats, the XAML specification describes a potentially open standard for describing user interface elements.

Regardless of whether XAML ever actually becomes an open standard, Microsoft has implemented WPF using a minimum of two XML namespaces. As noted in regard to the `Application.xaml` file, one namespace is focused on the definition of XAML, and the second is focused on WPF's custom classes. Returning to the ProVB_XAML `Application.xaml` file, the following namespace declaration is included:

```
xmlsn="http://schemas.microsoft.com/winfx/2006/xaml/presentation"
```

The preceding line is similar to an `Imports` statement for XML in that it indicates a set of nodes and keywords that will be used within the associated XML file. In this case, the `winfx/2006/xaml/presentation` namespace contains the definition of WPF—not the definition of XAML keywords, but rather the definition of WPF. The classes contained in the presentation namespace are the .NET implementation of WPF.

To start working with commands and controls that are part of the XAML standard, a second namespace reference is used:

```
xmlsn:x=http://schemas.microsoft.com/winfx/2006/xaml
```

This second reference is used in all XAML files to declare the actual XAML language standard. By convention, it is aliased as `x:`. For those of you who may not have done much XML development, this means that within the XAML you'll see things such as `x:Class`, `x:Code`, and other similar nodes. The `x:` is required to indicate that what follows is an element of the XAML languages, as opposed to, for example, WPF or some other .NET library. The `x:` nodes are the actual XAML declarations. What is important to remember is that the XAML namespace can be and is used for things other than just WPF. As you'll see in Chapter 26, Windows Workflow Foundation is based on XAML; it has its own workflows namespace.

One change with the introduction of the .NET 4 Framework is that unlike the original XAML classes, which were embedded within the `PresentationFramework.dll` library, with a dependency on the `WindowsBase` libraries, the core classes have now been moved into a separate `System.Xaml.dll` library of their own, with dependencies only on `MsCorLib`, `System`, and `System.XML`. This has helped extend the original syntax and capabilities of the core XAML language.

Note that as of this writing, there is no plan for all XAML language features to work with the Visual Studio 2010 compiler. If you are looking to leverage cutting-edge XAML 2010 features, you will need to leverage uncompiled XAML. This is possible by setting your project build action from Page to Resource and your XAML will be interpreted dynamically at runtime.

XAML Language Basics

XAML is defined as a language consisting of a collection of elements, attributes, and related objects. These objects are referenced from the XAML namespace, which by convention precedes each class with an `x:`. .NET extends and maps these declarative structures into .NET.

Before getting to the syntax, take a look at the three categories of XML statements you will find within the XAML namespace:

- ➤ attribute
- ➤ markup extension
- ➤ XAML directive

Each of the preceding items is a separate category of language element discussed in more detail in the sections which follow.

Attributes

Within XML, attributes refer to named properties that are associated with a given XML node. Thus, the XML node object might have several attributes such as `Name`, `Margin`, `Text`, and so on associated with it. These attributes in XML live within the definition of the XML node. They are not contained within the XML node, but in its definition, as shown here:

```
<object Name="anObject"></object>
```

Within XAML, the list of attributes includes those in Table 5-1. Be aware that the term "object" in the following example snippets can be replaced with one of several WPF objects, including `Application`, `Window`, `Button`, `Brush`, and so on.

TABLE 5-1: XAML Attributes

XAML ATTRIBUTES	DESCRIPTION AND EXAMPLE
`x:Class`	Used to reference the root class for an XAML document. Each document can be associated with a single root object. `<object x:Class="Window"></object>`
`x:ClassModifier`	Modifies the class definition for a given XAML document. Specifically, it enables you to indicate that a given class doesn't provide a public interface. Public is the default. `<object x:Class="Window" x:ClassModifier="Friend"></object>`

continues

TABLE 5-1 *(continued)*

XAML ATTRIBUTES	DESCRIPTION AND EXAMPLE
`x:FieldModifier`	Unlike classes, which are by default public, fields within objects are by default assigned with the modifier Friend. If you have added an object within XAML that you want available to other classes (within your code behind), then the FieldModifier needs to declare this field with the modifier of Friend. This property can only be used with objects that also have the `x:Name attribute` shown here: `<object x:Name="LoginWindow" x:FieldModifier="Public"></object>`
`x:Key`	Some objects, such as the Dictionary object and other collection objects, allow items to be indexed via a key. Such a key must be named, and this attribute is used to provide a unique key name. Note that most XAML applications leverage a resource dictionary, which is a common use of this attribute. Keys need to be unique within the scope of the object to which they are applicable. `<object.Resources> <SolidColorBrush x:Key="string"/></object.Resources>`
`x:Name`	Similar to a key, but used more for the naming of objects within the scope of an application. Such objects are not public by default, but typically represent the controls and related user interface objects used by your application. `<object x:Name="LoginWindow"></object>`
`x:Shared`	This actually maps to what Visual Basic users understand the keyword Shared to mean. By default, if your application requests an object from your XAML resources, then you will get the same instance of the requested resource. You can use this property such that each time a given object is requested, a new instance of that object is created. `<ResourceDictionary><object x:shared="false"/> </ResourceDictionary>`
`x:Subclass`	This attribute can be used in conjunction with an x:Class declaration. It essentially enables your XAML to inherit from another class; however, as a Visual Basic user you won't use this attribute because you can do this in a much more natural manner in the code-behind source file associated with your class. `<object x:Class="class" x:Subclass="namespace.subclass"></object>`
`x:TypeArguments`	This attribute enables you to create a collection of x:Type markup extensions. This collection acts as the parameters to the constructor for a generic class to ensure that the associated types are defined with the constructor. This attribute must be used with a class declaration, and the associated class must be a generic.
	This attribute is extended in XAML 2009, removing the restriction that this must be used with a class declaration.
	`<object x:class="PageFunction" x:TypeArguments= "{x:Type=type1}"></object>`

Notice that none of the preceding attributes are actually referenced as a node within XML. Instead, they modify the properties associated with a node. Thus, the attributes are modifiers, as opposed to the next category of elements: markup extensions. As implied by the word "extensible" in the name Extensible Application XML, one of the features of this model is that the format allows for the definition of extensions. These extensions expand on the base elements associated with that markup definition. XAML includes a limited number of such extensions. Unlike an attribute, a markup extension can be used to create an XML node or a collection of XML attributes. When used to create a node, the markup extension allows for the definition of property values within that node. When used to allow for the creation of a collection of attributes, it can be recognized by the surrounding curly braces, as shown in the preceding `TypeArguments` definition.

Markup Extensions

Markup extensions for XAML are shown in Table 5-2.

TABLE 5-2: XAML Markup Extensions

XAML MARKUP EXTENSION	DESCRIPTION AND EXAMPLE
`x:Array`	Used to provide support for arrays. The array declaration allows for the assignment of a data type, to support strong typing and the inclusion of a series of elements. `<x:Array Type="object"> <myObject1/> <myObject2/></x:Array>`
`x:Null`	Is equivalent to the term Nothing in Visual Basic, but the extension is implemented based on the C#/C++ keyword of `null`. Will set an object property to `null`, which may or may not be the default state when that object property is created. `x:Null` has no additional modifiers and is typically implemented as a node, as opposed to an attribute, as it references the value of its parent node. `<object><object.property><x:Null/></object.property></object>`
`x:Reference`	New with XAML 2010, this extension enables you to create references between XAML elements based on their named properties. This extension will allow you to target by name another object within the markup. More information is available as part of the implementation of the `Markup.Reference` class definition.
`x:Static`	Supports the reference of constant values, shared properties of objects, and enumeration values. Similar to an attribute, it is most commonly used as an attribute with the format `X:static "{namespace.class}"`. This extension is used to gain access to common values that are defaults for your application—for example, to the system colors used by the operating system. `<object Background="{x:Static SystemColors.ControlBrush}"></object>`
`x:Type`	As previously introduced with the `x:Typename` attribute, the `x:Type` extension allows for the specification of a type when creating an object that is a generic. However, it has a second use: the specification of a property type. Thus, if you create an object that has properties, then the `x:Type` extension is used to specify the type associated with that property. `<object><object.property> <x:Type TypeName="namespace.class"/></object.property></object>`

Don't let that last extension confuse you; there are two ways that markup extensions are used — either as attributes contained within curly braces or as nodes that may contain their own attributes and properties. Some, such as `x:Static`, always appear as attributes; others, such as `x:Null` and `x:Array`, always appear as nodes; and of course `x:Type` can be found in either location. Up until now, all the XAML language elements have been used to operate within the definition of XML. That is, they define attributes and nodes, and as long as you understand the definition of the keyword, you can understand the data it references.

XAML Directives

However, at times you need to truly reference data. For example, none of the preceding extensions would support embedding other XML data into your XAML file or referencing code directly from within your XAML file. These two capabilities are available based on XAML directives. XAML directives enable you to embed elements that don't follow the XML formatting rules. There are two such directives, as shown in Table 5-3.

TABLE 5-3: XAML Directives

XAML DIRECTIVE	DESCRIPTION AND EXAMPLE
x:Code	Enables you to embed Visual Basic code directly into your XAML file. However, although you can do it, you shouldn't: It's considered a very poor coding practice—not only because it isolates code outside of a code-behind file, but also because such code makes the XAML dependent on a language for compilation, and it is isolated and more difficult to debug and maintain. However, you may come across such an element. In general, it is considered best to further nest any embedded code within an x:Code block within a CDATA block, as shown in the following sample, so that the XAML parsing engine doesn't attempt to parse the code. Thus, a code block will look similar to this: `<object><x:Code> <![CDATA[ 'VB code can be enclosed by a CDATA directive` `Sub MyMethod() End Sub ]]></x:Code></object>`
x:XData	The second item that isn't standard XAML that you might want to embed within your XAML document is another XML document. For example, you might want to display an e-mail message or a Word document that has been converted to XML, so you might want this data to be within your XAML document. The key point is that you don't want this additional XML to accidentally use the same tag information associated with your XAML. Thus, you need to provide an x:XData directive containing your root data node, which contains your custom data. Note that in most cases the object node in this sample will be a System.Windows.Data.XMLDataProvider as opposed to a Window or some other object. A sample of this is shown here: `<object><x:XData> <dataItems xmlns="yourNamespace">…</dataItems><elementDataRoot>` `</x:XData></object>`

As shown here, the scope of the XML definition for what you're going to see within a XAML file is not that complex. You're probably wondering where all the controls, windows, and even the application object that we've already seen in action are. These items, while defined as part of the WPF implementation, are not part of the core XAML language definition. They are the WPF extensions, and the reason why you added a second namespace reference to the Presentation folder. Everything else you see in XAML that falls into this second category is also available for reference from your .NET application.

USING XAML TO DECLARE A WORKFLOW

In .NET 3.0 and 3.5, XAML was fairly tightly coupled to WPF. Starting with .NET 4.0 and beyond, Microsoft has placed a major focus on decoupling these two items and having the XAML syntax used across multiple different areas, for example WPF, WF, and WCF. After all, what better way to illustrate a complex workflow or interface than to create a XAML markup that defines the key interface elements for a WCF endpoint or to define the meta data when binding to data services?

With .NET Framework 4, the XAML used within workflows has been standardized on the same libraries used by WPF. To illustrate this, open Visual Studio and select File ➪ New Project. Then, from the resulting New Project dialog, shown in Figure 5-3, select the Workflow Console Application project type and assign the name ProVB_WFXAML to your new project.

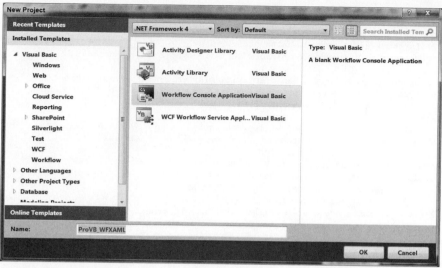

FIGURE 5-3

Creating this new project will place you back within Visual Studio with the default graphical view of your currently empty workflow. Because creating custom workflows isn't the goal of this chapter, close that view and right-click on `Workflow1.xaml` in your Solution Explorer. Select the Code view and you'll be greeted with the raw XAML shown in Figure 5-4.

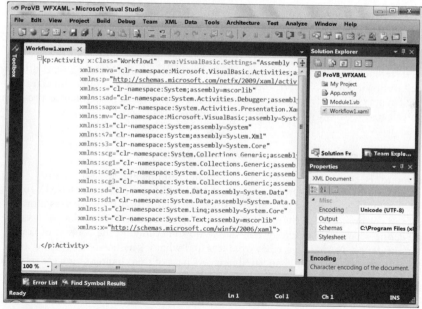

FIGURE 5-4

While this XAML is obviously not the same as what you saw earlier when creating a window, it is very similar. Note that at the top level, instead of an application that references a window, you have an activity. Like the listing which follows shows, it then references the class and a new library, `Microsoft` `.VisualBasic.Activities`:

```
<p:Activity x:Class="Workflow1"  mva:VisualBasic.Settings=
    "Assembly references and imported namespaces serialized as XML namespaces"
        xmlns:mva=
    "clr-namespace:Microsoft.VisualBasic.Activities;assembly=System.Activities"
        xmlns:p="http://schemas.microsoft.com/netfx/2009/xaml/activities"
        xmlns:s="clr-namespace:System;assembly=mscorlib"
        xmlns:sad=
            "clr-namespace:System.Activities.Debugger;assembly=System.Activities"
        xmlns:sapx="clr-namespace:System.Activities.Presentation.Xaml;assembly=
            System.Activities.Presentation"
        xmlns:mv="clr-namespace:Microsoft.VisualBasic;assembly=System"
        xmlns:s1="clr-namespace:System;assembly=System"
        xmlns:s2="clr-namespace:System;assembly=System.Xml"
        xmlns:s3="clr-namespace:System;assembly=System.Core"
        xmlns:scg="clr-namespace:System.Collections.Generic;assembly=System"
        xmlns:scg1=
    "clr-namespace:System.Collections.Generic;assembly=System.ServiceModel"
        xmlns:scg2="clr-namespace:System.Collections.Generic;assembly=System.Core"
        xmlns:scg3="clr-namespace:System.Collections.Generic;assembly=mscorlib"
        xmlns:sd="clr-namespace:System.Data;assembly=System.Data"
        xmlns:sd1="clr-namespace:System.Data;assembly=System.Data.DataSetExtensions"
        xmlns:sl="clr-namespace:System.Linq;assembly=System.Core"
        xmlns:st="clr-namespace:System.Text;assembly=mscorlib"
        xmlns:x="http://schemas.microsoft.com/winfx/2006/xaml">

</p:Activity>
```

Code snippet from workflow1

One of the new features related to workflows in .NET 4 is that they include some application-specific features related to Visual Basic. What you might want to be aware of is that this same Visual Basic library is also referenced for C# workflows. This feature is covered in more detail in Chapter 27.

However, aside from this difference, you should note that primarily the default XAML for a workflow looks similar to the XAML used for a window. This is, of course, the point; by creating a common declarative syntax, and expanding that syntax to support the necessary core language features, Microsoft is providing a standard way to create interfaces that are driven by functional requirements.

SUMMARY

This chapter introduced you to the concepts of both declarative programming and XAML as an implementation of a declarative programming language. As noted throughout the chapter, XAML focuses on information and the desired transformations to achieve results, whereas Visual Basic focuses more on implementing algorithms and custom logic for changes in state. XAML is used to define what you want as opposed to having you define what and how the system should do something. In the context of a new element of your user interface design, XAML describes what it is and what it's associated with and any transform that is applied to properly display the associated item. As part of this chapter you were introduced to the following:

➤ Declarative vs. imperative programming

➤ Visual Basic's native support for declarative programming

➤ Using XAML to define a window and simple user interface elements

➤ The XAML syntax

➤ Working with XAML to define a workflow process

XAML was designed to work side-by-side with an imperative language environment. As you'll see when you dig into WPF and Silverlight in Chapters 17 through 20 and WF covered in Chapter 26, you will bind your XAML to .NET Framework classes as well as to your custom application .NET classes. The underlying implementation of the XAML bindings is all native .NET classes and implementations, so no boundary needs to be crossed between the imperative and declarative implementation. At runtime your application is simply running within the common language runtime (CLR).

In fact, an early WPF book highlighted this dependence on the .NET Framework implementation by literally using C# to implement an entire WPF interface. The code in question was obscure, but it illustrated the "how" of XAML to readers being introduced to XAML in an almost painful manner. Even though you can, in theory, access everything within Silverlight, WPF, or Workflow using only VB or C#, but doing so is error prone, difficult, and time-consuming. XAML was introduced as a better way to handle some of the more complex interface and workflow tasks that you need to address.

As you'll see, once you master the basics of XAML in any of its common uses, you'll have syntax which is declarative, a way of asking for what is desired similar to the declarative Select, Insert, Update, and Delete statements of T-SQL. However, with XAML your declarative statements will be used to work across different environments and technologies.

Exception Handling
and Debugging

WHAT'S IN THIS CHAPTER

➤ The general principles behind exception handling

➤ The Try...Catch...Finally structure for trapping exceptions

➤ Obtaining information about an exception by using the exception object's methods and properties

➤ How to send exceptions to other code using the Throw statement

➤ Event logging and simple tracing, and how you can use these methods to obtain feedback about how your program is working

All professional-grade programs need to handle unexpected conditions. In older programming languages this was often called *error handling*. Unexpected conditions generated numeric error codes, which were trapped by programming logic that took appropriate action.

The common language runtime in .NET does not generate error codes. When an unexpected condition occurs, the CLR creates a special object called an *exception*. This object contains properties and methods that describe the unexpected condition in detail and provide various items of useful information about what went wrong.

Because the .NET Framework deals with exceptions instead of errors, the term *error handling* is rarely used in the .NET world. Instead, the term *exception handling* is preferred. This term refers to the techniques used in .NET to detect exceptions and take appropriate action.

This chapter covers how exception handling works in Visual Basic 2010. It discusses the common language runtime (CLR) exception handler in detail and the programming methods that are most efficient in catching errors.

NEW IN VISUAL STUDIO 2010 TEAM SYSTEM: HISTORICAL DEBUGGING

While this chapter does not cover features of the Visual Studio environment that are used for debugging, one new feature in Visual Studio 2010 should be mentioned. The Team System edition of Visual Studio 2010 has a new capability for debugging applications called *historical debugging*. It is also known informally as a "black box recorder."

Visual Studio's debugging capability has long included the capability to examine information about a running program using breakpoints and exceptions. When a program is halted, information about the present state of the program is available in Watch windows, the Locals window, and other parts of Visual Studio. This capability is part of every version of Visual Studio.

In the Team System edition only, historical debugging enables a tester to capture state information as a program is being run. If a program fails, then in addition to information about the current state of the program, other information captured at earlier points in the program's execution is available.

Because this capability is not available in all Visual Studio editions, details are not discussed here. If you have the Team System edition, you can access help information about how to use this feature.

NOTES ON COMPATIBILITY WITH VB6

For compatibility, Visual Basic 2010 and other .NET versions of Visual Basic still support the old-style syntax for error handling that was used in Visual Basic 6 and earlier versions. This includes support for the `On Error Goto` statement, the `Resume` statement, and the `Err` object. However, it is strongly recommended that you avoid using this old-style syntax in favor of the exception handling features that are native to .NET.

In case you need to interoperate with such older code, the section "Interoperability with VB6-Style Error Handling," later in this chapter, discusses the support in Visual Basic 2010 for interoperability between new exception handling logic and older "error handling" logic.

EXCEPTIONS IN .NET

As noted in the chapter introduction, .NET generates an *exception object* any time an unexpected condition is encountered. This enables a comprehensive, consistent approach to handling such conditions in any type of .NET module.

An exception object is an instance of a class that derives from a class named `System.Exception`. As shown later, a variety of subclasses of `System.Exception` are used for different circumstances, enabling different types of information about the exception to be exposed.

Important Properties and Methods of an Exception

The base `Exception` class has properties that contain useful information about typical exceptions, as shown in Table 6-1.

TABLE 6-1: Exception Class Properties

PROPERTY	DESCRIPTION
HelpLink	A string indicating the link to help for this exception
InnerException	Returns the exception object reference to an inner (nested) exception
Message	A string that contains a description of the error, suitable for displaying to users
Source	A string containing the name of an object that generated the error
StackTrace	A read-only property that holds the stack trace as a text string. The stack trace is a list of the pending method calls at the point at which the exception was detected. That is, if MethodA called MethodB, and an exception occurred in MethodB, then the stack trace would contain both MethodA and MethodB.
TargetSite	A read-only string property that holds the method that threw the exception

The `Exception` class also has two particularly helpful methods, as shown in Table 6-2.

TABLE 6-2: Useful Exception Class Methods

METHOD	DESCRIPTION
GetBaseException	Returns the first exception in the chain
ToString	Returns the error string, which might include as much information as the error message, the inner exceptions, and the stack trace, depending on the error

You will see these properties and methods used in the code examples shown later, after you have covered the syntax for detecting and handling exceptions.

There are many types of exception objects in the .NET Framework that derive from the base Exception class. Each is suited to a particular type of exception. For example, if a divide by zero is done in code, then an OverflowException is generated. In addition to the dozens of exception types available in the .NET Framework, you can inherit from a class called ApplicationException and create your own exception classes (see Chapter 3 for a discussion of inheritance).

Special-purpose exception classes can be found in many namespaces. Table 6-3 lists four representative examples of the classes that extend Exception.

TABLE 6-3: Examples of Classes Derived from the Exception Class

NAMESPACE	CLASS	DESCRIPTION
System	InvalidOperationException	Generated when a call to an object method is inappropriate because of the object's state
System	OutOfMemoryException	Results when there is not enough memory to carry out an operation
System.XML	XmlException	Often caused by an attempt to read invalid XML
System.Data	DataException	Represents errors in ADO.NET components

There are literally dozens of exception classes scattered throughout the .NET Framework namespaces. It is common for an exception class to reside in a namespace with the classes that typically generate the exception. For example, the DataException class is in System.Data, with the ADO.NET components that often generate a DataException instance.

Having many types of exceptions in VB 2010 enables different types of conditions to be trapped with different exception handlers. The syntax to accomplish that is discussed next.

STRUCTURED EXCEPTION-HANDLING KEYWORDS

Structured exception handling depends on several keywords in Visual Basic 2010:

➤ Try — Begins a section of code in which an exception might be generated from a code error. This section of code is often called a Try block. A trapped exception is automatically routed to a Catch statement (discussed next).

➤ Catch — Begins an exception handler for a type of exception. One or more Catch code blocks follow a Try block, with each Catch block catching a different type of exception. When an exception is encountered in the Try block, the first Catch block that matches that type of exception receives control.

➤ Finally — Contains code that runs when the Try block finishes normally, or when a Catch block receives control and then finishes. That is, the code in the Finally block always runs, regardless of whether an exception was detected. Typically, the Finally block is used to close or dispose of any resources, such as database connections, that might have been left unresolved by the code that had a problem.

➤ Throw — Generates an exception. It's often done in a Catch block when the exception should be kicked back to a calling routine, or in a routine that has itself detected an error such as a bad argument passed in. Another common place to throw an exception is after a test on the arguments passed to a method or property, if it is discovered that the argument is not appropriate and processing cannot continue, such as when a negative number is passed in for a count that must be positive.

The next section of the chapter covers the keywords in detail and includes code samples of the keywords in action. All the code in this section is included in the code download for this chapter.

The Try, Catch, and Finally Keywords

Here is an example showing some typical, simple structured exception-handling code in Visual Basic 2010. In this case, the most likely source of an error is the iItems argument. If it has a value of zero, then this would lead to dividing by zero, which would generate an exception.

First, create a Windows Forms Application in Visual Basic 2010 and place a button on the default Form1 created in the project. In the button's Click event, place the following two lines of code:

```
Dim sngAvg As Single
sngAvg = GetAverage(0, 100)
```

Code snippet from ExceptionHandlingSampleCodeForm

Then put the following function in the form's code:

```
Private Function GetAverage(iItems As Integer, iTotal As Integer) as Single
    ' Code that might throw an exception is wrapped in a Try block
    Try
        Dim sngAverage As Single
        ' This will cause an exception to be thrown if iItems = 0
        sngAverage = CSng(iTotal \ iItems)
        ' This only executes if the line above generated no error
        MessageBox.Show("Calculation successful")
        Return sngAverage
    Catch excGeneric As Exception
        ' If the calculation failed, you get here
        MessageBox.Show("Calculation unsuccessful - exception caught")
        Return 0
    End Try
End Function
```

Code snippet from ExceptionHandlingSampleCodeForm

This code traps all the exceptions with a single generic exception type, and doesn't include any Finally logic. Run the program and press the button. You will be able to follow the sequence better if you place a breakpoint at the top of the GetAverage function and step through the lines.

> *A breakpoint is a marker in a line of code indicating that you wish execution of the program to be suspended when execution reaches that line. When a breakpoint is reached, you have the opportunity to examine values of variables or perform other actions that may help you diagnose a problem. A breakpoint is set in Visual Studio by positioning the cursor on a line of code and choosing the appropriate option. Depending on your settings, you probably also have a shortcut key to set a breakpoint. The most common key used for that purpose is F9. You can also set a breakpoint by clicking next to the desired line in the vertical gray bar on the left side of the Code Editor window.*

Here is a more complex example that traps the divide-by-zero exception explicitly. This second version of the GetAverage function (notice that the name is GetAverage2) also includes a Finally block:

```vbnet
Private Function GetAverage2(iItems As Integer, iTotal As Integer) as Single
    ' Code that might throw an exception is wrapped in a Try block
    Try
        Dim sngAverage As Single
        ' This will cause an exception to be thrown.
        sngAverage = CSng(iTotal \ iItems)
        ' This only executes if the line above generated no error.
        MessageBox.Show("Calculation successful")
        Return sngAverage
    Catch excDivideByZero As DivideByZeroException
        ' You'll get here with an DivideByZeroException in the Try block
        MessageBox.Show("Calculation generated DivideByZero Exception")
        Return 0
    Catch excGeneric As Exception
        ' You'll get here when any exception is thrown and not caught in
        ' a previous Catch block.
        MessageBox.Show("Calculation failed - generic exception caught")
        Return 0
    Finally
        ' Code in the Finally block will always run.
        MessageBox.Show("You always get here, with or without an error")
    End Try
End Function
```

Code snippet from ExceptionHandlingSampleCodeForm

This code contains two `Catch` blocks for different types of exceptions. If an exception is generated, then .NET will go down the `Catch` blocks looking for a matching exception type. That means the `Catch` blocks should be arranged with specific types first and more generic types after.

Place the code for `GetAverage2` in the form, and place another button on `Form1`. In the `Click` event for the second button, place the following code:

```vbnet
Dim sngAvg As Single
sngAvg = GetAverage2(0, 100)
```

Code snippet from ExceptionHandlingSampleCodeForm

Run the program again and press the second button. As before, it's easier to follow if you set a breakpoint early in the code and then step through the code line by line.

The Throw Keyword

Sometimes a `Catch` block is unable to handle an error. Some exceptions are so unexpected that they should be "sent back up the line" to the calling code, so that the problem can be promoted to code that can decide what to do with it. A `Throw` statement is used for that purpose.

A `Throw` statement ends execution of the exception handler — that is, no more code in the `Catch` block after the `Throw` statement is executed. However, `Throw` does not prevent code in the `Finally` block from running. That code still runs before the exception is kicked back to the calling routine.

You can see the `Throw` statement in action by changing the earlier code for `GetAverage2` to look like this:

```vbnet
Private Function GetAverage3(iItems As Integer, iTotal as Integer) as Single
    ' Code that might throw an exception is wrapped in a Try block
    Try
        Dim sngAverage As Single
        ' This will cause an exception to be thrown.
        sngAverage = CSng(iTotal \ iItems)
        ' This only executes if the line above generated no error.
        MessageBox.Show("Calculation successful")
        Return sngAverage
```

```
    Catch excDivideByZero As DivideByZeroException
        ' You'll get here with an DivideByZeroException in the Try block.
        MessageBox.Show("Calculation generated DivideByZero Exception")
        Throw excDivideByZero
        MessageBox.Show("More logic after the throw - never executed")
    Catch excGeneric As Exception
        ' You'll get here when any exception is thrown and not caught in
        ' a previous Catch block.
        MessageBox.Show("Calculation failed - generic exception caught")
        Throw excGeneric
    Finally
        ' Code in the Finally block will always run, even if
        ' an exception was thrown in a Catch block.
        MessageBox.Show("You always get here, with or without an error")
    End Try
End Function
```

Code snippet from ExceptionHandlingSampleCodeForm

Here is some code to call `GetAverage3`. You can place this code in another button's `Click` event to test it:

Available for download on Wrox.com

```
Try
    Dim sngAvg As Single
    sngAvg = GetAverage3(0, 100)
Catch exc As Exception
    MessageBox.Show("Back in the click event after an error")
Finally
    MessageBox.Show("Finally block in click event")
End Try
```

Code snippet from ExceptionHandlingSampleCodeForm

Throwing a New Exception

`Throw` can also be used with exceptions that are created on-the-fly. For example, you might want your earlier function to generate an `ArgumentException`, as you can consider a value of `iItems` of zero to be an invalid value for that argument.

In such a case, a new exception must be instantiated. The constructor allows you to place your own custom message into the exception. To see how this is done, change the aforementioned example to throw your own exception instead of the one caught in the `Catch` block:

Available for download on Wrox.com

```
Private Function GetAverage4(iItems As Integer, iTotal as Integer) as Single
    If iItems = 0 Then
        Dim excOurOwnException As New _
            ArgumentException("Number of items cannot be zero")
        Throw excOurOwnException
    End If
    ' Code that might throw an exception is wrapped in a Try block.
    Try
        Dim sngAverage As Single
        ' This will cause an exception to be thrown.
        sngAverage = CSng(iTotal \ iItems)
        ' This only executes if the line above generated no error.
        MessageBox.Show("Calculation successful")
        Return sngAverage
    Catch excDivideByZero As DivideByZeroException
        ' You'll get here with an DivideByZeroException in the Try block.
        MessageBox.Show("Calculation generated DivideByZero Exception")
        Throw excDivideByZero
        MessageBox.Show("More logic after the thrown - never executed")
```

```
    Catch excGeneric As Exception
        ' You'll get here when any exception is thrown and not caught in
        ' a previous Catch block.
        MessageBox.Show("Calculation failed - generic exception caught")
          Throw excGeneric
    Finally
        ' Code in the Finally block will always run, even if
        ' an exception was thrown in a Catch block.
        MessageBox.Show("You always get here, with or without an error")
    End Try
End Function
```

Code snippet from ExceptionHandlingSampleCodeForm

This code can be called from a button with similar code for calling `GetAverage3`. Just change the name of the function called to `GetAverage4`.

This technique is particularly well suited to dealing with problems detected in property procedures. Property Set logic often includes a check to ensure that the property is about to be assigned a valid value. If not, then throwing a new `ArgumentException` (instead of assigning the property value) is a good way to inform the calling code about the problem.

The Exit Try Statement

The `Exit Try` statement will, under a given circumstance, break out of the `Try` or `Catch` block and continue at the `Finally` block. In the following example, you exit a `Catch` block if the value of `iItems` is 0, because you know that your error was caused by that problem:

Available for
download on
Wrox.com

```
Private Function GetAverage5(iItems As Integer, iTotal as Integer) As Single
    ' Code that might throw an exception is wrapped in a Try block.
    Try
        Dim sngAverage As Single
        ' This will cause an exception to be thrown.
        sngAverage = CSng(iTotal \ iItems)
        ' This only executes if the line above generated no error.
        MessageBox.Show("Calculation successful")
        Return sngAverage
    Catch excDivideByZero As DivideByZeroException
        ' You'll get here with an DivideByZeroException in the Try block.
        If iItems = 0 Then
            Return 0
            Exit Try
        Else
            MessageBox.Show("Error not caused by iItems")
        End If
        Throw excDivideByZero
        MessageBox.Show("More logic after the thrown - never executed")
    Catch excGeneric As Exception
        ' You'll get here when any exception is thrown and not caught in
        ' a previous Catch block.
        MessageBox.Show("Calculation failed - generic exception caught")
        Throw excGeneric
    Finally
        ' Code in the Finally block will always run, even if
        ' an exception was thrown in a Catch block.
        MessageBox.Show("You always get here, with or without an error")
    End Try
End Sub
```

Code snippet from ExceptionHandlingSampleCodeForm

In your first `Catch` block, you have inserted an `If` block so that you can exit the block given a certain condition (in this case, if the overflow exception was caused because the value of `iItems` was 0). The `Exit Try` goes immediately to the `Finally` block and completes the processing there:

```
If iItems = 0 Then
    Return 0
    Exit Try
Else
    MessageBox.Show("Error not caused by iItems")
End If
```

Code snippet from ExceptionHandlingSampleCodeForm

Now, if the overflow exception is caused by something other than division by zero, you'll get a message box displaying "Error not caused by iItems."

Nested Try Structures

Sometimes particular lines in a `Try` block may need special exception processing. Moreover, errors can occur within the `Catch` portion of the `Try` structures and cause further exceptions to be thrown. For both of these scenarios, nested `Try` structures are available. You can alter the example under the section "The Throw Keyword" to demonstrate the following code:

```
Private Function GetAverage6(iItems As Integer, iTotal as Integer) As Single
    ' Code that might throw an exception is wrapped in a Try block.
    Try
        Dim sngAverage As Single
        ' Do something for performance testing….
        Try
            LogEvent("GetAverage")
        Catch exc As Exception
            MessageBox.Show("Logging function unavailable")
        End Try
        ' This will cause an exception to be thrown.
        sngAverage = CSng(iTotal \ iItems)
        ' This only executes if the line above generated no error.
        MessageBox.Show("Calculation successful")
        Return sngAverage
    Catch excDivideByZero As DivideByZeroException
        ' You'll get here with an DivideByZeroException in the Try block.
        MessageBox.Show("Error not divide by 0")
        Throw excDivideByZero
        MessageBox.Show("More logic after the thrown - never executed")
    Catch excGeneric As Exception
        ' You'll get here when any exception is thrown and not caught in
        ' a previous Catch block.
        MessageBox.Show("Calculation failed - generic exception caught")
        Throw excGeneric
    Finally
        ' Code in the Finally block will always run, even if
        ' an exception was thrown in a Catch block.
        MessageBox.Show("You always get here, with or without an error")
    End Try
End Function
```

Code snippet from ExceptionHandlingSampleCodeForm

In the preceding example, you are assuming that a function exists to log an event. This function would typically be in a common library, and might log the event in various ways. You will look at logging exceptions in detail later in the chapter, but a simple `LogEvent` function might look like this:

```
Public Sub LogEvent(ByVal sEvent As String)
    FileOpen(1, "logfile.txt", OpenMode.Append)
    Print(1, DateTime.Now & "-" & sEvent & vbCrLf)
    FileClose(1)
End Sub
```

Code snippet from ExceptionHandlingSampleCodeForm

In this case, you don't want a problem logging an event, such as a "disk full" error, to crash the routine. The code for the GetAverage6 function triggers a message box to indicate trouble with the logging function.

A Catch block can be empty. In that case, the exception is ignored. However, execution does not pick up with the line after the line that generated the error, but instead picks up with either the Finally block or the line after the End Try if no Finally block exists.

Using Exception Properties

The previous examples have displayed hard-coded messages in message boxes, which is obviously not a good technique for production applications. Instead, a message box or log entry describing an exception should provide as much information as possible concerning the problem. To do this, various properties of the exception can be used.

The most brutal way to get information about an exception is to use the ToString method of the exception. Suppose that you modify the earlier example of GetAverage2 to change the displayed information about the exception like this:

```
Private Function GetAverage2(ByVal iItems As Integer, ByVal iTotal As Integer) _
    As Single
    ' Code that might throw an exception is wrapped in a Try block.
    Try
        Dim sngAverage As Single
        ' This will cause an exception to be thrown.
        sngAverage = CSng(iTotal \ iItems)
        ' This only executes if the line above generated no error.
        MessageBox.Show("Calculation successful")
        Return sngAverage
    Catch excDivideByZero As DivideByZeroException
        ' You'll get here with an DivideByZeroException in the Try block.
        MessageBox.Show(excDivideByZero.ToString)
        Throw excDivideByZero
        MessageBox.Show("More logic after the thrown - never executed")
    Catch excGeneric As Exception
        ' You'll get here when any exception is thrown and not caught in
        ' a previous Catch block.
        MessageBox.Show("Calculation failed - generic exception caught")
        Throw excGeneric
    Finally
        ' Code in the Finally block will always run, even if
        ' an exception was thrown in a Catch block.
        MessageBox.Show("You always get here, with or without an error")
    End Try
End Function
```

Code snippet from ExceptionHandlingSampleCodeForm

When the function is accessed with iItems = 0, a message box similar to the one in Figure 6-1 will be displayed.

The Message Property

The message shown in Figure 6-1 is helpful to a developer because it contains a lot of information, but it's not something you would typically want users to see. Instead, a user normally needs to see a short description of the problem, and that is supplied by the `Message` property.

If the previous code is changed so that the `Message` property is used instead of `ToString`, then the message box will provide something like what is shown in Figure 6-2.

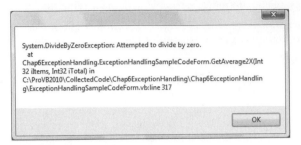

System.DivideByZeroException: Attempted to divide by zero.
at
Chap6ExceptionHandling.ExceptionHandlingSampleCodeForm.GetAverage2X(Int 32 iItems, Int32 iTotal) in
C:\ProVB2010\CollectedCode\Chap6ExceptionHandling\Chap6ExceptionHandlin g\ExceptionHandlingSampleCodeForm.vb:line 317

OK

Attempted to divide by zero.

OK

FIGURE 6-1　　　　　　　　　　　　　　　　　　　**FIGURE 6-2**

The InnerException and TargetSite Properties

The `InnerException` property is used to store an exception trail. This comes in handy when multiple exceptions occur. It's quite common for an exception to occur that sets up circumstances whereby further exceptions are raised. As exceptions occur in a sequence, you can choose to stack them for later reference by use of the `InnerException` property of your `Exception` object. As each exception joins the stack, the previous `Exception` object becomes the inner exception in the stack.

For simplicity, you'll start a new code sample, with just a subroutine that generates its own exception. You'll include code to add a reference to an `InnerException` object to the exception you are generating with the `Throw` method.

This example also includes a message box to show what's stored in the exception's `TargetSite` property. As shown in the results, `TargetSite` will contain the name of the routine generating the exception — in this case, `HandlerExample`. Here's the code:

Available for download on Wrox.com

```
Sub HandlerExample()
 Dim intX As Integer
 Dim intY As Integer
 Dim intZ As Integer
 intY = 0
 intX = 5
 ' First Required Error Statement.
 Try
   ' Cause a "Divide by Zero"
   intZ = CType((intX \ intY), Integer)
 ' Catch the error.
 Catch objA As System.DivideByZeroException
    Try
      Throw (New Exception("0 as divisor", objA))
    Catch objB As Exception
      Dim sError As String
      sError = "My Message: " & objB.Message & vbCrLf & vbCrLf
      sError &= "Inner Exception Message: " & _
          objB.InnerException.Message & vbCrLf & vbCrLf
      sError &= "Method Error Occurred: " & objB.TargetSite.Name
      MessageBox.Show(sError)
    End Try
 Catch
```

```
      Messagebox.Show("Caught any other errors")
    Finally
      Messagebox.Show(Str(intZ))
    End Try
End Sub
```

Code snippet from ExceptionHandlingSampleCodeForm

As before, you catch the divide-by-zero error in the first `Catch` block, and the exception is stored in `objA` so that you can reference its properties later.

You throw a new exception with a more general message ("0 as divisor") that is easier to interpret, and you build up your stack by appending `objA` as the `InnerException` object using an overloaded constructor for the `Exception` object:

```
Throw (New Exception("0 as divisor", objA))
```

You catch your newly thrown exception in another `Catch` statement. Note how it does not catch a specific type of error:

```
Catch objB As Exception
```

Then you construct an error message for the new exception and display it in a message box:

```
Dim sError As String
sError = "My Message: " & objB.Message & vbCrLf & vbCrLf
sError &= "Inner Exception Message: " & _
    objB.InnerException.Message & vbCrLf & vbCrLf
sError &= "Method Error Occurred: " & objB.TargetSite.Name
MessageBox.Show(sError)
```

Code snippet from ExceptionHandlingSampleCodeForm

The message box that is produced is shown in Figure 6-3.

First your own message is included, based on the new exception thrown by your own code. Then the `InnerException` gets the next exception in the stack, which is the divide-by-zero exception, and its message is included. Finally, the `TargetSite` property gives you the name of the method that threw the exception. `TargetSite` is particularly helpful in logs or error reports from users that are used by developers to track down unexpected problems.

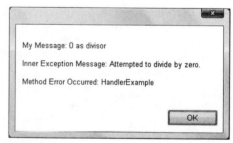

My Message: 0 as divisor

Inner Exception Message: Attempted to divide by zero.

Method Error Occurred: HandlerExample

FIGURE 6-3

After this message box, the `Finally` clause displays another message box that just shows the current value of `intZ`, which is zero because the divide failed. This second box also occurs in other examples that follow.

Source and StackTrace

The `Source` and `StackTrace` properties provide the user with information regarding where the error occurred. This supplemental information can be invaluable, as the user can pass it on to the troubleshooter in order to help resolve errors more quickly. The following example uses these two properties and shows the feedback when the error occurs:

```
Sub HandlerExample2()
Dim intX As Integer
Dim intY As Integer
Dim intZ As Integer
intY = 0
intX = 5
' First Required Error Statement.
Try
```

```
  ' Cause a "Divide by Zero"
  intZ = CType((intX \ intY), Integer)
' Catch the error.
Catch objA As System.DivideByZeroException
    objA.Source = "HandlerExample2"
    Messagebox.Show("Error Occurred at: " & _
        objA.Source & objA.StackTrace)
Finally
    Messagebox.Show(Str(intZ))
End Try
End Sub
```

Code snippet from ExceptionHandlingSampleCodeForm

The output from the `Messagebox` statement is very detailed, providing the entire path and line number where the error occurred, as shown in Figure 6-4.

Notice that this information is also included in the `ToString` method examined earlier (refer to Figure 6-1).

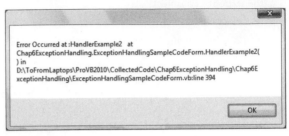

Error Occurred at :HandlerExample2   at
Chap6ExceptionHandling.ExceptionHandlingSampleCodeForm.HandlerExample2(
) in
D:\ToFromLaptops\ProVB2010\CollectedCode\Chap6ExceptionHandling\Chap6E
xceptionHandling\ExceptionHandlingSampleCodeForm.vb:line 394

GetBaseException

FIGURE 6-4

The `GetBaseException` method comes in very handy when you are deep in a set of thrown exceptions. This method returns the originating exception by recursively examining the `InnerException` until it reaches an exception object that has a null `InnerException` property. That exception is normally the exception that started the chain of unanticipated events.

In the following code, a chain of exceptions starts with a divide by zero, which results in exception object `objA`. The chain then continues with exception objects `objB` and `objC`, both created in code. Both of those last two exceptions are created by using a constructor on the `Exception` class that takes an argument for the `InnerException` of that new exception. Finally, the `GetBaseException` method is accessed on `objC`:

Available for download on Wrox.com

```
Sub HandlerExample3()
    Dim intX As Integer
    Dim intY As Integer
    Dim intZ As Integer
    intY = 0
    intX = 5
    ' First Required Error Statement.
    Try
        ' Cause a "Divide by Zero"
        intZ = CType((intX \ intY), Integer)
    ' Catch the error.
    Catch objA As System.DivideByZeroException
        Try
            Throw (New Exception("0 as divisor", objA))
        Catch objB As Exception
            Try
                Throw (New Exception("New error", objB))
            Catch objC As Exception
                Messagebox.Show(objC.GetBaseException.Message)
            End Try
        End Try
    Finally
        Messagebox.Show(Str(intZ))
    End Try
End Sub
```

Code snippet from ExceptionHandlingSampleCodeForm

The call `objC.GetBaseException` will trace back though the `InnerException`, for `ObjC`, which is `objB`, and then through `objB`'s `InnerException`, which is the original exception, `objA`. However, `objA` has a null `InnerException` because it's an original exception caused by the divide by zero. Thus, `objC.GetBaseException.Message` returns the `Message` property of the original `OverflowException` message even though you've thrown multiple errors since the original error occurred:

```
Messagebox.Show(objC.GetBaseException.Message)
```

To put it another way, the code traverses back to the exception caught as `objA` and displays the same message as the `objA.Message` property would, as shown in Figure 6-5.

HelpLink

The `HelpLink` property gets or sets the help link for a specific `Exception` object. It can be set to any string value, but it's typically set to a URL. If you create your own exception in code, you might want to set `HelpLink` to a URL (or a URN) describing the error in more detail. Then the code that catches the exception can go to that link. You could create and throw your own custom application exception with code like the following:

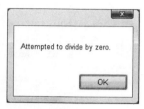

FIGURE 6-5

```
Dim exc As New ApplicationException("A short description of the problem")
exc.HelpLink = "http://mysite.com/somehtmlfile.htm"
Throw exc
```

Code snippet from ExceptionHandlingSampleCodeForm

When trapping an exception, the `HelpLink` can be used to launch a viewer so the user can see details about the problem. The following example shows this in action, using the built-in Explorer in Windows:

```
Sub HandlerExample4()
Try
    Dim exc As New ApplicationException("A short description of the problem")
    exc.HelpLink = "http://mysite.com/somehtmlfile.htm"
    Throw exc
    ' Catch the error.
Catch objA As System.Exception
    Shell("explorer.exe " & objA.HelpLink)
End Try
End Sub
```

Code snippet from ExceptionHandlingSampleCodeForm

This results in launching Internet Explorer to show the page specified by the URL. Most exceptions thrown by the CLR or the .NET Framework's classes have a blank `HelpLink` property. You should only count on using `HelpLink` if you have previously set it to a URL (or some other type of link information) yourself.

INTEROPERABILITY WITH VB6-STYLE ERROR HANDLING

Because Visual Basic 2010 still supports the older `On Error` statement from pre-.NET versions of VB, you may encounter code that handles errors with `On Error` instead of with structured exception handling. You can use both techniques in a single program, but it is not possible to use both in a single routine. If you attempt to use both `On Error` and `Try...Catch` in a single routine, you will get a syntax error.

The Visual Basic compiler does allow the two techniques for handling errors to communicate with each other. For example, suppose you have a routine that uses `Err.Raise` to promote the error to the calling code. Also suppose that the calling code makes the call in a `Try...Catch` block. In that case, the error created by `Err.Raise` becomes an exception in the calling code and is trapped by a `Catch` block just as a normal exception would be. Here's a code example to illustrate. First, create a subroutine that creates an error with `Err.Raise`, like this:

```
Private Sub RaiseErrorWithErrRaise()
    Err.Raise(53)    ' indicates File Not Found
End Sub
```

Code snippet from ExceptionHandlingSampleCodeForm

Then call this routine from a button's `Click` event, with the call inside a `Try...Catch` block:

```
Private Sub Button2_Click(ByVal sender As System.Object, _
    ByVal e As System.EventArgs) Handles Button2.Click
    Try
        RaiseErrorWithErrRaise()
    Catch ex As Exception
        MessageBox.Show(ex.Message)
    End Try
End Sub
```

Code snippet from ExceptionHandlingSampleCodeForm

When the button is clicked, it will display a message box with "File Not Found." Even though the File Not Found error is raised by `Err.Raise`, it is translated to a .NET exception automatically.

Similarly, exceptions that are generated by a `Throw` statement in a called routine can be trapped by `On Error` in a calling routine. The exception is then translated into an `Err` object that works like the VB6 `Err` object.

ERROR LOGGING

Error logging is important in many applications for thorough troubleshooting. It is common for end users of an application to forget exactly what an error said. Recording specific errors in a log enables you to get the specific error message without recreating the error.

While error logging is very important, you only want to use it to trap specific levels of errors because it carries overhead and can reduce the performance of your application. Specifically, log only errors that are critical to your application integrity — for instance, an error that would cause the data that the application is working with to become invalid.

There are three main approaches to error logging:

➤   Write error information in a text file or flat file located in a strategic location.

➤   Write error information to a central database.

➤   Write error information to the system's Event Logs, which are available on all versions of Windows supported by the .NET Framework 4. The .NET Framework includes a component that can be used to write to and read from the System, Application, and Security Logs on any given machine.

The type of logging you choose depends on the categories of errors you wish to trap and the types of machines on which you will run your application. If you choose to write to an Event Log, then you need to categorize the errors and write them in the appropriate log file. Resource-, hardware-, and system-level errors fit best into the System Event Log. Data access errors fit best into the Application Event Log. Permission errors fit best into the Security Event Log.

The Event Log

Three Windows Event Logs are available: the System, Application, and Security Logs. Events in these logs can be viewed using the Event Viewer, which is accessed from the Control Panel. Access Administrative Tools and then select the Event Viewer subsection to view events. Typically, your applications would use the Application Event Log.

Event logging is available in your program through an `EventLog` component, which can both read and write to all of the available logs on a machine. The `EventLog` component is part of the `System.Diagnostics` namespace. This component allows adding and removing custom Event Logs, reading and writing to and from the standard Windows Event Logs, and creating customized Event Log entries.

Event Logs can become full, as they have a limited amount of space, so you only want to write critical information to your Event Logs. You can customize each of your system Event Log's properties by changing the log size and specifying how the system will handle events that occur when the log is full. You can configure the log to overwrite data when it is full or overwrite all events older than a given number of days. Remember that the Event Log that is written to is based on where the code is running from, so if there are many tiers, then you must locate the proper Event Log information to research the error further.

There are five types of Event Log entries you can make. These five types are divided into event type entries and audit type entries.

Event type entries are as follows:

➤ **Information** — Added when events such as a service starting or stopping occurs

➤ **Warning** — Occurs when a noncritical event happens that might cause future problems, such as disk space getting low

➤ **Error** — Should be logged when something occurs that prevents normal processing, such as a startup service not being able to start

Audit type entries usually go into the Security Log and can be either of the following:

➤ **Audit Success** — For example, a success audit might be a successful login through an application to an SQL Server.

➤ **Audit Failure** — A failure audit might come in handy if a user doesn't have access to create an output file on a certain file system.

If you don't specify the type of Event Log entry, an information type entry is generated.

Each entry in an Event Log has a `Source` property. This required property is a programmer-defined string that is assigned to an event to help categorize the events in a log. A new source must be defined prior to being used in an entry in an Event Log. The `SourceExists` method is used to determine whether a particular source already exists on the given computer. Use a string that is relevant to where the error originated, such as the component's name. Packaged software often uses the software name as the source in the Application Log. This helps group errors that occur by specific software package.

The `EventLog` component is in the `System.Diagnostics` namespace. To use it conveniently, include an `Imports System.Diagnostics` statement in the declarations section of your code.

Certain security rights must be obtained in order to manipulate Event Logs. Ordinary programs can read all of the Event Logs and write to the Application Event Log. Special privileges, on the administrator level, are required to perform tasks such as clearing and deleting Event Logs. Your application should not normally need to do these tasks, or write to any log besides the Application Event Log.

The most common events, methods, and properties for the `EventLog` component are listed and described in the following tables.

Events, Methods, and Properties

Table 6-4 describes the relevant event of the `EventLog` component.

TABLE 6-4: Relevant EventLog Event

EVENT	DESCRIPTION
EntryWritten	Generated when an event is written to a log

Table 6-5 describes the relevant methods of the EventLog component.

TABLE 6-5: Relevant EventLog Methods

METHODS	DESCRIPTION
CreateEventSource	Creates an event source in the specified log
DeleteEventSource	Deletes an event source and associated entries
WriteEntry	Writes a string to a specified log
Exists	Used to determine whether a specific Event Log exists
SourceExists	Used to determine whether a specific source exists in a log
GetEventLogs	Retrieves a list of all Event Logs on a particular computer
Delete	Deletes an entire Event Log. Use this method with care.

Table 6-6 describes the relevant properties of the EventLog component.

TABLE 6-6: Relevant EventLog Properties

PROPERTIES	DESCRIPTION
Source	Specifies the source of the entry to be written
Log	Used to specify a log to write to. The three logs are System, Application, and Security. The Application Log is the default if not specified.

The following example illustrates some of these methods and properties:

Available for
download on
Wrox.com

```
Sub LoggingExample1()
  Dim objLog As New EventLog()
  Dim objLogEntryType As EventLogEntryType
  Try
    Throw (New EntryPointNotFoundException())
  Catch objA As System.EntryPointNotFoundException
    If Not EventLog.SourceExists("Example") Then
      EventLog.CreateEventSource("Example", "System")
    End If
    objLog.Source = "Example"
    objLog.Log = "System"
    objLogEntryType = EventLogEntryType.Information
    objLog.WriteEntry("Error: " & objA.Message, objLogEntryType)
  End Try
End Sub
```

Code snippet from ExceptionHandlingSampleCodeForm

The preceding code declares two variables: one to instantiate your log and one to hold your entry's type information. Note that you need to check for the existence of a source prior to creating it. The following two lines of code accomplish that:

Available for
download on
Wrox.com

```
If Not EventLog.SourceExists("Example") Then
  EventLog.CreateEventSource("Example", "System")
```

Code snippet from ExceptionHandlingSampleCodeForm

After you have verified or created your source, you can set the Source property of the EventLog object, set the Log property to specify which log you want to write to, and set EventLogEntryType to Information (other options are Warning, Error, SuccessAudit, and FailureAudit). If you attempt to write to a source that does not exist in a specific log, then you get an error. After you have set these three properties of the EventLog object, you can then write your entry. In this example, you concatenated the word Error with the actual exception's Message property to form the string to write to the log:

```
objLog.Source = "Example"
objLog.Log = "System"
objLogEntryType = EventLogEntryType.Information
objLog.WriteEntry("Error: " & objA.Message, objLogEntryType)
```

Code snippet from ExceptionHandlingSampleCodeForm

Writing to Trace Files

As an alternative to the event log, you can write your debugging and error information to trace files. A *trace file* is a text-based file that you generate in your program to track detailed information about an error condition. Trace files are also a good way to supplement your event logging if you want to track detailed information that would potentially fill the Event Log, or diagnosis of a problem requires analysis of a specific sequence of execution events.

This section covers using the StreamWriter interface in your development of a trace file. In this case, a trace file is a text file, so you need to understand the concepts involved in writing to text files by setting up streamwriters and debug listeners. The StreamWriter interface is handled through the System.IO namespace. It enables you to interface with the files in the file system on a given machine. The Debug class interfaces with these output objects through listener objects. The job of any listener object is to collect, store, and send the stored output to text files, logs, and the Output window. In the example, you will use the TextWriterTraceListener class.

As you will see, the StreamWriter object opens an output path to a text file, and by binding the StreamWriter object to a listener object you can direct debug output to a text file.

Trace listeners are output targets and can be a TextWriter or an EventLog, or can send output to the default Output window (which is DefaultTraceListener). The TextWriterTraceListener accommodates the WriteLine method of a Debug object by providing an output object that stores information to be flushed to the output stream, which you set up by the StreamWriter interface.

Table 6-7 lists some of the commonly used methods from the StreamWriter object.

TABLE 6-7: Common StreamWriter Methods

METHOD	DESCRIPTION
Close	Closes the StreamWriter
Flush	Flushes all content of the StreamWriter to the output file designated upon creation of the StreamWriter
Write	Writes byte output to the stream. Optional parameters allow location designation in the stream (offset).
WriteLine	Writes characters followed by a line terminator to the current stream object

Table 6-8 lists some of the methods associated with the Debug object, which provides the output mechanism for the text file example to follow.

TABLE 6-8: Common Debug Object Methods

METHOD	DESCRIPTION
Assert	Checks a condition and displays a message if False
Close	Executes a flush on the output buffer and closes all listeners
Fail	Emits an error message in the form of an Abort/Retry/Ignore message box
Flush	Flushes the output buffer and writes it to the listeners
Write	Writes bytes to the output buffer
WriteLine	Writes characters followed by a line terminator to the output buffer
WriteIf	Writes bytes to the output buffer if a specific condition is True
WriteLineIf	Writes characters followed by a line terminator to the output buffer if a specific condition is True

The following example shows how you can open an existing file (called `mytext.txt`) for output and assign it to the `Listeners` object of the `Debug` object so that it can catch your `Debug.WriteLine` statements:

Available for download on Wrox.com

```
Sub LoggingExample2()
  Dim objWriter As New _
     IO.StreamWriter("C:\mytext.txt", True)
  Debug.Listeners.Add(New TextWriterTraceListener(objWriter))
  Try
     Throw (New EntryPointNotFoundException())
  Catch objA As System.EntryPointNotFoundException
     Debug.WriteLine(objA.Message)
     objWriter.Flush()
     objWriter.Close()
     objWriter = Nothing
  End Try
End Sub
```

Code snippet from ExceptionHandlingSampleCodeForm

Looking in detail at this code, you first create a `StreamWriter` that is assigned to a file in your local file system:

```
Dim objWriter As New _
     IO.StreamWriter("C:\mytext.txt", True)
```

You then assign your `StreamWriter` to a debug listener by using the `Add` method:

```
Debug.Listeners.Add(New TextWriterTraceListener (objWriter))
```

This example forces an exception and catches it, writing the `Message` property of the `Exception` object (which is "Entry point was not found") to the debug buffer through the `WriteLine` method:

```
Debug.WriteLine(objA.Message)
```

Finally, you flush the listener buffer to the output file and free your resources:

```
objWriter.Flush()
objWriter.Close()
objWriter = Nothing
```

After running this code, you can examine the c:\mytext.txt file to see the trace output.

SUMMARY

This chapter reviewed the `Exception` object and the syntax available to work with exceptions. You have looked at the various properties of exceptions and learned how to use the exposed information. You have also seen how to promote exceptions to consuming code using the `Throw` statement, and how structured exception handling interoperates with the old-style `On Error`. As discussed, any new code you write should use structured exception handling. Avoid using the old-style `On Error` except for maintenance tasks in old code.

The chapter also covered writing to Event Logs to capture information about generated exceptions. While you should use Event Logs judiciously to avoid overloading them, having information about exceptions captured for after-the-face analysis is an invaluable tool for diagnosis.

The chapter covered a simple technique for generating trace output for programs. More sophisticated tracing features are available in .NET using the `Trace` and `TraceSwitch` classes, but a complete example is beyond the scope of this book. By using the full capabilities for exception handling that are now available in Visual Basic 2010, you can make your applications more reliable, and diagnose problems faster when they do occur. Proper use of event logging and tracing on can also help you tune your application for better performance.

7

Test-Driven Development

WHAT YOU WILL LEARN IN THIS CHAPTER

➤ What is test-driven development?

➤ Why should you test your applications?

➤ How to create unit tests in Visual Studio

➤ How to run automated tests in Visual Studio

➤ Testing in database applications

➤ How to create your classes from your tests

➤ Testing functionality in various editions of Visual Studio

➤ Third-party testing tools

Traditionally, testing has often been an afterthought in software development. Frequently, it was done at — or near — the end of the development cycle. In addition, it was typically the "junior developers" who were tasked with going through the application, testing everything. As a result of these two circumstances, testing often was rushed, incomplete, and led to the release of buggy software to the end users.

Into this mix, a number of developers began to use a new method that became known as *test-driven development (TDD)*. In TDD, you write the tests early (or before you write any real code), and test throughout the development cycle. This means that the code is tested more thoroughly, and by the developers themselves. The result should be fewer bugs, and code that works more closely to the design. It is this last point that causes many TDD proponents to describe TDD not as a testing strategy, but as a design strategy. By writing the tests first, you essentially encapsulate the desired behavior into the tests, meaning the code will follow.

One classic rationale of using this technique was that catching a bug earlier in the process was less expensive than finding one later. This makes sense; finding and fixing a bug as the code is first written is much less expensive than paying an additional developer to find and fix the bug after the code has been integrated into numerous other routines, incorporated into a multiform user interface, and so on.

Even more important than catching bugs, however, TDD gives you more confidence to change your code. If you have a solid suite of tests available for your classes, then you can dig in and make changes to your code with less worry that you might break something. If the tests still pass, then your code is still doing what it should.

This chapter looks at the tools available within Visual Studio for testing your applications. Most of the samples in this chapter will work with Visual Studio Professional and above (that is, the Express Editions of Visual Studio do not support these built-in testing tools). In addition, you will look at the additional features available within the Premium and Ultimate editions of Visual Studio, and some third-party tools that are available.

WHEN AND HOW TO TEST

Once you have decided that you want to do some form of TDD in your applications, you next need to decide when and how to test. The staunchest TDD proponents will say that you must use TDD with every application, and never write any code until you have written a test. The advice at the opposite end is the traditional "do all the testing at the end" methodology.

The right choice is likely somewhere in the middle; and where it fits in the continuum varies according to the target application, the abilities and desires of the development team, and the time allowed for the development. You might try going "full TDD" for a project or two to see how it fits you and your team, or you might simply create a number of tests to monitor an existing section of code that would benefit from TDD.

This chapter takes a pragmatic approach to testing, in which sometimes the test is written first, and in others the code is written first. While the latter is frowned upon by some TDD proponents, it still tests the code. In addition, if something changes in the code, the test will demonstrate whether it is still valid.

Using Assertions

Many developers have done a form of TDD in the past, creating test forms that contain various fields and many buttons to test various components of their application (see Figure 7-1). TDD formalizes this testing process into a cleaner, less error-prone, and more reliable methodology. The problem with the "test form" methodology is that the developer must remember the order of the various button clicks required for complete testing, as there may be side effects from testing the methods in a specific order. In addition, the maximum practical number of tests you can do with this style of testing is limited by the number of buttons that can fit on a screen.

FIGURE 7-1

With TDD, you can avoid these limitations by writing a series of small routines to test various aspects of your code. Each test is self-contained, so you do not have to test methods in a particular order to avoid one test affecting another. You may end up writing multiple routines to test a single method (for example, to test for edge cases, invalid input, etc.), but each test runs in relative isolation. Because each test is run within some sort of container and doesn't require a specific user interface, there is no limit to the number of tests you can create for a class.

At the core of each test are *assertions*. These are method calls that test for expected results from the code. For example, if you were testing some code that added two numbers — let's say 1 and 1 to keep it simple — you would have an assertion that the returned value be the expected result (we'll say 2 here). If the value is what is expected, then that part of the test succeeds. If any of the assertions in a test fail, then the whole test fails. There are three basic assert classes in the Microsoft.VisualStudio.TestTools.UnitTesting namespace: `Assert`, `StringAssert`, and `CollectionAssert`. The `Assert` class provides a number of basic tests via a series of static methods. Some of the more commonly used of these are described in Table 7-1.

TABLE 7-1: Common Assert Class Methods

METHOD	DESCRIPTION
IsTrue IsFalse	Assumes that some passed value is true or false. If it is not, then the assertion fails. Usually this is used to test the return values of methods that return `Boolean` values.
AreEqual AreNotEqual	Assumes that two values are equal (or not). This is typically used to check the return value of a method against the expected value. For example, you could use this method with a method that adds two numbers: `Assert.AreEqual(calc.Add(1,1), 2)` If the return value of `calc.Add(1,1)` is 2, then the test passes.
AreSame AreNotSame	Assumes that two objects are the same (or not). This means more than just having all of the properties have the same value; it means that the two values are pointing to the same object in memory.
IsNull	Assumes that the return value is `Nothing`.

IsInstanceOfType
IsNotInstanceOfType
	Assumes that the return value from the method is of a particular object type (or not). This is frequently used when the method might return a base class, or one of multiple child classes. For example, you might have a method that is defined as returning a `Stream`, but when called might return a `Stream`, `FileStream`, `NetworkStream`, or other class that inherits from `Stream`. You would then use this assertion if you expected a `FileStream` as follows:
	`Assert.IsInstanceOfType(obj.OpenStream(),`
	`    GetType(IO.FileStream))`

Fail	Immediately fails the current test. Typically, you would use this when catching an exception, so that rather than simply having the test blow up, you gracefully return a test failure instead.

The `StringAssert` class — as you might expect — is used to test `String` return values. Common methods of the `StringAssert` class are described in Table 7-2.

TABLE 7-2: Common StringAssert Class Methods

METHOD	DESCRIPTION

StartsWith
EndsWith
	Assumes that the return value starts (or ends) with a particular substring. For example, if you were testing a data access component method that should return the results of an alphabetic search, you could use the following assertion:
	`Dim dt As DataTable =`
	`    obj.GetEmployeesByLastName("D")`
	`Dim firstResult As String =`
	`    dt.Rows(0).Item("LastName").ToString()`
	`StringAssert.StartsWith(firstResult, "D")`

Contains	Assumes that the return value contains some substring.
Matches DoesNotMatch	Assumes that the tested value matches (or doesn't match) a given regular expression.

As described in Table 7-3, the `CollectionAssert` class provides static methods for testing instances of `ICollection`.

TABLE 7-3: Common CollectionAssert Class Methods

METHOD	DESCRIPTION
AreEqual AreNotEqual	Tests whether two collections are the same (or different). The two collections are the same if they contain the same number of entries, with the same values. For example, {1, 2, 3} is equal to {1, 2, 3}, but not {1, 3, 2}.
Contains DoesNotContain	Tests for the presence (or absence) of a particular item within the collection. For example, you might use it to test the results of a database query to ensure that an expected value is returned.
AllItemsAreNotNull	Assumes that all of the items in the collection are not Nothing.
AllItemsAreUnique	Assumes that there are no duplicates in the collection.
AreEquivalent AreNotEquivalent	Tests whether two collections are the same (or different). This differs from AreEqual in that the values do not need to be in the same order. Therefore, {1, 2, 3} is equivalent to both {1, 2, 3} and {1, 3, 2}.
IsSubsetOf IsNotSubsetOf	Tests one collection to see if it contains (or doesn't contain) the items of another collection.
AllItemsAreInstancesOfType	Assumes that the collection only includes items of the same type. This can be very useful when testing methods that return non-generic collections, or collections of Object.

Each of the preceding methods has a number of overloads. The simplest overload merely takes the appropriate parameters. Additional overloads return a string to provide additional information about the failure. This includes a method that allows you to insert additional parameters into the message. For example, you could call the Add method described earlier using any of these overloaded methods:

```
Assert.AreEqual(calc.Add(1,1), 2)
Assert.AreEqual(calc.Add(1,1), 2,
    "Values are not equal")
Assert.AreEqual(calc.Add(1,1), 2,
    "{0} does not equal {1}", calc.Add(1,1), 2)
```

TDD TOOLS IN VISUAL STUDIO

Originally, the testing tools were only available in the Team System editions of Visual Studio. Fortunately, Microsoft realized that more and more developers were starting to use testing in their development process, and so moved the tools into the Professional Edition. This means that nearly all Visual Basic developers have access to the basic tools for adding tests to their application. (So, unless you're running the Express Edition of Visual Basic, you don't have any excuses.)

The TDD tools provided by Visual Studio consist of the following:

➤ **New project types that can be added to your solution** — While you could add your tests to your existing projects, it's a better idea to add them to a separate project. This not only keeps the tests logically separated, but also keeps the code for the tests from swelling the size of your resulting applications and DLLs.

➤ **The Test View window (see Figure 7-2), which provides a simple means of viewing the tests in your solution** — You may or may not find this window valuable. This, and many of the other test-related windows, are accessed from the Test menu.

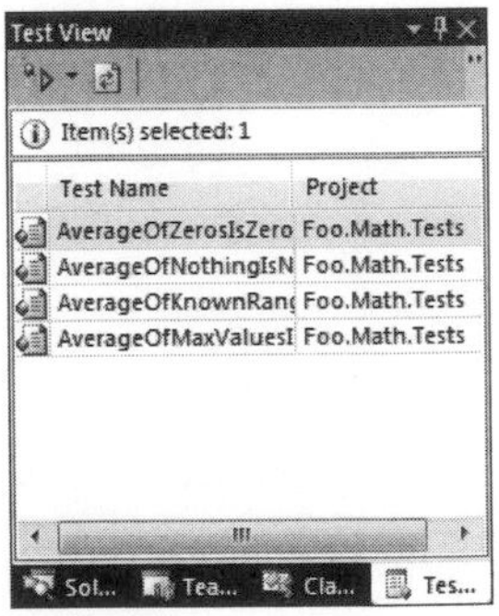

FIGURE 7-2

➤ The Test Results window (see Figure 7-3), which enables you to see the result of one or more tests — This is the main window you will work with when testing your applications. Ideally, you'll want to see all green symbols (indicating "passed") next to each of the tests; and if an error occurs, you will see a message to the right of the list of tests. Note that the green (or red) symbols do not appear until after you have run each test.

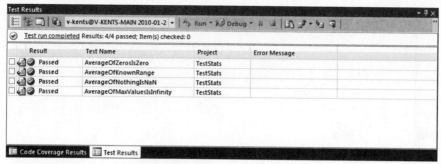

FIGURE 7-3

UNITTESTING WALK-THROUGH

As with any development, the best way to learn TDD is to actually try it, starting with a simple example. Create a new Class Library project called **Foo.Math**. Rename the `Class1` class to `Stats`. This project will use a few simple methods to help demonstrate TDD. Add an `Average` method that takes a `ParamArray` of `Double`, and returns a `Double`:

Available for
download on
Wrox.com

```vb
Public Class Stats
    Public Function Average(ByVal ParamArray values() As Double) As Double
        Dim result As Double
        Dim sum As Double
        For i As Integer = 0 To values.Count - 1
            sum += values(i)
        Next
        result = sum / values.Count
        Return result
    End Function
End Class
```

Code snippet from StatsTest

The code simply adds up the provided values and returns the average. Because each parameter is created as a `Double`, the values of any "smaller" numeric variable types (such as `Integer` or `Single`) will be upcast to a `Double`.

Creating a Test

Using the Test Project template, add a new project named **Foo.Math.Tests** to the solution, as shown in Figure 7-4. This will add a single class, `UnitTest1.vb`, to your solution (renamed to AverageTests.vb in Figure 7-5). Delete that class for now, as you will add your own in a moment. In addition, three solution items are added; these enable configuring how the testing will run. You will look at these later. For now, add a reference to the Foo.Math project.

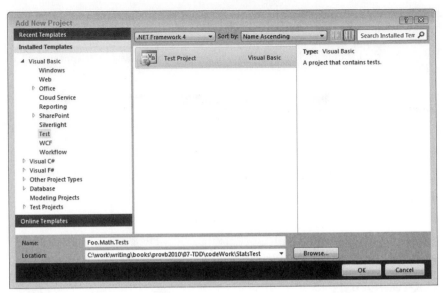

FIGURE 7-4

Right-click on the test project. Select Add ⇨ New Test. In the Add New Test dialog (see Figure 7-6), select Basic Unit Test and call the new file **AverageTests.vb**. Click OK to add the new test to your project. The initial code for the unit test provides the core structure needed by all tests:

```
Imports System.Text

<TestClass()> Public Class AverageTests

    <TestMethod()> Public Sub TestMethod1()
    End Sub

End Class
```

As you can see, the test class is simply a normal Visual Basic class, with the addition of a couple of attributes.

The `TestClass` attribute identifies this class to the testing functionality of Visual Studio; it has no other purpose beyond marking this as a class containing one or more tests.

FIGURE 7-5

The `TestMethod` attribute identifies one of those tests within the class. Like the `TestClass` attribute, this is primarily a marker attribute. Each of the tests will use this attribute to identify itself. This allows you to have other helper methods within the class that are not tests. Notice also that each of the tests is a `Sub`, not a `Function`.

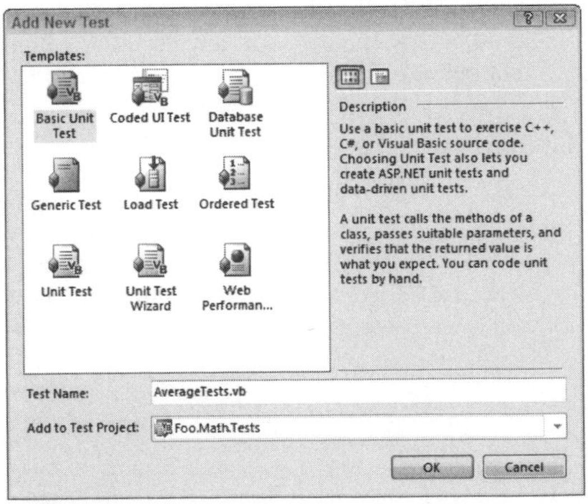

You're ready to begin to create some test methods. As with many other discussions regarding TDD, there are a number of opinions about the scope of each test. Some developers choose to test a number of separate cases within a single method, while others prefer to keep the scope of each test relatively simple. This book falls

FIGURE 7-6

into the second camp. Keeping your tests simple offers the same benefit as keeping any other method simple. That is, when your tests are simple and have a single purpose, there is less room for introducing errors.

Your test methods should be named such that you don't need to look into their code to understand what they are testing. For example, a test named `TestForDivideByZero` is a lot more meaningful than a test method called `Test1`. Again, this saves you time later should any of your tests fail.

For the simple `Average` method defined above, add the following tests (you could no doubt come up with more):

```vb
Imports System.Text

<TestClass()> Public Class AverageTests

    Dim obj As New Foo.Math.Stats

    <TestMethod()> Public Sub AverageOfKnownRange()
        Assert.AreEqual(obj.Average(1, 2, 3, 4, 5, 6, 7, 8, 9, 10),
                        5.5, "Average of 1-10 is not 5.5")
    End Sub

    <TestMethod()> Public Sub AverageOfZerosIsZero()
        Assert.AreEqual(obj.Average(0, 0), 0.0,
                        "Average of zeros is not zero")
    End Sub

    <TestMethod()> Public Sub AverageOfNothingIsNaN()
        Assert.AreEqual(obj.Average(), Double.NaN)
    End Sub

    <TestMethod()> Public Sub AverageOfMaxValuesIsInfinity()
        Assert.AreEqual(obj.Average(Double.MaxValue, Double.MaxValue),
                        Double.PositiveInfinity)
    End Sub
End Class
```

Code snippet from StatsTest

Here, four tests are defined; each tests for different combinations of good and bad parameters. The first test is an attempt to see if the function is working as designed, providing a set of values and checking the result. The `Assert.AreEqual` method used here takes three parameters:

➤ The method to test (or rather the result of that method)

➤ The expected result value

➤ A message to display in the user interface if an error occurs

The second test begins to examine some possible edge case scenarios — in this case, whether all zeros are passed to the `Average` method. Notice that the value to compare with the result has been written as 0.0, not just 0. This is because it would fail if it were written as 0, as you would be attempting to compare a `Double` with an `Integer`.

The final two tests check for two other edge cases: What happens if no values are passed in, and what happens if you use values that add up to greater than the capacity of the `Double` variable you are using to hold the temporary sum. Both simply check the result against a known value (`Double.NaN`, or Not a Number, and `Double.PositiveInfinity`).

Running a Test

Once you have created your tests, you are ready to run them. Select Test ➪ Run ➪ All Tests in Solution to run all of the tests. Alternately, you could select to run an individual test (Test ➪ Run ➪ Tests in Current

Context or from the Test View window). This will compile your solution and execute the tests. With a bit of luck, you should see the icon beside each test switch from Pending, through In Progress, to Passed in the Test Results window (see Figure 7-7).

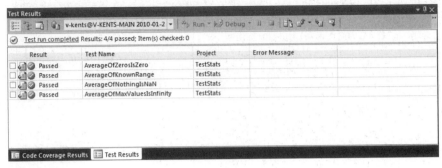

FIGURE 7-7

To see a failing test, make a change to the `Average` method that might reflect a simple, but common logic error:

Available for
download on
Wrox.com

```vb
Public Class Stats
    Public Function Average(ByVal ParamArray values() As Double) As Double
        Dim result As Double
        Dim sum As Double
        For i As Integer = 1 To values.Count - 1
            sum += values(i)
        Next
        result = sum / values.Count
        Return result
    End Function
End Class
```

Code snippet from StatsTest

This is a common error: You may forget when a collection is zero-based or one-based. If you build the solution and run all the tests, you will see that two succeed while two fail (see Figure 7-8).

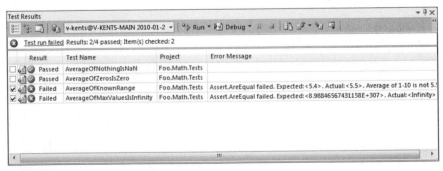

FIGURE 7-8

The `AverageOfKnownRange` test is failing because you are no longer adding up all the provided numbers. The error message returned also helps identify this problem. Notice that it includes the message you added to the test method:

```
Assert.AreEqual failed. Expected:<5.4>. Actual:<5.5>. Average of 1-10 is not 5.5
```

Similarly, the `AverageOfMaxValuesIsInfinity` test fails because you are only adding the first `Double.MaxValue` to the calculation, so no overflow occurs.

Change the code back to use the appropriate index and click the Run button in the Test Results window. By default, it will run only the checked tests. In this case, that means the two failing tests. You should now see the two tests pass.

Testing Data Access Code

While testing a class like the `Foo.Math.Stats` class shown earlier is relatively straightforward, other classes are less easy to test. Many classes require extensive setup or preparation before they can be used, or rely on additional code whose scope is beyond testing. The most common example is testing data access code. If you want to test against an actual database, you have a problem: After your tests are written, you must then create a database, put enough data in it to be representative of a "real" test, and then create the classes used to access the database. In addition, changes to this test database may affect the results of the tests, particularly over time. In other words, it requires a great deal of work to get from your original tests to something that approaches a working system.

Several techniques have been developed to work around this issue and still enable you to test your applications. This section looks at two of the more common techniques:

➤ Using a test database with a known state

➤ Using an interface with a fake test implementation

Initialization/Cleanup

Obviously, the best way to test data access code is to have it actually attempt to access a database. However, over time, the changes made to the database may affect the results of the tests. Therefore, it is best if the database is always in a known state at the beginning of the test run, and then reset at the end. Where should you add this code to your tests? Fortunately, the unit testing framework includes additional attributes you can add to the class containing your tests to cause the methods to act before and after your tests, as described in Table 7-4.

TABLE 7-4: Test Class Attributes

ATTRIBUTE	DESCRIPTION
`ClassInitialize`	A method marked with this attribute will be run when the test class itself is initialized, before any tests have run. This attribute must be applied to a `Shared` routine.
`ClassCleanup`	A method marked with this attribute will be run at the end of the test run, after all tests have completed. This is typically used to clean up any items created in the `ClassInitialize` method. The attribute must be applied to a `Shared` routine.
`TestInitialize`	A method marked with this attribute will be run before each test. This can be useful to refresh any values, or to prepare a variable for the test.
`TestCleanup`	A method marked with this attribute will be run after each test, typically to clean up something created during the `TestInitialize`, or that may have been affected by the test itself.

When working with a test database, these four attributes enable you to create a brand-new database populated with known data either at the beginning of the test run or just before (or after) each test. This means that your tests will always run with a database with known data, so the tests will act reliably.

Create a new Class Library project named **NorthwindData**. This project will represent a subset of the code you would use to manage the `Northwind` database. In this case, it will only access the employees table. Delete the default `Class1` that is added to the project and add the following interface:

```vb
Public Interface INorthwindRepository
    Function AllEmployees() As List(Of Employee)
    Function GetEmployeeByID(ByVal id As Integer) As Employee
    Function FindEmployeeByLastName(ByVal lastname As String) As Employee
    Sub InsertEmployee(ByVal value As Employee)
    Sub DeleteEmployee(ByVal id As Integer)
End Interface
```

Code snippet from NorthwindData

This interface represents the actions that the data access component will be able to perform. While it isn't a complete set of CRUD (Create, Retrieve, Update, and Delete) functions, it should provide you with enough to test. This is added as an interface to make it easier when you create the test implementation in the next section. Add a new class, `DbRepository`, that implements the preceding interface:

```vb
Imports System.Collections.Generic

Public Class DbRepository
    Implements INorthwindRepository

    Dim db As New NorthwindClassesDataContext

    Public Function AllEmployees() As List(Of Employee) _
        Implements INorthwindRepository.AllEmployees
        Dim result As List(Of Employee)
        result = (From e In db.Employees Select e).ToList
        Return result
    End Function

    Public Sub DeleteEmployee(ByVal id As Integer) _
        Implements INorthwindRepository.DeleteEmployee
        Dim emp As Employee
        emp = (From e In db.Employees
               Where e.EmployeeID = id
               Select e).FirstOrDefault
        db.Employees.DeleteOnSubmit(emp)
        db.SubmitChanges()
    End Sub

    Public Function FindEmployeeByLastName(ByVal lastname As String) As Employee _
        Implements INorthwindRepository.FindEmployeeByLastName
        Dim result As Employee
        result = (From e In db.Employees
                  Where e.LastName.StartsWith(lastname)
                  Select e).FirstOrDefault
        Return result
    End Function

    Public Function GetEmployeeByID(ByVal id As Integer) As Employee _
        Implements INorthwindRepository.GetEmployeeByID
        Dim result As Employee
        result = (From e In db.Employees
                  Where e.EmployeeID = id
                  Select e).FirstOrDefault
        Return result
    End Function

    Public Sub InsertEmployee(ByVal value As Employee) _
        Implements INorthwindRepository.InsertEmployee
        db.Employees.InsertOnSubmit(value)
```

```
        db.SubmitChanges()
    End Sub
End Class
```

Code snippet from NorthwindData

For this implementation, it actually uses LINQ to SQL to query the database. See Chapter 10 for more details on LINQ to SQL (if you're playing along, you can either come back after you've read Chapter 10 or just copy the `NorthwindClasses.dbml` and `app.config` files from the sample code).

Now it's time to turn to the tests (yes, we should have written the tests first, but we didn't). Add a new Test Project to the solution called **NorthwindData.Tests**. Rename the class created when you create the project to `TestDbTests`. As you will be using the SQL Server Management Objects (SMO), add a reference to `Microsoft.SqlServer.Smo.dll` and `Microsoft.SqlServer.ConnectionInfo.dll`. You will need to browse for these two DLLs; they are found at `c:\program files\microsoft sql server\100\sdk\assemblies`. Also add a reference to the `System.Configuration` namespace found on the .NET tab when adding a new reference. Add the following `Imports` statements to the test class:

Available for download on Wrox.com

```
Imports System.Text
Imports Microsoft.SqlServer.Management.Smo
Imports Microsoft.SqlServer.Management.Common
Imports System.Data.SqlClient
Imports System.Configuration

<TestClass()> Public Class TestDbTests
```

Code snippet from NorthwindData

Add a new method to the class that will be called when the test class is first instantiated. This method should have the attribute `ClassInitialize` added to it:

Available for download on Wrox.com

```
<ClassInitialize()> Public Shared Sub Setup(ByVal testContext As TestContext)
        'instantiate a new database
        'using the saved scripts and the
        'SQL Server Management Objects (SMO)

        'load create script
        Dim script As String
        Dim scriptPath As String =
            My.Application.Info.DirectoryPath &
            "\CreateTestDatabase.sql"
        script = IO.File.ReadAllText(scriptPath)

        'execute it using SMO
        ExecuteScript(script)
    End Sub
```

Code snippet from NorthwindData

The sample project includes the `CreateTestDatabase.sql` script. Add this file to your project if you are following along. This SQL script creates a new database, called `Testwind`, creates a new Employees table within the database, and adds a few records. Set the properties for the file so that the SQL script is marked as `Content`, and the `Copy to Output` property is set to `Copy if newer`. This ensures that the script is in the correct location defined in the preceding code.

The `ExecuteScript` method uses the SMO to actually execute the SQL script. Add this method to the TestDBTests class:

Available for download on Wrox.com

```
Private Shared Sub ExecuteScript(ByVal script As String)
    Dim dsn As String
    dsn = ConfigurationManager.ConnectionStrings("testdata").ConnectionString

    Using conn As New SqlConnection(dsn)
```

```
            Dim svr As New Server(New ServerConnection(conn))
            svr.ConnectionContext.ExecuteNonQuery(script)
        End Using
    End Sub
```

Code snippet from NorthwindData

The `Server` class from the SMO works similarly to the `SqlCommand` class you may have used when accessing SQL Server (and if not, you will in Chapter 10). It enables you to execute a SQL script to create database objects. As with other data access, it requires an open connection to the database: In this case, the `testdata` connection string is defined in an `app.config` file as follows:

```xml
<?xml version="1.0" encoding="utf-8" ?>
<configuration>
  <connectionStrings>
    <!-- the connection string should be on one line -->
    <add name="testdata"
        connectionString="server=.\sqlexpress;
                          database=master;
                          integrated security=true;"/>
  </connectionStrings>
</configuration>
```

Code snippet from NorthwindData

As you are creating the database in the `Setup` method, you should also delete it when testing is complete:

```
<ClassCleanup()> Public Shared Sub Cleanup()
    'drop the test database
    'load drop script
    Dim script As String
    Dim scriptPath As String =
        My.Application.Info.DirectoryPath &
        "\DropTestDatabase.sql"
    script = IO.File.ReadAllText(scriptPath)

    'execute it using SMO
    ExecuteScript(script)
End Sub
```

Code snippet from NorthwindData

The `ClassCleanup` attribute defines a method that is called after all tests have completed. In this case, it is used to execute a script that deletes the database. You can find this script in the sample code for this section.

Now that the database will be present, you are ready to create tests for it. For the purposes of this sample, just add three tests:

```
<TestMethod()> Public Sub AllEmployeesReturnsCount()
    Dim employees As List(Of Employee)
    employees = db.AllEmployees
    Assert.AreEqual(employees.Count, 9)
End Sub

<TestMethod()> Public Sub FindEmployeeReturnsItem()
    Dim emp As Employee = db.FindEmployeeByLastName("Dav")
    Assert.IsNotNull(emp)
    StringAssert.StartsWith(emp.LastName, "Dav")
End Sub

<TestMethod()> Public Sub InsertEmployeeIncreasesCount()
    Dim emp As New Employee
    With emp
```

```
            .EmployeeID = -1
            .FirstName = "Foo"
            .LastName = "deBar"
            .Title = "Vice President"
        End With
        Try
            Dim before As Integer = db.AllEmployees.Count
            db.InsertEmployee(emp)

            Dim after As Integer = db.AllEmployees.Count
            Assert.AreEqual(before + 1, after)
        Catch ex As Exception
            Assert.Fail(ex.Message)
        End Try
    End Sub
```

Code snippet from NorthwindData

The first test simply returns the full list of employees. As the create script creates nine employees, you can assert that value in the test. The second test does a search for one specific employee; it then asserts that the returned value is not null (that is, it returned the employee), then confirms that the returned employee matches the criteria. Finally, a new employee is created and saved to the database, and the test confirms that the count does increment by one. Notice that the code references a db variable. You need to add the following definition as a class-level variable:

Available for
download on
Wrox.com

```
<TestClass()> Public Class TestDbTests

    Dim db As INorthwindRepository = New DbRepository
```

Code snippet from NorthwindData

This sets the data access code for the tests to access the class you created earlier. You should now be able to run these tests and see three happy green icons. If you step through the tests, you should see the database created, and then removed after all the tests complete.

Using this method of testing requires a fair bit of setup, as you need to create the test database as well as the data access component before you can test. However, it does guarantee that your tests will behave like your actual code.

Test Implementation

An alternate approach to creating a test database is to provide an implementation of the interface that acts like the database should. That is, it returns the correct values, but rather than access a database to retrieve them, it simply creates them itself. This technique requires much less effort than creating the test database, but your fake data access may not behave completely like the live data access.

Add a new Unit Test (RepositoryTests) to your test project by selecting Add ➪ New Test ➪ Basic Unit Test and set the Name to RepositoryTests. The tests performed by this class will be similar to the ones you performed when using a test database earlier:

Available for
download on
Wrox.com

```
Imports System.Text

<TestClass()> Public Class RepositoryTests
    Dim db As INorthwindRepository = New TestRepository

    Private testContextInstance As TestContext

    '''<summary>
    '''Gets or sets the test context which provides
    '''information about and functionality for the current test run.
    '''</summary>
```

```vb
    Public Property TestContext() As TestContext
        Get
            Return testContextInstance
        End Get
        Set(ByVal value As TestContext)
            testContextInstance = Value
        End Set
    End Property

    <TestMethod()> Public Sub CreatedRepositoryIsTest()
        Assert.IsInstanceOfType(db, GetType(INorthwindRepository),
                                "Repository is not a TestRepository")
    End Sub

    <TestMethod()> Public Sub AllEmployeesReturnsCount()
        Dim employees As List(Of Employee)
        employees = db.AllEmployees
        Assert.AreEqual(employees.Count, 9)
    End Sub

    <TestMethod()> Public Sub FindEmployeeReturnsItem()
        Dim emp As Employee = db.FindEmployeeByLastName("6")
        Assert.IsNotNull(emp)
        StringAssert.Contains(emp.LastName, "6")
    End Sub

    <TestMethod()> Public Sub InsertEmployeeIncreasesCount()
        Dim emp As New Employee
        With emp
            .EmployeeID = -1
            .FirstName = "Foo"
            .LastName = "deBar"
            .Title = "Vice President"
        End With
        Try
            Dim before As Integer = db.AllEmployees.Count
            db.InsertEmployee(emp)
            Dim after As Integer = db.AllEmployees.Count
            Assert.AreEqual(before + 1, after)
        Catch ex As Exception
            Assert.Fail(ex.Message)
        End Try
    End Sub
End Class
```

Code snippet from NorthwindData

Note that rather than create a DbRepository, you create a TestRepository (you'll create that in a moment). The other differences between this test class and the earlier one is that there are no Setup or Cleanup methods. In addition, a new test confirms that the created repository is of the correct type; and the FindEmployeeReturnsItem is slightly different, as the returned data will be different.

The TestRepository class implements INorthwindRepository, but rather than access a database, it keeps the data in a private list. Add the TestRepository class to the NorthwindData project:

Available for download on Wrox.com

```vb
Imports System.Collections.Generic

Public Class TestRepository
```

```vbnet
    Implements INorthwindRepository

    Dim employeeList As List(Of Employee)

    Public Sub New()
        'setup employee list
        employeeList = New List(Of Employee)
        'add stock data
        For i As Integer = 1 To 9
            Dim emp As New Employee
            emp.EmployeeID = i
            emp.FirstName = "First" & i
            emp.LastName = "Last" & i
            emp.Title = "Consultant"
            emp.HireDate = DateTime.Today

            employeeList.Add(emp)
        Next
    End Sub
    Public Function AllEmployees() As List(Of Employee) _
        Implements INorthwindRepository.AllEmployees
        Return employeeList
    End Function

    Public Sub DeleteEmployee(ByVal id As Integer) _
        Implements INorthwindRepository.DeleteEmployee
        Dim emp As Employee
        emp = (From e In employeeList
                Where e.EmployeeID = id
                Select e).First
        employeeList.Remove(emp)
    End Sub

    Public Function FindEmployeeByLastName(ByVal lastname As String) As Employee _
        Implements INorthwindRepository.FindEmployeeByLastName
        Dim result As Employee
        result = (From e In employeeList
                Where e.LastName.Contains(lastname)
                Select e).FirstOrDefault
        Return result
    End Function

    Public Function GetEmployeeByID(ByVal id As Integer) As Employee _
        Implements INorthwindRepository.GetEmployeeByID
        Dim result As Employee
        result = (From e In employeeList
            Where e.EmployeeID = id
            Select e).First
        Return result
    End Function

    Public Sub InsertEmployee(ByVal value As Employee) _
        Implements INorthwindRepository.InsertEmployee
        employeeList.Add(value)
    End Sub

End Class
```

Code snippet from NorthwindData

The list is populated in the constructor with some nonsense data. The remaining methods are similar to their counterparts in the DbRepository, but rather than use the database connection, they retrieve elements from the employeeList.

You should now be able to run all the tests in both the `RepositoryTests` and `TestDbTests` to see that both of your implementations work and all tests pass.

As you can see, using the test implementation requires far less setup and code to implement than a test database. This means that it is easier to perform if you are simply experimenting with the functionality you might need to access your database. There is a slight chance that the behavior of the internal list may differ from the actual data access, but this can be controlled when defining the data types you return.

Using the Generate from Usage Feature

Visual Studio 2010 adds a very exciting testing feature: the capability to create your classes from the tests. This enables you to do "pure" test-first development, without the actual effort of creating the structure of your classes after you have tested them.

Using this method, you leverage IntelliSense to create the basic structure of the tested code while writing your tests. Initially, these tests will fail, as the tested class does not have any functionality. You then edit your class to add the needed functionality, and watch as your tests go from red to green.

Create a new Class Library project called **Person**. You can delete the initially created `Class1` from the project. Add a Test Project to the solution named **Person.Tests**. Rename the initially created class from `UnitTest1` to `EmployeeTests`, and the initial test from `TestMethod1` to `DefaultEmployeeInitializes`. This test will confirm that when you use the default constructor, the properties of the new object are set to default values. Of course, you haven't created this new class, or the properties, yet.

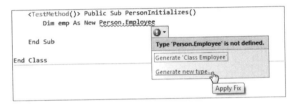

FIGURE 7-9

Add the line `Dim emp As New Person.Employee` to the method. You'll notice that the class name gets a blue, wavy line under it to mark it as unknown to IntelliSense. Open the smart tag menu for the item. Don't select the option to generate this type, as it will create the type within the Person.Tests project, rather than the Person project. Instead, select the "Generate new type" option (see Figure 7-9) to bring up the Generate New Type dialog.

In the Generate New Type dialog (see Figure 7-10) select to add the new type to the Person project, and change the `Access` to `Public`. When you click OK, the Class Library should contain a new file named `Employee.vb`.

FIGURE 7-10

Continue editing the test to add a few assertions about properties of the `Employee` object. For example, if the object has been created with the default constructor, then the properties should have a value appropriate for each type:

Available for
download on
Wrox.com

```
<TestMethod()> Public Sub DefaultEmployeeInitializes()
    Dim emp As New Person.Employee
    'ensure default property values
    Assert.AreEqual(emp.Name, String.Empty)
    Assert.AreEqual(emp.Salary, Decimal.Zero)
    Assert.AreEqual(emp.HireDate, DateTime.MinValue)
End Sub
```

Code snippet from Person

Blue, wavy lines should again appear under the three properties. You can open the smart tag menu and select to "Generate the property stub for `'Name'` in `Person.Employee`." This will add the method to the

Person class you created earlier. This time it automatically creates them in the correct project. Notice that you can also choose to add the new item as a method or field as well as a property.

Next, add a second test method to the test class. This second method, `ConstructorEmployeeInitializes`, will define a test that also constructs a new `Employee`, but this time using a constructor that takes the three parameters to populate the properties:

```vb
<TestMethod()> Public Sub ConstructorEmployeeInitializes()
    Dim emp As New Person.Employee("Foo deBar", 33000, DateTime.Today)
    'confirm the properties are set
    StringAssert.Contains(emp.Name, "Foo deBar")
    Assert.AreEqual(emp.Salary, 33000D)
    Assert.AreEqual(emp.HireDate, DateTime.Today)
End Sub
```

Code snippet from Person

Again the blue, wavy lines appear, and again you can use the smart tag menu to create the new constructor by selecting "Generate constructor stub in `Person.Employee`" from the smart tag menu. As you do this, however, more lines appear under the code in the earlier method. Now the creation of a new `Employee` using the default constructor has become invalid, as there is only the one constructor in the class: the one taking three parameters. Fortunately, to reduce the wear and tear on your typing fingers, the smart tag menu enables you to add a default constructor to the `Employee` class. The final structure of the test class is as follows:

```vb
<TestClass()> Public Class PersonTests
    <TestMethod()> Public Sub DefaultEmployeeInitializes()
        Dim emp As New Person.Employee
        'ensure default property values
        Assert.AreEqual(emp.Name, String.Empty)
        Assert.AreEqual(emp.Salary, Decimal.Zero)
        Assert.AreEqual(emp.HireDate, DateTime.MinValue)
    End Sub

    <TestMethod()> Public Sub ConstructorEmployeeInitializes()
        Dim emp As New Person.Employee("Foo deBar", 33000, DateTime.Today)
        'confirm the properties are set
        StringAssert.Contains(emp.Name, "Foo deBar")
        Assert.AreEqual(emp.Salary, 33000D)
        Assert.AreEqual(emp.HireDate, DateTime.Today)
    End Sub
End Class
```

Code snippet from Person

Of course, the code generated is not perfect. There is no easy way for Visual Studio to determine just what type each of the properties should be; and if you created methods, there is no way to determine the body of those methods. The generated `Employee` class looks as follows:

```vb
Public Class Employee

    Private _p1 As String
    Private _p2 As Integer
    Private _p3 As Date
    Sub New(ByVal p1 As String, ByVal p2 As Integer, ByVal p3 As Date)
        ' TODO: Complete member initialization
        _p1 = p1
        _p2 = p2
        _p3 = p3
    End Sub
    Sub New()
        ' TODO: Complete member initialization
    End Sub
```

```
        Property Name As Object
        Property Salary As Object
        Property HireDate As Object
    End Class
```

Notice that the three properties have all been created as Objects, and the parameters to the constructor — while correct — do not have very descriptive names. Therefore, the code for the class can be cleaned up a little: Give the parameters to the constructor more useful names, and apply the correct data types to the three properties. While you're in there, you might as well add a bit of validation to the Salary property, prohibiting negative values. After editing the Employee class, it should look as follows:

```
Public Class Employee
    Private _name As String
    Private _salary As Decimal
    Private _hireDate As Date

    Sub New(ByVal name As String,
            ByVal salary As Decimal,
            ByVal hireDate As Date)
        Me.Name = name
        Me.Salary = salary
        Me.HireDate = hireDate
    End Sub
    Sub New()
        Me.Name = String.Empty
        Me.Salary = Decimal.Zero
        Me.HireDate = DateTime.MinValue
    End Sub
    Property Name As String
        Get
            Return _name
        End Get
        Set(ByVal value As String)
            _name = value
        End Set
    End Property
    Property Salary As Decimal
        Get
            Return _salary
        End Get
        Set(ByVal value As Decimal)
            If value < 0 Then
                Throw New ArgumentOutOfRangeException("Salary cannot be negative")
            End If
            _salary = value
        End Set
    End Property
    Property HireDate As Date
        Get
            Return _hireDate
        End Get
        Set(ByVal value As Date)
            _hireDate = value
        End Set
    End Property
End Class
```

The short version of the properties for Name and HireDate could be left as is, because you don't perform any validation in them. Notice that rather than write directly to the private member variables, the constructor calls the properties. This ensures that whatever validation you add to the property also applies to the constructor. For the `Salary` property, it tests for a negative value passed in. If this happens, then a new exception is thrown.

Add a third test method to the test `PersonTests` class. This test will confirm that the validation added to the `Salary` property does actually throw an exception:

```
<TestMethod()> Public Sub SalaryCannotBeNegative()
    Try
        Dim emp As New Person.Employee("Foo deBar", -10, DateTime.Today)
        'if we get to this line, there is a problem
        'as the line should have triggered the exception
        Assert.Fail("Employee salary cannot be negative")
    Catch aex As ArgumentOutOfRangeException
        'this is caused by passing in a negative value
        'as it is expected, we'll ignore it
        'which will return a success for the test
    Catch ex As Exception
        'deal with other exceptions here
        Assert.Fail(ex.Message)
    End Try
End Sub
```

Code snippet from Person

This test is a little counterintuitive at first. Remember that you are attempting to cause an exception, so it is a little like coding a double negative. The method first attempts to create a new `Employee`, passing in the same `Name` and `HireDate` as before, but now with a negative `Salary`. If the class has been coded correctly, this should throw an `ArgumentOutOfRangeException`. Therefore, if the code doesn't throw an exception, it will continue on past the constructor, meaning that there is a problem in the code. The code then fails the test. If instead the correct exception was thrown, the code silently ignores it, meaning that the test will pass. This method of constructing a test enables you to ensure that your classes have been defined defensively. You should now be able to run the three tests and see them pass.

Using the Generate from Usage functionality in Visual Studio can be a great time saver when you create your tests, and the classes they test. It enables you to write the tests first, and then be able to execute the tests almost immediately, while giving you the core of the desired class.

OTHER VISUAL STUDIO EDITIONS

This chapter focuses on the testing functionality included in the Professional Edition of Visual Studio. Table 7-5 describes the Premium and Ultimate Editions, which include a great deal of additional functionality when testing.

TABLE 7-5: Functionality of the Premium and Ultimate Editions of Visual Studio

EDITION	FUNCTIONALITY	DESCRIPTION
Premium	Code coverage	This feature will analyze your code and tests and allows you to determine how much of the functionality of your classes is actually tested. Ideally, you would like this value to be as high as possible, as it means that you are testing most of the functionality of your application.
	Test impact analysis	This feature analyzes your code and tests and determines which tests are needed after a code change. This can be a great time saver if you have a large number of tests, as it means you will only need to execute a subset of them after updating your code.

continues

TABLE 7-5 *(continued)*

EDITION	FUNCTIONALITY	DESCRIPTION
	Coded UI test	This feature automates the testing of user interfaces (ASP.NET, Windows Forms or WPF applications). It records the steps you perform when manually executing a series of steps, and allows you to compare field values with desired values. While the merits of testing user interfaces have been debated for a while, this can be a useful step in validating your application.
Ultimate	Web performance testing	This feature allows you to test a Web application with a simulated number of requests. This allows you to do load testing and test how your application will perform with multiple simultaneous users accessing it, before you actually release the site. It works similarly to the Coded UI test in that you first record a series of steps. The test then executes these steps simulating multiple clients.

THIRD PARTY TESTING FRAMEWORKS

In addition to the testing tools in Visual Studio, a number of third-party testing tools are available. Some of these tools provide basically the same services provided by the built-in testing (albeit with a different syntax), while others provide functionality not available.

Several packages are available for adding functionality similar to the built-in testing. These can be used instead of, or in parallel with, the existing testing. In addition, they can be used when working with Visual Basic Express Edition, as the built-in testing is not available with that version. Some of these other testing frameworks include:

➤ **NUnit** — This was the first testing framework made available for .NET. It is an open-source framework, and originally a port of the JUnit library used by Java developers. Because of its age, you can find a great deal of material about understanding and working with this library. Available for download from www.nunit.org.

➤ **MbUnit** — MbUnit is an open-source testing framework that has become quite popular, and it is used by a number of projects. There are currently two actively updated versions of MbUnit. Version 2 is available from www.mbunit.com, while version 3 is part of the Gallio project at www.gallio.org.

➤ **xUnit.net** — An open-source project developed primarily by two Microsoft developers (including the original author of NUnit), this library attempts to enable developers to avoid some of the common errors users make with some of the other frameworks. It is quite stable and full-featured. Some developers argue that a few of the decisions made weren't the correct ones, but that's why we have choice, isn't it? Available for download from http://xunit.codeplex.com.

Another commonly used set of tools in testing are *mocking frameworks*. These enable you to create fake objects within your tests that have a set behavior. They serve to create something like the `TestRepository` you created earlier in this chapter, but without requiring you to actually create that class. They are particularly useful when you attempt to write your tests completely before creating your classes, or when your classes might require some setup or configuration tasks during the test. Some of the more commonly used mocking frameworks include:

➤ **RhinoMocks** — This is probably the most widely used mocking framework for .NET applications. Available from www.ayende.com/projects/rhino-mocks.aspx.

➤ **TypeMock** — This is a commercial package that provides a number of features not available in other mocking frameworks. Most notably, it enables you to mock existing classes and libraries without requiring that you have an interface. That is, you can mock classes directly. This can be useful when you want to mock an existing framework. Available from http://site.typemock.com.

➤ **Moq** — This is one of the more technically advanced mocking frameworks, written to target many modern .NET Framework features, such as lambda functions. Available from http://code.google.com/p/moq.

They may not all be in the box, but a wide variety of tools are available to help you test your code. It's worth trying them out on a small project to get a feel for them, and whether they will help you write better, more maintainable code.

SUMMARY

The unit testing features of Visual Studio enable you to verify your code, which gives you the confidence to change that code, as you have a set of tests available to verify that the code still works after you change it. While you might not become a full TDD convert, it is definitely worth taking a look at these tools to determine how they can fit into your development efforts.

This chapter looked at testing your Visual Basic applications using the unit testing functionality available with the Professional (and higher) edition of Visual Studio. In particular, it looked at how you create test classes and methods, and use Visual Studio to execute them and verify your code. You saw how to test both simple classes and classes that require setup, such as data access classes. In addition, it looked at some of the other products available to help you in your testing — both features of advanced editions of Visual Studio and third-party tools.

PART II
Business Objects and Data Access

8

Arrays, Collections, and Generics

WHAT YOU WILL LEARN IN THIS CHAPTER

➤ Working with arrays

➤ Iteration (looping)

➤ Working with collections

➤ Generics

➤ Nullable types

➤ Generic collections

➤ Generic methods

➤ Covariance and contravariance

In the beginning there were variables, and they were good. The idea that you map a location in memory to a value was a key to tracking a value. However, most of us want to work on data as a set. Taking the concept of a variable holding a value, we moved to the concept of a variable that could reference an array of values. Arrays improved what developers could build but they weren't the end of the line.

Over time certain patterns developed in how arrays were used. Instead of just collecting a set of values, we looked to use arrays to temporarily store values that were awaiting processing, or to provide sorted collections. Each of these patterns started as a best practice for how to build and manipulate array data or to build custom structures that replicate arrays.

The computing world was very familiar with these concepts — for example, using a linked list to enable more flexibility regarding how data is sorted and retrieved. Patterns such as the stack (first in, last out) or queue (first in, first out) were in fact created as part of the original base Class Libraries. Referred to as *collections*, they provide a more robust and feature-rich way to manage sets of data than arrays can provide. These were common patterns prior to the introduction of .NET, and .NET provided an implementation for each of these collection types.

However, the common implementation of these collection classes relied on the `Object` base class. This caused two issues. The first, which is discussed in this chapter, is called *boxing*. Boxing wasn't a big deal on any given item in a collection, but it caused a slight performance hit; and as your collection grew, it had the potential to impact your application's performance. The second issue was that having collections based only on the type `Object` went against the best practice of having a strongly typed environment. As soon as you started loading items into a collection, you lost all type checking.

Solving the issues with collections based on the `Object` type is called *generics*. Originally introduced as part of .NET 2.0, generics provide a way to create collection classes that are type-safe. The type of value that will be stored in the collection is defined as part of the collection definition. Thus .NET has taken the type-safe but limited capabilities of Arrays and combined them with the more powerful collection classes that were object-based to provide a set of collection classes which are type-safe.

This chapter looks at these three related ways to create sets of information. Starting with a discussion of arrays and the looping statements that process them. It next introduces collections and then moves to the use of generics, followed by a walk-through of the syntax for defining your own generic templates. Note that the sample code in this chapter is based on the ProVB_VS2010 project created in Chapter 1. Rather than step through the creation of this project again, this chapter makes reference to it. A copy of all of the code is also available as part of the download for this book.

ARRAYS

It is possible to declare any type as an array of that type. Because an array is a modifier of another type, the basic `Array` class is never explicitly declared for a variable's type. The `System.Array` class that serves as the base for all arrays is defined such that it cannot be created, but must be inherited. As a result, to create an `Integer` array, a set of parentheses is added to the declaration of the variable. These parentheses indicate that the system should create an array of the type specified. The parentheses used in the declaration may be empty or may contain the size of the array. An array can be defined as having a single dimension using a single index, or as having multiple dimensions by using multiple indices.

All arrays and collections in .NET start with an index of zero. However, the way an array is declared in Visual Basic varies slightly from other .NET languages such as C#. Back when the first .NET version of Visual Basic was announced, it was also announced that arrays would always begin at 0 and that they would be defined based on the number of elements in the array. In other words, Visual Basic would work the same way as the other initial .NET languages. However, in older versions of Visual Basic, it is possible to specify that an array should start at 1 by default. This meant that a lot of existing code didn't define arrays the same way.

To resolve this issue, the engineers at Microsoft decided on a compromise: All arrays in .NET begin at 0, but when an array is declared in Visual Basic, the index defines the upper limit of the array, not the number of elements. The challenge is to remember that all subscripts go from 0 to the upper bound, meaning that each array contains one more element than its upper bound.

The main result of this upper-limit declaration is that arrays defined in Visual Basic have one more entry by definition than those defined with other .NET languages. Note that it's still possible to declare an array in Visual Basic and reference it in C# or another .NET language. The following code examples illustrate five different ways to create arrays, beginning with a simple integer array as the basis for the comparison:

```
Dim arrMyIntArray1(20) as Integer
```

In the first case, the code defines an array of integers that spans from `arrMyIntArray1(0)` to `arrMyIntArray1(20)`. This is a 21-element array, because all arrays start at 0 and end with the value defined in the declaration as the upper bound.

Here is the second statement:

```
Dim arrMyIntArray2() as Integer = {1, 2, 3, 4}
```

The preceding statement creates an array with four elements numbered 0 through 3, containing the values 1 to 4.

In addition to creating arrays in one dimension it is possible to create arrays that account for multiple dimensions. Think of this as an array of arrays — where all of the contents are of the same type. Thus, in the third statement, we see an array of integers with two dimensions, a common representation of this is a grid:

```
Dim arrMyIntArray3(4,2) as Integer
```

The preceding declaration creates a multidimensional array containing five elements at the first level (or dimension). However, the second number 2 indicates that these five elements actually reference arrays of integers. In this case the second dimension for each of the first level dimensions contains three elements. Visual Basic provides this syntax as shorthand for consistently accessing these contained arrays. Thus, for each of the items in the first dimensions, you can access a second set of elements each containing three integers.

The fourth statement which follows shows an alternative way of creating a multidimensional array:

```
Dim arrMyIntArray4( , ) as Integer = _
    { {1, 2, 3},{4, 5, 6}, {7, 8, 9},{10, 11, 12},{13, 14 , 15} }
```

The literal array declaration creates a multidimensional array with five elements in the first dimension, each containing an array of three integers. The resulting array has 15 elements, but with the subscripts 0 to 4 at the first level and 0 to 2 for each second level dimension. An excellent way to think of this is as a grid or a table with five rows and three columns. In theory you can have any number of dimensions; however, while having three dimensions isn't too difficult to conceptualize, increasing numbers of dimensions in your arrays can significantly increase complexity, and you should look for a design that limits the number of dimensions.

The fifth example demonstrates that it is possible to simply declare a variable and indicate that the variable is an array, without specifying the number of elements in the array:

```
Dim arrMyIntArray5() as Integer
```

Note that the preceding declaration is not multidimensional, it is a single dimension array, just omitting the details for the number of elements defined. Similarly, if instead of creating arrMyIntArray5 with predefined values the goal had been to declare a two dimensional array placeholder, the declaration would have included a comma: `arrMyIntArray5(,)`. The usefulness of this empty declaration statement will become clearer as we look at various examples for using the preceding set of array declarations.

Multidimensional Arrays

The definition of arrMyIntArray3 and arrMyIntArray4 are multidimensional arrays. In particular, the declaration of arrMyIntArray4 creates an array with 15 elements (five in the first dimension, each of which contains three integers) ranging from arrMyIntArray4(0,0) through arrMyIntArray4(2,1) to arrMyIntArray4(4,2). As with all elements of an array, when it is created without specific values, the value of each of these elements is created with the default value for that type. This case also demonstrates that the size of the different dimensions can vary. It is possible to nest deeper than two levels, but this should be done with care because such code is difficult to maintain.

For example, the value of arrMyIntArray4(0,1) is 2, while the value of arrMyIntArray4(3,2) is 12. To demonstrate this, a method called SampleMD can be run from the ButtonTest_Click handler, which shows the elements of this multidimensional array's contents:

```
Private Sub SampleMD()
    Dim arrMyIntArray4(,) As Integer =
        {{1, 2, 3}, {4, 5, 6}, {7, 8, 9}, {10, 11, 12}, {13, 14, 15}}
    Dim intLoop1 As Integer
    Dim intLoop2 As Integer
    For intLoop1 = 0 To UBound(arrMyIntArray4)
        For intLoop2 = 0 To UBound(arrMyIntArray4, 2)
            TextBoxOutput.Text +=
                "{" & intLoop1 & ", " & intLoop2 & "} = " &
                arrMyIntArray4(intLoop1, intLoop2).ToString & vbCrLf
        Next
    Next
End Sub
```

Code snippet from Form1

The preceding sample, when run in the Test window from Chapter 1, results in the output shown in Figure 8-1. Note that Figure 8-1 is significantly simpler then what is in the code download. The code download includes additional samples, including an additional button which will be created later in this chapter. If you are working alongside the chapter with your own sample code your result will be similar to what is seen in Figure 8-1.

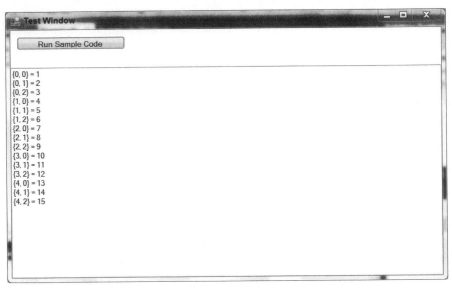

FIGURE 8-1

The UBound Function

Continuing to reference the arrays defined earlier, the declaration of `arrMyIntArray2` actually defined an array that spans from `arrMyIntArray2(0)` to `arrMyIntArray2(3)`. That's because when you declare an array by specifying the set of values, it still starts at 0. However, in this case you are not specifying the upper bound, but rather initializing the array with a set of values. If this set of values came from a database or other source, then the upper limit on the array might not be clear. To verify the upper bound of an array, a call can be made to the `UBound` function:

```
UBound(ArrMyIntArray2)
```

The preceding line of code retrieves the upper bound of the first dimension of the array and returns 3. However, as noted in the preceding section, you can specify an array with several different dimensions. Thus, this old-style method of retrieving the upper bound carries the potential for an error of omission. The better way to retrieve the upper bound is to use the `GetUpperBound` method on your array instance. With this call, you need to tell the array which dimension's upper-bound value you want, as shown here (also returning 3):

```
ArrMyIntArray2.GetUpperBound(0)
```

This is the preferred method of obtaining an array's upper bound because it explicitly indicates which upper bound is wanted when using multidimensional arrays, and it follows a more object-oriented approach to working with your array

The `UBound` function has a companion called `LBound`. The `LBound` function computes the lower bound for a given array. However, as all arrays and collections in Visual Basic are zero-based, it doesn't have much value anymore.

The ReDim Statement

The following code considers the use of a declared but not instantiated array. Unlike an integer value, which has a default of 0, an array waits until a size is defined to allocate the memory it will use. The following example revisits the declaration of an array that has not yet been instantiated. If an attempt were made to assign a value to this array, it would trigger an exception.

```
Dim arrMyIntArray5() as Integer
' The commented statement below would compile but would cause a runtime exception.
'arrMyIntArray5(0) = 1
```

The solution to this is to use the ReDim keyword. Although ReDim was part of Visual Basic 6.0, it has changed slightly. The first change is that code must first Dim an instance of the variable; it is not acceptable to declare an array using the ReDim statement. The second change is that code cannot change the number of dimensions in an array. For example, an array with three dimensions cannot grow to an array of four dimensions, nor can it be reduced to only two dimensions.

To further extend the example code associated with arrays, consider the following, which manipulates some of the arrays previously declared:

```
Dim arrMyIntArray3(4,2) as Integer
Dim arrMyIntArray4( , ) as Integer =
    { {1, 2, 3},{4, 5, 6}, {7, 8, 9},{10, 11, 12},{13, 14 , 15} }
ReDim arrMyIntArray5(2)
ReDim arrMyIntArray3(5,4)
ReDim Preserve arrMyIntArray4(UBound(arrMyIntArray4),1)
```

The ReDim of arrMyIntArray5 instantiates the elements of the array so that values can be assigned to each element. The second statement redimensions the arrMyIntArray3 variable defined earlier. Note that it is changing the size of both the first dimension and the second dimension. While it is not possible to change the number of dimensions in an array, you can resize any of an array's dimensions. This capability is required, as declarations such as Dim arrMyIntArray6(, , ,) As Integer are legal.

By the way, while it is possible to repeatedly ReDim a variable, for performance reasons this action should ideally be done only rarely, and never within a loop. If you intend to loop through a set of entries and add entries to an array, try to determine the number of entries you'll need before entering the loop, or at a minimum ReDim the size of your array in chunks to improve performance.

The Preserve Keyword

The last item in the code snippet in the preceding section illustrates an additional keyword associated with redimensioning. The Preserve keyword indicates that the data stored in the array prior to redimensioning should be transferred to the newly created array. If this keyword is not used, then the data stored in an array is lost. Additionally, in the preceding example, the ReDim statement actually reduces the second dimension of the array. Although this is a perfectly legal statement, this means that even though you have specified preserving the data, the data values 3, 6, 9, 12, and 15 that were assigned in the original definition of this array will be discarded. These are lost because they were assigned in the highest index of the second array. Because arrMyIntArray4(1,2) is no longer valid, the value that resided at this location (6) has been lost.

Arrays continue to be very powerful in Visual Basic, but the basic Array class is just that, basic. It provides a powerful framework, but it does not provide a lot of other features that would enable more robust logic to be built into the array. To achieve more advanced features, such as sorting and dynamic allocation, the base Array class has been inherited by the classes that make up the Collections namespace.

COLLECTIONS

The Collections namespace is part of the System namespace. It provides a series of classes that implement advanced array features. While the capability to make an array of existing types is powerful, sometimes more power is needed in the array itself. The capability to inherently sort or dynamically add dissimilar objects in an array is provided by the classes of the Collections namespace. This namespace contains a specialized set of objects that can be instantiated for additional features when working with a collection of similar objects. Table 8-1 defines several of the objects that are available as part of the System.Collections namespace.

TABLE 8-1: Collection Classes

CLASS	DESCRIPTION
ArrayList	Implements an array whose size increases automatically as elements are added.
BitArray	Manages an array of Booleans that are stored as bit values.
Hashtable	Implements a collection of values organized by key. Sorting is done based on a hash of the key.
Queue	Implements a first in, first out collection.
SortedList	Implements a collection of values with associated keys. The values are sorted by key and are accessible by key or index.
Stack	Implements a last in, first out collection.

Each of the objects listed focuses on storing a collection of objects. This means that in addition to the special capabilities each provides, it also provides one additional capability not available to objects created based on the Array class. Because every variable in .NET is based on the Object class, it is possible to have a collection that contains elements that are defined with different types. So a collection might contain an integer as its first item, a string as its second item, and a custom Person object as its third item. There is no guarantee of the type safety that is an implicit feature of an array.

Each of the preceding collection types stores an array of objects. All classes are of type Object, so a string could be stored in the same collection with an integer. It's possible within these collection classes for the actual objects being stored to be different types. Consider the following example code within ProVB_VS2010 download for Chapter 8:

Available for download on Wrox.com

```vb
Private Sub SampleColl()
    Dim objMyArrList As New System.Collections.ArrayList()
    Dim objItem As Object
    Dim intLine As Integer = 1
    Dim strHello As String = "Hello"
    Dim objWorld As New System.Text.StringBuilder("World")

    ' Add an integer value to the array list.
    objMyArrList.Add(intLine)

    ' Add an instance of a string object
    objMyArrList.Add(strHello)

    ' Add a single character cast as a character.
    objMyArrList.Add(" "c)

    ' Add an object that isn't a primitive type.
    objMyArrList.Add(objWorld)

    ' To balance the string, insert a break between the line
    ' and the string "Hello", by inserting a string constant.
    objMyArrList.Insert(1, ". ")

    For Each objItem In objMyArrList
        ' Output the values on a single line.
        TextBoxOutput.Text += objItem.ToString()
    Next
    TextBoxOutput.Text += vbCrLf
    For Each objItem In objMyArrList
        ' Output the types, one per line.
        TextBoxOutput.Text += objItem.GetType.ToString() & vbCrLf
    Next
End Sub
```

Code snippet from Form1

The preceding code is an example of implementing the `ArrayList` collection class. The collection classes, as this example shows, are versatile. The preceding code creates a new instance of an `ArrayList`, along with some related variables to support the demonstration. The code then shows four different types of variables being inserted into the same `ArrayList`. Next, the code inserts another value into the middle of the list. At no time has the size of the array been declared, nor has a redefinition of the array size been required. The output when run using the ProVB_V2010 project is shown in Figure 8-2.

Visual Basic has additional classes available as part of the `System.Collections.Specialized` namespace. These classes tend to be oriented around a specific problem. For example, the

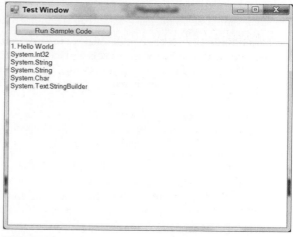

FIGURE 8-2

`ListDictionary` class is designed to take advantage of the fact that although a hash table is very good at storing and retrieving a large number of items, it can be costly when it contains only a few items. Similarly, the `StringCollection` and `StringDictionary` classes are defined so that when working with strings, the time spent interpreting the type of object is reduced and overall performance is improved. Each class defined in this namespace represents a specialized implementation that has been optimized for handling specific data types.

Iterative Statements

The preceding examples have relied on the use of the `For...Next` statement, which has not yet been covered. Since you've now covered both arrays and collections, it's appropriate to introduce the primary commands for working with the elements contained in those variable types. Both the `For` loop and `While` loop share similar characteristics, and which should be used is often a matter of preference.

For Each and For Next

The `For` structure in Visual Basic is the primary way of managing loops. It actually has two different formats. A standard `For Next` statement enables you to set a loop control variable that can be incremented by the `For` statement and custom exit criteria from your loop. Alternatively, if you are working with a collection in which the array items are not indexed numerically, then it is possible to use a `For Each` loop to automatically loop through all of the items in that collection. The following code shows a typical `For Next` loop that cycles through each of the items in an array:

```
For i As Integer = 0 To 10 Step 2
    arrMyIntArray1(i) = i
Next
```

The preceding example sets the value of every other array element to its index, starting with the first item, because like all .NET collections, the collection starts at 0. As a result, items 0, 2, 4, 6, 8, and 10 are set, but items 1, 3, 5, 7, and 9 are not explicitly defined because the loop doesn't address those values. In the case of integers, they'll default to a value of 0 because an integer is a value type; however, if this were an array of strings or other reference types, then these array nodes would actually be undefined, i.e., `Nothing`.

The `For Next` loop is most commonly set up to traverse an array, collection, or similar construct (for example, a data set). The control variable `i` in the preceding example must be numeric. The value can be incremented from a starting value to an ending value, which are 0 and 10, respectively, in this example. Finally, it is possible to accept the default increment of 1; or, if desired, you can add a `Step` qualifier to your command and update the control value by a value other than 1. Note that setting the value of `Step` to 0 means that your loop will theoretically loop an infinite number of times. Best practices suggest your control value should be an integer greater than 0 and not a decimal or other floating-point number.

Visual Basic provides two additional commands that can be used within the For loop's block to enhance performance. The first is Exit For; and as you might expect, this statement causes the loop to end and not continue to the end of the processing. The other is Continue, which tells the loop that you are finished executing code with the current control value and that it should increment the value and reenter the loop for its next iteration:

```
For i = 1 To 100 Step 2
    If arrMyIntArray1.Count <= i Then Exit For
    If i = 5 Then Continue For
    arrMyIntArray1 (i) = i - 1
Next
```

Both the Exit For and Continue keywords were used in the preceding example. Note how each uses a format of the If-Then structure that places the command on the same line as the If statement so that no End If statement is required. This loop exits if the control value is larger than the number of rows defined for arrMyIntArray1.

Next, if the control variable i indicates you are looking at the sixth item in the array (index of five), then this row is to be ignored, but processing should continue within the loop. Keep in mind that even though the loop control variable starts at 1, the first element of the array is still at 0. The Continue statement indicates that the loop should return to the For statement and increment the associated control variable. Thus, the code does not process the next line for item six, where i equals 5.

The preceding examples demonstrate that in most cases, because your loop is going to process a known collection, Visual Basic provides a command that encapsulates the management of the loop control variable. The For Each structure automates the counting process and enables you to quickly assign the current item from the collection so that you can act on it in your code. It is a common way to process all of the rows in a data set or most any other collection, and all of the loop control elements such as Continue and Exit are still available:

```
For Each item As Object In objMyArrList
    'Code A1
Next
```

While, Do While, and Do Until

In addition to the For loop, Visual Basic includes the While and Do loops, with two different versions of the Do loop. The first is the Do While loop. With a Do While loop, your code starts by checking for a condition; and as long as that condition is true, it executes the code contained in the Do loop. Optionally, instead of starting the loop by checking the While condition, the code can enter the loop and then check the condition at the end of the loop. The Do Until loop is similar to the Do While loop:

```
Do While blnTrue = True
    'Code A1
Loop
```

The Do Until differs from the Do While only in that, by convention, the condition for a Do Until is placed after the code block, thus requiring the code in the Do block to execute once before the condition is checked. It bears repeating, however, that a Do Until block can place the Until condition with the Do statement instead of with the Loop statement, and a Do While block can similarly have its condition at the end of the loop:

```
Do          .
    'Code A1
Loop Until (blnTrue = True)
```

In both cases, instead of basing the loop around an array of items or a fixed number of iterations, the loop is instead instructed to continue perpetually until a condition is met. A good use for these loops involves tasks that need to repeat for as long as your application is running. Similar to the For loop, there are Exit Do and

Continue commands that end the loop or move to the next iteration, respectively. Note that parentheses are allowed but are not required for both the While and the Until conditional expression.

The other format for creating a loop is to omit the Do statement and just create a While loop. The While loop works similarly to the Do loop, with the following differences. The While loop's endpoint is an End While statement instead of a loop statement. Second, the condition must be at the start of the loop with the While statement, similar to the Do While. Finally, the While loop has an Exit While statement instead of Exit Do, although the behavior is the same. An example is shown here:

```
While blnTrue = True
    If blnFalse Then
        blnTrue = False
    End if
    If not blnTrue Then Exit While
    System.Threading.Thread.Sleep(500)
    blnFalse = True
End While
```

The While loop has more in common with the For loop, and in those situations where someone is familiar with another language such as C++ or C#, it is more likely to be used than the older Do-Loop syntax that is more specific to Visual Basic.

Finally, before leaving the discussion of looping, note the potential use of endless loops. Seemingly endless, or infinite, loops play a role in application development, so it's worthwhile to illustrate how you might use one. For example, if you were writing an e-mail program, you might want to check the user's mailbox on the server every 20 seconds. You could create a Do While or Do Until loop that contains the code to open a network connection and check the server for any new mail messages to download. You would continue this process until either the application was closed or you were unable to connect to the server. When the application was asked to close, the loop's Exit statement would execute, thus terminating the loop. Similarly, if the code were unable to connect to the server, it might exit the current loop, alert the user, and probably start a loop that would look for network connectivity on a regular basis.

 One warning with endless loops: Always include a call to Thread.Sleep *so that the loop only executes a single iteration within a given time frame to avoid consuming too much processor time.*

Boxing

Normally, when a conversion (implicit or explicit) occurs, the original value is read from its current memory location, and then the new value is assigned. For example, to convert a Short to a Long, the system reads the two bytes of Short data and writes them to the appropriate bytes for the Long variable. However, under Visual Basic, if a value type needs to be managed as an object, then the system performs an intermediate step. This intermediate step involves taking the value on the stack and copying it to the heap, a process referred to as *boxing*. In Chapter 1, in the section titled "Value and Reference Types", a distinction was made regarding how certain types were stored. As noted then, Value types are stored on the stack, while reference values are stored on the heap. As noted earlier, the Object class is implemented as a reference type, so the system needs to convert value types into reference types for them to be objects. This doesn't cause any problems or require any special programming, because boxing isn't something you declare or directly control, but it does affect performance.

If you're copying the data for a single value type, this is not a significant cost, but if you're processing an array that contains thousands of values, the time spent moving between a value type and a temporary reference type can be significant. Thus, if when reviewing code you find a scenario where a value is boxed, it may not be of significant concern. When it becomes something to address is if that boxing is called within a loop that is executed thousands or millions of times. When considering best practices, boxing is something to address when working with large collections and calls that are made repeatedly.

Fortunately, there are ways to limit the amount of boxing that occurs when using collections. One method that works well is to create a class based on the value type you need to work with. This might seem counterintuitive at first because it costs more to create a class. The key is how often you reuse the data contained in the class. By repeatedly using the object to interact with other objects, you avoid creating a temporary boxed object.

Examples in two important areas will help illustrate boxing. The first involves the use of arrays. When an array is created, the portion of the class that tracks the element of the array is created as a reference object, but each element of the array is created directly. Thus, an array of integers consists of an `Array` object and a set of `Integer` value types. When you update one of the values with another integer value, no boxing is involved:

```
Dim arrInt(20) as Integer
Dim intMyValue as Integer = 1

arrInt(0) = 0
arrInt(1) = intMyValue
```

Neither of these assignments of an integer value into the integer array that was defined previously requires boxing. In each case, the array object identifies which value on the stack needs to be referenced, and the value is assigned to that value type. The point here is that just because you have referenced an object doesn't mean you are going to box a value. The boxing occurs only when the values being assigned are being transitioned from value types to reference types:

```
Dim strBldr as New System.Text.StringBuilder()
Dim mySortedList as New System.Collections.SortedList()
Dim count as Integer
For count = 1 to 100
    strBldr.Append(count)
    mySortedList.Add(count, count)
Next
```

The preceding snippet illustrates two separate calls to object interfaces. One call requires boxing of the value `intCount`, while the other does not. Nothing in the code indicates which call is which, but the `Append` method of `StringBuilder` has been overridden to include a version that accepts an integer, while the `Add` method of the `SortedList` collection expects two objects. Although the integer values can be recognized by the system as objects, doing so requires the runtime library to box these values so that they can be added to the sorted list.

When looking for boxing, the concern isn't that you are working with objects as part of an action, but that you are passing a value type to a parameter that expects an object, or you are taking an object and converting it to a value type. However, boxing does not occur when you call a method on a value type. There is no conversion to an object, so if you need to assign an integer to a string using the `ToString` method, there is no boxing of the integer value as part of the creation of the string. Conversely, you are explicitly creating a new string object, so the cost is similar.

GENERICS

Generics refer to the technology built into the .NET Framework (introduced originally with the .NET Framework version 2.0) that enables you to define a template and then declare variables using that template. The template defines the operations that the new type can perform; and when you declare a variable based on the template, you are creating a new type. The benefit of generics over untyped collections or arrays is that a generic template makes it easier for collection types to be strongly typed. The introduction of covariance in .NET Framework 4 makes it easier to reuse the template code in different scenarios.

The primary motivation for adding generics to .NET was to enable the creation of strongly typed collection types. Because generic collection types are strongly typed, they are significantly faster than the previous inheritance-based collection model. Anywhere you presently use collection classes in your code, you should consider revising that code to use generic collection types instead.

Visual Basic 2010 allows not only the use of preexisting generics, but also the creation of your own generic templates. Because the technology to support generics was created primarily to build collection classes, it naturally follows that you might create a generic collection anytime you would otherwise build a normal collection class. More specifically, anytime you find yourself using the `Object` data type, you should instead consider using generics.

Using Generics

There are many examples of generic templates in the .NET Base Class Library (BCL). Many of them can be found in the `System.Collections.Generic` namespace, but others are scattered through the BCL as appropriate. Many of the examples focus on generic collection types, but this is only because it is here that the performance gains, due to generics, are seen. In most cases, generics are used less for performance gains than for the strong typing benefits they provide. As noted earlier, anytime you use a collection data type, you should consider using the generic equivalent instead.

A generic is often written as something like `List(Of T)`. The type (or class) name in this case is `List`. The letter `T` is a placeholder, much like a parameter. It indicates where you must provide a specific type value to customize the generic. For instance, you might declare a variable using the `List(Of T)` generic:

```
Dim data As New List(Of Date)
```

In this case, you are specifying that the type parameter, `T`, is a `Date`. By providing this type, you are specifying that the list will only contain values of type `Date`. To make this clearer, let's contrast the new `List(Of T)` collection with the older `ArrayList` type.

When you work with an `ArrayList`, you are working with a type of collection that can store many types of values at the same time:

```
Dim data As New ArrayList()
data.Add("Hello")
data.Add(5)
data.Add(New Customer())
```

This `ArrayList` is loosely typed, internally always storing the values as type `Object`. This is very flexible but relatively slow because it is late bound. What this means is that when you determine something at runtime you are binding to that type. Of course, it offers the advantage of being able to store any data type, with the disadvantage that you have no control over what is actually stored in the collection.

The `List(Of T)` generic collection is quite different. It is not a type at all; it is just a template. A type is not created until you declare a variable using the template:

```
Dim data As New Generic.List(Of Integer)
data.Add(5)
data.Add(New Customer()) ' throws an exception
data.Add("Hello") ' throws an exception
```

When you declare a variable using the generic, you must provide the type of value that the new collection will hold. The result is that a new type is created — in this case, a collection that can hold only `Integer` values.

The important thing here is that this new collection type is strongly typed for `Integer` values. Not only does its external interface (its `Item` and `Add` methods, for instance) require `Integer` values, but its internal storage mechanism only works with type `Integer`. This means that it is not late bound like `ArrayList`, but rather is early bound. The net result is much higher performance, along with all the type-safety benefits of being strongly typed.

Generics are useful because they typically offer better performance than traditional collection classes. In some cases, they can also save you from writing code, as generic templates can provide code reuse, whereas traditional classes cannot. Finally, generics can sometimes provide better type safety compared to traditional classes, as a generic adapts to the specific type you require, whereas classes often must resort to working with a more general type such as `Object`.

Generics come in two forms: generic types and generic methods. For instance, `List(Of T)` is a generic type in that it is a template that defines a complete type or class. In contrast, some otherwise normal classes have single methods that are just method templates and that assume a specific type when they are called. We will look at both scenarios.

Nullable Types

In addition to having the option to explicitly check for the DBNull value, Visual Basic 2005 introduced the capability to create a nullable value type. In the background, when this syntax is used, the system creates a reference type containing the same data that would be used by the value type. Your code can then check the value of the nullable type before attempting to set this into a value type variable. Nullable types are built using generics. Note that while the Visual Basic keyword for null is Nothing, it is common to discuss this type as supporting a null value even in Visual Basic.

For consistency let's take a look at how nullable types work. The key, of course, is that value types can't be set to null (aka Nothing). This is why nullable types aren't value types. The following statements show how to declare a nullable integer:

```
Dim intValue as Nullable(Of Integer)
Dim intValue2 as Integer?
```

Both intValue and intValue2 act like integer variables, but they aren't actually of type Integer. As noted, the syntax is based on generics, but essentially you have just declared an object of type Nullable and declared that this object will, in fact, hold integer data. Thus, both of the following assignment statements are valid:

```
intValue = 123
intValue = Nothing
```

However, at some point you are going to need to pass intValue to a method as a parameter, or set some property on an object that is looking for an object of type Integer. Because intValue is actually of type Nullable, it has the properties of a nullable object. The Nullable class has two properties of interest when you want to get the underlying value. The first is the property value. This represents the underlying value type associated with this object. In an ideal scenario, you would just use the value property of the Nullable object in order to assign to your actual value a type of integer and everything would work. If the intValue.value wasn't assigned, you would get the same value as if you had just declared a new Integer without assigning it a value which would be 0.

Unfortunately, that's not how the nullable type works. If the intValue.value property contains Nothing and you attempt to assign it, then it throws an exception. To avoid getting this exception, you always need to check the other property of the nullable type: HasValue. The HasValue property is a Boolean that indicates whether a value exists; if one does not, then you shouldn't reference the underlying value. The following code example shows how to safely use a nullable type:

```
Dim intValue as Nullable(Of Integer)
Dim intI as Integer
If intValue.HasValue Then
    intI = intValue.Value
End If
```

Of course, you could add an Else statement to the preceding and use either Integer.MinValue or Integer.MaxValue as an indicator that the original value was Nothing. The key point here is that nullable types enable you to easily work with nullable columns in your database, but you must still verify whether an actual value or null was returned.

Generic Types

Now that you have a basic understanding of generics and how they compare to regular types, let's get into some more detail. To do this, you will make use of some other generic types provided in the .NET Framework. A generic type is a template that defines a complete class, structure, or interface. When you want to use such a generic, you declare a variable using the generic type, providing the real type (or types) to be used in creating the actual type of your variable.

Basic Usage

First, consider the `Dictionary(Of K, T)` generic. This is much like the `List(Of T)` discussed earlier, but this generic requires that you define the types of both the key data and the values to be stored. When you declare a variable as `Dictionary(Of K, T)`, the new `Dictionary` type that is created only accepts keys of the one type and values of the other.

Add the following method to the VBPro_VS2010 sample project and call it from the `ButtonTest_Click` event handler:

Available for
download on
Wrox.com

```
Private Sub SampleDict()
    Dim data As New Generic.Dictionary(Of Integer, String)
    data.Add(5, "Bill")
    data.Add(1, "Johnathan")
    For Each item As KeyValuePair(Of Integer, String) In data
        TextBoxOutput.AppendText("Data: " & item.Key & ", " &
                item.Value)
        TextBoxOutput.AppendText(Environment.NewLine)
    Next
    TextBoxOutput.AppendText(Environment.NewLine)

End Sub
```

Code snippet from Form1

As you type, watch the IntelliSense information on the `Add` method. Notice how the `key` and `value` parameters are strongly typed based on the specific types provided in the declaration of the data variable. In the same code, you can create another type of `Dictionary`:

Available for
download on
Wrox.com

```
Private Sub SampleDict()
    Dim data As New Generic.Dictionary(Of Integer, String)
    Dim info As New Generic.Dictionary(Of Guid, Date)
    data.Add(5, "Bill")
    data.Add(1, "Johnathan")
    For Each item As KeyValuePair(Of Integer, String) In data
        TextBoxOutput.AppendText("Data: " & item.Key & ", " &
                item.Value)
        TextBoxOutput.AppendText(Environment.NewLine)
    Next
    TextBoxOutput.AppendText(Environment.NewLine)
    info.Add(Guid.NewGuid, Now)
    For Each item As KeyValuePair(Of Guid, Date) In info
        TextBoxOutput.AppendText("Info: " & item.Key.ToString &
            ", " & item.Value)
        TextBoxOutput.AppendText(Environment.NewLine)
    Next
    TextBoxOutput.AppendText(Environment.NewLine)

End Sub
```

Code snippet from Form1

This code contains two completely different types. Both have the behaviors of a `Dictionary`, but they are not interchangeable because they have been created as different types.

Generic types may also be used as parameters and return types. For instance, add the following method to `Form1`:

```
Private Function LoadData() As Generic.Dictionary(Of Integer, String)
    Dim data As New Generic.Dictionary(Of Integer, String)
    data.Add(5, "William")
    data.Add(1, "Johnathan")
    Return data
End Function
```

To call this method from the btnDictionary_Click method, add this code:

```
Private Sub SampleDict()
    Dim data As New Generic.Dictionary(Of Integer, String)
    Dim info As New Generic.Dictionary(Of Guid, Date)
    data.Add(5, "Bill")
    data.Add(1, "Johnathan")
    For Each item As KeyValuePair(Of Integer, String) In data
        TextBoxOutput.AppendText("Data: " & item.Key & ", " &
            item.Value)
        TextBoxOutput.AppendText(Environment.NewLine)
    Next
    TextBoxOutput.AppendText(Environment.NewLine)
    info.Add(Guid.NewGuid, Now)
    For Each item As KeyValuePair(Of Guid, Date) In info
        TextBoxOutput.AppendText("Info: " & item.Key.ToString &
            ", " & item.Value)
        TextBoxOutput.AppendText(Environment.NewLine)
    Next
    TextBoxOutput.AppendText(Environment.NewLine)
    Dim results As Generic.Dictionary(Of Integer, String)
    results = LoadData()
    For Each item As KeyValuePair(Of Integer, String) In results
        TextBoxOutput.AppendText("Results: " & item.Key & ", " &
            item.Value)
        TextBoxOutput.AppendText(Environment.NewLine)
    Next
    TextBoxOutput.AppendText(Environment.NewLine)

End Sub
```

Code snippet from Form1

The results of running this code are shown in Figure 8-3.

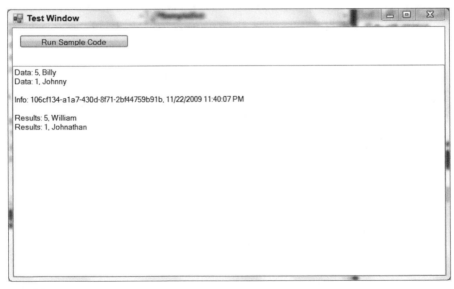

FIGURE 8-3

This works because both the return type of the function and the type of the data variable are exactly the same. Not only are they both Generic.Dictionary derivatives, they have exactly the same types in the declaration.

The same is true for parameters:

```
Private Sub DoWork(ByVal values As Generic.Dictionary(Of Integer, String))
  ' do work here
End Sub
```

Again, the parameter type is not only defined by the generic type, but also by the specific type values used to initialize the generic template.

Inheritance

It is possible to inherit from a generic type as you define a new class. For instance, the .NET BCL defines the `System.ComponentModel.BindingList(Of T)` generic type. This type is used to create collections that can support data binding. You can use this as a base class to create your own strongly typed, data-bindable collection. Add new classes named `Customer` and `CustomerList` to the sample project with the following code:

```
Public Class Customer
  Public Property Name() As String
End Class
```

Code snippet from Customer

```
Inherits System.ComponentModel.BindingList(Of Customer)

Private Sub CustomerList_AddingNew(ByVal sender As Object, _
  ByVal e As System.ComponentModel.AddingNewEventArgs) Handles Me.AddingNew
  Dim cust As New Customer()
  cust.Name = "<new>"
  e.NewObject = cust
End Sub
End Class
```

Code snippet from CustomerList

When you inherit from `BindingList(Of T)`, you must provide a specific type — in this case, `Customer`. This means that your new `CustomerList` class extends and can customize `BindingList(Of Customer)`. Here you are providing a default value for the `Name` property of any new `Customer` object added to the collection.

When you inherit from a generic type, you can employ all the normal concepts of inheritance, including overloading and overriding methods, extending the class by adding new methods, handling events, and so forth.

To see this in action, add a new `Button` control named `ButtonCustomer` to `Form1` and add a new form named `FormCustomerGrid` to the project. Add a `DataGridView` control to `FormCustomerGrid` and dock it by setting the Dock property to Fill in the parent container option.

Behind the `ButtonCustomer_Click` event handler, add the following code:

```
FormCustomerGrid.ShowDialog()
```

Then add the following code behind `FormCustomerGrid`:

```
Public Class FormCustomerGrid
  Dim list As New CustomerList()
  Private Sub FormCustomerGrid_Load(ByVal sender As System.Object,
                ByVal e As System.EventArgs) Handles MyBase.Load
    DataGridView1.DataSource = list
  End Sub
End Class
```

Code snippet from FormCustomerGrid

This code creates an instance of `CustomerList` and data binds the list as the `DataSource` for the `DataGridView` control. When you run the program and click the button to open the `CustomerForm`, notice that the grid contains a newly added `Customer` object. As you interact with the grid, new `Customer` objects are automatically added, with a default name of `<new>`. An example is shown in Figure 8-4.

All this functionality of adding new objects and setting the default `Name` value occurs because `CustomerList` inherits from `BindingList(Of Customer)`.

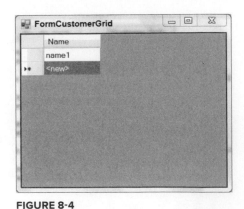

FIGURE 8-4

Generic Methods

A generic method is a single method that is called not only with conventional parameters, but also with type information that defines the method. Generic methods are far less common than generic types. Due to the extra syntax required to call a generic method, they are also less readable than a normal method.

A generic method may exist in any class or module; it does not need to be contained within a generic type. The primary benefit of a generic method is avoiding the use of `CType` or `DirectCast` to convert parameters or return values between different types.

It is important to realize that the type conversion still occurs; generics merely provide an alternative mechanism to use instead of `CType` or `DirectCast`.

Without generics, code often uses the `Object` type. Add the following method to `Form1`:

```
Public Function AreEqual(ByVal a As Object, ByVal b As Object) As Boolean
  Return a.Equals(b)
End Function
```

The problem with this code is that a and b could be anything. There is no restriction here, nothing to ensure that they are even the same type. An alternative is to use generics. Add the following method to `Form1`:

```
Public Function AreEqual(Of T)(ByVal a As T, ByVal b As T) As Boolean
  Return a.Equals(b)
End Function
```

Now a and b are forced to be the same type, and that type is specified when the method is invoked.

Create a new `Sub` method in `Form1` with the following code:

```
Private Sub CheckEqual()
    Dim result As Boolean
    ' use normal method
    result = AreEqual(1, 2)
    result = AreEqual("one", "two")
    result = AreEqual(1, "two")
    ' use generic method
    result = AreEqual(Of Integer)(1, 2)
    result = AreEqual(Of String)("one", "two")
    'result = AreEqual(Of Integer)(1, "two")
End Sub
```

Code snippet from Form1

However, why not just declare the method as a `Boolean`? This code will probably cause some confusion. The first three method calls are invoking the normal `AreEqual` method. Notice that there is no problem asking the method to compare an `Integer` and a `String`.

The second set of calls looks very odd. At first glance, they look like nonsense to many people. This is because invoking a generic method means providing two sets of parameters to the method, rather than the normal one set of parameters.

The first set of parameters contain the type or types required to define the method. This is much like the list of types you must provide when declaring a variable using a generic class. In this case, you're specifying that the `AreEqual` method will be operating on parameters of type `Integer`.

The second set of parameters contains the conventional parameters that you'd normally supply to a method. What is special in this case is that the types of the parameters are being defined by the first set of parameters. In other words, in the first call, the type is specified to be `Integer`, so 1 and 2 are valid parameters. In the second call, the type is `String`, so `"one"` and `"two"` are valid. Notice that the third line is commented out. This is because 1 and `"two"` aren't the same type; with Option Strict On, the compiler will flag this as an error. With Option Strict Off, the runtime will attempt to convert the string at runtime and fail, so this code will not function correctly.

CREATING GENERICS

Now that you have a good idea how to use preexisting generics in your code, let's take a look at how you can create generic templates. The primary reason to create a generic template instead of a class is to gain strong typing of your variables. Anytime you find yourself using the `Object` data type, or a base class from which multiple types inherit, you may want to consider using generics. By using generics, you can avoid the use of `CType` or `DirectCast`, thereby simplifying your code. If you can avoid using the `Object` data type, you will typically improve the performance of your code.

As discussed earlier, there are generic types and generic methods. A generic type is basically a class or structure that assumes specific type characteristics when a variable is declared using the generic. A generic method is a single method that assumes specific type characteristics, even though the method might be in an otherwise very conventional class, structure, or module.

Generic Types

Recall that a generic type is a class, structure, or interface template. You can create such templates yourself to provide better performance, strong typing, and code reuse to the consumers of your types.

Classes

A generic class template is created in the same way that you create a normal class, except that you require the consumer of your class to provide you with one or more types for use in your code. In other words, as the author of a generic template, you have access to the type parameters provided by the user of your generic.

For example, add a new class named `SingleLinkedList` to the project:

```
Public Class SingleLinkedList(Of T)
End Class
```

In the declaration of the type, you specify the type parameters that will be required:

```
Public Class SingleLinkedList(Of T)
```

In this case, you are requiring just one type parameter. The name, `T`, can be any valid variable name. In other words, you could declare the type like this:

```
Public Class SingleLinkedList(Of ValueType)
```

Make this change to the code in your project.

 By convention (carried over from C++ templates), the variable names for type parameters are single uppercase letters. This is somewhat cryptic, and you may want to use a more descriptive convention for variable naming.

Whether you use the cryptic standard convention or more readable parameter names, the parameter is defined on the class definition. Within the class itself, you then use the type parameter anywhere that you would normally use a type (such as `String` or `Integer`).

To create a linked list, you need to define a `Node` class. This will be a nested class:

```vb
Public Class SingleLinkedList(Of ValueType)
#Region " Node class "
  Private Class Node
    Private mValue As ValueType
    Public ReadOnly Property Value() As ValueType
      Get
          Return mValue
      End Get
    End Property
    Public Property NextNode() As Node

    Public Sub New(ByVal value As ValueType, ByVal newNode As Node)
        mValue = value
        NextNode = newNode
    End Sub
  End Class
#End Region
End Class
```

Code snippet from SingleLinkedList

Notice how the `mValue` variable is declared as `ValueType`. This means that the actual type of `mValue` depends on the type supplied when an instance of `SingleLinkedList` is created.

Because `ValueType` is a type parameter on the class, you can use `ValueType` as a type anywhere in the code. As you write the class, you cannot tell what type `ValueType` will be. That information is provided by the user of your generic class. Later, when someone declares a variable using your generic type, that person will specify the type, like this:

```vb
Dim list As New SingleLinkedList(Of Double)
```

At this point, a specific instance of your generic class is created, and all cases of `ValueType` within your code are replaced by the Visual Basic compiler with `Double`. Essentially, this means that for this specific instance of `SingleLinkedList`, the `mValue` declaration ends up as follows:

```vb
Private mValue As Double
```

Of course, you never get to see this code, as it is dynamically generated by the .NET Framework's JIT compiler at runtime based on your generic template code.

The same is true for methods within the template. Your example contains a constructor method, which accepts a parameter of type `ValueType`. Remember that `ValueType` will be replaced by a specific type when a variable is declared using your generic.

So, what type is `ValueType` when you are writing the template itself? Because it can conceivably be any type when the template is used, `ValueType` is treated like the `Object` type as you create the generic template. This severely restricts what you can do with variables or parameters of `ValueType` within your generic code.

The `mValue` variable is of `ValueType`, which means it is basically of type `Object` for the purposes of your template code. Therefore, you can do assignments (as you do in the constructor code), and you can call any methods that are on the `System.Object` type:

- ➤ `Equals()`
- ➤ `GetHashCode()`
- ➤ `GetType()`
- ➤ `ReferenceEquals()`
- ➤ `ToString()`

No operations beyond these basics are available by default. Later in the chapter, you will learn about the concept of *constraints*, which enables you to restrict the types that can be specified for a type parameter. Constraints have the added benefit that they expand the operations you can perform on variables or parameters defined based on the type parameter.

However, this capability is enough to complete the `SingleLinkedList` class. Add the following code to the class after the `End Class` from the `Node` class:

```vb
Private mHead As Node
Default Public ReadOnly Property Item(ByVal index As Integer) As ValueType
  Get
    Dim current As Node = mHead
    For index = 1 To index
      current = current.NextNode
      If current Is Nothing Then
        Throw New Exception("Item not found in list")
      End If
    Next
    Return current.Value
  End Get
End Property
Public Sub Add(ByVal value As ValueType)
  mHead = New Node(value, mHead)
End Sub
Public Sub Remove(ByVal value As ValueType)
  Dim current As Node = mHead
  Dim previous As Node = Nothing
  While current IsNot Nothing
    If current.Value.Equals(value) Then
      If previous Is Nothing Then
        ' this was the head of the list
        mHead = current.NextNode
      Else
        previous.NextNode = current.NextNode
      End If
      Exit Sub
    End If
    previous = current
    current = current.NextNode
  End While
  'got to the end without finding the item.
  Throw New Exception("Item not found in list")
End Sub

Public ReadOnly Property Count() As Integer
  Get
    Dim result As Integer = 0
    Dim current As Node = mHead
    While current IsNot Nothing
      result += 1
      current = current.NextNode
    End While
    Return result
  End Get
End Property
```

Code snippet from SingleLinkedList

Notice that the `Item` property and the `Add` and `Remove` methods all use `ValueType` as either return types or parameter types. More important, note the use of the `Equals` method in the `Remove` method:

```vb
If current.Value.Equals(value) Then
```

The reason why this compiles is because `Equals` is defined on `System.Object` and is therefore universally available. This code could not use the `=` operator because that is not universally available.

To try out the `SingleLinkedList` class, add the following method, which can be called from the `ButtonTest Click` method:

Available for
download on
Wrox.com

```vb
Private Sub CustomList()
    Dim list As New SingleLinkedList(Of String)
    list.Add("Nikita")
    list.Add("Elena")
    list.Add("Benajmin")
    list.Add("William")
    list.Add("Abigail")
    list.Add("Johnathan")
    TextBoxOutput.Clear()
    TextBoxOutput.AppendText("Count: " & list.Count)
    TextBoxOutput.AppendText(Environment.NewLine)
    For index As Integer = 0 To list.Count - 1
        TextBoxOutput.AppendText("Item: " & list.Item(index))
        TextBoxOutput.AppendText(Environment.NewLine)
    Next
End Sub
```

Code snippet from Form1

When you run the code, you will see a display similar to Figure 8-5.

FIGURE 8-5

Other Generic Class Features

Earlier in the chapter, you used the `Dictionary` generic, which specifies multiple type parameters. To declare a class with multiple type parameters, you use syntax like the following:

```vb
Public Class MyCoolType(Of T, V)
    Private mValue As T
    Private mData As V
    Public Sub New(ByVal value As T, ByVal data As V)
        mValue = value
        mData = data
    End Sub
End Class
```

In addition, it is possible to use regular types in combination with type parameters, as shown here:

```
Public Class MyCoolType(Of T, V)
  Private mValue As T
  Private mData As V
  Private mActual As Double
  Public Sub New(ByVal value As T, ByVal data As V, ByVal actual As Double)
    mValue = value
    mData = data
    mActual = actual
  End Sub
End Class
```

Other than the fact that variables or parameters of types T or V must be treated as type System.Object, you can write virtually any code you choose. The code in a generic class is really no different from the code you'd write in a normal class.

This includes all the object-oriented capabilities of classes, including inheritance, overloading, overriding, events, methods, properties, and so forth. However, there are some limitations on overloading. In particular, when overloading methods with a type parameter, the compiler does not know what that specific type might be at runtime. Thus, you can only overload methods in ways in which the type parameter (which could be any type) does not lead to ambiguity.

For instance, adding these two methods to MyCoolType before the .NET Framework 3.5 would have resulted in a compiler error:

```
Public Sub DoWork(ByVal data As Integer)
  ' do work here
End Sub
Public Sub DoWork(ByVal data As V)
  ' do work here
End Sub
```

Now this is possible due to the support for implicitly typed variables. During compilation in .NET, the compiler figures out what the data type of V should be. Next it replaces V with that type which allows your code to compile correctly. This was not the case prior to .NET 3.5. Before this version of the .NET Framework, this kind of code would have resulted in a compiler error. It wasn't legal because the compiler didn't know whether V would be an Integer at runtime. If V were to end up defined as an Integer, then you'd have two identical method signatures in the same class.

Classes and Inheritance

Not only can you create basic generic class templates, you can also combine the concept with inheritance. This can be as basic as having a generic template inherit from an existing class:

```
Public Class MyControls(Of T)
  Inherits Control
End Class
```

In this case, the MyControls generic class inherits from the Windows Forms Control class, thus gaining all the behaviors and interface elements of a Control.

Alternately, a conventional class can inherit from a generic template. Suppose that you have a simple generic template:

```
Public Class GenericBase(Of T)
End Class
```

It is quite practical to inherit from this generic class as you create other classes:

```
Public Class Subclass
  Inherits GenericBase(Of Integer)
End Class
```

Notice how the `Inherits` statement not only references `GenericBase`, but also provides a specific type for the type parameter of the generic type. Anytime you use a generic type, you must provide values for the type parameters, and this is no exception. This means that your new `Subclass` actually inherits from a specific instance of `GenericBase`, where `T` is of type `Integer`.

Finally, you can also have generic classes inherit from other generic classes. For instance, you can create a generic class that inherits from the `GenericBase` class:

```
Public Class GenericSubclass(Of T)
  Inherits GenericBase(Of Integer)
End Class
```

As with the previous example, this new class inherits from an instance of `GenericBase`, where `T` is of type `Integer`.

Things can get far more interesting. It turns out that you can use type parameters to specify the types for other type parameters. For instance, you could alter `GenericSubclass` like this:

```
Public Class GenericSubclass(Of V)
  Inherits GenericBase(Of V)
End Class
```

Notice that you're specifying that the type parameter for `GenericBase` is `V` — which is the type provided by the caller when declaring a variable of type `GenericSubclass`. Therefore, if a caller uses a declaration that creates an object as a `GenericSubclass(Of String)` then `V` is of type String. This means that the GenericSubclass is now inheriting from an instance of GenericBase, where its `T` parameter is also of type `String`. The point being that the type flows through from the subclass into the base class. If that is not complex enough, for those who just want a feel for how twisted this logic can become, consider the following class definition:

```
Public Class GenericSubclass(Of V)
  Inherits GenericBase(Of GenericSubclass(Of V))
End Class
```

In this case, the `GenericSubclass` is inheriting from `GenericBase`, where the `T` type in `GenericBase` is actually based on the declared instance of the `GenericSubclass` type. A caller can create such an instance with the simple declaration which follows:

```
Dim obj As GenericSubclass(Of Date)
```

In this case, the `GenericSubclass` type has a `V` of type `Date`. It also inherits from `GenericBase`, which has a `T` of type `GenericSubclass(Of Date)`.

Such complex relationships are typically not useful, in fact they are often counter productive making code difficult to follow and debug. The point was that it is important to recognize how types flow through generic templates, especially when inheritance is involved.

Structures

You can also define generic `Structure` types. The basic rules and concepts are the same as for defining generic classes, as shown here:

```
Public Structure MyCoolStructure(Of T)
  Public Value As T
End Structure
```

As with generic classes, the type parameter or parameters represent real types that are provided by the user of the `Structure` in actual code. Thus, anywhere you see a `T` in the structure, it will be replaced by a real type such as `String` or `Integer`.

Code can use the `Structure` in a manner similar to how a generic class is used:

```
Dim data As MyCoolStructure(Of Guid)
```

When the variable is declared, an instance of the `Structure` is created based on the type parameter provided. In this example, an instance of `MyCoolStructure` that holds `Guid` objects has been created.

Interfaces

Finally, you can define generic interface types. Generic interfaces are a bit different from generic classes or structures because they are implemented by other types when they are used. You can create a generic interface using the same syntax used for classes and structures:

```
Public Interface ICoolInterface(Of T)
  Sub DoWork(ByVal data As T)
  Function GetAnswer() As T
End Interface
```

Then the interface can be used within another type. For instance, you might implement the interface in a class:

```
Public Class ARegularClass
  Implements ICoolInterface(Of String)
  Public Sub DoWork(ByVal data As String) _
   Implements ICoolInterface(Of String).DoWork
  End Sub
  Public Function GetAnswer() As String _
    Implements ICoolInterface(Of String).GetAnswer
  End Function
End Class
```

Notice that you provide a real type for the type parameter in the `Implements` statement and `Implements` clauses on each method. In each case, you are specifying a specific instance of the `ICoolInterface` interface — one that deals with the `String` data type.

As with classes and structures, an interface can be declared with multiple type parameters. Those type parameter values can be used in place of any normal type (such as `String` or `Date`) in any `Sub`, `Function`, `Property`, or `Event` declaration.

Generic Methods

You have already seen examples of methods declared using type parameters such as `T` or `V`. While these are examples of generic methods, they have been contained within a broader generic type such as a class, a structure, or an interface.

It is also possible to create generic methods within otherwise normal classes, structures, interfaces, or modules. In this case, the type parameter is not specified on the class, structure, or interface, but rather directly on the method itself.

For instance, you can declare a generic method to compare equality like this:

```
Public Module Comparisons
  Public Function AreEqual(Of T)(ByVal a As T, ByVal b As T) As Boolean
    Return a.Equals(b)
  End Function
End Module
```

In this case, the `AreEqual` method is contained within a module, though it could just as easily be contained in a class or a structure. Notice that the method accepts two sets of parameters. The first set of parameters is the type parameter — in this example, just `T`. The second set of parameters consists of the normal parameters that a method would accept. In this example, the normal parameters have their types defined by the type parameter, `T`.

As with generic classes, it is important to remember that the type parameter is treated as a `System.Object` type as you write the code in your generic method. This severely restricts what you can do with parameters or variables declared using the type parameters. Specifically, you can perform assignment and call the various methods common to all `System.Object` variables.

In a moment you will look at constraints, which enable you to restrict the types that can be assigned to the type parameters and expand the operations that can be performed on parameters and variables of those types.

As with generic types, a generic method can accept multiple type parameters:

```
Public Class Comparisons
  Public Function AreEqual(Of T, R)(ByVal a As Integer, ByVal b As T) As R
    ' implement code here
  End Function
End Class
```

In this example, the method is contained within a class, rather than a module. Notice that it accepts two type parameters, T and R. The return type is set to type R, whereas the second parameter is of type T. Also, look at the first parameter, which is a conventional type. This illustrates how you can mix conventional types and generic type parameters in the method parameter list and return types, and by extension within the body of the method code.

Constraints

At this point, you have learned how to create and use generic types and methods, but there have been serious limitations on what you can do when creating generic type or method templates thus far. This is because the compiler treats any type parameters as the type System.Object within your template code. The result is that you can assign the values and call the various methods common to all System.Object instances, but you can do nothing else. In many cases, this is too restrictive to be useful.

Constraints offer a solution and at the same time provide a control mechanism. Constraints enable you to specify rules about the types that can be used at runtime to replace a type parameter. Using constraints, you can ensure that a type parameter is a Class or a Structure, or that it implements a certain interface or inherits from a certain base class.

Not only do constraints enable you to restrict the types available for use, but they also give the Visual Basic compiler valuable information. For example, if the compiler knows that a type parameter must always implement a given interface, then the compiler will allow you to call the methods on that interface within your template code.

Type Constraints

The most common kind of constraint is a *type constraint*. A type constraint restricts a type parameter to be a subclass of a specific class or to implement a specific interface. This idea can be used to enhance the SingleLinkedList to sort items as they are added. Create a copy of the class called ComparableLinkedList, changing the declaration of the class itself to add the IComparable constraint:

```
Public Class SingleLinkedList(Of ValueType As IComparable)
```

With this change, ValueType is not only guaranteed to be equivalent to System.Object, it is also guaranteed to have all the methods defined on the IComparable interface.

This means that within the Add method you can make use of any methods in the IComparable interface (as well as those from System.Object). The result is that you can safely call the CompareTo method defined on the IComparable interface, because the compiler knows that any variable of type ValueType will implement IComparable. Update the original Add method with the following implementation:

```
Public Sub Add(ByVal value As ValueType)
  If mHead Is Nothing Then
    ' List was empty, just store the value.
    mHead = New Node(value, mHead)
  Else
    Dim current As Node = mHead
    Dim previous As Node = Nothing
    While current IsNot Nothing
      If current.Value.CompareTo(value) > 0 Then
        If previous Is Nothing Then
          ' this was the head of the list
          mHead = New Node(value, mHead)
```

```
        Else
            ' insert the node between previous and current
            previous.NextNode = New Node(value, current)
        End If
        Exit Sub
    End If
    previous = current
    current = current.NextNode
End While
' you're at the end of the list, so add to end
previous.NextNode = New Node(value, Nothing)
    End If
End Sub
```

Code snippet from ComparableLinkedList

Note the call to the `CompareTo` method:

```
If current.Value.CompareTo(value) > 0 Then
```

This is possible because of the `IComparable` constraint on `ValueType`. Run the project and test this modified code. The items should be displayed in sorted order, as shown in Figure 8-6.

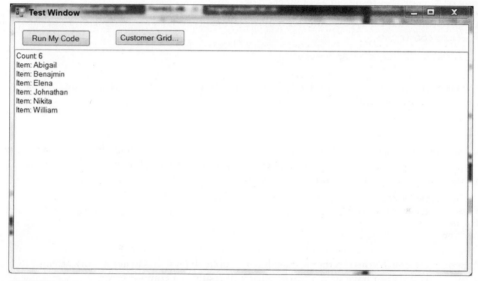

FIGURE 8-6

Not only can you constrain a type parameter to implement an interface, but you can also constrain it to be a specific type (class) or subclass of that type. For example, you could implement a generic method that works on any Windows Forms control:

```
Public Shared Sub ChangeControl(Of C As Control)(ByVal control As C)
    control.Anchor = AnchorStyles.Top Or AnchorStyles.Left
End Sub
```

The type parameter, C, is constrained to be of type `Control`. This restricts calling code to only specify this parameter as `Control` or a subclass of `Control` such as `TextBox`.

Then the parameter to the method is specified to be of type C, which means that this method will work against any `Control` or subclass of `Control`. Because of the constraint, the compiler now knows that the variable will always be some type of `Control` object, so it allows you to use any methods, properties, or events exposed by the `Control` class as you write your code.

Finally, it is possible to constrain a type parameter to be of a specific generic type:

```
Public Class ListClass(Of T, V As Generic.List(Of T))
End Class
```

The preceding code specifies that the V type must be a List(Of T), whatever type T might be. A caller can use your class like this:

```
Dim list As ListClass(Of Integer, Generic.List(Of Integer))
```

Earlier in the chapter, in the discussion of how inheritance and generics interact, you saw that things can get quite complex. The same is true when you constrain type parameters based on generic types.

Class and Structure Constraints

Another form of constraint enables you to be more general. Rather than enforce the requirement for a specific interface or class, you can specify that a type parameter must be either a reference type or a value type.

To specify that the type parameter must be a reference type, you use the Class constraint:

```
Public Class ReferenceOnly(Of T As Class)
End Class
```

This ensures that the type specified for T must be the type of an object. Any attempt to use a value type, such as Integer or Structure, results in a compiler error.

Likewise, you can specify that the type parameter must be a value type such as Integer or a Structure by using the Structure constraint:

```
Public Class ValueOnly(Of T As Structure)
End Class
```

In this case, the type specified for T must be a value type. Any attempt to use a reference type such as String, an interface, or a class results in a compiler error.

New Constraints

Sometimes you want to write generic code that creates instances of the type specified by a type parameter. In order to know that you can actually create instances of a type, you need to know that the type has a default public constructor. You can determine this using the New constraint:

```
Public Class Factories(Of T As New)
  Public Function CreateT() As T
    Return New T
  End Function
End Class
```

The type parameter, T, is constrained so that it must have a public default constructor. Any attempt to specify a type for T that does not have such a constructor will result in a compile error.

Because you know that T will have a default constructor, you are able to create instances of the type, as shown in the CreateT method.

Multiple Constraints

In many cases, you will need to specify multiple constraints on the same type parameter. For instance, you might want to require that a type be a reference type and have a public default constructor.

Essentially, you are providing an array of constraints, so you use the same syntax you use to initialize elements of an array:

```
Public Class Factories(Of T As {New, Class})
  Public Function CreateT() As T
    Return New T
  End Function
End Class
```

The constraint list can include two or more constraints, enabling you to specify a great deal of information about the types allowed for this type parameter.

Within your generic template code, the compiler is aware of all the constraints applied to your type parameters, so it allows you to use any methods, properties, and events specified by any of the constraints applied to the type.

Generics and Late Binding

One of the primary limitations of generics is that variables and parameters declared based on a type parameter are treated as type System.Object inside your generic template code. While constraints offer a partial solution, expanding the type of those variables based on the constraints, you are still very restricted in what you can do with the variables.

One key example is the use of common operators. There is no constraint you can apply that tells the compiler that a type supports the + or – operators. This means that you cannot write generic code like this:

```
Public Function Add(Of T)(ByVal val1 As T, ByVal val2 As T) As T
  Return val1 + val2
End Function
```

This will generate a compiler error because there is no way for the compiler to verify that variables of type T (whatever that is at runtime) support the + operator. Because there is no constraint that you can apply to T to ensure that the + operator will be valid, there is no direct way to use operators on variables of a generic type.

One alternative is to use Visual Basic's native support for late binding to overcome the limitations shown here. Recall that late binding incurs substantial performance penalties because a lot of work is done dynamically at runtime, rather than by the compiler when you build your project. It is also important to remember the risks that attend late binding — specifically, the code can fail at runtime in ways that early-bound code cannot. Nonetheless, given those caveats, late binding can be used to solve your immediate problem.

To enable late binding, be sure to add Option Strict Off at the top of the code file containing your generic template (or set the project property to change Option Strict projectwide from the project's properties). Then you can rewrite the Add function as follows:

```
Public Function Add(Of T)(ByVal value1 As T, ByVal value2 As T) As T
  Return CObj(value1) + CObj(value2)
End Function
```

By forcing the value1 and value2 variables to be explicitly treated as type Object, you are telling the compiler that it should use late binding semantics. Combined with the Option Strict Off setting, the compiler assumes that you know what you are doing and it allows the use of the + operator even though its validity can't be confirmed.

The compiled code uses dynamic late binding to invoke the + operator at runtime. If that operator does turn out to be valid for whatever type T is at runtime, then this code will work great. In contrast, if the operator is not valid, then a runtime exception will be thrown.

Covariance and Contravariance

As part of Visual Studio 2010, the concepts of covariance and contravariance have been brought forward into generics. The basic ideas are related to concepts associated with polymorphism. In short, prior to Visual Studio 2010 if you attempted to take, for example, an instance of a generic that inherits from the base class BindingList and assign that instance to an instance of its base class, you would get an error. The ability to take a specialized or sub class and do a polymorphic assignment to it's parent or base class describes covariance.

This topic can get complex so before moving on to discuss contravariance let's provide a very simple example of covariance in code. The following code declares two classes, Parent and ChildClass, and shows covariance in action:

```
Public Class Parent(Of T)

End Class

Public Class ChildClass(Of T)
    Inherits Parent(Of T)

End Class

Public Class CoVariance
    Public Sub MainMethod()
        Dim cc As New ChildClass(Of String)
        Dim dad As Parent(Of String)
        'Show me the covariance
        dad = cc
    End Sub
End Class
```

Code snippet from CoVariance

You'll note that ChildClass inherits from Parent. The snippet continues with a method extracted from a calling application. It's called MainMethod and you see that the code creates an instance of ChildClass and declares an instance of Parent. Next it looks to assign the instance cc of ChildClass to the instance dad of type Parent. It is this assignment which illustrates an example of covariance. There are, of course, dozens of different specializations that we could consider, but this provides the basis for all of those examples.

Note, if instead of declaring dad as being a Parent (Of String), the code had declared dad as a Parent (Of Integer), then the assignment of cc to dad would fail because dad would no longer be the correct Parent type. It is important to remember that the type assigned as part of the instantiation of a generic directly impacts the underlying class type of that generic's instance.

Contravariance refers to the ability to pass a derived type when a base type is called for. The reason these features are spoken of in a single topic is in fact that they are both specializations of the variance concept. The difference is mainly an understanding that in the case of contravariance you are passing an instance of ChildClass when a Parent instance was expected. Unfortunately contravariance could be called contra-intuitive. You are going to create a base method, and .NET will support its used by derived classes. To illustrate this concept the following code snippet creates two new classes (they are not generic classes), and then has another code snippet for a method that uses these new classes with generic methods to illustrate contravariance:

```
Public Class Base

End Class

Public Class Derived
    Inherits Base

End Class

Public Class ContraVariance

    Private baseMethod As Action(Of Base) = Sub(param As Base)
                                                'Do something.
                                            End Sub
    Private derivedMethod As Action(Of Derived) = baseMethod

    Public Sub MainMethod()
```

```
        ' Show the contra-syntax
        Dim d As Derived = New Derived()
        derivedMethod(d)
        baseMethod(d)
    End Sub

End Class
```

Code snippet from ContraVariance

As shown in the preceding example, you can have a method that expects an input parameter of type `Base` as its input parameter. In the past, this method would not accept a call with a parameter of type `Derived`, but with contravariance the method call will now accept a parameter of type `Derived` because this derived class will, by definition, support the same interface as the base class, just with additional capabilities that can be ignored. As a result, although at first glance it feels backwards, you are in fact able to pass a generic that implements a derived class to a method which is expecting a generic that is defined using a base class.

SUMMARY

This chapter took a look at the classes and language elements that target sets. We started with a look at arrays and the support for arrays within Visual Basic. The chapter then looked at collection classes. By default, these classes operate on the type `Object`, and it is this capability to handle any or all objects within their implementation that makes these classes both powerful and limited.

Following a quick review of the iterative language structures normally associated with these classes, the chapter moved on to looking at generics. Generics enable you to create class, structure, interface, and method templates. These templates gain specific types based on how they are declared or called at runtime. Generics provide you with another code reuse mechanism, along with procedural and object-oriented concepts.

Generics also enable you to change code that uses parameters or variables of type `Object` (or other general types) to use specific data types. This often leads to much better performance and increases the readability of your code.

Using XML with Visual Basic

WHAT YOU WILL LEARN IN THIS CHAPTER

➤ Learn the rationale behind XML

➤ Learn about the namespaces within the .NET Framework Class Library that deal with XML and XML-related technologies

➤ Look at some of the classes contained within these namespaces

➤ How to use *LINQ to XML* to read and edit XML

➤ How Visual Basic enables the use of XML literals within your code

➤ Learn how lambdas are used with Visual Basic and LINQ

➤ How you can create your own lambda expressions to create more generic code

This chapter describes how you can generate and manipulate *Extensible Markup Language (XML)* using Visual Basic 2010. The .NET Framework exposes many XML-specific namespaces that contain over 100 different classes. In addition, dozens of other classes support and implement XML-related technologies, such as those provided in ADO.NET, SQL Server, and BizTalk. Consequently, this chapter focuses on the general concepts and the most important classes.

Visual Basic relies on the classes exposed in the following XML-related namespaces to transform, manipulate, and stream XML documents:

➤ `System.Xml` provides core support for a variety of XML standards, including DTD (Document Type Definition), namespace, DOM (Document Object Model), XDR (XML Data Reduced – an old version of the XML schema standard), XPath, XSLT (XML Transformation), and SOAP (formerly Simple Object Access Protocol, now the acronym doesn't stand for anything).

➤ `System.Xml.Serialization` provides the objects used to transform objects to and from XML documents or streams using serialization.

➤ `System.Xml.Schema` provides a set of objects that enable schemas to be loaded, created, and streamed. This support is achieved using a suite of objects that support in-memory manipulation of the entities that compose an XML schema.

➤ `System.Xml.XPath` provides a parser and evaluation engine for the XML Path language (XPath).

➤ `System.Xml.Xsl` provides the objects necessary when working with Extensible Stylesheet Language (XSL) and XSL Transformations (XSLT).

➤ `System.Xml.Linq` provides the support for querying XML using LINQ (see the LINQ section later in this chapter for more details).

This chapter makes sense of this range of technologies by introducing some basic XML concepts and demonstrating how Visual Basic, in conjunction with the .NET Framework, can make use of XML.

At the end of this chapter, you will be able to generate, manipulate, and transform XML using Visual Basic.

AN INTRODUCTION TO XML

XML is a tagged markup language similar to HTML. In fact, XML and HTML are distant cousins and have their roots in the Standard Generalized Markup Language (SGML). This means that XML leverages one of the most useful features of HTML — readability. However, XML differs from HTML in that XML represents data, whereas HTML is a mechanism for displaying data. The tags in XML describe the data, as shown in the following example:

```
<?xml version="1.0" encoding="utf-8" ?>
<Movies>
  <FilmOrder name="Grease" filmId="1" quantity="21"></FilmOrder>
  <FilmOrder name="Lawrence of Arabia" filmId="2" quantity="10"></FilmOrder>
  <FilmOrder name="Star Wars" filmId="3" quantity="12"></FilmOrder>
  <FilmOrder name="Shrek" filmId="4" quantity="14"></FilmOrder>
</Movies>
```

This XML document represents a store order for a collection of movies. The standard used to represent an order of films would be useful to movie rental firms, collectors, and others. This information can be shared using XML for the following reasons:

➤ The data tags in XML are self-describing.

➤ XML is an open standard and supported on most platforms today.

XML supports the parsing of data by applications not familiar with the contents of the XML document. XML documents can also be associated with a description (a schema) that informs an application about the structure of the data within the XML document.

At this stage, XML looks simple: It is just a human-readable way to exchange data in a universally accepted format. The essential points that you should understand about XML are as follows:

➤ XML data can be stored in a plain text file.

➤ A document is said to be well-formed if it adheres to the XML standard (see www.w3.org/standards/xml/ for more details on the XML standard).

➤ Tags are used to specify the contents of a document — for example, `<FilmOrder>`.

➤ XML elements (also called *nodes*) can be thought of as the objects within a document.

➤ Elements are the basic building blocks of the document. Each element contains both a start tag and an end tag; and a tag can be both a start tag and an end tag in one — for example, `<FilmOrder/>`. In this case, the tag specifies that there is no content (or inner text) to the element (there isn't a closing tag because none is required due to the lack of inner-text content). Such a tag is said to be *empty*.

➤ Data can be contained in the element (the element content) or within attributes contained in the element.

➤ XML is hierarchical. One document can contain multiple elements, which can themselves contain child elements, and so on. However, an XML document can only have one root element.

This last point means that the XML document hierarchy can be thought of as a tree containing nodes:

> ➤ The example document has a root node, `<Movies>`.
> ➤ The branches of the root node are elements of type `<FilmOrder>`.
> ➤ The leaves of the XML element, `<FilmOrder>`, are its attributes: `name`, `quantity`, and `filmId`.

Of course, we are interested in the practical use of XML by Visual Basic. A practical manipulation of the example XML, for example, is to display (for the staff of a movie supplier) a particular movie order in an application so that the supplier can fill the order and then save the information to a database. This chapter explains how you can perform such tasks using the functionality provided by the .NET Framework Class Library.

XML SERIALIZATION

The simplest way to demonstrate Visual Basic's support for XML is to use it to serialize a class. The serialization of an object means that it is written out to a stream, such as a file or a socket. The reverse process can also be performed: An object can be deserialized by reading it from a stream and creating the XML from that stream. You may want to do this to save an object's data to a local file, or to transmit it across a network.

> *The type of serialization described in this chapter is XML serialization, whereby XML is used to represent a class in serialized form. You will see other forms of serialization in the WCF chapter (Chapter 13).*

To help you understand XML serialization, let's examine a class named `FilmOrder` in the FilmOrder project (which can be found in the code download from `www.wrox.com`). This class is implemented in Visual Basic and is used by the company for processing a movie order.

An instance of `FilmOrder` corresponding to each order could be serialized to XML and sent over a socket from a client's computer. We are talking about data in a proprietary form here: an instance of `FilmOrder` being converted into a generic form — XML — that can be universally understood.

The `System.Xml.Serialization` namespace contains classes and interfaces that support the serialization of objects to XML, and the deserialization of objects from XML. Objects are serialized to documents or streams using the `XmlSerializer` class.

Let's look at how you can use `XmlSerializer`. To make the sample simpler, we'll use a console application. This console application will use the class `FilmOrder`:

```vbnet
Public Class FilmOrder
    Public Name As String
    Public FilmId As Integer
    Public Quantity As Integer
    Public Sub New()
    End Sub
    Public Sub New(ByVal name As String, _
                   ByVal filmId As Integer, _
                   ByVal quantity As Integer)
        Me.Name = name
        Me.FilmId = filmId
        Me.Quantity = quantity
    End Sub
End Class
```

Code snippet from FilmOrder

From there, we can move on to the module.

To make the `XmlSerializer` object accessible, you need to make reference to the `System.Xml` `.Serialization` namespace:

```
Imports System.Xml.Serialization
```

In the `Sub Main`, create an instance of `XmlSerializer`, specifying the object to serialize and its type in the constructor:

```
Dim serialize As XmlSerializer = _
  New XmlSerializer(GetType(FilmOrder))
```

Create an instance of the same type passed as a parameter to the constructor of `XmlSerializer`. In a more complex application, you may have created this instance using data provided by the client, a database, or other source:

```
Dim MyFilmOrder As FilmOrder = _
  New FilmOrder("Grease", 101, 10)
```

Call the `Serialize` method of the `XmlSerializer` instance and specify the stream to which the serialized object is written (in this case it is `Console.Out`, so it will simply be displayed in the Console window) and the object to be serialized:

```
serialize.Serialize(Console.Out, MyFilmOrder)
Console.ReadLine()
```

Running the module, the following output is generated by the preceding code:

```
<?xml version="1.0" encoding="IBM437"?>
<FilmOrder xmlns:xsi="http://www.w3.org/2001/XMLSchema-instance"
       xmlns:xsd="http://www.w3.org/2001/XMLSchema">
  <Name>Grease</Name>
  <FilmId>101</FilmId>
  <Quantity>10</Quantity>
</FilmOrder>
```

This output demonstrates the default way in which the `Serialize` method serializes an object:

➤ Each object serialized is represented as an element with the same name as the class — in this case, `FilmOrder`.

➤ The individual data members of the class serialized are contained in elements named for each data member — in this case, `Name`, `FilmId`, and `Quantity`.

Also generated are the following:

➤ The specific version of XML generated — in this case, 1.0

➤ The encoding used for the text — in this case, IBM437

➤ The schemas used to describe the serialized object — in this case, just the two schemas defined by the XML schema specification, `www.w3.org/2001/XMLSchema-instance` and `www.w3.org/2001/XMLSchema`

A schema can be associated with an XML document and describe the data it contains (name, type, scale, precision, length, and so on). Either the actual schema or a reference to where the schema resides can be contained in the XML document. In either case, an XML schema is a standard representation that can be used by all applications that consume XML. This means that applications can use the supplied schema to validate the contents of an XML document generated by the `Serialize` method of the `XmlSerializer` object.

The code snippet that demonstrated the `Serialize` method of `XmlSerializer` displayed the XML generated to a stream displayed by `Console.Out`. Clearly, we do not expect an application to use

`Console.Out` when it would like to access a `FilmOrder` object in XML form. The point was to show how serialization can be performed in just two lines of code (one call to a constructor and one call to a method).

The `Serialize` method's first parameter is overridden so that it can serialize XML to a file (the filename is given as type `String`), a `Stream`, a `TextWriter`, or an `XmlWriter`. When serializing to `Stream`, `TextWriter`, or `XmlWriter`, adding a third parameter to the `Serialize` method is permissible. This third parameter is of type `XmlSerializerNamespaces` and is used to specify a list of namespaces that qualify the names in the XML-generated document.

An object is reconstituted using the `Deserialize` method of `XmlSerializer`. This method is overridden and can deserialize XML presented as a `Stream`, a `TextReader`, or an `XmlReader`. The output of the various `Deserialize` methods is a generic `Object`, so you need to cast the resulting object to the correct data type.

Before demonstrating the `Deserialize` method, we will introduce a new class, `FilmOrderList`. This class contains an array of film orders (actually an array of `FilmOrder` objects). `FilmOrderList` is defined as follows:

Available for download on Wrox.com

```
Public Class FilmOrderList
    Public FilmOrders() As FilmOrder
    Public Sub New()
    End Sub
    Public Sub New(ByVal multiFilmOrders() As FilmOrder)
        Me.FilmOrders = multiFilmOrders
    End Sub
End Class
```

Code snippet from FilmOrderList

The `FilmOrderList` class contains a fairly complicated object, an array of `FilmOrder` objects. The underlying serialization and deserialization of this class is more complicated than that of a single instance of a class that contains several simple types, but the programming effort involved on your part is just as simple as before. This is one of the great ways in which the .NET Framework makes it easy for you to work with XML data, no matter how it is formed.

To work through an example of the deserialization process, first create a sample order stored as an XML file called `Filmorama.xml`:

Available for download on Wrox.com

```xml
<?xml version="1.0" encoding="utf-8" ?>
<FilmOrderList xmlns:xsi="http://www.w3.org/2001/XMLSchema-instance"
 xmlns:xsd="http://www.w3.org/2001/XMLSchema">
  <FilmOrders>
    <FilmOrder>
      <Name>Grease</Name>
      <FilmId>101</FilmId>
      <Quantity>10</Quantity>
    </FilmOrder>
    <FilmOrder>
      <Name>Lawrence of Arabia</Name>
      <FilmId>102</FilmId>
      <Quantity>10</Quantity>
    </FilmOrder>
    <FilmOrder>
      <Name>Star Wars</Name>
      <FilmId>103</FilmId>
      <Quantity>10</Quantity>
    </FilmOrder>
  </FilmOrders>
</FilmOrderList>
```

Code snippet from FilmOrderList

In order for this to run, you should either have the .xml file in the location of the executable or load the file using the full path of the file within the code example. To have the XML in the same directory as the executable, add the XML file to the project, and set the Copy to Output Directory to "Copy if newer."

Once the XML file is in place, the next step is to change your console application so it will deserialize the contents of this file. First, ensure that your console application has made the proper namespace references:

```
Imports System.Xml
Imports System.Xml.Serialization
Imports System.IO
```

The following code in `Sub Main()` demonstrates an object of type `FilmOrderList` being deserialized (or rehydrated) from a file, `Filmorama.xml`. This object is deserialized using this file in conjunction with the `Deserialize` method of `XmlSerializer`:

Available for
download on
Wrox.com

```
' Open file Filmorama.xml
Dim dehydrated As FileStream = _
    New FileStream("Filmorama.xml", FileMode.Open)
' Create an XmlSerializer instance to handle deserializing,
' FilmOrderList
Dim serialize As XmlSerializer = _
    New XmlSerializer(GetType(FilmOrderList))
' Create an object to contain the deserialized instance of the object.
Dim myFilmOrder As FilmOrderList = _
    New FilmOrderList
' Deserialize object
myFilmOrder = serialize.Deserialize(dehydrated)
```

Code snippet from FilmOrderList

Once deserialized, the array of film orders can be displayed:

```
Dim SingleFilmOrder As FilmOrder
For Each SingleFilmOrder In myFilmOrder.FilmOrders
    Console.Out.WriteLine("{0}, {1}, {2}", _
        SingleFilmOrder.Name, _
        SingleFilmOrder.FilmId, _
        SingleFilmOrder.Quantity)
Next
Console.ReadLine()
```

This example is just code that serializes an instance of type `FilmOrderList`. The output generated by displaying the deserialized object containing an array of film orders is as follows:

```
Grease, 101, 10
Lawrence of Arabia, 102, 10
Star Wars, 103, 10
```

`XmlSerializer` also implements a `CanDeserialize` method. The prototype for this method is as follows:

```
Public Overridable Function CanDeserialize(ByVal xmlReader As XmlReader) _
    As Boolean
```

If `CanDeserialize` returns `True`, then the XML document specified by the `xmlReader` parameter can be deserialized. If the return value of this method is `False`, then the specified XML document cannot be deserialized. Using this method is usually preferable to attempting to deserialize and trapping the exception that may occur.

The `FromTypes` method of `XmlSerializer` facilitates the creation of arrays that contain `XmlSerializer` objects. This array of `XmlSerializer` objects can be used in turn to process arrays of the type to be serialized. The prototype for `FromTypes` is shown here:

```
Public Shared Function FromTypes(ByVal types() As Type) As XmlSerializer()
```

Before exploring the `System.Xml.Serialization` namespace, take a moment to consider the various uses of the term *attribute*.

Source Code Style Attributes

Thus far, you have seen attributes applied to a specific portion of an XML document. Visual Basic has its own flavor of attributes, as does C# and each of the other .NET languages. These attributes refer to annotations to the source code that specify information, or *metadata*, that can be used by other applications without the need for the original source code. We will call such attributes *Source Code Style attributes*.

In the context of the `System.Xml.Serialization` namespace, Source Code Style attributes can be used to change the names of the elements generated for the data members of a class or to generate XML attributes instead of XML elements for the data members of a class. To demonstrate this, we will change the `FilmOrder` class using these attributes to change the outputted XML.

To rename the XML generated for a data member, a Source Code Style attribute will be used. This Source Code Style attribute specifies that when `FilmOrder` is serialized, the `name` data member is represented as an XML element, `<Title>`. The actual Source Code Style attribute that specifies this is as follows:

```
<XmlElementAttribute("Title")> Public Name As String
```

The updated `FilmOrder` (contained in the `FilmOrderAttributes` project) also contains other Source Code Style attributes:

➤ `<XmlAttributeAttribute("ID")>` specifies that `FilmId` is to be serialized as an XML attribute named `ID`.

➤ `<XmlAttributeAttribute("Qty")>` specifies that `Quantity` is to be serialized as an XML attribute named `Qty`.

The complete modified `FilmOrder` is defined as follows:

Available for download on Wrox.com

```vb
Imports System.Xml.Serialization
Public Class FilmOrder
    <XmlElementAttribute("Title")> Public Name As String
    <XmlAttributeAttribute("ID")> Public FilmId As Integer
    <XmlAttributeAttribute("Qty")> Public Quantity As Integer
    Public Sub New()
    End Sub
    Public Sub New(ByVal name As String, _
                   ByVal filmId As Integer, _
                   ByVal quantity As Integer)
        Me.Name = name
        Me.FilmId = filmId
        Me.Quantity = quantity
    End Sub
End Class
```

Code snippet from FilmOrderAttributes

Note that you needed to include the `System.Xml.Serialization` namespace to bring in the Source Code Style attributes used.

The serialization code in `Sub Main()` doesn't change:

Available for download on Wrox.com

```vb
Dim serialize As XmlSerializer = _
    New XmlSerializer(GetType(FilmOrder))
Dim MyMovieOrder As FilmOrder = _
    New FilmOrder("Grease", 101, 10)
serialize.Serialize(Console.Out, MyMovieOrder)
Console.Readline()
```

Code snippet from FilmOrderAttributes

The console output generated by this code reflects the Source Code Style attributes associated with the class:

```
<?xml version="1.0" encoding="IBM437"?>
<FilmOrder xmlns:xsi="http://www.w3.org/2001/XMLSchema-instance"
           xmlns:xsd="http://www.w3.org/2001/XMLSchema" ID="101" Qty="10">
  <Title>Grease</Title>
</FilmOrder>
```

Compare this to the earlier version that does not include the attributes.

The example only demonstrates the Source Code Style attributes exposed by the `XmlAttributeAttribute` and `XmlElementAttribute` classes in the `System.Xml.Serialization` namespace. A variety of other Source Code Style attributes exist in this namespace that also control the form of XML generated by serialization.

SYSTEM.XML DOCUMENT SUPPORT

The `System.Xml` namespace implements a variety of objects that support standards-based XML processing. The XML-specific standards facilitated by this namespace include XML 1.0, Document Type Definition (DTD) support, XML namespaces, XML schemas, XPath, XQuery, XSLT, DOM Level 1 and DOM Level 2 (Core implementations), as well as SOAP 1.1, SOAP 1.2, SOAP Contract Language, and SOAP Discovery. The `System.Xml` namespace exposes over 30 separate classes in order to facilitate this level of the XML standard's compliance.

To generate and navigate XML documents, there are two styles of access:

➤ **Stream-based** — `System.Xml` exposes a variety of classes that read XML from and write XML to a stream. This approach tends to be a fast way to consume or generate an XML document because it represents a set of serial reads or writes. The limitation of this approach is that it does not view the XML data as a document composed of tangible entities, such as nodes, elements, and attributes. An example of where a stream could be used is when receiving XML documents from a socket or a file.

➤ **Document Object Model (DOM)-based** — `System.Xml` exposes a set of objects that access XML documents as data. The data is accessed using entities from the XML document tree (nodes, elements, and attributes). This style of XML generation and navigation is flexible but may not yield the same performance as stream-based XML generation and navigation. DOM is an excellent technology for editing and manipulating documents. For example, the functionality exposed by DOM could simplify merging your checking, savings, and brokerage accounts.

XML STREAM-STYLE PARSERS

Stream-based parsers read a block of XML in a forward-only manner, only keeping the current node in memory. When an XML document is parsed using a stream parser, the parser always points to the current node in the document (see Figure 9-1).

The following classes that access a stream of XML (read XML) and generate a stream of XML (write XML) are contained in the `System.Xml` namespace:

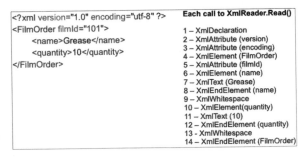

FIGURE 9-1

➤ `XmlWriter` — This abstract class specifies a non-cached, forward-only stream that writes an XML document (data and schema).

> ➤ XmlReader — This abstract class specifies a non-cached, forward-only stream that reads an XML document (data and schema).

The diagram of the classes associated with the XML stream-style parser refers to one other class, XslTransform. This class is found in the System.Xml.Xsl namespace and is not an XML stream-style parser. Rather, it is used in conjunction with XmlWriter and XmlReader. This class is covered in detail later.

The System.Xml namespace exposes a plethora of additional XML manipulation classes in addition to those shown in the architecture diagram. The classes shown in the diagram include the following:

> ➤ XmlResolver — This abstract class resolves an external XML resource using a Uniform Resource Identifier (URI). XmlUrlResolver is an implementation of an XmlResolver.

> ➤ XmlNameTable — This abstract class provides a fast means by which an XML parser can access element or attribute names.

Writing an XML Stream

An XML document can be created programmatically in .NET. One way to perform this task is by writing the individual components of an XML document (schema, attributes, elements, and so on) to an XML stream. Using a unidirectional write-stream means that each element and its attributes must be written in order — the idea is that data is always written at the end of the stream. To accomplish this, you use a writable XML stream class (a class derived from XmlWriter). Such a class ensures that the XML document you generate correctly implements the W3C Extensible Markup Language (XML) 1.0 specification and the namespaces in the XML specification.

Why is this necessary when you have XML serialization? You need to be very careful here to separate interface from implementation. XML serialization works for a specific class, such as the FilmOrder class used in the earlier samples. This class is a proprietary implementation and not the format in which data is exchanged. For this one specific case, the XML document generated when FilmOrder is serialized just so happens to be the XML format used when placing an order for some movies. You can use Source Code Style attributes to help it conform to a standard XML representation of a film order summary, but the eventual structure is tied to that class.

In a different application, if the software used to manage an entire movie distribution business wants to generate movie orders, then it must generate a document of the appropriate form. The movie distribution management software achieves this using the XmlWriter object.

Before reviewing the subtleties of XmlWriter, note that this class exposes over 40 methods and properties. The example in this section provides an overview that touches on a subset of these methods and properties. This subset enables the generation of an XML document that corresponds to a movie order.

The example builds the module that generates the XML document corresponding to a movie order. It uses an instance of XmlWriter, called FilmOrdersWriter, which is actually a file on disk. This means that the XML document generated is streamed to this file directly. Because the FilmOrdersWriter variable represents a file, you have to take a few actions against the file. For instance, you have to ensure the file is

> ➤ **Created** — The instance of XmlWriter, FilmOrdersWriter, is created by using the Create method, as well as by assigning all the properties of this object by using the XmlWriterSettings object.

> ➤ **Opened** — The file the XML is streamed to, FilmOrdersProgrammatic.xml, is opened by passing the filename to the constructor associated with XmlWriter.

> ➤ **Generated** — The process of generating the XML document is described in detail at the end of this section.

> ➤ **Closed** — The file (the XML stream) is closed using the Close method of XmlWriter or by simply making use of the Using keyword, which ensures that the object is closed at the end of the Using statement.

Before you create the `XmlWriter` object, you first need to customize how the object operates by using the `XmlWriterSettings` object. This object, introduced in .NET 2.0, enables you to configure the behavior of the `XmlWriter` object before you instantiate it:

```
Dim myXmlSettings As New XmlWriterSettings()
myXmlSettings.Indent = True
myXmlSettings.NewLineOnAttributes = True
```

Code snippet from FilmOrdersWriter

You can specify a few settings for the `XmlWriterSettings` object that define how XML creation will be handled by the `XmlWriter` object.

Once the `XmlWriterSettings` object has been instantiated and assigned the values you deem necessary, the next steps are to invoke the `XmlWriter` object and make the association between the `XmlWriterSettings` object and the `XmlWriter` object.

The basic infrastructure for managing the file (the XML text stream) and applying the settings class is either

```
Dim FilmOrdersWriter As XmlWriter = _
    XmlWriter.Create("..\FilmOrdersProgrammatic.xml", myXmlSettings)
FilmOrdersWriter.Close()
```

Code snippet from FilmOrdersWriter

or the following, if you are utilizing the `Using` keyword, which is the recommended approach:

```
Using FilmOrdersWriter As XmlWriter = _
    XmlWriter.Create("..\FilmOrdersProgrammatic.xml", myXmlSettings)
End Using
```

Code snippet from FilmOrdersWriter

With the preliminaries completed (file created and formatting configured), the process of writing the actual attributes and elements of your XML document can begin. The sequence of steps used to generate your XML document is as follows:

1. Write an XML comment using the `WriteComment` method. This comment describes from whence the concept for this XML document originated and generates the following code:

   ```
   <!-- Same as generated by serializing, FilmOrder -->
   ```

2. Begin writing the XML element, `<FilmOrder>`, by calling the `WriteStartElement` method. You can only begin writing this element because its attributes and child elements must be written before the element can be ended with a corresponding `</FilmOrder>`. The XML generated by the `WriteStartElement` method is as follows:

   ```
   <FilmOrder>
   ```

3. Write the attributes associated with `<FilmOrder>` by calling the `WriteAttributeString` method twice. The XML generated by calling the `WriteAttributeString` method twice adds to the `<FilmOrder>` XML element that is currently being written to the following:

   ```
   <FilmOrder FilmId="101" Quantity="10">
   ```

4. Using the `WriteElementString` method, write the child XML element `<Title>` contained in the XML element, `<FilmOrder>`. The XML generated by calling this method is as follows:

   ```
   <Title>Grease</Title>
   ```

5. Complete writing the `<FilmOrder>` parent XML element by calling the `WriteEndElement` method. The XML generated by calling this method is as follows:

   ```
   </FilmOrder>
   ```

Now you can put all this together in the VB module file shown here:

```vb
Imports System.Xml

Module Main
    Sub Main()
        Dim myXmlSettings As New XmlWriterSettings
        myXmlSettings.Indent = True
        myXmlSettings.NewLineOnAttributes = True
        Using FilmOrdersWriter As XmlWriter =
            XmlWriter.Create("..\FilmOrdersProgrammatic.xml", myXmlSettings)
            FilmOrdersWriter.WriteComment(" Same as generated " &
                "by serializing, FilmOrder ")
            FilmOrdersWriter.WriteStartElement("FilmOrder")
            FilmOrdersWriter.WriteAttributeString("FilmId", "101")
            FilmOrdersWriter.WriteAttributeString("Quantity", "10")
            FilmOrdersWriter.WriteElementString("Title", "Grease")
            FilmOrdersWriter.WriteEndElement() ' End  FilmOrder
        End Using
    End Sub
End Module
```

Code snippet from FilmOrdersWriter

Once this is run, you will find the XML file `FilmOrdersProgrammatic.xml` created in the same folder as the `Main.vb` file or in the `bin` directory. The content of this file is as follows:

```xml
<?xml version="1.0" encoding="utf-8"?>
<!-- Same as generated by serializing, FilmOrder -->
<FilmOrder
  FilmId="101"
  Quantity="10">
  <Title>Grease</Title>
</FilmOrder>
```

The previous XML document is the same in form as the XML document generated by serializing the `FilmOrder` class. Notice that in the previous XML document, the `<Title>` element is indented two characters and that each attribute is on a different line in the document. This was achieved using the `XmlWriterSettings` class.

The sample application covers only a small portion of the methods and properties exposed by the XML stream-writing class, `XmlWriter`. Other methods implemented by this class manipulate the underlying file, such as the `Flush` method; and some methods allow XML text to be written directly to the stream, such as the `WriteRaw` method.

The `XmlWriter` class also exposes a variety of methods that write a specific type of XML data to the stream. These methods include `WriteBinHex`, `WriteCData`, `WriteString`, and `WriteWhiteSpace`.

You can now generate the same XML document in two different ways. You have used two different applications that took two different approaches to generating a document that represents a standardized movie order. The XML serialization approach uses the "shape" of the class to generate XML, whereas the `XmlWriter` allows you more flexibility in the output, at the expense of more effort.

However, there are even more ways to generate XML, depending on the circumstances. Using the previous scenario, you could receive a movie order from a store, and this order would have to be transformed from the XML format used by the supplier to your own order format.

Reading an XML Stream

In .NET, XML documents can be read from a stream as well. Data is traversed in the stream in order (first XML element, second XML element, and so on). This traversal is very quick because the data is processed in one direction and features such as write and move backward in the traversal are not supported. At any given instance, only data at the current position in the stream can be accessed.

Before exploring how an XML stream can be read, you need to understand why it should be read in the first place. Returning to our movie supplier example, imagine that the application managing the movie orders can generate a variety of XML documents corresponding to current orders, preorders, and returns. All the documents (current orders, preorders, and returns) can be extracted in stream form and processed by a report-generating application. This application prints the orders for a given day, the preorders that are going to be due, and the returns that are coming back to the supplier. The report-generating application processes the data by reading in and parsing a stream of XML.

One class that can be used to read and parse such an XML stream is XmlReader. Other classes in the .NET Framework are derived from XmlReader, such as XmlTextReader, which can read XML from a file (specified by a string corresponding to the file's name), a Stream, or an XmlReader. This example uses an XmlReader to read an XML document contained in a file. Reading XML from a file and writing it to a file is not the norm when it comes to XML processing, but a file is the simplest way to access XML data. This simplified access enables you to focus on XML-specific issues.

In creating a sample, the first step is to make the proper imports:

Available for
download on
Wrox.com

```
Imports System.Xml
Imports System.Xml.Serialization
Imports System.IO
```

Code snippet from FilmOrdersReader

From there, the next step in accessing a stream of XML data is to create an instance of the object that will open the stream (the readMovieInfo variable of type XmlReader) and then open the stream itself. Your application performs this as follows (where MovieManage.xml is the name of the file containing the XML document):

```
Dim myXmlSettings As New XmlReaderSettings()
Using readMovieInfo As XmlReader = XmlReader.Create(fileName, myXmlSettings)
```

Note that like the XmlWriter class, the XmlReader also has a settings class. Though you can make assignments to the XmlReaderSettings object, in this case you do not. Later, this chapter covers the XmlReaderSettings object.

The basic mechanism for traversing each stream is to traverse from node to node using the Read method. Node types in XML include element and white space. Numerous other node types are defined, but this example focuses on traversing XML elements and the white space that is used to make the elements more readable (carriage returns, linefeeds, and indentation spaces). Once the stream is positioned at a node, the MoveToNextAttribute method can be called to read each attribute contained in an element. The MoveToNextAttribute method only traverses attributes for nodes that contain attributes (nodes of type element). An example of an XmlReader traversing each node and then traversing the attributes of each node follows:

Available for
download on
Wrox.com

```
While readMovieInfo.Read()
   ' Process node here.
   While readMovieInfo.MoveToNextAttribute()
      ' Process attribute here.
   End While
End While
```

Code snippet from FilmOrdersReader

This code, which reads the contents of the XML stream, does not utilize any knowledge of the stream's contents. However, a great many applications know exactly how the stream they are going to traverse is structured. Such applications can use XmlReader in a more deliberate manner and not simply traverse the stream without foreknowledge. This would mean you could use the GetAttribute method as well as the various ReadContentAs and ReadElementContentAs methods to retrieve the contents by name, rather than just walking through the XML.

Once the example stream has been read, it can be cleaned up using the `End Using` call:

```
End Using
```

This `ReadMovieXml` subroutine takes a string parameter that contains the filename of the file containing the XML. The code for the subroutine is as follows (and is basically the code just outlined):

Available for download on Wrox.com

```
Private Sub ReadMovieXml(ByVal fileName As String)
    Dim myXmlSettings As New XmlReaderSettings()
    Using readMovieInfo As XmlReader = XmlReader.Create(fileName, _
        myXmlSettings)
        While readMovieInfo.Read()
            ' Process node here.
            ShowXmlNode(readMovieInfo)
            While readMovieInfo.MoveToNextAttribute()
                ' Process attribute here.
                ShowXmlNode(readMovieInfo)
            End While
        End While
    End Using
End Sub
```

Code snippet from FilmOrdersReader

For each node encountered after a call to the `Read` method, `ReadMovieXml` calls the `ShowXmlNode` subroutine. Similarly, for each attribute traversed, the `ShowXmlNode` subroutine is called. This subroutine breaks down each node into its sub-entities:

➤ **Depth** — This property of `XmlReader` determines the level at which a node resides in the XML document tree. To understand depth, consider the following XML document composed solely of elements:

```
<A>
    <B></B>
    <C>
        <D></D>
    </C>
</A>.
```

Element `<A>` is the root element, and when parsed would return a depth of 0. Elements `<B>` and `<C>` are contained in `<A>` and hence reflect a depth value of 1. Element `<D>` is contained in `<C>`. The `Depth` property value associated with `<D>` (depth of 2) should, therefore, be one more than the `Depth` property associated with `<C>` (depth of 1).

➤ **Type** — The type of each node is determined using the `NodeType` property of `XmlReader`. The node returned is of enumeration type, `XmlNodeType`. Permissible node types include `Attribute`, `Element`, and `Whitespace`. (Numerous other node types can also be returned, including CDATA, Comment, Document, Entity, and DocumentType.)

➤ **Name** — The name of each node is retrieved using the `Name` property of `XmlReader`. The name of the node could be an element name, such as `<FilmOrder>`, or an attribute name, such as `FilmId`.

➤ **Attribute Count** — The number of attributes associated with a node is retrieved using the `AttributeCount` property of `XmlReader`'s `NodeType`.

➤ **Value** — The value of a node is retrieved using the `Value` property of `XmlReader`. For example, the element node `<Title>` contains a value of `Grease`.

The subroutine `ShowXmlNode` is implemented as follows:

Available for download on Wrox.com

```
Private Sub ShowXmlNode(ByVal reader As XmlReader)
    If reader.Depth > 0 Then
        For depthCount As Integer = 1 To reader.Depth
            Console.Write("  ")
        Next
```

```
      End If
      If reader.NodeType = XmlNodeType.Whitespace Then
          Console.Out.WriteLine("Type: {0} ", reader.NodeType)
      ElseIf reader.NodeType = XmlNodeType.Text Then
          Console.Out.WriteLine("Type: {0}, Value: {1} ", _
                                reader.NodeType, _
                                reader.Value)
      Else
          Console.Out.WriteLine("Name: {0}, Type: {1}, " & _
                                "AttributeCount: {2}, Value: {3} ", _
                                reader.Name, _
                                reader.NodeType, _
                                reader.AttributeCount, _
                                reader.Value)
      End If
  End Sub
```

Code snippet from FilmOrdersReader

Within the `ShowXmlNode` subroutine, each level of node depth adds two spaces to the output generated:

```
If reader.Depth > 0 Then
  For depthCount As Integer = 1 To reader.Depth
    Console.Write(" ")
  Next
End If
```

You add these spaces in order to create human-readable output (so you can easily determine the depth of each node displayed). For each type of node, `ShowXmlNode` displays the value of the `NodeType` property. The `ShowXmlNode` subroutine makes a distinction between nodes of type White space and other types of nodes. The reason for this is simple: A node of type White space does not contain a name or attribute count. The value of such a node is any combination of white-space characters (space, tab, carriage return, and so on). Therefore, it doesn't make sense to display the properties if the `NodeType` is `XmlNodeType.WhiteSpace`. Nodes of type Text have no name associated with them, so for this type, subroutine `ShowXmlNode` only displays the properties `NodeType` and `Value`. For all other node types (including elements and attributes), the `Name`, `AttributeCount`, `Value`, and `NodeType` properties are displayed.

To finalize this module, add a `Sub Main` as follows:

```
Sub Main(ByVal args() As String)
    ReadMovieXml("..\MovieManage.xml")
End Sub
```

Here is an example construction of the input `MovieManage.xml` file:

```
<?xml version="1.0" encoding="utf-8" ?>
<MovieOrderDump>
  <FilmOrderList>
    <multiFilmOrders>
      <FilmOrder filmId="101">
        <name>Grease</name>
        <quantity>10</quantity>
      </FilmOrder>
      <FilmOrder filmId="102">
        <name>Lawrence of Arabia</name>
        <quantity>10</quantity>
      </FilmOrder>
      <FilmOrder filmId="103">
        <name>Star Wars</name>
        <quantity>10</quantity>
      </FilmOrder>
    </multiFilmOrders>
  </FilmOrderList>
```

```
  <PreOrder>
    <FilmOrder filmId="104">
      <name>Shrek III - Shrek Becomes a Programmer</name>
      <quantity>10</quantity>
    </FilmOrder>
  </PreOrder>
  <Returns>
    <FilmOrder filmId="103">
      <name>Star Wars</name>
      <quantity>2</quantity>
    </FilmOrder>
  </Returns>
</MovieOrderDump>
```

Code snippet from FilmOrdersReader

Running this module produces the following output (a partial display, as it would be rather lengthy):

```
Name: xml, Type: XmlDeclaration, AttributeCount: 2, Value: version="1.0"
encoding="utf-8"
 Name: version, Type: Attribute, AttributeCount: 2, Value: 1.0
 Name: encoding, Type: Attribute, AttributeCount: 2, Value: utf-8
Type: Whitespace
Name: MovieOrderDump, Type: Element, AttributeCount: 0, Value:
Type: Whitespace
 Name: FilmOrderList, Type: Element, AttributeCount: 0, Value:
Type: Whitespace
  Name: multiFilmOrders, Type: Element, AttributeCount: 0, Value:
  Type: Whitespace
   Name: FilmOrder, Type: Element, AttributeCount: 1, Value:
    Name: filmId, Type: Attribute, AttributeCount: 1, Value: 101
    Type: Whitespace
    Name: name, Type: Element, AttributeCount: 0, Value:
     Type: Text, Value: Grease
    Name: name, Type: EndElement, AttributeCount: 0, Value:
    Type: Whitespace
    Name: quantity, Type: Element, AttributeCount: 0, Value:
     Type: Text, Value: 10
    Name: quantity, Type: EndElement, AttributeCount: 0, Value:
    Type: Whitespace
   Name: FilmOrder, Type: EndElement, AttributeCount: 0, Value:
   Type: Whitespace
```

This example managed to use three methods and five properties of XmlReader. The output generated was informative but far from practical. XmlReader exposes over 50 methods and properties, which means that we have only scratched the surface of this highly versatile class. The remainder of this section looks at the XmlReaderSettings class, introduces a more realistic use of XmlReader, and demonstrates how the classes of System.Xml handle errors.

The XmlReaderSettings Class

Just like the XmlWriter object, the XmlReader object requires settings to be applied for instantiation of the object. This means that you can apply settings specifying how the XmlReader object behaves when it is reading whatever XML you might have for it. This includes settings for dealing with white space, schemas, and other common options. An example of using this settings class to modify the behavior of the XmlReader class is as follows:

```
Dim myXmlSettings As New XmlReaderSettings()
myXmlSettings.IgnoreWhitespace = True
myXmlSettings.IgnoreComments = True
Using readMovieInfo As XmlReader = XmlReader.Create(fileName, myXmlSettings)
    ' Use XmlReader object here.
End Using
```

In this case, the `XmlReader` object that is created ignores the white space that it encounters, as well as any of the XML comments. These settings, once established with the `XmlReaderSettings` object, are then associated with the `XmlReader` object through its `Create` method.

Traversing XML Using XmlReader

An application can easily use `XmlReader` to traverse a document that is received in a known format. The document can thus be traversed in a deliberate manner. You just implemented a class that serialized arrays of movie orders. The next example takes an XML document containing multiple XML documents of that type and traverses them. Each movie order is forwarded to the movie supplier via fax. The document is traversed as follows:

```
Read root element: <MovieOrderDump>
    Process each <FilmOrderList> element
        Read <multiFilmOrders> element
            Process each <FilmOrder>
                Send fax for each movie order here
```

The basic outline for the program's implementation is to open a file containing the XML document to parse and to traverse it from element to element:

Available for
download on
Wrox.com

```
Dim myXmlSettings As New XmlReaderSettings()
Using readMovieInfo As XmlReader = XmlReader.Create(fileName, myXmlSettings)
    readMovieInfo.Read()
    readMovieInfo.ReadStartElement("MovieOrderDump")
    Do While (True)
        '*****************************************************
        '* Process FilmOrder elements here                   *
        '*****************************************************

    Loop
    readMovieInfo.ReadEndElement() ' </MovieOrderDump>
End Using
```

Code snippet from FilmOrdersReader2

The preceding code opened the file using the constructor of `XmlReader`, and the `End Using` statement takes care of shutting everything down for you. The code also introduced two methods of the `XmlReader` class:

➤   `ReadStartElement(String)` — This verifies that the current node in the stream is an element and that the element's name matches the string passed to `ReadStartElement`. If the verification is successful, then the stream is advanced to the next element.

➤   `ReadEndElement()` — This verifies that the current element is an end tab; and if the verification is successful, then the stream is advanced to the next element.

The application knows that an element, `<MovieOrderDump>`, will be found at a specific point in the document. The `ReadStartElement` method verifies this foreknowledge of the document format. After all the elements contained in element `<MovieOrderDump>` have been traversed, the stream should point to the end tag `</MovieOrderDump>`. The `ReadEndElement` method verifies this.

The code that traverses each element of type `<FilmOrder>` similarly uses the `ReadStartElement` and `ReadEndElement` methods to indicate the start and end of the `<FilmOrder>` and `<multiFilmOrders>` elements. The code that ultimately parses the list of movie orders and then faxes the movie supplier (using the `FranticallyFaxTheMovieSupplier` subroutine) is as follows:

Available for
download on
Wrox.com

```
Private Sub ReadMovieXml(ByVal fileName As String)
    Dim myXmlSettings As New XmlReaderSettings()
    Dim movieName As String
    Dim movieId As String
    Dim quantity As String

    XmlReader.Create(fileName, myXmlSettings)
```

```
            'position to first element
            readMovieInfo.Read()
            readMovieInfo.ReadStartElement("MovieOrderDump")
            Do While (True)
                readMovieInfo.ReadStartElement("FilmOrderList")
                readMovieInfo.ReadStartElement("multiFilmOrders")

                'for each order
                Do While (True)                        readMovieInfo.MoveToContent()
                  movieId = readMovieInfo.GetAttribute("filmId")
                    readMovieInfo.ReadStartElement("FilmOrder")

                    movieName = readMovieInfo.ReadElementString()
                    quantity = readMovieInfo.ReadElementString()
                    readMovieInfo.ReadEndElement() ' clear </FilmOrder>

                    FranticallyFaxTheMovieSupplier(movieName, movieId, quantity)

                    ' Should read next FilmOrder node
                    ' else quits
                    readMovieInfo.Read()
                    If ("FilmOrder" <> readMovieInfo.Name) Then
                        Exit Do
                    End If
                Loop
                readMovieInfo.ReadEndElement() ' clear </multiFilmOrders>
                readMovieInfo.ReadEndElement() ' clear </FilmOrderList>
                ' Should read next FilmOrderList node
                ' else you quit
                readMovieInfo.Read() ' clear </MovieOrderDump>
                If ("FilmOrderList" <> readMovieInfo.Name) Then
                    Exit Do
                End If
            Loop
            readMovieInfo.ReadEndElement() '  </MovieOrderDump>
        End Using
    End Sub
```

Code snippet from FilmOrderReader2

The values are read from the XML file using the `ReadElementString` and `GetAttribute` methods. Notice that the call to `GetAttribute` is done before reading the `FilmOrder` element. This is because the `ReadStartElement` method advances the location for the next read to the next element in the XML file. The `MoveToContent` call before the call to `GetAttribute` ensures that the current read location is on the element, and not on white space.

While parsing the stream, it was known that an element named `name` existed and that this element contained the name of the movie. Rather than parse the start tag, get the value, and parse the end tag, it was easier to get the data using the `ReadElementString` method.

The output of this example is a fax (left as an exercise for you). The format of the document is still verified by `XmlReader` as it is parsed.

The `XmlReader` class also exposes properties that provide more insight into the data contained in the XML document and the state of parsing: `IsEmptyElement`, `EOF`, `HasAttributes`, and `IsStartElement`.

.NET CLR-compliant types are not 100 percent interchangeable with XML types, so ever since the .NET Framework 2.0 was introduced, the new methods it made available in the `XmlReader` make the process of casting from one of these XML types to .NET types easier.

Using the `ReadElementContentAs` method, you can easily perform the necessary casting required:

```
Dim username As String = _
    myXmlReader.ReadElementContentAs(GetType(String), DBNull.Value)
Dim myDate As DateTime = _
    myXmlReader.ReadElementContentAs(GetType(DateTime), DBNull.Value)
```

In addition to the generic `ReadElementContentAs` method, there are specific `ReadElementContentAsX` methods for each of the common data types; and in addition to these methods, the raw XML associated with the document can also be retrieved, using `ReadInnerXml` and `ReadOuterXml`. Again, this only scratches the surface of the `XmlReader` class, a class quite rich in functionality.

Handling Exceptions

XML is text and could easily be read using mundane methods such as `Read` and `ReadLine`. A key feature of each class that reads and traverses XML is inherent support for error detection and handling. To demonstrate this, consider the following malformed XML document found in the file named `Malformed.xml`:

```
<?xml version="1.0" encoding="IBM437" ?>
<FilmOrder FilmId="101", Qty="10">
    <Name>Grease</Name>
<FilmOrder>
```

Code snippet from FilmOrdersReader2

This document may not immediately appear to be malformed. By wrapping a call to the method you developed (`ReadMovieXml`), you can see what type of exception is raised when `XmlReader` detects the malformed XML within this document as shown in `Sub Main()`. Comment out the line calling the MovieManage.xml file, and uncomment the line to try to open the malformed.xml file:

```
Try
    'ReadMovieXml("MovieManage.xml")
    ReadMovieXml("Malformed.xml")
Catch xmlEx As XmlException
    Console.Error.WriteLine("XML Error: " + xmlEx.ToString())
Catch ex As Exception
    Console.Error.WriteLine("Some other error: " + ex.ToString())
End Try
```

Code snippet from FilmOrdersReader2

The methods and properties exposed by the `XmlReader` class raise exceptions of type `System.Xml` `.XmlException`. In fact, every class in the `System.Xml` namespace raises exceptions of type `XmlException`. Although this is a discussion of errors using an instance of type `XmlReader`, the concepts reviewed apply to all errors generated by classes found in the `System.Xml` namespace. The `XmlException` extends the basic `Exception` to include more information about the location of the error within the XML file.

The error displayed when subroutine `ReadMovieXML` processes `Malformed.xml` is as follows:

```
XML Error: System.Xml.XmlException: The ',' character, hexadecimal value 0x2C,
    cannot begin a name. Line 2, position 49.
```

The preceding snippet indicates that a comma separates the attributes in element `<FilmOrder FilmId="101", Qty="10">`. This comma is invalid. Removing it and running the code again results in the following output:

```
XML Error: System.Xml.XmlException: This is an unexpected token. Expected
    'EndElement'. Line 5, position 27.
```

Again, you can recognize the precise error. In this case, you do not have an end element, `</FilmOrder>`, but you do have an opening element, `<FilmOrder>`.

The properties provided by the `XmlException` class (such as `LineNumber`, `LinePosition`, and `Message`) provide a useful level of precision when tracking down errors. The `XmlReader` class also exposes a level of precision with respect to the parsing of the XML document. This precision is exposed by the `XmlReader` through properties such as `LineNumber` and `LinePosition`.

Document Object Model (DOM)

The Document Object Model (DOM) is a logical view of an XML file. Within the DOM, an XML document is contained in a class named `XmlDocument`. Each node within this document is accessible and managed using `XmlNode`. Nodes can also be accessed and managed using a class specifically designed to process a specific node's type (`XmlElement`, `XmlAttribute`, and so on). XML documents are extracted from `XmlDocument` using a variety of mechanisms exposed through such classes as `XmlWriter`, `TextWriter`, `Stream`, and a file (specified by a filename of type `String`). XML documents are consumed by an `XmlDocument` using a variety of load mechanisms exposed through the same classes.

A DOM-style parser differs from a stream-style parser with respect to movement. Using the DOM, the nodes can be traversed forward and backward; and nodes can be added to the document, removed from the document, and updated. However, this flexibility comes at a performance cost. It is faster to read or write XML using a stream-style parser.

The DOM-specific classes exposed by `System.Xml` include the following:

➤ `XmlDocument` — Corresponds to an entire XML document. A document is loaded using the `Load` or `LoadXml` methods. The `Load` method loads the XML from a file (the filename specified as type `String`), `TextReader`, or `XmlReader`. A document can be loaded using `LoadXml` in conjunction with a string containing the XML document. The `Save` method is used to save XML documents. The methods exposed by `XmlDocument` reflect the intricate manipulation of an XML document. For example, the following creation methods are implemented by this class: `CreateAttribute`, `CreateCDataSection`, `CreateComment`, `CreateDocumentFragment`, `CreateDocumentType`, `CreateElement`, `CreateEntityReference`, `CreateNavigator`, `CreateNode`, `CreateProcessingInstruction`, `CreateSignificantWhitespace`, `CreateTextNode`, `CreateWhitespace`, and `CreateXmlDeclaration`. The elements contained in the document can be retrieved. Other methods support the retrieving, importing, cloning, loading, and writing of nodes.

➤ `XmlNode` — Corresponds to a node within the DOM tree. This is the base class for the other node type classes. A robust set of methods and properties is provided to create, delete, and replace nodes. The contents of a node can similarly be traversed in a variety of ways: `FirstChild`, `LastChild`, `NextSibling`, `ParentNode`, and `PreviousSibling`.

➤ `XmlElement` — Corresponds to an element within the DOM tree. The functionality exposed by this class contains a variety of methods used to manipulate an element's attributes.

➤ `XmlAttribute` — Corresponds to an attribute of an element (`XmlElement`) within the DOM tree. An attribute contains data and lists of subordinate data, so it is a less complicated object than an `XmlNode` or an `XmlElement`. An `XmlAttribute` can retrieve its owner document (property, `OwnerDocument`), retrieve its owner element (property, `OwnerElement`), retrieve its parent node (property, `ParentNode`), and retrieve its name (property, `Name`). The value of an `XmlAttribute` is available via a read-write property named `Value`. Given the diverse number of methods and properties exposed by `XmlDocument`, `XmlNode`, `XmlElement`, and `XmlAttribute` (and there are many more than those listed here), it's clear that any XML 1.0 or 1.1-compliant document can be generated and manipulated using these classes. In comparison to their XML stream counterparts, these classes offer more flexible movement within the XML document and through any editing of XML documents.

A similar comparison could be made between DOM and data serialized and deserialized using XML. Using serialization, the type of node (for example, attribute or element) and the node name are specified at compile time. There is no on-the-fly modification of the XML generated by the serialization process.

DOM Traversing XML

The first DOM example loads an XML document into an `XmlDocument` object using a string that contains the actual XML document. The example over the next few pages simply traverses each XML element (`XmlNode`) in the document (`XmlDocument`) and displays the data to the console. The data associated with this example is contained in a variable, `rawData`, which is initialized as follows:

```
Dim rawData  =
    <multiFilmOrders>
        <FilmOrder>
            <name>Grease</name>
            <filmId>101</filmId>
            <quantity>10</quantity>
        </FilmOrder>
        <FilmOrder>
            <name>Lawrence of Arabia</name>
            <filmId>102</filmId>
            <quantity>10</quantity>
        </FilmOrder>
    </multiFilmOrders>
```

Code snippet from DomReading

The XML document in `rawData` is a portion of the XML hierarchy associated with a movie order. Notice the lack of quotation marks around the XML: This is an XML literal. XML literals allow you to insert a block of XML directly into your VB source code. They can be written over a number of lines, and can be used.wherever you might normally load an XML file.

The basic idea in processing this data is to traverse each `<FilmOrder>` element in order to display the data it contains. Each node corresponding to a `<FilmOrder>` element can be retrieved from your `XmlDocument` using the `GetElementsByTagName` method (specifying a tag name of `FilmOrder`). The `GetElementsByTagName` method returns a list of `XmlNode` objects in the form of a collection of type `XmlNodeList`. Using the `For Each` statement to construct this list, the `XmlNodeList` (`movieOrderNodes`) can be traversed as individual `XmlNode` elements (`movieOrderNode`). The code for handling this is as follows:

```
Dim xmlDoc As New XmlDocument
Dim movieOrderNodes As XmlNodeList
Dim movieOrderNode As XmlNode
xmlDoc.LoadXml(rawData.ToString())
' Traverse each <FilmOrder>
movieOrderNodes = xmlDoc.GetElementsByTagName("FilmOrder")
For Each movieOrderNode In movieOrderNodes
    '*********************************************************
    ' Process <name>, <filmId> and <quantity> here
    '*********************************************************

Next
```

Code snippet from DomReading

Each `XmlNode` can then have its contents displayed by traversing the children of this node using the `ChildNodes` method. This method returns an `XmlNodeList` (`baseDataNodes`) that can be traversed one `XmlNode` list element at a time:

```
Dim baseDataNodes As XmlNodeList
Dim bFirstInRow As Boolean
baseDataNodes = movieOrderNode.ChildNodes
bFirstInRow = True
For Each baseDataNode As XmlNode In baseDataNodes
    If (bFirstInRow) Then
        bFirstInRow = False
    Else
        Console.Write(", ")
```

```
      End If
      Console.Write(baseDataNode.Name & ": " & baseDataNode.InnerText)
    Next
    Console.WriteLine()
```

Code snippet from DomReading

The bulk of the preceding code retrieves the name of the node using the `Name` property and the `InnerText` property of the node. The `InnerText` property of each `XmlNode` retrieved contains the data associated with the XML elements (nodes) `<name>`, `<filmId>`, and `<quantity>`. The example displays the contents of the XML elements using `Console.Write`. The XML document is displayed to the console as follows:

```
name: Grease, quantity: 10
name: Lawrence of Arabia, quantity: 10
```

Other, more practical, methods for using this data could have been implemented, including the following:

➤ The contents could have been directed to an ASP.NET `Response` object, and the data retrieved could have been used to create an HTML table (`<table>` table, `<tr>` row, and `<td>` data) that would be written to the `Response` object.

➤ The data traversed could have been directed to a `ListBox` or `ComboBox` Windows Forms control. This would enable the data returned to be selected as part of a GUI application.

➤ The data could have been edited as part of your application's business rules. For example, you could have used the traversal to verify that the `<filmId>` matched the `<name>`. Something like this could be done if you wanted to validate the data entered into the XML document in any manner.

Writing XML with the DOM

You can also use the DOM to create or edit XML documents. Creating new XML items is a two-step process, however. First, you use the containing document to create the new element, attribute, or comment (or other node type), and then you add that at the appropriate location in the document.

Just as there are a number of methods in the DOM for reading the XML, there are also methods for creating new nodes. The `XmlDocument` class has the basic `CreateNode` method, as well as specific methods for creating the different node types, such as `CreateElement`, `CreateAttribute`, `CreateComment`, and others. Once the node is created, you add it in place using the `AppendChild` method of `XmlNode` (or one of the children of `XmlNode`).

Create a new project that will be used to demonstrate writing XML with the DOM. Most of the work in this sample will be done in two functions, so the `Main` method can remain simple:

```
Sub Main()

    Dim data As String
    Dim fileName As String = "filmorama.xml"
    data = GenerateXml(fileName)

    Console.WriteLine(data)
    Console.WriteLine("Press ENTER to continue")
    Console.ReadLine()

End Sub
```

Code snippet from DomWriting

The `GenerateXml` function creates the initial `XmlDocument`, and calls the `CreateFilmOrder` function multiple times to add a number of items to the structure. This creates a hierarchical XML document that can then be used elsewhere in your application. Typically, you would use the `Save` method to write the XML to a stream or document, but in this case it just retrieves the OuterXml (that is, the full XML document) to display:

```vb
Private Function GenerateXml(ByVal fileName As String) As String
    Dim result As String
    Dim doc As New XmlDocument
    Dim elem As XmlElement

    'create root node
    Dim root As XmlElement = doc.CreateElement("FilmOrderList")
    doc.AppendChild(root)
    'this data would likely come from elsewhere
    For i As Integer = 1 To 5
        elem = CreateFilmOrder(doc, i)
        root.AppendChild(elem)
    Next
    result = doc.OuterXml
    Return result
End Function
```

Code snippet from DomWriting

The most common error made when writing an XML document using the DOM is to create the elements but forget to append them into the document. This step is done here with the AppendChild method, but other methods can be used, in particular InsertBefore, InsertAfter, PrependChild, and RemoveChild.

Creating the individual FilmOrder nodes uses a similar CreateElement/AppendChild strategy. In addition, attributes are created using the Append method of the Attributes collection for each XmlElement:

```vb
Private Function CreateFilmOrder(ByVal parent As XmlDocument,
    ByVal count As Integer) As XmlElement
    Dim result As XmlElement
    Dim id As XmlAttribute
    Dim title As XmlElement
    Dim quantity As XmlElement

    result = parent.CreateElement("FilmOrder")
    id = parent.CreateAttribute("id")
    id.Value = 100 + count

    title = parent.CreateElement("title")
    title.InnerText = "Some title here"

    quantity = parent.CreateElement("quantity")
    quantity.InnerText = "10"

    result.Attributes.Append(id)
    result.AppendChild(title)
    result.AppendChild(quantity)
    Return result
End Function
```

Code snippet from DomWriting

This generates the following XML (although it will all be on one line in the output):

```xml
<FilmOrderList>
  <FilmOrder id="101">
    <title>Some title here</title>
    <quantity> 10 </quantity>
  </FilmOrder>
```

```
        <FilmOrder id="102">
          <title>Some title here</title>
          <quantity> 10 </quantity>
        </FilmOrder>
        <FilmOrder id="103">
          <title>Some title here</title>
          <quantity> 10 </quantity>
        </FilmOrder>
        <FilmOrder id="104">
          <title>Some title here</title>
          <quantity>10</quantity>
        </FilmOrder>
        <FilmOrder id="105">
          <title>
            Some title here
          </title>
          <quantity>10</quantity>
        </FilmOrder>
      </FilmOrderList>
```

Once you get the hang of creating XML with the DOM (and forget to add the new nodes a few dozen times), it is quite a handy method for writing XML. If the XML you need to create can all be created at once, it is probably better to use the `XmlWriter` class instead. Writing XML with the DOM is best left for those situations when you need to either edit an existing XML document or move backwards through the document as you are writing. In addition, because the DOM is an international standard, it means that code using the DOM is portable to other languages that also provide a DOM.

In addition to the `XmlWriter`, the `XElement` shown later in this chapter provides yet another method for reading and writing XML.

XSL TRANSFORMATIONS

XSLT is used to transform XML documents into another format altogether. One popular use of XSLT is to transform XML into HTML so that XML documents can be presented visually. The idea is to use an alternate language (XSLT) to transform the XML, rather than rewrite the source code, SQL commands, or some other mechanism used to generate XML.

Conceptually, XSLT is straightforward. A file (a .xsl file) describes the changes (transformations) that will be applied to a particular XML file. Once this is completed, an XSLT processor is provided with the source XML file and the XSLT file, and performs the transformation. The `System.Xml.Xsl.XslTransform` class is such an XSLT processor. Another processor you will find (introduced in the .NET Framework 2.0) is the `XsltCommand` object found at `SystemXml.Query.XsltCommand`. This section looks at using both of these processors.

You can also find some features in Visual Studio that deal with XSLT. The IDE supports items such as XSLT data breakpoints and XSLT debugging. Additionally, XSLT stylesheets can be compiled into assemblies even more easily with the command-line stylesheet compiler, `XSLTC.exe`.

The XSLT file is itself an XML document. Dozens of XSLT commands can be used in writing an XSLT file. The first example explores the following XSLT elements (commands):

> `stylesheet` — This element indicates the start of the style sheet (XSL) in the XSLT file.

> `template` — This element denotes a reusable template for producing specific output. This output is generated using a specific node type within the source document under a specific context. For example, the text `<xsl: template match="/">` selects all root nodes ("/") for the specific transform template. The template is applied whenever the match occurs in the source document.

➤ for-each — This element applies the same template to each node in the specified set. Recall the example class (FilmOrderList) that could be serialized. This class contained an array of movie orders. Given the XML document generated when a FilmOrderList is serialized, each movie order serialized could be processed using

```
<xsl:for-each select = "FilmOrderList/multiFilmOrders/FilmOrder">.
```

➤ value-of — This element retrieves the value of the specified node and inserts it into the document in text form. For example, <xsl:value-of select="name" /> would take the value of the XML element <name> and insert it into the transformed document.

You can use XSLT to convert an XML document to generate a report that is viewed by the manager of the movie supplier. This report is in HTML form so that it can be viewed via the Web. The XSLT elements you previously reviewed (stylesheet, template, and for-each) are the only XSLT elements required to transform the XML document (in which data is stored) into an HTML file (data that can be displayed). An XSLT file DisplayOrders.xslt contains the following text, which is used to transform a serialized version, FilmOrderList found in Filmorama.xml:

```xml
<?xml version="1.0" encoding="UTF-8" ?>
<xsl:stylesheet xmlns:xsl="http://www.w3.org/1999/XSL/Transform" version="1.0">
  <xsl:template match="/">
    <html>
      <head><title>What people are ordering</title>
      </head>
      <body>
        <table border="1">
          <tr>
            <th>
              Film Name
            </th>
            <th>
              Film ID
            </th>
            <th>
              Quantity
            </th>
          </tr>
          <xsl:for-each select=
            "//FilmOrder">
            <tr>
              <td>
                <xsl:value-of select="Title" />
              </td>
              <td>
                <xsl:value-of select="@id" />
              </td>
              <td>
                <xsl:value-of select="Quantity" />
              </td>
            </tr>
          </xsl:for-each>
        </table>
      </body>
    </html>
  </xsl:template>
</xsl:stylesheet>
```

Code snippet from Transformation

In the preceding XSLT file, the XSLT elements are marked in bold. These elements perform operations on the source XML file containing a serialized `FilmOrderList` object, and generate the appropriate HTML file. Your generated file contains a table (marked by the table tag, `<table>`) that contains a set of rows (each row marked by a table row tag, `<tr>`). The columns of the table are contained in table data tags, `<td>`. Each row containing data (an individual movie order from the serialized object, `FilmOrderList`) is generated using the XSLT element, `for-each`, to traverse each `<FilmOrder>` element within the source XML document. In this case, a shorthand for the location of the `FilmOrder` element was used: `//FilmOrder` returns all `FilmOrder` elements, regardless of their depth in the XML file. Alternately, you could have specified the full path using `FilmOrderList/FilmOrders/FilmOrder` here.

The individual columns of data are generated using the `value-of` XSLT element, in order to query the elements contained within each `<FilmOrder>` element (`<Title>`, `<id>`, and `<Quantity>`).

The code in `Sub Main()` to create a displayable XML file using the `XslCompiledTransform` object is as follows:

Available for download on Wrox.com

```
Dim xslt As New XslCompiledTransform
Dim outputFile As String = "..\..\output.html"

xslt.Load("..\..\displayorders.xslt")
xslt.Transform("..\..\filmorama.xml", outputFile)

Process.Start(outputFile)
```

Code snippet from Transformation

This consists of only five lines of code, with the bulk of the coding taking place in the XSLT file. The previous code snippet created an instance of a `System.Xml.Xsl.XslCompiledTransform` object named `xslt`. The `Load` method of this class is used to load the XSLT file you previously reviewed, `DisplayOrders.xslt`. The `Transform` method takes a source XML file as the first parameter, which in this case was a file containing a serialized `FilmOrderList` object. The second parameter is the destination file created by the transform (`Output.html`). The `Start` method of the `Process` class is used to display the HTML file in the system default browser. This method launches a process that is best suited for displaying the file provided. Basically, the extension of the file dictates which application will be used to display the file. On a typical Windows machine, the program used to display this file is Internet Explorer, as shown in Figure 9-2.

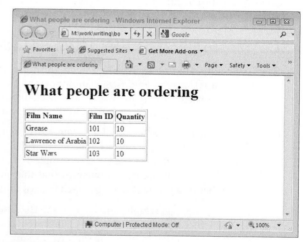

FIGURE 9-2

Don't confuse displaying this HTML file with ASP.NET. Displaying an HTML file in this manner takes place on a single machine without the involvement of a Web server.

As demonstrated, the backbone of the `System.Xml.Xsl` namespace is the `XslCompiledTransform` class. This class uses XSLT files to transform XML documents. `XslCompiledTransform` exposes the following methods and properties:

➤   `XmlResolver` — This get/set property is used to specify a class (abstract base class, `XmlResolver`) that is used to handle external references (import and include elements within the style sheet). These external references are encountered when a document is transformed (the method, `Transform`, is executed). The `System.Xml` namespace contains a class, `XmlUrlResolver`, which is derived from `XmlResolver`. The `XmlUrlResolver` class resolves the external resource based on a URI.

➤ `Load` — This overloaded method loads an XSLT style sheet to be used in transforming XML documents. It is permissible to specify the XSLT style sheet as a parameter of type `XPathNavigator`, filename of an XSLT file (specified as parameter type `String`), `XmlReader`, or `IXPathNavigable`. For each type of XSLT supported, an overloaded member is provided that enables an `XmlResolver` to also be specified. For example, it is possible to call `Load(String, XsltSettings, XmlResolver)`, where `String` corresponds to a filename, `XsltSettings` is an object that contains settings to affect the transformation, and `XmlResolver` is an object that handles references in the style sheet of type `xsl:import` and `xsl:include`. It would also be permissible to pass in a value of `Nothing` for the third parameter of the `Load` method (so that no `XmlResolver` would be specified).

➤ `Transform` — This overloaded method transforms a specified XML document using the previously specified XSLT style sheet. The location where the transformed XML is to be output is specified as a parameter to this method. The first parameter of each overloaded method is the XML document to be transformed. The most straightforward variant of the `Transform` method is `Transform(String, String)`. In this case, a file containing an XML document is specified as the first parameter, and a filename that receives the transformed XML document is specified as the second. This is exactly how the first XSLT example utilized the `Transform` method:

```
myXslTransform.Transform("..\FilmOrders.xml", destFileName)
```

The first parameter to the `Transform` method can also be specified as `IXPathNavigable` or `XmlReader`. The XML output can be sent to an object of type `Stream`, `TextWriter`, or `XmlWriter`. In addition, a parameter containing an object of type `XsltArgumentList` can be specified. An `XsltArgumentList` object contains a list of arguments that are used as input to the transform. These may be used within the XSLT file to affect the output.

XSLT Transforming between XML Standards

The first example used four XSLT elements to transform an XML file into an HTML file. Such an example has merit, but it doesn't demonstrate an important use of XSLT: transforming XML from one standard into another standard. This may involve renaming elements/attributes, excluding elements/attributes, changing data types, altering the node hierarchy, and representing elements as attributes, and vice versa.

Returning to the example, a case of differing XML standards could easily affect your software that automates movie orders coming into a supplier. Imagine that the software, including its XML representation of a movie order, is so successful that you sell 100,000 copies. However, just as you are celebrating, a consortium of the largest movie supplier chains announces that they are no longer accepting faxed orders and that they are introducing their own standard for the exchange of movie orders between movie sellers and buyers.

Rather than panic, you simply ship an upgrade that includes an XSLT file. This upgrade (a bit of extra code plus the XSLT file) transforms your XML representation of a movie order into the XML representation dictated by the consortium of movie suppliers. Using an XSLT file enables you to ship the upgrade immediately. If the consortium of movie suppliers revises their XML representation, then you are not obliged to change your source code. Instead, you can simply ship the upgraded XSLT file that ensures each movie order document is compliant.

The specific source code that executes the transform is as follows:

```
Dim xslt As New XslCompiledTransform
Dim outputFile As String = "..\..\output.html"

xslt.Load("..\..\displayorders.xslt")
xslt.Transform("..\..\filmorama.xml", outputFile)
```

Code snippet from Transformation

Those three lines of code accomplish the following:

➤ Create an `XslCompiledTransform` object

➤ Use the `Load` method to load an XSLT file (`ConvertLegacyToNewStandard.xslt`)

➤ Use the `Transform` method to transform a source XML file (`MovieOrdersOriginal.xml`) into a destination XML file (`MovieOrdersModified.xml`)

Recall that the input XML document (`MovieOrdersOriginal.xml`) does not match the format required by your consortium of movie supplier chains. The content of this source XML file is as follows:

```xml
<?xml version="1.0" encoding="utf-8" ?>
<FilmOrderList>
    <multiFilmOrders>
        <FilmOrder>
            <name>Grease</name>
            <filmId>101</filmId>
            <quantity>10</quantity>
        </FilmOrder>
        …
    </multiFilmOrders>
</FilmOrderList>
```

Code snippet from Transformation

The format exhibited in the preceding XML document does not match the format of the consortium of movie supplier chains. To be accepted by the collective of suppliers, you must transform the document as follows:

➤ Remove element `<FilmOrderList>`.

➤ Remove element `<multiFilmOrders>`.

➤ Rename element `<FilmOrder>` to `<DvdOrder>`.

➤ Remove element `<name>` (the film's name is not to be contained in the document).

➤ Rename element `<quantity>` to `HowMuch` and make `HowMuch` an attribute of `<DvdOrder>`.

➤ Rename element `<filmId>` to `FilmOrderNumber` and make `FilmOrderNumber` an attribute of `<DvdOrder>`.

➤ Display attribute `HowMuch` before attribute `FilmOrderNumber`.

Many of the steps performed by the transform could have been achieved using an alternative technology. For example, you could have used Source Code Style attributes with your serialization to generate the correct XML attribute and XML element name. Had you known in advance that a consortium of suppliers was going to develop a standard, you could have written your classes to be serialized based on the standard. The point is that you did not know, and now one standard (your legacy standard) has to be converted into a newly adopted standard of the movie suppliers' consortium. The worst thing you could do would be to change your working code and then force all users working with the application to upgrade. It is vastly simpler to add an extra transformation step to address the new standard.

The XSLT file that facilitates the transform is named `ConvertLegacyToNewStandard.xslt`. A portion of this file is implemented as follows:

```xml
<?xml version="1.0" encoding="utf-8"?>
<xsl:stylesheet version="1.0" xmlns:xsl="http://www.w3.org/1999/XSL/Transform">
  <xsl:template match="FilmOrder">
    <!-- rename <FilmOrder>  to <DvdOrder>
        -->
        <xsl:element name="DvdOrder">
          <!-- Make element Quantity attribute HowMuch
          Notice attribute HowMuch comes before attribute FilmOrderNumber -->
          <xsl:attribute name="HowMuch">
```

```
            <xsl:value-of select="Quantity"></xsl:value-of>
          </xsl:attribute>
          <!-- Make element id attribute FilmOrderNumber -->
          <xsl:attribute name="FilmOrderNumber">
            <xsl:value-of select="@id"></xsl:value-of>
          </xsl:attribute>
        </xsl:element>
        <!-- end of DvdOrder element -->
      </xsl:template>
    </xsl:stylesheet>
```

Code snippet from Transformation

In the previous snippet of XSLT, the following XSLT elements are used to facilitate the transformation:

➤ `<xsl:template match="FilmOrder">` — All operations in this template XSLT element take place on the original document's `FilmOrder` node.

➤ `<xsl:element name="DvdOrder">` — The element corresponding to the source document's `FilmOrder` element will be called `DvdOrder` in the destination document.

➤ `<xsl:attribute name="HowMuch">` — An attribute named `HowMuch` will be contained in the previously specified element, `<DvdOrder>`. This attribute XSLT element for `HowMuch` comes before the attribute XSLT element for `FilmOrderNumber`. This order was specified as part of your transform to adhere to the new standard.

➤ `<xsl:value-of select='Quantity'>` — Retrieve the value of the source document's `<Quantity>` element and place it in the destination document. This instance of XSLT element `value-of` provides the value associated with the attribute `HowMuch`.

Two new XSLT terms have crept into your vocabulary: `element` and `attribute`. Both of these XSLT elements live up to their names. Using the `element` node in an XSLT places an element in the destination XML document, while an `attribute` node places an attribute in the destination XML document. The XSLT transform found in `ConvertLegacyToNewStandard.xslt` is too long to review here. When reading this file in its entirety, remember that this XSLT file contains inline documentation to specify precisely what aspect of the transformation is being performed at which location in the XSLT document. For example, the following XML code comments indicate what the XSLT element `attribute` is about to do:

Available for
download on
Wrox.com

```
<!-- Make element 'Quantity' attribute HowMuch
     Notice attribute HowMuch comes before attribute FilmOrderNumber -->
<xsl:attribute name="HowMuch">
    <xsl:value-of select='Quantity'></xsl:value-of>
</xsl:attribute>
```

Code snippet from Transformation

The preceding example spans several pages but contains just three lines of code. This demonstrates that there is more to XML than learning how to use it in Visual Basic and the .NET Framework. Among other things, you also need a good understanding of XSLT, XPath, and XQuery. For more details on these standards, see Professional XML from Wrox.

Other Classes and Interfaces in System.Xml.Xsl

We just took a good look at XSLT and the `System.Xml.Xsl` namespace, but there is a lot more to it than that. Other classes and interfaces exposed by the `System.Xml.Xsl` namespace include the following:

➤ `IXsltContextFunction` — This interface accesses at runtime a given function defined in the XSLT style sheet.

➤ `IXsltContextVariable` — This interface accesses at runtime a given variable defined in the XSLT style sheet.

➤ XsltArgumentList — This class contains a list of arguments. These arguments are XSLT parameters or XSLT extension objects. The XsltArgumentList object is used in conjunction with the Transform method of XslTransform. Arguments enable you to use a single XSLT transformation for multiple uses, changing the parameters of the transformation as needed.

➤ XsltContext — This class contains the state of the XSLT processor. This context information enables XPath expressions to have their various components resolved (functions, parameters, and namespaces).

➤ XsltException, XsltCompileException — These classes contain the information pertaining to an exception raised while transforming data. XsltCompileException is derived from XsltException and is thrown by the Load method.

XML IN ASP.NET

Most Microsoft-focused Web developers have usually concentrated on either Microsoft SQL Server or Microsoft Access for their data storage needs. Today, however, a large amount of data is stored in XML format, so considerable inroads have been made in improving Microsoft's core Web technology to work easily with this format.

The XmlDataSource Server Control

ASP.NET contains a series of data source controls designed to bridge the gap between your data stores (such as XML) and the data-bound controls at your disposal. These new data controls not only enable you to retrieve data from various data stores, they also enable you to easily manipulate the data (using paging, sorting, editing, and filtering) before the data is bound to an ASP.NET server control.

With XML being as important as it is, a specific data source control is available in ASP.NET just for retrieving and working with XML data: XmlDataSource. This control enables you to connect to your XML data and use this data with any of the ASP.NET data-bound controls. Just like the SqlDataSource and the ObjectDataSource controls, the XmlDataSource control enables you to not only retrieve data, but also insert, delete, and update data items. With increasing numbers of users turning to XML data formats, such as Web services, RSS feeds, and more, this control is a valuable resource for your Web applications.

To show the XmlDataSource control in action, first create a simple XML file and include this file in your application. The following code reflects a simple XML file of Russian painters:

```xml
<?xml version="1.0" encoding="utf-8" ?>
<Artists>
    <Painter name="Vasily Kandinsky">
        <Painting>
            <Title>Composition No. 218</Title>
            <Year>1919</Year>
        </Painting>
    </Painter>
    <Painter name="Pavel Filonov">
        <Painting>
            <Title>Formula of Spring</Title>
            <Year>1929</Year>
        </Painting>
    </Painter>
    <Painter name="Pyotr Konchalovsky">
        <Painting>
            <Title>Sorrento Garden</Title>
            <Year>1924</Year>
        </Painting>
    </Painter>
</Artists>
```

Code snippet from XmlWeb

Now that the `Painters.xml` file is in place, the next step is to use an ASP.NET `DataList` control and connect this `DataList` control to an `<asp:XmlDataSource>` control, as shown here:

```
<%@ Page Language="vb" AutoEventWireup="false"
    CodeBehind="Default.aspx.vb" Inherits="XmlWeb._Default" %>

<!DOCTYPE html PUBLIC "-//W3C//DTD XHTML 1.0 Transitional//EN"
"http://www.w3.org/TR/xhtml1/DTD/xhtml1-transitional.dtd">
<html xmlns="http://www.w3.org/1999/xhtml">
<head runat="server">
    <title>Using XmlDataSource</title>
</head>
<body>
    <form id="form1" runat="server">
    <div>
        <asp:DataList ID="PainterList" runat="server"
            DataSourceID="PainterData">
            <ItemTemplate>
                <p>
                    <b>
                        <%# XPath("@name") %></b><br />
                    <i>
                        <%# XPath("Painting/Title") %></i><br />
                    <%# XPath("Painting/Year") %></p>
            </ItemTemplate>
        </asp:DataList>
        <asp:XmlDataSource ID="PainterData" runat="server"
            DataFile="~/Painters.xml" XPath="Artists/Painter" />
    </div>
    </form>
</body>
</html>
```

Code snippet from XmlWeb

This is a simple example, but it shows you the power and ease of using the `XmlDataSource` control. Pay attention to two attributes in this example. The first is the `DataFile` attribute. This attribute points to the location of the XML file. Because the file resides in the root directory of the Web application, it is simply `~/Painters.xml`. The next attribute included in the `XmlDataSource` control is the `XPath` attribute. The `XmlDataSource` control uses XPath for the filtering of XML data. In this case, the `XmlDataSource` control is taking everything within the `<Painter>` set of elements. The value `Artists/Painter` means that the `XmlDataSource` control navigates to the `<Artists>` element and then to the `<Painter>` element within the specified XML file.

The `DataList` control next must specify the `DataSourceID` as the `XmlDataSource` control. In the `<ItemTemplate>` section of the `DataList` control, you can retrieve specific values from the XML file by using XPath commands. The XPath commands filter the data from the XML file. The first value retrieved is an element attribute (`name`) contained in the `<Painter>` element. When you retrieve an attribute of an element, you preface the name of the attribute with an @ symbol. In this case, you simply specify `@name` to get the painter's name. The next two XPath commands go deeper into the XML file, getting the specific painting and the year of the painting. Remember to separate nodes with a /. When run in the browser, this code produces the results shown in Figure 9-3.

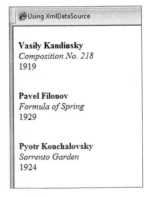

Using XmlDataSource

Vasily Kandinsky
Composition No. 218
1919

Pavel Filonov
Formula of Spring
1929

Pyotr Konchalovsky
Sorrento Garden
1924

FIGURE 9-3

Besides working from static XML files such as the `Painters.xml` file, the `XmlDataSource` file can work from dynamic, URL-accessible XML files. One popular XML format pervasive on the Internet today is *blogs*, or *weblogs*. Blogs can be viewed either in the browser (see Figure 9-4), through an RSS aggregator, or just as pure XML.

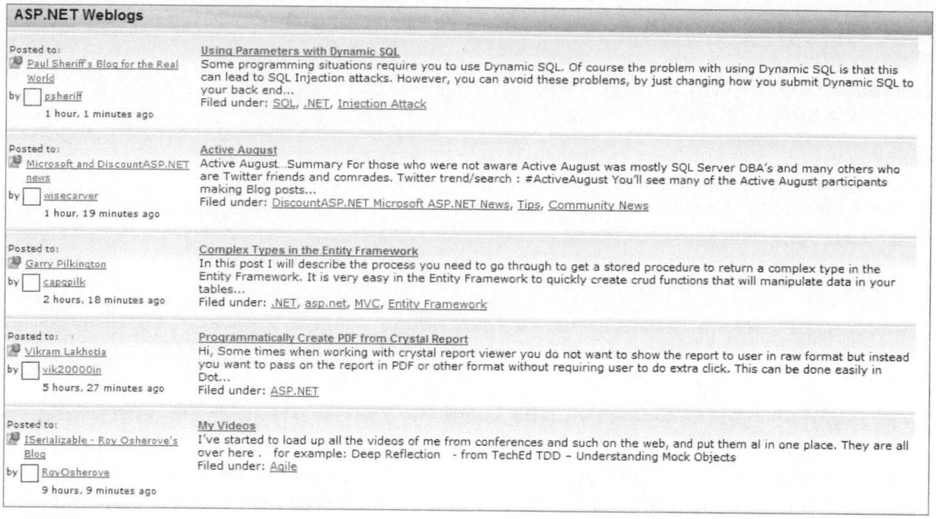

ASP.NET Weblogs

Posted to:	
Paul Sheriff's Blog for the Real World by [ ] psheriff 1 hour, 1 minutes ago	**Using Parameters with Dynamic SQL** Some programming situations require you to use Dynamic SQL. Of course the problem with using Dynamic SQL is that this can lead to SQL Injection attacks. However, you can avoid these problems, by just changing how you submit Dynamic SQL to your back end... Filed under: SQL, .NET, Injection Attack
Microsoft and DiscountASP.NET news by [ ] wisecarver 1 hour, 19 minutes ago	**Active August** Active August...Summary For those who were not aware Active August was mostly SQL Server DBA's and many others who are Twitter friends and comrades. Twitter trend/search : #ActiveAugust You'll see many of the Active August participants making Blog posts... Filed under: DiscountASP.NET Microsoft ASP.NET News, Tips, Community News
Garry Pilkington by [ ] capgpilk 2 hours, 18 minutes ago	**Complex Types in the Entity Framework** In this post I will describe the process you need to go through to get a stored procedure to return a complex type in the Entity Framework. It is very easy in the Entity Framework to quickly create crud functions that will manipulate data in your tables... Filed under: .NET, asp.net, MVC, Entity Framework
Vikram Lakhotia by [ ] vik20000in 5 hours, 27 minutes ago	**Programmatically Create PDF from Crystal Report** Hi, Some times when working with crystal report viewer you do not want to show the report to user in raw format but instead you want to pass on the report in PDF or other format without requiring user to do extra click. This can be done easily in Dot... Filed under: ASP.NET
ISerializable - Roy Osherove's Blog by [ ] RoyOsherove 9 hours, 9 minutes ago	**My Videos** I've started to load up all the videos of me from conferences and such on the web, and put them al in one place. They are all over here . for example: Deep Reflection - from TechEd TDD – Understanding Mock Objects Filed under: Agile

FIGURE 9-4

Now that you know the location of the XML from the blog, you can use this XML with the `XmlDataSource` control and display some of the results in a `DataList` control. The code for this example is shown here:

Available for download on Wrox.com

```vb
<%@ Page Language="vb" AutoEventWireup="false"
    CodeBehind="Default.aspx.vb" Inherits="ViewingRss._Default" %>

<!DOCTYPE html PUBLIC "-//W3C//DTD XHTML 1.0 Transitional//EN"
    "http://www.w3.org/TR/xhtml1/DTD/xhtml1-transitional.dtd">
<html xmlns="http://www.w3.org/1999/xhtml">
<head runat="server">
    <title>Viewing RSS</title>
</head>
<body>
    <form id="form1" runat="server">
    <div>
        <asp:DataList ID="RssList" runat="server"
            DataSourceID="RssData">
            <HeaderTemplate>
                <table border="1" cellpadding="3">
            </HeaderTemplate>
            <ItemTemplate>
                <tr>
                    <td>
                        <b>
                            <%# XPath("title") %></b><br />
                        <i>
                            <%# "published on " + XPath("pubDate") %></i><br />
                        <%# XPath("description").ToString().Substring(0,100) %>
                    </td>
                </tr>
            </ItemTemplate>
            <AlternatingItemTemplate>
                <tr style="background-color: #e0e0e0;">
                    <td>
                        <b>
                            <%# XPath("title") %></b><br />
                        <i>
                            <%# "published on " + XPath("pubDate") %></i><br />
                        <%# XPath("description").ToString().Substring(0,100) %>
```

```
            </td>
        </tr>
    </AlternatingItemTemplate>
    <FooterTemplate>
        </table>
    </FooterTemplate>
</asp:DataList>
<asp:XmlDataSource ID="RssData" runat="server"
    DataFile="http://weblogs.asp.net/mainfeed.aspx"
    XPath="rss/channel/item" />
        </div>
    </form>
</body>
</html>
```

Code snippet from ViewingRSS

This example shows that the `DataFile` points to a URL where the XML is retrieved. The `XPath` property filters out all the `<item>` elements from the RSS feed. The `DataList` control creates an HTML table and pulls out specific data elements from the RSS feed, such as the `<title>`, `<pubDate>`, and `<description>` elements. To make things a little more visible, only the first 100 characters of each post are displayed.

Running this page in the browser results in something similar to what is shown in Figure 9-5.

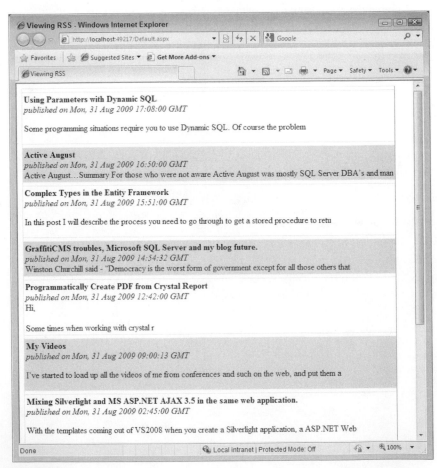

FIGURE 9-5

This approach also works with XML Web Services, even those for which you can pass in parameters using HTTP-GET. You just set up the `DataFile` value in the following manner:

```
DataFile="http://www.someserver.com/GetWeather.asmx/ZipWeather?zipcode=63301"
```

The XmlDataSource Control's Namespace Problem

One big issue with using the `XmlDataSource` control is that when using the XPath capabilities of the control, it is unable to understand namespace-qualified XML. The `XmlDataSource` control chokes on any XML data that contains namespaces, so it is important to yank out any prefixes and namespaces contained in the XML.

To make this a bit easier, the `XmlDataSource` control includes the `TransformFile` attribute. This attribute takes your XSLT transform file, which can be applied to the XML pulled from the `XmlDataSource` control. That means you can use an XSLT file, which will transform your XML in such a way that the prefixes and namespaces are completely removed from the overall XML document. An example of this XSLT document is illustrated here:

```xml
<?xml version="1.0" encoding="UTF-8"?>
<xsl:stylesheet version="1.0"
 xmlns:xsl="http://www.w3.org/1999/XSL/Transform">
    <xsl:output method="xml" version="1.0" encoding="UTF-8" indent="yes"/>
    <xsl:template match="*">
        <!-- Remove any prefixes -->
        <xsl:element name="{local-name()}">
            <!-- Work through attributes -->
            <xsl:for-each select="@*">
                <!-- Remove any attribute prefixes -->
                <xsl:attribute name="{local-name()}">
                    <xsl:value-of select="."/>
                </xsl:attribute>
            </xsl:for-each>
        <xsl:apply-templates/>
        </xsl:element>
    </xsl:template>
</xsl:stylesheet>
```

Now, with this XSLT document in place within your application, you can use the `XmlDataSource` control to pull XML data and strip that data of any prefixes and namespaces:

```
<asp:XmlDataSource ID="XmlDataSource1" runat="server"
 DataFile="NamespaceFilled.xml" TransformFile="~/RemoveNamespace.xsl"
 XPath="ItemLookupResponse/Items/Item"></asp:XmlDataSource>
```

The Xml Server Control

Since the very beginning of ASP.NET, there has always been a server control called the `Xml` server control. This control performs the simple operation of XSLT transformation upon an XML document. The control is easy to use: All you do is point to the XML file you wish to transform using the `DocumentSource` attribute, and the XSLT transform file using the `TransformSource` attribute.

To see this in action, use the `Painters.xml` file shown earlier. Create your XSLT transform file, as shown in the following example:

```xml
<?xml version="1.0" encoding="utf-8"?>
<xsl:stylesheet version="1.0"
     xmlns:xsl="http://www.w3.org/1999/XSL/Transform">
  <xsl:template match="/">
      <html>
      <body>
        <h3>List of Painters &amp; Paintings</h3>
        <table border="1">
          <tr bgcolor="LightGrey">
            <th>Name</th>
```

```
            <th>Painting</th>
            <th>Year</th>
          </tr>
          <xsl:apply-templates select="//Painter"/>
        </table>
      </body>
    </html>
  </xsl:template>
  <xsl:template match="Painter">
    <tr>
      <td>
        <xsl:value-of select="@name"/>
      </td>
      <td>
        <xsl:value-of select="Painting/Title"/>
      </td>
      <td>
        <xsl:value-of select="Painting/Year"/>
      </td>
    </tr>
  </xsl:template>
</xsl:stylesheet>
```

Code snippet from XmlControl

With the XML document and the XSLT document in place, the final step is to combine the two using the `Xml` server control provided by ASP.NET in `default.aspx`:

Available for download on Wrox.com

```
<%@ Page Language="vb" AutoEventWireup="false"
    CodeBehind="Default.aspx.vb" Inherits="XmlControl._Default" %>

<!DOCTYPE html PUBLIC "-//W3C//DTD XHTML 1.0 Transitional//EN"
    "http://www.w3.org/TR/xhtml1/DTD/xhtml1-transitional.dtd">

<html xmlns="http://www.w3.org/1999/xhtml" >
<head runat="server">
    <title>Using the Xml Control</title>
</head>
<body>
    <form id="form1" runat="server">
    <div>
        <asp:Xml ID="PainterView" runat="server"
            DocumentSource="~/Painters.xml"
            TransformSource="~/painters.xslt" />
    </div>
    </form>
</body>
</html>
```

Code snippet from XmlControl

The result is shown in Figure 9-6.

List of Painters & Paintings

Name	Painting	Year
Vasily Kandinsky	Composition No. 218	1919
Pavel Filonov	Formula of Spring	1929
Pyotr Konchalovsky	Sorrento Garden	1924

FIGURE 9-6

LINQ TO XML

With the introduction of LINQ to the .NET Framework, the focus was on easy access to the data that you want to work with in your applications. One of the main data stores in the application space is XML, so it was really a no-brainer to create the LINQ to XML implementation. With the inclusion of System.Xml.Linq, you now have a series of capabilities that make the process of working with XML in your code much easier to achieve.

LINQ HELPER XML OBJECTS

Even if the LINQ querying capability were not around, the new objects available to work with the XML are so good that they can even stand on their own outside LINQ. Within the new System.Xml.Linq namespace, you will find a series of new LINQ to XML helper objects that make working with an XML document in memory that much easier. The following sections describe the new objects that are available within this new namespace.

 Many of the examples in this chapter use a file called Hamlet.xml, *which you can find included in the file* http://metalab.unc.edu/bosak/xml/eg/shaks200.zip. *At this link you'll find all of Shakespeare's plays as XML files.*

XDocument

The XDocument class is a replacement of the XmlDocument object from the pre-LINQ world. While it does not comply with any international standards, the XDocument object is easier to work with when dealing with XML documents. It works with the other new objects in this space, such as the XNamespace, XComment, XElement, and XAttribute objects.

One of the more important members of the XDocument object is the Load method:

```
Dim xdoc As XDocument = XDocument.Load("C:\Hamlet.xml")
```

The preceding example loads the Hamlet.xml contents as an in-memory XDocument object. You can also pass a TextReader or XmlReader object into the Load method. From here, you can programmatically work with the XML:

```
Dim xdoc As XDocument = XDocument.Load("C:\Hamlet.xml")
Console.WriteLine(xdoc.Root.Name.ToString())
Console.WriteLine(xdoc.Root.HasAttributes.ToString())
```

Available for download on Wrox.com

Code snippet from LinqRead

This produces the following results:

```
PLAY
False
```

Another important member to be aware of is the Save method, which, like the Load method, enables you to save to a physical disk location or to a TextWriter or XmlWriter object. Note that you need to be running the application (or Visual Studio) as an administrator for this to work, as it writes to the root directory:

```
Dim xdoc As XDocument = XDocument.Load("C:\Hamlet.xml")
xdoc.Save("C:\CopyOfHamlet.xml")
```

XElement

Another common object that you will work with is the XElement object. With this object, you can easily create even single-element objects that are XML documents themselves, and even fragments of XML. For instance, here is an example of writing an XML element with a corresponding value:

```
Dim xe As XElement = New XElement("Company", "Wrox")
Console.WriteLine(xe.ToString())
```

When creating a new XElement object, you can define the name of the element as well as the value used in the element. In this case, the name of the element will be <Company>, while the value of the <Company> element will be Wrox. Running this in a console application, you will get the following result:

```
<Company>Wrox</Company>
```

You can also create a more complete XML document using multiple XElement objects, as shown here:

```
Imports System.Xml.Linq

Module Main

    Sub Main()

        Dim root As New XElement("Company",
                                New XAttribute("Type", "Publisher"),
                                New XElement("CompanyName", "Wrox"),
                                New XElement("CompanyAddress",
                                        New XElement("Steet", "111 River Street"),
                                        New XElement("City", "Hoboken"),
                                        New XElement("State", "NJ"),
                                        New XElement("Country", "USA"),
                                        New XElement("Zip", "07030-5774"))))
        Console.WriteLine(root.ToString())
        Console.WriteLine("Press ENTER to exit")
        Console.ReadLine()
    End Sub

End Module
```

Code snippet from XElementWriting

Running this application yields the results shown in Figure 9-7.

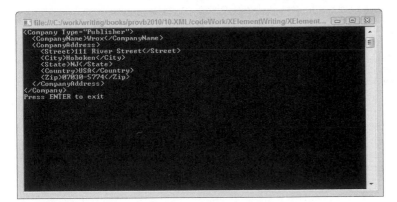

FIGURE 9-7

XNamespace

The XNamespace is an object that represents an XML namespace, and it is easily applied to elements within your document. For example, you can take the previous example and easily apply a namespace to the root element:

```
Imports System.Xml.Linq

Module Main

    Sub Main()
        Dim ns as Xnamespace = "http://www.example.com/somenamespace"
        Dim root As New Xelement(ns + "Company",
```

```
                            New XElement("CompanyName", "Wrox"),
                            New XElement("CompanyAddress",
                                New XElement("Street", "111 River Street"),
                                New XElement("City", "Hoboken"),
                                New XElement("State", "NJ"),
                                New XElement("Country", "USA"),
                                New XElement("Zip", "07030-5774")))
        Console.WriteLine(root.ToString())
        Console.WriteLine("Press ENTER to exit")
        Console.ReadLine()
    End Sub

End Module
```

In this case, an `XNamespace` object is created by assigning it a value of `http://www.example.com/somenamespace`. From there, it is actually used in the root element `<Company>` with the instantiation of the `XElement` object:

```
Dim root As New XElement(ns + "Company",
```

This will produce the results shown in Figure 9-8.

FIGURE 9-8

Besides dealing with the root element, you can also apply namespaces to all your elements:

Available for
download on
Wrox.com

```
Imports System.Xml.Linq

Module Main

    Sub Main()
        Dim ns1 As XNamespace = "http://www.example.com/ns/root"
        Dim ns2 As XNamespace = "http://www.example.com/ns/address"

        Dim root As New XElement(ns1 + "Company",
                        New XElement(ns1 + "CompanyName", "Wrox"),
                        New XElement(ns2 + "CompanyAddress",
                            New XElement(ns2 + "Street", "111 River Street"),
                            New XElement(ns2 + "City", "Hoboken"),
                            New XElement(ns2 + "State", "NJ"),
                            New XElement(ns2 + "Country", "USA"),
                            New XElement(ns2 + "Zip", "07030-5774")))
        Console.WriteLine(root.ToString())
        Console.WriteLine("Press ENTER to exit")
        Console.ReadLine()
    End Sub

End Module
```

Code snippet from XElementWritingNamespaces

This produces the results shown in Figure 9-9.

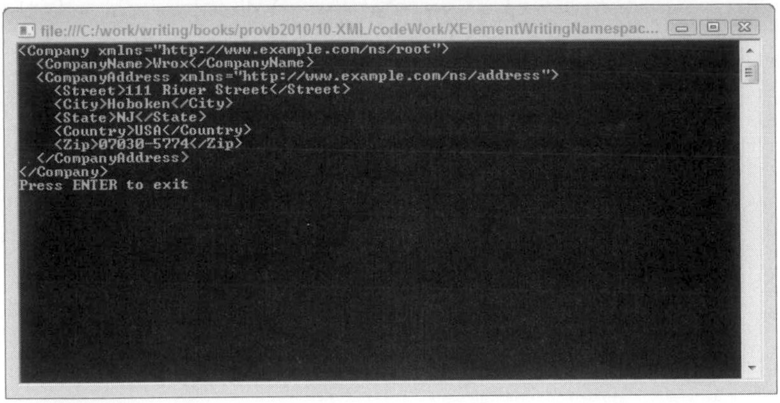

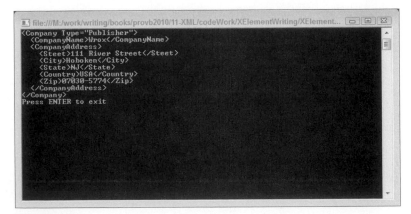

FIGURE 9-9

In this case, the subnamespace was applied to everything specified except for the `<Street>`, `<City>`, `<State>`, `<Country>`, and `<Zip>` elements, because they inherit from their parent, `<CompanyAddress>`, which has the namespace declaration.

XAttribute

In addition to elements, another important aspect of XML is attributes. Adding and working with attributes is done through the use of the `XAttribute` object. The following example adds an attribute to the root `<Company>` node:

```
Dim root As New Xelement("Company",
            New Xattribute("Type", "Publisher"),
                New XElement("CompanyName", "Wrox"),
                New XElement("CompanyAddress",
                    New XElement("Street", "111 River Street"),
                    New XElement("City", "Hoboken"),
                    New XElement("State", "NJ"),
                    New XElement("Country", "USA"),
                    New XElement("Zip", "07030-5774")))
```

Here, the attribute `MyAttribute` with a value of `MyAttributeValue` is added to the root element of the XML document, producing the results shown in Figure 9-10.

FIGURE 9-10

VISUAL BASIC AND XML LITERALS

Visual Basic takes LINQ to XML one step further, enabling you to place XML directly in your code. Using *XML literals*, you can place XML directly in your code for working with the XDocument and XElement objects. Earlier, the use of the XElement object was presented as follows:

```
Imports System.Xml.Linq

Module Main

    Sub Main()
        Dim root As New XElement("Company",
                            New XElement("CompanyName", "Wrox"),
                            New XElement("CompanyAddress",
                                New XElement("Street", "111 River Street"),
                                New XElement("City", "Hoboken"),
                                New XElement("State", "NJ"),
                                New XElement("Country", "USA"),
                                New XElement("Zip", "07030-5774")))
        Console.WriteLine(root.ToString())
        Console.WriteLine("Press ENTER to exit")
        Console.ReadLine()
    End Sub

End Module
```

Code snippet from XmlLiteral

Using XML literals, you can use the following syntax:

```
Module Main

    Sub Main()
        Dim root As XElement =
            <Company>
                <CompanyName>Wrox</CompanyName>
                <CompanyAddress>
                    <Street>111 River Street</Street>
                    <City>Hoboken</City>
                    <State>NJ</State>
                    <Country>USA</Country>
                    <Zip>07030-5774</Zip>
                </CompanyAddress>
            </Company>
        Console.WriteLine(root.ToString())
        Console.WriteLine("Press ENTER to exit")
        Console.ReadLine()
    End Sub

End Module
```

Code snippet from XmlLiteral

This enables you to place the XML directly in the code (see Figure 9-11). The best part about this is the IDE support for XML literals. Visual Studio 2010 has IntelliSense and excellent color-coding for the XML that you place in your code file.

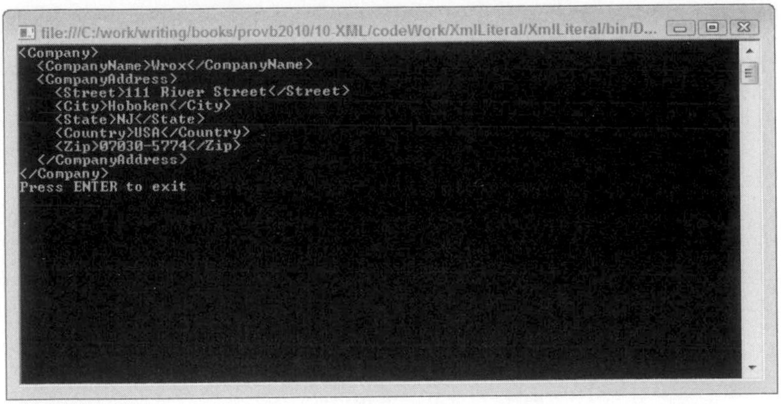

FIGURE 9-11

You can also use inline variables in the XML document. For instance, if you wanted to declare the value of the <CompanyName> element outside the XML literal, then you could use a construct similar to the following:

```
Module Module1
    Sub Main()
        Dim companyName As String = "Wrox"
        Dim xe As XElement = _
                <Company>
                <CompanyName><%= companyName %></CompanyName>
                    <CompanyAddress>
                    <Street>111 River Street</Street>
                    <City>Hoboken</City>
                    <State>NJ</State>
                    <Country>USA</Country>
                    <Zip>07030-5774</Zip>
                </CompanyAddress>
            </Company>
        Console.WriteLine(xe.ToString())
        Console.ReadLine()
    End Sub
End Module
```

In this case, the <CompanyName> element is assigned a value of `Wrox` from the `companyName` variable, using the syntax `<%= companyName %>`.

USING LINQ TO QUERY XML DOCUMENTS

Now that you can get your XML documents into an `XDocument` object and work with the various parts of this document, you can also use LINQ to XML to query your XML documents and work with the results.

Querying Static XML Documents

Notice that querying a static XML document using LINQ to XML takes almost no work at all. The following example makes use of the `hamlet.xml` file, querying for all the players (actors) who appear in a play. Each of these players is defined in the XML document with the <PERSONA> element:

Available for download on Wrox.com

```
Module Main
    Sub Main()
        Dim xdoc As XDocument = XDocument.Load("C:\hamlet.xml")
        Dim query = From people In xdoc.Descendants("PERSONA") _
                    Select people.Value
```

```
            Console.WriteLine("{0} Players Found", query.Count())
            Console.WriteLine()
            For Each item In query
                Console.WriteLine(item)
            Next
            Console.WriteLine("Press ENTER to exit")
            Console.ReadLine()
        End Sub
    End Module
```

Code snippet from LinqRead

In this case, an XDocument object loads a physical XML file (hamlet.xml) and then performs a LINQ query over the contents of the document:

```
Dim query = From people In xdoc.Descendants("PERSONA") _
            Select people.Value
```

The people object is a representation of all the <PERSONA> elements found in the document. Then the Select statement gets at the values of these elements. From there, a Console.WriteLine method is used to write out a count of all the players found, using query.Count. Next, each of the items is written to the screen in a For Each loop. The results you should see are presented here:

```
26 Players Found
CLAUDIUS, king of Denmark.
HAMLET, son to the late, and nephew to the present king.
POLONIUS, lord chamberlain.
HORATIO, friend to Hamlet.
LAERTES, son to Polonius.
LUCIANUS, nephew to the king.
VOLTIMAND
CORNELIUS
ROSENCRANTZ
GUILDENSTERN
OSRIC
A Gentleman
A Priest.
MARCELLUS
BERNARDO
FRANCISCO, a soldier.
REYNALDO, servant to Polonius.
Players.
Two Clowns, grave-diggers.
FORTINBRAS, prince of Norway.
A Captain.
English Ambassadors.
GERTRUDE, queen of Denmark, and mother to Hamlet.
OPHELIA, daughter to Polonius.
Lords, Ladies, Officers, Soldiers, Sailors, Messengers, and other Attendants.
Ghost of Hamlet's Father.
```

Querying Dynamic XML Documents

Numerous dynamic XML documents can be found on the Internet these days. Blog feeds, podcast feeds, and more provide XML documents by sending a request to a specific URL endpoint. These feeds can be viewed either in the browser, through an RSS aggregator, or as pure XML This code uses LINQ to XML to read a RSS feed:

```
Module Module1
    Sub Main()
        Dim xdoc As XDocument = _
                    XDocument.Load("http://weblogs.asp.net/mainfeed.aspx")
        Dim query = From rssFeed In xdoc.Descendants("channel") _
                    Select Title = rssFeed.Element("title").Value, _
```

```
                          Description = rssFeed.Element("description").Value, _
                          Link = rssFeed.Element("link").Value
            For Each item In query
                Console.WriteLine("TITLE: " + item.Title)
                Console.WriteLine("DESCRIPTION: " + item.Description)
                Console.WriteLine("LINK: " + item.Link)
            Next
            Console.WriteLine()
            Dim queryPosts = From myPosts In xdoc.Descendants("item") _
                      Select Title = myPosts.Element("title").Value, _
                          Published = _
                             DateTime.Parse(myPosts.Element("pubDate").Value), _
                          Description = myPosts.Element("description").Value, _
                          Url = myPosts.Element("link").Value
            For Each item In queryPosts
                Console.WriteLine(item.Title)
            Next
            Console.WriteLine("Press ENTER to exit")
            Console.ReadLine()
        End Sub
    End Module
```

Code snippet from LinqReadDynamic

Here, the Load method of the XDocument object points to a URL where the XML is retrieved. The first query pulls out all the main sub-elements of the <channel> element in the feed and creates new objects called Title, Description, and Link to get at the values of these sub-elements.

From there, a For Each statement is run to iterate through all the items found in this query. The second query works through all the <item> elements and the various sub-elements it contains (these are all the blog entries found in the blog). Though a lot of the items found are rolled up into properties, in the For Each loop, only the Title property is used. You will see results similar to that shown in Figure 9-12.

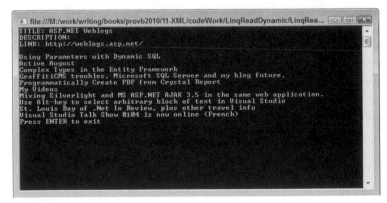

FIGURE 9-12

WORKING WITH THE XML DOCUMENT

If you have been working with the XML document hamlet.xml, you probably noticed that it is quite large. You've seen how you can query into the XML document in a couple of ways, and now this section takes a look at reading and writing to the XML document.

Reading from an XML Document

Earlier you saw just how easy it is to query into an XML document using the LINQ query statements, as shown here:

```
Dim query = From people In xdoc.Descendants("PERSONA") _
            Select people.Value
```

This query returns all the players found in the document. Using the Element method of the XDocument object, you can also get at specific values of the XML document you are working with. For instance, continuing to work with the hamlet.xml document, the following XML fragment shows you how the title is represented:

```
<?xml version="1.0"?>
<PLAY>
   <TITLE>The Tragedy of Hamlet, Prince of Denmark</TITLE>
   <!-- XML removed for clarity -->
</PLAY>
```

Code snippet from LinqRead

As you can see, the `<TITLE>` element is a nested element of the `<PLAY>` element. You can easily get at the title by using the following bit of code:

```
Dim xdoc As XDocument = XDocument.Load("C:\hamlet.xml")
Console.WriteLine(xdoc.Element("PLAY").Element("TITLE").Value)
```

This bit of code writes out the title, "The Tragedy of Hamlet, Prince of Denmark," to the console screen. In the code, you were able to work down the hierarchy of the XML document by using two Element method calls — first calling the `<PLAY>` element, and then the `<TITLE>` element found nested within the `<PLAY>` element.

Continuing with the hamlet.xml document, you can view a long list of players who are defined with the use of the `<PERSONA>` element:

```
<?xml version="1.0"?>
<PLAY>
   <TITLE>The Tragedy of Hamlet, Prince of Denmark</TITLE>
   <!-- XML removed for clarity -->
   <PERSONAE>
      <TITLE>Dramatis Personae</TITLE>
      <PERSONA>CLAUDIUS, king of Denmark. </PERSONA>
      <PERSONA>HAMLET, son to the late,
       and nephew to the present king.</PERSONA>
      <PERSONA>POLONIUS, lord chamberlain. </PERSONA>
      <PERSONA>HORATIO, friend to Hamlet.</PERSONA>
      <PERSONA>LAERTES, son to Polonius.</PERSONA>
      <PERSONA>LUCIANUS, nephew to the king.</PERSONA>
      <!-- XML removed for clarity -->
   </PERSONAE>
</PLAY>
```

Code snippet from LinqRead

Using that, review the following bit of the code's use of this XML:

```
Dim xdoc As XDocument = XDocument.Load("C:\hamlet.xml")
Console.WriteLine( _
   xdoc.Element("PLAY").Element("PERSONAE").Element("PERSONA").Value)
```

This piece of code starts at `<PLAY>`, works down to the `<PERSONAE>` element, and then makes use of the `<PERSONA>` element. However, using this you will get the following result:

```
CLAUDIUS, king of Denmark
```

Although there is a collection of `<PERSONA>` elements, you are dealing only with the first one that is encountered using the Element().Value call.

Writing to an XML Document

In addition to reading from an XML document, you can also write to the document just as easily. For instance, if you wanted to change the name of the first player of the hamlet file, you could make use of the code here to accomplish that task:

```
Module Module1
    Sub Main()
        Dim xdoc As XDocument = XDocument.Load("hamlet.xml")
        xdoc.Element("PLAY").Element("PERSONAE"). _
            Element("PERSONA").SetValue("Foo deBar, King of Denmark")
        Console.WriteLine(xdoc.Element("PLAY"). _
            Element("PERSONAE").Element("PERSONA").Value)
        Console.ReadLine()
    End Sub
End Module
```

Code snippet from LinqWrite

In this case, the first instance of the `<PERSONA>` element is overwritten with the value of `Foo deBar, King of Denmark` using the `SetValue` method of the `Element` object. After the `SetValue` is called and the value is applied to the XML document, the value is then retrieved using the same approach as before. Running this bit of code, you can indeed see that the value of the first `<PERSONA>` element has been changed.

Another way to change the document (by adding items to it in this example) is to create the element you want as `XElement` objects and then add them to the document:

```
Module Module1
    Sub Main()
        Dim xdoc As XDocument = XDocument.Load("hamlet.xml")
        Dim xe As XElement = New XElement("PERSONA", _
                "Foo deBar, King of Denmark")
        xdoc.Element("PLAY").Element("PERSONAE").Add(xe)
        Dim query = From people In xdoc.Descendants("PERSONA") _
                Select people.Value
        Console.WriteLine("{0} Players Found", query.Count())
        Console.WriteLine()
        For Each item In query
            Console.WriteLine(item)
        Next
        Console.ReadLine()
    End Sub
End Module
```

Code snippet from LinqAdd

In this case, an `XElement` document called `xe` is created. The construction of `xe` gives you the following XML output:

```
<PERSONA>Foo deBar, King of Denmark</PERSONA>
```

Then, using the `Element().Add` method from the `XDocument` object, you are able to add the created element:

```
xdoc.Element("PLAY").Element("PERSONAE").Add(xe)
```

Next, querying all the players, you will now find that instead of 26, as before, you now have 27, with the new one at the bottom of the list. Besides `Add`, you can also use `AddFirst`, which does just that — adds the player to the beginning of the list instead of the end, which is the default.

LAMBDA EXPRESSIONS IN VISUAL BASIC

While not specifically an XML feature, Visual Basic includes support for lambda expressions. These can be quite handy when dealing with XML, or other code that requires some function to be executed repeatedly.

Lambda expressions are at first glance similar to functions. You declare them with the `System.Func` generic, and then execute them as needed:

```
Dim Square As Func(Of Integer, Integer) =
        Function(x As Integer) x ^ 2
Dim value As Integer = 42
Console.WriteLine(Square(value))
```

This example creates a new lambda — called Square — that simply squares an integer. This expression takes an `Integer`, and returns an `Integer`. There are other `Func` generics available for a number of other combinations of parameters and return values. The `Function` keyword is used to define the expression (as you will see later, there is also now a `Sub` keyword).

In the preceding example, the actual function was written on one line, following the `Function` keyword. Many developers find this syntax a little confusing at first. Fortunately, in Visual Basic 2010, a more familiar form is available:

```
Dim SquareIt As Func(Of Integer, Integer) = Function(x As Integer)
                                        Return x ^ 2
                            End Function
Dim i As Integer = 42
Console.WriteLine(SquareIt(i))
```

In this sample, the lambda has been written more like a normal function, across multiple lines, and with a return statement. While this function has only a single line, you could include whatever processing you need to do within the lambda expression, just as you would do in a normal function.

These expressions differ from regular functions in that they are actually inherited from `Delegate`. This means that they are actually code objects. As such, you can even return them from a method. In addition, because they inherit from `Delegate`, they are interchangeable. For example, if you had two lambdas using the same signature, you could declare a method to return any lambda that uses that signature:

```
Dim Square As Func(Of Integer, Integer) = Function(x As Integer) x ^ 2
Dim Cube As Func(Of Integer, Integer) = Function(x As Integer) x ^ 3

Function GetMath(ByVal v As Integer) As Func(Of Integer, Integer)
    'square even numbers, cube odd ones
    If (v Mod 2) = 0 Then
        Return Square
    Else
        Return Cube
    End If

End Function
```

Code snippet from Lambdas

Your code will then run the appropriate method for the parameter(s):

```
Dim nums = {1, 2, 3, 4, 5, 6, 7, 8, 9, 10}
For Each x In nums
    Dim f As Func(Of Integer, Integer)
    f = GetMath(x)
    Console.WriteLine("{0}: {1}", x, f(x))
Next
```

Code snippet from Lambdas

Where do lambda expressions fit in with XML? The LINQ expressions you have been using are written internally as lambda expressions (LINQ is actually why lambda expressions were added to .NET).

In addition, you can use your own lambdas to simplify complex queries by replacing the queries with lambda expressions. For example, the following code prints off a subset of the lines from the hamlet.xml file that you've been using:

```vb
Dim doc As XElement = XElement.Load("..\..\hamlet.xml")
Dim speakers = {"OPHELIA", "LORD POLONIUS" }

Dim lines As List(Of String) =
        (From line In doc.Descendants("SPEECH") _
            .Where(Function(item As XElement)
                        Return (speakers.Contains(item.Descendants("SPEAKER").Value))
                  End Function) _
            .Select(Function(item As XElement)
                        Return String.Format("{0} said, {1}{2}{3}",
                        item.Descendants("SPEAKER").Value,
                        ControlChars.Quote,
                        item.Descendants("LINE").Value,
                        ControlChars.Quote)

                  End Function)).ToList()

lines.ForEach(Sub(line)
                    Console.WriteLine(line)
              End Sub)
```

Code snippet from Lambdas

The XML file is loaded into an XElement for processing, and an array of speakers is initialized. This uses the new syntax for initializing an array. You want to return the lines spoken by any of the people listed in the array. You could do this in regular LINQ syntax, but using a lambda reduces the where clause to a few lines. Notice that in this case, you still need to use statement completion characters to break up the long query.

In the previous examples, the lambda expression was written first, then used. However, in this example, the expressions are actually written where they will execute. Which form you should use depends on what you are attempting to accomplish, and the needs of the application, just as when you are trying to decide if a function should be written as a standalone function, or inline. For example, if you only need to access the lambda once or twice, writing it first is probably a good idea. In this case, the lambda is only used once, therefore putting it inline is a better choice. In addition, by having the lambda within the LINQ query, you get a better view of just what the lambda is doing (i.e. in the Where clause, the lambda returns the records desired, while in the Select clause, it formats the output)

A second lambda expression is used in the select clause to concatenate some of the child nodes of the <SPEECH> element in the XML. Finally, the entire result set is converted into a List(Of String). Each element in the list is a string containing the speaker and the line:

```
LORD POLONIUS said, "By the mass, and 'tis like a camel, indeed."
```

Next, the code prints off the selected lines (see Figure 9-13). In this case it uses the new Sub version of a lambda. This works exactly like the lambdas you've used earlier, except that it doesn't return any value.

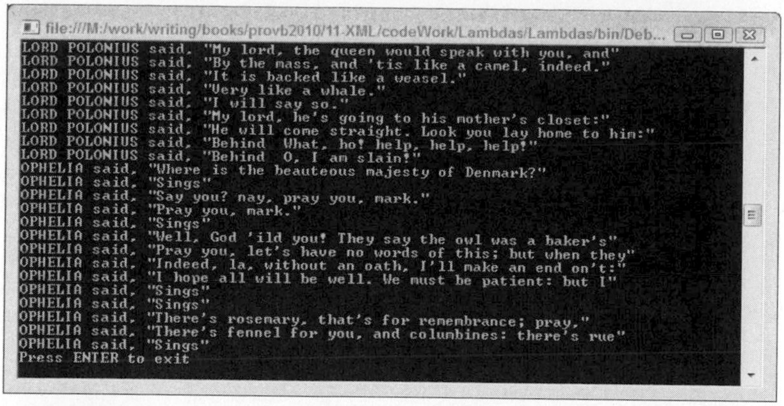

FIGURE 9-13

While most developers won't need to create lambda expressions, they provide powerful tools when working with XML or other code.

SUMMARY

The beauty of XML is that it isolates data representation from data display. Technologies such as HTML contain data that is tightly bound to its display format. XML does not suffer this limitation, and at the same time it has the readability of HTML. Accordingly, the XML facilities available to a Visual Basic application are vast, and a large number of XML-related features, classes, and interfaces are exposed by the .NET Framework.

This chapter showed you how to use `System.Xml.Serialization.XmlSerializer` to serialize classes. Source Code Style attributes were introduced in conjunction with serialization. This style of attributes enables the customization of the XML serialized to be extended to the source code associated with a class. What is important to remember about the direction of serialization classes is that a required change in the XML format becomes a change in the underlying source code. Developers should resist the temptation to rewrite serialized classes in order to conform to some new XML data standard (such as the example movie order format endorsed by the consortium of movie rental establishments). Technologies such as XSLT, exposed via the `System.Xml.Query` namespace, should be examined first as alternatives. This chapter demonstrated how to use XSLT style sheets to transform XML data using the classes found in the `System.Xml.Query` namespace.

The most useful classes and interfaces in the `System.Xml` namespace were reviewed, including those that support document-style XML access: `XmlDocument`, `XmlNode`, `XmlElement`, and `XmlAttribute`. The `System.Xml` namespace also contains classes and interfaces that support stream-style XML access: `XmlReader` and `XmlWriter`.

Next, you looked at how to use XML with ASP.NET. While you can use the `XmlReader` and `XmlDocument` (and related) classes with ASP.NET, there are included controls to make working with XML easier.

This chapter also described how to use LINQ to XML and some of the options available to you in reading from and writing to XML files and XML sources, whether the source is static or dynamic.

You were also introduced to the new LINQ to XML helper objects `XDocument`, `XElement`, `XNamespace`, `XAttribute`, and `XComment`. These outstanding new objects make working with XML easier than ever before.

Finally, you looked at lambda expressions. While lambda expressions are not specifically for use with XML, you saw how they can fit into a solution that processes XML.

10

ADO.NET and LINQ

WHAT YOU WILL LEARN IN THIS CHAPTER

- ➤ The architecture of ADO.NET
- ➤ How ADO.NET connects to databases
- ➤ Using ADO.NET to retrieve data
- ➤ Using ADO.NET to update databases
- ➤ Creating and using transactions
- ➤ Retrieving data with LINQ to SQL
- ➤ Updating databases using LINQ to SQL

ADO.NET 1.x was the successor to ActiveX Data Objects 2.6 (ADO). The main goal of ADO.NET 1.x was to enable developers to easily create distributed, data-sharing applications in the .NET Framework. The main goals of ADO.NET today are to improve the performance of existing features in ADO.NET 1.x, to provide easier use, and to add new features without breaking backward compatibility.

 Throughout this chapter, when ADO.NET is mentioned without a version number after it (that is, 1.x, 2.0, 3.5, or 4), the statement applies to all versions of ADO.NET.

ADO.NET 1.x was built upon industry standards such as XML, and it provided a data-access interface to communicate with data sources such as SQL Server and Oracle. ADO.NET 4 continues to build upon these concepts, while increasing performance. Applications can use ADO.NET to connect to these data sources and retrieve, manipulate, and update data. ADO.NET 4 does not break any compatibility with ADO.NET 2.0 or 1.x; it only adds to the stack of functionality.

In solutions that require disconnected or remote access to data, ADO.NET uses XML to exchange data between programs or with Web pages. Any component that can read XML can make use of ADO.NET components. A receiving component does not even have to be an ADO.NET component if a transmitting ADO.NET component packages and delivers a data set in an XML format. Transmitting information in XML-formatted data sets enables programmers to easily separate the data-processing and user interface components of a data-sharing application onto separate servers. This can greatly improve both the performance and the maintainability of systems that support many users.

For distributed applications, ADO.NET 1.x proved that the use of XML data sets provided performance advantages relative to the COM marshaling used to transmit disconnected data sets in ADO. Because transmission of data sets occurred through XML streams in a simple text-based standard accepted throughout the industry, receiving components did not require any of the architectural restrictions required by COM. XML data sets used in ADO.NET 1.x also avoided the processing cost of converting values in the `Fields` collection of a `Recordset` object to data types recognized by COM. Virtually any two components from different systems can share XML data sets, provided that they both use the same XML schema for formatting the data set. This continues to be true in ADO.NET 4, but the story gets better. The XML integration in ADO.NET today is even stronger, and extensive work was done to improve the performance of the `DataSet` object, particularly in the areas of serialization and memory usage.

ADO.NET also supports the scalability required by Web-based data-sharing applications. Web applications must often serve hundreds, or even thousands, of users. By default, ADO.NET does not retain lengthy database locks or active connections that monopolize limited resources. This enables the number of users to grow with only a small increase in the demands made on the resources of a system.

One of the issues some developers experience when working with ADO.NET and various databases is that you need to leverage at least two languages: Visual Basic and the version of SQL used by the database. To reduce this separation, Microsoft developed LINQ, (Language INtegrated Query). With LINQ, you can include the query within your Visual Basic code, and the query you add to your code is translated into the specific query language of the data store. One of the most common uses for LINQ is in working with databases (you will also see LINQ used in querying XML in the XML chapter) in its form as a "better" SQL.

The use of LINQ and SQL Server leads to one point of confusion: While LINQ can be used to query any database (or set of objects, XML, or other LINQ provider), there is also a specific technology known as LINQ to SQL. This is a SQL Server specific query tool that uses LINQ as its query mechanism. This chapter will look at both the generic LINQ query engine, as well as the LINQ to SQL tools.

In this chapter, you will see that ADO.NET is a very extensive and flexible API for accessing many types of data, and because ADO.NET 4 represents an incremental change to the previous versions of ADO.NET, all previous ADO.NET knowledge already learned can be leveraged. In fact, to get the most out of this chapter, you should be fairly familiar with earlier versions of ADO.NET and the entire .NET Framework.

This chapter demonstrates how to use the ADO.NET object model in order to build flexible, fast, and scalable data-access objects and applications. Specifically, it covers the following:

➤ The ADO.NET architecture

➤ Some of the specific features offered in ADO.NET, including batch updates, `DataSet` performance improvements, and asynchronous processing

➤ Working with the common provider model

➤ Using LINQ to query and edit your databases

ADO.NET ARCHITECTURE

The main design goals of ADO.NET are as follows:

➤ Customer-driven features that are still backwardly compatible with ADO.NET 1.x

➤ Improving performance on your data-store calls

➤ Providing more power for power users

➤ Taking advantage of SQL Server–specific features

ADO.NET addresses a couple of the most common data-access strategies used for applications today. When classic ADO was developed, many applications could be connected to the data store almost indefinitely. Today, with the explosion of the Internet as the means of data communication, a new data technology is required to make data accessible and updateable in a disconnected architecture.

The first of these common data-access scenarios is one in which a user must locate a collection of data and iterate through this data just a single time. This is a popular scenario for Web pages. When a request for data from a Web page that you have created is received, you can simply fill a table with data from a data store. In this case, you go to the data store, grab the data that you want, send the data across the wire, and then populate the table. In this scenario, the goal is to get the data in place as fast as possible.

The second way to work with data in this disconnected architecture is to grab a collection of data and use this data separately from the data store itself. This could be on the server or even on the client. Even though the data is disconnected, you want the capability to keep the data (with all of its tables and relations in place) on the client side. Classic ADO data was represented by a single table that you could iterate through; but ADO.NET can be a reflection of the data store itself, with tables, columns, rows, and relations all in place. When you are done with the client-side copy of the data, you can persist the changes that you made in the local copy of data directly back into the data store. The technology that gives you this capability is the `DataSet` class, which is covered shortly.

Although classic ADO was geared for a two-tiered environment (client-server), ADO.NET addresses a multi-tiered environment. ADO.NET is easy to work with because it has a unified programming model. This unified programming model makes working with data on the server similar to working with data on the client. Because the models are the same, you find yourself more productive when working with ADO.NET. This productivity increases even more when you use some of the more recent tools such as LINQ to SQL or Entity Framework.

BASIC ADO.NET FEATURES

This chapter begins with a quick look at the basics of ADO.NET and then provides an overview of ADO.NET capabilities, namespaces, and classes. It also reviews how to work with the `Connection`, `Command`, `DataAdapter`, `DataSet`, and `DataReader` classes. Later chapters will cover some of the more recently added ADO.NET features.

Common ADO.NET Tasks

Before jumping into the depths of ADO.NET, step back and make sure that you understand some of the common tasks you might perform programmatically within ADO.NET. This section looks at the process of selecting, inserting, updating, and deleting data.

 For all of the data-access examples in this chapter, you need the pubs database. As of this writing, you can find this link at www.microsoft.com/downloads/details .aspx?familyid=06616212-0356-46a0-8da2-eebc53a68034&displaylang=en. *Once installed, you will find the* pubs.mdf *file in the* C:\ SQL Server 2000 Sample Databases *directory. You can then attach this database to your SQL Server using SQL Server Management Studio.*

In addition, be sure to run the examples.sql file — available with the code download for this chapter — either using the examples.bat batch file, or with SQL Server Management Studio before running the code examples. This creates the necessary stored procedures and functions in the pubs database.

Selecting Data

After the connection to the data source is open and ready to use, you probably want to read the data from it. If you do not want to manipulate the data, but simply read it or transfer it from one spot to another, use the `DataReader` class (or one of the classes that inherit from `DataReader` for each database type).

The following example uses the `GetAuthorsLastNames` function to provide a list of company names from the pubs database: (You may need to update the connection string to match the location of the pubs database on your computer.)

```vb
Imports System.Data.SqlClient

Module Main

    Sub Main()

        Dim data As List(Of String)
        data = GetAuthorsLastNames()
        For Each author As String In data
            Console.WriteLine(author)
        Next

        Console.WriteLine("Press ENTER to exit")
        Console.ReadLine()
    End Sub

    Public Function GetAuthorsLastNames() As List(Of String)
        Dim conn As SqlConnection
        Dim cmd As SqlCommand
        Dim result As New List(Of String)
        'update to match the location of pubs on your computer
        Dim cmdString As String = "Select au_lname from authors"
        conn = New SqlConnection("Server=.\SQLEXPRESS;" & _
                "Database=pubs;" & _
                "Integrated Security=True;")
        cmd = New SqlCommand(cmdString, conn)
        conn.Open()
        Dim myReader As SqlDataReader
        myReader = cmd.ExecuteReader(CommandBehavior.CloseConnection)
        While myReader.Read()
            result.Add(myReader("au_lname").ToString())
        End While
        Return result
    End Function
End Module
```

Code snippet from SimpleDataReader project

In this example, you create an instance of both the `SqlConnection` and the `SqlCommand` classes. Then, before you open the connection, you simply pass the `SqlCommand` class a SQL statement selecting specific data from the pubs database. After your connection is opened (based upon the commands passed in), you create a `DataReader`. To read the data from the database, you iterate through the data with the `DataReader` by using the `myReader.Read` method. Each time you call the `Read` method, the current position of the reader is set to point to the next line returned by the SQL statement. Once the position moves to the end, the `Read` method returns false, exiting the loop. After the `List(Of String)` object is built, the connection is closed and the object is returned from the function. In the sample application, this data is displayed in the console window.

Inserting Data

When working with data, you often insert the data into the data source, in this case a SQL Server database. The next code sample shows you how to do this:

```vb
Imports System.Data.SqlClient

Module Main
    Sub Main()
        InsertData()
```

```
            Console.WriteLine("Press ENTER to exit")
            Console.ReadLine()
    End Sub

    Sub InsertData()
        Dim conn As SqlConnection
        Dim cmd As SqlCommand
        Dim cmdString As String = "Insert authors(au_id, au_fname, au_lname, " &
            "phone, contract) " &
            "Values ('555-12-1212', 'Foo', 'deBar', '212-555-1212', 1)"
        conn = New SqlConnection("Server=.\SQLEXPRESS;" & _
                                    "database=pubs;Integrated Security=True;")
        cmd = New SqlCommand(cmdString, conn)
        conn.Open()
        cmd.ExecuteNonQuery()
        'confirm we have it inserted by displaying the data
        cmdString = "SELECT au_fname, au_lname, phone" &
            "FROM authors WHERE au_lname='deBar'"
        cmd = New SqlCommand(cmdString, conn)
        Using reader As SqlDataReader = cmd.ExecuteReader
            While (reader.Read)
                Console.WriteLine("{0} {1}: {2}",
                                    reader.GetString(0),
                                    reader.GetString(1),
                                    reader.GetString(2))
            End While
        End Using
        conn.Close()
    End Sub

End Module
```

Code snippet from SimpleDataInsert project

Inserting data into SQL is pretty straightforward and simple. Using the SQL command string, you insert specific values for specific columns. The actual insertion is initiated using the ExecuteNonQuery command. This executes a command on the data when you don't want anything in return. If you were expecting data back from the insert, you could use ExecuteScalar (if a single value — such as the inserted record ID — is returned) or ExecuteReader (if data — such as the complete inserted record — is returned).

Updating Data

In addition to inserting new records into a database, you frequently need to update existing rows of data in a table. Imagine a table in which you can update multiple records at once. In the next example, you want to update the royalty schedule table in pubs (roysched) by changing the royalty terms for those titles currently at 10%:

```
Imports System.Data.SqlClient

Module Main

    Sub Main()
        Dim records As Integer
        records = UpdateRoyaltySchedule(10, 8)
        Console.WriteLine("{0} records affected", records)

        Console.WriteLine("Press ENTER to exit.")
        Console.ReadLine()

    End Sub

Public Function UpdateRoyaltySchedule(ByVal currentPercent As Integer,
                                        ByVal newPercent As Integer) As Integer
```

```
            Dim cmd As SqlCommand
            Dim result As Integer
            Dim cmdString As String =
                String.Format("UPDATE roysched SET royalty={0} where royalty={1}",
                                                newPercent,
                                                currentPercent)
            'update to match the location of pubs on your computer
            Using conn As New SqlConnection("Server=(local)\sqlexpress;" &
                                "database=pubs;Integrated Security=true;")
                conn.Open()
                'display the record before updating
                DisplayData(conn, "before")
                cmd = New SqlCommand(cmdString, conn)
                result = cmd.ExecuteNonQuery()
                'display the record after updating
                DisplayData(conn, "after")
            End Using


        Return result
    End Function
    Private Sub DisplayData(ByVal conn As SqlConnection,
                        ByVal direction As String)
        Dim cmdString As String = "SELECT * FROM roysched ORDER BY title_id"
        Dim cmd As New SqlCommand(cmdString, conn)

        Console.WriteLine("Displaying data ({0})", direction)
        Using reader As SqlDataReader = cmd.ExecuteReader
            While reader.Read
                Console.WriteLine("Title: {0} {1}-{2} Royalty: {3}%",
                                    reader.GetString(0),
                                    reader.GetInt32(1),
                                    reader.GetInt32(2),
                                    reader.GetInt32(3))

            End While
        End Using
    End Sub
End Module
```

Code snippet from SimpleDataUpdate project

This update function changes the royalty percentage for authors from 10% to 8%. This is done with the SQL command string. The great thing about these update capabilities is that you can capture the number of records that were updated by assigning the result of the ExecuteNonQuery command to the records variable. The total number of affected records is then returned by the function.

Notice that in this case the connection was wrapped in a Using statement. The Using statement creates a scope for an object, and the object is properly disposed of at the close of the statement. This guarantees that the connection will be closed when the Using clause completes.

Deleting Data

Along with reading, inserting, and updating data, you sometimes need to delete data from the data source. Deleting data is a simple process of using the SQL command string and then the ExecuteNonQuery command as you did in the update example. The following bit of code illustrates this:

```
Imports System.Data.SqlClient

Module Main

    Sub Main()
        Dim deletes As Integer
```

```vb
        deletes = DeleteAuthor("deBar")
        Console.WriteLine("{0} author(s) deleted", deletes)

        Console.WriteLine("Press ENTER to exit.")
        Console.ReadLine()
    End Sub

    Public Function DeleteAuthor(ByVal lastName As String) As Integer
        Dim result As Integer
        Dim cmd As SqlCommand
        Dim cmdString As String =
            String.Format("DELETE authors WHERE au_lname='{0}'",
                          lastName)

        Using conn As New SqlConnection("server=(local)\sqlexpress;" &
                                        "database=pubs;integrated security=true;")
            cmd = New SqlCommand(cmdString, conn)
            conn.Open()
            DisplayData(conn, "before")
            result = cmd.ExecuteNonQuery()
            DisplayData(conn, "after")
        End Using

        Return result
    End Function
    Private Sub DisplayData(ByVal conn As SqlConnection,
                            ByVal direction As String)
        Dim cmdString As String = "SELECT count(*) FROM authors"
        Dim cmd As New SqlCommand(cmdString, conn)
        Dim count As Integer = CType(cmd.ExecuteScalar(), Integer)
        Console.WriteLine("Number of authors {0}: {1}",
                          direction,
                          count)
    End SubEnd Module
```

Code snippet from SimpleDelete project

You can assign the `ExecuteNonQuery` command to an `Integer` variable (just as you did for the update function) to return the number of records deleted in order to verify that the records are deleted.

Basic ADO.NET Namespaces and Classes

The core ADO.NET namespaces are shown in Table 10-1. In addition to these namespaces, each new data provider will have its own namespace. For example, the Oracle .NET data provider adds a namespace of `System.Data.OracleClient` (for the Microsoft-built Oracle data provider).

TABLE 10-1: Core ADO.NET Namespaces

NAMESPACE	DESCRIPTION
`System.Data`	This namespace is the core of ADO.NET. It contains classes used by all data providers. Its classes represent tables, columns, rows, and the `DataSet` class. It also contains several useful interfaces, such as `IDbCommand`, `IDbConnection`, and `IDbDataAdapter`. These interfaces are used by all managed providers, enabling them to plug into the core of ADO.NET.
`System.Data.Common`	This namespace defines common classes that are used as base classes for data providers. All data providers share these classes. Two examples are `DbConnection` and `DbDataAdapter`.

continues

TABLE 10-1 *(continued)*

NAMESPACE	DESCRIPTION
System.Data.OleDb	This namespace defines classes that work with OLE-DB data sources using the .NET OLE DB data provider. It contains classes such as `OleDbConnection` and `OleDbCommand`.
System.Data.Odbc	This namespace defines classes that work with the ODBC data sources using the .NET ODBC data provider. It contains classes such as `OdbcConnection` and `OdbcCommand`.
System.Data.SqlClient	This namespace defines a data provider for the SQL Server 7.0 or later database. It contains classes such as `SqlConnection` and `SqlCommand`.
System.Data.SqlTypes	This namespace defines classes that represent specific data types for the SQL Server database.
System.Data.Linq	This namespace provides support for connecting, querying, and editing databases using LINQ (Language Integrated Query).
System.Data.Services	This namespace provides support for ADO.NET Data Services, a server-side method of providing data using a REST-like syntax. It is covered in Chapter 12.
System.Data.EntityClient	This namespace provides support for the Entity Framework for working with data. It is covered in Chapter 11.

ADO.NET has three distinct types of classes commonly referred to as:

➤ **disconnected** — These provide the basic structure for the ADO.NET Framework. A good example of this type of class is the `DataTable` class. The objects created from these disconnected class types are capable of storing data without any dependency on a specific data provider.

➤ **shared** — These form the base classes for data providers and are shared among all data providers.

➤ **data providers** — These are meant to work with different kinds of data sources. They are used to perform all data-management operations on specific databases. The `SqlClient` data provider, for example, works only with the SQL Server database.

A *data provide*r contains `Connection`, `Command`, `DataAdapter`, and `DataReader` objects. Typically, in programming ADO.NET, you first create the `Connection` object and provide it with the necessary information, such as the connection string. You then create a `Command` object and provide it with the details of the SQL command that is to be executed. This command can be an inline SQL text command, a stored procedure, or direct table access. You can also provide parameters to these commands if needed.

After you create the `Connection` and the `Command` objects, you must decide whether the command returns a result set. If the command doesn't return a result set, then you can simply execute the command by calling one of its several `Execute` methods. Conversely, if the command returns a result set, you must decide whether you want to retain the result set for future use without maintaining the connection to the database. If you want to retain the result set but not the connection, then you must create a `DataAdapter` object and use it to fill a `DataSet` or a `DataTable` object. These objects are capable of maintaining their information in a disconnected mode. However, if you don't want to retain the result set, but rather simply process the command in a swift fashion, then you can use the `Command` object to create a `DataReader` object. The `DataReader` object needs a live connection to the database, and it works as a forward-only, read-only cursor.

ADO.NET Components

To better support the disconnected model as defined above, the ADO.NET components separate data access from data manipulation. This is accomplished via two main components: the `DataSet` and the .NET data provider. Figure 10-1 illustrates the concept of separating data access from data manipulation.

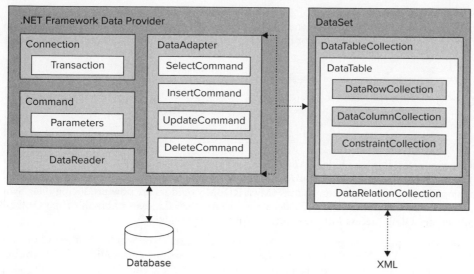

FIGURE 10-1

The `DataSet` is the core component of the disconnected architecture of ADO.NET. It is explicitly designed for data access independent of any data source. As a result, it can be used with multiple and differing data sources, with XML data, or even to manage data local to an application such as an in-memory data cache. The `DataSet` contains a collection of one or more `DataTable` objects made up of rows and columns of data, as well as primary key, foreign key, constraint, and relation information about the data in the `DataTable` objects. It is basically an in-memory database, but what sets it apart is that it doesn't care whether its data is obtained from a database, an XML file, a combination of the two, or somewhere else. You can apply inserts, updates, and deletes to the `DataSet` and then push the changes back to the data source, no matter where the data source lives! This chapter offers an in-depth look at the `DataSet` object family.

The other core element of the ADO.NET architecture is the .NET data provider, whose components are designed for data manipulation (as opposed to data access with the `DataSet`). These components are listed in Table 10-2.

The `DataAdapter` uses `Command` objects to execute SQL commands at the data source, both to load the `DataSet` with data and to reconcile changes made to the data in the `DataSet` with the data source. You will take a closer look at this later in the detailed discussion of the `DataAdapter` object.

 .NET data providers can be written for any data source, though this is a topic beyond the scope of this chapter.

TABLE 10-2: .NET Data Provider Components

OBJECT	ACTIVITY
`Connection`	Provides connectivity to a data source
`Command`	Enables access to database commands to return and modify data, run stored procedures, and send or retrieve parameter information
`DataReader`	Provides a high-performance, read-only stream of data from the data source
`DataAdapter`	Provides the bridge between the `DataSet` object and the data source

The .NET Framework 4 ships with a number of .NET data providers, including ones for accessing SQL Server and Oracle databases, as well as more generic data providers, such as the ODBC and OLE DB data providers. Other data providers are available for just about every other database out there, for example, a MySQL database.

> *Do not confuse the OLE DB .NET data provider with generic OLE DB providers. The OLE DB .NET data provider connects to specific OLE DB providers to access each data source.*

The rule of thumb when deciding which data provider to use is to first use a .NET Relational Database Management System (RDBMS)–specific data provider if it is available, and to use the .NET OLE DB provider when connecting to any other data source. (Most RDBMS vendors are now producing their own .NET data providers in order to encourage .NET developers to use their databases.) Finally, if no OLE DB provider is available, try ODBC access using the .NET ODBC data provider.

For example, if you were writing an application that uses SQL Server, then you would want to use the SQL Server .NET data provider. The .NET OLE DB provider is used to access any data source exposed through OLE DB, such as Microsoft Access. You will be taking a closer look at these later.

.NET DATA PROVIDERS

.NET data providers are used for connecting to a RDBMS-specific database (such as SQL Server or Oracle), executing commands, and retrieving results. Those results are either processed directly (via a `DataReader`) or placed in an ADO.NET `DataSet` (via a `DataAdapter`) in order to be exposed to the user in an ad hoc manner, combined with data from multiple sources, or passed around between tiers. NET data providers are designed to be lightweight, to create a minimal layer between the data source and the .NET programmer's code, and to increase performance while not sacrificing any functionality.

Connection Object

To connect to a specific data source, you use a data connection object. To connect to Microsoft SQL Server 7.0 or later, you need to use the `SqlConnection` object of the SQL Server .NET data provider. You need to use the `OleDbConnection` object of the OLE DB .NET data provider to connect to an OLE DB data source, or the OLE DB provider for SQL Server (SQLOLEDB) to connect to versions of Microsoft SQL Server earlier than 7.0.

Connection String Format — OleDbConnection

For the OLE DB .NET data provider, the connection string format is the same as the connection string format used in ADO, with the following exceptions:

➤ The `Provider` keyword is required.

➤ The `URL`, `Remote Provider`, and `Remote Server` keywords are not supported.

Here is an example `OleDbConnection` connection string connecting to an Access database:

```
Provider=Microsoft.Jet.OLEDB.4.0;Data Source=
"C:\Program Files\Microsoft Expression\Web 2\WebDesigner\1033\FPNWIND.MDB";
```

Connection-String Format — SqlConnection

The SQL Server .NET data provider supports a connection-string format that is similar to the OLE DB (ADO) connection-string format. The only thing that you need to omit, obviously, is the provider name-value pair, as you know you are using the SQL Server .NET data provider. Here is an example of a `SqlConnection` connection string:

```
Data Source=(local);Initial Catalog=pubs;Integrated Security=SSPI;
```

Alternately, you can use a connection-string format that is more specific to SQL Server. This sample would connect to the same database as the previous one:

```
Server=(local);Database=pubs;Trusted Connection=true;
```

Command Object

After establishing a connection, you can execute commands and return results from a data source (such as SQL Server) using a Command object. A Command object can be created using the Command constructor, or by calling the CreateCommand method of the Connection object. When creating a Command object using the Command constructor, you need to specify a SQL statement to execute at the data source, and a Connection object. The Command object's SQL statement can be queried and modified using the CommandText property. The following code is an example of executing a SELECT command and returning a DataReader object:

```
' Build the SQL and Connection strings.
Dim sql As String = "SELECT * FROM authors"
Dim connectionString As String = "Database=pubs;"
 & "Server=(local)\sqlexpress;Trusted Connection=true;"
' Initialize the SqlCommand with the SQL
' and Connection strings.
Dim command As SqlCommand = New SqlCommand(sql,
    New SqlConnection(connectionString))
' Open the connection.
command.Connection.Open()
' Execute the query, return a SqlDataReader object.
' CommandBehavior.CloseConnection flags the
' DataReader to automatically close the DB connection
' when it is closed.
Dim dataReader As SqlDataReader = _
    command.ExecuteReader(CommandBehavior.CloseConnection)
```

The CommandText property of the Command object executes all SQL statements in addition to the standard SELECT, UPDATE, INSERT, and DELETE statements. For example, you could create tables, foreign keys, primary keys, and so on, by executing the applicable SQL from the Command object.

The Command object exposes several Execute methods to perform the intended action. When returning results as a stream of data, ExecuteReader is used to return a DataReader object. ExecuteScalar is used to return a singleton value ExecuteNonQuery is used to execute commands that do not return rows, which usually includes stored procedures that have output parameters and/or return values. (You will learn about stored procedures later in this chapter.) Finally, the ExecuteXmlReader returns an XmlReader, which can be used to read a block of XML returned from the database. (You will see how this is used in the XML chapter.)

When using a DataAdapter with a DataSet, Command objects are used to return and modify data at the data source through the DataAdapter object's SelectCommand, InsertCommand, UpdateCommand, and DeleteCommand properties.

 Note that the DataAdapter *object's* SelectCommand *property must be set before the* Fill *method is called.*

The InsertCommand, UpdateCommand, and DeleteCommand properties must be set before the Update method is called. You will take a closer look at this when you look at the DataAdapter object.

Using Stored Procedures with Command Objects

The motivation for using stored procedures is simple. Imagine you have the following code:

```
SELECT au_lname FROM authors WHERE au_id='172-32-1176'
```

If you pass that to SQL Server using `ExecuteReader` on `SqlCommand` (or any execute method, for that matter), SQL Server has to compile the code before it can run it, in much the same way that VB .NET applications have to be compiled before they can be executed. This compilation takes up SQL Server's time, so it is easy to deduce that if you can reduce the amount of compilation that SQL Server has to do, database performance should increase. (Compare the speed of execution of a compiled application against interpreted code.)

That's what stored procedures are all about: You create a procedure, store it in the database, and because the procedure is recognized and understood ahead of time, it can be compiled ahead of time and ready for use in your application.

One other benefit of using stored procedures in your code is that it is generally safer. When using SQL without stored procedures, there is always the temptation to build the SQL statement by concatenating strings. With this, there is the danger — particularly if some of those strings are user generated — that the resulting SQL is invalid or malicious; for example, if you had a text box where a user could type in search criteria, that you then concatenated into a query, using code such as:

```
Dim sql As String = "SELECT * FROM myTable WHERE field LIKE '" & query & "%'"
```

This looks innocent enough, but you could get into trouble very quickly if the user entered something like:

```
Bob;delete * from systables;
```

Using stored procedures prevent an attack like this from happening.

Stored procedures are very easy to use, but the code to access them is sometimes a little verbose. The next section demonstrates some code that can make accessing stored procedures a bit more straightforward, but to make things clearer, let's start by building a simple application that demonstrates how to create and call a stored procedure.

Creating a Stored Procedure

To create a stored procedure, you can either use the tools in Visual Studio .NET or you can use the tools in SQL Server's Enterprise Manager if you are using SQL Server 2000, or in SQL Server Management Studio if you are using SQL Server 2005/2008. (Technically, you can use a third-party tool or just create the stored procedure in a good, old-fashioned SQL script.)

This example builds a stored procedure that returns all of the columns for a given author ID. The SQL to do this looks like the following:

```
SELECT
    au_id, au_lname, au_fname, phone,
    address, city, state, zip, contract
FROM
    authors
WHERE
    au_id = whatever author ID you want
```

The "whatever author ID you want" part is important. When using stored procedures, you typically have to be able to provide parameters into the stored procedure and use them from within code. This is not a book about SQL Server, so this example focuses only on the principle involved. You can find many resources on the Web about building stored procedures (they have been around a very long time, and they are most definitely not a .NET-specific feature).

Variables in SQL Server are prefixed by the @ symbol, so if you have a variable called au id, then your SQL will look like this:

```
SELECT
    au_id, au_lname, au_fname, phone,
    address, city, state, zip, contract
FROM
    authors
WHERE
    au_id = @au_id
```

In Visual Studio, stored procedures can be accessed using the Server Explorer. Simply add a new data connection (or use an existing data connection), and then drill down into the `Stored Procedures` folder in the management tree. A number of stored procedures are already loaded. The `byroyalty` procedure is a stored procedure provided by the sample pubs database developers. Figure 10-2 illustrates the stored procedures of the pubs database in Visual Studio.

To create a new stored procedure, just right-click the `Stored Procedures` folder in the Server Explorer and select Add New Stored Procedure to invoke the editor window.

A stored procedure can be either a single SQL statement or a complex set of statements. T-SQL supports branches, loops, and other variable declarations, which can make for some pretty complex stored procedure code. However, your stored procedure is just a single line of SQL. You need to declare the parameter that you want to pass in (`@au_id`) and the name of the procedure: `usp_authors_Get_By_ID`. Here's code for the stored procedure:

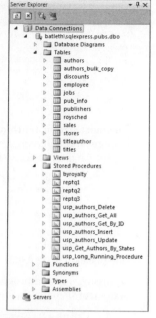

FIGURE 10-2

```
CREATE PROCEDURE usp_authors_Get_By_ID
    @au_id varchar(11)
AS
SELECT
    au_id, au_lname, au_fname, phone,
    address, city, state, zip, contract
FROM
    authors
WHERE
    au_id = @au_id
```

Click OK to save the stored procedure in the database. You are now able to access this stored procedure from code.

Calling the Stored Procedure

Calling the stored procedure is just a matter of creating a `SqlConnection` object to connect to the database, and a `SqlCommand` object to run the stored procedure.

Now you have to decide what you want to return by calling the stored procedure. In this case, you return an instance of the `SqlDataReader` object. The `TestForm.vb` file contains a method called `GetAuthorSqlReader` that takes an author ID and returns an instance of a `SqlDataReader`. Here is the code for the method:

```
Private Function GetAuthorSqlReader(ByVal authorId As String) As SqlDataReader
    ' Build a SqlCommand
    Dim command As SqlCommand = New SqlCommand("usp_authors_Get_By_ID",
        GetPubsConnection())
    ' Tell the command we are calling a stored procedure
    command.CommandType = CommandType.StoredProcedure
    ' Add the @au_id parameter information to the command
    command.Parameters.Add(New SqlParameter("@au_id", authorId))
    ' The reader requires an open connection
    command.Connection.Open()
    ' Execute the sql and return the reader
    Return command.ExecuteReader(CommandBehavior.CloseConnection)
End Function
```

Code snippet from AdoNetFeaturesTest project

Notice that in the `SqlCommand`'s constructor call, you have factored out creating a connection to the pubs database into a separate helper method. This is used later in other code examples in your form.

Here is the code for the `GetPubsConnection` helper method:

```
Private Function GetPubsConnection() As SqlConnection
    ' Build a SqlConnection based on the config value.
    Return New
        SqlConnection(ConfigurationSettings. _
            ConnectionStrings("db").ConnectionString)
End Function
```

Code snippet from AdoNetFeaturesTest project

The most significant thing this code does is grab a connection string to the database from the application's configuration file, `app.config`. Here is what the entry in the `app.config` file looks like (update to match the location of pubs on your computer):

```
<connectionStrings>
    <add name="db" value="server=(local)\sqlexpress;
        database=pubs;trusted_connection=true;" />
</connectionStrings>
```

Although the helper method doesn't do much, it is nice to place this code in a separate method. This way, if the code to get a connection to the databases needs to be changed, the code only has to be changed in one place.

Accessing a stored procedure is more verbose (but not more difficult) than accessing a normal SQL statement through the methods discussed thus far. The approach is as follows:

1. Create a `SqlCommand` object.

2. Configure it to access a stored procedure by setting the `CommandType` property.

3. Add parameters that exactly match those in the stored procedure itself.

4. Execute the stored procedure using one of the `SqlCommand` object's `ExecuteX` methods.

There is no real need to build an impressive UI for this application, as we're about to add a button named `getAuthorByIdButton` that calls the `GetAuthorSqlRecord` helper method and displays the selected author's name. Here is the button's `Click` event handler:

```
Private Sub _getAuthorByIdButton_Click(ByVal sender As System.Object, _
    ByVal e As System.EventArgs) Handles _getAuthorByIdButton.Click
    Dim reader As SqlDataReader = Me. GetAuthorSqlReader ("409-56-7008")
    If reader.Read()
        MessageBox.Show(reader("au_fname").ToString() & "  "
            & reader("au_lname").ToString())
    End If
    reader.Close()
End Sub
```

Code snippet from AdoNetFeaturesTest project

This has hard-coded an author ID of 409-56-7008. Run the code now and you should see the result shown in Figure 10-3.

DataReader Object

You can use the `DataReader` to retrieve a read-only, forward-only stream of data from the database. Using the `DataReader` can increase application performance and reduce system overhead because only one buffered row at a time is ever in memory. With the `DataReader` object, you are getting as close to the raw data as possible in ADO.NET; you do not have to go through the overhead of populating a `DataSet` object, which sometimes may be expensive if the `DataSet` contains a lot of data. The disadvantage of using a `DataReader` object is that it requires an open database connection and increases network activity.

FIGURE 10-3

After creating an instance of the Command object, a DataReader is created by calling the ExecuteReader method of the Command object. Here is an example of creating a DataReader and iterating through it to print out its values to the screen:

```vb
Private Sub TraverseDataReader()
    ' Build the SQL and Connection strings.
    Dim sql As String = "SELECT * FROM authors"
    Dim connectionString As String = "database=pubs;" _
        & "server=(local)\sqlexpress;trusted_connection=true;"
    ' Initialize the SqlCommand with the SQL query and connection strings.
    Dim command As SqlCommand = New SqlCommand(sql, _
        New SqlConnection(connectionString))
    ' Open the connection.
    command.Connection.Open()
    ' Execute the query, return a SqlDataReader object.
    ' CommandBehavior.CloseConnection flags the
    ' DataReader to automatically close the DB connection
    ' when it is closed.
    Dim reader As SqlDataReader = _
        command.ExecuteReader(CommandBehavior.CloseConnection)
    ' Loop through the records and print the values.
    Do While reader.Read
        Console.WriteLine(reader.GetString(1) & " " & reader.GetString(2))
    Loop
    ' Close the DataReader (and its connection).
    reader.Close()
End Sub
```

Code snippet from AdoNetFeaturesTest project

This code snippet uses the SqlCommand object to execute the query via the ExecuteReader method. This method returns a populated SqlDataReader object, which you loop through and then print out the author names. The main difference between this code and looping through the rows of a DataTable is that you have to stay connected while you loop through the data in the DataReader object; this is because the DataReader reads in only a small stream of data at a time to conserve memory space.

> *At this point, an obvious design question is whether to use the DataReader or the DataSet. The answer depends upon performance and how you will use the data. If you want high performance and you only need to access the data you are retrieving once, then the DataReader is the way to go. If you need access to the same data multiple times, or if you need to model a complex relationship in memory, or if you need to use the data when not connected to the database, then the DataSet is the way to go. As always, test each option thoroughly before deciding which one is the best.*

The Read method of the DataReader object is used to obtain a row from the results of the query. Each column of the returned row may be accessed by passing the name or ordinal reference of the column to the DataReader; or, for best performance, the DataReader provides a series of methods that enable you to access column values in their native data types (GetDateTime, GetDouble, GetGuid, GetInt32, and so on). Using the typed accessor methods when the underlying data type is known reduces the amount of type conversion required (converting from type Object) when retrieving the column value.

The DataReader provides a nonbuffered stream of data that enables procedural logic to efficiently process results from a data source sequentially. The DataReader is a good choice when retrieving large amounts of data; only one row of data is loaded in memory at a time. You should always call the Close method when you are through using the DataReader object, as well as close the DataReader object's database connection; otherwise, the connection will be open until the garbage collector gets around to collecting the object. Alternately, use the Using statement to automatically close the database connection at the end of the Using clause.

Note how you use the `CommandBehavior.CloseConnection` enumeration value on the `SqlDataReader` `.ExecuteReader` method. This tells the `SqlCommand` object to automatically close the database connection when the `SqlDataReader.Close` method is called.

> *If your command contains output parameters or return values, they will not be available until the* `DataReader` *is closed.*

Executing Commands Asynchronously

In ADO.NET, additional support enables `Command` objects to execute their commands asynchronously, which can result in a huge perceived performance gain in many applications, especially in Windows Forms applications. This can come in very handy, especially if you ever have to execute a long-running SQL statement. This section examines how this functionality enables you to add asynchronous processing to enhance the responsiveness of an application.

The `SqlCommand` object provides three different asynchronous call options: `BeginExecuteReader`, `BeginExecuteNonQuery`, and `BeginExecuteXmlReader`. Each of these methods has a corresponding "end" method — that is, `EndExecuteReader`, `EndExecuteNonQuery`, and `EndExecuteXmlReader`. Now that you are familiar with the `DataReader` object, let's look at an example using the `BeginExecuteReader` method to execute a long-running query.

In the AdoNetFeaturesTest project, I have added a button and an associated `Click` event handler to the form that will initiate the asynchronous call to get a `DataReader` instance:

```
Private Sub _testAsyncCallButton_Click(ByVal sender As System.Object,
    ByVal e As System.EventArgs) Handles _testAsyncCallButton.Click

    ' Build a connection for the async call to the database
    Dim connection As SqlConnection = GetPubsConnection()
    connection.ConnectionString &= "Asynchronous Processing=true;"

    ' Build a command to call the stored procedure
    Dim command As New SqlCommand("usp_Long_Running_Procedure", connection)

    ' Set the command type to stored procedure
    command.CommandType = CommandType.StoredProcedure

    ' The reader requires an open connection
    connection.Open()

    ' Make the asynchronous call to the database
    command.BeginExecuteReader(AddressOf Me.AsyncCallback,
    command, CommandBehavior.CloseConnection)
End Sub
```

Code snippet from AdoNetFeaturesTest project

The first thing you do is reuse your helper method `GetPubsConnection` to get a connection to the pubs database. Next, and this is very important, you append the statement `"Asynchronous Processing=true"` to your `Connection` object's connection string. This must be set in order for ADO.NET to make asynchronous calls to SQL Server.

After getting the connection set, you then build a `SqlCommand` object and initialize it to be able to execute the `usp_Long_Running_Procedure` stored procedure. This procedure simulates a long-running query by using the SQL Server `WAITFOR DELAY` statement to create a 20-second delay before it executes the `usp_Authors_Get_All` stored procedure. As you can probably guess, the `usp_authors_Get_All` stored procedure simply selects all of the authors from the authors table. The delay is added simply to demonstrate that while this stored procedure is executing, you can perform other tasks in your Windows Forms application. Here is the SQL code for the `usp_Long_Running_Procedure` stored procedure:

```
CREATE PROCEDURE usp_Long_Running_Procedure
AS
SET NOCOUNT ON
WAITFOR DELAY '00:00:20'
EXEC usp_authors_Get_All
```

Available for download on Wrox.com

Code snippet from Examples.sql

The last line of code in the Button's `Click` event handler is the call to `BeginExecuteReader`. In this call, the first thing you are passing in is a delegate method (`Me.AsyncCallback`) for the `System.AsyncCallback` delegate type. This is how the .NET Framework calls you back once the method is finished running asynchronously. You then pass in your initialized `SqlCommand` object so that it can be executed, as well as the `CommandBehavior` value for the `DataReader`. In this case, you pass in the `CommandBehavior.CloseConnection` value so that the connection to the database will be closed once the `DataReader` has been closed. You will look at the `DataReader` in more detail in the next section.

Now that you have initiated the asynchronous call, and have defined a callback for your asynchronous call, let's look at the actual method that is being called back, the `AsyncCallback` method:

```
Private Sub AsyncCallback(ByVal ar As IAsyncResult)
    ' Get the command that was passed from the AsyncState of the IAsyncResult.
    Dim command As SqlCommand = CType(ar.AsyncState, SqlCommand)
    ' Get the reader from the IAsyncResult.
    Dim reader As SqlDataReader = command.EndExecuteReader(ar)
    ' Get a table from the reader.
    Dim table As DataTable = Me.GetTableFromReader(reader, "Authors")
    ' Call the BindGrid method on the Windows main thread,
    ' passing in the table.
    Me.Invoke(New BindGridDelegate(AddressOf Me.BindGrid),
        New Object() {table})
End Sub
```

Available for download on Wrox.com

Code snippet from AdoNetFeaturesTest project

The first line of the code is simply retrieving the `SqlCommand` object from the `AsyncState` property of the `IAsyncResult` that was passed in. Remember that when you called `BeginExecuteReader` earlier, you passed in your `SqlCommand` object. You need it so that you can call the `EndExecuteReader` method on the next line. This method gives you your `SqlDataReader`. On the next line, you then transform the `SqlDataReader` into a `DataTable` (covered later when the `DataSet` is discussed).

The last line of this method is probably the most important. If you tried to just take your `DataTable` and bind it to the grid, it would not work, because right now you are executing on a thread other than the main Windows thread. The helper method named `BindGrid` can do the data binding, but it must be called only in the context of the Windows main thread. To bring the data back to the main Windows thread, it must be marshaled via the `Invoke` method of the `Form` object. Invoke takes two arguments: the delegate of the method you want to call and (optionally) any parameters for that method. In this case, you define a delegate for the `BindGrid` method, called `BindGridDelegate`. Here is the delegate declaration:

```
Private Delegate Sub BindGridDelegate(ByVal table As DataTable)
```

Notice how the signature is exactly the same as the `BindGrid` method shown here:

```
Private Sub BindGrid(ByVal table As DataTable)
    ' Clear the grid.
    Me._authorsGridView.DataSource = Nothing
    ' Bind the grid to the DataTable.
    Me._authorsGridView.DataSource = table
End Sub
```

Here is another look at the call to the form's `Invoke` method:

```
Me.Invoke(New BindGridDelegate(AddressOf Me.BindGrid), _
    New Object() {table})
```

You pass in a new instance of the `BindGridDelegate` delegate and initialize it with a pointer to the `BindGrid` method. As a result, the .NET worker thread that was executing your query can now safely join up with the main Windows thread.

DataAdapter Objects

Each .NET data provider included with the .NET Framework has a `DataAdapter` object. A `DataAdapter` is used to retrieve data from a data source and populate `DataTable` objects and constraints within a `DataSet`. The `DataAdapter` also resolves changes made to the `DataSet` back to the data source. The `DataAdapter` uses the `Connection` object of the .NET data provider to connect to a data source, and `Command` objects to retrieve data from, and resolve changes to, the data source from a `DataSet` object.

This differs from the `DataReader`, in that the `DataReader` uses the `Connection` object to access the data directly, without having to use a `DataAdapter`. The `DataAdapter` essentially decouples the `DataSet` object from the actual source of the data, whereas the `DataReader` is tightly bound to the data in a read-only fashion.

The `SelectCommand` property of the `DataAdapter` is a `Command` object that retrieves data from the data source. A nice, convenient way to set the `DataAdapter`'s `SelectCommand` property is to pass in a `Command` object in the `DataAdapter`'s constructor. The `InsertCommand`, `UpdateCommand`, and `DeleteCommand` properties of the `DataAdapter` are `Command` objects that manage updates to the data in the data source according to modifications made to the data in the `DataSet`. The `Fill` method of the `DataAdapter` is used to populate a `DataSet` with the results of the `SelectCommand` of the `DataAdapter`. It also adds or refreshes rows in the `DataSet` to match those in the data source. The following example code demonstrates how to fill a `DataSet` object with information from the authors table in the pubs database:

Available for download on Wrox.com

```
Private Sub TraverseDataSet()
    ' Build the SQL and Connection strings.
    Dim sql As String = "SELECT * FROM authors"
    Dim connectionString As String = "database=pubs;" _
        & "server=(local)\sqlexpress;trusted_connection=true;"
    ' Initialize the SqlDataAdapter with the SQL
    ' and Connection strings, and then use the
    ' SqlDataAdapter to fill the DataSet with data.
    Dim adapter As New SqlDataAdapter(sql, connectionString)
    Dim authors As New DataSet
    adapter.Fill(authors)

    ' Iterate through the DataSet's table.
    For Each row As DataRow In authors.Tables(0).Rows
        Console.WriteLine(row("au_fname").ToString _
            & " " & row("au_lname").ToString)
    Next

    ' Print the DataSet's XML.
    Console.WriteLine(authors.GetXml())
    Console.ReadLine()
End Sub
```

Code snippet from AdoNetFeaturesTest project

Note how you use the constructor of the `SqlDataAdapter` to pass in and set the `SelectCommand`, as well as pass in the connection string in lieu of a `SqlCommand` object that already has an initialized `Connection` property. You then just call the `SqlDataAdapter` object's `Fill` method and pass in an initialized `DataSet` object. If the `DataSet` object is not initialized, then the `Fill` method raises an exception (`System. ArgumentNullException`).

Ever since ADO.NET 2.0, a significant performance improvement was made in the way that the
`DataAdapter` updates the database. In ADO.NET 1.x, the `DataAdapter`'s `Update` method would loop
through each row of every `DataTable` object in the `DataSet` and subsequently make a trip to the database
for each row being updated. In ADO.NET 2.0, batch update support was added to the `DataAdapter`.
This means that when the `Update` method is called, the `DataAdapter` batches all of the updates from the
`DataSet` in one trip to the database.

Now let's take a look at a more advanced example. Here, you use a `DataAdapter` to insert, update, and
delete data from a `DataTable` back to the pubs database:

Available for
download on
Wrox.com

```
Private Sub _batchUpdateButton_Click(ByVal sender As System.Object,
        ByVal e As System.EventArgs) Handles _batchUpdateButton.Click
    ' Build insert, update, and delete commands.
    ' Build the parameter values.
    Dim insertUpdateParams() As String = {"@au_id", "@au_lname",
        "@au_fname",
        "@phone", "@address", "@city", "@state", "@zip", "@contract"}
```

Code snippet from AdoNetFeaturesTest project

The preceding code begins by initializing a string array of parameter names to pass into the
`BuildSqlCommand` helper method:

```
' Insert command.
Dim insertCommand As SqlCommand =
    BuildSqlCommand("usp_authors_Insert",
    insertUpdateParams)
```

Next, you pass the name of the stored procedure to execute and the parameters for the stored procedure to
the `BuildSqlCommand` helper method. This method returns an initialized instance of the `SqlCommand` class.
Here is the `BuildSqlCommand` helper method:

Available for
download on
Wrox.com

```
Private Function BuildSqlCommand(ByVal storedProcedureName As String,
        ByVal parameterNames() As String) As SqlCommand
    ' Build a SqlCommand.
    Dim command As New SqlCommand(storedProcedureName, GetPubsConnection())
    ' Set the command type to stored procedure.
    command.CommandType = CommandType.StoredProcedure
    ' Build the parameters for the command.
    ' See if any parameter names were passed in.
    If Not parameterNames Is Nothing Then
        ' Iterate through the parameters.
        Dim parameter As SqlParameter = Nothing
        For Each parameterName As String In parameterNames
            ' Create a new SqlParameter.
            parameter = New SqlParameter()
            parameter.ParameterName = parameterName
            ' Map the parameter to a column name in the DataTable/DataSet.
            parameter.SourceColumn = parameterName.Substring(1)
            ' Add the parameter to the command.
            command.Parameters.Add(parameter)
        Next
    End If
    Return command
End Function
```

Code snippet from AdoNetFeaturesTest project

This method first initializes a `SqlCommand` class and passes in the name of a stored procedure; it then
uses the `GetPubsConnection` helper method to pass in a `SqlConnection` object to the `SqlCommand`. The
next step is to set the command type of the `SqlCommand` to a stored procedure. This is important because
ADO.NET uses this to optimize how the stored procedure is called on the database server. You then check
whether any parameter names have been passed (via the `parameterNames` string array); if so, you iterate

through them. While iterating through the parameter names, you build up SqlParameter objects and add them to the SqlCommand's collection of parameters.

The most important step in building up the SqlParameter object is setting its SourceColumn property. This is what the DataAdapter later uses to map the parameter name to the name of the column in the DataTable when its Update method is called. An example of such a mapping is associating the @au_id parameter name with the au_id column name. As shown in the code, the mapping assumes that the stored procedure parameters all have exactly the same names as the columns, except for the mandatory @ character in front of the parameter. That's why when assigning the SqlParameter's SourceColumn property value, you use the Substring method to strip off the @ character to ensure that it maps correctly.

You then call the BuildSqlCommand method two more times to build your update and delete SqlCommand objects:

Available for
download on
Wrox.com

```
' Update command.
Dim updateCommand As SqlCommand =
    BuildSqlCommand("usp_authors_Update",
    insertUpdateParams)
' Delete command.
Dim deleteCommand As SqlCommand = _
    BuildSqlCommand("usp_authors_Delete",
    New String() {"@au_id"})
```

Code snippet from AdoNetFeaturesTest project

Now that the SqlCommand objects have been created, the next step is to create a SqlDataAdapter object. Once the SqlDataAdapter is created, you set its InsertCommand, UpdateCommand, and DeleteCommand properties with the respective SqlCommand objects that you just built:

Available for
download on
Wrox.com

```
' Create an adapter.
Dim adapter As New SqlDataAdapter()
' Associate the commands with the adapter.
adapter.InsertCommand = insertCommand
adapter.UpdateCommand = updateCommand
adapter.DeleteCommand = deleteCommand
```

Code snippet from AdoNetFeaturesTest project

The next step is to get a DataTable instance of the authors table from the pubs database. You do this by calling the GetAuthorsSqlReader helper method to first get a DataReader and then the GetTableFromReader helper method to load a DataTable from a DataReader:

Available for
download on
Wrox.com

```
' Get the authors reader.
Dim reader As SqlDataReader = GetAuthorsSqlReader()
' Load a DataTable from the reader.
Dim table As DataTable = GetTableFromReader(reader, "Authors")
```

Code snippet from AdoNetFeaturesTest project

Once you have your DataTable filled with data, you begin modifying it so you can test the new batch update capability of the DataAdapter. The first change to make is an insert in the DataTable. In order to add a row, you first call the DataTable's NewRow method to give you a DataRow initialized with the same columns as your DataTable:

```
' Add a new author to the DataTable.
Dim row As DataRow = table.NewRow
```

Once that is done, you can set the column values of the DataRow:

Available for
download on
Wrox.com

```
row("au_id") = "335-22-0707"
row("au_fname") = "Foo"
row("au_lname") = "deBar"
row("phone") = "800-555-1212"
row("contract") = 0
```

Code snippet from AdoNetFeaturesTest project

Then you call the Add method of the DataTable's DataRowCollection property and pass in the newly populated DataRow object:

```
table.Rows.Add(row)
```

Now that there is a new row in the DataTable, the next test is to update one of its rows:

```
' Change an author in the DataTable.
table.Rows(0)("au_fname") = "Updated Name!"
```

Finally, you delete a row from the DataTable. In this case, it is the second-to-last row in the DataTable:

```
' Delete the second to last author from the table
table.Rows(table.Rows.Count - 2).Delete()
```

Now that you have performed an insert, update, and delete action on your DataTable, it is time to send the changes back to the database. You do this by calling the DataAdapter's Update method and passing in either a DataSet or a DataTable. Note that you are calling the GetChanges method of the DataTable; this is important, because you only want to send the changes to the DataAdapter:

```
' Send only the changes in the DataTable to the database for updating.
adapter.Update(table.GetChanges())
```

To prove that the update worked, you get back a new DataTable from the server using the same technique as before, and then bind it to the grid with your helper method to view the changes that were made:

```
' Get the new changes back from the server to show that the update worked.
    reader = GetAuthorsSqlReader()
    table = GetTableFromReader(reader, "Authors")
    ' Bind the grid to the new table data.
    BindGrid(table)
End Sub
```

Code snippet from AdoNetFeaturesTest project

SQL Server .NET Data Provider

The SQL Server .NET data provider uses Tabular Data Stream (TDS) to communicate with the SQL Server. This offers a great performance increase, as TDS is SQL Server's native communication protocol. As an example of how much of an increase you can expect, when I ran some simple tests accessing the authors table of the pubs database, the SQL Server .NET data provider performed about 70 percent faster than the OLE DB .NET data provider.

> *This is very important, as going through the OLE DB or ODBC layers means that the CLR has to marshal (convert) all of the COM data types to .NET CLR data types each time data is accessed from a data source. When using the SQL Server .NET data provider, everything runs within the .NET CLR, and the TDS protocol is faster than the other network protocols previously used for SQL Server.*

To use this provider, you need to include the System.Data.SqlClient namespace in your application. Note that it works only for SQL Server 7.0 and later. I highly recommend using the SQL Server .NET data provider anytime you are connecting to a SQL Server 7.0 and later database server. The SQL Server .NET data provider requires the installation of MDAC 2.6 or later.

OLE DB .NET Data Provider

The OLE DB .NET data provider uses native OLE DB through COM interop to enable data access. The OLE DB .NET data provider supports both manual and automatic transactions. For automatic transactions, the OLE DB .NET data provider automatically enlists in a transaction and obtains transaction details from

Windows 2000 Component Services. The OLE DB .NET data provider does not support OLE DB 2.5 interfaces. OLE DB providers that require support for OLE DB 2.5 interfaces will not function properly with the OLE DB .NET data provider. This includes the Microsoft OLE DB provider for Exchange and the Microsoft OLE DB provider for Internet Publishing. The OLE DB .NET data provider requires the installation of MDAC 2.6 or later. To use this provider, you need to include the System.Data.OleDb namespace in your application.

THE DATASET COMPONENT

The DataSet is central to supporting disconnected, distributed data scenarios with ADO.NET. The DataSet is a memory-resident representation of data that provides a consistent relational programming model regardless of the data source. The DataSet represents a complete set of data, including related tables, constraints, and relationships among the tables; basically, it's like having a small relational database residing in memory.

 Because the DataSet *contains a lot of metadata, you need to be careful about how much data you try to stuff into it, as it consumes memory.*

The methods and objects in a DataSet are consistent with those in the relational database model. The DataSet can also persist and reload its contents as XML, and its schema as XSD. It is completely disconnected from any database connections, so it is totally up to you to fill it with whatever data you need in memory.

Ever since ADO.NET 2.0, several new features have been added to the DataSet and the DataTable classes, as well as enhancements to existing features. The features covered in this section are as follows:

➤ The binary serialization format option

➤ Additions to make the DataTable more of a standalone object

➤ The capability to expose DataSet and DataTable data as a stream (DataReader), and to load stream data into a DataSet or DataTable

DataTableCollection

An ADO.NET DataSet contains a collection of zero or more tables represented by DataTable objects. The DataTableCollection contains all of the DataTable objects in a DataSet.

A DataTable is defined in the System.Data namespace and represents a single table of memory-resident data. It contains a collection of columns represented by the DataColumnCollection, which defines the schema and rows of the table. It also contains a collection of rows represented by the DataRowCollection, which contains the data in the table. Along with the current state, a DataRow retains its original state and tracks changes that occur to the data.

DataRelationCollection

A DataSet contains relationships in its DataRelationCollection object. A relationship (represented by the DataRelation object) associates rows in one DataTable with rows in another DataTable. The relationships in the DataSet can have constraints, which are represented by UniqueConstraint and ForeignKeyConstraint objects. It is analogous to a JOIN path that might exist between the primary and foreign key columns in a relational database. A DataRelation identifies matching columns in two tables of a DataSet.

Relationships enable you to see what links information within one table to another. The essential elements of a DataRelation are the name of the relationship, the two tables being related, and the related columns in each table. Relationships can be built with more than one column per table, with an array of `DataColumn` objects for the key columns. When a relationship is added to the `DataRelationCollection`, it may optionally add `ForeignKeyConstraints` that disallow any changes that would invalidate the relationship.

ExtendedProperties

The `DataSet` (as well as the `DataTable` and `DataColumn`) has an `ExtendedProperties` property. `ExtendedProperties` is a `PropertyCollection` in which a user can place customized information, such as the `SELECT` statement that is used to generate the result set, or a date/time stamp indicating when the data was generated. Because the `ExtendedProperties` contains customized information, this is a good place to store extra user-defined data about the `DataSet` (or `DataTable` or `DataColumn`), such as a time when the data should be refreshed. The `ExtendedProperties` collection is persisted with the schema information for the `DataSet` (as well as `DataTable` and `DataColumn`). The following code example adds an expiration property to a `DataSet`:

Available for download on Wrox.com

```
Private Sub _extendedDataSetButton_Click(ByVal sender As System.Object, _
        ByVal e As System.EventArgs) Handles _extendedDataSetButton.Click
    ' Build the SQL and Connection strings.
    Dim cmdString As String = "SELECT * FROM authors"
    Dim connection As SqlConnection = GetPubsConnection()
    ' Initialize the SqlDataAdapter with the SQL
    ' and Connection strings, and then use the
    ' SqlDataAdapter to fill the DataSet with data.
    Dim adapter As SqlDataAdapter = _
        New SqlDataAdapter(cmdString, connection)
    Dim authors As New DataSet
    adapter.Fill(authors)
    ' Add an extended property called "expiration."
    ' Set its value to the current date/time + 1 hour.
    authors.ExtendedProperties.Add("expiration", _
        DateAdd(DateInterval.Hour, 1, Now))
    MessageBox.Show(authors.ExtendedProperties("expiration").ToString, _
                    "Authors Expiration")

End Sub
```

Code snippet from AdoNetFeaturesTest project

This code begins by filling a `DataSet` with the authors table from the pubs database. It then adds a new extended property, called `expiration`, and sets its value to the current date and time plus one hour. You then simply read it back. As you can see, it is very easy to add extended properties to `DataSet` objects. The same pattern also applies to `DataTable` and `DataColumn` objects.

Creating and Using DataSet Objects

The ADO.NET `DataSet` is a memory-resident representation of the data that provides a consistent relational programming model, regardless of the source of the data it contains. A `DataSet` represents a complete set of data, including the tables that contain, order, and constrain the data, as well as the relationships between the tables. The advantage to using a `DataSet` is that the data it contains can come from multiple sources, and it is fairly easy to get the data from multiple sources into the `DataSet`. In addition, you can define your own constraints between the `DataTables` in a `DataSet`.

There are several methods for working with a `DataSet`, which can be applied independently or in combination:

➤ Programmatically create `DataTables`, `DataRelations`, and constraints within the `DataSet` and populate them with data.

➤ Populate the `DataSet` or a `DataTable` from an existing RDBMS using a `DataAdapter`.

➤ Load and persist a `DataSet` or `DataTable` using XML.

➤ Load a `DataSet` from an XSD schema file.

➤ Load a `DataSet` or a `DataTable` from a `DataReader`.

Here is a typical usage scenario for a `DataSet` object:

1. A client makes a request to a Web service.

2. Based on this request, the Web service populates a `DataSet` from a database using a `DataAdapter` and returns the `DataSet` to the client.

3. The client then views the data and makes modifications.

4. When finished viewing and modifying the data, the client passes the modified `DataSet` back to the Web service, which again uses a `DataAdapter` to reconcile the changes in the returned `DataSet` with the original data in the database.

5. The Web service may then return a `DataSet` that reflects the current values in the database.

6. Optionally, the client can then use the `DataSet` class's `Merge` method to merge the returned `DataSet` with the client's existing copy of the `DataSet`; the `Merge` method will accept successful changes and mark with an error any changes that failed.

The design of the ADO.NET `DataSet` makes this scenario fairly easy to implement. Because the `DataSet` is stateless, it can be safely passed between the server and the client without tying up server resources such as database connections. Although the `DataSet` is transmitted as XML, Web services and ADO.NET automatically transform the XML representation of the data to and from a `DataSet`, creating a rich, yet simplified, programming model.

In addition, because the `DataSet` is transmitted as an XML stream, non-ADO.NET clients can consume the same Web service consumed by ADO.NET clients. Similarly, ADO.NET clients can interact easily with non-ADO.NET Web services by sending any client `DataSet` to a Web service as XML and by consuming any XML returned as a `DataSet` from the Web service. However, note the size of the data; if your `DataSet` contains a large number of rows, it will eat up a lot of bandwidth.

Programmatically Creating DataSet Objects

You can programmatically create a `DataSet` object to use as a data structure in your programs. This could be quite useful if you have complex data that needs to be passed around to another object's method. For example, when creating a new customer, instead of passing 20 arguments about the new customer to a method, you could just pass the programmatically created `DataSet` object with all of the customer information to the object's method. In addition, this helps maintain your software as instead of having to maintain all those functions dealing with the multiple parameters, they simply need to receive a dataset. If the structure of the data changes, your functions do not need to change.

Here is the code for building an ADO.NET `DataSet` object that is comprised of related tables:

Available for
download on
Wrox.com

```
Private Sub _buildDataSetButton_Click(ByVal sender As System.Object,
              ByVal e As System.EventArgs) _
              Handles _buildDataSetButton.Click
    Dim customerOrders As New Data.DataSet("CustomerOrders")
    Dim customers As Data.DataTable = customerOrders.Tables.Add("Customers")
    Dim orders As Data.DataTable = customerOrders.Tables.Add("Orders")
    Dim row As Data.DataRow
    With customers
        .Columns.Add("CustomerID", Type.GetType("System.Int32"))
        .Columns.Add("FirstName", Type.GetType("System.String"))
        .Columns.Add("LastName", Type.GetType("System.String"))
        .Columns.Add("Phone", Type.GetType("System.String"))
        .Columns.Add("Email", Type.GetType("System.String"))
    End With
    With orders
```

```
                .Columns.Add("CustomerID", Type.GetType("System.Int32"))
                .Columns.Add("OrderID", Type.GetType("System.Int32"))
                .Columns.Add("OrderAmount", Type.GetType("System.Double"))
                .Columns.Add("OrderDate", Type.GetType("System.DateTime"))
            End With
            customerOrders.Relations.Add("Customers_Orders",
            customerOrders.Tables("Customers").Columns("CustomerID"),
            customerOrders.Tables("Orders").Columns("CustomerID"))
            row = customers.NewRow()
            row("CustomerID") = 1
            row("FirstName") = "Foo"
            row("LastName") = "deBar"
            row("Phone") = "555-1212"
            row("Email") = "foo@debar.com"
            customers.Rows.Add(row)
            row = orders.NewRow()
            row("CustomerID") = 1
            row("OrderID") = 22
            row("OrderAmount") = 0
            row("OrderDate") = #11/10/1997#
            orders.Rows.Add(row)
            MessageBox.Show(customerOrders.GetXml, "Customer Orders")
        End Sub
```

Code snippet from AdoNetFeaturesTest project

Here is what the resulting XML of the `DataSet` looks like:

```
<CustomerOrders>
  <Customers>
    <CustomerID>1</CustomerID>
    <FirstName>Foo</FirstName>
    <LastName>deBar</LastName>
    <Phone>555-1212</Phone>
    <Email>foo@debar.com</Email>
  </Customers>
  <Orders>
    <CustomerID>1</CustomerID>
    <OrderID>22</OrderID>
    <OrderAmount>0</OrderAmount>
    <OrderDate>1997-11-10T00:00:00.0000</OrderDate>
  </Orders>
</CustomerOrders>
```

You begin by first defining a `DataSet` object named `CustomerOrders`. You then create two tables: one for customers (customers) and one for orders (orders). Then you define the columns of the tables. Note that you call the `Add` method of the `DataSet`'s `Tables` collection. You then define the columns of each table and create a relation in the `DataSet` between the customers table and the orders table on the CustomerID column. Finally, you create instances of `DataRows` for the tables, add the data, and then append the rows to the `Rows` collection of the `DataTable` objects.

> *If you create a `DataSet` object with no name, it is given the default name of `NewDataSet`.*

ADO.NET DataTable Objects

A `DataSet` is made up of a collection of tables, relationships, and constraints. In ADO.NET, `DataTable` objects are used to represent the tables in a `DataSet`. A `DataTable` represents one table of in-memory relational data. The data is local to the .NET application in which it resides, but it can be populated from a data source such as SQL Server using a `DataAdapter`.

The `DataTable` class is a member of the `System.Data` namespace within the .NET Framework Class Library. You can create and use a `DataTable` independently or as a member of a `DataSet`, and `DataTable` objects can be used by other .NET Framework objects, including the `DataView`. You access the collection of tables in a `DataSet` through the `DataSet` object's `Tables` property.

The schema, or structure, of a table is represented by columns and constraints. You define the schema of a `DataTable` using `DataColumn` objects as well as `ForeignKeyConstraint` and `UniqueConstraint` objects. The columns in a table can map to columns in a data source, contain calculated values from expressions, automatically increment their values, or contain primary key values.

If you populate a `DataTable` from a database, it inherits the constraints from the database, so you don't have to do all of that work manually. A `DataTable` must also have rows in which to contain and order the data. The `DataRow` class represents the actual data contained in the table. You use the `DataRow` and its properties and methods to retrieve, evaluate, and manipulate the data in a table. As you access and change the data within a row, the `DataRow` object maintains both its current and original state.

You can create parent-child relationships between tables within a database, such as SQL Server, using one or more related columns in the tables. You create a relationship between `DataTable` objects using a `DataRelation`, which can then be used to return a row's related child or parent rows.

Advanced ADO.NET Features of the DataSet and DataTable Objects

One of the main complaints developers had about ADO.NET 1.x was related to the performance of the `DataSet` and its `DataTable` children — in particular, when they contained a large amount of data. The performance hit comes in two different ways. The first way is the time it takes to actually load a `DataSet` with a lot of data. As the number of rows in a `DataTable` increases, the time to load a new row increases almost proportionally to the number of rows. The second way is when the large `DataSet` is serialized and remoted. A key feature of the `DataSet` is the fact that it automatically knows how to serialize itself, especially when you want to pass it between application tiers. Unfortunately, the serialization is quite verbose and takes up a lot of memory and network bandwidth. Both of these performance problems have been addressed since ADO.NET 2.0.

Indexing

The first improvement made since ADO.NET 2.0 to the `DataSet` family was a complete rewrite of the indexing engine for the `DataTable`, which now scales much better for large `DataSets`. The addition of the new indexing engine results in faster basic inserts, updates, and deletes, which also means faster `Fill` and `Merge` operations. Just as in relational database design, if you are dealing with large `DataSets`, then it pays big dividends if you first add unique keys and foreign keys to your `DataTable`. Even better, you don't have to change any of your code at all to take advantage of this new feature.

Serialization

The second improvement made to the `DataSet` family was adding new options to the way the `DataSet` and `DataTable` are serialized. The main complaint about retrieving `DataSet` objects from Web services and remoting calls was that they were way too verbose and took up too much network bandwidth. In ADO.NET 1.x, the `DataSet` serializes as XML, even when using the binary formatter. Using ADO.NET, you can also specify true binary serialization by setting the newly added `RemotingFormat` property to `SerializationFormat.Binary`, rather than (the default) `SerializationFormat.XML`. In the `AdoNetFeaturesTest` project of the Examples solution, I have added a Button (`serializationButton`) to the form and its associated `Click` event handler that demonstrates how to serialize a `DataTable` in binary format:

```vb
Private Sub _serializationButton_Click(ByVal sender As System.Object, _
    ByVal e As System.EventArgs) Handles _serializationButton.Click
    ' Get the authors reader.
    Dim reader As SqlDataReader = GetAuthorsSqlReader()
```

```
' Load a DataTable from the reader
Dim table As DataTable = GetTableFromReader(reader, "Authors")
```

The preceding code begins by calling the helper methods `GetAuthorsSqlReader` and `GetTableFromReader` to get a `DataTable` of the authors from the pubs database. The next code block, shown here, is where you are actually serializing the `DataTable` out to a binary format:

```
' Save the table in a binary format
Dim filename As String = FileIO.SpecialDirectories.MyDocuments & _
    "\authors.dat"
Using fs As New FileStream(filename, FileMode.Create)
    table.RemotingFormat = SerializationFormat.Binary
    Dim format As New BinaryFormatter
    format.Serialize(fs, table)
End Using
' Tell the user what happened
MessageBox.Show(
    String.Format("Successfully serialized the DataTable to {0}",
    filename))
```

This code takes advantage of the `Using` statement for Visual Basic to wrap up creating and disposing of a `FileStream` instance that will hold your serialized `DataTable` data. The next step is to set the `DataTable`'s `RemotingFormat` property to the `SerializationFormat.Binary` enumeration value. Once that is done, you simply create a new `BinaryFormatter` instance, and then call its `Serialize` method to serialize your `DataTable` into the `FileStream` instance. You then finish by showing users a message box indicating that the data has been serialized.

DataReader Integration

Another nice feature of the `DataSet` and `DataTable` classes is the capability to both read from and write out to a stream of data in the form of a `DataReader`. You will first take a look at how you can load a `DataTable` from a `DataReader`. To demonstrate this, I have added a Button (`loadFromReaderButton`) and its associated `Click` event handler to `TestForm.vb` of the AdoNetFeaturesTest project in the Examples solution:

```
Private Sub _loadFromReaderButton_Click(ByVal sender As System.Object, _
    ByVal e As System.EventArgs) Handles _loadFromReaderButton.Click

    ' Get the authors reader.
    Dim reader As SqlDataReader = GetAuthorsSqlReader()

    ' Load a DataTable from the reader.
    Dim table As DataTable = GetTableFromReader(reader, "Authors")

    ' Bind the grid to the table.
    BindGrid(table)
End Sub
```

This method is a controller method, meaning that it only calls helper methods. It begins by first obtaining a `SqlDataReader` from the `GetAuthorsSqlReader` helper method. It then calls the `GetTableFromReader` helper method to transform the `DataReader` into a `DataTable`. The `GetTableFromReader` method is where you actually get to see the `DataTable`'s new load functionality:

```
Private Function GetTableFromReader(ByVal reader As SqlDataReader, _
    ByVal tableName As String) As DataTable
    ' Create a new DataTable using the name passed in.
    Dim table As New DataTable(tableName)
```

```
        ' Load the DataTable from the reader.
        table.Load(reader)
        ' Close the reader.
        reader.Close()
        Return table
    End Function
```

Code snippet from AdoNetFeaturesTest project

This method begins by first creating an instance of a `DataTable` and initializing it with the name passed in from the `tableName` argument. Once the new `DataTable` has been initialized, you call the new `Load` method and pass in the `SqlDataReader` that was passed into the method via the `reader` argument. This is where the `DataTable` takes the `DataReader` and populates the `DataTable` instance with the column names and data from the `DataReader`. The next step is to close the `DataReader`, as it is no longer needed; and finally, you return the newly populated `DataTable`.

DataTable Independence

One of the most convenient capabilities in ADO.NET is the inclusion of several methods from the `DataSet` class in the `DataTable` class. The `DataTable` is now much more versatile and useful than it was in the early ADO.NET days. The `DataTable` now supports all of the same read and write methods for XML as the `DataSet` — specifically, the `ReadXml`, `ReadXmlSchema`, `WriteXml`, and `WriteXmlSchema` methods.

The `Merge` method of the `DataSet` has now been added to the `DataTable` as well; and in addition to the existing functionality of the `DataSet` class, some of the new features of the `DataSet` class have been added to the `DataTable` class — namely, the `RemotingFormat` property, the `Load` method, and the `GetDataReader` method.

WORKING WITH THE COMMON PROVIDER MODEL

In ADO.NET 1.x, you could code to either the provider-specific classes, such as `SqlConnection`, or the generic interfaces, such as `IDbConnection`. If there was a possibility that the database you were programming against would change during your project, or if you were creating a commercial package intended to support customers with different databases, then you had to use the generic interfaces. You cannot call a constructor on an interface, so most generic programs included code that accomplished the task of obtaining the original `IDbConnection` by means of their own factory method, such as a `GetConnection` method that would return a provider-specific instance of the `IDbConnection` interface.

ADO.NET today has a more elegant solution for getting the provider-specific connection. Each data provider registers a `ProviderFactory` class and a provider string in the .NET `machine.config` file. A base `ProviderFactory` class (`DbProviderFactory`) and a `System.Data.Common.ProviderFactories` class can return a `DataTable` of information (via the `GetFactoryClasses` method) about different data providers registered in `machine.config`, and can return the correct `ProviderFactory` given the provider string (called `ProviderInvariantName`) or by using a `DataRow` from this `DataTable`. Instead of writing your own framework to build connections based on the name of the provider, ADO.NET now makes it much more straightforward, flexible, and easy to solve this problem.

Let's look at an example of using the common provider model to connect to the pubs database and display some rows from the authors table. In the AdoNetFeaturesTest project, on the `TestForm.vb` form, the `providerButton` button's `Click` event handler shows this functionality. The code is broken down into six steps. The first step is to get the provider factory object based on a configuration value of the provider's invariant name:

```
Private Sub _providerButton_Click(ByVal sender As System.Object, _
  ByVal e As System.EventArgs) Handles _providerButton.Click
        ' 1. Factory
```

```
' Create the provider factory from config value.
Dim factory As DbProviderFactory = DbProviderFactories.GetFactory( _
    ConfigurationSettings.AppSettings("providerInvariantName"))
```

Code snippet from AdoNetFeaturesTest project

You are able to get the factory via the `DbProviderFactories` object's `GetFactory` method and pass in the string name of the provider invariant that you are storing in the project's `app.config` file. Here is the entry in the `app.config` file:

```
<add key="providerInvariantName" value="System.Data.SqlClient" />
```

In this case, you are using the SQL Server data provider. Once you have the factory object, the next step is to use it to create a connection:

Available for download on Wrox.com

```
' 2. Connection
' Create the connection from the factory.
Dim connection As DbConnection = factory.CreateConnection()
' Get the connection string from config.
connection.ConnectionString = _
    ConfigurationSettings.ConnectionStrings("db").ConnectionString
```

Code snippet from AdoNetFeaturesTest project

The connection is created by calling the `DbProviderFactory`'s `CreateConnection` method. In this case, the factory is returning a `SqlConnection`, because you chose to use the `System.Data.SqlClient` provider invariant. To keep your code generic, you will not be directly programming against any of the classes in the `System.Data.SqlClient` namespace. Note how the connection class you declare is a `DbConnection` class, which is part of the `System.Data` namespace.

The next step is to create a `Command` object so you can retrieve the data from the authors table:

Available for download on Wrox.com

```
' 3. Command
' Create the command from the connection.
Dim command As DbCommand = connection.CreateCommand()
' Set the type of the command to stored procedure.
command.CommandType = CommandType.StoredProcedure
' Set the name of the stored procedure to execute.
command.CommandText = "usp_authors_Get_All"
```

Code snippet from AdoNetFeaturesTest project

You begin by declaring a generic `DbCommand` class variable and then using the `DbConnection`'s `CreateCommand` method to create the `DbCommand` instance. Once you have done that, you set the command type to `StoredProcedure` and then set the stored procedure name.

This example uses a `DbDataAdapter` to fill a `DataTable` with the authors' data. Here is how you create and initialize the `DbDataAdapter`:

Available for download on Wrox.com

```
' 4. Adapter
' Create the adapter from the factory.
Dim adapter As DbDataAdapter = factory.CreateDataAdapter()
' Set the adapter's select command.
adapter.SelectCommand = command
```

Code snippet from AdoNetFeaturesTest project

Just as you did when you created your `DbConnection` instance, you use the factory to create your `DbDataAdapter`. After creating it, you then set the `SelectCommand` property's value to the instance of the previously initialized `DbCommand` instance.

After finishing these steps, the next step is to create a `DataTable` and fill it using the `DataAdapter`:

Available for
download on
Wrox.com

```
' 5. DataTable
' Create a new DataTable.
Dim authors As New DataTable("Authors")
' Use the adapter to fill the DataTable.
adapter.Fill(authors)
```

Code snippet from AdoNetFeaturesTest project

The final step is to bind the table to the form's grid:

```
' 6.  Grid
' Populate the grid with the data.
BindGrid(authors)
```

You already looked at the `BindGrid` helper method in the asynchronous example earlier. In this example, you are simply reusing this generic method again:

Available for
download on
Wrox.com

```
Private Sub BindGrid(ByVal table As DataTable)
      ' Clear the grid.
      Me._authorsGridView.DataSource = Nothing
      ' Bind the grid to the DataTable.
      Me._authorsGridView.DataSource = table
End Sub
```

Code snippet from AdoNetFeaturesTest project

The main point to take away from this example is that you were able to easily write database-agnostic code with just a few short lines. ADO.NET 1.x required a lot of lines of code to create this functionality; you had to write your own abstract factory classes and factory methods in order to create instances of the generic database interfaces, such as `IDbConnection`, `IDbCommand`, and so on.

CONNECTION POOLING IN ADO.NET

Pooling connections can significantly enhance the performance and scalability of your application. Both the SQL Client .NET data provider and the OLE DB .NET data provider automatically pool connections using Windows Component Services and OLE DB session pooling, respectively. The only requirement is that you must use the exact same connection string each time if you want a pooled connection.

ADO.NET now enhances the connection pooling functionality offered in ADO.NET 1.x by enabling you to close all of the connections currently kept alive by the particular managed provider that you are using. You can clear a specific connection pool by using the shared `SqlConnection.ClearPool` method or clear all of the connection pools in an application domain by using the shared `SqlConnection.ClearPools` method. Both the SQL Server and Oracle managed providers implement this functionality.

TRANSACTIONS AND SYSTEM.TRANSACTIONS

While you can do simple transaction support with ADO.NET, Visual Basic includes a set of classes specifically designed for working with transactions: the `System.Transactions` namespace. As the name implies, these classes allow you to define and work with transactions in your code.

You may well be wondering at this point why we need two methods of working with transactions. The classes of `System.Transaction`, particularly the `Transaction` class itself, abstract the code from the resource managers participating in the transaction. Transactions in ADO.NET are specific to each database you may access. There is no unified method of creating a transaction, nor is there a standard way of sharing a database transaction across multiple databases or other transaction supporters. The `Transaction` class provides for these limitations, and can coordinate multiple resource managers itself.

The classes of System.Transaction also provide the means to create your own resource managers. These resource managers may then participate in transactions. At first, you may balk at this prospect, wondering how you could write something that manages all the details of a transactional data store. Aren't the details enormous? Fortunately, the classes make it easy to enlist in a transaction and report on your results.

Creating Transactions

System.Transaction supports two means of working with transactions: *implicit* and *explicit*. With implicit transactions, you define a boundary for the transaction. Any resource managers you use within this boundary become part of the transaction. That is, if you have defined a boundary and then call a database such as SQL Server, the actions performed on the database are part of the transaction. If the code reaches the boundary without incident, then the transaction is committed. If an exception occurs during this implicit transaction, then the transaction is rolled back. Explicit transactions, as you may have guessed, mean that you explicitly commit or roll back the transaction as needed.

Using the implicit model can greatly simplify the code involved in a transaction. The following code demonstrates inserting multiple records using implicit transactions:

Available for
download on
Wrox.com

```vb
Private Sub MultipleInsertImplicit()
    'insert a number of records into the sales table
    'using implicit transactions
    Dim cmdString As String = "INSERT INTO Sales(stor_id, ord_num, " &
        "ord_date, qty, payterms, title_id) " &
        "VALUES (@storeID, @ordNum, @ordDate, " &
        "@qty, @payterms, @titleID)"
    Dim cmd As New SqlCommand(cmdString, connection)
    'add the parameters to the command. We'll set the values later
    With cmd.Parameters
        .Add("@storeID", SqlDbType.Char, 4)
        .Add("@ordNum", SqlDbType.VarChar, 20)
        .Add("@ordDate", SqlDbType.DateTime)
        .Add("@qty", SqlDbType.Int)
        .Add("@payterms", SqlDbType.VarChar, 12)
        .Add("@titleID", SqlDbType.VarChar, 6)
    End With
    'start implicit transaction
    Using txn As New TransactionScope
        Try
            'insert 10 random records
            For i As Integer = 1 To 10
                cmd.Parameters("@storeID").Value = PickRandomStore()
                cmd.Parameters("@ordNum").Value = PickRandomOrderNumber()
                cmd.Parameters("@ordDate").Value = (DateTime.Now)
                cmd.Parameters("@qty").Value = (New Random().Next(1, 100))
                cmd.Parameters("@payterms").Value = ("NET 30")
                cmd.Parameters("@titleID").Value = (PickRandomTitle())

                cmd.ExecuteNonQuery()
            Next
        Catch ex As Exception
            Console.WriteLine(ex.Message)
        End Try

    End Using
    'if no exceptions occur, transaction will commit here

End
```

Code snippet from SubSimpleTransactions

This code inserts multiple sales orders into the sales table. The bulk of the code is setting up the query to insert the record, and creating random parameters to insert. The `Using` clause wraps the inserts within an implicit transaction. All resource managers that recognize transactions participate in this transaction. The `Using` clause guarantees that the `TransactionScope` object is disposed of when the transaction is complete. If something happens, the transaction is automatically rolled back, otherwise it is committed.

Using explicit transactions requires a bit more code but provides greater control over the transaction. You can use either the `Transaction` class or the `CommittableTransaction` class to wrap transactions in this model. `CommittableTransaction` is a child class of `Transaction`, and adds the capability to commit a transaction, as the name implies.

Using a `CommittableTransaction` in the above scenario changes it as follows:

```
Private Sub MultipleInsertExplicit()
    'insert a number of records into the sales table
    'using explicit transactions

    Dim cmdString As String = "INSERT INTO Sales(stor_id, ord_num, " &
"ord_date, qty, payterms, title_id) " &
"VALUES (@storeID, @ordNum, @ordDate, " &
"@qty, @payterms, @titleID)"
    Dim cmd As New SqlCommand(cmdString, connection)
    'add the parameters to the command. We'll set the values later
    With cmd.Parameters
        .Add("@storeID", SqlDbType.Char, 4)
        .Add("@ordNum", SqlDbType.VarChar, 20)
        .Add("@ordDate", SqlDbType.DateTime)
        .Add("@qty", SqlDbType.Int)
        .Add("@payterms", SqlDbType.VarChar, 12)
        .Add("@titleID", SqlDbType.VarChar, 6)
    End With
    'start implicit transaction
    Using txn As New CommittableTransaction
        Try
            'insert 10 random records
            For i As Integer = 1 To 10
                cmd.Parameters("@storeID").Value = PickRandomStore()
                cmd.Parameters("@ordNum").Value = PickRandomOrderNumber()
                cmd.Parameters("@ordDate").Value = (DateTime.Now)
                cmd.Parameters("@qty").Value = (New Random().Next(1, 100))
                cmd.Parameters("@payterms").Value = ("NET 30")
                cmd.Parameters("@titleID").Value = (PickRandomTitle())

                cmd.ExecuteNonQuery()
            Next

            'commit the transaction
            txn.Commit()
        Catch ex As Exception
            'if an exception occurs, we rollback the attempt
            'this could also have been done elsewhere
            txn.Rollback()
            Console.WriteLine(ex.Message)
        End Try

    End Using
End
```

Code snippet from SubSimpleTransactions

Notice that the transaction must now be explicitly committed or rolled back. You could also pass the transaction variable to other methods to vote on the transaction. If you do this, you can enlist other transaction containers using the `EnlistTransaction` method (or `EnlistDistributedTransaction` if the transaction will span multiple computers). Once it is a part of the transaction, it can then use the transaction methods to commit or roll back each part of the transaction.

Using the `TransactionScope` and `Transaction` classes can greatly decrease the amount of effort involved in creating and working with transactions in your applications. Generally, using implicit transactions using `TransactionScope` is easier and less error prone, and should be your first choice.

Creating Resource Managers

In addition to using the classes in `System.Transactions` for managing transactions, you can also use them to define your own resource managers. These resource managers can then participate in transactions with databases, MSDTC, message queues, and more. There are three basic steps to defining a resource manager:

1. Create an enlistment class. This class is used to track the resource manager's participation in the transaction. That is, this is the class that will vote on whether the transaction should complete or be rolled back. This class should implement the `IEnlistmentNotification` interface.

2. Enlist the new enlistment class in the transaction. There are two main ways the class may participate in the transaction: `EnlistDurable` or `EnlistVolatile`. You use `EnlistDurable` if your resource manager stores data permanently, such as in a file or database. `EnlistVolatile` is used if your resource manager stores its information in memory or in some other nonrecoverable location.

3. Implement the methods of the `IEnlistmentNotification` interface to react to the states of the transaction. The `IEnlistmentNotification` interface provides four methods: `Prepare`, `Commit`, `Rollback`, and `InDoubt`. `Commit` and `Rollback` are self-explanatory, used at t`hese two phases of the transaction. `Prepare` is called before `Commit`, to determine whether it is possible to commit the transaction. Finally, `InDoubt` is called if the transaction is questionable. This can happen if the transaction coordinator has lost track of one of the resource managers.

Why would you define your own resource managers, rather than simply use an existing one such as SQL Server? You might need to store data in another database that does not directly participate in transactions. Alternately, you may want to enable a normally nontransactional component with transactional behavior. For example, the cache in ASP.NET doesn't support the addition of items using transactions. You could create a resource manager that wraps the ASP.NET cache and adds support for commit and rollback of entries. This might be part of a system in which you want to use the cache as an in-memory data store. While this would work without the transactions, adding transactional support would ensure that if the database write fails for any reason, then the entry could be rolled back out of the cache.

LINQ TO SQL

There has always been a logical disconnect for developers working with databases. Most of your application is written in one language (Visual Basic), while the data access (or at least the queries) is written in SQL. In Visual Basic, programming with objects means a wonderful, strongly typed ability to work with code. You can navigate very easily through the namespaces, work with a debugger in the Visual Studio IDE, and more. However, when you have to access data, you will notice that things are dramatically different. You end up in a world that is not strongly typed, and debugging is a pain or even nonexistent. You end up spending most of the time sending strings to the database as commands. As a developer, you also have to be aware of the underlying data and how it is structured or how all the data points relate.

Microsoft has provided LINQ as a lightweight façade that provides a strongly typed interface to the underlying data stores. LINQ provides the means for developers to stay within the coding environment they're used to and access the underlying data as objects that work with the IDE, IntelliSense, and even debugging.

With LINQ, the queries that you create now become first-class citizens within the .NET Framework alongside everything else you are used to. When you begin to work with queries for the data store you're working with, you will quickly realize that they now work and behave as if they were types in the system. This means that you can now use any .NET-compliant language and query the underlying data store as you never have before.

LINQ TO SQL AND VISUAL BASIC

LINQ to SQL in particular is a means to have a strongly typed interface against a SQL Server database. You will find that the approach that LINQ to SQL provides is by far the easiest approach there is at present for querying SQL Server. It's not simply about querying single tables within the database; for instance, if you call the authors table of the Microsoft sample pubs database and want to pull a title for each author from the same database, then LINQ will use the relations of the tables and make the query on your behalf. LINQ will query the database and load up the data for you to work with from your code (again, strongly typed).

Keep in mind that LINQ to SQL is not only about querying data; you can also perform the INSERT, UPDATE, and DELETE statements that you need to perform.

In addition, you can interact with the entire process and customize the operations performed to add your own business logic to any of the CRUD operations (CREATE/READ/UPDATE/DELETE).

Visual Studio is highly integrated with LINQ to SQL in that it offers an extensive user interface that enables you to design the LINQ to SQL classes you will work with.

The following section demonstrates how to set up a LINQ to SQL instance and pull items from the pubs database.

Retrieving Data Using LINQ to SQL: Creating the Console Application

To illustrate using LINQ to SQL, the LinqReading example begins by calling a single table from the pubs database and using this table to populate some results to the screen.

The next step is to add a LINQ to SQL class. When working with LINQ to SQL, one of the big advantages is that Visual Studio does an outstanding job of making it as easy as possible. Visual Studio provides an object-relational mapping designer, called the Object Relational Designer (O/R Designer), that enables you to visually design the object-to-database mapping.

To start this task, right-click on your solution and select Add] New Item from the provided menu. From the items in the Add New Item dialog, select the LINQ to SQL Classes option, as shown in Figure 10-4.

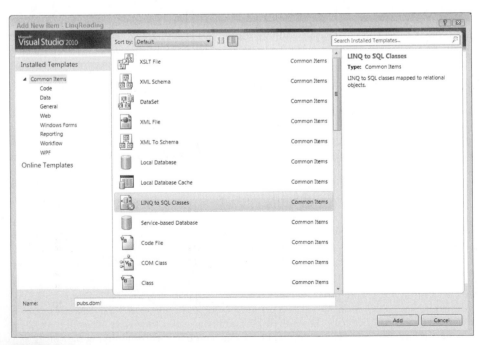

FIGURE 10-4

Because this example uses the pubs database, name the file `pubs.dbml`. Click the Add button, which will create a couple of files for you. The Solution Explorer, after adding the `pubs.dbml` file, is shown in Figure 10-5.

A number of items were added to your project with this action. First, the `pubs.dbml` file was added, which contains two components. Because the LINQ to SQL class that was added works with LINQ, the `System.Data.Linq` reference was also added on your behalf.

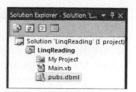

FIGURE 10-5

Introducing the O/R Designer

Another big addition to the IDE that appeared when you added the LINQ to SQL class to your project (the `pubs.dbml` file) was a visual representation of the .dbml file. The new O/R Designer appears as a tab within the document window directly in the IDE. Figure 10-6 shows a view of the O/R Designer when it is first initiated.

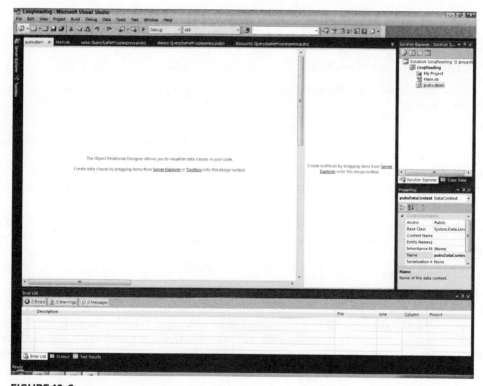

FIGURE 10-6

The O/R Designer consists of two parts. The first is for data classes, which can be tables, classes, associations, and inheritances. Dragging such items on this design surface will give you a visual representation of the object that can be worked with. The second part (on the right) is for methods, which map to the stored procedures within a database.

When viewing your .dbml file within the O/R Designer, you also have an Object Relational Designer set of controls in the Visual Studio Toolbox, as shown in Figure 10-7.

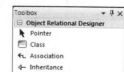

FIGURE 10-7

Creating the Product Object

For this example, you will work with the Titles table from the pubs database, which means you need to create a titles table that will use LINQ to SQL to map to this table. Accomplishing this task is simply a matter of opening a view of the tables contained within the database from the Server Explorer dialog within Visual Studio and dragging and dropping the Titles table onto the left-hand design surface of the O/R Designer. The results of this action are illustrated in Figure 10-8.

With this action, a bunch of code is added to the designer files of the .dbml file on your behalf. These classes give you strongly typed access to the titles table. For a demonstration of this, turn your attention to the console application's `Main.vb` file. Following is the code required for this example:

FIGURE 10-8

```vb
Module Main
    Sub Main()
        Dim dc As New pubsDataContext
        Dim query = dc.titles
        For Each item In query
            Console.WriteLine("{0}: {1}",
                item.title_id, item.title)
        Next
        Console.WriteLine("Press ENTER to exit")
        Console.ReadLine()
    End Sub
End Module
```

Code snippet from LinqReading Project

This short bit of code is querying the Titles table within the pubs database and pulling out the data to display. It is useful to step through this code starting with the first line in the `Main` method:

```vb
Dim dc As New pubsDataContext()
```

The `pubsDataContext` object is an object of type `DataContext`. You can view this as a class that maps to a `Connection` type object. This object works with the connection string and connects to the database for any required operations.

The next line is quite interesting:

```vb
Dim query = dc.titles
```

Here, you are using an implicitly typed variable. If you are unsure of the output type, you can assign a type to the query variable and the type will be set into place at compile time. Actually, the code `dc.titles` returns a `System.Data.Linq.Table(Of LinqReading.titles)` object, and this is what the query type is set as, when the application is compiled. Therefore, you could have also just as easily written the statement as follows:

```vb
Dim query As Table(Of title) = dc.titles
```

This approach is actually better because programmers who look at the application's code later will find it easier to understand what is happening, as just using the `Dim` query by itself has so much of a hidden aspect to it. To use `Table(Of title)`, which is basically a generic list of `Title` objects, you should make a reference to the `System.Data.Linq` namespace (using `Imports System.Data.Linq`).

The value assigned to the `Query` object is the value of the `titles` property, which is of type `Table(Of title)`. From there, the next bit of code iterates through the collection of `Title` objects found in `Table(Of title)`:

```vb
For Each item In query
    Console.WriteLine("{0}: {1}",
        item.title_ID, item.title)
Next
```

In this case, the iteration pulls out the `title_id` and `title` properties from the `Title` object and writes them out to the program. Because you are using only a few of the items from the table, the O/R Designer enables you to delete the columns that you are not interested in pulling from the database. This example demonstrates just how easy it is to query a SQL Server database using LINQ to SQL.

HOW OBJECTS MAP TO LINQ OBJECTS

The great thing about LINQ is that it gives you strongly typed objects to use in your code (with IntelliSense), and these objects map to existing database objects. Again, LINQ is nothing more than a thin façade over these pre-existing database objects. Table 10-3 shows the mappings that exist between the database objects and the LINQ objects.

TABLE 10-3: Database to LINQ Object Mappings

DATABASE OBJECT	LINQ OBJECT
Database	DataContext
Table	Class and Collection
View	Class and Collection
Column	Property
Relationship	Nested Collection
Stored Procedure	Method

On the left side you are dealing with your database. The database is the entire entity: the tables, views, triggers, stored procedures — everything that makes up the database. On the right, or LINQ side, you have an object called the `DataContext` object. A `DataContext` object is bound to the database. For the required interaction with the database, it contains a connection string that handles all of the transactions that occur, including any logging. It also manages the output of the data. In short, the `DataContext` object completely manages the transactions with the database on your behalf.

Tables, as you saw in the example, are converted to classes. This means that if you have a Products table, you will have a `Product` class. Note that LINQ is name-friendly in that it changes plural tables to singular to provide the proper name to the class that you are using in your code. In addition to database tables being treated as classes, database views are treated the same. Columns, conversely, are treated as properties. This enables you to manage the attributes (names and type definitions) of the column directly.

Relationships are nested collections that map between these various objects. This enables you to define relationships that are mapped to multiple items.

It's also important to understand the mapping of stored procedures. These actually map to methods within your code off the `DataContext` instance. The next section takes a closer look at the `DataContext` and the table objects within LINQ.

Looking at the architecture of LINQ to SQL, you will notice that there are actually three layers: your application, the LINQ to SQL layer, and the SQL Server database. As shown in the previous examples, you can create a strongly typed query in your application's code:

```
dc.titles
```

This in turn is translated to a SQL query by the LINQ to SQL layer, which is then supplied to the database on your behalf:

```
SELECT [t0].[title_id], [t0].[title], [t0].[type], [t0].[pub_id],
[t0].[price], [t0].[advance], [t0].[royalty], [t0].[ytd_sales],
[t0].[notes], [t0].[pubdate]
FROM [titles] AS [t0]
```

In return, the LINQ to SQL layer takes the rows coming out of the database from this query and turns them into a collection of strongly typed objects that you can easily work with.

The DataContext Object

In the preceding section, you learned that the `DataContext` object manages the transactions that occur with the database you are working with when working with LINQ to SQL. There is actually a lot that you can do with the `DataContext` object.

Using the Connection Property

The `Connection` property actually returns an instance of the `System.Data.SqlClient.SqlConnection` that is used by the `DataContext` object. This is ideal if you need to share this connection with other ADO.NET code that you might be using in your application, or if you need to get at any of the `SqlConnection` properties or methods that it exposes. For instance, getting at the connection string is a simple matter:

```
Dim dc As New pubsDataContext()
Console.WriteLine(dc.Connection.ConnectionString)
```

Using the Transaction Property

If you have an ADO.NET transaction that you can use, you are able to assign that transaction to the `DataContext` object instance using the `Transaction` property. You can also use `Transaction` using the `TransactionScope` object from the .NET Framework. You would need to make a reference to the `System.Transactions` namespace in your `References` folder for this example to work:

```
Imports System.Transactions

Module Main

    Sub Main()
        Dim dc As New PubsDataContext
        Using theScope As New TransactionScope
            Dim title1 As New title With {
                .title_id = "777779",
                .title = "Professional XML",
                .type = "programming",
                .pubdate = "April 15, 2007"}
            dc.titles.InsertOnSubmit(title1)
            Dim title2 As New title With {
                .title_id = "502242",
                .title = "Professional VB 2010",
                .type = "programming",
                .pubdate = "June 15, 2010"}
            dc.titles.InsertOnSubmit(title2)

            Try
                Console.WriteLine("Before insert: {0} titles",
                                dc.titles.Count)

                dc.SubmitChanges()
                Console.WriteLine("After insert: {0} titles",
                                dc.titles.Count)

            Catch ex As Exception
                Console.WriteLine("ERROR: {0}", ex.Message)
            End Try
            theScope.Complete()
        End Using

        Console.WriteLine("Press ENTER to exit")
```

```
        Console.ReadLine()
    End Sub

End Module
```

Code snippet from LinqTransactions project

In this case, the `TransactionScope` object is used within a `Using` clause. This means that everything contained within that clause will happen as a single transaction; if one of the operations on the database fails, everything will be rolled back to the original state. Within this transaction, two records are submitted. The actual changes will not happen until the call to `SubmitChanges`.

Other Methods and Properties of the DataContext Object

In addition to the items just described, several other methods and properties are available from the `DataContext` object. Table 10-4 shows some of the available methods from `DataContext`.

TABLE 10-4: Partial List of DataContext Methods

METHOD	DESCRIPTION
CreateDatabase	Enables you to create a database on the server
DatabaseExists	Enables you to determine whether a database exists and can be opened
DeleteDatabase	Deletes the associated database
ExecuteCommand	Enables you to pass in a command to the database to be executed
ExecuteQuery	Enables you to pass queries directly to the database
GetChangeSet	The `DataContext` object keeps track of changes occurring in the database on your behalf. This method enables you to access those changes.
GetCommand	Provides access to the commands that are performed
GetTable	Provides access to a collection of tables from the database
Refresh	Enables you to refresh your objects from the data stored within the database
SubmitChanges	Executes the `INSERT`, `UPDATE`, and `DELETE` commands that have been established in your code
Translate	Converts an `IDataReader` to objects

In addition to these methods, the `DataContext` object exposes some of the properties shown in Table 10-5.

TABLE 10-5: Partial List of DataContext Properties

PROPERTY	DESCRIPTION
ChangeConflicts	Provides a collection of objects that caused concurrency conflicts when the `SubmitChanges` method was called
CommandTimeout	Enables you to set the timeout period for commands against the database. You should set this to a higher value if your query needs more time to execute.
Connection	Enables you to work with the `System.Data.SqlClient.SqlConnection` object used by the client
DeferredLoadingEnabled	Enables you to specify whether or not to delay the loading of one-to-many or one-to-one relationships
LoadOptions	Enables you to specify or retrieve the value of the `DataLoadOptions` object

continues

TABLE 10-5 *(continued)*

PROPERTY	DESCRIPTION
Log	Enables you to specify the output location of the command that was used in the query
Mapping	Provides the metamodel on which the mapping is based. That is, this defines how the tables will be translated to VB classes.
ObjectTrackingEnabled	Specifies whether or not to track changes to the objects within the database for transactional purposes. If you are dealing with a read-only database, then you should set this property to false.
Transaction	Enables you to specify the local transaction used with the database

The Table(TEntity) Object

The Table(TEntity) object is a representation of the tables that you are working with from the database. For instance, you saw the use of the Product class, which is a Table(Of Product) instance. As you will see throughout this chapter, several methods are available from the Table(TEntity) object. Some of these methods are defined in Table 10-6.

TABLE 10-6: Partial List of Table(TEntity) Object Methods

METHOD	DESCRIPTION
Attach	Enables you to attach an entity to the DataContext instance
AttachAll	Enables you to attach a collection of entities to the DataContext instance
DeleteAllOnSubmit(TSubEntity)	Enables you to put all the pending actions into a state of readiness for deletion. Everything here is enacted when the SubmitChanges method is called off of the DataContext object.
DeleteOnSubmit	Enables you to put a pending action into a state of readiness for deletion. Everything here is enacted when the SubmitChanges method is called off of the DataContext object.
GetModifiedMembers	Provides an array of modified objects. You will be able to access their current and changed values.
GetNewBindingList	Provides a new list for binding to the data store
GetOriginalEntityState	Provides an instance of the object as it appeared in its original state
InsertAllOnSubmit(TSubEntity)	Enables you to put all the pending actions into a state of readiness for insertion. Everything here is enacted when the SubmitChanges method is called off of the DataContext object.
InsertOnSubmit	Enables you to put a pending action into a state of readiness for insertion. Everything here is enacted when the SubmitChanges method is called off of the DataContext object.

QUERYING THE DATABASE

As you have seen so far in this chapter, there are a number of ways in which you can query the database from the code of your application. In some of the simplest forms, your queries looked like the following:

```
Dim query As Table(Of title) = dc.titles
```

This command retrieved the entire Titles table to your Query object instance.

Using Query Expressions

In addition to pulling down a straight table using dc.titles, you are about to use a strongly typed query expression directly in your code:

```
Sub SimpleSelect()
    Dim dc As New PubsDataContext
    Dim query = From p In dc.titles Select p
    For Each item In query
        Console.WriteLine(item.title_id & ": " & item.title)
    Next
End Sub
```

Code snippet from LinqExpressions project

In this case, a Query object (again, a Table(Of title) object) is populated with the query value of From p in dc.titles Select p.

Query Expressions in Detail

You can use several query expressions from your code. The preceding example is a simple select statement that returns the entire table. Table 10-7 shows some of the other query expressions that you have at your disposal.

TABLE 10-7: Common Query Expressions

EXPRESSION TYPE	DESCRIPTION
Project	Select *<expression>*
Filter	Where *<expression>*, Distinct
Test	Any(*<expression>*), All(*<expression>*)
Join	*<expression>* Join *<expression>* On *<expression>* Equals *<expression>*
Group	Group By *<expression>*, Into *<expression>*, *<expression>* Group Join <decision> On *<expression>* Equals *<expression>* Into *<expression>*
Aggregate	Count(*<expression>*), Sum(*<expression>*), Min(*<expression>*), Max(*<expression>*), Avg(*<expression>*)
Partition	Skip [While] *<expression>*, Take [While] *<expression>*
Set	Union, Intersect, Except
Order	Order By *<expression>*, *<expression>*[Ascending	Descending]

Filtering Using Expressions

In addition to straight queries for the entire table, you can filter items using the Where and Distinct options. The following example queries the Products table for a specific type of record:

```
Dim query = From p In dc.titles
            Where p.title.StartsWith("S")
            Select p
```

Here, this query is selecting all the records from the Titles table that start with the letter "S." This is done via the Where p.title.StartsWith("S") expression. You will find a large selection of methods available off the ProductName property that enable you to fine-tune the filtering you need.

You can add as many of these expressions to the list as you need. For instance, the next example adds two Where statements to your query:

```
Dim query = From p In dc.titles
            Where p.title.StartsWith("S")
```

```
Where p.title.EndsWith("?")
    Select p
```

In this case, a filter expression looks for items with a product name starting with the letter "S," and then a second expression is included to ensure that a second criterion is also applied, which states that the items must also end with a question mark.

Performing Joins

In addition to working with one table, you can work with multiple tables and perform joins with your queries. If you add the sale, store and title tables onto the pubs.dbml design surface, you will get the result shown in Figure 10-9.

After you drag and drop these elements onto the design surface, Visual Studio knows that there is a relationship between them and creates the relationship for you in the code, represented by the black arrow.

From here, you can use a Join statement in your query to work with these tables, as shown in the following example:

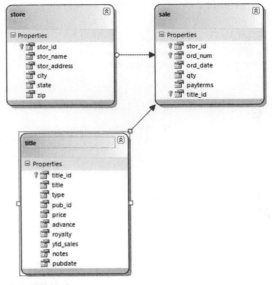

FIGURE 10-9

Available for download on Wrox.com

```
Module Main
    Sub Main()
        Dim dc As New PubsDataContext
        'display the generated SQL in the console
        dc.Log = Console.Out

        'returned data includes only three properties
        'from different tables
        Dim query = From t In dc.titles
                    Join s In dc.sales
                    On s.title_id Equals t.title_id
                    Join st In dc.stores
                    On st.stor_id Equals s.stor_id
                    Order By st.stor_id
                    Select st.stor_name, t.title, s.qty

        For Each item In query
            Console.WriteLine("{0} sold {1} copies of '{2}'",
                              item.stor_name,
                              item.qty,
                              item.title)
        Next

        Console.WriteLine("Press ENTER to exit")
        Console.ReadLine()
    End Sub
End Module
```

Code snippet from LinqJoins project

This example is pulling from the three tables and joining on the key columns in those tables. The DataContext's log is redirected to the console to enable you to see the generated SQL statement:

```
SELECT [t2].[stor_name], [t0].[title], [t1].[qty]
FROM [dbo].[titles] AS [t0]
```

```
INNER JOIN [dbo].[sales] AS [t1] ON [t0].[title_id] = [t1].[title_id]
INNER JOIN [dbo].[stores] AS [t2] ON [t1].[stor_id] = [t2].[stor_id]
ORDER BY [t2].[stor_id]
```

From here, a new object is created with the Select statement; and this new object is comprised of the stor_ name title, and qty columns from the three tables.

When it comes to iterating through the collection of this new object, note that the For Each statement does not define the variable item with a specific type, as the type is not known yet. The item object here has access to all the properties specified in the class declaration.

Grouping Items

You can easily group items with your queries. In the pubs.dbml example that you have been working with so far, you can see that there is a relationship between the title table and the sales table. The following example demonstrates how to group products by category:

```vbnet
Module Main

    Sub Main()
        Dim dc As New PubsDataContext

        Dim query = From t In dc.titles
                    Join s In dc.sales
                    On s.title_id Equals t.title_id
                    Order By s.store.state Ascending
                    Group s By Key = s.store.state
                    Into Group
                    Select Key, Group

        For Each item In query
            Console.WriteLine("Sales for {0}", item.Key)
            For Each s In item.Group
                Console.WriteLine("{0} - {1} copies",
                                    s.title.title,
                                    s.qty)
            Next
        Next

        Console.WriteLine("Press ENTER to exit")
        Console.ReadLine()
    End Sub

End Module
```

Code snippet from LinqGrouping project

This example creates a new object, which is a group of key values (the states where the sales occur), and packages the entire sales table into this new table, called Group. Before that, the states are ordered by name using the Order By statement, and the order provided is Ascending (the other option being Descending). The output is the State code (renamed to Key) and the Sales instance. The iteration with the For Each statements is done once for the Key and again for each of the Sales that are found in the category.

A partial output of this program is presented here:

```
Sales for CA
Secrets of Silicon Valley - 50 copies
Is Anger the Enemy? - 75 copies
Is Anger the Enemy? - 10 copies
Onions, Leeks, and Garlic: Cooking Secrets of the Mediterranean - 40 copies
Fifty Years in Buckingham Palace Kitchens - 20 copies
Sushi, Anyone? - 20 copies
```

```
Straight Talk About Computers - 15 copies
Silicon Valley Gastronomic Treats - 10 copies
You Can Combat Computer Stress! - 35 copies
Sales for OR
The Gourmet Microwave - 15 copies
The Busy Executive's Database Guide - 10 copies
Cooking with Computers: Surreptitious Balance Sheets - 25 copies
But Is It User Friendly? - 30 copies
Sales for WA
The Busy Executive's Database Guide - 5 copies
Is Anger the Enemy? - 3 copies
Is Anger the Enemy? - 20 copies
The Gourmet Microwave - 25 copies
Computer Phobic AND Non-Phobic Individuals: Behavior Variations - 20 copies
Life Without Fear - 25 copies
Prolonged Data Deprivation: Four Case Studies - 15 copies
Emotional Security: A New Algorithm - 25 copies
```

Many more commands and expressions are available to you beyond what has been presented in this chapter.

STORED PROCEDURES

So far, you have been querying the tables directly and leaving it up to LINQ to create the appropriate SQL statement for the operation. When working with pre-existing databases that make heavy use of stored procedures (and for those who want to follow the best practice of using stored procedures within a database), LINQ is still a viable option.

LINQ to SQL treats working with stored procedures as a method call. As shown earlier in Figure 11-6, the design surface called the O/R Designer enables you to drag and drop tables onto it so that you can then programmatically work with the table. On the right side of the O/R Designer is a pane in which you can drag and drop stored procedures.

Any stored procedures that you drag and drop onto this part of the O/R Designer become available methods to you off the DataContext object. For this example, drag and drop the usp_Get_Authors_By_States stored procedure onto this part of the O/R Designer (see Figure 10-10). You can rename it to GetAuthorsByStates using the property window. The following code shows how you would call this stored procedure within the pubs database:

```vb
Imports System.Data.Linq
Module Main
    Sub Main()
        Dim dc As New PubsDataContext
        'wraps the GetAuthorsByStates stored procedure
        'first parameter is the delimited list of states
        'second parameter is the delimiter
        Dim query = dc.GetAuthorsByStates("OR|UT", "|")
        For Each item In query
            Console.WriteLine("{0} {1} from {2}, {3}",
                              item.au_fname,
                              item.au_lname,
                              item.city,
                              item.state)
        Next
    End Sub
End Module
```

Code snippet from LinqSproc project

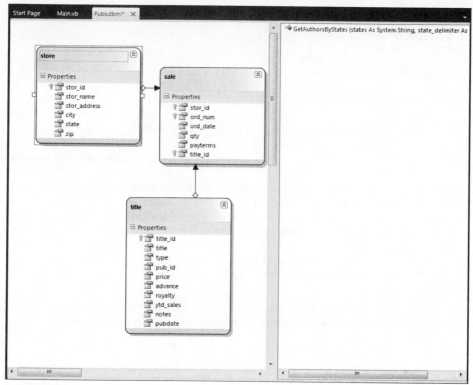

FIGURE 10-10

The stored procedure takes two parameters. The first one is a delimited list of state abbreviations. Authors from those states will be returned. The second parameter is the delimiter used to separate the elements in the first parameter. This is a common way of querying for an unknown number of values.

The return value for the query is a new type — named GetAuthorsByStatesResult — that wraps the fields returned. From here, iteration through this object is simple. As you can see from this example, calling your stored procedures is a straightforward process.

UPDATING THE DATABASE

LINQ to SQL is not just for querying your database. You can also use it to insert, update, and delete records from the query. As you saw above in the LinqTransactions project, this is done using the DataContext object. The short version of updating the database is that you make one or more changes to the data returned from the database, then you submit those changes to save them.

To insert a new record, you create a new instance of the class created by the LINQ to SQL designer, and insert it into the appropriate collection. This does not add it to the database, however. Only once you execute the SubmitChanges method of the DataContext does the record get sent to the database as the following code shows:

```vb
Private Sub InsertTitle()
    Console.WriteLine("Titles before insert: {0}", dc.titles.Count)
    Dim newTitle As New title
    With newTitle
        .title_id = "NU1234"
        .title = "Some new title"
```

```
                .type = "test"
                .pubdate = New DateTime(2010, 1, 1)
                .notes = "Added via LINQ"
                .price = 50.0
        End With
        dc.titles.InsertOnSubmit(newTitle)

        Console.WriteLine("Titles after insert, but before submit: {0}",
            dc.titles.Count)
        dc.SubmitChanges()
        Console.WriteLine("Titles after submit: {0}", dc.titles.Count)
    End Sub
```

Code snippet from LinqUpdates project

In the code, you create a new title. As the DataContext is connected to the database, you do not need to query first to return a collection to add the new record. Instead, you can add to the titles collection created by the designer. Once the new title is created, you then set the properties as desired. All required properties will need to be set, or an exception will occur when you attempt to submit the record(s) to the database. You then add the newly created record to the collection with the InsertOnSubmit method. At this point the record has not been added to either the database or the collection as the second Console.WriteLine demonstrates. Finally, once the SubmitChanges method is called, the newly added record exists in both the collection and the database.

Updating a record is similar, with the main difference that you start with an existing record. This record could be in an existing collection you are working with, or retrieved specifically to be updated.

```
        Private Sub UpdateTitle()
            'retrieve record to update
            Dim aTitle As title = (From t In dc.titles
                                    Where t.title_id = "NU1234"
                                    Select t).Single

            Console.WriteLine("Record before update: {0}", aTitle.title)

            'change values
            aTitle.title = "Updated title"
            aTitle.price = 45.95
            'submit
            dc.SubmitChanges()

            Console.WriteLine("Record after update: {0}", aTitle.title)
        End Sub
```

Code snippet from LinqUpdates project

In the code above, a single record is returned from the database by including the `Single` clause in the LINQ query. Alternately, you could already have a collection returned (as we will do with the delete) and update one or more records from it. As with the insert, you then can set the properties as desired. Changes are not sent to the database until the `SubmitChanges` method is called. While only a single record is changed here, there may be multiple records changed. All will be submitted when `SubmitChanges` is called.

Finally, deleting records using LINQ to SQL mirrors the method used to insert. Rather than adding the new item into the collection with `InsertOnSubmit`, you mark it for deletion with `DeleteOnSubmit`.

```
        Private Sub DeleteTitle()
            Console.WriteLine("Titles before delete: {0}", dc.titles.Count)
            'retrieve all records
            Dim theTitles = From t In dc.titles
                            Order By t.title_id Select t
            'find and delete the desired record(s)
```

```
        For Each t As title In theTitles
            If t.title_id = "NU1234" Then
                dc.titles.DeleteOnSubmit(t)
            End If
        Next
        Console.WriteLine("Titles after delete, but before submit: {0}",
                          dc.titles.Count)
        'submit
        dc.SubmitChanges()
        Console.WriteLine("Titles after delete: {0}", dc.titles.Count)

    End Sub
```

Code snippet from LinqUpdates project

This sample retrieves the entire collection to demonstrate the scenario where you have a collection, and you want to delete some of them. There is a simpler method if you know the records you want to delete and can create a LINQ query to return them all. In this case you can use the method as shown below (not in the code sample):

```
    Dim theTitles = From t In dc.titles Where t.type = "test"
                        Order By t.title_id Select t
    dc.titles.DeleteAllOnSubmit(theTitles)
    dc.SubmitChanges()
```

This retrieves all the titles in the test category and marks them all for deletion. As with the other samples, the actual deletion occurs when SubmitChanges is called.

SUMMARY

This chapter looked at ADO.NET and some of its more advanced features. You have seen and used the main objects in ADO.NET that you need to quickly get up and running in order to build data-access into your .NET applications. You took a fairly in-depth look at the DataSet and DataTable classes, as these are the core classes of ADO.NET.

This chapter also looked at stored procedures, including how to create them in SQL Server and how to access them from your code. Finally, you looked at the new Language Integrated Query (LINQ) features that enable you to use a more natural (to VB developers) syntax to query and edit your databases.

11

Data Access with the Entity Framework

WHAT YOU WILL LEARN IN THIS CHAPTER

➤ What is Object-Relational Mapping?

➤ What is the Entity Framework

➤ How the Entity Framework works with databases

➤ Using the Entity Framework to edit data

➤ Using the Entity Framework to create new databases

In the past, Microsoft has been known to change the recommended data access strategy relatively frequently. For example, Data Access Objects (DAO) was released in the Visual Basic 3.0 time frame, followed by RDO (Remote Data Objects) as an option in the Visual Basic 4 days, and ADO (Active Database Objects) with Visual Basic 6. Of course, all of these were COM libraries, so it was no surprise when they were superseded by ADO.NET when the .NET Framework shipped. There have been remarkably few changes to ADO.NET since then.

Now, when I see Microsoft recommending a new data access strategy, I start to get nervous. However, in this case there is good news. The Entity Framework (EF) does not replace ADO.NET. You can continue to use ADO.NET without fear of it going away, even as a recommended data access tool. The Entity Framework simply provides a different — richer and more flexible — model for working with data sources.

Beyond simply being a set of classes you use to access your data, Entity Framework enables you to work naturally with the data using the classes you have designed, while saving the data to the underlying database schema. The Entity Framework provides the mapping necessary to convert the data structures, variable types, and relationships between the Visual Basic data you work with in your applications to the SQL Server, Oracle, or other database. It offers a means of working with your database more easily and more naturally than with ADO.NET, without requiring you to manually build your own data access layer.

Compared to LINQ to SQL, Entity Framework provides most of the same functionality for rapidly accessing your data. Where it differs is that Entity Framework provides a great deal of functionality not provided by LINQ to SQL, such as the ability to use databases other than SQL Server, and the ability to use client-side classes that don't directly map to database tables.

OBJECT-RELATIONAL MAPPING

While ADO.NET allows a certain degree of abstraction between databases, at its heart it mirrors the database structure. You use a database `Connection` object that accesses a command that either returns data in the form of a `DataReader` or populates a `DataSet`. You work with stored procedures or the database tables to maintain your database. However, as many developers discover, the data types used in the various databases are not the same, and they definitely do not match the data types you use in your Visual Basic applications. This can lead to errors in your application, such as when a database `NULL` is passed to a Visual Basic type. In addition, some of the interactions may be clumsy, such as when saving the contents of an object to the database, where you may need to map properties to the data in one or more database rows or tables.

To solve this object-to-database mismatch, a number of strategies have been developed. Many developers struggle with this process manually, handwriting a data access layer to convert between .NET and SQL. Another common strategy — and one requiring less work — is to use tools known as Object-Relational Mapping (ORM) tools. These tools either manually or automatically map the data types used in a database to those used by the client program, and vice versa. The best of these enable the actual structure of the database to be hidden from the client program, providing a more natural interaction between the program and the database. In the .NET world, the oldest and most used is nHibernate, itself a port of the Hibernate library developed first for Java development. However, there are many other ORMs, including SubSonic, LightSpeed, OpenAccess, and nowMicrosoft's Entity Framework. Even LINQ to SQL could be viewed as an ORM, in that it converts between Visual Basic types and SQL types.

While still a relatively young framework, the Entity Framework provides many of the capabilities available in the older, more mature frameworks. This includes the capability to split an object across multiple tables, map multiple objects to the same table, perform "lazy loading" (a performance optimization whereby an object is not loaded into memory until it is actually accessed), and much more. In addition, we will likely see Microsoft continue to improve it over time, so it is definitely a strong competitor in the ORM space.

ENTITY FRAMEWORK ARCHITECTURE

Figure 11-1 shows the architecture used within the Entity Framework.

As you can see from the diagram, the Entity Framework is composed of a number of logical layers. The lowest layer is related to the actual data access, and involves the familiar ADO.NET data providers. This should be expected from the earlier description of the Entity Framework not as an entirely new method of retrieving data, but as an extension of your existing knowledge of ADO.NET. The additional layers are intended to make your development experience easier and more flexible. At this layer, Entity Framework does not differ from ADO.NET or LINQ to SQL, as it deals with the tables directly.

Above the actual data access layer is the storage layer. This is basically a representation of the structure of the database, using an XML syntax. It includes any of the tables you've added to your model, as well as the relationships between them.

Above the storage layer is the mapping layer. This serves as a means of translating between the storage layer below and the conceptual layer above. You can think of it as a relatively thin layer, responsible for mapping the fields of the database tables to the appropriate properties of the classes used by your application.

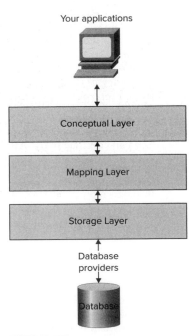

FIGURE 11-1

Next is the conceptual layer. This is the layer that provides the entities of your model, providing you with the classes you will work with in your applications — either the classes generated by the Entity Framework designer or your own classes, as you'll see later.

Finally, there is the object services layer. This serves to provide LINQ and Entity Query Language (Entity SQL) syntax over your conceptual model.

When you see a diagram like the one shown in Figure 11-1, your first instinct might be to worry about the performance penalties that these additional layers cause to your application. Of course, every mapping, abstraction, or communication adds to the query and/or update time, this is to be expected. However, the decision to use Entity Framework should not entirely be based on whether it is faster or slower than classic ADO.NET. Rather, it should depend on a combination of "Is it fast enough for my needs?" and "How much more productive does it make me?" Because Entity Framework uses the core ADO.NET objects, there is no way it can be faster than, or even as fast as, using those classes themselves. However, working with Entity Framework can be a much more natural development process, meaning you can be much more productive in creating — and, more important, maintaining — your data access code.

Conceptual Model

Your Entity Framework applications deal directly with the conceptual models you either generate or create. To see how these are constructed, create a simple console application (`SimpleEF`) and add an ADO.NET Entity Data Model to the application by selecting Project ➪ Add New Item (see Figure 11-2).

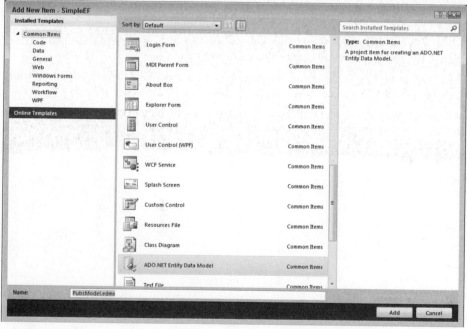

FIGURE 11-2

When you add an Entity Framework model to your application, it starts a wizard to generate the classes. The first step is to decide if you will generate your classes initially from a database or from a blank slate. For now, select to generate the classes from the database (see Figure 11-3). Select the `pubs` database.

The connection string generated at this stage (see Figure 11-4) can look a little foreboding to anyone used to the more simple SQL Server or Access connection strings.

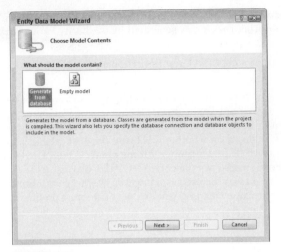

FIGURE 11-3

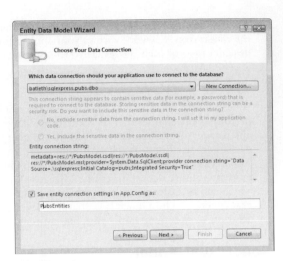

FIGURE 11-4

```
metadata=res://*/PubsModel.csdl|res://*/PubsModel.ssdl|
res://*/PubsModel.msl;provider=System.Data.SqlClient;
provider connection string=&quot;Data Source=.\sqlexpress;
Initial Catalog=pubs;Integrated Security=True;MultipleActiveResultSets=True&quot;
```

Ignoring the first few sections, you can see the "normal" connection string contained within this connection. The reason it has the additional sections is because this connection string will be used by all three layers (storage, conceptual, and mapping), not just the connection to the database. The three additional parts of the connection string identify the files that will define the structure of each layer.

Next, just as with LINQ to SQL, you can choose the database objects you would like to include in your model. For now, just select the `authors`, `titleauthor`, and `titles` tables (see Figure 11-5) and click Finish.

Figure 11-6 shows the resulting model in Visual Studio. Notice that it includes the relationships between the three tables in the model in addition to creating properties that represent the columns in the database.

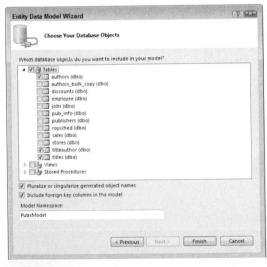

FIGURE 11-5

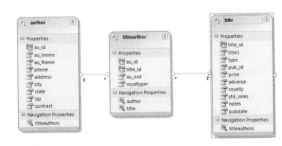

FIGURE 11-6

Finally, the wizard has created a number of *navigation properties* that represent the foreign key relationships. You can explore your model within this designer window or use the Model Browser pane that opens in Visual Studio (see Figure 11-7) which you can view by selecting View ⇨ Other Windows ⇨ Entity Data Model Browser.

Build the application but don't run it yet. Once you have it built, select the Show All Files option in the Solution Explorer (see Figure 11-8). If you navigate into the generated obj folder, you will find the three generated XML files. The following code shows a portion of the CSDL file, which is the conceptual model:

FIGURE 11-7

```xml
<?xml version="1.0" encoding="utf-8"?>
<Schema Namespace="PubsModel"
Alias="Self"
        xmlns:annotation="http://schemas.microsoft.com/ado/2009/02/edm/annotation"
        xmlns="http://schemas.microsoft.com/ado/2008/09/edm">
  <EntityContainer Name="PubsEntities" annotation:LazyLoadingEnabled="true">
    <EntitySet Name="authors" EntityType="PubsModel.author" />
    <EntitySet Name="titleauthors" EntityType="PubsModel.titleauthor" />
    <EntitySet Name="titles" EntityType="PubsModel.title" />
    <AssociationSet Name="FK__titleauth__au_id__0CBAE877"
       Association="PubsModel.FK__titleauth__au_id__0CBAE877">
      <End Role="authors" EntitySet="authors" />
      <End Role="titleauthor" EntitySet="titleauthors" />
    </AssociationSet>
    <AssociationSet Name="FK__titleauth__title__0DAF0CB0"
       Association="PubsModel.FK__titleauth__title__0DAF0CB0">
      <End Role="titles" EntitySet="titles" />
      <End Role="titleauthor" EntitySet="titleauthors" />
    </AssociationSet>
  </EntityContainer>
  <EntityType Name="author">
    <Key>
      <PropertyRef Name="au_id" />
    </Key>
    <Property Name="au_id" Type="String" Nullable="false" MaxLength="11"
      Unicode="false" FixedLength="false" />
    <Property Name="au_lname" Type="String" Nullable="false" MaxLength="40"
      Unicode="false" FixedLength="false" />
    <Property Name="au_fname" Type="String" Nullable="false" MaxLength="20"
      Unicode="false" FixedLength="false" />
    <Property Name="phone" Type="String" Nullable="false" MaxLength="12"
      Unicode="false" FixedLength="true" />
    <Property Name="address" Type="String" MaxLength="40"
      Unicode="false" FixedLength="false" />
    <Property Name="city" Type="String" MaxLength="20" Unicode="false"
      FixedLength="false" />
    <Property Name="state" Type="String" MaxLength="2" Unicode="false"
      FixedLength="true" />
    <Property Name="zip" Type="String" MaxLength="5" Unicode="false"
      FixedLength="true" />
    <Property Name="contract" Type="Boolean" Nullable="false" />
    <NavigationProperty Name="titleauthors"
      Relationship="PubsModel.FK__titleauth__au_id__0CBAE877"
                      FromRole="authors" ToRole="titleauthor" />
  </EntityType>
  ...
```

Code snippet from SimpleEF

This snippet shows some of the main terms you will see repeatedly throughout your work with the Entity Framework. The `EntityType` defines one of your objects — in this case, the `author` class. The collection of authors is defined as an `EntitySet`. There are `AssociationSets` that define the relationships between the various `EntityTypes`. Finally, there is an `EntityContainer` that groups everything. One point to notice is that each of the Property elements in the XML file has a Type attribute. This attribute uses Visual Basic data types, rather than database-specific types. This XML file will be updated as you change your conceptual model.

If you look at one of the generated types in the Class View window (see Figure 11-9), you will see that it inherits from `EntityObject`. The `EntityObject` class in turn inherits from `StructuralObject` and implements three interfaces (`IEntityWithChangeTracker`, `IEntityWithKey` and `IEntityWithRelationships`). The names of these three interfaces give you some idea of what the generated classes are capable of:

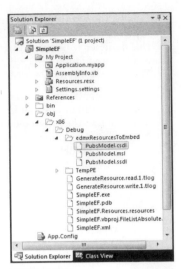

FIGURE 11-8

➤ They are able to identify one another via one or more key properties.

➤ They are aware of changes to their properties; therefore, you will be able to identify changed objects and/or properties without requiring a trip back to the database.

➤ They track their relationship to one or more other `EntityObjects`.

Storage Model

The storage model XML initially looks similar to the conceptual model XML (see the generated `PubsModel.ssdl` file in the Solution Explorer View):

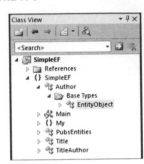

FIGURE 11-9

```xml
<?xml version="1.0" encoding="utf-8"?>
<Schema Namespace="PubsModel.Store" Alias="Self" Provider="System.Data.SqlClient"
ProviderManifestToken="2008"
xmlsn:store="http://schemas.microsoft.com/ado/2007/12/edm/EntityStoreSchemaGenerator"
xmlsn="http://schemas.microsoft.com/ado/2009/02/edm/ssdl">
  <EntityContainer Name="PubsModelStoreContainer">
    <EntitySet Name="authors" EntityType="PubsModel.Store.authors"
store:Type="Tables" Schema="dbo" />
    <EntitySet Name="titleauthor" EntityType="PubsModel.Store.titleauthor"
store:Type="Tables" Schema="dbo" />
    <EntitySet Name="titles" EntityType="PubsModel.Store.titles"
store:Type="Tables" Schema="dbo" />
    <AssociationSet Name="FK__titleauth__au_id__0CBAE877"
Association="PubsModel.Store.FK__titleauth__au_id__0CBAE877">
      <End Role="authors" EntitySet="authors" />
      <End Role="titleauthor" EntitySet="titleauthor" />
    </AssociationSet>
    <AssociationSet Name="FK__titleauth__title__0DAF0CB0"
Association="PubsModel.Store.FK__titleauth__title__0DAF0CB0">
      <End Role="titles" EntitySet="titles" />
      <End Role="titleauthor" EntitySet="titleauthor" />
    </AssociationSet>
  </EntityContainer>
  <EntityType Name="authors">
```

```
      <Key>
        <PropertyRef Name="au_id" />
      </Key>
      <Property Name="au_id" Type="varchar" Nullable="false" MaxLength="11" />
      <Property Name="au_lname" Type="varchar" Nullable="false" MaxLength="40" />
      <Property Name="au_fname" Type="varchar" Nullable="false" MaxLength="20" />
      <Property Name="phone" Type="char" Nullable="false" MaxLength="12" />
      <Property Name="address" Type="varchar" MaxLength="40" />
      <Property Name="city" Type="varchar" MaxLength="20" />
      <Property Name="state" Type="char" MaxLength="2" />
      <Property Name="zip" Type="char" MaxLength="5" />
      <Property Name="contract" Type="bit" Nullable="false" />
    </EntityType>
  ...
```

Code snippet from SimpleEF

One major difference between this file and the earlier conceptual model is that the types in the storage model are SQL Server data types. In addition, unlike the conceptual model file, this file will not change as you update your Entity Framework model, as it is tied to the database structure.

Mapping Model

Finally, you have the third XML file, the mapping schema language (MSL) file:

```
<?xml version="1.0" encoding="utf-8"?>
<Mapping Space="C-S" xmlns="http://schemas.microsoft.com/ado/2008/09/mapping/cs">
  <EntityContainerMapping StorageEntityContainer="PubsModelStoreContainer"
  CdmEntityContainer="PubsEntities">
    <EntitySetMapping Name="authors">
      <EntityTypeMapping TypeName="PubsModel.author">
        <MappingFragment StoreEntitySet="authors">
          <ScalarProperty Name="au_id" ColumnName="au_id" />
          <ScalarProperty Name="au_lname" ColumnName="au_lname" />
          <ScalarProperty Name="au_fname" ColumnName="au_fname" />
          <ScalarProperty Name="phone" ColumnName="phone" />
          <ScalarProperty Name="address" ColumnName="address" />
          <ScalarProperty Name="city" ColumnName="city" />
          <ScalarProperty Name="state" ColumnName="state" />
          <ScalarProperty Name="zip" ColumnName="zip" />
          <ScalarProperty Name="contract" ColumnName="contract" />
        </MappingFragment>
      </EntityTypeMapping>
    </EntitySetMapping>
  ...
```

Code snippet from SimpleEF

This may seem like a great deal of overhead, as it appears to map properties of the classes to the identical fields of tables. However, as you customize the conceptual model, the mapping model will change to reflect the new structure. As the Entity Framework supports mapping a single object to multiple tables, or vice versa, this mapping model increases in importance, and is the core benefit of using a framework such as Entity Framework.

LINQ to Entities

Just as there is LINQ to SQL, LINQ to XML, and LINQ to objects, there is also a LINQ syntax for working with Entity Framework models. The syntax is very similar to that used by LINQ to SQL, in that a context object is used as your access point to the exposed classes. You first create an instance of that context object and then use it to access the entities in your model. The following shows a LINQ query to retrieve authors in California:

```vbnet
Sub Main()
    Dim db As New PubsEntities
    Dim authors = From a In db.authors
                  Where a.state = "CA"
                  Order By a.au_lname, a.au_fname
                  Select a
    For Each author In authors.ToList
        Console.WriteLine("{0} {1}: {2}",
                          author.au_fname,
                          author.au_lname,
                          author.phone)
    Next

    Console.WriteLine("Press ENTER to exit")
    Console.ReadLine()
End Sub
```

Code snippet from SimpleEF

Here, the new context object (`PubsEntities`) is defined within the routine, but you are more likely to create it once and use it throughout your application. The remainder of the query defines a restriction and a sort, and returns all the properties.

Another complaint many developers have with a tool like Entity Framework is that they don't trust an application to generate T-SQL. Unlike LINQ to SQL, Entity Framework context does not support a `Log` property to view the generated T-SQL. However, you can use SQL Server Profiler to view the T-SQL for this query:

```sql
SELECT
[Extent1].[au_id] AS [au_id],
[Extent1].[au_lname] AS [au_lname],
[Extent1].[au_fname] AS [au_fname],
[Extent1].[phone] AS [phone],
[Extent1].[address] AS [address],
[Extent1].[city] AS [city],
[Extent1].[state] AS [state],
[Extent1].[zip] AS [zip],
[Extent1].[contract] AS [contract]
FROM [dbo].[authors] AS [Extent1]
WHERE 'CA' = [Extent1].[state]
ORDER BY [Extent1].[au_lname] ASC, [Extent1].[au_fname] ASC
```

Admittedly, this is a very simple query. However, with a slightly more complex query, you can see that the generated T-SQL is generally comparable to a hand-coded query:

```vbnet
Dim titles = From ta In db.titleauthors
             Where ta.author.state = "CA"
             Order By ta.author.au_lname
             Select New With {.Title = ta.title.title1,
                              .FirstName = ta.author.au_fname,
                              .LastName = ta.author.au_lname,
                              .PublishDate = ta.title.pubdate}

For Each title In titles
    Console.WriteLine("{0} by {1} {2}, published {3:d}",
                      title.Title,
                      title.FirstName,
                      title.LastName,
                      title.PublishDate)
```

The above query also retrieves the authors from California, but rather than returning the values from the `TitleAuthors` entity, it creates a new object to return. This new object returns the properties of the associated `Title` entity. This results in the following T-SQL (from SQL Server Profiler):

```
SELECT
[Project1].[C1] AS [C1],
[Project1].[title] AS [title],
[Project1].[au_fname] AS [au_fname],
[Project1].[au_lname] AS [au_lname],
[Project1].[pubdate] AS [pubdate]
FROM ( SELECT
    [Extent2].[au_lname] AS [au_lname],
    [Extent2].[au_fname] AS [au_fname],
    [Extent3].[title] AS [title],
    [Extent3].[pubdate] AS [pubdate],
    1 AS [C1]
  FROM    [dbo].[titleauthor] AS [Extent1]
  INNER JOIN [dbo].[authors] AS [Extent2]
    ON [Extent1].[au_id] = [Extent2].[au_id]
  INNER JOIN [dbo].[titles] AS [Extent3]
    ON [Extent1].[title_id] = [Extent3].[title_id]
  WHERE 'CA' = [Extent2].[state]
)  AS [Project1]
ORDER BY [Project1].[au_lname] ASC
```

The ObjectContext

As you have seen from the preceding queries, you use a context object as the root of all your queries. This context is the logical equivalent of the `Connection` object in ADO.NET, but it does much more. The context object is a class that inherits from `ObjectContext`. In addition to providing access to the database, the `ObjectContext` is also responsible for allowing you to retrieve metadata about the entities within your model and helping the objects track their changes.

Once you have made changes to one or more objects tracked by an object context, you can apply those changes back to the database using the `ObjectContext`. The `SaveChanges` method submits the changes you have made to the database. It iterates over all the added, updated, and deleted objects and submits these changes, and returns the number of records updated.

At this point, the objects do not know that they have been saved, so you must set them back to their unchanged state. There are two ways you can do this. First, you can call the `SaveChanges` method with a single `Boolean` parameter set to `SaveOptions.AcceptAllChangesAfterSave`. This automatically updates the changed objects. Alternately, you can call the `AcceptAllChanges` method of the `ObjectContext`. This also iterates through all the successful updates, resetting the change tracking. The following code shows these steps while adding and updating authors in the database:

```
'add a new author
Dim newAuthor As Author = Author.CreateAuthor(
        "555-55-5555",
        "deBar",
        "Foo",
        "555-555-1212",
        True)
db.Authors.AddObject(newAuthor)
'update an existing author
Dim authorKey As New EntityKey("PubsEntities.Authors",
                                "AuthorID", "527-72-3246")
Dim editAuthor As Author = CType(db.GetObjectByKey(authorKey), Author)
        'note: if you use this routine before renaming the
        '      properties in the model, comment this line
        '      and uncomment the other below
        editAuthor.LastName = "Green"
```

```
          ' before renaming properties
         'editAuthor.au_lname = "Green"Console.WriteLine("Author state after edit: {0}",
    editAuthor.EntityState.ToString())
'submit all changes, setting EntityState to unchanged
Dim recs As Integer = db.SaveChanges(Objects.SaveOptions.AcceptAllChangesAfterSave)
Console.WriteLine("{0} records changed", recs)
'alternately, you could call
'db.AcceptAllChanges()
'after SubmitChanges
Console.WriteLine("Author state after save: {0}",
    editAuthor.EntityState.ToString())
```

Code snippet from SimpleEF

The output of this routine should be as follows:

```
Author state after edit: Modified
2 records changed

Author state after save: Unchanged
```

The update process operates within a single transaction, so if any of the changes fail, the entire SaveChanges will fail.

MAPPING OBJECTS TO ENTITIES

Once you have completed the Entity Data Model wizard, you have a basic Entity Framework model that enables you to query your database. As you have seen, this gives you basically everything that is available with LINQ to SQL. However, you have definitely not seen all the benefits of using the Entity Framework. Exploring these benefits involves improving the conceptual model to better map to the desired structure.

Simple Mapping

The mapping created above left you with a very thin layer over the database. Each of the generated properties were identical to the field names, and the field names in the pubs database are not exactly "friendly." Changing these to create more "Visual Basic-like" property names is a simple matter.

Select the author table in the model and open the Mapping Details pane of Visual Studio. If it is closed, you can open it by selecting View ➪ Other Windows ➪ Entity Data Model Mapping Details.

As shown in the Mapping Details pane in Figure 11-10, the author object maps to the authors table, and each property maps to the field with the same name. By changing the Name property for each field in the Properties pane, you can create a mapping that better explains what some of the fields represent.

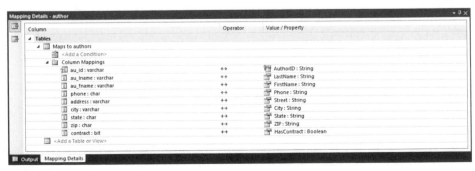

FIGURE 11-10

In addition, once you've changed the mapping, the code used to access the types reflects the new mapping (see Figure 11-11):

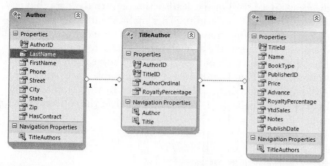

FIGURE 11-11

```
Dim db As New PubsEntities
Sub SimpleQuery()
    Dim authors = From a In db.Authors
            Where a.State = "CA"
            Order By a.LastName, a.FirstName
            Select a

    For Each author In authors.ToList
        Console.WriteLine("{0} {1}: {2}",
        author.FirstName,
        author.LastName,
        author.Street)
    Next
End Sub
```

Code snippet from SimpleEF

Recall that the Entity Framework model included a number of navigation properties that represented the relationships between the defined classes, such as the `titleauthors` property on the `title` and `author` classes. These navigation properties — as their name implies — enable you to navigate between the classes in your queries. For example, you can query and return the books written by authors from California with the following query:

```
Dim titles = From ta In db.TitleAuthors
Where ta.Author.State = "CA"
Order By ta.Author.LastName
Select New With {.Title = ta.Title.Name,
.FirstName = ta.Author.FirstName,
.LastName = ta.Author.LastName,
.PublishDate = ta.Title.PublishDate}

For Each title In titles
    Console.WriteLine("{0} by {1} {2}, published {3:d}",
    title.Title,
    title.FirstName,
    title.LastName,
    title.PublishDate)
Next
```

Code snippet from SimpleEF

The process of navigating the query is made much easier if you start in the middle with the join table. In this case, we query the titleauthors table to retrieve the titles that have one or more authors from California.

The titleauthors table does not have fields for author; these properties are the navigation properties, which enable you to traverse the relationships relatively naturally.

This query also demonstrates the use of projections in a LINQ query. Rather than return the data that is queried, a new object is created using the `Select New With {}` syntax. This enables you to define a new object to be returned as a result of the query. Each of the properties in the new object are defined by including them in the braces, starting with a dot. In the preceding query, the new object will have four properties: `Title`, `FirstName`, `LastName` and `PublishDate`, and the values of these properties come from the results of the query. This returned object is an anonymous object. That is, it does not have a usable name within the system (if you look at it in the debugger, it will have a name that has been generated by the compiler. Still, the returned object can be used normally: Because it is a collection, you can iterate over the collection using a `For Each` loop to display the list (see Figure 11-12).

FIGURE 11-12

Using a Single Table for Multiple Objects

Within your application design, you may have one or more classes that inherit from another. For example, you might have a `Contact` base class, with employees and customers that inherit from them. The `Contact` base class has the standard `FirstName`, `LastName`, and so on, properties. The `Employee` child class might add properties for department or manager, while the Customer would have a shipping address, customer ID, or other properties. These types of designs are traditionally very difficult to map to a database. If you were to save this structure to a database, you would have a couple of options. One, you might include all the properties, and add a property to identify the type of the resulting object, as shown in Figure 11-13.

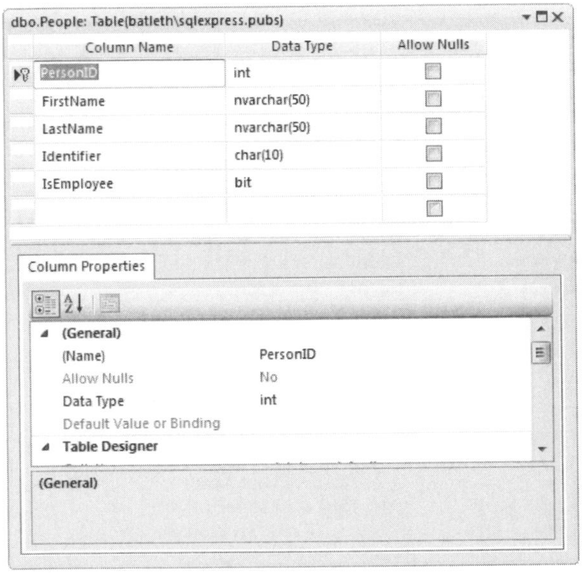

In this table, the `IsEmployee` field is true if the person is an employee, and false if not.

FIGURE 11-13

The identifier will indicate either an employee number or a customer number. Figure 11-14 shows the desired conceptual model (see the `EmployeeModel` in the `SimpleEF` project).

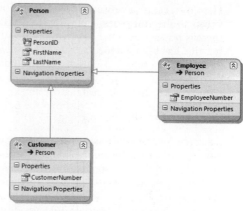

In this model, `Customer` and `Employee` inherit from `Person`. Notice that the `IsEmployee` and `Identifier` fields are not on the model, and the `Employee` and `Customer` entities have their own unique properties.

To create this structure, you use the Mapping Details pane of Visual Studio. After you have generated a model based on the People table (refer to Figure 11-14), add two new entities that will represent the `Employee` and `Customer` entities. Change the `Id` property that is created by default to the `EmployeeNumber` and `Customer` number properties. Set the `Type` property to `String`, and the `Max Length` property to `10`. Select the `Inheritance` item

FIGURE 11-14

from the Toolbox, and drag an inheritance from `Employee` to `Person`, and `Customer` to `Person`.

Once the basic model is done, you're ready to add the mapping. Select the `Person` entity and delete the `IsEmployee` and `Identifier` properties by right-clicking on them and selecting Delete. This will remove

the mapping of these properties to the `Person` object. At the same time, as you will not be creating new people using this type (as someone needs to be either an `Employee` or a `Customer`), set the `Abstract` property of the `Person` entity to `True`.

Select the `Employee` entity. Select the Person table under the `Tables` collection. Map the `Identifier` field to the `EmployeeNumber` property. Notice that above the field mappings is a Condition mapping. This is how you will distinguish employees from customers. Select the `IsEmployee` field, and set the Condition's value to true (see Figure 11-15).

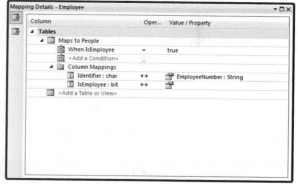

FIGURE 11-15

Do a similar mapping for the `Customer` entity, but set the Condition to select the `IsEmployee=false` records. You should now be able to validate the model by right-clicking the designer and selecting Validate.

You can now work with the three tables as you would expect from the model. For example, you can create a new employee with the following code:

```vb
Dim ctx As New EmployeeEntities
Dim newEmployee As New Employee
With newEmployee
    .FirstName = "Augustus"
    .LastName = "Caesar"
    .EmployeeNumber = "LIVXXIII"
End With
ctx.People.AddObject(newEmployee)
ctx.SaveChanges(Objects.SaveOptions.AcceptAllChangesAfterSave)
```

Code snippet from SimpleEF

Here, you create a new employee, assign some values to the properties, and save. Recall that there is no `EmployeeNumber` field in the database, but this has been mapped to the `Identifier` field in the `Person` table. Also notice that you do not directly set the `IsEmployee` field. Instead, it is set based on whether you create either an `Employee` or a `Customer`. Figure 11-16 shows the newly added record in the `Person` table.

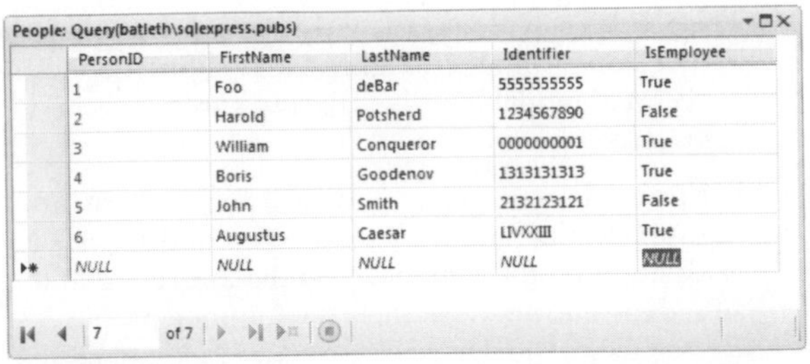

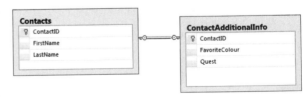

FIGURE 11-16

Selecting records when using these types of models can be slightly confusing the first few times, as you will find that the context does not have an `Employees` or `Customers` collection on them. If you look at the properties for these entities, it makes more sense; you will see that the `EntitySetName` property for these entities is `People` (how I defined the `EntitySetName` for the `Person` collection). Therefore, you still query them as people, but you add an additional qualifier to the query to select for the desired child class:

```
Dim ctx As New EmployeeEntities
Dim employees = From e In ctx.People.OfType(Of Employee)()
                Order By e.LastName Select e
For Each emp In employees
    Console.WriteLine("{0} {1}: {2}",
        emp.FirstName,
        emp.LastName,
        emp.EmployeeNumber)
Next
```

Code snippet from SimpleEF

In this code, the `OfType(Of Employee)` clause defines the type you are retrieving. Of course, you could have had multiple types here, rather than just the two, and the `OfType` clause would limit the returned records to just those with the correct value in the Condition mappings you created.

Using Multiple Tables for an Object

Alternately, there are instances when you would like to store parts of a single entity on different tables. This is typically when you know that only some of the records in a database will need certain fields and you prefer a more normalized database. For example, if you are creating a contact management application, you will have some fields that every record will contain, such as `FirstName`, `LastName`, etc. However, some of the contacts may have additional properties, such as a `BirthDate`, `Department`, etc. At this point in your design, you have two options: Include those properties as columns in your table (and have many of them null), or split your table into two tables — one for the core contact information and the other for the additional information for each contact (see Figure 11-17).

FIGURE 11-17

However, splitting the tables like that can be awkward for the client developer. Rather than work with a simple object, they now would have to navigate through the join to retrieve the additional information. Fortunately, Entity Framework enables you to simplify the scenario by mapping an entity to the two tables.

The Entity Framework enables the creation of these split entities as long as the two objects share their primary key. That way, when an object is inserted or updated, the correct data will be inserted in the additional table. In this case, the two tables were defined as follows:

TABLE	FIELD	DATA TYPE
Contact	ContactID	int, identity
	FirstName	varchar(50)
	LastName	varchar(50)
ContactAdditionalInfo	ContactID	int
	FavoriteColour	varchar(50)
	Quest	varchar(255)

Create a new Entity Data Model (called `ContactModel`) and drag the two tables over. Copy the two additional properties from the `ContactAdditionalInfo` table and paste them into the `Contact` table.

Now you will need to set up the mapping for the combined entity. In the Mapping Details pane, click the space next to Add a table or view and select the `ContactAdditionalInfo` table. It should automatically select the correct fields, but you may have to select them manually. Once you have done this, you can delete the `ContactAdditionalInfo` entity from the model (see Figure 11-18).

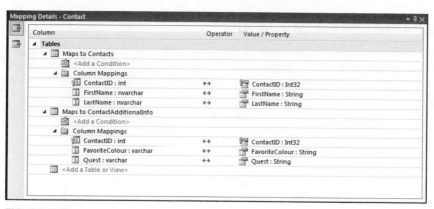

FIGURE 11-18

The final mapping should appear as shown in Figure 11-19.

Once this mapping is complete, you can treat the entity as though it were a single object, and the Entity Framework will handle the database. Add a few entries to the two tables, making sure that some (not necessarily all) of the records in the `ContactAdditionalInfo` table have values:

FIGURE 11-19

```vb
Dim ctx As New ContactEntities
Dim faves = From c In ctx.Contacts
            Where c.FavoriteColor IsNot Nothing
            Order By c.LastName
            Select New With {.Name = c.FirstName & " " & c.LastName,
                             .Color = c.FavoriteColour}

For Each fav In faves
    Console.WriteLine("{0} likes {1}", fav.Name, fav.Color)
Next
```

Code snippet from SimpleEF

Here the contacts are queried based on one of the properties that actually resides in the secondary table. However, from this code you wouldn't know that, thinking instead that it was a single table. In addition, notice that you again create a simple projection for the display of the data.

In addition to querying the data, using the merged tables is also transparent when inserting data:

```
Dim ctx As New ContactEntities
Dim newContact As New Contact
With newContact
    .FirstName = "Foo"
    .LastName = "deBar"
    .FavoriteColor = "Blue"
    .Quest = "To seek the holy data access layer"
End With
ctx.Contacts.AddObject(newContact)
ctx.SaveChanges()
```

Code snippet from SimpleEF

This is an example of one of the core benefits of using something like the Entity Framework: The client developer does not know the database contains two tables, nor do they care. They simply use the classes provided to them by the framework, and tell them to save the data. The DBA, meanwhile, is happy that his or her database is normalized, with no series of NULL columns cluttering up the database model.

GENERATING THE DATABASE FROM A MODEL

Sometimes it is better to work with a conceptual model, and then use that to build your database. This fits better with a design process in which you design the classes — using either UML or simply a whiteboard — and then once you're comfortable with the model, use the model to build your database. Obviously, this is really only an option for brand-new development, where you have the flexibility to create whatever database you desire. Many developers prefer to design and communicate just the conceptual model between themselves before "formalizing" it by actually building out the database.

Working in this model with Entity Framework is a two-stage process: First you design the desired model, then you create the database from it. Once the database is in place, you can then continue to work with the model or the database, refining each as appropriate. Visual Studio includes the tools to keep the two in sync.

To explore the process of model-first design, add a new Entity Framework model called BlogModel to an application by selecting Project ⇨ Add New Item and selecting the ADO.NET Entity Data Model template (See the ModelFirst project in the sample code). Rather than generate the model from a database, choose "Empty model" from the Entity Data Model Wizard (see Figure 11-20).

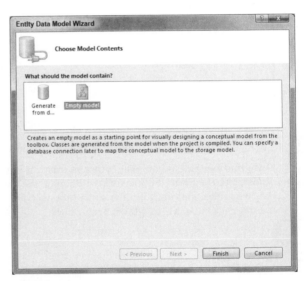

FIGURE 11-20

You will be returned to Visual Studio with a blank slate you can use to define your model. You add new entities (and other Entity Framework constructs) from the Toolbox. Drag two entities onto the designer; name one Post, and the other Comment. These will be used to create a very basic blogging engine. Add properties as described in the following table. To add a new property, right-click on the entity and select Add ⇨ Scalar Property.

ENTITY	PROPERTY	DEFINITION
Post	PostID	`Int32`. In addition, set the `Entity Key` property to `True`, the `StoreGeneratedPattern` to `Identity`, and `Nullable` to `False`. (Note: this replaces the Id field created when you create this new entity.)
	Title	String. Set `Max Length` to something reasonable, such as 512, and set `Nullable` to `False`.
	Body	String. Set `Max Length` to `Max`, and `Nullable` to `False`.
	PublishDate	`DateTimeOffset`. Set `Nullable` to `False`.
	Entity Set Name	`Posts`
Comment	CommentID	`Int32`. In addition, set the `Entity Key` property to `True`, the `StoreGeneratedPattern` to `Identity`, and `Nullable` to `False`. (Note: this replaces the Id field created when you create this new entity.)
	Body	String. Set `Max Length` to something reasonable, perhaps 512, and set `Nullable` to `False`.
	Author	String. Set `Max Length` to 50, and set `Nullable` to `False`.
	PostID	`Int32`. This will be used to relate the two tables.
	Entity Set Name	`Comments`

Once you have the two entities defined, select the association item from the Toolbox. Right-click on the designer, and select Add ⇨ Association to add an association from the Post entity to the Comment entity (see Figure 11-21). Note: uncheck the Add foreign key properties to the Comment entity, as you have already included the `PostID` property.

In addition, navigation properties will be added to the two entities. Select the `Referential Constraint` property of the association and click the ellipses to bring up the Referential Constraint dialog. This dialog identifies the properties used to map between the two entities — in this case, the `PostID` property. Select Post in the Principal drop-down. The Comment item should already be selected in the Dependant field. Finally (see Figure 11-22), select the `PostID` property as the `DependantProperty`. If you fail to create this mapping, Entity Framework will add an additional property to the Comment table when you generate your database.

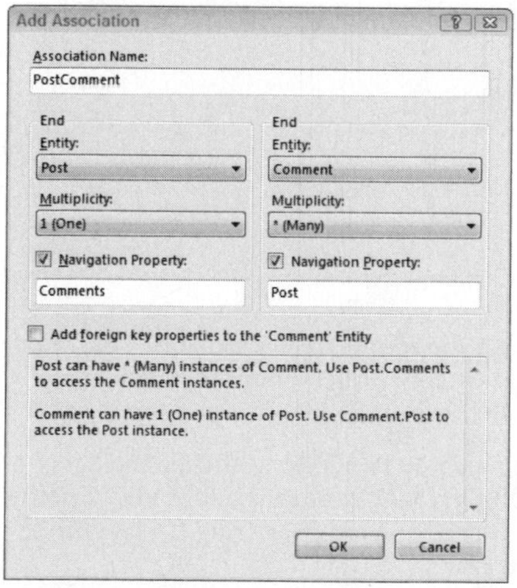

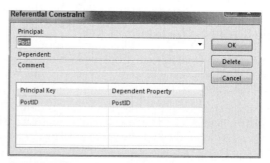

FIGURE 11-21

FIGURE 11-22

Right-click on the white space of the designer to display the context menu. Select Generate Database from the Model. As you have not yet assigned this to a database, warnings will appear in the Error List, telling you that the three items have not been mapped (the Post and Comment entities, and the PostComment association). In addition, the Generate Database Wizard will run. The first step is to either select an existing database connection or create a new one. Select your target and click Next. This will display the DDL that will be applied to the database (see Figure 11-23). While the SQL in this dialog is not editable, it is a good idea to review it to ensure that you've set up the model correctly. If so, click Finish to send this command to the database. This will build the tables in the database, apply any constraints (e.g., for the primary keys), and create the relationships.

 If Visual Studio is not connected to your database, it will just add the newly created DDL to a new window. Select Execute SQL to run this query and create your database.

You can now use the model just as though you generated it from a database.

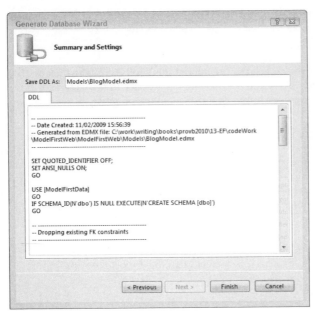

FIGURE 11-23

Updating the Model

Eventually, you will have to make changes to your model, whether you model first or generate your model from a database. If you make the changes to your model, you can usually just resubmit the DDL to the database. However, this typically drops the tables first, so you will likely lose data.

Another alternative is to make the changes at the database. You may add new tables, change the data types of columns, or add new columns to your database using T-SQL, SQL Management Studio, or other methods. You can then update your model by right-clicking on the designer and selecting Update Model from Database. This will start up the Update Wizard (see Figure 11-24).

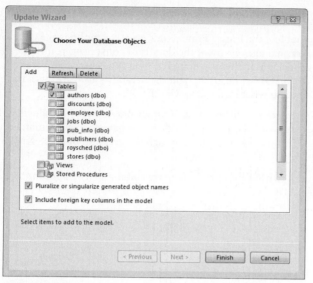

FIGURE 11-24

This dialog has three tabs, depending on what you'd like to update from your database. The Add and Delete tabs enable you to identify database items you'd like to add or delete from your model. The Refresh tab enables you to identify structures that may have changed in the database. The wizard will update the corresponding entities in your model.

For example, add a new column called CommentDate to the Comments table that will be used to track when the comment is made. Set the data type to `DateTimeOffset`. Save that change to the database and run the Update Wizard, selecting to refresh the existing tables. The result should add a new property to your Comment entity (see Figure 11-25).

 If you get an error saving the changes to the database, it may be because Visual Studio is configured to not allow changes that require re-creating tables. To enable this functionality, go to the Visual Studio options dialog Tools ➪ Options ➪ Designers ➪ Table and Database Designers and uncheck the property Prevent saving changes that require table re-creation.

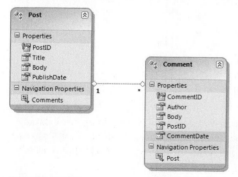

FIGURE 11-25

SUMMARY

Using an Object-Relational Mapping (ORM) tool like the Entity Framework greatly simplifies the creation of a database application. The Entity Framework manages many of the details of converting your logical application model into the physical database model, automatically mapping data types between Visual Basic and T-SQL. It provides the ease of use of LINQ to SQL while giving you the flexibility to work with the entities as designed, rather than being constrained to what is possible with T-SQL.

This chapter looked at how you can connect to a database using Entity Framework. One of the benefits of the Entity Framework is that the model you use to work with your data does not have to exactly match the tables in your database. As you saw, the Entity Framework does this through the creation of three XML files to manage the mapping between the two.

In addition, you saw how the Entity Framework greatly simplifies editing the database. The amount of code required to update a database "by hand" using ADO.NET (i.e. using `DataReader` and/or `DataSet`) is much larger than the amount you need to write when working with the Entity Framework.

12

Working with SQL Server

WHAT YOU WILL LEARN IN THIS CHAPTER

➤ How to use SQL Server Compact to create local copies of your SQL Server databases to create a local cache

➤ How to use SQL Server Compact and the Sync Framework to create a local synchronized cache of your SQL Server databases

➤ How to use SQL Server's XML features to return data as XML

➤ How to create CLR objects within your SQL Server databases

➤ How to create and use WCF Data Services to expose your data as a RESTful service

Most of the relationship between a developer and SQL Server relates to querying or saving data, and we've spent the last couple of chapters examining the two main ways of doing this with Visual Basic. However, Visual Studio 2010 provides a few other ways to work with databases: SQL Server Compact, SQL CLR, and WCF Data Services.

While Visual Basic has always included tools for working with the various server editions and versions of SQL Server, there exists a much smaller version: SQL Server Compact. SQL Server Compact is a lightweight version of the database that requires minimal installation and configuration to use. It runs on both Windows and devices running Windows CE. SQL Server Compact is particularly well suited for creating local caches of a larger remote database, which may be used to improve performance when querying rarely changing tables or for the creation of partially connected solutions when working with data. In combination with various synchronization scenarios, SQL Server Compact provides developers with a powerful tool for enabling their applications to work both connected to the main database and offline (still storing records until the next connection).

SQL Server 2005 was the first version to add integration with the .NET Framework. This provided two main benefits. One, you can use Visual Basic to create elements in the database, such as user-defined types, stored procedures, and functions. These objects may work alone or in concert with Transact-SQL (T-SQL) objects. Two, you can expose Web services from your databases, enabling .NET and other client applications to execute code on the database. SQL Server 2008 continues this feature, and includes new data types that leverage this feature to manipulate rich data in your applications.

Transact-SQL, while full-featured, lacks a number of features that are common in general-purpose languages such as Visual Basic. Visual Basic includes better support for looping and conditional statements than T-SQL. In addition to these language features, the .NET Framework is available for use with Visual Basic, meaning you have access to tools for network access, string handling, mathematical processing, internationalization, and more. Therefore, if your stored procedures need access to features such as these, it may be beneficial to look at using Visual Basic as the language, not T-SQL.

While ADO.NET and the Entity Framework are intended for communicating directly with a database, you frequently need to share this data across networks. While you can pass some of the objects from these frameworks across network boundaries — or use custom-serialized .NET objects — WCF Data Services (formerly ADO.NET Data Services) makes this remarkably easy. WCF Data Services enables access to databases over the Internet using standard protocols, such as HTTP, JSON, and AtomPub.

This chapter describes how you can use Visual Basic to create applications that save data to SQL Server Compact databases. It covers some of the synchronization methods you can take advantage of to create partially connected applications. This chapter also covers the capability to host CLR objects and Web services within SQL Server, and how you can create these objects using Visual Basic. Finally, you will learn how to leverage WCF Data Services to access your data across the Internet.

SQL SERVER COMPACT

The main benefits of SQL Server Compact over its larger cousins are size and ease of deployment. Even SQL Server Express Edition requires that you install a Windows service before working with data. The database engine of SQL Server Compact consists of a set of DLLs with a total size of less than 2MB. Installation can be done either by including these DLLs in the output of your project or by including the SQL Server Compact MSI file as part of your deployment project. This MSI can be included when deploying your application with ClickOnce. After it is installed, you get most of the benefits of SQL Server, including multi-user access, the query processor, and referential integrity. All the data and log files for the database are stored in a single file (with the extension .SDF). This file can be encrypted for security purposes with a simple password. The database file will grow as needed to support the stored data and may be compacted if necessary. If these benefits remind you of "the old days" of storing your data in Jet (Microsoft Access) databases, it should. SQL Server Compact provides the same rapid development and deployment model you used to enjoy, along with better compatibility and upgradeability between the server and client databases.

SQL Server Compact is not without its limitations, however. Designed to be small and portable, it does place restrictions on the size and types of data you can store. Those limitations include the following:

➤ By default, the maximum database size for SQL Server Compact is 256MB (128MB on devices). However, you can configure the maximum database size to be as high as 4GB if you change the connection string.

➤ Maximum row size is 8060 bytes, although, as with the other editions of SQL Server, this does not include the size of blob or text fields.

➤ By default, SQL Server Compact does not work with ASP.NET. This can be enabled, but it is not recommended except in cases of simple sites with limited data access needs. This is primarily for concurrency. While SQL Server Compact supports multiple users, the types used by SQL Server Compact are not thread-safe, and having them in use by multiple threads may lead to collisions. However, it is fine for small sites where multiple users will not be accessing the file at the same time. To enable SQL Server Compact on ASP.NET, you should make the following method call before attempting to open a connection to the SQL Server Compact database:

```
AppDomain.CurrentDomain.SetData("SQLServerCompactEditionUnderWebHosting",
true)
```

➤ SQL Server Compact does not support the use of stored procedures, views, functions, or user-defined types.

When it is working in a standalone situation, SQL Server Compact is almost identical to its larger SQL versions. You still connect to the database with a class that inherits DbConnection and use classes that inherit from DbDataAdapter and DbCommand to query it. SQL Server Compact differs, however, in that you don't use the classes in System.Data.SqlClient. Instead, you use the classes in the namespace System.Data.SqlServerCe. There you will find SQL Server CompactConnection, SQL Server CompactCommand, and SQL Server CompactDataAdapter. The code that follows shows a simple example of accessing a SQL Server Compact database:

```
Using conn As New SqlCeConnection(My.Settings.productsConnectionString)
    conn.Open()
    Using cmd As _
      New SqlCeCommand("SELECT ProductName, UnitPrice FROM Products", conn)
        Using reader As SqlCeDataReader = cmd.ExecuteReader
            While reader.Read
                Console.WriteLine("{0}: {1:c}",
                    reader.GetString(0),
                    reader.GetDecimal(1))
            End While
        End Using
    End Using
End Using
```

If you use the provider-agnostic classes, then the code becomes even more like the SQL Server equivalent:

```
Dim fact As DbProviderFactory
Dim prov As String = My.Settings.productsProvider
fact = DbProviderFactories.GetFactory(prov)
Using conn As DbConnection = fact.CreateConnection()
    conn.ConnectionString = My.Settings.productsConnectionString
    conn.Open()
    Using cmd As DbCommand = fact.CreateCommand
        With cmd
            .CommandText = "SELECT ProductName, UnitPrice FROM Products"
            .CommandType = CommandType.Text
            .Connection = conn
            Using reader As DbDataReader = cmd.ExecuteReader
                While reader.Read
                    Console.WriteLine("{0}: {1:c}", _
                        reader.GetString(0), _
                        reader.GetDecimal(1))
                End While
            End Using
        End With
    End Using
End Using
```

The simplest possible way to use a SQL Server Compact database in your application is to use it as a standalone database. While you get none of the benefits of synchronization, you do get the benefit of the simpler (and smaller) deployment for SQL Server Compact. However, the true power of SQL Server Compact comes into play when you use it along with synchronization with a full SQL Server database. This enables you to more easily create applications that work both offline and online.

Connecting to a SQL Server Compact Database

As with other editions of SQL Server, the key to connecting to a SQL Server Compact database is in the connection string. However, because SQL Server Compact does not have the same features in terms of server and integrated security, different options are used to connect to the database, the most important of which are described in Table 12-1. Only the data source and password values can be set within the IDE.

TABLE 12-1: SQL Server Compact Connection Options

OPTION	DESCRIPTION
Provider name	`System.Data.SqlServerCe`
Data source	Points to the SDF file. As this file is normally included in the project, the value can be written using the `DataDirectory` shortcut: `DataSource=|DataDirectory|\ DatabaseName.sdf;`

continues

TABLE 12-1 *(continued)*

OPTION	DESCRIPTION
Password	The password used to encrypt the database.
Max buffer size	The maximum amount of memory that is used before SQL Server Compact flushes the changes to disk, measured in kilobytes. The default value is 640, which should be enough for everyone.
Max database size	The maximum size for the database, measured in megabytes. The default value is 256MB (128MB when SQL Server Compact is running on devices), and the maximum value is 4096MB (4GB).
Mode	How the database file will be opened. This value can be Read Only, Read Write, Exclusive, or Shared Read. The default, Read Write, should be used, unless you have particular needs for your database.
Autoshrink threshold	As SQL Server Compact databases will grow on demand, there may be situations when you need them to shrink on demand as well, such as when a large amount of data is deleted or a complex operation needing temporary tables completes. When this occurs, this setting identifies when, and by how much, the database should shrink. By default, SQL Server Compact will shrink a database when 60 percent of the available space is empty. Normally, you will not need to change this setting unless space is at a premium.

Using SQL Server Compact as a local standalone database can be useful when creating small, easily deployed applications. You can see this by creating a simple application to store contact data in a SQL Server Compact database:

1. Create a new Windows Forms Application project named **LocalDatabase** and add a new local database to your application by right-clicking the project and selecting Add Item (see Figure 12-1).

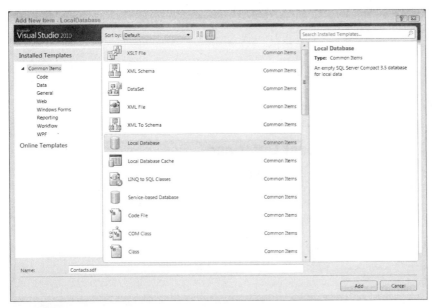

FIGURE 12-1

2. Once you have added the new database, Visual Studio will also add a new data set to the project and start the Data Source Configuration Wizard. As you are not using the database to retrieve server data, the DataSet will initially be blank (see Figure 12-2). Click Finish to add the new DataSet. You will add the tables later.

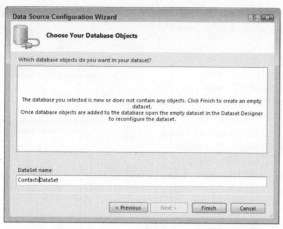

FIGURE 12-2

3. Double-click on the Contacts.sdf file in your project to open it in the Server Explorer window. You can now add a new table named Contacts to the database, as shown in Figure 12-3 and described in the following table.

COLUMN	DATA TYPE	DESCRIPTION
id	Int	This should be set to not allow null values, and as the primary key for the table. Remember to set Identity to true.
FirstName	NVarChar(50)	Allow Nulls should be set to false.
LastName	NVarChar(50)	Allow Nulls should be set to false.
EMail	NVarChar(100)	Allow Nulls should be set to true.

FIGURE 12-3

4. In Solution Explorer, double-click the `ContactsDataSet` added earlier to open the designer and drag the newly created table onto the surface (see Figure 12-4).

5. Open the Data Sources window in Visual Studio by clicking the Data Sources tab. You should see the ContactsDataSet, with the Contacts table. Drag the Contacts table onto the form to create a `DataGridView` control and a navigator (see Figure 12-5). You should now be able to run the application and add some data.

6. If you look at the contents of the `Contacts.sdf` file, you may be dismayed, as no data is visible. This is because it is not the database actually being written to. If you look in the `/bin/debug` folder for the application, you will see the actual database, which contains the data added (see Figure 12-6).

FIGURE 12-4

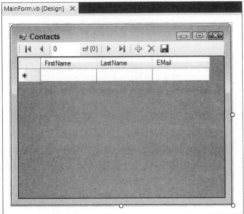

FIGURE 12-5

FIGURE 12-6

Synchronizing Data

As mentioned earlier, although you can use SQL Server Compact as a standalone database, it really shines when it is used in combination with a remote database and synchronization. Synchronization enables you to reduce the network traffic required when querying the database, while still keeping up-to-date data on the client. It may be one-way synchronization, pulling the most recent server changes down to the client, or it may be bidirectional, keeping both client and server synchronized. The best choice depends on the situation. You would want to use synchronization in your applications in a number of scenarios:

➤ **Remote data mirror applications** — These applications use the local database only as a local copy of the master database, likely as a subset of data. In this scenario, shown in Figure 12-7, data flows only one way: from the server database to the client. Most commonly, this would be product information, news, or customer data that the clients would read but not change.

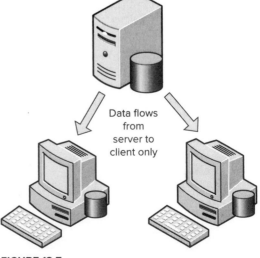

Data flows from server to client only

FIGURE 12-7

➤ **Remote data entry applications** — These include Sales or Field Force Automation (SFA and FFA) applications, such as the classic "traveling sales agent" applications. In this scenario, a given data row goes only in a single direction: reference data down to the client, inserts up to the server, as shown in Figure 12-8. As with the remote data mirror applications, a subset of data is typically installed on the client workstation, generally the catalog information and any reference data required, before the application goes off the network. The sales agent then goes out, making sales. Occasionally, the application is reconnected to the network, when new customer and sales data are uploaded to the main database, and updated catalog data is sent to the client.

➤ **Simple queuing applications** — These applications are a special case of the preceding scenario. The applications write exclusively to the local database and use synchronization to push the changed data to the server database. The difference here is partly intent; here the local database on the client is used as a temporary holding space. A periodic synchronization moves data between server and client when the two are connected. This scenario, shown in Figure 12-9, improves the overall performance of the application, particularly when you have a slow connection between server and client. It also provides access to the application even when the network is not available.

➤ **Remote database applications** — These applications treat the remote database as though it were a "master" copy of the data. In this scenario, shown in Figure 12-10, data may be changed either at the client or at the server, and the changes flow in both directions. This is the most dangerous scenario for synchronization clients because the data may have been changed differently in two (or more) locations. Therefore, some form of conflict resolution is required, as well as policies that specify which changes take precedence (e.g., last change overrides the data, someone must manually process all conflicts to select the valid data, or the data change made by the highest person in the organization chart wins). It is best to avoid or limit this scenario if possible when building a synchronization solution.

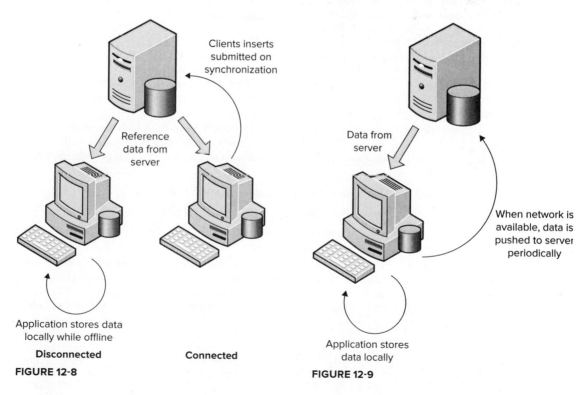

FIGURE 12-8

FIGURE 12-9

Because each synchronization scenario requires different decisions, SQL Server Compact supports three different technologies for defining the synchronization:

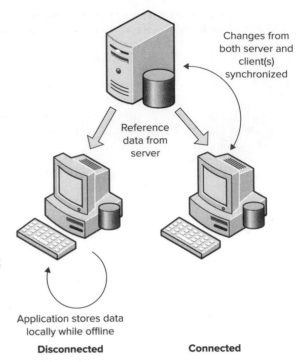

➤ **Remote Data Access (RDA)** — RDA is the simplest means of configuring synchronization between SQL Server Compact and one of its larger brethren. With RDA, you create a new virtual directory under IIS. The virtual directory includes the SQL Server CE Agent DLL. Client applications then initiate the synchronization. Data can be pulled or pushed out of a single table, and you can query for a subset of the data. While this method is tempting, Microsoft has announced that further support for this technology is unlikely; they won't be adding any additional features to it. Instead, developers are encouraged to make use of Sync Services.

➤ **Merge replication** — This is the replication system built into SQL Server. It is a DBA-centric model, whereby the database administrator configures the data shared between the applications. The SQL Server Agent then schedules the synchronization between server and client(s). This form of synchronization is powerful, but it is also the most complex to configure. It requires permissions to create the publications and synchronization schedule on the server, as well as to create the subscriptions on the client. Creating merge replication publications is supported only on SQL Server Standard Edition and higher, so you can't create a merge replication between SQL Server Express and SQL Server Compact.

FIGURE 12-10

➤ **Sync Framework** — The Sync Framework provides the simplicity of RDA with the robustness of merge replication. They make it incredibly easy to create an application that uses the SQL Server Compact database as a local cache. With a bit of additional code, you can also use it for bidirectional synchronization.

Here's an example of using Sync Framework to create a one-way synchronization:

1. Create a new Windows Forms Application project (here it is called LocalCache).

2. Add a new Local Database Cache item to the project (see Figure 12-11). As this will be used to cache data from the pubs database, it is called PubsCache.

3. The Local Database Cache item enables you to easily configure the Sync Framework, as it starts the Data Synchronization Wizard. The first step of the wizard is to configure the two connection strings: for server and client. Create a new server connection string to the pubs database used in Chapter 10. Once this is done, the wizard will add a new SQL Server Compact database to the project and create the client connection (see Figure 12-12).

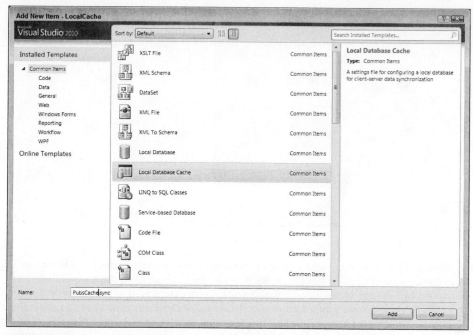

FIGURE 12-11

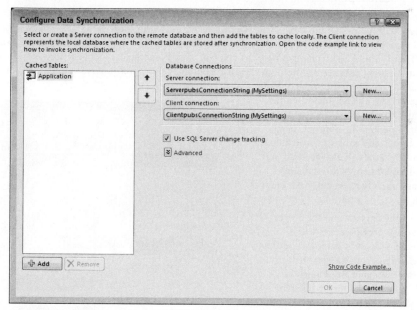

FIGURE 12-12

4. The next step in configuring the synchronization is to add the tables that will be synchronized. Click the Add button in the lower-left corner of the dialog and select the stores and titles tables (see Figure 12-13).

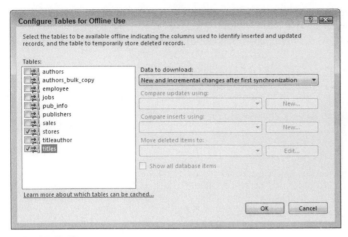

FIGURE 12-13

5. The Sync Framework may need to make changes to your database to enable some of its functionality. In order to identify new or updated records, it needs to add fields. By default, these are called `CreationDate` and `LastEditDate`. In addition, deleted records are moved to a tombstone table, rather than completely deleted. If you already have columns defined for these purposes, you can select them instead. Alternatively, you can have the synchronization pull down the full copy of the table with each synchronization, which may be a useful alternative if the tables are fairly small. Click OK to return to the Configure Data Synchronization dialog.

6. Clicking OK on the Configure Data Synchronization dialog opens a new dialog, the Data Source Configuration Wizard. This allows you to define whether you will access your local data using a data set, or using an Entity Framework model. Select the data set, and click Next. The next step confirms the local connection string. There should be no changes here, so you can click Next again. The next step is to select the tables that the local data set will hold; in this case you want the stores and titles tables. Select them and click Finish to complete the wizard. Note a number of changes to the project, including the newly added sync file, as well as the local SQL Server Compact database and the data set. If you chose to add the columns and tables for tracking the changes to the database, you will also see two SQL files per table added: one to apply those changes to the database (this has already been run) and one to remove those changes.

7. Open the designer for the data set and the Server Explorer. If you have not previously created a connection to the server-side pubs database, add one now. Drag the `sales` table from the server-side `pubs` database to the Dataset designer (see Figure 12-14). In this case, you will write to the server-side table, but use the data in the local database as a cache for the less frequently changing stores and titles data. This should improve the overall performance of the application, as it reduces the need to constantly retrieve the data for those two tables.

8. Before adding a control to display the sales data on the form, you must make a few changes to the data source. Select the form as the active window, and

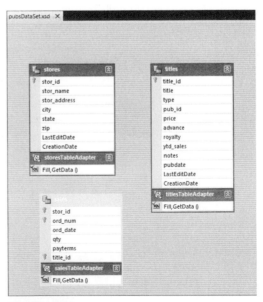

FIGURE 12-14

open the Data Sources window. At this point, you can change the controls that will be used to edit the data. Change the control used to display the sales table to a `DetailsView`, the control for the `ord_num` column to a `Label`, and the controls for the `stor_id` and `title_id` to a `ComboBox` (see Figure 12-15). This enables you to create a form displaying a single record at a time, with drop-down fields for the two columns being synchronized.

FIGURE 12-15

9. You can now drag the `sales` table onto the form from the Data Sources window. This creates the `DetailsView` control, as well as a `BindingNavigator`. It also creates the connections necessary for navigating through the data. Drag the `stores` table from the Data Sources window onto the `stor_id` `ComboBox`. This adds a connection to the local data. It also sets the visible text of the `ComboBox` to the name of each store, rather than simply displaying the store's id value. Repeat this with the `titles` table and the `title_id` `ComboBox`. The form should now look similar to what is shown in Figure 12-16, and you should be able to run the application and navigate through the data.

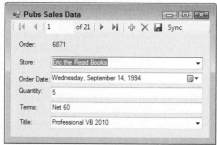

FIGURE 12-16

10. You're ready to add the synchronization code to the application, but there needs to be some way to trigger it. Add a new button to the toolbar at the top of the form by clicking just after the Save button. Set the properties of the new button as shown in the following table:

PROPERTY	VALUE
Name	SyncButton
DisplayStyle	Text
Text	Sync

11. Double-click the newly created `SyncButton` to add the code to perform the synchronization. What code do you need to add? Fortunately, the developers have written the majority of it for you. Right-click the PubsCache.sync file and select View Designer to see the designer. Click the Show Code Example link in the lower-right corner to display the required code (see Figure 12-17).

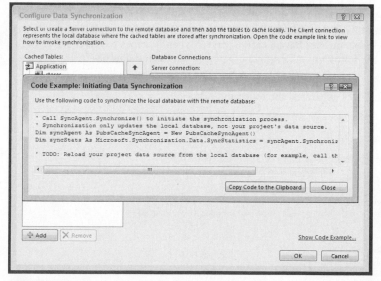

FIGURE 12-17

12. Click the Copy Code to the Clipboard button to copy the code. Add the code to the SyncButton click event as shown in the following code. In addition to the code that performs the actual synchronization, you need to add the lines to reload your data into the `DataSet`:

```
Private Sub SyncButton_Click(ByVal sender As System.Object, _
  ByVal e As System.EventArgs) Handles SyncButton.Click
    Dim syncAgent As PubsCacheSyncAgent = New PubsCacheSyncAgent()
    Dim syncStats As Microsoft.Synchronization.Data.SyncStatistics = _
        syncAgent.Synchronize()
    Me.TitlesTableAdapter.Fill(Me.PubsDataSet.titles)
    Me.StoresTableAdapter.Fill(Me.PubsDataSet.stores)
End Sub
```

Code snippet from LocalCache

13. Run the application (see Figure 12-18). You should be able to view and edit the sales data. Make a change to one of the stores or titles on the server. You should be able to see the change only after you have clicked the Sync button.

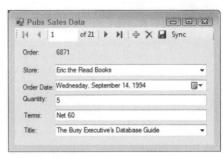

FIGURE 12-18

The addition of Sync Services and SQL Server Compact provide the Visual Basic developer with yet another client-side tool for configuration and data. You get a powerful and well-tested data storage and query mechanism without sacrificing much in terms of disk or memory overhead.

SQL SERVER'S BUILT-IN XML FEATURES

Two of the major XML-related features exposed by SQL Server are as follows:

➤ FOR XML — The FOR XML clause of a T-SQL SELECT statement enables a rowset to be returned as an XML document. The XML document generated by a FOR XML clause is highly customizable with respect to the document hierarchy generated, per-column data transforms, representation of binary data, XML schema generated, and a variety of other XML nuances.

➤ OPENXML — The OPENXML extension to Transact-SQL enables a stored procedure call to manipulate an XML document as a rowset. Subsequently, this rowset can be used to perform a variety of tasks, such as SELECT, INSERT INTO, DELETE, and UPDATE.

SQL Server's support for OPENXML is a matter of calling a stored procedure. A developer who can execute a stored procedure call using Visual Basic in conjunction with ADO.NET can take full advantage of SQL Server's support for OPENXML. FOR XML queries have a certain caveat when it comes to ADO.NET. To understand this caveat, consider the following FOR XML query of the Northwind database:

```
SELECT ShipperID, CompanyName, Phone FROM Shippers FOR XML RAW
```

The output for this FOR XML RAW query generated the following XML:

```
<row ShipperID="1" CompanyName="Speedy Express" Phone="(314) 555-9831" />
<row ShipperID="2" CompanyName="United Package" Phone="(314) 555-3199" />
<row ShipperID="3" CompanyName="Federal Shipping" Phone="(314) 555-9931" />
```

The same FOR XML RAW query can be executed from ADO.NET as follows:

```
Dim adapter As New _
    SqlDataAdapter("SELECT ShipperID, CompanyName, Phone " & _
                   "FROM Shippers FOR XML RAW",
                   "SERVER=localhost;UID=sa;PWD=sa;Database=Northwind;")
Dim ds As New DataSet
adapter.Fill(ds)
Console.Out.WriteLine(ds.GetXml())
```

The caveat with respect to a FOR XML query is that all data (the XML text) must be returned via a result set containing a single row and a single column named XML_F52E2B61-18A1-11d1-B105- 00805F49916B. The output from the preceding code snippet demonstrates this caveat (where . . . represents similar data not shown for reasons of brevity):

```
<NewDataSet>
  <Table>
    <XML_F52E2B61-18A1-11d1-B105-00805F49916B>
      /&lt;row ShipperID="1" CompanyName="Speedy Express"
      Phone="(503) 555-9831"/&gt;
      ...
    </XML_F52E2B61-18A1-11d1-B105-00805F49916B>
  </Table>
</NewDataSet>
```

The value of the single row and single column returned contains what looks like XML, but it contains /< instead of the less-than character, and /> instead of the greater-than character. The symbols < and > cannot appear inside XML data, so they must be entity-encoded — that is, represented as /> and /<. The data returned in element <XML_F52E2B61-18A1-11d1-B105-00805F49916B> is not XML, but data contained in an XML document.

To fully utilize FOR XML queries, the data must be accessible as XML. The solution to this quandary is the ExecuteXmlReader method of the SQLCommand class. When this method is called, a SQLCommand object assumes that it is executed as a FOR XML query and returns the results of this query as an XmlReader object. An example of this follows:

```
Dim connection As New _
    SqlConnection("SERVER=localhost;Integrated Security=True;Database=Northwind;")
Dim command As New _
    SqlCommand("SELECT ShipperID, CompanyName, Phone " &
               "FROM Shippers FOR XML RAW")
Dim memStream As MemoryStream = New MemoryStream
Dim xmlReader As New XmlTextReader(memStream)
connection.Open()
command.Connection = connection
xmlReader = command.ExecuteXmlReader()
' Extract results from XMLReader
```

You need to import the System.Data.SqlClient namespace for this example to work.

The XmlReader created in this code is of type XmlTextReader, which derives from XmlReader. The XmlTextReader is backed by a MemoryStream; hence, it is an in-memory stream of XML that can be traversed using the methods and properties exposed by XmlTextReader. Streaming XML generation and retrieval was discussed in Chapter 9.

Using the ExecuteXmlReader method of the SQLCommand class, it is possible to retrieve the result of FOR XML queries. What makes the FOR XML style of queries so powerful is that it can configure the data retrieved. The three types of FOR XML queries support the following forms of XML customization:

➤   FOR XML RAW — This type of query returns each row of a result set inside an XML element named <row>. The data retrieved is contained as attributes of the <row> element. The attributes are named for the column name or column alias in the FOR XML RAW query.

➤   FOR XML AUTO — By default, this type of query returns each row of a result set inside an XML element named for the table or table alias contained in the FOR XML AUTO query. The data retrieved is contained as attributes of this element. The attributes are named for the column name or column alias in the FOR XML AUTO query. By specifying FOR XML AUTO, ELEMENTS, it is possible to retrieve all data inside elements, rather than inside attributes. All data retrieved must be in attribute or element form. There is no mix-and-match capability.

➤ FOR XML EXPLICIT — This form of the FOR XML query enables the precise XML type of each column returned to be specified. The data associated with a column can be returned as an attribute or an element. Specific XML types, such as CDATA and ID, can be associated with a column returned. Even the level in the XML hierarchy in which data resides can be specified using a FOR XML EXPLICIT query. This style of query is fairly complicated to implement.

FOR XML queries are flexible. Using FOR XML EXPLICIT, it would be possible to generate any form of XML standard. The decision that needs to be made is where XML configuration takes place. Using Visual Basic, a developer could use XmlTextReader and XmlTextWriter to create any style of XML document. Using the XSLT language and an XSLT file, the same level of configuration can be achieved. SQL Server and, in particular, FOR XML EXPLICIT, enable the same level of XML customization, but this customization takes place at the SQL level and may even be configured to stored procedure calls. Choosing between these three options should be made based on your relative comfort levels with the three languages involved. That is, using the FOR XML EXPLICIT query would be a good choice for those who like to work in T-SQL, while others who prefer XSLT or Visual Basic would choose those tools.

CLR INTEGRATION IN SQL SERVER

As the Developer Division within Microsoft works on the .NET Framework and Visual Basic, other teams within SQL Server work on the new version of SQL Server. The SQL teams wanted to leverage the .NET Framework, so they set about integrating the common language runtime (CLR) into SQL Server 2005. This integration means that developers can use Visual Basic code within the context of SQL Server. Success as a DBA is not dependent on knowing only T-SQL. In addition, complex data access code needn't be written outside the database. The benefit to both developers and DBAs is more flexibility in choosing a development language, and more capabilities for your database programming.

CLR integration is disabled by default in SQL Server. This is a safety measure, as most users won't need the features it provides. Not enabling it means one less avenue for attack by hackers. In order to enable creating SQL objects using Visual Basic, you need to enable the integration. This is done by executing the following SQL statement in a query window in the SQL Server Management Studio console:

```
sp_configure 'clr enabled', 1
GO
RECONFIGURE WITH OVERRIDE
GO
```

This is not a decision that should be made lightly. Enabling any feature means that hackers potentially have the feature available to them too, and if a feature as powerful as CLR integration is compromised, your server can become a dangerous tool. There are limits to the features of the .NET Framework available, however.

Now that you've likely been scared away from enabling CLR integration, be aware that it is an incredibly useful tool in some circumstances. T-SQL, for all of its power, is a relatively limited language compared with Visual Basic. It lacks many of the conditional or looping constructs that developers are used to, such as the WITH statement. In addition, debugging has traditionally been fairly weak with T-SQL. Finally, the ability to use external libraries in T-SQL is limited. You can get around these limits by using Visual Basic to replace T-SQL when appropriate.

Deciding between T-SQL and Visual Basic

Once you have enabled CLR integration with your database, your next set of decisions revolves around when to use T-SQL and the native services of SQL Server versus when to use Visual Basic and the .NET Framework. Your final choice should be based on the needs of the application, rather than because a technology is new or interesting. Table 12-2 outlines some common application-building scenarios and which option would be most appropriate.

TABLE 12-2: Using T-SQL versus Visual Basic

SCENARIO	T-SQL	VISUAL BASIC
User-defined types (UDT)	Generally should be the first, if not the only, choice	Can be used if you need to integrate with other managed code, or if the UDT needs to provide additional methods. Also a good idea if the UDT will be shared with external Visual Basic code.
Functions and stored procedures	Use if the code is to process data in bulk, or with little procedural code	Use if the code requires extensive procedural processing or calculations, or if you need access to external libraries, such as the .NET Framework
Extended stored procedures	Typically, the main method used to provide new functionality to SQL Server. For example, the xp_sendmail procedure enables sending e-mail from T-SQL. Generally, extended stored procedures should be avoided in favor of creating the procedures in managed code. This is partly due to the complexity of creating secure extended procedures, but mostly because they may be removed from a future version of SQL Server.	Use if you need access to external code or libraries, such as the .NET Framework. Depending on your needs, the code may be limited to working within the context of SQL Server, or it may access external resources, such as network services. The benefits of better memory management and security make Visual Basic a better choice for creating these extended stored procedures.
Code location	T-SQL code can exist only within SQL Server. This enables optimizations of queries.	Visual Basic code may exist either within SQL Server or on the client. This may mean that you can take code from the client and adapt it for running within SQL Server. In this case, the code would execute closer to the data, generally increasing performance. In addition, the hardware running SQL Server typically performs better than the average desktop, again meaning that the code will execute faster.
Web services	T-SQL supports the creation of Web services to make any function or stored procedure available via SOAP.	Functions and stored procedures written in Visual Basic may be exposed as Web services from SQL Server. The better support for XML handling and procedural logic may mean that it is easier to create these Web services in Visual Basic.
XML handling	T-SQL has been extended to provide some capability for reading and writing XML. These extensions provide the capability to work with the XML only as a whole, however.	Provides excellent XML handling, both for working with the document as a whole and via streaming APIs. Generally, if you need to do a lot of XML handling, using Visual Basic will make your life a lot easier.

Creating User-Defined Types

One feature of SQL Server that does not usually get the attention it deserves is the capability to create user-defined types (UDTs). These enable developers to define new data types that may be used in columns, functions, stored procedures, and so on. They can make database development easier by applying specific constraints to values, or simply to better identify the intent of a column. For example, when presented with a table containing a column of data type varchar(11), you may still be unsure as to the purpose of the value; but if that column is instead of type ssn, you would recognize this (if you are in the U.S.) as a social security number.

With SQL Server 2005 and later, you can create UDTs using Visual Basic. In addition to the normal benefits of user-defined types, UDTs written in Visual Basic have another benefit — they may also provide functionality in the form of methods, which means that you can extend the functionality of your database by providing these methods.

UDTs written using Visual Basic are implemented as structures or classes. Since Visual Studio defaults to creating UDTs as structures, this will be assumed here, but keep in mind that you can create them as classes as well. The properties or fields of the structure become the subtypes of the UDT. Public methods are also accessible, just as they would be in a Visual Basic application.

In addition to the normal code used when writing structures, you must also implement other items to make your UDT work with SQL Server. First, your structure should have the attribute `Microsoft .SqlServer.Server.SqlUserDefinedType`. This attribute identifies the structure as being a SQL Server UDT. In addition, marking the class with the `Serializable` attribute is highly recommended. The `SqlUserDefinedType` attribute has a number of parameters that provide information affecting how SQL Server works with the type. These parameters are described in Table 12-3.

TABLE 12-3: SqlUserDefinedType Attribute Parameters

PARAMETER	VALUE	DESCRIPTION
Format	Native or UserDefined	Identifies the serialization format. If you use `Native` (the default when you create your UDT with Visual Studio), then it uses the SQL Server serialization model. If you set it to `UserDefined`, you must also implement `Microsoft .SqlServer.Server.IBinarySerialize`. This interface includes methods for reading and writing your data type. Generally, using `Native` is safe enough unless your data type requires special handling to avoid saving it incorrectly. For example, if you were storing a media stream, you would likely set it as `UserDefined` to avoid writing the stream incorrectly.
IsByteOrdered	Boolean	True if the data is stored in byte order, false if it is stored using some other order. If this is true, then you can use the default comparison operators with the type, as well as use it as a primary key. The capability to compare two values is a great indicator of how you should use this parameter. If it is possible to define one instance of this UDT as being larger than another, then `IsByteOrdered` is likely true. If it is not, such as with a latitude value, then `IsByteOrdered` is false.
IsFixedLength	Boolean	This should be set to true if all instances of this type are the same size. If the UDT includes only fixed-size elements, such as `int`, `double`, or `char(20)`, then this is true. If it includes variable-size elements, such as `varchar(50)` or `text`, then it should be false. This is a marker to enable optimizations by the SQL Server query processor.
ValidationMethodName	String	Name of a method to be used to validate the data in the UDT. This method is used when loading the UDT, and should return true if the data is valid.
MaxByteSize	Integer, with a maximum of 8000	Defines the maximum size of the UDT, in bytes

In addition to this attribute, each user-defined type also needs to implement the shared method `Parse`, and the instance method `ToString`. These methods enable conversion between your new data type and the interim format, `SqlString`. Finally, you should also implement `INullable` in your structure, although this is not a requirement. This interface requires the addition of the `IsNull` property, which enables your UDT to deal with null values, either stored in the database or passed from the client.

> *If you are using Visual Studio to create your UDTs, then it's best to create and debug all of your UDTs before you begin to use them, especially if you need to use them in any table columns. This is because Visual Basic drops all of the objects you create in a SQL Server project when deploying the project. If you have any tables that use any user-defined types, then you will be unable to drop the UDT, and therefore deploy the changes you've made. If you need to make changes, you may receive an error similar to "Cannot drop type 'Location' because it is currently in use." This error causes the deploy step of your project to fail. If this happens, then change the column type or temporarily drop the table. You can then redeploy the UDT as needed. Don't forget to change the column back, or recreate the table.*

While you can write code that integrates with SQL Server using any DLL, Visual Studio provides the Visual Basic SQL CLR Database Project (see Figure 12-19). This project type generates a DLL but also connects the DLL to the database.

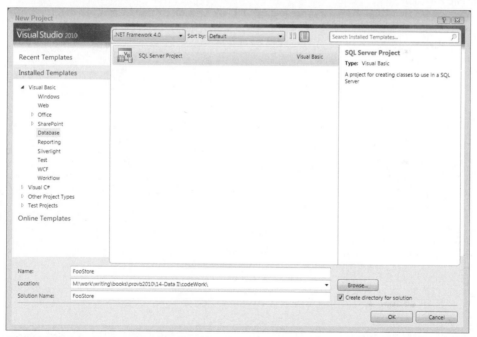

FIGURE 12-19

> *SQL Server 2008 only supports .NET 4 assemblies if you have installed the cumulative update 5 for Service Pack 1.*

When you create a new SQL Server Project, Visual Studio prompts you to identify the database that will host the DLL. At this point, you can either select an existing database connection or create a new one. For the sample project, create a new database called FooStore. Visual Studio also asks whether you want to enable SQL/CLR debugging on the connection. Typically, you will want to enable this on development servers, but keep in mind that when debugging, the server is limited to the single connection. Once the project is created, you can add the various database types via the Project menu. Deploying the project (via the Deploy option on the Build menu) loads the created DLL into the database. You can confirm that it is loaded by looking at the Assemblies folder in the Server Explorer (see Figure 12-20).

FIGURE 12-20

The following code example shows a simple `Location` user-defined type written in Visual Basic. This type identifies a geographic location. We will use it throughout the remainder of the chapter to track the location of customers and stores. The `Location` type has two main properties: `Latitude` and `Longitude`. Create this file by selecting Add User-defined Type from the Project menu.

Available for
download on
Wrox.com

```vb
Imports System
Imports System.Data
Imports System.Data.SqlClient
Imports System.Data.SqlTypes
Imports Microsoft.SqlServer.Server
<Serializable()> _
<Microsoft.SqlServer.Server.SqlUserDefinedType(Format.Native)> _
Public Structure Location
    Implements INullable
    Public ReadOnly Property IsNull() As Boolean Implements INullable.IsNull
        Get
            If Me.Latitude = Double.NaN OrElse Me.Longitude = Double.NaN Then
                _isNull = True
            Else
                _isNull = False
            End If
            Return _isNull
        End Get
    End Property
    Public Shared ReadOnly Property Null As Location
        Get
            Dim result As Location = New Location
            result._isNull = True
            result.Latitude = Double.NaN
            result.Longitude = Double.NaN
            Return result
        End Get
    End Property
    Public Overrides Function ToString() As String
        Return String.Format("{0}, {1}", Latitude, Longitude)
    End Function
    Public Shared Function Parse(ByVal s As SqlString) As Location
        If s.IsNull Then
            Return Null
        End If
        Dim result As Location = New Location
        Dim temp() As String = s.Value.Split(CChar(","))
        If (temp.Length > 1) Then
            result.Latitude = Double.Parse(temp(0))
            result.Longitude = Double.Parse(temp(1))
        End If
        Return result
    End Function
End Function
```

```
    Public Function Distance(ByVal loc As Location) As Double
        Dim result As Double
        Dim temp As Double
        Dim deltaLat As Double
        Dim deltaLong As Double
        Const EARTH_RADIUS As Integer = 6378 'kilometers
        Dim lat1 As Double
        Dim lat2 As Double
        Dim long1 As Double
        Dim long2 As Double
        'convert to radians
        lat1 = Me.Latitude * Math.PI / 180
        long1 = Me.Longitude * Math.PI / 180
        lat2 = loc.Latitude * Math.PI / 180
        long2 = loc.Longitude * Math.PI / 180
        'formula from http://mathforum.org/library/drmath/view/51711.html
        deltaLong = long2 - long1
        deltaLat = lat2 - lat1
        temp = (Math.Sin(deltaLat / 2)) * 2 + _
            Math.Cos(lat1) * Math.Cos(lat2) * (Math.Sin(deltaLong / 2)) * 2
        temp = 2 * Math.Atan2(Math.Sqrt(temp), Math.Sqrt(1 - temp))
        result = EARTH_RADIUS * temp
        Return result
    End Function

    Private _lat As Double
    Private _long As Double
    Private _isNull As Boolean
    Public Property Latitude() As Double
        Get
            Return _lat
        End Get
        Set(ByVal value As Double)
            _lat = value
        End Set
    End Property
    Public Property Longitude() As Double
        Get
            Return _long
        End Get
        Set(ByVal value As Double)
            _long = value
        End Set
    End Property
End Structure
```

Code snippet from FooStore

In addition to the Latitude and Longitude properties, the Location type also defines a Distance method. This is used to identify the distance between two locations. It uses the formula for calculating the distance between two points on a sphere to calculate the distance. This formula is clearly described at the "Ask Dr. Math" forum (see http://mathforum.org/library/drmath/view/51879.html). As the Earth is not a perfect sphere, this calculation is only an estimate, but it should be close enough for our needs.

Look at the properties for the project; on the Database tab for the properties, ensure that the connection string has been set to the FooStore database. For now, select Safe for the Permission Level. Right-click the project in the Solution Explorer and select Deploy; this will build the project and copy the DLL to the database.

Now that you have created the Location type, you can use it in the definition of a table. Here we will create part of an e-commerce application to demonstrate the use of Location and other SQL Server features.

Imagine that you are creating an application for an online store that also has physical locations. When a customer orders a product, you must obviously ship it from some location. Major online sellers typically have large warehouses that they can use to fulfill these orders. However, they are usually limited to shipping from these warehouses. Other companies have physical stores that stock many of the items available for order. Wouldn't it make sense that if one of those stores has stock and is closer to the customer, you would use the stock in the store to fulfill the order from the website? It would save on shipping costs, and it would get the product to the customer faster. This would save you money, and lead to happier customers who are more likely to order from you again. This hypothetical scenario would likely be called into play many times throughout the day; therefore, moving it to a stored procedure would be useful to improve performance. The calculations would be closer to the data, and the database server itself could perform optimizations on it if needed.

Open the database using SQL Server Management Studio or the Server Explorer in Visual Studio. Create a table called `Stores`. This table will be used to track the physical store locations. Figure 12-21 shows the layout of this table. Note that the new `Location` data type should appear at the bottom of the list of data types; it is not inserted in alphabetical order.

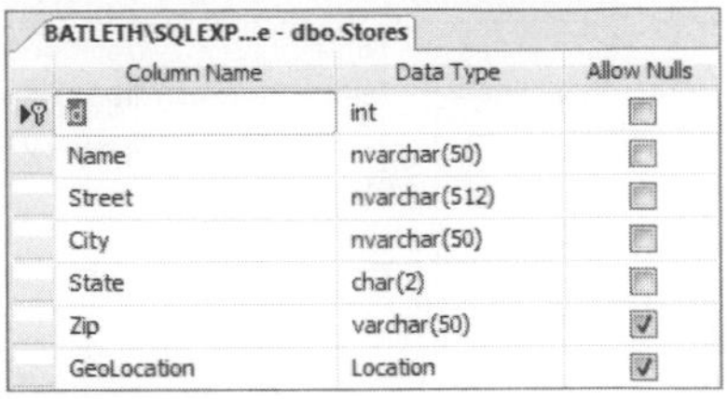

The `id` column is defined as an identity column and is the primary key. Don't bother adding any data to the table yet, unless you know the appropriate latitude and longitude for each location. We'll create a function for calculating the location in a moment.

FIGURE 12-21

In addition to the `Stores` table, create two other tables: one for products (see Figure 12-22), and the other to track the stock (see Figure 12-23) available in each store.

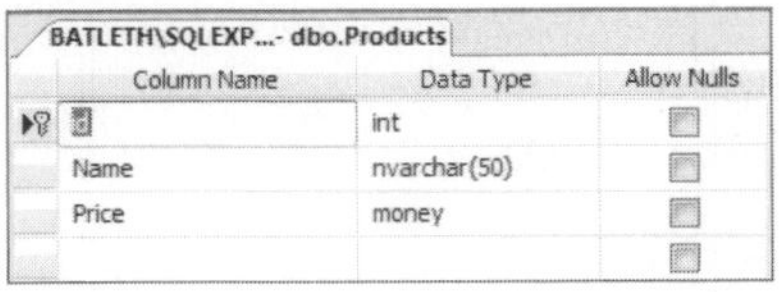

FIGURE 12-22

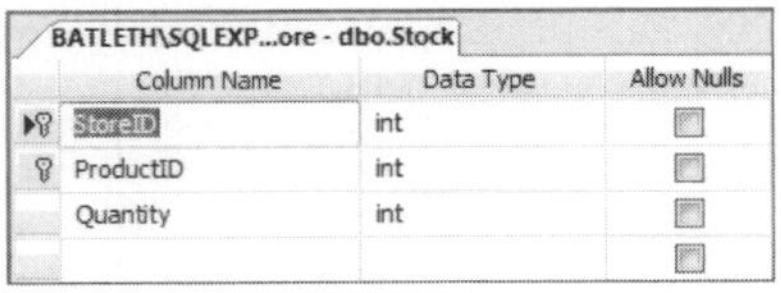

FIGURE 12-23

As with the `Stores` table, the `id` column for the `Products` table is an identity field. The `Name` field will contain the name of the product, and `Price` reflects the unit price of each item. A typical product table would likely have other columns as well; this table has been kept as simple as possible for this example.

The `Stock` table will provide the connection between the `Stores` and `Products` tables. It uses the combination of the two primary keys as its key (refer to Figure 12-23). This means that each combination of store and product has a single entry, with the quantity of the product per store.

Now that the tables are in place for the sample, we'll turn our attention to creating a way to determine the location, using a SQL Server function written in Visual Basic.

Creating Functions

Functions are a feature of SQL Server that enable a simple calculation that returns either a scalar value or a table of values. These functions differ from stored procedures in that they are typically used to perform some calculation or action, rather than specifically act on a table. You can create functions in either T-SQL or Visual Basic.

When creating functions with Visual Basic, you define a class with one or more methods. Methods that you want to make available as SQL Server functions should be marked with the `Microsoft.SqlServer .Server.SqlFunctionAttribute` attribute. SQL Server will then register the methods, after which they may be used in your database. The `SqlFunction` attribute takes a number of optional parameters, shown in Table 12-4.

TABLE 12-4: SqlFunctionAttribute Optional Parameters

PARAMETER	VALUE	DESCRIPTION
DataAccess	Either `DataAccessKind.None` or `DataAccessKind.Read`	Set to `DataAccessKind.Read` if the function will access data stored in the database.
SystemDataAccess	Either `SystemDataAccessKind.None` or `SystemDataAccessKind.Read`	Set to `SystemDataAccessKind.Read` if the function will access data in the system tables of the database.
FillRowMethodName	String	The name of the method that will return each row of data. This is used only if the function returns tabular data.
IsDeterministic	Boolean	Set to true if the function is deterministic — that is, if it will always produce the same result, given the same input and database output. (A random function would obviously not be deterministic.) The default is false.
IsPrecise	Boolean	Set to true if the function does not use any floating-point calculations. The default is false.
TableDefinition	String	Provides the table definition of the return value. Only needed if the function returns tabular data.

By default, SQL Server loads Visual Basic objects into a safe environment. This means that they cannot call external code or resources. In addition, Code Access Security (CAS) limits the access of SQL Server to some aspects of the .NET Framework. You can change this behavior by explicitly setting the permission level under which the code will run. Table 12-5 outlines the available permission levels.

TABLE 12-5: CAS Permission Levels

PERMISSIONS	SAFE	EXTERNAL	UNSAFE
Code access	Limited to code running within the SQL Server context	Ability to access external resources	Unlimited
Framework access	Limited	Limited	Unlimited
Native code	No	No	Yes

You should use the minimum permission level needed to get your code to run. Typically, this means only the Safe level, which enables access to the libraries providing data access, XML handling, mathematic calculations, and other commonly needed capabilities.

If you need access to other network resources, such as the capability to call out to external Web services or SMTP servers, then you should enable the External permission level. This also provides all the capabilities provided by the Safe permission level.

Only enable the Unsafe permission level in the rarest of circumstances, when you need access to native code. Code running within this permission level has full access to any code available to it, so it may represent a potential security hole for your application.

If you attempt to deploy a Visual Basic DLL that requires external access, you will receive this lengthy — but not entirely helpful — error message:

```
CREATE ASSEMBLY for assembly 'FooStore' failed because assembly 'FooStore' is not
authorized for PERMISSION_SET = EXTERNAL_ACCESS. The assembly is authorized
when either of the following is true: the database owner (DBO) has EXTERNAL ACCESS
ASSEMBLY permission and the database has the TRUSTWORTHY database property on; or
the assembly is signed with a certificate or an asymmetric key that has a
corresponding login with EXTERNAL ACCESS ASSEMBLY permission.
```

The error message provides the steps required to enable external access. At this point, you have two options:

➤ **Provide the External Access Assembly permission to the user account associated with the database owner** — You should not do this unless the second option is not possible. This creates a dangerous security hole in your database. It would mean that any Visual Basic code running on the server has external access permissions, and complete access to the database.

➤ **Sign the assembly, create an account that uses this signature, and then provide the External Access Assembly permission to that account** — This is the preferred method for enabling safe external access by a Visual Basic assembly. By signing your assembly and giving the assembly (and the user id associated with the signature) permission, you are limiting the amount of code that can access other servers.

The following steps outline how to provide external access permissions to a Visual Basic assembly using Visual Studio. First, set the permission level to External, as shown in Figure 12-24, and provide a name for the owner of the assembly. This is done using the Database page of the project's property pages.

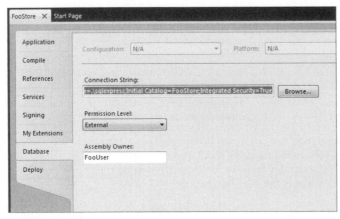

FIGURE 12-24

Once you have enabled external access for your Visual Basic code, you also need to sign your assembly. Sign the assembly on the Signing tab of the properties dialog (see Figure 12-25). Use an existing key file or create a new one.

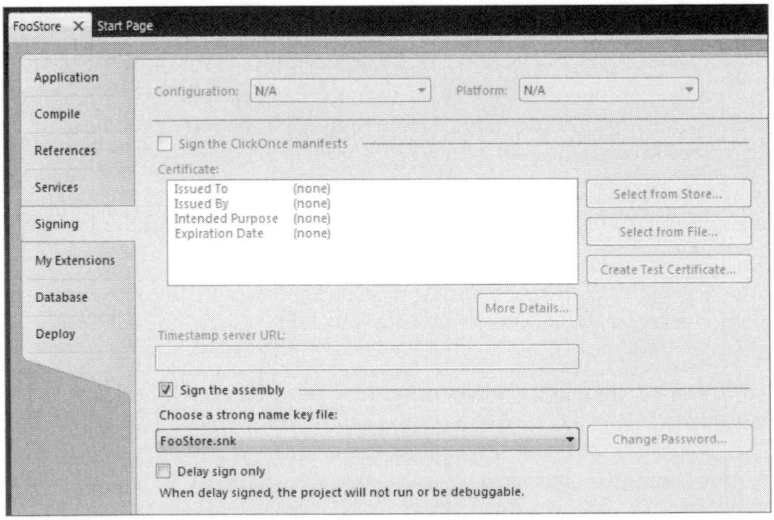

FIGURE 12-25

Once you have signed and built the assembly, the next steps are to create a key in the database based on the signature of the assembly and create a user who will be associated with the key. This is done using a T-SQL query. Run the following query in SQL Management Studio (update the path to the DLL as appropriate for your machine):

```
USE master
GO
CREATE ASYMMETRIC KEY FooStoreKey
  FROM EXECUTABLE FILE = 'C:\FooStore.dll'
GO
CREATE LOGIN FooUser
  FROM ASYMMETRIC KEY FooStoreKey
GRANT EXTERNAL ACCESS ASSEMBLY TO FooUser
GO
```

Creating a new asymmetric key must be done from the master database. The DLL listed in the FROM EXECUTABLE FILE clause should be the DLL you have just created in Visual Basic; adjust the path in the SQL statement to match the location of your DLL. Once the key is created, you can create a new login based on this key and provide that user with external access. You should also add that login to the database and give it permission to access the desired objects.

Now that the assembly is capable of accessing external sites, we are ready to begin coding the function that will convert the addresses to latitude and longitude (that is, geocode the address). Several companies sell databases or services that provide this capability. However, Yahoo! has a free Web service that will geocode addresses. It can be called up to 5,000 times a day, more than enough for this sample (but probably not enough for a real store).

The Geocode service is accessed by sending a GET request to http://api.local.yahoo.com/MapsService/V1/geocode with the parameters provided in Table 12-6.

TABLE 12-6: Parameters for Accessing the Geocode Service

PARAMETER	DESCRIPTION
appid	(Required) The unique string used to identify each application using the service. Note that this parameter name is case-sensitive. For testing purposes, you can use YahooDemo (used by the Yahoo samples themselves). However, your own applications should have unique application IDs. You can register them at http://api.search.yahoo.com/webservices/register_application.
street	(Optional) The street address you are searching for. This should be URL-encoded. That is, spaces should be replaced with + characters, and high ASCII or characters such as < , /, > , etc., should be replaced with their equivalent using '%##' notation.
city	(Optional) The city for the location you are searching for. This should be URL-encoded, although this is really only necessary if the city name contains spaces or high ASCII characters.
state	(Optional) The U.S. state (if applicable) you are searching for. Either the two-letter abbreviation or the full name (URL-encoded) will work.
zip	(Optional) The U.S. zip code (if applicable) you are searching for. This can be in either 5-digit or 5+4-digit format.
location	(Optional) A free-form field of address information containing the URL-encoded and comma-delimited request. This provides an easier method for querying, rather than setting, the individual values listed above. For example: location=1600+Pennsylvania+Avenue+NW,+Washington,+DC

The following code shows the full source for the `fnGetLocation` function:

```vb
Imports System
Imports System.Data
Imports System.Data.SqlClient
Imports System.Data.SqlTypes
Imports Microsoft.SqlServer.Server
Imports System.Xml
Imports System.Text
Partial Public Class UserDefinedFunctions
    'Replace YahooDemo with your key
    Private Const YAHOO_APP_KEY As String = "YahooDemo"
    Private Const BASE_URL As String = _
        "http://api.local.yahoo.com/MapsService/V1/geocode"
    <Microsoft.SqlServer.Server.SqlFunction()> _
    Public Shared Function fnGetLocation(ByVal street As SqlString, _
        ByVal city As SqlString, _
        ByVal state As SqlString, _
        ByVal zip As SqlString) As Location
        Dim result As New Location
        Dim query As New StringBuilder
        'uses Yahoo geocoder to geocode the location
        'limited to 5000 calls/day
        'construct URL
        ' URL should look like:
        '    http://api.local.yahoo.com/MapsService/V1/geocode?
        '        appid=YahooDemo&street=701+First+Street&city=Sunnyvale&state=CA

        query.AppendFormat("{0}?appid={1}", BASE_URL, YAHOO_APP_KEY)
        If Not street.IsNull Then
            query.AppendFormat("&street={0}", street)
        End If
        If Not city.IsNull Then
            query.AppendFormat("&city={0}", city)
        End If
        If Not state.IsNull Then
            query.AppendFormat("&state={0}", state)
        End If
        If Not zip.IsNull Then
            query.AppendFormat("&zip={0}", zip)
        End If
        'Debug.Print(query.ToString())
        'send request
        Using r As XmlReader = XmlReader.Create(query.ToString())
            'parse output
            While r.Read
                If r.IsStartElement("Latitude") Then
                    ' longitude directly follows latitude in the result xml
                    result.Latitude = Double.Parse(r.ReadElementString)
                    result.Longitude = Double.Parse(r.ReadElementString)
                    Exit While
                End If
            End While
        End Using
        Return result
    End Function
End Class
```

Code snippet from FooStore

Most of the code in the preceding example is used to create the appropriate URL to create the query. The query should look as follows:

```
http://api.local.yahoo.com/MapsService/V1/geocode?appid=YahooDemo&street=
701+First+Street&city=Sunnyvale&state=CA&country=USA
```

While the `YahooDemo appid` will work for testing, there is a good chance that it will not work at times. The query is limited to 5,000 requests for each `appid`, so if several people call the geocoder in a day, the request will fail. Therefore, you should request your own `appid` for testing, and replace the preceding `appid` with your own, which you can obtain at the following Web page:

```
http://api.search.yahoo.com/webservices/register_application
```

> *Notice that the preceding code uses a* `StringBuilder` *to construct the query. Why not simply concatenate strings to create the query? There are several reasons, but the most important is performance. Because strings in Visual Basic are immutable, concatenation requires the creation of new strings each time. For example, the simple expression* `Dim s As String = "Hello" & "world"` *actually requires three strings, two of which would be immediately discarded. The* `StringBuilder` *class was built to avoid this repeated creation and disposal of objects, and the resulting code offers much better performance than simple concatenation.*

Once the query is constructed, an `XmlReader` is used to execute the query. The resulting XML from a call to Yahoo!'s geocoder looks like the following:

```
<?xml version="1.0" ?>
<ResultSet xmlns:xsi="http://www.w3.org/2001/XMLSchema-instance"
    xmlns="urn:yahoo:maps"
    xsi:schemaLocation="urn:yahoo:maps
        http://api.local.yahoo.com/MapsService/V1/GeocodeResponse.xsd">
  <Result precision="address"
      warning="The exact location could not be found,
        here is the closest match: 701 First Ave, Sunnyvale, CA 94089">
    <Latitude>37.416384</Latitude>
    <Longitude>-122.024853</Longitude>
    <Address>701 FIRST AVE</Address>
    <City>SUNNYVALE</City>
    <State>CA</State>
    <Zip>94089-1019</Zip>
    <Country>US</Country>
  </Result>
</ResultSet>
```

While you could load all of this into an `XmlDocument` for processing, the `XmlReader` is generally faster. In addition, because all that is really needed are the two values for latitude and longitude, using the `XmlReader` enables the code to extract these two values quickly, and without the overhead of loading all the other data. As the `XmlReader` class implements `IDisposable`, you should ensure the correct handling and disposal of the class by either setting the object to nothing in a `Try ... Finally` block, or by using the `Using` statement:

Available for download on Wrox.com

```
Using r As XmlReader = XmlReader.Create(query.ToString())
    'parse output
    While r.Read
        If r.IsStartElement("Latitude") Then
            ' longitude directly follows latitude in the result xml
            result.Latitude = Double.Parse(r.ReadElementString)
            result.Longitude = Double.Parse(r.ReadElementString)
            Exit While
        End If
    End While
End Using
```

Code snippet from FooStore

As shown in Chapter 9, you create the XmlReader using the shared Create method. This method has a number of overridden versions. In this case, the string version of the URL is used to create the XmlReader. The code then loops through the resulting XML until the start element for the Latitude element is found. As you know, the two values are next to each other; the code may then access them and stop reading. Figure 12-26 shows testing this new function in SQL Server Management Studio.

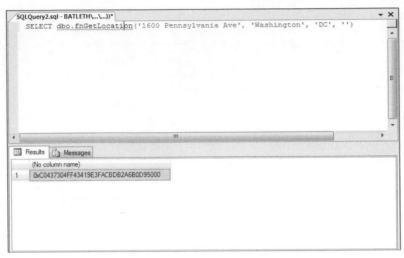

FIGURE 12-26

Using the User-Defined Function

Even though the fnGetLocation function is written in Visual Basic, you can still use this function from T-SQL. This means that you can use either Visual Basic or T-SQL for a given SQL Server object, whichever is better suited to the scenario. The following code shows the procedure used to insert new stores. This procedure is written in T-SQL, but it calls the function written in Visual Basic. Alternately, you could create an insert trigger that calls the function to determine the store's location.

```
CREATE PROCEDURE dbo.procInsertStore
(
    @name nvarchar(50),
    @street nvarchar(512),
    @city nvarchar(50),
    @state char(2),
    @zip varchar(50)
)
AS
    /* need to populate location */
    DECLARE @loc AS Location;
    SET @loc = dbo.fnGetLocation(@street, @city, @state, @zip);
    INSERT INTO Stores (Name, Street, City, State, Zip, GeoLocation)
        OUTPUT INSERTED.id
    VALUES (@name, @street, @city, @state, @zip, @loc);
    RETURN @@IDENTITY
```

Code snippet from FooStore

The stored procedure uses the function and user-defined type just as it would use the same objects written in T-SQL. Before storing the store data, it calls the Web service to determine the latitude and longitude of the location, and then stores the data in the table.

We are now ready to add data to the three tables. Add a few stores (see Figure 12-27) using the stored procedure. The actual data is not that important, but having multiple stores relatively close to one another will be useful later.

BATLETH\SQLEXP...e - dbo.Stores

id	Name	Street	City	State	Zip	GeoLocation
1	Store #50	357 108th Aven...	Bellevue	WA	NULL	47.613388, -122.196374
2	Store #63	15703 NE 56th ...	Redmond	WA	98052	47.658078, -122.130854
3	Store #11	611 Broadway	New York	NY	10012	40.725679, -73.996744
4	Store #23	23 W 60th St	New York	NY	10010	40.76931, -73.982725
5	Store #34	340 W North Av...	Chicago	IL	NULL	41.911249, -87.637928
6	Store #26	2550 N Clark St.	Chicago	IL	NULL	41.928935, -87.642653
NULL	NULL	NULL	NULL	NULL	NULL	NULL

FIGURE 12-27

Similarly, add a number of items to the Products table (see Figure 12-28). Once again, the data itself is not important, only that you have a variety of items from which to choose.

BATLETH\SQLEXP...- dbo.Products

id	Name	Price
1	Widget	3.5000
2	Doodad	12.9900
3	Thingie	4.9500
4	Whatchamacallit	52.9800
5	Macguffin	99.9900
NULL	NULL	NULL

FIGURE 12-28

Finally, add the data to the Stock table (see Figure 12-29). Use a single entry for each combination of store and product. Make certain that you have a variety of quantities on hand for testing.

BATLETH\SQLEXP...ore - dbo.Stock

StoreID	ProductID	Quantity
1	1	0
1	2	0
1	3	0
1	4	4
1	5	2
2	1	0
2	2	2
2	3	0
2	4	0
2	5	1
3	1	1
3	2	4
3	3	2
3	4	4
3	5	2
4	1	0
4	2	2
4	3	3
4	4	0
4	5	1
5	1	4
5	2	0
5	3	4
5	4	2
5	5	0
NULL	NULL	NULL

FIGURE 12-29

Now that we have some data to work with, and a function for determining the latitude and longitude of any address, we're ready to examine how to create a stored procedure in Visual Basic to locate the nearest store with available stock to the customer.

Creating Stored Procedures

Just as with user-defined types and functions, you identify methods as being stored procedures with an attribute. In the case of stored procedures, this is `Microsoft.SqlServer.Server.SqlProcedureAttribute`. This attribute is basically a marker attribute; no additional parameters have any dramatic effect on the behavior of the code.

When creating a stored procedure in Visual Basic, you should keep a few considerations in mind. First, and likely most important, is the context. Your code is no longer running as a separate application, but within SQL Server. Tasks that require long processing mean that whatever resources you are using will be unavailable to other code, which could cause your database to become less responsive, leading to more slowdowns. Therefore, always remain conscious of the resources you are using, and the amount of time you lock them.

The second major consideration when creating stored procedures in Visual Basic is the connection to the data. When writing standalone Visual Basic code that accesses data, you need to create a connection to a class that implements `IDbConnection`, frequently `SqlConnection` or `OleDbConnection`. The connection string used then identifies the database, user id, and so on. However, in a stored procedure, you are running within the context of SQL Server itself, so most of this information is superfluous, which makes connecting to the data source much easier.

```
Using connection As New SqlConnection("context connection=true")
...'work with the data here
End Using
```

The connection string is now reduced to the equivalent of "right where the code is running." The user id, database, and other parameters are implied by the context under which the code is running.

Once you have connected to the database, the rest of the code is basically the same as you are used to performing with other ADO.NET code. This means that migrating code that accesses SQL Server to run as a stored procedure is fairly easy: Change the connection string used to connect to the database, and add the `SqlProcedure` attribute.

Returning Data from the Stored Procedure

Once you have performed the manipulations required to get your data, you obviously need to send it back to the user. With normal ADO.NET, you would create a `DataSet` or `SqlDataReader`, and use the methods and properties of the class to extract the data. However, the data access code running within a stored procedure is running in the context of SQL Server, and the stored procedure must behave in the same way as other stored procedures. In addition, your stored procedure may actually be called from T-SQL, which has no knowledge of either the `DataSet` or `IDataReader` data types. Therefore, you must change your code slightly to achieve this behavior.

When returning data using ADO.NET, you typically have a few options. The first option depends on whether you need to return a single value or one or more rows of data.

Returning a Single Value

If you are returning a single value from the stored procedure, then you create your stored procedure as a subroutine. The data you return should be a `ByRef` parameter of the subroutine. Finally, you need to mark this parameter as an out parameter using the `System.Runtime.InteropServices.Out` attribute. For example, if you were attempting to create a stored procedure that returned the total value of all the items available at a selected store, then you would create something similar to the following procedure:

Available for download on Wrox.com

```
Imports System
Imports System.Data
Imports System.Data.SqlClient
Imports System.Data.SqlTypes
Imports Microsoft.SqlServer.Server
Imports System.Runtime.InteropServices
Partial Public Class StoredProcedures
    <Microsoft.SqlServer.Server.SqlProcedure()>
    Public Shared Sub procGetStoreInventoryValue(ByVal storeID As Int32,
        <Out()> ByRef totalValue As SqlMoney)
        Dim query As String =
            "SELECT SUM(Products.Price * Stock.Quantity) as total" &
            "FROM Products INNER JOIN Stock ON " &
            "Products.id = Stock.ProductID " &
            "WHERE Stock.StoreID = @storeID"
        Using conn As New SqlConnection("context connection = true")
            Using cmd As New SqlCommand(query, conn)
                cmd.Parameters.Add("@storeID", SqlDbType.Int).Value = storeID
                totalValue = CSng(cmd.ExecuteScalar(), SqlMoney)
            End Using
        End Using
    End Sub
End Class
```

Code snippet from FooStore

Because this stored procedure doesn't really do any processing of the data, or mathematical calculations, it would probably be best created using T-SQL.

The procedure is fairly basic: It uses the current connection to execute a block of SQL and returns the value from that SQL. As before, the `SqlConnection` and `SqlCommand` values are created using the new `Using` statement. This ensures that they are disposed of, freeing the memory used, when the code block is completed.

Just as when working with `ByRef` parameters in other code, any changes made to the variable within the procedure are reflected outside the method. The `Out` attribute extends this to identify the parameter as a value that needs to be marshaled out of the application. It is needed to change the behavior of the `ByRef` variable. Normally, the `ByRef` variable is an `In/Out` value. You must at least have it available when you make the call. By marking it with the `Out` attribute, you mark it as not having this requirement.

Returning Multiple Values

Things become slightly more complex if you want to return one or more rows of data. In a sense, your code needs to replicate the data transfer that would normally occur when a stored procedure is executed within SQL Server. The data must somehow be transferred to the TDS (Tabular Data Stream). How do you create this TDS? Fortunately, SQL Server provides you with a way, via the `SqlPipe` class. The `SqlContext` class provides access to the `SqlPipe` class via its `Pipe` property. As shown in Table 12-7, the `SqlPipe` class has several methods that may be used to return data to the code that called the stored procedure:

TABLE 12-7: SqlPipe Class Methods Used to Return Data

METHOD	DESCRIPTION
ExecuteAndSend	Takes a `SqlCommand`, executes it, and returns the result. This is the most efficient method that may be used to return data, as it does not need to generate any memory structures.
Send(SqlDataReader)	Takes a `SqlDataReader` and streams out the resulting data to the client. This is slightly slower than the preceding method, but recommended if you need to perform any processing on the data before returning.
Send(SqlDataRecord)	Returns a single row of data to the client. This is a useful method if you are generating the data and need to send back only a single row.
Send(String)	Returns a message to the client. This is not the same as a scalar string value, however. Instead, this is intended for sending informational messages to the client. The information sent back may be retrieved using the `InfoMessage` event of the `SqlConnection`.
SendResultsStart	Used to mark the beginning of a multi-row block of data. This method takes a `SqlDataRecord` that is used to identify the columns that will be sent with subsequent `SendResultsRow` calls. This method is most useful when you must construct multiple rows of data before returning to the client.
SendResultsRow	Used to send a `SqlDataRecord` back to the client. You must already have called `SendResultsStart` using a matching `SqlDataRecord`; otherwise, an exception will occur.
SendResultsEnd	Marks the end of the transmission of a multi-row block of data. This can only be called after first calling `SendResultsStart`, and likely one or more calls to `SendResultsRow`. If you fail to call this method, then any other attempts to use the `SqlPipe` will cause an exception.

If all you want to do is execute a block of SQL and return the resulting data, then use the `ExecuteAndSend` method. (Actually, in this case, you should probably be using T-SQL, but there may be cases that justify doing this in Visual Basic). This method avoids the overhead involved in creating any memory structures to hold the data in an intermediate form. Instead, it streams the data just as it would if the procedure were written in T-SQL.

The next most commonly used method for returning data is the version of the `Send` method that takes a `SqlDataReader`. With this method, your code can return a block of data pointed at by a `SqlDataReader`. This method, as well as the version of `Send` that takes a `SqlDataRecord`, are commonly used when some processing of the data is needed before returning. They do require that some memory structures be created, so they do not return data as fast as the `ExecuteAndSend` method.

The version of `Send` taking a `SqlDataRecord` object can be a handy method for constructing and returning a single row of data (or when using `SendResultsRow`).

The `SqlDataRecord` class is new with the `Microsoft.SqlServer.Server` namespace, and represents a single row of data. Why a new data type? Why not just leverage `DataSet`? The creators needed an object that was capable of being converted into the tabular data stream format used by SQL Server, and the `DataSet` would need to have this functionality added to it.

There are two ways to return a `SqlDataRecord`. If only a single row of data needs to be returned, then you use the `Send(SqlDataRecord)` method. If multiple records will be returned, then you use the `SendResultsStart`, `SendResultsRow`, and `SendResultsEnd` methods (see below). In each case, you are responsible for creating and populating the values for each column in the `SqlDataRecord`.

Columns within a `SqlDataRecord` are defined using the `SqlMetaData` class. Each column requires the definition of an instance of a separate `SqlMetaData` object, with the constructor of `SqlDataRecord` taking a parameter array of these objects. Each `SqlMetaData` object defines the type, size, and maximum length (if appropriate) of the data for the column. The following code creates a `SqlDataRecord` with four columns:

```
Dim rec As SqlDataRecord
rec = New SqlDataRecord(
    new SqlMetaData("col1", SqlDbType.Int),
    new SqlMetaData("col2", SqlDbType.VarChar, 25),
    new SqlMetaData("col3", SqlDbType.Float),
    new SqlMetaData("col4", SqlDbType.Text, 512))
```

You can retrieve data from each of the columns in two ways. You can use the `GetValue` method, which returns the value stored in the nth column of the `SqlDataRecord` as an object, or you can return the data as a particular data type using one of the many `GetPNG` methods, where `PNG` is the type required. For example, to return the value stored in the second column of the preceding example as a string, you would use `GetString(1)`. Similarly, there are `SetValue` and `SetPNG` methods for setting the value of each column. Once you have created your `SqlDataRecord` and populated its values, you return it to the client by passing it to the `Send` method of the `SqlPipe`, as shown in the following code:

```
rec.SetInt32(0, 42)
rec.SetString(1, "Some string")
rec.SetFloat(2, 3.14)
rec.SetString(3, "Some longer string")
SqlContext.Pipe.Send(rec)
```

The version of the `Send` method that takes a string is slightly different from the other two variants. Rather than return data, the intent of the `Send(String)` version is to return information back to the calling application; it's the equivalent of the T-SQL `print` statement. You can receive this data by adding a handler to the `InfoMessage` event of the `SqlConnection`.

The final three methods of the `SqlPipe` used for returning multiple rows of data are used together. `SendResultsStart` marks the beginning of a set of rows, `SendResultsRow` is used to send each row, and `SendResultsEnd` marks the end of the set of rows.

In addition to marking the start of the block of data, `SendResultsStart` is used to define the structure of the returned data. This is done by using a `SqlDataRecord` instance. Once you have called `SendResultsStart`, the only valid methods of `SqlPipe` that you can use are `SendResultsRow` and `SendResultsEnd`. Calling any other method will cause an exception. The records you send back with each call of `SendResultsRow` should match the structure defined in the `SendResultsStart` method. In fact, to conserve server resources, it's a good idea to use the same `SqlDataRecord` instance for all of these calls. If you create a new `SqlDataRecord` with each row, then you are wasting memory, as each of these objects will be marked for garbage collection. Therefore, the basic process for using these three methods would work similarly to the following (the `cols` variable points to a prepared collection of `SqlMetaData` objects):

```
Dim rec As New SqlDataRecord(cols)
SqlContext.Pipe.SendResultsStart(rec)
For I As Integer = 1 To 10
    'populate the record
    rec.SetInt32(0, I)
    rec.SetString(1, "Row #" & I.ToString())
    rec.SetFloat(2, I * Math.PI)
    rec.SetString(3, "Information about row #" & I.ToString())
    SqlContext.Pipe.SendResultsRow(rec)
Next

SqlContext.Pipe.SendResultsEnd()
```

The following code shows the complete class, including the stored procedure for determining the nearest store with available stock:

```
Imports System
Imports System.Data
Imports System.Data.SqlClient
Imports System.Data.SqlTypes
Imports Microsoft.SqlServer.Server
Imports System.Collections.Generic
Partial Public Class StoredProcedures
    <Microsoft.SqlServer.Server.SqlProcedure()>
    Public Shared Sub procGetClosestStoreWithStock(ByVal street As SqlString,
        ByVal city As SqlString,
        ByVal state As SqlString,
        ByVal zip As SqlString,
        ByVal productID As SqlInt32,
        ByVal quantity As SqlInt32)
        Dim loc As Location
        Dim query As String = "SELECT id, Name, Street, City, " &
            "State, Zip, GeoLocation " &
            "FROM Stores INNER JOIN Stock on Stores.id = Stock.StoreId " &
            "WHERE Stock.ProductID = @productID " &
            "AND Stock.Quantity > @quantity " &
            "ORDER BY Stock.Quantity DESC"
        Dim dr As SqlDataReader
        Dim result As SqlDataRecord = Nothing
        'get location of requested address
        loc = UserDefinedFunctions.fnGetLocation(street, city, state, zip)
        Using connection As New SqlConnection("context connection=true")
            connection.Open()
            'pipe is used to return data to the user
            Dim pipe As SqlPipe = SqlContext.Pipe
            'get stores with stock
            Using cmd As New SqlCommand(query, connection)
                With cmd.Parameters
                    .Add("@productID", SqlDbType.Int).Value = productID
                    .Add("@quantity", SqlDbType.Int).Value = quantity
                End With
                dr = cmd.ExecuteReader()
                'find the closest store
                Dim distance As Double
                Dim smallest As Double = Double.MaxValue
                Dim storeLoc As Location
                Dim rowData(6) As Object
```

```
                While (dr.Read)
                        dr.GetSqlValues(rowData)
                        storeLoc = DirectCast(rowData(6), Location)
                        distance = loc.Distance(storeLoc)
                        If distance < smallest Then
                                result = CopyRow(rowData)
                                smallest = distance
                        End If
                End While
                pipe.Send(result)
            End Using
        End Using
    End Sub
    Private Shared Function CopyRow(ByVal data() As Object) As SqlDataRecord
        Dim result As SqlDataRecord
        Dim cols As New List(Of SqlMetaData)
        'set up columns
        cols.Add(New SqlMetaData("id", SqlDbType.Int))
        cols.Add(New SqlMetaData("Name", SqlDbType.NVarChar, 50))
        cols.Add(New SqlMetaData("Street", SqlDbType.NVarChar, 512))
        cols.Add(New SqlMetaData("City", SqlDbType.NVarChar, 50))
        cols.Add(New SqlMetaData("State", SqlDbType.Char, 2))
        cols.Add(New SqlMetaData("Zip", SqlDbType.VarChar, 50))
        result = New SqlDataRecord(cols.ToArray())
        'copy data from row to record
        result.SetSqlInt32(0, DirectCast(data(0), SqlInt32))
        result.SetSqlString(1, DirectCast(data(1), SqlString))
        result.SetSqlString(2, DirectCast(data(2), SqlString))
        result.SetSqlString(3, DirectCast(data(3), SqlString))
        result.SetSqlString(4, DirectCast(data(4), SqlString))
        result.SetSqlString(5, DirectCast(data(5), SqlString))
        Return result
    End Function
End Class
```

Code snippet from FooStore

There are three basic steps to the stored procedure. First, it needs to determine the location of the inputted address. Next, it needs to find stores with available stock — that is, with stock greater than the requested amount. Finally, it needs to find the store on that list that is closest to the inputted address.

Getting the location of the address is probably the easiest step, as you already have the fnGetLocation function. Rather than needing to create and use a SqlConnection, however, because the function is a shared method of the UserDefinedFunctions class, you can use it directly from your code. Here you can see another benefit in the way that the Visual Basic-SQL interaction was designed. The code is the same that you would have used in a system written completely in Visual Basic, but in this case it is actually calling a SQL Server scalar function.

Obtaining the list of stores with stock is simply a matter of creating a SqlCommand and using it to create a SqlDataReader. Again, this is basically the same step you would take in any other Visual Basic application. The difference here is that the code will execute within SQL Server. Therefore, the SqlConnection is defined using the connection string "context connection=true".

The final step in the stored procedure — finding the nearest store — requires some mathematical calculations (within the Location.Distance method). While the previous two steps could have been performed easily in straight T-SQL, it is this step that would have been the most awkward to perform using that language. The code loops through each row in the list of stores with available stock. Because all of the values from each row are needed, the GetSqlValues method copies the current row to an array of Object values. Within this array is the GeoLocation column, and you can cast this value to a Location object. After this is done, the Distance method may be used to determine the distance between the input address and the store's address.

When the minimum distance has been determined, the `Send(SqlDataRecord)` method of the `SqlPipe` class is used to write the data to the output stream, returning it to the calling function.

The `CopyRow` function is used to create the `SqlDataRecord` to return. The first step in creating a `SqlDataRecord` is to define the columns of data. The constructor for the `SqlDataRecord` requires an array of `SqlMetaData` objects that define each column. The preceding code uses the `List` generic collection to make defining this array easier. Once the columns are defined, the data returned from the `GetValues` method is used to populate the columns of the new `SqlDataRecord`.

Exposing Web Services from SQL Server

Another feature of SQL Server is the capability to expose Web services directly from the server. This means there is no requirement for IIS on the server, as the requests are received and processed by SQL Server. You define what ports will be used to host the Web service. The structure of the Web service is defined based on the parameters and return data of the function or stored procedure you use as the source of the Web service.

 Exposing Web services directly from SQL Server is supported only on the Standard and higher editions. The Express and Compact editions do not support creating Web services in this manner.

When you are architecting a scenario and plan to expose Web services from SQL Server, keep in mind at least one important question: Why do you think you need to expose this database functionality outside of the SQL Server? It's not a trivial question. It means that you plan on hanging data off of the server, possibly for public access. That's a potentially dangerous scenario not to be taken lightly. Most of the scenarios for which it makes sense to provide Web services directly from a SQL Server involve systems entirely behind a firewall, where Web services are used as the conduit between departments (typical A2A integration). This would be useful if the target departments were using another platform or database, or where security considerations prevented them from directly accessing the SQL Server.

Following is the basic syntax of the `CREATE ENDPOINT` command. Although both `AS HTTP` and `AS TCP` are shown, only one can occur per `CREATE ENDPOINT` command.

```
CREATE ENDPOINT endPointName [ AUTHORIZATION login ]
STATE = { STARTED | STOPPED | DISABLED }
AS HTTP (
  PATH = 'url',
  AUTHENTICATION =( { BASIC | DIGEST | INTEGRATED | NTLM | KERBEROS } [ ,. . .n ] ),
  PORTS = ( { CLEAR | SSL} [ ,. . . n ] )
  [ SITE = {'*' | '+' | 'webSite' },]
  [, CLEAR_PORT = clearPort ]
  [, SSL_PORT = SSLPort ]
  [, AUTH_REALM = { 'realm' | NONE } ]
  [, DEFAULT_LOGON_DOMAIN = { 'domain' | NONE } ]
  [, COMPRESSION = { ENABLED | DISABLED } ]
  )
AS TCP (
  LISTENER_PORT = listenerPort
  [ , LISTENER_IP = ALL | (<4-part-ip> | <ip_address_v6> ) ]
  )
FOR SOAP(
  [ { WEBMETHOD [ 'namespace' .] 'method_alias'
    (   NAME = 'database.owner.name'
      [ , SCHEMA = { NONE | STANDARD | DEFAULT } ]
      [ , FORMAT = { ALL_RESULTS | ROWSETS_ONLY } ]
    )
  } [ ,. . .n ] ]
  [   BATCHES = { ENABLED | DISABLED } ]
```

```
[ , WSDL = { NONE | DEFAULT | 'sp_name' } ]
[ , SESSIONS = { ENABLED | DISABLED } ]
[ , LOGIN_TYPE = { MIXED | WINDOWS } ]
[ , SESSION_TIMEOUT = timeoutInterval | NEVER ]
[ , DATABASE = { 'database_name' | DEFAULT }
[ , NAMESPACE = { 'namespace' | DEFAULT } ]
[ , SCHEMA = { NONE | STANDARD } ]
[ , CHARACTER_SET = { SQL | XML }]
[ , HEADER_LIMIT = int ]
)
```

The main points to consider when creating an endpoint are as follows:

➤ What stored procedure or function (or UDF) will you be exposing as a Web service? This is identified in the `WebMethod` clause. There may be multiple Web methods exposed from a single endpoint. If so, each will have a separate `WebMethod` parameter listing. This parameter identifies the database object you will expose, and allows you to give it a new name.

➤ What authentication will clients need to use? Typically, if your clients are part of the same network, then you use integrated or NTLM authentication. If clients are coming across the Internet or from non-Windows, then you may want to use Kerberos, Digest, or Basic authentication.

➤ What network port will the service use? The two basic options when creating an HTTP endpoint are CLEAR (using HTTP, typically on port 80) or SSL (using HTTPS, typically on port 443). Generally, use SSL if the data transmitted requires security, and you are using public networks. Note that Internet Information Services (IIS) and other Web servers also use these ports. If you have both IIS and SQL Server on the same machine, you should alternate ports (using `CLEAR_PORT` or `SSL_PORT`) for your HTTP endpoints. When creating TCP endpoints, select a `LISTENER_PORT` that is unused on your server. HTTP offers the broadest reach and largest number of possible clients, while TCP offers better performance. If you are making the Web service available over the Internet, you would generally use HTTP and TCP within the firewall, where you can control the number and type of clients.

To continue our example, you can make the `procGetClosestStoreWithStock` procedure available as a Web service using the following code:

```
CREATE ENDPOINT store_endpoint
  STATE = STARTED
AS
HTTP(
  PATH = '/footsore',
  AUTHENTICATION = (INTEGRATED),
  PORTS = (CLEAR),
  CLEAR_PORT = 8888,
  SITE = 'localhost'
  )
FOR
SOAP(
  WEBMETHOD 'GetNearestStore' (name = 'fooStore.dbo.procGetClosestStoreWithStock'),
  WSDL = DEFAULT,
  SCHEMA = STANDARD,
  DATABASE = 'fooStore', NAMESPACE = 'http://fooStore.com/webmethods'
);
```

Endpoints are created within the master database, as they are part of the larger SQL Server system, and not stored within each database. The endpoint defined in the preceding code creates a SOAP wrapper around the `procGetClosestStoreWithStock` stored procedure, making it available as `GetNearestStore`. Integrated security is used, which means that any users need network credentials on the SQL Server. If this service were available over the Internet, you might use Digest or Basic instead. As the server is also running IIS, this example moved the port for the service to 8888.

Once the service has been created you can create clients based on the WSDL of the service.

Accessing the Web Service

SQL Server makes some of the work easier when hosting Web services. The WSDL for the service is automatically generated. Many SOAP tools, such as Visual Studio, enable the creation of wrapper classes based on the WSDL for the service.

The WSDL for a SQL Server Web service may be a little daunting when you first see it, as it's quite lengthy. This is primarily because the WSDL includes definitions for the various SQL Server data types as well as for the Web services you create. Figure 12-30 shows part of the WSDL, the part created for the `procGetClosestStoreWithStock` procedure. You can view this WSDL by including the query `?WSDL` to the end of the URL for the Web Service.

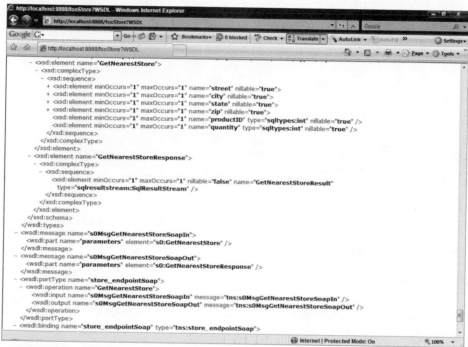

FIGURE 12-30

As you can see from the WSDL, two main structures are defined: `GetNearestStore` and `GetNearestStoreResponse`. The `GetNearestStore` document is what is sent to the Web service. It includes definitions of each of the columns sent, along with the expected data types and sizes.

`GetNearestStoreResponse` is the return document. In the preceding sample, you can see that it is of type `SqlResultStream`. This type, also defined in the WSDL, is the tabular data stream returned from SQL Server. It consists of the return value from the stored procedure and any result sets of data. This will be converted to an `Object` array by the SOAP wrapper classes. You can then convert these data blocks to other types.

When creating a Web service, it's a good idea to create a simple form that can be used to test the service. Add a new Windows Forms Application project to the solution (or create a new Project/Solution). Select the Add Service Reference command from the Solution Explorer. Click the Advanced button on the Add Service Reference dialog and select Add Web Reference. From the Add Web Reference dialog, select the fooStore service (see Figure 12-31).

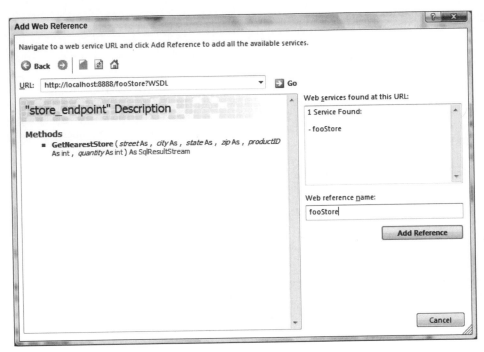

FIGURE 12-31

Once you have the connection to the Web service, you're ready to begin laying out the fields of the test form. Most of the fields are TextBox controls, with the exception of the Product ComboBox and the DataGridView on the bottom. The Table 12-8 describes the properties set on the controls:

TABLE 12-8: Control Properties

CONTROL	PROPERTY	VALUE
TextBox	Name	StreetField
TextBox	Name	CityField
TextBox	Name	StateField
	MaxLength	2
TextBox	Name	ZipField
ComboBox	Name	ProductList
TextBox	Name	QuantityField
Button	Name	GetNearestStoreButton
	Text	&Get NearestStore
DataGridView	Name	ResultGrid
	AllowUserToAddRows	False
	AllowUserToDeleteRows	False
	ReadOnly	True

Organize the controls on the form in any way you find aesthetically pleasing. Figure 12-32 shows one example.

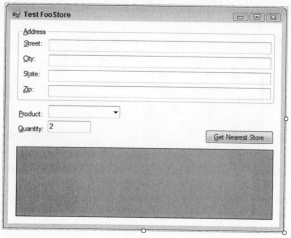

FIGURE 12-32

The code for the test form is as follows:

```vb
Imports System.Data
Imports System.Data.SqlClient
Public Class MainForm
    Private Sub GetNearestStoreButton_Click(ByVal sender As System.Object, _
        ByVal e As System.EventArgs) Handles GetNearestStoreButton.Click
        Using svc As New fooStore.store_endpoint
            Dim result() As Object
            Dim data As New DataSet
            svc.Credentials = System.Net.CredentialCache.DefaultCredentials
            result = svc.GetNearestStore(Me.StreetField.Text,
                Me.CityField.Text,
                Me.StateField.Text,
                Me.ZipField.Text,
                CInt(Me.ProductList.SelectedValue),
                CInt(Me.QuantityField.Text))
            If result IsNot Nothing Then
                data = DirectCast(result(0), DataSet)
                Me.ResultGrid.DataSource = data.Tables(0)
            End If
        End Using
    End Sub
    Private Sub MainForm_Load(ByVal sender As System.Object, _
        ByVal e As System.EventArgs) Handles MyBase.Load
        Dim ds As New DataSet
        Using conn As New SqlConnection(My.Settings.FooStoreConnectionString)
            Using da As New SqlDataAdapter("SELECT id, Name FROM PRODUCTS", conn)
                da.Fill(ds)
                With Me.ProductList
                    .DataSource = ds.Tables(0)
                    .ValueMember = "id"
                    .DisplayMember = "Name"
                End With
            End Using
        End Using
    End Sub
End Class
```

Code snippet from FooStore

The test form consists of two methods. The `Load` method is used to retrieve the data that populates the product drop-down. The call to the Web service takes place in the `Button` click event. This method calls the Web service wrapper, passing in the values entered on the form. Recall that the Web service returns two result sets: the data and the return value.

Run the test application. Enter an address close to one of the stores, and select a product and quantity you know to be available. Click the Get Nearest Store button. After a brief delay, the store's address should appear (see Figure 12-33). Try again with a larger quantity or different product so that another store is returned. Depending on the stock available at each of the store locations, the nearest store may not be all that near.

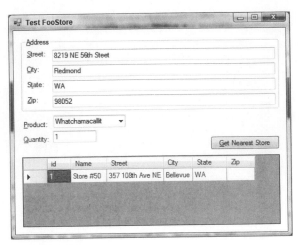

FIGURE 12-33

SQL Server 2008 Features

Now that you've expended the effort to create your own geospatial data type, it's time to tell you that you wasted your time. SQL Server 2008 includes a number of new data types, including two geospatial data types: `geometry` and `geography`. The `geometry` type is designed for smaller areas, when the curvature of the Earth is not significant, whereas the `geography` type is "curve aware."

There are a couple of benefits to using these types over creating your own. First, they are much more fully designed than the type you created earlier in this chapter. The `geography` data type includes a number of standard methods defined by the Open Geospatial Consortium. This standard ensures that your code is portable across multiple implementations. In the case of distance, this can be calculated using the `STDistance` method (all of the methods defined in the standard begin with "ST"). The geospatial types include methods for defining areas, calculating distances and areas, indicating whether areas intersect, and many others.

Second, and probably more important, these types are defined within the `Microsoft.SqlServer.Types` namespace. As Microsoft created this namespace, they could do a little bit of "cheating" behind the scenes. This namespace does not require you to enable SQL CLR on your server to use them. This means you don't need to do any additional configuration, and that a potential security hole is not activated.

Converting the FooStore application to use the new types is relatively easy. First, you can change the data type of the GeoLocation column from the `Location` type created earlier to `geography` (see Figure 12-34). You should drop the table and recreate this, as the internal representation of the data in the column does not match the new data type.

The second major change is that you no longer need the calculations behind the `Distance` method of the `location` object. This (rather ugly) calculation is encapsulated within the `STDistance` method, which takes a `geography` type and returns the distance as a `SqlDouble`.

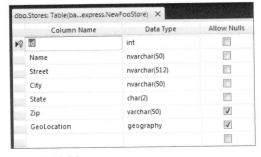

FIGURE 12-34

WCF DATA SERVICES

In the previous two chapters, you have seen two of the major data access methods in the .NET Framework: "classic" ADO.NET and the Entity Framework. Deciding when to use one over the other depends on whether you're working on new code versus existing code, and/or your desire to work with the latest and greatest technologies. In both cases, however, you can choose to access your data using either types specifically designed for each data access technology or your own types. Either way, it is assumed that you're working on a network, and you can expect a .NET class at the other end. WCF Data Services (formerly ADO.NET Data Services) attempts to change that model. Rather than take a traditional .NET or network model to your data access, WCF Data Services (DS) provides a REST model for your data.

REST

REST, or REpresentational State Transfer, is an application model first defined by Roy Fielding in his doctoral thesis. While you may have never heard of Roy Fielding in the past, you likely use one of his creations daily; he was one of the principal authors of the HTTP specification. In his thesis, he described a way to create applications that "work the way the Internet works":

➤ Every piece of data (or resource) is uniquely identified by some address within the system.

➤ You use a consistent interface for accessing these resources.

➤ You process these resources through representations of the resources, in known data formats.

➤ The entire system is stateless.

Applying these principals to the Internet, you can see how they work in action:

➤ Every Web page is defined using a unique URL (Uniform Resource Locator).

➤ The HTTP protocol defines a number of verbs that may be used to act on those URLs. While the two most commonly used verbs are GET and POST, many others are available (e.g., PUT and DELETE).

➤ When you request a specific resource, you receive the content along with the MIME type of that content.

➤ HTTP is very stateless (as many new ASP.NET developers painfully discover).

WCF Data Services provides this mechanism for working with your data. It adds an additional layer to your applications that enables you to manipulate an Entity Framework model (or other data, as you'll see below) using this RESTful model:

➤ Each query, record, or field within your database can be uniquely identified using a URL, such as http://example.com/PubsService.svc/authors('172-32-1176')

➤ You use the same HTTP verbs to access your data (GET to retrieve an item, POST to insert new records, PUT to update them, and DELETE to delete them).

➤ When requesting data, you receive it in Atom or JSON format.

➤ The entire system remains stateless, typically with optimistic concurrency when changing records.

Atom and JSON

As described above, the data returned by Data Services is in the form of either Atom or JSON. These are both standard data formats: Atom (an official IETF standard – RFC 4287), while JSON (JavaScript Object Notation) is really just using JavaScript's object definition syntax.

Atom is an XML format that was initially proposed as a "better RSS," but it has grown into a flexible format for defining objects of any syntax. Figure 12-35 shows an example of this format. The `<content>` element holds the actual data, while the rest of the XML is used to provide metadata (data about the data).

```
<?xml version="1.0" encoding="utf-8" standalone="yes" ?>
- <entry xml:base="http://localhost:49191/PubsService.svc/"
    xmlns:d="http://schemas.microsoft.com/ado/2007/08/dataservices"
    xmlns:m="http://schemas.microsoft.com/ado/2007/08/dataservices/metadata"
    xmlns="http://www.w3.org/2005/Atom">
    <id>http://localhost:49191/PubsService.svc/authors('172-32-1176')</id>
    <title type="text" />
    <updated>2009-10-18T22:17:16Z</updated>
  - <author>
      <name />
    </author>
    <link rel="edit" title="author" href="authors('172-32-1176')" />
    <link rel="http://schemas.microsoft.com/ado/2007/08/dataservices/related/titleauthors"
      type="application/atom+xml;type=feed" title="titleauthors" href="authors('172-32-
      1176')/titleauthors" />
    <category term="PubsModel.author"
      scheme="http://schemas.microsoft.com/ado/2007/08/dataservices/scheme" />
  - <content type="application/xml">
    - <m:properties>
        <d:au_id>172-32-1176</d:au_id>
        <d:au_lname>White</d:au_lname>
        <d:au_fname>Johnson</d:au_fname>
        <d:phone>408 496-7223</d:phone>
        <d:address>10932 Bigge Rd.</d:address>
        <d:city>Menlo Park</d:city>
        <d:state>CA</d:state>
        <d:zip>94025</d:zip>
        <d:contract m:type="Edm.Boolean">true</d:contract>
      </m:properties>
    </content>
  </entry>
```

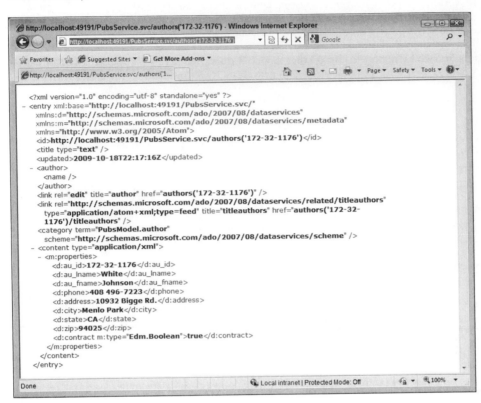

FIGURE 12-35

The root element of Atom is either a `<feed>` node, or an `<entry>` node. Feed elements are used to contain multiple entry elements, whereas an entry element represents a single item.

JSON is a subset of JavaScript that has become a popular syntax for passing data across the Internet (see Figure 12-36). It is a very concise format for describing data. Individual objects are wrapped in braces ({}); and within an object, the properties are defined using name:value pairs, each in quotes. Collections are defined by wrapping the child objects with brackets ([]).

{ "d" : { "__metadata": { "uri": "http://127.0.0.1:49191/PubsService.svc/authors(\'172-32-1176\')", "type": "PubsModel.author" }, "au_id": "172-32-1176", "au_lname": "White", "au_fname": "Johnson", "phone": "408 496-7223", "address": "10932 Bigge Rd.", "city": "Menlo Park", "state": "CA", "zip": "94025", "contract": true, "titleauthors": { "__deferred": { "uri": "http://127.0.0.1:49191/PubsService.svc/authors(\'172-32-1176\')/titleauthors" } } } }

FIGURE 12-36

The benefit of JSON over Atom is this conciseness. For the single author shown in Figures 12-35 and 12-36, the JSON version is 459 bytes, whereas the Atom format is 1,300 bytes. Obviously, the more objects you have here, the more the XML format would increase this difference. Conversely, the Atom format retains more information about the record than the bare-bones JSON format.

Exposing Data Using WCF Data Services

WCF Data Services is a specialized WCF library that converts the HTTP requests to some provider. Currently, DS supports the Entity Framework as well as custom objects.

Adding DS support to a project containing an Entity Framework model is as simple as adding a new WCF Data Service class to the project (see Figure 12-37). This adds a new class to the project that represents the actual service:

```vb
Imports System.Data.Services
Imports System.Linq
Imports System.ServiceModel.Web

Public Class PubsService
    ' TODO: replace [[class name]] with your data class name
    Inherits DataService(Of [[class name]])

    ' This method is called only once to initialize service-wide policies.
    Public Shared Sub InitializeService(ByVal config As IDataServiceConfiguration)
        ' TODO: set rules to indicate which entity sets
        ' and service operations are visible, updatable, etc.
        ' Examples:
        ' config.SetEntitySetAccessRule("MyEntityset", EntitySetRights.AllRead)
        ' config.SetServiceOperationAccessRule("MyServiceOperation",
                ServiceOperationRights.All)
    End Sub

End Class
```

Code snippet from SimpleDataService

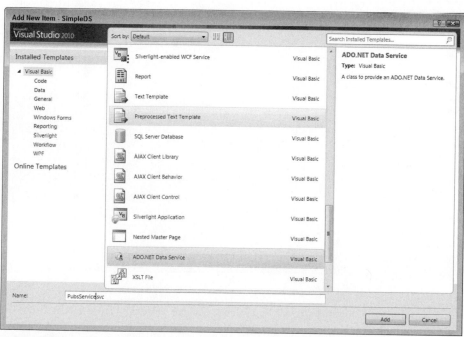

FIGURE 12-37

As shown in the preceding code, you must perform a number of steps before the project will compile. First, you need to identify the class providing the data. Second, by default, DS does not allow any data access. You need to explicitly identify the objects that may be queried, and what users may do with them. When exposing an Entity Framework model, the class is your entities. You can apply multiple security rules, depending on how you have separated the entities in your model. Alternately, you can take the easy route and expose all the objects in your model, as shown in the following code:

```
Public Class PubsService
    Inherits DataService(Of PubsEntities)

    ' This method is called only once to initialize service-wide policies.
    Public Shared Sub InitializeService(ByVal config As IDataServiceConfiguration)
        config.SetEntitySetAccessRule("*", EntitySetRights.All)
        config.UseVerboseErrors = True
    End Sub

End Class
```

Once you have configured your data service, you can browse to the service to view the available resources (see Figure 12-38).

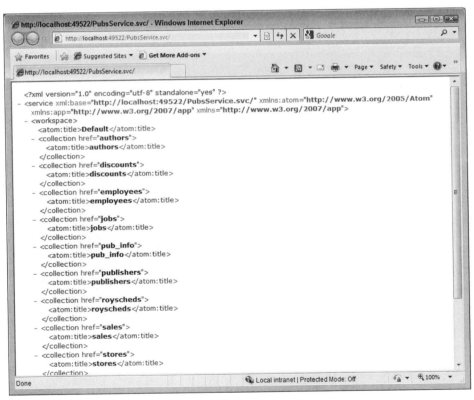

FIGURE 12-38

Each of the collections returned represents an additional query you can perform. Figure 12-39 shows the results of querying the authors table.

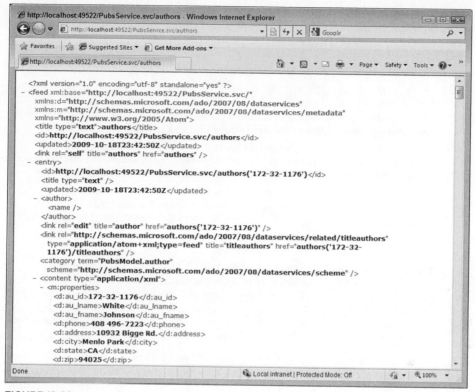

FIGURE 12-39

As shown in Table 12-9, you can perform a number of different queries using any browser:

TABLE 12-9: Query Examples and Results

QUERY	QUERY EXAMPLE	RESULT
/entity	/authors	Returns a list of all the entities in that table
/entity(KEY)	/authors('213-46-8915')	Returns a single entity, identified by the provided key
/entity(KEY)/related	/titles('BU1032')/sales	Returns the data in the related table (in this case, the sales for a specific title)
/entity(KEY)/field	/authors('213-46-8915')/ address	Returns the data for a specific column (Note: This can be combined with any of the queries to return specific column data.)
/entity(multiple keys)	/sales(ord_num='6871', stor_id='6380',title_ id='BU1032')/store/	Returns an item defined by multiple query values

These queries can be combined, enabling you to extract just the data you want. For example, /sales(ord_num='6871',stor_id='6380',title_id='BU1032')/store/stor_name would return the store name for one specific order of one specific title. When using a browser to explore the data service, the `<link>` elements in each entry shows you other queries you can perform.

In addition to the entity-specific queries, you can use several additional operators to compose your queries. In each case, the operator can be appended to the query as a query parameter. Some of these parameters are listed in Table 12-10:

TABLE 12-10: Operators Used as Query Parameters

OPERATOR	EXAMPLE
$value	Returns just the data for a field, without any containing XML. This can be used in much the same way you might query a database to get a single value using `ExecuteScalar`.
$orderby	Sorts the returned data. You can include multiple sort items by separating them with commas. For example: `/authors/?$orderby=state,city` would sort first by state, then by city to return the authors. Adding "desc" to the end will sort in descending order.
$top, $skip	Typically used together to enable paging data. `Top` returns the top '*n*' elements, while `skip` ignores that many items before returning data. For example, `/authors/?$orderby=state,city&$top=4&$skip=4` would return the second set of four authors.
$expand	When querying for data that includes child data (e.g., order detail rows when retrieving orders), `$expand` returns the child data as well.
$filter	Enables you to more flexibly query the data. This includes a number of operations for comparison, string, date and mathematical functions, and more. Some example queries include `/authors/?$filter=(state eq 'CA')`, `/authors/?$filter=startswith(au_lname, 'S')`, and `/sales/?$filter=year(ord_date) gt 1993&$orderby=ord_date desc`. Of course, these can also be combined with the usual AND, OR and NOT operations to create very rich queries.

Although working with the Data Service using the browser provides you with an easy way to query the data, you are limited in what you can do with it. You cannot query to retrieve the JSON representation, for example. To get more flexibility, you should download the free Fiddler tool (www.fiddlertool.com) to work with DS. This tool provides a great deal of support for working with HTTP, including monitoring requests made via a browser, as well as the capability to make requests from Fiddler itself. By adding the Accept:application/json header to the request, you can view the JSON output of the data service. Fiddler also enables you to build requests for working with the other HTTP verbs.

Any client that can generate the appropriate URL can query the data service. As the resulting data is in standard data formats, you should be able to work with the data, even on non-.NET clients. The following code shows a simple console application that queries the PubsDataService to retrieve and display a list of the authors, sorted by state and city. The client could be an ASP.NET application, using jQuery or ASP.NET AJAX to retrieve the data, a Silverlight application, a WPF application, or even an application running on another platform.

```
Module Main

    'replace this with the address of your service
    Const ADDRESS As String =
     "http://localhost:49233/PubsService.svc/authors/?$orderby=state,city"

    Sub Main()
        Dim doc As New XDocument()
        Dim schemaNS As XNamespace =
         "http://schemas.microsoft.com/ado/2007/08/dataservices/metadata"
        Dim schemaDS As XNamespace =
         "http://schemas.microsoft.com/ado/2007/08/dataservices"

        doc = XDocument.Load(ADDRESS)
        Dim authors = (From prop In doc.Descendants(schemaNS + "properties")
                       From a In prop.Descendants(schemaDS + "au_lname")
```

```
                    Select a).ToList()

        For Each author In authors
            Console.WriteLine(author.Value)
        Next

        Console.WriteLine("Press ENTER to exit")
        Console.ReadLine()
    End Sub

End Module
```

Code snippet from SimpleDataService

While this URL format makes it relatively easy to query the database, it is less helpful when editing the data. You use the same URL syntax, but you manipulate the database using some of the other HTTP verbs (see the following table).

VERB	DESCRIPTION
POST	Used to create new entries. You need to include the new entry in the body of the request, using the same format you receive when you query the entry.
PUT	Used to update entries. The updated entry is included in the body of the request.
DELETE	Used to delete a record

WCF Data Services Client Library

The flexibility of querying WCF Data Services using an URL is attractive, but you hardly want to build an application that creates URLs whenever you want to query or edit a database. Fortunately, WCF Data Services also provides the capability to manipulate the data using LINQ. DS converts the LINQ requests into the appropriate URL.

To use the client library, you need to add a Service Reference to your data service (see Figure 12-40).

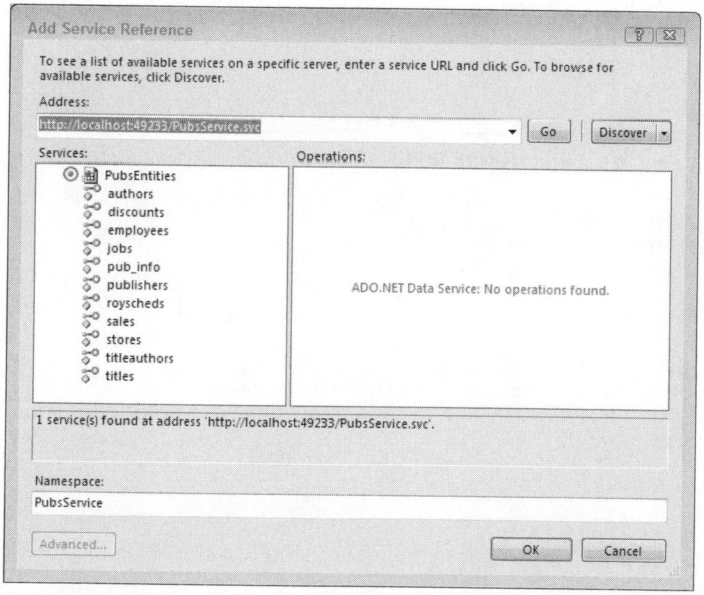

FIGURE 12-40

Just as with other WCF services, adding the service reference creates a client-side proxy of your service. You can then query the objects directly, and DS creates the appropriate URL from your LINQ query. You first instantiate a context to your service, and then make the query:

```
Dim context As New PubsEntities(URL)
Dim authors = From a In context.authors
              Where a.state = "CA"
              Order By a.city Select a
For Each author In authors
    'do something with the author type here
Next
```

Code snippet from SimpleDataService

This provides a much more natural means of querying the service, regardless of whether it's using JSON, Atom, or HTTP to make the request.

Add a new Windows Forms application to act as a client for the data service, and add a Service Reference to the project. Figure 12-41 shows one possible user interface. In this case, the list box on the left will be populated with the authors. Selecting an author will allow you to edit the properties using the fields on the right, or you can clear the fields to create a new author (see Figure 12-42).

FIGURE 12-41

FIGURE 12-42

```
Imports System.Data.Services.Client
Imports SimpleDataServiceClient.PubsService

Public Class MainForm

    'update this to match your service
    Dim ServiceUri As Uri = New Uri("http://localhost:49233/PubsService.svc")
    Dim isNew As Boolean = True
    Dim isDirty As Boolean = False

    Dim context As PubsEntities

    Private Sub MainForm_Load(ByVal sender As Object,
                    ByVal e As System.EventArgs) Handles Me.Load
```

```vbnet
        context = New PubsEntities(ServiceUri)

        InitializeList()
    End Sub

    Private Sub RefreshButton_Click(ByVal sender As System.Object,
                ByVal e As System.EventArgs) Handles RefreshButton.Click
        'retrieves the list of authors
        'and updates the list
        InitializeList()
    End Sub

    Private Sub InitializeList()
        Me.AuthorsList.Items.Clear()

        Dim authors = From a In context.authors
                    Where a.state = "CA"
                    Order By a.city Select a
        For Each author In authors
            Me.AuthorsList.Items.Add(author)
        Next
    End Sub

    Private Sub ClearButton_Click(ByVal sender As System.Object,
                ByVal e As System.EventArgs) Handles ClearButton.Click
        isNew = True
        Au_fnameTextBox.Text = String.Empty
        Au_lnameTextBox.Text = String.Empty
        PhoneTextBox.Text = String.Empty
        AddressTextBox.Text = String.Empty
        CityTextBox.Text = String.Empty
        StateTextBox.Text = String.Empty
        ZipTextBox.Text = String.Empty
        ContractCheckBox.Checked = False
    End Sub

    Private Sub Field_TextChanged(ByVal sender As Object,
                ByVal e As System.EventArgs) _
            Handles ZipTextBox.TextChanged, _
            StateTextBox.TextChanged, _
            PhoneTextBox.TextChanged, _
            CityTextBox.TextChanged, _
            Au_lnameTextBox.TextChanged, _
            Au_fnameTextBox.TextChanged, _
            AddressTextBox.TextChanged
        isDirty = True
    End Sub

    Private Sub SaveButton_Click(ByVal sender As System.Object,
                ByVal e As System.EventArgs) Handles SaveButton.Click
        Dim selectedAuthor As author = Nothing

        If isNew Then
            'saving a new entity
            selectedAuthor = New author
        ElseIf isDirty Then
            'updating an existing entity
            selectedAuthor = Me.AuthorsList.SelectedItem
        End If
        'update fields
```

```
        With selectedAuthor
            .au_id = Au_idTextBox.Text
            .au_fname = Au_fnameTextBox.Text
            .au_lname = Au_lnameTextBox.Text
            .phone = PhoneTextBox.Text
            .address = AddressTextBox.Text
            .city = CityTextBox.Text
            .state = StateTextBox.Text
            .zip = ZipTextBox.Text
            .contract = ContractCheckBox.Checked
        End With
        If isNew Then
            context.AddToauthors(selectedAuthor)
        ElseIf isDirty Then
            context.UpdateObject(selectedAuthor)
        End If

        context.SaveChanges()

        isNew = False
        isDirty = False

    End Sub

    Private Sub AuthorsList_SelectedIndexChanged(ByVal sender As System.Object, _
            ByVal e As System.EventArgs) _
        Handles AuthorsList.SelectedIndexChanged

        'fill fields
        Dim SelectedAuthor As author =
          DirectCast(Me.AuthorsList.SelectedItem, author)
        With SelectedAuthor
            Au_idTextBox.Text = .au_id
            Au_fnameTextBox.Text = .au_fname
            Au_lnameTextBox.Text = .au_lname
            PhoneTextBox.Text = .phone
            AddressTextBox.Text = .address
            CityTextBox.Text = .city
            StateTextBox.Text = .state
            ZipTextBox.Text = .zip
            ContractCheckBox.Checked = .contract
        End With
        isNew = False
    End Sub
End Classs
```

Code snippet from SimpleDataService

Most of the preceding code should be fairly self-explanatory. Two routines probably need explanation, however.

The `InitializeList` routine is a simple LINQ query to retrieve the list of authors. It then adds them to the list box. The `DisplayMember` of the list box is set to the Last Name field (au_lname), while the `ValueMember` is set to the key (au_id).

The `SaveButton` code is divided into three logical parts. First, you must identify the author you want to save. As this may be either an existing author or a new one, the `isNew` and `isDirty` flags are used to determine if this is an insert or an update. Next, the fields are set to the new values. Finally, the magic happens: The proxy method `Addtoauthors` is used to add a new author to the list if you are performing an insert, while `UpdateObject` is used to mark for an update. We could have made a number of changes here, and the context tracks these. Once the `SaveChanges` method is called, they are sent to the server.

A couple of options are available when calling `SaveChanges` using the `SaveChangesOptions` enumeration. By default, each request is sent individually. If an error occurs, the save will end, but any saves that have already occurred will remain in place. If you use the `ContinueOnError` option, DS will continue to save items. You can use the return value from the `SaveChanges` method to determine the result of each update. Alternately, the `SaveChangesOptions.Batch` will send all of the requests within a single `ChangeSet`. While not technically a transaction, the `ChangeSet` behaves similarly: Either all the updates will happen or none will. Again, the return from the `SaveChanges` method will identify where the errors occurred.

SUMMARY

The addition of SQL Server Compact to the SQL family gives you a new, but familiar, place to store data. Rather than create yet another XML file to store small amounts of data, you can make use of the powerful storage and query functionality of SQL Server. In addition, when you combine it with Sync Framework, disconnected and partly connected applications become remarkably easy to create and deploy. One of the most potentially useful changes made to SQL Server lately is the capability to move your code into the database. By integrating the common language runtime (CLR) with SQL Server, developers now have a choice when creating data access code between T-SQL and Visual Basic.

While the implications of having your database run Visual Basic code can be a little unnerving, the benefits you receive in terms of flexibility and power may be just what you need in some applications. Visual Basic provides several tools that are not normally available when working with T-SQL, such as access to the .NET Framework's classes. While you should only use Visual Basic in stored procedures and other database structures when it's appropriate, in those cases you can dramatically improve the scalability, performance, and functionality of your database applications.

WCF Data Services is still a relatively new technology, but it holds a great deal of promise: enabling developers to easily provide Web-style APIs over their applications. By leveraging existing standards, it holds the promise to be the cross-platform, easy to use communication tools that Web services were intended to be.

13

Services (XML/WCF)

WHAT YOU WILL LEARN IN THIS CHAPTER

- ➤ Review of distributed communication technologies
- ➤ Introduction to Web services and remoting
- ➤ Overview of service-oriented architecture
- ➤ WSDL, SOAP and WS-* protocols
- ➤ Creating a WCF service
- ➤ Creating a WCF TCP host
- ➤ Creating a WCF client
- ➤ Testing a WCF service with Visual Studio over HTTP
- ➤ Creating a WCF client with a data contract
- ➤ Testing a WCF service over TCP

Over the years there has been an ongoing effort to make communication between distributed components as easy as communication between components and objects within a single executable. Microsoft's first foray into distributed computing involved a technology known as Distributed COM (DCOM). With the introduction of .NET, Microsoft replaced COM, and by extension DCOM, with two new emergent technologies: ASP.NET Web Services and .NET Remoting.

Most people recognized Remoting as the next generation of DCOM, as it was primarily a binary protocol tied to a Microsoft implementation. As such, its use was limited in a heterogeneous environment, which limited adoption. Conversely, XML Web services proved to be a more emergent technology, one which has continued to evolve, changing the face of distributed computing.

However, the initial release of XML Web Services (known within the .NET community as ASP.NET Web Services), didn't have sufficient support for advanced security and related features that were built into binary protocols like Remoting.

Thus, in the .NET 2.0 time frame you could have used ASP.NET Web Services, Web Service Enhancements 3.0 (WSE), MSMQ, Enterprise Services, .NET Remoting, and even the System .Messaging namespace. Each one of these technologies has pros and cons associated with it. ASP.NET Web Services (also known as ASMX Web Services) provided the capability to easily build interoperable Web services. The WSE enabled you to easily build services that took advantage of some of the WS-* message protocols. MSMQ enabled the queuing of messages, making it easy to work with solutions that were only intermittently connected. Enterprise Services, provided as a successor to COM+, offered an easy means to build distributed applications. .NET Remoting provided a fast way to move messages from one .NET application to another. Moreover, this is only the Microsoft world — it does not include all the options available in other environments, such as the Java world.

With all these options for a Microsoft developer, it became difficult to decide on the best technology for a solution. Another problematic issue was that almost no one had mastered all of the preceding technologies. While XML Web Services were becoming something of an interoperability standard, under the heading service-oriented architecture (SOA), that still left multiple different solutions and all sorts of interoperability issues. With these challenges in mind, Microsoft brought forth the Windows Communication Foundation (WCF).

WCF is a framework for building services. Originally introduced as part of the .NET 3.0 enhancements, WCF combines support for several different protocols. Microsoft wanted to provide its developers with a framework that would offer the fastest means to getting a service solution in place, while remaining somewhat agnostic of the underlying transport protocol. Using the WCF, you can take advantage of a variety of powerful protocols under the covers — everything from binary to basic XML Web Services can be supported with the same implementation. WCF is the successor to a series of different distributed communication technologies.

INTRODUCTION TO SERVICES

Understanding the history of the search for a decent *remote method invocation (RMI)* protocol is imperative to an understanding of why Web services are so important. Each of the RMI systems, created before the current Web services model, solved a particular set of problems. In this section, you will see how current WCF services represent the next stage in the evolution of these cross-platform boundaries. While each of these technologies managed to address one or more issues, all ultimately failed to fully provide a solution.

The Network Angle

Throughout the history of computing, networking operations were largely handled by the operating system. UNIX, the networking host of early computing, featured a body of shell operations that provided remarkable user control over network operations. Personal computing was slower to catch up: Microsoft and Apple software didn't inherently support networking protocols until the mid-1990s. Third-party add-ons by Novell and Banyan were available earlier, but they were only an adjunct to the operating system. The concept of the network being the computer did not fully infiltrate the development community until the expansion of the World Wide Web.

Application Development

Let's break away from networking for a minute and look at how application development evolved until now. Early time-sharing operating systems enabled several people to use the same application with its built-in data. These single-tier systems didn't allow for growth in the system's size, and data redundancy became the standard, with nightly batch jobs to synchronize the data becoming commonplace through the 1970s and early 1980s.

Eventually, the opportunity presented by networks became the overriding factor in systems development, and enterprise network developers began offering the loosely termed *Object Request Brokers (ORBs)* on their systems: *Microsoft's Transaction Server (MTS)*, *Common Object Request Broker Architecture (CORBA)*, and the like. These ORBs enabled the separation of the user interface from the business logic using tightly coupled method pooling. This three-tier architecture brings you to the present in development terms, so let's step back and let networking catch up.

Merging the Network and Application Development

The HTTP protocol was born in 1990. There were several other information delivery protocols before, such as Gopher, but HTTP was different because of the extensibility of the related language, HTML, and the flexibility of the transport layer, TCP/IP. Suddenly, the movement of many data formats was possible in a stateless, distributed way. Software as a service was born.

Over the next decade, low-level protocols supported by network systems and the Internet became a staple in applications, with SMTP and FTP providing file and information transfer among distributed servers. *Remote procedure calls (RPCs)* took things to the next level, but they were platform specific, with UNIX implementations in CORBA and Microsoft's Distributed COM (DCOM) leading the pack.

Enterprise development took a cue from the emerging technologies in wide area network (WAN) networking and personal computing, and development for these large-scale business systems began to mature. As usage of networks grew, developers began to solve problems of scalability, reliability, and adaptability with the traditional flat-format programming model. Multi-tier development began to spread the data, processing, and user interface of applications over several machines connected by local area networks (LANs).

This made applications more scalable and reliable by accommodating growth and providing redundancy. Gradually, vendor compliance and the Java programming language provided adaptability, enabling applications to run in a variety of circumstances on a variety of platforms.

However, there was a dichotomy between the capabilities of the network and the features of the programming environment. Specifically, after the introduction of XML, there still existed no "killer app" using its power. XML is a subset of Standard Generalized Markup Language (SGML), an international standard that describes the relationship between a document's content and its structure. It enables developers to create their own tags for hierarchical data transport in an HTML-like format. With HTTP as a transport and Simple Object Access Protocol SOAP as a protocol, still needed was an interoperable, ubiquitous, simple, broadly supported system for the execution of business logic throughout the world of Internet application development.

The Foundations of Web Services

The hunt began with a look at the existing protocols. As had been the case for years, the Microsoft versus Sun Alliance debate was heating up among RPC programmers. CORBA versus DCOM was a source of continuing debate for developers using those platforms for distributed object development. After Sun added Remote Method Invocation to Java with Java-RMI, there were three distributed object protocols that fit none of the requirements.

Because DCOM and RMI are manufacturer-specific, it makes sense to start with those. CORBA is centrally managed by the Object Management Group, so it is a special case and should be considered separately.

RMI and DCOM provide distributed object invocation for their respective platforms — extremely important in this era of distributed networks. Both accommodate enterprise-wide reuse of existing functionality, which dramatically reduces cost and time-to-market. Both provide encapsulated object methodology, preventing changes made to one set of business logic from affecting another. Finally, similar to ORB-managed objects, maintenance and client weight are reduced by the simple fact that applications using distributed objects are by nature multi-tier.

DCOM

DCOM's best feature is the fact that it is based on COM, one of the most prevalent desktop object models in use today. COM components are shielded from one another, and calls between them are so well defined by the OS-specific languages that there is practically no overhead to the methods. Each COM object is instantiated in its own space, with the necessary security and protocol providers. When an object in one process needs to call an object in another process, COM handles the exchange by intercepting the call and forwarding it through one of the network protocols.

When you use DCOM, all you are doing is making the wire a bit longer. With Windows NT4, Microsoft added the TCP/IP protocol to the COM network architecture and essentially made DCOM Internet-savvy. Aside from the setup on the client and server, the inter-object calls are transparent to the client, and even to the programmer.

Any Microsoft programmer can tell you, though, that DCOM has its problems. First, because there is a customer wire transport function, most firewalls do not allow DCOM calls to get through, even though they are by nature quite benign. There is no way to query DCOM about the methods and properties available, unless you have the opportunity to get the source code or request the remote component locally. In addition, there is no standard data transfer protocol (though that is less of a problem because DCOM is mostly for Microsoft networks).

As noted, DCOM essentially transitioned to Remoting with the launch of .NET. A fully binary communication protocol that allowed communication across the wire between .NET components. Remoting did what it was designed to do, but being limited to .NET-enabled solutions on both ends of the connection also limited its usefulness in the same way that all of the other binary communication protocols were limited. As part of .NET 3.0 and the introduction of WCF, Remoting is essentially encapsulated in that communication framework.

Remote Method Invocation in Java

RMI is Sun's answer to DCOM. Java relies on a really neat, but very proprietary, protocol called *Java Object Serialization*, which protects objects marshaled as a stream. The client and server both need to be constructed in Java for this to work, but it further simplifies RMI because Java doesn't care whether the serialization takes place on one machine or across a continent. Similarly to DCOM, RMI enables the object developer to define an interface for remote access to certain methods.

CORBA

CORBA uses the *Internet Inter-ORB Protocol* to provide remote method invocation. It is remarkably similar to Java Object Serialization in this regard. Because it is only a specification, though, it is supported by a number of languages on diverse operating systems. With CORBA, the ORB does all the work, such as finding the pointer to the parent, instantiating it so that it can receive remote requests, carrying messages back and forth, and disputing arbitration and garbage collecting. The CORBA objects use specially designed sub-ORB objects called *basic* (or *portable*) *object adapters* to communicate with remote ORBs, giving developers more leeway in code reuse.

At first glance, CORBA would seem to be your ace in the hole. Unfortunately, it doesn't actually work that way. CORBA suffers from the same problem Web browsers do — poor implementations of the standards, which causes lack of interoperability between ORBs. With IE and Netscape, minor differences in the way pages are displayed is written off as cosmetic. When there is a problem with the CORBA standard, however, it is a *real* problem. Not only is appearance affected, but also network interactions, as if there were 15 different implementations of HTTP.

The Problems

The principal problem of the DCOM/CORBA/RMI methods is complexity of implementation. The transfer protocol of each is based on vendor-specific standards, generally preventing interoperability. In essence, the left hand has to know what the right hand is doing. This prevents a company using DCOM from communicating with a company using CORBA.

First, there is the problem of wire format. Each of these three methods uses an OS-specific wire format that encompasses information supplied only by the operating system in question. This means two diverse machines cannot usually share information. The benefit is security: Because the client and server can make assumptions about the availability of functionality, data security can be managed with API calls to the operating system.

The second problem is the number of issues associated with describing the format of the protocol. Apart from the actual transport layer, there must be a schema, or layout, for the data that moves back and forth. Each of the three contemporary protocols makes numerous assumptions between the client and server. DCOM, for instance, provides ADO/RDS for data transport, whereas RMI has JDBC. While we can endlessly debate the merits of one over the other, we can at least agree that they don't play well together.

The third problem is knowing where to find broadly available services, even within your own network. We have all faced the problem of having to call up the COM + MMC panel so that we could remember how to spell this component or that method. When the method is resident on a server ten buildings away and you don't have access to the MMC console, the next step is digging through the text documentation, if there is any.

Some Other Players

On a path to providing these services, we stumble across a few other technologies. While Java applets and Microsoft's client-side ActiveX technically are not distributed object invocations, they do provide distributed computing and provide important lessons. Fortunately, we can describe both in the same section because they are largely the same, with different operating systems as their backbone.

Applets and client-side ActiveX are both attempts to use the HTTP protocol to send thick clients to the end user. In circumstances where a user can provide a platform previously prepared to maintain a thicker-than-HTML client base to a precompiled binary, the ActiveX and applet protocols pass small applications to the end user, usually running a Web browser. These applications are still managed by their servers, at least loosely, and usually provide custom data transmission, utilizing the power of the client to manage the information distributed, as well as display it.

This concept was taken to the extreme with *Distributed Applet-Based Massively Parallel Processing*, a strategy that used the power of the Internet to complete processor-intense tasks, such as 3-D rendering or massive economic models, with a small application installed on the user's computer. If you view the Internet as a massive collection of parallel processors, sitting mostly unused, you have the right idea.

In short, HTTP can provide distributed computing. The problem is that the tightly coupled connection between the client and server has to go, given the nature of today's large enterprises. The HTTP angle did show developers that using an industry-recognized transport method solved problem number one, wire format. Using HTTP meant that regardless of the network, the object could communicate. The client still had to know a lot about the service being sent, but the network did not.

The goal? Distributed Object Invocation meets the World Wide Web. The problems are wire format, protocol, and discovery. The solution is a standards-based, loosely coupled method invocation protocol with a huge catalog. Microsoft, IBM, and Ariba set out in 1999 to create just that, and generated the RFC for Web services.

Web Services

A Web service is a means of exposing application logic or data via standard protocols such as XML or SOAP (Simple Object Access Protocol). A Web service comprises one or more function endpoints, packaged together for use in a common framework throughout a network. Web services provide access to information through standard Internet protocols, such as HTTP/HTTPS. A Web Services Description Language (WSDL) contract is used to detail the input and output requirements for calling the interface. Consumers of the Web service can learn about the structure of the data the Web service provides, as well as all the details about how to actually consume this data, from the WSDL. A WSDL provides a detailed description of the remote interface offered from the Web service.

This simple concept provides for a very wide variety of potential uses by developers of Internet and intranet applications alike. Today, the Web services model is often the heart of the next generation of systems architecture because it is all of the following:

➤ **Architecturally neutral** — Web services do not depend on a proprietary wire format, schema description, or discovery standard.

➤ **Ubiquitous** — Any service that supports the associated Web service standards can support the service.

➤ **Simple** — Creating Web services is quick and easy. The data schema is human readable. Any programming language can participate.

➤ **Interoperable** — Because the Web services all conform to the same standards, and use common communication protocols, they are not concerned about the technology of the application calling them.

In basic terms, a Web service is an interface with an XML document describing all of the methods and properties available for use by the caller. Any body of code written in just about any programming language can be described with this XML document, and any application that understands XML (or SOAP) over the assigned protocol (such as HTTP) can access the object. That's because the parameters you type after the function name are passed via XML to the Web service, and because SOAP is an open standard.

Web services are remarkably easy to deploy. The power of Web services comes from the use of the WSDL contract. In addition, Web services are inherently cross-platform, even when created with Microsoft products. The standard XML schemas are part of the WSDL specification.

The key is that even though this protocol may not be as efficient or fast as some of the binary protocols of the past, its implementation-agnostic contracts make it more useful. Given that you can create a communication protocol that is either available for use by 50% of users and which runs superfast versus one that is available to 100% of users and runs fast, the tendency will be to adopt the solution with greater reach. Thus, Web services became the interoperability baseline for service communication.

For this reason, they best represent where the Internet is heading — toward an architecturally neutral collection of devices, rather than millions of PCs surfing the World Wide Web. Encapsulating code so that you can simply and easily enable cell phones to use your logic is a major boon to developers, even if they do not realize it yet.

How This All Fits Together

Microsoft's support for Web services really took off with the introduction of .NET. However, support was available to have Web services run on older operating systems like Windows NT4 SP6, with the SOAP Toolkit installed.

The .NET Framework encapsulated the Web service protocol into objects. This was great initially, but as noted earlier, over time it was generally agreed that not every communication needed to be put up as a HTTP/HTTPS-based service. WCF was the result of Microsoft taking a look at the common concepts from all of the preceding communication technologies and seeking a unified solution.

While Web services remain one of the most common underlying implementations for WCF services, the reality is that they are now a subset of what you can do with WCF. Things like the WS-* protocols become configuration settings; similarly, you can have a single interface that supports multiple different communication protocols. Thus, the same service that is used with a client that supports a binary transfer protocol like Remoting can communicate via HTTP protocol for a client that doesn't support those binary protocols.

WCF is now an integrated part of the service-oriented architecture strategy. Historically, the starting place on MSDN for Web Services was http://msdn.microsoft.com/webservices, but that link now takes you directly to http://msdn.microsoft.com/wcf. It's not that Web services have gone away or become less important, it's simply that Web services are a subset of the complete WCF communication framework.

The goal of WCF is to provide a loosely coupled, ubiquitous, universal information exchange format. Toward that end, SOAP is not the only mechanism for communicating with WCF services.

What Makes a WCF Service

A WCF service consists of three parts: the service, one or more endpoints, and an environment in which to host the service.

A service is a class that is written in (or in the case of Interop, wrapped by) one of the .NET-compliant languages. The class can contain one or more methods that are exposed through the WCF service. A service can have one or more endpoints, which are used to communicate through the service to the client.

Endpoints themselves are also made up of three parts. These parts are usually defined by Microsoft as the "ABC" of WCF. Each letter of WCF means something in particular in the WCF model. Similarly,

- ➤ "A" is for address
- ➤ "B" is for binding
- ➤ "C" is for contract

Basically, you can think of this as follows: "A" is the *where*, "B" is the *how*, and "C" is the *what*. Finally, a hosting environment is where the service is contained. This constitutes an application domain and process. All three of these elements (the service, the endpoints, and the hosting environment) together create a WCF service offering, as depicted in Figure 13-1.

The core idea is that when you want to create an enterprise architecture supporting multiple different applications, the most appropriate protocol will vary depending on how a service is currently being used. Having a unified strategy that allows you, as a developer, to specify a given endpoint and how that endpoint communicates means that the same underlying implementation can power multiple different endpoints. Thus, questions of security and performance can be viewed on a per-connection basis. This enables an organization to create a service-oriented architecture (SOA).

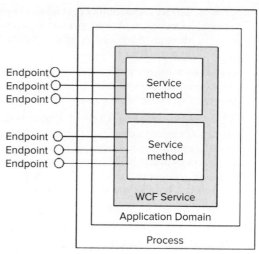

FIGURE 13-1

THE LARGER MOVE TO SOA

Looking at what WCF provides, you will find that it is supporting of a larger move that organizations are making to the much-discussed SOA. Keep in mind that an SOA is a message-based service architecture that is vendor-agnostic. This means you have the capability to distribute messages across a system, and the messages are interoperable with other systems that would otherwise be considered incompatible with the provider system.

Looking back, you can see the gradual progression to the service-oriented architecture model. In the 1980s, the revolutions arrived amid the paradigm of everything being an object. When object-oriented programming came on the scene, it was enthusiastically accepted as the proper means to represent entities within a programming model. The 1990s took that one step further, and the component-oriented model was born. This enabled objects to be encapsulated in a tightly coupled manner. It was only recently that the industry turned to a service-oriented architecture, once developers and architects needed to distribute components to other points in an organization, to their partners, or to their customers. This distribution system needed to have the means to transfer messages between machines that were generally incompatible with one another. In addition, the messages had to include the capability to express the metadata about how a system should handle a message.

If you ask 10 people what an SOA is, you'll probably get 11 different answers, but there are some common principles that are considered to be the foundation of a service-oriented architecture:

➤ **Boundaries are explicit** — Any data store, logic, or entity uses an interface to expose its data or capabilities. The interface provides the means to hide the behaviors within the service, and the interface front-end enables you to change this behavior as required without affecting downstream consumers.

➤ **Services are autonomous** — All the services are updated or versioned independently of one another. This means that you don't upgrade a system in its entirety; instead, each component of these systems is an individual entity within itself and can move forward without waiting for other components to progress forward. Note that with this type of model, once you publish an interface, that interface must remain unchanged. Interface changes require new interfaces (versioned, of course).

➤ **Services are based upon contracts** — All services developed require a contract regarding what is needed to consume items from the interface (usually done through a WSDL document).

➤ **Schemas are used to define the data formats** — Along with a contract, schemas are required to define the items passed in as parameters or delivered through the service (using XSD schemas).

➤ **Service compatibility that is based upon policy** — The final principle enables services to define policies (decided at runtime) that are required to consume the service. These policies are usually expressed through WS-Policy. A policy provides consumers with an understanding of what is actually required to consume a service.

If your own organization is considering establishing an SOA, the WCF is a framework that works on these principles and makes it relatively simple to implement. The next section looks at what the WCF offers. Then you can dive into building your first WCF service.

As stated, the Windows Communication Foundation is a means to build distributed applications in a Microsoft environment. Though the distributed application is built upon that environment, this does not mean that the consumers are required to be Microsoft clients; nor is any Microsoft component or technology necessary to accomplish the task of consumption. Conversely, building WCF services means you are also building services that abide by the principles set forth in the aforementioned SOA discussion, and that these services are vendor-agnostic — that is, they can be consumed by almost anyone.

WCF is part of the .NET Framework and is available to applications targeting .NET 3.0 or later.

Capabilities of WCF

WCF provides you with the capability to build all kinds of distributed applications. You can build Web services just as you could previously in earlier .NET Framework releases. This means that your services will support SOAP, and therefore will be compatible with older .NET technologies, older Microsoft technologies, and even non-Microsoft technologies (such as any Java-based consumers).

WCF is not limited to pure SOAP over a wire; you can also work with an InfoSet, and create a binary representation of your SOAP message that can then be sent along your choice of protocol. This is for folks who are concerned about the performance of their services and have traditionally turned to .NET Remoting for this binary-based distribution system.

The WCF framework can also work with a message through its life cycle, meaning that WCF can deal with transactions. Along with distributed transactions, WCF can deal with the queuing of messages, and it allows for the intermittent connected nature that an application or process might experience across the web. Of course, what WCF truly provides is a framework to communicate with tools that support many of these capabilities. It's not that WCF provides a message store and forward capability so much as it supports the protocols used in message store and forward.

When you need to get messages from one point to another, the WCF is the big gun in your arsenal to get the job accomplished. For instance, many developers might consider using WCF primarily to communicate ASP.NET Web Service-like messages (SOAP) from one disparate system to another, but you can use WCF for much more than this. For instance, WCF can be used to communicate messages to components contained on the same machine on which the WCF service is running.

This means you can use WCF to communicate with components contained in different processes on the same machine. For example the same service might be called by a WPF application using a binary format within your organization, while the same service may expose an endpoint hosted on a web server and accessible over the Web via HTTP and SOAP. You use WCF to communicate with components on the same machine or on another machine — even accepting calls from a client that is not a Microsoft-based machine.

Contracts and Metadata

Probably the biggest and most exciting part of the WCF model is that it enables you to develop a service once and then expose that service via multiple endpoints (even endpoints on entirely different protocols) via simple configuration changes. These changes start with the interface definition. As part of creating a service you'll be able to define an Interface and that interface has two top level contracts.

From an implementation standpoint a contract is an attribute that is associated with either an interface or a class definition. The `<Service Contract>` is used as part of an interface definition. That interface will expose a series of `<OperationContract>` method definitions, which describe what services this service provides.

A Service Contract with at least one operation is required in order to have a service. Without this minimum definition there isn't anything to call. The methods within the `ServiceContract` interface are attributed with the `<OperationContract>` to define the various interfaces.

Optionally, if your service is going to accept data types other than primitive types, it needs to provide metadata to define these data types. A `<DataContract>` attribute can be associated with one or more classes to define these custom data structures. An interface does not need to expose any custom data structures, but if it does, it needs to determine which properties of the class to include in the interface. Each property to be exposed is associated with a `<DataMember>` attribute to identify it as part of the `DataContract`.

Working with the WS-* Protocols

WCF understands and can work with the full set of WS-* specifications, and these specifications can be enabled to create messages that meet defined ways of dealing with security, reliability, and transactions. A few of these protocols and an understanding of how messages are managed are important enough to take a closer look at their implementation details.

Messages, as defined by the Messaging layer, rely on SOAP (sent as open text or in a binary format). The advanced WS-* specifications make heavy use of the SOAP header, enabling messages to be self-contained and not have any real reliance on the transport protocol to provide items such as security, reliability, or any other capability beyond the simple transmission of the message itself. *Message Transmission Optimization Mechanism (MTOM)* is a capability to replace *Direct Internet Message Encapsulation (DIME)* as a means to transmit binary objects along with a SOAP message. An example binary object would be a JPEG image that you want to expose through a WCF service.

The security implementation in WCF enables you to work with WS-Security. Before WS-Security came along, the initial lack of a security model in Web services kept many companies from massively adopting them companywide and moving to a service-oriented architecture. WS-Security addresses the main areas that are required to keep messages secure — credential exchange, message integrity, and message confidentiality.

To do this WS-Security supports implementing security at two levels. The first is at the message level. WS-Security enables entities to provide and validate credentials within the messages that are exchanged. Alternatively WS-Security also enables transport level security. This form of security focuses on establishing credentials based on the transport protocol, for example using HTTPS to securely transmit data.

With message level security WS-Security enables two entities to exchange their security credentials from within the message itself (actually, from the SOAP header of the message). The great thing about WS-Security is that it doesn't require a specific type of credential set to be used. Instead, it allows any type of credentials to be used. In addition, it is possible to send messages through multiple routers. In effect, this allows your solution to bounce messages from here to there before they reach their final destination while ensuring that the messages are not tampered with in transport. As messages move from one SOAP router to another, these SOAP nodes can make additions to or subtractions from the messages. If such SOAP nodes were to get into the hands of malicious parties, the integrity of the messages could be compromised. This is where WS-Security comes into play.

The other area in which WS-Security helps is when you need to have WS-Security encrypt all or part of your SOAP messages. When your messages are zipping across the virtual world, there is a chance that they might be intercepted and opened for viewing by parties who should not be looking at their contents. That's why it is often beneficial to scramble the contents of the message. When it reaches the intended receiver, the application can then use your encryption key and unscramble the message to read the contents.

WS-SecureConversation works to establish a connection that enables entities to exchange multiple messages and maintain their established security arrangements. WS-Trust, conversely, works in conjunction with WS-Security and allows for the issuance of security tokens and a way in which entities can exchange these tokens. This specification also deals with establishing trust relationships between two entities.

WS-ReliableMessaging allows for reliable end-to-end communications of messages to ensure that they are delivered.

The Transactions section allows for the use of WS-Coordination and WS-AtomicTransaction. WS-Coordination is there for the purpose of addressing the description of the relationships that multiple services have to one another. As a company starts developing a multitude of services within its enterprise, it realizes that many of the services developed have a relationship with one another, and that's where WS-Coordination comes into play. This specification is meant to be expanded by other specifications that will further define particular coordination types.

WS-AtomicTransaction uses WS-Coordination and WS-Security to allow for the definition of a service transaction process. An atomic transaction is a way of creating a transaction process that works on an all-or-nothing basis. These are meant to be short-lived transactions, so when you use them you are locking data resources and holding onto physical resources such as connections, threads, and memory.

The main point of this discussion is to emphasize the slew of WS-* specifications at your disposal. Even better, when working with WCF you really don't have to be aware that these specifications are even there — you can access the capabilities these specifications offer through programmatic or declarative programming.

BUILDING A WCF SERVICE

Building a WCF service is not hard to accomplish. Using Visual Studio 2010, you'll see the WCF new project templates shown in Figure 13-2. One word of warning however, in order to host a WCF service you'll need to have started Visual Studio with the Run as Administrator menu link. Before attempting to replicate all of the steps in the sample, make sure you've started Visual Studio using the 'Run as Administrator' option from the context menu.

FIGURE 13-2

When you build a WCF project in this manner, the idea is that you build a traditional Class Library that is compiled down to a DLL that can then be added to another project. The separation of code and use of multiple projects is a powerful tool for managing complexity on larger projects. That said, though, you can also just as easily build a WCF service directly in your .NET project, whether that is a console application or a Windows Forms application.

This example will first create a new WCF service in a Service Library. It then demonstrates how to host the WCF service inside a console application. Start by creating a new Service Library with the name ProVB_WCFCalculatorService.

Once you have created your new library project, Visual Studio will look similar to what is shown in Figure 13-3.

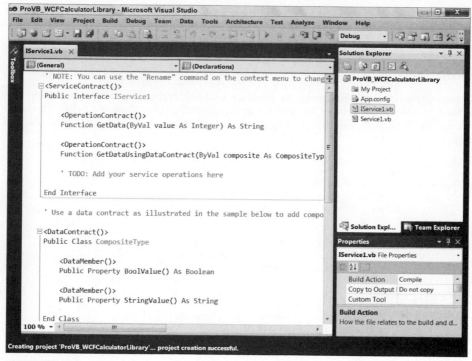

FIGURE 13-3

This example first demonstrates how to build the WCF service. It then demonstrates how to build a console application that will host this service, and finally demonstrates how to leverage Visual Studio 2010 to test this service.

Creating the Interface

To create your service, you need a service contract, which is the interface of the service. This consists of all the methods exposed, as well as the input and output parameters that are required to invoke the methods. To accomplish this task, rename the file `IService1.vb` to `ICalculator.vb`. Then replace the contents of the generated file with the code presented here:

```
<ServiceContract()>
Public Interface ICalculator
    <OperationContract()>
    Function Add(ByVal a As Integer, ByVal b As Integer) As Integer
    <OperationContract()>
    Function Subtract(ByVal a As Integer, ByVal b As Integer) As Integer
    <OperationContract()>
    Function Multiply(ByVal a As Integer, ByVal b As Integer) As Integer
    <OperationContract()>
    Function Divide(ByVal a As Integer, ByVal b As Integer) As Integer
End Interface
```

Code snippet from ICalculator.vb

This is pretty much the normal interface definition you would expect, but with a couple of new attributes included. The `<ServiceContract()>` attribute is used to define the class or interface as the service class, and it needs to precede the opening declaration of the class or interface.

Within the interface, four methods are defined. Each of these methods is going to be exposed through the WCF service as part of the service contract, so they all require that the `<OperationContract()>` attribute be applied to them.

Utilizing the Interface

The next step is to create a class that implements the interface. Not only is the new class implementing the interface defined, it is also implementing the service contract. From Solution Explorer, right-click on the generated `Service1.vb` file and rename this file as `Calculator.vb`. Next, replace the code in this file with the code that follows:

Available for download on Wrox.com

```vb
Public Class Calculator
    Implements ICalculator
    Public Function Add(ByVal a As Integer,
                        ByVal b As Integer) As Integer _
                    Implements ICalculator.Add
        Return (a + b)
    End Function
    Public Function Subtract(ByVal a As Integer,
                            ByVal b As Integer) As Integer _
                        Implements ICalculator.Subtract
        Return (a - b)
    End Function
    Public Function Multiply(ByVal a As Integer,
                            ByVal b As Integer) As Integer _
                        Implements ICalculator.Multiply
        Return (a * b)
    End Function
    Public Function Divide(ByVal a As Integer,
                          ByVal b As Integer) As Integer _
                      Implements ICalculator.Divide
        Return (a / b)
    End Function
End Class
```

Code snippet from Calculator.vb

From these new additions, you can see that nothing is done differently with the `Calculator` class than what you might do otherwise. It is a simple class that implements the `ICalculator` interface and provides implementations of the `Add`, `Subtract`, `Multiply`, and `Divide` methods.

With the interface and the class available, you now have your WCF service built and ready to go. The next step is to get the service hosted. This is a simple service. One of the simplicities of the service is that it exposes only simple types, rather than a complex type. This enables you to build only a service contract and not have to deal with construction of a data contract. Constructing data contracts is presented later in this chapter.

Hosting the WCF Service in a Console Application

The next step is to take the service just developed and host it in some type of application process. You have many available hosting options, including the following:

➤ Console applications
➤ Windows Forms applications
➤ Windows Presentation Foundation applications
➤ Managed Windows Services

➤ Internet Information Services (IIS) 5.1

➤ Internet Information Services (IIS) 6.0

➤ Internet Information Services (IIS) 7.0 and the Windows Activation Service (WAS)

As stated earlier, this example hosts the service in a simple console application. There are a couple of ways to activate hosting — either through the direct coding of the hosting behaviors or through declarative programming (usually done via the configuration file).

For this example, the console application will define the host through coding the behaviors of the host environment directly. As mentioned at the start of this sample, in order to host a WCF service this way, you need to have started Visual Studio with the Run as Administrator menu link. If you are not running as administrator, you will get a permissions error when the console application attempts to start.

Using the File menu in Visual Studio, select Add ➡ New Project to add a new Console Application to your solution. Name the new console application ProVB_ServiceHost. After creating the new project, right-click the project name in Solution Explorer and set this project to be the startup project.

Next, right-click the project and select Add Reference. You need to add two references for this console application to act as a service host. The first will be shown when the Add Reference dialog opens — it will open to the Projects tab and you'll want to add a reference to the ProVB_WCFCalculatorLibrary. After adding this reference, open the dialog a second time and switch to the .NET tab. Scroll down and select System .ServiceModel.dll as shown in Figure 13-4.

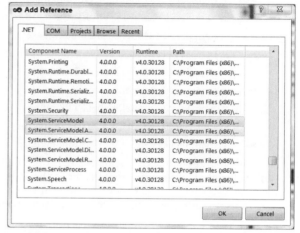

FIGURE 13-4

You are now ready to start making changes to the code. The following is the code for the console application:

Available for download on Wrox.com

```vb
Imports System.ServiceModel
Imports System.ServiceModel.Description

Module Module1
    Sub Main()
        Using svcHost As New ServiceHost( _
                GetType(ProVB_WCFCalculatorLibrary.Calculator))
            Dim netBind As New NetTcpBinding(SecurityMode.None)
            svcHost.AddServiceEndpoint( _
                GetType(ProVB_WCFCalculatorLibrary.ICalculator),
                netBind,
                New Uri("net.tcp://localhost:8080/Calculator/"))
            Dim smb As New ServiceMetadataBehavior()
            smb.HttpGetEnabled = True
            smb.HttpGetUrl = New Uri("http://localhost:8000/Calculator")
            svcHost.Description.Behaviors.Add(smb)
            svcHost.Open()
            Console.WriteLine("Press <Enter> to close and end the Service Host")
            Console.ReadLine()
        End Using
    End Sub
End Module
```

Code snippet from Module1.vb

A couple of things are going on in this file. First, in order to gain access to work with any of the WCF framework pieces, you need a reference to the System.ServiceModel and the System.ServiceModel .Description namespaces in the file. The System.ServiceModel gives you access to defining things such as the endpoints that you need to create, while the System.ServiceModel.Description namespace reference gives you access to defining things such as the WSDL file.

Remember that creating endpoints uses the ABC model (address, binding, and contract). The address part here is net.tcp://localhost:8080/Calculator. The binding is a TCP binding — NetTcpBinding — while the contract part is the ICalculator interface.

Many different bindings are available to you when coding WCF services. Here, this example makes use of the NetTcpBinding. The full list of available bindings is as follows:

- ➤ System.ServiceModel.BasicHttpBinding
- ➤ System.ServiceModel.Channels.CustomBinding
- ➤ System.ServiceModel.MsmqBindingBase
- ➤ System.ServiceModel.NetNamedPipeBinding
- ➤ System.ServiceModel.NetPeerTcpBinding
- ➤ System.ServiceModel.NetTcpBinding
- ➤ System.ServiceModel.WebHTTPBinding
- ➤ System.ServiceModel.WSDualHttpBinding
- ➤ System.ServiceModel.WSHttpBindingBase

Clearly, several bindings are available. In the preceding example, the NetTcpBinding class is the transport pipe being used. This means that the service being built will be delivered over TCP. At this point your development environment should look similar to what is shown in Figure 13-5. However, before running the new console, let's look at the various commands it will use to host your custom service.

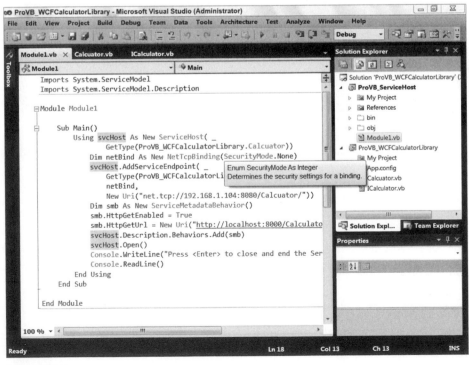

FIGURE 13-5

In the first step of the example, for the console-application code, a `ServiceHost` object is established:

```
Using svcHost As New ServiceHost( _
          GetType(ProVB_WCFCalculatorLibrary.Calculator))
```

By working with the `Using` keyword, when the `End Using` statement is encountered, the `ServiceHost` object is destroyed. In the creation of the host, the `Calculator` type is assigned. From there, the endpoint is established. In this case, a `NetTcpBinding` object is created with a security setting of `None` through the command `SecurityMode.None`:

```
Dim netBind = New NetTcpBinding(SecurityMode.None)
```

This means that no security is applied to the message. The other options include `Message`, `Transport`, and `TransportWithMessageCredential`. The `Message` option signifies that the security credentials will be included in the message (in the SOAP header, for instance), whereas the `Transport` option indicates that the transport protocol provides the security implementation. The last option, `TransportWithMessageCredential`, means that the message contains some security credentials along with the transport protocol security provided by the transport protocol.

Once the `NetTcpBinding` object is in place, the next step is to finalize the endpoint creation. This is done through the use of the `ServiceHost` object's `AddServiceEndpoint` method:

```
svcHost.AddServiceEndpoint( _
    GetType(ProVB_WCFCalculatorLibrary.ICalculator),
    netBind,
    New Uri("net.tcp://localhost:8080/Calculator/"))
```

From this, you can see that the entire ABC statement is used in the creation of the endpoint, although not necessarily in ABC order; in fact, the first item defined is actually the "C" — the contract. This is done through the `GetType(ICalculator)` setting. The "B" is next (the binding) with the reference to the `NetTcpBinding` object. Then, finally, the "A" is defined through an instantiation of a `Uri` object pointing to `net.tcp://localhost:8080/Calcuator/`.

The next step is a process to bring forth the WSDL document so that it can be viewed by the developer consuming this service:

```
Dim smb As New ServiceMetadataBehavior()
smb.HttpGetEnabled = True
smb.HttpGetUrl = New Uri("http://localhost:8000/calculator")
serviceHost.Description.Behaviors.Add(smb)
```

This bit of code is the reason why the `System.ServiceModel.Description` namespace is imported into the file at the beginning. Here, a `ServiceMetadataBehavior` object is created, the object's `HttpGetEnabled` property is set to `True`, and the `HttpGetUrl` property is provided an address of `http://localhost:8000/calculator`. The documents can be located anywhere you like.

After the `ServiceMetadataBehavior` object is created as you wish, the next step is to associate this object with the `ServiceHost` through the `serviceHost.Description.Behaviors.Add` method.

After all of these items are defined — you only need to open the `ServiceHost` for business, using the `serviceHost.Open` method. The console application is kept alive through the use of a `Console.ReadLine` method call, which waits for the end user to press the Enter key before shutting down the application. You want the `Console.ReadLine` command there because you want to keep the host open.

Compiling and running this application produces the results illustrated in Figure 13-6. Note that you may initially get a firewall warning when you run this application, but you'll want to allow access for this application to communicate (at least locally) through your local firewall. Additionally, if you didn't start Visual Studio with Administrator rights as noted at the beginning of this step, you'll get a runtime error related to permissions.

FIGURE 13-6

Keep in mind that your service is only available for as long as that console window is open and active; when you close the console you are stopping the listener for your new service.

Reviewing the WSDL Document

The preceding console-application code provides an instantiation of the ServiceMetadataBehavior object and defines a Uri object for it as well. You can simply type in that address to get at the WSDL file for the service you just built. Therefore, calling http://localhost:8000/calculator from your browser provides the WSDL file shown in Figure 13-7.

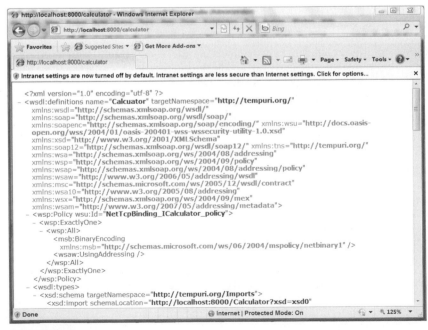

FIGURE 13-7

With this WSDL file, you can now consume the service it defines through TCP. Note the following element at the bottom of the document:

```
<wsdl:service name="Calculator">
    <wsdl:port name="NetTcpBinding_ICalculator"
     binding="tns:NetTcpBinding_ICalculator">
        <soap12:address location="net.tcp://localhost:8080/Calculator/" />
        <wsa10:EndpointReference>
            <wsa10:Address>net.tcp://localhost:8080/Calculator/</wsa10:Address>
        </wsa10:EndpointReference>
    </wsdl:port>
</wsdl:service>
```

This element in the XML document indicates that in order to consume the service, the end user needs to use SOAP 1.2 over TCP. This is presented through the use of the `<soap12:address>` element in the document. The `<wsa10:EndpointReference>` is a WS-Addressing endpoint definition.

Using this simple WSDL document, you can now build a consumer that makes use of this interface. Just as important, you have created not only a service that meets the standards for a Web service, but also a custom host that is communicating via standard protocols.

BUILDING A WCF CONSUMER

Now that a TCP service is out there, which you built using the WCF framework, the next step is to build a consumer application that uses the simple Calculator service. The consumer sends its request via TCP using SOAP. Using TCP means that the consumption can actually occur with a binary encoding of the SOAP message on the wire, substantially decreasing the size of the payload being transmitted.

This section describes how to consume this service. You have two options at this point: You can open a second instance of Visual Studio 2010 and create a new Windows Forms project to reference your service or you can add a new Windows Forms project to your current solution. For simplicity, this example uses the latter.

The only difference in terms of what is needed occurs as part of adding a reference to the service. If you create your application in a new solution, then in order to add the reference you'll need to have a copy of the service running. To that end, after you add a new solution called ProVB_WCFCalculatorClient you can start the add reference process.

Adding a Service Reference

Right-click on the project name in the Solution Explorer and select Add Service Reference from the dialog.

After selecting Add Service Reference, you are presented with the dialog shown in Figure 13 8. The selections you make within this dialog, and to some extent what you'll get at the other end, depends on how you've approached creating your project. Let's start with what you need to do if you have your client in a separate solution.

The Add Service Reference dialog asks you for two things: the Service URI (basically a pointer to the WSDL file) and the name you want to give to the reference. The name you provide the reference is the name that will be used for the instantiated object that enables you to interact with the service.

Referring to Figure 13-8, you can see that the name provided for the Address text box is `http://localhost:8000/calculator`. Remember that this is the location you defined earlier when you built the service. This URI was defined in code directly in the service:

```
Dim smb As New ServiceMetadataBehavior()
smb.HttpGetEnabled = True
smb.HttpGetUrl = New Uri("http://localhost:8000/calculator")
serviceHost.Description.Behaviors.Add(smb)
```

Manually entering that URL is the difference between having your client in a separate solution and what we are about to do for a client in the same solution. Since in this case you are working with a service within the same solution, you are going to use the Discover button. The Discover button has a single option: Services in Solution. Using this button will trigger Visual Studio to look at the current solution, locate any services, and dynamically create a host for that service.

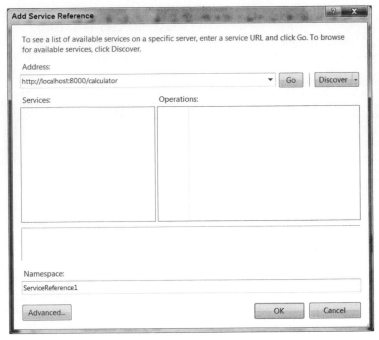

FIGURE 13-8

This is a great feature of Visual Studio 2010, as it recognizes and supports the developer who needs to implement and test a WCF Service. Instead of needing that production URL, which you would need to track, it will simply create a runtime reference. Figure 13-9 illustrates the Add Service Reference dialog after having located the local service using the Discover button.

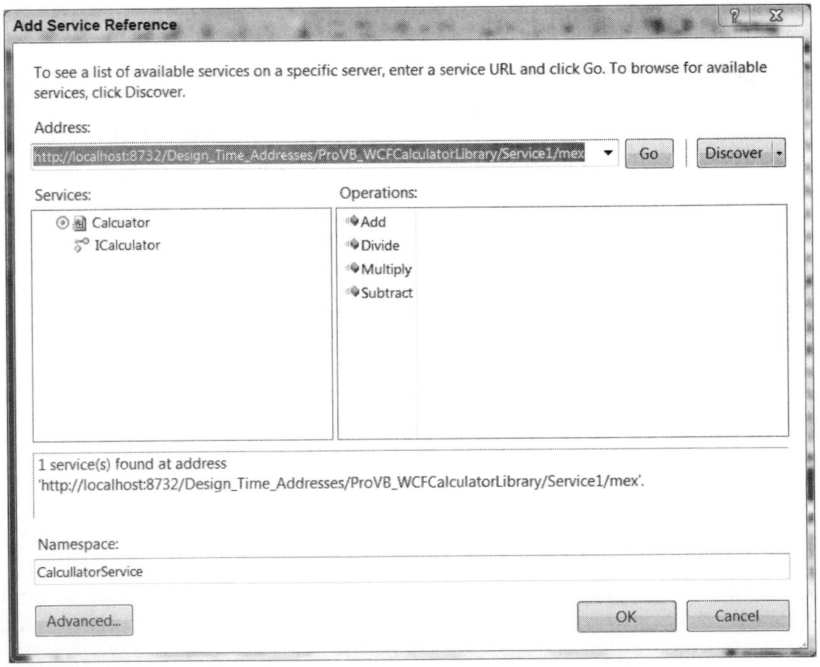

FIGURE 13-9

The port shown in Figure 13-9 was randomly generated by Visual Studio. Running this code locally, you can expect to see a different port generated.

Notice that by expanding the top-level Calculator node within the Services pane in Figure 13-9, a single interface is exposed, and selecting that interface populates the available operations in the Operations pane.

Rename the service reference to CalculatorService from ServiceReference1 (refer to Figure 13-9). Press the OK button in the Add Service Reference dialog.

Finally, a quick best practices note concerning the address. For this example and as a tester, you will of course have a generated or test URI. When the application is ready to deploy, you want this URI to reflect production. The best practice is to have a custom configuration setting in your `app.config` (or `web.config`) file that is updated with the production URI. This application setting is read at runtime, and then after the service reference is created, its `uri` property is updated with the correct value from the application configuration file.

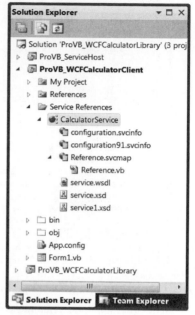

FIGURE 13-10

Reviewing the Reference

You've now added a Service References folder to your project, which contains the proxy details for your Calculator service. This proxy is a collection of files, as shown in Figure 13-10. Note that you'll need to show all the files in order to see the files shown in Figure 13-10.

Digging down into these files, you will find `Reference.svcmap` and `Reference.vb`. The other important addition to note is the `System.ServiceModel` reference, made for you in the References folder.

Looking at the `Reference.svcmap` file, you can see that it is a simple XML file that provides some information about where the WSDL file is located, as well as the location of the service (referenced through the `configuration.svcinfo` file):

Available for
download on
Wrox.com

```xml
<?xml version="1.0" encoding="utf-8"?>
<ReferenceGroup xmlns:xsi="http://www.w3.org/2001/XMLSchema-instance"
 xmlns:xsd="http://www.w3.org/2001/XMLSchema"
 ID="db9d4ff8-090f-433b-880e-617eee3924ed"
 xmlns="urn:schemas-microsoft-com:xml-wcfservicemap">
  <ClientOptions>
    <GenerateAsynchronousMethods>false</GenerateAsynchronousMethods>
    <EnableDataBinding>true</EnableDataBinding>
    <ExcludedTypes />
    <ImportXmlTypes>false</ImportXmlTypes>
    <GenerateInternalTypes>false</GenerateInternalTypes>
    <GenerateMessageContracts>false</GenerateMessageContracts>
    <NamespaceMappings />
    <CollectionMappings />
    <GenerateSerializableTypes>true</GenerateSerializableTypes>
    <Serializer>Auto</Serializer>
    <UseSerializerForFaults>true</UseSerializerForFaults>
    <ReferenceAllAssemblies>true</ReferenceAllAssemblies>
    <ReferencedAssemblies />
    <ReferencedDataContractTypes />
    <ServiceContractMappings />
  </ClientOptions>
```

```
<MetadataSources>
  <MetadataSource Address="http://localhost:8732/Design_Time_Addresses/
                                 ProVB_WCFCalculatorLibrary/Service1/mex"
 Protocol="mex" SourceId="1" />
</MetadataSources>
<Metadata>
  <MetadataFile FileName="service.wsdl" MetadataType="Wsdl"
                  ID="849df155-c852-41ae-99cf-730f184b9b72" SourceId="1"
                  SourceUrl="http://localhost:8732/Design_Time_Addresses/
                                 ProVB_WCFCalculatorLibrary/Service1/mex" />
  <MetadataFile FileName="service.xsd" MetadataType="Schema"
                  ID="10793301-16af-4981-ac16-b09e798357a6" SourceId="1"
                  SourceUrl="http://localhost:8732/Design_Time_Addresses/
                                 ProVB_WCFCalculatorLibrary/Service1/mex" />
  <MetadataFile FileName="service1.xsd" MetadataType="Schema"
                  ID="669fdea8-5375-4987-8922-bc2910d40492" SourceId="1"
                  SourceUrl="http://localhost:8732/Design_Time_Addresses/
                                 ProVB_WCFCalculatorLibrary/Service1/mex" />
</Metadata>
<Extensions>
  <ExtensionFile FileName="configuration91.svcinfo" Name="configuration91.svcinfo" />
  <ExtensionFile FileName="configuration.svcinfo" Name="configuration.svcinfo" />
</Extensions>
</ReferenceGroup>
```

Code snippet from Reference.svcmap

This file provides the capability to later update the reference to the service if needed, due to a change in the service interface. You can see this capability by right-clicking on the CalculatorService reference; an Update Service Reference option appears in the provided menu.

The other file in the reference collection of files, the Reference.vb file, is your proxy to interact with the service. This file is presented here:

```
Option Strict On
Option Explicit On
Namespace CalculatorService

    <System.CodeDom.Compiler.GeneratedCodeAttribute("System.ServiceModel", "4.0.0.0"), _
     System.ServiceModel.ServiceContractAttribute( _
        ConfigurationName:="CalculatorService.ICalculator")> _
    Public Interface ICalculator

        <System.ServiceModel.OperationContractAttribute( _
        Action:="http://tempuri.org/ICalculator/Add", _
        ReplyAction:="http://tempuri.org/ICalculator/AddResponse")> _
        Function Add(ByVal a As Integer, ByVal b As Integer) As Integer

        <System.ServiceModel.OperationContractAttribute( _
        Action:="http://tempuri.org/ICalculator/Subtract", _
        ReplyAction:="http://tempuri.org/ICalculator/SubtractResponse")> _
        Function Subtract(ByVal a As Integer, ByVal b As Integer) As Integer

        <System.ServiceModel.OperationContractAttribute( _
        Action:="http://tempuri.org/ICalculator/Multiply", _
        ReplyAction:="http://tempuri.org/ICalculator/MultiplyResponse")> _
        Function Multiply(ByVal a As Integer, ByVal b As Integer) As Integer

        <System.ServiceModel.OperationContractAttribute( _
        Action:="http://tempuri.org/ICalculator/Divide", _
        ReplyAction:="http://tempuri.org/ICalculator/DivideResponse")> _
        Function Divide(ByVal a As Integer, ByVal b As Integer) As Integer
```

```vb
        End Interface

        <System.CodeDom.Compiler.GeneratedCodeAttribute("System.ServiceModel", "4.0.0.0")> _
        Public Interface ICalculatorChannel
            Inherits CalculatorService.ICalculator, System.ServiceModel.IClientChannel
        End Interface

        <System.Diagnostics.DebuggerStepThroughAttribute(), _
         System.CodeDom.Compiler.GeneratedCodeAttribute("System.ServiceModel", "4.0.0.0")> _
        Partial Public Class CalculatorClient
            Inherits System.ServiceModel.ClientBase(Of CalculatorService.ICalculator)
            Implements CalculatorService.ICalculator

            Public Sub New()
                MyBase.New
            End Sub

            Public Sub New(ByVal endpointConfigurationName As String)
                MyBase.New(endpointConfigurationName)
            End Sub

            Public Sub New(ByVal endpointConfigurationName As String,
               ByVal remoteAddress As String)
                MyBase.New(endpointConfigurationName, remoteAddress)
            End Sub

            Public Sub New(ByVal endpointConfigurationName As String,
               ByVal remoteAddress As System.ServiceModel.EndpointAddress)
                MyBase.New(endpointConfigurationName, remoteAddress)
            End Sub

            Public Sub New(ByVal binding As System.ServiceModel.Channels.Binding,
               ByVal remoteAddress As System.ServiceModel.EndpointAddress)
                MyBase.New(binding, remoteAddress)
            End Sub

            Public Function Add(ByVal a As Integer, ByVal b As Integer) As Integer
                Implements CalculatorService.ICalculator.Add
                Return MyBase.Channel.Add(a, b)
            End Function

            Public Function Subtract(ByVal a As Integer, ByVal b As Integer) As Integer
                Implements CalculatorService.ICalculator.Subtract
                Return MyBase.Channel.Subtract(a, b)
            End Function

            Public Function Multiply(ByVal a As Integer, ByVal b As Integer) As Integer
                Implements CalculatorService.ICalculator.Multiply
                Return MyBase.Channel.Multiply(a, b)
            End Function

            Public Function Divide(ByVal a As Integer, ByVal b As Integer) As Integer
                Implements CalculatorService.ICalculator.Divide
                Return MyBase.Channel.Divide(a, b)
            End Function
        End Class
    End Namespace
```

Code snippet from Reference.vb

Here, an interface is defining the four methods and the implementing class `CalculatorClient`, which contains the functions that, in turn, call the service built earlier in the chapter.

Configuration File Changes

Another addition to your project is the `app.config` file. After the service reference is made, the `app.config` file contains several new configuration settings. These configuration settings were automatically added by the Visual Studio WCF extensions. The new `app.config` file is presented in the following code block:

```xml
<?xml version="1.0" encoding="utf-8" ?>
<configuration>
    <startup>
        <supportedRuntime version="v4.0" sku=".NETFramework,Version=v4.0,Profile=Client" />
    </startup>
    <system.serviceModel>
        <bindings>
            <wsHttpBinding>
                <binding name="WSHttpBinding_ICalculator" closeTimeout="00:01:00"
                    openTimeout="00:01:00" receiveTimeout="00:10:00"
                                                        sendTimeout="00:01:00"
                    bypassProxyOnLocal="false" transactionFlow="false"
                                    hostNameComparisonMode="StrongWildcard"
                    maxBufferPoolSize="524288" maxReceivedMessageSize="65536"
                    messageEncoding="Text" textEncoding="utf-8" useDefaultWebProxy="true"
                    allowCookies="false">
                    <readerQuotas maxDepth="32" maxStringContentLength="8192"
                                                        maxArrayLength="16384"
                        maxBytesPerRead="4096" maxNameTableCharCount="16384" />
                    <reliableSession ordered="true" inactivityTimeout="00:10:00"
                        enabled="false" />
                    <security mode="Message">
                        <transport clientCredentialType="Windows"
                                                    proxyCredentialType="None"
                            realm="" />
                        <message clientCredentialType="Windows"
                                            negotiateServiceCredential="true"
                            algorithmSuite="Default" />
                    </security>
                </binding>
            </wsHttpBinding>
        </bindings>
        <client>
            <endpoint address= "http://localhost:8732/Design_Time_Addresses/
                            ProVB_WCFCalculatorLibrary/Service1/"
                            binding="wsHttpBinding" bindingConfiguration=
                            "WSHttpBinding_ICalculator"
                            contract="CalculatorService.ICalculator"
                            name="WSHttpBinding_ICalculator">
                <identity>
                    <dns value="localhost" />
                </identity>
            </endpoint>
        </client>
    </system.serviceModel>
</configuration>
```

Code snippet from app.config

There are two important parts to this file. First, the information in the `wsHttpBinding` section is important because this defines behaviors such as the timeouts and the maximum amount of data that can be placed in a message. It is not uncommon for these defaults to prevent people from successfully sending messages and cause great confusion. Note that if you right-click on your service reference, another context menu option is to Configure Your Service Reference. This key dialog enables you to edit these values to reflect your service's specific needs.

The second important part of this configuration document is the `<client>` element. This element contains a child element called `<endpoint>` that defines the *where* and *how* of the service consumption process.

The `<endpoint>` element provides the address of the service — and it specifies which binding of the available WCF bindings should be used. In this case, the `wsHttpBinding` is the required binding. Although you are using an established binding from the WCF framework, from the client side you can customize how this binding behaves. As noted, the settings that define the behavior of the binding are specified using the `bindingConfiguration` attribute of the `<endpoint>` element. In this case, the value provided to the `bindingConfiguration` attribute is `WSHttpBinding_ICalculator`, which is a reference to the `<binding>` element contained within the `<wsHttpBinding>` element:

```
<binding name="WSHttpBinding_ICalculator" closeTimeout="00:01:00"
    openTimeout="00:01:00" receiveTimeout="00:10:00" sendTimeout="00:01:00"
    bypassProxyOnLocal="false" transactionFlow="false"
    hostNameComparisonMode="StrongWildcard"
    maxBufferPoolSize="524288" maxReceivedMessageSize="65536"
    messageEncoding="Text" textEncoding="utf-8" useDefaultWebProxy="true"
    allowCookies="false">
    <readerQuotas maxDepth="32" maxStringContentLength="8192" maxArrayLength="16384"
        maxBytesPerRead="4096" maxNameTableCharCount="16384" />
    <reliableSession ordered="true" inactivityTimeout="00:10:00" enabled="false" />
    <security mode="Message">
        <transport clientCredentialType="Windows" proxyCredentialType="None"
            realm="" />
        <message clientCredentialType="Windows" negotiateServiceCredential="true"
            algorithmSuite="Default" />
    </security>
</binding>
```

Note one important distinction here. If instead of using the built-in Visual Studio test engine to test your service declaration, you bound to the custom client, you would find that this configuration file would be subtly different. Instead of having a `wsHttpBinding`, you would have a `netTCP` binding. This binding would have different setting defaults and, more important, indicate a different transport protocol for your requests. If you play with these two different bindings, you'll find that the binary format used by `netTCP` responds much more quickly than the `wsHttpBinding` that Visual Studio has generated for you.

As demonstrated, the Visual Studio 2010 capabilities for WCF make the consumption of these services fairly trivial. The next step is to code the Windows Forms project to test the consumption of the service interface.

Writing the Consumption Code

The code to consume the interface is quite minimal. End users will merely select the radio button of the operation they want to perform. The default radio button selected is Add. The user places a number in each of the two text boxes provided and clicks the Calculate button to call the service to perform the designated operation on the provided numbers.

To accomplish this, add two text boxes, four radio buttons, one button, and one label to your form. The display (for labeling the controls) should look similar to what is shown in Figure 13-11. Next, you want to create two event handlers; the first is on `Form Load` to pre-populate the text boxes with default numbers (to speed testing), and the second is an event handler for the button you've labeled Calculate.

Clicking the Calculate button will create an instance of the service and then open a connection and make the appropriate call. In a production environment, you might keep a static instance of the service available in your application so you could create it once instead of for each event. Similarly, you'll want to follow the best practice mentioned earlier of assigning the URI at runtime based on an application setting.

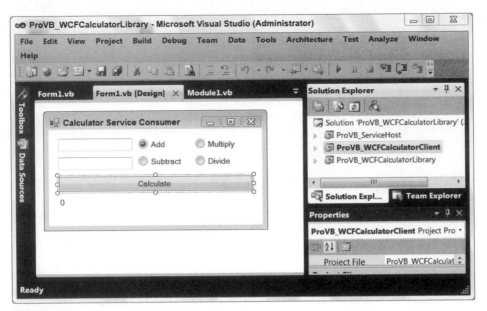

FIGURE 13-11

The code for the form is as follows:

Available for
download on
Wrox.com

```vb
Public Class Form1
    Private Sub Form1_Load(ByVal sender As System.Object,
                           ByVal e As System.EventArgs) Handles MyBase.Load
        TextBox1.Text = 21
        TextBox2.Text = 21
    End Sub

    Private Sub Button1_Click(ByVal sender As System.Object,
                    ByVal e As System.EventArgs) Handles Button1.Click
        Dim result As Integer
        Dim ws As New CalculatorService.CalculatorClient()
        ws.Open()
        If RadioButton1.Checked = True Then
            result = ws.Add(Integer.Parse(TextBox1.Text), Integer.Parse(TextBox2.Text))
        ElseIf RadioButton2.Checked = True Then
            result = ws.Subtract(Integer.Parse(TextBox1.Text),
                                 Integer.Parse(TextBox2.Text))
        ElseIf RadioButton3.Checked = True Then
            result = ws.Multiply(Integer.Parse(TextBox1.Text),
                                 Integer.Parse(TextBox2.Text))
        ElseIf RadioButton4.Checked = True Then
            result = ws.Divide(Integer.Parse(TextBox1.Text),
                               Integer.Parse(TextBox2.Text))
        End If
        ws.Close()
        Label1.Text = result.ToString()
    End Sub

End Class
```

Code snippet from Form1.vb

This is quite similar to the steps taken when working with Web references from the XML Web Services world. First is an instantiation of the proxy class, as shown with the creation of the svc object:

```vb
Dim ws As New CalculatorService.CalculatorClient()
```

Working with the ws object now, the IntelliSense options provide you with the appropriate Add, Subtract, Multiply, and Divide methods. Running this application provides results similar to those presented in Figure 13-12.

In this case, the Add method is invoked from the service when the form's Calculate button is pressed.

Another best practice is to get a tool such as Fiddler2 to track communication with your service. (www.fiddler2.com/fiddler2/) This free tool enables you to view messages sent across a HTTP/HTTPS.

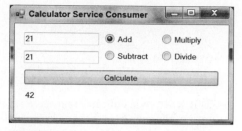

FIGURE 13-12

Note that while this tool will work if you've used Visual Studio to configure your testing to be transported via HTTP, if you've relied on the custom client, you'll find that the requests are instead sent as binary data over TCP and are not available to Fiddler2.

Using a binding to the custom client means the requests and responses are sent over TCP as binary, dramatically decreasing the size of the payload for large messages. This is something that .NET Remoting was used for prior to the release of the WCF framework.

This concludes the short tutorial demonstrating how to build a single service that can support two different endpoints. Visual Studio 2010 can generate one such endpoint, which is based on the same XML and open standards as a traditional Web service. The other you built manually into your command-line application to support the TCP protocol and binary data transfer. Depending on how you map that service to your client, you can consume the service as either an XML-based data transfer or a binary data transfer that can map directly into your .NET Windows Forms application.

WORKING WITH DATA CONTRACTS

In the preceding sample WCF service, the data contract depended upon simple types or primitive data types. A .NET type of Integer was exposed, which in turn was mapped to an XSD type of int. You might not have noticed the input and output types actually defined in the WSDL document that was provided via the WCF-generated one, but they are there. These types are exposed through an imported .xsd document (a dynamic document). This bit of the WSDL document is presented here:

```
<wsdl:types>
  <xsd:schema targetNamespace="http://tempuri.org/Imports">
    <xsd:import schemaLocation="http://localhost:8000/calculator?xsd=xsd0"
     namespace="http://tempuri.org/" />
    <xsd:import schemaLocation="http://localhost:8000/calculator?xsd=xsd1"
     namespace="http://schemas.microsoft.com/2003/10/Serialization/" />
  </xsd:schema>
</wsdl:types>
```

Typing in the XSD location of http://localhost:8000/calculator?xsd=xsd0 gives you the input and output parameters of the service. For instance, looking at the definition of the Add method, you will see the following bit of XML:

Available for download on Wrox.com

```
<xs:element name="Add">
  <xs:complexType>
    <xs:sequence>
      <xs:element minOccurs="0" name="a" type="xs:int" />
      <xs:element minOccurs="0" name="b" type="xs:int" />
    </xs:sequence>
  </xs:complexType>
</xs:element>
<xs:element name="AddResponse">
  <xs:complexType>
```

```
        <xs:sequence>
          <xs:element minOccurs="0" name="AddResult" type="xs:int" />
        </xs:sequence>
      </xs:complexType>
    </xs:element>
```

Code snippet from ProVB_WCFCalculatorClient\Service References\CalculatorService\service.xsd

This XML code indicates that there are two required input parameters (a and b) that are of type int; in return, the consumer gets an element called `<AddResult>`, which contains a value of type int.

As a builder of this WCF service, you didn't have to build the data contract, mainly because this service uses simple types. When using complex types, you have to create a data contract in addition to your service contract.

Building a Service with a Data Contract

For an example of working with data contracts, you can create a new WCF service (again within a Console Application project) called ProVB_WCFWithDataContract. As with the other samples this solution is available as part of the online code download. In this case, you still need an interface that defines your service contract, and then another class that implements that interface. In addition to these items, you need another class that defines the data contract.

Like the service contract, which makes use of the `<ServiceContract()>` and the `<OperationContract()>` attributes, the data contract uses the `<DataContract()>` and `<DataMember()>` attributes. To gain access to these attributes, you have to make a reference to the `System.Runtime.Serialization` namespace in your project and import this namespace into the file.

The full WCF interface definition located in `IHelloCustomer.vb` in the code download is presented here:

Available for
download on
Wrox.com

```
<ServiceContract()> _
Public Interface IHelloCustomer
    <OperationContract()> _
    Function HelloFirstName(ByVal cust As Customer) As String
    <OperationContract()> _
    Function HelloFullName(ByVal cust As Customer) As String
End Interface

<DataContract()> _
Public Class Customer
    <DataMember()> _
    Public FirstName As String
    <DataMember()> _
    Public LastName As String
End Class
```

Code snippet from IHelloCustomer.vb

Similarly, the project contains the file `HelloCustomer.vb`, which contains the implementation class. The code for that file follows:

Available for
download on
Wrox.com

```
Public Class HelloCustomer
    Implements IHelloCustomer
    Public Function HelloFirstName(ByVal cust As Customer) As String _
      Implements IHelloCustomer.HelloFirstName
        Return "Hello " & cust.FirstName
    End Function
    Public Function HelloFullName(ByVal cust As Customer) As String _
      Implements IHelloCustomer.HelloFullName
        Return "Hello " & cust.FirstName & " " & cust.LastName
    End Function
End Class
```

Code snippet from HelloCustomer.vb

This class, the `Customer` class, has two members: `FirstName` and `LastName`. Both of these properties are of type `String`. You specify a class as a data contract as part of the interface definition through the use of the `<DataContract()>` attribute:

```
<DataContract()> _
Public Class Customer
    ' Code removed for clarity
End Class
```

Now, any of the properties contained in the class are also part of the data contract through the use of the `<DataMember()>` attribute:

```
<DataContract()> _
Public Class Customer
    <DataMember()> _
    Public FirstName As String
    <DataMember()> _
    Public LastName As String
End Class
```

Finally, the `Customer` object is used in the interface, as well as the class that implements the `IHelloCustomer` interface.

NAMESPACES

Note that the services built in the chapter have no defined namespaces. If you looked at the WSDL files that were produced, you would see that the namespace provided is `http://tempuri.org`. Obviously, you do not want to go live with this default namespace. Instead, you need to define your own namespace.

To accomplish this task, the interface's `<ServiceContract()>` attribute enables you to set the namespace:

```
<ServiceContract(Namespace:="http://www.Wrox.com/ns/")> _
Public Interface IHelloCustomer
    <OperationContract()> _
    Function HelloFirstName(ByVal cust As Customer) As String
    <OperationContract()> _
    Function HelloFullName(ByVal cust As Customer) As String
End Interface
```

Code snippet from ProVB_WCFWithDataContract\IHelloCustomer.vb

Here, the `<ServiceContract()>` attribute uses the `Namespace` property to provide a namespace.

Building the Host

The next step is the same as before: Create a new Console Application project to act as the WCF service host. Name the new project **ProVB_WCFWithDataContractHost** and change the `Module1.vb` file so that it becomes the host of the WCF service you just built. Keep in mind that you'll need to add the appropriate project reference and `System.ServiceModel` references to the code. Once that is complete, the updated code will look similar to the following:

```
Imports System.ServiceModel
Imports System.ServiceModel.Description

Module Module1
    Sub Main()
        Using svcHost =
            New ServiceHost(GetType(ProVB_WCFWithDataContract.HelloCustomer))
                Dim netBind = New NetTcpBinding(SecurityMode.None)
        svcHost.AddServiceEndpoint(GetType(ProVB_WCFWithDataContract.IHelloCustomer),
                    netBind,
```

```
                    New Uri("net.tcp://localhost:8080/HelloCustomer/"))
            Dim smb = New ServiceMetadataBehavior()
            smb.HttpGetEnabled = True
            smb.HttpGetUrl = New Uri("http://localhost:8000/HelloCustomer")
            svcHost.Description.Behaviors.Add(smb)
            svcHost.Open()
            Console.WriteLine("Press the <ENTER> key to close the host.")
            Console.ReadLine()
        End Using
    End Sub
End Module
```

Code snippet from ProVB_WCFWithDataContractHost \module1.vb

This host uses the `IHelloCustomer` interface and builds an endpoint at `net.tcp://localhost:8080/ HelloCustomer`. This time, however, we'll have this running when we map our interface so you can see an example of the TCP binding. Build your solution and show all files in the Solution Explorer for your host project. You can then see the bin folder for your project, which contains the Debug folder. Right-click the Debug folder and from the context menu select Open Folder in Windows Explorer.

This should give you a view similar to what is shown in Figure 13-13. Right-click on ProVB_ WCFWithDataContractHost and run your application as Administrator (you may be prompted to resolve a firewall issue and to confirm that you want to elevate the privileges of this process) to start your WCF host outside of Visual Studio. By starting this application outside of Visual Studio, you can directly reference the TCP-based binding you created as part of your host console from the Add Service Reference dialog. Just leave this running in the background as you continue this example.

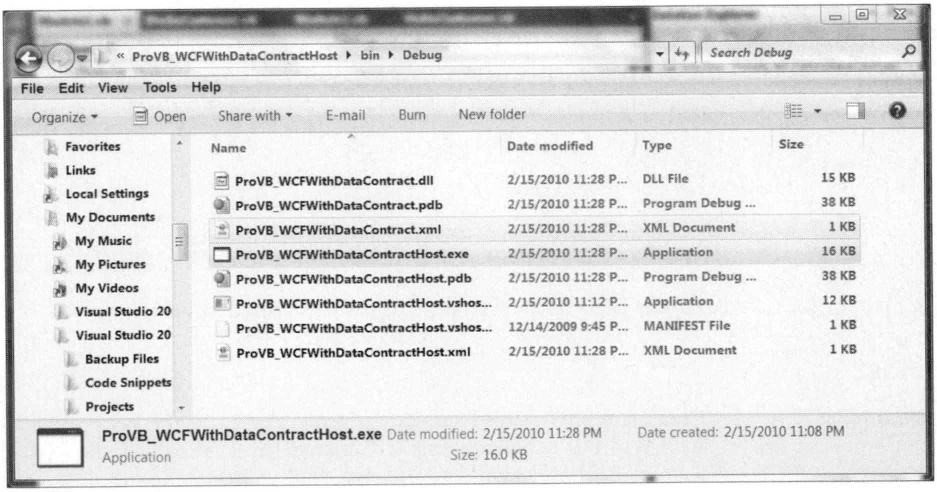

FIGURE 13-13

Building the Consumer

Now that the service is running and in place, the next step is to build the consumer. To begin, add a new Console Application project to your Service Library solution called **ProVB_HelloWorldConsumer**. Right-click on the project and select Add Service Reference from the options provided. In short you are going to create another copy of the service host created in the previous example.

From the Add Service Reference dialog, target your custom service host by entering `http:// localhost:8000/HelloCustomer` as the service URI. Then simply rename the default `ServiceReference1` with the name `HelloCustomerService` as shown in Figure 13-14.

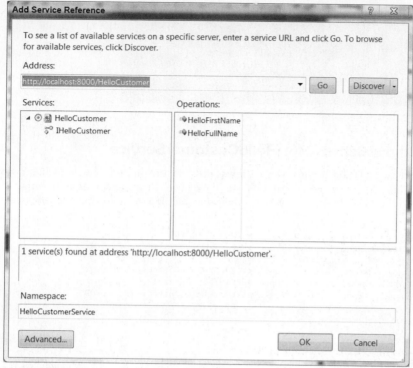

FIGURE 13-14

This will add the changes to the references and the `app.config` file just as before, enabling you to consume the service. You can use the steps to create the service host from the first sample, but update the connections to reference the new service. The following code shows what is required:

Available for
download on
Wrox.com

```
Module Module1
    Sub Main()
        Dim svc As New HelloCustomerService.HelloCustomerClient()
        Dim cust As New HelloCustomerService.Customer()
        Dim result As String
        svc.Open()
        Console.WriteLine("What is your first name?")
        cust.FirstName = Console.ReadLine()
        Console.WriteLine("What is your last name?")
        cust.LastName = Console.ReadLine()
        result = svc.HelloFullName(cust)
        svc.Close()
        Console.WriteLine(result)
        Console.ReadLine()
    End Sub
End Module
```

Code snippet from ProVB_HelloWorldConsumer\Module1.vb

As a consumer, once you make the reference, the service reference doesn't just provide a `HelloCustomerClient` object; you will also find the `Customer` object that was defined through the service's data contract.

Therefore, the preceding code block just instantiates both of these objects and builds the `Customer` object before it is passed into the `HelloFullName` method provided by the service. Running this bit of code will return the results shown in Figure 13-15.

FIGURE 13-15

Looking at WSDL and the Schema for HelloCustomerService

After you made the reference to the HelloCustomer service, it was possible for you to review the WSDL in your new reference. With the Solution Explorer showing all files, you'll see the `HelloCustomer1.wsdl` within your solution. You can open this file to look at the WSDL, where you will find the following XSD imports:

Available for
download on
Wrox.com

```
<wsdl:types>
  <xsd:schema targetNamespace="http://www.Wrox.com/ns/Imports">
    <xsd:import schemaLocation="http://localhost:8000/HelloCustomer?xsd=xsd0"
    namespace="http://www.Wrox.com/ns/" />
    <xsd:import schemaLocation="http://localhost:8000/HelloCustomer?xsd=xsd1"
     namespace="http://schemas.microsoft.com/2003/10/Serialization/" />
    <xsd:import schemaLocation="http://localhost:8000/HelloCustomer?xsd=xsd2"
     namespace="http://schemas.datacontract.org/2004/07/
     ProVB_WCFWithDataContract" />
  </xsd:schema>
</wsdl:types>
```

Code snippet from ProVB_HelloWorldConsumer\Service References\HelloCustomerService\HelloCustomer1.wsdl

`http://localhost:8000/HelloCustomer?xsd=xsd2` provides the details about your `Customer` object. The code from the file `HelloCustomer2.xsd`, which is part of your reference definition, is shown here:

Available for
download on
Wrox.com

```
<?xml version="1.0" encoding="utf-8"?>
<xs:schema
    xmlns:tns="http://schemas.datacontract.org/2004/07/ProVB_WCFWithDataContract"
    elementFormDefault="qualified"
    targetNamespace=
            "http://schemas.datacontract.org/2004/07/ProVB_WCFWithDataContract"
    xmlns:xs="http://www.w3.org/2001/XMLSchema">
  <xs:complexType name="Customer">
    <xs:sequence>
      <xs:element minOccurs="0" name="FirstName" nillable="true"
                                            type="xs:string" />
      <xs:element minOccurs="0" name="LastName" nillable="true"
                                            type="xs:string" />
    </xs:sequence>
  </xs:complexType>
  <xs:element name="Customer" nillable="true" type="tns:Customer" />
</xs:schema>
```

Code snippet from ProVB_HelloWorldConsumer\Service References\HelloCustomerService\HelloCustomer2.xsd

This is an XSD description of the `Customer` object. Making a reference to the WSDL that includes the XSD description of the `Customer` object causes the auto-generated proxy class (located in the file `Reference.vb`) to create the following class as part of the proxy (this code follows the `Namespace` declaration in the downloadable sample):

Available for
download on
Wrox.com

```
<System.Diagnostics.DebuggerStepThroughAttribute(), _
System.CodeDom.Compiler.GeneratedCodeAttribute("System.Runtime.Serialization" _
, "4.0.0.0"), _
    System.Runtime.Serialization.DataContractAttribute(Name:="Customer", _
```

```vb
    [Namespace]:= _
   "http://schemas.datacontract.org/2004/07/ProVB_WCFWithDataContract"), _
    System.SerializableAttribute()> _
   Partial Public Class Customer
       Inherits Object
       Implements System.Runtime.Serialization.IExtensibleDataObject, _
                System.ComponentModel.INotifyPropertyChanged
       <System.NonSerializedAttribute()> _
       Private extensionDataField As _
                   System.Runtime.Serialization.ExtensionDataObject


       <System.Runtime.Serialization.OptionalFieldAttribute()> _
       Private FirstNameField As String


       <System.Runtime.Serialization.OptionalFieldAttribute()> _
       Private LastNameField As String


       <Global.System.ComponentModel.BrowsableAttribute(false)> _
       Public Property ExtensionData() As _
       System.Runtime.Serialization.ExtensionDataObject _
   Implements System.Runtime.Serialization.IExtensibleDataObject.ExtensionData
           Get
               Return Me.extensionDataField
           End Get
           Set
               Me.extensionDataField = value
           End Set
       End Property


       <System.Runtime.Serialization.DataMemberAttribute()> _
       Public Property FirstName() As String
           Get
               Return Me.FirstNameField
           End Get
           Set
               If (Object.ReferenceEquals(Me.FirstNameField, value) <> _
                                                   true) Then
                   Me.FirstNameField = value
                   Me.RaisePropertyChanged("FirstName")
               End If
           End Set
       End Property

       <System.Runtime.Serialization.DataMemberAttribute()> _
       Public Property LastName() As String
           Get
               Return Me.LastNameField
           End Get
           Set
               If (Object.ReferenceEquals(Me.LastNameField, value) <> _
                                                   true) Then
                   Me.LastNameField = value
                   Me.RaisePropertyChanged("LastName")
               End If
           End Set
       End Property
```

Code snippet from ProVB_HelloWorldConsumer\Service References\HelloCustomerService\Reference.vb

As you can see, Visual Studio and WCF provide the tools you need to define and share complex data types across a distributed system. Combined with the other powerful features supported by WCF, you have the tools to build robust, enterprise-quality distributed solutions.

SUMMARY

This chapter looked at one of the more outstanding capabilities provided to the Visual Basic world. Visual Studio 2010 and .NET 4 are a great combination for building advanced services that take your application to a distributed level.

Though not exhaustive, this chapter broadly outlined the basics of the WCF framework. As you begin to dig more deeply into the technology, you will find strong and extensible capabilities.

PART III
Smart Client Applications

14

Windows Forms

WHAT YOU WILL LEARN IN THIS CHAPTER

➤ How to construct a Windows Forms application

➤ How to control the startup and organization of your forms

➤ Important controls available in Windows Forms and how to take advantage of their capabilities

➤ Usage of special families of controls and components, such as extender providers, common dialogs, and the ToolStrip

➤ Programming tips for a variety of programming scenarios

Windows Forms is a part of the .NET Framework that is used to create user interfaces for local applications, often called Win32 clients. Windows Forms does not change when moving from Visual Basic 2005 or Visual Basic 2008 to Visual Basic 2010. Accordingly, the version number used for Windows Forms in Visual Studio 2010 is still 2.0.

The pace of change in Windows Forms is slowing because of the advent of Windows Presentation Foundation (WPF). Going forward, you can expect continued innovation in WPF, but not much in Windows Forms. However, that does not imply that you should abandon Windows Forms or be reluctant to write programs in it. Windows Forms still has many advantages over WPF.

Those advantages include a more complete set of controls and a mature, easy-to-use designer. The result is often faster development in Windows Forms compared to WPF. WPF has advantages of its own, of course. These are discussed in Chapter 17, which provides an introduction to WPF.

Chapter 15 includes more advanced treatment of certain aspects of Windows Forms. After gaining a basic understanding of the key capabilities in this chapter, you'll be ready to go on to the more advanced concepts in that chapter.

THE SYSTEM.WINDOWS.FORMS NAMESPACE

You've already seen how namespaces are used to organize related classes in the .NET Framework. The main namespace used for Windows Forms classes is System.Windows.Forms. The classes in this namespace are contained in the System.Windows.Forms.dll assembly.

If you choose a Windows Forms Application project or Windows Forms Control Library project in VS.NET, a reference to `System.Windows.Forms.dll` is added by default. In some other cases, such as creating a library that will work with controls, you need to add that reference manually. (You can learn more about creating controls in Windows Forms in Chapter 15.)

USING FORMS

A window on the desktop is created in Windows Forms by using a form. Thus, a form is the outer container for your application's interface.

A form is just a special kind of class in Windows Forms. A class becomes a form based on inheritance. It must have the `System.Windows.Forms` class in its inheritance tree, which causes the form to have the behavior and object interface a form requires.

The preferred technique to create a form is to create an instance with the `New` keyword, just as you would with any other class. Typical code would look like this:

```
Dim f As New Form1
f.Show()
```

Setting a Startup Form

If you create a new Windows Forms application in Visual Studio, by default it will contain a form class named `Form1`. The properties for the project will be set to use that form as the startup form for the application — that is, it will be the initial form displayed when the application begins.

To change the startup form, open the Properties dialog for the project. Do this using the Project ⇨ Properties menu. You can also invoke the window by right-clicking the project name in the Solution Explorer and selecting Properties from the context menu. The Properties dialog for a Windows Forms application is shown in Figure 14-1.

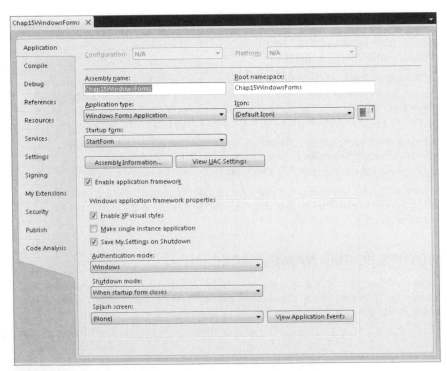

FIGURE 14-1

If the Properties menu item doesn't appear under your Project menu, open the Solution Explorer (Ctrl+Alt+L), highlight the project name (it will be in bold font), and then try again.

The Startup form drop-down will contain the available forms in your application. Selecting a form in this drop-down will cause that form to be the first form displayed when your application begins.

You can also use this dialog to specify other startup tasks, such as showing a splash screen. To control these additional options, the check box labeled "Enable application framework" must be checked.

Showing Forms via Sub Main

If you do not wish to use the default way to load your Windows Forms application, you can take explicit control of the startup process in code. You might do this, for example, because you have logic you must run for authentication before the first form is loaded.

To take control of the startup process, first create an empty subroutine named Sub Main in a code module. If your project does not yet contain a code module, you may need to create one. Code modules are discussed in Chapter 2.

Uncheck the check box labeled "Enable application framework" in the project properties dialog. The drop-down for Startup form will change its label to Startup object, and it will contain a new entry: Sub Main.

Finally, create your logic for Sub Main. Typical logic looks like this:

```
Sub Main()
    ' Do start up work here
    Dim f As New Form1
    Application.Run(f)
End Sub
```

Note that you do not use the earlier technique to show a form with the Show method when you are creating your Sub Main logic. The object reference to the form would immediately fall out of scope. The form would briefly appear, then the application would terminate. Instead, in Sub Main, your logic should use the Application object's Run method to load your starting form.

More about the Application Class

The Application class contains a number of shared methods and properties that are useful in managing your Windows Forms application. In addition to the Run method shown earlier, the Application class has an Exit method to end an application, and a Restart method to cause an application to shut down and immediately restart.

The Application class also has useful events to manage your application. For example, the ApplicationExit event fires when your application is about to shut down.

Startup Location for a Form

Often, you'll want a form to be centered on the screen when it first appears. VB.NET does this automatically for you when you set the StartPosition property. Table 14-1 shows the settings and their meanings.

TABLE 14-1: Options for Starting Position of a Form

STARTPOSITION VALUE	EFFECT
Manual	Shows the form positioned at the values defined by the form's Location property
CenterScreen	Shows the form centered on the screen
WindowsDefaultLocation	Shows the form at the window's default location
WindowsDefaultBounds	Shows the form at the window's default location, with the window's default bounding size
CenterParent	Shows the form centered in its owner

Form Borders

Forms have a number of border options in Windows Forms. The `FormBorderStyle` property is used to set the border option, and the options can affect the way a form can be manipulated by the user. The options available for `FormBorderStyle` include the following:

➤   `None` — No border, and the user cannot resize the form

➤   `FixedSingle` — Single 3-D border, and the user cannot resize the form

➤   `Fixed3D` — 3-D border, and the user cannot resize the form

➤   `FixedDialog` — Dialog-box-style border, and the user cannot resize the form

➤   `Sizeable` — Same as `FixedSingle`, except that the user can resize the form

➤   `FixedToolWindow` — Single border, and the user cannot resize the form

➤   `SizeableToolWindow` — Single border, and the user can resize the form

Each of these has a different effect on the buttons that appear in the title bar of the form. For details, check the help topic for the `FormBorderStyle` property.

Always on Top — the TopMost Property

Some forms need to remain visible at all times, even when they don't have the focus, such as floating toolbars and tutorial windows. In Windows Forms, forms have a property called `TopMost`. Set it to `True` to have a form overlay other forms even when it does not have the focus.

Note that a form with `TopMost` set to `True` is on top of all applications, not just the hosting application. If you need a form to only be on top of other forms in the application, then this capability is provided by an owned form.

Owned Forms

As with the `TopMost` property, an owned form floats above the application but it does not interfere with using the application. An example is a search-and-replace box. However, an owned form is not on top of all forms, just the form that is its owner.

When a form is owned by another form, it is minimized and closed with the owner form. Owned forms are never displayed behind their owner form, but they do not prevent their owner form from gaining the focus and being used. However, if you want to click on the area covered by an owned form, the owned form has to be moved out of the way first.

A form can only have one "owner" at a time. If a form that is already owned by Form1 is added to the owned forms collection for Form2, then the form is no longer owned by Form1.

There are two ways to make a form owned by another form. It can be done in the owner form or in the owned form.

AddOwnedForm Method

In the owner form, another form can be made owned with the `AddOwnedForm` method. The following code makes an instance of Form2 become owned by Form1. This code would reside somewhere in Form1 and would typically be placed just before the line that shows the instance of Form2 to the screen:

```
Dim frm As New Form2
Me.AddOwnedForm(frm)
```

Owner Property

The relationship can also be set up in the owned form. This is done with the `Owner` property of the form. Here is a method that would work inside Form2 to make it owned by a form that is passed in as an argument to the function:

```
Public Sub MakeMeOwned(frmOwner As Form)
    Me.Owner = frmOwner
End Sub
```

Because this technique requires a reference to the owner inside the owned form, it is not used as often as using the `AddOwnedForm` method in the owner form.

OwnedForms Collection

The owner form can access its collection of owned forms with the `OwnedForms` property. Here is code to loop through the forms owned by a form:

Available for
download on
Wrox.com

```
Dim frmOwnedForm As Form
For Each frmOwnedForm In Me.OwnedForms
    Console.WriteLine(frmOwnedForm.Text)
Next
```

Code snippet from StartForm

The owner form can remove an owned form with the `RemoveOwnedForm` property. This could be done in a loop like the previous example, with code like the following:

Available for
download on
Wrox.com

```
Dim frmOwnedForm As Form
For Each frmOwnedForm In Me.OwnedForms
    Console.WriteLine(frmOwnedForm.Text)
    Me.RemoveOwnedForm(frmOwnedForm)
Next
```

Code snippet from StartForm

This loop would cause an owner form to stop owning all of its slaved forms. Note that those "deslaved" forms would not be unloaded, they would simply no longer be owned.

Making Forms Transparent and Translucent

Windows Forms offers advanced capabilities to make forms translucent, or parts of a form transparent. You can even change the entire shape of a form.

The Opacity Property

The `Opacity` property measures how opaque or transparent a form is. A value of 0 percent makes the form fully transparent. A value of 100 percent makes the form fully visible. Any value greater than 0 and less than 100 makes the form partially visible, as if it were a ghost. Note that an opacity value of 0 percent disables the capability to click the form.

Very low levels of opacity, in the range of 1 or 2 percent, make the form effectively invisible, but still allow the form to be clickable. This means that the `Opacity` property has the potential to create mischievous applications that sit in front of other applications and "steal" their mouse clicks and other events.

 Percentage values are used to set opacity in the Properties window, but if you want to set the `Opacity` property in code, you must use values between 0 and 1 instead, with 0 equivalent to 0 percent and 1 equivalent to 100 percent.

Tool and dialog windows that should not completely obscure their background are one example of a usage for `Opacity`. Setting expiration for a "free trial" by gradually fading out the application's user interface is another.

The following block of code shows how to fade a form out and back in when the user clicks a button named Button1. You may have to adjust the Step value of the array, depending on your computer's performance:

```
Private Sub Button1_Click(ByVal sender As System.Object, _
                          ByVal e As System.EventArgs) _
                          Handles Button1.Click
    Dim i As Double
    For i = -1 To 1 Step 0.005
      ' Note - opacity is a value from 0.0 to 1.0 in code
      ' Absolute value is used to keep us in that range
      Me.Opacity = System.Math.Abs(i)
      Me.Refresh
    Next i
End Sub
```

Code snippet from StartForm

The TransparencyKey Property

Instead of making an entire form translucent or transparent, the TransparencyKey property enables you to specify a color that will become transparent on the form. This enables you to make some sections of a form transparent, while other sections are unchanged.

For example, if TransparencyKey is set to a red color and some areas of the form are that exact shade of red, then they will be transparent. Whatever is behind the form shows through in those areas; and if you click in one of those areas, you are actually clicking the object behind the form.

TransparencyKey can be used to create irregularly shaped "skin" forms. A form can have its BackgroundImage property set with an image, and by just painting a part of the image with the TransparencyKey color, you can make parts of the form disappear.

The Region Property

Another way to gain the capability of "skins" is by using the Region property of a form. The Region property allows a shape for a form to be encoded as a "graphics path," thereby changing the shape from the default rectangle to another shape. A path can contain line segments between points, curves, and arcs, and outlines of letters, in any combination.

The following example changes the shape of a form to an arrow. Create a new Windows application. Set the FormBorderStyle property of Form1 to None. Then place the following code in the Load event for Form1:

```
Dim PointArray(6) As Point
PointArray(0) = New Point(0, 40)
PointArray(1) = New Point(200, 40)
PointArray(2) = New Point(200, 0)
PointArray(3) = New Point(250, 100)
PointArray(4) = New Point(200, 200)
PointArray(5) = New Point(200, 160)
PointArray(6) = New Point(0, 160)
Dim myGraphicsPath As _
System.Drawing.Drawing2D.GraphicsPath = _
        New System.Drawing.Drawing2D.GraphicsPath
myGraphicsPath.AddPolygon(PointArray)
Me.Region = New Region(myGraphicsPath)
```

Code snippet from ArrowShapedForm

When the program is run, Form1 will appear in the shape of a right-pointing arrow. If you lay out the points in the array, you will see that they have become the vertices of the arrow.

Visual Inheritance

By inheriting from `System.Windows.Forms.Form`, any class automatically gets all the properties, methods, and events that a form based on Windows Forms is supposed to have. However, a class does not have to inherit directly from the `System.Windows.Forms.Form` class to become a Windows form. It can become a form by inheriting from another form, which itself inherits from `System.Windows .Forms.Form`. In this way, controls originally placed on one form can be directly inherited by a second form. Not only is the design of the original form inherited, but also any code associated with these controls (the processing logic behind an Add New button, for example). This means you can create a base form with processing logic required in a number of forms, and then create other forms that inherit the base controls and functionality.

VB 2010 provides an Inheritance Picker tool to aid in this process. Note, however, that a form must be compiled into either an `.exe` or `.dll` file before it can be used by the Inheritance Picker. Once that is done, adding a form that inherits from another form in the project can be achieved by selecting Project ➪ Add Windows Form and then choosing the template type of Inherited Form in the resulting dialog.

Scrollable Forms

Some applications need fields that will fit on a single screen. While you could split the data entry into multiple screens, an alternative is a scrollable form.

You can set your forms to automatically have scrollbars when they are sized smaller than the child controls they contain. To do so, set the `AutoScroll` property of your form to True. When you run your program, resize the form to make it smaller than the controls require and presto — instant scrolling.

MDI Forms

MDI (Multiple Document Interface) forms are forms that are created to hold other forms. The MDI form is often referred to as the *parent*, and the forms displayed within the MDI parent are often called *children*. Figure 14-2 shows a typical MDI parent with several children displayed within it.

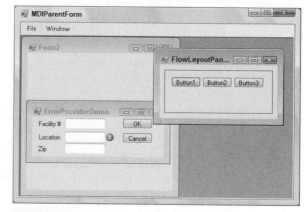

Creating an MDI Parent Form

In Windows Forms, a regular form is converted to an MDI parent form by setting the `IsMdiContainer` property of the form to True. This is normally done in the Properties window at design time.

FIGURE 14-2

A form can also be made into an MDI parent at runtime by setting the `IsMdiContainer` property to True in code, but the design of an MDI form is usually different from that of a normal form, so this approach is not often needed.

 You cannot have both `Autoscroll` *and* `IsMdiContainer` *set to True at the same time. MDI containers have their own scrolling functionality. If you set* `Autoscroll` *to True for an MDI container, then the* `IsMdiContainer` *property will be set to False, and the form will cease to be an MDI container.*

MDI Child Forms

In Windows Forms, a form becomes an MDI child at runtime by setting the form's `MDIParent` property to point to an MDI parent form. This makes it possible to use a form as either a standalone form or an MDI child in different circumstances. In fact, the `MDIParent` property cannot be set at design time — it must be set at runtime to make a form an MDI child.

Any number of MDI child forms can be displayed in the MDI parent-client area. The currently active child form can be determined with the `ActiveForm` property of the MDI parent form.

An MDI Example in VB 2010

To see these changes to MDI forms in action, try the following exercise. It shows the basics of creating an MDI parent and having it display an MDI child form:

1. Create a new Windows application. It will have an empty form named Form1. Change both the name of the form and the form's `Text` property to **MDIParentForm**.

2. In the Properties window, set the `IsMDIContainer` property for `MDIParentForm` to True. This designates the form as an MDI container for child windows. (Setting this property also causes the form to have a different default background color.)

3. From the Toolbox, drag a `MenuStrip` control to the form. Create a top-level menu item called File with submenu items called New MDI Child and Quit. In addition, create a top-level menu item called Window. The File ⇨ New MDI Child menu option creates and shows new MDI child forms at runtime; the Window menu keeps track of the open MDI child windows.

4. In the component tray at the bottom of the form, click the MenuStrip item and select Properties. In the Properties window, set the `MDIWindowListItem` property to `WindowToolStripMenuItem`. This enables the Window menu to maintain a list of open MDI child windows, with a check mark next to the active child window.

5. Create an MDI child form to use as a template for multiple instances. Select Project ⇨ Add Windows Form and click the Add button in the Add New Item dialog. That results in a new blank form named Form2. Place any controls you like on the form. As an alternative, you can reuse any of the forms created in previous exercises in this chapter.

6. Return to the MDIParentForm. In the menu editing bar, double-click the New MDI Child option under File. The Code Editor will appear, with the cursor in the event routine for that menu option. Place the following code in the event:

```
' This line may change if you are using a form with a different name.
Dim NewMDIChild As New Form2()
'Set the Parent Form of the Child window.
NewMDIChild.MDIParent = Me
'Display the new form.
NewMDIChild.Show()
```

Code snippet from MDIParentForm

7. In the menu editing bar for the MDIParentForm, double-click the Quit option under File. The Code Editor will appear, with the cursor in the event routine for that menu option. Place the following code in the event:

```
Protected Sub QuitToolStripMenuItem_Click(ByVal sender As Object, _
                        ByVal e As System.EventArgs)
        End
End Sub
```

Code snippet from MDIParentForm

8. Run and test the program. Use the File ⇨ New MDI Child option to create several child forms. Note how the Window menu option automatically lists them with the active one checked and allows you to activate a different one.

Arranging Child Windows

MDI parent forms have a method called `LayoutMDI` that automatically arranges child forms in the familiar cascade or tile layout. For the preceding example, add a menu item to your Windows menu called **Tile Vertical** and insert the following code into the menu item's `Click` event to handle it:

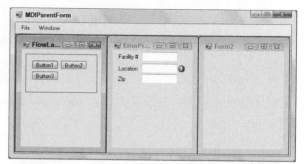

```
Me.LayoutMdi(MDILayout.TileVertical)
```

To see an example of the rearrangement, suppose that the MDI form in Figure 14-2 is rearranged with the `MDILayout.TileVertical` option. It would then look similar to the image in Figure 14-3.

FIGURE 14-3

Dialog Forms

The `Show` method of a form displays *modeless forms*, which are forms that enable users to click off them onto another form in the application.

Applications also sometimes need forms that retain control until their operation is finished. That is, you can't click off such a form onto another form. Such a form is called a *modal form*.

Showing a form modally is done with the `ShowDialog` method. The following code shows a modal dialog in Windows Forms, assuming the project contains a form with a type of `DialogForm`:

```
Dim frmDialogForm As New DialogForm
frmDialogForm.ShowDialog()
```

DialogResult

When showing a dialog form, you'll often need to get information about what action the user selected. Windows Forms has a built-in property for that purpose. When a form is shown with the `ShowDialog` method, the form has a property called `DialogResult` to indicate its state.

The `DialogResult` property can take the following enumerated results:

- ➤ `DialogResult.Abort`
- ➤ `DialogResult.Cancel`
- ➤ `DialogResult.Ignore`
- ➤ `DialogResult.No`
- ➤ `DialogResult.None`
- ➤ `DialogResult.OK`
- ➤ `DialogResult.Retry`
- ➤ `DialogResult.Yes`

When the `DialogResult` property is set, the dialog is hidden as a result. That is, setting the `DialogResult` property causes an implicit call to the `Hide` method of the dialog form, so that control is released back to the form that called the dialog.

The DialogResult property of a dialog box can be set in two ways. The most common way is to associate a DialogResult value with a button. Then, when the button is pressed, the associated value is automatically placed in the DialogResult property of the form.

To set the DialogResult value associated with a button, use the DialogResult property of the button. If this property is set for the button, then it is unnecessary to set the DialogResult in code when the button is pressed.

The following example uses this technique. In Visual Studio 2010, start a new VB Windows application. On the automatic blank form that appears (named Form1), place a single button and set its Text property to Dialog.

Now add a new Windows form by selecting Project ➪ Add Windows Form and name it **DialogForm.vb**. Place two buttons on DialogForm and set the properties for the buttons as shown in the following table.

PROPERTY	VALUE FOR FIRST BUTTON	VALUE FOR SECOND BUTTON
Name	OKButton	CancelButton
Text	OK	Cancel
DialogResult	OK	Cancel

Do not put any code in DialogForm at all. The form should look like the one shown in Figure 14-4.

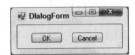

FIGURE 14-4

On the first form, Form1, place the following code in the Click event for Button1:

```
Dim frmDialogForm As New DialogForm()
frmDialogForm.ShowDialog()
' You're back from the dialog - check user action.
Select Case frmDialogForm.DialogResult
  Case DialogResult.OK
    MsgBox("The user pressed OK")
  Case DialogResult.Cancel
    MsgBox("The user pressed cancel")
End Select
frmDialogForm = Nothing
```

Run and test the code. When a button is pressed on the dialog form, a message box should be displayed (by the calling form) indicating the button that was pressed.

The second way to set the DialogResult property of the form is in code. In a Button_Click event, or anywhere else in the dialog form, a line like the following can be used to set the DialogResult property for the form and simultaneously hide the dialog form, returning control to the calling form:

```
Me.DialogResult = DialogResult.Ignore
```

This particular line sets the dialog result to DialogResult.Ignore, but setting the dialog result to any of the permitted values also hides the dialog form.

Forms at Runtime

The life cycle of a form is like that of all objects: It is created and later destroyed. Forms have a visual component, so they use system resources, such as handles. These are created and destroyed at interim stages within the lifetime of the form. Forms can be created and will hold state as a class, but will not appear until they are activated.

Table 14-2 summarizes the typical states of a form's existence. For each state, it includes how you get the form to that state, the events that occur when the form enters a state, and a brief description of each.

TABLE 14-2: Typical States during the Lifecycle of a Form

CODE	EVENTS FIRED	NOTES
MyForm = New Form1	Load	The form's New method will be called (as will InitializeComponent).
MyForm.Show or MyForm.ShowDialog	HandleCreated	Use Show for modeless display.
	Load	Use ShowDialog for modal display.
	VisibleChanged	The HandleCreated event only fires the first time the form is shown or after it has previously been closed.
	Activated	
MyForm.Activate	Activated	A form can be activated when it is visible but does not have the focus.
MyForm.Hide	Deactivate	Hides the form (sets the Visible property to False)
	VisibleChanged	
MyForm.Close	Deactivate	Closes the form and calls Dispose to release the window's resources
	Closing	During the Closing event, you can set the CancelEventArgs.Cancel property to True to abort the close.
	Closed	
	VisibleChanged	
	HandleDestroyed	Also called when the user closes the form using the control box or the X button
	Disposed	The Deactivate event will only fire if the form is currently active.
		Note: There is no longer an Unload event. Use the Closing or Closed event instead.
MyForm.Dispose	None	Use the Close method to finish using your form.
MyForm = Nothing	None	Releasing the reference to the form flags it for garbage collection. The garbage collector calls the form's Finalize method.

Default Instances of Forms

There is one additional way to display a form to the screen. It is included in Windows Forms for compatibility with VB6 and earlier versions, and is not recommended in code you create. However, you may see it in code you maintain.

A form can be shown to the screen with a shared Show method, like this:

```
Form1.Show()
```

Showing a form without instancing it is referred to as using the default instance of the form. That default instance is available from anywhere in a project containing a form. There is only one default instance, and any reference to it will bring up the same underlying instance of the form.

Another way to get to the default instance of a form is through the My namespace. The following line has exactly the same effect, showing the default instance of a form:

```
My.Forms.Form1.Show()
```

CONTROLS

The controls included in Windows Forms provide basic functionality for a wide range of applications. This section covers the features that all controls use (such as docking) and summarizes the standard controls available to you.

Control Tab Order

The VS 2010 design environment enables you to set the tab order of the controls on a form simply by clicking them in sequence. To activate the feature, open a form in the designer and select View ➪ Tab Order. This will place a small number in the upper-left corner of each control on your form, representing the tab index of that control.

FIGURE 14-5

To set the values, simply click each control in the sequence you want the tab flow to operate. Figure 14-5 shows a simple form with the tab order feature enabled.

 In Windows Forms 2.0, it is possible to have two or more controls with the same tab index value. At runtime, Visual Basic will break the tie by using the z-order of the controls. The control that is highest in the z-order receives the focus first. The z-order is a ranking number that determines which controls are in front of or behind other controls. (The term comes from the z-axis, which is an axis perpendicular to the traditional x-axis and y-axis.) The z-order can be changed by right-clicking the control and selecting Bring to Front.

Properties for All Controls

The base `Control` class, which is a base class for all Windows Forms controls, has many properties that affect all types of controls. `Height`, `Width`, `Top`, `Left`, `BackColor`, and `ForeColor` are examples. Because all controls inherit from this class, all Windows Forms controls have these properties and the functionality they provide.

Most of these properties are self-explanatory or familiar to experienced developers. However, you may not be familiar with some properties that were added for the 2.0 version of Windows Forms: `MaximumSize`, `MinimumSize`, and `UseWaitCursor`.

MaximumSize and MinimumSize Properties

The `MaximumSize` and `MinimumSize` properties specify the control's maximum and minimum height and width, respectively. Forms had these properties in Windows Forms 1.0 and 1.1, but in 2.0 all controls have them.

If the maximum height and width are both set to the default value of 0, then there is no maximum. Similarly, if the minimum height and width are set to zero, then there is no minimum. The form or control can be any size.

If these properties are set to anything else, then the settings become limits on the size of the control. For example, if the `MaximumSize` height and width are both set to 100, then the control cannot be bigger than 100 × 100 pixels. The visual designer will not make the control any larger on the form design surface. Attempting to set the height or width of the control in code at runtime to a value greater than 100 will cause it to be set to 100 instead.

The MaximumSize and MinimumSize properties can be reset at runtime to enable sizing of the controls outside the limits imposed at design time. However, the properties have a return type of Size, so resetting either property requires creating a Size structure. For example, you can reset the MinimumSize property for a button named Button1 with the following line of code:

```
Button1.MinimumSize = New Size(20, 20)
```

This sets the new minimum width and height to 20 pixels.

The Size structure has members for Height and Width, which can be used to fetch the current minimum or maximum sizes for either height or width. For example, to find the current minimum height for Button1, use the following line of code:

```
Dim n As Integer = Button1.MinimumSize.Height
```

UseWaitCursor Property

Windows Forms interfaces can use threading or asynchronous requests to allow tasks to execute in the background. When a control is waiting for an asynchronous request to finish, it is helpful to indicate that to the user by changing the mouse cursor when the mouse is inside the control. Normally, the cursor used is the familiar hourglass, which is called the WaitCursor in Windows Forms.

For any control, setting the UseWaitCursor property to True causes the cursor to change to the hourglass (or whatever is being used for the WaitCursor) while the mouse is positioned inside the control. This enables a control to visually indicate that it is waiting for something. The typical usage is to set UseWaitCursor to True when an asynchronous process is begun and then set it back to False when the process is finished and the control is ready for normal operation again.

Dynamic Sizing and Positioning of Controls

Windows Forms 2.0 includes a variety of ways to enable dynamic user interfaces. Not only can controls be set to automatically stretch and reposition themselves as a form is resized, they can also be dynamically arranged inside some special container controls intended for that purpose. This section covers all these ways of enabling dynamic sizing and positioning of controls.

Docking

Docking refers to "gluing" a control to the edge of a parent control. Good examples of docked controls are menu bars and status bars, which are typically docked to the top and bottom of a form, respectively. All visual controls have a Dock property.

To work through an example, create a new Windows application and place a TextBox control on a form. Set the Text property of the TextBox to "I'm Getting Docked." The result when you show the form should look something like Figure 14-6.

Suppose that you need to glue this TextBox to the top of the form. To do this, view the Dock property of the label. If you pull it down, you'll see a small graphic showing several sections, like the one shown in Figure 14-7.

Simply click the top section of the graphic to stick the label at the top of the form. The other sections give you other effects. (A status bar would use the bottom section, for example. Clicking the box in the middle causes the control to fill the form.) The TextBox control will immediately "stick" to the top of your form. When you run your program and stretch the window sideways, you'll see the effect shown in Figure 14-8.

FIGURE 14-6

FIGURE 14-7

FIGURE 14-8

If you try to dock multiple controls to the same edge, Windows Forms must decide how to break the tie. Precedence is given to controls in reverse z-order. That is, the control that is furthest back in the z-order will be the first control next to the edge. If you dock two controls to the same edge and want to switch them, then right-click the control you want docked first and select Send to Back.

If you want a gap between the edge of your form and the docked controls, set the `DockPadding` property of the parent control. You can set a different value for each of the four directions (Left, Right, Top, Bottom); and you can set all four properties to the same value using the All setting.

Anchoring

Anchoring is similar to docking except that you can specifically define the distance that each edge of your control will maintain from the edges of a parent. To see it in action, add a button to the form in the docking example. The result should look like what is shown in Figure 14-9.

Dropping down the `Anchor` property of the button gives you the graphic shown in Figure 14-10.

The four rectangles surrounding the center box enable you to toggle the anchor settings of the control. Figure 14-10 shows the default anchor setting of Top, Left for all controls.

When the setting is on (dark gray), the edge of the control maintains its original distance from the edge of the parent as the parent is resized. If you set the anchor to two opposing edges (such as the left and right edges), the control stretches to accommodate this, as shown in Figure 14-11.

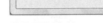

FIGURE 14-9   **FIGURE 14-10**   **FIGURE 14-11**

One of the most common uses of anchoring is to set the `Anchor` property for buttons in the lower-right portion of a form. Setting the `Anchor` property of a button to `Bottom`, `Right` causes the button to maintain a constant distance from the bottom-right corner of the form.

You can also set the `Anchor` property in code. The most common scenario for this would be for a control created on-the-fly. To set the `Anchor` property in code, you must add the anchor styles for all the sides to which you need to anchor. For example, setting the `Anchor` property to `Bottom`, `Left` would require a line of code like this:

```
MyControl.Anchor = Ctype(AnchorStyles.Bottom + AnchorStyles.Right, AnchorStyles)
```

Sizable Containers

Early versions of Windows Forms used the `Splitter` control to allow resizing of containers. This control is still available in Windows Forms 2.0 but it doesn't appear by default in the Toolbox. In its place is a replacement control, `SplitContainer`, that provides the same functionality with less work on your part.

A single `SplitContainer` acts much like two panels with an appropriately inserted `Splitter`. You can think of it as a panel with two sections separated by a movable divider so that the relative sizes of the sections can be changed by a user.

To use a `SplitContainer`, simply drop it on a form, resize it, and position the draggable divider to the appropriate point. If you want the divider to be horizontal instead of vertical, you change the `Orientation` property. Then you can place controls in each subpanel in any way you like. It is common to insert a control such as a `TreeView` or `ListBox`, and then dock it to its respective subpanel. This enables users to resize such contained controls. A typical example of a SplitContainer in action is shown in Figure 14-12.

The cursor in Figure 14-12 shows that the mouse is hovering over the divider, allowing repositioning of the divider by dragging the mouse. A SplitContainer may be nested inside another SplitContainer. This enables you to build forms in which several parts are resizable relative to each other.

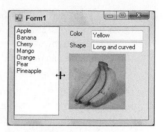

FIGURE 14-12

FlowLayoutPanel Control

The FlowLayoutPanel control enables the dynamic layout of controls contained within it, based on the size of the FlowLayoutPanel.

FlowLayoutPanel works conceptually much like a simple HTML page shown in a browser. The controls placed in the FlowLayoutPanel are positioned in sequence horizontally until there's not enough space for the next control, which then wraps further down for another row of controls. The following walk-through demonstrates this capability.

Start a new Windows Application project. On the blank Form1 included in the new project, place a FlowLayoutPanel control toward the top of the form, making it a bit less wide than the width of the form. Set the Anchor property for the FlowLayoutPanel to Top, Left, and Right. Set the BorderStyle property for the FlowLayoutPanel to FixedSingle so it's easy to see.

Place three Button controls in the FlowLayoutPanel, keeping their default sizes. The form you create should look like the one shown in Figure 14-13.

Run the application. The initial layout will be similar to the design-time layout. However, if you resize the form to about two thirds of its original width, the layout of the buttons changes. Because there is no longer enough room for them to be arranged side by side, the arrangement automatically switches. Figure 14-14 shows the form in three configurations: first with its original width, then narrower so that only two buttons fit in the FlowLayoutPanel, and finally so narrow that the buttons are all stacked in the FlowLayoutPanel.

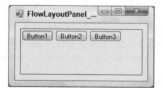

FIGURE 14-13

FIGURE 14-14

Note that no logic of any kind was added to the form — the FlowLayoutPanel handles the repositioning of the buttons automatically. In fact, any position information you set for the button controls is ignored if they are placed in a FlowLayoutPanel.

Padding and Margin Properties

To assist in positioning controls in the FlowLayoutPanel, all controls have a property called Margin. There are settings for Margin.Left, Margin.Right, Margin.Top, and Margin.Bottom. These settings determine how much space is reserved around a control when calculating its automatic position in a FlowLayoutPanel.

You can see the Margin property in action by changing the Margin property for one or more of the buttons in the previous example. If you change all the Margin settings for the first button to 10 pixels, for example, and run the application, the form will look like the one shown in Figure 14-15.

The first button now has a 10-pixel separation from all the other controls in the FlowLayoutPanel, as well as a 10-pixel separation from the edges of the FlowLayoutPanel itself.

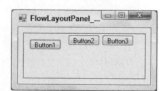

FIGURE 14-15

The Padding property is for the FlowLayoutPanel or other container control. When a control is embedded into a FlowLayoutPanel, the Padding.Left, Padding.Right, Padding.Top, and Padding.Bottom properties of the FlowLayoutPanel determine how far the control should be positioned from the inside edge of the container.

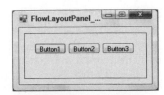

FIGURE 14-16

You can see the Padding property in action by changing the Padding property for the FlowLayoutPanel in the previous example. If you set all Padding settings to 15 pixels, and reset the Margin property for the first button back to the default, then the form will look like what is shown in Figure 14-16 in the visual designer.

Notice that all the controls in the FlowLayoutPanel are now at least 15 pixels from the edges.

The Padding property is also applicable to other container controls if the contained controls have their Dock property set. If the settings for Padding are not zero, then a docked control will be offset from the edge of the container by the amount specified by the Padding property.

TableLayoutPanel Control

Another control that uses dynamic layout of child controls is the TableLayoutPanel. This control consists of a table of rows and columns, resulting in a rectangular array of cells. You can place one control in each cell. However, that control can itself be a container, such as a Panel or FlowLayoutPanel.

You can control the dimensions of the columns and rows by setting some key properties. For columns, set the number of columns with the ColumnCount property, and then control each individual column with the ColumnStyles collection. When you click the button for the ColumnStyles collection, you get a designer window that enables you to set two key properties for each column: SizeType and Width.

SizeType can be set to one of the following enumerations:

➤   Absolute — Sets the column width to a fixed size in pixels

➤   AutoSize — Indicates that the size of the column should be managed by the TableLayoutPanel, which allocates width to the column depending on the widest control contained in the column

➤   Percent — Sets what percentage of the TableLayoutPanel to use for the width of the column

The Width property is only applicable if you do not choose a SizeType of AutoSize. It sets either the number of pixels for the width of the column (if the SizeType is Absolute) or the percentage width for the column (if the SizeType is Percent).

Similarly, for rows, there is a RowCount property to set the number of rows, and a RowStyles collection to manage the size of the rows. Each row in RowStyles has a SizeType, which works the same way as SizeType does for columns except that it manages the height of the row instead of the width of a column. The Height property is used for rows instead of a Width property, but it works in a corresponding way. Height is either the number of pixels (if SizeType is Absolute) or a percentage of the height of the TableLayoutPanel (if SizeType is Percent). If SizeType is AutoSize, then a row is sized to the height of the tallest control in the row.

An advanced UI layout technique is to first create a TableLayoutPanel, and then embed a FlowLayoutPanel in some of the cells of the TableLayoutPanel. This enables several controls to be contained in a cell and repositioned as the size of the cell changes.

A step-by-step example of using a TableLayoutPanel with an embedded FlowLayoutPanel is included in the next chapter in the section "Creating a Composite UserControl."

Panel and GroupBox Container Controls

Of course, not all applications need the dynamic layout of the containers just discussed. Windows Forms includes two controls that are static containers, in which the positions and layout of the contained controls are not adjusted at all.

These two containers, which have only minor differences, are the GroupBox control and the Panel control.

These two controls are similar in the following ways:

➤   They can serve as a container for other controls.

➤   If they are hidden or moved, then the action affects all the controls in the container.

The `GroupBox` control always has a border, and it can have a title, if needed. The border is always set the same way. Figure 14-17 shows a form with a `GroupBox` control containing three `RadioButton` controls.

The `Panel` control has three major differences from the `GroupBox` control:

➤   It has options for displaying its border in the `BorderStyle` property, with a default of no border.

➤   It has the capability to scroll if its `AutoScroll` property is set to `True`.

➤   It cannot set a title or caption.

Figure 14-18 shows a form containing a `Panel` control with its `BorderStyle` property set to `FixedSingle`, with scrolling turned on by setting `AutoScroll` to `True`, and with a `CheckedListBox` that is too big to display all at once (which forces the panel to show a scrollbar).

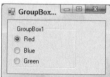

FIGURE 14-17

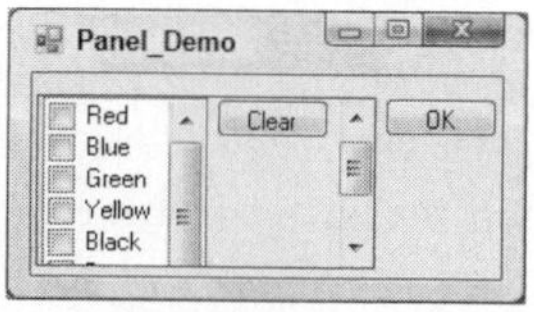

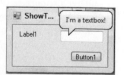

FIGURE 14-18

Extender Providers

Windows Forms has a family of components that can only be used in association with visual controls. These components are known as *extender providers*. They work with the Visual Studio IDE to cause new properties to appear in the Properties window for controls on the form.

Extender providers have no visible manifestation except in conjunction with other controls, so they appear in the component tray. The three extender providers available with Windows Forms 2.0 are the `HelpProvider`, the `ToolTip`, and the `ErrorProvider`. All three work in basically the same way. Each extender provider implements the properties that are "attached" to other controls. The best way to see how this works is to go through an example, so let's do that with a `ToolTip` component.

ToolTip

The `ToolTip` is the simplest of the built-in extender providers. It adds just one property to each control: `ToolTip` on ToolTip1 (assuming the `ToolTip` control has the default name of ToolTip1). This property works in very much the same way the `ToolTipText` property works in VB6, and in fact replaces it.

To see this in action, create a Windows Forms application. On the blank Form1 that is created for the project, place a couple of buttons. Take a look at the Properties window for Button1. Notice that it does not have a `ToolTip` property of any kind.

Drag over the `ToolTip` control, which will be placed in the component tray. Go back to the Properties window for Button1. A property named `ToolTip` on ToolTip1 is now present. Set any string value you like for this property.

Run the project and hover the mouse pointer over Button1. You will see a ToolTip containing the string value you entered for the `ToolTip` on ToolTip1 property.

Other properties of the `ToolTip` component enable you to control other characteristics of the ToolTip, such as the initial delay before the ToolTip appears.

New in Windows Forms 2.0 is the capability to change the shape of ToolTips to a "balloon." This is done by setting the `IsBalloon` property of the `ToolTip` component to `True`. Instead of a hovering rectangular ToolTip, the ToolTip has a rounded rectangular outline with a pointer to the control it is associated with, not unlike the dialog balloons in a comic strip. Figure 14-19 shows an example.

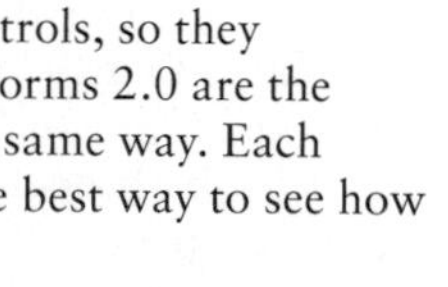

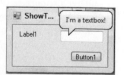

FIGURE 14-19

HelpProvider

The `HelpProvider` enables controls to have associated context-sensitive help available by pressing F1. When a `HelpProvider` is added to a form, all controls on the form get the new properties shown in Table 14-3, which show up in the controls' Properties window.

TABLE 14-3: Properties of the HelpProvider Component

PROPERTY	USAGE
HelpString on HelpProvider1	Provides a pop-up ToolTip for the control when F1 is pressed while the control has the focus. If the `HelpKeyword` and `HelpNavigator` properties (described later) are set to provide a valid reference to a help file, then the `HelpString` value is ignored in favor of the help file information.
HelpKeyword onHelpProvider1	Provides a keyword or other index to use in a help file for context-sensitive help for this control. The `HelpProvider1` control has a property that indicates which help file to use. This replaces the `HelpContextID` property in VB6.
HelpNavigator onHelpProvider1	Contains an enumerated value that determines how the value in `HelpKeyword` is used to refer to the help file. There are several possible values for displaying elements such as a topic, an index, or a table of contents in the help file.
ShowHelp onHelpProvider1	Determines whether the `HelpProvider` control is active for this control

Filling in the `HelpString` property immediately causes the control to provide ToolTip help when F1 is pressed while the control has the focus. The `HelpProvider` control has a property to point to a help file (either an HTML help file or a Win32 help file), and the help topic in the `HelpTopic` property points to a topic in this file.

ErrorProvider

The `ErrorProvider` component presents a simple, visual way to indicate to a user that a control on a form has an error associated with it. The added property for controls on the form when an `ErrorProvider` is used is called `Error` on ErrorProvider1 (assuming the `ErrorProvider` has the default name of ErrorProvider1). Setting this property to a string value causes the error icon to appear next to a control. In addition, the text appears in a ToolTip if the mouse hovers over the error icon.

Figure 14-20 shows a screen with several text boxes, one of which has an error icon next to it (with a ToolTip). The error icon and ToolTip are displayed and managed by an `ErrorProvider`.

The `ErrorProvider` component's default icon is a red circle with an exclamation point. When the `Error` property for the text box is set, the icon blinks for a few moments, and hovering over the icon causes the ToolTip to appear. Writing your own code to set the `Error` property is explained in the section "Working with Extender Providers in Code."

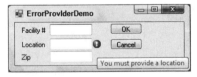

FIGURE 14-20

Properties of Extender Providers

In addition to providing other controls with properties, extender providers also have properties of their own. For example, the `ErrorProvider` has a property named `BlinkStyle`. When it is set to `NeverBlink`, the blinking of the icon is stopped for all controls affected by the `ErrorProvider`.

Other properties of the `ErrorProvider` enable you to change things such as the icon used and where the icon appears in relation to the field containing the error. For instance, you might want the icon to appear on the left side of a field instead of the default right side. You can also have multiple error providers on your form. For example, you might wish to give users a warning, rather than an error. A second error provider with a yellow icon could be used for this feature.

Working with Extender Providers in Code

You can set the `Error` property in the previous example with the Properties window, but this is not very useful for on-the-fly error management. However, setting the `Error` property in code is not done with typical property syntax. By convention, extender providers have a method for each extended property they need to set, and the arguments for the method include the associated control and the property setting. To set the `Error` property in the previous example, the following code was used:

```
ErrorProvider1.SetError(txtName, "You must provide a location!")
```

The name of the method to set a property is the word `Set` prefixed to the name of the property. The preceding line of code shows that the `Error` property is set with the `SetError` method of the `ErrorProvider`.

There is a corresponding method to get the value of the property, and it is named with `Get` prefixed to the name of the property. To determine the current `Error` property setting for `txtName`, you would use the following line:

```
sError = ErrorProvider1.GetError(txtName)
```

Similar syntax is used to manipulate any of the properties managed by an extender provider. The discussion of the `ToolTip` provider earlier mentioned setting the `ToolTip` property in the Properties window. To set that same property in code, the syntax would be as follows:

```
ToolTip1.SetToolTip(Button1, "New tooltip for Button1")
```

Advanced Capabilities for Data Entry

Windows Forms 2.0 includes some advanced capabilities for data entry that were not available in earlier versions. `TextBox` and `ComboBox` controls in 2.0 have autocompletion capabilities, and a `MaskedTextbox` control allows entry of formatted input such as phone numbers.

Autocompletion

Responsive user interfaces help users accomplish their purposes, thereby making them more productive. One classic way to do this is with *autocompletion*.

An example of autocompletion is IntelliSense in Visual Studio. Using IntelliSense, a user only has to type in a few letters, and Visual Studio presents a list of probable entries matching those letters. If the desired entry is found, the user only needs to select it, rather than type the entire entry.

Autocompletion is available in Windows Forms 2.0 with text boxes and combo boxes. Both use a set of properties to control how autocompletion works and from where the list of entries available to the user comes.

To see autocompletion in action, create a Windows application project. Drag a `TextBox` control from the Toolbox onto the blank Form1 created for the project. Set the AutoCompleteMode for the text box to Suggest in the Properties window. Then set the AutoCompleteSource to CustomSource. Finally, click the button in the settings window for AutoCompleteCustomSource. You'll see a window for adding entries that is very similar to the window for entering items for a list box or combo box.

Enter the following items into the dialog:

```
Holder
Holland
Hollis
Holloway
Holly
Holstein
Holt
```

Start the project and type **Hol** into the text box. As soon as you start typing, a drop-down will appear that contains entries matching what you've typed, including all seven elements in the list. If you then type another 1, the list will decrease to the four elements that begin with Holl. If you then type an o, the list will contain only the entry Holloway.

The `AutoCompleteMode` has two other modes. The `Append` mode does not automatically present a drop-down, but instead appends the rest of the closest matching entry to the text in the `Textbox` or `ComboBox`, and highlights the untyped characters. This allows the closest matching entry to be placed in the text area without the user explicitly selecting an entry.

The `SuggestAppend` mode combines `Suggest` and `Append`. The current best match is displayed in the text area, and the drop-down with other possibilities is automatically displayed. This mode is the one most like IntelliSense.

You can also set the list of items to be included in the autocompletion list at runtime, which is the most common usage scenario. A list of items from a database table would typically be loaded for autocompletion. Here is typical code to create a list of items and attach the list to a `ComboBox`:

Available for download on Wrox.com

```
Dim autoCompleteStringCollection1 As New AutoCompleteStringCollection
Dim nReturn As Integer
nReturn = autoCompleteStringCollection1.Add("Holder")
nReturn = autoCompleteStringCollection1.Add("Holland")
nReturn = autoCompleteStringCollection1.Add("Hollis")
nReturn = autoCompleteStringCollection1.Add("Holloway")
ComboBox1.AutoCompleteCustomSource = autoCompleteStringCollection1
```

Code snippet from AutoComplete

For this sample to work properly, the `ComboBox` control's `AutoCompleteSource` property must be set to `CustomSource`.

Several built-in lists are available for use with autocompletion. Instead of setting `AutoCompleteSource` to `CustomSource`, you can set it to sources such as files in the file system, or URLs recently used in Internet Explorer. See the documentation for `AutoCompleteSource` for additional options; or, if you are using `AutoCompleteSource` in code, IntelliSense will show the options available.

MaskedTextbox Control

The `MaskedTextbox` control allows entry of information that conforms to a "mask" which determines what is and is not valid in each character position. You can set the `Mask` property in the Properties window, but you can also click the smart tag (right-pointing arrow) on the right side of the `MaskedTextbox`. In both cases, you can either construct a mask manually or select one of the commonly used masks from a list.

If you want to create your own mask, you need to design it based on the set of formatting characters described in Table 14-4.

TABLE 14-4: Mask Characters Available in the MaskedTextBox Control

MASK CHARACTER	DESCRIPTION
#	Digit placeholder
.	Decimal placeholder. The actual character used is the one specified as the decimal placeholder in your international settings. This character is treated as a literal for masking purposes.
,	Thousands separator. The actual character used is the one specified as the thousands separator in your international settings. This character is treated as a literal for masking purposes.
:	Time separator. The actual character used is the one specified as the time separator in your international settings. This character is treated as a literal for masking purposes.
/	Date separator. The actual character used is the one specified as the date separator in your international settings. This character is treated as a literal for masking purposes.

MASK CHARACTER	DESCRIPTION
\	Treat the next character in the mask string as a literal. This enables you to include the #, &, A, and ? characters in the mask. This character is treated as a literal for masking purposes.
&	Character placeholder. Valid values for this placeholder are ANSI characters in the following ranges: 32–126 and 128–255.
>	Converts all the characters that follow to uppercase
<	Converts all the characters that follow to lowercase
A	Alphanumeric character placeholder (entry required); e.g., a–z, A–Z, or 0–9
a	Alphanumeric character placeholder (entry optional)
9	Digit placeholder (entry optional); e.g., 0–9
C	Character or space placeholder (entry optional). This operates exactly like the & placeholder and ensures compatibility with Microsoft Access.
?	Letter placeholder; e.g., a–z or A–Z
Literal	All other symbols are displayed as literals — that is, as themselves.

Literal characters are simply inserted automatically by the `MaskedTextbox` control. If you have literal characters for the parentheses in a phone number, for example, the user need not type these in order for them to show up in the text area of the control.

As an example of a mask, suppose that you have an account number that must consist of exactly two uppercase letters and five digits. You could construct a mask of >??00000. The first character forces all letters to uppercase. The two question marks specify two required alphabetic characters, and the five zeros specify five required digits.

Once you have set the `Mask` for the `MaskedTextbox`, all entries in the control will be coerced to the mask pattern. Keystrokes that don't conform will be thrown away.

Validating Data Entry

Most controls that you place on a form require that its content be validated in some way. A `TextBox` might require a numeric value only or simply require that the user provide any value and not leave it blank.

The `ErrorProvider` component discussed earlier makes this task significantly easier than it was in previous versions. To illustrate the use of an `ErrorProvider` in data validation, create a new Windows Application project and change the `Text` property for the blank `Form1` to `Data Validation Demo`. Then place two `TextBox` controls on the form that will hold a user ID and password, as shown in Figure 14-21.

FIGURE 14-21

Name the first text box `UserNameTextBox` and name the second text box `PasswordTextBox`. Drag an `ErrorProvider` onto the form, which will cause it to appear in the component tray. In the next section, you'll add the code that simply verifies that the user has filled in both text boxes and then provides a visual indication, via the `ErrorProvider`, if either of the fields has been left blank.

The Validating Event

The `Validating` event fires when your control begins its validation. It is here that you need to both place the code that validates your control and set a visual indication for an error. Insert the following code to see this in action:

Available for download on Wrox.com

```
Private Sub UserNameTextBox_Validating(ByVal sender As Object, _
                    ByVal e As System.ComponentModel.CancelEventArgs) _
                    Handles UserNameTextBox.Validating
    If userNameTextbox.Text = "" Then
        ErrorProvider1.SetError(UserNameTextBox, "User Name cannot be blank")
```

```
        Else
            ErrorProvider1.SetError(UserNameTextBox, "")
        End If
    End Sub
    Private Sub PasswordTextBox_Validating(ByVal sender As Object, _
                        ByVal e As System.ComponentModel.CancelEventArgs) _
                        Handles PasswordTextBox.Validating
        If passwordTextbox.Text = "" Then
            ErrorProvider1.SetError(PasswordTextBox, "Password cannot be blank")
        Else
            ErrorProvider1.SetError(PasswordTextBox, "")
        End If
    End Sub
```

Code snippet from Data_Validation

Run the program and then tab between the controls without entering any text to get the error message. You'll see an icon blink next to each of the `TextBox` controls; and if you hover over an error icon, you'll see the appropriate error message.

There is also a `Validated` event that fires after a control's `Validating` event. It can be used, for example, to do a final check after other events have manipulated the contents of the control.

The CausesValidation Property

The `CausesValidation` property determines whether the control will participate in the validation events on the form. A control with a `CausesValidation` setting of `True` (it is `True` by default) has two effects:

➤ The control's `Validating`/`Validated` events fire when appropriate.

➤ The control triggers the `Validating`/`Validated` events for other controls.

It is important to understand that the validation events fire for a control not when the focus is lost but when the focus shifts to a control that has a `CausesValidation` value of `True`.

To see this effect, set the `CausesValidation` property of the Password text box in your application to `False` (be sure to leave it `True` for the User ID and OK button). When you run the program, tab off the User ID text box and again to the OK button. Notice that it isn't until the focus reaches the OK button that the validating event of the User ID text box fires. Also notice that the validating event of the Password field never fires.

Ultimately, if you determine that the control is not valid, you need to specify what happens. That may include setting the focus to the control that needs attention (as well as indicating the error with an `ErrorProvider`).

Toolbars and the ToolStrip Control

Earlier versions of Windows Forms (prior to 2.0) had a control named `Toolbar`, but this has been superseded by the `ToolStrip` control in Windows Forms 2.0. `ToolStrip` has many improvements. It supports movement to sides of a form other than the place where it was laid out, and you have much more flexibility in placing items on the toolbar. It also integrates better with the IDE to assist in creating toolbars and manipulating the many settings available.

The `ToolStrip` does not sit alone on a form. When a `ToolStrip` is dragged onto a form, the container that actually sits on the form is called a `RaftingContainer`. This container handles the positioning so that the toolbar created by a `ToolStrip` can be dragged to other parts of the form.

The `ToolStrip` sits inside the `RaftingContainer` and is the container for toolbar elements. It handles the sizing of the toolbar, movement of toolbar elements, and other general toolbar functions.

The items on the toolbar must be from a set of controls specially designed to serve as toolbar items. All of these items inherit from the `ToolStripItem` base class. The controls available for toolbar items are described in Table 14-5.

TABLE 14-5: Controls Available for Inclusion in a ToolStrip Control

CONTROL	DESCRIPTION
ToolStripButton	Replicates the functionality of a regular Button for a toolbar
ToolStripLabel	Replicates the functionality of a regular Label for a toolbar
ToolStripSeparator	A visual toolbar element that displays a vertical bar to separate other groups of elements (no user interaction)
ToolStripComboBox	Replicates the functionality of a regular ComboBox for a toolbar. This item must be contained within a ToolStripControlHost (see below).
ToolStripTextBox	Replicates the functionality of a regular TextBox for a toolbar. This item must be contained within a ToolStripControlHost (see below).
ToolStripControlHost	A hosting container for other controls that reside on a ToolStrip. It can host any of the following controls: ToolStripComboBox, ToolStripTextBox, other Windows Forms controls, or user controls.
ToolStripDropDownItem	A hosting container for toolbar elements that feature drop-down functionality. It can host a ToolStripMenuItem, a ToolStripSplitButton, or a ToolStripDropDownButton.
ToolStripDropDownButton	A button that supports drop-down functionality. Clicking the button shows a list of options from which the user must select the one desired. This item is used when the user needs to select from a group of options, none of which is used a large majority of the time.
ToolStripSplitButton	A combination of a regular button and a drop-down button. This item is often used when there is a frequently used option to click but you also need to offer users other options that are less frequently used.
ToolStripMenuItem	A selectable option displayed on a menu or context menu. This item is typically used with the menu controls that inherit from the ToolStrip, discussed later in this chapter in the section "Menus."

Note that almost any control can be hosted on a toolbar using the ToolStripControlHost. However, for buttons, text boxes, labels, and combo boxes, it is much easier to use the ToolStrip version instead of the standard version.

Creating a ToolStrip and Adding Toolbar Elements

Try an example to see how to build a toolbar using the ToolStrip control. Create a new Windows application. Add a ToolStrip control to the blank Form1 that is included with the new project. Make the form about twice its default width so that you have plenty of room to see the ToolStrip as you work on it.

The ToolStrip is positioned at the top of the form by default. It does not contain any elements, although if you highlight the ToolStrip control in the component tray, a "menu designer" will appear in the ToolStrip.

The easiest way to add multiple elements to the ToolStrip is to use the Items Collection Editor for the ToolStrip. Highlight the ToolStrip in the component tray and click the button in the Properties window for the Items property. You'll see the Items Collection Editor as a dialog, as shown in Figure 14-22.

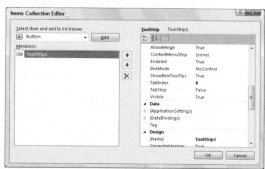

FIGURE 14-22

The drop-down in the upper-left corner contains the different types of items that can be placed on the toolbar. The names in the drop-down are the same as the names in the table of controls except that the "Toolstrip" prefix is not present. Add one each of the following types, with the setting specified:

➤ `Button` — Set the `Text` property to `Go`. Set the `DisplayStyle` property to `Text`.

➤ `ComboBox` — Leave the `Text` property blank. Set `DropDownStyle` to `DropDownList`. Open the Items dialog and add the names of some colors.

➤ `SplitButton` — Set the `Text` property to `Options`. Set the `DisplayStyle` property to `Text`.

➤ `TextBox` — Leave the `Text` property blank.

Click OK. The `ToolStrip` on the design surface will look like the one shown in Figure 14-23.

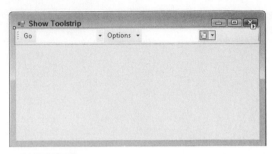

You can now handle events on any of these toolbar elements the same way you would any other controls. You can double-click to get a Click event routine or access the event routines through the drop-downs in the Code Editor.

To make the `ToolStrip` more dynamic, it must be embedded in a `ToolStripContainer`. You can do that manually by dragging one over and putting the `ToolStrip` in it, but it's easier to click the smart tag

FIGURE 14-23

on the `ToolStrip` and then select Embed in ToolStripContainer. This causes a `ToolStripContainer` to appear on your form. Set the `Dock` property for the `ToolStripContainer` to `Fill` and it will provide a surface for the `ToolStrip` that includes all four edges of the form.

Run your program. Using the mouse, grab the dotted handle on the far left edge of the toolbar. If you drag this to the right, then the toolbar will be repositioned. If you drag it to other positions on the form, then the entire toolbar will dock to different edges of the form.

Allowing Users to Move Toolbar Elements

By default, the `AllowItemReorder` property of the `ToolStrip` is set to `False`. If you change that to `True`, then the elements on the toolbar can be moved around in relation to one another (reordered) at runtime.

Change the `AllowItemReorder` property to `True` for the `ToolStrip` and run your program again. Hold down the Alt key and drag elements on the toolbar around. They will assume new positions on the toolbar when you drop them.

Creating a Standard Set of Toolbar Elements

If you need a toolbar that has the typical visual elements for cut, copy, paste, and so on, it is not necessary to create the elements. The designer will do it for you.

Create a new form in your project and drag a `ToolStrip` onto it. As before, it will be positioned at the top and will not contain any elements. With the `ToolStrip` highlighted in the component tray, click the `Item` property. Below the properties in the Properties window, a link named Insert Standard Items will appear. Click that link; elements will be inserted into the `ToolStrip`, making it look like the one shown in Figure 14-24.

FIGURE 14-24

Menus

Menus are added to a form in Windows Forms 2.0 by dragging controls called `MenuStrip` or `ContextMenuStrip` onto your form. `MenuStrip` implements a standard Windows-style menu at the top of the form. `ContextMenuStrip` enables a pop-up menu with a right mouse button click.

These controls are actually subclasses of the `ToolStrip`, so much of the information you learned earlier in this chapter about working with the `ToolStrip` also applies to the `MenuStrip` and `ContextMenuStrip`. When dragged onto the form, these controls appear in the component tray just as the `ToolStrip` does, and you access the designer for these controls the same way you do for the `ToolStrip`. However, because these are menus, the most common way to add items is to type them directly into the menu designer that appears when the control is highlighted.

The menu designer is extremely intuitive — the menu appears on your form just as it would at runtime, and you simply fill in the menu items you need. Each item can be renamed, and each can have a Click event associated with it.

Adding Standard Items to a Menu

If your form's menu needs to have the standard top-level options (File, Edit, and so on) and the typical options under these items, then you can have all these usual options inserted for you automatically.

To see this capability in action, drag a `MenuStrip` to a form and then click the smart tag (the right arrow at the right edge) for the `MenuStrip` to bring up the Items Collection Editor. Click the Insert Standard Items link at the bottom of the dialog.

Icons and Checkmarks for Menu Items

Each menu item has an `Image` property. Setting this property to an image causes the image to appear on the left side of the text for the menu option. You can see this property in use by looking at the standard items inserted in the preceding example. The File ➪ Save option has an icon of a diskette, which is produced by setting the image property of that item.

Items can also have check marks beside them. This is done by changing the `Checked` property of the item to `True`. You can do this at design time or runtime, enabling you to manipulate the check marks on menus as necessary.

Context Menus

To implement a context menu for a form or any control on a form, drag a `ContextMenuStrip` to the form and add the menu items. Items are added and changed the same way as they are with the `MenuStrip`.

To hook a context menu to a control, set the control's `ContextMenuStrip` property to the `ContextMenuStrip` menu control you want to use. Then, when your program runs and you right-click in the control, the context menu will pop up.

Dynamically Manipulating Menus at Runtime

Menus can be adjusted at runtime using code. Context menus, for instance, may need to vary according to the state of your form. The following walk-through shows how to add a new menu item to a context menu and how to clear the menu items.

Create a new Windows application. On the blank Form1 for the project, drag over a `MenuStrip` control. Using the menu designer, type in a top-level menu option of File. Under that option, type in options for Open and Save.

Now place a button on the form. Double-click the button to get its Click event, and place the following code into the event:

```
Dim NewItem As New ToolStripMenuItem
NewItem.Text = "Save As"
' Set any other properties of the menu item you like.
FileToolStripMenuItem.DropDownItems.Add(NewItem)
AddHandler NewItem.Click, _
    AddressOf Me.NewMenuItem_Click
```

Code snippet from AddMenuItem

Add the event handler referenced in this code at the bottom of the form's code:

```
Private Sub NewMenuItem_Click(ByVal sender As System.Object, _
                             ByVal e As System.EventArgs)
    MessageBox.Show("New menu item clicked!")
End Sub
```

Code snippet from AddMenuItem

If you now run the program and look at the menu, it will only have File and Save options. Clicking the button will cause a new Save As item to be added to the menu, and it will be hooked to the event routine called `NewMenuItem_Click`.

Common Dialogs

Windows Forms provides you with seven common dialog controls. Each control opens a predefined form that is identical to the one used by the operating system.

These dialogs cannot be shown modeless. They have a `ShowDialog` method to show them modally. That method returns one of the standard `DialogResult` values, as discussed earlier in this chapter.

OpenFileDialog and SaveFileDialog

These two controls open the standard dialog control that enables users to select files on the system. They are quite similar except for the buttons and labels that appear on the actual dialog box when it is shown to the user. Each prompts the user for a file on the system by allowing the user to browse the files and folders available.

Use the properties described in Table 14-6 to set up the dialogs.

TABLE 14-6: Important Properties of the OpenFileDialog and SaveFileDialog Controls

PROPERTY	DESCRIPTION
InitialDirectory	Defines the initial location that is displayed when the dialog opens, e.g., `OpenFileDialog1.InitialDirectory = "C:\Program Files"`
Filter	String that defines the Files of Type list. Separate items using the pipe character. Items are entered in pairs; the first of each pair is the description of the file type, and the second half is the file wildcard, e.g., `OpenFileDialog1 .Filter = "All Files$|*.* |Text Files|*.txt|Rich Text Files|*.rtf"`
FilterIndex	Integer that specifies the default filter item to use when the dialog box opens. For example, with the preceding filter used, defaults to text files as follows: `OpenFileDialog1.FilterIndex = 2`
RestoreDirectory	Boolean value that, when `True`, forces the system's default directory to be restored to the location it was in when the dialog was first opened. This is `False` by default.
Filename	Holds the full name of the file that the user selected, including the path
ShowDialog	Displays the dialog

The following code opens the standard dialog box, asking the user to select a file that currently exists on the system, and simply displays the choice in a message box upon return:

```
OpenFileDialog1.InitialDirectory = "C:\"
OpenFileDialog1.Filter = "Text files|*.txt|All files|*.*"
OpenFileDialog1.FilterIndex = 1
OpenFileDialog1.RestoreDirectory = True
If OpenFileDialog1.ShowDialog() = Windows.Forms.DialogResult.OK Then
    MessageBox.Show("You selected """ & OpenFileDialog1.FileName & """")
End If
```

Code snippet from CommonDialogDemo

ColorDialog Control

As the name implies, this control gives the user a dialog box from which to select a color. Use the properties described in Table 14-7 to set up the dialog boxes as follows:

```
ColorDialog1.Color = TextBox1.BackColor
ColorDialog1.AllowFullOpen = True
If ColorDialog1.ShowDialog()= Windows.Forms.DialogResult.OK Then
    TextBox1.BackColor = ColorDialog1.Color
End If
```

Code snippet from CommonDialogDemo

TABLE 14-7: Important Properties of the ColorDialog Control

PROPERTY	DESCRIPTION
Color	The System.Drawing.Color that the user selected. You can also use this to set the initial color selected when the user opens the dialog.
AllowFullOpen	Boolean value that when True, allows the user to select any color. If False, then the user is restricted to the set of default colors.
ShowDialog	Displays the dialog

FontDialog Control

This control displays the standard dialog box, allowing users to select a font. Use the properties described in Table 14-8 to set up the dialog boxes.

TABLE 14-8: Important Properties of the FontDialog Control

PROPERTY	COMMENTS
Font	The System.Drawing.Font that the user selected. Also used to set the initial font.
ShowEffects	Boolean value that when True, makes the dialog box display the text effects options of underline and strikeout
ShowColor	Boolean value that when True, makes the dialog box display the combo box of the font colors. The ShowEffects property must be True for this to have an effect.
FixedPitchOnly	Boolean value that when True, limits the list of font options to only those that have a fixed pitch (such as Courier or Lucida console).
ShowDialog	Displays the dialog

Using these properties looks like this:

```
FontDialog1.Font = TextBox1.Font
FontDialog1.ShowColor = True
FontDialog1.ShowEffects = True
FontDialog1.FixedPitchOnly = False
If FontDialog1.ShowDialog()= Windows.Forms.DialogResult.OK Then
    TextBox1.Font = FontDialog1.Font
End If
```

Printer Dialog Controls

There are three more common dialog controls: PrintDialog, PrintPreviewDialog, and PageSetup-Dialog. They can all be used to control the output of a file to the printer, and you can use these in conjunction with the PrintDocument component to run and control print jobs.

Drag and Drop

Implementing a drag-and-drop operation in the .NET Framework is accomplished by a short sequence of events. Typically, it begins in a `MouseDown` event of one control, and always ends with the `DragDrop` event of another.

To demonstrate the process, begin with a new Windows application. Add two list boxes to your form, and add three items to the first using the Items Property Designer. This application enables you to drag the items from one list box into the other.

The first step in making drag and drop work is specifying whether or not a control will accept a drop. By default, all controls reject such behavior and do not respond to any attempt by the user to drop something onto them. In this case, set the `AllowDrop` property of the second list box (the one without the items added) to `True`.

The next item of business is to invoke the drag-and-drop operation. This is typically done in the `MouseDown` event of the control containing the data you want to drag (although you're not restricted to it). The `DoDragDrop` method is used to start the operation. This method defines the data that will be dragged and the type of dragging that is allowed. Here, you'll drag the text of the selected list box item, and permit both a move and a copy of the data to occur.

Switch over to the code window of your form and add the following code to the `MouseDown` event of ListBox1:

```vb
Private Sub ListBox1_MouseDown(ByVal sender As Object, _
                    ByVal e As System.Windows.Forms.MouseEventArgs) _
                    Handles ListBox1.MouseDown
    Dim DragDropResult As DragDropEffects
    If e.Button = MouseButtons.Left Then
        DragDropResult = ListBox1.DoDragDrop( _
                    ListBox1.Items(ListBox1.SelectedIndex), _
                    DragDropEffects.Move Or DragDropEffects.Copy)
        ' Leave some room here to check the result of the operation
        ' (You'll fill it in next).
    End If
End Sub
```

Code snippet from DragAndDropSampleScreen

Notice the comment about leaving room to check the result of the operation. You'll fill that in shortly. For now, calling the `DoDragDrop` method has gotten you started.

The next step involves the recipient of the data — in this case, ListBox2. Two events here are important to monitor: `DragEnter` and `DragDrop`.

As you can guess by the name, the `DragEnter` event occurs when the user first moves over the recipient control. The `DragEnter` event has a parameter of type `DragEventArgs` that contains an `Effect` property and a `KeyState` property.

The `Effect` property enables you to set the display of the drop icon for the user to indicate whether a move or a copy occurs when the mouse button is released. The `KeyState` property enables you to determine the state of the Ctrl, Alt, and Shift keys. It is a Windows standard that when both a move or a copy can occur, a user indicates the copy action by holding down the Ctrl key. Therefore, in this event, you check the `KeyState` property and use it to determine how to set the `Effect` property.

Add the following code to the `DragEnter` event of ListBox2:

```vb
Private Sub ListBox2_DragEnter(ByVal sender As Object, _
                    ByVal e As DragEventArgs) _
                    Handles ListBox2.DragOver
    If e.KeyState = 9 Then ' Control key
        e.Effect = DragDropEffects.Copy
```

```
    Else
        e.Effect = DragDropEffects.Move
    End If
End Sub
```

Code snippet from DragAndDropSampleScreen

Note that you can also use the `DragOver` event if you want, but it will fire continuously as the mouse moves over the target control. In this situation, you only need to trap the initial entry of the mouse into the control.

The final step in the operation occurs when the user lets go of the mouse button to drop the data at its destination. This is captured by the `DragDrop` event. The parameter contains a property holding the data that is being dragged. It's now a simple process of placing it into the recipient control as follows:

Available for download on Wrox.com

```
Private Sub ListBox2_DragDrop(ByVal sender As Object, _
                        ByVal e As System.Windows.Forms.DragEventArgs) _
                        Handles ListBox2.DragDrop
    ListBox2.Items.Add(e.Data.GetData(DataFormats.Text))
End Sub
```

Code snippet from DragAndDropSampleScreen

One last step: You can't forget to manipulate ListBox1 if the drag and drop was a move. Here's where you'll fill in the hole you left in the `MouseDown` event of ListBox1. Once the `DragDrop` has occurred, the initial call that invoked the procedure returns a result indicating what ultimately happened. Go back to the `ListBox1_MouseDown` event and enhance it to remove the item from Listbox1 if it was moved (and not simply copied):

Available for download on Wrox.com

```
Private Sub ListBox1_MouseDown(ByVal sender As Object, _
                ByVal e As System.Windows.Forms.MouseEventArgs) _
                Handles ListBox1.MouseDown
    Dim DragDropResult As DragDropEffects
    If e.Button = MouseButtons.Left Then
        DragDropResult = ListBox1.DoDragDrop( _
                    ListBox1.Items(ListBox1.SelectedIndex), _
                    DragDropEffects.Move Or DragDropEffects.Copy)
        ' If operation is a move (and not a copy), then remove then
        ' remove the item from the first list box.
        If DragDropResult = DragDropEffects.Move Then
            ListBox1.Items.RemoveAt(ListBox1.SelectedIndex)
        End If
    End If
End Sub
```

Code snippet from DragAndDropSampleScreen

When you're done, run your application and drag the items from Listbox1 into Listbox2. Try a copy by holding down the Ctrl key when you do it. The screenshot in Figure 14-25 shows the result after Item1 has been moved and Item3 has been copied a few times.

FIGURE 14-25

Summary of Standard Windows.Forms Controls

This section lists the basic controls that are generally quite intuitive and don't warrant a full example to explain.

➤ Button

➤ Can display both an icon and text simultaneously. The image is set using the `Image` property (instead of `Picture`). The image position can be set using the `ImageAlign` property (left, right, center, and so on).

➤ Text on the button can be aligned using the `TextAlign` property.

> ➤ Can have different appearances using the FlatStyle property

> ➤ Has AcceptButton and CancelButton properties to allow a button click on an Enter keypress or an Escape keypress, respectively

➤ CheckBox

> ➤ Can appear as a toggle button using the Appearance property

> ➤ Check box and text can be positioned within the defined area using the CheckAlign and TextAlign properties.

> ➤ Checked value is stored in the CheckState property.

> ➤ Has a FlatStyle property controlling the appearance of the check box

➤ CheckedListBox

> ➤ A list box that has check boxes beside each item (see ListBox)

➤ ComboBox

> ➤ Like the new ListBox control, it can now hold a collection of objects instead of an array of strings (see ListBox).

> ➤ Now has a MaxDropDownItems property that specifies how many items to display when the list opens

➤ DateTimePicker

➤ DomainUpDown

> ➤ A simple one-line version of a list box

> ➤ Can hold a collection of objects and will display the ToString result of an item in the collection

> ➤ Can wrap around the list to give a continuous scrolling effect using the Wrap property

➤ HScrollBar

➤ ImageList

➤ Label

> ➤ Can display an image and text

> ➤ Has automatic sizing capability. Set the AutoSize property to True for automatic horizontal sizing (this is the default value of the property).

> ➤ Can specify whether a mnemonic should be interpreted (If UseMnemonic is True, then the first ampersand (&) in the Text property specifies underlining the following character and having it react to the Alt key shortcut, placing the focus on the next control in the tab order that can hold focus, such as a text box.)

➤ LinkLabel

> ➤ Identical to a label, but behaves like a hyperlink with extra properties, such as LinkBehavior (for example, HoverUnderline), LinkColor, and ActiveLinkColor

➤ ListBox

> ➤ A list box can now hold a collection of objects, instead of an array of strings. Use the DisplayMember property to specify what property of the objects to display in the list, and the ValueMember property to specify what property of the objects to use as the values of the list items. (This is similar to the ItemData array from previous versions.) For example, a combo box could store a collection of employee objects, and display to the user the Name property of each, as well as retrieve the EmployeeId as the value of the item currently selected.

➤ ListView

> ➤ Sub-items can have their own font display properties.

➤ MonthCalendar

➤ NotifyIcon

> ➤ Gives a form an icon in the system tray

> ➤ ToolTip of the icon is set by the Text property of the control.

> ➤ Pop-up menus are set using a ContextMenu control (see the "Menus" section earlier in chapter).

➤ NumericUpDown

> ➤ A single-line text box that displays a number and up/down buttons that increment/decrement the number when clicked

➤ PictureBox

> ➤ Image property defines the graphic to display instead of Picture.

> ➤ Use the SizeMode property to autostretch or center the picture.

➤ ProgressBar

> ➤ Has a Step method that automatically increments the value of the progress bar by the amount defined in the Step property

➤ RadioButton

> ➤ Use CheckAlign and TextAlign to specify where the radio button and text appear in relation to the area of the control.

➤ RichTextBox

> ➤ Use the Lines array to get or set specific individual lines of the control's text.

➤ TabControl

> ➤ Has a TabPages collection of TabPage objects. A TabPage object is a subclass of the Panel control specialized for use in the TabControl.

> ➤ Uses the Appearance property to display the tabs as buttons, if desired (formerly the Style property of the TabStrip control)

➤ TextBox

> ➤ Now has a CharacterCasing property that can automatically adjust the text entered into uppercase or lowercase

> ➤ The ReadOnly property is used to prevent the text from being edited.

> ➤ Now has Cut, Copy, Paste, Undo, and ClearUndo methods

➤ Timer

> ➤ Special version of Timer that conforms to the Windows Forms threading model (Don't use Timer classes from other namespaces in Windows Forms.)

➤ TrackBar

➤ TreeView

➤ VScrollBar

➤ WebBrowser

> ➤ Even smart client applications often need to display HTML or browse websites. The WebBrowser control is in an intelligent wrapper around the browsing control built in to Windows.

Handling Groups of Related Controls

Occasionally it is necessary for a set of controls to be treated as a group. For example, a set of RadioButton controls might be related, and you might want to channel the Click event for all the controls in the group to the same event handler.

To have a single method handle multiple events from controls, you must attach those controls' events to the handler. You can do that with multiple controls specified in a `Handles` clause or by using `AddHandler` for each control. Unless controls are being added to your form on-the-fly, using additional controls in the `Handles` clause is usually preferable. Here is an example of a declaration for a Click event that handles three `RadioButton` controls:

```
Private Sub RadioButton3_Click(ByVal sender As Object, _
        ByVal e As EventArgs) _
        Handles RadioButton1.Click, _
        RadioButton2.Click, RadioButton3.Click
```

There is no `Index` property as in old-style control arrays in VB6. Instead, simply use the `Sender` parameter of the event handler to determine which control originated the event.

A simple example is helpful to see how to set this up. Create a new Windows application and set the `Text` property of the blank Form1 to Add Dynamic Control Demo. Then add two buttons to the form, as shown in Figure 14-26.

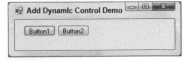

FIGURE 14-26

Double-click Button1 to switch over to the code that handles the `Button1.Click` event. To make this method respond to the `Button2.Click` event as well, simply add the `Button2.Click` event handler to the end of the `Handles` list, and then add some simple code to display a message box indicating what button triggered the event:

Available for download on Wrox.com

```
' Note the change in the method name from Button1_Click. Since
' two objects are hooked up, it's a good idea to avoid having the
' method specifically named to a single object.
Private Sub Button_Click(ByVal sender As System.Object, _
            ByVal e As System.EventArgs) _
        Handles Button1.Click, Button2.Click
    Dim buttonClicked As Button
    buttonClicked = CType(sender, Button)
    ' Tell the world what button was clicked
    MessageBox.Show("You clicked " & buttonClicked.Text)
End Sub
```

Code snippet from AddDynamicControl

Run the program and click the two buttons. Each one will trigger the event and display a message box with the appropriate text from the button that was clicked.

Adding Controls at Runtime

You may add controls to a form at runtime. Here is an example that enhances the preceding program to add a third button dynamically at runtime. Add another button to your form that will trigger the addition of Button3, as shown in Figure 14-27.

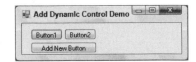

FIGURE 14-27

Name the new button **AddNewButton** and add the following code to handle its `Click` event:

Available for download on Wrox.com

```
Private Sub AddNewButton_Click(ByVal sender As System.Object, _
                ByVal e As System.EventArgs) _
                Handles addNewButton.Click
    Dim newButton As Button
    ' Create the new control
    newButton = New Button()
    ' Set it up on the form
    newButton.Location = New System.Drawing.Point(184, 12)
    newButton.Size = New System.Drawing.Size(75, 23)
    newButton.Text = "Button3"
    ' Add it to the form's controls collection
```

```
    Me.Controls.Add(newButton)
    ' Hook up the event handler.
    AddHandler newButton.Click, AddressOf Me.Button_Click
End  Sub
```

Code snippet from AddDynamicControl

When the `AddNewButton` button is clicked, the code creates a new button, sets its size and position, and then does two essential things. First, it adds the button to the form's controls collection; second, it connects the `Click` event of the button to the method that handles it.

With this done, run the program and click the `AddNewButton` button. `Button3` will appear. Then, simply click `Button3` to prove that the `Click` event is being handled. You should get the result shown in Figure 14-28.

FIGURE 14-28

OTHER HANDY PROGRAMMING TIPS

Here are some other handy programming tips for using Windows Forms:

➤ **Switch the focus to a control** — Use the `.Focus` method. To set the focus to TextBox1, for example, use the following code:

```
TextBox1.Focus()
```

➤ **Quickly determine the container control or parent form** — With the use of group boxes and panels, controls are often contained many times. You can now use the `FindForm` method to immediately get a reference to the form. Use the `GetContainerControl` method to access the immediate parent of a control.

➤ **Traverse the tab order** — Use the `GetNextControl` method of any control to get a reference to the next control on the form in the tab order.

➤ **Convert client coordinates to screen coordinates (and back)** — Want to know where a control is in screen coordinates? Use the `PointToScreen` method. Convert back using the `PointToClient` method.

➤ **Change the z-order of controls at runtime** — Controls now have both `BringToFront` and `SendToBack` methods.

➤ **Locate the mouse pointer** — The `Control` class now exposes a `MousePosition` property that returns the location of the mouse in screen coordinates.

➤ **Manage child controls** — Container controls, such as a group box or panel, can use the `HasChildren` property and `Controls` collection to determine the existence of, and direct references to, child controls, respectively.

➤ **Maximize, minimize, or restore a form** — Use the form's `WindowState` property.

➤ **Create a global exception handler** — On the Project Properties dialog, click the button labeled View Application Events. (This button is available only if the Use Application Framework check box is checked.) A new code module will be created named ApplicationEvents.vb, and you can handle the `UnhandledException` event in that module. Any exceptions that are not handled in other code cause this event to fire.

SUMMARY

Windows Forms is still an excellent technology for the development of rich client and smart client interfaces. While Windows Presentation Foundation will experience more innovation in coming generations of the .NET platform, at present it's significantly easier to develop on Windows Forms. The maturity of the designer and control set in Windows Forms makes it a good choice for many client-based applications, and Windows Forms will be supported indefinitely on the .NET platform.

Becoming a capable Windows Forms developer requires becoming familiar with the controls that are available, including their properties, events, and methods. This takes time. If you are inexperienced with form-based interfaces, you can expend a fair amount of time using the reference documentation to find the control capabilities you need. However, that investment is worthwhile, both because it enables you to be a proficient Windows Forms developer and because many of the concepts will carry over into WPF.

Many professional Windows Forms developers need to go beyond just creating forms and laying out controls. Complex applications often also require creating new controls or enhancing built-in controls. Accordingly, the next chapter discusses how to create and modify Windows Forms controls, along with some additional advanced Windows Forms topics.

15

Advanced Windows Forms

WHAT YOU WILL LEARN IN THIS CHAPTER

➤ How to inherit from existing Windows Forms controls and extend them for your own purposes

➤ How to create UserControls that combine controls into a reusable surface

➤ How to create Windows Forms controls that draw their own interface

The previous chapter discussed the basics of Windows Forms 2.0. These capabilities are sufficient for straightforward user interfaces for systems written in VB 2010; but as applications become larger and more complex, it becomes more important to use the advanced capabilities of the .NET environment to better structure the application. Poorly structured large systems tend to have redundant code. Repeated code patterns end up being used (in slightly different variations) in numerous places in an application, which has numerous bad side effects: longer development time, less reliability, more difficult debugging and testing, and tougher maintenance.

Examples of needs that often result in repeated code include ensuring that fields are entered by the user, that the fields are formatted correctly, and that null fields in the database are handled correctly. Proper object-oriented design can encapsulate such functionality, making it unnecessary to use repeated code. Using the full object-oriented capabilities of the .NET environment, plus additional capabilities specific to Windows Forms programming, you can componentize your logic, enabling the same code to be used in numerous places in your application.

This chapter discusses techniques for componentizing code in Windows Forms applications. It is assumed that you have already read Chapters 2 and 3 on inheritance and other object-oriented techniques available in .NET before working with this chapter.

PACKAGING LOGIC IN VISUAL CONTROLS

As shown in the last chapter, Windows Forms user interfaces are based on using controls. A control is simply a special type of .NET class (just as forms are). As a fully object-oriented programming environment, VB 2010 gives you the capability to inherit and extend classes, and controls are no exception. Therefore, it is possible to create new controls that extend what the built-in controls can do.

There are four primary sources of controls for use on Windows Forms interfaces:

➤ Controls packaged with the .NET Framework (referred to in this chapter as *built-in controls*)

➤ Existing ActiveX controls that are imported into Windows Forms (These are briefly discussed in Chapter 30.)

➤ Third-party .NET-based controls from a software vendor

➤ Custom controls that are created for a specific purpose in a particular project or organization

If you can build your application with controls from the first three categories, so much the better. Using prewritten functionality that serves the purpose is generally a good idea. However, this chapter assumes you need more than such prepackaged functionality.

CUSTOM CONTROLS IN WINDOWS FORMS

There are three basic techniques for creating custom Windows Forms controls in .NET, corresponding to three different starting points. This range of options offers the flexibility to choose a technique that offers an appropriate balance between simplicity and flexibility:

➤ You can inherit from an existing control.

➤ You can build a composite control (using the UserControl class as your starting point).

➤ You can write a control from scratch (using the very simple Control class as your starting point).

These options are in rough order of complexity, from simplest to most complex. Let's look at each one with a view to understanding the scenarios in which each one is useful.

Inheriting from an Existing Control

The simplest technique starts with a complete Windows Forms control that is already developed. A new class is created that inherits the existing control. This new class has all the functionality of the base class from which it inherits, and the new logic can be added to create additional functionality in this new class or, indeed, to override functionality from the parent (when permitted).

Here are some typical scenarios where it might make sense to extend an existing Windows Forms control:

➤ A text box used for entry of American-style dates

➤ A self-loading list box, combo box, or data grid

➤ A ComboBox control that had a mechanism to be reset to an unselected state

➤ A NumericUpDown control that generates a special event when it reaches 80 percent of its maximum allowed value

Each of these scenarios starts with an existing control that simply needs some additional functionality. The more often such functionality is needed in your project, the more sense it makes to package it in a custom control. If a text box that needs special validation or editing will be used in only one place, then it probably doesn't make sense to create an inherited control. In that case, it's probably sufficient to simply add some logic in the form where the control is used to handle the control's events and manipulate the control's properties and methods.

Building a Composite Control

In some cases, a single existing control does not furnish the needed functionality, but a combination of two or more existing controls does. Such a combination is called a composite control. Here are some typical examples:

➤ A set of buttons with related logic that are always used together (such as Save, Delete, and Cancel buttons on a file maintenance form)

➤ A set of text boxes to hold a name, address, and phone number, with the combined information formatted and validated in a particular way

➤ A set of option buttons with a single property exposed as the chosen option

As with inherited controls, composite controls are only appropriate for situations that require the same functionality in multiple places. If the functionality is only needed once, then simply placing the relevant controls on the form and including appropriate logic right in the form is usually better.

Composite controls in Windows Forms are most often created using the `UserControl` class as a base class. Composite controls can be created using other classes as a base, however, and a later section entitled Embedding Controls in Other Controls shows an example.

Writing a Control from Scratch

If a control needs special functionality not available in any existing control, then it can be written from scratch to draw its own visual interface and implement its own logic. This option requires more work, but it enables you to do just about anything within .NET and Windows Forms, including very sophisticated user interfaces.

To write a control from scratch, it is necessary to inherit from the `Control` class, which provides basic functionality such as properties for colors and size. With this basic functionality already built in, your required development tasks include adding any specific properties and methods needed for the control, writing rendering logic that will paint the control to the screen, and handling mouse and keyboard input to the control.

INHERITING FROM AN EXISTING CONTROL

With this background on the options for creating custom controls, the next step is to look in depth at the procedures used for their development. First up is creating a custom control by inheriting from an existing control and extending it with new functionality. This is the simplest method for the creation of new controls, and the best way to introduce generic techniques that apply to all custom controls.

After you look at the general steps needed to create a custom control via inheritance, an example illustrates the details. It is important to understand that many of the techniques described for working with a control created through inheritance also apply to the other ways that a control can be created. Whether inheriting from the `Control` class, the `UserControl` class, or from an existing control, a control is a .NET class. Creating properties, methods, and events, and coordinating these members with the Visual Studio designers, is done in a similar fashion, regardless of the starting point.

Process Overview

Here are the general stages involved in creating a custom control via inheritance from an existing control. This is not a step-by-step recipe, just an overview. A subsequent example provides more detail on the specific steps, but those steps follow these basic stages:

1. Create or open a Windows Control Library project and add a new custom control to the project. The class that is created will inherit from the `System.Windows.Forms.Control` base class. The line that specifies the inherited class must be changed to inherit from the control that is being used as the starting point.

2. The class file gets new logic added as necessary to add new functionality. Then the project is compiled with a `Build` operation in order to create a DLL containing the new control's code.

3. The control is now ready to be used. It can be placed in the Windows Forms Toolbox with the Choose Items option in Visual Studio 2010. From that point forward, it can be dragged onto forms like any other control.

Stage 2, of course, is where the effort lies. New logic for the custom control may include new properties, methods, and events. It may also include intercepting events for the base control and taking special actions as necessary. These tasks are done with standard .NET coding techniques.

Several coding techniques are specific to developing Windows Forms controls, such as using particular .NET attributes. While our example includes adding routine properties and events, we focus on these special techniques for programming controls.

Writing Code for an Inherited Control

This section discusses how to place new logic in an inherited control, with special emphasis on techniques that go beyond basic object orientation. A detailed example using the techniques follows this section.

Creating a Property for a Custom Control

Creating a property for a custom control is just like creating a property for any other class. It is necessary to write a property procedure, and to store the value for the property somewhere, most often in a module-level variable, which is often called a *backing field*.

Properties typically need a default value — that is, a value the property takes on automatically when the control is instantiated. Typically, this means setting the backing field that holds the property value to some initial value. That can be done when the backing field is declared, or it can be done in the constructor for the control.

Here's the code for a typical simple property for a custom control:

Available for download on Wrox.com

```
Dim _nMaxItemsSelected As Integer = 10
Public Property MaxItemsSelected() As Integer
  Get
    Return _nMaxItemsSelected
  End Get
  Set(ByVal Value As Integer)
    If Value < 0 Then
      Throw New ArgumentException("Property value cannot be negative")
    Else
      _nMaxItemsSelected = Value
    End If
  End Set
End Property
```

Code snippet from LimitedCheckedListBox

After a property is created for a control, it automatically shows up in the Properties window for the control. If your Properties window is arranged alphabetically, you will see it in the list. If your window is arranged by category, then the new property will appear in the Misc category. However, you can use some additional capabilities to make the property work better with the designers and the Properties window in Visual Studio.

Coordinating with the Visual Studio IDE

Controls are normally dragged onto a visual design surface, which is managed by the Visual Studio IDE. In order for your control to work effectively with the IDE, it must be able to indicate the *default value* of its properties. The IDE needs the default value of a property for two important capabilities:

➤ To reset the value of the property (done when a user right-clicks the property in the Properties window and selects Reset)

➤ To determine whether to set the property in designer-generated code. A property that is at its default value does not need to be explicitly set in the designer-generated code.

There are two ways for your control to work with the IDE to accomplish these tasks. For properties that take simple values, such as integers, Booleans, floating-point numbers, or strings, .NET provides an attribute. For properties that take complex types, such as structures, enumerated types, or object references, two methods need to be implemented.

Attributes

You can learn more about attributes in Chapter 4, but a short summary of important points is included here. Attributes reside in namespaces, just as components do. The attributes used in this chapter are in the `System.ComponentModel` namespace. To use attributes, the project must have a reference to the assembly containing the namespace for the attributes. For `System.ComponentModel`, that's no problem — the project automatically has the reference.

However, the project will not automatically have an `Imports` statement for that namespace. Attributes could be referred to with a full type name, but that's a bit clumsy. To make it easy to refer to the attributes in code, put the following line at the beginning of all modules that need to use the attributes discussed in this chapter:

```
Imports System.ComponentModel
```

That way, an attribute can be referred to with just its name. For example, the `DefaultValue` attribute, discussed in detail below, can be declared like this:

```
<DefaultValue(4)> Public Property MyProperty() As Integer
```

> *All the examples in this chapter assume that the* `Imports` *statement has been placed at the top of the class, so all attributes are referenced by their short name. If you get a compile error on an attribute, then it's likely that you've omitted that line.*

Unlike earlier versions of Visual Basic, Visual Basic 2010 allows such lines of code to be split into separate lines, without the need for line continuation characters. For example, the last example could also be written as follows:

```
<DefaultValue(4)>
Public Property MyProperty() As Integer
```

Setting a Default Value with an Attribute

The .NET Framework contains many attributes. Most are used to tag classes, properties, and methods with metadata — that is, information that some other entity, such as a compiler or the Visual Studio IDE, might need to know.

For example, the `DefaultValue` attribute tells the Visual Studio IDE the default value of a property. You can change the preceding code for a simple property to include a `DefaultValue` attribute. Here are the first few lines, showing the change to the property declaration that applies the attribute:

Available for
download on
Wrox.com

```
Dim mnMaxItemsSelected As Integer = 10
<DefaultValue(10)> Public Property MaxItemsSelected() As Integer
   Get
      Return mnMaxItemsSelected
...
```

Code snippet from LimitedCheckedListBox

Including the `DefaultValue` attribute enables the Properties window to reset the value of the property back to the default value. That is, if you right-click the property in the Properties window and select Reset from the pop-up context menu, the value of the property returns to 10 from any other value to which it was set.

Another effect of the attribute can be seen in the code generated by the visual designer. If the preceding property is set to any value that is not the default, a line of code appears in the designer-generated code to set the property value. This is called *serializing* the property.

For example, if the value of MaxItemsSelected is set to 5, then a line of code something like this appears in the designer-generated code:

```
MyControl.MaxItemsSelected = 5
```

If the property has the default value of 10 (because it was never changed or it was reset to 10), then the line to set the property value is not present in the designer-generated code. That is, the property does not need to be serialized in code if the value is at the default.

To see serialized code, you need to look in the partial class that holds the Windows Forms designer-generated code. This partial class is not visible in the Solution Explorer by default. To see it, press the Show All Files button in the Solution Explorer.

Alternate Techniques for Working with the IDE

The last sample property returned an Integer. Some custom properties return more complex types, such as structures, enumerated types, or object references. These properties cannot use a simple DefaultValue attribute to take care of resetting and serializing the property. An alternate technique is needed.

For complex types, designers check to see whether a property needs to be serialized by using a method on the control containing the property. The method returns a Boolean value that indicates whether a property needs to be serialized (True if it does, False if it does not).

For the following examples, suppose a control has a property named MyColor, which is of type Color. The Color type is a structure in Windows Forms, so the normal DefaultValue attribute can't be used with it. Further suppose the backing variable for the property is named _MyColor.

In this case, the method to check serialization would be called ShouldSerializeMyColor. It would typically look something like the following code:

```
Public Function ShouldSerializeMyColor() As Boolean
   If Color.Equals(_MyColor, Color.Red) Then
      Return False
   Else
      Return True
   End If
End Function
```

Code snippet from LimitedCheckedListBox

This is a good example of why a DefaultValue attribute can't work for all types. There is no equality operator for the Color type, so you have to write appropriate code to perform the check to determine whether the current value of the MyColor property is the default. In this case, that's done with the Equals method of the Color type.

If a property in a custom control does not have a related ShouldSerializeXXX method or a DefaultValue attribute, then the property is always serialized. Code for setting the property's value is always included by the designer in the generated code for a form, so it's a good idea to always include either a ShouldSerializeXXX method or a DefaultValue attribute for every new property created for a control.

Providing a Reset Method for a Control Property

The ShouldSerialize method only takes care of telling the IDE whether to serialize the property value. Properties that require a ShouldSerialize method also need a way to reset a property's value to the default. This is done by providing a special reset method. In the case of the MyColor property, the reset method is named ResetMyColor. It would look something like the following:

```
Public Sub ResetMyColor()
   _MyColor = Color.Red
End Sub
```

Code snippet from LimitedCheckedListBox

Other Useful Attributes

`DefaultValue` is not the only attribute that is useful for properties. The `Description` attribute is also one that should be used consistently. It contains a text description of the property, and that description shows up at the bottom of the Properties windows when a property is selected. To include a `Description` attribute, the declaration of the preceding property would appear as follows:

```
<DefaultValue(100),
Description("This is a pithy description of my property")>
Public Property MyProperty() As Integer
```

Code snippet from LimitedCheckedListBox

Such a property will look like Figure 15-1 when highlighted in the Properties window.

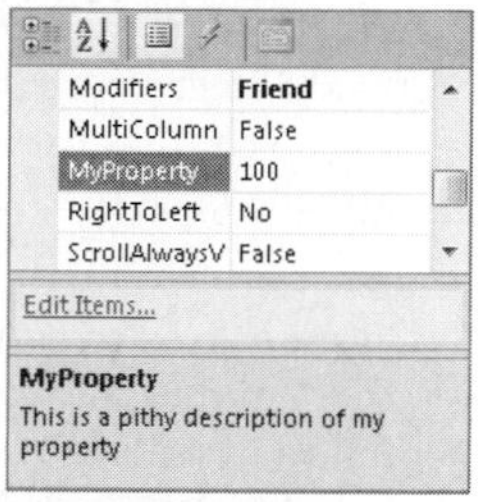

Another attribute you will sometimes need is the `Browsable` attribute. As mentioned earlier, a new property appears in the Properties window automatically. In some cases, you may need to create a property for a control that you do not want to show up in the Properties window. In that case, you use a `Browsable` attribute set to `False`. Here is code similar to the last, making a property nonbrowsable in the Properties window:

```
<Browsable(False)>
Public Property MyProperty() As Integer
```

FIGURE 15-1

One additional attribute you may want to use regularly is the `Category` attribute. Properties can be grouped by category in the Properties window by pressing a button at the top of the window. Standard categories include Behavior, Appearance, and so on. You can have your property appear in any of those categories, or you can make up a new category of your own. To assign a category to a property, use code like this:

```
<Category("Appearance")>
Public Property MyProperty() As Integer
```

There are other attributes for control properties that are useful in specific circumstances. If you understand how the common ones discussed here are used, then you can investigate additional attributes for other purposes in the documentation.

Defining a Custom Event for the Inherited Control

Events in .NET are covered in Chapter 2. To recap, for controls, the process for creating and handling an event includes these steps:

1. Declare the event in the control. The event can have any arguments that are appropriate, but it cannot have named arguments, optional arguments, or arguments that are `ParamArrays`. Though not required, normally you will want to follow the same convention as events in the .NET Framework, which means an event declaration similar to this:

    ```
    Public Event MyEvent(ByVal sender As Object, e As EventArgs)
    ```

2. Elsewhere in the control's code, implement code to raise the event. The location and circumstances of this code vary depending on the nature of the event, but a typical line that raises the preceding event looks like the following code:

    ```
    RaiseEvent MyEvent(Me, New EventArgs)
    ```

3. The form that contains the control can now handle the event. The process for doing that is the same as handling an event for a built-in control.

As the preceding example shows, the standard convention in .NET is to use two arguments for an event: `Sender`, which is the object raising the event, and e, which is an object of type `EventArgs` or a type that inherits from `EventArgs`. This is not a requirement of the syntax (you can actually use any arguments you like when you declare your event), but it's a consistent convention throughout the .NET Framework, so it is used in this chapter. It is suggested that you follow this convention as well, because it will make your controls consistent with the built-in controls in their operation.

The following example illustrates these concepts. In this example, you create a new control that contains a custom property and a custom event. The property uses several of the attributes discussed.

A CheckedListBox Limiting Selected Items

This example inherits the built-in `CheckedListBox` control and extends its functionality. If you are not familiar with this control, it works just like a normal `ListBox` control except that selected items are indicated with a check in a check box at the front of the item, rather than by highlighting the item.

To extend the functionality of this control, the example includes the creation of a property called `MaxItemsToSelect`. This property holds a maximum value for the number of items that a user can select. The event that fires when a user checks an item is then monitored to determine whether the maximum has already been reached.

If selection of another item would exceed the maximum number, then the selection is prevented, and an event is fired to let the consumer form know that the user has tried to exceed the maximum limit. The code that handles the event in the form can then do whatever is appropriate. In this case, a message box is used to tell the user that no more items can be selected.

The `DefaultValue`, `Description`, and `Category` attributes are placed on the `MaxItemsToSelect` property to coordinate with the IDE.

Here is the step-by-step construction of our example:

1. Start a new Windows Control Library project in Visual Studio and name it **MyControls**. In the Solution Explorer, select the `UserControl1.vb` file, right-click it, and delete it.

2. Select Project ⇨ Add New Item, and select the item template called Custom Control. Name the item **LimitedCheckedListBox**.

3. Click the button in the Solution Explorer to show all files for the project. Bring up the file `LimitedCheckedListBox.Designer.vb`, which is found by clicking the plus sign next to `LimitedCheckedListBox.vb`. (If you don't see a plus sign next to `LimitedCheckedListBox.vb`, click the Show All Files button at the top of the Solution Explorer.)

4. At the top of the `LimitedCheckedListbox.Designer.vb` code, look for the line that reads as follows:

   ```
   Inherits System.Windows.Forms.Control
   ```

5. Change that line to the following:

   ```
   Inherits System.Windows.Forms.CheckedListbox
   ```

6. Close `LimitedCheckedListbox.Designer.vb` and open `LimitedCheckedListBox.vb` in the Code Editor. Add the following declarations at the top of the code (before the line declaring the class):

   ```
   Imports System.ComponentModel
   ```

   This enables you to utilize the attributes required from the `System.ComponentModel` namespace.

7. The code for `LimitedCheckedListBox.vb` will contain an event for painting the control. Since you are not using a control that draws its own surface, delete that event. (It won't hurt to leave it, but you don't need it.)

8. Begin adding code specifically for this control. First, implement the `MaxItemsToSelect` property. A module-level variable is needed to hold the property's value, so insert this line just under the class declaration line:

   ```
   Private _nMaxItemsToSelect As Integer = 4
   ```

9. Create the code for the property itself. Insert the following code into the class just above the line that says `End Class`:

```
<DefaultValue(4), Category("Behavior"),
Description("The maximum number of items allowed to be checked")>
Public Property MaxItemsToSelect() As Integer
  Get
    Return _nMaxItemsToSelect
  End Get
  Set(ByVal Value As Integer)
    If Value < 0 Then
      Throw New ArgumentException("Property value cannot be negative")
    Else
      _nMaxItemsToSelect = Value
    End If
  End Set
End Property
```

Code snippet from LimitedCheckedListBox

This code sets the default value of the `MaxItemsToSelect` property to 4, and sets a description for the property to be shown in the Properties window when the property is selected there. It also specifies that the property should appear in the Behavior category when properties in the Properties window are sorted by category.

10. Declare the event that will be fired when a user selects too many items. The event is named `MaxItemsExceeded`. Just under the code for step 9, insert the following line:

```
Public Event MaxItemsExceeded(Sender As Object, e As EventArgs)
```

11. Insert code into the event routine that fires when the user clicks on an item. For the `CheckedListBox` base class, this is called the `ItemCheck` property. Open the left-hand drop-down box in the code window and select the option `LimitedCheckedListBox` Events. Then, select the `ItemCheck` event in the right-hand drop-down box of the code window. The following code will be inserted to handle the `ItemCheck` event:

```
Private Sub LimitedCheckedListBox_ItemCheck(ByVal sender As Object,
        ByVal e As System.Windows.Forms.ItemCheckEventArgs) _
        Handles Me.ItemCheck
End Sub
```

Code snippet from LimitedCheckedListBox

12. The following code should be added to the `ItemCheck` event to monitor it for too many items:

```
Private Sub LimitedCheckedListBox_ItemCheck(ByVal sender As Object,
        ByVal e As System.Windows.Forms.ItemCheckEventArgs) _
        Handles MyBase.ItemCheck
If (Me.CheckedItems.Count >= _nMaxItemsToSelect) _
  And (e.NewValue = CheckState.Checked) Then
    RaiseEvent MaxItemsExceeded(Me, New EventArgs)
    e.NewValue = CheckState.Unchecked
End If

End Sub
```

Code snippet from LimitedCheckedListBox

13. Build the project to create a DLL containing the `LimitedCheckedListBox` control.

14. Add a new Windows Application project to the solution (using the File ➪ Add Project ➪ New Project menu) to test the control. Name the new project anything you like. Right-click the project in the Solution Explorer, and select Set as Startup Project in the pop-up menu. This will cause your Windows application to run when you press F5 in Visual Studio.

15. Scroll to the top of the controls in the Toolbox. The `LimitedCheckedListBox` control should be there.

16. The Windows Application project will have a Form1 that was created automatically. Drag a `LimitedCheckedListBox` control onto Form1, just as you would a normal list box. Change the

CheckOnClick property for the LimitedCheckedListBox to True (to make testing easier). This property was inherited from the base CheckedListBox control.

FIGURE 15-2

17. In the Items property of the LimitedCheckedListBox, click the button to add some items. Insert the following list of colors: Red, Yellow, Green, Brown, Blue, Pink, and Black. At this point, your Windows Application project should have a Form1 that looks something like Figure 15-2.

18. Bring up the code window for Form1. In the left-hand drop-down box above the code window, select LimitedCheckedListBox1 to get to its events. Then, in the right-hand drop-down box, select the MaxItemsExceeded event. The empty event will look like the following code:

Available for download on Wrox.com

```
Private Sub LimitedCheckedListBox1_MaxItemsExceeded(
        ByVal sender As System.Object, e As System.EventArgs) _
        Handles LimitedCheckedListBox1.MaxItemsExceeded

    End Sub
```

Code snippet from LimitedCheckedListBox

19. Insert the following code to handle the event:

Available for download on Wrox.com

```
MsgBox("You are attempting to select more than " &
        LimitedCheckedListBox1.MaxItemsToSelect &
        " items. You must uncheck some other item " &
        " before checking this one.")
```

Code snippet from LimitedCheckedListBox

20. Start the Windows Application project. Check and uncheck various items in the list box to verify that the control works as intended. You should get a message box whenever you attempt to check more than four items. (Four items is the default maximum, which was not changed.) If you uncheck some items, then you can check items again until the maximum is once again exceeded. When finished, close the form to stop execution.

21. If you want to check the serialization of the code, look at the designer-generated code in the partial class for Form1 (named LimitedCheckedListBox.Designer.vb), and examine the properties for LimitedCheckedListBox1. Note that there is no line of code that sets MaxSelectedItems. Remember that if you don't see the partial class in the Solution Explorer, then you'll need to press the Show All button at the top of the Solution Explorer.

22. Go back to the Design view for Form1 and select LimitedCheckedListBox1. In the Properties window, change the MaxSelectedItems property to 3.

23. Return to the partial class and look again at the code that declares the properties for LimitedCheckedListBox1. Note that there is now a line of code that sets MaxSelectedItems to the value of 3.

24. Go back to the Design view for Form1 and select LimitedCheckedListBox1. In the Properties window, right-click the MaxSelectedItems property. In the pop-up menu, select Reset. The property will change back to a value of 4, and the line of code that sets the property you looked at in the last step will be gone.

These last few steps showed that the DefaultValue attribute is working as it should.

THE CONTROL AND USERCONTROL BASE CLASSES

In the earlier example, a new control was created by inheriting from an existing control. As is standard with inheritance, this means the new control began with all the functionality of the control from which it inherited. Then new functionality was added.

This chapter didn't discuss the base class for this new control (CheckedListBox) because you probably already understand a lot about the properties, methods, events, and behavior of that class. However, you are not likely to be as familiar with the base classes used for the other techniques for creating controls, so it's appropriate to discuss them now.

Two generic base classes are used as a starting point to create a control. It is helpful to understand something about the structure of these classes to know when the use of each is appropriate.

The classes discussed in this chapter are all in the System.Windows.Forms *namespace. There are similarly named classes for some of these in the* System.Web.UI *namespace (which is used for Web Forms), but these classes should not be confused with anything discussed in this chapter.*

The Control Class

The Control class is contained within the System.Windows.Forms namespace and contains base functionality to define a rectangle on the screen, provide a handle for it, and process routine operating system messages. This enables the class to perform such functions as handling user input through the keyboard and mouse. The Control class serves as the base class for any component that needs a visual representation on a Win32-type graphical interface. Besides built-in controls and custom controls that inherit from the Control class, the Form class also ultimately derives from the Control class.

In addition to these low-level windowing capabilities, the Control class also includes such visually related properties as Font, ForeColor, BackColor, and BackGroundImage. The Control class also has properties that are used to manage layout of the control on a form, such as docking and anchoring.

The Control *class does not contain any logic to paint to the screen except to paint a background color or show a background image. While it does offer access to the keyboard and mouse, it does not contain any actual input processing logic except for the ability to generate standard control events such as* Click *and* KeyPress. *The developer of a custom control based on the* Control *class must provide all of the functions for the control beyond the basic capabilities provided by the* Control *class.*

A standard set of events is also furnished by the Control class, including events for clicking the control (Click, DoubleClick), for keystroke handling (KeyUp, KeyPress, KeyDown), for mouse handling (MouseUp, MouseHover, MouseDown, etc.), and drag-and-drop operations (DragEnter, DragOver, DragLeave, DragDrop). Also included are standard events for managing focus and validation in the control (GotFocus, Validating, Validated). See the help files on the Control class for details about these events and a comprehensive list.

The UserControl Class

The built-in functionality of the Control class is a great starting point for controls that will be built from scratch, with their own display and keyboard handling logic. However, the Control class has limited capability for use as a container for other controls.

That means that composite controls do not typically use the Control class as a starting point. Composite controls combine two or more existing controls, so the starting point must be able to manage contained controls. The class that is most often used to meet this requirement is the UserControl class. Because it ultimately derives from the Control class, it has all of the properties, methods, and events discussed earlier for that class.

However, the UserControl class does not derive directly from the Control class. It derives from the ContainerControl class, which, in turn, derives from the ScrollableControl class.

As the name suggests, the ScrollableControl class adds support for scrolling the client area of the control's window. Almost all the members implemented by this class relate to scrolling. They include AutoScroll, which turns scrolling on or off, and controlling properties such as AutoScrollPosition, which gets or sets the position within the scrollable area.

The ContainerControl class derives from ScrollableControl and adds the capability to support and manage child controls. It manages the focus and the capability to tab from control to control. It includes properties such as ActiveControl to point to the control with the focus, and Validate, which validates the most recently changed control that has not had its validation event fired.

Neither ScrollableControl nor ContainerControl are usually inherited from directly; they add functionality that is needed by their more commonly used child classes: Form and UserControl.

The UserControl class can contain other child controls, but the interface of UserControl does not automatically expose these child controls in any way. Instead, the interface of UserControl is designed to present a single, unified interface to outside clients such as forms or container controls. Any object interface that is needed to access the child controls must be specifically implemented in your custom control. The following example demonstrates this.

A COMPOSITE USERCONTROL

Our earlier example showed inheriting an existing control, which was the first of the three techniques for creating custom controls. The next step up in complexity and flexibility is to combine more than one existing control to become a new control. This is similar to the process of creating a UserControl in VB6, but it is easier to do in Windows Forms.

The main steps in the process of creating a UserControl are as follows:

1. Start a new Windows Control Library project and assign names to the project and the class representing the control.

2. The project will contain a design surface that looks a lot like a form. You can drag controls onto this surface just as you would a form. Writing code that works with the controls, such as event routines, is done the same way as with a form, but with a few extra considerations that don't apply to most forms. In particular, it is important to handle resizing when the UserControl is resized. This can be done by using the Anchor and Dock properties of the constituent controls, or you can create resize logic that repositions and resizes the controls on your UserControl when it is resized on the form containing it. Another option is to use FlowLayoutPanel and/or TableLayoutPanel controls to do automatic layout.

3. Create properties of the UserControl to expose functionality to a form that will use it. This typically means creating a property to load information into and get information out of the control. Sometimes properties to handle cosmetic elements are also necessary.

4. Build the control and use it in a Windows application exactly as you did for the inherited controls discussed earlier.

> *There is a key difference between this type of development and inheriting a control, as shown in the preceding examples. A* UserControl *will not by default expose the properties of the controls it contains. It exposes the properties of the* UserControl *class plus any custom properties that you give it. If you want properties for contained controls to be exposed, then you must explicitly create logic to expose them.*

Creating a Composite UserControl

To demonstrate the process of creating a composite UserControl, the next exercise builds one that is similar to what is shown in Figure 15-3. The control is named ListSelector.

This type of layout is common in wizards and other user interfaces that require selection from a long list of items. The control has one list box holding a list of items that can be chosen (on the left), and another list box containing the items chosen so far (on the right). Buttons enable items to be moved back and forth.

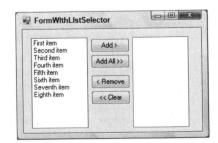

FIGURE 15-3

Loading this control means loading items into the left list box, which we will call SourceListBox. Getting selected items back out involves exposing the items that are selected in the right list box, named TargetListBox.

The buttons in the middle that transfer elements back and forth are called AddButton, AddAllButton, RemoveButton, and ClearButton, from top to bottom, respectively.

There are several ways to handle this kind of interface element in detail. A production-level version would have the following characteristics:

➤ Buttons would gray out (disable) when they are not appropriate. For example, btnAdd would not be enabled unless an item were selected in lstSource.

➤ Items could be dragged and dropped between the two list boxes.

➤ Items could be selected and moved with a double-click.

Such a production-type version contains too much code to discuss in this chapter. For simplicity, the exercise has the following limitations:

➤ Buttons do not gray out when they should be unavailable.

➤ Drag-and-drop is not supported. (Implementation of drag-and-drop is discussed in Chapter 14, if you are interested in adding it to the example.)

➤ No double-clicking is supported.

This leaves the following general tasks to make the control work, which are detailed in the step-by-step exercise that follows:

1. Create a UserControl and name it ListSelector.

2. Add the list boxes and buttons to the ListSelector design surface, using a TableLayoutPanel and a FlowLayoutPanel to control layout when the control is resized.

3. Add logic to transfer elements back and forth between the list boxes when buttons are pressed. (More than one item may be selected for an operation, so several items may need to be transferred when a button is pressed.)

4. Expose properties to enable the control to be loaded, and for selected items to be fetched by the form that contains the control.

Resizing the Control

As shown in Figure 15-3, there are three main areas of the control: the two ListBox controls and a vertical strip between them that holds the buttons. As the control is resized, these areas need to also be appropriately resized.

If the ListSelector control gets too small, then there won't be enough room for the buttons and the list boxes to display properly, so it needs to have a minimum size. That's enforced by setting the MinimumSize property for the UserControl in the designer. The MinimumSize property is inherited from the Control class (as discussed in the previous chapter).

The rest of the resizing is handled by using a TableLayoutPanel that contains three columns, one for each of the three areas. That is, the first column of the TableLayoutPanel will hold SourceListBox, the second column will hold the buttons, and the third column will hold TargetListBox. The capabilities of the TableLayoutPanel enable the middle column to be a fixed size, and the left and right columns to share all remaining width.

The middle column could contain a standard Panel to hold the buttons, but it's a bit easier to use a FlowLayoutPanel because it automatically stacks the buttons.

Exposing Properties of Contained Controls

Most of the controls contained in the composite control in this exercise do not need to expose their interfaces to the form that will use the composite control. The buttons, for example, are completely private to the ListSelector — none of their properties or methods need to be exposed.

The easiest way to load up the control is to expose the `Items` property of the source list box. Similarly, the easiest way to allow access to the selected items is to expose the `Items` property of the target list box. The `Items` property exposes the entire collection of items in a list box, and can be used to add, clear, or examine items. No other properties of the list boxes need to be exposed.

The exercise also includes a `Clear` method that clears both list boxes simultaneously. This allows the control to be easily flushed and reused by a form that consumes it.

Stepping through the Example

Here is the step-by-step procedure to build the composite `UserControl`:

1. Start a new Windows Control Library project and name it **ListSelector**.

2. Right-click on the `UserControl1.vb` module that is generated for the project and select Rename. Change the name of the module to `ListSelector.vb`. The resulting dialog asks if you wish to rename all references in the project. Click Yes. This automatically changes the name of your class to `ListSelector`.

3. Go to the design surface for the control. Increase the size of the control to about 300 × 200. Then drag a `TableLayoutPanel` onto the control and set the `Dock` property of the `TableLayoutPanel` to `Fill`.

4. Click the smart tag (the triangular glyph in the upper-right corner) of the `TableLayoutPanel`. A menu will appear. Select Edit Rows and Columns.

5. Highlight Column2 and click the Insert button. The `TableLayoutPanel` will now have three columns. In the new column just inserted (the new Column2), the width will be set to an absolute size of 20 pixels. Change that width to 100 pixels. The dialog containing your column settings should now look like Figure 15-4.

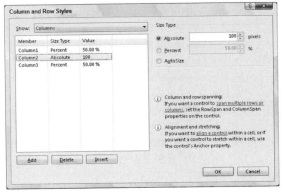

6. Click the Show drop-down menu in the upper-left corner and select Rows. Press the Delete button to delete a row because you need only one row in the control. Click OK. The design surface for the control should now look similar to Figure 15-5.

FIGURE 15-4

7. Drag a `ListBox` into the first cell and another one into the third cell. Drag a `FlowLayoutPanel` into the middle cell. For all three of these, set the `Dock` property to `Fill`.

8. Drag four buttons into the `FlowLayoutPanel` in the middle. At this point your control should look like the one shown in Figure 15-6.

FIGURE 15-5

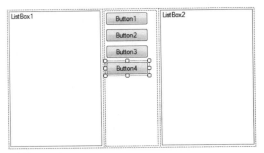

FIGURE 15-6

9. Change the names and properties of these controls as shown in the following table:

ORIGINAL NAME	NEW NAME	PROPERTIES TO SET FOR CONTROL
ListBox1	SourceListBox	
ListBox2	TargetListBox	
Button1	AddButton	Text = "Add >" Size.Width = 90
Button2	AddAllButton	Text = "Add All >>" Size.Width = 90
Button3	RemoveButton	Text = "< Remove" Margin.Top = 20 Size.Width = 90
Button4	ClearButton	Text = "<< Clear" Size.Width = 90

10. In the Properties window, click the drop-down at the top and select ListSelector so that the properties for the `UserControl` itself appear in the Properties window. Set the `MinimumSize` height and width to 200 pixels each.

11. Create the public properties and methods of the composite control. In this case, you need the following members:

MEMBER	DESCRIPTION
Clear method	Clears both list boxes of their items
SourceItems property	Exposes the Items collection for the source list box
SelectedItems property	Exposes the Items collection for the target list box

The code for these properties and methods is as follows:

```
<Browsable(False)>
Public ReadOnly Property SourceItems() As ListBox.ObjectCollection
    Get
        Return SourceListBox.Items
    End Get
End Property
<Browsable(False)>
Public ReadOnly Property SelectedItems() As ListBox.ObjectCollection
    Get
        Return TargetListBox.Items
    End Get
End Property
Public Sub Clear()
    SourceListBox.Items.Clear()
    TargetListBox.Items.Clear()
End Sub
```

Remember that your class must have an `Imports` for `System.ComponentModel` at the top so that the attributes can be identified by the compiler.

12. Put logic in the class to transfer items back and forth between the list boxes and clear the target list box when the Clear button is pressed. This logic manipulates the collections of items in the list boxes, and is fairly brief. You need one helper function to check whether an item is already in a list box before adding it (to avoid duplicates). Here are the `Click` events for each of the buttons, with the helper function at the top:

```
Private Function ItemInListBox(ByVal ListBoxToCheck As ListBox,
                    ByVal ItemToCheck As Object) As Boolean
    Dim bFound As Boolean = False
```

```
        For Each Item As Object In ListBoxToCheck.Items
            If Item Is ItemToCheck Then
                bFound = True
                Exit For
            End If
        Next
        Return bFound
    End Function
    Private Sub AddButton_Click(ByVal sender As System.Object, _
                           ByVal e As System.EventArgs) _
                           Handles AddButton.Click
        For Each SelectedItem As Object In SourceListBox.SelectedItems
            If Not ItemInListBox(TargetListBox, SelectedItem) Then
                TargetListBox.Items.Add(SelectedItem)
            End If
        Next
    End Sub
    Private Sub AddAllButton_Click(ByVal sender As System.Object, _
                           ByVal e As System.EventArgs) _
                           Handles AddAllButton.Click
        For Each SelectedItem As Object In SourceListBox.Items
            If Not ItemInListBox(TargetListBox, SelectedItem) Then
                TargetListBox.Items.Add(SelectedItem)
            End If
        Next
    End Sub
    ' For both the following operations, we have to go through the
    ' collection in reverse because we are removing items.
    Private Sub RemoveButton_Click(ByVal sender As System.Object, _
                           ByVal e As System.EventArgs) _
                           Handles RemoveButton.Click
        For iIndex As Integer = TargetListBox.SelectedItems.Count - 1 To 0 _
                Step -1
            TargetListBox.Items.Remove(TargetListBox.SelectedItems(iIndex))
        Next iIndex
    End Sub
    Private Sub ClearButton_Click(ByVal sender As System.Object, _
                           ByVal e As System.EventArgs) _
                           Handles ClearButton.Click
        For iIndex As Integer = TargetListBox.Items.Count - 1 To 0 Step -1
            TargetListBox.Items.Remove(TargetListBox.Items(iIndex))
        Next iIndex
    End Sub
```

Code snippet from ListSelector

The logic in the Click events for RemoveButton and ClearButton needs a bit of explanation. Because items are being removed from the collection, it is necessary to go through the collection in reverse. Otherwise, the removal of items will confuse the looping enumeration and a runtime error will be generated.

13. Build the control. Then create a Windows Application project to test it in. You can drag the control from the top of the Toolbox, add items in code (via the Add method of the SourceItems collection), resize, and so on. For testing, you should arrange for some items to be added to SourceItems, and the easiest way to do this is to use the Add method to add some items in the form's Load event. When the project is run, the buttons can be used to transfer items back and forth between the list boxes, and the items in the target list box can be read with the SelectedItems property.

Keep in mind that you can also use the techniques for inherited controls in composite controls, too. You can create custom events, apply attributes to properties, and create ShouldSerialize and Reset methods to make properties work better with the designer. (That wasn't necessary here because our two properties were ReadOnly.)

BUILDING A CONTROL FROM SCRATCH

If your custom control needs to draw its own interface, you should use the `Control` class as your starting point. Such a control gets a fair amount of base functionality from the `Control` class. A partial list of properties and methods of the `Control` class was included earlier in the chapter. These properties arrange for the control to automatically have visual elements such as background and foreground colors, fonts, window size, and so on.

However, such a control does not automatically use any of that information to actually display anything (except for a `BackgroundImage`, if that property is set). A control derived from the `Control` class must implement its own logic for painting the control's visual representation. In all but the most trivial examples, such a control also needs to implement its own properties and methods to gain the functionality it needs.

The techniques used in the earlier example for default values and the `ShouldSerialize` and `Reset` methods all work fine with the controls created from the `Control` class, so that capability is not discussed again. Instead, this section focuses on the capability that is very different in the `Control` class — the logic to paint the control to the screen.

Painting a Custom Control with GDI+

The base functionality used to paint visual elements for a custom control is in the part of .NET called GDI+. A complete explanation of GDI+ is too complex for this chapter, but an overview of some of the main concepts is needed here.

What Is GDI+?

GDI+ is an updated version of the old GDI (Graphics Device Interface) functions provided by the Windows API. GDI+ provides a new API for graphics functions, which then takes advantage of the Windows graphics library.

The System.Drawing Namespace

The GDI+ functionality can be found in the `System.Drawing` namespace and its subnamespaces. Some of the classes and members in this namespace will look familiar if you have used the Win32 GDI functions. Classes are available for such items as pens, brushes, and rectangles. Naturally, the `System.Drawing` namespace makes these capabilities much easier to use than the equivalent API functions.

With the `System.Drawing` namespace, you can manipulate bitmaps and use various structures for dealing with graphics such as Point, Size, Color, and Rectangle. Also included are numerous classes for use in drawing logic. The first three such classes you need to understand represent the surface on which drawing takes place, and the objects used to draw lines and fill shapes:

- `Graphics` — Represents the surface on which drawing is done. Contains methods to draw items to the surface, including lines, curves, ellipses, text, and so on.
- `Pen` — Used for drawing line-based objects
- `Brush` — Used for filling shapes (includes its subclasses)

The `System.Drawing` namespace includes many other classes and some subsidiary namespaces. Let's look at the `Graphics` class in a bit more detail.

The System.Drawing.Graphics Class

Many of the important drawing functions are members of the `System.Drawing.Graphics` class. Methods such as `DrawArc`, `FillRectangle`, `DrawEllipse`, and `DrawIcon` have self-evident actions. More than 40 methods provide drawing-related functions in the class.

Many drawing members require one or more points as arguments. A point is a structure in the `System.Drawing` namespace. It has X and Y values for horizontal and vertical positions, respectively. When a variable number of points are needed, an array of points may be used as an argument. The next example uses points.

The `System.Drawing.Graphics` class cannot be directly instantiated. It is only supposed to be manipulated by objects that can set the `Graphics` class up for themselves. There are several ways to get a reference to a `Graphics` class, but the one most commonly used in the creation of Windows controls is to get one out of the arguments in a `Paint` event. That technique is used in a later example. For now, to understand the capabilities of GDI+ a little better, let's do a quick example on a standard Windows Form.

Using GDI+ Capabilities in a Windows Form

Here is an example of a form that uses the `System.Drawing.Graphics` class to draw some graphic elements on the form's surface. The example code runs in the `Paint` event for the form, and draws an ellipse, an icon (which it gets from the form itself), and two triangles: one in outline and one filled.

Start a Windows Application project in VB 2010. On the Form1 that is automatically created for the project, place the following code in the `Paint` event for the form:

```
' Need a pen for the drawing. We'll make it violet.
Dim penDrawingPen As New _
           System.Drawing.Pen(System.Drawing.Color.BlueViolet)
' Draw an ellipse and an icon on the form
e.Graphics.DrawEllipse(penDrawingPen, 30, 100, 30, 60)
e.Graphics.DrawIcon(Me.Icon, 90, 20)
' Draw a triangle on the form.
' First have to define an array of points.
Dim pntPoint(2) As System.Drawing.Point
pntPoint(0).X = 150
pntPoint(0).Y = 100
pntPoint(1).X = 150
pntPoint(1).Y = 150
pntPoint(2).X = 50
pntPoint(2).Y = 70
e.Graphics.DrawPolygon(penDrawingPen, pntPoint)
' Do a filled triangle.
' First need a brush to specify how it is filled.
Dim bshBrush As System.Drawing.Brush
bshBrush = New SolidBrush(Color.Blue)
' Now relocate the points for the triangle.
' We'll just move it 100 pixels to the right.
pntPoint(0).X += 100
pntPoint(1).X += 100
pntPoint(2).X += 100
e.Graphics.FillPolygon(bshBrush, pntPoint)
```

Code snippet from GDIScreenShot

Start the program. The form that appears will look like the one shown in Figure 15-7.

To apply GDI+ to control creation, you create a custom control that displays a "traffic light," with red, yellow, and green signals that can be displayed via a property of the control. GDI+ classes will be used to draw the traffic light graphics in the control.

Start a new project in VB 2010 of the Windows Control Library type and name it **TrafficLight**. The created module has a class in it named `UserControl1`. We want a different type of control class, so you need to get rid of this one. Right-click on this module in the Solution Explorer and select Delete.

Next, right-click on the project and select Add New Item. Select the item type of Custom Control and name it `TrafficLight.vb`.

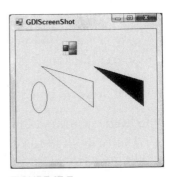

FIGURE 15-7

As with the other examples in this chapter, it is necessary to include the `Imports` statement for the namespace containing the attribute you will use. This line should go at the very top of the code module for `TrafficLight.vb`:

```
Imports System.ComponentModel
```

The `TrafficLight` control needs to know which "light" to display. The control can be in three states: red, yellow, or green. An enumerated type will be used for these states. Add the following code just below the previous code:

Available for
download on
Wrox.com

```
Public Enum TrafficLightStatus
    statusRed = 1
    statusYellow = 2
    statusGreen = 3
End Enum
```

Code snippet from TrafficLight

The example also needs a module-level variable and a property procedure to support changing and retaining the state of the light. The property is named `Status`. To handle the `Status` property, first place a declaration directly under the last enumeration declaration that creates a module-level variable to hold the current status:

```
Private mStatus As TrafficLightStatus = TrafficLightStatus.statusGreen
```

Then, insert the following property procedure in the class to create the `Status` property:

Available for
download on
Wrox.com

```
<Description("Status (color) of the traffic light")>
Public Property Status() As TrafficLightStatus
    Get
        Status = mStatus
    End Get
    Set(ByVal Value As TrafficLightStatus)
        If mStatus <> Value Then
            mStatus = Value
            Me.Invalidate()
        End If
    End Set
End Property
```

Code snippet from TrafficLight

The `Invalidate` method of the control is used when the `Status` property changes, which forces a redraw of the control. Ideally, this type of logic should be placed in all of the events that affect rendering of the control.

Now add procedures to make the property serialize and reset properly:

Available for
download on
Wrox.com

```
Public Function ShouldSerializeStatus() As Boolean
    If mStatus = TrafficLightStatus.statusGreen Then
        Return False
    Else
        Return True
    End If
End Function
Public Sub ResetStatus()
    Me.Status = TrafficLightStatus.statusGreen
End Sub
```

Code snippet from TrafficLight

Place code to do painting of the control, to draw the "traffic light" when the control repaints. We will use code similar to that used previously. The code generated for the new custom control will already have a blank `OnPaint` method inserted. You just need to insert the following highlighted code into that event, below the comment line that says "Add your custom paint code here":

Available for
download on
Wrox.com

```
Protected Overrides Sub OnPaint(ByVal pe As _
                    System.Windows.Forms.PaintEventArgs)
    MyBase.OnPaint(pe)
    'Add your custom paint code here
    Dim grfGraphics As System.Drawing.Graphics
    grfGraphics = pe.Graphics
    ' Need a pen for the drawing the outline. We'll make it black.
```

```
    Dim penDrawingPen As New _
        System.Drawing.Pen(System.Drawing.Color.Black)
    ' Draw the outline of the traffic light on the control.
     ' First have to define an array of points.
     Dim pntPoint(3) As System.Drawing.Point
    pntPoint(0).X = 0
    pntPoint(0).Y = 0
    pntPoint(1).X = Me.Size.Width - 2
    pntPoint(1).Y = 0
    pntPoint(2).X = Me.Size.Width - 2
    pntPoint(2).Y = Me.Size.Height - 2
    pntPoint(3).X = 0
    pntPoint(3).Y = Me.Size.Height - 2
    grfGraphics.DrawPolygon(penDrawingPen, pntPoint)
    ' Now ready to draw the circle for the "light"
    Dim nCirclePositionX As Integer
    Dim nCirclePositionY As Integer
    Dim nCircleDiameter As Integer
    Dim nCircleColor As Color = Color.LightGreen
    nCirclePositionX = Me.Size.Width * 0.02
    nCircleDiameter = Me.Size.Height * 0.3
    Select Case Me.Status
        Case TrafficLightStatus.statusRed
            nCircleColor = Color.OrangeRed
            nCirclePositionY = Me.Size.Height * 0.01
        Case TrafficLightStatus.statusYellow
            nCircleColor = Color.Yellow
            nCirclePositionY = Me.Size.Height * 0.34
        Case TrafficLightStatus.statusGreen
            nCircleColor = Color.LightGreen
            nCirclePositionY = Me.Size.Height * 0.67
    End Select
    Dim bshBrush As System.Drawing.Brush
    bshBrush = New SolidBrush(nCircleColor)
    ' Draw the circle for the signal light
     grfGraphics.FillEllipse(bshBrush, nCirclePositionX,
            nCirclePositionY, nCircleDiameter, nCircleDiameter)
End Sub
```

Code snippet from TrafficLight

Build the control library by selecting Build from the Build menu. This will create a DLL in the /bin directory where the Control Library solution is saved.

Next, start a new Windows Application project. Drag a TrafficLight control from the top of the Toolbox onto the form in the Windows Application project. Notice that its property window includes a Status property. Set that to statusYellow. The rendering on the control on the form's design surface will change to reflect this new status. Change the background color of the TrafficLight control to a darker gray to improve its contrast. (The BackColor property for TrafficLight was inherited from the Control class.)

At the top of the code for the form, place the following line to make the enumerated value for the traffic light's status available:

```
Imports TrafficLight.TrafficLight
```

Add three buttons (named btnRed, btnYellow, and btnGreen) to the form to make the TrafficLight control display as red, yellow, and green. The logic for the buttons looks something like the following:

```
Private Sub btnRed_Click(ByVal sender As System.Object,
                ByVal e As System.EventArgs) Handles btnRed.Click
    TrafficLight1.Status = TrafficLightStatus.statusRed
End Sub
Private Sub btnYellow_Click(ByVal sender As System.Object,
                ByVal e As System.EventArgs) Handles btnYellow.Click
```

Available for
download on
Wrox.com

```
        TrafficLight1.Status = TrafficLightStatus.statusYellow
    End Sub
    Private Sub btnGreen_Click(ByVal sender As System.Object,
            ByVal e As System.EventArgs) Handles btnGreen.Click
        TrafficLight1.Status = TrafficLightStatus.statusGreen
    End Sub
```

Code snippet from TrafficLight

In the Solution Explorer, right-click your test Windows Application project and select Set as Startup Project. Then press F5 to run. When your test form appears, you can change the "signal" on the traffic light by pressing the buttons. Figure 15-8 shows a sample screen.

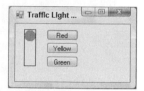

Of course, you can't see the color in a black-and-white screenshot; but as you can tell from its position, the circle is red. The "yellow light" displays in the middle of the control, and the "green light" displays at the bottom. These positions are all calculated in the Paint event logic, depending on the value of the Status property.

FIGURE 15-8

For a complete example, it would be desirable for the control to allow the user to change the Status by clicking on a different part of the "traffic light." That means including logic to examine mouse clicks, calculate whether they are in a given area, and change the Status property if appropriate. In the code available for download for this book, the TrafficLight example includes such functionality.

ATTACHING AN ICON FOR THE TOOLBOX

By default, the icon that appears in the Toolbox next to your control's name is a gear-shaped icon. However, you can attach an icon to a control for the Toolbox to display. There are two ways to do that.

Windows Forms includes a ToolboxBitmap attribute that can specify an icon for a class. It can be used in several ways, and you can see examples in the help file for the ToolboxBitmap attribute.

The easy way to attach an icon to your control is to let Visual Studio do it for you. Simply locate or draw the icon you want to use and add it to the project containing your control. Then rename the icon so that it has the same name as your control but an extension of .ico instead of vb.

For example, to attach an icon to the TrafficLight control in the preceding example, find an icon you like, place it in your project, and name it **TrafficLight.ico**. Then Visual Studio will attach the icon to your control during the compilation process; and when your control is added to the Toolbox, your icon will be used instead of the gear-shaped one.

> *Custom icons are displayed for a control in the Toolbox only when the control is added with the Toolbox's Choose Items option. Controls that appear in the Toolbox at the top because their project is currently loaded do not exhibit custom icons. They always have a blue, gear-shaped icon.*

EMBEDDING CONTROLS IN OTHER CONTROLS

Another valuable technique for creating custom controls is to embed other controls. In a sense, the UserControl does this; but when a UserControl is used as the base class, by default it only exposes the properties of the UserControl class. Instead, you may want to use a control such as TextBox or Grid as the starting point, but embed a Button in the TextBox or Grid to obtain some new functionality.

The embedding technique relies on the fact that in Windows Forms, all controls can be containers for other controls. Visual Basic developers are familiar with the idea that Panels and GroupBoxes can be containers, but in fact a TextBox or a Grid can also be a container of other controls.

This technique is best presented with an example. The standard ComboBox control does not have a way for users to reset to a "no selection" state. Once an item is selected, setting to that state requires code that sets the SelectedIndex to -1.

This exercise creates a ComboBox that has a button to reset the selection state back to "no selection." That enables users to access that capability directly. Now that you have worked with several controls in the examples, rather than proceed step by step, we'll just show the code for such a ComboBox and discuss how the code works:

```vb
Public Class SpecialComboBox
    Inherits ComboBox
    Dim WithEvents btnEmbeddedButton As Button
    Public Sub New()
        Me.DropDownStyle = ComboBoxStyle.DropDownList
        ' Fix up the embedded button.
        btnEmbeddedButton = New Button
        btnEmbeddedButton.Width = SystemInformation.VerticalScrollBarWidth
        btnEmbeddedButton.Top = 0
        btnEmbeddedButton.Height = Me.Height - 4
        btnEmbeddedButton.BackColor = SystemColors.Control
        btnEmbeddedButton.FlatStyle = FlatStyle.Popup
        btnEmbeddedButton.Text = "t"
        Dim fSpecial As New Font("Wingdings 3", Me.Font.Size - 1)
        btnEmbeddedButton.Font = fSpecial
        btnEmbeddedButton.Left = Me.Width - btnEmbeddedButton.Width - _
            SystemInformation.VerticalScrollBarWidth
        Me.Controls.Add(btnEmbeddedButton)
        btnEmbeddedButton.Anchor = CType(AnchorStyles.Right _
            Or AnchorStyles.Top Or AnchorStyles.Bottom, AnchorStyles)
        btnEmbeddedButton.BringToFront()
    End Sub

    Private Sub btnEmbeddedButton_Click(ByVal sender As Object, _
            ByVal e As System.EventArgs) Handles btnEmbeddedButton.Click
        Me.SelectedIndex = -1
        Me.Focus
    End Sub
    Private Sub BillysComboBox_DropDownStyleChanged(ByVal sender As Object, _
            ByVal e As System.EventArgs) Handles MyBase.DropDownStyleChanged
        If Me.DropDownStyle <> ComboBoxStyle.DropDownList Then
            Me.DropDownStyle = ComboBoxStyle.DropDownList
            Throw New _
                InvalidOperationException("DropDownStyle must be DropDownList")
        End If
    End Sub
End Class
$$
```

Code snippet from SpecialCombo

Like the first example in the chapter, this example inherits from a built-in control. Thus, it immediately gets all the capabilities of the standard ComboBox. All you need to add is the capability to reset the selected state.

To do that, you need a button for the user to press. The class declares the button as a private object named btnEmbeddedButton. Then, in the constructor for the class, the button is instantiated, and its properties are set as necessary. The size and position of the button need to be calculated. This is done using the size of the ComboBox and a special system parameter called SystemInformation.VerticalScrollBarWidth. This parameter is chosen because it is also used to calculate the size of the button used to drop down a combo box. Thus, your new embedded button will be the same width as the button that the regular ComboBox displays for dropping down the list.

Of course, you need to display something in the new button to indicate its purpose. For simplicity, the preceding code displays a lowercase "t" using the WingDings 3 font (which all Windows systems should have installed). This causes a left-pointing triangle to appear, as shown in Figure 15-9, which is a screenshot of the control in use.

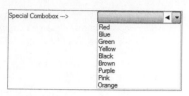

The button is then added to the `Controls` collection of the `ComboBox`. You may be surprised to learn that a `ComboBox` even has a `Controls` collection for embedded controls, but all controls in Windows Forms have one.

FIGURE 15-9

Finally, the `Anchor` property of the new button is set to maintain the position if the `SpecialComboBox` is resized by its consumer.

Besides the constructor, only a couple of small routines are needed. The `Click` event for the button must be handled, and in it the `SelectedIndex` must be set to -1. In addition, because this functionality is only for combo boxes with a style of `DropDownList`, the `DropDownStyleChanged` event of the `ComboBox` must be trapped, and the style prevented from being set to anything else.

SUMMARY

This chapter discussed how to create custom controls in Windows Forms, enabling you to consolidate logic used throughout your user interfaces. The full inheritance capabilities in .NET and the classes in the Windows Forms namespace enable several options for creating controls. It is probably best to start by overriding these controls in order to learn the basics of creating properties and coordinating them with the designer, building controls and testing them, and so on. These techniques can then be extended by creating composite controls, as illustrated by the examples in this chapter.

We also discussed creating a control from scratch, using the base `Control` class. In the course of writing a control from scratch, it was necessary to discuss the basics of GDI+, but if you are going to do extensive work with GDI+, you need to seek out additional resources to aid in that effort.

The key concept that you should take away from this chapter is that Windows Forms controls are a great way both to package functionality that will be reused across many forms and to create more dynamic, responsive user interfaces much more quickly with much less code.

16

User Controls Combining WPF and Windows Forms

WHAT YOU WILL LEARN IN THIS CHAPTER

➤ The Windows Forms Integration Library
➤ Using WPF controls in Windows Forms
➤ Using Windows Forms controls in WPF
➤ Integration library limitations

Chapter 15 looked at advanced features of Windows Forms. One of these features goes well beyond Windows Forms: user controls. User controls are used in Windows Forms, ASP.NET, WPF, and Silverlight. The concepts around user controls reflect a best practice for encapsulating application logic within a reusable component. Within an application, smaller components that encapsulate functionality and communicate via a method such as events provide a robust architecture. This chapter acts as a bridge to the next chapter which deals with WPF and also references using a user control.

The same concept is used to provide a migration path from Windows Forms to Windows Presentation Foundation (WPF). WPF was first introduced in .NET 3.0 as Microsoft's next-generation solution to graphical user-interface development. In terms of user interfaces, the transition to this new model will be similar in significance and paradigm shift to the shift from COM-based Visual Basic to Visual Basic .NET. The core paradigms and syntax familiar to developers of Windows applications are changing, and most of the changes are not backwardly compatible.

As a result, developers will need to transition existing application source code to a new technology paradigm. Perhaps not this year or next, but at some point the WPF paradigm will be used to update the look and feel of existing applications. How will this transition compare to the last major .NET-related transition — the one from COM? The original version of Visual Studio .NET included a tool to aid in migrating code from the COM-based world to .NET. No migration tool will be provided to transition existing user interfaces to WPF, which should be considered a good thing, considering the history of the current migration tools.

Instead, Microsoft learned the lesson that migration is both difficult and time consuming and is best done at the developer's pace. Therefore, instead of trying to automatically process code based on a procedural paradigm to work under a declarative paradigm, the tool of choice is one that enables components built in the respective paradigms to communicate. After all, in some cases a change like this results in a complete rewrite of an application or the application UI, and the migration library will never be used.

This same interoperability paradigm is repeated in the Power Pack tools for Visual Basic, which Microsoft first released in 2006. These tools, covered in Appendix B, are similar in concept to the Interop methodology that Microsoft has chosen to follow with WPF.

Microsoft is providing libraries that enable user-interface developers to integrate these two user-interface models (WPF and Windows Forms). In the long run, Windows Forms to WPF integration will probably go the way of COM-Interop, which is to say it will be available for many years, but its limitations and ties to an older technology will reduce its influence, and eventually it will be forced into retirement with the older technology.

The focus of this chapter is how to use the Windows Forms Integration Library to best enable you to both leverage WPF with your existing code and leverage your existing code and related forms-based code with your new WPF applications. Just as with COM-Interop, the point of the integration library is to help you, the developer, transition your application from Windows Forms to WPF gradually, while working with the time and budget constraints that all developers face and potentially waiting for a control that isn't available in WPF.

THE INTEGRATION LIBRARY

WindowsFormsIntegration library enables WPF applications to host Windows Forms controls and vice versa. The library is contained in the `WindowFormsIntegration.dll` which supports the `System.Windows.Forms.Integration` namespace. This namespace provides the tools necessary for using WPF and Windows Forms in a single application. At the core of this namespace are the two classes `ElementHost` and `WindowsFormsHost`. These two classes provide for interoperability in the WPF and the Windows Forms environment, respectively.

The `WindowsFormsIntegration.dll` is located with the other .NET assemblies and is imported like any other common namespace. After you add a reference and import the namespace you'll find the appropriate control class for your project type — `ElementHost` or `WindowsFormsHost` — in the list of tools in the Toolbox window for the designer.

Table 16-1 describes the classes and the delegate that make up the `Windows.Forms.Integration` namespace, a similar list is available from MSDN: `http://msdn.microsoft.com/en-us/library/system.windows .forms.integration.aspx`.

TABLE 16-1: Windows.Forms.Integration Classes and Delegate

CLASS	DESCRIPTION
ChildChangedEventArgs	This class is used when passing event arguments to the `ChildChanged` event. This event occurs on both the `WindowsFormsHost` and `ElementHost` classes when the content of the `Child` property is changed.
ElementHost	This is the core class for embedding WPF controls within Windows Forms. Using the `Child` property, you identify the top-level object (probably some type of panel) that will be hosted, and via this object define an area that will be controlled by that object. The object referenced by the host can contain other controls but the host references only this one.
IntegrationExceptionEventArgs	This is the base class for the `Integration` and `Property Mapping` exception classes. It provides the common implementation used by these classes.
LayoutExceptionEventArgs	This class enables you to return information related to a Layout error within a host class to the hosting environment, Windows Forms, or WPF.

CLASS	DESCRIPTION
PropertyMap	A property on each of the host classes. It provides a way for a Windows Form to handle a change that occurs to one of the properties of a hosted control — for example, if the size of the ElementHost control has changed, causing the form to carry out some other action. The same capability exists for WPF applications hosting a WindowsFormsHost control.
PropertyMappingExceptionEventArgs	Similar to the layout exception class, this enables a hosted control to return information related to an exception to the hosting environment.
WindowsFormsHost	This is the primary control when a WPF application wants to host Windows Forms controls. Similar to ElementHost, the actual WindowsFormsHost object contains only a single child — typically, a user control. This control can then contain an array of controls, but it is this class that acts as the virtual Windows Form that is referencing the user control.
PropertyTranslator	This is the only delegate in this namespace. It is used within your Visual Basic code to enable you to translate properties from a WindowsFormsHost control to a WPF ElementHost control (and vice versa). Essentially, you provide it with the property to be updated and the value to update that property with, and this method passes that value across the boundary from one UI model to the other. It works in conjunction with the PropertyMap class.

These classes enable your application to host controls within its display area. As noted, when you add the appropriate host class to your display area, the host class contains a child control. Each host contains only a single child control. The one-to-one relationship enables the integration library to assign the display area allocated to the host directly to the child and not be concerned with maintaining positioning multiple children, but instead be focused on a single target child. Thus, when you assign a control to a WindowsFormsHost, behind the scenes the Margin, Docking, AutoSizing, and Location properties of the WindowsFormsHost control are automatically applied to the child control. The host controls don't contain a great deal of logic about the workings of what they are hosting; instead, they just act as an interop layer. The properties of the child are controlled via the host, and that child control can, via user controls and panels, act as a native host for other controls you want to display within the host control.

Similar to the WindowsFormsHost, the ElementHost control automatically controls the display characteristics, including the following properties: Height, Width, Margin, HorizontalAlignment, and VerticalAlignment. In both cases, the host control acts as the virtual display area for the hosted control, and you should manage that display area via the host control, not the child it contains. Even though both controls are targeted at area controls such as user controls and panels, their purpose is to access controls and features across the UI display models.

HOSTING WPF CONTROLS IN WINDOWS FORMS

Hosting WPF controls within your existing Windows Forms–based applications enables you to introduce new functionality that requires the capabilities of WPF without forcing you to entirely rewrite your application. This way, even as you work on upgrading an existing application to WPF, you aren't forced to take on a single large project. As for the integration itself, it isn't page- or window-based, although you can introduce new WPF windows to an existing application. The integration is focused on enabling you to incorporate new user controls into your existing Windows Forms application.

Accordingly, the model is based around the idea that you can encapsulate the functionality of a set of WPF UI features as a user control. This has a couple of key advantages, the first being that if you've been working with .NET, you are already familiar with user controls and how they function. Once again, the paradigms of previous user-interface models appear and are reused within WPF. The second big advantage to modeling this around user controls is that as more of your application moves to WPF, you don't have to rewrite the user controls you create today when later they are used within a pure WPF environment.

With this goal in mind of creating a control that can later be moved from being hosted within a Windows Form application to running unchanged within a WPF application, you can turn your attention to creating a sample solution.

Creating a WPF Control Library

The first step is to open Visual Studio 2010 and go to the New Project dialog. From here, select the Windows category of templates and create a new Windows Forms Application. For example purposes, you can name this ProVBWinform_Interop — the name used for the downloadable sample. As discussed in Chapter 1, Visual Studio uses the template to create a new Windows Forms project, and you can accept the default of targeting .NET 4. At this point, using the File menu, add a second project to your solution (File ⇨ Add ⇨ New Project).

Again select the Windows category of templates and create a new WPF user control library. You could add a WPF control to your Windows Forms project, but this would limit the portability of the control when you wanted to transition to a WPF project and reuse it. For demonstration purposes, use the name **WpfInteropCtrl**. When you are done, the Visual Studio Solution Explorer will look similar to what is shown in Figure 16-1.

The next step is to add customization to the newly created WPF library, after which the Windows Forms application will be updated to reference the integration library and the new WPF user control. The first customization is to the grid, which is by default in the display area. For this example, you will change the background color of the grid that fills your control's display. You will also add a new `Image` control to the grid and bind it to the edges using the `Margin` property, not the `Height` or `Width` properties.

FIGURE 16-1

The complete XAML is shown in the following code block. You can replace the default XAML for `UserControl1` with the code shown in the following snippet:

```
<UserControl x:Class="UserControl1"
             xmlns:="http://schemas.microsoft.com/winfx/2006/xaml/presentation"
             xmlns:x="http://schemas.microsoft.com/winfx/2006/xaml"
             xmlns:mc="http://schemas.openxmlformats.org/markup-compatibility/2006"
             xmlns:d="http://schemas.microsoft.com/expression/blend/2008"
             mc:Ignorable="d"
             d:DesignHeight="300" d:DesignWidth="300">
    <Grid Background="LightSteelBlue">
        <Image Margin="10,10,10,10" Name="Image1" />
    </Grid>
</UserControl>
```

Code snippet from UserControl1.xaml

One important change to this XAML with .NET 4.0 is the inclusion of the `Expression/blend/2008` namespace and the `DesignHeight` and `DesignWidth` properties. These attributes provide a new feature for Visual Studio 2010. It is common to want the size of a user control to be defined by the area within the parent. However, traditionally, without declaring a default height and width for a control, your design surface was unusable. Because data isn't typically available in Design view, controls resize down to nothing visually. These attributes enable you to define the design surface such that at runtime the control will respond dynamically to the area available.

Now that you have completed your work in XAML, it's time for some code to accompany your control. As you can imagine, this WPF control is fairly simple in that you merely want it to display an image. This means you need a property that represents the path to the image to be displayed, some logic to load that image, the capability to respond to changes in size, and, for the purposes of custom code, the capability to prevent increasing the size of the image beyond its original size.

To meet these requirements you add a public property `Image` to your control that represents the path to the image that will be loaded. Within the `Set` logic for this property, you load the image. As noted in the following code block, the internal value has been set to a specific picture, but to be thorough, take a minute to review the accessors.

The `Get` and `Set` property accessors have been defined, and the `Set` accessor is customized. Note that after assigning the path for the current image to the internal value, this accessor then creates a new local image object and attempts to load the selected image path as a bitmap. WPF comes with converters for several common image types, but because this is demo code, no real checking is done to ensure the validity of the path passed in.

Thus, this logic is located within a `Try...Catch` block; and if the image load fails, the image value in the control is set to nothing. However, if a valid image path is provided, then the code loads the image and calls the local `ResizeMargins` method to handle adding margins based on the size of the image. Similarly, the `SizeChanged` event is handled in this code, and it calls the same private method to ensure that the image is not stretched beyond its original size:

```vb
Public Class UserControl1
    ' The default directory and image path are native to Windows 7.
    ' On other operating system's you'll need to select an appropriate directory.
    Private imageSource As String = "C:\Users\Public\Pictures\Sample Pictures "

    Public Property Image() As String
        Get
            Return imageSource
        End Get
        Set(ByVal value As String)
            imageSource = value
            Dim image As BitmapImage
            Try
                image = New Windows.Media.Imaging.BitmapImage( _
                    New Uri("file:///" + imageSource))
                ' Add any path validation prior to trying to load the selected file...
                Image1.Source = image
                ' resize Margins if appropriate
                ResizeMargins(image)
            Catch
                Image1.Source = Nothing
                Return
            End Try
        End Set
    End Property

    Private Sub UserControl1_SizeChanged(ByVal sender As Object,
            ByVal e As System.Windows.SizeChangedEventArgs) Handles Me.SizeChanged
        If Image1.Source IsNot Nothing Then
            ResizeMargins(CType(Image1.Source, Windows.Media.Imaging.BitmapImage))
        End If
    End Sub

    Public Sub ResizeMargins(ByVal image As Windows.Media.Imaging.BitmapImage)
        ' actualheight and actualwidth represent the size of the image control
```

```
' whether margin is set or not. if the actual size is greater than the
' size of the image reset margins to the max size of the image.
Dim imgH As Double = image.Height
Dim ctrlH As Double = Me.ActualHeight
Dim marginHorizontal As Double
If imgH > ctrlH Then
    marginHorizontal = 0
Else
    marginHorizontal = (ctrlH - imgH) / 2
End If

Dim imgW As Double = image.Width
Dim ctrlW As Double = Me.ActualWidth
Dim marginSide As Double
If imgW > ctrlW Then
    marginSide = 0
Else
    marginSide = (ctrlW - imgW) / 2
End If
Image1.Margin = New Thickness(marginSide, marginHorizontal,
                              marginSide, marginHorizontal)

    End Sub
End Class
```

Code snippet from UserControl1.xaml

The remaining custom code is in fact the `ResizeMargins` method. This method is reasonably simple. It takes the size of the image itself and compares this to the size of the control `Image1`. Note that this code references the `ActualHeight` property. Unlike the `Height` property, which for controls that are docked doesn't provide a valid size, the `ActualHeight` property reflects the current size of the `Image1` control. If the control size is larger than the original size of the image, then the code adjusts the margins to fill in around the image.

This completes the definition of your sample WPF control library, so compile your application to ensure that no errors are pending.

The Windows Forms Application

The next step is to customize the Windows Forms application. Begin by adding the five required references that enable you to embed and manipulate this control. They are the four framework libraries — `WindowsFormsIntegration`, `PresentationCore`, `PresentationFramework`, and `WindowsBase` — and a project reference to your custom WpfInteropCtrl library. Open the project properties for your ProVBWinForm_Interop project and go to the References tab.

Choose Add References, and in the list of available .NET libraries you'll find all four framework references available. Other presentation libraries are also available from this screen; and depending on what you intend to do in your application, you can choose to add other library references to your project as well. Finally, switch to the Project References tab and add a reference to your local project.

Laying Out Controls on the Form

Now go to the Design mode for the `Form1.vb` file that was created by the Windows Forms template when you created this project. Extend the default size of the design surface with the size of your control in mind, allocating enough room to align three rows of Windows Forms controls above your custom user control.

Starting at the top, you are going to add a new `Button` control to the upper-left corner of the form. The label on this button will be "Select Folder"; to change this you will update the Text property on the control. Ensure the button is sized to display fully . Next, add a `FolderBrowserDialog` control to your window; this control doesn't have a display element and will be shown below your form. Now add a `Label` control below your button and change its text property to "Image:." Once this is in place, add a `ComboBox` control to the right of this label. Accept the default name of `ComboBox1`, and using the properties for the control, select the `anchor` property and add a binding to the right side of the container in addition to the default top and left bindings. This tells the control to expand as the containing form is widened.

Next, add a `Label` control to the right of your button, and use the text "Mask:." To the right of the "Mask:" label, add a new combo box, `ComboBox2`, in the sample code. Go to the context menu for this `ComboBox` and select Edit Items to open the edit window. Within this screen add the three options that will make up the image mask options: No Mask, Ellipse, and Rectangle. Ensure that this control is also bound to the form's width.

Below the image `ComboBox`, in a third row on your Windows Form. add a `Label` control with the text "Margin:" and a `TextBox` control with the name `TextBoxMargin`. Set the default value for this `TextBox` to 10 and limit its length to 4 characters in the properties display. Similarly, alongside this text box, add another `Label` control with the text "Corner Radius," and a second `TextBox` control called `TextBoxRounding`. Set the default value for this second text box to 50.

At this point, drag and drop your `UserControl1` directly onto the form surface. This is a change from Visual Studio 2008. With Visual Studio 2010, you drag the targeted WPF control onto the form and the designer automatically encapsulates the WPF control with an Element Host control. The controls then allow you to resize the Element Host to fill the available area, and then using the anchor property of the element host, anchor it to all four sides to ensure it resizes with the form.

The Design view for `Form1` should look similar to the one shown in Figure 16-2. Note the expanded Properties pane. This is currently set to display/edit the properties for ElementHost1, focusing on its reference to the user control.

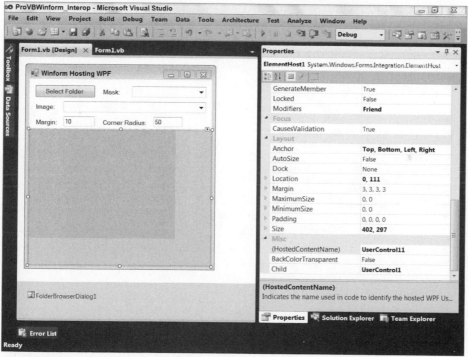

FIGURE 16-2

Adding Custom Code to the Form

The next step is to add some custom code to this form. The form will allow you to select a folder containing images and then display any of those images. Additionally, you will have the capability to place a mask over the image to provide a custom "frame" around the displayed image. The goal is to demonstrate not only adding a control, but also a scenario in which you need to map one of the ElementHost's properties within your code.

The next listing provides the basis for your customization. The first item is to hold onto the current directory path. The private value is defined on the form class, and a default path for images on Windows 7 is assigned to this property. Next, the Load event for the form is handled. Within the Load event, the code will get the list of files from the default directory and then load ComboBox1 with this list of files. It will select the first file from the list, and then ensure that no mask is selected. Finally, the sample code calls the method AddPropertyMapping. This call is currently commented on, and you will uncomment it after the reason for mapping a property is illustrated.

The next method shown in this code block is the event handler for the button's Click event. This event handler opens a folder browsing dialog using the control FolderBrowserDialog1. It uses the current path as the default for this dialog, and if the user selects a new directory for images, it loads the new list of files into the ComboBox. Note that it doesn't change the selected image, so a user won't see a new image automatically displayed when the list of files is loaded. You should update Form1.vb with the code in the following snippet:

```vb
Public Class Form1
    ' The default directory path is native to Windows 7.
    ' On other operating systems select an appropriate directory.
    Private m_path As String = "C:\Users\Public\Pictures\Sample Pictures"
    Private Sub Form1_Load(ByVal sender As System.Object, _
                           ByVal e As System.EventArgs) _
                           Handles MyBase.Load
        For Each filename As String In System.IO.Directory.GetFiles(m_path)
            ComboBox1.Items.Add(filename)
        Next
        ComboBox1.SelectedIndex = 0
        Me.ComboBox2.SelectedIndex = 0
        'AddPropertyMapping()
    End Sub
    Private Sub Button1_Click(ByVal sender As System.Object, _
                              ByVal e As System.EventArgs) _
                              Handles Button1.Click
        FolderBrowserDialog1.SelectedPath = m_path
        If (FolderBrowserDialog1.ShowDialog() = _
                                    Windows.Forms.DialogResult.OK) Then
            If Not m_path = FolderBrowserDialog1.SelectedPath Then
                m_path = FolderBrowserDialog1.SelectedPath
                ComboBox1.Items.Clear()
                For Each filename As String In _
                                    System.IO.Directory.GetFiles(m_path)
                    ComboBox1.Items.Add(filename)
                Next
            End If
        End If
    End Sub
    Private Sub ComboBox1_SelectedIndexChanged( _
              ByVal sender As System.Object, ByVal e As System.EventArgs) _
              Handles ComboBox1.SelectedIndexChanged
        Dim x As WpfInteropCtrl.UserControl1 = _
                    CType(ElementHost1.Child, WpfInteropCtrl.UserControl1)
        x.Image = ComboBox1.SelectedItem.ToString
    End Sub
End Class
```

Code snippet from Form1

Finally, the preceding code includes the SelectedIndexChanged event handler, which is called when a user selects a new item from the list of available image files. This event handler retrieves the selected image path and passes this path to the child of the `ElementHost1` control. Because the child object is in fact an instance of the class `WpfInteropCtrl.UserControl1`, the generic child property can be cast to this object, which supports the public property defined as part of the user control's definition, discussed earlier.

At this point, if you are following along with the text, you should save, build, and run your project. The project will work, although to be honest at this point it isn't doing too much. It illustrates that you can, in fact, host classes from the `System.Windows.Controls` namespace in an `ElementHost` control.

Custom Display Masking

The next part of this demonstration involves altering the display of the `ElementHost` content based on code located within the Windows Form. Accordingly, the next block of code uses a geometric shape to overlay a mask above the selected display, making it possible to round the corners or the entire image. The application of the mask occurs based on the second `ComboBox` control you added to the form.

This control was assigned three values, and when one of the values is selected, it triggers the `ComboBox2` `.SelectedIndexChanged` event, which has been handled in this code. The code follows a best practice and calls a private method that implements the appropriate action based on which value was selected. The method `ApplyMask` uses a `Select Case` statement to identify which of the three fixed maps has been selected and then either disables the clipping region or enables a clipping region of the appropriate shape.

The clipping region is a WPF property available on WPF controls. The `Clip` property enables you to overlay a given control with a geometric shape that masks out portions of the targeted control. This example implements two simple masks: an ellipse and a rectangle. Selecting to not have a mask sets the `Clip` property for the `Child` object within the control `ElementHost1` to `Nothing`. However, selecting a mask to screen out a portion of the display results in the code calling one of a pair of methods, `EllipseMask` and `RectMask`, each of which is focused on a single geometric shape.

These two methods share the majority of their logic, first getting the available display area from `ElementHost1`'s `Child` property. Both then use the `TextBoxMargin` to allow the user to change the size of the margin surrounding the clip region. Note that in both cases the margin isn't applied in the same manner as setting a margin in WPF was.

Under WPF, a `Margin` property is defined as a thickness or distance between the edge of the control and the edge of the display for each of the four sides. Thus, both the left and right or top and bottom values are the same. However, in the case of a clipping region, the code is defining the size of a rectangle. Thus, the size of the rectangle needs to account for the fact that moving the top of the image 10 pixels lower means that the box needs to be 20 pixels smaller on the length of the side so that the 10 pixels from the top balance the 10 matching pixels on the bottom. This is why the margin is doubled when describing the height and width, but not doubled when defining the upper-left corner location. To get this feature you'll want to create an event handler with an implementation similar to what is shown in the following snippet:

```
Private Sub ComboBox2_SelectedIndexChanged(ByVal sender As System.Object, _
                        ByVal e As System.EventArgs) _
                        Handles ComboBox2.SelectedIndexChanged
    ApplyMask()
End Sub
Private Sub ApplyMask()
    Select Case ComboBox2.SelectedIndex
        Case 0
            ElementHost1.Child.Clip = Nothing
            TextBoxMargin.Enabled = False
            TextBoxRounding.Enabled = False
        Case 1
            EllipseMask()
            TextBoxMargin.Enabled = True
            TextBoxRounding.Enabled = False
        Case 2
            RectMask()
```

```vb
                TextBoxMargin.Enabled = True
                TextBoxRounding.Enabled = True
            Case Else
                ' Can occur if the textbox controls load before the combo box.
                ' Nothing needs to be done in that case.
        End Select
    End Sub
    Private Sub EllipseMask()
        Dim width As Double = ElementHost1.Child.RenderSize.Width
        Dim height As Double = ElementHost1.Child.RenderSize.Height
        Dim margin As Double = Convert.ToDouble(TextBoxMargin.Text)
        If width = 0 Then
            width = ElementHost1.Width
        End If
        If height = 0 Then
            height = ElementHost1.Height
        End If
        If (margin * 2) > height Or (margin * 2) > width Then
            ElementHost1.Child.Clip = Nothing
        Else
            ElementHost1.Child.Clip = New Windows.Media.EllipseGeometry( _
                            New Windows.Rect(margin, margin, _
                            width - (margin * 2), height - (margin * 2)))
        End If
    End Sub
    Private Sub RectMask()
        Dim width As Double = ElementHost1.Width
        Dim height As Double = ElementHost1.Height
        Dim margin As Double = Convert.ToDouble(TextBoxMargin.Text)
        If (margin * 2) > height Or (margin * 2) > width Then
            ElementHost1.Child.Clip = Nothing
        Else
            Dim rect As New Windows.Media.RectangleGeometry( _
                            New Windows.Rect(margin, margin, _
                            width - (margin * 2), height - (margin * 2)))
            rect.RadiusX = Convert.ToDouble(TextBoxRounding.Text)
            rect.RadiusY = rect.RadiusX
            ElementHost1.Child.Clip = rect
        End If
    End Sub
    Private Sub TextBoxMargin_TextChanged(ByVal sender As System.Object, _
                                ByVal e As System.EventArgs) _
                                Handles TextBoxMargin.TextChanged

        Dim margin As Double
        If Double.TryParse(TextBoxMargin.Text, margin) Then
            ApplyMask()
        Else
            TextBoxMargin.Text = 0
        End If
    End Sub
    Private Sub TextBoxRounding_TextChanged(ByVal sender As System.Object, _
                                ByVal e As System.EventArgs) _
                                Handles TextBoxRounding.TextChanged

        Dim margin As Double
        If Double.TryParse(TextBoxRounding.Text, margin) Then
            ApplyMask()
        Else
            TextBoxRounding.Text = 0
        End If
    End Sub
```

Code snippet from Form1

Aside from the margin, note that in the `RectMask` function the code also applies the value from the `TextBoxRounding` control to the `RadiusX` and `RadiusY` properties on the rectangle. These properties cause the corners of the rectangle to be rounded, so when the rectangle mask is selected, the user is able to apply a value that changes the amount of corner rounding.

Finally, the preceding code block includes two additional event handlers, one for each of the two text boxes on the form. The first one handles events related to the margin's width, and the second event is related to the radius for rounded corners on your rectangle map. In both cases they call the same `ApplyMask` method, which is called when you select a mask.

Now it's time to build and run your application. After building and running your control, you should see a display similar to the one shown in Figure 16-3. Superficially, this application works, allowing you to apply different masks and resize them. Notice that you are now modifying your WPF controls from within your Windows Forms application.

However, apply a mask and then resize your main frame. Notice how even though the image was resized, the mask remained static. Your application isn't recognizing a change in the size of control `ElementHost1` or the need to recalculate the size and location of the mask.

FIGURE 16-3

Using a Mapped Property of a WPF Control

There are a couple of potential solutions to this problem; however, for the purposes of this chapter, which focuses on demonstrating the features of the Windows Forms Integration library, the solution described here uses a mapped property on your control. The capability to access the mapped properties of WPF controls is one of the features of this library that provides you with greater flexibility. One of the available properties on control `ElementHost1`, the `PropertyMap` collection, enables you to select one or more of the `ElementHost1` properties and essentially register for a custom event handler. This is not an event handler in the traditional Windows Forms sense of the word, but rather the assignment of a delegate that is called when that property is changed.

The first step is to go to the load event described earlier in this chapter and uncomment the line that is calling the method `AddPropertyMapping`. Once you have uncommented this line, add the functions shown in the block of code that follows. The first of these is, in fact, the custom function `AddPropertyMapping`. This function simply calls the `Add` method on the `PropertyMap` collection to assign a new delegate in the form of a `PropertyTranslator` from the `Windows.Forms.Integration` library that will be called when the `Size` property of control `ElementHost1` is changed. Note that by assigning this value at the end of the `Form1_Load` event handler, your application will now make this call whenever the size of the control changes:

Available for download on Wrox.com

```
' The AddPropertynMapping method assigns a custom
' mapping for the Size property.
Private Sub AddPropertyMapping()
    ElementHost1.PropertyMap.Add( _
        "Size", _
        New Integration.PropertyTranslator(AddressOf OnEHSizeChange))
End Sub
''' <summary>
''' Called when the ElementHost control's size is changed
''' </summary>
''' <param name="h"></param>
```

```
''' <param name="propertyName"></param>
''' <param name="value"></param>
''' <remarks>A change of this property requires the form hosting this
''' control to adjust the clipping region, so the Property Mapper
''' in the Integration library is used to map an "event" handler.</remarks>
Private Sub OnEHSizeChange(ByVal h As Object, _
            ByVal propertyName As String, ByVal value As Object)
    ApplyMask()
End Sub
```

Code snippet from Form1

The second method in the preceding block of code is the actual `OnEHSizeChange` method. Note that this method has three parameters:

➤ The first is the actual object that has been changed.

➤ The second is the name of the property, so multiple properties could call the same delegate in your Windows Forms code.

➤ The third is the new value of that property.

For the purposes of this demonstration, because this method will only be called for a single property on a single object, and because the new value will already be assigned within the control, the only thing this method needs to do is call the same `ApplyMask` method that is called elsewhere to correctly apply the mask to the image.

Save, build, and run your example code again and notice how the mapping of the property has enabled your form to detect when a property on control `ElementHost1`, or potentially even on one of the WPF controls within your `ElementHost` control, has changed. As an exercise, consider changing this example to detect when the image hosted in control `Image1` changes.

This example illustrates how you can create a new WPF component that can be incorporated into an existing Windows Forms application. You can start the process of migrating your application to WPF while still focusing the majority of your available resources on adding new capabilities to your existing application. Migration in this context means you are not forced to spend the majority of your cycles rewriting your entire existing interface. Instead, you can integrate these two display methodologies. The preceding example demonstrates one way of working with a WPF control within a Windows Forms application.

Other methods for carrying out the same tasks, including adding WPF controls within the context of the same project, are also possible. However, defining WPF controls within a Windows Forms project reduces your ability to migrate your control into a larger WPF model. Using the method demonstrated in this chapter makes that transition easy, as you'll just be hosting Windows Forms controls in WPF.

HOSTING WINDOWS FORMS CONTROLS IN WPF

In the case of WPF hosting Windows Forms controls, you might choose to do this if you have an existing application that relies on certain controls that have not yet been implemented in WPF. For example, the following table lists some of the controls that are not directly supported in WPF:

BindingNavigator	DataGridView	DateTimePicker
ErrorProvider	HelpProvider	ImageList
LinkLabel	MaskedTextBox	MonthCalendar
NotifyIcon	PrintDocument	PropertyGrid

In addition to these controls that aren't directly supported, still other controls may behave differently in this release. For example, the `ComboBox` control in WPF doesn't provide built-in support for autocomplete. In other cases, such as the `HelpProvider` (F1 Help), a control isn't supported because WPF provides an alternative implementation. Even if you have an application in which the existing user interface takes advantage of one of the preceding control's features, it is understandable that you might be interested in integrating your existing investment in the next version of your application.

However, there is a real possibility that if you have heavily leveraged a `DataGridView` control, you will want to reuse your existing control, rather than attempt to design a custom replacement.

To walk through the process of using the `WindowsFormsHost` control, create a new WPF Application called ProVB_WPFInterop; a copy of the completed project is available with this name as part of the code download. Once you have done that, select File ➪ Add to add a second project to this solution. This time, pick a Windows Control Library and give it the name WinFormInteropCtrl. Again, Visual Studio will execute the template to create a new project. At this point you will have access to a new control called `UserControl1`. Go to the designer for this new user control and add a `Button` control and a `DataGridView` control to the design surface, as shown in Figure 16-4.

Figure 16-4 shows one way to arrange these controls. For the purposes of this demonstration, the `Button` control is static; it is there to demonstrate a formatting issue. Next, manually add the two columns shown in the grid through Visual Studio 2010. You can do this using the context menu available in the upper-right corner of the control's display. Simply select Add Column for each of the two columns, calling the first

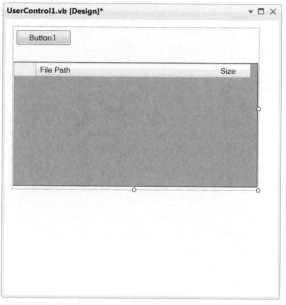

FIGURE 16-4

File Path and the second Size. The first column will wind up holding lengthy string values representing the available images, so ensure you add a decent default length to this column. This control represents a complex grid but it is not meant to be one. Resize the grid to fit within the display area of your user control. This demonstration focuses on display characteristics, so there is no need to edit the default code-behind or provide an action for the click event of the button.

After you have created a new `UserControl1`, build the project so that the WinFormInteropCtrl has been compiled and then close this window. The next step is to update your WPF project with the appropriate references. Three references need to be added. From the Project Settings window, select the References tab. Add references to the .NET assemblies `System.Windows.Forms` and `WindowsFormsIntegration`. Finally, add a reference to the WinFormInteropCtrl project. After adding these three references, close the Project Settings window and recompile the project.

Having created a new user control and added the references, open the `MainWindow.xaml` file that's created with this template. In that XAML file you'll see the "Window" declaration. This declaration in Visual Studio imports a few namespaces, as discussed in Chapter 17. You'll want to change the title attribute of the window in XAML to reflect the new form title, Pro VB WPF Interop.

Next, switch to Design view and add a button to the upper-left corner of the display. This button will illustrate two concepts. First, just like the Windows Forms example, where the code leveraged some of the WPF classes outside the context of the interop form, this WPF form is going to leverage the same `FolderBrowseDialog` that was used in the preceding Windows form. Second, it will help show that although WPF and Windows Forms share the same control, a button, the default display of that control is very different, a problem that can be corrected. Label this button "Select Folder." Note technically the text shown on the button is part of the content property. In this case you can implicitly reference that property by putting the desired text directly into the XAML between the open and close tags of the buttons.

Next, add a second button to the upper-right corner of the display. Align the buttons, label this as a Close button. Next, drag and drop a `WindowsFormsHost` control onto the display. The control should be docked to the bottom bounds of the display below the two buttons.

Unlike the Windows Forms project earlier in this chapter, the WPF design surface currently does not support adding your custom user control to this display. At this point you can review the XAML view within Visual Studio to compare your XAML to the XAML shown in the following listing. Your overall display should look similar to Figure 16-5.

```xaml
<Window x:Class="MainWindow"
    xmlns="http://schemas.microsoft.com/winfx/2006/xaml/presentation"
    xmlns:x="http://schemas.microsoft.com/winfx/2006/xaml"
    Title="ProVB WPF Interop" Height="350" Width="525">
    <Grid>
    <Button Height="23" HorizontalAlignment="Left" Margin="14,14,0,0"
            Name="Button1" VerticalAlignment="Top"
            Width="100">Select Folder</Button>
    <Button Height="23" HorizontalAlignment="Right" Margin="0,14,26,0"
            Name="Button2" VerticalAlignment="Top"
            Width="75">Close</Button>
    <my:WindowsFormsHost Margin="0,50,0,0" Name="WindowsFormsHost1"
            xmlns:my="clr-namespace:System.Windows.Forms.Integration;
                                    assembly=WindowsFormsIntegration" />
    </Grid>
</Window>
```

Code snippet from MainWindow.xaml

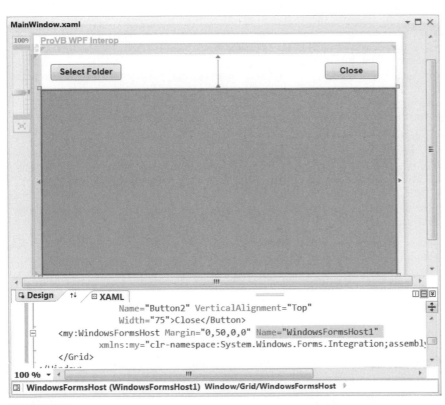

FIGURE 16-5

Once you have set up your application's look, it's time to start handling some of the code. You'll notice in the code that follows there is again a default directory that is the Images directory on Windows 7. The next method is the `Window1_Loaded` method. This method is called once when your form is initially loaded, and it's a great place to create an instance of your custom user control and assign it as the child of `WindowsFormsHost1`. There is also a line that has been commented out in this initial listing; you will uncomment that line after the first time you test run your application.

Both of the buttons need event handlers. In this case you can use the Visual Basic `Handles` clause to associate the method shown in the sample code with the button. Both Button1 and Button2 have associated handlers in the code snippet which follows.

The majority of this code is associated with the `Button1.Click` event handler. In this case, for brevity, the application doesn't automatically load the contents of the directory. Instead when you first click `Button1`, you'll be allowed to select the default folder and then have it load the contents of that folder. Notice that although the grid was created with two columns, this sample code merely loads the document name for demonstration purposes into the grid that is part of your custom user control:

```vb
Class MainWindow
    'Private Sub Window1_Initialized(ByVal sender As Object,
                        ByVal e As System.EventArgs) Handles Me.Initialized
    '   Me.WindowStyle = Windows.WindowStyle.None
    '   Me.AllowsTransparency = True
    'End Sub

    Private Sub Window1_Loaded(ByVal sender As System.Object,
                    ByVal e As System.Windows.RoutedEventArgs) Handles MyBase.Loaded
        WindowsFormsHost1.Child = New WinFormInteropCtrl.UserControl1()
        PopulateGrid("C:\Users\Public\Pictures\Sample Pictures")
        System.Windows.Forms.Application.EnableVisualStyles()
    End Sub

    Private Sub Button1_Click(ByVal sender As System.Object,
                    ByVal e As System.Windows.RoutedEventArgs) Handles Button1.Click
        Dim FolderBrowserDialog1 As New System.Windows.Forms.FolderBrowserDialog()
        FolderBrowserDialog1.SelectedPath = "C:\Users\Public\Pictures\Sample Pictures"
        If (FolderBrowserDialog1.ShowDialog() = Windows.Forms.DialogResult.OK) Then
            PopulateGrid(FolderBrowserDialog1.SelectedPath)
        End If
    End Sub

    Private Sub PopulateGrid(ByVal path As String)
        Dim uc As WinFormInteropCtrl.UserControl1 =
                    CType(WindowsFormsHost1.Child, WinFormInteropCtrl.UserControl1)
        Dim roid As Integer
        For Each control As System.Windows.Forms.Control In uc.Controls
            If TypeOf control Is System.Windows.Forms.DataGridView Then
                Dim grid As System.Windows.Forms.DataGridView = control
                grid.Rows.Clear()
                For Each filename As String In System.IO.Directory.GetFiles(path)
                    roid = grid.Rows.Add()
                    grid.Rows(roid).Cells(0).Value = filename
                    grid.Rows(roid).Cells(1).Value = New System.IO.FileInfo(filename).Length
                Next
            End If
        Next
    End Sub

    Private Sub Button2_Click(ByVal sender As System.Object,
                    ByVal e As System.Windows.RoutedEventArgs) Handles Button2.Click
        Me.Close()
```

```
      End Sub
   End Class
```

Code snippet from MainWindow.xaml

Finally, note that the last method is the event handler for the `Button2.Click` event. As you might expect, this event handles closing the window, an important capability if you hide the outer frame of your window.

At this point you can run the application. If you are using the downloadable package, you should see the results shown in Figure 16-6. If you are creating your own copy of the project, you should see similar results; however, the button in `WindowsFormsHost1` should have the incorrect styling.

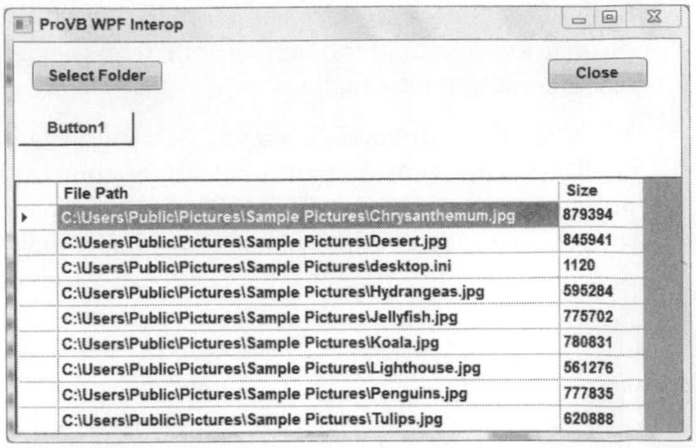

The first item that should jump out at you is that the `WinFormInteropCtrl` has lost the Windows XP visual styling. Referring back to Figure 16-6, you can confirm that this styling was present in the designer for this control. To resolve this issue, go to the code-behind file for your `Window1.xaml` file, `Window1.xaml.vb`. Within the `Window1_Loaded` method, either before or after the call to create your user control as the child of the control `WindowsFormsHost1`, add the following line of code:

FIGURE 16-6

```
        System.Windows.Forms.Application.EnableVisualStyles()
```

Rerun the application. The visual styling is now correct, but you should also be able to see that WPF and Windows Forms render this style differently on a similar control. Thus, you'll want to ensure that you minimize the number of similar controls you reference on different sides of the host boundary. In this case, you simply needed to manually reset the display settings for your control to indicate that it should use the Windows XP styling; however, this styling issue provides an excellent introduction to the next topic.

Note Windows 7 users may experience an added display issue. For some reason Windows 7 and the WPF Interop libraries cause a display issue. The issue goes away when the window is resized, but if you see a ghost image, resize the running window and it will go away. This issue is not shown in Figure 16-6.

One of the options discussed in the preceding chapter that focused on WPF was the capability to change the window style so that the traditional border and controls in the frame were hidden. Once this is done, it is possible to enable transparency and really work on creating a custom look and feel for your application. However, you'll note that the following code is commented out in the online materials. That's because this code is there to illustrate one of the limitations of the `WindowsFormsHost` control.

```
        Private Sub Window1_Initialized(ByVal sender As Object, _
                          ByVal e As System.EventArgs) Handles Me.Initialized
            Me.WindowStyle = Windows.WindowStyle.None
            Me.AllowsTransparency = True
        End Sub
```

If you enable this code, you'll find that instead of getting your interop control to display, the WPF rendering engine does not render anything. Thus, while the limitations include not being able to use certain types of transparency with the control, this provides a much better illustration of how using a `WindowsFormsHost` control can affect your application's overall look and feel.

INTEGRATION LIMITATIONS

The challenge with integration is that these two display models don't operate under the same paradigm. The Windows Forms world and the `WindowsFormsHost` are based on window handles, also known as `HWnd` structures. WPF, conversely, has only a single `HWnd` to define its display area for the operating system and then avoids using HWnds. Keep in mind, then, that when you are working with encapsulating a control, that control — be it WPF or Windows Forms — will be affected by the environment in which it is hosted.

For example, if you host a WPF control inside a Windows Forms application, then the ability to control low-level graphical display characteristics such as opacity or background will be limited by the rules for Windows Forms. Unlike WPF, which layers control characteristics supporting the display of a control at a layer below the current control, Windows Forms controls are contained in an HWnd; when the HWnd doesn't paint a background for your WPF control, the display may show that region as not painted and use a black or white background instead. Note that setting the AllowTransparency property for a control is supported when hosting WPF controls on a Windows Form. You can play with the background color used for the ElementHost control introduced earlier in this chapter to get a feel for this issue.

Recognizing that the host control is often limited by the underlying environment containing it is a good guide to predicting limitations. Although sometimes the actual characteristics of the parent application framework might come as a surprise, as you gain more experience with WPF you'll be able to predict where issues are likely to exist. For example, you can create both window- and page-based WPF applications, but these applications work on entirely different models. For example, a page-based WPF application is stateless. To support this stateless nature in those instances where it finds itself used in a page-based WPF application, the WindowsFormsHost control fully refreshes the contained control each time the page is refreshed — losing any user input that you might expect to remain within a Windows Forms control.

Another issue can arise with the advanced scaling capabilities of WPF. Although Windows Forms controls are scalable, Windows Forms doesn't support the concept of scaling down to 0 and then restoring properly.

Similarly, be aware of the message loop, current control focus, and property mapping of hosted controls. The host controls support passing messages to the controls they contain, but across the application the ordering of messages may not occur in the expected order. Similarly, when a WindowsFormsHost control has passed focus to a contained control and then the form is minimized, the host control may lose track of which control within its child has that focus. As a result, even though the unseen host has the current focus within your WPF application, there is no visible control with that focus.

Finally, there are additional potential issues with property mapping other than the background color issue described earlier, so you need to watch the behavior of these controls carefully and be prepared to manually map properties as shown in this chapter's first example.

This is not a complete list of potential issues you may encounter when attempting to integrate these two distinct user-interface implementations. One final warning is that you can't nest host controls. Both Windows Forms and WPF can contain multiple-host controls within a given window, but each of these host controls must be separate and of the same type. Thus, you can't create a WPF application containing a WindowsFormsHost control that contains an ElementHost control. If you're integrating controls, try to minimize the number of panels containing the host controls so that you don't accidentally attempt to nest the embedded host controls in another layer of integration.

SUMMARY

This chapter extended the coverage of user controls with regard to how you can leverage them to encapsulate application logic across disparate display systems. The chapter introduced the Windows .Forms.Integration library and the capability to have WPF and Windows Forms components provide an application user interface. This library is similar to other transitional libraries in that the focus is on supporting business needs and not on complete support for the features of WPF by Windows Forms components within the WPF environment. Key points from this chapter include the following:

➤ It is possible to start a migration to a WPF-based application interface using the Windows.Forms .Integration library and the ElementHost class.

➤ Such an interface enables you to embed enhanced image processing into an existing Windows Forms application.

➤ Using the `WindowsFormsHost` class enables you to embed a complex business or third-party control that you are not ready to replace within a WPF application.

➤ Using the integration library, you can support key business-driven components, but it may affect the visual appeal of your user interface.

While this chapter introduced the Windows Forms integration library, you may have noticed that the overall tone isn't describing this as the next great feature. This isn't because the integration library didn't require significant effort to create or wasn't well designed. This library is an excellent resource — in the limited area for which it was designed: to support your transition from Windows Forms to WPF. Using this library across a few releases of your application as you migrate to a WPF-based user interface is an excellent way to manage complexity, but always remember that you want to fully commit to the WPF-based paradigms, which means moving beyond this library.

Finally, if you do have the opportunity to create a complete new user interface and can avoid the added complexity associated with using multiple different display technologies via these integration classes, then you should. While user controls are a best practice, so is building an application that can fully leverage all of the new features of declarative programming, as you'll see in the next chapter on WPF.

17

WPF Desktop Applications

WHAT YOU WILL LEARN IN THIS CHAPTER

- ➤ The WPF strategy
- ➤ Why you should use WPF
- ➤ Creating a WPF application
- ➤ Implementing a custom WPF application
- ➤ Dynamic properties
- ➤ Customizing the user interface
- ➤ Data binding

Windows Presentation Foundation (WPF) — previously known as Avalon — is the next-generation presentation library and development paradigm for user interfaces. It was introduced with Windows Vista as a key architectural component in the .NET 3.0 Framework. This chapter introduces you to the WPF programming model and discusses key elements you'll need to know in order to work with WPF. Rest assured you will be creating applications that leverage the features of WPF in the future. Visual Studio introduces a fully enabled development environment for creating and customizing WPF-based applications.

The libraries that make up WPF were released in conjunction with the release of Windows Vista — not the commercial and much-publicized public launch of Vista in January 2007, but the initial release of Vista to enterprise partners in November 2006. The libraries shipped with Vista and coincidentally with Microsoft Office 2007, but what you may have noticed at the time was the lack of development tools.

However, with Visual Studio 2010, there are tools for not only the .NET 4 libraries, but also for all of the .NET 3.0 libraries. In fact, one of the main focuses of Visual Studio 2010 is the introduction of a WPF-based user interface and better support for developing WPF applications. Prior to Visual Studio 2010 it was a given that you would need to have someone, either a designer or a developer, use a design tool to build your user interface. Microsoft's Expression suite of tools — in particular Expression Blend, was considered a requirement to create a custom WPF application.

This chapter introduces a basic WPF application. It goes through a series of steps to build a custom WPF Windows framework application that you can leverage. The goal is to introduce you to WPF in a manner that should be familiar to Windows Forms developers and then expand on what additional items WPF brings to the equation, such as declarative data binding. This chapter will not make you an expert WPF developer — WPF is too large a topic to fully cover in a single chapter — but it does provide a good starting place.

WHAT, WHERE, WHY, HOW — WPF STRATEGY

When .NET was released, most people realized that in terms of application development, a paradigm shift was occurring. The release of WPF was the first step in yet another paradigm shift, this one focusing on how user interfaces are designed and implemented. Therefore, it's appropriate to take a little time to look at not only where the user interface models are coming from, but also where they are going. Understanding that will enable you to see how WPF fits in, and not only why you'll want WPF in the future, but also how you can start leveraging it today.

The original user interfaces were punch cards for input and hard-copy text for output. OK, maybe that's going a little too far back. Instead, let's jump ahead to the part of the user interface's resume that applies to where we're going today. In the 1980s and 1990s, several computer and software manufacturers introduced the graphical user interface (GUI). These GUI environments, while implemented differently on different platforms, became a part of the operating system. For Windows, this is the User32.dll and its companion UI classes. The original Visual Basic 1.0 was designed to enable developers to interact in a simple manner with these files, unlike C++, which referenced the raw User32.dll interfaces for everything.

Over time, Visual Basic's simple drag-and-drop approach to creating the forms that users would access as part of an application in that GUI environment helped make it the most popular development language. However, with Web migrations, the paradigm started to shift. The Web introduced its own way of creating forms — one that used HTML. The HTML model is more declarative and doesn't guarantee the behavior of the components in the user interface. For example, the HTML page may declare it wants a text box, but it's up to the browser to interpret and provide the code that creates the actual object. The HTML control model is supported on Windows by Internet Explorer, and by third-party tools such as Firefox and Netscape.

.NET ushered in the next stage of client UI implementation with ASP.NET and Windows Forms. Changing the UI model wasn't a primary focus of .NET; .NET introduced new tools for the UI. .NET shipped with two user-interface implementations: ASP.NET's HTML-based UI and the desktop-centric Windows Forms. It's important to realize that Windows Forms isn't based on the same code that User32 windows are, even though the programming model whereby the designer adds the code to a portion of the application's source is similar. The managed environment represents both the second and third programming models for developing user interfaces under Windows. Of course, other platforms include still other GUI models, but these three GUI models — User32.dll, ASP.NET, and Windows Forms — represent the ones Microsoft supported as of .NET 2.0.

Thus, Microsoft was creating many user-interface controls with three distinct implementations, a cost noticeable to even an organization as large as Microsoft. For developers, including those at Microsoft, the pain starts with the fact that a user interface can't be transported seamlessly between a Web-based version of an application and a local desktop version of the same application, or across platforms. For example, Microsoft can't design a UI for Outlook and reuse it for Outlook Web Access (OWA). Instead, it needs a different team of developers with different skills to create the OWA interface, and have you seen a remotely downloadable Windows Forms–based OWA application?

Having pointed out how some applications are designed with dual interfaces, that's certainly not the norm. Let's face it: There often isn't much economic incentive to create both a Windows Forms-based and ASP.NET-based user interface for the same application. There are certainly cases where an application is successful, and a follow-up task may be to attempt to reproduce the user interface for another target UI, but that is the exception, not the rule.

This is where the WPF model comes in. WPF is a declarative way of designing interfaces. The idea is that you can use a declaration to describe your user interface and then compile or include that definition with either a desktop or Web or even another operating system version of your application. WPF uses XML to declare the user-interface elements, relying on a standard known as the *Extensible Application Markup Language (XAML)*. Taken a step further consider that going forward an application could be built using Silverlight and that same XAML used for a WPF version.

RASTER GRAPHICS AND VECTOR GRAPHICS

Currently, when you create a Windows Forms control you decide how large, in pixels, that button should be. A similar action is taken with regard to HTML forms, where you can specify either a size in pixels or a percentage of the screen. In both cases, the computer simply lays out a square or rounded square based on a flat set of pixels. It does the same with other images you use, working with what are known as *raster graphics*. Raster graphics are a collection of points on the surface of a screen that represent an image.

The alternative form of graphics is known as *vector graphics*. A vector is a line with a point of origin that continues forward in space from that point of origin. Vector graphics aren't based on a collection of points, but rather on a series of vectors. A plane representing the surface of your screen is placed in the path of these vectors, which define a set of points, and that is what you see on your screen. Vector graphics provide much better and more realistic image manipulation. Note that you can incorporate a raster image with vector graphics because you can place the raster image in your virtual plane, but the reverse isn't feasible.

WPF is the first forms-based engine that relies on this vector-based model. The good news is that you can create user interfaces that truly look fantastic. The bad news is that you need to account for the fact that computing a series of vectors and the plane that intersects those vectors requires more CPU or graphical processing unit (GPU) cycles. Thus, like Vista or Windows 7 UI, all WPF user interfaces require a bit more computing horsepower. However, unlike Vista or Windows 7, for which certain graphical features are disabled if your computer doesn't natively have that horsepower, for WPF, that isn't the case.

Because WPF is compatible with Windows XP, it isn't limited to those scenarios in which a powerful GPU is available to offload that processing. After all, Windows Vista was the first operating system to support leveraging the GPU, so system performance only degrades when you run a WPF application on Windows XP or an older computer that isn't able to support something like the Glass display settings.

However, those concerns aside, one of the main appeals of the WPF model is its graphical capabilities. Because WPF is built around vector graphics and enhanced GPU processor support, it enables a much more appealing user interface. You can hide the native Windows frame, as you'll see later in this chapter, make round buttons, and essentially begin to create a truly custom user interface, one that in an artistically designed application has users saying "wow" in a truly memorable experience.

SHOULD YOUR NEXT WINDOWS PROJECT USE WPF?

Microsoft will, of course, need to support all its previous GUI models in addition to WPF for the foreseeable future. However, Microsoft is motivated by the same factors that the rest of us can leverage — better graphics and a single application that can have a UI that runs in multiple environments. Accordingly, Microsoft announced that enhancements to the .NET-based Windows Forms Class Libraries would not be occurring. While this UI model will receive maintenance and security-related updates, there will be no future new development on that set of libraries.

Does this mean you should automatically plan on moving to WPF for your next Windows application? Prior to Visual Studio 2010 the answer to that depended on several factors. If you need to target a client who is limited to .NET 2.0, then the answer is obviously no. However, now that Visual Studio 2010 is available, the answer consistently looks more and more like yes. Of course, there are always mitigating factors — for example, if your clients are on an older operating system, then the enhanced graphics can incur a performance hit. While Windows Forms still has a more mature control set, the WPF control gallery has made gains such that it is almost on a par with it. The bigger challenge is the shift in development paradigm.

While WPF provides a great deal of flexibility, we're only now getting past the point where using it also meant a lot of manual implementation. With Visual Studio 2010, it is much easier to do many of the tasks we expect to be easy. For example, whereas originally a simple setting such as Transparency might have required a lot of consideration to incorporate standard Windows behavior, now that is better understood; and the enhanced capability to manage it can make WPF development faster than the equivalent Windows Forms development. The challenge, of course, is experience in dealing with the new declarative development paradigm for your UI.

Coincidentally, this is the main reason why you should consider starting to switch to WPF. At this point, even Visual Studio is using WPF. If you want to maintain your skills, then you need to start down the WPF path. In fact, while most of the demos in this book still leverage Windows Forms, the next edition, which will target the next version of WPF, will request that authors migrate to WPF-based demo applications. An increasing amount of development is moving to WPF, and job postings are looking for developers with WPF and Silverlight experience. While you may have a large investment in a Windows Forms application (and therefore need to start with the `ElementHost` control discussed in Chapter 16), you should still start the process of moving from Windows Forms to WPF.

CREATING A WPF APPLICATION

Chapter 5 introduced you to declarative concepts and XAML so this chapter focuses on WPF specifics. The first time this book looked at WPF, in *Professional Visual Basic 2005 with .NET 3.0* Evjen et al., 2007, the focus was on going through the manual steps of both creating a basic WPF application and updating the build file to create that application. These steps were appropriate because at the time WPF didn't have a native IDE and code-generation toolset. Most early WPF applications were built by hand or with limited conversion tools that could output graphics as XAML.

With Visual Studio 2010 we've come a long way in a relatively short time. Visual Studio now includes a true WPF IDE, support for XAML-based IntelliSense, and a robust designer in the form of Expression Blend, a powerful option (not a requirement) for building a compelling WPF application.

Be aware that while working in WPF, whether you are in Visual Studio or Expression Blend, it is very easy to spend a lot of time adjusting colors or fades, or adding simple animations. In an ideal scenario the idea is that the UI design will be handled by a UI designer and those costs will be accounted for separately. However, if you are doing the design as a developer this can chew up an application development budget in nothing flat. Accordingly, it is recommended that you define the initial application layout and then get the application operational. Only after you have completed the business integration and gotten the control elements working as required should you return to the design surface to provide complex graphics and behavior on top of your application.

Thus, the next step is to use Visual Studio to generate your WPF application. This chapter will take an application through three phases, so the code download contains three different projects. For now we will create the first project, after which we transition to either the _Step2 or _Step3 version of the sample project. In each case, the project contains the completed code for the previous phase, but because this code is transformed rather dramatically, with some elements disappearing completely over the course of the chapter, this format provides you with a series of checkpoints while going through this chapter yourself.

Create a .NET 4 WPF application called ProVB_WPF_Step1. This application could also be created as a .NET 3.0 application, but in that case you wouldn't have access to .NET 4 Class Libraries. Additionally, note that the list of available templates for WPF applications disappears if you choose to target a .NET 2.0 baseline.

As shown in Figure 17-1, Visual Studio opens in the main window you've just declared. One thing to notice is that there isn't a line of VB code in this project, just a few XAML snippets.

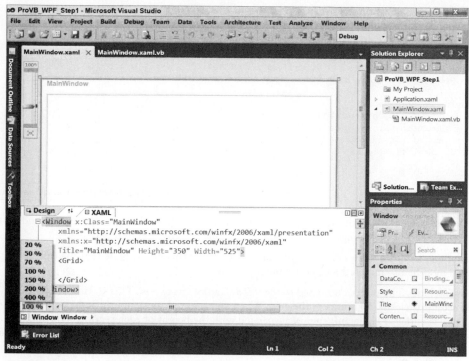

FIGURE 17-1

You'll also note a new feature of Visual Studio 2010 has been highlighted in Figure 17-1. In the lower-left corner is a drop-down showing a series of percentages. Changing the value here changes the default size of the text in the XAML code window. Thus, at 200% the text in the text editor is shown at 200% normal size. This is one of the benefits of having a WPF-based editor; the vector graphics allow for scaling on-the-fly without needing to change a font size to change the size of the displayed text.

Chapter 5 also introduced the XAML that is generated with a new project, so the next step is to start customizing this newly created project.

Implementing a Custom WPF Application

It is possible to do much of your WPF programming using XAML, but the next step is to examine how XAML can be integrated with code. After all, at some point you probably expect to start seeing some Visual Basic code again. Until now the ProVB_WPF_Step1 sample has been a pure XAML application, so first we will make a quick plan for what this application will do and then we will create a first-cut implementation. For demonstration purposes, we will create a simple photo-viewing application. The user should be able to select a folder containing one or more images and then view those images, moving forward and backward through the list.

For now, that will be the extent of the requirements; later, after the basic application is operational, you can expand the scope to customize the look and feel further. Begin by modifying the "empty" window. Of course, it's not really empty. The window actually has a grid within it, so you can start with that and create three sections. After selecting the grid, hover over the left-hand border of your window. You'll see a point appear within the border that sends a guide line horizontally across the window. Select a point about 40 pixels from the top and a second point approximately 40 pixels from the bottom, dividing your grid into three sections.

Don't worry about being exactly on 40, because after you've selected your two points you are going to switch to the XAML view. Now, instead of the previous display, you have code similar to what appears here:

```xaml
<Window x:Class="MainWindow"
    xmlns="http://schemas.microsoft.com/winfx/2006/xaml/presentation"
    xmlns:x="http://schemas.microsoft.com/winfx/2006/xaml"
    Title="ProVB_WPF" Height="350" Width="525" Name="MainWindow">
    <Grid>
        <Grid.RowDefinitions>
            <RowDefinition Height="45" />
            <RowDefinition Height="215*" />
            <RowDefinition Height="40" />
        </Grid.RowDefinitions>
    </Grid>
</Window>
```

Code snippet from MainWindow.xaml

Note if instead of working along with the text you are looking at the sample download, keep in mind that the download includes all of the changes that will be made during the creation of this first step.

The preceding snippet includes a few edits that you can reproduce at this point. Note that the title of the window has been modified to match the project name.

The XAML now includes a new section related to the `Grid.RowDefinitions`. This section contains the specification of sections within the points in the grid. When you selected those points in the designer, you were defining these sections. The default syntax associated with the height of each section is the number of pixels followed by an asterisk. The asterisk indicates that when the window is resized, this row should also resize. For this application, only the center section should resize, so the asterisk has been removed from the top and bottom row definitions.

This provides a set of defined regions that can be used to align controls within this form. Thus, the next step is to add some controls to the form and create a basic user interface. In this scenario, the actions should be very familiar to any developer who has worked with either Windows Forms or ASP.NET forms.

Controls

WPF provides an entirely different set of libraries for developing applications. However, although these controls exist in a different library, how you interact with them from Visual Basic is generally the same. Each control has a set of properties, events, and methods that you can leverage. The XAML file may assign these values in the declarative format of XML, but you can still reference the same properties on the instances of the objects that the framework creates within your Visual Basic code.

Starting with the topmost section of the grid, `Grid.Row 0`, drag the following controls from the Toolbox onto the form: a `Label`, a `TextBox`, and a `Button`. These can be aligned into this region in the same order they were added. Ensure that the label is bound to the left side and top of the window, while the button is bound to the right side and top of the window. Meanwhile, the text box should be bound to the top and both sides of the window so that as the window is stretched, the width of the text box increases. The resulting XAML should be similar to this:

```xaml
<Window x:Class="MainWindow"
    xmlns="http://schemas.microsoft.com/winfx/2006/xaml/presentation"
    xmlns:x="http://schemas.microsoft.com/winfx/2006/xaml"
    Title="ProVB_WPF" Height="350" Width="525" Name="MainWindow">
    <Grid>
        <Grid.RowDefinitions>
            <RowDefinition Height="45" />
            <RowDefinition Height="215*" />
            <RowDefinition Height="40" />
        </Grid.RowDefinitions>
```

```xaml
        <Label Margin="0,11,0,0" Name="Label1" HorizontalAlignment="Left" Width="80"
Height="23" VerticalAlignment="Top">Image Path:</Label>

        <TextBox Margin="81,13,92,0" Name="TextBox1" Height="21"
VerticalAlignment="Top" />

        <Button HorizontalAlignment="Right" Margin="0,11,9,11" Name="ButtonBrowse"
Width="75">Images . . .</Button>
    </Grid>
</Window>
```

Code snippet from MainWindow.xaml

As shown in the newly added lines (in bold), each control is assigned a name and defines a set of editable properties. Note that these names can be addressed from within the code and that you can handle events from each control based on that control's named instance. For now, however, just adjust the text within the label to indicate that the text box to its immediate right will contain a folder path for images, and adjust the button control. Rename the Button control to `ButtonBrowse` and use the text `Images...` to label the button. There is obviously more to do with this button, but for now you can finish creating the initial user interface.

Next, add the following controls in the following order. First, add an `Image` control. To achieve a design surface similar to the one shown in Figure 17-2, drop the `Image` control so that it overlaps both the middle and bottom sections of the grid display. Now add three buttons to the bottom portion of the display. At this point the controls can be aligned. You can do this through a combination of editing the XAML directly and positioning things on the screen. For example, expand the `Image` control to the limits of the two bottom grid rows using the design surface; similarly, align the buttons visually on the design surface.

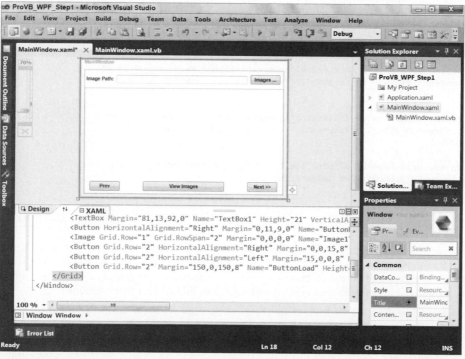

FIGURE 17-2

As shown in the figure, the separations for the two row definitions are described in the design surface, and each of the buttons has a custom label. Note that the Next button is followed by a pair of greater than symbols, but the Prev button is missing a matching set of less than symbols. They could have been added as the < symbol but instead one of the changes to be made in the Visual Basic code is the addition of these symbols to the button label.

First, however, review the XAML code and ensure that, for example, the Image control is assigned to Grid.Row 1 and that the property Grid.RowSpan is 2. Unlike the items that were in Grid.Row 0, the items in other rows of the grid must be explicitly assigned. Similarly, the name and caption of each button in the bottom row of the grid are modified to reflect that control's behavior. These and similar changes are shown in the following XAML:

```xaml
<Window x:Class="MainWindow"
  xmlns="http://schemas.microsoft.com/winfx/2006/xaml/presentation"
  xmlns:x="http://schemas.microsoft.com/winfx/2006/xaml"
    Title="ProVB_WPF" Height="350" Width="525" Name="MainWindow">
    <Grid>
        <Grid.RowDefinitions>
            <RowDefinition Height="45" />
            <RowDefinition Height="215*" />
            <RowDefinition Height="40" />
        </Grid.RowDefinitions>
        <Label Margin="0,11,0,0" Name="Label1" HorizontalAlignment="Left" Width="80"
Height="23" VerticalAlignment="Top">Image Path:</Label>

        <TextBox Margin="81,13,92,0" Name="TextBox1" Height="21"
VerticalAlignment="Top" />

        <Button HorizontalAlignment="Right" Margin="0,11,9,11" Name="ButtonBrowse"
Width="75">Images . . .</Button>

        <Image Grid.Row="1" Grid.RowSpan="2" Margin="0,0,0,0" Name="Image1"
Stretch="Fill" />

        <Button Grid.Row="2" HorizontalAlignment="Right" Margin="0,0,15,8"
Name="ButtonNext" Width="75" Height="23" VerticalAlignment="Bottom">Next >>
</Button>

        <Button Grid.Row="2" HorizontalAlignment="Left" Margin="15,0,0,8"
Name="ButtonPrev" Width="75" Height="23" VerticalAlignment="Bottom">
Prev</Button>

        <Button Grid.Row="2" Margin="150,0,150,8" Name="ButtonLoad" Height="23"
VerticalAlignment="Bottom">View Images</Button>
    </Grid>
</Window>
```

Code snippet from MainWindow.xaml

Note in the bold sections the description of the new controls. The Image control is first, and it is positioned in Grid.Row number 1, which, because .NET arrays are always zero-based, is the second row. The second attribute on this node indicates that it will span more then a single row in the grid. For now, this control uses the default name, and it has been set so that it will stretch to fill the area that contains it.

Following the Image control are the definitions for the three buttons along the bottom of the display. For now, these buttons will control the loading of images; over the course of this chapter, these buttons will be either removed or redone significantly. The order of these buttons isn't important, so following their order in the file, the first button is like the others positioned in the final row of the grid. This button has been placed on the right-hand side of this area and is bound to the bottom and right corners of the display. Its name has been changed to "ButtonNext" and its label is "Next >>."

The next button is the Prev button, which has been placed and bound to the left-hand side and bottom of the display. Its name has been changed to "ButtonPrev," and its display text has been changed to read "Prev." As noted earlier, the arrow symbols are not in the button name; and, as you can test in your own code, attempting to add them here causes an error.

Finally, there is the ButtonLoad button, which is centered in the display area. It has been bound to both sides of the display to maintain its position in the center. The label for this button is "View Images," which is, of course, the goal of this application. However, in order for that to happen, you need an event handler for this button; in fact, you need several event handlers in order to get the basic behavior of the application in place.

Event Handlers

In previous versions of Visual Studio you could click on a control and Visual Studio would automatically generate the default event handler for that control in your code. Fortunately, WPF also provides this behavior, so generate the following event handlers:

➤ Double-click on the title bar of the form to generate the `MainWindow_Loaded` event handler.

➤ Double-click on the Images button to create the `ButtonBrowse_Click` handler.

➤ Double-click on the Load button to create the `ButtonLoad_Click` handler.

➤ Double-click on the Prev button to create the `ButtonPrev_Click` handler.

➤ Double-click on the Next button to create the `ButtonNext_Click` handler.

To create each of these handlers, you need to return to the Design view and click on the associated control, but after they are created you can stay in Code view for most of this section. Take a look at the `ButtonBrowse_Click` event handler's method stub:

```
Private Sub ButtonBrowse_Click(ByVal sender As System.Object, _
    ByVal e As System.Windows.RoutedEventArgs) _
    Handles ButtonBrowse.Click
End Sub
```

The preceding code was reformatted with line extension characters to improve readability, but this is essentially what each of your event handlers looks like. As a Visual Basic developer, you should find this syntax very familiar. Note that the method name has been generated based on the control name and the event being handled. The parameter list is generated with the "sender" and e parameter values, although the e value now references a different object in the System.Windows namespace. Finally, defined here is the VB-specific Handles syntax that indicates this method is an event handler, and which specific event or events it handles.

While this is a very familiar, powerful, and even recommended way of defining event handlers with VB and WPF, it isn't the only way. WPF allows you to define event handlers within your XAML code. To be honest, if this were a book on C#, we would probably spend a fair amount of time covering the advantages of that type of event handler declaration. After all, C# doesn't support the direct association of the event handler declaration with the method handling the event; as a result, C# developers prefer to declare their event handlers in XAML.

 Visual Basic provides a default implementation of WPF that encourages less coupling of the UI to the application code than C# does.

However, one of the goals of XAML is the separation of the application logic from the UI, and placing the names of event handlers in the UI actually couples the UI to the application logic. It shouldn't matter to the UI whether the Click event or the DoubleClick or any other event is being handled by custom logic. Therefore, although this section introduces the way to define events directly in XAML, the recommendation is to define event handlers with the code that implements the handler.

In order to demonstrate this in the code, return to the Design view for your form. Select the Images button and position your cursor just after the word Button, which names this node. Press the spacebar. You'll see that you have IntelliSense, indicating which properties and events are available on this control. Typing a c adjusts the IntelliSense display so that you see the Click event. Select this event by pressing Tab and you'll see the display shown in Figure 17-3.

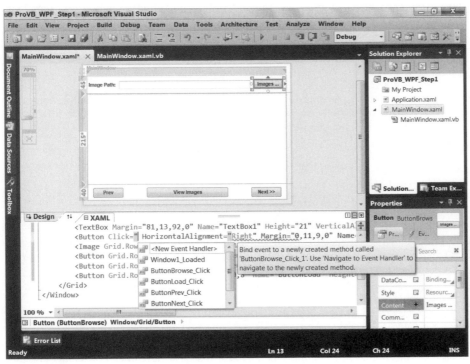

FIGURE 17-3

As shown here, not only does the XAML editor support full IntelliSense for selecting properties and events on a control, when an event is selected, it displays a list of possible methods that can handle this event. Of particular note is the first item in the list, which enables you to request that a new event handler be created in your code. Selecting this item tells Visual Studio to generate the same event handler stub that you created by double-clicking on the control; however, instead of placing the Handles clause on this method, the definition of this method as an event handler is kept in the XAML.

This causes two issues. First, if you are looking only at the code, then nothing explicitly indicates whether a given method in your code is in fact an event handler. This makes maintaining the code a bit (not a lot) more difficult to maintain. Second, if you have handled an event that is specific to Windows as opposed to the Web, then your XAML won't be portable. Neither of these side effects is desirable. Thus, given the VB syntax for defining events as part of the method declaration, the code in this chapter avoids the embedded XAML style of declaring standard Windows event handlers.

At this point, you could run your application. It won't do anything except allow you to close it, but you can verify that it behaves as expected and save your work.

Adding Behavior

It's almost time to make this UI do something, but there is one more step before you start working with code. As part of this application, you want to allow users to select the directory from which images should be displayed. In theory, you could (and in practice, at some time probably would) write a custom interface for selecting or navigating to the images directory. However, for this application that isn't important, and you want a quick and easy solution.

Unfortunately, WPF doesn't offer any native control that supports providing a quick and easy view into the file system. However, Windows Forms does, and in this case you want to leverage this control. The good news is that you can, and the even better news is that you don't need the Windows interop library in order to do so. Because something like the Browse Folders dialog isn't a control hosted on your form, you can reference it from your code. Thus, although you need the Windows Forms Integration Library and the `WindowsFormsHost` control discussed in Chapter 16 for any UI-based controls, in this case the code just needs to reference the `System.Windows.Forms` library.

Because the `System.Windows.Forms` library isn't automatically included as a reference in a WPF application, you need to manually add a reference to this library. Keep in mind that this library isn't going to be available to you outside of WPF's rich client implementation. Thus, this feature is limited to WPF running on the client; for other scenarios you would change out how you select an image. Open the My Project display and select the References tab. Click the Add button to open the Add Reference dialog and then select the `System.Windows.Forms` library, as shown in Figure 17-4. You can't add controls to your WPF form without leveraging the `Windows.Forms.Integration` library, but you can, behind the scenes, continue to reference controls and features of Windows Forms.

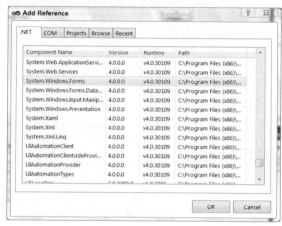

FIGURE 17-4

With this additional reference, you can begin to place some code into this application. Start with the `window_loaded` event. This event is where you'll define the default path for the image library, set up the label for the Prev button, and change the default property of the grid control so that it handles the images the way you want:

Available for download on Wrox.com

```vb
Private Sub MainWindow_Loaded(ByVal sender As System.Object, _
                    ByVal e As System.Windows.RoutedEventArgs) _
                    Handles MyBase.Loaded
    ' Append the << to the text for the button since these are _
    ' reserved characters within XAML
    ButtonPrev.Content = "<< " + ButtonPrev.Content.ToString()
    ' Set the default path from which to load images
    TextBox1.Text = _
        Environment.GetFolderPath(Environment.SpecialFolder.MyPictures)
    ' Have the images maintain their aspect ration
    Image1.Stretch = Stretch.Uniform
End Sub
```

Code snippet from MainWindow.vb

The preceding implementation handles these three tasks. It takes the content of the `ButtonPrev` control and appends the two less than symbols to the front of the string so that both buttons are displayed uniformly. Of course, long term, this code is going to be disposed of, but for now it helps to illustrate that while controls such as `Button` may seem familiar from Windows Forms, these controls are in fact different. The WPF version of the `Button` control doesn't have a `text` property; it has a `content` property. The `content` property is, in fact, an untyped object reference. In the case of this application, you know this content is a string to which you can append additional text. However, this code is neither a good idea nor easily maintained, so this is just a temporary solution.

Next, the code updates the `text` property of the `TextBox` control used on the form. This text box displays the folder for the images to display. In order to provide a dynamic path, the code leverages the `Environment` class to get a folder path. To this shared method the code passes a shared environment variable: `Environment.SpecialFolder.MyPictures`. This variable provides the path to the current user's My Pictures folder (or the User's Pictures folder on Windows 7 and Vista). By using this value, the code automatically points to a directory where the current user would be expected to have images.

Finally, to again demonstrate that any of the WPF classes can be modified within your code, this code sets a property on the `Image` control. Specifically, it updates the `Stretch` property of the `Image` control to ensure that images are resized with their aspect maintained. Thus, if an image is square, then when your image control becomes a rectangle, the image remains square. The `Stretch.Uniform` value indicates that the aspect should be maintained, while other members of the `Windows.Stretch` enumeration provide alternative behavior.

The next step is to implement your first button handler, the `ButtonBrowse_Click` handler. When this button is clicked, the application should open the Folder Browse dialog, displaying the currently selected folder as the default. The user should be allowed to navigate to an existing folder or create a new folder. When the dialog is closed, the application should, if the user selected a new folder, update the folder's text box to display this new location:

```vb
Private Sub ButtonBrowse_Click(ByVal sender As System.Object, _
                        ByVal e As System.Windows.RoutedEventArgs) _
                        Handles ButtonBrowse.Click
    Dim folderDialog As System.Windows.Forms.FolderBrowserDialog = _
                        New System.Windows.Forms.FolderBrowserDialog()
    folderDialog.Description = "Select the folder for images."
    folderDialog.SelectedPath = TextBox1.Text
    Dim res As System.Windows.Forms.DialogResult = _
                        folderDialog.ShowDialog()
    If res = System.Windows.Forms.DialogResult.OK Then
        TextBox1.Text = folderDialog.SelectedPath
    End If
End Sub
```

Code snippet from MainWindow.vb

The preceding code block declares an instance of the `System.Windows.Forms.FolderBrowserDialog` control. As noted when the reference was added, this control isn't part of your primary window display, so you can create an instance of this dialog without needing the `Windows.Forms.Interface` library. It then sets a description, indicating to users what they should do while in the dialog, and updates the current path for the dialog to reflect the currently selected folder. The dialog is then opened and the result assigned directly into the variable `res`. This variable is of type `System.Windows.Forms.DialogResult` and is checked to determine whether the user selected the OK button or the Cancel button. If OK was selected, then the currently selected folder is updated.

Now it's time to start working with the images. That means you need to retrieve a list of images and manipulate that list as the user moves forward and backward through it. You could constantly return to the source directory to find the next and previous images, but you will get much better performance by capturing the list locally and keeping your current location in the list. This implies two local variables; and because you want these variables available across different events, you need to declare them as member variables to your class:

```vb
Class MainWindow
    Private m_imageList As String() = {}
    Private m_curIndex As Integer = 0
    Private Sub MainWindow_Loaded(ByVal sender As System.Object, _
                        ByVal e As System.Windows.RoutedEventArgs) _
                        Handles MyBase.Loaded
        ' Append the << to the text for the button since these are _
        ' reserved characters within XAML
        ButtonPrev.Content = "<< " + ButtonPrev.Content.ToString()
```

```vb
' Set the default path from which to load images
TextBox1.Text = _
        Environment.GetFolderPath(Environment.SpecialFolder.MyPictures)
' Have the images maintain their aspect ration
Image1.Stretch = Stretch.Uniform
End Sub
Private Sub ButtonBrowse_Click(ByVal sender As System.Object, _
                    ByVal e As System.Windows.RoutedEventArgs) _
                    Handles ButtonBrowse.Click
    Dim folderDialog As System.Windows.Forms.FolderBrowserDialog = _
                New System.Windows.Forms.FolderBrowserDialog()
    folderDialog.Description = "Select the folder for images."
    folderDialog.SelectedPath = TextBox1.Text
    Dim res As System.Windows.Forms.DialogResult = _
                                        folderDialog.ShowDialog()
    If res = System.Windows.Forms.DialogResult.OK Then
        TextBox1.Text = folderDialog.SelectedPath
    End If
End Sub
Private Sub ButtonLoad_Click(ByVal sender As System.Object, _
                    ByVal e As System.Windows.RoutedEventArgs) _
                    Handles ButtonLoad.Click
    Image1.Source = Nothing
    m_imageList = System.IO.Directory.GetFiles(TextBox1.Text, "*.jpg")
    m_curIndex = 0
    If m_imageList.Count > 0 Then
        Image1.Source = _
                New System.Windows.Media.Imaging.BitmapImage( _
                    New System.Uri(m_imageList(m_curIndex)))
    End If
End Sub
```

Code snippet from MainWindow.vb

The beginning of the preceding code adds two new properties to the class MainWindow. Both values are private variables that have not been exposed as public properties. They are being made available for use in the image-handling buttons. Your code should look similar to the preceding code. The second bold section is an implementation of the ButtonLoad Click event handler. This event handler is called when the user clicks the button, ButtonLoad, and the first thing it does is clear the current image from the display. It then leverages the System.IO.Directory class, calling the shared method GetFiles to retrieve a list of files. For simplicity, this call screens out all files that don't have the extension .jpg. In a full production application, this call would probably use a much more complex screening system to gather all types of images and potentially feed a folder navigation control so that users could change the selected folder or even add multiple folders at once.

Once the list of files is retrieved and assigned to the private variable m_imageList, the code clears the current index and determines whether any files were returned for the current directory. The screenshots in this chapter have three images in the folder in order to obtain a small array; however, if no images are present, then the code exists without displaying anything. Here, presume an image is available. The code uses the System.Windows.Media.Imaging class to load an image file as a bitmap. It does this by accepting the URI or path to that image, a path that was returned as an array from your call to GetFiles. Note that the BitmapImage call doesn't need an image formatted as a bitmap, but instead converts the chosen image to a bitmap format that can then be directly referenced by the source property of the Image control:

Available for download on Wrox.com

```vb
Private Sub ButtonPrev_Click(ByVal sender As System.Object, _
                    ByVal e As System.Windows.RoutedEventArgs) _
                    Handles ButtonPrev.Click
    If m_imageList.Count > 0 Then
        m_curIndex -= 1
        If m_curIndex < 0 Then
            m_curIndex = m_imageList.Count - 1
```

```
                End If
                Image1.Source = New System.Windows.Media.Imaging.BitmapImage( _
                                        New System.Uri(m_imageList(m_curIndex)))
            End If
        End Sub
        Private Sub ButtonNext_Click(ByVal sender As System.Object, _
                            ByVal e As System.Windows.RoutedEventArgs) _
                            Handles ButtonNext.Click
            If m_imageList.Count > 0 Then
                m_curIndex += 1
                If m_curIndex > m_imageList.Count - 1 Then
                    m_curIndex = 0
                End If
                Image1.Source = New System.Windows.Media.Imaging.BitmapImage( _
                                        New System.Uri(m_imageList(m_curIndex)))
            End If
        End Sub
    End Class
```

Code snippet from MainWindow.vb

After the code to load an image has been added, implementing the `ButtonPrev` and `ButtonNext` event handlers is fairly simple. In both cases the code first checks to ensure that one or more images are available in the `m_imageList`. If so, then the code either decrements or increments the `m_curIndex` value, indicating the image that should currently be displayed. In each case the code ensures that the new index value is within the limits of the array. For example, if it is below 0, then it is reset to the last image index; and if it is greater than the last used index, the counter is reset to 0 to return it to the start of the list.

The next logical step is to run the application. If you have images loaded in your Pictures folder, then you can open the first of these images in the application. If not, then you can navigate to another directory such as the Samples folder using the Images button. At this point, you'll probably agree that the sample application shown in Figure 17-5 looks just like a typical Windows Forms application — so much so in fact that the next steps are included to ensure that this doesn't look like a Windows Forms application.

However, before adding new features, there is a possibility that when you loaded your image, your application didn't display the image quite like the one shown in Figure 17-5; in fact, it might look more like Figure 17-6. If, when you worked on your own code, you added the `Image` control after adding the View, Prev, and Next buttons, then your buttons — in particular, the View Images button — might be completely

FIGURE 17-5

FIGURE 17-6

hidden from view. This is caused by the way in which WPF layers and loads controls, and to resolve it you need to change the order in which the controls are loaded in your XAML. Before doing that, however, this is a good place to discuss layers and the WPF layering and layout model.

Layout

WPF supports a very robust model for control layout, which it achieves by leveraging the capability to layer controls and by providing a set of controls directly related to layout. Combined with the capability to define a reasonable set of layout information for each control, what you wind up with is an adaptable environment that can, at the extreme, provide unique behavior.

How does the process work? Within each control are the basic elements associated with the sizing of that control. As with past versions of Windows Forms, included is the concept of height and width and the four associated limitations: MaxHeight, MaxWidth, MinHeight, and MinWidth. Additionally, as shown in this chapter, it is possible to bind controls to window borders.

The layout properties aren't the focus of this section, however. More important is the concept of *layered controls*. What happens when you layer an image on top of something such as a grid? Recall how the Image control you defined was bound to the four borders of its display area. In fact, the control isn't bound to the limits of the window per se; it is bound to the limits of the grid control upon which it is explicitly layered. This layering occurs because the Image control is defined as part of the content of the grid. That content is actually a collection containing each of the layered controls for the selected control.

When it comes to layout and layering, keep in mind that if a control is explicitly layered on top of another control as part of its content, then its display boundaries are by default limited by the containing control's boundaries. This layering is as much about containing as it is layering.

However, you can override this behavior using the combination of the ClipToBounds property, the LayoutClip property, and the GetLayoutClip method of the container. Note, however, that the default behavior of WPF controls is to set ClipToBounds to false and then use the LayoutClip property and the GetLayoutClip method to specify the actual clipping bounds. Resetting and manually managing the clipping behavior enables a control to be drawn outside the bounds of its parent container. That behavior is beyond the scope of this chapter, as the process is somewhat involved; the preferred behavior, when available, is to clip within the region of the parent control.

The fact that your control can be drawn beyond the limits of its container is an important concept. It means your controls are no longer "contained," but rather are truly layered. This may sound trivial, but the implications are significant. Under previous UI models, an object had a container of some sort. For example, a panel could contain other controls of certain types, but not necessarily all types. A button's content was generally text unless you had a button configured for images, but you couldn't really find a button configured to contain, for example, a drop-down list box, unless you wrote a custom display implementation.

By moving to a more layered approach, it's possible to create a single control that handles text, images, and other controls. Controls that support layering encapsulate a *content presenter control*. Thus, when you indicated that the Image control in ProVB_WPF should stretch, it stretched in accordance with the grid control. Were you to change the XAML definition of the grid control and give it a fixed height or width, then even though the window might change, the Image control would still be bound to the limits of the grid control.

This behavior is explicit layering, and it is only available with certain control types. For example, WPF provides a series of different "panel" controls that are used to provide a framework for control layout. The grid is probably the one most familiar to .NET Windows Forms developers because it maps most closely to the default behavior of Windows Forms. Other similar controls include StackPanel, Canvas, DockPanel, ToolBar, and Tab-related controls. Each of these provides unique layout behavior. Because these are available as controls, which you can nest, you can combine these different layout paradigms within different sections of a single form, which enables you to group controls and achieve a common layout behavior of related controls.

To be clear, however, explicit layering or nesting isn't just available with `Panel` controls; another WPF example is the `Button` control. The button has a layer of generic button code — background color, border, size, and so on — that is managed within the display for the button. The button also has a content presenter within its definition that takes whatever was placed into the button's `content` property and calls the presentation logic for that control. This enables the button and many other controls to contain other controls of any type.

You can place a button on a form and bind it to the form's borders, and then place other controls on the form. Because the button exposes a `content` property, it supports explicit layering, and other controls can in fact be placed within the content of the button. Thus, whenever a user clicks on the surface of the form, a `Click` event is raised to the underlying button that is the owner of that content. The fact that WPF controls forward events up the chain of containers is an important factor to consider when capturing events and planning for application behavior. The formal name for this behavior is *routed events*.

Routed events are a key new concept introduced with WPF, and they are important in the sense that as you add controls to your UI, you create a hierarchy. In the example thus far, this hierarchy is rather flat: There is a window, and then a grid, and each of the controls is a child of the grid. However, you can make this hierarchy much deeper, and routed events enable the controls at the top of the hierarchy to be notified when something changes in the controls that are part of their content structure.

In addition to these explicit concepts of layering, hierarchy, and routed events, WPF also has the concept of implicit layering. An *implicit layer* describes the scenario when you have two different controls defined to occupy the same space on your form. In the case of the example code, recall that the image was defined to overlay both of the row definitions, including the one containing the three `Image` control buttons. Thus, these controls were defined to display in the same area, which isn't a problem for WPF, but which in the current design isn't ideal for display purposes either.

The key point is that layering can be either implicit or explicit. In case you didn't see the same behavior that's been described in terms of the loaded image hiding the control buttons, you'll need to modify the XAML code. Note that the code available for download implements the solution correctly, so if you are following along with the sample code you'll need to modify the XAML in `MainWindow.xaml`. The *incorrect* version of this XAML is as follows:

```
<Grid>
    <Grid.RowDefinitions>
        <RowDefinition Height="45" />
        <RowDefinition Height="215*" />
        <RowDefinition Height="40" />
    </Grid.RowDefinitions>
    <Label Margin="0,11,0,0" Name="Label1" HorizontalAlignment="Left" Width="80"
Height="23" VerticalAlignment="Top">Image Path:</Label>
    <TextBox Margin="81,13,92,0" Name="TextBox1" Height="21"
VerticalAlignment="Top" />
    <Button HorizontalAlignment="Right" Margin="0,11,9,0" Name="ButtonBrowse"
Width="75" Height="23" VerticalAlignment="Top">Images ...</Button>
    <Button Grid.Row="2" HorizontalAlignment="Right" Margin="0,0,15,8"
Name="ButtonNext" Width="75" Height="23" VerticalAlignment="Bottom">Next >></Button>
    <Button Grid.Row="2" HorizontalAlignment="Left" Margin="15,0,0,8"
Name="ButtonPrev" Width="75" Height="23" VerticalAlignment="Bottom"> Prev</Button>
    <Button Grid.Row="2" Margin="150,0,150,8" Name="ButtonLoad" Height="23"
VerticalAlignment="Bottom">View Images</Button>
    <Image Grid.Row="1" Grid.RowSpan="2" Margin="0,0,0,0" Name="Image1"
Stretch="Fill" />
</Grid>
```

In the preceding XAML, the buttons are defined and loaded, and the `Image` control isn't defined until later. As a result, the `Image` control is considered to be layered on top of the `Button` controls. When the application starts, you might expect that Image control to immediately block the buttons, but it doesn't. That's because there is no image to display, so the Image control essentially stays out of the way, enabling the controls that would otherwise be behind it to both be displayed and receive input. WPF fully supports the concept of transparency, as demonstrated later in this chapter.

When there is something to display, the resulting image can block the same buttons that were used to load it (refer to Figure 17-6). Because the image isn't part of the content for any of these buttons, none of the click events that would occur on the image at this point are raised to those buttons, so the buttons that are hidden don't respond. This is different behavior from what you get when you layer controls, and much closer to what a Windows Forms developer might expect. As a result, you need to be aware, just as with other user interfaces, of the order in which controls overlap in the same display area that's loaded.

Thus, everything you've done in the past, both with Windows Forms and ASP.NET, is still possible. On the surface, the WPF controls have more in common with existing programming models than might at first seem apparent.

Now that we have uttered heresy against this new UI paradigm, it's time to examine what is meant by a paradigm shift with the XAML model. As noted, it starts with a new set of classes and a new declarative language, but it continues with being able to have much finer control over your application's UI behavior.

Customizing the User Interface

While you can create a user interface that looks disappointingly similar to a Windows Forms application, the real power of WPF is the customization it enables you to create for your application. At this point, our example moves from the ProVB_WPF application to the second application, ProVB_WPF_Step2. The goal here is to provide, through Visual Studio 2010, an even cleaner interface — not one that leverages all of WPF's power, but one that at least reduces the Windows Forms look and feel of this application.

The first step is to change some of the application. For starters, a text box with the name of the selected directory is redundant. You don't expect users to type that name, but rather to select it, so you can instead display the currently selected directory on the actual button label. Accordingly, the current Label and TextBox controls in the form can be removed. Additionally, both at load and following a change to the selected folder, instead of waiting for the user to request the image folder, the application should just query and pull the initial image.

Carrying out these changes is relatively simple. The first step is to adjust the existing button handler for the View Images button. Because this button will be deleted but the actions that the handler implements are still needed, change the method definition from being an event handler with associated parameters to being a private method that doesn't require any parameters:

```
Private Sub LoadImages()
```

Next, this method needs to be called when a new directory is chosen, so update the event handler for ButtonBrowse_Click to include a call to this method when the name of the directory is updated.

Now you can get rid of the Label and TextBox controls. Eliminating the Label control is easy, as it isn't referenced in the code, but the TextBox poses a challenge. You can replace the TextBox control with a reference to the content of the Button control, but in this case you've jumped from the frying pan into the fire in terms of maintenance. Face it: The button content over time could be anything.

From a coding standpoint, it makes much more sense to store the current path as part of your local business data. Then, if the goal is to have the label of that button display the current path, fine; but if for some reason that changes, then you can minimize the changes required to your application code. Therefore, add a new private value to your class:

```
Private m_curImagePath As String = ""
```

Now replace all of the references to TextBox1.Text with the new value of m_curImagePath in your code. There are likely more than you would expect, and not using the button's label for this task should make more sense at this point. Next, you need to update the button label for when the m_curImagePath value changes. This occurs only in two places: in the MainWindow_Loaded event handler and in the ButtonBrowse_Click event handler.

Finally, update the code in the MainWindow_Loaded event handler. There are three actions in the current method, and two of them should be eliminated. The first is where the code is adding the "<<" to the ButtonPrev label. This label is going to become an image, so get rid of this assignment statement. Similarly, setting the Stretch property of the Image control within this event is a duplicate effort. Instead, update the XAML by directly setting that property to the desired value. When you are done, the code for your class and its first three methods should look similar to the following, given that there were no changes to the event handlers for ButtonPrev and ButtonNext:

```vbnet
Class MainWindow
    Private m_imageList As String() = {}
    Private m_curIndex As Integer = 0
    Private m_curImagePath As String = ""

    Private Sub MainWindow_Loaded(ByVal sender As System.Object, _
                                  ByVal e As System.Windows.RoutedEventArgs) _
                                  Handles MyBase.Loaded
        ' Set the default path from which to load images and load them
        m_curImagePath = _
               Environment.GetFolderPath(Environment.SpecialFolder.MyPictures)
        ButtonBrowse.Content = m_curImagePath
        LoadImages()
    End Sub

    Private Sub ButtonBrowse_Click(ByVal sender As System.Object, _
                                   ByVal e As System.Windows.RoutedEventArgs) _
                                   Handles ButtonBrowse.Click
        Dim folderDialog As System.Windows.Forms.FolderBrowserDialog = _
                          New System.Windows.Forms.FolderBrowserDialog()
        folderDialog.Description = "Select the folder for images."
        folderDialog.SelectedPath = m_curImagePath
        Dim res As System.Windows.Forms.DialogResult = _
                                                  folderDialog.ShowDialog()
        If res = System.Windows.Forms.DialogResult.OK Then
            m_curImagePath = folderDialog.SelectedPath
            ButtonBrowse.Content = m_curImagePath
            LoadImages()
        End If
    End Sub

    Private Sub LoadImages()
        Image1.Source = Nothing
        m_imageList = System.IO.Directory.GetFiles(m_curImagePath, "*.jpg")
        m_curIndex = 0
        If m_imageList.Count > 0 Then
            Image1.Source = New System.Windows.Media.Imaging.BitmapImage( _
                                    New System.Uri(m_imageList(m_curIndex)))
        End If
    End Sub
End Sub
```

Code snippet from MainWindow.vb

Now that you have updated your code, it's time to clean up the XAML. First, delete the Label and TextBox controls and move the button that is currently on the right-hand side of the top section to the left-hand side. Next, bind the window to both sides of the display and expand its size to allow it to display the full path. (Of course, this is ugly, which means it will be changed as part of the upcoming UI changes.)

Next, delete the button labeled View Images from the design surface. At this point you could stop, but to help prepare for other design changes you are going to make, review the placement of the Prev and Next buttons. Currently, these buttons are tied to the bottom portion of the grid; instead, get rid of that third grid row definition and center the Prev and Next buttons on the side of the image. At this point, the designer should look similar to what is shown in Figure 17-7.

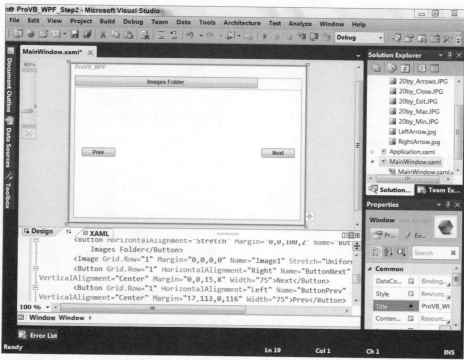

FIGURE 17-7

This is a much simpler and cleaner interface. The XAML is as follows:

Available for download on Wrox.com

```
<Grid>
    <Grid.RowDefinitions>
        <RowDefinition Height="25" />
        <RowDefinition Height="215*" />
    </Grid.RowDefinitions>
    <Button HorizontalAlignment="Stretch" Margin="0,0,100,2" Name="ButtonBrowse" >
Images Folder</Button>
    <Image Grid.Row="1" Margin="0,0,0,0" Name="Image1" Stretch="Uniform" />
    <Button Grid.Row="1" HorizontalAlignment="Right" Name="ButtonNext"
VerticalAlignment="Center" Margin="0,0,15,8" Width="75">Next</Button>
    <Button Grid.Row="1" HorizontalAlignment="Left" Name="ButtonPrev"
VerticalAlignment="Center" Margin="17,113,0,116" Width="75"> Prev</Button>
    </Grid>
```

Code snippet from MainWindows.vb

This indicates that the Grid now has only two row definitions, and the Image control was updated to be located in row 1, as were the Prev and Next buttons.

Now you are ready to address the next set of changes to make this application look and behave more like a WPF application. One is to get rid of the "ugly" Windows frame around the application. (Your designer may want to skin this application later, and that frame just won't support the look desired.) Second, the designer wants the Prev and Next buttons modified so that they are circular instead of square and use images instead of text; and just to be consistent, the designer would like those buttons hidden except when the user hovers over them.

Removing the Frame

Removing the Windows frame from your application is actually fairly easy to do, as you only need to set two properties on your form. The first is WindowStyle, which is set to None; the second is AllowTransparency, which is set to True. You can accomplish that by adding the following line before the closing bracket of your window attributes:

```
WindowStyle="None" AllowsTransparency="True"
```

Once you've added this line to your XAML, run the application in the debugger. This is a good point to test not only what happens based on this change, but also the other changes you made to reduce the number of controls in your application. The result is shown in Figure 17-8. You probably notice that there are no longer any controls related to moving, resizing, closing, or maximizing your window. In fact, if you don't start the application within the Visual Studio debugger, you'll need to go to the Task Manager in order to end the process, as you haven't provided any way to end this application through the user interface.

In order to be able to skin this application, you need to provide some controls that implement many of the baseline window behaviors that most form developers take for granted. This isn't as hard as it might sound. The main challenge is to add a series

FIGURE 17-8

of buttons for maximizing and restoring your application window, closing the application, and, of course, resizing the application. Because your designer wants to skin the application, you decide that the best way to handle the resize capability is with a single hotspot in the bottom-right corner that represents the resize capability.

However, your first task is to provide a way to move the window. To do that you are going to add a rectangular area that maps to the top Grid.Row. This rectangle supports capturing the MouseDown event and then responds if the user drags the window with the mouse button down. Because moving the window is essentially a mouse down and drag activity, as opposed to a Click event, the Rectangle is a quick and easy way to implement this feature. It takes only a single line of XAML added as the first control in the grid:

```
<Rectangle Name="TitleBar" HorizontalAlignment="Stretch" Margin="0,0,0,0"
   Stroke="Black" Fill="Green" VerticalAlignment="Stretch" />
```

Now, of course, you've filled the default rectangle with a beautiful green color to help with visibility, leaving the black border around the control. These two elements help you see where the rectangle is prior to taking this XAML into a designer and cleaning it up. Aside from this, however, having a control is only half the equation; the other half is detecting and responding to the DragMove event.

This is done with the following event handler, which is added using VB:

```
Private Sub Rectangle_MouseLeftButtonDown(ByVal sender As Object, _
            ByVal e As System.Windows.Input.MouseButtonEventArgs) _
            Handles TitleBar.MouseLeftButtonDown
    Me.DragMove()
End Sub
```

To recap, that's a single line of code in the handler — calling the built-in method on the Window base class, DragMove. This method handles dragging the window to a new location. Right now the handler only looks for the dragging to occur from a control named TitleBar, but you could change this to something else or even change which control was called Titlebar.

Having resolved the first issue, you can move to the second: implementing the three buttons required for minimize, maximize, and close. In each case the action required only occurs after a Click event. One of the unique characteristics of a button is that it detects a Click event, so it is the natural choice for implementing these actions. The buttons in this case should be images, so the first step is to create a few simple images.

Four image references have been added to the example project. Yes, these images are ugly, but the goal here isn't to create flashy design elements. You can literally spend days tweaking minor UI elements, which shouldn't be your focus. The focus here is on creating the elements that can be used in the UI. The color of the buttons, whether the Close button looks like the Windows icon, and so on are irrelevant at this point. What you care about here is providing a button with basic elements that a designer can later customize. As a rule, don't mix design and implementation.

The simplest way for an engineer to create graphics is with the world-famous Paint program. Not that it's the best way or even the only way, after all, even Visual Studio includes a basic image editor. The goal here isn't something fancy but something reasonably meaningful. Create the four necessary .jpg files as 24×24 pixel images, and include an image for the resize handle for the window. Next, access the MyProject page and select the Resources tab. Then, select each of your .jpg files and add them as Image resources to the project, as shown in Figure 17-9.

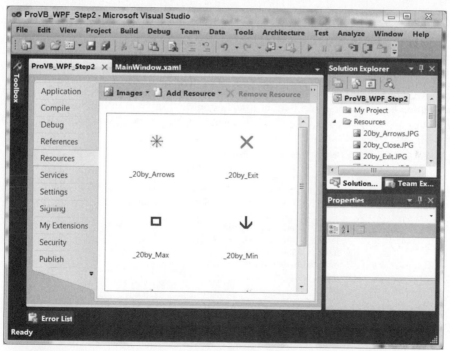

FIGURE 17-9

Note that Visual Studio automatically places these items in the Resources folder for your project. Next, verify that in the properties for each file, the BuildAction property is set to Resource. In order for these resources to be referenced from within your XAML, they need to be designated as resources, not just located in this folder. Now do a complete build of your project so the resources are compiled.

At this point you can move back to the XAML designer and add the three buttons for minimize, maximize, and close. For your purposes, they should reside in the upper-right corner of the display and be around the same size as your new graphics. Drag a button onto the design surface and then edit the XAML to place it in the upper-right corner and size it to a height and width of 20 pixels. After doing this, one easy way to proceed is to simply copy that first button and paste two more buttons just like it into the XAML. Then all you need to do is change the button names and locations. Voilà — three buttons.

Of course, your goal is for these buttons to have images on them, so you need to add an Image control to the form and then move it so that it becomes the content for the first button. In this case, just bind the image control to the borders of the button using the Margin attribute and then add a source to the button. Here, the source is the local reference to your .jpg resource, so in the case of ButtonClose, the source value is set to /Resources/20by_Exit.jpg. Add an Image control to the other two buttons and reference the associated resource in order to get the XAML here:

Available for download on Wrox.com

```xml
<Button Height="20" Width="20" HorizontalAlignment="Right" Margin="0,1,1,0"
                        Name="ButtonClose" VerticalAlignment="Top">
    <Image Margin="0,0,0,0" Name="Image2" Stretch="Fill"
            Source="/Resources/20by_Exit.JPG"/>
</Button>
<Button Height="20" Width="20" HorizontalAlignment="Right" Margin="0,1,25,0"
                        Name="ButtonMax" VerticalAlignment="Top" >
    <Image Margin="0,0,0,0" Name="Image3" Stretch="Fill"
                        Source="/Resources/20by_Max.JPG"/>
</Button>
<Button Height="20" Width="20" HorizontalAlignment="Right" Margin="0,1,47,0"
                        Name="ButtonMin" VerticalAlignment="Top" >
    <Image Margin="0,0,0,0" Name="Image4" Stretch="Fill"
                        Source="/Resources/20by_Min.JPG"/>
</Button>
```

Code snippet from MainWindow.xaml

At this point the basic XAML elements needed in order to implement a custom shell on this application are in place. Note that each button has a specific name: ButtonClose, ButtonMax, and ButtonMin. You'll need these, and the design can't change them because you'll use the button names to handle the Click event for each button. In each case, you need to carry out a simple action:

Available for download on Wrox.com

```vb
Private Sub ButtonMin_Click(ByVal sender As Object, _
                        ByVal e As RoutedEventArgs) _
                        Handles ButtonMin.Click
    Me.WindowState = WindowState.Minimized
End Sub

Private Sub ButtonMax_Click(ByVal sender As Object, _
                        ByVal e As RoutedEventArgs) _
                        Handles ButtonMax.Click
    If (Me.WindowState = WindowState.Maximized) Then
        Me.WindowState = WindowState.Normal
    Else
        Me.WindowState = WindowState.Maximized
    End If
End Sub

Private Sub ButtonClose_Click(ByVal sender As Object, _
                        ByVal e As RoutedEventArgs) _
                        Handles ButtonClose.Click
    Me.Close()
End Sub
```

Code snippet from MainWindow.vb

The code is fairly simple. After all, it's not as if the methods you need aren't still available; all you are doing is providing part of the plumbing that will enable your custom UI to reach these methods. Thus, to minimize the button's `Click` event, merely reset the window state to minimized. The real plumbing, however, was prebuilt for you as part of the way WPF layers controls. Keep in mind that when users click the minimize button, they are actually clicking on an image. WPF routes the `Click` event that occurred on that image.

When you hear about routed events and how powerful they are, remember that they are a capability built into the way that WPF layers and associates different controls. The routing mechanism in this case is referred to as *bubbling* because the event bubbles up to the parent; however, routed events can travel both up and down the control hierarchy.

For the `ButtonMax` event handler, the code is significantly more complex. Unlike minimizing a window, which has only one action when the button is pressed, the maximize button has two options. The first time it is pressed it takes the window from its current size and fills the display. If it is then pressed again, it needs to detect that the window has already been maximized and instead restore that original size. As a result, this event handler has an actual `If` statement that checks the current window state and then determines which value to assign.

Finally, the `ButtonClose` event handler has that one line of code that has been with VB developers pretty much since the beginning, `Me.Close`, which tells the current window it's time to close. As noted, there isn't much magic here; the actual "magic" occurs with resizing.

Up until this point, changing the default window frame for a set of custom controls has been surprisingly easy. Now, however, if you are working on your own, you are about to hit a challenge. You need a control that will respond to the user's drag action and enable the user to drag the window frame while providing you with updates on that status.

There isn't a tool in the Visual Studio Toolbox for WPF that does this, but there are things such as splitter windows and other resizable controls that have this behavior. WPF was written in such a way that most of what you consider "controls" are actually an amalgamation of primitive single-feature controls. In this case, the primitive you are looking for is called a `Thumb`. The `Thumb` control is a WPF control, and it is located in the `System.Windows.Controls.Primitives` namespace.

Fortunately, you can directly reference this control from within your XAML; and once you have added it to your XAML, handling the events is just as simple as it is with your other custom UI elements. However, this control can't contain another control, and its default look is blank. For the moment, examine the XAML that is used to create an instance of this control on your form:

```
<Thumb Grid.Row="1" Cursor="ScrollAll" Name="ThumbResize" Height="20" Width="20"
HorizontalAlignment="Right" VerticalAlignment="Bottom" Margin="0,0,0,0" />
```

Note a few items of customization. Because the typical location to resize from in most UI models is the lower-right corner, this control is placed in the lower-right corner and aligned to the bottom and right edges of the bottom grid row. The control itself is sized to match the other buttons used to control the window's behavior. The name `ThumbResize` is used to indicate the control, and in this case the property `Cursor` is set. The `Cursor` property enables you to control the display of the mouse cursor when it moves over the control. There are several options in the enumeration of standard mouse cursors, and for this control arrows are displayed in every direction.

Before you change the default display any further, it makes sense to wire up an event handler. This enables you to test the control's behavior. Just as with the other event handlers, double-clicking on the control in the designer generates a default event handler for the control. In this case, the event to be handled is the `DragDelta` event. As the name implies, this event fires every time the potential size of the display area is changed. There are multiple ways to handle resizing. For this application, having the window redisplay as the user drags the mouse is feasible because the amount of time to update the display is short.

If that weren't the case, then you would want to override two additional events: `DragStarted` and `DragOver`. These events enable you to catch the window's start size and the final size based on the end of the user's action. You would then only resize the form in the `DragOver` event instead of in the `DragDelta` event.

You would still need to override `DragDelta` because it is in this event that you monitor whether the window's minimum and/or maximum size constraints have been met:

```
Private Sub ThumbResize_DragDelta(ByVal sender As System.Object, _
                                  ByVal e As Primitives.DragDeltaEventArgs) _
                                  Handles ThumbResize.DragDelta
      Me.Height += e.VerticalChange
      If (Me.Height < Me.MinHeight) Then
          Me.Height = Me.MinHeight
      End If
      Me.Width += e.HorizontalChange
      If (Me.Width < Me.MinWidth) Then
          Me.Width = Me.MinWidth
      End If
  End Sub
```

Code snippet from MainWindow.vb

The preceding block of code illustrates the code for this event handler. Notice that in this case the parameter `e` is specific to the `DragDeltaEventArgs` structure. This structure enables you to retrieve the current totals for both the vertical and horizontal change of the current drag location from the current window's frame.

This code enables you to see the visible window as the window is dragged because each time the event is fired, the `Height` and `Width` properties of the window are updated with the changes so that the window is resized. Note that this code handles checking the minimum height and width of your window. The code to check for the maximum size is similar. At this point, you can rerun the application to verify that the event is handled correctly and that as you drag the thumb, the application is resized.

Once you have the `ThumbResize` control working, the next step is to customize the display of this control. Unlike a button or other more advanced controls, this control won't allow you to associate it with an image or have content. As one of the primitive control types, you are limited to working with aspects such as the background color; and just assigning a color to this control really doesn't meet your needs. Thus, this is an excellent place to talk about another WPF feature: resources.

Resources

Typically, there comes a point where you want to include one or more resources with your application. A resource can be anything, including a static string, an image, a graphics element, and so on. In this case, you want to associate an image with the background of a control that would otherwise not support an image. Resources enable you to set up a more complex structure than just a color, which can then be assigned to a control's property. For this simple example you'll create a basic application-level resource that uses an image brush, and then have your control reference this resource.

As noted in the introduction to XAML syntax, the definition for `x:Key` included the label `object.Resources`. The implication is that objects of different types can include resources. The scope of a resource, then, is defined by the scope of the object with which it is defined. For a resource that will span your application, you can in fact define that resource within your application XAML. Resources that are to be available within a given window are defined in the XAML file for that window. The following XAML demonstrates adding a resource to the application file of the sample application created earlier:

```xml
<Application x:Class="Application"
    xmlns="http://schemas.microsoft.com/winfx/2006/xaml/presentation"
    xmlns:x="http://schemas.microsoft.com/winfx/2006/xaml"
        StartupUri="MainWindow.xaml">
    <Application.Resources>
        <ImageBrush x:Key="ResizeImage"
                         ImageSource="/Resources/20by_Arrows.JPG">
```

```
  </ImageBrush>
 </Application.Resources>
</Application>
```

Code snippet from Application.xaml

Here, you are going to create a new `ImageBrush`. An image brush, as you would expect, accepts an image source and then it "paints" this image onto the surface where it is applied. In the XAML, notice that you assign an `x:Key` value. As far as XAML is concerned, this name is the identity of the resource. Once this has been assigned, other controls and objects within your XAML can reference this resource and apply it to an object or property. Thus, you need to add a reference to this resource to your definition of the `ThumbResize` control. This should result in a change to your XAML similar to this:

```
<Thumb Grid.Row="1" Cursor="ScrollAll" HorizontalAlignment="Right" Height="20"
Background="{StaticResource ResizeImage}" Name="ThumbResize"
Margin="0,0,0,0" Width="20" VerticalAlignment="Bottom" />
```

This change involves what is assigned to the `Background` property of your `Thumb` control. As you look through XAML files, you will often see references to items such as `StaticResources`, and these can become fairly complex when you start to work with a tool such as Expression Blend. However, this example should help you recognize what you are seeing when you look at more complex XAML files. You will also see references to dynamic resources, which are discussed later in this chapter in conjunction with dependency properties.

Resources can be referenced by several different controls and even other resources. However, resources aren't the only, or most maintainable, resource in all instances. Because a resource must be referenced within each object that uses it, it doesn't scale well across several dozen controls. In addition, during maintenance, each time someone edited a XAML file that applies resources to every control, they would also need to be careful to add that resource to any new controls. Fortunately, XAML borrows other resource types based on the basic idea of style sheets. WPF supports other types of resources, including templates and styles, which are discussed later in this chapter. Unlike styles and resources, templates are applied to all objects of the same type. Coverage of templates is beyond the scope of this chapter, but they work similarly to resources except that the settings they define are automatically applied to every control of a given type.

This juncture is an excellent point to test your application. When you start it, you should see something similar to Figure 17-10. As noted earlier, at this point the application isn't exactly going to win a beauty contest (although the baby might). What you have achieved is a custom framework that enables you to literally treat an application UI as a blank slate, while still providing the standard Windows services that users have come to expect. This is important as you start to create applications that truly push the UI design envelope.

FIGURE 17-10

Customizing the Buttons

Your next task is to adjust the buttons in the application. Recall that the `ButtonPrev` and `ButtonNext` controls need to be round and only appear when the mouse is over them. This requires both XAML updates and new event handlers to hide the buttons. The second task results from the fact that when the mouse hovers over a button, Windows automatically changes the color of that button. This is a problem because the graphic guru doesn't want Windows changing the color of elements in the display.

We'll begin with making the current buttons round and changing them to use images instead of text. Making the buttons round in Visual Studio isn't as hard as it sounds. You can clip the button display and thus quickly create a round button. The easiest way to do this is to place the button on a `Panel` control and then clip the display region of the panel. You might be tempted to clip the button or place it within a border region, but neither of these actions will work as expected.

What you need to leverage is the capability to layer controls and a `Panel` control for each of these buttons. In this case, placing a panel on the display and then telling the panel that its contents have been clipped to fit within a geometric shape enables the clipped control to be displayed with the desired shape. Additionally, when it comes to hiding the button and only showing it when the mouse is over the control, the container is the control you need to detect the `MouseEnter` event. Instead of adding a panel to your application window, you are welcome to try the following: Go to the `ButtonPrev` XAML and set its visibility to `Hidden`. Next, from within the XAML, add a new event handler for the `MouseEnter` event and generate the stub. Within this stub, add a single line of code to make the button visible and set a breakpoint on this line of code.

Now start your application. Do you see any good way of knowing when the mouse is over the area where the control should be? No matter how many times you move across the area where the control should be, your `MouseEnter` event handler isn't called. Similarly, you can stop your application and change the visibility setting on the button from Hidden to Collapsed. Restart the application. You'll get the same result. In fact, short of attempting to track where the mouse is over your entire application and then computing the current location of the buttons to determine whether the mouse's current position happens to fall in that region, there isn't a good way to handle this aside from adding another control. If you chose to run this experiment, you should remove the reference to the event handler from your XAML — you can leave the button visibility set to either Hidden or Collapsed — and the event handler code.

The UI trick is that the `Panel`, or in this case the `StackPanel`, control that you use supports true background transparency. Thus, even though it doesn't display, it does register for handling events. Thus, the `StackPanel` acts not only as a way to clip the display area available to the button, but also as the control that knows when the button should be visible. You'll create `MouseEnter` and `MouseLeave` event handlers for the `StackPanel`, and these will then tell `ButtonNext` when to be visible and when to be hidden.

First, add a `StackPanel` control to your display. This stack panel, once it has been added to your design surface, will be easier to manipulate from within the XAML display. Ensure that the `StackPanel` was created in the second grid row. Then ensure that it has both an open and a close tag, and position these tags so they encapsulate your existing `ButtonNext` declaration. At this point, the `ButtonNext` declaration is constrained by the `StackPanel`'s display region. Next, ensure that most of the layout settings previously associated with the button are instead associated with the `StackPanel`:

```
<StackPanel Background="Transparent" Margin="0,0,25,0" Height="75" Width="75"
Name="StackPanelNext" Grid.Row="1" HorizontalAlignment="Right"
VerticalAlignment="Center" >
    <Button Grid.Row="1" Height="75" Width="75" HorizontalAlignment="Center"
VerticalAlignment="Center" Name="ButtonNext" Visibility="Hidden">Next</Button>
</StackPanel>
```

Code snippet from MainWindow.xaml

The preceding snippet shows how the `Margin` property that was set on the button is now associated with the `StackPanel`. Similarly, the `StackPanel` has the `VerticalAlignment` and `HorizontalAlignment` settings that were previously defined on the button. The `Button` now places both its vertical and horizontal alignment settings to `Stretch` because it is mainly concerned with filling the available area. Finally, note that both the `ButtonNext` control and the `StackPanelNext` control are given `Height` and `Width` properties of 75 pixels, making them square.

Before you address that issue, it makes sense to set up the event handlers to show and hide `ButtonNext`; otherwise, there won't be anything in the display. Within the code you can create an event handler for the MouseLeave event and associate it with Handles StackPanelNext.MouseLeave. If you previously attempted to capture the MouseEnter event with the button itself, you already have that method and all you need to do is add the Handles clause to the event definition:

```
Private Sub StackPanelNext_MouseEnter(ByVal sender As System.Object, _
                         ByVal e As System.Windows.Input.MouseEventArgs) _
                     Handles StackPanelNext.MouseEnter
    ButtonNext.Visibility = Windows.Visibility.Visible
End Sub

Private Sub StackPanelNext_MouseLeave(ByVal sender As System.Object, _
                         ByVal e As System.Windows.Input.MouseEventArgs) _
                     Handles StackPanelNext.MouseLeave
    ButtonNext.Visibility = Windows.Visibility.Hidden
End Sub
```

Code snippet from MainWindow.vb

At this point, test your code and ensure that it compiles. If so, make a test run and see whether the button is hidden and reappears as you mouse over the area where it should be located. If everything works, you are almost ready to repeat this logic for ButtonPrev. First, however, add the clip region to your StackPanel control so that the button displays as a circle instead of as a square.

The Clip property needs a geometry for the display region. Creating this requires that you define another object and then assign this object to that property. Since you'll want to report this geometric definition for both buttons, the most efficient way of doing this is to add a resource to your window. Go to the top of your MainWindow XAML, just below the attributes for the window. Add a new XML node for <Window.Resources></Window.Resources>. Between the start and end tags, create a new EllipseGeometry object. A radius is the distance from the center to the edge of a circle, so define your X and Y radius properties as 34. This is less than the distance between any edge and the center of your StackPanel.

Next, center the ellipse on the point 36, 36 — placing it near the center of your StackPanel and far enough from the edges that neither radius reaches all the way to one of the edges. The resulting XAML is shown in the following code block:

```
<Window.Resources>
    <EllipseGeometry x:Key="RoundPanel" Center="36, 36" RadiusX="34" RadiusY="34">
</EllipseGeometry>
    </Window.Resources>
```

Code snippet from MainWindow.xaml

Define the Clip property for your StackPanel to reference this new resource. As shown in the sample code, the name for this resource is RoundPanel. Then, add the following property definition to your StackPanelNext control:

```
Clip="{StaticResource RoundPanel}"
```

Next, add the images that will be used on these buttons. From the Resources tab of the MyProject screen, add two new images: LeftArrow.jpg and RightArrow.jpg. The images here were created with Microsoft Paint. Of course, both images are also square, but from the standpoint of what will be visible this doesn't matter. Once the images have been loaded, the last step is to add an Image control to the ButtonNext content, similar to what was done earlier for your minimize, maximize, and close buttons:

```
<Image Margin="0,0,0,0" Stretch="Fill"
                        Source="/Resources/RightArrow.jpg"></Image>
```

Once you have defined this you can then copy the StackPanel definition you've set up around ButtonNext and replicate it around ButtonPrev. You'll need to customize the location settings and then create event handlers for the StackPanelPrev mouse events that update the visibility of the ButtonPrev control. The code block that follows shows the complete XAML file to this point:

```xml
<Window x:Class="MainWindow"
    xmlns="http://schemas.microsoft.com/winfx/2006/xaml/presentation"
    xmlns:x="http://schemas.microsoft.com/winfx/2006/xaml"
    Title="ProVB_WPF" Height="335" Width="415" Name="MainWindow"
    WindowStyle="None" AllowsTransparency="True">
    <Window.Resources>
        <EllipseGeometry x:Key="RoundPanel" Center="36, 36" RadiusX="34" RadiusY="34">
</EllipseGeometry>
    </Window.Resources>
    <Grid>
        <Grid.RowDefinitions>
            <RowDefinition Height="25" />
            <RowDefinition Height="215*" />
        </Grid.RowDefinitions>
        <Rectangle Name="TitleBar" HorizontalAlignment="Stretch" Margin="0,0,0,0"
Stroke="Black" Fill="Green" VerticalAlignment="Stretch" />
        <Button HorizontalAlignment="Stretch" Margin="0,0,130,2" Name="ButtonBrowse">
Images Folder</Button>
        <Button Height="20" Width="23" HorizontalAlignment="Right" Margin="0,1,1,0"
Name="ButtonClose" VerticalAlignment="Top">
            <Image Margin="0,0,0,0" Name="Image2" Stretch="Fill" Source="/Resources/
20by_Exit.JPG"/>
        </Button>
        <Button Height="20" Width="20" HorizontalAlignment="Right" Margin="0,1,25,0"
Name="ButtonMax" VerticalAlignment="Top" >
            <Image Margin="0,0,0,0" HorizontalAlignment="Center" Name="Image3"
Stretch="Fill" Source="/Resources/20by_Max.JPG"/>
        </Button>
        <Button Height="20" Width="20" HorizontalAlignment="Right" Margin="0,1,47,0"
Name="ButtonMin" VerticalAlignment="Top" >
            <Image Margin="0,0,0,0" Name="Image4" Stretch="Fill" Source="/Resources/
20by_Min.JPG"/>
        </Button>
        <Image Grid.Row="1"  Margin="0,0,0,0" Name="Image1" Stretch="Uniform" />
        <StackPanel Background="Transparent" VerticalAlignment="Center"
Margin="0,0,25,0" Height="75" Name="StackPanelNext" Grid.Row="1"
HorizontalAlignment="Right" Width="75" Clip="{StaticResource RoundPanel}">
            <Button Grid.Row="1" HorizontalAlignment="Stretch"
VerticalAlignment="Stretch" Name="ButtonNext" Height="75" Width="75"
Visibility="Hidden">
                <Image Margin="0,0,0,0" Stretch="Fill" Source="/Resources/
RightArrow.jpg"></Image>
            </Button>
        </StackPanel>
        <StackPanel Background="Transparent" VerticalAlignment="Center"
Margin="25,0,0,0" Height="75" Name="StackPanelPrev" Grid.Row="1"
HorizontalAlignment="Left" Width="75" Clip="{StaticResource RoundPanel}">
            <Button Grid.Row="1" HorizontalAlignment="Left" VerticalAlignment="Center"
Name="ButtonPrev" Height="75" Width="75" Visibility="Hidden">
                <Image Margin="0,0,0,0" Stretch="Fill"
                    Source="/Resources/LeftArrow.jpg"></Image>
            </Button>
        </StackPanel>
        <Thumb Grid.Row="1" Cursor="ScrollAll"  Background="{StaticResource
ResizeImage}" Height="20" Width="20" HorizontalAlignment="Right" Margin="0,0,0,0"
Name="ThumbResize" VerticalAlignment="Bottom" />
    </Grid>
</Window>
```

Code snippet from MainWindow.xaml

Next, test run the application. Figure 17-11 shows the application with the mouse over the Next button, causing that button to appear.

That completes the steps for the code in the ProVB_WPF_Step2 project. The next step is to separate out the custom window framework that was the focus of the ProVB_WPF_Step2. This can act as a base set of window classes that can be reused across multiple different applications. You can leverage the main application window and move the current logic associated with displaying images into a user control.

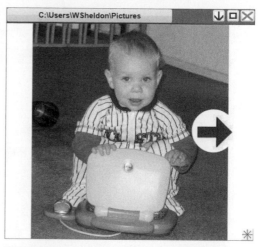

FIGURE 17-11

WPF User Controls

As for the specific controls available in WPF, you've seen in this chapter that several are available, although even those like the button that seem familiar may not work as expected. WPF controls need to fit a different paradigm than the old Windows Forms model. In that model, a control could be associated with data, and in some cases undergo minor customization to its look and feel. Under WPF, the concept of a grid is used. It isn't, however, similar to the old Windows Forms DataGridView in any way. The WPF grid is a much more generic grid that enables you to truly customize almost every aspect of its behavior.

Part of the goal of WPF is to make it immaterial which environment your application will work in, Web or desktop. For most of us, our code will either be on the desktop for WPF or running under Silverlight if on the Web. Thus, in most cases you'll want to make your XAML portable.

A Page control is, of course, the base UI element for a WPF-based Web application, so it's easy to see how this paradigm of the content area can support the layering of two different user-interface implementations. Once you have defined the base elements of your user interface you can leverage user controls, which are equally happy on the desktop or in the browser. Of course, creating applications that flexible is a bit more challenging, unless you are leveraging services. In other words, instead of targeting the file system, you would target a service, which might be local or remote, and that would be focused on the appropriate file system. Then the application is running on a local computer. It can encapsulate the pages in a Window control; and when hosted in a browser, it can use those same user controls within the framework of a Page.

Aside from some standard user interface controls, the WPF Toolbox contains nearly all of the controls that you can find in every other Windows-based user interface model, such as tabs, toolbars, tooltips, text boxes, drop downs, expanders, and so on. It should also be noted that the WPF namespace consists of several graphics, ink, and even data and data-bound controls.

Accordingly, the key to working with WPF is taking these basic controls and using WPF user control projects to create the building blocks that you will then use to create your custom user interfaces. If the example in this chapter demonstrated anything, it is how time-consuming making changes to the XAML can be. If you open ProVB_WPF_Step3, you'll find that this is exactly what was done with all of the image handling from ProVB_WPF_Step2.

The newly created user control is called ImageRotator. This control contains not only the Image control and the buttons associated with moving to the next and previous image, but also the button to select the correct folder. The main changes that were made to implement this control involve that button. Figure 17-12 shows the updated control within the designer.

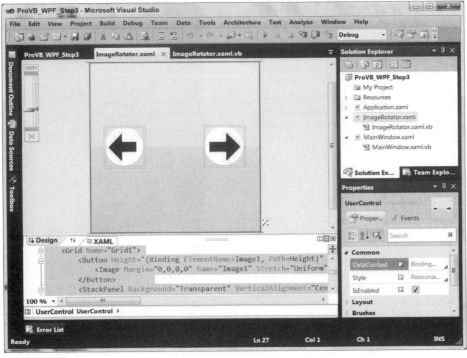

FIGURE 17-12

During Step 2 of the project, that button was "conveniently" located in the custom title bar. What might not be obvious as you look at a black-and-white copy of Figure 17-12 is that the background of the control is in fact covered by `ButtonBrowse`. `ButtonBrowse` now needs to be within the control, and the goal is to still keep it from overlying the screen real estate available to the image. As strange as it sounds having the button over the full control display allows you to minimize its display impact by covering it with the image and removing its explicit visual presence. The key takeaway as you look within the following updated XAML is that the `Image` control is now the button's content:

Available for
download on
Wrox.com

```xaml
<UserControl x:Class="ImageRotator"
             xmlns=
"http://schemas.microsoft.com/winfx/2006/xaml/presentation"
             xmlns:x="http://schemas.microsoft.com/winfx/2006/xaml"
             xmlns:mc=
"http://schemas.openxmlformats.org/markup-compatibility/2006"
             xmlns:d=
"http://schemas.microsoft.com/expression/blend/2008"
             mc:Ignorable="d"
             d:DesignHeight="300" d:DesignWidth="300">
    <UserControl.Resources>
        <EllipseGeometry x:Key="RoundPanel" Center="36, 36"
 RadiusX="34" RadiusY="34"></EllipseGeometry>
    </UserControl.Resources>
    <Grid Name="Grid1" MinWidth="100" MinHeight="100">
        <Button Height="{Binding ElementName=Image1, Path=Height}"
Width="{Binding ElementName=Image1, Path=Width}" Name="ButtonBrowse" >
            <Image Margin="0,0,0,0" Name="Image1" Stretch="Uniform" />
        </Button>
        <StackPanel Background="Transparent" VerticalAlignment="Center"
 Margin="0,0,25,0" Height="75" Name="StackPanelNext"
```

```
                HorizontalAlignment="Right" Width="75"
                Clip="{StaticResource RoundPanel}">
                        <Button HorizontalAlignment="Stretch"
                VerticalAlignment="Stretch" Name="ButtonNext"
                Height="75" Width="75" Visibility="Hidden">
                            <Image Margin="0,0,0,0" Stretch="Fill"
                Source="/Resources/RightArrow.jpg"></Image>
                        </Button>
                    </StackPanel>
                    <StackPanel Background="Transparent" VerticalAlignment="Center"
                Margin="25,0,0,0" Height="75" Name="StackPanelPrev"
                HorizontalAlignment="Left" Width="75"
                Clip="{StaticResource RoundPanel}">
                        <Button HorizontalAlignment="Left"
                VerticalAlignment="Center" Name="ButtonPrev"
                Height="75" Width="75" Visibility="Hidden">
                            <Image Margin="0,0,0,0" Stretch="Fill"
                Source="/Resources/LeftArrow.jpg"></Image>
                        </Button>
                    </StackPanel>
                </Grid>
            </UserControl>
```

Code snippet from ImageRotator.xaml

The preceding XAML should look familiar. The main differences from the last time we looked at this code as part of the `MainWindow` class are the changes related to the user control declaration and to `ButtonBrowse`.

In terms of the `UserControl`, it has several attributes that should be very familiar in terms of class and namespace definitions. One which may not be familiar is the one labeled `mc` and associated with markup compatibility. This library is also used within the attributes of the user control declaration. `mc:Ignorable="d"` indicates that attribute values which are namespaced within the "d" namespace can be ignored when processing this XAML.

`DesignHeight` and `DesignWidth` are the two attributes prefaced with `d:`. In this context it should be relatively clear what is occurring: We are introducing the idea that when designing this user control, it is useful to have a visible design surface. However, at deployment, this user control should be sized to the needs of the containing object. Since the design surface has no containing object, this could cause an issue because the height and width would default to 0. The only way to prevent that would be to introduce an element to force a size on the user control, and of course that would carry forward into the deployment and affect use of the control.

What `mc:Ignorable` provides is a way within XAML to describe aspects of the UI that are specific to design time. That way, at runtime it isn't necessary to remember to remove these attributes; instead they are ignored.

In addition to the elements used to define the new user control class, the other change of interest involves `ButtonBrowse`. As noted, `ButtonBrowse` is now included in the same display area as the image. You'll note that the button's height and width are now data bound, as explained in more detail shortly.

Before discussing data binding and leaving the majority of this XAML behind, notice how the image has been placed as the content of the button. Placing the image into the button's content allows the code to leverage the built-in command routing of WPF. When someone clicks on the image, the image doesn't handle the `Click` event. It is therefore passed to the UI element layered below the image, the button. The button, of course, handles the `Click` event. Thus, unlike the days of Windows Forms, when you would attach the image to the button which had some knowledge about using an image as its surface, in WPF the button is blissfully unaware that an image is acting as its content. However, this decoupling of the image from the button leaves a gap in relation to the sizing of the button, and that's where data binding the button's height and width to those of the image comes in.

Data Binding in WPF

WPF includes significant support for binding, whether it is between controls or to a data source. Binding to a source is a very declarative method for associating an external value with a control. Because you specify what is bound, if the bound item changes, then WPF knows to automatically reflect that change in your control. Thus, you aren't managing state and attempting to track and update changes; that becomes part of the "plumbing" and you can just expect it to work.

In order to manage some of the complexity of data binding, this chapter looks at binding between controls, the use of dependency properties, and then binding to external data sources.

Binding between WPF Controls

As noted in the updated XAML for the `ImageRotator` control, the size of `ButtonBrowse` has been bound to the size of the control `Image1`. Control `Image1` conveniently is the contents of `ButtonBrowse`, which creates an interesting dependency when you think about it. However, the size of the image is constrained by the available space within the control's display area and the scaling of the image being displayed. Thus, if the control is sized at 300×300 and an image is loaded, the control will compute its scale based on the available space. For an image which has a greater height than width, that might be 250×300. Notice how all of this is handled automatically.

In the past your next step would have been to detect that the `Image` control changed size, communicating this size change to the button to keep it "hidden" behind the image. The code would also need to capture when a new image was loaded, since this would result in resizing the image and another notification to the button. To this also add another notification each time the control was resized, etc. In other words, you would be attempting to ensure that your plumbing captured every change in the `Image` control's size.

With WPF you can simply associate the height of the button with the same value that the `Image` control is using for its height, and step back. It doesn't matter how or when the `Image` control changes size; when the height changes, it changes for both controls. The same is done for the `Width` property and that's it; no custom code, no custom event — nothing.

The format used in the `ButtonBrowse` control is what might be called an inline format for binding:

```
<Button Height="{Binding ElementName=Image1, Path=Height}"
Width="{Binding ElementName=Image1, Path=Width}" Name="ButtonBrowse" >
```

Notice that the `Height` and `Width` properties remain as attributes of the `Button`'s XML node. This method is convenient when you have only a couple of properties to bind. A second method for binding is discussed later in the chapter.

Binding between controls is, of course, not the only form of binding; nor are you limited to binding to just another named control. In fact, in some cases it's not realistic to bind to a named control. For example, if you are working with a data grid, you'll want to bind to the current row, and that implies an associative binding. In that case you want to use a `RelativeSource` binding so that you can indicate that the row associated with your control in the data grid is the one to which you are binding. That row won't have a name, just a direct parent relationship. Keep in mind that this example shows only one set of binding parameters; several others are available in order to support the disparate needs of different requirements.

In terms of limitations, you can bind to any object that inherits from `DependencyObject`. This class is in the class hierarchy for all of the controls in the `System.Windows.Controls` namespace. It can also be in the class hierarchy of your own customer classes. However, your property also needs to be implemented as a dependency property, the subject of the next section.

Dependency Properties

Not all properties are dependency properties, but any property used where the design allows for data binding is typically implemented as a dependency property. For the purposes of this chapter, it's only necessary to understand a few things about dependency properties. First, they are often used to reference resources and styles as dynamic resources, not static resources. Second, they are identified in the documentation of the WPF components. Finally, to help expand your concept of binding, keep in mind that the `Style` property is in fact a dependency property.

Every control can be associated with one or more styles. As part of your development, you can create a style just as you create a resource. Styles can be assigned similarly to resources — that is, either by referencing them by name when assigning a new style to an instance of a control, or by creating a style that is associated with all instances of a given type. In either case, the `Style` property of a control is what is known as a *dependency property*.

When you hear the term *dependency* you may initially assume this means the property has a dependency on some other item. However, in the context of WPF, a better way to think of the term *dependency* is that "it depends on who set that specific value in the object that defines that property." A dependency property isn't dependent on some external item; the property's value varies over time depending upon the last update to the property.

Going into the details of why this occurs is beyond the scope of this chapter. However, dependency properties are coupled with change notification logic, and play a significant role in things such as animation and 3-D layout. For our purposes, the goal is to demonstrate the usefulness of dependency properties and how to create a custom dependency property.

To this end, start by assuming that you would like the `ImageRotator` control to notify its parent container whenever the path for images changes. The traditional way to do this, using a custom event, is illustrated in the code for the `ImageRotator` control:

Available for download on Wrox.com

```vb
Public Class ImageRotator

    Private m_imageList As String() = {}
    Private m_curIndex As Integer = 0
    Private m_curImagePath As String = ""
    Private thename As String

    Public Event ImagePathChanged(ByVal sender As Object, ByVal e As String)


    Private Sub Grid1_Loaded(ByVal sender As System.Object,
            ByVal e As System.Windows.RoutedEventArgs) Handles
        Grid1.Loaded
        m_curImagePath = Environment.GetFolderPath(Environment.SpecialFolder.MyPictures)
        RaiseEvent ImagePathChanged(Me, m_curImagePath)
        LoadImages()
    End Sub

    Private Sub ButtonBrowse_Click(ByVal sender As System.Object,
            ByVal e As System.Windows.RoutedEventArgs) Handles
        ButtonBrowse.Click
        Dim folderDialog As System.Windows.Forms.FolderBrowserDialog =
            New System.Windows.Forms.FolderBrowserDialog()
        folderDialog.Description = "Select the folder for images."
        folderDialog.SelectedPath = m_curImagePath
        Dim res As System.Windows.Forms.DialogResult = folderDialog.ShowDialog()
        If res = System.Windows.Forms.DialogResult.OK Then
            m_curImagePath = folderDialog.SelectedPath
            RaiseEvent ImagePathChanged(Me, m_curImagePath)
            LoadImages()
        End If
    End Sub

    Private Sub LoadImages()
        Image1.Source = Nothing
```

```vb
        m_imageList = System.IO.Directory.GetFiles(m_curImagePath, "*.jpg")
        m_curIndex = 0
        If m_imageList.Count > 0 Then
            Image1.Source = New System.Windows.Media.Imaging.BitmapImage(
            New System.Uri(m_imageList(m_curIndex)))
        End If
    End Sub

    Private Sub ButtonPrev_Click(ByVal sender As System.Object,
            ByVal e As System.Windows.RoutedEventArgs) Handles
        ButtonPrev.Click
        If m_imageList.Count > 0 Then
            m_curIndex -= 1
            If m_curIndex < 0 Then
                m_curIndex = m_imageList.Count - 1
            End If
            Image1.Source = New System.Windows.Media.Imaging.BitmapImage(
            New System.Uri(m_imageList(m_curIndex)))
        End If
    End Sub

    Private Sub ButtonNext_Click(ByVal sender As System.Object,
            ByVal e As System.Windows.RoutedEventArgs) Handles
        ButtonNext.Click
        If m_imageList.Count > 0 Then
            m_curIndex += 1
            If m_curIndex > m_imageList.Count - 1 Then
                m_curIndex = 0
            End If
            Image1.Source = New System.Windows.Media.Imaging.BitmapImage(
            New System.Uri(m_imageList(m_curIndex)))
        End If
    End Sub

    Private Sub StackPanelPrev_MouseEnter(ByVal sender As System.Object,
        ByVal e As System.Windows.Input.MouseEventArgs) Handles StackPanelPrev.MouseEnter
            ButtonPrev.Visibility = Windows.Visibility.Visible
    End Sub

    Private Sub StackPanelPrev_MouseLeave(ByVal sender As System.Object,
        ByVal e As System.Windows.Input.MouseEventArgs) Handles StackPanelPrev.MouseLeave
            ButtonPrev.Visibility = Windows.Visibility.Hidden
    End Sub

    Private Sub StackPanelNext_MouseEnter(ByVal sender As System.Object,
        ByVal e As System.Windows.Input.MouseEventArgs) Handles StackPanelNext.MouseEnter
            ButtonNext.Visibility = Windows.Visibility.Visible
    End Sub

    Private Sub StackPanelNext_MouseLeave(ByVal sender As System.Object,
        ByVal e As System.Windows.Input.MouseEventArgs) Handles StackPanelNext.MouseLeave
            ButtonNext.Visibility = Windows.Visibility.Hidden
    End Sub
End Class
```

Code snippet from ImageRotator.vb

The preceding code block is mostly the same code which previously existed in the MainWindow.vb class. The changes to support a custom event have been highlighted in bold. Notice that in addition to the declaration of the custom event and the custom property, which is passed with the event, the only other change is to raise that event as required.

Now that we have a custom event, let's take the updated (and much shorter) code for the main window and add a handler for this event. You'll find the new event handler at the bottom of the following code block:

```vb
Class MainWindow

    'Move Window
    Private Sub Rectangle_MouseLeftButtonDown(ByVal sender As Object,
            ByVal e As System.Windows.Input.MouseButtonEventArgs) _
            Handles TitleBar.MouseLeftButtonDown
        Me.DragMove()
    End Sub

    'Minimize
    Private Sub ButtonMin_Click(ByVal sender As Object,
            ByVal e As RoutedEventArgs) Handles ButtonMin.Click
        Me.WindowState = WindowState.Minimized
    End Sub

    Private Sub ButtonMax_Click(ByVal sender As Object,
            ByVal e As RoutedEventArgs) Handles ButtonMax.Click
        If (Me.WindowState = WindowState.Maximized) Then
            Me.WindowState = WindowState.Normal
        Else
            Me.WindowState = WindowState.Maximized
        End If
    End Sub

    Private Sub ButtonClose_Click(ByVal sender As Object,
            ByVal e As RoutedEventArgs) Handles ButtonClose.Click
        Me.Close()
    End Sub

    'Resize
    Private Sub ThumbResize_DragDelta(ByVal sender As System.Object,
            ByVal e As Primitives.DragDeltaEventArgs) Handles ThumbResize.DragDelta

        If (Me.Height + e.VerticalChange < Me.MinHeight) Then
            Me.Height = Me.MinHeight
        Else
            Me.Height += e.VerticalChange
        End If

        If (Me.Width + e.HorizontalChange < Me.MinWidth) Then
            Me.Width = Me.MinWidth
        Else
            Me.Width += e.HorizontalChange
        End If
    End Sub

    Private Sub ImageRotater_UpdatedPath(ByVal sender As Object,
            ByVal e As String) Handles imageRotator1.ImagePathChanged
        labelWindowTitle.Content = e
    End Sub
End Class
```

Code snippet from MainWindow.vb

The new event handler is shown at the bottom of the code handling the new `ImagePathChanged` event from the `ImageRotator` control (instance `imageRotator1` is shown within the window). At this point the view in the designer for the updated window is shown in Figure 17-13. There have been a couple of changes related to the display, including the addition of a `Label` control, as referenced in the event hander.

FIGURE 17-13

In moving the previous `Image` controls into a user control, other changes were made. First, as previously discussed, the stylish button on the title rectangle was removed and placed in the control. In its place, although not visible, is the `Label` control `labelWindowTitle`. This label is the target of the new event and will display the image folder. Next, note that the buttons on the title rectangle have been updated. These updated graphics were imported from the Visual Studio 10 image library. You'll find the library under the Visual Studio 10 installation folder within the Common7 folder.

FIGURE 17-14

Within the main portion of the display, the control `imageRotator1` is only a portion of the display. Two labels and two buttons have been added. These are currently unused but will be before this phase of the application is complete. In fact, if you just download and run the sample code you'll find that the current image doesn't match the final display. However, the goal here is to run the application, and if everything is working correctly you'll see something similar to what is shown in Figure 17-14.

Creating a Custom Dependency Property

At this point we have a tool that supports one-way communication. In transforming this to a dependency property, the first example is going to use a read-only dependency property. Thus, in the sample code all of the event-specific code is now commented out. In its place a new read-only region is added. (Note that in the final sample code that region is also commented out, replaced by a new read-write dependency property.)

The place to start is back within the code for the `ImageRotator` control. Once you have commented out the single line that defines the custom event, you are going to add all of the following code to define a read-only dependency property:

```vb
Public ReadOnly Property ImageURI As String
    Get
        Try
            If Image1 IsNot Nothing AndAlso Image1.Source IsNot Nothing Then
                Return Image1.Source.ToString()
            Else
                Return "No Selection"
            End If
        Catch ex As Exception
            Return ""
        End Try
        Return ""
    End Get
End Property

Private Shared ReadOnly ImageProp As DependencyPropertyKey =
    DependencyProperty.RegisterAttachedReadOnly("ImageURI",
                            GetType(String),
                            Type.GetType("ProVB_WPF_Step3.ImageRotator"),
                            New FrameworkPropertyMetadata(
                                        "Can you see me now?"))
```

Code snippet from ImageRotator.vb

At this point, you are likely wondering why you are substituting more code. There are two elements to that answer. One, you are creating something that can be referenced directly in XAML in a declarative fashion. Two, and more important, when you transform this to a read-write property, you'll be able to replace that one-way communication, which is the event pattern, with a two-way communication pattern that supports all the same decoupling provided by the custom event.

For now you should review each of these two new property declarations. From the top, the first one should look reasonably familiar in that it is a standard class property definition. This property is mapping to the source property within the `Image` control for now, but in the big picture this is just the property that would need to be exposed. As you'll soon see, you can map this to a property on the user control, as opposed to one of the controls in the user control, and this will be more valuable.

Next up is a line that is marked `Private`, and it defines a `Shared ReadOnly` field called `ImageProp`. `ImageProp` will be the name of the read-only property; and because it is read only, instead of being created as a true dependency property, you need to create a `DependencyPropertyKey`. This is a read-only version of a dependency property, and the main parameters are the name of the property to be exposed and the type of that property. In this case, we are using the `GetType` method to get that type. Next is the type of the object that provides this property. Note that here we switch to the less precise `Type.GetType()` method. Note that this method accepts a string, and that string must include the full namespace of the object. Thus, the `GetType` method is preferred.

The final parameter to the `RegisterAttachedReadOnly` method is a `FrameworkPropertyMetadata` object. The first parameter of this object is a default value for the property. It includes other attributes related to where setters should call and defines potential dependencies for the system when a property value is changed. These are not required for this example.

If you did nothing else for your new property and jumped ahead to the mapping in the main window, then you would be able to go to the designer for `MainWindow` and see this in the Design view. That's a tip in case you are doing this on your own and face any issues; you can step back to this point for debugging purposes.

I say that because the next step before leaving this code is to replace the locations where you previously called `RaiseEvent` and instead set your new dependency property. You'll see that next to each of the now commented `RaiseEvent` calls in the code is a new line that reads as follows:

```vb
SetValue(ImageProp, m_curImagePath)
```

Hopefully, at this point you are thinking that this is just like a custom event. When new concepts are introduced, such as something like XAML, users often need a familiar point of reference on which to base their understanding. Here you can see that the dependency property's behavior is much like the combination of a custom property with a custom event.

The remaining step in implementing this dependency property is "listening" for updates. Of course, in reality the event handler in the final `MainWindow.vb` source file is commented out. Instead of replacing that custom event handler with more VB code, you are going to modify the XAML. What follows is the XAML for the main window (highlighted in bold are the changes that were made to the baseline XAML when it was brought over to the Step 3 version of the project):

```xaml
<Window x:Class="MainWindow"
    xmlns="http://schemas.microsoft.com/winfx/2006/xaml/presentation"
    xmlns:x="http://schemas.microsoft.com/winfx/2006/xaml"
    Title="ProVB_WPF" Height="363" Width="444" Name="MainWindow"
    WindowStyle="None" AllowsTransparency="True"
    xmlns:my="clr-namespace:ProVB_WPF_Step3">
    <Grid>
        <Grid.RowDefinitions>
            <RowDefinition Height="25" />
            <RowDefinition Height="215*" />
        </Grid.RowDefinitions>
        <Rectangle Name="TitleBar" HorizontalAlignment="Stretch" Margin="0,0,0,0"
            Stroke="Black" Fill="Green" VerticalAlignment="Stretch" />
        <Label Grid.Row="0" Height="28" HorizontalAlignment="Left" Margin="10,0,0,0"
            Name="labelWindowTitle" VerticalAlignment="Top" ></Label>
        <Button Height="20" Width="23" HorizontalAlignment="Right" Margin="0,1,1,0"
            Name="ButtonClose" VerticalAlignment="Top" >
            <Image Margin="0,0,0,0" Name="Image2" Stretch="Fill"
            Source="/ProVB_WPF_Step3;component/Resources/1385_Disable_24x24_72.png"/>
        </Button>
        <Button Height="20" Width="20" HorizontalAlignment="Right" Margin="0,1,25,0"
            Name="ButtonMax" VerticalAlignment="Top" >
            <Image Margin="0,0,0,0" HorizontalAlignment="Center" Name="Image3"
                Stretch="Fill"
        Source="/ProVB_WPF_Step3;component/Resources/112_Plus_Green_24x24_72.png"/>
        </Button>
        <Button Height="20" Width="20" HorizontalAlignment="Right" Margin="0,1,47,0"
                Name="ButtonMin" VerticalAlignment="Top" >
            <Image Margin="0,0,0,0" Name="Image4" Stretch="Fill"
    Source="/ProVB_WPF_Step3;component/Resources/112_DownArrowShort_Green_24x24_72.png"/>
        </Button>
        <my:ImageRotator Grid.Row="1" HorizontalAlignment="Center" x:Name="imageRotator1"
            VerticalAlignment="Top" Margin="0,0,0,100" />
        <Thumb Grid.Row="1" Cursor="ScrollAll" Background="{StaticResource ResizeImage}"
            Height="20" Width="20" HorizontalAlignment="Right" Margin="0,0,0,0"
            Name="ThumbResize" VerticalAlignment="Bottom" />
        <Label Content="Name:" Grid.Row="1" HorizontalAlignment="Left" Margin="12,0,0,48"
            Name="label1" Height="28" VerticalAlignment="Bottom" />
        <TextBox Grid.Row="1" Margin="81,0,86,53" Name="textBox1" Height="23"
            VerticalAlignment="Bottom" />
        <Label Content="Job Title:" Grid.Row="1" Height="28" HorizontalAlignment="Left"
            Margin="10,0,0,12" Name="label2" VerticalAlignment="Bottom" />
        <TextBox Grid.Row="1" Height="23" Margin="81,0,86,17" Name="textBox2"
            VerticalAlignment="Bottom" />
    </Grid>
</Window>
```

Code snippet from MainWindow.xaml

The first changed line adds a new namespace, which references the current project. One of the nice integrations with .NET is the ability to reference any .NET namespace from within WPF. In this case the `my` alias is assigned to the current project and is then used in the XAML when the `ImageRotator` control is referenced. Near the bottom of the XAML are the declarations for the new labels and text boxes, which are located at the bottom of the window.

Of particular interest here, however, is the second highlighted code section, which describes the new `Label` control. Keep in mind that the goal is to have this label display the path for the images, the same path that is now represented with a dependency object. To make this association you could add XAML similar to what was done for `ButtonBrowse` in the `ImageRotator` XAML. However, this is an opportunity to bind with an alternate XAML syntax.

In this case, between the `<Label>` and `</Label>` tags you'll want to add the following XAML:

```
<Label.Content>
    <Binding ElementName="imageRotator1" Path="ImageURI"></Binding>
</Label.Content>
```

Code snippet from MainWindow.xaml

The preceding XAML should look familiar, as it has the same attributes that you embedded within the `ButtonBrowse` binding. However, in this case you'll see that you have a very readable binding declaration, and if you were going to bind several different properties, this format might be a bit more readable. However, at this point, instead of having custom code to listen for a custom event, you've simply bound the label to the user control's `ImageURI` property.

This causes only one visible change to how the application behaves, and it occurs within the designer. Unlike Figure 17-13, where the title bar's label isn't visible, once you have mapped the dependency property, the path to the default image that is shown in the figure is displayed on the title bar. However, at runtime, you get what is shown in Figure 17-14.

Before departing this section, let's shift over to the Properties window for the label control. Now that you've manually added this XAML you can use the Properties window to examine this binding. The Properties window for WPF has been greatly enhanced, as you can see in Figure 17-15, which shows the `Content` property for the `labelWindowTitle` control. Notice that this property's binding definition is accurately reflected within the Properties window, which shows the source as the `imageRotator1` control, and that the `ImageURI` property is the path for the binding within that control.

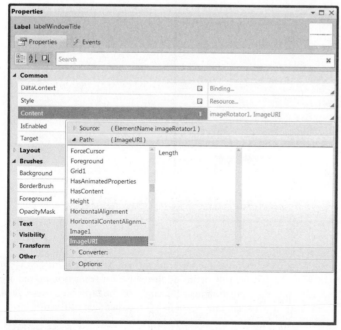

FIGURE 17-15

The properties haven't just been updated for WPF bindings. Updates and several enhancements related to the design and styles in the application have been applied. It is now possible to do much more core design of your application from within Visual Studio. Unlike in the past where the use of Expression Blend was an expectation, for business applications that need minimal customization it is likely that a developer can add some simple styling to update the application look and feel.

Modifying the Look of the User Interface

As noted earlier, one of the primary uses for binding is to bind styles and design changes. To demonstrate both this and a new feature of Visual Studio 2010, it is time to make some additional design changes to the application. Prior to Visual Studio 2010, creating a gradient color for a control was easy to do in Expression Blend but difficult to manage in Visual Studio. Thus, the next change that you can make to have your project match the final version of ProVB_WPF_Step3 is to change that green bar acting as a header.

Figure 17-16 shows the new Properties window containing the `Rectangle`, which is used as a title bar. Here, the background property is being customized. Unlike with Windows Forms, the color-based properties enable you to specify that you want to use a gradient brush. To do so, select the third button above the color window, which is a black-white gradient. Once that is done, you can start adding gradient points in the same manner that a user of Word can add tabs to a document.

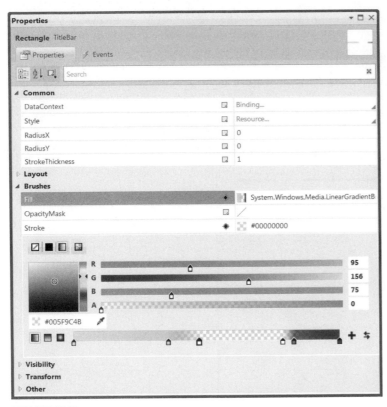

FIGURE 17-16

Replicating what was done in ProVB_WPF_Step3 requires six tags on your gradient bar, and to add those tags you simply click on the bar. Just like adding tabs in Word, you can easily define additional color transition points. By defining the two inner tags as transparent and adjusting their position near the edges of the `ButtonBrowse` display, you can create a transparent background for the button while creating a gradient on either side of the title bar.

For the three control buttons, I first created a blue gradient background below the buttons. Finally, to mimic some of the glass styling, I modified the `Opacity` property within the Visibility portion of the properties window and set the opacity of the rectangle to 50% (aka .5). This setting enables you to see both the colors and what is in back of the control.

At this point I also ensured that the border, or "Stroke," of the rectangle was transparent (refer to Figure 17-16). However, if you ran the application now, you would find that instead of being transparent, the newly transparent areas are instead white. This is because the underlying window's background is painted with a white brush by default.

Therefore, the next step is to access the window properties and set the background brush to transparent. This is good to know because you might be tempted to change the window's opacity property. After all, if the opacity allows you to see through, then wouldn't setting that to 0 allow you to see through the window? The answer is yes, but that property is applied to the contents of the window as well as the background. As a result, your entire application disappears. Instead, you want only the background to disappear; and the correct way to handle that is to set the background brush.

At this point, if you run the application you'll have something that looks similar to what is shown in Figure 17-17. Of course, Figure 17-17 also shows how difficult making your background transparent can be when looking for the controls that are part of your application. However, you might want this capability in some situations.

Notice how if you click outside one of the colored regions your window allows that click to pass through. This gives you an opportunity to explore some of the advantages and challenges of having a completely transparent surface. You might want to test what happens by setting just the background brush to have an almost imperceptible presence.

However, by now you've probably noticed that it's not only difficult to see the controls, but moving the window is tricky because the new label doesn't respond to the mouse down by allowing you to drag the window. Returning to Visual Studio, select the `Label` control. Then, in the Properties window, select the Events tab. Find the MouseDown event and click in the area where it is defined to get the drop down list of available events. Select the existing event handler for the `Rectangle` control.

FIGURE 17-17

This is where Visual Studio 2010 does something awesome: Instead of mapping this handler within the XAML, as it does for C#, it recognizes that you have a `Handles` clause and adds the `Label` control's `MouseDown` event to the list of events on your `Handles` clause in the code. In other words, it recognizes what you are doing and handles the event appropriately based on how you have chosen to handle events in your existing code.

Now it's time to make the final UI changes for the application, the ones which you actually see in the sample code. Notice that the `ImageRotator` has been shifted to the left side of the display and it's margin is tied to the bottom of the window. A new `Label` control that has its text property set to "Name List" is placed to the right of the `ImageRotator`. Below the label is a new `List` control. At this point the user interface should look similar to the final UI.

Note in order to give the application some coherence, the experimental background has been eliminated and some of the visibility of the background has been restored. This is why when you run the code download it doesn't have a completely invisible background. The final design within Visual Studio should look similar to what is shown in Figure 17-18. This image shows the final layout of the ProVB_WPF_Step3 look and feel.

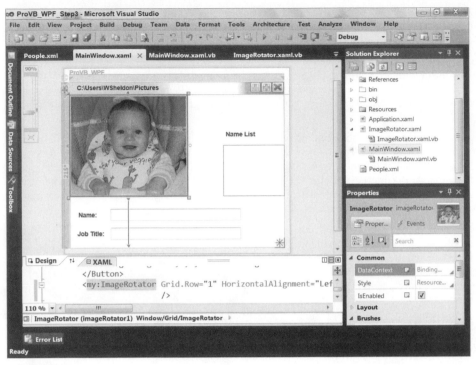

FIGURE 17-18

Before leaving the design discussion, a quick introduction to styles is in order. It may not be obvious, but every WPF application has an implicit style definition if you don't override it. For example, when you added a button to your form, how did it know that its background should be a gradient silver-like color? Where did those hover-over and mouse-down effects come from?

Styles

Styles essentially leverage the concept of resources. With a style you have the option of either referencing all objects of a common type and setting the default style for that control type or creating a custom style that is specific to those control instances that reference it. In short, styles provide a mechanism for you to apply a theme across an application and to override that theme in those specific instances where you want to. If another developer later adds new elements to your application, the default styles are automatically applied.

Styles are defined like resources; in fact, they are defined within the same section of your XAML file in which resources are defined. As with resources, when you define a style at the application level, the style can be applied across all of the windows in the application. Conversely, if a style is meant to target only the objects in a given window, page, or user control, then it makes sense to define them at that level.

Rather than provide a simple example of a style, let's look at a complex style that focuses on the hover effect for a standard button. This effect is defined within the default style, and the following code block provides the default style for the control of type `Button`. Note that generating this style information in XAML format is best done with Expression Blend, as discussed in Chapter 18.

```
<Style x:Key="ButtonFocusVisual">
  <Setter Property="Control.Template">
    <Setter.Value>
      <ControlTemplate>
        <Rectangle SnapsToDevicePixels="true" Stroke="Black" StrokeDashArray="1 2"
StrokeThickness="1" Margin="2"/>
```

```
        </ControlTemplate>
      </Setter.Value>
    </Setter>
  </Style>
  <LinearGradientBrush x:Key="ButtonNormalBackground" EndPoint="0,1" StartPoint="0,0">
    <GradientStop Color="#F3F3F3" Offset="0"/>
    <GradientStop Color="#EBEBEB" Offset="0.5"/>
    <GradientStop Color="#DDDDDD" Offset="0.5"/>
    <GradientStop Color="#CDCDCD" Offset="1"/>
  </LinearGradientBrush>
  <SolidColorBrush x:Key="ButtonNormalBorder" Color="#FF707070"/>
  <Style x:Key="ButtonStyle1" TargetType="{x:Type Button}">
    <Setter Property="FocusVisualStyle" Value="{StaticResource ButtonFocusVisual}"/>
    <Setter Property="Background" Value="{StaticResource ButtonNormalBackground}"/>
    <Setter Property="BorderBrush" Value="{StaticResource ButtonNormalBorder}"/>
    <Setter Property="BorderThickness" Value="1"/>
    <Setter Property="Foreground" Value="{DynamicResource {x:Static SystemColors.
ControlTextBrushKey}}"/>
    <Setter Property="HorizontalContentAlignment" Value="Center"/>
    <Setter Property="VerticalContentAlignment" Value="Center"/>
    <Setter Property="Padding" Value="1"/>
    <Setter Property="Template">
      <Setter.Value>
        <ControlTemplate TargetType="{x:Type Button}">
          <Microsoft_Windows_Themes:ButtonChrome SnapsToDevicePixels="true"
          x:Name="Chrome" Background="{TemplateBinding Background}" BorderBrush="{
          TemplateBinding BorderBrush}" RenderDefaulted="{TemplateBinding IsDefaulted}"
RenderMouseOver="{TemplateBinding IsMouseOver}" RenderPressed="{TemplateBinding
          IsPressed}">
            <ContentPresenter SnapsToDevicePixels="{TemplateBinding
              SnapsToDevicePixels}" HorizontalAlignment="{TemplateBinding
              HorizontalContentAlignment}" Margin="{TemplateBinding Padding}"
              VerticalAlignment="{TemplateBinding VerticalContentAlignment}"
              RecognizesAccessKey="True"/>
          </Microsoft_Windows_Themes:ButtonChrome>
          <ControlTemplate.Triggers>
            <Trigger Property="IsKeyboardFocused" Value="true">
              <Setter Property="RenderDefaulted" TargetName="Chrome" Value="true"/>
            </Trigger>
            <Trigger Property="ToggleButton.IsChecked" Value="true">
              <Setter Property="RenderPressed" TargetName="Chrome" Value="true"/>
            </Trigger>
            <Trigger Property="IsEnabled" Value="false">
              <Setter Property="Foreground" Value="#ADADAD"/>
            </Trigger>
          </ControlTemplate.Triggers>
        </ControlTemplate>
      </Setter.Value>
    </Setter>
  </Style>
```

There are two lines of interest in the preceding code block. The first concerns the actual button style defined. Styles often reference other resources; and similar to early C compilers, references must be defined before they are actually referenced. Thus, the style defined in the preceding code block is actually the last style entry:

```
<Style x:Key="ButtonStyle1" TargetType="{x:Type Button}">
```

This line, which is highlighted in bold in the code block, indicates that this set of resources defines a style with the key ButtonStyle1. Because this style is defined with a key, it is not a default style applied to all controls of the target type. Styles always define a target type because different control types expect different specific values defined within all of the detailed elements of a style.

To have every control button use the same style, instead of providing a key for the style `ButtonStyle1`, you provide only the type definition. If at some point you want objects of different types to share certain characteristics, this can be done by defining a resource and then applying it to the style for each of the types. If these styles are then designated without a key, then they are by default applied to every object of that type.

Next, if you want to find a way to remove the default highlight that occurs as you mouse over a button, then you need to determine how the style specifies that effect. The good news is that the hook that causes that behavior is in fact included in this file; the bad news is that it references a template that is then assigned to that behavior. The following line of XAML shows that the `RenderMouseOver` property is being associated with the template `IsMouseOver`:

```
RenderMouseOver="{TemplateBinding IsMouseOver}"
```

It is this template that causes the button to change its look to reflect this state. Thus, to have a button without this default behavior, you need to either define a new template or delete this XAML element from your custom style.

You could, of course, take the preceding code block, make the necessary change, and paste it into your application's XAML. Certainly that will work if you also carry out the other steps that you need. However, long term, the preceding block of XAML is specific to controls of the type `Button`. Moreover, all of the preceding code was in fact generated. If you need to customize the runtime behavior of another control type, you'll need to generate the default style for that control. Expression Blend although no longer a requirement is still a good option for doing this.

Data Binding to a Data Source

The final item to look at in this chapter is binding to a data source. For brevity, this example uses a simple XML file `People.xml`, which is part of the ProVB_WPF_Step3 project. The contents of this file are as follows:

```xml
<?xml version="1.0" encoding="utf-8" ?>
<People xmlns="">
    <Person PersonID="187012">
        <FirstName>Johnny</FirstName>
        <LastName>Climber</LastName>
        <JobTitle>Danger Boy</JobTitle>
        <working_folder>C:\Users\WSheldon\Pictures\Johnny</working_folder>
    </Person>
    <Person PersonID="181810">
        <FirstName>Billy</FirstName>
        <LastName>Karate</LastName>
        <JobTitle>Gold Belt</JobTitle>
        <working_folder>C:\Users\WSheldon\Pictures\Billy</working_folder>
    </Person>
</People>
```

Code snippet from People.xml

The contents of this file are fairly simple, and represent a human resource-style application. Each entry has an internal ID and a series of fields. The `working_folder` node is machine specific, so when you consider running this application you'll need to map that to folders that exist on your local machine. Otherwise, you won't see any images.

While this file will be data-bound in the main window, the first step is to update the `ImageRotator` control. The first part of its transformation involves taking the read-only `ImageURI` property and transforming it into a read-write dependency property. As noted, the previously referenced read-only property was commented out and in a collapsed region in the sample download code. The final code begins similarly to the original in that it defines a standard class property. In this case, however, the property supports a `Set` method, which calls the local method to update the displayed image in the `Image` control.

The updated property code follows, starting with the updated `ImageURI` property:

```vb
Public Property ImageURI As String
    Get
        Return m_curImagePath
    End Get
    Set(ByVal value As String)
        m_curImagePath = value
        LoadImages()
    End Set
End Property

Private Shared ImageProp As DependencyProperty =
  DependencyProperty.RegisterAttached("ImageURI",
              GetType(String),
              GetType(ProVB_WPF_Step3.ImageRotator),
              New FrameworkPropertyMetadata(Nothing,
                  FrameworkPropertyMetadataOptions.AffectsRender,
                  New PropertyChangedCallback(AddressOf UriChanged)))

Public Shared Sub UriChanged(ByVal prop As DependencyObject,
            ByVal args As DependencyPropertyChangedEventArgs)
    CType(prop, ImageRotator).ImageURI = args.NewValue
End Sub
```

Code snippet from ImageRotator.vb

The original call to reference a `DependencyPropertyKey` has also been updated and the code now references a true `DependencyProperty` update. However, your focus should be on the fourth parameter to the `RegisterAttached` method. While the first three parameters are unchanged, the fourth parameter is now passing two new properties.

The new constructor for the `FrameworkPropertyMetadata` has a `null` parameter for the "default" value. It then passes an option flag indicating that when this property is updated, the rendering of the window is affected and will need to be updated. This is true because an update to this property will result in the selection of a new image, which will need to be sized and displayed.

However, it is the final parameter, the new `PropertyChangedCallback`, that is important. This is registering with the property what method should be notified when a change is made for this property. As noted earlier, when you think of a dependency property as a property plus an event with two-way communication, you need a place that will accept the inbound communications. This callback method is essentially an event handler for the `PropertyChanged` event when it is fired outside of the local class.

In this case, the address of the `UriChanged` method is passed. That method is the remaining new code. As you'll note by looking at the code, the `UriChanged` method is a `Shared` method, which means it can't just reference the local property. Fortunately, the first parameter is the instance of the `DependencyObject` which needs to be updated, and one of the values passed within the `EventArgs` parameter is in fact the new value. As a result, the method only requires a single line which casts the inbound dependency object to the local type and then calls the appropriate property on the local class, passing the new value.

This creates an infrastructure that supports two-way communication whereby your object will notify those who are interested in the value of this property about changes to it, and those who need to update this property can notify your object of a new proposed value. Note that if, for example, someone passed a path which wasn't valid, then you could reject the assignment of that value. If you are looking at the download code, then you know there is one last set of changes to comment out, some of the lines in the `Load` event of this class; however, that change is covered as the last step in this process.

The code now supports a bi-directional property associated with the image path, allowing updates to be sent to the control via binding within the XAML of the main window. Note that there are no updates to the `ImageRotator.xaml` file or the `MainWindow.xaml.vb` file. The data binding is focused on the

`MainWindow.xaml` file, which has again grown in length, and accordingly complexity. To help manage this, the next code block addresses the changes to this file which occur in the resources and data context for the file, while the updates to individual control binding are the focus of the second block.

The XAML which follows shows a couple of minor modifications to the window, but it is the bold lines which are of interest for the purposes of data binding. Because these lines are located near the top, we'll discuss them before the code. The first is a new `DataContext` assigned to the top-level grid. This grid, which isn't given a name but which is parent to all of the other controls, acts as the central clearing for the binding contexts.

The first highlighted line, which creates a data context for the grid, actually binds it to the new `ListBox` control. The selected item in the `ListBox` is then bound to the grid. By referencing this context across all of the other controls in the window, these controls can use this data context as their current context. Because updates to the selected item in the list are automatically updated to this context, each control can thus be kept in sync with the selected item in the grid, with no further code.

What may then interest you is the next highlighted section, which contains the grid resources. Most of the time developers would traditionally take these resources and map them to the selected item in the `ListBox`. However, as just discussed with WPF, the grid is binding to the selected item in the `ListBox`; thus, all of the other controls can inherit that context for the data context.

The implication is that the one control that won't inherit is the `ListBox`. Instead, as you'll see later, the `ListBox` explicitly binds to the first of the grid resources, the `XmlDataProvider`. This class is available to provide a way for XAML to load an XML file and bind to its contents. Either the provider can use a `Source` property, or you could embed the data within an `x:Data` block. Once bound, the provider is assigned a key so that it can be referenced from other controls. In this example, only the `ListBox` control will actually bind to this data source, but in theory other controls could bind to it. Additionally, the top-level node for XPath queries is defined as People. When the code asks for a property, it will get one based on entries under People. This is the starting point for the very simple XPath that the application will use.

The creation of the data provider is short and sweet; what comes next, however, is a data template. Called the `PersonName` template, this template defines an output format. It is also used by the `ListBox` control, although it could be used, for example, to populate the window title if you wanted a different title on the window. Within is a short snippet of WPF that describes a container — in this case, a `StackPanel` and the controls which are on the `StackPanel`. This means that a `DataTemplate` can be an extremely powerful way to format complex data structures. The controls within map directly to the default data source, in this case referencing two of the nodes from the `Person` structure in the XML.

These represent the only highlighted areas for binding in the first section of XML. The block which follows includes the top-level window showing a partially transparent background, through the buttons that are on the title bar rectangle:

```
<Window x:Class="MainWindow"
    xmlns="http://schemas.microsoft.com/winfx/2006/xaml/presentation"
    xmlns:x="http://schemas.microsoft.com/winfx/2006/xaml"
    Title="ProVB_WPF" Height="363" Width="444" Name="MainWindow"
    WindowStyle="None" AllowsTransparency="True" xmlns:my="clr-namespace:ProVB_WPF_Step3"
    WindowStartupLocation="CenterScreen" Background="#B4FFFFFF">
    <Grid OpacityMask="Black" Opacity="1"
        DataContext="{Binding ElementName=ListBox1, Path=SelectedItem}">
        <Grid.RowDefinitions>
            <RowDefinition Height="25" />
            <RowDefinition Height="215*" />
        </Grid.RowDefinitions>
        <Grid.Resources>
            <XmlDataProvider Source="People.xml" x:Key="People"
                        XPath="People">
            </XmlDataProvider>
            <DataTemplate x:Key="PersonName">
```

```xml
<StackPanel Orientation="Horizontal">
    <TextBlock>
        <TextBlock.Text>
            <Binding XPath="FirstName"></Binding>
        </TextBlock.Text>
    </TextBlock>
        <TextBlock Text=" "></TextBlock>
    <TextBlock>
        <TextBlock.Text>
            <Binding XPath="LastName"></Binding>
        </TextBlock.Text>
    </TextBlock>
    </StackPanel>
    </DataTemplate>
</Grid.Resources>
<Rectangle Name="TitleBar" HorizontalAlignment="Stretch" Margin="0,0,0,0"
        Stroke="#00000000" VerticalAlignment="Stretch" Opacity="0.5">
    <Rectangle.Fill>
        <LinearGradientBrush EndPoint="1,0.5" StartPoint="0,0.5">
            <GradientStop Color="#FF0AFF0A" Offset="0" />
            <GradientStop Color="Blue" Offset="1" />
            <GradientStop Color="#005F9C4B" Offset="0.474" />
            <GradientStop Color="#00638F54" Offset="0.785" />
            <GradientStop Color="#9D0000FF" Offset="0.826" />
            <GradientStop Color="#FF00ED00" Offset="0.359" />
        </LinearGradientBrush>
    </Rectangle.Fill>
</Rectangle>
<Label Grid.Row="0" Height="28" HorizontalAlignment="Left"
    Margin="10,0,0,0" Name="labelWindowTitle" VerticalAlignment="Top">
    <Label.Content>
        <Binding ElementName="imageRotator1" Path="ImageURI"></Binding>
    </Label.Content>
</Label>
<Button Height="20" Width="23" HorizontalAlignment="Right"
        Margin="0,1,1,0" Name="ButtonClose" VerticalAlignment="Top" >
    <Image Margin="0,0,0,0" Name="Image2" Stretch="Fill"
Source="/ProVB_WPF_Step3;component/Resources/1385_Disable_24x24_72.png"/>
</Button>
<Button Height="20" Width="20" HorizontalAlignment="Right"
        Margin="0,1,25,0" Name="ButtonMax" VerticalAlignment="Top" >
    <Image Margin="0,0,0,0" HorizontalAlignment="Center" Name="Image3"
        Stretch="Fill" Source=
        "/ProVB_WPF_Step3;component/Resources/112_Plus_Green_24x24_72.png"/>
</Button>
<Button Height="20" Width="20" HorizontalAlignment="Right"
        Margin="0,1,47,0" Name="ButtonMin" VerticalAlignment="Top" >
    <Image Margin="0,0,0,0" Name="Image4" Stretch="Fill" Source=
"/ProVB_WPF_Step3;component/Resources/112_DownArrowShort_Green_24x24_72.png"/>
</Button>
```

Code snippet from MainWindows.xaml

Note that a couple of minor changes to the preceding XAML aren't covered here — for example, the gradient information for the LinearGradientBrush. In addition, note something that has not been changed. The first step in the binding process was to have the labelWindowTitle control bind to the ImageURI property of the ImageRotator. With the changes you are about to make, it would make sense to have this property bind locally instead of to the control. This is not changed in the sample in order to reduce the complexity of the changes to the code, but it's something you can do on your own.

The focus is on the highlighted sections and the changes to support data binding. You can see that the changes to support data binding in the XAML are relatively minor. The second half of the MainWindow.xaml file starts with the `ImageRotator` control declaration. Note that this is now being bound to the `working_folder` node of the imported XML. By binding to this property, as you shift from one entry to another, the location for the available images will automatically update and a new image will be loaded for each entry.

Below that are the two new text boxes, which have each been bound to a node in the data. Note that similar to the `ImageRotator`, each is inheriting the binding source from a parent control in the hierarchy: the grid. As such, they are all focused on the currently selected entry in the list box — which, by the way, is the first entry. Changing what is selected, changes what is editable in the control.

No, this isn't one-way binding; this is full two-way, editable binding. Start the application and type in a new name, and you'll see the display in the list box updated once you leave the text box. The updates occur on the change in focus and it should be noted that this sample code does not include any persistence mechanism to save your edits before you close the window, but from the standpoint of binding you have full two-way binding.

The only remaining question involves the changes to the `ListBox` control, which are discussed following the XAML block:

```xml
<my:ImageRotator Grid.Row="1" HorizontalAlignment="Left"
        x:Name="imageRotator1" Margin="0,0,0,100"
        ImageURI="{Binding XPath=working_folder}"/>
<Thumb Grid.Row="1" Cursor="ScrollAll"
        Background="{StaticResource ResizeImage}" Height="20"
        Width="20" HorizontalAlignment="Right" Margin="0,0,0,0"
        Name="ThumbResize" VerticalAlignment="Bottom" />
<Label Content="Name:" Grid.Row="1" HorizontalAlignment="Left"
        Margin="12,0,0,48" Name="label1" Height="28"
        VerticalAlignment="Bottom" />
<TextBox Grid.Row="1" Margin="81,0,86,53" Name="textBox1" Height="23"
        VerticalAlignment="Bottom"
        Text="{Binding XPath=FirstName}" >
</TextBox>
<Label Content="Job Title:" Grid.Row="1" Height="28"
        HorizontalAlignment="Left" Margin="10,0,0,12" Name="label2"
        VerticalAlignment="Bottom" />
<TextBox Grid.Row="1" Height="23" Margin="81,0,86,17" Name="textBox2"
        VerticalAlignment="Bottom"
        Text="{Binding XPath=JobTitle}"/>
<ListBox Grid.Row="1" Height="100" Margin="0,99,0,0"
        Name="ListBox1" VerticalAlignment="Top"
        HorizontalAlignment="Right" Width="120"
        IsSynchronizedWithCurrentItem="True"
        ItemTemplate="{StaticResource PersonName}">
    <ListBox.ItemsSource>
        <Binding Source="{StaticResource People}"
        XPath="Person[*]"/>
    </ListBox.ItemsSource>
</ListBox>
<Label Content="Name List" Grid.Row="1" Height="28"
    HorizontalAlignment="Left" Margin="302,66,0,0" Name="Label3"
    VerticalAlignment="Top" />
        </Grid>
    </Window>
```

Code snippet from MainWindow.xaml

The final highlighted section of code is for the data that will be shown in the `ListBox`. The list box itself is relatively standard but it has two key bindings. The `ItemTemplate` is a property of the `ListBox` control that enables you to apply a data template to the items that will be displayed. As noted earlier, this XAML defines a data template that combines the `FirstName` and `LastName` data elements from the XML. For example, if your application needed to place `LastName` first or change the separator to a comma instead of a space, you would edit the data template. Having these changes encapsulated in a template enables you to make them in one place and then apply them anywhere they are needed.

Finally, there is the binding for the source of items in the ListBox. Notice that in this case the control isn't defining a data source, but instead is binding to a source that will be used for the items that it contains. You'll probably recognize the People resource as the XML data source defined as one of the grid resources. The ListBox has access to this resource as a child of the grid. The resource could also have been defined at the window or application level and still be accessible by any of the controls on the grid. Within the binding to this data source is the remaining XPath statement, which simply asks the grid to display all of the available Person items.

Without the data template this display would simply take each of those items and serialize the results into the display. However, by applying the data template, what you see as a result are the names of each entry. Note that you could add or reduce the amount of information provided by the data template to the ListBox item display by changing the data template.

With the MainWindow updates in place, only one change remains. Up until now you have consistently seen a default image in the ImageRotator based on the use of a default path. In fact, if you've mapped the first entry in your copy of the XML data file to a folder that varies from this, you might be thinking that the image data binding isn't working. That's because right now the ImageRotator.vb control's Load event loads a default path. This path interferes with the data binding from the XML file. Thus, in the final version of the sample code, you'll find that all of the lines within the Load event have been commented out as shown here:

Available for
download on
Wrox.com

```
Private Sub Grid1_Loaded(ByVal sender As System.Object,
        ByVal e As System.Windows.RoutedEventArgs) Handles Grid1.Loaded
    'm_curImagePath = Environment.GetFolderPath(
                            Environment.SpecialFolder.MyPictures)
    'RaiseEvent ImagePathChanged(Me, m_curImagePath)
    'SetValue(ImageProp, m_curImagePath)
    'LoadImages()
End Sub
```

Code snippet from MainWindow.xaml

That's it. At this point your design surface should show an image associated with the first entry in your People.xml data file. When you run the application, you'll see the screen shown in Figure 17-19. Not only can you switch between entries, more important, everything is editable. If you change the first name of an entry and move to the Job Title field, you'll see the name updated within the list box.

Note that the code didn't implement any persistence for changes made on the screen that would require additional code to take the XML and save it back to the system. However, you have an example that demonstrates how to create a data-bound set of controls that are dependent on each other such that an item selected from a list or grid becomes available to controls that are completely unaware of that list or grid.

You could continue to make several changes and enhancements to this sample code. However, this example focused on ensuring that you are exposed to the power, and accordingly some of the complexity, of data binding with WPF.

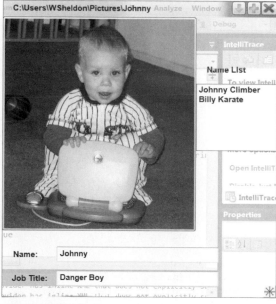

FIGURE 17-19

SUMMARY

A good exercise moving forward with the demonstration code from this chapter is to combine this code with one of the examples provided in Expression Blend. For example, the original version of Blend included a Photo Book application which provided a XAML layer you could use in the `Image` control to provide a better UI feel to that control. The Photo Book sample application includes an excellent user control, `Photobook.xaml`, that encapsulates the page-turning effect. The challenge isn't just to leverage a control but to enhance it, such as extending the full `Windows.Media.MediaPlayer` control so that you could display not only saved images, but also recordings.

This chapter focused on familiarizing you with WPF. WPF implements a new application development paradigm for user interfaces. You can start designing and planning the next versions of your applications to use these new controls. Keep in mind that this single chapter hasn't covered all the new features you can potentially leverage with WPF — that would require an entire book. Instead, you should now have an understanding of the base principals of the WPF programming model and how it integrates with Visual Basic.

WPF is the user interface paradigm of the future for .NET developers. However, while the graphic support is more powerful, certain elements of this model require you to handle more of what traditionally was thought of as standard window behavior. It is hoped that this chapter has clarified several key concepts that you need to know when working with WPF:

➤ WPF-based applications leverage traditional programming languages such as Visual Basic.

➤ Creating the custom window behaviors, while sometimes required, is not especially difficult.

➤ Visual Basic is uniquely positioned with literal XML strings to dynamically generate and display XAML elements as part of your application.

➤ Data binding in WPF is an extremely powerful concept that is used at multiple layers of the application interface to create many of the dynamic elements of the user interface.

➤ The updates in Visual Studio 2010 make it possible for a developer to create visually compelling business applications with WPF.

This chapter focused on the WPF libraries within the context of building new applications. At this point you are probably wondering about your existing applications. Unlike the early releases, unless you are tied to a production environment capped at .NET 2.0, you should be working with WPF and Silverlight. The next chapter is going to take you into Expression Blend and from there onto Silverlight. Expression Blend will still be the place to go to get beyond the current capabilities for UI design in Visual Studio. Then there is Silverlight, the new XAML based UI for cutting-edge Web hosted applications.

18

Expression Blend 3

WHAT YOU WILL LEARN IN THIS CHAPTER

- ➤ Getting to know Expression Blend
- ➤ How to create a new project
- ➤ Blend's Toolbox and Assets tab
- ➤ Objects and Timeline
- ➤ Visual State Manager
- ➤ How to use Resources
- ➤ Getting started with SketchFlow
- ➤ Documenting SketchFlow

While Visual Studio 2010 has introduced several new features for editing both WPF and Silverlight applications, Microsoft has another very essential tool called Microsoft Expression Blend. With Blend, Microsoft has introduced a more designer-friendly tool that enables designers to be involved in the development process by editing the same Solution and Project files that Visual Studio creates. While Blend is primarily targeted toward designers, this is not a tool that developers should shy away from, because it will enable you to do much more than you could do in just Visual Studio.

Through the use of both Visual Studio 2010 and Expression Blend 3, you can create rich user experiences that enable you to do more than just drop some text boxes on a form. Although everything you can do in Blend you can do in Visual Studio by just editing your XAML, Blend simply offers a much better format for editing complex concepts such as the following:

- ➤ Visual State Manager
- ➤ Styling
- ➤ Behaviors

With Blend 3, Microsoft also introduced a powerful feature called *SketchFlow*. With SketchFlow you can build quick and powerful mock-ups of an application's user interface with little or no code. SketchFlow provides an informal look and feel that enables your users to see an interactive design that is not as formal as a finalized application. We will show you some examples of this later in the chapter. Unlike previous chapters, this chapter has very little code and focuses primarily on the user interface.

GETTING TO KNOW BLEND

While Blend has many similarities with Visual Studio, it is not exactly the same application. The most notable difference is that Blend uses a dark UI schema. The dark UI schema helps when designing many applications because it seems to make the design pop against the darker background. As we go through the UI of Blend, you will notice several other things that differ from Visual Studio besides the dark UI schema. After working through this chapter, you should be comfortable enough with Blend that you know when to use it versus when to use Visual Studio.

Since Blend is not included with Visual Studio, you will need to download it from `www.microsoft.com/Expression/try-it/default.aspx#PageTop -DCP`.

Creating a New Project

When you start Blend for the first time you are welcomed with a screen that has three tabs. The Projects tab is shown in Figure 18-1; also included are a Help tab and a Samples tab, which you can use to jump to several examples that come with Expression Blend 3.

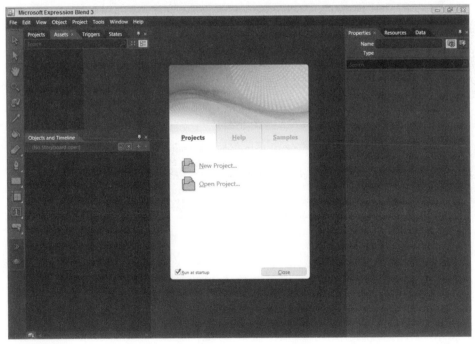

FIGURE 18-1

To create a new project, click New Project; the dialog shown in Figure 18-2 will appear.

This dialog gives you four project type options: two Silverlight project types and two WPF project types. This chapter primarily covers creating a Silverlight 3 application in Expression Blend, so select Silverlight 3 Application + Website. This has the exact same effect that it would if you were doing it in Visual Studio; it will create both a Silverlight 3 application and an ASP.NET application in which to host the Silverlight application.

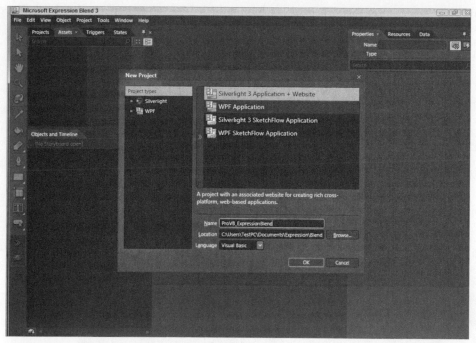

FIGURE 18-2

After the application is created you will see several things you are accustomed to in Visual Studio, and many new options. The following sections describe the various parts of the user interface.

Projects and Solutions Tab

One of the greatest things about the integration between Blend and Visual Studio is that both use the same project and solution files, thus enabling both a designer and a developer to work in the same project. If you aren't working with a designer, you can seamlessly switch between Visual Studio and Blend to edit the same project files. In Visual Studio you can simply right-click a file in your solution explorer and click Edit in Expression Blend. Or in Expression Blend you can right-click a file and select Edit in Visual Studio.

Just like Visual Studio, you have a Projects window; but by default it is in the top-left corner, rather than the top-right corner in Visual Studio. Figure 18-3 shows the default view of the Projects window with a new Silverlight application loaded.

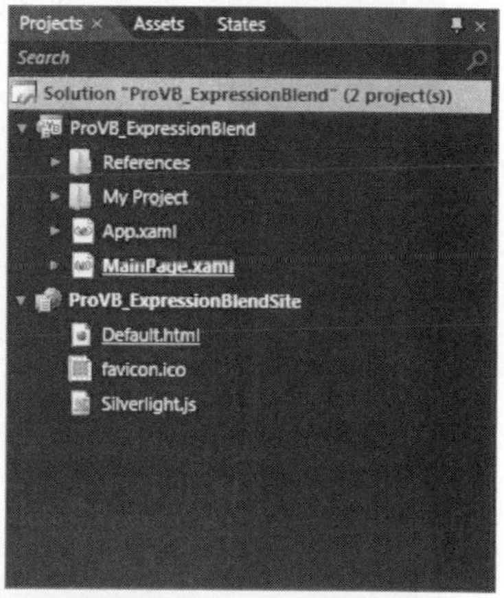

Blend's Toolbox and the Assets Tab

One of the first things you will want to do is add controls to your design surface. Blend actually has two windows for finding controls. One is the Toolbox, which is very similar to Visual Studio's Toolbox except that it shows only one column of controls; these are the most common controls. If you have ever used Adobe Photoshop it will remind you more of that application's Toolbox than the one in Visual Studio. The other way to access controls is via the Assets window, which

FIGURE 18-3

shows controls by category and enables you to search by control name. This search feature is tremendously useful when you have large projects with hundreds of user controls and you want to find one quickly. Figure 18-4 shows both the Toolbox and the Assets window.

Design Surface

Visual Studio and Expression Blend also share a similar design surface. The design surface is the area onto which you can drag your controls. For example, you can drag a `Button` control onto the design surface from the Toolbox or the Assets window. Just as in Visual Studio, you can drag any control to any location on the layout.

Before delving too deeply into the design surface, drag a few controls onto it. For this example, you'll build a simple login screen by dragging two `TextBlocks`, a `TextBox`, a `PasswordBox`, and a `Button` onto the design surface. Position your controls as shown in Figure 18-5.

FIGURE 18-4

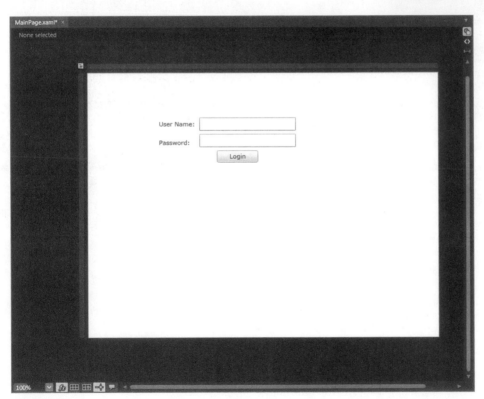

FIGURE 18-5

Three buttons in the top-right corner of the design surface are very similar to the design surface in Visual Studio, and enable you to select the view of the design surface. The top button is the Design button, and when this button is selected it will show the visual design of your control. The next button is the XAML view, and when this button is selected it will show the XAML view of the control. The last button is the Split view, which shows both the Design view and the XAML view. This is the default view in Visual Studio.

In the bottom-left corner of the design surface are a few buttons that enable you to adjust the view and how the design surface reacts. The first button, and one of the most useful, is the Zoom button. Unlike the zoom in Visual Studio, you can actually use your mouse wheel to zoom in on and out of a control. This is very helpful when you are laying out a lot of controls and fine-tuning their placement.

The next button on the bottom is the fx button, which will turn off any effects you have applied to any controls. You will sometimes find this necessary when you have a large number of controls that have different effects applied and you want to return to the raw design.

The next three buttons on the bottom all relate to the gridline placement options. The first button will make the gridlines visible or hidden — previously, in Visual Studio you had to use the Options menu to turn this feature on and off. The next button enables you to turn on gridline snapping. This is great if you want most items to be consistently spaced or similarly aligned.

The design surface also has a number of visual cues that indicate when controls are placed in alignment with each other or are spaced as desired. This is great for creating controls of the same height or horizontally aligning them. These suggestions are very subtle, and most you will not notice until you drag a control around; and most of them you will use without even realizing. Microsoft has outdone itself in making Blend the ideal layout tool for both WPF and Silverlight.

The last button on the bottom will hide and show annotations that are placed on your controls. Annotations are covered in more detail later in this chapter.

Objects and Timeline

One of the greatest things about Blend is the Objects and Timeline window. This window provides you with a visual insight into the hierarchy of your XAML, as well as giving you insight into the animation timeline. Figure 18-6 shows a basic hierarchy of the login control you created earlier.

While this login control is very simple, the information provided here offers some great insight into what is going on in the XAML. Here is the XAML for the same control:

FIGURE 18-6

Available for
download on
Wrox.com

```xml
<UserControl
 xmlns="http://schemas.microsoft.com/winfx/2006/xaml/presentation"
 xmlns:x="http://schemas.microsoft.com/winfx/2006/xaml"
 x:Class="ProVB_ExpressionBlend.MainPage"
 Width="640" Height="480">
 <Grid x:Name="LayoutRoot" Background="White">

  <TextBlock HorizontalAlignment="Left" VerticalAlignment="Top" Text="User Name:"
TextWrapping="Wrap" Margin="130,85,0,0"/>
  <TextBlock HorizontalAlignment="Left" Margin="130,119,0,0" VerticalAlignment="Top"
Text="Password:" TextWrapping="Wrap"/>
  <TextBox VerticalAlignment="Top" TextWrapping="Wrap" Margin="204,83,260,0"/>
  <PasswordBox VerticalAlignment="Top" Margin="204,111,260,0"/>
  <Button VerticalAlignment="Top" Content="Login" Margin="236,141,0,0"
HorizontalAlignment="Left" Width="75"/>
 </Grid>
</UserControl>
```

Code snippet from MainPage.xaml

Although it is important to dig into the XAML and truly understand it, sometimes you just need a visual representation of a control's hierarchy. This is what the Objects and Timeline window provides.

Sometimes when designing a complex control you need to hide or show controls just at design time, perhaps because you have several controls or graphics overlapping and need to get to one of the controls in the background. The Objects and Timeline window enables you to hide controls by clicking the eye icon to the right of the controls. When you change a control to be hidden at design time, Blend will add the following as a parameter to the actual XAML of the control:

```
d:IsHidden="True"
```

While this does change your XAML, it does not change the runtime experience of the control. Therefore, if you have the control hidden at design time but have the `Visibility` set to visible, the control will still show when you run the application. This can be confusing because this setting is not a runtime setting.

Next to the eye icon you will see a little circle with which you can lock the position of the control. This is great when you have a number of controls you may want to move at once while keeping one in place, or you want to avoid accidently moving the control.

The other main feature of the Objects and Timeline window is, you guessed it, the timeline. This is where you can add storyboard animations to your control by adding key frames for placement. You can see an example blank storyboard in Figure 18-7.

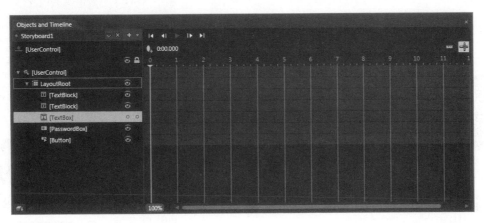

FIGURE 18-7

While the timeline feature opens a whole other world for the designer, it is a world that many developers will shy away from. It is also a complex topic requiring a complete book of its own, so we will not dive any deeper into this feature.

States

The next window in the top left is the States window. This window provides two major functions: the capability to edit the state of an existing control and the capability to add custom states to your own controls. Later in this chapter we will go into much more detail about editing states and customizing states. For example, Figure 18-8 shows some of the basic visual states when editing a button.

While all the controls that ship with Silverlight have basic states, such as `MouseOver` and `Disabled`, some have more complex states, such as `Invalid` and `Valid`, which interact with the validation features of Silverlight. Later in this chapter you will learn how to both customize existing controls and create your own controls.

FIGURE 18-8

In the States window you can also customize the transition between states. By adjusting both time and the easing function between states, you can provide rich flowing animations without the need for storyboards. In addition, this window will save you a lot of time learning the XAML to do these animations.

Properties

As with many of the other windows, you will find the Properties window to be almost identical to the functionality provided by the Properties window in Visual Studio. While this window is very similar, it also gives you greater insight into what is actually going on in your XAML than Visual Studio does. Figure 18-9 shows the properties for a button.

Just as in Visual Studio, a search box at the top of the dialog enables you to quickly find a property by typing its name. Then you have the properties grouped by category below the search. Note that Blend gives you much finer control of the appearance-related properties than Visual Studio provides.

The other thing you may notice is a small square box to the right of every property. This small box looks insignificant at first, but it offers a lot of insight into your XAML. It also enables you to do some significant tasks without having to dive too deeply into editing your XAML. By clicking this box you can specify whether this property is data bound or associated with a resource or just a plain old local value.

This box will also change colors based on what has been applied to the property. If the box is white, that simply means that the property has a local value applied to it. If is green, then a resource has been applied to it. Finally, if it is yellow, then the property has been data bound. If you click on the box when it is a color, you have the option to reset the value, which will completely remove the setting in your XAML. This is useful for keeping your XAML really clean. In Blend, you will find that it's very easy to reset properties of controls without even knowing it when trying to get them placed exactly where you want. Once you have finished working with a control or a set of controls, it isn't a bad idea to look them over to see if these boxes have changed colors because you can quickly see what has changed and to what.

FIGURE 18-9

Resources

The Resources window is one of the simplest windows and it can provide you with insight about many things, such as the static resources in your application or your control. Resources are most commonly used like Cascading Style Sheets in an ASP.NET application for setting common design properties. From the Resources window you can edit these values easily without having to switch to your `app.xaml` file to find a property.

Using the Resources window, you can also manage and create new resource dictionaries. This is ideal for large projects for which you may want to organize your resources into individual resource dictionaries so that you can share them, or to simplify finding them later.

Data

The Data window is a great tool for creating things like sample data for SketchFlow mock-ups or to organize XML and object data sets. If you click the first button on the right of the Data screen it will ask you if you want to create a sample data set. Figure 18-10 shows what you will see when you create a sample data set.

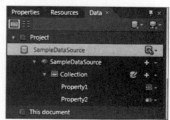

FIGURE 18-10

SKETCHFLOW

One of the most important innovations introduced by Microsoft with Blend 3 is SketchFlow. With SketchFlow you can create detailed prototypes of an application, website, or nearly anything that needs to be visualized on a computer screen. This capability to rapidly prototype user interfaces enables you to communicate with your customers or users before investing a large amount of time implementing a design.

The name SketchFlow comes from the informal look of the prototype, which resembles a manually drawn sketch. This hand-drawn look helps convey to your customer the idea that it is a prototype and not a finished product. This informal approach helps cut the cost of developing working designs in other applications.

While communicating to a customer is just a small piece of the puzzle when initially designing an application, there is a greater need for the customer to relay changes back to the developers and the designer. Using the *SketchFlow Player*, the end user can add comments and make drawings right on top of the working prototype, exporting this feedback and e-mailing it to the developer or the designer, who can then import it directly into Blend. This feedback is then overlaid directly onto the design surface of the controls they made comments on.

One of the other great things about a SketchFlow application is that you can create rich documentation of your controls by simply exporting it to Word. This enables you to use the content of your SketchFlow application and layout in a professional manner, such as for a presentation, a proposal, or a sales contract.

With rich interactivity, SketchFlow takes you beyond just writing a few wireframes on a napkin. It provides a robust application that demonstrates everything from sample data to animations — and all this is done through a Silverlight or WPF application.

Your First SketchFlow

In this section, you'll start using Blend by creating a new Silverlight 3 SketchFlow application. You will quickly find that this is simply a Silverlight application with a few extras, including SketchFlow Map and SketchFlow Animations. As shown in Figure 18-11, the application also includes `Sketch.Flow` and `SketchStyles.xaml` files.

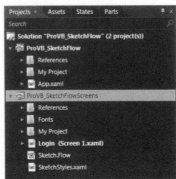

FIGURE 18-11

SketchFlow Map

The best place to start when beginning a SketchFlow application is the SketchFlow Map window, shown in Figure 18-12. This window enables you to create various screens and components that you may use in your application. As you create these screens, Blend will actually create physical user controls in your SketchFlow application. In this example we have mapped out a simple sales dashboard.

This SketchFlow is very similar to a site map or an application flow diagram. From the map, you can click a control to be taken directly to that control in your project.

Using SketchFlow Map, you can also add component screens, which can be used for things like navigation or other common controls such as a header. If you have a component screen, you can simply drag the component screen to connect to another screen and Blend will place

FIGURE 18-12

that control in the top-left corner of the window. This is really powerful when quickly mocking up a large number of controls and their relationships.

Adding Sketch Controls

Now that you have controls created, you will want to place something on them. Instead of dragging controls from the Toolbox onto the design surface, go to the Assets window. In the Assets window you will see a category Styles, which has a SketchStyles subcategory under it. This subcategory contains all the hand-drawn styled controls as shown in Figure 18-13.

Put the following controls on the login screen by dragging them to the design surface: two `TextBlock-Sketchs`, one `Button-Sketch`, one `TextBox-Sketch`, and a `PasswordBox-Sketch`. When you are done, instead of having the traditional-looking text boxes and controls, you have controls that look hand drawn, as shown in Figure 18-14.

FIGURE 18-13

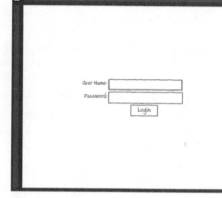

FIGURE 18-14

This simple method of creating an informal look for a prototype helps to keep your customers from getting too concerned about the application's actual look and feel, and instead focus on its functionality. Providing customers with an informal prototype enables you to deliver a final product that offers both a rich experience and correct functionality, rather than initially focusing on, for example, the color of a button.

SketchFlow provides you with 33 controls that have the SketchFlow style applied to them. Many of them you will recognize as standard controls, including items such as `ListBox`, `TabControl`, and others; but you will also notice a few controls that are not in the standard control set. One such control is the `Note-Sketch`, which provides a Post-it-style note that you can place on a control. This control is useful for describing some functionality in an unfinished screen in your prototype, or for relaying notes to your customer for a specific screen. Many of the other controls are just specialized styles of controls, such as the `TitleCenter-Sketch`, which is just a styled version of the `TextBlock` that is centered and a little larger than the standard `TextBlock`.

Adding Simple Behaviors to Navigate

One of the main goals in SketchFlow is to create a prototype with no code, and one of the ways you do this is through behaviors. Behaviors offer you a number of out-of-the-box actions you can apply to any object. The behaviors that are included with SketchFlow are shown in Table 18-1.

TABLE 18-1: SketchFlow Behaviors

BEHAVIOR	DESCRIPTION
ActivateStateAction	Activates a specific state for the active screen or a specific control on the current screen
ChangePropertyAction	Changes a property of a specific control and can optionally animate the change with an easing function
ControlStoryboardAction	Performs basic actions such as play, stop, and pause on a storyboard
FluidMoveBehavior	Animates the change of an object's properties inside a panel
GoToStateAction	Applies a specific state to the current control
HyperlinkAction	A simple navigation behavior for changing the URI of the browser
MouseDragElementBehavior	Allows an object to be moved by the mouse
NavigateForwardAction	Acts much like the forward button on the browser to move forward in your SketchFlow
NavigateToScreenAction	Navigates to a specific screen
NavigateBackAction	Acts like the Back button would in the browser but within your SketchFlow screens
PlaySketchFlowAnimationAction	Plays a SketchFlow Animation
PlaySoundAction	Plays a specified sound
RemoveElementAction	Removes an element from your control

Clearly, you can choose from a wide variety of behaviors to create a very interactive prototype; and if these don't completely suit your needs, you can also develop your own simply by clicking File ➪ New Item ➪ Behavior. A large number of behaviors are also available on CodePlex at http://expressionblend.codeplex.com.

The easiest way to add navigation is simply by right-clicking the Login button you created and selecting Navigate To ➪ Sales Dashboard. This will create a NavigateToScreenAction behavior for your button, as shown in Figure 18-15.

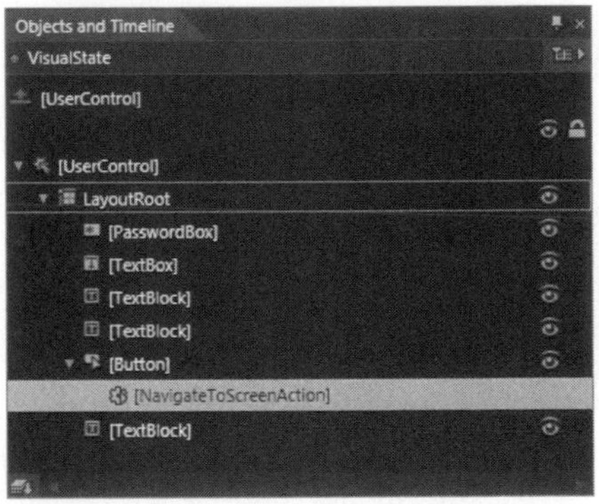

SketchFlow Player

So far, you have only seen half of the SketchFlow prototyping tool; the second half is the actual SketchFlow Player. This player

FIGURE 18-15

does much more than just play back your SketchFlow: It also allows user feedback that can be directly layered over the design surface in Expression Blend. This powerful form of communication enables your users to interact with the design process in a way they have never been able to with previous Microsoft products.

To view the SketchFlow Player, simply press F5 just as you would in Visual Studio to run an application. Once it is running, it will bring up your web browser. SketchFlow Player is shown in Figure 18-16.

The SketchFlow Player UI is very minimal so that your users can understand it without much training, and they can focus on your prototype. With a SketchFlow prototype, users can interact with it just as if it were a real application. Things like buttons work based on the behaviors you applied in Blend, and other controls such as list boxes and text boxes give the appearance of actually working. As mentioned earlier, the prototype's informal look and feel helps users to focus on the functionality and the user experience.

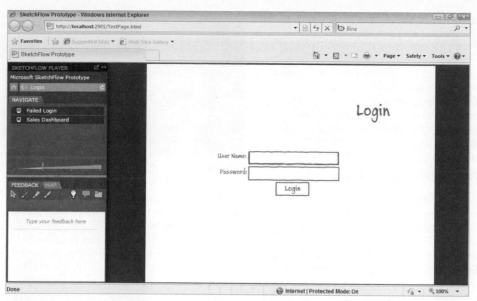

FIGURE 18-16

User Feedback

Recall that the SketchFlow Player enables users to give you rich feedback by two methods. The first method is simply by typing in a message in the left panel under the Feedback tab. The other method is by actually drawing on the design surface, as shown in Figure 18-17.

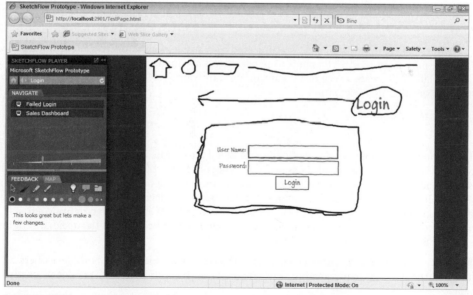

FIGURE 18-17

After users have entered this type of feedback, they can simply click the folder icon under the Feedback tab and select Export Feedback. This will create a feedback file that users can e-mail to you for your use in Blend. Once you have the feedback file, you can pull it into Blend by going to the Feedback window.

You can show the Feedback window by clicking Window ➪ Feedback. Once the window appears, click the plus icon to import your feedback file. This will overlay the user's feedback directly over the design of the control, as well as put their comments in the Feedback window. When working on a large SketchFlow for which a user may have commented on several screens, you will see a lightbulb icon just above any screen that contains feedback in the SketchFlow Map, as shown in Figure 18-18.

FIGURE 18-18

Documenting Your SketchFlow

At this point, you have seen the interactive portion of the SketchFlow Player, but there is also a very rich documentation feature that enables you to put annotations directly into your control. While annotations have always been a great way to make comments in your application, they have typically been used for communicating with other developers or your designer. With SketchFlow you can use this for actual documentation through the Word Export feature. Combining both of these features provides an ideal solution for tasks such as proposal requirements or specification documentation.

Annotations

Creating annotations is fairly simple. From any screen you can simply select Tools ➪ Create Annotation. This will give you a nice little yellow box into which you can type your annotation. Once you have created a few annotations you can run your SketchFlow prototype again. You will notice that the annotation does not show by default. To show the annotations, simply click the icon to the left of the Export Feedback button. This is a great place to communicate the functionality of a screen that doesn't interact with the screen. For example, if you wanted to describe the screen's function for later documentation, place that in an annotation.

Exporting to Word

Once you have created a SketchFlow prototype, documented it by using annotations, and received feedback from your users, you may want to actually put it to paper. Blend has made this very easy to do: Select File ➪ Export To Word. This will create a very rich documentation of your SketchFlow prototype that you could include in a proposal or other documentation.

SUMMARY

This chapter has demonstrated how to leverage Expression Blend 3 to create richer user experiences. Along the way, you have also seen the similarities and differences between Blend and Visual Studio. While Microsoft has designed Blend to be optimized for the designer, this is not a tool that developers should shy away from. Many users have become accustomed to more advanced and richer user experiences than what was really capable in previous versions of .NET. With the advent of both WPF and Silverlight, Microsoft has opened the door to creating applications that engage the user as never before, and the optimal tool for designing the interfaces of these applications is Blend.

Blend is also a great tool for quickly creating prototypes with zero code. This enables both developers and designers to focus on the business requirements, rather than interactive technologies to produce a costly, showy prototype.

19

Silverlight

WHAT YOU WILL LEARN IN THIS CHAPTER

- ➤ General Silverlight Overview
- ➤ Silverlight Media Features
- ➤ Starting a Silverlight Project
- ➤ Silverlight Navigation Application
- ➤ Silverlight Class Library
- ➤ What makes up a Silverlight Solution
- ➤ How to use layout controls
- ➤ Using Silverlight out of the browser

Rich internet application (RIA) is growing at a fast pace with new technologies coming out every day. Many of these technologies begin to widen the gap between the traditional application developer and Web developers. At the same time, Web development continues to be a conglomerate of many different technologies, including things like CSS, JavaScript, PHP, Flash, Action Scripting, and a dozen other languages and technologies. Silverlight was introduced by Microsoft so that .NET developers could leverage their existing skill set. By leveraging the skills you have already learned in this book, you can create complex applications without all the various Web technologies.

This chapter takes a comprehensive look at Silverlight and its similarities to WPF. Many of the things you learned in Chapter 17 about layout and design will also apply to this chapter.

WHAT IS SILVERLIGHT?

Microsoft introduced Silverlight in September 2007 as a rich media plug-in alternative to other platforms like Flash, but Silverlight has quickly matured to a powerful rich internet application platform. Silverlight 3, introduced in July 2009, enables .NET developers to create powerful line-of-business (LOB) applications that can be distributed on the Web. This cross-browser and cross-platform plug-in enables you to develop Web applications that are completely built in .NET for both the server-side and client-side code.

This unified experience across multiple platforms enables you, as a developer, to focus on the needs of your user, rather than why your JavaScript won't run in Firefox but will run in Internet Explorer. For most Web developers, the frustration of many loosely coupled technologies can create more support than it is worth; for most developers this frustration leads to creating simpler applications. While many things in ASP.NET have helped simplify this concern, it still lacks the rich design capabilities that Silverlight can offer.

Microsoft has also created a rich media experience in Silverlight that includes things like true HD video as well as digital rights management (DRM) for protecting media. This chapter primarily focuses on the development environment of Silverlight, but it is important to be familiar with some of the rich media features.

Smooth Streaming

One of the most common problems when delivering HD video across the Web is the varying access speeds of users. We have all seen the results of this when watching various online videos; while you are watching, suddenly the video decides to buffer. This is why Microsoft has added the Smooth Streaming feature to Silverlight; it enables a much smoother user experience. With Smooth Streaming, instead of buffering, the video quality is briefly lowered until the buffer can catch up. As a result, most users won't notice the lower video quality because it is both minimal and short.

Industry Standard Video

With the introduction of true high-definition video into Silverlight, Microsoft has also introduced many industry standard formats, as well as the capability to create your own. The provided formats include the very popular H.264, which is what popular sites like YouTube have begun to use.

Because Silverlight enables you to use your own custom codecs, you can create streaming media with proprietary media files. This is actually what NetFlix uses to deliver their streaming movies.

Digital Rights Management

When creating an application in which you deliver copyrighted video and audio, it is always necessary to protect that data. This is where digital rights management (DRM) comes into play — by providing a way to secure that content from anyone trying to convert it to a format that they can then copy. Silverlight provides this protection through several different methods, including PlayReady, Windows Media DRM 10, or third-party DRM extensibility.

STARTING A SILVERLIGHT PROJECT

Now that you have seen some of the benefits of Silverlight and what it has to offer on the media side, let's dive into some Silverlight development. Silverlight is much more than a Flash alternative; it is one of the best platforms for delivering line-of-business (LOB) applications.

When creating a Silverlight application, you are presented with three options: Silverlight Application, Silverlight Navigation Application, and Silverlight Class Library, as shown in Figure 19-1.

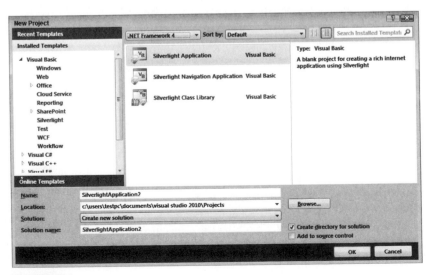

FIGURE 19-1

Silverlight Application

The Silverlight Application project is a baseline application that serves as a very common starting point for most developers. When you create a Silverlight Application solution, it will create both an ASP.NET application that will host the Silverlight application and the actual Silverlight application, as shown in Figure 19-2.

The Silverlight application contains an `App.xaml` file, which is covered in greater detail later in the chapter, and the `MainPage.xaml` file, which is the first control that loads. This would be similar to your main form in a Windows application and what is shown in your edit window after creating the project. Much like Windows development, you can simply copy controls from the Toolbox to the design surface.

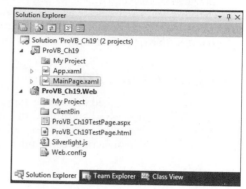

FIGURE 19-2

Unlike the Silverlight Navigation application, the Silverlight application does not support deep linking right out-of-the-box. It is therefore ideal when you don't need your users to bookmark sections of your app like they would in a Web application.

Silverlight Navigation Application

When working with Web applications, we have all become accustomed to doing things like bookmarking or forwarding links to friends. Silverlight 3 features a built-in navigation framework that enables users to create deep linking, such as `www.mywebsite.com/default.aspx#/Home`. When you create a navigation framework application, you will see the page highlighted in Figure 19-3 in your solution folder.

The `MainPage.xaml` in this project is actually a container control for Silverlight pages. A Silverlight page is simply a variation of the `UserControl` but runs in the navigation frame. You can also see that the project contains a Views folder that contains a `Home.xaml` and an `About.xaml`. These are similar to your pages in an ASP.NET application.

The navigation framework relies on a control called a `Frame`. This frame is similar to the frameset in HTML, but unlike framesets you can define various ways of mapping content to them through the `UriMapper`. The navigation frame that is created with the Navigation Application's XAML looks like this:

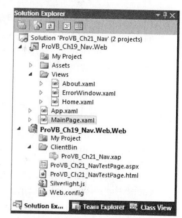

FIGURE 19-3

Available for download on Wrox.com

```
<navigation:Frame x:Name="ContentFrame" Style="{StaticResource ContentFrameStyle}"
                   Source="/Home"
Navigated="ContentFrame_Navigated" NavigationFailed="ContentFrame_NavigationFailed">
    <navigation:Frame.UriMapper>
      <uriMapper:UriMapper>
        <uriMapper:UriMapping Uri="" MappedUri="/Views/Home.xaml"/>
        <uriMapper:UriMapping Uri="/{pageName}"
          MappedUri="/Views/{pageName}.xaml"/>
      </uriMapper:UriMapper>
    </navigation:Frame.UriMapper>
  </navigation:Frame>
```

Code snippet from MainPage.xaml

As you can see, there are two defined mappings: one for when no URI is mapped and one for when someone specifies a page like `default.aspx#/About`, in which case it will load the `About.xaml` page in the Views folder. Later in this chapter, you will learn more about how to add pages and see what their code actually looks like.

Silverlight Class Library

The Silverlight Class Library template provides a way to consolidate various items into their own assembly. This is exactly the same as adding a Class Library to a Windows Forms Application project, but Visual Studio knows to target a Silverlight application. This is important because Silverlight runs a subset of the .NET Framework.

SILVERLIGHT SOLUTION

While we have described the various types of solutions you can create in Silverlight, there are many common items between the Silverlight Application solution and the Silverlight Navigation Application solution. This section covers their commonality, including the common files in a Silverlight application. Both solution types have similar structures containing a Web Application and a Silverlight Application.

Web Application

The Web application that is created is simply an ASP.NET application with a page to host your Silverlight controls. It also contains a `Silverlight.js` file that contains the JavaScript that helps assist users if they do not have Silverlight installed. It also creates a *<project name>*TestPage.aspx file and a *<project name>*TestPage.html file, both of which serve the same purpose of displaying the Silverlight application but give you two different ways of doing it. The only difference is that one is an ASP.NET page and the other is an HTML page.

The ClientBin Folder and .xap File

Also in your Web project is a ClientBin folder. When you compile your Silverlight application, this is where it is actually placed. When a Silverlight application is compiled, it creates a `.xap` file — a compressed file that contains your Silverlight application. You can change the `.xap` extension to `.zip` to view its contents in Windows Explorer.

Application Library Caching

Now that you have seen where Visual Studio stores the compiled version of your Silverlight application, let's look at one way to optimize what it stores in that folder. As you build larger applications that contain references to third-Party controls and other assemblies, you may find that your `.xap` file's size has grown very large. If you know that several assemblies or libraries it contains will not change, you might like to just cache the individual assemblies but update others. You can do this with *application library caching*.

To enable application library caching, simply right-click on the Silverlight project and select Properties. This will bring up the Silverlight build options shown in Figure 19-4.

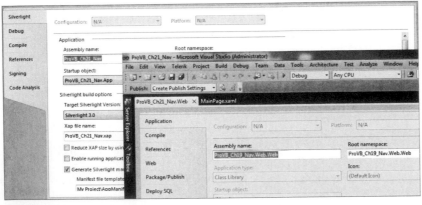

FIGURE 19-4

Simply check the "Reduce XAP size by using application library caching" field. Now when you compile the Navigation example, it will create three files in your ClientBin folder: the .xap for your application, and two zip files that contain the additional assemblies so they can be cached on the client side.

> *If you are developing an application that will use the "Enable running application out of the browser" option, you will not be able to use application library caching.*

Silverlight Application

The Silverlight project contains all your client-side logic that makes up the Silverlight application. This section describes several files you should be familiar with and why they are there.

App.xaml

Much like a Windows Forms application, you have a starting point for the application, which is contained in the App.xaml file. This file also contains the logic for unhandled exceptions. Here is the App.xaml code:

```vb
Partial Public Class App
    Inherits Application

    Public Sub New()
        InitializeComponent()
    End Sub

    Private Sub Application_Startup(ByVal o As Object, ByVal e As StartupEventArgs)
        Handles Me.Startup
        Me.RootVisual = New MainPage()
    End Sub

    Private Sub Application_UnhandledException(ByVal sender As Object,
        ByVal e As ApplicationUnhandledExceptionEventArgs)
            Handles Me.UnhandledException

    ' If the app is running outside of the debugger then report the exception using
    ' the browser's exception mechanism. On IE this will display it a yellow alert
    ' icon in the status bar and Firefox will display a script error.
        If Not System.Diagnostics.Debugger.IsAttached Then

    ' NOTE: This will allow the application to continue running after an exception has been thrown
            ' but not handled.
    ' For production applications this error handling should be replaced with something that will
            ' report the error to the website and stop the application.
            e.Handled = True
            Dim errorWindow As ChildWindow = New ErrorWindow(e.ExceptionObject)
            errorWindow.Show()
        End If
    End Sub

End Class
```

Code snippet from App.xaml.vb

As you can see, the Application_Startup event is first called when your Silverlight Application is loaded. The StartupEventArgs property can have parameters passed from the ASP.NET or HTML page if needed. Then, it uses the me.RootVisual property to tell the Silverlight runtime what control to show.

Using the Application_UnhandledException function, you can add global error handling for your application. This is the optimal place for putting logging logic for unhandled exceptions.

MainPage.xaml

Now that you have an understanding of how the application starts, this section looks at what it will use to display. By default, it will be a `UserControl` that is set to the `RootVisual` in the `app.xaml`. A user control consists of two files: a `.xaml` file containing the layout information and a `.vb` file containing the class associated with the UI. Here is the sample `MainPage.xaml` from the Navigation application:

```xml
<UserControl
    x:Class="SilverlightApplication1.MainPage"
    xmlns="http://schemas.microsoft.com/winfx/2006/xaml/presentation"
    xmlns:x="http://schemas.microsoft.com/winfx/2006/xaml"
    xmlns:navigation="clr-namespace:System.Windows.Controls;assembly=System.Windows
.Controls.Navigation"
    xmlns:uriMapper="clr-namespace:System.Windows.Navigation;assembly=System.Windows
.Controls.Navigation"
    xmlns:d="http://schemas.microsoft.com/expression/blend/2008" xmlns:
mc="http://schemas.openxmlformats.org/markup-compatibility/2006"
    mc:Ignorable="d" d:DesignWidth="640" d:DesignHeight="480">

  <Grid x:Name="LayoutRoot" Style="{StaticResource LayoutRootGridStyle}">

    <Border x:Name="ContentBorder" Style="{StaticResource ContentBorderStyle}">

      <navigation:Frame x:Name="ContentFrame"
        Style="{StaticResource ContentFrameStyle}"
                        Source="/Home"
Navigated="ContentFrame_Navigated" NavigationFailed="ContentFrame_NavigationFailed">
          <navigation:Frame.UriMapper>
            <uriMapper:UriMapper>
              <uriMapper:UriMapping Uri="" MappedUri="/Views/Home.xaml"/>
              <uriMapper:UriMapping Uri="/{pageName}"
                MappedUri="/Views/{pageName}.xaml"/>
            </uriMapper:UriMapper>
          </navigation:Frame.UriMapper>
      </navigation:Frame>
    </Border>

    <Grid x:Name="NavigationGrid" Style="{StaticResource NavigationGridStyle}">

      <Border x:Name="BrandingBorder" Style="{StaticResource BrandingBorderStyle}">
        <StackPanel x:Name="BrandingStackPanel"
            Style="{StaticResource BrandingStackPanelStyle}">

          <ContentControl Style="{StaticResource LogoIcon}"/>
          <TextBlock x:Name="ApplicationNameTextBlock"
              Style="{StaticResource ApplicationNameStyle}"
                        Text="Application Name"/>

        </StackPanel>
      </Border>

      <Border x:Name="LinksBorder" Style="{StaticResource LinksBorderStyle}">
        <StackPanel x:Name="LinksStackPanel"
            Style="{StaticResource LinksStackPanelStyle}">

          <HyperlinkButton x:Name="Link1" Style="{StaticResource LinkStyle}"
                              NavigateUri="/Home"
              TargetName="ContentFrame" Content="home"/>

          <Rectangle x:Name="Divider1" Style="{StaticResource DividerStyle}"/>

          <HyperlinkButton x:Name="Link2" Style="{StaticResource LinkStyle}"
                              NavigateUri="/About"
```

```
                        TargetName="ContentFrame" Content="about"/>

                </StackPanel>
            </Border>

        </Grid>

    </Grid>

</UserControl>
```

The code-behind file is as follows:

```vb
Imports System.Windows.Navigation

Partial Public Class MainPage
    Inherits UserControl

    Public Sub New()
        InitializeComponent()
    End Sub

    Private Sub ContentFrame_Navigated(ByVal sender As Object,
            ByVal e As NavigationEventArgs) Handles ContentFrame.Navigated
        For Each child As UIElement In LinksStackPanel.Children
            Dim hb As HyperlinkButton = TryCast(child, HyperlinkButton)
            If hb IsNot Nothing AndAlso hb.NavigateUri IsNot Nothing Then
                If hb.NavigateUri = e.Uri Then
                    VisualStateManager.GoToState(hb, "ActiveLink", True)
                Else
                    VisualStateManager.GoToState(hb, "InactiveLink", True)
                End If
            End If
        Next
    End Sub

    Private Sub ContentFrame_NavigationFailed(ByVal sender As Object,
        ByVal e As NavigationFailedEventArgs) Handles ContentFrame.NavigationFailed
        e.Handled = True
        Dim errorWindow As ChildWindow = New ErrorWindow(e.Uri)
        errorWindow.Show()
    End Sub
End Class
```

You probably noticed that this is very similar to what you learned about WPF. The general idea is the same. You can add controls to the XAML and then modify the code for the control. This separation of UI and code helps create a simple architecture for managing the application design. This separation is very useful when using both Visual Studio and Microsoft Expression Blend.

CONTROLS

Just as in Windows forms development, Silverlight offers a large collection of controls that give you a lot of options for developing rich interfaces. In addition, you will find Silverlight development to be almost identical to WPF development, as both user interfaces use XAML as the layout method.

Layout Management

When developing Silverlight applications, you are given a few different options for placing controls on the primary design surface: Grid, StackPanel, Canvas, ScrollViewer and Border. Each one of these layouts has its own set of features that reflect when to use it; and you are not limited to just one type of layout control because you can actually nest them inside of each other to create a variety of layout options.

Grid

By default, when creating any Silverlight control, you will have a Grid as your root layout control. The Grid control gives you the most flexibility, supporting options like rows and columns. If you are familiar with HTML tables, you will feel pretty comfortable with this option. The Grid control enables you to define rows and columns using the Grid.RowDefinitions and Grid.ColumnDefinitions properties. In the row definitions, you can set two primary options, Height and MinHeight, but most of the time you will just set the Height. Similarly, you have the option to set the Width and MinWidth properties in the ColumnDefinitions. The following example sets a grid with four rows that are 50 pixels high, along with four columns that are 100 pixels wide:

```xaml
<UserControl x:Class="SilverlightApplication1.SilverlightControl1"
    xmlns="http://schemas.microsoft.com/winfx/2006/xaml/presentation"
    xmlns:x="http://schemas.microsoft.com/winfx/2006/xaml"
    xmlns:d="http://schemas.microsoft.com/expression/blend/2008"
    xmlns:mc="http://schemas.openxmlformats.org/markup-compatibility/2006"
    mc:Ignorable="d"
    d:DesignHeight="300" d:DesignWidth="400">

    <Grid x:Name="LayoutRoot" Background="White">
        <Grid.RowDefinitions>
            <RowDefinition Height="50" />
            <RowDefinition Height="50" />
            <RowDefinition Height="50" />
            <RowDefinition Height="50" />
        </Grid.RowDefinitions>
        <Grid.ColumnDefinitions>
            <ColumnDefinition Width="100" />
            <ColumnDefinition Width="100" />
            <ColumnDefinition Width="100" />
            <ColumnDefinition Width="100" />
        </Grid.ColumnDefinitions>
    </Grid>
</UserControl>
```

Code snippet from SilverlightControl1.xaml

Figure 19-5 shows what you would see on your design surface.

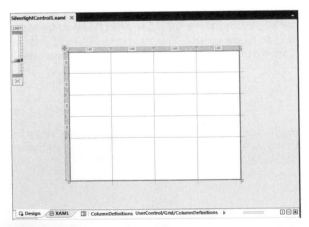

FIGURE 19-5

Here is where the Silverlight grid begins to differ from the HTML grid, as you do not have to place controls inside of something, such as the `<td>` in the XAML; you merely have to set the properties of `Grid.Column` and `Grid.Row` on your controls. So, for example, if you wanted to place a button on the second row and third column, you would set it like this:

```xml
<UserControl x:Class="SilverlightApplication1.SilverlightControl1"
    xmlns="http://schemas.microsoft.com/winfx/2006/xaml/presentation"
    xmlns:x="http://schemas.microsoft.com/winfx/2006/xaml"
    xmlns:d="http://schemas.microsoft.com/expression/blend/2008"
    xmlns:mc="http://schemas.openxmlformats.org/markup-compatibility/2006"
    mc:Ignorable="d"
    d:DesignHeight="300" d:DesignWidth="400">

    <Grid x:Name="LayoutRoot" Background="White">
        <Grid.RowDefinitions>
            <RowDefinition Height="50" />
            <RowDefinition Height="50" />
            <RowDefinition Height="50" />
            <RowDefinition Height="50" />
        </Grid.RowDefinitions>
        <Grid.ColumnDefinitions>
            <ColumnDefinition Width="100" />
            <ColumnDefinition Width="100" />
            <ColumnDefinition Width="100" />
            <ColumnDefinition Width="100" />
        </Grid.ColumnDefinitions>
        <Button Content="Button" Grid.Column="2" Grid.Row="1" />
    </Grid>
</UserControl>
```

Code snippet from SilverlightControl1.xaml

Here, the `Grid.Column` and `Grid.Row` are a zero-based index. In addition to just setting the position of your button this way, the layout manager will have your button fill the designated cell of the grid. Your button should look like the one shown in Figure 19-6.

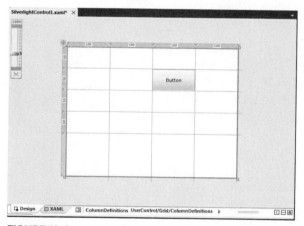

FIGURE 19-6

Two other control placement options are the `Grid.ColumnSpan` and `Grid.RowSpan` properties. These can be used to have controls span multiple columns or rows, respectively. For example, you could set the button in the preceding example to be defined like this:

```xml
<UserControl x:Class="SilverlightApplication1.SilverlightControl1"
    xmlns="http://schemas.microsoft.com/winfx/2006/xaml/presentation"
    xmlns:x="http://schemas.microsoft.com/winfx/2006/xaml"
```

```
    xmlns:d="http://schemas.microsoft.com/expression/blend/2008"
    xmlns:mc="http://schemas.openxmlformats.org/markup-compatibility/2006"
    mc:Ignorable="d"
    d:DesignHeight="300" d:DesignWidth="400">

    <Grid x:Name="LayoutRoot" Background="White">
        <Grid.RowDefinitions>
            <RowDefinition Height="50" />
            <RowDefinition Height="50" />
            <RowDefinition Height="50" />
            <RowDefinition Height="50" />
        </Grid.RowDefinitions>
        <Grid.ColumnDefinitions>
            <ColumnDefinition Width="100" />
            <ColumnDefinition Width="100" />
            <ColumnDefinition Width="100" />
            <ColumnDefinition Width="100" />
        </Grid.ColumnDefinitions>
    <Button Content="Button" Grid.Column="2" Grid.Row="1"
            Grid.ColumnSpan="2" Grid.RowSpan="2" />
    </Grid>
</UserControl>
```

Code snippet from SilverlightControl1.xaml

The `Grid` control also offers proportional sizing, so you can size the grid's rows and columns proportionally. To enable proportional sizing, you simply set the `Height` or `Width` to a value like `2*`, which specifies that a given column should be twice the size of the other columns that are set to `1*`. For example, you could define your grid's rows and columns like this:

```
<UserControl x:Class="SilverlightApplication1.SilverlightControl1"
    xmlns="http://schemas.microsoft.com/winfx/2006/xaml/presentation"
    xmlns:x="http://schemas.microsoft.com/winfx/2006/xaml"
    xmlns:d="http://schemas.microsoft.com/expression/blend/2008"
    xmlns:mc="http://schemas.openxmlformats.org/markup-compatibility/2006"
    mc:Ignorable="d"
    d:DesignHeight="300" d:DesignWidth="400">

    <Grid x:Name="LayoutRoot" Background="White">
        <Grid.RowDefinitions>
            <RowDefinition Height="1*" />
            <RowDefinition Height="1*" />
            <RowDefinition Height="2*" />
            <RowDefinition Height="2*" />
        </Grid.RowDefinitions>
        <Grid.ColumnDefinitions>
            <ColumnDefinition Width="1*" />
            <ColumnDefinition Width="2*" />
            <ColumnDefinition Width="2*" />
            <ColumnDefinition Width="1*" />
        </Grid.ColumnDefinitions>
        <Button Content="Button" Grid.Column="2" Grid.Row="1"
                Grid.ColumnSpan="2" Grid.RowSpan="2" />
    </Grid>
</UserControl>
```

Code snippet from SilverlightControl1.xaml

The preceding code would result in a layout that looks something like what is shown in Figure 19-7.

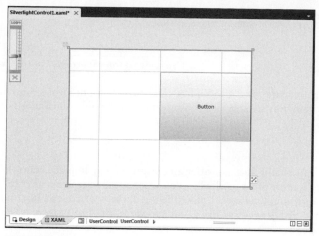

FIGURE 19-7

As you can see, there is a lot of power in the `Grid` control; but it is not just limited to a column and row structure. One thing that the `Grid` control can offer that none of the other layout controls can offer is *anchoring*. As you saw in Chapter 15, anchoring is extremely useful for placing controls on user controls that may be resized. For example, if you wanted to place a button in the center of the grid, you would define it like this:

```
<UserControl x:Class="SilverlightApplication1.SilverlightControl1"
    xmlns="http://schemas.microsoft.com/winfx/2006/xaml/presentation"
    xmlns:x="http://schemas.microsoft.com/winfx/2006/xaml"
    xmlns:d="http://schemas.microsoft.com/expression/blend/2008"
    xmlns:mc="http://schemas.openxmlformats.org/markup-compatibility/2006"
    mc:Ignorable="d"
    d:DesignHeight="300" d:DesignWidth="400">

    <Grid x:Name="LayoutRoot" Background="White">
            <Button Content="Button" Width="100" Height="30" HorizontalAlignment="Center"
        VerticalAlignment="Center" />
    </Grid>
</UserControl>
```

Code snippet from SilverlightControl1.xaml

Once you have the button centered, you can set the `HorizontalAlignment` option to Center, Left, Right, or Stretch; and you can set the `VerticalAlignment` option to Center, Top, Bottom, or Stretch. This will place your button in relation to the `Grid` control. This is great for placing the control in the bottom-right corner, but sometimes you may not want it directly on the bottom and all the way to the right. This is where margins come into play. For example, if you want to place the button in the bottom-right corner and offset it by 12 pixels from the bottom and the right, you would define it like this:

```
<UserControl x:Class="SilverlightApplication1.SilverlightControl1"
    xmlns="http://schemas.microsoft.com/winfx/2006/xaml/presentation"
    xmlns:x="http://schemas.microsoft.com/winfx/2006/xaml"
    xmlns:d="http://schemas.microsoft.com/expression/blend/2008"
    xmlns:mc="http://schemas.openxmlformats.org/markup-compatibility/2006"
    mc:Ignorable="d"
    d:DesignHeight="300" d:DesignWidth="400">

    <Grid x:Name="LayoutRoot" Background="White">
```

```
                    <Button Content="Button" Width="100" Height="30"
                HorizontalAlignment="Right" VerticalAlignment="Bottom" Margin="0,0,12,12" />
            </Grid>
        </UserControl>
```

Code snippet from SilverlightControl1.xaml

From what you have seen of the `Grid` control's capabilities, it should be clear that it will fit most situations. However, although it is probably the most commonly used layout control, it is not the only one and it does not fit every situation.

StackPanel

One frequently overlooked aspect of the `Grid` is that it does not offer an optimized way to place controls that actually stack. The `StackPanel` control is most often used when you want to arrange items next to each other or on top of each other in a row or column manner. Unlike the `Grid`, the `StackPanel` does not have to have the rows and columns defined; it simply needs its `Orientation` value set. The `Orientation` value can be set to either `Horizontal` or `Vertical`.

You might use the `StackPanel` to define elements such as a menu on which you would place several buttons, as shown in this example:

```
<UserControl x:Class="SilverlightApplication1.SilverlightControl1"
    xmlns="http://schemas.microsoft.com/winfx/2006/xaml/presentation"
    xmlns:x="http://schemas.microsoft.com/winfx/2006/xaml"
    xmlns:d="http://schemas.microsoft.com/expression/blend/2008"
    xmlns:mc="http://schemas.openxmlformats.org/markup-compatibility/2006"
    mc:Ignorable="d"
    d:DesignHeight="300" d:DesignWidth="400">

    <StackPanel x:Name="LayoutRoot" Background="White">
        <Button Content="Menu Item 1" Width="100" Height="30" Margin="5"/>
        <Button Content="Menu Item 1" Width="100" Height="30" Margin="5"/>
        <Button Content="Menu Item 1" Width="100" Height="30" Margin="5"/>
        <Button Content="Menu Item 1" Width="100" Height="30" Margin="5"/>
    </StackPanel>
</UserControl>
```

Code snippet from SilverlightControl1.xaml

This will create a stack panel for which the menu items are stacked on top of each other. Alternatively, you could have the menu items stack beside one another by setting the `Orientation` property as shown in this example:

```
<UserControl x:Class="SilverlightApplication1.SilverlightControl1"
    xmlns="http://schemas.microsoft.com/winfx/2006/xaml/presentation"
    xmlns:x="http://schemas.microsoft.com/winfx/2006/xaml"
    xmlns:d="http://schemas.microsoft.com/expression/blend/2008"
    xmlns:mc="http://schemas.openxmlformats.org/markup-compatibility/2006"
    mc:Ignorable="d"
    d:DesignHeight="300" d:DesignWidth="400">

    <StackPanel x:Name="LayoutRoot" Background="White" Orientation="Horizontal">
        <Button Content="Menu Item 1" Width="100" Height="30" Margin="5"/>
        <Button Content="Menu Item 1" Width="100" Height="30" Margin="5"/>
        <Button Content="Menu Item 1" Width="100" Height="30" Margin="5"/>
        <Button Content="Menu Item 1" Width="100" Height="30" Margin="5"/>
    </StackPanel>
</UserControl>
```

Code snippet from SilverlightControl1.xaml

This will place the menu items side-by-side.

As you have seen, this simple control is very powerful for various layout options; and it is used as the layout method for things like list views and combo boxes.

Canvas

The `Canvas` control is very basic compared to the previous layout controls. It enables you to place controls by defining coordinates relative to the parent control, as shown in the following example:

```
<UserControl x:Class="SilverlightApplication1.SilverlightControl1"
    xmlns="http://schemas.microsoft.com/winfx/2006/xaml/presentation"
    xmlns:x="http://schemas.microsoft.com/winfx/2006/xaml"
    xmlns:d="http://schemas.microsoft.com/expression/blend/2008"
    xmlns:mc="http://schemas.openxmlformats.org/markup-compatibility/2006"
    mc:Ignorable="d"
    d:DesignHeight="300" d:DesignWidth="400">

    <Canvas x:Name="LayoutRoot" Background="White" >
        <Button Content="Menu Item 1" Width="100" Height="30" Canvas.Left="100"
        Canvas.Top="200" />
        <Button Content="Menu Item 2" Width="100" Height="30" Canvas.Left="100"
        Canvas.Top="100"/>
    </Canvas>
</UserControl>
```

Code snippet from SilverlightControl1.xaml

You can set the positions of any controls inside of the `Canvas` control based on `Canvas.Top`, `Canvas.Left`, `Canvas.Right`, and `Canvas.Bottom`. The `Canvas` control offers the least amount of flexibility and creates your controls in a static position, unlike the `Grid` and `StackPanel`. In other words, if your canvas is resized at runtime, then your controls will not move, a result that is only appropriate in certain scenarios. Most of the time you will find it easier to use the `Grid` or `StackPanel` controls.

ScrollViewer

The `ScrollViewer` control is most commonly used with other layout controls, and most commonly the `StackPanel`. The `ScrollViewer` is simply a container element that provides horizontal and vertical scrollbars in case the content within it exceeds the size of the `ScrollViewer`. Note that the `ScrollViewer` can only contain one child control, which is why you would want to use it in conjunction with another layout control. Typically, you would place either a `StackPanel` or a `Grid` as the main child of the `ScrollViewer`, and then place more controls inside of them. Here is an example in which 10 buttons are specified inside of the `StackPanel`:

```
<UserControl x:Class="SilverlightApplication1.SilverlightControl1"
    xmlns="http://schemas.microsoft.com/winfx/2006/xaml/presentation"
    xmlns:x="http://schemas.microsoft.com/winfx/2006/xaml"
    xmlns:d="http://schemas.microsoft.com/expression/blend/2008"
    xmlns:mc="http://schemas.openxmlformats.org/markup-compatibility/2006"
    mc:Ignorable="d"
    d:DesignHeight="300" d:DesignWidth="400">

    <ScrollViewer x:Name="LayoutRoot" Background="White" >
        <StackPanel>
            <Button Content="Menu Item 1" Width="100" Height="30" Margin="5" />
            <Button Content="Menu Item 2" Width="100" Height="30" Margin="5" />
            <Button Content="Menu Item 3" Width="100" Height="30" Margin="5" />
            <Button Content="Menu Item 4" Width="100" Height="30" Margin="5" />
            <Button Content="Menu Item 5" Width="100" Height="30" Margin="5" />
```

```
                    <Button Content="Menu Item 6" Width="100" Height="30" Margin="5" />
                    <Button Content="Menu Item 7" Width="100" Height="30" Margin="5" />
                    <Button Content="Menu Item 8" Width="100" Height="30" Margin="5" />
                    <Button Content="Menu Item 9" Width="100" Height="30" Margin="5" />
                    <Button Content="Menu Item 10" Width="100" Height="30" Margin="5" />
            </StackPanel>
        </ScrollViewer>
    </UserControl>
```

Code snippet from SilverlightControl1.xaml

As you can see from this example, the `StackPanel` would grow outside of your design surface, but instead it creates the necessary scrollbars for your content. This gives you the flexibility to put controls inside an area that might be smaller than the area required to display them.

Border

Last but not least is the `Border` control, which simply adds a border to a control. Like the `ScrollViewer`, the `Border` control only allows one child control. One common use of the `Border` control would be to add rounded corners using the curved `CornerRadius` property, as shown in this example:

Available for download on Wrox.com

```
<UserControl x:Class="SilverlightApplication1.SilverlightControl1"
    xmlns="http://schemas.microsoft.com/winfx/2006/xaml/presentation"
    xmlns:x="http://schemas.microsoft.com/winfx/2006/xaml"
    xmlns:d="http://schemas.microsoft.com/expression/blend/2008"
    xmlns:mc="http://schemas.openxmlformats.org/markup-compatibility/2006"
    mc:Ignorable="d"
    d:DesignHeight="300" d:DesignWidth="400">

    <Grid x:Name="LayoutRoot" Background="White" >
        <Border BorderBrush="Silver" BorderThickness="1" Height="263"
        HorizontalAlignment="Left" Margin="12,25,0,0"
        Name="Border1" VerticalAlignment="Top" Width="376"
        Background="Gray" CornerRadius="20">
            <Grid Name="Grid1">
                <Button Content="Button" Height="23" Name="Center"
                    VerticalAlignment="Center" Width="75" />
            </Grid>
        </Border>
    </Grid>
</UserControl>
```

Code snippet from SilverlightControl1.xaml

Although the `Border` control is simple, it does help add a small improvement to the overall look and feel of your content.

ADDING ITEMS TO THE SILVERLIGHT PROJECT

As with all other .NET projects, you will need to add more than just the basic items provided when you first create a Silverlight project, and Silverlight offers several different options. Most are very similar to what you will find in other project types in Visual Studio, but many are unique to Silverlight.

You will find all of these options when you right-click on your Silverlight project and select Add New Item, as shown in Figure 19-8.

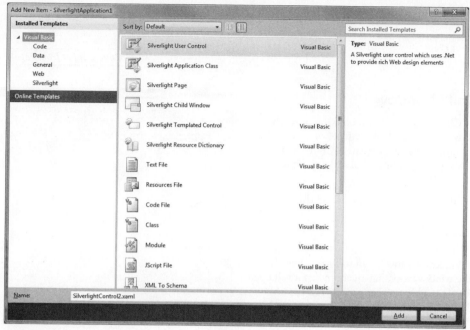

FIGURE 19-8

The following sections provide a brief overview of each item type and when to use it.

Silverlight User Control

The Silverlight User Control is probably the most common item you will add to your Silverlight project. It is almost exactly like adding a user control in a Windows Forms application or a WPF project. Selecting it will provide you with both a XAML and .vb code-behind file. This is where you can create the user interface for your controls.

Silverlight Application Class

The Silverlight Application Class is similar to what you have learned earlier in the chapter about the App.xaml because this is exactly what the App.xaml is. The only time you would probably create a Silverlight Application Class is when you have created a Silverlight project and removed your App.xaml, or you created a Silverlight Class Library and wanted to convert it to a complete application.

Silverlight Page

The Silverlight Page is very similar to a page in ASP.NET and is what works with the navigation framework described earlier in the chapter. The only real difference is the capability to set the Page title that will show in the browser title bar. For a basic page the code looks like this:

```
<navigation:Page x:Class="SilverlightApplication1.Page1"
        xmlns="http://schemas.microsoft.com/winfx/2006/xaml/presentation"
        xmlns:x="http://schemas.microsoft.com/winfx/2006/xaml"
        xmlns:d="http://schemas.microsoft.com/expression/blend/2008"
        xmlns:mc="http://schemas.openxmlformats.org/markup-compatibility/2006"
        mc:Ignorable="d"
        xmlns:navigation="clr-namespace:System.Windows.Controls;
            assembly=System.Windows.Controls.Navigation"
        d:DesignWidth="640" d:DesignHeight="480"
        Title="Page1 Page" >
```

```
<Grid x:Name="LayoutRoot">

</Grid>
</navigation:Page>
```

Code snippet from Page1.xaml

Silverlight Child Window

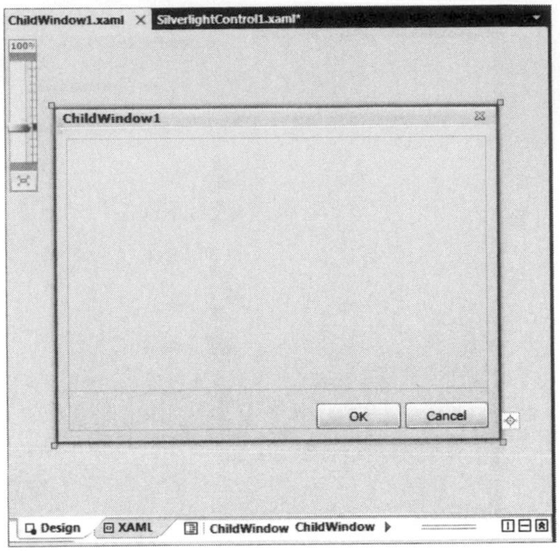

The Silverlight Child Window is a modal dialog within Silverlight that gives you the look and feel of a Windows Forms modal dialog. When you create a Child Window you will get a design surface that looks like the one shown in Figure 19-9.

To show this Child Window you would use the following code:

```
Dim nWnd as New ChildWindow1
nWnd.Show()
```

When a Child Window is shown, you will see a nice animation of the window zooming in; and when it is hidden, it will zoom out. This adds a nice touch to your application.

FIGURE 19-9

Silverlight Template Control

A Silverlight Template Control is a class that has an existing control as its base class. It is similar to a control template in Windows Forms or WPF. Unlike a User Control, it does not have a design surface, but when compiled it does create a class which is available in the Toolbox window for use as a control.

Silverlight Resource Dictionary

Last but not least is the Silverlight Resource Dictionary. This class enables you to centralize things like templates, styles, and more. It also creates a simple way to organize these items into separate files for better manageability.

SILVERLIGHT OUT OF THE BROWSER

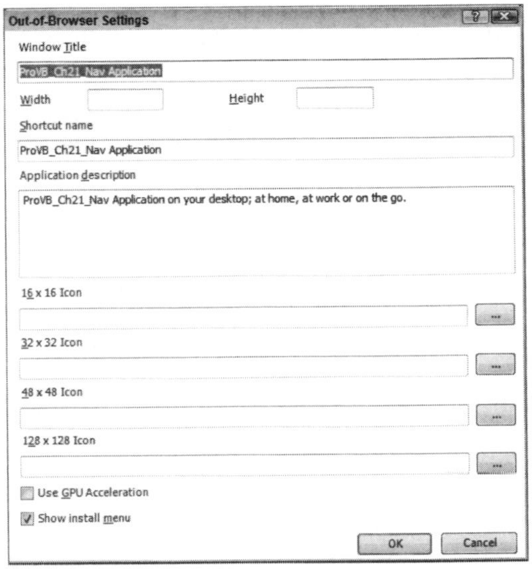

One of the features introduced in Silverlight 3 is "out of the browser" capabilities. This feature allows your users to create a desktop and start menu icon for your application. It also enables your application to run out of the browser even when there is no Internet connection. These features are not just limited to the PC, but also work on the Mac, so now you can build cross-platform .NET applications without having to use something like the Mono Project to develop them.

To enable Out of the Browser options, simply right-click on your Silverlight project and click Properties. Then you can simply check "Enable running application out of the browser." That's it — you have just made your Silverlight application capable of running out of the browser on both a PC and a Mac. To set up a few more options, you can click the Out-of-Browser Settings button, which will bring up the dialog shown in Figure 19-10.

FIGURE 19-10

From here you can set several additional options, including the title of the window, window size, and icon options. When you define these settings under the Properties window, you are actually creating an `OutOfBrowserSettings.xml` file under the My Project folder, which can be viewed by clicking the Show Hidden Files button on the Solution Explorer. Here is a sample `OutOfBrowserSettings.xml` file:

```
<OutOfBrowserSettings
ShortName="SilverlightApplication1 Application"
EnableGPUAcceleration="False"
ShowInstallMenuItem="True">
  <OutOfBrowserSettings.Blurb>SilverlightApplication1 Application on your desktop;
         at home, at work or on the go.
</OutOfBrowserSettings.Blurb>
  <OutOfBrowserSettings.WindowSettings>
    <WindowSettings Title="SilverlightApplication1 Application" />
  </OutOfBrowserSettings.WindowSettings>
  <OutOfBrowserSettings.Icons>
    <Icon Size="16,16">MyIcon.png</Icon>
    <Icon Size="32,32">MyIcon.png</Icon>
    <Icon Size="48,48">MyIcon.png</Icon>
    <Icon Size="128,128">MyIcon.png</Icon>
  </OutOfBrowserSettings.Icons>
</OutOfBrowserSettings>
```

Of course, this just describes the setup for running your application out of the browser. To actually install the application, there are two options for installing the application: by right-clicking the application and selecting install or by initiating it from the code.

Let's take a look at the first option. After setting your application to run out of the browser, actually run your application. You will see that it runs just as you expect. Now right-click the application. You will be presented with the dialog shown in Figure 19-11.

Once you have installed the application, it will run the Silverlight application in what seems to be a standalone application. This application will automatically update itself to the version hosted on in your Asp.NET appication. To uninstall the running application, right-click on it.

FIGURE 19-11

The second way of installing the application, from code, is actually very simple — only one line of code:

```
App.Current.Install()
```

That's it! You can create a button and call the `Install` function to install the application locally.

SUMMARY

This chapter has only briefly described a diverse set of features from Silverlight, as entire books could be written about Silverlight and its various elements. In this chapter you have learned how to do basic layout and design, and have seen how it relates to other technologies that you have learned in previous chapters. We will continue with Silverlight in the next chapter to dig deeper into building more complex applications, and how to interact with Web services, including SOAP and WCF to interact with data. We will also build on your knowledge of Visual Basic and Silverlight to create a Model View View-Model application which enables better separation of concerns for your application.

PART IV
Internet Applications

20

Silverlight and Services

WHAT YOU WILL LEARN IN THIS CHAPTER

➤ ASMX Web Service

➤ ADO.NET Data Service

➤ WCF Ria Services

➤ Model-View-ViewModel

As you have seen in the previous chapter, Silverlight offers developers a familiar environment for developing applications. However, Silverlight offers a lot more than the capability to make great-looking websites. Silverlight has a rich line-of-business applications too. With Silverlight 3, Microsoft enabled developers to easily create a variety of business applications, including new `DataForm` controls and `Validation` controls. Silverlight 4, now in beta and soon to be released, will continue to strengthen Silverlight's line-of-business support by adding additional features such as trusted offline capabilities and finer control on the offline.

Throughout this chapter you will learn both how to leverage existing Web service technologies and how to use some of the newer technologies targeted toward Silverlight. As with all line-of-business applications, it is important to be able to get to data and then update it back on the server. Silverlight can do this through existing Web services like SOAP or WCF with little modification, or you can use some of the new offerings of ADO.NET Data Services and RIA Services.

This chapter also offers a high-level overview of a commonly suggested best practice for developing Silverlight line-of-business applications called *Model-View-ViewModel (MVVM)*. This suggested best practice is ideal for creating software that is easy to test and maintain.

SERVICES AND SILVERLIGHT

In previous chapters, you saw how to use various Web Service technologies to get data into Windows Forms applications, and we will continue to use these concepts with regard to Silverlight. For the most part, this chapter is a review of what you already learned in the previous service chapters, but it points out the differences between calling these services in Silverlight compared to any other type of application.

ASMX Web Service

One of the first Web service types made available in .NET was the ASMX Web service sometimes referred to as SOAP. This simple protocol uses XML to send messages back and forth between the server and the client. ASMX Web services are designed to handle synchronous calls between the client and the server, but with Silverlight you must take a slightly different approach because all calls in Silverlight have to be asynchronous in order to prevent your web browser from locking up while waiting on the Silverlight application to get a response from the server.

To get started, we'll create a new Silverlight application in Visual Studio and then add a new Web service to the ASP.NET project by right-clicking the project and selecting Add New Item. From the list that appears, select Web Service as shown in Figure 20-1.

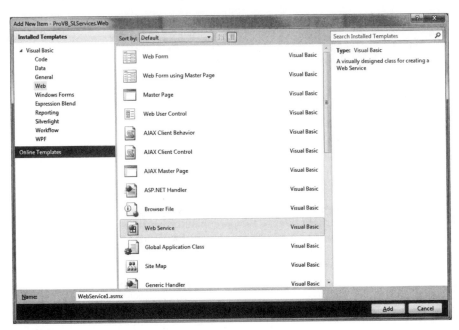

FIGURE 20-1

Once you have created a Web service you will be presented with the following code:

```
Imports System.Web.Services
Imports System.Web.Services.Protocols
Imports System.ComponentModel

' To allow this Web Service to be called from script,
' using ASP.NET AJAX, uncomment the following line.
' <System.Web.Script.Services.ScriptService()> _
<System.Web.Services.WebService(Namespace:="http://tempuri.org/")> _
<System.Web.Services.WebServiceBinding(ConformsTo:=WsiProfiles.BasicProfile1_1)> _
<ToolboxItem(False)> _
Public Class WebService1
    Inherits System.Web.Services.WebService

    <WebMethod()> _
    Public Function HelloWorld() As String
       Return "Hello World"
    End Function

End Class
```

This is about as basic as you can get for a Web service — a simple `HelloWorld` function that returns a string. The next step is to reference the Web service from your Silverlight application. Right-click the Silverlight project and select Add Service Reference. The Add Service Reference dialog shown in Figure 20-2 will appear.

Build your project then, click the Discover button on the right side. When it finds the Web service you just created, click OK. Once you have done this, your Silverlight project will now contain a reference to your service, as well as a new file called `ServiceReferences.ClientConfig` that contains similar code:

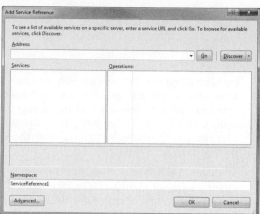

FIGURE 20-2

```
<configuration>
    <system.serviceModel>
        <bindings>
            <basicHttpBinding>
                <binding name="WebService1Soap" maxBufferSize="2147483647"
                maxReceivedMessageSize="2147483647">
                    <security mode="None" />
                </binding>
            </basicHttpBinding>
        </bindings>
        <client>
            <endpoint address="http://localhost:38588/WebService1.asmx"
              binding="basicHttpBinding"
                bindingConfiguration="WebService1Soap"
              contract="ServiceReference1.WebService1Soap"
                name="WebService1Soap" />
        </client>
    </system.serviceModel>
</configuration>
```

This file is added when using most of the various Web services. As shown in the code, it defines the endpoint address as your local test Web server. When moving a Silverlight application from development to production, you need to change that property to point to your production address.

In addition, when creating a Web service reference, Visual Studio auto-generates a proxy class to make calling the Web service much easier. In this example it is called `WebService1SoapClient` and you can reference it by `ServiceReference1.WebService1SoapClient`. This works the same as adding Web services to other project types except that it generates a function called `<functioname>Async` for every function that is exposed in the Web service, as well as an event called `<functionname>Completed`. This event is where you will receive the results from the Web service function call.

To call that from the Silverlight application, open the code view of the `MainPage.xaml` and create the following code:

```
Private WithEvents svc As New ServiceReference1.WebService1SoapClient

Private Sub MainPage_Loaded(ByVal sender As Object,
ByVal e As System.Windows.RoutedEventArgs) Handles Me.Loaded
    TestSoapCall()
End Sub

Private Sub TestSoapCall()
    svc.HelloWorldAsync()
End Sub

Private Sub svc_HelloWorldCompleted(ByVal sender As Object,
```

```
ByVal e As ServiceReference1.HelloWorldCompletedEventArgs) Handles svc.HelloWorldCompleted
      MessageBox.Show(e.Result)
End Sub
```

Code snippet from WebService1SoapClient

Unlike calling the Web service from another type of application, with Silverlight you need to create an event handler to handle the `HelloWorldComplete` function, due to the asynchronous limitations of Silverlight. This is a little different from what you may have done with other Web services, and it does require keeping some things in mind when using this method. This includes updating your user interface to notify the user that you are waiting on something from the server, and disabling buttons that may require the data you are getting back from the server.

With an ASMX Web service, you can also pass more complex objects than just strings to Silverlight. This opens a large set of possibilities for passing data from a database or other server system. While ASMX Web services are simple, they are not always the optimal way of sending data back and forth, as each object is serialized to XML and is not compressed. As you will see in the next example, WCF services offer some of these options with no special configuration or coding.

WCF Service

The WCF service is almost identical to the ASMX Web service method of creating a connection to the server, but it offers many performance and security benefits over ASMX Web services.

Begin by creating another service: Right-click your ASP.NET application and select Add New Item. Under the Silverlight category you will find a Silverlight-enabled WCF service, as shown in Figure 20-3.

FIGURE 20-3

Creating a Silverlight-enabled WCF service is nearly identical to creating a normal WCF service; the only difference is the following option:

```
<AspNetCompatibilityRequirements(
RequirementsMode:=AspNetCompatibilityRequirementsMode.Allowed)>
```

Just as you did earlier for the ASMX Web service, make a `HelloWorld` function in your WCF service as shown here:

Available for download on Wrox.com

```
Imports System.ServiceModel
Imports System.ServiceModel.Activation

<ServiceContract(Namespace:="")>
<AspNetCompatibilityRequirements(
RequirementsMode:=AspNetCompatibilityRequirementsMode.Allowed)>
Public Class Service1

    <OperationContract()>
    Public Function HelloWorld() As String
        Return "Hello from WCF Service"
    End Function

End Class
```

Code snippet from Service1

As you can see, there is very little difference between the ASMX and WCF services so far, and you also add the reference the same way.

Now add the WCF service by right-clicking the Silverlight application, selecting Add Service Reference, and then clicking the Discover button, as you did before. You will see both services on the ASP.NET project: `Service1.svc` and `WebService1.asmx`. Select `Service1.asmx` and click OK. Now add the following code to the `MainPage.xaml.vb`:

Available for download on Wrox.com

```
Partial Public Class MainPage
    Inherits UserControl

    Public Sub New()
        InitializeComponent()
    End Sub


    Private WithEvents svc As New ServiceReference1.WebService1SoapClient
    Private WithEvents svc2 As New ServiceReference2.Service1Client
    Private Sub MainPage_Loaded(ByVal sender As Object,
      ByVal e As System.Windows.RoutedEventArgs) Handles Me.Loaded
        TestSoapCall()

    End Sub

    Private Sub TestSoapCall()
        svc.HelloWorldAsync()
        svc2.HelloWorldAsync()
    End Sub

    Private Sub TestWCFCall()
        TestWCFCall()
    End Sub

    Private Sub svc_HelloWorldCompleted(ByVal sender As Object,
        ByVal e As ServiceReference1.HelloWorldCompletedEventArgs)
            Handles svc.HelloWorldCompleted
        MessageBox.Show(e.Result)
    End Sub
```

```
        Private Sub svc2_HelloWorldCompleted(ByVal sender As Object,
            ByVal e As ServiceReference2.HelloWorldCompletedEventArgs)
            Handles svc.HelloWorldCompleted
             MessageBox.Show(e.Result)
        End Sub
    End Class
```

Code snippet from MainPage.xaml

This appears to be exactly the same as the ASMX Web service, but this is only an appearance of similarities. The way the code is actually executed is in fact much different because of the way in which WCF binds to the Web service. You can see where it defines this in the `ServiceReferences.ClientConfig`:

Available for download on Wrox.com

```
<configuration>
    <system.serviceModel>
        <bindings>
            <basicHttpBinding>
                <binding name="WebService1Soap" maxBufferSize="2147483647"
                maxReceivedMessageSize="2147483647">
                    <security mode="None" />
                </binding>
            </basicHttpBinding>
            <customBinding>
                <binding name="CustomBinding_Service1">
                    <binaryMessageEncoding />
                    <httpTransport maxReceivedMessageSize="2147483647"
                     maxBufferSize="2147483647" />
                </binding>
            </customBinding>
        </bindings>
        <client>
            <endpoint address="http://localhost:38588/WebService1.asmx"
              binding="basicHttpBinding"
                bindingConfiguration="WebService1Soap"
             contract="ServiceReference1.WebService1Soap"
             name="WebService1Soap" />
            <endpoint address="http://localhost:38588/Service1.svc"
              binding="customBinding"
                bindingConfiguration="CustomBinding_Service1"
    contract="ServiceReference2.Service1"
                name="CustomBinding_Service1" />
        </client>
    </system.serviceModel>
</configuration>
```

Code snippet from ServiceReferences.ClientConfig

Unlike the `basicHttpBinding` that the ASMX service assigned to its endpoint, WCF-based services bind using a `customBinding`. The `customBinding` is actually defined slightly above the endpoints, and you can see that it is defined to use `binaryMessageEncoding`. This is what tells Silverlight to use binary messaging to communicate with the Web service, but this only half the story; this binding is also defined in the `web.config`, as shown here:

Available for download on Wrox.com

```
        <?xml version="1.0"?>
<configuration>

    <system.web>
        <compilation debug="true" strict="false" explicit="true"
targetFramework="4.0" />
    </system.web>
    <system.webServer>
      <modules runAllManagedModulesForAllRequests="true"/>
    </system.webServer>
```

```
        <system.serviceModel>
            <behaviors>
                <serviceBehaviors>
                    <behavior name="">
                        <serviceMetadata httpGetEnabled="true" />
                        <serviceDebug includeExceptionDetailInFaults="false" />
                    </behavior>
                </serviceBehaviors>
            </behaviors>
            <bindings>
                <customBinding>
                    <binding name="ProVB_SLServices.Web.Service1.customBinding0">
                        <binaryMessageEncoding />
                        <httpTransport />
                    </binding>
                </customBinding>
            </bindings>
            <serviceHostingEnvironment aspNetCompatibilityEnabled="true" />
            <services>
                <service name="ProVB_SLServices.Web.Service1">
                    <endpoint address="" binding="customBinding"
    bindingConfiguration="ProVB_SLServices.Web.Service1.customBinding0"
                        contract="ProVB_SLServices.Web.Service1" />
                    <endpoint address="mex" binding="mexHttpBinding"
    contract="IMetadataExchange" />
                </service>
            </services>
        </system.serviceModel>
    </configuration>
```

Code snippet from web.config

This not only converts your message to binary, but gives you a significant boost to performance, as the binary objects are also compressed. This method also results in a slight security improvement because the objects are not sent across in plain text, where a network monitoring tool could see the data. It is not, however, secure enough to rely on this as your only method of security — you would still want to rely on SSL and other levels of security for highly secured applications.

While both WCF and ASMX Web services provide a great way to access your data, you still have to define all your function calls between the server and the client. For smaller applications this is not an issue, but imagine applications for which you may have 300 or more database tables that you need to send data back and forth. These types of situations lead us into the next type of service.

ADO.NET Data Service

Now that you have seen the two most classic examples of Web services, this section looks at one of the latest Microsoft technologies for getting to your data. Microsoft has created ADO.NET Data Services to provide a REST-based Web service to expose LINQ to SQL, Entity Framework, or other ORM technology classes. REST (Representational state transfer) uses traditional Web-based standards to expose data for create, read, update, and delete (CRUD) operations. To do this with WCF, you would have to build your own CRUD operations for every table in your database, which for a large application can be impractical to implement.

To get started with ADO.NET Data Services, we'll set up a few things in our project that we will use throughout the rest of the chapter. Rather than use the traditional Northwind database, we are going to build our own. We are going to create a basic "issue management system" where we keep track of customers and their issues. To begin, first add a SQL Server Database to the ASP.NET project as shown in Figure 20-4.

FIGURE 20-4

Visual Studio will create an App_Data folder and place your database in it. Now double-click your database and add two tables, beginning with the Customers table shown in Table 20-1.

TABLE 20-1: Customers

COLUMN NAME	TYPE	DESCRIPTION
CustomerID	Int	Unique identity for customers
Name	Varchar(50)	Name of customer
PhoneNumber	Varchar(50)	Phone number of customer
EMailAddress	Varchar(50)	E-mail address of customer
Address	Varchar(50)	Address of customer
City	Varchar(50)	City of customer
State	Varchar(50)	State of customer

Now that we have a customer table, we'll also add an Issues table to keep track of issues for the customer. This will build a basic issue-tracking database. Add the structure for the Issues table as shown in Table 20-2.

TABLE 20-2: Issues

COLUMN NAME	TYPE	DESCRIPTION
IssueID	Int	Unique identity for issues
CustomerID	Int	ID of customer to whom the issue belongs
IssueDate	Datetime	Date of issue
ResolvedDate	Datetime	Date the issue was resolved
Description	Varchar(5000)	Description of issue
Resolution	Varchar(5000)	Resolution of issue

Now that we have the tables, we can also add a foreign key between the Issues and Customers table by using the following script:

```
/* To prevent any potential data loss issues,
 you should review this script in detail before
running it outside the context of the database designer.*/
BEGIN TRANSACTION
SET QUOTED_IDENTIFIER ON
SET ARITHABORT ON
SET NUMERIC_ROUNDABORT OFF
SET CONCAT_NULL_YIELDS_NULL ON
SET ANSI_NULLS ON
SET ANSI_PADDING ON
SET ANSI_WARNINGS ON
COMMIT
BEGIN TRANSACTION
GO
COMMIT
BEGIN TRANSACTION
GO
ALTER TABLE dbo.Issues ADD CONSTRAINT
        FK_Issues_Customers FOREIGN KEY
        (
        CustomerID
        ) REFERENCES dbo.Customers
        (
        CustomerID
        ) ON UPDATE  NO ACTION
           ON DELETE  NO ACTION

GO
COMMIT
```

Code snippet from CreateTable.sql

Once we have the tables, we need some data in them, so use the following script to generate the data:

```
Insert Into Customers (Name,PhoneNumber,EmailAddress,Address,City,State,Zip)
Values ('ACME Corp','(123) 123-1234','jonathan@acme.com','123 Main Street',
'Beverly Hills','CA', '90210')
Insert Into Customers (Name,PhoneNumber,EmailAddress,Address,City,State,Zip)
Values ('East Coast Computers','(311) 123-1235',
'jonathan@acme.com','123 Broadway', 'New York','NY', '10249')


Insert Into Issues (CustomerID,IssueDate,ResolvedDate,Description)
 Values (1,GetDate(),null,'I can''t login into my program')
Insert Into Issues (CustomerID,IssueDate,ResolvedDate,Description)
Values (1,GetDate() - 5 ,GetDate(),'What is a mouse?')
Insert Into Issues (CustomerID,IssueDate,ResolvedDate,Description)
Values (1,GetDate() - 10 ,GetDate() - 9,'My computer came in how do I open the box?')
Insert Into Issues (CustomerID,IssueDate,ResolvedDate,Description)
Values (2,GetDate(),null,'My computer is saying I need Silverlight, what do I do?')
Insert Into Issues (CustomerID,IssueDate,ResolvedDate,Description)
Values (2,GetDate() - 5 ,GetDate() - 4,'How do I hook up my internet connection?')
```

Code snippet from InsertData.sql

Now that we have some data, we can use it for the rest of the chapter. Right-click your ASP.NET project, add a new item, select ADO.NET Entity Data Model, and name it CustomerIssueModel.edmx, as shown in Figure 20-5.

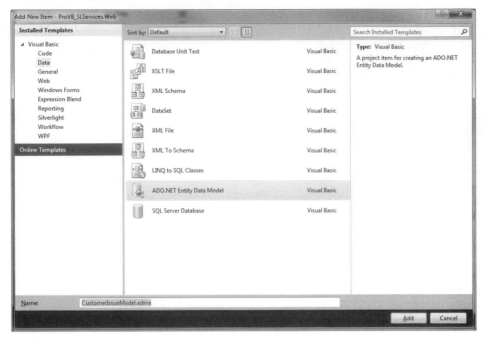

FIGURE 20-5

When the Entity Data Model Wizard appears, select Generate from Database and click Next. When it asks you to choose the database connection, select the ProVB_DB.mdf that we created earlier and enter **CustomerIssueEntities** as the name for the connection string. Select Next. When the Choose Your Database Objects dialog appears, check Tables, and enter CustomerIssueEntitiesModel in the Model Namespace text box, as shown in Figure 20-6.

Click Finish. You have just created your first ADO.NET Entity Data model. See Figure 20-7.

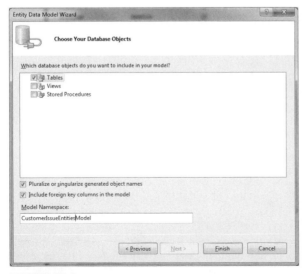

FIGURE 20-6

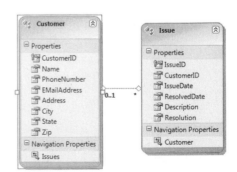

FIGURE 20-7

As you can see, table names are converted to singular versions of the table names and automatic links are created to the other tables based on the foreign key. This model is all you need to access your database from the server-side code, but now we must create an ADO.NET Data Service so that Silverlight can also access this data. To do so, add an item of ADO.NET Data Service to your ASP.NET application. This will create the following code:

```
Imports System.Data.Services
Imports System.Data.Services.Common
Imports System.Linq
Imports System.ServiceModel.Web

Public Class WebDataService1
    ' TODO: replace [[class name]] with your data class name
    Inherits DataService(Of [[class name]])

    ' This method is called only once to initialize service-wide policies.
    Public Shared Sub InitializeService(ByVal config As DataServiceConfiguration)
        ' TODO: set rules to indicate which entity sets and service operations
        ' are visible, updatable, etc.
        ' Examples:
        ' config.SetEntitySetAccessRule("MyEntityset", EntitySetRights.AllRead)
        ' config.SetServiceOperationAccessRule("MyServiceOperation",
        ServiceOperationRights.All)
        config.DataServiceBehavior.MaxProtocolVersion =
        DataServiceProtocolVersion.V2
    End Sub

End Class
```

There is an error with the code and it contains several to-do comments. We need to set the class to inherit a `DataService(Of CustomerIssueEntities)` so that it will compile. We also need to set up the security on the ADO.NET Data Service, so the final version of the code should look like this:

```
Imports System.Data.Services
Imports System.Data.Services.Common
Imports System.Linq
Imports System.ServiceModel.Web

Public Class WebDataService1
    ' TODO: replace [[class name]] with your data class name
    Inherits DataService(Of CustomerIssueEntities)

    ' This method is called only once to initialize service-wide policies.
    Public Shared Sub InitializeService(ByVal config As DataServiceConfiguration)

        config.SetEntitySetAccessRule("*", EntitySetRights.AllRead)
        config.SetServiceOperationAccessRule("*", ServiceOperationRights.All)
        config.DataServiceBehavior.MaxProtocolVersion =
        DataServiceProtocolVersion.V2
    End Sub

End Class
```

As you can tell from the security settings, you probably wouldn't want to do this from a production application, but rather make it more secure than this.

You have just created your first REST API, which is accessible not only by Silverlight, but also by other Web technologies such as PHP, ASP.NET, and many more. The great thing about ADO.NET Data Services is that it takes your model and creates a standard based API that almost any Web developer could consume. To see how this actually works, set the `WebDataService1.svc` as your start page in your Web project and run your project. You will see the following XML:

```
<?xml version="1.0" encoding="utf-8" standalone="yes" ?>
<service xml:base="http://localhost:38588/WebDataService1.svc/"
xmlns:atom="http://www.w3.org/2005/Atom"
xmlns:app="http://www.w3.org/2007/app"
```

```
xmlns="http://www.w3.org/2007/app">
<workspace>
  <atom:title>Default</atom:title>
 <collection href="Customers">
  <atom:title>Customers</atom:title>
  </collection>
 <collection href="Issues">
  <atom:title>Issues</atom:title>
  </collection>
  </workspace>
  </service>
```

This tells you that there are two collections in the ADO.NET Data Service, so, for example, you can navigate to WebDataService1.svc/Customers, which will return all the customers in the Customers table and return the following XML:

```
<?xml version="1.0" encoding="iso-8859-1" standalone="yes"?>
<feed xml:base="http://localhost:38588/WebDataService1.svc/"
xmlns:d="http://schemas.microsoft.com/ado/2007/08/dataservices"
xmlns:m="http://schemas.microsoft.com/ado/2007/08/dataservices/metadata"
xmlns="http://www.w3.org/2005/Atom">
  <title type="text">Customers</title>
  <id>http://localhost:38588/WebDataService1.svc/Customers</id>
  <updated>2009-11-21T01:47:49Z</updated>
  <link rel="self" title="Customers" href="Customers" />
  <entry>
    <id>http://localhost:38588/WebDataService1.svc/Customers(1)</id>
    <title type="text"></title>
    <updated>2009-11-21T01:47:49Z</updated>
    <author>
      <name />
    </author>
    <link rel="edit" title="Customer" href="Customers(1)" />
    <link
       rel="http://schemas.microsoft.com/ado/2007/08/dataservices/related/Issues"
       type="application/atom+xml;type=feed" title="Issues" href="Customers(1)/Issues" />
    <category term="CustomerIssueEntitiesModel.Customer"
scheme="http://schemas.microsoft.com/ado/2007/08/dataservices/scheme"
/>
    <content type="application/xml">
      <m:properties>
        <d:CustomerID m:type="Edm.Int32">1</d:CustomerID>
        <d:Name>ACME Corp</d:Name>
        <d:PhoneNumber>(123) 123-1234</d:PhoneNumber>
        <d:EMailAddress>jonathan@acme.com</d:EMailAddress>
        <d:Address>123 Main Street</d:Address>
        <d:City>Beverly Hills</d:City>
        <d:State>CA</d:State>
        <d:Zip>90210</d:Zip>
      </m:properties>
    </content>
  </entry>
  <entry>
    <id>http://localhost:38588/WebDataService1.svc/Customers(2)</id>
    <title type="text"></title>
    <updated>2009-11-21T01:47:49Z</updated>
    <author>
      <name />
    </author>
    <link rel="edit" title="Customer" href="Customers(2)" />
    <link
       rel="http://schemas.microsoft.com/ado/2007/08/dataservices/related/Issues"
       type="application/atom+xml;type=feed" title="Issues" href="Customers(2)/Issues" />
```

```
      <category term="CustomerIssueEntitiesModel.Customer"
   scheme="http://schemas.microsoft.com/ado/2007/08/dataservices/scheme"
   />
       <content type="application/xml">
         <m:properties>
           <d:CustomerID m:type="Edm.Int32">2</d:CustomerID>
           <d:Name>East Coast Computers</d:Name>
           <d:PhoneNumber>(311) 123-1235</d:PhoneNumber>
           <d:EMailAddress>jonathan@acme.com</d:EMailAddress>
           <d:Address>123 Broadway</d:Address>
           <d:City>New York</d:City>
           <d:State>NY</d:State>
           <d:Zip>10249</d:Zip>
         </m:properties>
       </content>
     </entry>
   </feed>
```

And if you wanted to return the first customer, you could simply change the address to `WebDataService1.svc/Customers(1)`, which will return the following:

```
<?xml version="1.0" encoding="iso-8859-1" standalone="yes"?>
<entry xml:base="http://localhost:38588/WebDataService1.svc/"
xmlns:d="http://schemas.microsoft.com/ado/2007/08/dataservices"
xmlns:m="http://schemas.microsoft.com/ado/2007/08/dataservices/metadata"
xmlns="http://www.w3.org/2005/Atom">
  <id>http://localhost:38588/WebDataService1.svc/Customers(1)</id>
  <title type="text"></title>
  <updated>2009-11-21T02:05:05Z</updated>
  <author>
    <name />
  </author>
  <link rel="edit" title="Customer" href="Customers(1)" />
  <link rel="http://schemas.microsoft.com/ado/2007/08/dataservices/related/Issues"
type="application/atom+xml;type=feed" title="Issues" href="Customers(1)/Issues" />
  <category term="CustomerIssueEntitiesModel.Customer"
scheme="http://schemas.microsoft.com/ado/2007/08/dataservices/scheme" />
  <content type="application/xml">
    <m:properties>
      <d:CustomerID m:type="Edm.Int32">1</d:CustomerID>
      <d:Name>ACME Corp</d:Name>
      <d:PhoneNumber>(123) 123-1234</d:PhoneNumber>
      <d:EMailAddress>jonathan@acme.com</d:EMailAddress>
      <d:Address>123 Main Street</d:Address>
      <d:City>Beverly Hills</d:City>
      <d:State>CA</d:State>
      <d:Zip>90210</d:Zip>
    </m:properties>
  </content>
</entry>
```

If you wanted to get the issues for the first customer, then you would change the address to `WebDataService1.svc/Customers(1)/Issues`:

```
<?xml version="1.0" encoding="iso-8859-1" standalone="yes"?>
<feed xml:base="http://localhost:38588/WebDataService1.svc/"
xmlns:d="http://schemas.microsoft.com/ado/2007/08/dataservices"
xmlns:m="http://schemas.microsoft.com/ado/2007/08/dataservices/metadata"
xmlns="http://www.w3.org/2005/Atom">
  <title type="text">Issues</title>
  <id>http://localhost:38588/WebDataService1.svc/Customers(1)/Issues</id>
  <updated>2009-11-21T02:06:12Z</updated>
  <link rel="self" title="Issues" href="Issues" />
```

```
<entry>
  <id>http://localhost:38588/WebDataService1.svc/Issues(1)</id>
  <title type="text"></title>
  <updated>2009-11-21T02:06:12Z</updated>
  <author>
    <name />
  </author>
  <link rel="edit" title="Issue" href="Issues(1)" />
  <link rel="http://schemas.microsoft.com/ado/2007/08/dataservices/related/Customer"
type="application/atom+xml;type=entry"
title="Customer" href="Issues(1)/Customer" />
  <category term="CustomerIssueEntitiesModel.Issue"
scheme="http://schemas.microsoft.com/ado/2007/08/dataservices/scheme" />
  <content type="application/xml">
    <m:properties>
      <d:IssueID m:type="Edm.Int32">1</d:IssueID>
      <d:CustomerID m:type="Edm.Int32">1</d:CustomerID>
      <d:IssueDate m:type="Edm.DateTime">2009-11-20T16:50:18.43</d:IssueDate>
      <d:ResolvedDate m:type="Edm.DateTime" m:null="true" />
      <d:Description>I can't login into my program</d:Description>
      <d:Resolution m:null="true" />
    </m:properties>
  </content>
</entry>
<entry>
  <id>http://localhost:38588/WebDataService1.svc/Issues(2)</id>
  <title type="text"></title>
  <updated>2009-11-21T02:06:12Z</updated>
  <author>
    <name />
  </author>
  <link rel="edit" title="Issue" href="Issues(2)" />
  <link
      rel="http://schemas.microsoft.com/ado/2007/08/dataservices/related/Customer"
      type="application/atom+xml;type=entry" title="Customer" href="Issues(2)/Customer" />
  <category term="CustomerIssueEntitiesModel.Issue"
scheme="http://schemas.microsoft.com/ado/2007/08/dataservices/scheme" />
  <content type="application/xml">
    <m:properties>
      <d:IssueID m:type="Edm.Int32">2</d:IssueID>
      <d:CustomerID m:type="Edm.Int32">1</d:CustomerID>
      <d:IssueDate m:type="Edm.DateTime">2009-11-15T16:50:18.43</d:IssueDate>
      <d:ResolvedDate m:type="Edm.DateTime">2009-11-20T16:50:18.43
      </d:ResolvedDate>
      <d:Description>What is a mouse?</d:Description>
      <d:Resolution m:null="true" />
    </m:properties>
  </content>
</entry>
<entry>
  <id>http://localhost:38588/WebDataService1.svc/Issues(3)</id>
  <title type="text"></title>
  <updated>2009-11-21T02:06:12Z</updated>
  <author>
    <name />
  </author>
  <link rel="edit" title="Issue" href="Issues(3)" />
  <link
      rel="http://schemas.microsoft.com/ado/2007/08/dataservices/related/Customer"
      type="application/atom+xml;type=entry" title="Customer" href="Issues(3)/Customer" />
  <category term="CustomerIssueEntitiesModel.Issue"
scheme="http://schemas.microsoft.com/ado/2007/08/dataservices/scheme" />
```

```xml
      <content type="application/xml">
        <m:properties>
          <d:IssueID m:type="Edm.Int32">3</d:IssueID>
          <d:CustomerID m:type="Edm.Int32">1</d:CustomerID>
          <d:IssueDate m:type="Edm.DateTime">2009-11-10T16:50:18.43</d:IssueDate>
          <d:ResolvedDate m:type="Edm.DateTime">2009-11-11T16:50:18.43</d:ResolvedDate>
          <d:Description>My computer came in how do I open the box?</d:Description>
          <d:Resolution m:null="true" />
        </m:properties>
      </content>
    </entry>
  </feed>
```

Through all these requests, you can start to see how REST works. It's just as easy to update the data. For example, if you wanted to update the first customer, you could post the field names to `WebDataService1 .svc/Customers(1)` from any Web form. This creates a very powerful API that you could expose to other third parties and such. But how does this apply to Silverlight? To see that, add a reference to the ADO.NET Data Service just as you have done with the other services.

Now that you have the reference, add a `DataGrid` to your `MainPage.xaml` as shown here:

Available for download on Wrox.com

```xml
<UserControl xmlns:my="clr-
namespace:System.Windows.Controls;assembly=System.Windows.Controls.Data"
x:Class="ProVB_SLServices.MainPage"
    xmlns="http://schemas.microsoft.com/winfx/2006/xaml/presentation"
    xmlns:x="http://schemas.microsoft.com/winfx/2006/xaml"
    xmlns:d="http://schemas.microsoft.com/expression/blend/2008"
    xmlns:mc="http://schemas.openxmlformats.org/markup-compatibility/2006"
    mc:Ignorable="d"
    d:DesignHeight="300" d:DesignWidth="400">

    <Grid x:Name="LayoutRoot" Background="White">
        <my:DataGrid x:Name="dtGrid"></my:DataGrid>
    </Grid>
</UserControl>
```

Code snippet from MainPage.xaml

Now let's see how you get the data and bind it to the grid. This is actually very simple. You will leverage what you have learned about LINQ to make a LINQ call directly to the Web service; but because ADO.NET Data Services is asynchronous, you need to have a function to receive the data. Here is what the code looks like:

Available for download on Wrox.com

```vb
Imports System.Data.Services.Client

Partial Public Class MainPage
    Inherits UserControl

    Public Sub New()
        InitializeComponent()
    End Sub

    Private Sub MainPage_Loaded(ByVal sender As Object,
       ByVal e As System.Windows.RoutedEventArgs) Handles Me.Loaded
        TestADODS()
    End Sub

    Private Sub TestADODS()

        Dim entities As New
  ServiceReference3.CustomerIssueEntitiesModel.CustomerIssueEntities(New
Uri("WebDataService1.svc", UriKind.Relative))
```

```
            Dim customers As DataServiceQuery(Of
    ServiceReference3.CustomerIssueEntitiesModel.Customer) = _
                From e In entities.Customers _
                Select e

            customers.BeginExecute(
    New AsyncCallback(AddressOf OnCustomersLoaded), customers)
        End Sub

        Private Sub OnCustomersLoaded(ByVal result As IAsyncResult)

            Dim customerQuery As DataServiceQuery(Of
        ServiceReference3.CustomerIssueEntitiesModel.Customer) = result.AsyncState

            Dim customers = customerQuery.EndExecute(result)

            dtGrid.ItemsSource = customers.ToList
        End Sub

    End Class
```

Code snippet from MainPage.xaml

Now that you have seen how easy it is to get data from an ADO.NET Data Service, you are ready to look at the last service type, RIA Services, which offers the best options for Silverlight developers.

MODEL-VIEW-VIEWMODEL

Now that you know how to develop Web services to interact with data on the server, let's take a look at a suggested best practice regarding how to interact with the data. Silverlight (and WPF for that matter) caters to using a pattern called Model-View-ViewModel (MVVM), which highly isolates the individual parts of a line-of-business application into pieces that are easily tested and maintained. This section provides a high-level overview of MVVM and what it means for you.

Separation of Concerns

Traditionally, developers have done a poor job of designing applications that keep a true separation of concerns. For example, if you have a business rule saying that the Customer name is required on customer, then, in the past, you might put code on every user control in which you let someone edit customer to validate that they entered the name. This is not too bad on small projects, but what happens when that project grows, and you give users various ways to edit the same data, and you need to add a new business rule; must you edit every user control to handle that business rule? Not with MVVM, which simplifies your project by isolating these needs into discrete testable units.

While MVVM does not reduce the amount of code you need to write, and in most cases can actually mean more code, it creates very manageable code in the long run. It is also a pattern that can be a little intimidating to jump into at first, to do it in the true MVVM fashion. Throughout this section, we will describe how to build the MVVM pattern for the database we created, highlighting the true strengths of MVVM.

The Model

The Model is the first M in the MVVM pattern, and this is very similar, if not identical, to what you have learned about the MVC pattern for ASP.NET. A model class is a simple class that merely handles the description of the data and validation of the data. For example, if we created a Model for the Customer in our database, it might look something like this:

```vbnet
Imports System.ComponentModel.DataAnnotations

Namespace Models
    Public Class Customer
        Inherits ModelBase

        <Display(AutoGenerateField:=False)>
        Public Property CustomerID As Integer

        Private _Name As String
        <Display(Name:="Customer Name", Order:=0, Description:="This is the Customer's Name")>
        <Required()>
        Public Property Name As String
            Get
                Return _Name
            End Get
            Set(ByVal value As String)
                _Name = value
                RaisePropertyChange("Name")
            End Set
        End Property

        Private _PhoneNumber As String
        <Display(Name:="Phone Number", Order:=1)>
        <RegularExpression("^0{0,1}[1-9]{1}[0-9]{2}[\s]{0,1}[\-]{0,1}[\s]{0,1}[1-9]
{1}[0-9]{6}$",
ErrorMessage:="Please enter valid Phone Number (xxx) xxx-xxxx")>
        Public Property PhoneNumber As String
            Get
                Return _PhoneNumber
            End Get
            Set(ByVal value As String)
                _PhoneNumber = value
                RaisePropertyChange("PhoneNumber")
            End Set
        End Property

        Private _EMailAddress As String
        <Display(Name:="EMail Address", Order:=2)>
        <Required()>
        <RegularExpression("^([0-9a-zA-Z]([-.\w]*[0-9a-zA-Z])*@([0-9a-zA-Z][-\w]*[0
-9a-zA-Z]\.)+[a-zA-Z]{2,9})$", ErrorMessage:="Please enter valid email address")>
        Public Property EMailAddress As String
            Get
                Return _EMailAddress
            End Get
            Set(ByVal value As String)
                _EMailAddress = value
                RaisePropertyChange("EMailAddress")
            End Set
        End Property

        Private _Address As String
        <Display(Name:="Address", Order:=3)>
        Public Property Address As String
            Get
                Return _Address
            End Get
            Set(ByVal value As String)
                _Address = value
                RaisePropertyChange("Address")
            End Set
```

```
            End Property

            Private _City As String
            <Display(Name:="City", Order:=4)>
            Public Property City As String
                Get
                    Return _City
                End Get
                Set(ByVal value As String)
                    _City = value
                    RaisePropertyChange("City")
                End Set
            End Property

            Private _State As String
            <Display(Name:="State", Order:=5)>
            Public Property State As String
                Get
                    Return _State
                End Get
                Set(ByVal value As String)
                    _State = value
                    RaisePropertyChange("State")
                End Set
            End Property

            Private _Zip As String
            <Display(Name:="Zip", Order:=6)>
            Public Property Zip As String
                Get
                    Return _Zip
                End Get
                Set(ByVal value As String)
                    _Zip = value
                    RaisePropertyChange("Zip")
                End Set
            End Property


        End Class
    End Namespace
```

Code snippet from MyModels

As you can see, this model simply describes the data. You can also do custom validation in the model by using the `CustomValidation` attribute — for example, to do more complex validation you may need to use the regular expression validation.

Through such a simple model class you have centralized all of your business logic for the `Customer` class. This makes the class very simple to test and very reusable. If you create a `List(Of Customer)` and bind it to a data grid, it will use this logic to validate the rows; or if you bind one instance of the `Customer` class to a `DataForm`, it will also use the same validation. Clearly, centralizing this logic in one place creates powerful code.

The other part of the implementation for the model is the model base. All models in your project should inherit from a `ModelBase` class. This is how you can centralize how you implement the `INotifyPropertyChanged` needs of a model. Here is the sample `ModelBase` for this project:

```
Imports System
Imports System.Collections.Generic
Imports System.ComponentModel
Imports System.ComponentModel.DataAnnotations

Namespace Models
```

```
    Public MustInherit Class ModelBase
        Implements INotifyPropertyChanged

        Private Property validationResults() As List(Of ValidationResult)

        Protected Sub RaisePropertyChange(ByVal ParamArray propertyname() As String)
            For Each s As String In propertyname
                RaiseEvent PropertyChanged(Me, New PropertyChangedEventArgs(s))
            Next

        End Sub

        Protected Sub Validate(ByVal value As Object, ByVal propertyName As String)
            Validator.ValidateProperty(value,
                New ValidationContext(Me, Nothing, Nothing))
        End Sub

        Public Function IsValid() As Boolean
            Return Validator.TryValidateObject(Me,
                New ValidationContext(Me, Nothing, Nothing), Me.validationResults, True)
        End Function


        Public Event PropertyChanged(ByVal sender As Object,
    ByVal e As System.ComponentModel.PropertyChangedEventArgs)
    Implements System.ComponentModel.INotifyPropertyChanged.PropertyChanged

        End Class
    End Namespace
```

Code snippet from MyModels

The `PropertyChanged` event is what lets the View know that something changed in your model. This is the most basic model implementation for MVVM.

The View

The View is simply the user interface to which you will bind your ViewModel. The ViewModel should simply be a description of where fields are placed to display data. If you read various references outlining the ways to do MVVM, you will find many highly opinionated developers who believe that there should be zero code in your code-behind for your views. While this is a noble goal, it is not always practical.

The View is generally just a simple user control to place controls on the form; but there is also an out-of-the-box view called DataForm that will use the metadata from the model to generate the form. This is great for building applications quickly and easily.

That is just one way to create a View; the other is to actually define the fields directly on the user control. To bind a text field to a model, you would do the following:

```
<TextBox Text="{Binding CompanyName,Mode=TwoWay,ValidatesOnDataErrors=True,
NotifyOnValidationError=True}" />
```

This will allow the View to receive validation errors directly from the model. For you, this means that there is no business logic in your View — it is self-contained in the Model, which creates an ideal way of testing your UI also.

The ViewModel

The final part of the MVVM puzzle is the ViewModel. You can think of this as the glue that binds the Model and the View together. It is what will go and get the data from the Web service and fill a collection of your model class to bind to other controls.

In addition, you will bind the View's data context to an instance of the ViewModel. This basically becomes the code-behind for your view except that it is loosely tied to the view so you can reuse it for multiple views. This also gives you great flexibility for testing and much more.

SUMMARY

In this chapter you saw how to interact with various types of Web services, and used that knowledge to build a basic MVVM application. This will give you a foundation for building stronger Silverlight line-of-business applications. The lessons you have learned throughout this chapter, Chapter 18, and Chapter 19 should enable you to build very powerful Silverlight applications with rich interfaces. There are also many new technologies coming with Silverlight 4 that will continue to make it easier to build applications, and using less code.

21

Working with ASP.NET

WHAT YOU WILL LEARN IN THIS CHAPTER

➤ Overview of ASP.NET

➤ Introduction to Web Forms

➤ Using server controls

➤ Working with events

➤ Understanding ViewState

➤ Adding validation

➤ Building data-driven applications

ASP.NET is a Web application framework (built on top of the .NET framework) that enables you to build powerful, secure, and dynamic applications in a highly productive environment. This chapter introduces ASP.NET and helps get you started building applications for the Web.

THE HISTORY OF ASP.NET

The technologies and practices around Web development have changed considerably since .NET was first released in 2002, and ASP.NET has evolved to keep up. The additions of the provider model, ASP.NET AJAX, ASP.NET MVC, ASP.NET Dynamic Data, Silverlight, and SharePoint have enabled Web developers on the Microsoft platform to build applications that meet the needs and expectations of today's consumer.

Here's a brief summary of the versions of ASP.NET and some of the key features introduced with each version.

VERSION	FEATURES
1.0/1.1	Web Forms
2.0	Master pages
	Themes and skins
	DataSource controls

continues

(continued)

VERSION	FEATURES
	Provider model
	Membership and profiles
	Navigation controls
	ASP.NET AJAX extensions
3.5	ASP.NET AJAX integrated in .NET Framework
	Support for REST and JSON in Web services
3.5 SP1	ASP.NET MVC
	ASP.NET Routing
	ASP.NET Dynamic Data
4.0	Web application deployment
	Web Forms additions (control over client IDs, support for routing, enhanced support for standards, integration with Dynamic Data)
	Microsoft Ajax Library additions (templates, observer, script loader)

KEY FEATURES OF ASP.NET

As you can see, there's a lot to cover to fully understand ASP.NET. We're not going to be able to get through all of it in this book so it's worth spending some time summarizing the key features before we get into the mechanics of building Web applications.

Developer Productivity

Much of ASP.NET's focus is on developer productivity. Huge gains were made with the move from Classic ASP to ASP.NET Web Forms. Server controls and the underlying framework removed the need for much of the tedious coding required when using existing Web development technologies.

Web Forms continues to evolve with each new version of the framework. ASP.NET AJAX makes it easy to handle user interactions with client-side JavaScript and Web service calls. Automated view generation (or scaffolding) and `HtmlHelper` classes assist in building ASP.NET MVC applications.

The ASP.NET development team is continually striving to add capabilities to the framework and to Visual Studio so that developers can focus on solving business problems, rather than "plumbing."

Performance and Scalability

The Microsoft team set out to provide the world's fastest Web application server. One of the most exciting performance features of ASP.NET is the caching capability aimed at exploiting Microsoft's SQL Server. This feature is called *SQL cache invalidation*. Before ASP.NET 2.0, it was possible to cache the results that came from SQL Server and to update the cache based on a time interval — for example, every 15 seconds or so. This meant that end users might see stale data if the result set changed sometime during that 15-second interval.

In some cases, this time interval result set is unacceptable. Ideally, the result set stored in the cache is destroyed if any underlying change occurs in the source from which the result set is retrieved — in this case, SQL Server. Ever since ASP.NET 2.0, you can make this happen with the use of SQL cache invalidation. When the result set from SQL Server changes, the output cache is triggered to change, and the end user always sees the latest result set. The data presented is never stale.

ASP.NET 4 provides 64-bit support, which means you can run your ASP.NET applications on 64-bit Intel or AMD processors. In addition, because ASP.NET 4 is fully backwardly compatible with ASP.NET 1.0/1.1

and 2.0, you can now take any former ASP.NET application, recompile it on the .NET Framework 4, and run it on a 64-bit processor.

Localization

ASP.NET and Visual Studio make it easy (well, relatively easy) to localize applications. Through the use of resource files (.resx), strongly typed resource access, and locale-aware data binding, you can build pages that will dynamically change based on the culture settings of the requester.

Health Monitoring

The built-in health-monitoring capabilities are rather significant features designed to make it easier to manage a deployed ASP.NET application. ASP.NET health monitoring is built around various health-monitoring events (referred to as *Web events*) occurring in your application. Using the health-monitoring system enables you to perform event logging for Web events such as failed logins, application starts and stops, or any unhandled exceptions. The event logging can occur in more than one place, so you can log to the Event Log or even back to a database. In addition to performing this disk-based logging, you can also use the system to e-mail health-monitoring information.

Besides working with specific events in your application, you can use the health-monitoring system to take health snapshots of a running application. As with many of the features built into ASP.NET, you can extend the health-monitoring system and create your own events for recording application information.

Easy Access to Data

ASP.NET Web Forms include a set of server controls designed to enable you to easily bind data to user interface elements on a page. Using these data controls can significantly reduce the amount of VB code you would need to write to manually retrieve data and bind to it — sometimes they eliminate the need for VB code altogether. Even better, this functionality is not limited to data coming from a relational database. In fact, several data-source server controls are at your disposal; and you can even create your own.

ASP.NET AJAX 4 adds client-side data-binding with the addition of the DataView control and client-side templates. These tools enable JSON (JavaScript Object Notation) objects to be bound to the values or attributes of elements in a page using a notation similar to that of WPF.

Administration and Management

The initial release of ASP.NET focused on the developer, and little thought was given to the people who had to administer and manage all the ASP.NET applications. Instead of working with consoles and wizards as they did in the past, administrators and managers of these new applications now had to work with unfamiliar XML configuration files such as machine.config and web.config.

To remedy this situation, if you are using Windows XP or Windows Server 2003, ASP.NET includes a Microsoft Management Console (MMC) snap-in that enables Web application administrators to edit configuration settings easily on-the-fly through IIS. If you are using one of the newer versions of Windows that include IIS 7.0, the IIS Manager has been enhanced to give you the same capabilities of the MMC snap-in.

VISUAL STUDIO SUPPORT FOR ASP.NET

Visual Studio 2010 offers a wide range of features to assist you in building applications; IntelliSense, code snippets, integrated debugging, CSS style support, and the ability to target multiple versions of the .NET framework are a few examples. When working with ASP.NET you'll see that many of these productivity features also apply when working with inline code, client-side JavaScript code, XML, and HTML markup.

Web Site and Web Application Projects

Visual Studio gives you two models for ASP.NET projects: Web site projects and Web application projects.

The Web site project model was added with Visual Studio 2005. This model is designed to be very lightweight and familiar to Web developers and designers coming to Visual Studio from other tools. It uses a folder structure to define the contents of a project, enabling you to open a website just by pointing Visual Studio at a folder or a virtual directory. The default deployment model uses dynamic compilation whereby VB source files are deployed along with markup and other content files. Alternatively, the project can be precompiled, which creates an assembly per folder or an assembly per page depending on settings passed to the complier. You can create a new website by selecting File ➪ New ➪ Web Site from the main menu in Visual Studio.

The Web application project model is very similar to other project types. The structure is based on a project file (.vbproj) and all VB code in the project compiles into a single assembly. To deploy, the assembly along with markup and static content files are copied to the server. You can create a new Web application project by selecting File ➪ New ➪ Project from the main menu in Visual Studio.

ASP.NET Application Folders

ASP.NET 2.0 added a set of special folders that have specific meaning to ASP.NET applications. By using these folders, you can have your code automatically compiled for you, your application themes accessible throughout your application, and your globalization resources available whenever you need them. The following sections show how these defined folders work. For additional information you can visit the ASP.NET Web Site Layout page on MSDN (http://msdn.microsoft.com/en-us/library/ex526337.aspx).

\App_Code Folder (Web Site Projects Only)

The \App_Code folder is meant to store your classes, .wsdl files, and typed data sets. Any of these items stored in this folder are then automatically available to all the pages within your solution. The nice thing about the \App_Code folder is that when you place something inside it, Visual Studio automatically detects this and compiles it if it is a class (such as a .vb file), automatically creates your XML Web service proxy class (from the .wsdl file), or automatically creates a typed data set for you from your .xsd files.

\App_Data Folder

The \App_Data folder holds the data stores used by the application. It is a good spot to centrally store all the data stores your application might use. The \App_Data folder can contain Microsoft SQL Express files (.mdf files), Microsoft Access files (.mdb files), XML files, and more.

The user account utilized by your application has read and write access to any of the files contained within the \App_Data folder. By default, this is the ASP.NET account. Another reason to store all your data files in this folder is that much of the ASP.NET system — from the membership and role management systems to the GUI tools such as the ASP.NET MMC snap-in, the new IIS Manager, and the ASP.NET Web Site Administration Tool — is built to work with the \App_Data folder.

\App_Themes Folder

Themes are a way of providing a common look and feel to your site across every page. You implement a theme by using a .skin file, CSS files, and images used by the server controls of your site. All these elements can make a *theme*, which is then stored in the \App_Themes folder of your solution. By storing these elements within the \App_Themes folder, you ensure that all the pages within the solution can take advantage of the theme and easily apply its elements to the controls and markup of the page.

\App_GlobalResources Folder

Resource files are string tables that can serve as data dictionaries for your applications when they require changes to content based on things such as changes in culture. You can add Assembly Resource files (.resx) to the \App_GlobalResources folder, and they are dynamically compiled and made part of the solution for use by all your .aspx pages in the application.

\App_LocalResources

Even if you are not interested in constructing application-wide resources using the \App_GlobalResources folder, you may want resources that can be used for a single .aspx page. You can do this very simply by using the \App_LocalResources folder.

Add page-specific resource files to the \App_LocalResources folder by constructing the name of the .resx file in the following manner:

➤ Default.aspx.resx

➤ Default.aspx.fi.resx

➤ Default.aspx.ja.resx

➤ Default.aspx.en-gb.resx

\App_WebReferences

The \App_WebReferences folder is a new name for the Web References folder used in earlier versions of ASP.NET. Using the \App_WebReferences folder, you have automatic access to the remote Web services referenced from your application.

\App_Browsers

The \App_Browsers folder holds .browser files, which are XML files used both to identify the browsers making requests to the application and to understand the capabilities of these browsers. You can find a list of globally accessible .browser files at C:\Windows\Microsoft.NET\Framework\v4.0.21006\ CONFIG\Browsers. If you want to change any part of these default browser definition files, just copy the appropriate .browser file from the Browsers folder to your application's \App_Browsers folder and change the definition.

Web Server Options

ASP.NET gives you several options to host your Web projects. The two most popular by far are IIS and the ASP.NET Development Server (also known as Cassini) that comes with Visual Studio. The ASP.NET Development Server is lightweight and convenient but it only allows you to run and test pages locally, and it does not include all the features of IIS. This is the default server for both Web site and Web application projects.

The mechanism used to select which server will be used depends on the project type. For Web site projects, you can choose in the New Web Site dialog by selecting an option from the Web Location drop-down. Selecting File System will use the development server, while selecting HTTP will use IIS.

For Web application projects you can set which server to use after the project has been created. This is done through the Web tab of the project properties. You can even switch back and forth, enabling you to do most of your development with the development server but switching to IIS when you want to test in an environment closer to production.

BUILDING ASP.NET APPLICATIONS USING WEB FORMS

ASP.NET offers two models for building Web applications: Web Forms and ASP.NET MVC (or just MVC for short). Web Forms has been around since .NET 1.0, and MVC was added with .NET 3.5 SP1 in late 2007. MVC is covered in detail in Chapter 23 so this chapter and the next focus on Web Forms.

Pages, Forms, Controls, and Events

When viewed as a whole, Web Forms is an abstraction that enables you to develop an ASP.NET application in almost exactly the same way you would develop a Windows Forms (or Classic VB) application. You build pages by dragging and dropping controls on a design surface, you set properties of those controls though the Properties window, you add event handlers by double-clicking the controls, and you have separation between the code generated by the designer and the code you write.

As you will see, this abstraction can be a little leaky, but on the whole it makes the transition from building client applications to building Web applications much more inviting than it was before .NET.

Server Controls

ASP.NET provides two distinct types of controls: HTML controls and Web server controls. Each type of control is quite different; and as you work with ASP.NET, you will see that much of the focus is on the Web server controls. This does not mean that HTML server controls have no value. They do provide you with many capabilities — some that Web server controls do not.

If you are wondering which is the better control type to use, it depends on what you are trying to achieve. HTML server controls map to specific HTML elements. You can place an `HtmlTable` server control on your ASP.NET page that works dynamically with a `<table>` element. On the other hand, Web server controls map to specific functionality that you want on your ASP.NET pages. This means an `<asp:Panel>` control might use a `<table>` or an `<IFrame>` element — it depends on the capability of the requesting browser.

The following list summarizes some advice regarding when to use HTML server controls and when to use Web server controls:

➤ Use HTML server:

   ➤ When converting traditional ASP 3.0 Web pages to ASP.NET Web pages and speed of completion is a concern. It is a lot easier to change your HTML elements to HTML server controls than it is to change them to Web server controls.

   ➤ When you prefer a more HTML-type programming model

   ➤ When you want to explicitly control the code that is generated for the browser

➤ Use Web server

   ➤ When you require a richer set of functionality to achieve complicated page requirements

   ➤ When you are developing Web pages that will be viewed by a multitude of browser types and therefore require different code based upon these types

   ➤ When you prefer a more Visual Basic–type programming model that is based on the use of controls and control properties

You have a couple of ways to use these controls to construct pages. You can use tools that enable you to visually drag and drop controls onto a design surface or you can work with server controls directly in the markup for the page.

To experience working with a page you can follow along with the instructions below or you can examine the sample project included with the book. The instructions below have you working with a single page over several steps while the sample project has a page including the work done up to the end of each step.

Create a folder named BasicWebForms somewhere in your file system. This folder will be used to store the files that make up the sample Web site we are about to build. Open Visual Studio 2010 and select File ➪ New ➪ Web Site. In the New Web Site dialog that comes up, select the Empty Web Site template, click the Browse button to navigate to the folder you just created and then click the Open button and the OK button to create the Web site (see Figure 21-1). Then create a page by right-clicking on the project and selecting Add New Item, selecting the Web Forms item template, setting the Name to Default.aspx (see Figure 21-2).

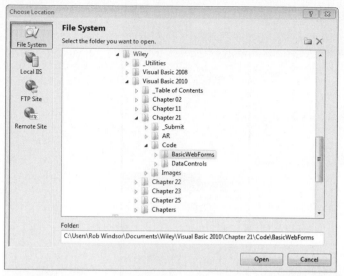

FIGURE 21-1

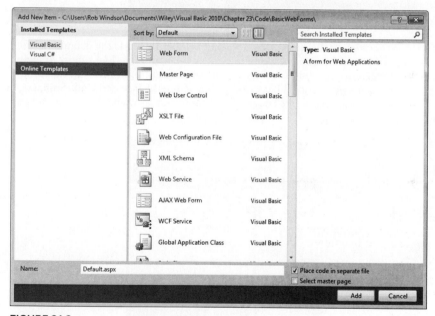

FIGURE 21-2

In the sample application, Step01-ServerControls.aspx contains all the code and markup you will add in this section.

With the project created, we can return to the discussion of controls. To use the drag-and-drop technique to build your page, click the Design or Split tab at the bottom of the design area in the IDE. When either of these views is active, you can drag and drop controls from the Toolbox onto the design surface, or you can place the cursor in the location where you want the control to appear and then double-click the control in the Toolbox (see Figure 21-3).

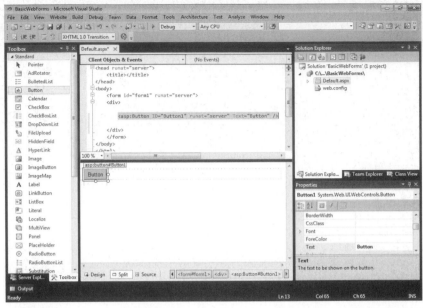

FIGURE 21-3

You also can work directly in the markup. Because many developers prefer this, it is the default view of a page. Hand-coding your own ASP.NET pages may seem to be a slower approach than simply dragging and dropping controls onto a design surface, but it isn't as slow as you might think. Many of the same productivity features available when editing Visual Basic code, such as IntelliSense and Code Snippets, are also available when editing page markup. Also, like Design view, the Source view enables you to drag and drop controls from the Toolbox into the markup itself (see Figure 21-4).

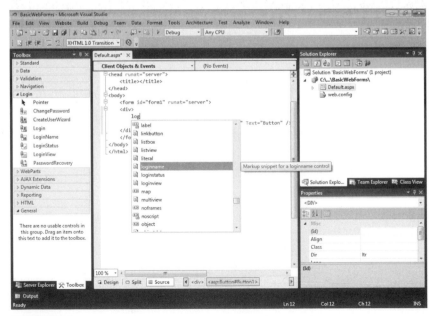

FIGURE 21-4

Whether you are in Design view or Source view, you can highlight a control to edit its properties in the Properties window. Changing the properties will change the appearance or behavior of the highlighted control. Because all controls inherit from a specific base class (`WebControl`), you can highlight multiple controls at the same time and change the base properties of all the controls at once by holding down the Ctrl key as you make your control selections.

Use the techniques described above to add controls to Default.aspx so that it looks like Figure 21-5 in split view. This is a simple form that will allow users to enter their name and e-mail address and submit them to some process by clicking a Submit button. The markup for the body of the page should look something like this:

Available for
download on
Wrox.com

```
<body>
    <form id="form1" runat="server">
    <div>
        <asp:Label ID="Label1" runat="server" Text="Name: "></asp:Label>
        <asp:TextBox ID="NameTextBox" runat="server" Width="200px"></asp:TextBox>
        <br />
        <asp:Label ID="Label2" runat="server" Text="Email: "></asp:Label>
        <asp:TextBox ID="EmailTextBox" runat="server" Width="200px"></asp:TextBox>
        <br />
        <asp:Button ID="SubmitButton" runat="server" Text="Submit" />
        <br />
        <br />
        <asp:Label ID="ResultsLabel" runat="server" Text="Label"></asp:Label>
    </div>
    </form>
</body>
```

Code snippet from Step01-ServerControls.aspx

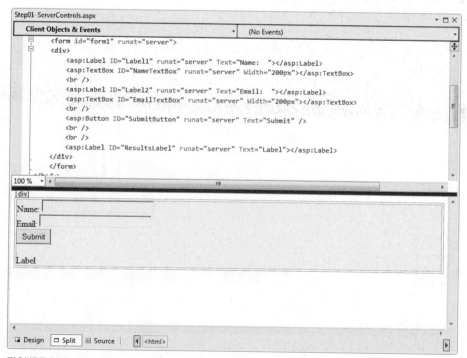

FIGURE 21-5

Events

ASP.NET Web Forms uses an event-driven model similar to that used with Windows Forms. Developers can handle events generated by the page or the controls that appear on the page. For example, the code to handle the Click event of the Submit button would look like this:

```
Protected Sub SubmitButton_Click(ByVal sender As Object, ByVal e As EventArgs)
    Handles SubmitButton.Click
    'Code actions here
End Sub
```

The key difference between ASP.NET Web Forms events and those of Windows Forms is what happens when an event occurs. The objects that make up a Windows Form exist as long as the form; thus, they maintain state across user interactions. Because of the stateless model of the Web, the objects that make up the page (in the sample project that means the page, the labels, the text boxes, and the button) only live long enough to generate the markup for that page. Once a request is complete and the final markup has been sent to the client browser, the objects that comprise the page are orphaned and they await garbage collection.

Since the original objects are no longer available, new objects will need to be created for the event code to run. Therefore, when a user interaction triggers a server-side event, a request is sent to the server, which includes information about the event; the page and the control objects are created on the server; the internal state of these objects is set using information passed in the request; the event handler executes; and an updated version of the page is sent back to the client browser. This process is called a *postback*.

The code for an event handler can use the traditional ASP style and be placed inline in the same page as your markup, as shown here:

```
<script runat="server">
    Protected Sub SubmitButton_Click(ByVal sender As Object, ByVal e As EventArgs)
    Handles SubmitButton.Click
        'Code actions here
    End Sub
</script>
```

However, the more common approach is to use a *code-behind file* (sometimes called a *code-beside file*). The idea of using the code-behind model is to separate the business logic and presentation logic into their own files. This makes it easier to work with your pages, especially if you are working in a team environment where visual designers work on the UI of the page and coders work on the business logic that sits behind the presentation pieces. The code-behind file is associated with the ASPX file through attributes of the Page directive. Note that the Page directive will differ slightly depending on whether you are using the Web site or Web application project type.

```
<%@ Page Language="vb" AutoEventWireup="false"
    CodeBehind="Default.aspx.vb" Inherits="BasicWebForms._Default" %>
```

How do you hook up these events for server controls? Again, the model is similar to that seen in Windows Forms. You can double-click a control in the Design view to add the handler for the default event for that control, you can use Event view in the Properties window (see Figure 21-6), or you can use the drop-downs at the top of the Code Editor (see Figure 21-7).

FIGURE 21-6

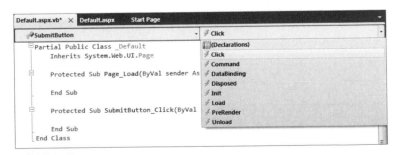

FIGURE 21-7

In the sample application, Step02-Events.aspx is the completed version of the page up to the end of this section.

Add an event handler for the Click event of the Submit button. In the event handler show the values for the name and e-mail entered by the user in the Result label. The code shown here will accomplish this:

```vb
Protected Sub SubmitButton_Click(ByVal sender As Object, ByVal e As EventArgs)
    Handles SubmitButton.Click
    ResultsLabel.Text = String.Format("You entered Name: {0} and Email: {1}",
        NameTextBox.Text, EmailTextBox.Text)
End Sub
```

Code snippet from Step02-Events.aspx.vb

Figure 21-8 shows the page before the Submit button is clicked and Figure 21-9 shows the page after.

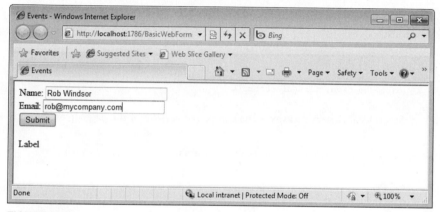

FIGURE 21-8

FIGURE 21-9

Page Life Cycle

In addition to handling the events of controls, you will often want to handle the events raised during the life cycle of the page. This enables you to tailor the generation of the page to suit your needs.

Here is a list of the commonly used events in the page life cycle. Additional events are possible, but those are primarily used by developers creating custom server controls.

1. PreInit
2. Init
3. InitComplete
4. PreLoad
5. Load
6. LoadComplete
7. PreRender
8. SaveStateComplete
9. Unload

Of these, the most frequently used is the Load event, which is generally used to initialize the properties of the page and its child controls:

```
Protected Sub Page_Load(ByVal sender As Object, ByVal e As System.EventArgs)
    Handles Me.Load
    ' Retrieve data from a database or service
    ' Use data to populate the properties of controls
End Sub
```

In the sample application, Step03-PageLifecycle.aspx is the completed version of the page up to the end of this section.

Go back to your application and add a drop-down list to enable users to enter the state in which they live:

```
<asp:Label ID="Label3" runat="server" Text="State: "></asp:Label>
<asp:DropDownList ID="StateDropDown" runat="server" Width="200px">
</asp:DropDownList>
```

Code snippet from Step03-PageLifecycle.aspx

In the Load event for the page, we'll populate this control with a few state names. We'll also update the Submit button's Click event handler to output the selected state:

```
Protected Sub Page_Load(ByVal sender As Object, ByVal e As System.EventArgs)
    Handles Me.Load
    ResultsLabel.Text = String.Empty
    StateDropDown.Items.Add("New York")
    StateDropDown.Items.Add("California")
    StateDropDown.Items.Add("Florida")
End Sub

Protected Sub SubmitButton_Click(ByVal sender As Object, ByVal e As EventArgs)
    Handles SubmitButton.Click
    ResultsLabel.Text = String.Format(
        "You entered Name: {0}, Email: {1}, and State: {2}",
        NameTextBox.Text, EmailTextBox.Text, StateDropDown.Text)
End Sub
```

Code snippet from Step03-PageLifecycle.aspx.vb

Running the sample now seems to work correctly, but if you inspect the items in the State drop-down after clicking the Submit button at least once, you'll notice that they appear multiple times (see Figure 21-10). It seems that the values in the control are being persisted across page requests and that the code in the Page_Load event handler is adding to the existing items instead of populating the item collection from scratch.

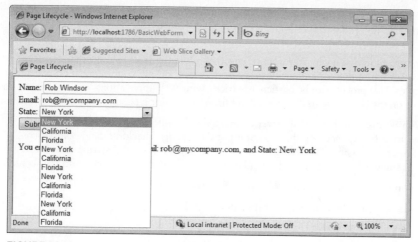

FIGURE 21-10

ViewState

As previously mentioned, the `Page` object and each of its child controls are constructed on each request. The ASP.NET team needed a way to persist some of the properties of the controls across postbacks to maintain the illusion that pages were living across requests. What they came up with is a somewhat ingenious trick called ViewState.

The properties that need to be persisted across calls are packaged up and encoded and then placed in a hidden field within the page. When a postback occurs, these values are unpackaged and placed into the properties of the newly created server controls. The ViewState for a page looks something like this:

```
<input type="hidden" name="__VIEWSTATE" id="__VIEWSTATE" value="/
wEPDwUKMjAxNDUzMTQ4NA9kFgICAw9kFgQCEQ8QZA8WA2YCAQICFgMQBQhOZXcgWW9yawUI
TmV3IFlvcmtnEAUKQ2FsaWZvcm5pYQUKQ2FsaWZvcm5pYWcQBQdGbG9yaWRhBQdGbG9yaWRhZ2Rk
AhUPDxYCHgRUZXh0ZWRkZFU1smgJJtYR8JfiZ/9yASSM5EIp" />
```

ViewState can be turned off at the page or the control level via the `EnableViewState` property. The ASP .NET team has gone to great lengths to keep the size of ViewState as small as possible but it still needs to be monitored and managed. Unchecked, ViewState can get large enough to affect the load times of your pages.

With these facts in mind, a simple adjustment is all that is required to address the issue with the sample project. In the `Page_Load` event handler, we need to check if the current request is a postback. If it is, the items will be populated automatically from the ViewState; otherwise, we need to execute our code to get the items into the control:

Available for download on Wrox.com

```
Protected Sub Page_Load(ByVal sender As Object, ByVal e As System.EventArgs)
    Handles Me.Load
    ResultsLabel.Text = String.Empty
    If Not Me.IsPostBack Then
        StateDropDown.Items.Add("New York")
        StateDropDown.Items.Add("California")
        StateDropDown.Items.Add("Florida")
    End If
End Sub
```

Code snippet from Step04-ViewState.aspx.vb

Now, no matter how many times you click the button, the list will have the proper number of items.

In the sample application, Step04-ViewState.aspx is the completed version of the page up to this point.

Field Validation

Validating user input is important in two ways: You want to effectively communicate to users that they have entered invalid data, and you want to prevent a malicious user from compromising your application (via a SQL injection attack, for example). This process can be particularly tricky with Web applications, as you want to do as much validation as possible on the client side so that users don't have to wait for a postback to see potential issues.

Fortunately, ASP.NET Web Forms include a set of server controls that handle common validation needs, including checking for required fields, checking the type of input data, range checking, field comparison, and data validation by regular expression. By adding these controls to your page and setting the required properties, the ASP.NET Framework will add code to validate input on both the client side and the server side.

The key properties common to the validation controls are as follows:

➤ `ControlToValidate` — The control whose state will be validated

➤ `Text` — The message to show beside the control

➤ `ErrorMessage` — Detailed information to show in a summary

➤ `SetFocusOnError` — Move the focus to the target control when invalid

In addition to the controls that perform validation, a `ValidationSummary` control will display a summary of the appropriate error messages when the user attempts to submit invalid values.

Continuing with your project, add validation controls to ensure that the user enters a value for the Name and E-mail fields (using the `RequiredFieldValidator`) and that the e-mail address is in the proper format (using the `RegularExpressionValidator`). Figure 21-11 shows the Design view of the page. The updated markup is shown here:

Available for
download on
Wrox.com

```
<body>
    <form id="form1" runat="server">
    <div>
        <asp:Label ID="Label1" runat="server" Text="Name: "></asp:Label>
        <asp:TextBox ID="NameTextBox" runat="server" Width="200px"></asp:TextBox>
         
        <asp:RequiredFieldValidator
            ID="RequiredFieldValidator1" runat="server"
            ControlToValidate="NameTextBox"
            ErrorMessage="You must enter a name"
            SetFocusOnError="True">*</asp:RequiredFieldValidator>
        <br />
        <asp:Label ID="Label2" runat="server" Text="Email: "></asp:Label>
        <asp:TextBox ID="EmailTextBox" runat="server" Width="200px"></asp:TextBox>
         
        <asp:RequiredFieldValidator
            ID="RequiredFieldValidator2" runat="server"
            ControlToValidate="EmailTextBox"
            ErrorMessage="You must enter an email address"
            SetFocusOnError="True">*</asp:RequiredFieldValidator>
         
        <asp:RegularExpressionValidator
            ID="RegularExpressionValidator1" runat="server"
            ControlToValidate="EmailTextBox"
            ErrorMessage="The email address has an invalid format"
            ValidationExpression="\w+([-+.']\w+)*@\w+([-.]\w+)*\.\w+([-.]\w+)*">
            *
            </asp:RegularExpressionValidator>
        <br />
        <asp:Label ID="Label3" runat="server" Text="State: "></asp:Label>
        <asp:DropDownList ID="StateDropDown" runat="server" Width="200px">
        </asp:DropDownList>
        <br />
```

```
            <asp:Button ID="SubmitButton" runat="server" Text="Submit" />
            <br />
            <br />
            <asp:Label ID="ResultsLabel" runat="server" Text="Label"></asp:Label>
            <asp:ValidationSummary ID="ValidationSummary1" runat="server" />
        </div>
        </form>
</body>
```

Code snippet from Step05-Validation.aspx

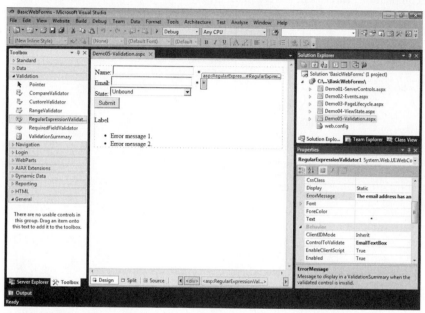

FIGURE 21-11

Figure 21-12 shows the page after an attempt to submit with an invalid name and an improperly formatted e-mail address.

In the sample application, Step05-Validation.aspx is the completed version of the page.

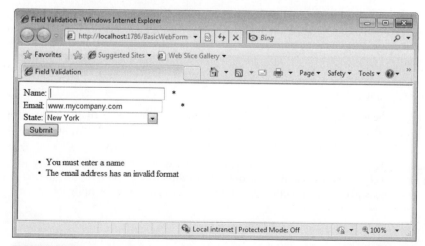

FIGURE 21-12

Compilation

One of the big advantages that ASP.NET has over other Web development tools is that it uses compiled code. You can observe the effects of the compilation process when you navigate to a page the first time after an update; it will take noticeably longer because the page is being parsed and compiled. When an ASP.NET page is hit for the first time, the request is passed to the ASP.NET page parser, which takes the markup for the page and converts it into a VB class (see Figure 21-13). ASP.NET then compiles the class (and the code-behind if you are using a Web site project) and caches the DLL in the Framework folders. Subsequent requests for the page will use the compiled code from the cached DLL. If an updated version of the page is deployed, the dynamic compilation process will be repeated.

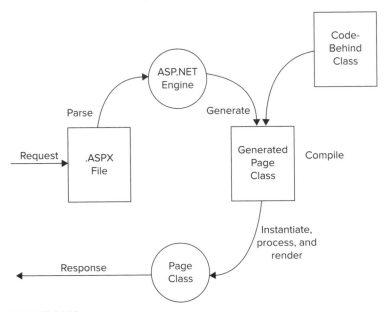

FIGURE 21-13

If you are using the Web site project model, ASP.NET allows you to precompile your site (both Web pages and code) prior to deployment, thus avoiding the cost of dynamic compilation. This is discussed further in the next section.

Deployment

Like many other areas of .NET and Visual Studio, you have several options when it is time to deploy your website to the server on which it will be hosted.

If you have network access to the server, you can just copy the required files using Windows Explorer. If you are using the Web site project model and you haven't precompiled your site, you copy the VB source code files to the server; otherwise, you will not.

The next option (traditionally the most common) is to copy the files via FTP. Several available programs make this easy. If you are using the Web site project model, you can use the Copy Web Site utility built into Visual Studio. Just select Website ➪ Copy Web Site from the main menu.

Another option for those using the Web site project model is the Publish Web Site utility. This utility precompiles the content of the website and then copies the output to a directory or server location that you specify. You can publish directly as part of the precompilation process or you can precompile locally and then copy the files yourself using Windows Explorer or FTP. The Publish Web Site utility can be accessed by selecting Build ⇨ Publish Web Site from the main menu.

For those that are using Web application projects, Visual Studio 2010 adds some interesting new capabilities when it comes to deployment: Web.config Transformations, an integrated Web Deployment Tool, and Web One-Click Deployment. Due to space limitations, we are not going to be able to cover this topic here. For more information, you can check out the Making Web Deployment Easier episode of the 10-4 Show on Channel 9 (http://channel9.msdn.com/shows/10-4/10-4-Episode-10-Making-Web- Deployment-Easier/).

DATA-DRIVEN APPLICATIONS

ASP.NET provides several server controls that make it easy for you to work with data in your pages. As data for your applications finds itself in more and more types of data stores, it can sometimes be a nightmare to figure out how to get at and aggregate these information sets onto a Web page in a simple and logical manner. ASP.NET data source controls are meant to work with a specific type of data store by connecting to them and performing operations such as inserts, updates, and deletes — all on your behalf. The following table details the data source controls included in .NET 4:

DATA SOURCE CONTROL	DESCRIPTION
SqlDataSource	Enables you to work with any SQL-based database, such as Microsoft SQL Server or Oracle
AccessDataSource	Enables you to work with a Microsoft Access file (.mdb)
ObjectDataSource	Enables you to work with custom business objects
LinqDataSource	Enables you to use LINQ to query everything — from in-memory collections to databases
EntityDataSource	Enables you to work with an Entity Data Model
XmlDataSource	Enables you to work with the information from an XML source (e.g., a file or an RSS feed)
SiteMapDataSource	Enables you to work with the hierarchical data represented in the site map file (.sitemap)

In tandem with the data source controls, ASP.NET provides a number of server controls that you can use to display and interact with data on a page. These controls have sophisticated two-way data-binding, enabling you to attach to the data source controls by setting a few properties. In addition to the standard controls such as the TextBox, ListBox, and CheckBox, there are more complex controls such as the GridView, FormView, and ListView.

Data Binding with the SqlDataSource Control

The instructions in this section assume you have a SQL Server 2005 or 2008 Express instance named SqlExpress. If you have the full version of SQL Server or are using a differently named instance, you will need to modify the connection strings shown accordingly. If you do not have SQL Server at all, the easiest way to get the Express version is to use Microsoft's Web Platform Installer (www.microsoft.com/web/downloads/platform.aspx).

To explore the use of the data controls, let's turn to Visual Studio. Create a new Web application project named DataControls by selecting File ⇨ New Project and completing the New Project dialog as shown in Figure 21-14. Once the project has been created, add a new page named Step01-Sql.aspx.

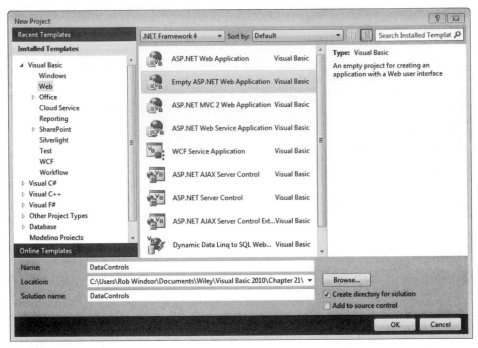

FIGURE 21-14

For all of the data-access examples in this chapter and the next, you will need the Northwind database. To get this database you have two options. If you are using SQL Express, you can use the local version included with the book's sample code. Just copy Northwind.mdb from the sample code into the App_Data folder of your Web project. The other option, whether you are using SQL Express or the full version of SQL Server, is to add the Northwind database to a SQL instance. Do a search for "Northwind and pubs Sample Databases for SQL Server 2000." This should take you to www.microsoft.com/downloads/ details.aspx?familyid=06616212-0356-46a0-8da2-eebc53a68034&displaylang=en. Even though the download page indicates the databases are for SQL Server 2000, they will work with newer versions of the product. Once installed, you will find the Northwind.mdf file in the C:\ SQL Server 2000 Sample Databases directory.

Assuming you now have a sample database available, you can return to the Visual Studio project. Add a `SqlDataSource` control from the Data tab of the Toolbox to the page created earlier. This control is nonvisual, so it appears as a gray box on the design surface. Use the smart tag on the `SqlDataSource` control to access the Configure Data Source Wizard. Working through the wizard, you must choose your data connection and then indicate whether you want to store this connection in the `web.config` file which is highly advisable. Figure 21-15 shows the configuration process for a local Northwind database.

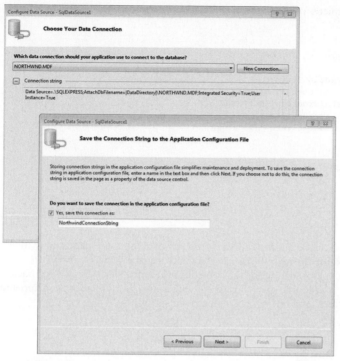

FIGURE 21-15

Within this configuration process, you also choose the table you are going to work with, and test out the queries that the wizard generates. For this example, choose the Customers table and select every row by checking the * check box, as shown in Figure 21-16.

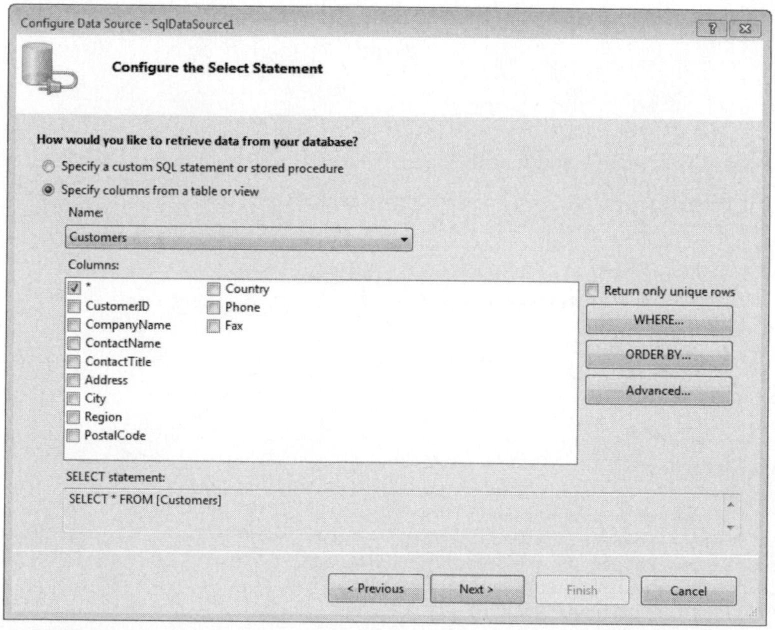

FIGURE 21-16

When the configuration process is complete, you will notice that your `web.config` file has changed to include the connection string:

```
<configuration>

    <connectionStrings>
        <add name="NorthwindConnectionString"
        connectionString="Data Source=.\SQLEXPRESS;
            AttachDbFilename=|DataDirectory|\NORTHWND.MDF;
            Integrated Security=True;User Instance=True"
        providerName="System.Data.SqlClient" />
    </connectionStrings>

    <system.web>
        . . .
    </system.web>
</configuration>
```

Code snippet from Web.config

Once you have configured the `SqlDataSource` control, add a `GridView` control to the page and connect it to the `SqlDataSource`. This can be done through the `GridView` control's smart tag, as shown in Figure 21-17. You can also enable paging and sorting for the control in the same form. Finally, go back to the smart tag and click the Auto Format link to give your `GridView` control a more appealing appearance than the default provided. Choose the look and feel that best suits your mood.

FIGURE 21-17

The code generated by the wizard (it is also how you would code it yourself) is shown here:

```
<%@ Page Language="vb" AutoEventWireup="false" CodeBehind="Step01-Sql.aspx.vb"
    Inherits="DataControls.Step01_Sql" %>

<!DOCTYPE html PUBLIC "-//W3C//DTD XHTML 1.0 Transitional//EN"
    "http://www.w3.org/TR/xhtml1/DTD/xhtml1-transitional.dtd">

<html xmlns="http://www.w3.org/1999/xhtml">
<head runat="server">
    <title>SqlDataSource Example</title>
</head>
<body>
    <form id="form1" runat="server">
    <div>
        <asp:GridView ID="GridView1" runat="server"
            AllowPaging="True" AllowSorting="True"
            AutoGenerateColumns="False" DataKeyNames="CustomerID"
            DataSourceID="SqlDataSource1" CellPadding="4"
            ForeColor="#333333" GridLines="None">
            <AlternatingRowStyle BackColor="White" />
            <Columns>
```

```
            <asp:BoundField DataField="CustomerID" HeaderText="CustomerID"
                ReadOnly="True" SortExpression="CustomerID" />
            <asp:BoundField DataField="CompanyName" HeaderText="CompanyName"
                SortExpression="CompanyName" />
            <asp:BoundField DataField="ContactName" HeaderText="ContactName"
                SortExpression="ContactName" />
            <asp:BoundField DataField="ContactTitle" HeaderText="ContactTitle"
                SortExpression="ContactTitle" />
            <asp:BoundField DataField="Address" HeaderText="Address"
                SortExpression="Address" />
            <asp:BoundField DataField="City" HeaderText="City"
                SortExpression="City" />
            <asp:BoundField DataField="Region" HeaderText="Region"
                SortExpression="Region" />
            <asp:BoundField DataField="PostalCode" HeaderText="PostalCode"
                SortExpression="PostalCode" />
            <asp:BoundField DataField="Country" HeaderText="Country"
                SortExpression="Country" />
            <asp:BoundField DataField="Phone" HeaderText="Phone"
                SortExpression="Phone" />
            <asp:BoundField DataField="Fax" HeaderText="Fax"
                SortExpression="Fax" />
        </Columns>
        <EditRowStyle BackColor="#2461BF" />
        <FooterStyle BackColor="#507CD1" Font-Bold="True"
            ForeColor="White" />
        <HeaderStyle BackColor="#507CD1" Font-Bold="True"
            ForeColor="White" />
        <PagerStyle BackColor="#2461BF"
            ForeColor="White" HorizontalAlign="Center" />
        <RowStyle BackColor="#EFF3FB" />
        <SelectedRowStyle BackColor="#D1DDF1"
            Font-Bold="True" ForeColor="#333333" />
        <SortedAscendingCellStyle BackColor="#F5F7FB" />
        <SortedAscendingHeaderStyle BackColor="#6D95E1" />
        <SortedDescendingCellStyle BackColor="#E9EBEF" />
        <SortedDescendingHeaderStyle BackColor="#4870BE" />
    </asp:GridView>
    <asp:SqlDataSource ID="SqlDataSource1" runat="server"
        ConnectionString=
            "<%$ ConnectionStrings:NorthwindConnectionString %>"
        SelectCommand="SELECT * FROM [Customers]"></asp:SqlDataSource>
</div>
</form>
</body>
</html>
```

Code snippet from Step01-Sql.aspx

Looking at the markup for the `SqlDataSource`, notice that the `SelectCommand` attribute contains the query you built when configuring the data source. Also note that the `ConnectionString` attribute points at a setting placed inside the `web.config` file. You could put the connection string directly in the page but that would likely make maintenance more difficult if you ever needed to make a change.

Looking now at the `GridView` control, you can see how easy it is to add paging and sorting capabilities. It is simply a matter of adding the attributes `AllowPaging` and `AllowSorting` to the control and setting their values to `True` (they are set to `False` by default):

Available for
download on
Wrox.com

```
<asp:GridView ID="GridView1" runat="server"
    AllowPaging="True" AllowSorting="True"
    AutoGenerateColumns="False" DataKeyNames="CustomerID"
    DataSourceID="SqlDataSource1" CellPadding="4"
```

```
    ForeColor="#333333" GridLines="None">
  <!-- Inner content removed for clarity -->
</asp:GridView>
```

Code snippet from Step01-Sql.aspx

Each of the columns from the Customers table of the Northwind database is defined in the control through the use of the `<asp:BoundField>` control, a subcontrol of the `GridView`. The `BoundField` control enables you to specify the header text of the column through the use of the `HeaderText` attribute. The `DataField` attribute actually ties the values displayed in this column to a particular value from the Customers table, and the `SortExpression` attribute should use the same values for sorting — unless you are sorting on a different value than what is being displayed.

Ultimately, when your run your page it should look similar to what is shown in Figure 21-18.

CustomerID	CompanyName	ContactName	ContactTitle	Address	City	Region	PostalCode	Country	Phone	Fax
ALFKI	Alfreds Futterkiste	Maria Anders	Sales Representative	Obere Str. 57	Berlin		12209	Germany	030-0074321	030-0076545
ANATR	Ana Trujillo Emparedados y helados	Ana Trujillo	Owner	Avda. de la Constitución 2222	México D.F.		05021	Mexico	(5) 555-4729	(5) 555-3745
ANTON	Antonio Moreno Taqueria	Antonio Moreno	Owner	Mataderos 2312	México D.F.		05023	Mexico	(5) 555-3932	
AROUT	Around the Horn	Thomas Hardy	Sales Representative	120 Hanover Sq.	London		WA1 1DP	UK	(171) 555-7788	(171) 555-6750
BERGS	Berglunds snabbköp	Christina Berglund	Order Administrator	Berguvsvägen 8	Luleå		S-958 22	Sweden	0921-12 34 65	0921-12 34 67
BLAUS	Blauer See Delikatessen	Hanna Moos	Sales Representative	Forsterstr. 57	Mannheim		68306	Germany	0621-08460	0621-08924
BLONP	Blondesddsl père et fils	Frédérique Citeaux	Marketing Manager	24, place Kléber	Strasbourg		67000	France	88.60.15.31	88.60.15.32
BOLID	Bólido Comidas preparadas	Martin Sommer	Owner	C/ Araquil, 67	Madrid		28023	Spain	(91) 555 22 82	(91) 555 91 99
BONAP	Bon app'	Laurence Lebihan	Owner	12, rue des Bouchers	Marseille		13008	France	91.24.45.40	91.24.45.41
BOTTM	Bottom-Dollar Markets	Elizabeth Lincoln	Accounting Manager	23 Tsawassen Blvd.	Tsawassen	BC	T2F 8M4	Canada	(604) 555-4729	(604) 555-3745

1 2 3 4 5 6 7 8 9 10

FIGURE 21-18

Now let's expand upon the previous example by allowing for the editing and deletion of records that are displayed in the `GridView`. If you are using the Visual Studio `SqlDataSource` Configuration Wizard to accomplish these tasks, then you need to take some extra steps beyond what was shown in the preceding `GridView` example.

You can continue working the page created earlier. The sample project contains a new page, Demo02-SqlWithUpdate.aspx, with the code and markup you are about to add.

Go back to the `SqlDataSource` control on the design surface of your page and pull up the control's smart tag. Select the Configure Data Source option to reconfigure the `SqlDataSource` control to enable the editing and deletion of data from the Customers table of the Northwind database.

To do this, go through the wizard again, but when you get to the Configure the Select Statement screen click the Advanced button. This will pull up the Advanced SQL Generation Options dialog, shown in Figure 21-19.

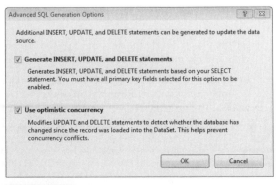

FIGURE 21-19

As shown in this dialog, select both of the check boxes. This will instruct the `SqlDataSource` control to not only handle the simple SELECT query, but also the UPDATE and DELETE queries. Press OK and then work through the rest of the wizard.

Click the Yes button in the dialog that appears asking if you want to refresh the fields and keys used by the `GridView`.

Return to the `GridView` control's smart tag. You will also now find check boxes in the smart tag for editing and deleting rows of data. Make sure both of these check boxes are checked.

Now look at what changed in the code. First, the `SqlDataSource` control has changed to allow for the updating and deletion of data:

Available for download on Wrox.com

```
<asp:SqlDataSource ID="SqlDataSource1" runat="server"
    ConnectionString="<%$ ConnectionStrings:NorthwindConnectionString %>"
    SelectCommand="SELECT * FROM [Customers]"
    ConflictDetection="CompareAllValues"
    DeleteCommand="DELETE FROM [Customers] WHERE ... "
    InsertCommand="INSERT INTO [Customers] ... "
    UpdateCommand="UPDATE [Customers] ... ">
    <DeleteParameters>
        <asp:Parameter Name="original_CustomerID" Type="String" />
        <asp:Parameter Name="original_CompanyName" Type="String" />
        <asp:Parameter Name="original_ContactName" Type="String" />
        <asp:Parameter Name="original_ContactTitle" Type="String" />
        <asp:Parameter Name="original_Address" Type="String" />
        <asp:Parameter Name="original_City" Type="String" />
        <asp:Parameter Name="original_Region" Type="String" />
        <asp:Parameter Name="original_PostalCode" Type="String" />
        <asp:Parameter Name="original_Country" Type="String" />
        <asp:Parameter Name="original_Phone" Type="String" />
        <asp:Parameter Name="original_Fax" Type="String" />
    </DeleteParameters>
    <InsertParameters>
        <asp:Parameter Name="CustomerID" Type="String" />
        <asp:Parameter Name="CompanyName" Type="String" />
        <asp:Parameter Name="ContactName" Type="String" />
        <asp:Parameter Name="ContactTitle" Type="String" />
        <asp:Parameter Name="Address" Type="String" />
        <asp:Parameter Name="City" Type="String" />
        <asp:Parameter Name="Region" Type="String" />
        <asp:Parameter Name="PostalCode" Type="String" />
        <asp:Parameter Name="Country" Type="String" />
        <asp:Parameter Name="Phone" Type="String" />
        <asp:Parameter Name="Fax" Type="String" />
    </InsertParameters>
    <UpdateParameters>
        <asp:Parameter Name="CompanyName" Type="String" />
        <asp:Parameter Name="ContactName" Type="String" />
        <asp:Parameter Name="ContactTitle" Type="String" />
        <asp:Parameter Name="Address" Type="String" />
        <asp:Parameter Name="City" Type="String" />
        <asp:Parameter Name="Region" Type="String" />
        <asp:Parameter Name="PostalCode" Type="String" />
        <asp:Parameter Name="Country" Type="String" />
        <asp:Parameter Name="Phone" Type="String" />
        <asp:Parameter Name="Fax" Type="String" />
        <asp:Parameter Name="original_CustomerID" Type="String" />
        <asp:Parameter Name="original_CompanyName" Type="String" />
        <asp:Parameter Name="original_ContactName" Type="String" />
        <asp:Parameter Name="original_ContactTitle" Type="String" />
```

```
                <asp:Parameter Name="original_Address" Type="String" />
                <asp:Parameter Name="original_City" Type="String" />
                <asp:Parameter Name="original_Region" Type="String" />
                <asp:Parameter Name="original_PostalCode" Type="String" />
                <asp:Parameter Name="original_Country" Type="String" />
                <asp:Parameter Name="original_Phone" Type="String" />
                <asp:Parameter Name="original_Fax" Type="String" />
            </UpdateParameters>
        </asp:SqlDataSource>
```

Code snippet from Step02-SqlWithUpdate.aspx

Second, additional queries have been added to the control. Using the `DeleteCommand`, `InsertCommand`, and `UpdateCommand` attributes of the `SqlDataSource` control, these functions can now be performed just as `SELECT` queries were enabled through the use of the `SelectCommand` attribute. As you can see, each of these new queries has parameters that are assigned through the `<DeleteParameters>`, `<UpdateParameters>`, and `<InsertParameters>` elements. Within each of these subsections, the actual parameters are defined through the use of the `<asp:Parameter>` control.

Besides these changes to the `SqlDataSource`, only one small change has been made to the `GridView` control:

Available for
download on
Wrox.com

```
<Columns>
    <asp:CommandField ShowDeleteButton="True" ShowEditButton="True" />
    <asp:BoundField DataField="CustomerID" HeaderText="CustomerID"
        ReadOnly="True" SortExpression="CustomerID" />
    <asp:BoundField DataField="CompanyName" HeaderText="CompanyName"
        SortExpression="CompanyName" />
    <asp:BoundField DataField="ContactName" HeaderText="ContactName"
        SortExpression="ContactName" />
    <asp:BoundField DataField="ContactTitle" HeaderText="ContactTitle"
        SortExpression="ContactTitle" />
    <asp:BoundField DataField="Address" HeaderText="Address"
        SortExpression="Address" />
    <asp:BoundField DataField="City" HeaderText="City"
        SortExpression="City" />
    <asp:BoundField DataField="Region" HeaderText="Region"
        SortExpression="Region" />
    <asp:BoundField DataField="PostalCode" HeaderText="PostalCode"
        SortExpression="PostalCode" />
    <asp:BoundField DataField="Country" HeaderText="Country"
        SortExpression="Country" />
    <asp:BoundField DataField="Phone" HeaderText="Phone"
        SortExpression="Phone" />
    <asp:BoundField DataField="Fax" HeaderText="Fax"
        SortExpression="Fax" />
</Columns>
```

Code snippet from Step02-SqlWithUpdate.aspx

The only change needed for the `GridView` control is the addition of a new column from which editing and deleting commands can be initiated. This is done with the `<asp:CommandField>` control. From this control, you can see that we also enabled the Edit and Delete buttons through a Boolean value. Once built and run, your new page will look like the one shown in Figure 21-20.

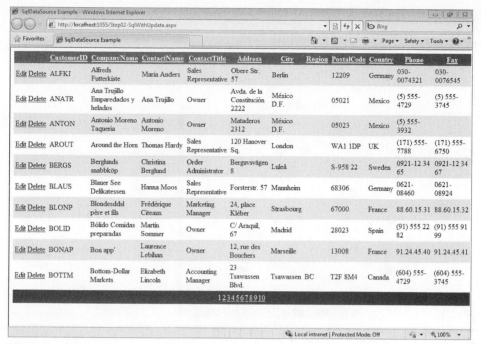

FIGURE 21-20

Data Binding with the LinqDataSource Control

It is hoped that while we were building the sample something jumped out at you as being odd or out of place. For the vast majority of applications, accessing the database directly from the user interface is an anti-pattern. Architectural best practices dictate that there should be one or more logical layers (e.g., data access layer, business logic layer, service layer) between the two. In an effort to keep this book from getting so large it would have to be sold in volumes, we will bypass the discussion of application architecture here and limit ourselves to building a data access layer using LINQ to SQL. Once we have the model, we will build a new page that emulates the behavior of the one we just built.

Returning to your project, create a new LINQ to SQL model called **Northwind.dbml** and add the Customers table to it. Saving the model will create the NorthwindDataContext and the Customer entity we are about to use. Create a new page named Step03-Linq.aspx and add a GridView and a LinqDataSource to it. Build the project to ensure that the NorthwindDataContext will be visible to the LinqDataSource. Use the LinqDataSource control's smart tag to access the data source configuration.

The first page of the wizard allows selection of the data context. This will generally be a LINQ to SQL model but it could also be a collection or array. Select the NorthwindDataContext (see Figure 21-21) and click the Next button.

FIGURE 21-21

You want to emulate what you did previously, so in the second page choose the values that will select all columns from the Customers table, as shown in Figure 21-22. Click the Advanced button and enable inserts, updates, and deletes as shown in Figure 21-23. Click the OK button to close the Advanced Options dialog and click the Finish button to close the wizard.

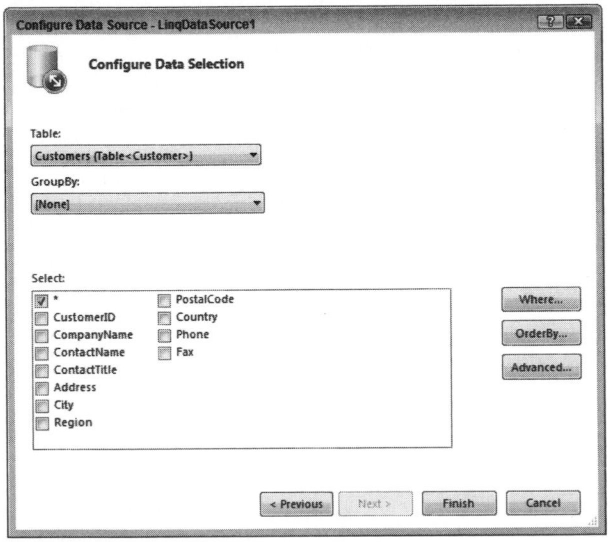

FIGURE 21-22

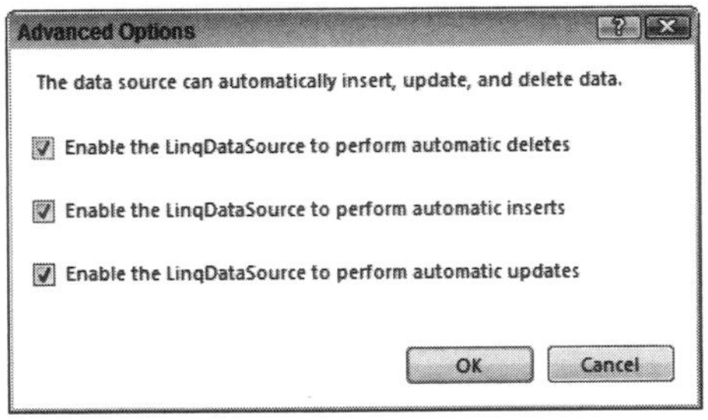

FIGURE 21-23

Now use the smart tag on the GridView control to bind to the LinqDataSource and to enable paging, sorting, editing, and deleting, as shown in Figure 21-24. Also use the smart tag to Auto Format your GridView control.

Notice that except for some minor differences in the configuration wizard for the data source, the process of designing this page was the same as that used for the SqlDataSource. Additionally, when you run the page you should see the same content and behavior as before. This consistency of design is one of the big advantages of the data source controls.

Taking a look at the markup for the LinqDataSource, you can see that it is quite simple:

FIGURE 21-24

Available for download on Wrox.com

```
<asp:LinqDataSource ID="LinqDataSource1" runat="server"
    ContextTypeName="DataControls.NorthwindDataContext" EnableDelete="True"
    EnableInsert="True" EnableUpdate="True" EntityTypeName="" TableName="Customers">
</asp:LinqDataSource>
```

Code snippet from Step03-Linq.aspx

Let's extend it a little bit by adding the capability to filter the customers by country. In the sample project, the filter is added in a new page named Step04-LinqWithParameter.aspx. You can continue working with the page you created earlier.

Run the Configure Data Source Wizard for the LinqDataSource. In the second page, click the Where button and enter the options shown in Figure 21-25 to add the filter based on a parameter coming from the query string.

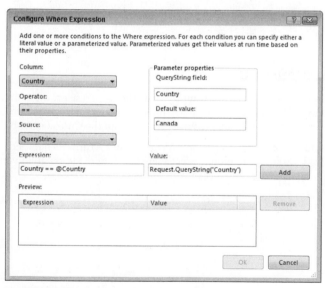

FIGURE 21-25

Taking another look at the markup for the LinqDataSource, you can see that there is now a Where attribute representing your filter, and a QueryStringParameter that takes the name of the country on which to filter:

Available for download on Wrox.com

```
<asp:LinqDataSource ID="LinqDataSource1" runat="server"
    ContextTypeName="DataControls.NorthwindDataContext" EnableDelete="True"
    EnableInsert="True" EnableUpdate="True" EntityTypeName=""
    TableName="Customers" Where="Country == @Country">
    <WhereParameters>
```

```
            <asp:QueryStringParameter DefaultValue="Canada" Name="Country"
                QueryStringField="Country" Type="String" />
        </WhereParameters>
    </asp:LinqDataSource>
```

Code snippet from Step04-LinqWithParameter.aspx

Run the page and add "?Country=Mexico" to the end of the URL to set the query string parameter. You should see a page similar to the one shown in Figure 21-26.

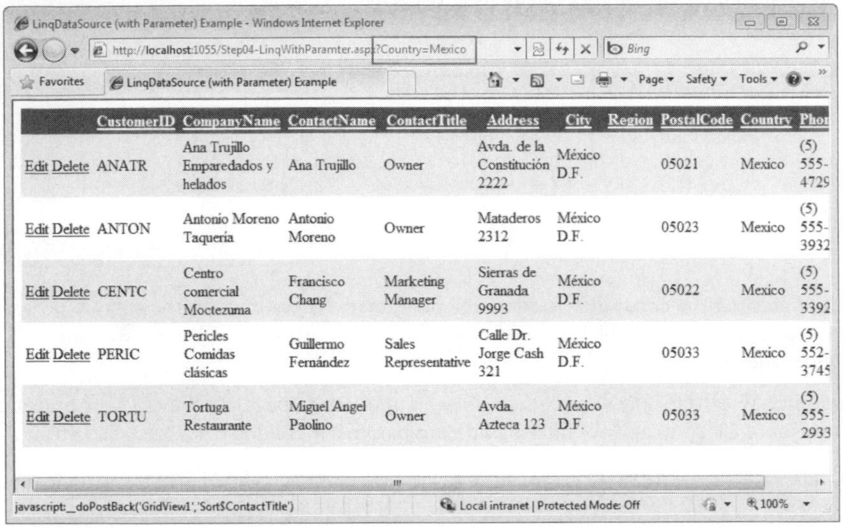

FIGURE 21-26

Data Binding with the ObjectDataSource Control

Passing the country on the query string works fine, but what if you want to allow the user to select the country in a drop-down instead? The Northwind database does not have a Country table, so you need to get the possible values using a query. Specifically, you need to find the distinct set of country names from the Customers table.

You can easily add a method to the `NorthwindDataContext` to perform the query and return the names of the countries. Right-click on `Northwind.dbml` in the Solution Explorer, select View Code, and add the following:

Available for download on Wrox.com

```
Public Function GetCountryNames() As String()
    Dim query = From cust In Customers
                Select cust.Country Distinct
                Order By Country

    Return query.ToArray()
End Function
```

Code snippet from Northwind.vb

With this method in place, you can now add a `DropDown` control and bind it to the method using the `ObjectDataSource`. The `ObjectDataSource` enables you to use any object that has methods that expose standard CRUD functionality as a data source. Add a `DropDown` control above the `GridView` and add an `ObjectDataSource` control to the bottom of the page. Use the smart tag on the `ObjectDataSource` to open the Configure Data Source Wizard.

On the first page, choose the NorthwindDataContext as the business object that will supply the data, as show in Figure 21-27.

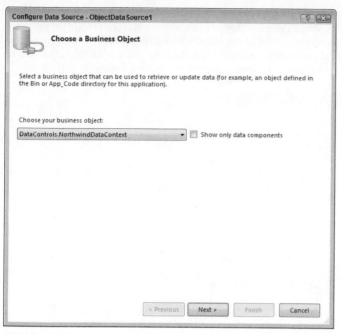

FIGURE 21-27

In the second page you can set the methods of the business object that will be called when attempting to select, insert, update or delete. You don't need to update data, so only choose a select method. On the Select tab, choose GetCountryNames and click the Finish button to complete the wizard (see Figure 21-28).

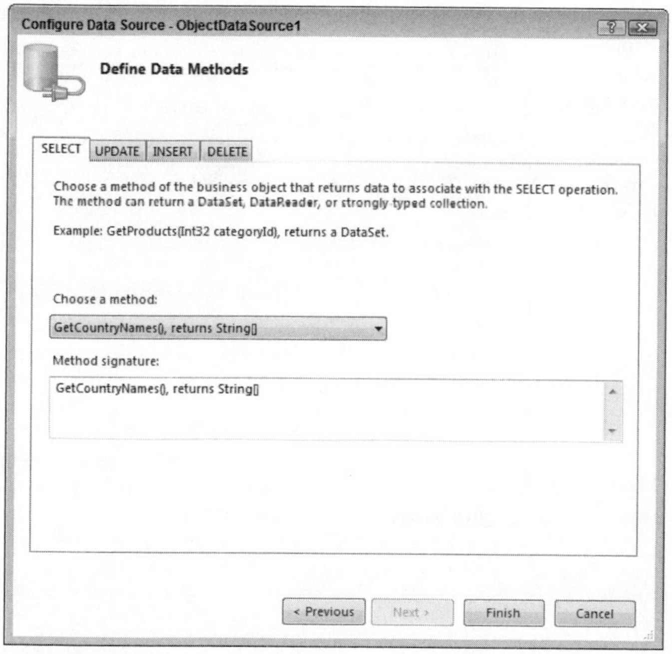

FIGURE 21-28

Configuring the `DropDown` control to bind to the `ObjectDataSource` gets a little tricky when using an array of simple types (i.e., string, integers, dates), as the Choose Data Source Wizard (available via the smart tag) assumes that you want to bind to properties of the objects being returned by the select method, not the objects themselves. For example, if you run the wizard to bind to the array of strings returned by GetCountryNames, it will try to get you to display the length of each string (see Figure 21-29)

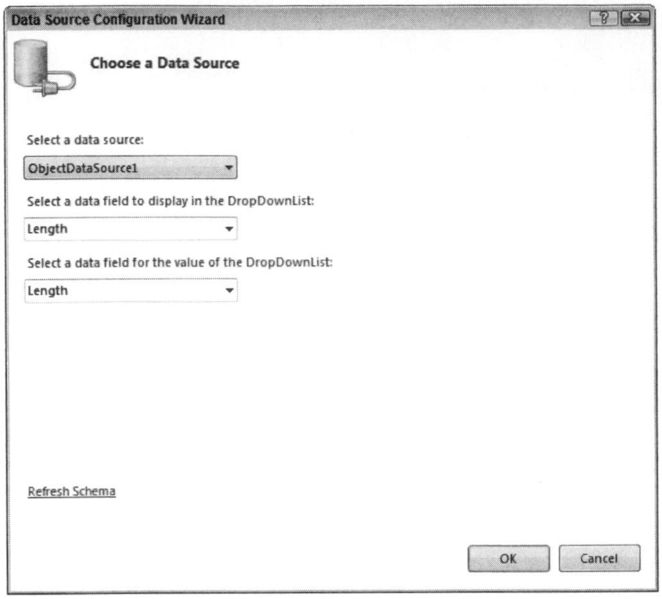

FIGURE 21-29

In this case, we'll go a little bit more "old school" and set the properties of the `DropDown` control using the Properties window, rather than use a wizard in the designer. Hooking up the data binding just requires that you set the `DataSourceID` attribute to `ObjectDataSource1`. You also need to set the `AutoPostBack` property to `True` so that the page will rebind when a new country name is selected.

Finally, you want to update the `LinqDataSource` to use the value coming from the `DropDown` control instead of one being passed on the query string. Open the Configure Data Source Wizard for the `LinqDataSource` control, and on the second page click the Where button. In the dialog that pops up, remove the existing expression and add a new one using the values shown in Figure 21-30.

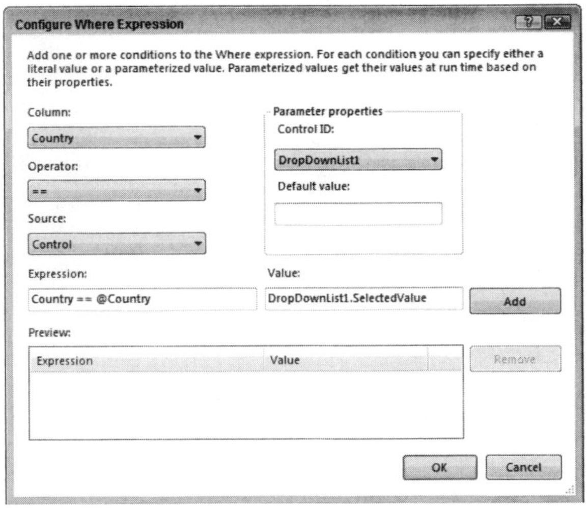

FIGURE 21-30

When you run the project you should see only the customers from the country selected in the drop-down. The page should look something like the one show in Figure 21-31.

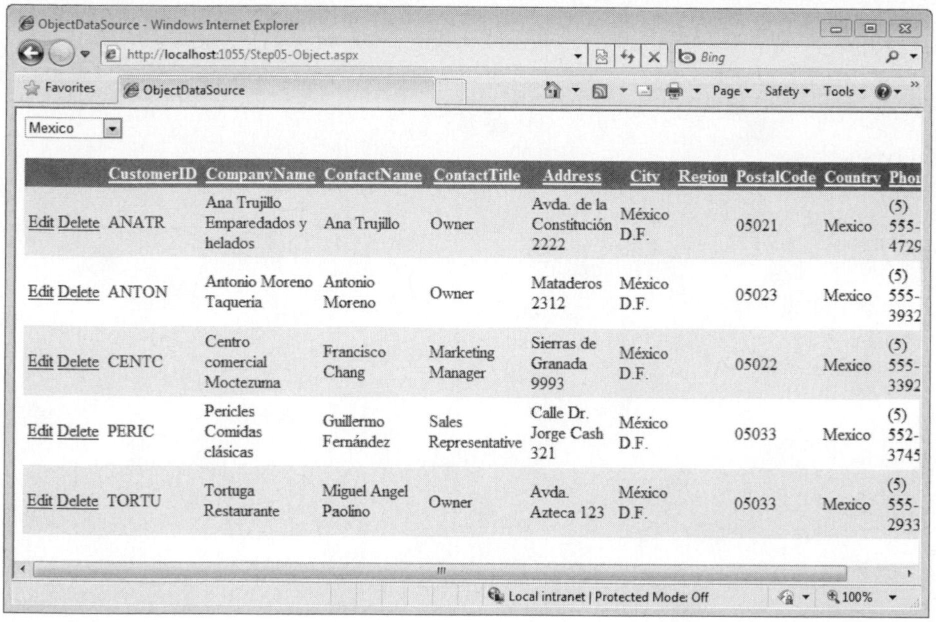

FIGURE 21-31

SUMMARY

This chapter covered a lot of ground. It discussed many aspects of ASP.NET applications as a whole and the options you have when building and deploying these applications. With the skills learned in this chapter you should be able to build and deploy simple applications that allow you to display and edit data from a database. For many of you, these skills will be enough to solve a good deal of the tasks assigned to you.

However, that doesn't mean there isn't a lot more to cover. The next chapter delves into some of the more advanced features available to you when building Web applications with ASP.NET and WebForms.

22

ASP.NET Advanced Features

WHAT YOU WILL LEARN IN THIS CHAPTER

➤ The purpose and use of master pages

➤ Quickly and easily adding navigation to your site

➤ Securing access to your site with membership and roles

➤ Adding persistent profiles for users of your site

➤ Working with the ASP.NET provider model

➤ Adding richness and interactivity with Microsoft Ajax

ASP.NET is an exciting technology. It enables the creation and delivery of remotely generated applications (Web applications) accessible via a simple browser — a container that many are rather familiar with. The purpose of Web-based applications (in our case, ASP.NET applications) is to deliver only a single instance of the application to the end user over HTTP. This means that the end users viewing your application will always have the latest version at their disposal. Because of this, many companies today are looking at ASP.NET to not only deliver the company's website, but also to deliver some of their latest applications for their employees, partners, and customers.

The last chapter looked at some of the basics of ASP.NET. This chapter continues that exploration, showing you some additional and exciting technologies, including master pages, navigation, personalization, AJAX and more.

MASTER PAGES

Many Web applications are built so that each page of the application has a similar look and feel; and there may be common page elements such as a header, navigation sections, advertisements, footers, and more. Most people prefer uniformity in their applications in order to give end users a consistent experience across pages.

ASP.NET 2.0 introduced a feature called *master pages* that enable you to create a template (or a set of templates) that define the common elements for a set of pages. Once a master page is created, you can then create a *content page* (with an .aspx extension), and that defines the content specific to a single page. The content page and the master page are associated by attributes in the Page directive so ASP.NET can combine the two files into a single Web page to display in a browser (see Figure 22-1).

The following sections describe how you make this work, beginning with the master page.

Creating a Master Page

The first step is to create a template that will end up being your master page. You can build a master page using any text editor (such as Notepad), but it is far easier to use Visual Studio.

The sample code included with the book contains a Web site project named **MasterPages**. We will use this project to explore the use of master pages in ASP.NET. If you wish to follow along, create the project and add a master page by right-clicking on the project in the Solution Explorer, and selecting Add New Item. In the Add New Item dialog is an option to add a master page to the solution, as shown in Figure 22-2.

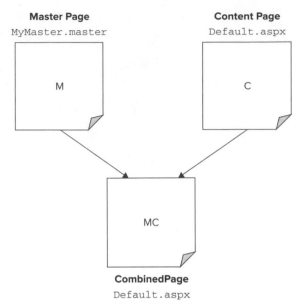

Master Page
MyMaster.master

M

Content Page
Default.aspx

C

CombinedPage
Default.aspx

MC

FIGURE 22-1

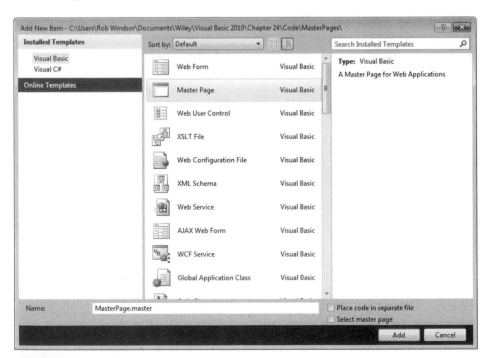

FIGURE 22-2

The options available when creating a master page are quite similar to those when creating a standard .aspx page. You can create master pages to be inline or you can have master pages that utilize the code-behind model. If you wish to use the code-behind model, then make sure that you have the Place code in a separate file check box checked in the dialog — otherwise, leave it blank. Creating an inline master page produces a single `.master` file. Using the code-behind model produces a `.master` file in addition to a `.master.vb` file. The master page in the sample project was created to use the inline model. You also have the option to nest your master page within another master page by selecting the Select master page field.

A master page should be built so that it contains one or more `ContentPlaceHolder` controls. The content for these controls will be "filled in" by the associated content pages. The master page item template includes two place holders: one for the main content of the page and one for the page head.

```
<%@ Master Language="VB" %>

<!DOCTYPE html PUBLIC ... >

<script runat="server">

</script>

<html xmlns="http://www.w3.org/1999/xhtml">
<head runat="server">
    <title></title>
    <asp:ContentPlaceHolder id="head" runat="server">
    </asp:ContentPlaceHolder>
</head>
<body>
    <form id="form1" runat="server">
    <div>
        <asp:ContentPlaceHolder id="ContentPlaceHolder1" runat="server">

        </asp:ContentPlaceHolder>
    </div>
    </form>
</body>
</html>
```

Update the master page so that it contains three place holder controls. Leave the existing control inside the head tag. In the body, create a table with the other two place holders contained within. The modified master page should look similar to the following:

```
<%@ Master Language="VB" %>

<!DOCTYPE html PUBLIC "-//W3C//DTD XHTML 1.0 Transitional//EN"
    "http://www.w3.org/TR/xhtml1/DTD/xhtml1-transitional.dtd">

<script runat="server">
</script>

<html xmlns="http://www.w3.org/1999/xhtml">
<head runat="server">
    <title>My Company Master Page</title>
    <asp:ContentPlaceHolder id="head" runat="server">
    </asp:ContentPlaceHolder>
</head>
<body>
    <form id="form1" runat="server">
    <div>
        <table cellpadding="3" border="1">
            <tr bgcolor="silver">
                <td colspan="2"><h1>My Company Home Page</h1></td>
            </tr>
            <tr>
                <td>
                    <asp:contentplaceholder id="ContentPlaceHolder1"
                     runat="server">
```

```
                      </asp:contentplaceholder>
                  </td>
                  <td>
                      <asp:contentplaceholder id="ContentPlaceHolder2"
                       runat="server">
                      </asp:contentplaceholder>
                  </td>
              </tr>
              <tr>
                  <td colspan="2">Copyright 2010 - My Company</td>
              </tr>
          </table>
      </div>
      </form>
</body>
</html>
```

Code snippet from MasterPage.master

The first thing to notice is the `<% Master %>` directive at the top of the page instead of the standard `<% Page %>` directive. This specifies that this is a master page and cannot be navigated to in the browser. In this case, the Master directive simply uses the Language attribute and nothing more, but it has a number of other attributes at its disposal to fine-tune the behavior of the page.

The idea is to code the master page as you would any other .aspx page. This master page contains a simple table and three areas that are meant for the content pages. It is *only* in these three specified areas that content pages are allowed to inject content into the dynamically created page (as shown shortly).

The nice thing about working with master pages is that you are not limited to working with them in the Source view of the IDE; Visual Studio also enables you to work with them in Design view, shown in Figure 22-3. In this view, you can work with the master page by simply dragging and dropping controls onto the design surface, just as you would with any typical .aspx page.

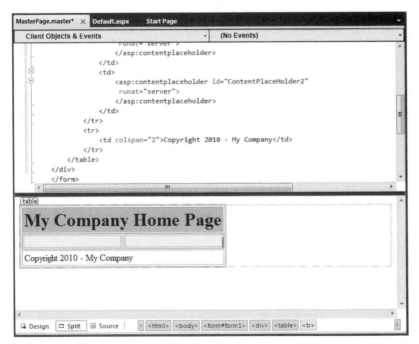

FIGURE 22-3

Creating the Content Page

Now that you have a master page you can start creating content pages associated with it. To create a content page, right-click on the solution in the Solution Explorer and select Add New Item. Select the Web Form template, and check the Select master page check box. The settings used to create the content page in the sample project are shown in Figure 22-4. Clicking the Add button brings up a dialog that enables you to select a master page to associate with this new file, as shown in Figure 22-5.

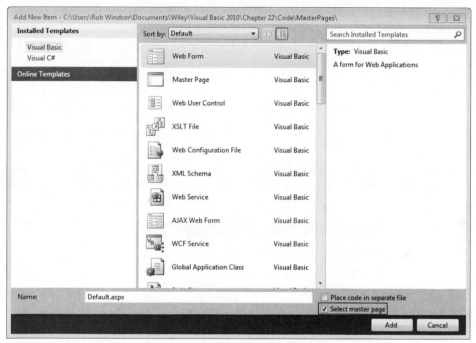

FIGURE 22-4

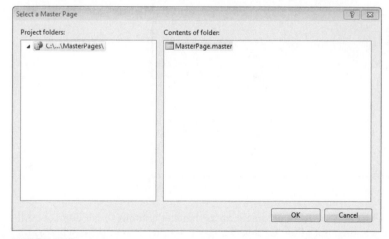

FIGURE 22-5

In this case you should only have a single master page available in the dialog, though it is possible to have as many master pages as you wish in a single project. Select the `MasterPage.master` page and click OK.

The page created should have one `Content` control for each of the `ContentPlaceHolder` controls in the selected master page:

```
<%@ Page Title="" Language="VB" MasterPageFile="~/MasterPage.master" %>

<script runat="server">
</script>

<asp:Content ID="Content1" ContentPlaceHolderID="head" Runat="Server">
</asp:Content>
<asp:Content ID="Content2" ContentPlaceHolderID="ContentPlaceHolder1" Runat="Server">
</asp:Content>
<asp:Content ID="Content3" ContentPlaceHolderID="ContentPlaceHolder2" Runat="Server">
</asp:Content>
```

This file is quite a bit different from a typical .aspx page. First, there is none of the default HTML code, script tags, and DOCTYPE declarations. Second, note the addition of the `MasterPageFile` attribute in the `Page` directive. This new attribute makes the association to the master page that will be used for this content page. In this case, it is the `MasterPage.master` file created earlier.

There isn't much to show while in the Source view of Visual Studio when looking at a content page; the real power of master pages can be seen when you work with the page in the designer by switching to the Design or Split view (see Figure 22-6).

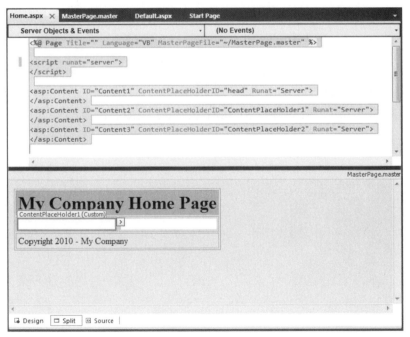

FIGURE 22-6

This view shows you the entire template and the two content areas that can contain server controls. All the grayed-out areas are off-limits and do not allow for any changes from the content page, whereas the available areas allow you to deal with any type of content you wish. For instance, not only can you place raw text in these content areas, you can also add anything that you would normally place into a typical .aspx page. The page in the sample application includes a simple form as shown below. If you're following along you can use the Design or Source view to build a similar user interface. If you want to build an identical interface you will need to get the wrox.jpg file from the sample code included with the book and put it in a folder named Images in your project.

```vb
<%@ Page Title="" Language="VB" MasterPageFile="~/MasterPage.master" %>

<script runat="server">
    Sub Button1_Click(ByVal sender As Object, ByVal e As System.EventArgs)
        Label1.Text = "Hello " & TextBox1.Text
    End Sub
</script>

<asp:Content ID="Content1" ContentPlaceHolderID="head" Runat="Server">
</asp:Content>
<asp:Content ID="Content2" ContentPlaceHolderID="ContentPlaceHolder1" Runat="Server">
    <b>Enter in your name:<br />
    <asp:TextBox ID="TextBox1" Runat="server"></asp:TextBox>
    <asp:Button ID="Button1" Runat="server" Text="Submit" OnClick="Button1_Click" />
    <br />
    <br />
    <asp:Label ID="Label1" Runat="server"></asp:Label>
    </b>
</asp:Content>
<asp:Content ID="Content3" ContentPlaceHolderID="ContentPlaceHolder2" Runat="Server">
    <asp:Image ID="Image1" Runat="server" ImageUrl="~/Images/wrox.jpg" />
</asp:Content>
```

Code snippet from Default.aspx

Just as with typical .aspx pages, you can create any event handlers you may need for your content page. This particular example uses a button-click event for when the end user submits the form. Running this example produces the results shown in Figure 22-7.

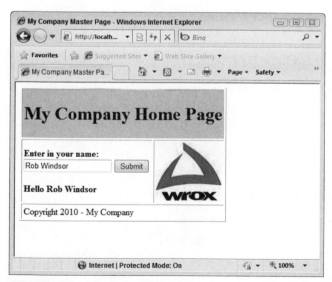

FIGURE 22-7

Providing Default Content in Your Master Page

Earlier, you saw how to use a basic `ContentPlaceHolder` control. In addition to using it as shown, you can also create `ContentPlaceHolder` controls that contain default content:

```
<asp:ContentPlaceHolder ID="ContentPlaceHolder1" runat="server">
   Here is some default content!
</asp:ContentPlaceHolder>
```

For default content, you can again use whatever you want, including any other ASP.NET server controls. A content page that uses a master page containing one of these `ContentPlaceHolder` controls can then either override the default content — by just specifying other content (which overrides the original content declared in the master page) — or keep the default content contained in the control.

NAVIGATION

Developers rarely build single-page Web applications. Instead, applications are usually made up of multiple pages that are related to each other in some fashion. Some applications have a workflow through which end users can work from page to page, while other applications have a navigation structure that allows for free roaming throughout the pages. Sometimes the navigation structure of a site becomes complex, and managing this complexity can be rather cumbersome.

ASP.NET includes a way to manage the navigational structure of your Web applications by defining it in an XML file and then binding the XML data to server controls focused on navigation. You maintain your navigational structure in a single file, and the data-binding mechanism ensures that any changes are instantaneously reflected throughout your application.

The sample projects included with the book contain a Web site project named Navigation. You can open this project and follow along with the existing code or you can build your own project as we go.

The first step in working with the ASP.NET navigation system is to create a sitemap file, the XML file that will contain the complete site structure. For instance, suppose you want the following navigation:

```
Home
        Books
        Magazines
                U.S. Magazines
                European Magazines
```

This site structure has three levels to it, with multiple items in the lowest level. You can reflect this in the `web.sitemap` file as follows:

```
<?xml version="1.0" encoding="utf-8" ?>
<siteMap xmlns="http://schemas.microsoft.com/AspNet/SiteMap-File-1.0" >
   <siteMapNode url="default.aspx" title="Home"
     description="The site homepage">
       <siteMapNode url="books.aspx" title="Books"
        description="Books from our catalog" />
       <siteMapNode url="magazines.aspx" title="Magazines"
        description="Magazines from our catalog">
          <siteMapNode url="magazines_us.aspx" title="U.S. Magazines"
           description="Magazines from the U.S." />
          <siteMapNode url="magazines_eur.aspx" title="European Magazines"
           description="Magazines from Europe" />
       </siteMapNode>
   </siteMapNode>
</siteMap>
```

Code snippet from Web.sitemap

To create a sitemap file in Visual Studio, go to the Add New Item dialog and select the Site Map option. You can place the preceding content in this file. To move a level down in the hierarchy, nest `<siteMapNode>`

elements within other `<siteMapNode>` elements. A `<siteMapNode>` element can contain several different attributes, as defined in Table 22-1.

TABLE 22-1: siteMapNode Element Attributes

ATTRIBUTE	DESCRIPTION
Title	Provides a textual description of the link. The `String` value used here is the text used for the link.
Description	This attribute not only reminds you what the link is for, it is also used for the `ToolTip` attribute on the link. The `ToolTip` attribute is the yellow box that appears next to the link when the user hovers the cursor over the link for a couple of seconds.
Url	Describes where the file is located in the solution. If the file is in the root directory, then simply use the filename, such as `default.aspx`. If the file is located in a subfolder, then be sure to include the folders in the `String` value used for this attribute, e.g., `MySubFolder/MyFile.aspx`.
Roles	If ASP.NET security trimming is enabled, you can use the `Roles` attribute to define which roles are allowed to view and click the provided link in the navigation.

Using the SiteMapPath Server Control

One of the available server controls that can bind to a site map is the `SiteMapPath` control. This control provides a popular structure found on many Internet websites. Sometimes called *breadcrumb navigation*, this feature is simple to implement in ASP.NET.

To see an example of this control at work, we'll need a page that would be at the bottom of the site map structure. Within the project that contains your site map file, create a Web Form named **magazines_us.aspx** (this page name is included in the site map file) and drag and drop a `SiteMapPath` control from the Navigation section of the Toolbox onto it. This control's markup looks as follows:

```
<asp:SiteMapPath ID="SiteMapPath1" runat="server"></asp:SiteMapPath>
```

What else do you need to do to get this control to work? Nothing. Simply build and run the page to see the results shown in Figure 22-8.

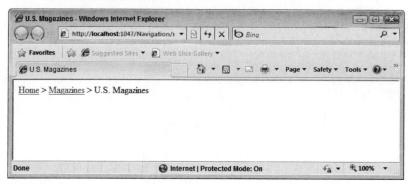

FIGURE 22-8

The `SiteMapPath` control defines the end user's place in the application's site structure. It shows the current page the user is on (U.S. Magazines), as well as the two pages above it in the hierarchy.

The `SiteMapPath` control requires no `DataSource` control, as it automatically binds itself to any `.sitemap` file it finds in the project; nothing is required on your part to make this happen. The `SiteMapPath`'s smart tag enables you to customize the control's appearance too, so you can produce other results, as shown in Figure 22-9.

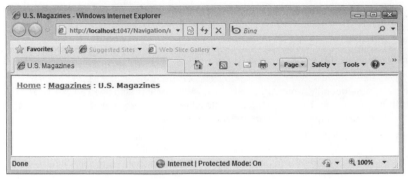

FIGURE 22-9

The code for this version of the SiteMapPath control is as follows:

Available for
download on
Wrox.com

```
<asp:SiteMapPath ID="SiteMapPath1" runat="server" Font-Names="Verdana"
    Font-Size="0.8em" PathSeparator=" : " >
    <CurrentNodeStyle ForeColor="#333333" />
    <NodeStyle Font-Bold="True" ForeColor="#284E98" />
    <PathSeparatorStyle Font-Bold="True" ForeColor="#507CD1" />
    <RootNodeStyle Font-Bold="True" ForeColor="#507CD1" />
</asp:SiteMapPath>
```

Code snippet from magazines_us.aspx

This example illustrates that a lot of style elements and attributes can be used with the SiteMapPath control. Many options at your disposal enable you to create breadcrumb navigation that is unique.

Menu Server Control

Another navigation control enables end users of your application to navigate throughout the pages based upon information stored within the web.sitemap file. The Menu server control produces a compact navigation system that pops up sub-options when the user hovers the mouse over an option. The result of the Menu server control when bound to the site map is shown in Figure 22-10.

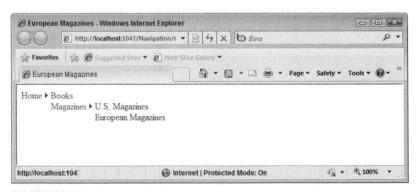

FIGURE 22-10

To see this, examine the Web Form named **magazines_eur.aspx**. It has both a Menu and a SiteMapDataSource control on the page:

```
<asp:SiteMapDataSource ID="SiteMapDataSource1" runat="server" />
<asp:Menu ID="Menu1" runat="server" DataSourceID="SiteMapDataSource1">
</asp:Menu>
```

Code snippet from magazines_eur.aspx

The `SiteMapDataSource` control automatically works with the application's `web.sitemap` file and the `Menu` control to bind to the `SiteMapDataSource` (just like a `GridView` can bind to a `SqlDataSource`). Like many of the other visual controls in ASP.NET, you can easily modify the appearance of the `Menu` control by clicking the Auto Format link in the control's smart tag. Choosing Classic produces the result shown in Figure 22-11.

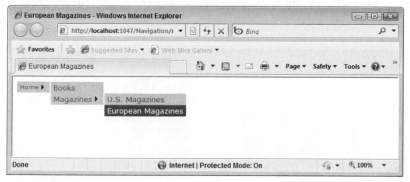

FIGURE 22-11

As with the other controls, a lot of sub-elements contribute to the changed look of the control's style:

```
<asp:Menu ID="Menu1" runat="server" DataSourceID="SiteMapDataSource1"
    BackColor="#B5C7DE" DynamicHorizontalOffset="2" Font-Names="Verdana"
    Font-Size="0.8em" ForeColor="#284E98" StaticSubMenuIndent="10px">
    <DynamicHoverStyle BackColor="#284E98" ForeColor="White" />
    <DynamicMenuItemStyle HorizontalPadding="5px" VerticalPadding="2px" />
    <DynamicMenuStyle BackColor="#B5C7DE" />
    <DynamicSelectedStyle BackColor="#507CD1" />
    <StaticHoverStyle BackColor="#284E98" ForeColor="White" />
    <StaticMenuItemStyle HorizontalPadding="5px" VerticalPadding="2px" />
    <StaticSelectedStyle BackColor="#507CD1" />
</asp:Menu>
```

Code snippet from magazines_eur.aspx

WORKING WITH THE ASP.NET PROVIDER MODEL

Ever since the beginning days of ASP.NET, users wanted to be able to store sessions by means other than the three traditional storage modes: `InProc`, `StateServer`, and `SQLServer`. One such request was for a new storage mode that could store sessions in an Oracle database. This might seem like a logical thing to add, but if the team added a storage mode for Oracle they would soon get requests to add additional modes for other databases and data storage methods. For this reason, instead of building storage modes for specific scenarios, the ASP.NET team made the system extensible by designing a plugable *provider model* that enables anyone to add new modes as needed.

In addition to session state, there are several other features included in ASP.NET that require state storage of some kind. In addition, instead of recording state in a fragile mode (the way sessions are stored by default), many of these features require their state to be stored in more concrete data stores such as databases or XML files. This also enables a longer-lived state for the users visiting an application — something else that is required by these new systems.

The features found in ASP.NET today that require advanced state management include the following:

➤ Membership

➤ Role management

➤ Site navigation

➤ Personalization

➤ Health-monitoring Web events

➤ Web parts personalization

➤ Configuration file protection

For each of the features one or more providers are available by default to define the way the state of that system is recorded. Figure 22-12 illustrates these providers.

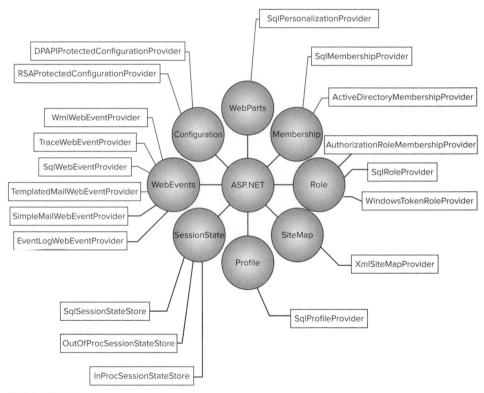

FIGURE 22-12

The next section describes how to set up SQL Server to work with several of the providers presented in this chapter. You can use SQL Server 7.0, 2000, 2005, or 2008 for the back-end data store for many of the providers presented (although not all of them).

Creating an Application Services Database

The instructions in this section and the next assume you have a SQL Server 2005 or 2008 Express instance named SqlExpress. If you have differently named instances available, you will need to modify the connection strings shown accordingly. If you do not have SQL Server at all, the easiest way to get the Express version is to use Microsoft's Web Platform Installer (www.microsoft.com/web/downloads/platform.aspx).

There are two mechanisms you can use to create an application services database. Let Visual Studio or another .NET framework tool do it for you, or do it yourself.

The first option is only available when you have configured your application to use a local (or user instance) database for application services. Unfortunately the tools are inconsistent, sometimes the database will be created automatically, and sometimes you will need to create it. We'll see two examples where the database is created automatically in this chapter: by Visual Studio when we add profile properties to an application, and by the Web Site Administration Tool when we configure membership and role information.

To create the database explicitly, you can use a tool named aspnet_regsql.exe that comes with the .NET Framework. This tool can create the necessary tables, roles, stored procedures, and other items needed by the providers. To access this tool, open the Visual Studio 2010 command prompt by selecting Start ⇨ All Programs ⇨ Microsoft Visual Studio 2010 ⇨ Visual Studio Tools ⇨ Visual Studio Command Prompt (2010). Make sure you run the command prompt as administrator. You will likely need the additional privilege to be able to create the application services database. With the command prompt open, you can access aspnet_regsql.exe, which can be run as a command-line tool or a GUI interface.

The ASP.NET SQL Server Setup Wizard Command-Line Tool

The command-line version gives developers optimal control over how the database is created. Working from the command line using this tool is not difficult, so don't be intimidated by it.

At the command prompt, type **aspnet_regsql.exe -?** to get a list of all the command-line options at your disposal for working with this tool.

Table 22-2 describes some of the available options for setting up your SQL Server instance to work with the ASP.NET application services.

TABLE 22-2: Frequently Used Setup Wizard Command-Line Options

COMMAND OPTION	DESCRIPTION
-?	Displays a list of available option commands.
-W	Uses the Wizard mode. This is the default if no other parameters are used.
-S *<server>*	Specifies the SQL Server instance to work with.
-U *<login>*	Specifies the username for logging in to SQL Server. If you use this, then you also use the -P command.
-P *<password>*	Specifies the password to use for logging in to SQL Server. If you use this, then you also use the -U command.
-E	Provides instructions for using the current Windows credentials for authentication.
-C	Specifies the connection string for connecting to SQL Server. If you use this, then you don't need to use the -U and -P commands because they are specified in the connection string itself.
-A all	Adds support for all the available SQL Server operations provided by ASP.NET, including membership, role management, profiles, site counters, and page/control personalization.
-A p	Adds support for working with profiles.
_R all	Removes support for all the available SQL Server operations that have been previously installed. These include membership, role management, profiles, site counters, and page/control personalization.
-R p	Removes support for the profile capability from SQL Server.
-d *<database>*	Specifies the database name to use with the application services. If you don't specify a database name, then aspnetdb is used.
-sqlexportonly *<filename>*	Instead of modifying an instance of a SQL Server database, use this command in conjunction with the other commands to generate a SQL script that adds or removes the features specified. This command creates the scripts in a file that has the name specified in the command.

One advantage of using the command-line tool, rather than the GUI-based version of the ASP.NET SQL Server Setup Wizard, is that you can install in the database just the features you're interested in working with, instead of installing everything (as the GUI-based version does). For instance, if you want only the membership system to interact with SQL Server — not any of the other systems (such as role management and personalization) — then you can configure the setup so that only the tables, roles, stored procedures, and other items required by the membership system are established in the database.

The ASP.NET SQL Server Setup Wizard GUI Tool

To access the GUI version, type the following at the Visual Studio command prompt:

```
aspnet_regsql.exe
```

At this point, the ASP.NET SQL Server Setup Wizard welcome screen appears, as shown in Figure 22-13.

Clicking the Next button gives you a new screen that offers two options: one to configure SQL Server for application services and the other to remove existing tables used by the application services (see Figure 22-14).

FIGURE 22-13

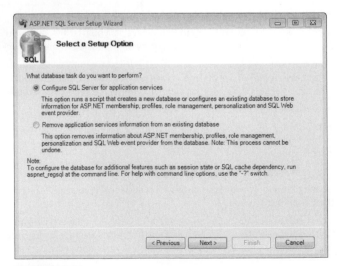

FIGURE 22-14

From here, choose Configure SQL Server for application services and click Next. The third screen (see Figure 22-15) asks for the login credentials to SQL Server and the name of the database to perform the operations. The Database option is <default> — meaning the wizard creates a database called aspnetdb. If you want to add application services to an existing database you can select it from the drop-down at the bottom on the page.

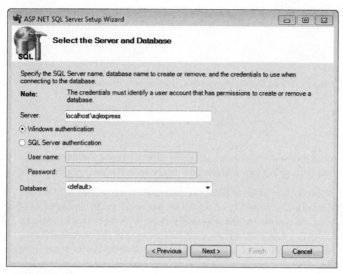

FIGURE 22-15

After you have made your server and database selections, click Next. The screen shown in Figure 22-16 asks you to confirm your settings. If everything looks correct, click the Next button — otherwise, click Previous and correct your settings.

FIGURE 22-16

When this is complete, you get a notification that everything was set up correctly.

Connecting the Built-In Providers to a Database

The built-in providers that require storage will look in the `web.config` file for a connection string entry named `LocalSqlServer` to determine how they should connect to the database. If this entry does not exist in `web.config`, they will use the default entry from `machine.config` which indicates a local database should be used. Here is an example connection string that is configured to use the database created by the wizard in the last section:

```
<configuration>

  <connectionStrings>
    <clear />
    <add name="LocalSqlServer"
         connectionString="Data Source=localhost\sqlexpress;Database=aspnetdb;
             Integrated Security=SSPI" />
  </connectionStrings>

</configuration>
```

Notice the `<clear>` element. This is required as the `machine.config` file already has an entry named `LocalSqlServer`. This entry must be cleared first, so we can add the new entry with the proper connection string.

Just like the default connection string, the built-in providers have their default settings defined in the `machine.config` file. In most cases the defaults are suitable, and you do not need to do any application specific configuration. However, if you want to customize the way individual providers work, you can override their default settings in the `web.config` file. For instance, if you are using the membership provider, and you want a minimum password length of 12 characters and login to fail after three invalid password attempts, then you would add the following:

```
<configuration>
  <system.web>

    <membership>
    <providers>
      <clear />
      <add name="AspNetSqlMembershipProvider"
           type="System.Web.Security.SqlMembershipProvider, ..."
           connectionStringName="LocalSqlServer"
           enablePasswordRetrieval="false"
           enablePasswordReset="true"
           requiresQuestionAndAnswer="true"
           applicationName="/"
           requiresUniqueEmail="false"
           passwordFormat="Hashed"
           maxInvalidPasswordAttempts="3"
           minRequiredPasswordLength="12"
           minRequiredNonalphanumericCharacters="1"
           passwordAttemptWindow="10"
           passwordStrengthRegularExpression=""/>
    </providers>
    </membership>

  </system.web>
</configuration>
```

MEMBERSHIP AND ROLE MANAGEMENT

ASP.NET contains a built-in membership and role management system that can be initiated either through code or through the ASP.NET Web Site Administration Tool. This is an ideal system for authenticating users to access a page or even your entire site. This management system not only provides a new API suite for managing users, but also provides you with some server controls that interact with this API.

The sample code contains a Web site project called **Membership** that we will use as an example for this section. It's based on the Empty Web site project template. After the project was created, a couple of pages were added to help demonstrate the security features of the Membership provider. If you want to build your own project, you'll need to create a folder called Secret and then create a page in this folder called **Payroll .aspx**. Also, create a **Default.aspx** page in the root folder. Add a line of text (something like "This is the payroll page") to both the payroll and default pages.

As mentioned previously, the membership and role-management providers access their data by finding a connection string named `LocalSqlServer`. The Web Site Administration Tool uses these providers so the connection string must be properly configured before using the tool. Also recall that if you do not have an entry for `LocalSqlServer` in the `web.config` file, the tool will create and use a local database in your application for storage. The sample application included with this book uses a local database that was automatically created when membership was configured. It is named `aspnetdb.mdb` and it is located in the `App_Data` folder.

Let's walk through the process of using the ASP.NET Web Site Administration Tool to set up security and user roles. You can launch this tool through a button in the Solution Explorer or by selecting ASP.NET Configuration under Website (Web site projects) or Project (Web application projects) in the main menu. When the tool opens, click the Security tab and then click the link to start the Security Setup Wizard as shown in Figure 22-17.

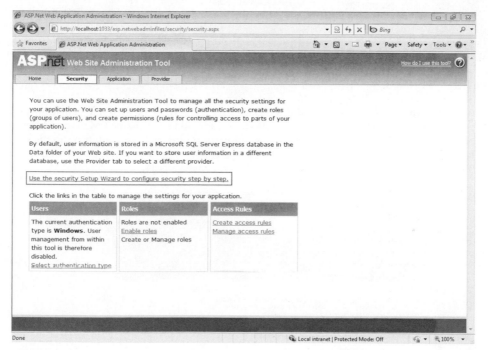

FIGURE 22-17

You'll be greeted with the Welcome page for the wizard. This page describes how the wizard will help you set up security for your site. Clicking the Next button will take you to the page where you can choose which authentication you will use.

The options presented ask whether your application will be available on the public Internet or hosted on an intranet. These options are misleading because you can use either of them regardless of where the site is being hosted. What the wizard is really asking is what kind of authentication you wish to use. If you select Internet, then your website will be enabled with forms authentication. If you select local network, then your site will be configured to work with Windows Integrated Authentication. For our example, select the Internet option as shown in Figure 22-18.

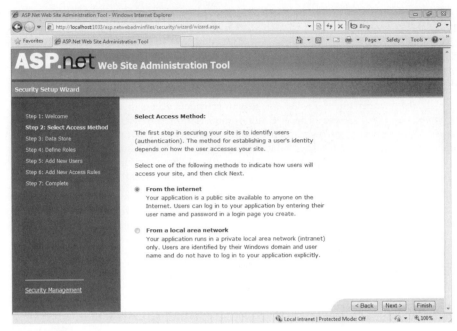

FIGURE 22-18

Working through the wizard, you are also asked whether you are going to work with role management. Enable role management by checking the appropriate check box and add a role named Manager. After this step, you can begin to enter users into the system. Fill out information for each user you want in the system, as shown in Figure 22-19. The database used in the sample application has three users: Rob Windsor, Bill Sheldon, and Billy Hollis. The password is the same for all users: pass@word1.

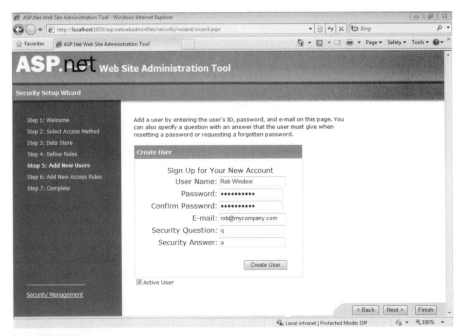

FIGURE 22-19

The next step is to create the access rules for your site. You can pick specific folders and apply the rules for the folder. Click the Membership folder on the left and then add an access rule to deny anonymous users to the folder (see Figure 22-20). Now click the Secret folder and add two access rules, one to allow people in the Manager role and one to deny all users (see Figure 22-21). The order is important, as the rules are applied in the order in which they appear in the `web.config` file(s). If the order of the rules were reversed, users in the Manager role would be denied access to the Secret folder.

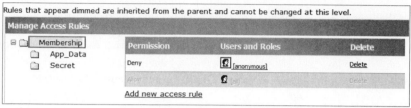

FIGURE 22-20

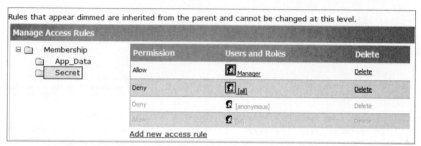

FIGURE 22-21

Click the Finish button to exit the wizard. You should be redirected back to the Security tab. The last step is to add at least one of the users you created to the Manager role. Click the Manage users link, and then click the Edit roles link for one or more of the users and add them to the Manager role as shown in Figure 22-22.

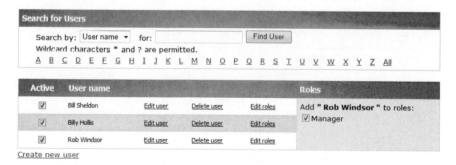

FIGURE 22-22

The contents added to the `web.config` file in the root folder include the following:

```
<?xml version="1.0" encoding="utf-8"?>
<configuration>
    <system.web>
        <authorization>
            <allow roles="Manager" />
```

```
            <deny users="?" />
        </authorization>
        <roleManager enabled="true" />
        <authentication mode="Forms" />
    </system.web>
</configuration>
```

Code snippet from web.config

This shows all the settings that were added by the wizard. The `<authorization>` section allows for users who are in the role of Manager, and denies all anonymous users (defined with a question mark). The `<roleManager>` element turns on the role management system, while the `<authentication>` element turns on forms authentication.

Note that there is a second `web.config` in the `Secret` folder. This defines the security for the folder and the pages inside:

```
<configuration>
    <system.web>
        <authorization>
            <allow roles="Manager" />
            <deny users="*" />
        </authorization>
    </system.web>
</configuration>
```

Code snippet from Secret\web.config

Now, add a page called `Login.aspx`. This page will be used when users need to enter their credentials. On the login page place a `Login` server control. This is one of the many server controls that are designed to work with the `Membership` and `Role` providers. Each one requires little or no configuration because they are aware of the methods and properties of the providers to which they are connected. For example, the `Login` control natively knows how to ask the `Membership` provider to validate credentials entered by a user.

Now run the application trying to access the `Default.aspx` page. You will start out as an anonymous user. Because anonymous users have been denied access to all pages in the site, you will be redirected to the `Login.aspx` page so you can enter your credentials, as shown in Figure 22-23.

FIGURE 22-23

Entering the credentials for any of the users you created earlier should get you to the `Default.aspx` page. However, only the credentials for users in the Manager role will be sufficient to allow you to navigate to the `Payroll.aspx` page.

PROFILE PROPERTIES

Many Web applications have features that allow for personalization of some kind. This might be as simple as greeting a user by name, or it might deal with more advanced issues such as content placement. Whatever the case, personalization techniques have always been tricky. Developers have used anything from cookies, sessions, or database entries to control the personalization that users can perform on their pages.

ASP.NET includes a personalization system that is easy to use. It is as simple as making entries in the web.config file to get the personalization system started. Like the membership and role management systems, the personalization system uses the provider model so it can be customized to suit your needs.

Continuing with the Membership project created in the last section, we'll create two profile properties, FirstName and LastName, both of type String. To get started, alter the web.config file in the root folder as shown here:

```xml
<?xml version="1.0"?>
<configuration>
    <system.web>
        <profile>
            <properties>
                <add name="FirstName" type="System.String" />
                <add name="LastName" type="System.String" />
            </properties>
        </profile>
    </system.web>
</configuration>
```

Code snippet from web.config

When you are using a Web site project, which makes use of dynamic compilation, ASP.NET will create a class in the background with strongly typed properties matching those you just defined. When you are using a Web application project you have to get and set the properties using methods of the Profile property of the current HttpContext.

Update the Default.aspx page by adding the controls and code required to allow the user to enter a first name and last name, and then save these values to the corresponding Profile properties. In addition, add controls and code required to show the values of the Profile properties when the page loads and when their values are updated. You should end up with something similar to this:

```vb
<%@ Page Language="VB" %>

<script runat="server">
    Protected Sub Page_Load(ByVal sender As Object, _
        ByVal e As System.EventArgs)

        If Not IsPostBack Then
            ' Web Application projects
            'Dim prof = HttpContext.Current.Profile
            'TextBox1.Text = prof.GetPropertyValue("FirstName")
            'TextBox2.Text = prof.GetPropertyValue("LastName")

            ' Web Site projects
            TextBox1.Text = Profile.FirstName
            TextBox2.Text = Profile.LastName
        End If
        PopulateLabel()
    End Sub

    Protected Sub Button1_Click(ByVal sender As Object, _
        ByVal e As System.EventArgs)

        ' Web Application projects
        'Dim prof = HttpContext.Current.Profile
```

```
            'prof.SetPropertyValue("FirstName", TextBox1.Text)
            'prof.SetPropertyValue("LastName", TextBox2.Text)

            ' Web Site projects
            Profile.FirstName = TextBox1.Text
            Profile.LastName = TextBox2.Text
            PopulateLabel()
        End Sub

        Private Sub PopulateLabel
            ' Web Application projects
            'Dim prof = HttpContext.Current.Profile
            'Label1.Text = "First name: " & prof.GetPropertyValue("FirstName") & _
            '"<br/>Last name: " & prof.GetPropertyValue("LastName")

            ' Web Site projects
            Label1.Text = "First name: " & Profile.FirstName & _
            "<br/>Last name: " & Profile.LastName
        End Sub
    </script>

    <html xmlns="http://www.w3.org/1999/xhtml" >
    <head id="Head1" runat="server">
        <title>Welcome Page</title>
    </head>
    <body>
        <form id="form1" runat="server">
        <div>
            <asp:LoginName ID="LoginName1" runat="server" />
            <br /><br />
            First name:<br />
            <asp:TextBox ID="TextBox1" Runat="server"></asp:TextBox>
            <br />
            Last name:<br />
            <asp:TextBox ID="TextBox2" Runat="server"></asp:TextBox>
            <br />
            <asp:Button ID="Button1" Runat="server" Text="Submit Information"
             OnClick="Button1_Click" />
            <br />
            <br />
            <asp:Label ID="Label1" Runat="server"></asp:Label>
        </div>
        </form>
    </body>
    </html>
```

Code snippet from Default.aspx

When this page is posted back to itself, the values entered into the two text boxes are placed into the personalization engine and associated with this particular user through the Profile object. Once stored in the personalization engine, they are then available to you on any page within the application through the use of the same Profile object.

MICROSOFT AJAX (ASP.NET AJAX)

In Web development, Ajax (asynchronous JavaScript and XML) is a term that signifies the capability to build rich, interactive applications. These applications contain client-side code that responds to user interactions by making asynchronous Web service calls via the XMLHttpRequest object and then updating areas of the page using the Document Object Model (DOM). Because the Web service calls are made asynchronously, the page remains responsive to the user throughout the process.

The creation and inclusion of the `XMLHttpRequest` object in JavaScript and the fact that most upper-level browsers support it led to the creation of the Ajax model. Ajax applications, although they have been around for a few years, gained popularity after Google released a number of notable, Ajax-enabled applications such as Google Maps and Google Suggest. These applications clearly demonstrated the value of Ajax.

Shortly thereafter, Microsoft released a beta for a new toolkit that enabled developers to incorporate Ajax features in their Web applications. This toolkit has had several names — initially it was code-named *Atlas*, at release it was renamed to ASP.NET AJAX, and with the release of .NET 4 Beta 2 it has been renamed again to Microsoft Ajax. Whatever the name, this toolkit abstracts away the low-level coding previously required, making it extremely simple to start using Ajax features in your applications today.

Understanding the Need for Ajax

To understand what Ajax is doing to your Web application, it would be instructive to first take a look at what a Web page does when it *does not* use Ajax. Figure 22-24 shows a typical request and response activity for a Web application.

In this case, end user interactions cause a full page postback. The Web server processes the request, ASP.NET generates the updated page (including ViewState), and the full page is sent to the end user's browser where it is rendered. During this process the page is unresponsive to additional user interactions and the user generally experiences a "flicker" as the page is being updated.

Conversely, an Ajax-enabled Web page includes JavaScript that takes care of issuing the calls to the Web server. It does this when it is possible to send a request and get a response for just part of the page and using script; the client library only updates the parts of the page that have changed due to the request. With only part of the page being processed, the end user experiences what some people term "fluidity" in the page, which makes the page seem more responsive. Less code is required to update just a portion of a page, and it produces the responsiveness the end user expects. Figure 22-25 shows a diagram of how this works.

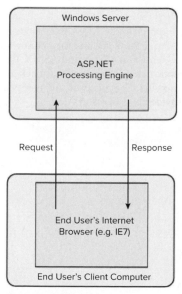

FIGURE 22-24

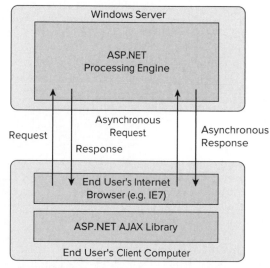

FIGURE 22-25

Microsoft Ajax Implementation

There are actually two parts to Microsoft Ajax: a client-side JavaScript library and a set of server controls.

The Microsoft Ajax Library is a set of JavaScript files that expose an object-oriented interface that is designed to be familiar to those who have used the .NET Framework (see Figure 22-26). Even though many of the namespaces, types, and calling conventions are similar to those found in .NET, the client-side library has no dependency on the .NET Framework. Thus, it can be used in Web pages of any kind: ASPX, HTML, PHP, JSP and so on. This fact was the primary motivation for removing ASP.NET from the name of the toolkit. The toolkit is also designed with browser compatibility in mind; anything you build using the library should work consistently across recent versions of the popular browsers.

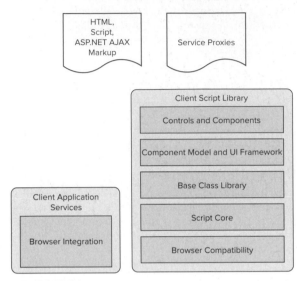

FIGURE 22-26

The server-side framework is mostly made up of a set of server controls that appear in the AJAX Extensions tab of the Toolbox (see Figure 22-27). The most commonly used controls are the ScriptManager and the UpdatePanel (you'll see both of these later). In addition, the server-side framework adds extensions to WCF and ASMX Web services that enable the automatic creation of JavaScript proxies and automatic marshalling of objects back and forth between JavaScript objects (JSON) and the .NET objects, significantly easing the process of calling services from client-side code. Figure 22-28 illustrates the server-side framework provided by Microsoft Ajax.

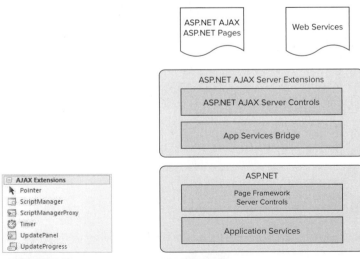

FIGURE 22-27   **FIGURE 22-28**

UpdatePanel Control vs. Client-Side Service Calls

Like many things in the .NET arena, Microsoft gives you options for adding Ajax behavior to your applications. Using the `UpdatePanel` control enables you to continue to develop with server controls and the Web Forms model. It has a small learning curve and is great when working with existing applications, but it is somewhat limited in functionality. The alternative is to move to a more architecturally pure Ajax implementation whereby you use client-side JavaScript to make Web service calls and update pages using the DOM or using the new `DataView` control and client templates. Because this changes the development process for many, it has a steeper learning curve; but it offers greater flexibility in implementation.

Introducing the Sample Project

For this example you will build an application similar to something you built earlier. You will have a page that displays customers from the Northwind database, filtered by country. The big difference will be the introduction of a Web service that sits between the user interface code and the data model. You will start with an application that does not make use of Microsoft Ajax and then update it first to use the `UpdatePanel` control and then to use client-side service calls and client templates.

The solution will contain two projects, a Class Library project named Service that will have the data model and the implementation of the service operations, and a Web application project named Client that will expose the Web service and the pages with which end users interact. The data model and the solution structure are shown in Figure 22-29.

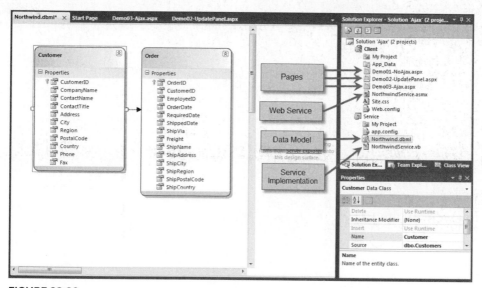

FIGURE 22-29

The code for the service implementation (`Service.NorthwindService`) is shown below. You'll need to add the LINQ to SQL model shown in Figure 22-29 before adding this code.

Available for download on Wrox.com

```
Public Class CustomerDto
    Property CustomerID As String
    Property CompanyName As String
    Property ContactName As String
    Property ContactTitle As String
    Property OrderCount As Integer
End Class
```

```vb
Public Class NorthwindService
    Public Function GetCountryNames() As String()
        Dim dc As New NorthwindDataContext
        Dim query = From cust In dc.Customers
                    Select cust.Country Distinct
                    Order By Country
        Return query.ToArray()
    End Function

    Public Function GetCustomersByCountry(ByVal country As String) _
        As CustomerDto()
        Dim dc As New NorthwindDataContext
        Dim query = From cust In dc.Customers
                    Where cust.Country = country
                    Select New CustomerDto With {
                        .CustomerID = cust.CustomerID,
                        .CompanyName = cust.CompanyName,
                        .ContactName = cust.ContactName,
                        .ContactTitle = cust.ContactTitle,
                        .OrderCount = cust.Orders.Count
                        }
        Return query.ToArray()
    End Function
End Class
```

Code snippet from Service\NortwindService.vb

The code for the Web service (`Client.NorthwindService`) is shown next (note that it just delegates calls to the service implementation class):

```vb
Imports System.Web.Services
Imports System.Web.Services.Protocols
Imports System.ComponentModel

<System.Web.Script.Services.ScriptService()> _
<System.Web.Services.WebService(Namespace:="http://mycompany.com/Northwind")> _
<System.Web.Services.WebServiceBinding(ConformsTo:=WsiProfiles.BasicProfile1_1)> _
<ToolboxItem(False)> _
Public Class NorthwindService
    Inherits System.Web.Services.WebService

    <WebMethod()> _
    Public Function CountryNames() As String()
        Dim svc As New Service.NorthwindService()
        Return svc.GetCountryNames()
    End Function

    <WebMethod()> _
    Public Function GetCustomersByCountry(ByVal country As String) _
        As Service.CustomerDto()
        Dim svc As New Service.NorthwindService()
        Return svc.GetCustomersByCountry(country)
    End Function
End Class
```

Code snippet from Client\NorthwindService.asmx.vb

Finally, the markup for the page (`Client.Demo01-NoAjax`) is shown here. It uses the `ObjectDataSource` control to communicate with the Web service to get data, and uses standard data binding to populate the `DropDownList` and `GridView` controls:

```
<%@ Page Language="vb" AutoEventWireup="false" CodeBehind="Demo01-NoAjax.aspx.vb"
Inherits="Client.Demo01_NoAjax" %>

<!DOCTYPE html PUBLIC "-//W3C//DTD XHTML 1.0 Transitional//EN"
"http://www.w3.org/TR/xhtml1/DTD/xhtml1-transitional.dtd">

<html xmlns="http://www.w3.org/1999/xhtml" >
<head id="Head1" runat="server">
    <title>No Ajax</title>
</head>
<body>
    <form id="form1" runat="server">
    <div>
        <asp:ObjectDataSource ID="ObjectDataSource1" runat="server"
            SelectMethod="CountryNames" TypeName="Client.NorthwindService">
        </asp:ObjectDataSource>
        <asp:DropDownList ID="DropDownList1" runat="server"
            DataSourceID="ObjectDataSource1" AutoPostBack="True">
        </asp:DropDownList>
        <br /><br />

        <asp:ObjectDataSource ID="ObjectDataSource2" runat="server"
            SelectMethod="GetCustomersByCountry"
            TypeName="Client.NorthwindService">
            <SelectParameters>
                <asp:ControlParameter ControlID="DropDownList1"
                    Name="country"
                    PropertyName="SelectedValue" Type="String" />
            </SelectParameters>
        </asp:ObjectDataSource>
        <asp:GridView ID="GridView1" runat="server"
            AutoGenerateColumns="False"
            DataSourceID="ObjectDataSource2">
            <Columns>
                <asp:BoundField DataField="CustomerID"
                    HeaderText="Customer ID"
                    SortExpression="CustomerID" />
                <asp:BoundField DataField="CompanyName"
                    HeaderText="Company Name"
                    SortExpression="CompanyName" />
                <asp:BoundField DataField="ContactName"
                    HeaderText="Contact Name"
                    SortExpression="ContactName" />
                <asp:BoundField DataField="ContactTitle"
                    HeaderText="Contact Title"
                    SortExpression="ContactTitle" />
                <asp:BoundField DataField="OrderCount"
                    HeaderText="Order Count"
                    SortExpression="OrderCount" />
            </Columns>
        </asp:GridView>
    </div>
    </form>
</body>
</html>
```

Code snippet from Client\Demo01-NoAjax.aspx

Figure 22-30 shows the Demo01-NoAjax.aspx page running. What can't be captured in an image is that there is a full-page postback each time the user selects a new country. However, you can see the communication with the server when a new country is selected using a tracing tool like Fiddler (www.fiddlertool.com). Figure 22-31 shows the request in the upper pane (1,590 bytes) and the response in the lower pane (4,374 bytes).

FIGURE 22-30

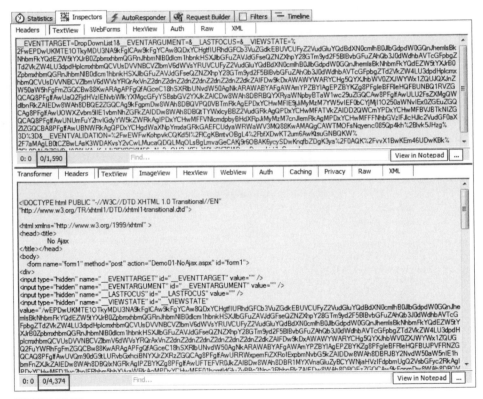

FIGURE 22-31

Adding the UpdatePanel Control

One of the drawbacks to the current implementation is that the markup for the drop-down list containing the countries is sent with every response even though the list of countries rarely changes. When a country is selected from the list, all you really need to update is the grid containing the customer data.

The previously mentioned `UpdatePanel` control enables you to do this quite easily. The `UpdatePanel`, along with the rest of the Microsoft Ajax framework, allows for *partial-page rendering*. In other words, you can indicate a section of a page that you want to be updated when a user interaction occurs, leaving the remainder of the page unchanged. An added benefit is that this process will be done asynchronously, so the page remains responsive while the update is in progress. To achieve this goal, you need to use the properties of the `UpdatePanel` to indicate which events of which controls will trigger an *asynchronous postback* instead of a regular full-page postback.

In our example, we want to wrap the `GridView` control in an `UpdatePanel` and indicate that a `SelectedIndexChanged` event on the `DropDownList` control should cause an asynchronous postback. To do this, add a `ScriptManager` control to the top of the page, and then update the part of the page (or create a modified copy) that includes the markup for the `GridView` to look like this from the Demo02-UpdatePanel.aspx page:

```
<asp:ScriptManager ID="ScriptManager1" runat="server">
</asp:ScriptManager>

<asp:ObjectDataSource ID="ObjectDataSource1" runat="server"
    SelectMethod="CountryNames" TypeName="Client.NorthwindService">
</asp:ObjectDataSource>
<asp:DropDownList ID="DropDownList1" runat="server"
    DataSourceID="ObjectDataSource1" AutoPostBack="True">
</asp:DropDownList>
<br /><br />

<asp:ObjectDataSource ID="ObjectDataSource2" runat="server"
    SelectMethod="GetCustomersByCountry"
    TypeName="Client.NorthwindService">
    <SelectParameters>
        <asp:ControlParameter ControlID="DropDownList1"
            Name="country"
            PropertyName="SelectedValue" Type="String" />
    </SelectParameters>
</asp:ObjectDataSource>
<asp:UpdatePanel ID="UpdatePanel1" runat="server">
<ContentTemplate>
    <asp:GridView ID="GridView1" runat="server"
        AutoGenerateColumns="False"
        DataSourceID="ObjectDataSource2">
        <Columns>
            <asp:BoundField DataField="CustomerID" HeaderText="Customer ID"
                SortExpression="CustomerID" />
            <asp:BoundField DataField="CompanyName" HeaderText="Company Name"
                SortExpression="CompanyName" />
            <asp:BoundField DataField="ContactName" HeaderText="Contact Name"
                SortExpression="ContactName" />
            <asp:BoundField DataField="ContactTitle" HeaderText="Contact Title"
                SortExpression="ContactTitle" />
            <asp:BoundField DataField="OrderCount" HeaderText="Order Count"
                SortExpression="OrderCount" />
        </Columns>
    </asp:GridView>
</ContentTemplate>
<Triggers>
    <asp:AsyncPostBackTrigger ControlID="DropDownList1"
        EventName="SelectedIndexChanged" />
</Triggers>
</asp:UpdatePanel>
```

Code snippet from Client\Demo02-UpdatePanel.aspx

Figure 22-32 shows the page running. In this case, when a new country is selected the page is asynchronously posted back to the server and the page-lifecycle runs, but only the markup for the grid is sent to the client. Looking at the trace in Figure 22-33, you can see that the request is virtually the same as before (1,668 bytes) but the response is significantly smaller (2,625 bytes).

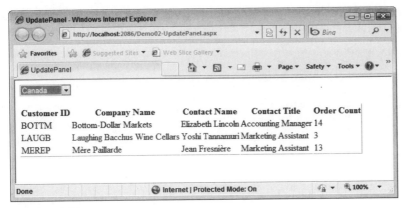

FIGURE 22-32

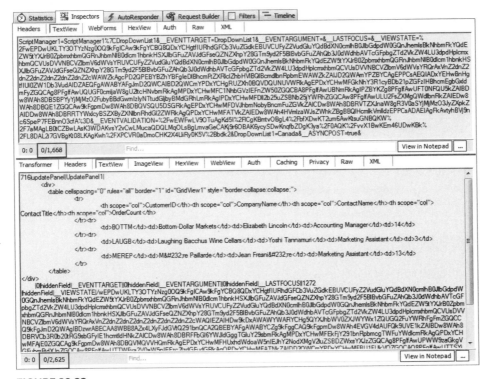

FIGURE 22-33

Using Client-Side Service Calls and Client Templates

As you've seen, refactoring the page to add Ajax-like behavior with the UpdatePanel is fairly easy and doesn't require a significant change in the way you develop pages. You also get the benefit of reduced traffic, as only the markup for the area of the page that is contained in the UpdatePanel is sent in the response.

Unfortunately, there are some drawbacks. The main drawback is that the full page life cycle is running for each request. This means that markup for the entire page is being generated on the server even though some of it is going to be discarded because it is outside the UpdatePanel. The second drawback is the size of the request and response. Even though we reduced it significantly from the full-page postback, we can do much, much better (as you will see shortly).

Let's modify the application to use a purer Ajax implementation in which we are calling Web services from the client-side JavaScript. This is done in Demo03-Ajax.aspx in the sample application.

The first thing we need to do is ensure that the Web service we are going to call is able to generate a JavaScript proxy. If you are using ASMX Web Services, all that is required is the addition of the `System.Web.Script.Services.ScriptService` attribute to your service type. If you look back at the sample code, our service type (NorthwindService.asmx.vb) already has that attribute so we are good to go. If we were using a WCF service, we would need an endpoint that used the `webHttpBinding` and had the `enableWebScript` element in its endpoint behavior.

Next, we need to add a service reference and a couple of script references to the `ScriptManager`. Since we'll be calling our service from the client-side, we need to ensure that the JavaScript proxy is added to our page; the service reference will take care of this. The script references ensure that the page has access to the required client-side libraries. Traditionally, the client-side libraries have been deployed as embedded resources in the `System.Web.Extensions` assembly. With the release of .NET 4 Beta 2, Microsoft decided to take the Microsoft Ajax Library out of band, allowing the library to be updated more frequently than the .NET Framework. The most recent version of the Microsoft Ajax Library can be downloaded from CodePlex (`http://ajax.codeplex.com`).

For the sample application, the ASP.NET Ajax Library 0911 Beta was downloaded and the JavaScript files were added to the Client project in a folder named Scripts.

```
<asp:ScriptManager ID="ScriptManager1" runat="server">
    <Scripts>
        <asp:ScriptReference Path="~/Scripts/MicrosoftAjax.js" />
        <asp:ScriptReference Path="~/Scripts/MicrosoftAjaxTemplates.js" />
    </Scripts>
    <Services>
        <asp:ServiceReference Path="NorthwindService.asmx" />
    </Services>
</asp:ScriptManager>
```

Code snippet from Client\Demo03-Ajax.aspx

If you know your application will have reliable access to the Internet, you have the option of using the Microsoft Ajax Content Delivery Network (CDN). This allows your application to load the required JavaScript files directly from the Microsoft site instead of having to include them with each project. An additional benefit is that the `ScriptManager` control is aware of the CDN so all you need to do is set one property and the `ScriptManager` automatically ensures that the required JavaScript files are included with each response.

```
<asp:ScriptManager EnableCdn="true" ID="ScriptManager1" runat="server">
    <Services>
        <asp:ServiceReference Path="NorthwindService.asmx" />
    </Services>
</asp:ScriptManager>
```

Since we will be calling the service to get the customer data from the client side, we will also be rendering the customer data on the client side. We'll replace the `UpdatePanel`, the `GridView`, and its associated `ObjectDataSource` with a HTML table. What will be a little unusual about the table is that we will use the client template features to enable client-side data binding. This allows us to define a template for the table body that includes placeholders for properties of the objects that will be bound to the template. For simple binding, the name of the property is surrounded in double curly braces (e.g., `{{ CustomerID }}`); however, more complex binding scenarios are supported using a syntax similar to that used in WPF (e.g., `{binding RequiredDate, convert=dateConverter}`). In a moment you will create a `DataView` control and attach it to the `tbody` element. The `DataView` will act like the server-side `DataSource` controls we used earlier. It will be the object that receives the data and populates the target element via the data-binding mechanism.

The last important point to note is the class attribute on the `tbody` element. It needs to have the value `"sys-template"` for the data binding to work:

```
<table id="customersTable" cellspacing="0" border="1">
<thead>
  <tr>
     <th>Customer ID</th>
     <th>Company Name</th>
     <th>Contact Name</th>
     <th>Contact Title</th>
     <th>Order Count</th>
  </tr>
</thead>
<tbody id="customersBody" class="sys-template">
  <tr>
    <td>{{CustomerID}}</td>
    <td>{{CompanyName}}</td>
    <td>{{ContactName}}</td>
    <td>{{ContactTitle}}</td>
    <td align="right">{{OrderCount}}</td>
  </tr>
</tbody>
</table>
```

Code snippet from Client\Demo03-Ajax.aspx

Finally, we need to add the JavaScript code to populate the table we just created. Let's start with what happens when the page loads. Just as we have a `Page_Load` event hander on the server side, we can create a `pageLoad` function in JavaScript and the framework will call it for us when the client-side elements have been initialized.

When the page loads, we want to create the `DataView` that will be used to populate the body of the table; then we want to populate the table; and finally we want to hook up an event handler so that when the user selects a different country, the table is refreshed. When we create the `DataView` we will pass a string parameter that uses CSS selector syntax to identify the element to attach to. In this case, that element is the table body. To show the customers we will call a custom `showCustomers` function, which we'll add shortly. To add the event handler to the `DropDownList`, we will use the `$addhandler` shortcut method, indicating that when the change event happens we want to call the `showCustomers` function:

```
var custView;

function pageLoad() {
    custView = Sys.create.dataView("#customersBody");
    showCustomers();
    $addHandler($get("DropDownList1"), "change", showCustomers);
}
```

Code snippet from Client\Demo03-Ajax.aspx

The code to show the customers is fairly simple. First, we get the name of the country the user has selected from the `DropDownList`. Then we call the Web service to get the customers for the selected country. This is done asynchronously, so the Web service call takes two parameters: the country and the name of the function we want to call when the service operation is complete (this is generally known as the *callback function*). When the service operation returns, the callback function will be passed the data representing the customers as a JavaScript array. All we need to do to update the table is to give the `DataView` the array; it will take care of the data binding and rendering:

```
function showCustomers() {
    var country = $get("DropDownList1").value;
    Client.NorthwindService.GetCustomersByCountry(country, showCustomersComplete);
}

function showCustomersComplete(data) {
    custView.set_data(data);
}
```

Code snippet from Client\Demo03-Ajax.aspx

Our page is now complete and ready for testing. The complete code and markup is shown here:

```
<%@ Page Language="vb" AutoEventWireup="false" CodeBehind="Demo03-Ajax.aspx.vb"
Inherits="Client.Demo03_Ajax" %>

<!DOCTYPE html PUBLIC "-//W3C//DTD XHTML 1.0 Transitional//EN"
"http://www.w3.org/TR/xhtml1/DTD/xhtml1-transitional.dtd">

<html xmlns="http://www.w3.org/1999/xhtml">
<head id="Head1" runat="server">
    <title>Ajax</title>
    <link href="Site.css" rel="stylesheet" type="text/css" />

    <script type="text/javascript">
        var custView;

        function pageLoad() {
            custView = Sys.create.dataView("#customersBody");
            showCustomers();
            $addHandler($get("DropDownList1"), "change", showCustomers);
        }

        function showCustomers() {
            var country = $get("DropDownList1").value;
            Client.NorthwindService.GetCustomersByCountry(
                country, showCustomersComplete);
        }

        function showCustomersComplete(data) {
            custView.set_data(data);
        }
    </script>
</head>
<body>
    <form id="form1" runat="server">
    <div>
        <asp:ScriptManager ID="ScriptManager1" runat="server">
            <Scripts>
                <asp:ScriptReference Path="~/Scripts/MicrosoftAjax.js" />
                <asp:ScriptReference Path="~/Scripts/MicrosoftAjaxTemplates.js" />
            </Scripts>
            <Services>
                <asp:ServiceReference Path="NorthwindService.asmx" />
            </Services>
        </asp:ScriptManager>

        <asp:ObjectDataSource ID="ObjectDataSource1" runat="server"
```

```
            SelectMethod="CountryNames" TypeName="Client.NorthwindService">
        </asp:ObjectDataSource>
        <asp:DropDownList ID="DropDownList1" runat="server"
            DataSourceID="ObjectDataSource1">
        </asp:DropDownList>
        <br /><br />

        <table id="customersTable" cellspacing="0" border="1">
        <thead>
          <tr>
              <th>Customer ID</th>
              <th>Company Name</th>
              <th>Contact Name</th>
              <th>Contact Title</th>
              <th>Order Count</th>
          </tr>
        </thead>
        <tbody id="customersBody" class="sys-template">
          <tr>
            <td>{{CustomerID}}</td>
            <td>{{CompanyName}}</td>
            <td>{{ContactName}}</td>
            <td>{{ContactTitle}}</td>
            <td align="right">{{OrderCount}}</td>
          </tr>
        </tbody>
        </table>
    </div>
    </form>
  </body>
  </html>
```

Code snippet from Client\Demo03-Ajax.aspx

Figure 22-34 shows the page running. Looking at the trace in Figure 22-35, you can see that the request is a simple JavaScript object that represents the country selected (20 bytes); and the response is a JavaScript array that represents the customer data from the selected country (538 bytes). That's an 87% savings in network traffic when compared to the example using the `UpdatePanel`.

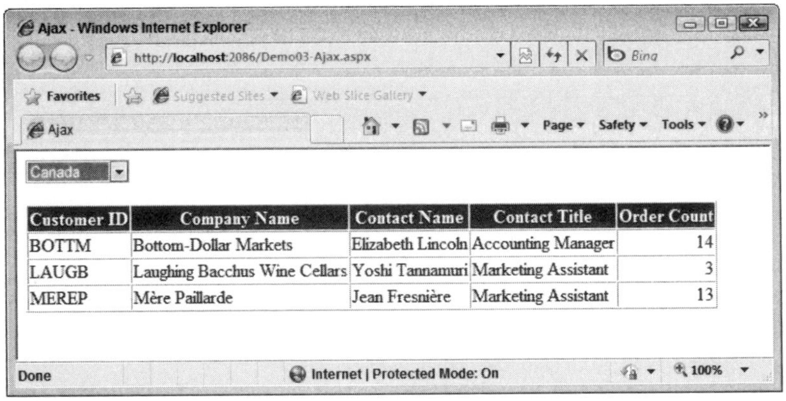

FIGURE 22-34

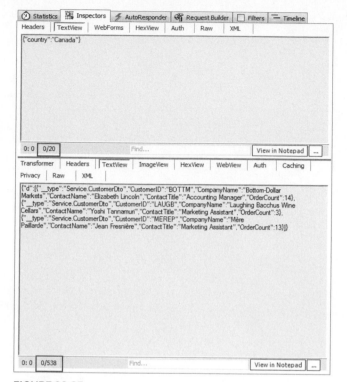

FIGURE 22-35

SUMMARY

This chapter and the previous chapter offered a whirlwind tour of ASP.NET and some of the features that you can provide in the projects you develop. ASP.NET is highly focused on the area of developer productivity, and it works very hard at providing you access to functionality expected in websites today.

A nice aspect of most of the features presented is that you can either utilize the wizards that are built into the underlying technology or skip these wizards and employ the technologies by editing markup. Either way is fine. Another useful aspect of the technologies introduced is that they all enable a huge amount of customization. You can alter the behavior and output of these technologies to achieve exactly what you need. If you want to dig deeper into ASP.NET, be sure to take a look at *Professional ASP.NET 4* (Evjen et al., Wiley, 2010).

23

ASP.NET MVC

WHAT YOU WILL LEARN IN THIS CHAPTER

➤ The Model-View-Controller (MVC) Pattern

➤ The goals of ASP.NET MVC

➤ How the MVC pattern has been applied to ASP.NET MVC

➤ Working with controllers and actions

➤ Using scaffolding to help generate views

➤ Validation in ASP.NET MVC 2

ASP.NET MVC is a Web framework that was originally released in March 2009 as an alternative to ASP.NET Web Forms. It was designed to limit abstractions and give developers a great deal of control over the creation of pages in an application. Specifically, ASP.NET MVC was designed to do the following:

➤ **Provide complete control over HTML markup** — With Web Forms, the final markup is mostly determined by the server controls on a page.

➤ **Have intuitive website URLs** — With Web Forms, the URL is determined by the location and name of the file being addressed.

➤ **Have a clear separation of concerns** — The Web Forms programming model encourages developers to put business logic and database access code in the code-behind for a page.

➤ **Be testable by default** — Several aspects of the Web Forms model make it difficult to write unit tests for user interface layer logic.

It's important to repeat that ASP.NET MVC is an alternative to Web Forms, not its replacement. MVC will suit the style of some developers, and seem a step backward for others. Many have used the analogy of manual versus automatic transmission. Manual (MVC) gives you complete control but requires more effort; automatic (Web Forms) may be slightly less efficient but it does the work for you. Ultimately, the choice of framework is yours. Choose the one that best suits your development style.

As this book is being written, ASP.NET MVC 2 is in Beta and is projected to be complete with the release of Visual Studio 2010. The contents of this chapter are based on the version of ASP.NET MVC 2 included with the Beta 2 versions of Visual Studio 2010 and .NET 4.

MODEL-VIEW-CONTROLLER AND ASP.NET

The Model-View-Controller pattern was conceived in the late 1970s by Trygve Reenskaug, a Norwegian computer scientist. It provides a powerful and elegant means of separating concerns within an application, and it applies extremely well to Web development.

The pattern separates an application into three components:

➤ **Model** — The business objects in the application

➤ **View** — The user interface

➤ **Controller** — Classes that handle user requests and manage application logic and flow

In the ASP.NET implementation of the pattern, requests are routed to controller classes that generally apply application logic (authorization, for example), interact with the model to retrieve or update data, determine the data that needs to be rendered in the response, and then pass control to a view to format the data and render the final markup to the user.

Another important aspect of the implementation of ASP.NET MVC is the use of convention over configuration. As we build an application in the next section, you will see that conventions are used to determine the names and locations of files in a project or to determine which class or file to load at runtime. You are not forced to follow these conventions, but doing so allows for a consistent experience across ASP.NET MVC applications.

BUILDING AN ASP.NET MVC APPLICATION

ASP.NET MVC is a new addition to the ASP.NET family and is likely new to most of you reading this book. Following the premise that the most effective way to learn a new framework is to use it, we will spend the remainder of this chapter building an ASP.NET MVC 2 application.

Creating the Project

Open Visual Studio and create a new ASP.NET MVC 2 Web Application named **MvcDemo**. You will immediately be asked if you want to create an associated unit test project (see Figure 23-1). Because testability is one of the core tenets of ASP.NET MVC it makes sense that the project template would encourage you to do so. Keep the default test project name and click OK to create the projects.

If you look at the MVC project in the Solution Explorer (see Figure 23-2), you'll see that several files and folders have been created by default. Three of the folders should jump out at you immediately: Models, Views, and Controllers. These folders map to the three components of the pattern on which this style of application is based.

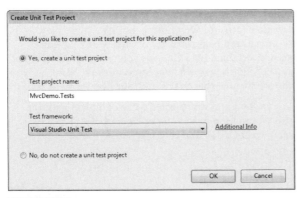

FIGURE 23-1

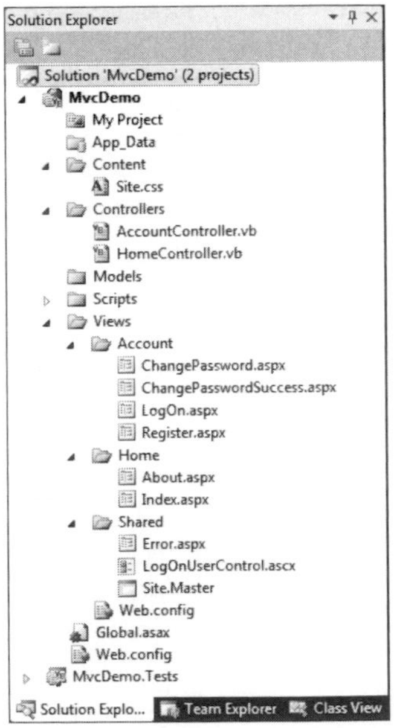

FIGURE 23-2

Currently, there are no out-of-the-box Web site project templates for ASP.NET MVC.

If you run the application, you will see that a few pages (including the master page) are included as part of the project template (see Figure 23-3). While not exactly the same, the site will be similar in look and feel to one created when you use the non-empty Web Forms project templates.

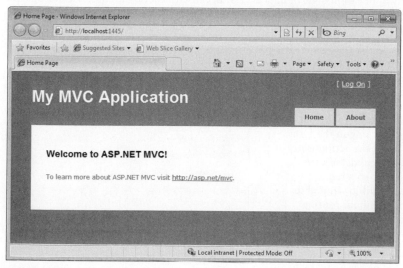

FIGURE 23-3

Controllers and Actions

In traditional Web application frameworks, requests are mapped to files containing markup for pages. In ASP.NET MVC, requests are mapped to methods on classes. The classes are the previously mentioned controller classes, and the methods are known as actions. Action methods are responsible for receiving user input, retrieving or saving data to the model, and passing control to the appropriate view. The view will typically return the markup for a page but it could also return other content types such as a binary file or JSON formatted data. Typical actions will handle requests to list, add, edit, or delete entities from the model.

Let's examine these concepts further by creating a new controller. In the Solution Explorer, right-click on the Controllers folder and select Add ➪ Controller. By convention, the names of controller classes should end with "Controller." The Add Controller dialog even encourages the use of this convention, as shown in Figure 23-4. Set the name to **SimpleController** and click the Add button.

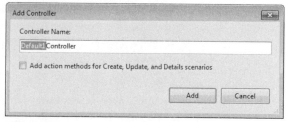

FIGURE 23-4

The class that's created will inherit from the base `Controller` class (`System.Web.Mvc.Controller`) and will have the shell for a default action method named `Index`:

```
Public Class SimpleController
    Inherits System.Web.Mvc.Controller
```

```
' GET: /Simple/

Function Index() As ActionResult
    Return View()
End Function

End Class
```

The `Index` action method is about as simple as it gets. When a request comes in for this action it just passes control to a view without any application logic or data access. Because the action method has not specified which view to show, convention states that ASP.NET MVC should look for a file matching the pattern `/Views/{Controller}/{Action}.aspx`. In the case of the `Index` action, that would be `/Views/Simple/Index.aspx`, which does not exist at this point.

The comment above the method is not required but it is something you'll typically see in code generated by Visual Studio. It indicates that this action will be accessed via an `HTTP GET` request to `/Simple`. This illustrates another convention. The default routing rules used by MVC expect something in the form of `/{Controller}/{Action}`. If the action is not specified, then ASP.NET MVC will default to calling the `Index` action method, so a request to `/Simple` or `/Simple/Index` will be routed to the `Index` action. You will learn about routing and how to add or modify routing rules later in this chapter.

Because the view for the `Index` action does not exist, let's create it. We could do this rather easily by hand, but there's no need to; Visual Studio will create it for us. In the Code Editor, right-click anywhere in the code for the `Index` method and select the Add View option in the context menu. In the Add View dialog, leave the default values as they are (see Figure 23-5) and click the Add button. You should be presented with a new content page that looks something like the following:

FIGURE 23-5

```
<%@ Page Title="" Language="VB" MasterPageFile="~/Views/Shared/Site.Master"
    Inherits="System.Web.Mvc.ViewPage" %>

<asp:Content ID="Content1" ContentPlaceHolderID="TitleContent" runat="server">
        Index
</asp:Content>

<asp:Content ID="Content2" ContentPlaceHolderID="MainContent" runat="server">
    <h2>Index</h2>
</asp:Content>
```

Note two things about the page: It was created in the proper folder by default (that is, `\Views\Simple`) and it inherits from `System.Web.Mvc.ViewPage` instead of `System.Web.UI.Page`. At this point you should be able to run the application. Once it is loaded in the browser, navigate to `/Simple` and you'll see a page like the one shown in Figure 23-6.

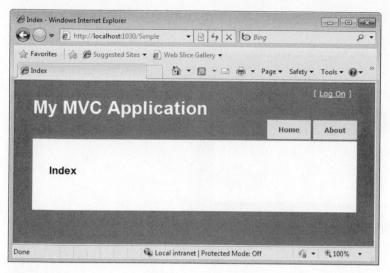

FIGURE 23-6

Now we'll look at an example in which data is passed from the action method to the view. Back in the SimpleController class, add a new action method called SayHello that takes a string parameter called name. When a request is made, ASP.NET will match parameters on the query string to parameters of the method. The action method can pass the value of the parameter to the view by adding it to the built-in ViewData collection.

```
' GET: /Simple/SayHello?name=Rob

Function SayHello(ByVal name As String) As ActionResult
    ViewData("Name") = name
    Return View()
End Function
```

Code snippet from \Controllers\SimpleController.vb

Create the view by right-clicking anywhere in the code for the SayHello function, selecting Add View in the context menu, and clicking the Add button. In the content page that's created, modify the value of the <h2> element to output the value of the name parameter stored in the ViewData:

```
<asp:Content ID="Content2" ContentPlaceHolderID="MainContent" runat="server">
    <h2>Hello <%: ViewData("Name")%></h2>
</asp:Content>
```

Note the use of the new <%: %> syntax. This is the same as <%= %> except that it automatically HTML encodes the output. This new syntax works in both Web Forms and MVC.

If you run the application and navigate to /Simple/SayHello?name=Rob, you should see a page similar to the one shown in Figure 23-7.

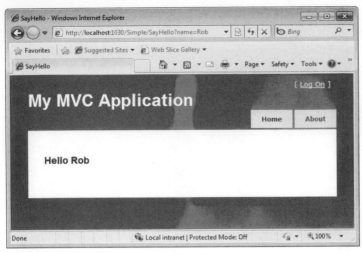

FIGURE 23-7

Adding the Model

In MVC, the model typically refers to the business or domain objects. These are classes that represent the data in the application, along with the corresponding business rules and validation. For our sample application we will use LINQ to SQL to create a simple domain model over data from the Northwind database.

If you don't have the Northwind database available, get the one included in the sample code for the book and add it to the App_Data folder of your project. In the Models folder, create a new LINQ to SQL model called **Northwind.dbml** and add the Categories and Products table to it as shown in Figure 23-8. Saving the model will create the `NorthwindDataContext` and the domain objects for categories and products.

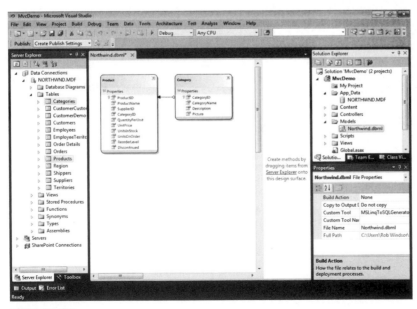

FIGURE 23-8

We could stop here and have our controllers access the data model directly, but doing so will reduce testability and lead to duplication of queries across the application. To avoid these issues, we will create a class that encapsulates access to the data model.

In the Models folder, create a new class called `NorthwindRepository`. In it create three methods: one that returns all categories, one that returns all products, and one that returns products in a specific category. In all three of the methods, sort the results by the name of the product or category.

```vb
Public Class NorthwindRepository
    Private _context As New NorthwindDataContext()

    Public Function GetCategories() As IQueryable(Of Category)
        Dim query = From cat In _context.Categories
                    Order By cat.CategoryName
                    Select cat
        Return query
    End Function

    Public Function GetProducts() As IQueryable(Of Product)
        Dim query = From prod In _context.Products
                    Order By prod.ProductName
                    Select prod
        Return query
    End Function

    Public Function GetProductsForCategory(ByVal categoryName As String) _
        As IQueryable(Of Product)
        Dim query = From prod In _context.Products
                    Where prod.Category.CategoryName = categoryName
                    Order By prod.ProductName
                    Select prod
        Return query
    End Function
End Class
```

Code snippet from \Models\NorthwindRepository.vb

Views

Now that we have a model, we can create some controllers, actions, and views that are more like those you would create in a traditional business application. To start off, we will look at views that display data from the database; later in the chapter we add views that let us modify the data.

Create a new controller called `ProductsController`. The `Index` action should be modified to get the list of categories and return a view that will display them:

```vb
Public Class ProductsController
    Inherits System.Web.Mvc.Controller

    Private _repository As New NorthwindRepository()

    '
    ' GET: /Products/

    Function Index() As ActionResult
        Dim categories = _repository.GetCategories().ToList()
        Return View(categories)
    End Function

End Class
```

Code snippet from \Controllers\ProductsController.vb

Notice that instead of passing the list of categories to the view using the `ViewData` collection (which would be weakly typed), we pass them as the first parameter to the `View` method. This enables us to create a strongly typed view, one that is aware that it is rendering category objects. Bring up the Add View dialog as before, but this time check the Create a Strongly-Typed View check box and select MvcDemo.Category from the View data class drop-down. For now we'll keep the default value of Empty in the View content drop-down. You'll see the effect of using the other values in this drop-down later in the chapter.

In the resulting view page, you show the category names in an unordered list:

```
<%@ Page Title="" Language="VB" MasterPageFile="~/Views/Shared/Site.Master"
    Inherits="System.Web.Mvc.ViewPage(Of IEnumerable(Of MvcDemo.Category))" %>

<asp:Content ID="Content1" ContentPlaceHolderID="TitleContent" runat="server">
        Product Categories
</asp:Content>

<asp:Content ID="Content2" ContentPlaceHolderID="MainContent" runat="server">
    <h2>Product Categories</h2>

    <ul>
    <% For Each category In Model %>
    <li><%: category.CategoryName %></li>
    <% Next %>
    </ul>
</asp:Content>
```

The first thing to note is the value of the `Inherits` attribute of the `Page` directive. `ViewPage` is a generic type, so setting the `type` parameter to the name of the type of data used in the page enables that data to be accessed in a strongly typed fashion. When this page was generated by Visual Studio, the type parameter was set to `MvcDemo.Category` (the type name we provided in the Add View dialog). Since we are working with a list of categories instead of an individual category, this needs to be manually changed to `IEnumerable(Of MvcDemo.Category)`.

The other thing that might jump out is the code used to generate the unordered list. If you've done Classic ASP programming, this style of mixing HTML markup with VB code will bring back memories (probably scary ones). Yes, this style of programming does return when building views in ASP.NET MVC, but its potentially negative effect on readability and maintainability is greatly reduced because the view pages will contain minimal logic and no data access code.

If you run the application and navigate to `/Products`, you should see a page similar to the one shown in Figure 23-9.

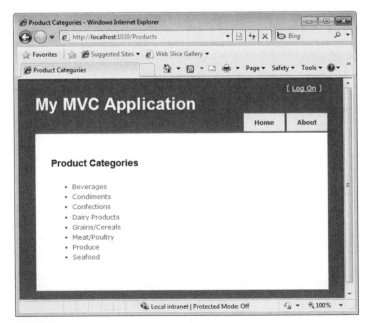

FIGURE 23-9

Now that we have a way to create a list a categories, let's repeat the process to create a list of products. Because there are a lot of products, we can show them by category to limit the number shown on a page. In the `ProductsController`, create a new action method called `Browse`. It should use the repository to get the products for the category passed in as a parameter and then pass control to the `Browse` view:

```vb
' GET: /Products/Browse?category=beverages

Function Browse(ByVal category As String) As ActionResult
    Dim products = _repository.GetProductsForCategory(category)
    Return View(products.ToList())
End Function
```

Code snippet from \Controllers\ProductsController.vb

Create the strongly typed view for this action using the same steps you used for the `Index` action. In this case, set the View data class option to `MvcDemo.Product` as shown in Figure 23-10.

FIGURE 23-10

As before, the `Inherits` attribute of the `Page` directive in the generated view page must be manually modified (the type parameter needs to be `IEnumerable(Of MvcDemo.Product)`). This view will show an unordered list of products and their corresponding unit prices:

```aspx
<%@ Page Title="" Language="VB" MasterPageFile="~/Views/Shared/Site.Master"
    Inherits="System.Web.Mvc.ViewPage(Of IEnumerable (Of MvcDemo.Product))" %>

<asp:Content ID="Content1" ContentPlaceHolderID="TitleContent" runat="server">
        Browse Products
</asp:Content>

<asp:Content ID="Content2" ContentPlaceHolderID="MainContent" runat="server">

    <h2>Browse Products</h2>

    <ul>
    <% For Each prod In Model%>
        <%  Dim item = String.Format("{0}   (${1:F})",
                prod.ProductName, prod.UnitPrice)%>
        <li><%: item%></li>
    <% Next%>
    </ul>

</asp:Content>
```

Code snippet from \Views\Products\Browse.aspx

Running the application and navigating to `/Products/Browse?category=beverages` should render a page similar to the one shown in Figure 23-11.

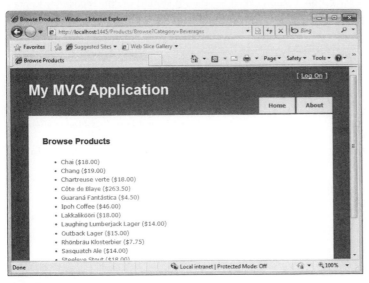

FIGURE 23-11

To complete this section, we'll tie the list of categories and products together. We'll modify the `Index` view (i.e., the list of categories), changing the items in the unordered list to links that will take us to the page showing the products for the selected category. Instead of creating anchor tags directly, we'll use the `ActionLink` *HTML Helper* to build the links for us; specifically, we'll use the overloaded version that takes the link text, the target action, and the parameters to pass to the action:

Available for
download on
Wrox.com

```
<ul>
<% For Each category In Model%>
<li>
    <%: Html.ActionLink(category.CategoryName,
        "Browse", New With {.Category = category.CategoryName}) %>
</li>
<% Next%>
</ul>
```

Code snippet from \Views\Products\Index.aspx

You should now be able to navigate to the list of categories, click one of the links, and get the list of products for the category you selected.

Routing

One of the goals of ASP.NET MVC is to enable developers to create "friendly" URLs for their users. In our application, it would be nice to get a list of products in the beverage category by navigating to `/Products/Browse/Beverages` instead of using the query string as we are now.

This change can be accomplished through the routing engine included in ASP.NET. This engine enables us to map a URL template to a controller (and potentially an action and parameters). When a request comes in, the engine uses pattern-matching algorithms to find a template that matches the "shape" of the request and then routes the request to the corresponding controller.

Open the `Global.asax` file and look for the method named `RegisterRoutes`. In it you will see the code that has been routing the requests we've been making so far to controllers and actions:

```
routes.MapRoute( _
    "Default", _
    "{controller}/{action}/{id}", _
    New With {.controller = "Home", .action = "Index", .id = ""} _
)
```

The first parameter is the route name used as the key in the route table. The second parameter is the URL template. This template indicates there are potentially three segments: the first mapping to the controller name, the second mapping to the action name, and the third mapping to an id. The final parameter is an anonymous type that defines the default values of the segments.

Add the following code (above the existing call to `MapRoute`) to add a mapping that allows us to include the category name as part of the URL when we browse products:

```
routes.MapRoute("BrowseProducts", _
    "Products/Browse/{Category}", _
    New With {.controller = "Products", .action = "Browse", .Category = ""})
```

Code snippet from Global.asax

You should now be able to run the application and navigate to `/Products/Browse/Beverages` or `/Products/Browse/Condiments` to see products in those categories.

Scaffolding and CRUD Operations

We've used the tooling in Visual Studio to assist us in creating controllers and views but we haven't explored these tools fully. They have additional functionality to assist in creating the action methods and views for a slightly modified version of the CRUD (create, read, update and delete) operations.

Before we get into creating new MVC elements, however, we need to revisit the `NorthwindRepository` class. Two new methods will be needed: one to retrieve a single product by ID, and the second to enable us to save any changes to the LINQ to SQL entities:

```
Public Function GetProduct(ByVal id As Integer) As Product
    Dim query = From prod In _context.Products
                Where prod.ProductID = id
                Select prod
    Return query.SingleOrDefault()
End Function

Public Sub Save()
    _context.SubmitChanges()
End Sub
```

Code snippet from \Models\NorthwindRepository.vb

With these changes complete, we are now able to properly explore the scaffolding tools in Visual Studio. These work in a very similar way to the data server controls in Web Forms. By indicating the type of data to render and the type of view you desire (list, edit, create, etc.), Visual Studio can use reflection to determine the properties of the object being rendered and generate the appropriate markup and code.

To see this in action, create a new controller called `AdminController` but this time check the option to "Add action methods for Create, Update and Details scenarios," as shown in Figure 23-12. The generated code contains base implementations of `Index`, `Details`, `Create` and `Edit` action methods.

We'll start by modifying the `Index` action method. When it is requested we'll return a view showing a grid with the data for all products. Modify the

FIGURE 23-12

action method to both get all products from the `NorthwindRepository` and pass the resulting list to the `Index` view:

```
Private _repository As New NorthwindRepository()

'
' GET: /Admin/

Function Index() As ActionResult
    Dim products = _repository.GetProducts()
    Return View(products.ToList())
End Function
```

Add a strongly typed view for the `Index` action, choosing List from the View content drop-down, as shown in Figure 23-13.

FIGURE 23-13

Choosing List will cause Visual Studio to generate a table to show the product data along with links to create, edit, or display the product data. Because the generated table will be too wide for the page, we'll delete some of the columns. The modified view should look something like the following:

```
<h2>Product Index</h2>

<p><%=Html.ActionLink("Create New", "Create")%></p>

<table>
    <tr>
        <th></th>
        <th>ProductName</th>
        <th>Category</th>
        <th>UnitPrice</th>
        <th>UnitsInStock</th>
        <th>Discontinued</th>
    </tr>

<% For Each item In Model%>
    <tr>
        <td>
            <%=Html.ActionLink("Edit", "Edit", New With {.id = item.ProductID})%> |
            <%=Html.ActionLink("Details", "Details", New With {.id = item.ProductID})%>
        </td>
```

```
        <td>
            <%= Html.Encode(item.ProductName) %>
        </td>
        <td>
            <%= Html.Encode(item.CategoryID) %>
        </td>
        <td>
            <%= Html.Encode(String.Format("{0:F}", item.UnitPrice)) %>
        </td>
        <td>
            <%= Html.Encode(item.UnitsInStock) %>
        </td>
        <td>
            <%= Html.Encode(item.Discontinued) %>
        </td>
    </tr>
<% Next%>

</table>
```

Code snippet from \Views\Admin\Index.aspx

Notice the assumptions based on the ASP.NET MVC conventions. The Create link assumes you will have a `Create` action method, the Edit link assumes you have an `Edit` action method that takes the `ProductID` as a parameter, and so on. Without the conventions in place, these links would not be able to be code generated.

Running the application and navigating to /Admin should render a page similar to the one shown in Figure 23-14.

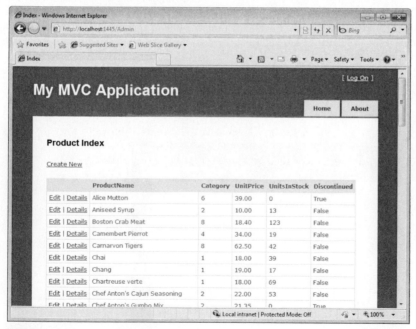

FIGURE 23-14

Moving to the `Details` action method, modify the code to get the requested product from the repository and pass it on to the `Details` view:

```
'
' GET: /Admin/Details/5

Function Details(ByVal id As Integer) As ActionResult
```

```
        Dim product = _repository.GetProduct(id)
        Return View(product)
    End Function
```

Code snippet from \Controllers\AdminController.vb

Generate the strongly typed view, this time selecting Details from the View content drop-down menu.

```
<h2>Product Details</h2>

<fieldset>
    <legend>Fields</legend>
    <p>ProductID: <%= Html.Encode(Model.ProductID) %></p>
    <p>ProductName: <%= Html.Encode(Model.ProductName) %></p>
    <p>SupplierID: <%= Html.Encode(Model.SupplierID) %></p>
    <p>CategoryID: <%= Html.Encode(Model.CategoryID) %></p>
    <p>QuantityPerUnit: <%= Html.Encode(Model.QuantityPerUnit) %></p>
    <p>UnitPrice: <%= Html.Encode(String.Format("{0:F}", Model.UnitPrice)) %></p>
    <p>UnitsInStock: <%= Html.Encode(Model.UnitsInStock) %></p>
    <p>UnitsOnOrder: <%= Html.Encode(Model.UnitsOnOrder) %></p>
    <p>ReorderLevel: <%= Html.Encode(Model.ReorderLevel) %></p>
    <p>Discontinued: <%= Html.Encode(Model.Discontinued) %></p>
</fieldset>
<p>
    <%=Html.ActionLink("Edit", "Edit", New With {.id = Model.ProductID})%> |
    <%=Html.ActionLink("Back to List", "Index") %>
</p>
```

Code snippet from \Views\Admin\Details.aspx

Run the application, navigate to /Admin, and click the Details link for one of the items. You should be taken to a page similar to the one shown in Figure 23-15. Clicking the Back to List link at the bottom of the page will take you back to the list of products.

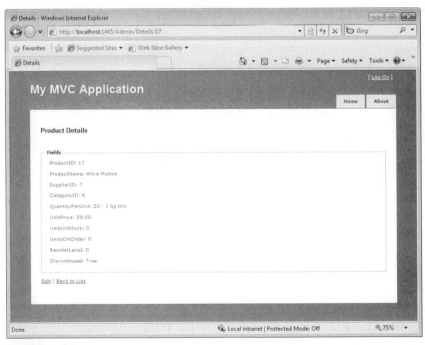

FIGURE 23-15

We'll look at the `Edit` action in two parts. The first part involves generating a form that allows editing of product data; the second involves receiving the updated data when the user submits the form.

The `Edit` action method will have the same implementation as the `Details` action method. Modify it so that it retrieves the requested product and returns the `Details` view:

```
'
' GET: /Admin/Edit/5

Function Edit(ByVal id As Integer) As ActionResult
    Dim product = _repository.GetProduct(id)
    Return View(product)
End Function
```

Code snippet from \Controllers\AdminController.vb

Generate a strongly typed view, selecting Edit from the View content drop-down, as shown in Figure 23-16.

```
<h2>Edit Product</h2>

<script src="../../Scripts/jquery-1.3.2.min.js" type="text/javascript"></script>
<script src="../../Scripts/jquery.validate.min.js" type="text/javascript"></script>
<script src="../../Scripts/MicrosoftMvcJQueryValidation.js" type="text/javascript">
</script>

<%=Html.ValidationSummary("Edit was unsuccessful. Please correct the errors ... ")%>
<% Html.EnableClientValidation()%>

<% Using Html.BeginForm() %>

    <fieldset>
        <legend>Fields</legend>
        <p>
            <label for="ProductName">ProductName:</label>
            <%= Html.TextBox("ProductName", Model.ProductName) %>
            <%= Html.ValidationMessage("ProductName", "*") %>
        </p>
        <p>
            <label for="SupplierID">SupplierID:</label>
            <%= Html.TextBox("SupplierID", Model.SupplierID) %>
            <%= Html.ValidationMessage("SupplierID", "*") %>
        </p>
        <!-- Some fields removed for brevity -->
        <p>
            <%= Html.LabelFor(Function(p) p.Discontinued)%>
            <%= Html.EditorFor(Function(p) p.Discontinued)%>
            <%= Html.ValidationMessage("Discontinued", "*") %>
        </p>
        <p>
            <input type="submit" value="Save" />
        </p>
    </fieldset>

<% End Using %>

<div>
    <%=Html.ActionLink("Back to List", "Index") %>
</div>
```

Code snippet from \Views\Admin\Edit.aspx

A few things in the generated view require further discussion. Note that several elements in the code snippet deal with validation. ASP.NET MVC 1.0 supported server-side validation, and ASP.NET MVC 2 adds native support for client-side validation. The links to the script files include the required JavaScript to implement the client-side validation framework. One of these files is the jQuery base library, and the second is a jQuery validation plug-in. Microsoft is including jQuery as part of ASP.NET 4, and the jQuery base library as part of many of the out-of-the-box project templates (including the one we are currently using). It's a safe bet that we'll see jQuery being used regularly as part of Visual Studio project and item templates in the future. The ValidationSummary and ValidationMessage HTML Helpers act very similarly to the validation server controls in the Web Forms framework. You'll learn how to implement rules to populate these controls more deeply in the next section.

FIGURE 23-16

The next item of note is the use of the TextBox helper. Several HTML Helpers can be used to render intrinsic elements such as text boxes, check boxes, buttons, drop-downs, and so on. The current implementation of the auto-scaffolding uses these kinds of helpers in the generated code.

ASP.NET MVC 2 adds new strongly typed helper methods that enable better compile-time checking and IntelliSense. The markup and code for the Discontinued property have been modified to use the new LabelFor and EditorFor helpers. Both these methods expect a lambda expression returning the value for the property as parameters. Reflection is used to determine the name of the property, so it can be shown in the label, and the type of property, so the proper HTML element can be rendered to display and edit. In our example, the Discontinued property is a Boolean, so a check box is rendered in the form. It seems a foregone conclusion that the scaffolding mechanism will be modified to generate these strongly typed helpers in the near future.

The final item of note is the BeginForm helper. This method is responsible for rendering the HTML form tag that will determine how updated data is sent to the client when the user submits the form. Calling BeginForm without any parameters will cause the form data to be sent via an HTTP POST to the current URL. To handle the POST, we have a second Edit action method:

```vb
' POST: /Admin/Edit/5

<AcceptVerbs(HttpVerbs.Post)> _
Function Edit(ByVal id As Integer, ByVal collection As FormCollection) As ActionResult
    Dim product = _repository.GetProduct(id)
    Try
        UpdateModel(product)
        _repository.Save()
        Return RedirectToAction("Index")
    Catch
        Return View(product)
    End Try
End Function
```

Code snippet from \Controllers\AdminController.vb

Using the `AcceptVerbs` attribute enables differentiation between action methods of the same name. Think of it as an additional form of method overloading.

Also note the parameter list. The `id` will be populated from the query string parameter of the same name, and the `FormCollection` will be populated from the payload of the `POST`. We can retrieve the values entered by the user via the `Request.Form` collection or the collection parameter. It is not difficult to write the code to go through each property of the entity object being edited and update the property value from the form parameters, but it is tedious and verbose. Fortunately, the framework includes a helper method on the controller base class called `UpdateModel` that will do this for us. It uses reflection to determine the property names on the object, and then automatically converts and assigns values to them based on the input values submitted by the client. It will also add any validation errors encountered when assigning property values to the `ModelState` property of the controller class.

Therefore, when the user submits the form, we need to do the following: Get the product object being edited from the repository, use `UpdateModel` to update its properties from the form parameters, save to properties of the updated entity to the database, and then redirect to the `Index` view. If the update fails, we want to return the `Edit` view for the product so that any validation errors contained in the `ModelState` will be rendered via the `ValidationMessage` and `ValidationSummary` helpers.

Run the application, navigate to `/Admin`, and click the Edit link for one of the items. You should be taken to a page similar to the one shown in Figure 23-17. Update a field or two and click the Save button. Confirm that the values were actually updated by opening the table via the Server Explorer in Visual Studio (see Figure 23-18).

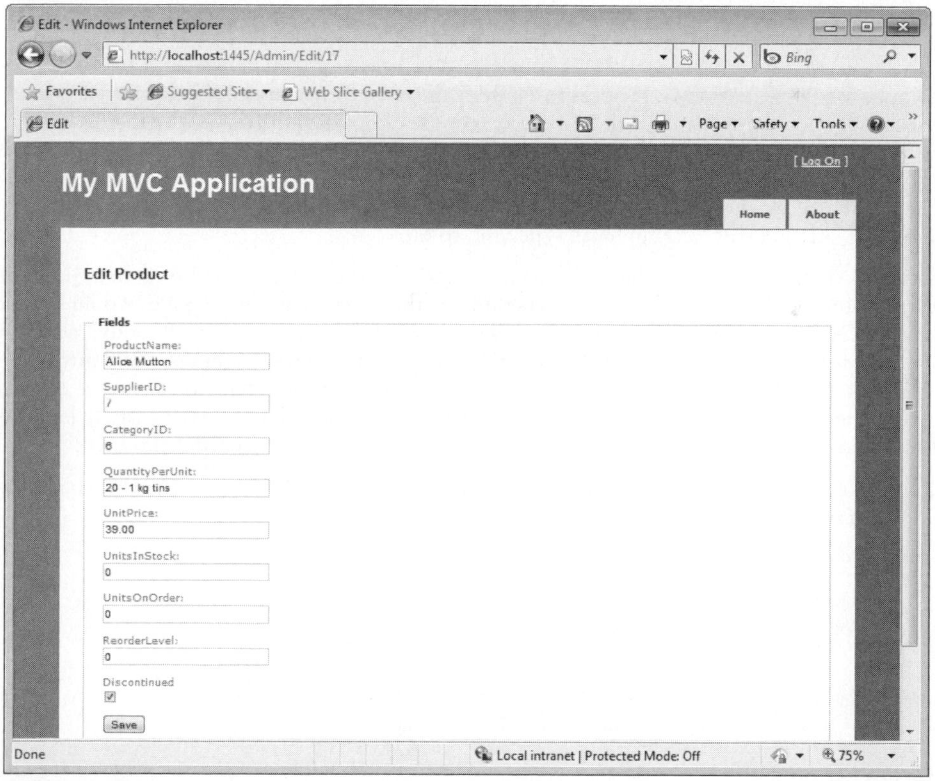

FIGURE 23-17

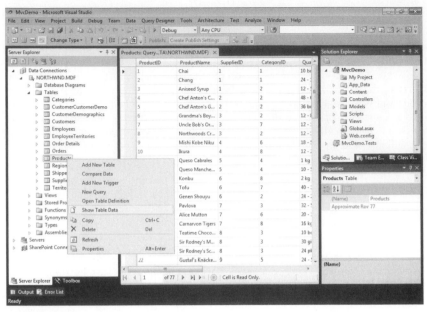

FIGURE 23-18

Validation

So far you've seen how to use the HTML Helpers to render validation information in your views. What we have yet to look at is how to define the validation rules for the properties in your entities. ASP.NET MVC 2 makes this easy by adding support for data annotation validation attributes. You can use the built-in attributes in System.ComponentModel.DataAnnotations or you can create your own custom attributes. You can use these attributes to indicate several things about a value: that it is required, that it should be in a specified range, that it should be of a certain data type, and so on.

Your first instinct is likely to put these attributes on the properties of the entities in our LINQ to SQL model. Unfortunately, these properties are part of the code generated by the designer, so any changes would be lost if the model were updated. Instead, we will create a metadata class (often referred to as a "buddy" class) that has properties that match the name and type of the properties on an entity from the model. We'll attribute the properties in the metadata class to indicate their validation requirements, and then associate the metadata class to the entity in the model using the MetadataType attribute. This last step can be done safely because the classes representing the entities in the LINQ to SQL model are implemented as partial classes.

To add the validation rules for the Product entity, create a new class called Product.vb in the Model folder and add the following implementation:

```vb
Imports System.ComponentModel.DataAnnotations

<MetadataType(GetType(ProductValidation))> _
Public Class Product
End Class

Friend Class ProductValidation
    Private Const MoneyMaxValue As Double = 922227203685477.62

    <Required()> _
    Public Property ProductID As Integer

    <Required()> _
    <StringLength(40)> _
```

```vb
    Public Property ProductName As String

    <Required()> _
    <Range(1, Integer.MaxValue)> _
    Public Property SupplierID As Integer

    <Required()> _
    <Range(1, Integer.MaxValue)> _
    Public Property CategoryID As Integer

    <StringLength(20)> _
    Public Property QuantityPerUnit As String

    <Range(0.0, MoneyMaxValue)> _
    Public Property UnitPrice As Nullable(Of Decimal)

    <Range(0, Short.MaxValue)> _
    Public Property UnitsInStock As Nullable(Of Short)

    <Range(0, Short.MaxValue)> _
    Public Property UnitsOnOrder As Nullable(Of Short)

    <Range(0, Short.MaxValue)> _
    Public Property ReorderLevel As Nullable(Of Short)
End Class
```

Code snippet from \Models\Product.vb

Run the application, navigate to /Admin, and click the Edit link for one of the items. Update a field or two with values that will fail validation and click the Save button. Because we have client validation implemented, you should see the error messages without posting back to the server (see Figure 23-19). Correcting the errors and tabbing out of the fields should remove the error messages.

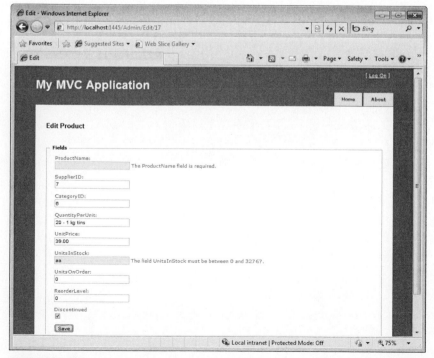

FIGURE 23-19

SUMMARY

This chapter only scratches the surface of ASP.NET MVC, but it covered enough of the fundamentals to enable you to start building applications using the framework. Hopefully, this chapter also gives you enough of a sense of what ASP.NET MVC is about to know whether it is something that suits your style. For more on ASP.NET MVC, be sure to check out *Professional ASP.NET MVC 2* (Galloway et al., Wiley, 2010).

24

SharePoint 2010 Development

WHAT YOU WILL LEARN IN THIS CHAPTER

- ➤ Introduction to SharePoint
- ➤ Using Features to componentize functionality
- ➤ Packaging and deployment with the Solutions Framework
- ➤ Setting up a development environment
- ➤ Using the SharePoint tools in Visual Studio 2010
- ➤ Building visual Web Parts

It's fair to say that SharePoint has been a wildly successful product for Microsoft. If you are doing Web development on the ASP.NET platform, it is very likely that you are already doing development for SharePoint or will be given the opportunity to do so in the near future.

To successfully build customizations for SharePoint, you need to understand several fundamental concepts before starting to write code. The component, packaging, and deployment model used in SharePoint is significantly different from that used in other areas of ASP.NET. In addition, there are several object models (or APIs) used to interact with SharePoint depending on what type of application you're building and where it will be deployed.

This chapter is designed to teach you the fundamental concepts and enough about the tools in Visual Studio 2010 and the developer object models to enable you to start developing for SharePoint 2010.

INTRODUCTION

So, what is SharePoint? There are many answers to this question. From a technical aspect, SharePoint is a Web application that is hosted in IIS and runs on top of ASP.NET. For end users, SharePoint is an information collaboration and management system. For developers, SharePoint is an application development platform.

SharePoint 2010, which is the focus of this chapter, runs on 64-bit versions of Windows Server 2008 or Windows Server 2008 R2. A deployment of SharePoint 2010 also requires a 64-bit instance of Microsoft SQL Server to store configuration information and content. One additional aspect, which is key for developers, is that SharePoint 2010 runs on .NET 3.5, not .NET 4 as you might expect.

What we refer to as SharePoint is really a set of products and technologies. These are grouped into a set of services and a set of products built on top of those services. In SharePoint 2003, the services were referred to as Windows SharePoint Services 2.0 and the products were referred to as SharePoint Portal Server 2003. In SharePoint 2007, it was Windows SharePoint Services 3.0 and Microsoft Office SharePoint Server 2007. Now, in SharePoint 2010, we have Microsoft SharePoint Foundation 2010 and Microsoft SharePoint Server 2010.

SharePoint Foundation 2010

Microsoft SharePoint Foundation 2010 is a free add-on to Windows Server 2008 or Windows Server 2008 R2. It provides the core features (or the foundation) for the SharePoint platform. It implements the provisioning engine that enables end users to create sites, lists, and libraries and the security model to ensure that access to these resources is protected. It also implements the information collaboration and management features mentioned previously. SharePoint Foundation is a powerful piece of software on its own and has enough functionality to meet the needs of many small to mid-size organizations.

SharePoint Server 2010

SharePoint Server 2010 is a retail product that sits on top of SharePoint Foundation, adding functionality commonly desired by larger organizations. At a high level, the Server product editions are separated into two groups depending on whether you plan to use SharePoint internally on an intranet or externally on the Internet. Enterprise search, Web content management, social networking, InfoPath and Excel services, and access to external applications through Business Connectivity Services are just a few of the features offered by SharePoint Server 2010.

SharePoint Terminology

You should be familiar with several terms and concepts when working with SharePoint. The most important of these are the architectural concepts: farm, Web application, site collection, site, list, and library.

A SharePoint deployment is called a *farm*. The farm is made up of one or more front-end Web servers and a SQL Server database used to store configuration information. A simple deployment can be done on a single server using SQL Server 2008 Express.

A farm may contain one or more SharePoint Web applications. A Web application is an IIS website extended for use with SharePoint. In general, you will segregate Web applications by authentication mode. For example, you may have one Web application for internal use that uses integrated Windows authentication, and another that acts as an extranet that uses ASP.NET forms authentication.

A SharePoint Web application is made up of several *site collections*. These are portions of the application that are isolated from each other in terms of administrative privilege and visibility of data. For example, a company intranet could have site collections for individual departments (Sales, Marketing, HR, and so on). One or more end users can be designated as owners of a site collection, giving them administrative privilege within its boundaries. Within a site collection, the owner can create new sites, pages, lists of data, or libraries of documents, and they can give rights to other users to view or contribute to these resources.

A site collection contains a hierarchy of sites. The root of this hierarchy acts as the entry point for the collection. The root may contain many child sites, and they in turn may have child sites of their own. For example, the site at the root of the Sales site collection may have child sites named North Division and South Division.

Within each site, owners can provision lists, libraries, and pages. The *list*, which consists of rows and columns of data, is the basic storage mechanism in SharePoint. It is similar to an Excel worksheet or a database table. SharePoint has several built-in list templates, including contacts, announcements, and events. A special form of a list is the *library*. The library has the same features but it is centralized around a document (Word, Excel, InfoPath, image, etc.). Both lists and libraries have built-in collaboration features, including major and minor versioning, content approval, and check in/out policy.

The SharePoint Development Environment

To effectively do SharePoint development you need an isolated environment in which to work — in other words, a single machine with both SharePoint and Visual Studio installed. The development process requires files to be added or removed from common areas of the file system, the Web server to be reset regularly, and functionality to be added and removed from SharePoint sites and site collections. Trying to do this on a shared SharePoint Web application in a team environment can easily cause havoc.

It is a common practice in the SharePoint community to do your work in a virtualized environment using products like Virtual PC, Hyper-V, VMware, or VirtualBox. One of the main reasons for this practice had been that SharePoint would only run on Windows Server. This changes with SharePoint 2010, which can be run on 64-bit versions of Windows 7 or Windows Vista SP1 for development purposes. This doesn't mean that developers will stop running a virtualized environment, it just removes one of the motivating factors. If you do decide to go the virtualized route, make sure you give your environment at least 1GB of RAM and 40GB of disk space.

You can find additional details about setting up a development environment for SharePoint 2010 in *Setting Up the Development Environment for SharePoint Server* (http://msdn.microsoft.com/en-us/library/ee554869(office.14).aspx).

In addition to SharePoint and Visual Studio, you will want to have Microsoft SharePoint Designer 2010 installed on your development machine. This free tool is mostly used by power users and designers to customize SharePoint sites. It is quite powerful and can do many of the tasks developers can do with Visual Studio. They key difference is that the customizations made with SharePoint Designer are meant to be done on the live site and are not meant to be reusable. The big benefit of SharePoint Designer is the immediate results. Since you are working on the live site you see your changes as soon as you save them. This makes SharePoint Designer an excellent prototyping tool for markup and styles that you will ultimately copy into your Visual Studio solutions.

FEATURES AND THE SOLUTIONS FRAMEWORK

Visual Studio 2010 includes tooling that aids you when doing SharePoint development. These tools automatically generate and manage the documents required to properly componentized, package, and deploy your customizations. This is great for experienced SharePoint developers, as it reduces their workload. It's not so great for those new to SharePoint development, as it hides or obfuscates some of the very important tasks being performed. The following sections should help to provide you with a clear understanding of the foundational topics of Features and the Solutions Framework, without which you will not be able to effectively work with the tools and designers available in Visual Studio.

Features

Features are, in effect, the component model in SharePoint. They enable you to define a set of functionality as a logical group of elements. The elements may include menu items, pages, event handlers, Web Parts, list definitions, and more. For example, you could create a feature that creates and populates a list, provisions a page to show data from the list, and adds a link to the page somewhere in the site.

Once a Feature has been installed, it needs to be activated in order for the elements to be used. Features can be activated at four different scopes: site, site collection, Web application, or farm. End users interact with Features scoped only to the site or site collection level; the other two scopes are the domain of the administrator. Features may also be deactivated. This will generally remove elements added at activation, although that is not always the case.

Creating a Site Collection

To explore how to work with Features, we'll create a site collection to use for testing. Creating a site collection can be done is several ways: using SharePoint 2010 Central Administration, using the stsadm.exe command-line utility, or using the new PowerShell administration commands (also known as *cmdlets*). The

Stsadm utility has been around for several versions of SharePoint and will be familiar to those who have done SharePoint development in the past. However, it won't be long before the PowerShell cmdlets become the standard for command-line administration of SharePoint (just as PowerShell is becoming the standard administration tool for other Microsoft server products); thus, examples in this chapter will use them in favor of the other options.

To create the site collection and its root site, select All Programs ➪ Microsoft SharePoint 2010 Products ➪ SharePoint 2010 Management Shell from the Start menu. When the command window opens, enter the following command, replacing the placeholder with your full user name (see Figure 24-1):

```
New-SPSite http://localhost/sites/demo -Name "Demo"
    -OwnerAlias "<Machine Name>\<User Name>" -Template "STS#0"
```

FIGURE 24-1

For more information on this or any of the other available PowerShell cmdlets, use the `Get-Help` command — for example:

```
Get-Help New-SPSite
```

You should now be able to navigate to `http://localhost/sites/demo` and see a page similar to that shown in Figure 24-2.

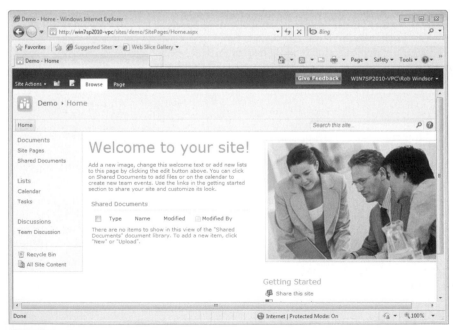

FIGURE 24-2

Building a Feature

With the site and site collection in place, you can move on to building a Feature. At the core of a Feature are XML documents that define the Feature and its elements. In fact, simple Features can be created with the XML documents alone.

You'll create just such a Feature, one that does the following: creates a list of contacts and populates it with some data, provisions a page that displays the contacts in the list, and adds a link to the page to the containing site. Using Windows Explorer, create a folder named **SimpleFeature**. This folder will contain the files that define the Feature, along with the page that displays the list of contacts. The first document you'll create is known as the Feature *manifest*. Using any text or XML editor you like, create a new file named `feature.xml` and save it into the SimpleFeature folder created earlier. Add the following Collaborative Application Markup Language to the file:

Available for download on Wrox.com

```xml
<Feature
    xmlns="http://schemas.microsoft.com/sharepoint/"
    Id="BEAE3C0D-EF1F-4341-B7C4-6BF3C59D2162"
    Title="Simple Feature"
    Description="No Visual Studio here"
    Scope="Web"
    Hidden="FALSE">

    <ElementManifests>
      <ElementManifest Location="elements.xml" />
      <ElementFile Location="Contacts.aspx" />
    </ElementManifests>

</Feature>
```

Code snippet from feature.xml

> ### COLLABORATIVE APPLICATION MARKUP LANGUAGE (CAML)
>
> Collaborative Application Markup Language is XML that conforms to specific schemas defined by SharePoint. It is used in configuration files and code to define features and elements, to query data contained in lists, to define how data is rendered to the browser, and much more. We'll explore several uses of CAML in this chapter. More information is available in this article from the SharePoint Foundation SDK: `http://msdn.microsoft.com/en-us/library/ms426449(office.14).aspx`

When copying a sample like the one above, it is considered a best practice to replace any GUIDs you find. In this case, replace the `Id` attribute of the Feature with a freshly generated GUID. This eliminates the chance that you will have multiple Features with the same unique identifier in your farm. You can generate a GUID using the `guidgen.exe` command-line utility from the Windows SDK (see Figure 24-3). You can also access this utility from Visual Studio by selecting Tools ➪ Create GUID from the main menu.

Several aspects of the Feature are defined by the attributes of the Feature XML element. The Title and Description are the text displayed on the page where the Feature will be activated or deactivated, and the Scope determines the level at which the Feature will be activated.

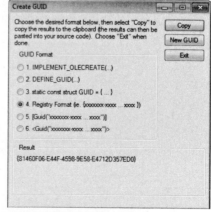

FIGURE 24-3

SITE COLLECTIONS, SITES, AND WEBS

In regard to scope, you should be aware of a naming inconsistency. This issue will also be apparent when you begin to write code against the SharePoint object models. What we call site collections and sites today were formerly called sites and webs, respectively. These legacy terms remain in the XML schemas and developer object models we use today. Therefore, when you want to activate a Feature at the site level, you set the scope to Web. When you want to activate it at the site collection level, you set the scope to Site. This will be somewhat confusing when you first start developing on the SharePoint platform but it will become second nature in no time.

Also contained in the feature manifest are references to the associated element manifests which describe the contents of the Feature. For our sample Feature there will only be one element manifest but it will define three elements. The first (a `ListInstance`) will create the list of contacts and populate it with some data. The second (a `Module`) will add the page you will create shortly to the target site, and the third (a `CustomAction`) will add a link to the page in the Site Actions menu.

Creating the Element Maniftest

To create the element manifest, create a new file named `elements.xml`, save it to the SimpleFeature folder, and add the following code:

```xml
<Elements xmlns="http://schemas.microsoft.com/sharepoint/">

  <!-- Create the contacts list -->
  <ListInstance
    FeatureId="00BFEA71-7E6D-4186-9BA8-C047AC750105"
    TemplateType="105"
    Title="Contacts"
    Url="Contacts"
    QuickLaunchUrl="Contacts/Forms/AllItems.aspx">
    <Data>
      <Rows>
        <Row>
          <Field Name="ID">1</Field>
          <Field Name="Last Name">Anders</Field>
          <Field Name="First Name">Maria</Field>
          <Field Name="Company">Alfreds Futerkiste</Field>
          <Field Name="Business Phone">030-0074321</Field>
        </Row>
        <Row>
          <Field Name="ID">2</Field>
          <Field Name="Last Name">Hardy</Field>
          <Field Name="First Name">Thomas</Field>
          <Field Name="Company">Around the Horn</Field>
          <Field Name="Business Phone">(171) 555-7788</Field>
        </Row>
        <Row>
          <Field Name="ID">3</Field>
          <Field Name="Last Name">Lebihan</Field>
          <Field Name="First Name">Laurence</Field>
          <Field Name="Company">Bon app'</Field>
          <Field Name="Business Phone">91.24.45.40</Field>
        </Row>
        <Row>
          <Field Name="ID">4</Field>
          <Field Name="Last Name">Ashworth</Field>
          <Field Name="First Name">Victoria</Field>
          <Field Name="Company">B's Beverages</Field>
          <Field Name="Business Phone">(171) 555-1212</Field>
        </Row>
```

```
        <Row>
          <Field Name="ID">5</Field>
          <Field Name="Last Name">Mendel</Field>
          <Field Name="First Name">Roland</Field>
          <Field Name="Company">Ernst Handel</Field>
          <Field Name="Business Phone">7675-3425</Field>
        </Row>
      </Rows>
    </Data>
  </ListInstance>

  <!-- Provision the page to display the contacts -->
  <Module Url="MySitePages" >
    <File Url="Contacts.aspx" Type="Ghostable" />
  </Module>

  <!-- Add the menu option that links to Contacts.aspx -->
  <CustomAction
    Id="SiteActionsToolbar"
    GroupId="SiteActions"
    Location="Microsoft.SharePoint.StandardMenu"
    Sequence="100"
    Title="Contacts"
    Description="A page showing some sample data">
      <UrlAction Url="~site/MySitePages/Contacts.aspx"/>
  </CustomAction>

</Elements>
```

Code snippet from elements.xml

You can add many types of elements, far more than can be covered in this chapter. The three used here (`ListInstance`, `Module`, and `CustomAction`) are among the most common. Additional information is available in this section of the SharePoint Foundation SDK: `http://msdn.microsoft.com/en-us/library/ms414322(office.14).aspx`

One important aspect of the definition of an element is the use of what are commonly called *magic* numbers and strings. These are hard-coded values that have specific meaning. For example, the string "FF0000" is used to represent the color Red in certain contexts. The use of magic strings and numbers are quite common in CAML.

The preceding file demonstrates two examples. First, the combination of the `FeatureId` and `TemplateType` in the `ListInstance` element indicate the type of list you wish to create. Second, the combination of the `GroupId` and `Location` attributes in the `CustomAction` element indicate where the menu option or link will be placed within the SharePoint site.

The final file to create is the page that will show the data from the contacts list. This is a standard ASP.NET content page that will fill two of the several content placeholders in the default master page for the site. It will use SharePoint-specific versions of the ASP.NET `DataSource` and `GridView` controls to retrieve and display data from the contacts list.

The `SPDataSource` is specifically designed to work with data coming from SharePoint lists, and the `SPGridView` is designed to respect the CSS styles used in a SharePoint site. Using these controls together provide a simple, no-code method to surface data from your SharePoint site.

Create a file named `Contacts.aspx`, add the following code, and save it to the SimpleFeature folder:

```
<% Assembly Name="Microsoft.SharePoint, Version=14.0.0.0, ..." %>

<% Page MasterPageFile="~masterurl/default.master"
    meta:progid="SharePoint.WebPartPage.Document" %>

<% Register TagPrefix="SharePoint"
    Namespace="Microsoft.SharePoint.WebControls"
```

```
        Assembly="Microsoft.SharePoint, Version=14.0.0.0, ..." %>

<asp:Content runat="server" ContentPlaceHolderID="PlaceHolderPageTitle">
    Contacts
</asp:Content>

<asp:Content runat="server" ContentPlaceHolderID="PlaceHolderMain">
    <h3>Contacts</h3>

    <SharePoint:SPDataSource runat="server"
        ID="ContactsDataSource" DataSourceMode="List"
        UseInternalName="false">
        <SelectParameters>
            <asp:Parameter Name="ListName" DefaultValue="Contacts" />
        </SelectParameters>
    </SharePoint:SPDataSource>

    <SharePoint:SPGridView runat="server"
        ID="ContactsGridView" DataSourceID="ContactsDataSource"
        AutoGenerateColumns="false" RowStyle-BackColor="#DDDDDD"
        AlternatingRowStyle-BackColor="#EEEEEE">
        <Columns>
            <asp:BoundField HeaderText="Company"
                HeaderStyle-HorizontalAlign="Left" DataField="Company" />
            <asp:BoundField HeaderText="First Name"
                HeaderStyle-HorizontalAlign="Left" DataField="First Name" />
            <asp:BoundField HeaderText="Last Name"
                HeaderStyle-HorizontalAlign="Left" DataField="Last Name" />
            <asp:BoundField HeaderText="Phone"
                HeaderStyle-HorizontalAlign="Left" DataField="Business Phone" />
        </Columns>
    </SharePoint:SPGridView>
</asp:Content>
```

Code snippet from Contacts.aspx

Manually Deploying and Installing the Feature

Now that you have all the files in place, you need to deploy the Feature. We'll start by looking at a manual technique, and later you'll learn how to properly package your Feature for production deployment. Manual deployment is a two-step process:

1. Copy the Feature files to the SharePoint system folders.
2. Install the Feature.

The SharePoint system folders are found under the system root, which is located at `C:\Program Files\ Common Files\Microsoft Shared\web server extensions\14\`. (You may hear of this referred to as the "14 Hive," although Microsoft and the SharePoint community are moving away from using the term.) It is in the system folders that files common across the farm are stored, which include the files that define Features. For the remainder of this chapter, the short form of `[14]` will be used to represent the path to the system root.

Features are stored in `[14]\TEMPLATES\FEATURES`. Each Feature has its own subfolder that contains the feature and element manifests, along with other supporting files. The first step in deploying your sample Feature is to copy the SimpleFeature folder here. Use Windows Explorer (or some other technique) to do so.

To install the feature, open the SharePoint 2010 Management Shell and enter the following command, which is the relative path from `[14]\TEMPLATES\FEATURES` to the folder containing the Feature manifest:

```
Install-SPFeature -path SimpleFeature
```

Activating the Feature

You are now ready to activate the sample Feature. Navigate to the team site you created earlier (http:// localhost/sites/demo) and select Site Settings ➪ Manage site features from the Site Actions menu located at the top-left corner of the page. The sample Feature, named Simple Feature, should appear in the list, as shown in Figure 24-4.

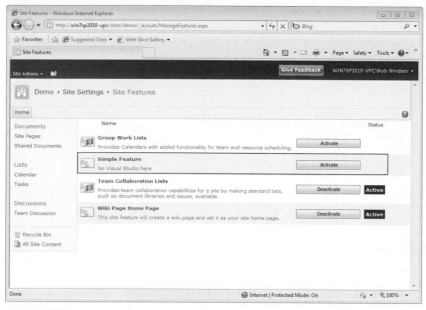

FIGURE 24-4

Before you activate the Feature, note the two list names shown in the Quick Launch area on the left of the page; there should be Calendar and Tasks. Click the Activate button for the Simple Feature. Activating the Feature creates the Contacts list, which should appear in the Lists area as shown in Figure 24-5. You can click on the Contacts link to see the data that was added when the list was created.

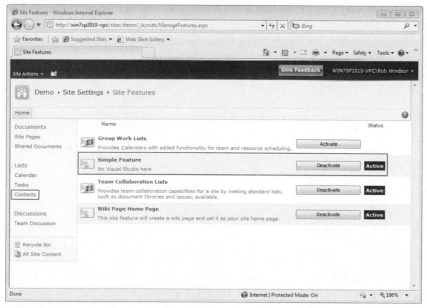

FIGURE 24-5

The other way to see the list data is to navigate to the `Contacts.aspx` page. Opening the Site Actions menu and selecting Contacts (see Figure 24-6) should get you to the page (see Figure 24-7).

FIGURE 24-6

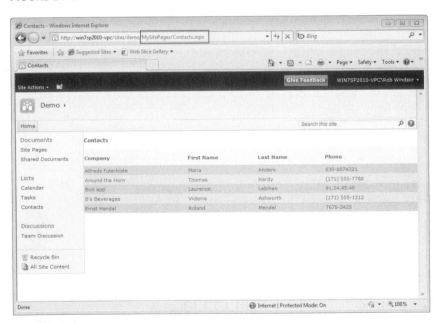

FIGURE 24-7

Deactivating and Removing the Feature

To remove the Feature, just reverse the process used to deploy it. First deactivate the Feature by selecting Site Settings ⇨ Manage site features from the Site Actions menu and clicking the appropriate Deactivate button. You'll be redirected to a page asking you confirm that you want to deactivate the Feature. Click the Deactivate This Feature link to do so.

Note that deactivating the Feature removes the menu option that was added to the Site Actions menu but it does not remove the contacts list or the page that displays its data. This emphasizes that some elements are automatically removed, whereas other elements require code to be removed.

The next step in removing the Feature is to open the SharePoint 2010 Management Shell and enter the following command:

```
Uninstall-SPFeature -Identity SimpleFeature -Confirm:$False
```

Finally, delete the SimpleFeature folder from [14]\TEMPLATE\FEATURES and you are done.

While this deployment process works well enough for a simple example, it is not suitable for a production environment. For production purposes, you will package the files that comprise your Feature, including a solution manifest, into a solution package.

Solution Framework

The Solution Framework included with SharePoint Foundation provides a mechanism for you to package Features for deployment. The package is a CAB file that includes the files that make up the Features to be deployed, along with a solution manifest. The process used to deploy a package depends on the type: farm or sandbox.

Farm solutions are deployed using a two-step process. The package is copied into the solution store and then timer jobs are set up on the front-end Web servers to retrieve the package and deploy the files based on instructions contained in the solution manifest. Most of the files will be deployed to folders under the system root. Only administrators may deploy a farm solution.

Sandboxed solutions, which are new to SharePoint 2010, allow a non-administrator to deploy a solution within the context of a site collection. As the name implies, these solutions run in a sandbox. That is, they are restricted to using a subset of the server object model and are restricted in the number of resources they may use.

Creating a Solution Package

To begin we will deploy the package as a farm solution. The first step is to create the solution manifest. The manifest won't be a very complex document because there isn't much the automated deployment mechanism needs to know to deploy our Feature. Create a file named manifest.xml, add the following CAML, and save it to the SimpleFeature folder. Be sure to replace the value of the SolutionId attribute with a freshly generated GUID.

Available for download on Wrox.com

```
<Solution
  SolutionId="361A1DD0-E8A1-4559-A429-A381B4CC9A90"
  xmlns="http://schemas.microsoft.com/sharepoint/">

  <FeatureManifests>
    <FeatureManifest Location="SimpleFeature\feature.xml" />
  </FeatureManifests>

</Solution>
```

Code snippet from manifest.xml

Now you need to build the package. The package is a CAB file, so you'll use a command-line tool named makecab.exe to build it. This utility, which is included with all recent versions of Windows, takes a text file describing the contents and structure of the CAB as input. Create a file named Cab.ddf, add the following text, and save it to the SimpleFeature folder (key aspects of the file are shown in bold):

```
;
.OPTION EXPLICIT      ; Generate errors
.Set CabinetNameTemplate=SimpleFeature.wsp
.set DiskDirectoryTemplate=CDROM ; All cabinets go in a single directory
.Set CompressionType=MSZIP;** All files are compressed in cabinet files
.Set UniqueFiles="ON"
.Set Cabinet=on
.Set DiskDirectory1=Package

manifest.xml

.Set DestinationDir=SimpleFeature
```

```
feature.xml
elements.xml
Contacts.aspx

;***
```

Note that the filename is `SimpleFeature.wsp`, it should be output to a folder named Package, and the contents of the file should include the solution manifest and the files that comprise the Feature.

You are now ready to build the package. Open the SharePoint 2010 Management Shell from the Start menu and navigate to the SimpleFeature folder. Then execute the following command to build the package:

```
Makecab /f Cab.ddf
```

You should see output similar to that shown in Figure 24-8. Note that the package has been created in the `SimpleFeature\Package` folder.

```
Administrator: SharePoint 2010 Management Shell

PS C:\DevProjects\Features\SimpleFeature> Makecab /f Cab.ddf
Cabinet Maker - Lossless Data Compression Tool

4,707 bytes in 4 files
Total files:           4
Bytes before:      4,707
Bytes after:       1,447
After/Before:         30.74% compression
Time:                  0.09 seconds ( 0 hr  0 min  0.09 sec)
Throughput:           49.43 Kb/second
PS C:\DevProjects\Features\SimpleFeature>
```

FIGURE 24-8

Before deploying the package, let's start fresh by deleting and recreating our test site collection. Open the SharePoint 2010 Management Shell and execute the following two commands. Remember that you need to replace the placeholder with your full user name:

```
Remove-SPSite http://localhost/sites/demo -Confirm:$False
New-SPSite http://localhost/sites/demo -Name "Demo"
    -OwnerAlias "<Machine Name>\<User Name>" -Template "STS#0"
```

Deploying a Farm Solution

As mentioned previously, deploying a package to the farm is a two-step process, so you need to use calls to two PowerShell cmdlets to achieve it. Open a new SharePoint 2010 Management Shell, this time as Administrator, and execute the following commands (note that the `LiteralPath` parameter to the first command requires the absolute path to the package). You should see output similar to that shown in Figure 24-9.

```
Add-SPSolution -LiteralPath <Path>\SimpleFeature\Package\SimpleFeature.wsp
Install-SPSolution -Identity SimpleFeature.wsp
```

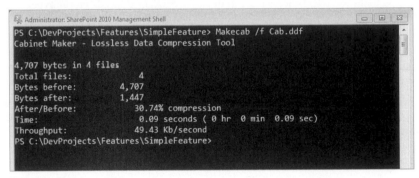

```
Administrator: SharePoint 2010 Management Shell

PS C:\Users\Rob Windsor> Add-SPSolution -LiteralPath C:\DevProjects\Features\Sim
pleFeature\Package\SimpleFeature.wsp

Name                          SolutionId                            Deployed
----                          ----------                            --------
simplefeature.wsp             361a1dd0-e8a1-4559-a429-a381b4cc9a90  False


PS C:\Users\Rob Windsor> Install-SPSolution -Identity SimpleFeature.wsp
PS C:\Users\Rob Windsor>
```

FIGURE 24-9

At this point, your Feature should be available not only to your test site but to all sites in the farm.

To confirm that everything worked as expected, use the same steps you did previously to activate the Feature. Ensure that the Contacts list was created and populated with data and that you can navigate to `Contacts.aspx` using the menu option that was added to the Site Actions menu.

To clean up, deactivate the Feature and use the following to PowerShell commands to uninstall it and remove it from the solution store:

```
Uninstall-SPSolution -Identity SimpleFeature.wsp -Confirm:$False
Remove-SPSolution -Identity SimpleFeature.wsp -Confirm:$False
```

Deploying a Sandboxed Solution

Now that you've seen how deployment of a farm solution works, this section takes a look at deploying a sandboxed solution. Recall that sandboxed solutions are designed to be deployed and administered by site collection owners rather than SharePoint administrators.

Start fresh by deleting and recreating your test site. Open the SharePoint 2010 Management Shell and execute the following two commands. Remember to replace the placeholder with your full user name:

```
Remove-SPSite http://localhost/sites/demo -Confirm:$False
New-SPSite http://localhost/sites/demo -Name "Demo"
    -OwnerAlias "<Machine Name>\<User Name>" -Template "STS#0"
```

If you didn't do this previously, run the following two additional PowerShell commands to uninstall and remove the package deployed to the farm:

```
Uninstall-SPSolution -Identity SimpleFeature.wsp
Remove-SPSolution -Identity SimpleFeature.wsp
```

Navigate to the demo site (`http://localhost/sites/demo`) and then to the Solutions Gallery by selecting Site Actions ➪ Site Settings ➪ Solutions (the Solutions link is at the bottom of the Galleries group). At the top of the page, click the Solutions tab, and click the Upload Solution button in the ribbon. In the Upload Solution dialog, browse to `SimpleFeature.wsp` in the `SimpleFeature\Package` folder and click OK (see Figure 24-10). In the Activate Solution dialog that pops up, click the Activate button in the ribbon and then click the Close button (see Figure 24-11).

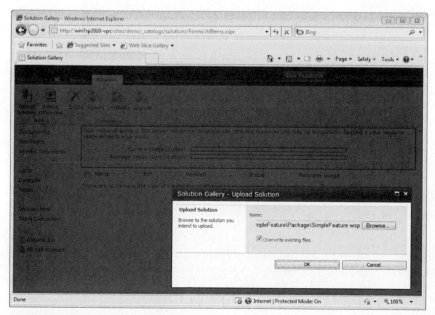

FIGURE 24-10

At this point the package has been deployed to the test site collection. The Simple Feature is now available to be activated by any site in the collection, but the deployment process would need to be repeated to make it available to sites in other site collections. The overloaded use of the term activate may be confusing; activating the solution does not activate the Features contained within. Therefore, you need to go to the Site Features page and activate the Simple Feature.

Once the Feature has been activated, check that the Contacts list was created and populated with data and that you can navigate to `Contacts .aspx` using the menu option that was added to the Site Actions menu.

FIGURE 24-11

To remove the sandboxed solution, deactivate the Feature and return to the Solutions Gallery. Click the check box beside the SimpleFeature item and then click the Deactivate button in the ribbon (see Figure 24-12). In the Deactivate Solution dialog that pops up, click the Deactivate button to confirm. Now click the check box beside the SimpleFeature item once more and click the Delete button in the ribbon to remove the solution from the gallery.

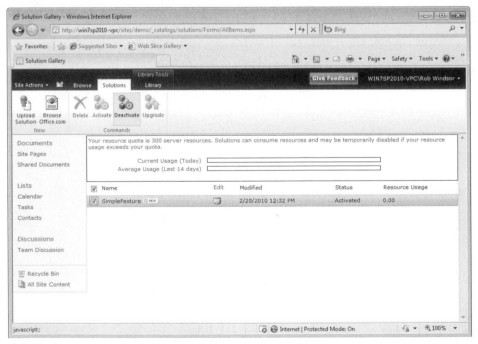

FIGURE 24-12

At this point you should have enough of an understanding of Features and the Solution Framework to move forward and start using Visual Studio. From this point forward, you'll no longer need to manually manage the files we created by hand — but if something goes wrong you'll have enough of a background to know where to look.

VISUAL STUDIO TOOLS FOR SHAREPOINT DEVELOPMENT

One of the things that was clearly missing from previous versions of Visual Studio was tooling to assist in SharePoint development. Out-of-the-box, Visual Studio 2005 had none and Visual Studio 2008 only had templates for building SharePoint workflows. To attempt to address this issue, Microsoft and members of the community built extensions to Visual Studio. The three most popular of these were the Visual Studio Extensions for Windows SharePoint Services 3.0 (VSeWSS), WSPBuilder, and STSDev.

As SharePoint rose in popularity, the need for more and better tooling for SharePoint development became glaringly obvious. It's clear that this was understood by Microsoft because they've added extensive support for SharePoint development to Visual Studio 2010. Multiple project and item templates, solution and Feature explorers and designers, the capability to use visual designers when creating Web Parts, and the capability to deploy and debug using F5 are just some of the features that were added.

This section takes a look at some of these tools by recreating the Feature used in the last example with Visual Studio 2010. You'll start fresh by recreating your test site. Open the SharePoint 2010 Management Shell and execute the following two commands:

```
Remove-SPSite http://localhost/sites/demo -Confirm:$False
New-SPSite http://localhost/sites/demo -Name "Demo"
   -OwnerAlias "<Machine Name>\<User Name>" -Template "STS#0"
```

Start Visual Studio 2010 as Administrator and select File ➪ New Project from the main menu. In the New Project dialog, pick the Visual Basic ➪ SharePoint ➪ 2010 node from the Installed Templates, select Empty SharePoint Project, set the target framework to .NET Framework 3.5, set the Name to **SimpleFeatureVisualStudio**, and click the OK button (see Figure 24-13). Recall that SharePoint 2010 runs on .NET 3.5, not .NET 4, so it's important to set the target framework.

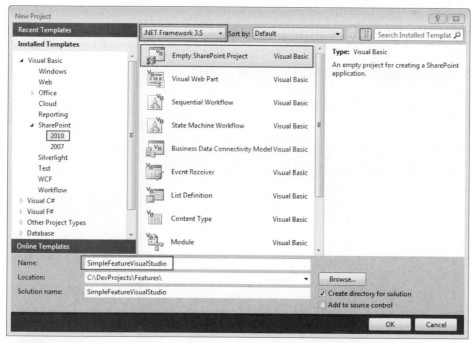

FIGURE 24-13

A dialog will appear asking you which local site you wish to use for debugging and whether you want to deploy the solution as a farm or sandboxed solution when testing (see Figure 24-14). Set the site to `http://localhost/sites/demo`, choose to deploy as a farm solution, and click the Finish button. The

Visual Studio project created for you represents the SharePoint solution; now you need to add your Feature and its elements.

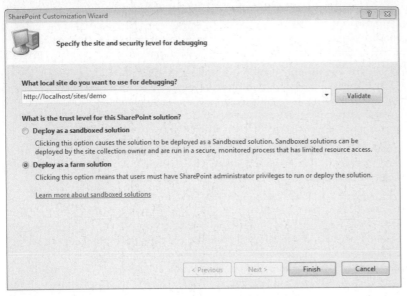

FIGURE 24-14

To create the Feature, right-click on the Features node in the Solution Explorer and select Add Feature. In the Feature designer, set the Title to **Simple Feature 2**, and the Description to something that indicates this Feature was built with Visual Studio (see Figure 24-15). Now you are ready to create the elements.

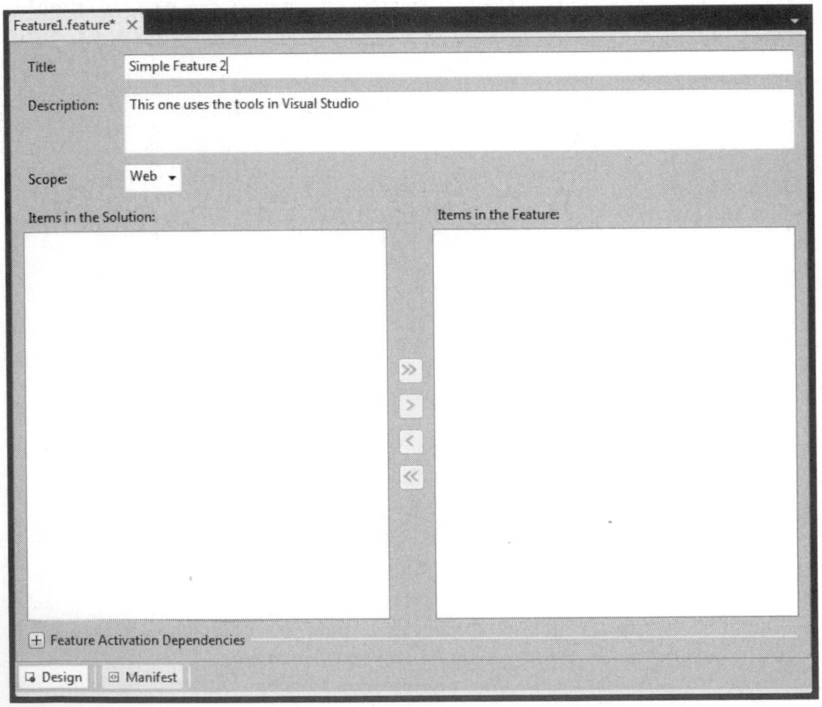

FIGURE 24-15

We'll start with the Contacts list. Right-click on the project in the Solution Explorer, select Add ➪ New Item, select the List Instance item template, set the Name to **Contacts**, and click the Add button. Visual Studio will examine the test site you selected when you created the project to see what kinds of lists are available. It will then present a dialog allowing you to select the list type, and give your list a name and description. Complete the dialog as shown in Figure 24-16 and click the Finish button.

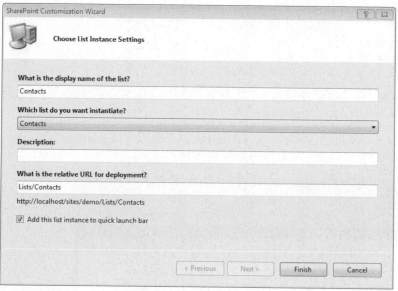

FIGURE 24-16

Two things should happen: A new folder containing the elements.xml file for the list instance should be added to the project, and the new element should be added to the Feature created earlier (see Figure 24-17).

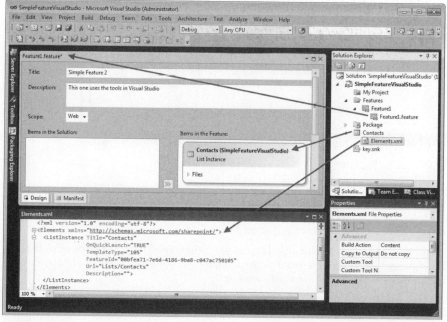

FIGURE 24-17

The CAML generated for the list instance is sufficient to create the Contacts list but it will not populate the data. You'll need to add that by copying the `Data` element from the last example into the `Elements.xml` file.

```
<Elements xmlns="http://schemas.microsoft.com/sharepoint/">
  <ListInstance Title="Contacts"
                OnQuickLaunch="TRUE"
                TemplateType="105"
                FeatureId="00bfea71-7e6d-4186-9ba8-c047ac750105"
                Url="Lists/Contacts"
                Description="">
  <!-- Insert Data element here -->
  </ListInstance>
</Elements>
```

Next, you want to add the `Contacts.aspx` page. If you recall, this page was provisioned into the site using a Module. Right-click on the project in the Solution Explorer, select Add ➪ New Item, select the Module item template, and click the Add button. A new folder will be created in the project for the Module, a sample file will be created for the Module to provision, and the new element will be added to the Feature (see Figure 24-18).

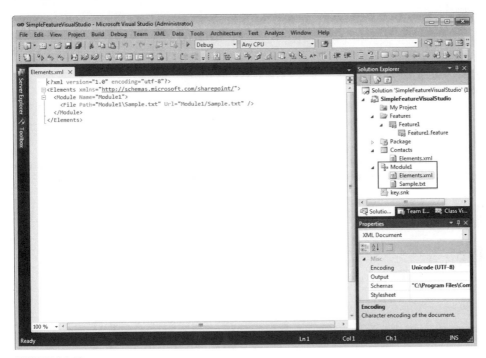

FIGURE 24-18

The `Contacts.aspx` page from the last example can be used as-is, so right-click on the Module1 folder in the Solution Explorer, select Add ➪ Existing Item, navigate to and select `Contacts.aspx` used previously, and click the Add button. A new `File` element should be added to the `Module`. We don't need the sample file, so right-click on it in the Solution Explorer and select Delete.

The last step is to modify the generated CAML. Update the `URL` property of the `File` element so that the `Contacts.aspx` page is provisioned into a virtual folder named `MySitePages` (instead of Module1). The completed `Elements.xml` should look like the following:

```xml
<Elements xmlns="http://schemas.microsoft.com/sharepoint/">
  <Module Name="Module1">
    <File Path="Module1\Contacts.aspx" Url="MySitePages/Contacts.aspx" />
  </Module>
</Elements>
```

Code snippet from Module1\Elements.xml

The final element to add is the option in the Site Actions menu that enables you to navigate to the `Contacts.aspx` page. This is defined by a `CustomAction` element. Right-click on the project in the Solution Explorer, select Add ➪ New Item, and look through the list of item templates. You won't find a template for a custom action, so select the Empty Element template instead. Copy and paste the CAML for the `CustomAction` used in the previous example into the newly created `Elements.xml` (see Figure 24-19).

FIGURE 24-19

At this point you've replicated everything done in the previous example. To confirm that you're ready to move forward, examine the generated Feature and solution manifests. Double-click `Feature1.feature` in the Solution Explorer and select the Manifest tab at the bottom of the designer to see the generated CAML. You should see something similar to the following (also shown in Figure 24-20):

```xml
<Feature
  xmlns="http://schemas.microsoft.com/sharepoint/"
  Title="Simple Feature 2"
  Description="This one uses the tools in Visual Studio"
  Id="fabe1b4b-5a99-4d06-80d0-30922bb53322"
  Scope="Web">
  <ElementManifests>
    <ElementManifest Location="Contacts\Elements.xml" />
    <ElementFile Location="Module1\Contacts.aspx" />
    <ElementManifest Location="Module1\Elements.xml" />
    <ElementManifest Location="EmptyElement1\Elements.xml" />
  </ElementManifests>
</Feature>
```

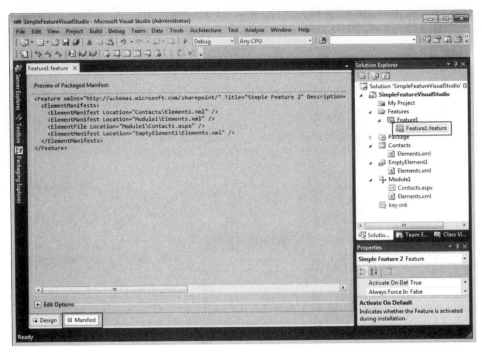

FIGURE 24-20

This is effectively the same as the Feature manifest from the previous example except that the elements are split into three manifests, rather than being included in one.

To see the solution manifest, double-click `Package.package` in the Solution Explorer (you may need to expand the Package folder) and select the Manifest tab at the bottom of the designer. You should see something similar to the following (also shown in Figure 24-21):

```
<Solution
  xmlns="http://schemas.microsoft.com/sharepoint/"
  SolutionId="7aa00dc0-bd83-4bff-a99b-271ddd6e713e">
  <Assemblies>
    <Assembly
      Location="SimpleFeatureVisualStudio.dll"
      DeploymentTarget="GlobalAssemblyCache" />
  </Assemblies>
  <FeatureManifests>
    <FeatureManifest Location="SimpleFeatureVisualStudio_Feature1\Feature.xml" />
  </FeatureManifests>
</Solution>
```

The big difference between this manifest and the one used in the previous example is the inclusion of the `Assembly` element. This directs SharePoint to deploy the assembly for this project into the global assembly cache (GAC). This project does not include any Visual Basic code so the presence of the element is inconsequential.

You are now ready to test. Press F5 and several things will happen: Visual Studio will build the package and deploy it, it will activate the Feature in the site you indicated you want to use for testing, it will attach the debugger to the appropriate worker process, and it will launch the site in your browser. To confirm that everything worked as expected, ensure that the Contacts list was created and populated with data and that you can navigate to `Contacts.aspx` using the menu option that was added to the Site Actions menu. Close the browser to stop your debugging section.

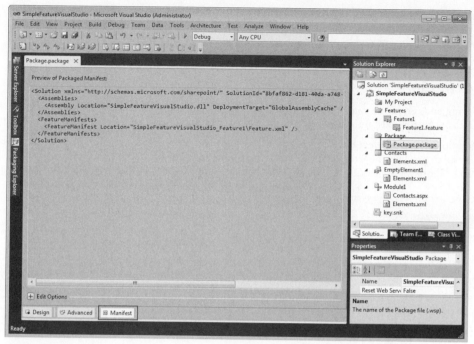

FIGURE 24-21

Now let's deploy and use the project as a sandboxed solution. Select the project in the Solution Explorer and set the Sandboxed Solution property to True in the Properties Window. Pressing F5 this time will remove the farm solution deployed previously and then deploy the sandboxed solution and activate the Feature. The end-user experience from this point should be exactly the same as before.

Those of you who are new to SharePoint development may not appreciate it, but this is a huge improvement over anything that was available in the past. To sweeten the story even further, Microsoft has gone to great lengths to make tooling for SharePoint extensible, so you can look forward to additional tools being released by Microsoft and the SharePoint developer community.

THE SHAREPOINT 2010 OBJECT MODELS

It's quite likely that by this point in the chapter you are wondering whether any actual coding is done when customizing SharePoint. Of course, the answer is yes. Developers can use the server object model, the client object models, or the SharePoint Web services to interact with the functionality and data exposed by SharePoint 2010. Which one of these mechanisms you use will depend on the type of application you are building and where it will run.

The server object model is designed to be used when writing code that will run as part of a SharePoint Web application. If you create a Web Part, site or application page, or write an event handler to work with a Feature or a list, you'll be using the server object model. You may also use the server object model in a client application as long as it runs on a server that is part of the SharePoint farm. This practice is not common and is generally restricted to custom administration utilities.

The client object models (.NET managed, JavaScript, and Silverlight) are designed to be used in situations where you cannot use the server object model. The .NET managed object model can be used in client or ASP.NET Web applications targeting .NET 3.5 or later. The JavaScript object model can be used in client-side code running in pages or Web parts that are hosted in SharePoint. The Silverlight object model can be used in Silverlight applications or controls that run inside or outside the context of SharePoint.

The final option is to use the SharePoint Web services. These can be used in all of the places we've discussed so far (on the server, on the client, in JavaScript, and in Silverlight). Because the need for the Web services has, for the most part, been replaced by the client object models, the SharePoint Web services are not covered in this chapter.

Server Object Model

You've waited long enough to see some code so let's dive right in. The canonical "Hello, World" example for SharePoint is a console application that loops through the lists in a site and displays the items for each list.

Open Visual Studio 2010 and select File ⇨ New Project from the main menu. Select the Visual Basic node in the Installed Templates, select the Console Application item template, set the Name to **ServerObjectModel**, and click OK (see Figure 24-22).

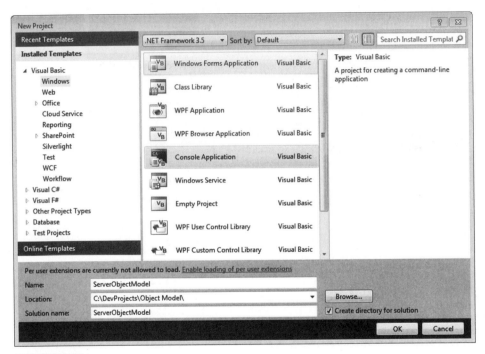

FIGURE 24-22

Two other project settings need to be set to ensure that this application is compatible with SharePoint 2010. Because this application will be using the server object model, it will only be able to be run on a server in the SharePoint farm and will effectively run in the context of SharePoint; therefore, it needs to target the .NET Framework 3.5 and a 64-bit CPU. Right-click on the project in the Solution Explorer and select Properties, select the Compile tab, scroll down to the bottom of the settings and click the Advanced Compile Options button, and configure the Advanced Compiler Settings dialog as shown in Figure 24-23.

The server object model contains types that map to the common architectural concepts in SharePoint. The types we will use in the example are SPSite, SPWeb, SPList, and SPListItem, which map to a site collection, a site, a list, and a list item, respectively.

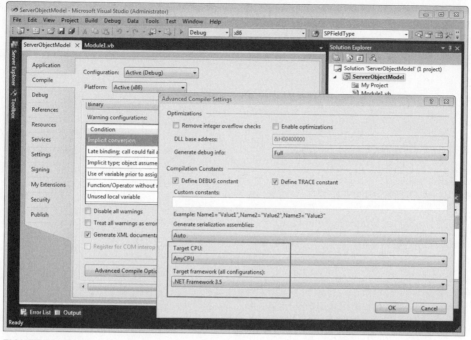

FIGURE 24-23

The server object model is implemented in the `Microsoft.SharePoint.dll`. Add a reference to this assembly, which you'll find on the .NET tab of the Add Reference dialog.

Getting back to the code for the console application, the first thing you need to do is get access to the site you want to inspect. You can't create a `SPWeb` object directly, so you need to get an object representing the parent site collection and use one of its properties or methods. Because the site we want is the root site in the collection, we'll use the `RootWeb` property.

Update `Module1.vb` to look like the following:

```vb
Imports Microsoft.SharePoint

Module Module1
    Sub Main()
        Dim siteUrl = "http://localhost/sites/demo/"
        Using site As New SPSite(siteUrl)
            Dim web = site.RootWeb

        End Using
    End Sub
End Module
```

Code snippet from Module1.vb

Note that the `SPSite` object is instantiated with a `Using` statement. Both the `SPSite` and `SPWeb` objects hold references to unmanaged resources that need to be cleaned up in a timely manner. Not doing so can have significant adverse effects on the performance and resource usage of your applications. The rule of thumb is that if you create an instance of an `SPSite` or `SPWeb`, you should ensure that it is disposed. If you get a reference to the `SPSite` or `SPWeb` from a property of another object, you should not dispose.

Inside the `Using` statement, loop through the lists contained in the site and write out the name of the list to the console. Hidden lists and document libraries should be skipped:

```vb
For Each list As SPList In web.Lists
    If Not list.Hidden AndAlso _
        list.BaseType <> SPBaseType.DocumentLibrary Then

        Console.WriteLine(list.Title)
    End If
Next
```

Code snippet from Module1.vb

After you display the title of the list to the console, display the title of each item in the list:

```vb
For Each item As SPListItem In list.Items
    Console.WriteLine(vbTab + item.Title)
Next
```

The completed code should look like the following.

```vb
Imports Microsoft.SharePoint

Module Module1
    Sub Main()
        Dim siteUrl = "http://localhost/sites/demo/"
        Using site As New SPSite(siteUrl)
            Dim web = site.RootWeb

            For Each list As SPList In web.Lists
                If Not list.Hidden AndAlso _
                    list.BaseType <> SPBaseType.DocumentLibrary Then
                    Console.WriteLine(list.Title)

                    For Each item As SPListItem In list.Items
                        Console.WriteLine(vbTab + item.Title)
                    Next
                End If
            Next
        End Using
    End Sub
End Module
```

Code snippet from Module1.vb

Press Ctrl+F5 to run the application. If your test site still has the Contacts list created in one of the previous sample Features, you should see output similar to that shown in Figure 24-24.

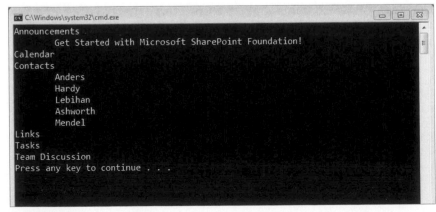

FIGURE 24-24

Now let's see how you can build the same application using the managed client object model.

Client Object Models

The client object models are a new addition to SharePoint 2010. They can be used in most (but not all) places where the SharePoint Web services were used previously. As mentioned, there are three client object models: one used with .NET managed code, one used with JavaScript, and one used with Silverlight. These three are very similar (disregarding the differences of the hosts in which they operate). Once you have learned how to use one, picking up the other two is not difficult. This section focuses on the managed client object model.

The biggest difference between the server and client object models is the batching used to access resources in the client object models. Recall that applications written with the client object model are running outside the context of SharePoint. That means that access to resources crosses a process or machine boundary, and that means service calls. While it may not be obvious from the code, when you make requests for resources from code in the client object models, a call to a WCF service is being made. To make this as efficient as possible, the client object models allow you to batch the requests for resources together.

For this sample application, open Visual Studio 2010 and select File ➪ New Project from the main menu. Select the Console Application item template, set the Name to **ClientObjectModel**, and click OK. The restrictions on the target version of the .NET Framework and CPU do not apply to applications built using the managed client object model.

Like the server object model, the managed client object model contains types that map to the common architectural concepts in SharePoint, but the names of the types are not prefixed with SP. The managed client object model is implemented in `Microsoft.SharePoint.Client.dll` and `Microsoft.SharePoint.Client.Runtime.dll`. Add a reference to these assemblies, which you'll find on the .NET tab of the Add Reference dialog.

Also like the server object model, the client object model has a context object that is central to many operations. These context objects are conceptually similar to the `HttpContext` object in ASP.NET. On the server side, this is the `SPContext`; on the client side, it is the `ClientContext`.

Moving to the code, the first thing you need to do is get access to the site you want to inspect. This will be done through the `ClientContext`, which has properties that allow access to the site collection and the site associated with the URL passed into the constructor of the `ClientContext`.

Accessing properties does not actually get their values. As mentioned previously, retrieving the values is done in batches. Therefore, once you have the `ClientContext` constructed, you'll create variables to hold a reference to the site and its collection of lists. To populate those variables, you pass references to them to the context via the `Load` method and then retrieve their values via the `ExecuteQuery` method. It's the `ExecuteQuery` method that calls the WCF service mentioned earlier. Add this code to the Main method of Module1:

```vb
Imports Microsoft.SharePoint.Client

Module Module1
    Sub Main()
        Dim siteUrl = "http://localhost/sites/demo/"
        Using context As New ClientContext(siteUrl)
            Dim web = context.Web
            Dim lists = web.Lists
            context.Load(web)
            context.Load(lists)
            context.ExecuteQuery()

        End Using
    End Sub
End Module
```

Code snippet from Module1.vb

After the call to `ExecuteQuery`, loop through the lists you just retrieved and write out the name of the list to the console. Hidden lists and document libraries should be skipped:

```
For Each list As List In lists
    If Not list.Hidden AndAlso _
        list.BaseType <> BaseType.DocumentLibrary Then

        Console.WriteLine(list.Title)
    End If
Next
```

Code snippet from Module1.vb

After you display the title of the list to the console, display the title of each item in the list. This needs to be done a little differently than the last example. Instead of the `List` type having an `Items` property, the client object model encourages you to limit the information crossing the wire by exposing a `GetItems` method that executes a CAML query. You only need the value of the `Title` property for each item, so that is all you will retrieve:

```
Dim xml = <View>
              <ViewFields>
                  <FieldRef Name="Title"/>
              </ViewFields>
          </View>

Dim query As New CamlQuery()
query.ViewXml = xml.ToString()
Dim items = list.GetItems(query)
context.Load(items)
context.ExecuteQuery()

For Each item In items
    Console.WriteLine(vbTab + item("Title"))
Next
```

Code snippet from Module1.vb

The completed code should look like the following:

```
Imports Microsoft.SharePoint.Client

Module Module1
    Sub Main()
        Dim siteUrl = "http://localhost/sites/demo/"
        Using context As New ClientContext(siteUrl)
            Dim web = context.Web
            Dim lists = web.Lists
            context.Load(web)
            context.Load(lists)
            context.ExecuteQuery()

            For Each list As List In lists
                If Not list.Hidden AndAlso _
                    list.BaseType <> BaseType.DocumentLibrary Then
                    Console.WriteLine(list.Title)

                    Dim xml = <View>
                                  <ViewFields>
                                      <FieldRef Name="Title"/>
                                  </ViewFields>
                              </View>

                    Dim query As New CamlQuery()
                    query.ViewXml = xml.ToString()
```

```
                    Dim items = list.GetItems(query)
                    context.Load(items)
                    context.ExecuteQuery()

                    For Each item In items
                        Console.WriteLine(vbTab + item("Title"))
                    Next
                End If
            Next
        End Using
    End Sub
End Module
```

Code snippet from Module1.vb

Press Ctrl+F5 to run the application. Unless you added, edited, or deleted items since running the last example, you should get identical output to Figure 24-24.

BUILDING WEB PARTS

Web Parts are one of the core elements used to build user interfaces in SharePoint. They are a special type of server control that support customizable properties and personalization.

From a development aspect, there are two types of Web Parts: SharePoint and ASP.NET. That is, you can build Web Parts specifically for SharePoint using types found in the SharePoint server object model, or you can build Web Parts that will work in both ASP.NET and SharePoint using types found in ASP.NET 3.5. The SharePoint-specific Web Part framework is really there for backward compatibility; any new work should be done using the ASP.NET Web Part framework.

Like any server control in ASP.NET, Web Parts are built with code only. That is, there is no design-time experience during development. The user interface is expressed in Visual Basic code and you only see the result when the page hosting the control is executed.

To address this issue, Web Part developers have begun to build the user interface for Web Parts with user controls (which do have a design-time experience), and then the Web Part hosts the user control. This type of Web Part is commonly called a Visual Web Part.

To see how to build a Visual Web Part with Visual Studio 2010, open Visual Studio 2010, select File ➪ New Project, select the Visual Web Part project template, set the Name to **ContactsEditorWebPart**, and click the Add button.

A folder named VisualWebPart1 will be added to the project. This folder will contain four files (see Figure 24-25):

FIGURE 24-25

➤ Elements.xml — The element manifest that provisions the Web Part definition to the Web Part gallery of the target site collection

➤ VisualWebPart.vb — The code file for the Web Part

➤ VisualWebPart1.webpart — The Web Part definition file

➤ VisualWebPart1UserControl.ascx — The user control that represents the user interface for the Web Part

Add the following markup to VisualWebPart1UserControl.ascx to implement the user interface for a form that allows users to select and edit an existing contact. The Design view for the completed form should look similar to the one shown in Figure 24-26.

```
<asp:DropDownList ID="ContactsDropDownList" runat="server" AutoPostBack="True">
</asp:DropDownList>
<br /><br />

<asp:Label ID="Label1" runat="server" Text="First Name"></asp:Label>
  
<asp:TextBox ID="FirstNameTextBox" runat="server"></asp:TextBox>
<br />
<asp:Label ID="Label2" runat="server" Text="Last Name"></asp:Label>
  
<asp:TextBox ID="LastNameTextBox" runat="server"></asp:TextBox>
<br />
<asp:Label ID="Label3" runat="server" Text="Company"></asp:Label>
  
<asp:TextBox ID="CompanyTextBox" runat="server"></asp:TextBox>
<br />
<asp:Label ID="Label4" runat="server" Text="Business Phone"></asp:Label>
  
<asp:TextBox ID="BusinessPhoneTextBox" runat="server"></asp:TextBox>
<br /><br />

<asp:Button ID="SaveButton" runat="server" Text="Save" />
```

Code snippet from VisualWebPart1UserControl.ascx

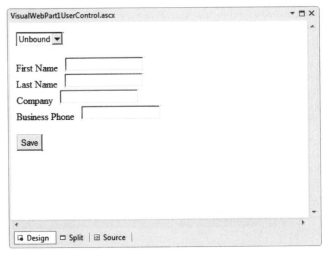

FIGURE 24-26

Right-click in the Code Editor (away from any text) and select View Code. Add the following code to populate the drop-down list that shows the existing items in the Contacts list:

```
Protected Sub Page_Load(ByVal sender As Object, ByVal e As EventArgs)
    Handles Me.Load
    If Not IsPostBack Then
        LoadContactsDropDown()
    End If
End Sub

Private Sub LoadContactsDropDown()
    Dim web = SPContext.Current.Web
    Dim list = web.Lists.TryGetList("Contacts")
    If list IsNot Nothing Then
        Dim data = list.Items.GetDataTable()
        ContactsDropDownList.DataSource = data
        ContactsDropDownList.DataTextField = "Title"
```

```
            ContactsDropDownList.DataValueField = "ID"
            ContactsDropDownList.DataBind()
        End If
    End Sub
```

To get the items, you must first get access to the current site using the SPContext object. Then you attempt to get a reference to the Contacts list. If the list exists, then you can use a very handy helper method to get the item data for the list as a DataTable. Once you have the DataTable, you can use standard ASP.NET data-binding techniques to populate the drop-down.

> *Although we want to show the last names of the contacts in the drop-down, we bind to the Title column. In SharePoint, the first column in any list is named Title internally. A complete explanation of why this is the case is beyond the scope of this chapter.*

Now you need some code to populate the text boxes in the form. This needs to be done when the page is first loaded and when the selected item in the drop-down list changes. Add a method that gets the appropriate item from the Contacts list and populates the text boxes with the values of its properties. Update the Load event handler for the page to call this method. Also, add an event handler for the SelectedIndexChanged event of the drop-down and call the method within:

```
Protected Sub Page_Load(ByVal sender As Object, ByVal e As EventArgs)
    Handles Me.Load
    If Not IsPostBack Then
        LoadContactsDropDown()
        LoadTextBoxes()
    End If
End Sub

Protected Sub ContactsDropDownList_SelectedIndexChanged(...)
    Handles ContactsDropDownList.SelectedIndexChanged
    LoadTextBoxes()
End Sub

Private Sub LoadTextBoxes()
    Dim web = SPContext.Current.Web
    Dim list = web.Lists.TryGetList("Contacts")
    If list IsNot Nothing Then
        Dim id = CInt(ContactsDropDownList.SelectedValue)
        Dim item = list.Items.GetItemById(id)

        LastNameTextBox.Text = item("Title").ToString()
        FirstNameTextBox.Text = item("First Name").ToString()
        CompanyTextBox.Text = item("Company").ToString()
        BusinessPhoneTextBox.Text = item("Business Phone").ToString()
    End If
End Sub
```

Again, you will go to the SPContext to get the current site and then attempt to get the Contacts list. You get the ID of the selected item from the drop-down and then get that item from the list. Once you have the item, you populate the text boxes in the form with the item's properties. Finally, you need to be able to save the new values for the properties when the Save button is clicked:

```
Protected Sub SaveButton_Click() Handles SaveButton.Click
    Dim web = SPContext.Current.Web
    Dim list = web.Lists.TryGetList("Contacts")
    If list IsNot Nothing Then
        Dim id = CInt(ContactsDropDownList.SelectedValue)
```

```
        Dim item = list.Items.GetItemById(id)

        item("Title") = LastNameTextBox.Text
        item("First Name") = FirstNameTextBox.Text
        item("Company") = CompanyTextBox.Text
        item("Business Phone") = BusinessPhoneTextBox.Text
        item.Update()

        LoadContactsDropDown()
        LoadTextBoxes()
    End If
End Sub
```

Code snippet from VisualWebPart1UserControl.ascx.vb

This code will be similar to the code that populates the form but instead of populating the values of the text boxes, you'll be updating the properties of the item. Once the item has been updated, you'll repopulate the drop-down (in case the last name was changed for the item being edited) and repopulate the form.

The completed code-behind for the user control should look similar to the following:

```
Partial Public Class VisualWebPart1UserControl
    Inherits UserControl

    Protected Sub Page_Load() Handles Me.Load
        If Not IsPostBack Then
            LoadContactsDropDown()
            LoadTextBoxes()
        End If
    End Sub

    Protected Sub ContactsDropDownList_SelectedIndexChanged()
        Handles ContactsDropDownList.SelectedIndexChanged
        LoadTextBoxes()
    End Sub

    Protected Sub SaveButton_Click() Handles SaveButton.Click
        Dim web = SPContext.Current.Web
        Dim list = web.Lists.TryGetList("Contacts")
        If list IsNot Nothing Then
            Dim id = CInt(ContactsDropDownList.SelectedValue)
            Dim item = list.Items.GetItemById(id)

            item("Title") = LastNameTextBox.Text
            item("First Name") = FirstNameTextBox.Text
            item("Company") = CompanyTextBox.Text
            item("Business Phone") = BusinessPhoneTextBox.Text
            item.Update()

            LoadContactsDropDown()
            LoadTextBoxes()
        End If
    End Sub

    Private Sub LoadContactsDropDown()
        Dim web = SPContext.Current.Web
        Dim list = web.Lists.TryGetList("Contacts")
        If list IsNot Nothing Then
            Dim data = list.Items.GetDataTable()
            ContactsDropDownList.DataSource = data
            ContactsDropDownList.DataTextField = "Title"
            ContactsDropDownList.DataValueField = "ID"
            ContactsDropDownList.DataBind()
        End If
    End Sub

    Private Sub LoadTextBoxes()
```

```vb
        Dim web = SPContext.Current.Web
        Dim list = web.Lists.TryGetList("Contacts")
        If list IsNot Nothing Then
            Dim id = CInt(ContactsDropDownList.SelectedValue)
            Dim item = list.Items.GetItemById(id)

            LastNameTextBox.Text = item("Title").ToString()
            FirstNameTextBox.Text = item("First Name").ToString()
            CompanyTextBox.Text = item("Company").ToString()
            BusinessPhoneTextBox.Text = item("Business Phone").ToString()
        End If
    End Sub

End Class
```

Code snippet from VisualWebPart1UserControl.ascx.vb

The last thing to do before testing out the Web Part is to set the name and description that will be shown to the user in the Web Part Gallery. Double-click `VisualWebPart1.webpart` in the Solution Explorer and update the two `property` elements as shown here:

```xml
<properties>
  <property name="Title" type="string">Contacts Editor Part</property>
  <property name="Description" type="string">This is a test</property>
</properties>
```

Oh, it appears there is one more last thing to do before testing your Web Part. Make sure you have a Contacts list with some data in it. If you don't, then install and activate one of the Simple Features created in the Features section. The easiest way to do this is to open the SimpleFeatureVisualStudio solution, right-click on the project in the Solution Explorer, and select Deploy. This will deploy the solution and activate the Feature contained within.

Press F5 to deploy your Web Part and bring up the test site in the browser. You'll be directed to a page that will let you create a page with which you can test your work. Name the page `TestPage.aspx`, choose the Full Page, Vertical Layout Template, and scroll down to find and click the Create button (see Figure 24-27).

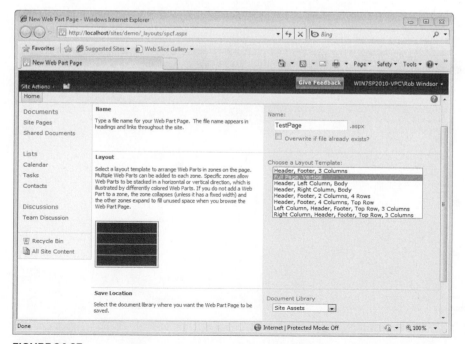

FIGURE 24-27

You should be directed to the newly created `TestPage.aspx`. Once there, click the Add a Web Part link in the main body of the page, select the Custom Category and the Contacts Editor Part in the ribbon, and click the Add button (see Figure 24-28). Click the Stop Editing button in the ribbon and the page with your Web Part will be added (you may need to refresh the page for the data to be populated). The final page should look similar to that shown in Figure 24-29.

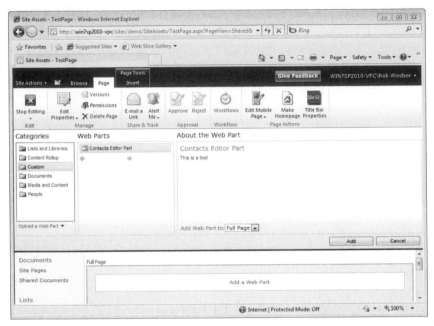

FIGURE 24-28

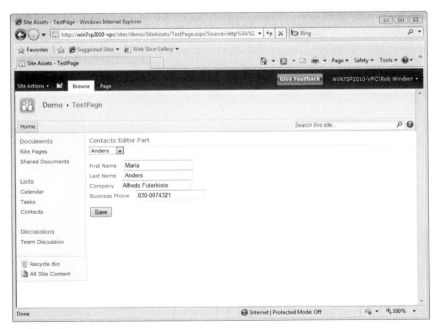

FIGURE 24-29

SUMMARY

At this point, while you may not be an expert SharePoint developer, you should understand the important foundational concepts and have enough of a familiarity with the tools in Visual Studio 2010 to continue your own exploration of the subject.

SharePoint development is not as easy to pick up as ASP.NET. There are many quirks and oddities that will have you pulling your hair out at times. Fortunately, the platform and the tools in Visual Studio have matured to the point that many of the issues faced in the past have been addressed or can easily be avoided.

As someone who has gone through the learning curve, I cannot stress enough how important it is to learn the fundamentals. This chapter covered Features, Solutions, and deployment but there is much more to learn. Site columns, content types, field types, master pages, list and site definitions, event handlers and more still await you. The investment in learning these concepts will pay off many times over when architecting, developing, and debugging your SharePoint applications.

For more information on this subject, be sure to check out *Professional SharePoint 2010 Development* (Rizzo et al. Wiley, 2010).

PART V
Libraries and Specialized Topics

25

Visual Studio Tools for Office

WHAT YOU WILL LEARN IN THIS CHAPTER

➤   VSTO releases and Office Automation

➤   Office business application architecture

➤   VBA-VSTO interop

➤   Creating a document template (Word)

➤   Creating an Office add-in (Excel)

➤   Outlook form regions

This chapter introduces the Visual Studio Tools for Office (VSTO) project templates. VSTO was originally available as an add-in to Visual Studio for several releases, and then became part of the core product with Visual Studio 2008. Visual Studio 2010 continues to include it as part of the standard installation of all versions of Visual Studio Professional and above. The VSTO package isn't so much a set of new menus as it is templates and DLLs that enable you to integrate custom business logic into Microsoft Office products.

VSTO was somewhat neglected in the .NET development world prior to Visual Studio 2008. The main Office client applications that most people think about targeting, Word and Excel, have supported customization through Visual Basic for Applications (VBA) since long before .NET. Visual Studio 2008 expanded the list of supported applications, and support for customization of the full Office System, including SharePoint, continues with the latest version of Visual Studio, which enables full-featured Office Business Application (OBA) development.

This chapter focuses on using Visual Studio 2010 with the Office 2010 Beta — the existing code demos for Office 2007 released with Professional Visual Basic 2008 are still functional with Visual Studio 2010 and available as part of the code download. In addition to introducing you to the role of the VSTO family of tools, this chapter demonstrates three different implementation examples. Everything covered in this chapter can be targeted at both Office 2007 and Office 2010.

VSTO is available as part of Visual Studio 2010 Professional and is focused on enabling you to move from a goal of "this project will create a custom grid with the following capabilities" to a goal of "this project will enable users to leverage Excel 2007/2010 and surface our business application data in the robust Excel table management system, where users can customize and save the data back into our custom line-of-business data store." Developers and customers often talk about how nice it would be to embed Excel in their application. Now, as you'll see in this chapter, the real solution is the reverse — your application can be embedded in Excel.

EXAMINING THE VSTO RELEASES

With Visual Studio 2005, the VSTO package was available as an add-in to Visual Studio. VSTO has been around since early in the .NET tools life cycle. That original package targeted Office 2003, which was the most recent version of Office at the time Visual Studio 2007 was released. There were five templates, two each for Word and Excel document-level customizations and then a single template for creating Outlook add-ins.

With the release of Office 2007, Microsoft provided an update to the Visual Studio 2005 environment called VSTO 2005 SE, where SE stood for Second Edition. This update essentially enabled VSTO to access some of the same templates for Office 2007; however, access to other features, such as the Office 2007 Ribbon, was limited in this set of tools. The requirement to manually create and edit an XML file to define a custom Ribbon bar made approaching this solution somewhat intimidating. However, VSTO 2005 SE was just an interim release until the VSTO team could put together a more complete package for Visual Studio 2008.

With the release of Visual Studio 2008, the number of available options enabling you to extend the standard features of Office VSTO expanded. This continues with the release of Visual Studio 2010, although with Visual Studio 2010 the templates targeting SharePoint have been moved out of the Office category and into a new SharePoint category. Note that for Office 2003 support, you need to continue to leverage Visual Studio 2008.

Office Automation versus VSTO

In any discussion of VSTO, it's important to distinguish between Office automation and VSTO. *Office automation* is a term that actually refers to the capability to create a custom application that references Word or Excel or some other Office application. In this case, the user of your custom application can start and send data to your application. This type of automation does not necessarily involve VSTO or VBA.

Office automation relies on the custom application having a reference to Office and then sending information into or retrieving information from that application without Office being customized. This type of automation leverages COM-based interop to the Office components and doesn't fall into the same category of application as VSTO. A VSTO application is one in which the actual Office application is aware of and connected to the custom logic. Thus, when a user of an application that supports Office automation wants to retrieve data from an Excel spreadsheet, that user exits Excel, goes to that custom application, asks it to connect to the currently running instance of Excel, and attempts to retrieve the data. This type of automation tends to treat Office as more of a black box.

VSTO applications are built into Office. They can and do display UI elements directly within applications such as Word, and they can and do leverage the same automation elements and interop assemblies that Office automation clients leverage. The key difference is that VSTO applications are directly integrated with the application process (threads) and have direct access to UI elements that are part of the application.

PIA-Free Deployment

One of the key new features related to Visual Studio 2010 and .NET Framework 4 is support for assemblies that don't require Primary Interop Assembly (PIA). A PIA encapsulates the metadata that defines the .NET types needed to take an external and often COM-based interface and expose that interface within .NET. Traditionally, to work with VSTO you were required to ensure that the client would have the appropriate PIA for the targeted version of Office.

Visual Studio 2010 makes this unnecessary. Instead, when you reference an Office assembly such as those used in VSTO, you can choose to have Visual Studio generate those portions of the PIA that you actually reference as part of your assembly. Thus, instead of needing to ship and reference an external assembly to get the metadata that defines the Office interfaces, you can now have that metadata embedded into your executable. The result is a smaller package for deployment, as it is no longer necessary to ship the entire set of PIA assemblies with your application.

There is one item to check, however, especially when migrating a project from a previous version of Visual Studio. Embedding of interop types is optional. By default, when you create a new VSTO solution, the assemblies will be marked to embed the interop types within your assemblies. However, you should check referenced assemblies on your migrated projects by selecting referenced Office assemblies within Visual Studio Solution Explorer and reviewing the reference properties. As shown in Figure 25-1, the Embed Interop Types property should be set to `True`. This will allow Visual Studio 2010 to remove your external assembly references.

Because this capability is specific to Visual Studio 2010, which doesn't support Office 2003, it isn't available for projects targeting Office 2003. Additionally, when it comes to the Office Primary Interop Assemblies (PIA) for Office 2003, the Office installer did not automatically include these when Office 2003 was installed. As a result, if at some point you choose to do either a VSTO or an Office automation project for an Office 2003 project, you'll want to include the redistributable for these assemblies. The PIA for Office 2003 is available from Microsoft Downloads, currently located at `www.microsoft.com/downloads/details`

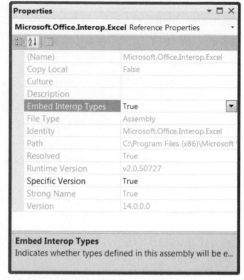

FIGURE 25-1

`.aspx?familyid=3c9a983a-ac14-4125-8ba0-d36d67e0f4ad&displaylang=en`. If it moves, you'll want to Bing Office 2003 PIA and proceed to the new MSDN download page. You should only download these assemblies directly from Microsoft.

VSTO Project Types

While the difference between a Word project and an Excel project is no doubt self-evident to you, the difference between an Add-In project and a Document project might not be. In short, each of the different VSTO project types targets not only a given client or server Office application, but also a different way of customizing that application. In the case of Add-In projects, the project type enables you to customize the application. The main project types for VSTO are as follows:

➤ **Add-In** — This template enables you to create an extension to an Office product that is loaded every time that product is started. Add-ins, as with Visual Studio add-ins, are code that is registered with the application and started every time that application is started. Add-ins are needed for some applications such as Outlook in which an inbound customized message would need the add-in support on the client to recognize the customizations in order to load the document (mail message) correctly.

➤ **Document/Workbook** — These are two separate templates, associated with Word and Excel, respectively. The key aspect of these templates is that the code associated with your custom logic is embedded in a specific document file. The model is much closer to the model exposed by the original VBA customization in these products. In fact, there is even a way to interoperate between Document/Workbook projects and VBA projects. If you open Word or Excel and select a new document or a document that doesn't include this logic, the custom code isn't loaded. On the one hand, this makes these projects lower risk in that you are less likely to disable a client's system. On the other hand, without a central location such as SharePoint to host these custom documents, the application model is much weaker.

➤ **Template** — These projects are similar to the Document/Workbook model in that you are defining code that lives in a single template. This template and code are loaded only when a user chooses to use it from within Office.

A Word add-in is built using a project template that enables you to create a custom actions pane and a custom menu and/or ribbon bar for Word. The Add-In project types host code that will run each time that Word (or the selected application) is started. Thus, it doesn't matter which document the user chooses to open or the underlying template that is part of the current document — the code in the Add-In will be loaded.

This doesn't mean that an Add-In template can't be document specific. In the case of Outlook, the only available template is an Add-In template. This is because of the nature of the extensions to Outlook, which loads a complete collection of "documents" (i.e., e-mail messages) when it is started. As such, the document model isn't directly used in Outlook, although Outlook does support custom *Outlook Form Regions*.

What makes an Outlook Form Region (OFR) different from a Document or Template model VSTO extension? The OFR is part of an add-in to Outlook, so if a new message is received that references that custom OFR, Outlook is ready to load the custom application logic. The potential challenges of OFR messages are discussed later in this chapter. The OFR customization provides a very powerful, compelling application model, but it also has key requirements in order for it to function correctly.

OFFICE BUSINESS APPLICATION ARCHITECTURE

The Office Business Application (OBA) model is one that Microsoft promotes as a product. Indeed, if you go to www.microsoft.com/office/oba, you'll find yourself redirected to the OBA product site at Microsoft. However, there isn't a license or a product called OBA that you can order in a box. Rather, the OBA model is conceptual, explaining how you can leverage the components that make up Microsoft Office to create a custom business logic solution. Instead of building applications from scratch, you can integrate the functionality of Excel for managing table data into your business logic using VSTO (not that VSTO is the only enabling technology associated with an OBA).

The OBA model has been made possible by a combination of several changes to Microsoft Office that have occurred over the years. When products such as Word and Excel were originally rolled into the larger "Office" product group, it was primarily a licensing arrangement. The original Office designation was a little like MSDN in that it enabled you to purchase a group of products for a lower price than purchasing each independently. Aside from some limited integration points, such as using the Word engine to edit Outlook messages, these products were independent.

However, over time, integration has gone beyond COM-based document integration. Arguably one of the key enabling technologies within the Office integration and collaboration framework is SharePoint. Other servers in the Office suite also fill this role in specialized areas — for example, Office Communication Server. This chapter doesn't cover SharePoint in depth, or its far more functional upgrade, Microsoft Office SharePoint Server (MOSS).

SharePoint provides a central location from which you can host customized Office documents. It also enables you to host custom workflow logic and provides a central location for e-mail and notification messages related to business processes. Feature-rich versions of MOSS include capabilities such as Excel Services and other advanced capabilities.

Because of these benefits, the OBA model builds around a central server. As noted, this might be a SharePoint server if the goal is to create a custom workflow to monitor an internal business process, but it doesn't have to be SharePoint. As shown in Figure 25-2, you might choose to create your OBA to leverage data stored in a line-of-business (LOB) system such as SAP, PeopleSoft, SQL Server, or any of several other business and data systems. Often these systems have either limited or no custom user interface. As a result, the user interface may or may not include features that your customers are familiar with from Office. Given that millions of people are familiar with Office and its interface, the OBA model enables taking this data and placing it into that interface.

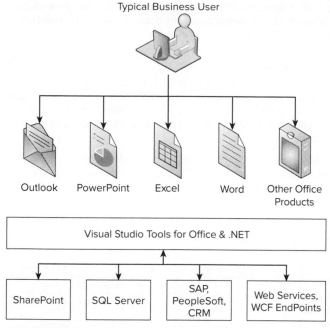

FIGURE 25-2

This brings up the second key enabling technology: the ease with which you can now import and export data and behavior to the Office client applications via VSTO. In fact, even with SharePoint it is the VSTO piece that truly enables you to integrate your custom business application into the Office client tools. VSTO enables you to retrieve data from a database via ADO.NET or LINQ or to communicate with XML Web Services and WCF. Once you have the data, you can enable your users to leverage their experience with the Office user interface to manipulate that data. As you'll see in this chapter, VSTO allows you to interface your LOB processes and data into every one of the Microsoft Office client applications.

This should give you a better idea of what an OBA is and how it provides an architectural pattern that you can use to create a business application using VSTO. In addition to the URL provided at the start of this section, you can also find more information at the Microsoft-sponsored site www.obacentral.com.

Finally, to see an example of an OBA consider TFS, and what was known as Team System. The Team Explorer install not only provides a set of add-ins for Visual Studio, but also provides support for a set of custom VSTO document applications. Every time you create a new Team Foundation Server (TFS) project, a new SharePoint project site is created. The site will contain several VSTO-based documents for Word and Excel. These illustrate one example of how to use VSTO and the OBA model for your custom applications.

Of course, VSTO wasn't the original — or even now the only — way to create custom logic within an Office client application. Since the early days of COM, both Microsoft Word and Microsoft Excel have supported Visual Basic for Applications (VBA). Fortunately, ongoing improvements occurring within VSTO can be integrated with existing VBA.

WORKING WITH BOTH VBA AND VSTO

The VBA model for Office document customization was limited at best. For starters, it is only available in Word and Excel. However, the VBA application model is not yet retired. That bears repeating: VBA is still a viable and supported set of tools for customizing the Microsoft Office experience. As with all such changes in technology, there are certain things that VSTO does that VBA wasn't designed to do, and to a certain degree is not capable of doing. However, there are also certain VBA optimizations within the existing tools with which VSTO can't currently compete.

Office 2007 is also known as Office version 12. Because Microsoft is committed to keeping VBA through Office 2010 (aka version 14), instead of doing a blanket conversion you'll be able to interoperate with existing code. Just like the WPF interop library and the Visual Basic 6.0 interop library, VSTO and VBA have an interop library. Microsoft suggests that companies with complex VBA solutions will probably want to update these Document/Workbook-style solutions with VSTO features, but not necessarily attempt to convert working code and features. Thus, your new VSTO code may call existing VBA functions; and similarly your existing VBA code may start calling your VSTO objects.

There are, of course, limitations to this model, and it isn't one that's recommended for new development. When it comes to the capability to call VBA from VSTO, you can call the Run method on the Office object model. This method accepts the name of a VBA method and a list of parameters. There is no IntelliSense, as what you are doing is making a dynamic runtime call. An example of this call is as follows:

```
Dim result As Integer = Me.Application.Run("MyFunctionAdd", 1, 2)
```

That's it — no special steps or hoops, just a standard call. Of course, your document or workbook needs to actually include the VBA function MyFunctionAdd, but that should be apparent. Also note that when you combine VBA and VSTO, you have to handle permissions for both, so plan to spend a little more time building your installation package and permissions. In addition, when you create your first custom VSTO Document or Workbook project, you'll get the warning shown in Figure 25-3.

FIGURE 25-3

At this point, you may not know whether you want to enable VBA interop within Visual Studio and your VSTO projects. If you've worked with VBA in the past or think you might need to do any VBA, consider enabling access to the VBA project system. As noted in the dialog, while turning this off completely is meant to act as a first layer of defense against the spread of macro viruses, your project will still maintain protection via other layers of security. Keep in mind that this option is available only to Word Document and Excel Workbook templates.

While this chapter isn't going to focus on security, sometimes — such as when you are enabling VBA macro interop — you do require a few specific settings. While it's possible to call VSTO from VBA in Office 2007/2010, it isn't the default. Starting with Office 2007, it's possible to enable macros, and as part of the creation of a VSTO project on a macro-enabled document, by changing a couple of document properties in your VSTO project, you can reference your VSTO methods and properties from VBA code. This process only begins after you have enabled macros within your document.

Your first step in enabling macros in a document is to ensure that the file is saved as a .docm file instead of a .docx file. The same is true for Excel, where the file type needs to be .xlsm as opposed to .xlsx. By default, documents saved with the extension .docx do not allow macros. Open Word 2007/2010 with your .docm file and press Alt+F11 to open the VBA editor for your document. You can add an actual macro or something as simple as a comment inside a default event handler. Alternatively, you can select a document that already contains a macro.

The demo document has a single macro ProVB, which was created to open a user form and insert the text "Hello World" at the start of the document. Once this is complete, you need to save your document. For this example, call your document **VBAInterop**. Then, select the Word Macro-Enabled Document type, as shown in Figure 25-4.

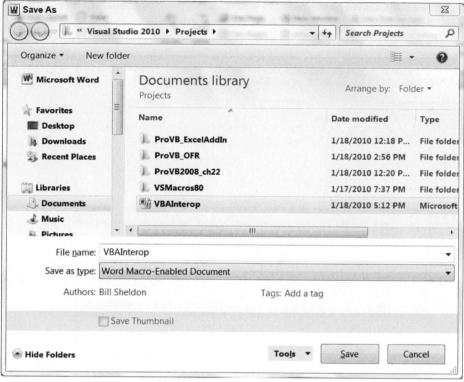

FIGURE 25-4

If you accidentally attempt to save your document as a .docx, the file system should warn you that it is about to clear your macros. The message box allows you to return to the Save As window and change the document type to a macro-enabled document.

Next, you need to ensure that Word considers your macro available whenever the document is opened. This demo was written on the Windows 7 operating system with Office 2010. In this environment you need to change your Trust settings for Office. Once you have added your comment macro and saved your .docm file, within Word (you may need to reopen the document) you should see a notification that a macro in the document has been prevented from running.

At this point you can choose to enable the macro. However, that choice is for the currently running instance only. If you closed and reopened the document, you would again be presented with that prompt. To make it possible to always run macros, you need to access the Trust Center for Word.

To traverse the menus, go to the File tab in the upper-left corner of your document and select Options. On the left side of the Word Options dialog is an item labeled Trust Center. This opens the Trust Center dialog, shown in Figure 25-5.

For the VBA interop to work, go to the Macro Settings in the Word/Excel Trust Center and select Enable all macros. Yes, you essentially need to turn off the security for macros on your development machine (unless you are using digitally signed macros — which isn't the case for this example).

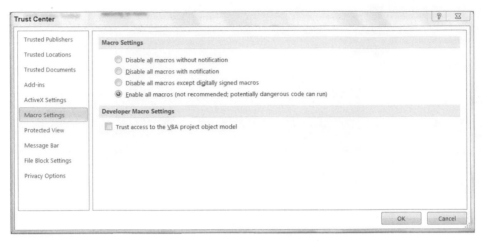

FIGURE 25-5

Once you have saved your document, it's time to open Visual Studio 2010 and create a new Office 2010 Word Document project, which in this case you can also name VBAInterop, as shown in Figure 25-6.

FIGURE 25-6

This brings up a second dialog, which is where you need to change from the default process. Normally, you would create a new document in the dialog shown in Figure 25-7. However, in this case you actually want to import your macro-enabled document VBAInterop.docm. By default, the Browse button limits the display of available files to those with the .docx extension, so you need to change the default in the file browse window to .docm in order to see your document.

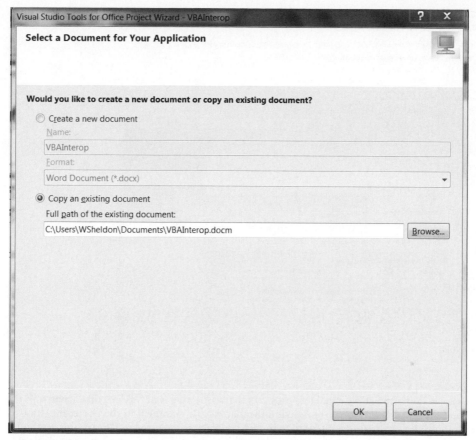

FIGURE 25-7

Clicking OK triggers Visual Studio to generate your project. When the generation is complete, Visual Studio will display your Word document within the main window, and in the lower right-hand corner you should have your Properties window. This window, shown in Figure 25-8, has two new Interop properties at the bottom. These properties are specific to macro-enabled documents and are not available if you didn't start your project with a macro-enabled document. You need to modify both these properties from their default of False to the new value of True.

These properties cause your VSTO project to regenerate and insert a new property within your project's macro file. To test this, you can start your project; once the project builds, Word will start and open your custom document. Once your document is open, press Alt+F11 to open the Macro Editor. Within the source for the

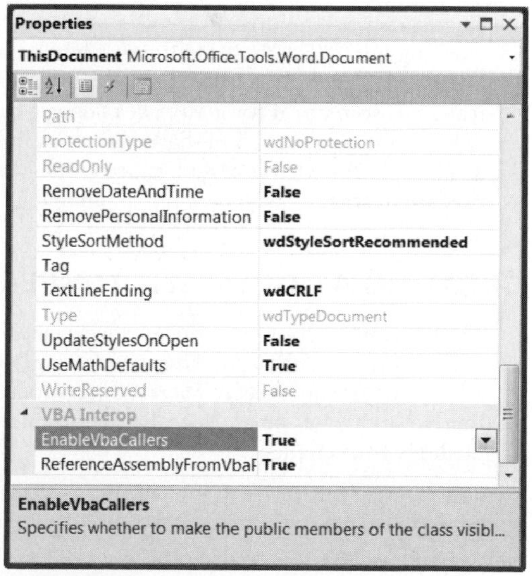

FIGURE 25-8

ThisDocument code should be the newly generated property value, as shown in Figure 25-9. The resulting code should look similar to the following:

```
Property Get CallVSTOAssembly() As VBAInterop.ThisDocument
    Set CallVSTOAssembly = GetManagedClass(Me)
End Property
```

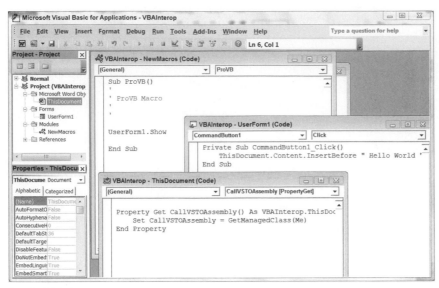

FIGURE 25-9

The code in this block shows the newly generated property that associates your VBA environment with the VSTO code you are creating. You can then proceed to the placeholder comment in the Document_New method where you initially entered a comment to maintain your macro's existence. Within this method, on a new line, make a call to CallVSTOAssembly, and you'll have IntelliSense for the list of available methods and properties.

There are a few additional steps in order to enable VBA to connect to VSTO, but for those who are already working with VBA these steps won't be a significant challenge. After all, it is development experience and the ability to continue to leverage existing resources that really drive this interop feature. The fact that this feature is so natural for a VBA developer — who may want to leverage key new capabilities such as WCF, WF, or possibly even WPF-based graphics in Excel — means that you can expect to be able to leverage your existing VBA code for several more years. When you do "migrate," the process is one that you control and execute in stages based on your requirements and decisions, not some overriding conversion process.

CREATING A DOCUMENT TEMPLATE (WORD)

The previous section introduced you to creating a document template from the standpoint of interoperating with VBA; but unless you have an existing VBA application, in most cases you'll just create a new, clean Word Document project. These projects focus on a specific document. They are self-contained in the sense that your changes only affect the user's system when the user chooses to open a document that specifically includes your changes.

This is great, as it isolates your changes. When users open Word or Excel they don't automatically load your customization. This way, your code won't affect the overall performance of their system (not that most developers care about this). The model also means that customizations for Application A aren't competing with Application B, which is in some ways a bigger challenge with add-ins.

However, this model (shared by VBA) has a limitation. The user must open a copy of the correct document to access your custom code. In an uncontrolled environment it may be difficult for a user to find the most recent version of that code. Sure, the first time your document customization is sent out to 10, 20, or 200,000 users, it's easy to locate and update the source documents. However, when you need to update some element of that standalone document, you have a problem.

Fortunately, this is where the OBA model and SharePoint become invaluable. By placing your documents onto SharePoint, you now have a controlled location from which users can access your VSTO application. In fact, with SharePoint 3.0, MOSS 2007, and SharePoint 2010 you can actually create a library for copies of your custom document that uses your document as what is known as a *content type*. By using your VSTO document as a SharePoint content type, when users access that SharePoint library and request a "new" document, they'll automatically open a new document that leverages your customizations.

An alternative to leveraging SharePoint is illustrated by another way to leverage document-based VSTO solutions. Your document might be included in a Microsoft or Windows Installer (MSI) package that is part of a larger installed application. In fact, you might not want users to directly open your customizations. Instead, your custom application might install your custom document via an MSI so that updates can occur in conjunction with your application updates. For example, when a user needs to modify data in a grid, you might open a custom Excel document, which, rather then save data in Excel automatically, places the data back into your application data store when the user asks to save.

The first step in creating such a solution is to create a new project. In this case the sample project will be named **ProVB_WordDocument**. Once you have changed the default name, click OK in the New Project dialog. This will take you to the Office Project Wizard dialog shown in Figure 25-10.

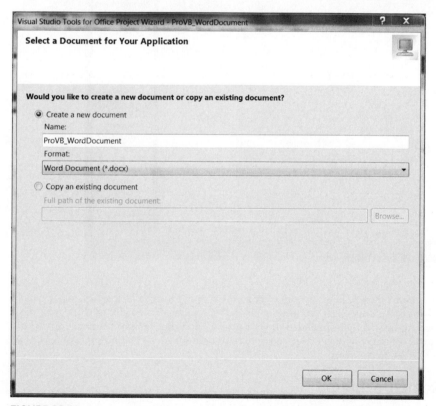

FIGURE 25-10

Note that you can specify a name for the document but it defaults to the project name you've chosen. That's because as part of this process, Visual Studio is going to generate a new Office 2007/2010 document and place that .docx file in your solution directory. When you work on this project, you'll be customizing that document. Thus, in many cases you may want to give the document that will host your customization an end-user-friendly name instead of your project name.

Once this is complete you are returned to the main Visual Studio window with a new project. Unlike other project types, however, in this case the template creates a Word document and then opens that document within Visual Studio. As shown in Figure 25-11, within the Solution Explorer, on the upper-right side of the display, your project contains a .docx file. The full name of the ProVB_WordDocument.docx file is shown in the tab in the upper-left corner. Associated with this file is a second .vb file, which is where some of your custom code may be placed. As shown in the figure, the Visual Studio user interface actually encapsulates this document. The Properties window shows the properties for this document. Note that unlike when you created your VSTO project from an existing VBA document, there are no properties to support integration with VBA.

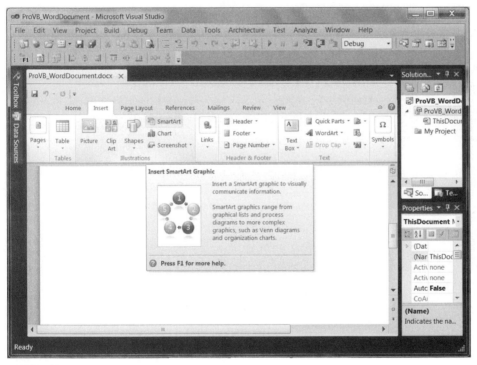

FIGURE 25-11

Also noteworthy (although not shown) is that if you were to open your project's properties and review the references, you'd find that all the Office Primary Interop assemblies you need in order to work with the Office object model have automatically been added to your project, and that the Embed Interop Types property has been set to True. You no longer need to try to figure out which COM interop assemblies are needed to access that interface from Word.

Adding Content to the Document

Of course, the main visual feature in Figure 25-11 is that Visual Studio has fully encapsulated the Word user interface. Note how the Insert tab has been selected in the document. You have full access to all the features in Word in this mode; and to demonstrate this, let's adjust the default contents of this document. Choose the

Smart Art ribbon bar button. Then, from within its dialogs, go to the Process tab of the SmartArt Graphic dialog, scroll down, and select the circular equation image. This will add that item to your document and automatically open an equation editor, as shown in Figure 25-12.

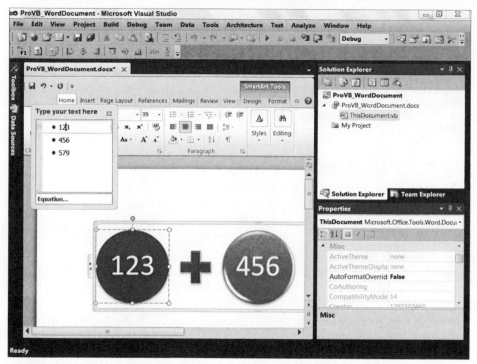

FIGURE 25-12

You can enter some numbers into the text box for this equation but there is no built-in adding logic. Close that text window and return to Visual Studio. Of course, at this point you haven't actually added any code to your document, so switch to the Code view. By default, VSTO inserts two event handlers when your project is created. Note that as long as the .docx file is displayed, you can't access the ThisDocument .vb file for that document. To switch the view, close the default .docx display and then right-click on the ThisDocument.vb file in the Solution Explorer and select Code View from the context menu. Now you should be able to see the code that was created as part of your project:

```vb
Public Class ThisDocument

    Private Sub ThisDocument_Startup(ByVal sender As Object, _
                        ByVal e As System.EventArgs) Handles Me.Startup

    End Sub

    Private Sub ThisDocument_Shutdown(ByVal sender As Object, _
                        ByVal e As System.EventArgs) Handles Me.Shutdown

    End Sub

End Class
```

Code snippet from ThisDocument.vb

As the preceding code illustrates, the document has two events available within VSTO. The first handles the startup event; the second handles the shutdown event. These are the only two events that are added to your project by default. You'll learn more about these shortly, but first add another event. This is the `BeforeSave` event; and as you might expect, it fires just before your document is saved:

Available for download on Wrox.com

```vb
Private Sub ThisDocument_BeforeSave(ByVal sender As Object, _
                  ByVal e As Microsoft.Office.Tools.Word.SaveEventArgs) _
                  Handles Me.BeforeSave
    Dim res As DialogResult = MessageBox.Show( _
                  "Should I save?", "Before Save", _
                  MessageBoxButtons.YesNo)
    If res = DialogResult.No Then
        ' This code could call a backend data store and then
        ' not save the associated document so the document would remain
        ' unchanged.
        e.Cancel = True
    Else
        ' This code would allow you to encourage the user to
        ' always save a new copy of the document
        e.ShowSaveAsDialog = True
    End If
End Sub
```

Code snippet from ThisDocument.vb

The preceding code illustrates a custom override of the `BeforeSave` event on the document. Note that after the event handler is declared, the code creates a local variable to hold a dialog result. It then shows a message box asking the user if it should save. Normally this isn't something you would do on this event, but in this case it enables you to see two of the attributes of the `SaveEventArgs` class.

If the user chooses not to save, then you have the option to not save data. Alternatively, you don't have to offer a choice to the user; instead, you can simply add code ensuring that the user simultaneously saves data to a back-end data store. Whether you need to call a Web service or update a database, this is a good place to call that logic. You then can save to the database and decide whether or not you actually want to update the underlying document. In some cases you might quietly save the data to the database and never save the document; then, when the document is next opened, you retrieve the data from the database as part of the startup. This is a particularly useful trick if you don't trust the file system's read-only privileges or you want to ensure that data from multiple different users is properly refreshed each time the document is opened.

Alternatively, you can force the user to perform a "save as" instead of a typical save. This uses the self-explanatory `ShowSaveAsDialog` property. The idea, again, is that you might not want the user to replace the original document; to keep that from happening, you can have Word automatically prompt the user to save the document with a different name. You can also save data to a database or other data store during this process.

Adding a Ribbon and an Actions Pane

The preceding work provides some baseline code in your application but it doesn't provide either a custom ribbon or a custom task pane. Therefore, before testing this, let's add one of each of these items to the project. To add either of these controls, right-click on your project in the Solution Explorer and then select the Add button to open the Add New Item dialog.

As shown in Figure 25-13, when this dialog opens you can select from one or more categories. In order to manage the available selections, select the Office category. This will reduce the number of available options from dozens to the three that are appropriate for a Word Document project. Start by adding a new ribbon bar. There are two options: XML and visual designer. Select visual designer and enter **DocRibbon** for your control's name.

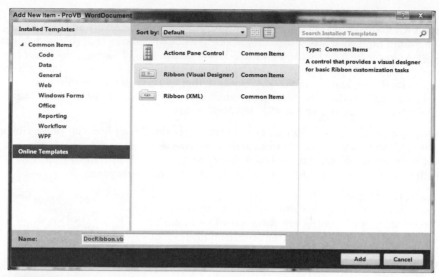

FIGURE 25-13

Figure 25-13 shows two alternatives for the Ribbon control, for backward compatibility. Previously, if you were customizing a ribbon bar for Office 2007 under Visual Studio 2005 and VSTO 2005 SE, then you didn't have access to a visual designer for the ribbon bar. Instead, you needed to create and edit an XML file, which would define your ribbon and the controls that were placed on it. There was neither a designer nor a tool customized for this task.

With the release of Visual Studio 2008, the VSTO team had an opportunity to create a visual designer for the ribbon bar. Thus, unless you are working with a legacy XML definition file, you should always select the ribbon with visual design support. Once you have modified the name of the new control to DocRibbon, select OK and return to Visual Studio. The control template will generate the control and open in Design view.

In Design mode, note that if you open the control Toolbox, you have a new category of controls available at the top. The Office Ribbon Controls, shown on the left in Figure 25-14, provide a list of controls that you can add to the default ribbon. Note that these controls are Windows Forms controls, not WPF controls.

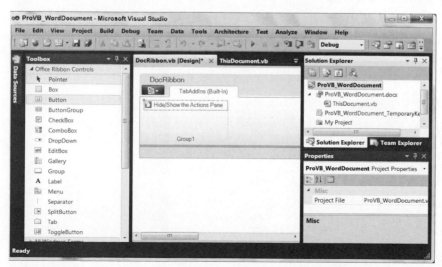

FIGURE 25-14

Add a button to the default Group1 in the designer. Once the button has been added, go to its properties and change the label for the button to "Hide/Show the Actions Pane." You can optionally add an icon to the button. For this I went into the Visual Studio directory to retrieve one of the icons that ship with Visual Studio 2010. If you navigate to the folder where you installed Visual Studio 10 and navigate the folder tree `Common7\VS2010ImageLibrary\1033`, within this folder you'll find a zip file: `VS2010ImageLibrary.zip`. Within this zip file are several thousand different images and icons that you can leverage within your application. Figure 25-14 shows the updated button display which includes an icon on the left side. The icon named `NewDocument.bmp` was taken from the VS2010ImageLibrary.

For now, skip implementing a handler for this button, as you want to see the default behavior of the ribbon and the actions pane. Instead, right-click on your project and again request to add a new item. In the Add New Item dialog, select an actions pane and name it **DocActionPane**. Once you have created your new actions pane you'll again be in Visual Studio, this time in the designer for your new pane.

Unlike the Ribbon control, the designer for the actions pane doesn't require a special set of controls and by default has a white background. Unfortunately, I've had trouble delineating the edges of the control in a white-on-white scenario. Therefore, before doing anything else, I proceed to the properties for the control and select the BackColor property. Visual Studio 2010 opens a small window with three tabs, Custom, Web, and System, as shown in Figure 25-15.

FIGURE 25-15

This illustrates the default setting for the background, which is the system-defined color for control surfaces. Specifically, the System tab colors are those defined for your system based on setting your own visual preferences. The other two tabs present color options the developer has selected. If you only want to change the display color while you are working on the design and layout, it's good to capture the original color and then go to the highlighted Custom tab and select a nice bright color such as red to highlight the actual surface area of your actions pane.

Now it's time to add a simple control to this panel. Once again, drag a button onto the design surface. Orient it in the upper-left corner and change the label to "Load." Eventually this button will be used to load some data into the document, but this is a good time to test run your project using F5. Your project will start and Visual Studio will start Microsoft Word. When Word opens, your document will display the image that you've embedded, as shown in Figure 25-16.

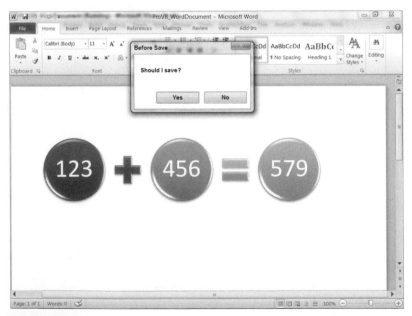

FIGURE 25-16

Figure 25-16 shows your custom document in Word. Note a few things about the running application at this point. First, the tab Add-Ins is set to display the custom ribbon bar. This isn't an error; even though you have created a custom VSTO Document solution, the customizations you made to the ribbon bar were automatically placed in this section.

Next, Figure 25-16 also captures the message box that was added to the BeforeSave event earlier. Because the Save button in the upper-left corner of the title bar was selected, the event was fired. Below this you see the custom smart graphics that were added to the document itself. So far, so good, but where is the document's actions pane?

Unlike the ribbon bar, which is automatically associated with your custom document when you add it to your project, the document actions pane needs to be manually associated with your document. As a result, Figure 25-16 does not show your custom actions pane, so your next step is to add that pane to your document, and in this case have it shown or hidden based on the selection of the toggle button added to the ribbon bar. Close the running document and return to Visual Studio once the debugger has stopped.

Activating the Actions Pane

If you choose to view all files in your project, you can select and open your DocActionPane.Designer .vb source file. Within this file you'll find that your DocActionPane class inherits from System.Windows .Forms.UserControl. That's right; the document actions pane is just a customized user control.

Knowing this tells you that you can in fact include not only individual controls, but also panel controls, such as a tab panel, or other custom user controls in this display area. More important, you can take a user control that you might be using in your current application logic and use it with no significant changes within the document's actions pane. However, anticipating your probable question, the reason the panel didn't show up is that both Word and Excel expect you to associate a user control with the ActionsPane property of your document.

Because the actions pane is actually open for use by any user control in your project, it is up to you to tell Word which control to assign. View the code for your document in the ThisDocument.vb file. Earlier you saw that the template created the Startup event handler by default. Add to this handler the following line:

```
Private Sub ThisDocument_Startup() Handles Me.Startup

    ActionsPane.Controls.Add(New DocActionPane())
End Sub
```

Code snippet fromThisDocument.vb

That line of code takes the built-in actions pane associated with your document and adds a control to that pane. Of course, you could also add items such as buttons and text boxes directly to your document's actions pane. However, as the control you added demonstrated, the preferred method is to create a custom user control and add this one control to the embedded actions pane in your document. The New DocActionPane() literally creates a new instance of your user control and places it onto the actions pane.

However, this isn't very flexible, in that you want users to be able to show or hide that pane. Instead of relying on the built-in controls for displaying or hiding the pane, you want to be able to toggle the actions pane on and off, which is why you have already added a button to the ribbon. That means customizing the Click handler for your toggle button. Before leaving the ThisDocument.vb display, make sure you close this file's editor so that later you'll be able to get to the document itself.

Next, select DocRibbon and double-click your button to add an event handler for your ToggleButton1 control's Click event. This is where you want to alter the status of your actions pane's display. The way to access the actions pane from the ribbon bar is through the application's Globals collection. Within VSTO you'll find a reference to the current document or workbook within this collection. From here you have access to objects such as the actions pane. In fact, you can type **Globals.ThisDocument.ActionsPane** to get access to the actions pane to which you assigned your user control.

However, while this does give you access to the user control, that control in your display is hosted by a frame, so even if you add code that sets the `Visibility` property on the `ActionsPane` attribute of your document, it probably won't have the desired effect. Setting the visibility status on the control only hides the control; it does not hide the now empty frame that was hosting the control. However, keep in mind that you can access the actions pane directly, as there may be a point when you want to do more than just hide and show the actions pane. For example, if you wanted to pass data or set a custom property on your user control, then you would leverage this object and retrieve your control from the `Controls` collection.

For this task you want to hide the entire Document Actions frame, not just the control it contains. The secret to this is the fact that the frame is considered by Word to be a `CommandBar`. Therefore, you need to access the `CommandBars` collection. However, the `CommandBars` collection has multiple different controls in it, so you need to retrieve the Document Actions pane from this collection. The most reliable way to do that is by name, so your `Click` event handler code should look similar to the following:

```vb
Private Sub ToggleButton1_Click(ByVal sender As System.Object, _
        ByVal e As Microsoft.Office.Tools.Ribbon.RibbonControlEventArgs) _
        Handles ToggleButton1.Click
    If ToggleButton1.Checked = True Then
        Globals.ThisDocument.CommandBars("Document Actions").Visible = _
                                                          True

        ToggleButton1.Label = "Hide Action Pane"
    Else
        Globals.ThisDocument.CommandBars("Document Actions").Visible = _
                                                          False

        ToggleButton1.Label = "Show Action Pane"
    End If
End Sub
```

Code snippet from DocRibbon.vb

The preceding code is called when the toggle button on your ribbon is clicked. It first determines whether the toggle button is selected or unselected. The `Checked` property provides this; and if the button is being selected, then the next step is to ensure that the Document Actions command bar is visible. Next, the code updates the text label on the button to "Hide Action Pane." This provides the user with initial feedback regarding what the button will do if it is clicked again.

Similarly, the code does the reverse, hiding the command bar and updating the text on the toggle button to indicate that in order to restore the command bar, the user should press the button again.

Now there is only one other thing to do. By default, because you are assigning a control to the actions pane, your pane should be displayed. However, it may not be; the user might load an add-in that suppresses the Document Actions command bar. Additionally, your toggle button is by default not selected, which is the state normally associated with the command bar being hidden.

To resolve these issues, you can override the `Load` event on your ribbon. Within the `Load` event, check the visibility status of the command bar and set the appropriate values for the display text and checked status of your toggle button:

```vb
Private Sub DocRibbon_Load(ByVal sender As System.Object, _
                    ByVal e As RibbonUIEventArgs) _
                    Handles MyBase.Load
    If Globals.ThisDocument.CommandBars("Document Actions").Visible Then
        ToggleButton1.Checked = True
        ToggleButton1.Label = "Hide Action Pane"
    Else
        ToggleButton1.Label = "Show Action Pane"
    End If
End Sub
```

Code snippet from DocRibbon.vb

Now that you have created the appropriate handlers for your ribbon bar, which will enable you to show and hide the actions pane, it's a good time to again test your application. Figure 25-17 shows your custom document. It displays the Add-Ins ribbon, and your Show/Hide toggle button is selected with the caption "Hide Action Pane." This correctly reflects that the next time that button is toggled, the display of the actions pane will be hidden. Although you can't see it in the book, notice how the toggle button indicates its visual state by applying the Office color scheme for a selected control. When working with a custom Office application, it's often said that your UI will be more intuitive to a user familiar with the behavior of Office; this example demonstrates that.

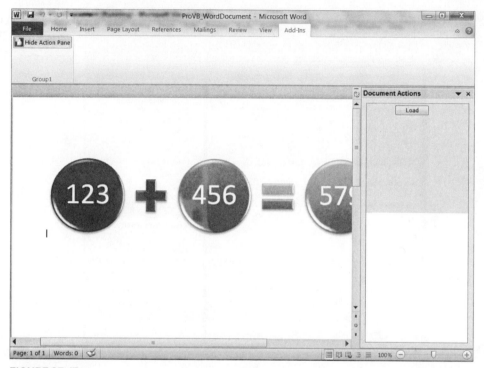

FIGURE 25-17

The other item that Figure 25-17 displays is the actual Document Actions window with your actions pane. You may recall that I changed the background color of the DocActionPane control to red. This should leave you a little concerned about why that red background (not apparent in Figure 25-17) is near only the top of the window. This challenge is one for which there is only a partial resolution.

Unfortunately, the layout of a .NET control within the Document Actions host is limited. You can request that your control fill the display, but this value is ignored. You can request that it stretch, but this setting determines whether the size of the control should by default match the display area of its contents. There simply isn't a good way to automatically resize your custom display area.

You can return to Visual Studio and increase the height of your background. In fact, you can make the background tall enough and wide enough to account for a display area of almost any size, but the real challenge is related to the controls that you place in your display. Unfortunately, you can't be certain that as the user resizes Word, the key controls you've chosen to place on the actions pane will always be displayed. However, right now there is only a single button on this control and it isn't doing anything, so it's time to add some logic for placing data into the Word document.

Updating a Content Control

Until now the only thing placed in your Word document was a simple graphic. While this made it apparent that you can in fact customize the content of this VSTO document, it didn't really demonstrate the capability to dynamically update the content of the document. The first step is to look at what was one of the new features of Office 2007 — content controls. Return to the Design view of your Word document, as shown in Figure 25-18, and notice the Toolbox. Within this Toolbox is a section titled Word Controls, which has been expanded.

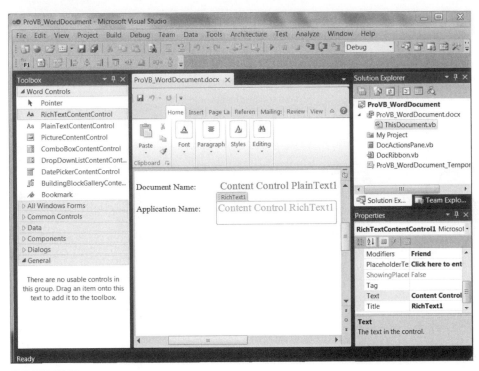

FIGURE 25-18

The controls shown in this section of the Toolbox are controls that you can apply to your document. Let's look at a couple of simple examples. Add some text similar to what is shown in Figure 25-18 (the actual content isn't that important). Then, on a new line within the document, add the text **Document Name:** followed by a tab or two. Drag a `PlainTextContentControl` onto your document. On the next line, add the label **Application Name:** followed by a tab. Then drag a `RichTextContentControl` onto the document. These two controls will provide a simple example of working with content controls.

On the lower right-hand side of Figure 25-18, you'll notice the Properties window. It is currently selected for the second control, but it provides an illustration of a few key content control properties. The first two are the capability to lock the control or to lock the contents of the control. Locking the control prevents users of your document from being able to delete the control. Locking the contents enables you to ensure that the text within the control can't be modified by the user. Of the other properties shown, the `Text` property represents the text that should be displayed in the control, which is customized along with the `Title` property.

The `Title` property was customized to demonstrate how you can reference these controls within your code. Keep in mind that these are controls, which means you can data bind these controls to data you have retrieved, and you can handle events on these controls. Several chapters have already covered handling events, so this demo code focuses on having the actions pane interface with these controls.

With that in mind, switch to the Design view for your `DocActionPane` control. Not that you are going to make changes to this beautiful design — you just want to double-click your Load button to create an event handler for the `Click` event. This will take you to the Code view, where you can enter the custom code to update your content controls. The code block that follows includes two methods for accessing these controls, one of which has been commented out:

```vb
Public Class DocActionPane
    Private Sub Button1_Click(ByVal sender As System.Object, _
                        ByVal e As System.EventArgs) _
                        Handles Button1.Click
        'This code could make database calls, process user input etc.
        'For Each ctrl As Word.ContentControl In _
        '                        Globals.ThisDocument.ContentControls
        '    'This will retrieve all of the embedded content controls.
        '    'Cycle through the list looking for those of interest
        '    Select Case ctrl.Title
        '        Case "PlainText1"
        '            ctrl.Range.Text = My.User.Name
        '        Case "RichText1"
        '            ctrl.Range.Text = My.Application.Info.ProductName
        '        Case Else
        '    End Select
        'Next
        Globals.ThisDocument.PlainTextContentControl1.Text = _
                                        Globals.ThisDocument.Name
        Globals.ThisDocument.PlainTextContentControl1.LockContentControl = _
                                        True
        Globals.ThisDocument.PlainTextContentControl1.LockContents = True
        Globals.ThisDocument.RichTextContentControl1.Text = _
                                        My.Application.Info.ProductName
    End Sub
End Class
```

Code snippet from DocActionPane.vb

The event handler starts with a comment related to the fact that at this point you are essentially working within the confines of a user control. Thus, you can add any data access code or XML processing code you want into this class. (Because those have already been covered in other chapters, this code focuses on the content controls.)

The first block of code, which is associated with a `For` loop, has been commented out because it isn't needed or even the preferred solution in this scenario. However, if instead of working with Word this solution were focused on Excel, and if you were working with cells, each of which might contain a content control, then the odds are good you would want an efficient way to access this large array of controls. This loop leverages the `ContentControls` collection. It also serves to illustrate a couple of key idiosyncrasies of this control collection.

Unlike what you might expect after the controls are retrieved from the collection, they do not directly expose all of their properties. In fact, the first missing property is the `Name` property. Thus, for this code to work based on identifying specific controls, you would need to use a separate identifier such as `Title`. In fact, a title has been added to each of the controls in the document, so if you want to you can uncomment and run this code. However, in typical scenarios where you use this code, you would be processing an array of controls and be primarily interested in control type and control location.

Control location would be related in Excel to the range associated with that control. Specifically, the `Range` property and its property `Cells` would tell you where on the spreadsheet you were. The `Range` property is important for a second reason. Like the control's `Name` property, the controls in this array don't expose a `Text` property. Instead, you can access the `Text` property of the `Range` in order to update the text in that control. As noted, however, this code has been commented out because there is a more direct way to access named properties.

The uncommented lines of code leverage the `Globals.ThisDocument` object to access by name the controls in your document. This code is not limited to Word and will work for Excel if you have only a small number of controls in your workbook. Note that the first line updates the value displayed in the `PlainTextContentControl`. It replaces the default text (which was formatted with a larger font and colored red) with the current document name.

Next, the code locks the control and its content. Not that you would necessarily wait until this point to set those properties, but this is just an illustration of accessing these properties and seeing the results when you run your document. The final line updates the `RichTextContentControl` using the `My` namespace, this time to retrieve the application name for your project.

At this point you can build and run your code. Once your document is displayed, go to the actions pane and use the Load button. Your results should look similar to what is shown in Figure 25-19. Note that the formatting for both the plain-text controls and the rich-text controls, which was applied in your source code, has remained unchanged.

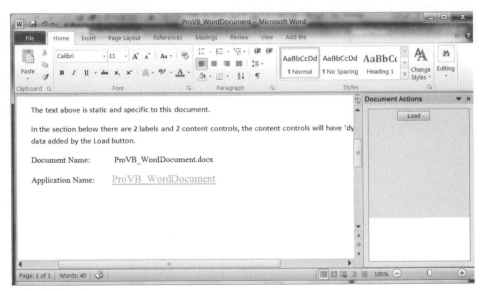

FIGURE 25-19

Note also that the highlight around your content control is by default visible to the end user. This is why you may want to lock these controls. In fact, you can attempt to delete or edit the document name to get a feel for the end-user experience. In case it wasn't clear, the work shown in this section can be replicated in an Excel workbook. In fact, the next section looks at using Excel, but instead of creating another VSTO document, the focus is on creating an add-in.

CREATING AN OFFICE ADD-IN (EXCEL)

Unlike the Document/Workbook project, the Add-In project type is installed on the user's computer and then loaded for every document that is opened. This introduces a set of different issues and concerns. For starters, unlike the document project, where you focus on the content of the document or workbook, in an add-in scenario you don't have an associated document in your project. Nor can you access the actions pane, although the Add-In project allows you to access not only the ribbon bar but also a similar UI feature called the task pane.

Of course, the most important difference is the fact that once your add-in is registered, it will be loaded for every document that the user accesses. This means that even if the user opens a VSTO document project, your add-in will be loaded alongside the customizations associated with that document. Similarly, if the user has multiple add-ins installed, then each one will be loaded for every document the user accesses. In short, your code has to play well with others and should load with minimal delay. When working with an add-in, keep in mind that it is unlikely to be the user's only one.

Create a new project of the type Excel 2010 Add-In. While in the New Project dialog, name your project **ProVB_ExcelAddIn** and click OK. You'll notice that, unlike when you created a document project and were deposited within your Office client inside Visual Studio, you are now in a code page. As shown in Figure 25-20, the code associated with your document looks very similar to what you had with your document project. However, unlike that project, you don't have access to the document itself.

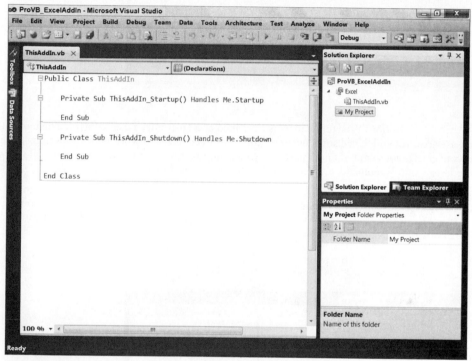

FIGURE 25-20

Just like the document-based project, you have the `Startup` and `Shutdown` event handlers and no others, but you can create any that are available for your application. To begin, access the ribbon bar and task pane by right-clicking on your project. Select Add New Item to open the Add New Item dialog, and select the Office category. This is where the next difference for an Add-In project becomes apparent: As illustrated in Figure 25-21, only the two Ribbon templates are available.

Select the Ribbon (visual designer) template and name your new control **RibbonAddIn**. Selecting Add will add this control to your project; and just as with the document project, you'll be in the designer for your ribbon. Leaving the ribbon alone for now, return to your project and again select Add New Item and return to the dialog shown in Figure 25-21. This time select the Common Items category.

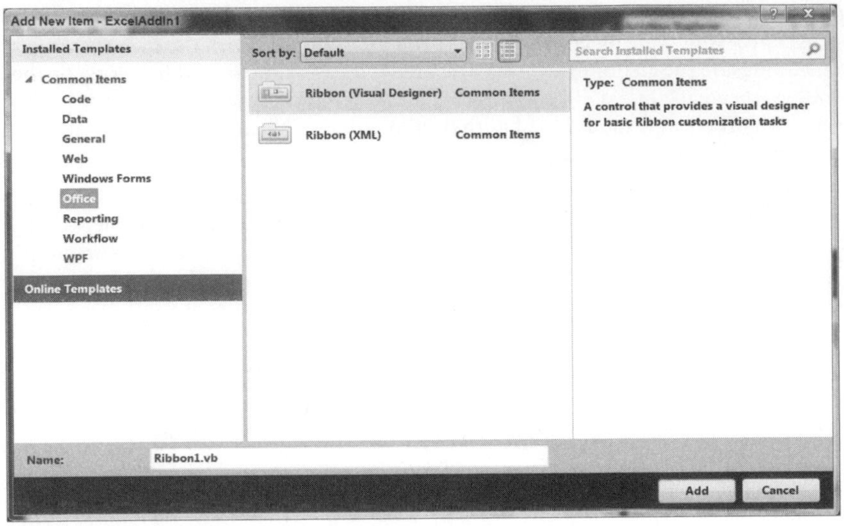

FIGURE 25-21

Earlier in this chapter, the Actions Pane template was described as a customized user control. The template took a common user control and added some custom properties to enable it to work with the actions pane. The task pane, conversely, doesn't need much in the way of customization for the user control it will use, so simply select the User Control template, use **TaskPaneUC** for your control name, and click Add.

After you are returned to Visual Studio, drag a button and a label into your new user control's design surface. The result should look similar to what is displayed in Figure 25-22. You can provide a custom label for your button if you choose, and after you have reviewed the layout of your controls, go ahead and double-click your button to create the event handler for the Click event.

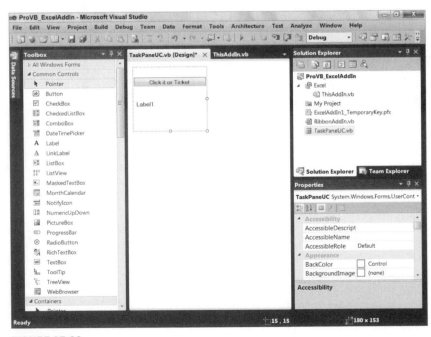

FIGURE 25-22

After adding the event handler, add a simple call to reset the text displayed by the label control, which is in your user control. In theory, you could add any code you wanted, but in keeping with the idea that you don't want to necessarily target or count on anything existing within your document, the goal is just to ensure that your code is accessible:

```vb
Public Class TaskPaneUC
    Private Sub Button1_Click(ByVal sender As System.Object,
                              ByVal e As System.EventArgs)
                              Handles Button1.Click
        Label1.Text = "Clicked it."
    End Sub
End Class
```

Code snippet from TaskPaneUC.vb

You could run your project and look for your custom task pane at this point, but by now you can probably guess that you won't find it. Just as with the actions pane, you need to associate your custom control with the collection of available task panes. Unlike the actions pane, for which there is only a single instance, each Add-In project could in theory want access to its own task pane. To resolve this, when you create an instance of a task pane, you create an item in a collection and assign it a unique name. This is significant, because although it wasn't mentioned earlier, regardless of how badly you want to change the name of the Document Actions pane, it isn't possible.

To associate your control with the task pane, switch to your Add-In and take two steps. First, declare a property for your Add-In that will hold a copy of your task pane. Note that this property has been declared as a "Friend" member so that other classes in the same project can access it. This will be important when you want to reference that control from within your ribbon bar.

Second, code is added to the Startup event handler. The first line assigns your custom user control as a new entry in the list of available task panes, and passes a copy of that control to the member variable you created. The second line is temporary; it indicates that your task pane should be visible, so you can ensure that you are seeing what you expect:

```vb
Public Class ThisAddIn
    Private m_ProVBTaskPane As Microsoft.Office.Tools.CustomTaskPane
    Friend Property ProVBTaskPane() As Microsoft.Office.Tools.CustomTaskPane

        Get
            Return m_ProVBTaskPane
        End Get
        Set(ByVal value As Microsoft.Office.Tools.CustomTaskPane)
            m_ProVBTaskPane = value
        End Set
    End Property

    Private Sub ThisAddIn_Startup(ByVal sender As Object,
                                  ByVal e As System.EventArgs)
                                  Handles Me.Startup
        ProVBTaskPane = Me.CustomTaskPanes.Add(New TaskPaneUC(),
                                               "Do Not Push Me")
        ProVBTaskPane.Visible = True
    End Sub
```

Code snippet from ThisAddIn.vb

Once you've added the preceding code to your project, it's time to test run your application. Using F5, build and start your project. Excel 2007 will open and then a blank spreadsheet will open. Your custom task pane should appear on the right-hand side; and once you click the button, your display should look similar to Figure 25-23.

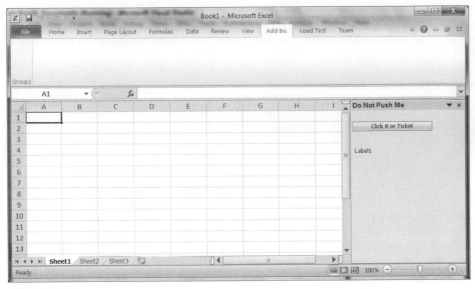

FIGURE 25-23

Notice that your custom title for the task pane is displayed. Of course, you could exit Visual Studio right now and open an Excel spreadsheet that was completely unrelated to your current project. However, your code has been registered for COM interop, so if you do this your custom task pane appears within your totally unrelated spreadsheet. This would quickly become annoying, which is why you'll want to display your custom task pane only when the user asks for it.

The next step is to customize your ribbon so that it can control your task pane. First, within your `ThisAddIn.vb` logic, remove the following line:

```
ProVBTaskPane.Visible = True
```

Next, go to the designer for your ribbon and add a new `ToggleButton`. You can label this button with some descriptive text. Additionally, select the group control that is already on your ribbon and change the text shown as the label for that control to something such as "ProVB Add-In." Double-click your new button and add the event handler for the `Click` event. Within this event you are going to again hide and show the control and update the display text of the button:

Available for
download on
Wrox.com

```vb
Private Sub ToggleButton1_Click(ByVal sender As System.Object,
        ByVal e As Microsoft.Office.Tools.Ribbon.RibbonControlEventArgs)
                                        Handles ToggleButton1.Click
    If ToggleButton1.Checked = True Then
        Globals.ThisAddIn.ProVBTaskPane.Visible = True
        ToggleButton1.Label = "Hide Push Me Pane"
    Else
        Globals.ThisAddIn.ProVBTaskPane.Visible = False
        ToggleButton1.Label = "Show Push Me Pane"
    End If
End Sub
```

Code snippet from RibbonAddIn.vb

The preceding code block should in fact look very similar to what you did within your Document project earlier in this chapter. However, there is a key difference when it comes to referencing the task pane. Notice that instead of accessing the `CommandBars` collection to make the entire pane display clear correctly, you are instead referencing the local `ProVBTaskPane` property that you declared in your `ThisAddIn` class. In addition, instead of a global reference to `ThisDocument`, you access the `ThisAddIn` object.

Similar to working with the earlier project, you will want to modify the Load event. However, there is an additional consideration here. When your add-in is loaded by Excel, the ribbon bar is loaded before the core add-in's Startup event fires. This is important because you can't just check to see whether your task pane is visible. First you need to determine whether the task pane exists. Then, if it does, you check whether it is visible. To do this you create an If statement, which as shown in the following code block leverages the conditional AndAlso:

```vb
Imports Microsoft.Office.Tools.Ribbon

Public Class RibbonAddIn

    Private Sub RibbonAddIn_Load(ByVal sender As System.Object, _
                                 ByVal e As RibbonUIEventArgs) _
                             Handles MyBase.Load
        If Globals.ThisAddIn.ProVBTaskPane IsNot Nothing AndAlso _
           Globals.ThisAddIn.ProVBTaskPane.Visible Then
            ToggleButton1.Checked = True
            ToggleButton1.Label = "Hide Push Me Pane"
        Else
            ToggleButton1.Label = "Show Push Me Pane"
        End If

    End Sub
    Private Sub ToggleButton1_Click(ByVal sender As System.Object, _
        ByVal e As Microsoft.Office.Tools.Ribbon.RibbonControlEventArgs) _
                                        Handles ToggleButton1.Click
        If ToggleButton1.Checked = True Then
            Globals.ThisAddIn.ProVBTaskPane.Visible = True
            ToggleButton1.Label = "Hide Push Me Pane"
        Else
            Globals.ThisAddIn.ProVBTaskPane.Visible = False
            ToggleButton1.Label = "Show Push Me Pane"
        End If
    End Sub
End Class
```

Code snippet from RibbonAddIn.vb

If you fail to add that check, then you'll throw an exception as Excel is trying to load. Excel won't appreciate this, and it remembers. The next time Excel starts it will warn the user that your add-in caused an error the last time it tried to load it, and suggest that the user disable your add in — not exactly the result you want for your code.

If your code is working, then your display should look similar to what is shown in Figure 25-24, which shows the user interface with the mouse hovering over your new ribbon bar button. Note you can't actually see the mouse, but can see the hover over effect in the button coloring and the Office tip on the screen. By leaving the mouse over your button, you'll get an Office tip telling you that you can select F1 for help about this control. Using the F1 key starts the help system and Excel opens a help page describing how you can manage add-ins within Excel.

The F1 help page is a good resource for assistance if you need a bit of help on a topic. You can test your add-in at this point to ensure that it opens and closes the task pane correctly. However, just as you can manage add-ins from Excel, it is difficult to dispose of them from within Excel. This is important, because if you start creating add-ins for several different customers, you could wind up with ten or twenty such add-ins taking up residence on your system. Excel would open only after a longer and longer delay.

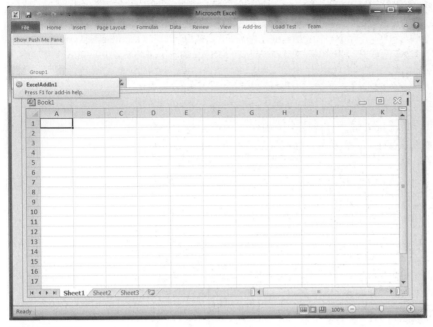

FIGURE 25-24

Of course, it's bad enough that during testing, every time you debug, you're paying a price to ensure that your current code is registered properly. Having add-ins piling up could be even more of a problem. Fortunately, Visual Studio has an easy solution, as shown in Figure 25-25.

FIGURE 25-25

This same menu option is available across all the different Add-In project types. Selecting this enables you to easily remove from your system the test add-ins that you make. As annoying as this might be for Excel or Word, when you see the implications of an Outlook Form Region, which relies on an Outlook add-in, you'll understand why this clean option is important.

OUTLOOK FORM REGIONS

As previously noted, Visual Studio 2010 VSTO provides templates for every client application in the Microsoft Office suite. Some of these, such as Word and Excel, are the traditional favorites for customization. Others, such as PowerPoint, may see very little automation. However, there is a new kid on the block. Outlook supports an add-in template that includes what is sure to become one of the more popular extension models.

Outlook form regions (OFRs) provide you with the capability to customize what users see when they open an e-mail message or a contact or any of several other components within Outlook. As you'll see in this section, OFRs provide a very flexible framework that enables you to embed anything from an HTML view to a custom WPF user control in Outlook. Because Outlook is as popular as almost any other Office client application, this feature will have a broad reach.

Using an OFR provides a canvas that isn't simply visible alongside your primary focus; the OFR provides a very configurable UI that enables you to extend or replace the default interface associated with typical components in Outlook. Because e-mail has become the ubiquitous office and home communication tool, being able to customize how key business data is presented in this medium is powerful.

To get started, create a new Outlook add-in project named **ProVB_OFR**. (Not shown here are screenshots of the New Project dialog or the initial view in Visual Studio after the template has run, as the Outlook add-in looks very similar to the Excel add-in discussed earlier.) You'll find yourself in the code view for your add-in, with the `Startup` and `Shutdown` event handlers.

At this point, add your OFR to your project. Right-click on your project and select the Add option from the context menu to open the Add New Item dialog. As before, go to the Office category to review the available templates, where you'll find an Outlook Form Region template (see Figure 25-26). Give it a meaningful name, such as **AdjoiningOFR,** to reflect the type of form region you'll create.

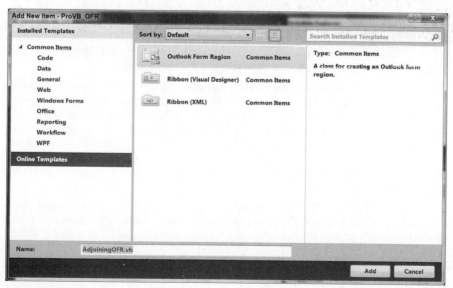

FIGURE 25-26

After clicking the Add button, instead of being returned to Visual Studio, you'll be presented with the first screen in the wizard for the New Outlook Form Region. This wizard walks you through several different options related to your OFR. The first choice, shown in Figure 25-27, is whether you want to generate your form from scratch or would like to import one of the standard templates that ship with Outlook.

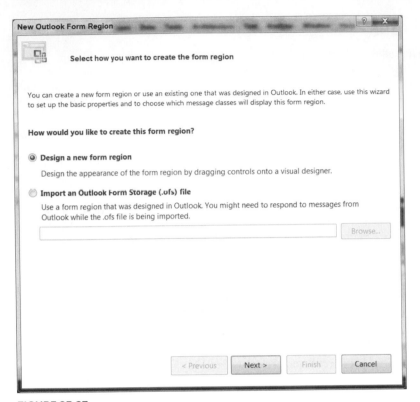

FIGURE 25-27

The current example will go through the steps to create a new form region. (Take some time to explore one or more of the standard forms on your own, as a complete discussion is beyond the scope of this chapter.) Click Next to be taken to the second step of the wizard — selecting a type of form.

The dialog shown in Figure 25-28 lists four different types of potential regions. As you move between the different options, the wizard displays a graphic that illustrates how each one affects the default display. These four options can actually be grouped into two sets. The first two options — Separate and Adjoining — are form types that modify the built-in components of Outlook. When displayed, these forms keep their default display and then add your customization. So for example an e-mail message will be displayed with the original body plus your customization shown either adjoining or available as a separate tab. The second group consists of the Replacement and Replace-all regions. These form types replace the object that would normally display within Outlook.

As noted in the naming of your OFR, the plan is to demonstrate creating an Adjoining form region, but to demonstrate how Replacement and Replace-all forms work, select one of these two options and click Next. This will take you to a screen where you can name and set some options related to your OFR. You will return to this screen when you revert to the Adjoining OFR type. Instead of discussing this now, click Next a second time and move to the next step in the wizard. This will take you to the screen shown in Figure 25-29, defining the classes that can be associated with your OFR.

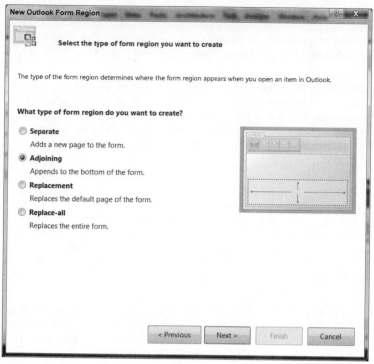

FIGURE 25-28

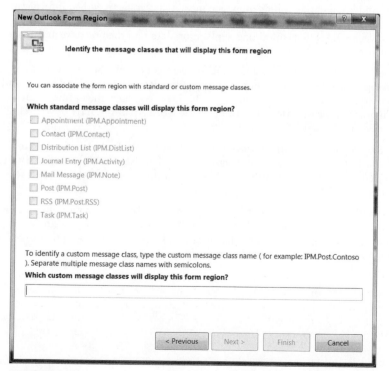

FIGURE 25-29

Keep in mind that Figure 25-29 shows this dialog as it looks when you have selected either a Replacement or a Replace-all OFR type. As noted, these form types replace the underlying class. In Figure 25-29, each of the built-in classes has been disabled, so you can't ask to apply your change to one of those existing types. Instead, your only option is to define a custom class or classes; the best practice is to define a single class.

This custom message class is one that you would define within your custom add-in. To better explain what is occurring, let's use a mail message as an example. Typically, when Outlook receives a mail message, the message is assigned to the class IPM.Note. The IPM.Note class is what provides all of the typical display elements that you see in a message within Outlook. If you create a replacement form, then when that form is sent it is flagged not as a typical message, but instead as an instance of your custom class.

In other words, the sender of the message needs to be aware of the class name used for this type of OFR. In theory, this is all that the sender needs to be aware of — however, that's only in theory. The Replacement and Replace-all form types work fine as long as the initial message is sent to the Microsoft Exchange Server. If, however, you are attempting to trigger a message from, say, SharePoint, there is a problem. Typically, when SharePoint is installed and configured, the e-mail options are set up such that SharePoint handles its own messages. However, SharePoint doesn't allow for sending messages with custom message types, so when your code attempts to trigger this custom message type from within SharePoint, the message is sent only if you have configured your SharePoint server to communicate with an Exchange Server.

There are other unique features to Replacement and Replace-all forms. On the positive side, unlike the OFRs that modify an existing object type, Replacement and Replace-all forms are instantiated only when a message of that specific class is received. As discussed later in this section, Adjoining and Separate forms need to have custom code added that screens when that OFR should be displayed.

Another advantage of Replacement and Replace-all forms is that they give you more control over the message content. Any text in the underlying body is hidden, which means that you can embed information in the message body that will later be used in the form. In addition, these form types also hide enclosures, so it is possible to enclose, for example, an XML file containing application data and then retrieve and process this data when the message is opened.

However, for this example you are creating a new Adjoining OFR, so use the Previous button twice in order to return to the screen shown in Figure 25-28. Change your OFR type from Replacement to Adjoining and click Next. This should bring you to the screen shown in Figure 25-30. Here you have the option to provide a display name for your OFR. In order to see the effect of this, place the word **An** at the start of your class name so that you'll be able to see where this value is used.

The three check boxes in this dialog represent situations when this OFR will, by default, be available in Outlook. In the case of the first one at least, you might not want to accept that default. "Inspectors that are in compose mode," enables you to determine whether someone who is creating a new message or contact should also see your OFR region by default.

Although the setting is present for all OFR types, it in fact is not applicable to Replacement and Replace-all. In the case of Replacement and Replace-all forms, Outlook doesn't automatically offer these as an option for creating a new message. Instead, users need to access the File menu and select the Forms option to tell Outlook that they are attempting to send a message defined by the custom type.

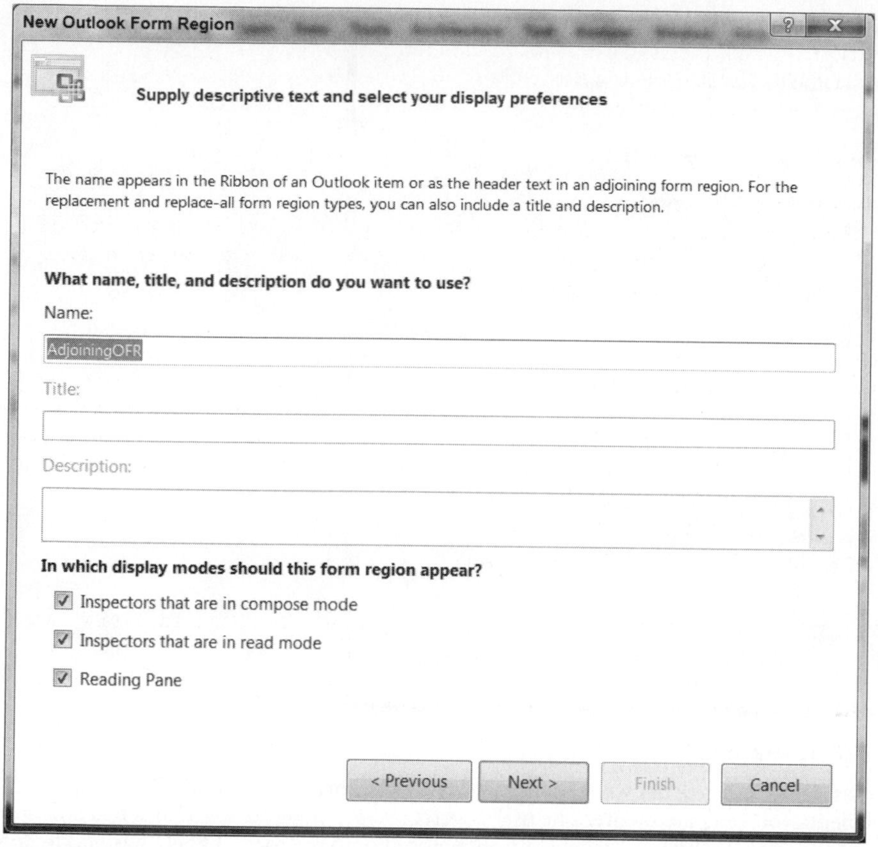

FIGURE 25-30

However, for Separate and Adjoining forms, Outlook will, if you leave this checked, automatically add your custom region to the standard new message, contact, appointment, and so on, window. This could get quite annoying if your users aren't going to be placing data into that OFR and it is for display only. Thus, in many cases you'll clear this first check box. However, if you are customizing a contact to capture and update new data elements, you would probably want to leave this check box selected.

As for the other two check boxes in Figure 25-30, these refer to displaying your custom OFR, and typically these remain selected so that your OFR will be visible to display data.

Clicking Next takes you to the dialog shown in Figure 25-31. This dialog enables you to select from any of the standard classes that are used within Outlook. The goal is to enable you to create a custom OFR for one or more of these classes, although typically you'll select just one. For now, select just Mail Message and click Finish to complete the creation of your OFR and return to Visual Studio.

After returning to Visual Studio, you'll be in the designer for your AdjoiningOFR user control. That's right, once again you are working with a Windows Forms user control that has been customized by the VSTO team to provide the characteristics you defined in the preceding wizard. At this point you can open the Toolbox and drag and drop controls onto the form.

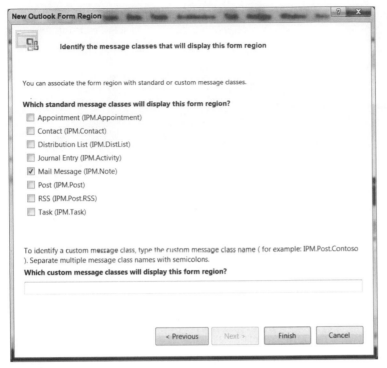

FIGURE 25-31

Figure 25-32 illustrates a few changes that you can make so that your form will be both visible and have some simple elements you can manipulate. The user control shown in Figure 25-32 has had a new background color assigned, and has had two label controls dragged onto the form. Label1 has had its font changed to a much larger size and the background changed to white. The default text in Label1 is now a zero. To the left of Label1 is Label2, which has had its text updated to read "Attachment Count."

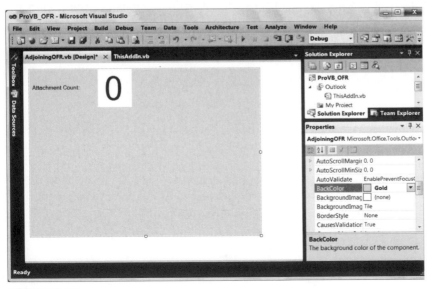

FIGURE 25-32

You still haven't written any actual code, so this is a great time to test your application. Use F5 to build and run it. Once the build is complete, Outlook will automatically open. You should see something similar to what is shown in Figure 25-33.

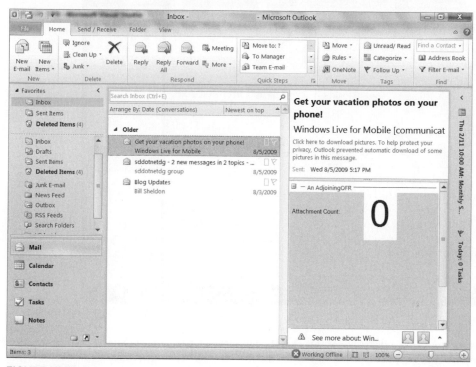

FIGURE 25-33

Note that even the original Outlook test message, which was received two days previously, now includes your custom OFR. In fact, you'll find that every message you open includes the OFR — which could easily become annoying, given that in a real application your OFR would probably be targeting a single message type. Similarly, if you choose to create a new message, there it is again — an OFR that has only display information. Once you have satisfied yourself with the impact of this region on Outlook, close Outlook and return to Visual Studio.

Figure 25-34 provides a view of the default generated code for your OFR. Your goal is to carry out two tasks: First, make this OFR display only if the associated message includes one or more attachments. Second, update Label1 so that the number of attachments is shown in the OFR.

The first item to note is the Form Region Factory code block, which has been collapsed. There are actually three generated methods, and it is the method hidden inside this code block where you'll want to put the custom logic specifying when this OFR should be visible. When expanded, as shown in the following code, not only do you have your AdjoiningOFR class, but within this collapsed block is a second partial class definition that defines an implementation to create your OFR as part of a factory. Factories are a well-known software pattern wherein the calling application might not know the details of which class is being created, but only the base-class OFR and the methods and properties exposed at the base-class level.

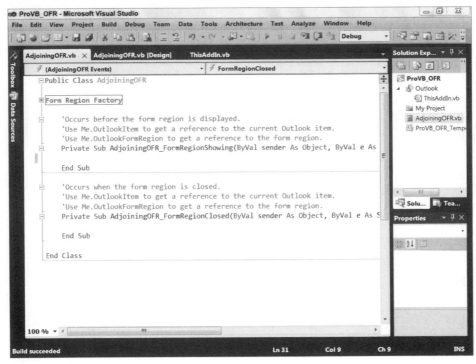

FIGURE 25-34

Software patterns are outside the scope of this chapter, but in short, the factory patterns indicate that there will be a `FormRegionInitializing` event handler, and that the calling application will be able to create several different types of OFRs based on which factory has been implemented within each OFR. Here is the code:

```
Public Class AdjoiningOFR
#Region "Form Region Factory"
    <Microsoft.Office.Tools.Outlook.FormRegionMessageClass
    (Microsoft.Office.Tools.Outlook.FormRegionMessageClassAttribute.Note)> _
    <Microsoft.Office.Tools.Outlook.FormRegionName("ProVB_OFR.AdjoiningOFR")> _
    Partial Public Class AdjoiningOFRFactory

    ' Occurs before the form region is initialized.
    ' To prevent the form region from appearing, set e.Cancel to true.
    ' Use e.OutlookItem to get a reference to the current Outlook item.
        Private Sub AdjoiningOFRFactory_FormRegionInitializing( _
                ByVal sender As Object, _
                ByVal e As _
            Microsoft.Office.Tools.Outlook.FormRegionInitializingEventArgs) _
                Handles Me.FormRegionInitializing
    End Sub

    End Class

#End Region

    'Occurs before the form region is displayed.
    'Use Me.OutlookItem to get a reference to the current Outlook item.
    'Use Me.OutlookFormRegion to get a reference to the form region.
    Private Sub AdjoiningOFR_FormRegionShowing(ByVal sender As Object, _
```

Available for download on Wrox.com

```
                                       ByVal e As System.EventArgs) _
                                       Handles MyBase.FormRegionShowing
        End Sub
        'Occurs when the form region is closed.
        'Use Me.OutlookItem to get a reference to the current Outlook item.
        'Use Me.OutlookFormRegion to get a reference to the form region.
        Private Sub AdjoiningOFR_FormRegionClosed(ByVal sender As Object, _
                                       ByVal e As System.EventArgs) _
                                       Handles MyBase.FormRegionClosed
        End Sub

    End Class
```

Code snippet from AdjoiningOFR.vb

In order to prevent your OFR from being displayed, you need to add custom code to the
FormRegionInitializing event handler. In this case you simply want to determine whether the message
has one or more attachments. If it doesn't have any attachments, then you want the OFR to remain hidden:

```
        Private Sub AdjoiningOFRFactory_FormRegionInitializing( _
                            ByVal sender As Object, _
    ByVal e As Microsoft.Office.Tools.Outlook.FormRegionInitializingEventArgs) _
                            Handles Me.FormRegionInitializing
            Try
                Dim mail = CType(e.OutlookItem, Outlook.MailItem)
                If Not mail.Attachments.Count > 0 Then
                    e.Cancel = True
                    Return
                End If
            Catch
                e.Cancel = True
            End Try
        End Sub
```

Code snippet from AdjoiningOFR.vb

The preceding code illustrates some of the key elements to screening your OFR. The first thing to note is
that you can access the inbound e-mail message by retrieving the OutlookItem object from the parameter
e. Of course, you need to cast this item, as it is passed as type Object. Once you've done this, you have full
access to the Outlook object model for e-mail messages. Thus, you can quickly determine the number of
attachments; and if there are none, you can set the Cancel property to True.

The next task is getting the number of attachments in your message into the OFR. This is a fairly easy task.
Unlike the decision about whether to display the OFR, which occurs when the code is about to create that
OFR, your ability to influence what is displayed doesn't occur until the FormRegionShowing event handler
is called. In the code block that follows, instead of retrieving the current e-mail object from a parameter,
it is one of the member values for your OFR:

```
        Private Sub AdjoiningOFR_FormRegionShowing(ByVal sender As Object, _
                                       ByVal e As System.EventArgs) _
                                       Handles MyBase.FormRegionShowing
            Dim mail = CType(Me.OutlookItem, Outlook.MailItem)
            Me.Label1.Text = mail.Attachments.Count
        End Sub
```

Code snippet from AdjoiningOFR.vb

Thus, the code to get the number of attachments and assign that as the contents of the label boils down
to two lines of custom code. At this point you can rerun the application to test your code. Once Outlook
opens, you should see that the AnAdjoiningPane, which was previously displayed for all messages, is now
gone except in the case of those that have attachments.

This means that when you now create a new message, the OFR is still not shown. However, if you add an attachment and then save that message before sending, you can reopen the saved message and you'll see the OFR displayed. Keep in mind that the determination of whether the OFR should be displayed occurs during the creation of the OFR, and once the OFR has been hidden you can't change that setting while the object remains open.

SUMMARY

This chapter looked at VSTO and introduced many of its new features. It didn't spend a lot of time talking about how you can add controls and logic to user controls, but instead focused on how to work with the custom task pane or actions pane, and how to leverage new capabilities such as content controls.

VSTO isn't just a simple set of extensions that mirrors what you could do in VBA. In fact, VSTO extends every client in the Office system and provides multiple templates. It provides flexibility with Word and Excel to customize either at the document level or by creating a custom add-in; and if you do customize at the document level, it provides the option to interoperate with any existing VBA code you have in your document.

In addition to Word and Excel, you've been introduced to Windows Outlook form regions. The OFR model enables you to send business data directly into the application that everyone uses. The various OFR models have differing advantages and disadvantages, but each is based on an underlying user control, which enables you to leverage everything that is available via Windows Forms, including WPF interop.

You also learned that the OBA model is becoming an increasingly important focus for Microsoft. The ability to tie your business logic into applications such as Word, Excel, and Outlook means that your developers can spend less time creating and maintaining custom grid controls, and your end users can get started with less time spent in training.

26

Windows Workflow Foundation

WHAT YOU WILL LEARN IN THIS CHAPTER

➤ What is workflow?

➤ How Windows Workflow Foundation abstracts workflow in your applications

➤ How you build workflows with Windows Workflow Foundation

➤ How you can extend Windows Workflow Foundation by creating custom activities

➤ How you can integrate Windows Workflow Foundation into your applications

Windows Workflow Foundation (WF) is a powerful tool when developing applications, as it provides a standard means of adding workflow to an application. *Workflow* refers to the steps involved in an application. Most business applications contain one or more workflows, such as the approval steps in an expense-tracking application or the steps involved in paying for a cart full of items at an online store. Normally, a workflow is created in code and is an integral part of the application. WF enables developers to graphically build the workflow, keeping it logically separated from the code itself. It also enables the workflow to change as the needs of the business change. These workflows may be as complex as needed and may integrate child workflows, human processes, or Web services.

This chapter looks at how you can take advantage of WF in your applications: how you can add and edit workflows, how you can integrate workflows into an existing business process, and how the graphical tools used to build workflows with Visual Studio can help you communicate with business users and avoid errors caused by mistakes in the workflow.

 The method of building workflows with WF changed with Visual Basic 2010. If you are working with an earlier version of the .NET Framework, see the samples in Appendix C.

WORKFLOW IN APPLICATIONS

Just what is workflow? It's a very heavily used word, and many developers use it in multiple contexts. For our purposes, it is the description of the steps involved in some process performed at least partially by a computer. Workflows are common in many types of business applications. For example, if you were building an application for tracking employee expense reports, the workflow might look something like the following:

1. The employee completes a form and submits it into the system.
2. The system examines the data in the expense report:
   a. Depending on the rules defined by the company, it may be automatically approved, require management approval, or require investigation by the accounting department. Some of the rules that may come into play would likely be the expense types, the amount of each expense, how the expense was paid, the level of the employee, and so on.
   b. Copies of the expense report are e-mailed if additional approval is required.
   c. If approved, the expense report continues in the workflow; otherwise, it is returned to the submitting employee for correction (or to complain to the employee's manager).
3. Expense report values are recorded in the accounting system.
4. A check is printed and sent to the happy employee.

The steps in a workflow may be carried out by a human or a computer; they may require custom code or calculations, or they may need to integrate with an external application. Building workflows into an application is frequently a process that can lead to a number of errors in the system. Unless a developer completely understands the business process (and they rarely do), identifying the true workflow used for a process requires interviewing multiple people at one or more companies. This often results in conflicting descriptions of the steps involved, or of the actions required at each step, requiring someone to decide on the actual intent. WF reduces the risk of building errors into the system by providing a graphical tool that can be better understood by nontechnical analysts and users of the system to validate the workflow.

Even after the exact workflow has been defined, it frequently changes. This may be due to some new legal requirements, a company merger, or even (frequently) the whims of management. In traditional applications, this would likely mean that a developer would have to change the code for one or more steps of the process, ideally without introducing any new bugs into the system. In short, developing workflow applications using traditional tools can be a difficult, time-consuming process. WF makes building and maintaining these workflows easier by abstracting away the logic of the workflow, and by providing several of the common services required.

BUILDING WORKFLOWS

The actual workflow files in WF are typically XML files written in a version of XAML. This is the same XAML used to describe Windows Presentation Foundation (WPF) files. (See Chapter 17 for more details on WPF.) The XAML files describe the actions to perform within the workflow, and the relationship between those actions. You could create a workflow using only a text editor, but Visual Studio makes creating these workflows much easier. It provides a graphical designer that enables developers to visually design the workflow, creating the XAML in the background.

A workflow comprises a number of activities, although even the top-level workflow is itself an activity. This should give you the (correct) idea that you can nest many activities within one another, which provides a natural-feeling composition model to building up a workflow from smaller components.

Adding Workflow with Windows Workflow Foundation

Workflow Foundation is composed of a number of components that work together with your application to carry out the desired workflow. Six main components make up any WF application:

➤ **Host process** — The executable that will host the workflow. Typically, this is your application, and usually a Windows Form, Silverlight, WPF, ASP.NET, or Windows service application. The workflow is hosted and runs within this process. All normal rules of application design apply here: If another application needs to communicate with the workflow, then you need to use Web services to enable communication between the two applications.

➤ **Runtime services** — WF provides several essential services to your application. Most notable, of course, is the capability to execute workflows. This service is responsible for loading, scheduling, and executing your workflows within the context of the host process. In addition to this service, WF provides services for persistence and tracking. The persistence service enables saving the state of a workflow as needed. Because a workflow may take a long time to complete, having multiple workflows in process can use a lot of the computer's memory. The persistence services enable the workflow to be saved for later use. When there is more to complete, the workflow can be reactivated and continue, even after weeks of inactivity. The tracking services enable the developer to monitor the state of the workflows. This is particularly useful when you have multiple workflows active at any given time (such as in a shopping checkout workflow). The tracking services enable the creation of applications to monitor the health of your workflow applications. This layer will also be extended in the future through Windows Server AppFabric, which will provide a number of management and tracking services for WF and WCF services.

➤ **Workflow invoker** — Responsible for executing each workflow instance. It runs in process within the host process. Each engine may execute multiple workflow instances simultaneously, and multiple engines may be running concurrently within the same host process.

➤ **Workflow** — The list of steps required to carry out a process. The workflow may be created graphically using a tool such as Visual Studio, or manually using a text editor. Each workflow is composed of one or more activities, and may consist of workflow markup and/or code. Multiple instances of a workflow may be active at any given moment in an application.

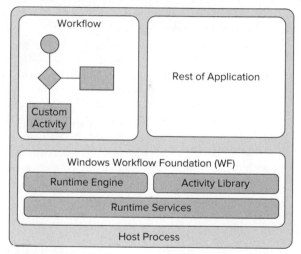

➤ **Activity library** — A collection of the standard actions used to create workflows. If you are familiar with flowcharts, the activities are the individual elements you use to draw the flowchart. There are several different types of activities. Some are used to communicate with outside processes, while others affect the flow of a workflow.

➤ **Custom activities** — In addition to the standard activities that exist within the activity library, developers can create custom activities. This may be to support a particular application you need to integrate with WF, or as a simplification of a complex composite activity. Creating custom activities is done mostly through attributes and inheritance.

FIGURE 26-1

Figure 26-1 shows how the main components of WF fit together.

WF supports two main styles of creating workflows: *sequential* and *flowchart*. Sequential workflows (see Figure 26-2) are the classic style of process. They begin when some action initiates the workflow, such as the submission of an expense report or a user decision to check out a shopping cart. The workflow then continues stepwise through the activities until it reaches the end. There may be branching or looping, but generally the flow moves down the workflow. Sequential workflows are best when a set series of steps is needed for the workflow, and the workflow proceeds in a single direction until completed.

FIGURE 26-2

Flowchart workflows (see Figure 26-3) are less linear than sequential workflows. They provide a more familiar metaphor for most developers, as they work similarly to the classic model of a flowchart in application design. They are typically used when the data moves through a series of steps toward completion. Typically, the flow goes in a single direction, but branching is more common in this style of workflow.

While any workflow can contain elements of each of these workflow types, a good way to decide between the two is the linearity of the desired workflow. If it is a linear series of steps, then the bulk of the workflow likely would fit into the sequential model, while more branching processes would likely be better modeled as a flowchart. For example, browsing a shopping site is a classic example of a flowchart. Users are either in browse mode or cart view mode, and they may move between the two modes in either direction. Selecting checkout would likely initiate a sequential workflow, as the steps in that process are more easily described in a linear fashion.

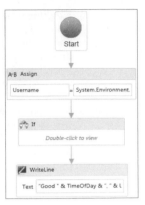

FIGURE 26-3

A Simple Workflow

As with any other programming endeavor, the best way to understand WF is to create a simple workflow and extend it with additional steps. Start Visual Studio and create a new Workflow Console Application called **HelloWorkflow**.

This project creates three files: a module that includes the main file for the application (originally Module1.vb, renamed to Main.vb in the sample), the application configuration file (app.config), and the workflow (workflow1.xaml). The workflow begins life blank, but you can drag activities from the Toolbox onto the design surface. This design surface is the equivalent of the designers you use when creating Windows Forms or WPF applications: Dragging activities onto the WF design surface edits the underlying XAML files.

To begin, drag a `WriteLine` activity (from the Primitives category of activities) onto the surface. This is a very simple activity that simply writes some text to the console (or other class that inherits the `TextWriter` class). Set the `Text` property of the `WriteLine` activity to something appropriate like `"Hello Workflow"` (with the quotes). In order to better see this, you can add some code to the `Main` method to pause the console when the application is running:

```
Shared Sub Main()
    WorkflowInvoker.Invoke(New Workflow1())
    Console.WriteLine("Press ENTER to exit")
    Console.ReadLine()
End Sub
```

Code snippet from HelloWorkflow

Run the project to see the console window (see Figure 26-4), along with the message you are expecting.

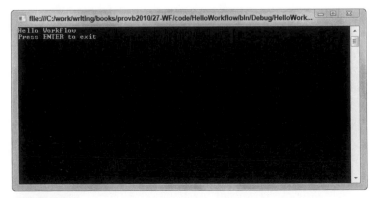

FIGURE 26-4

While trivial, the project makes a useful test bed for experimenting with the various activities. Delete the `WriteLine` activity and replace it with a `Flowchart` activity. Add an `If` activity to the designer and a `WriteLine` activity. As you hover your mouse over the Start icon on the flowchart, you will see a number of handles appear on the icon (see Figure 26-5). Drag an arrow from these handles from the start icon to a handle on the `If` activity. Add a similar arrow between the `If` activity and the `WriteLine` activity. Notice the red exclamation icons that are added to the `If` and `Flowchart` icons, as shown in Figure 26-6 (without the color). This is used throughout the workflow designer to indicate that either there is an error in an activity's settings or you still have to make a change to one or more settings. This bubbles up to any container of the activity. In this case, as you haven't set any condition on the `If` statement, it indicates the error. This is also the cause of the error marker on the `Flowchart`.

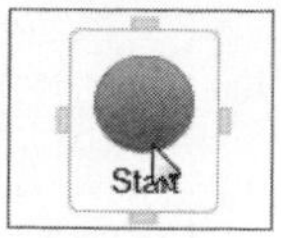

FIGURE 26-5

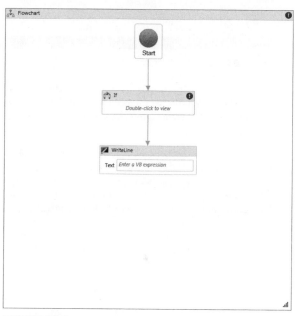

FIGURE 26-6

Double-click the `If` activity to open its designer (see Figure 26-7). Notice that you have three areas to edit. First, a condition must be set. This is similar to the code you would use in any normal `If` statement. Then you can add other activities to the `Then` and `Else` areas. While these two areas can accept only a single activity, if you have a complex chain of events you can drag a `Sequence` activity to wrap the steps required.

You can either type the expression into the field or bring up the Expression Editor dialog (see Figure 26 -8) by clicking the ellipses next to the Condition property in the Properties Window of Visual Studio. Set the Condition to `System.DateTime.Now.Hour < 12`.

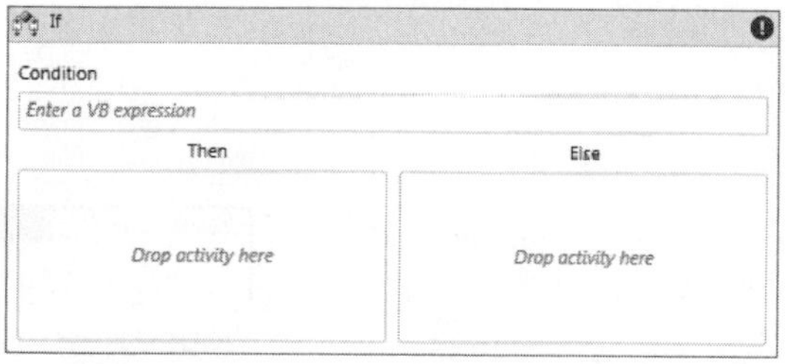

FIGURE 26-7

FIGURE 26-8

This will return `True` before noon. In this case, the `WriteLine` activity should display a greeting for morning. You therefore need a way for this activity to supply a value to the `WriteLine` activity. In WF, this is done through the use of variables and arguments. Variables are used within a workflow, while arguments provide the means to send data into and extract data from a workflow. In this case, you want a variable to provide the time of day to the `WriteLine` activity.

You create new variables using the Variables pane of the workflow designer. Open this by clicking the Variables link at the bottom-left corner of the designer. Create a new string variable called `TimeOfDay` (see Figure 26-9)

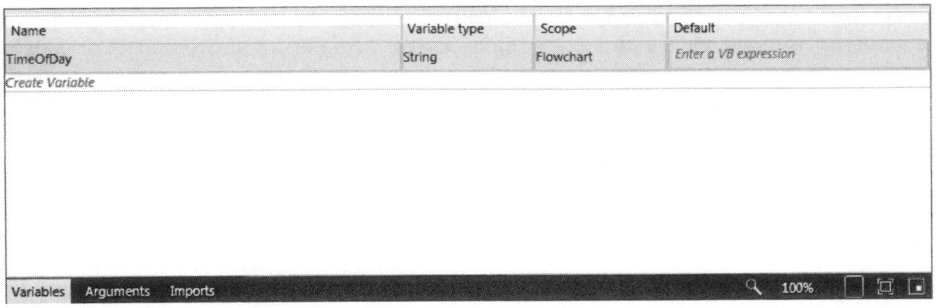

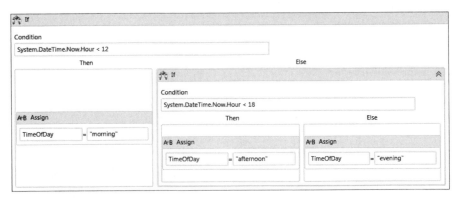

FIGURE 26-9

Now you can drag an `Assign` activity to the `Then` section of the `If` activity designer. The `To` property is the name of the variable you'll assign a value into (in this case the `TimeOfDay` variable) and the `Expression` property is a VB expression to assign to the variable. In this case, something like "morning" should work (with the quotes).

For cases when the time of day is not before noon, it would be best if the message were a little more variable. Drag another `If` activity into the `Else` area of the `If` activity designer. Set the condition of this activity to `System.DateTime.Now.Hour < 18`, and add an `Assign` activity to each of the `Then` and `Else` areas of this activity. They should assign the value of "afternoon" and "evening" to the `TimeOfDay` variable. The completed `If` activity should look similar to Figure 26-10.

FIGURE 26-10

Return to the main flowchart by clicking the Flowchart item in the breadcrumb at the top of the workflow designer (see Figure 26-11). Before you update the `WriteLine` activity, drag a new `Assign` activity onto the designer. This will be used to hold the current user's name. Delete the arrow connecting the Start icon and the `If` activity and connect the Start icon to the new `Assign` activity and then to the `If` activity. Create a new string variable called `UserName` to hold the user name, and set the value to `System.Environment.UserName`. Set the `Text` property of the `WriteLine` activity to `"Good " & TimeOfDay & ", " & Username`. The final workflow should appear as shown in Figure 26-12. Run the workflow to see the resulting message.

FIGURE 26-11

While this workflow is probably overkill to generate a simple message, the example does show many of the common steps used in defining a workflow. Workflows are composed of multiple activities. Many activities can in turn be composed of other activities. Activities may use declarative properties, or code may be executed as needed.

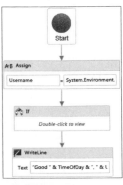

FIGURE 26-12

Standard Activities

The standard WF activities can be divided into five major categories:

➤ **Low-level activities** — These activities perform some minor task, usually as part of a larger process.

ACTIVITY	DESCRIPTION
Assign	Assigns a new value to a workflow variable
Delay	Causes a delay in the workflow. This may be useful in cases where you would like a timed event to occur, or you want to provide some sort of timeout for a long-running process.
InvokeMethod	Calls a method on a class or object. You can supply parameters as needed.
WriteLine	Writes a message to either the console or any TextWriter class. In addition to using it for debugging purposes, this is also useful as a logging mechanism, or to create text files to be used elsewhere in the workflow.
AddToCollection<T>	Adds an item into a collection managed by the workflow. For example, it might add an item into a processing queue for other parts of the workflow. This is a generic activity, and you need to assign the type for the objects stored in the collection.
ClearCollection<T>	Clears the items from the collection managed by the workflow
ExistsInCollection<T>	Determines whether a given object is already stored in the collection managed by the workflow
RemoveFromCollection<T>	Removes an item from the collection managed by the workflow

➤ **Control of flow activities** — These activities are the equivalent of Visual Basic's If statement or While loop. They enable the workflow to branch or repeat as needed to carry out a step.

ACTIVITY	DESCRIPTION
DoWhile	Works like the VB do...while loop. Performs a child activity (use a sequence if you need multiple steps) while a condition is true. Will run at least once.
ForEach<T>	Works like the VB for each...next loop. Performs a child activity on each of the items in a collection. You need to define the type used in the iteration.
If	Chooses a child activity based on a given condition. If you need multiple children, then use a sequence.
Parallel	Performs two or more child activities on the input simultaneously. For example, you might define a Parallel to write to a log, submit to a Web service, and add to a collection at the same time.
ParallelForEach<T>	Like the ForEach<T>, but the child activities are executed in parallel, rather than sequentially.
Pick	Schedules two or more PickBranch activities. These activities will wait until one of them is triggered, and the flow will follow that branch from then on. This can be used to provide routing for a system, such as where the data is submitted to multiple Web services. Once one of the Web services has been selected using the Pick, you can then continue with the workflow. Alternately, if you had a manual process in a workflow (e.g., a pause waiting for an e-mail to be returned), you could use a Pick activity to select between the manual process and a Delay, with the process timing out if the Delay is triggered first.
PickBranch	Used with the Pick activity to provide new branches for the stage
Sequence	Container for multiple steps in a workflow. This may be the parent of the workflow, or it may be used within another activity when you need multiple children at a given step.

continues

(continued)

ACTIVITY	DESCRIPTION
Switch<T>	Works like the VB `case` statement. Switches the flow through a workflow based on the value of a variable or condition.
While	Works like the VB `while...end while` loop. Performs a child activity (use a sequence if you need multiple steps) while a condition is true.
TerminateWorkflow	Stops the workflow before the end of the workflow is reached. This is useful in the event of errors in the workflow, or if the data input doesn't allow for completion. Also used for flowchart workflows as a means of completion.

➤ **Activities that communicate with external code** — These activities are either called by external code to initiate a workflow or used to call to external code as part of a workflow. This category also includes activities that communicate with external systems to persist the workflow state.

ACTIVITY	DESCRIPTION
Receive	Receives a one-way WCF message
ReceiveAndSendReply	Receives a WCF message and sends back a result
Send	Sends a one-way WCF message
SendAndReceiveReply	Sends a WCF message and waits for a result
Persist	Saves the current state of the workflow. This is very useful for long-running workflows, as it enables you to save the current state of the workflow, saving memory. You can then reload the workflow as it was persisted as needed later.

➤ **Transaction activities** — These activities group a number of other activities together into some logical element. This is usually done to mark a number of activities that participate in a transaction.

ACTIVITY	DESCRIPTION
CancellationScope	Marks the boundaries of a set of activities to perform if a process is cancelled. Typically, this would be used to close any handles, undo any partially completed steps, etc.
CompensableActivity	Marks the boundaries of an activity that may be "undone." This activity groups one or more actions to be performed. In addition, it contains actions to undo whatever steps may have already been performed. This is typically to enable rollback of a partially failed transaction. This activity is used as an alternative to transactions when you don't necessarily control the success of each of the steps in a process. For example, if you send a request to a Web service, and then fail another step, the `CompensableActivity` can send a cancel request to the Web service.
Compensate	Invokes the compensation activity in a `CompensableActivity` activity. That is, it "undoes" whatever activity was performed.
Confirm	Performs the equivalent of a commit on the `CompensableActivity`
TransactionScope	Marks the boundaries of a transaction within the workflow
Rethrow	Rethrows an existing exception. This is typically done within the `Catch` clause of a `Try...Catch` activity to propagate the exception to another part of the workflow.
Throw	Creates an exception within a workflow
TryCatch	Wraps an activity (use a sequence if you need multiple children) within a `Try...Catch` block to handle exceptions
CorrelationScope	Marks the boundaries of a set of Web services that will share a correlation handle
InitializeCorrelation	Allows you to initialize a correlation. Typically, this is done using a message, but this activity allows you to start it without an explicit correlation message.
TransactedReceiveScope	Allows you to flow a transaction into a WCF communication

➤ **Flowchart activities** — These activities are used in flowchart-style workflows and allow for the organization of the steps, simple decisions, and other stages.

ACTIVITY	DESCRIPTION
Flowchart	This activity is used to create a flowchart workflow. It is a container for all the steps involved in the workflow.
FlowDecision	A simple If statement within a flowchart workflow. This is used to control the actions of a workflow based on a condition.
FlowSwitch	A switch statement within a flowchart workflow. This works similar to the VB case statement in that you have multiple cases that work based on the assigned condition. You also define a default condition if none of the cases apply.

A Less Simple Workflow

To see a few of these activities together, create a new Workflow Console Application named Fulfillment. This will be used to create part of a workflow for an order fulfillment application. The workflow will collect an XML file from a directory on disk, validate it using a few simple rules, and add it to a collection representing the order queue. Other workflows might then retrieve items from this collection for actual processing. Figure 26-13 shows the final workflow.

As you can see from the figure, the workflow is a flowchart consisting of four stages. The DisplayName property of each of these stages has been set to better describe the contents of the stage. As you would expect, this is invaluable in improving the understanding of the workflow when you come back to it later (or try to explain it to end users). The basic outline of the workflow is as follows:

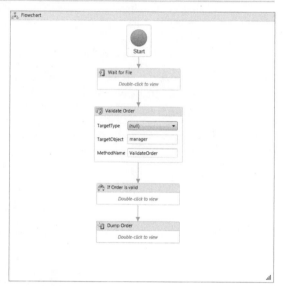

FIGURE 26-13

➤ The workflow begins a loop to monitor a directory for XML files. This file will represent an order, with one or more details. This is a DoWhile activity.

➤ Once an order is received, a few simple validations are performed by calling a method on a .NET class. This is an InvokeMethod activity.

➤ If the order is valid, it is added to a collection for later processing. If not, the validation errors are displayed and the workflow completes. This is an If activity.

➤ To demonstrate additional processing, the orders collection is simply displayed to the console. Of course, in a real application, this stage would send the orders on to another application for actual fulfillment and shipping. This is a ForEach<T> activity.

Before you begin building the workflow, there are some helper classes that you need to build. These represent an order, an order detail line, and a manager class for processing the order. Add a new Class Library project to the solution, named **OrderManager**. This has three classes: Order, OrderDetail, and OrderSystem.

The Order class represents an order in the system. For this example, it consists of a few properties, including the collection of order details.:

```
Public Class Order
    Public Property OrderID As Integer
    Public Property OrderDate As Date
    Public Property CustomerName As String
    Public Property ShipAddress As String
```

```
        Public Property Details As List(Of OrderDetail)

        Public Sub New()
            Details = New List(Of OrderDetail)
        End Sub
    End Class
```

The `OrderDetail` class is an individual line item within an order. Again, for this example it is greatly simplified:

```
Public Class OrderDetail
    Public Property Parent As Order
    Public Property ItemName As String
    Public Property Quantity As Integer
End Class
```

The `OrderSystem` class is a general manager class for the orders. In addition to the functionality for this demo, it would likely be responsible for saving orders to a database, and so on:

```
Public Class OrderSystem

    Public Function GetOrderFromDropFile(ByVal path As String) As Order
        Dim result As Order = Nothing
        Dim files As String()
        Dim doc As New XDocument
        Dim detail As OrderDetail

        files = IO.Directory.GetFiles(path)
        If files.Length > 0 Then
            doc = XDocument.Load(files(0))
            'load header
            result = New Order
            With result
                .OrderID = CInt(doc.Root.Attribute("id").Value)
                .CustomerName = doc.Root.Element("customerName").Value
                .OrderDate = CDate(doc.Root.Element("orderDate").Value)
                .ShipAddress = doc.Root.Element("shipAddress").Value
            End With
            'load detail rows
            Dim details As List(Of XElement) = (From item In doc.Descendants
                        Where item.Name = "orderDetail"
                        Select item).ToList

            For Each d In details
                detail = New OrderDetail
                With detail
                    .Parent = result
                    .ItemName = d.Element("itemName").Value
                    .Quantity = CDec(d.Element("quantity").Value)
                End With
                result.Details.Add(detail)
            Next
            'delete file to avoid calling this again
            'likely you would move to a backup directory instead
            '           IO.File.Delete(files(0))
        End If

        Return result
```

```
    End Function

    Public Function ValidateOrder(ByVal anOrder As Order) As String()
        Dim result As New List(Of String)

        'check for OrderID
        If Not IsNumeric(anOrder.OrderID) Then
            result.Add("Order ID is not valid")
        End If
        'check for ship address
        If Not String.IsNullOrEmpty(anOrder.ShipAddress) Then
            result.Add("No ship address")
        End If
        'check for at least one OrderDetail
        If anOrder.Details.Count < 1 Then
            result.Add("Must have at least one item in order")
        End If
        'other checks here

        Return result.ToArray
    End Function

End Class
```

Code snippet from OrderManager

For this example, the `OrderSystem` class exposes two methods. The first attempts to load an XML file from an assigned directory. Once a file has been loaded, it converts the contents of the XML file into an `Order` object, and one or more `OrderDetail` objects. LINQ to XML is used to retrieve the rows containing order details.

The second method does a few simple validations on the order, and returns a list of validation errors (as strings) to the calling program.

The following code shows a sample order XML file (also included in the source code for the `OrderManager` project):

```xml
<?xml version="1.0" encoding="utf-8" ?>
<order id="1234">
  <orderDate>2009-12-01</orderDate>
  <customerName>Moe's Family Diner</customerName>
  <shipAddress>1313 Mockingbird Lane, Springfield, AK</shipAddress>
  <orderDetails>
    <orderDetail>
      <itemName>Mango puree</itemName>
      <quantity>2</quantity>
    </orderDetail>
    <orderDetail>
      <itemName>Everso Sharp Knives</itemName>
      <quantity>15</quantity>
    </orderDetail>
    <orderDetail>
      <itemName>Mega frier</itemName>
      <quantity>1</quantity>
    </orderDetail>
    <orderDetail>
      <itemName>Case of sparklers</itemName>
      <quantity>200</quantity>
    </orderDetail>
  </orderDetails>
</order>
```

Code snippet from OrderManager

Build the project to ensure you have no errors, and then you're ready to build the workflow to use these classes. Add a new `Flowchart` activity to the designer, and add the four activities shown in Figure 26-12, connecting them as shown.

The workflow will make use of the objects in the `OrderManager` project. As such, you should import that namespace into your workflow. First, add a reference to the `OrderManager` project: Right click on the `Fulfillment` project and select Add Reference. Select the `OrderManager` project on the Projects tab. Next, click the Imports link at the bottom of the workflow designer on the `FulfillmentWorkflow`. This displays the current list of namespaces available to your workflow. Add the `OrderManager` namespace by entering it in the space at the top of the list and pressing Enter to save it to the list.

The `DoWhile` loop consists of a `Sequence`, which in turn contains a `Delay` activity and an `InvokeMethod` activity (see Figure 26-14). The `DoWhile` activity requires that you set a condition that will end the loop. In this case, it will be when an order has been picked up by the `InvokeMethod`.

FIGURE 26-14

The following table describes the property settings for the added activities.

ACTIVITY	PROPERTY	VALUE	DESCRIPTION
DoWhile	Condition	theOrder Is Nothing	You will create the `theOrder` variable shortly. This variable will hold an instance of an `Order` class for processing.
Delay	Duration	00:00:10	The `Duration` property is a `TimeSpan`. In this case, the delay is set for 10 seconds. In a real-world application, you would set this based on the frequency of orders being processed.
InvokeMethod	TargetObject	manager	This is an instance of an `OrderSystem` class.
	MethodName	GetOrderFromDropFile	A method on the `OrderSystem` class
	Result	theOrder	Once a new file has been processed, the resulting order is saved for processing within the workflow.
	Parameters	System .Configuration .ConfigurationManager .AppSettings("dropFilePath") .ToString()	The directory to monitor will be set using the application configuration file.

The `InvokeMethod` activity is used to call the `ValidateOrder` method on the `manager` object. Set the properties on this activity as shown in this table:

ACTIVITY	PROPERTY	VALUE	DESCRIPTION
InvokeMethod	TargetObject	manager	This is an instance of an OrderSystem class.
	MethodName	ValidateOrder	A method on the OrderSystem class
	Result	ValidationErrors	A variable that will be added to the workflow shortly
	Parameters	theOrder	The instance of the Order class created by the GetOrderFromDropFile method above

FIGURE 26-15

Next, the processing branches based on whether errors are encountered in the order. If the order is valid, then it is added to a collection for further processing. If, however, there are any validation errors, they are displayed and the workflow ends (see Figure 26-15). Set the properties for these activities as follows:

ACTIVITY	PROPERTY	VALUE	DESCRIPTION
If	Condition	ValidationErrors.Length > 0	The condition will return true if any errors were added to the collection by the earlier ValidateOrder call.
AddToCollection<T>	TypeArgument	OrderManager.Order	This defines the type of objects stored in the collection.
	Collection	Orders	This is a variable of the workflow that will store the orders.
	Item	theOrder	The item to add to the collection. In this case it is a workflow variable.
ForEach<T>	TypeArgument	String	This will iterate over each of the items in the ValidationErrors collection to display them.
	Values	ValidationErrors	This is the collection to iterate over.
WriteLine	Text	ValidationError	This is the value of the current iteration in the loop.
TerminateWorkflow	Reason	"One or more orders have errors"	This will be available to the calling application to determine why the workflow terminated.

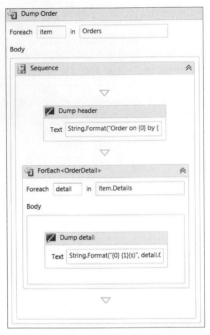

FIGURE 26-16

Finally, the orders are simply displayed on the console to confirm they have been processed. This is done with another ForEach<T> activity that writes the order's information, followed by each of the detail rows in the order (see Figure 26-16). The properties of these activities are defined as follows:

ACTIVITY	PROPERTY	VALUE	DESCRIPTION
ForEach<T>	TypeArgument	OrderManager.Order	This will iterate over each of the orders in the collection to display them.
	Values	Orders	This is a workflow variable containing the orders submitted.
WriteLine	Text	String .Format("Order on {0} by {1} for:", item .OrderDate, item .CustomerName)	Displays the contents of the order's header information
ForEach<T>	TypeArgument	OrderManager .OrderDetails	This will iterate over the detail rows contained within the submitted order.
	Values	item.Details	This is the collection of order details within the current order.
WriteLine	Text	String .Format("{0} {1}(s)", detail .Quantity, detail .ItemName)	Displays the contents of the fields of each order detail row

As described above, you will use a number of workflow variables needed to store data during processing. These are described in the following table:

VARIABLE	TYPE	DESCRIPTION
theOrder	OrderManager.Order	Will hold the current submitted order
Orders	List<Order>	Represents the current queue of orders for processing. Set the default to New List(Of Order) to ensure that the collection is initialized.
ValidationErrors	String()	Will hold any validation errors in the current submitted order

In addition to those variables, an instance of the OrderSystem class will be passed into the workflow as an argument. Open the Arguments pane and add the following item.

ARGUMENT	TYPE	DESCRIPTION
manager	OrderManager.OrderSystem	Will hold the object that provides the processing for the loading and validating of the orders

All that remains is to update the host application. As described above, you will provide an instance of the OrderSystem class to the workflow. This is done in the Main method for the Console application:

Available for
download on
Wrox.com

```
Shared Sub Main()
    Dim inputs As New Dictionary(Of String, Object)
    'Workflow expects the OrderSystem as parameter
    Dim sys As New OrderManager.OrderSystem
    inputs.Add("manager", sys)
    WorkflowInvoker.Invoke(New FulfilmentWorkflow(), inputs)

    Console.WriteLine("Press ENTER to exit")
    Console.ReadLine()
End Sub
```

Code snippet from Fulfillment

Recall that the input for a workflow is a Dictionary(Of String, Object), and that the key in this dictionary must match the name of an argument in the system — in this case, manager.

Before running the application, you also need to add an application configuration file. This will include a single application setting named dropFilePath that should be set to the location where you will add the XML files.

Run the application and copy an XML file to the monitored directory. After a brief delay, you should see the contents of the order displayed on the console (see Figure 26-17).

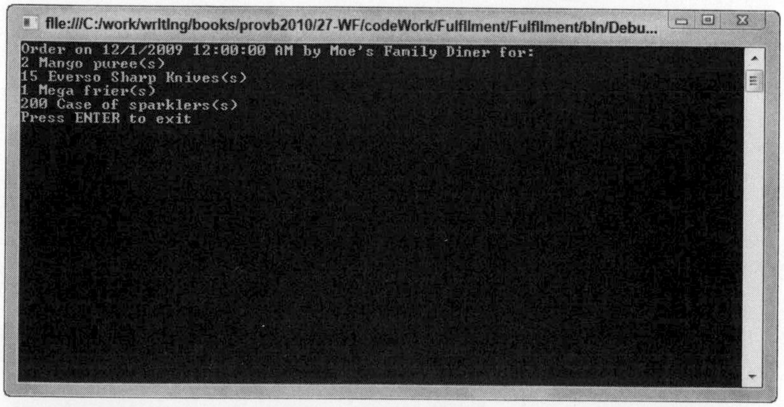

```
file:///C:/work/writing/books/provb2010/27-WF/codeWork/Fulfilment/Fulfilment/bin/Debu...

Order on 12/1/2009 12:00:00 AM by Moe's Family Diner for:
2 Mango puree(s)
15 Everso Sharp Knives(s)
1 Mega frier(s)
200 Case of sparklers(s)
Press ENTER to exit
```

FIGURE 26-17

Building Custom Activities

In addition to the standard activity library, WF supports extensibility through the creation of custom activities. Creating custom activities is a matter of creating a new class that inherits from `Activity` (or one of the existing child classes). Creating custom activities is the primary means of extending WF. You might use custom activities to simplify a complex workflow, grouping a number of common activities into a single new activity. Alternatively, custom activities can create a workflow that is easier to understand, using terms that are more familiar to the developers and business experts. Finally, custom activities can be used to support software used within the business, such as activities to communicate with a Customer Relationship Management (CRM) or Enterprise Resource Planning (ERP) system.

Creating custom activities with WF 4 is much easier than it was with earlier releases. To create a custom activity, you inherit from `Activity`, or one of the existing children of `Activity`, and override the appropriate methods. The most common classes you will inherit from are as follows:

➤ `Activity` — The base class. Use only if one of the other following three classes are too specific for your needs.

➤ `CodeActivity` — Use when your activity performs some action. You override the `Execute` method to carry out your action. This activity works synchronously (as opposed to the `AsyncCodeActivity` below), so the entire activity must complete before the workflow continues.

➤ `AsyncCodeActivity` — Similar to `CodeActivity`, but the work is performed asynchronously. This is the most commonly used class to inherit from when creating custom activities.

➤ `NativeActivity` — Use this when your activity needs to interact with the workflow engine itself. For example, the flow control activities inherit from this class.

When defining properties for your custom activities, you do not use the standard types. Instead, you use a generic class to wrap the type. This enables your properties to communicate with the running workflow. There are three wrappers you should use in your activities:

➤ `InArgument(Of type)` — Used to wrap a property that will be provided to the workflow

➤ `OutArgument(Of type)` — Used to wrap a property that the workflow will expose to the calling code

➤ `InOutArgument(Of type)` — Used to wrap a property that will be provided to the workflow, as well as returned

To see how you can easily create a new activity and use it within a workflow, create a new Workflow Console application (`CustomActivity`). Add a new class (`EncryptActivity`) to the project for your new activity. This new activity will be used to encrypt a string within a workflow (you'll also be creating an activity to decrypt the text):

```
Imports System.Activities
Imports System.Security.Cryptography
Imports System.Text

Public Class EncryptActivity
    Inherits CodeActivity

    Public Property Input As InArgument(Of String)
    Public Property Password As InArgument(Of String)
    Public Property Output As OutArgument(Of String)

    Protected Overrides Sub Execute(ByVal context As CodeActivityContext)
        Dim aes As New AesCryptoServiceProvider
        Dim hash As New MD5CryptoServiceProvider

        'load the properties from the current workflow context
        Dim plaintext As String = Input.Get(context)
```

```
        Dim pwd As String = Password.Get(context)

        Dim inBuffer As Byte()
        Dim outBuffer As Byte()

        'the key is the input to the encryptor
        'we can only decrypt using the same password
        aes.Key = hash.ComputeHash(Encoding.ASCII.GetBytes(pwd))
        'Electronic CodeBook format (each block is encrypted individually)
        aes.Mode = CipherMode.ECB

        Dim encrypt As ICryptoTransform = aes.CreateEncryptor
        inBuffer = Encoding.ASCII.GetBytes(plaintext)

        'here's the actual encryption
        outBuffer = encrypt.TransformFinalBlock(inBuffer,
            0, inBuffer.Length)

        'store the output in the current workflow context
        'Base64 to avoid any high ASCII issues
        Output.Set(context, Convert.ToBase64String(outBuffer))

    End Sub
End Class
```

Code snippet from CustomActivity

The encryption uses the AES encryption, although you could use any of the encryption methods in the `System.Security.Cryptography` namespace. You can see Chapter 34 for more details on the classes in this namespace, but the mechanics of using them are as follows:

1. Create an instance of one of the cryptography service providers.

2. Set the `Key` (and optionally `IV`, or initialization vector, properties) on the service provider. This is the value used to provide the encryption (i.e., the password).

3. Create an actual encryptor using the service provider.

4. Encrypt the text. Note that the encryption method (`TransformFinalBlock`) does not take a string, but an array of bytes, so you need to convert your input (and output).

Add another class (`DecryptActivity`) to the project. The code for the `DecryptActivity` is basically a mirror image of the `EncryptActivity`:

Available for
download on
Wrox.com

```
Imports System.Activities
Imports System.Security.Cryptography
Imports System.Text

Public Class DecryptActivity
    Inherits CodeActivity

    Public Property Input As InArgument(Of String)
    Public Property Password As InArgument(Of String)
    Public Property Output As OutArgument(Of String)

    Protected Overrides Sub Execute(ByVal context As CodeActivityContext)
        Dim aes As New AesCryptoServiceProvider
        Dim hash As New MD5CryptoServiceProvider

        'convert the input parameters from the current context
        Dim encryptedtext As String = Input.Get(context)
        Dim pwd As String = Password.Get(context)

        Dim inBuffer As Byte()
```

```
            Dim outBuffer As Byte()

            'generate security hash from the password
            aes.Key = hash.ComputeHash(Encoding.ASCII.GetBytes(pwd))
            aes.Mode = CipherMode.ECB

            'create decryptor
            Dim decrypt As ICryptoTransform = aes.CreateDecryptor
            inBuffer = Convert.FromBase64String(encryptedtext)

            'do actual decryption
            outBuffer = decrypt.TransformFinalBlock(inBuffer, 0, inBuffer.Length)

            'Save the decrypted text to the current workflow context
            Output.Set(context, Encoding.ASCII.GetString(outBuffer))

        End Sub

    End Class
```

Code snippet from CustomActivity

The main difference between the two activities is that rather than create an encryptor, you create a decryptor. In addition, because the output of the encryptor was converted to a base 64 string, it is converted to a byte array using `FromBase64String`.

New activities will not appear in the Toolbox until they have been compiled, so build the project to ensure that everything is working. Once you have done that, you can build your workflow to test the two activities. Switch to the workflow designer. You should see the new activities in the Toolbox (see Figure 26-18).

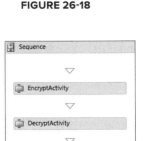

FIGURE 26-18

Drag a `Sequence` activity onto the designer, and then add an `EncryptActivity`, `DecryptActivity`, and `WriteLine` activity to it. The final workflow should look like Figure 26-19.

The input parameters will be provided by the host console application. To do this, you need to configure the workflow with the desired parameters. You then provide them to the workflow by including a `Dictionary` containing those parameters. Click the Arguments link on the workflow designer. You will use two input parameters (for the text to encrypt and the password) and an output parameter (for the decrypted text). The names of these parameters do not need to match the properties of the custom activities, but the case is significant in the `Dictionary`, so you need to ensure that they are added correctly (see Figure 26-20).

FIGURE 26-19

Name	Direction	Argument type	Default value
inputText	In	String	*Enter a VB expression*
password	In	String	*Enter a VB expression*
outputText	Out	String	*Default value not supported*
Create Argument			

FIGURE 26-20

Similarly, you need a variable to hold the temporary value after the encryption, so add a new variable using the Variables pane of the designer. The name is not important, but it should be a `String`. In the table below, this variable is called `tempText`.

Now you're ready to set the properties for the activities. The following table shows how they should be set:

ACTIVITY	PROPERTY	VALUE
EncryptActivity	Input	inputText
	Password	password
	Output	tempText
DecryptActivity	Input	tempText
	Password	password
	Output	outputText
WriteLine	Text	String .Format("{0} encrypted is {1} . Decrypted to {2}", inputText, tempText, outputText)

You can now turn your attention to the main routine that will call the workflow. The input to the workflow and the output of the `Invoke` method are both of type `Dictionary(Of String, Object)`. The key you use to add the item to the `Dictionary` is important, as it should match the names of the arguments you added to the workflow, including the case of the name. The following code shows the `Main` method of the console application:

```vb
Shared Sub Main()
    Dim parms As New Dictionary(Of String, Object)
    Dim output As New Dictionary(Of String, Object)

    'add the input parameters
    parms.Add("inputText", "Some text to encrypt")
    parms.Add("password", "5up3r53cr3t!")

    Console.WriteLine("The original text is: {0}",
        parms.Item("inputText").ToString())

    output = WorkflowInvoker.Invoke(New Workflow1(), parms)

    Console.WriteLine("The decrypted string is: {0}",
        output.Item("outputText").ToString())

    Console.WriteLine("Press ENTER to exit")
    Console.ReadLine()

End Sub
```

Code snippet from CustomActivity

You could reuse the `Dictionary` for both input and output, but in this case two dictionaries are created to avoid any confusion. The two input parameters are added to the input dictionary, keeping in mind that case is significant and should match the arguments you created earlier on the workflow. This input dictionary is added as a parameter in the call to the `WorkflowInvoker.Invoke`. This also populates the output dictionary with any `OutArgument` arguments of the workflow — in this case, the `outputText` value. Running this workflow should display the same text for input and output.

Dynamically Loading Workflows

As each workflow is a self-contained block of XAML, you might want to dynamically load your workflows, rather than compile them into the application. This gives you easier access to changing or extending your application by creating or editing the XAML and making it available to your application.

In order to have the XAML files left "loose" when you compile them, you need to change the properties for the XAML file. Select the workflow file in the Solution Explorer and set the Build Action to Content and the Copy to Output Directory to Copy if newer. This will move the XAML files to the output directory when you build the application. The `DynamicallyLoadingWorkflows` sample includes three sample workflows.

To load one of the workflows, you use the `ActivityXamlServices.Load` method. This is from the `System.Activities.XamlIntegration` namespace. The method takes a path to a XAML file and loads it. You can then pass it on to the `WorkflowInvoker` to execute as normal:

```vb
Shared Sub Main()
        'load a workflow
        ' in this case based on the current tick
        ' of the clock
        ' (( in this case 0 to 2 ))
        Dim pick As Integer = DateTime.Now.Second Mod 3
        Dim filename As String =
                String.Format("Workflow{0}.xaml", pick + 1)
        WorkflowInvoker.Invoke(ActivityXamlServices.Load(filename))

        Console.WriteLine("Press ENTER to exit")
        Console.ReadLine()
End Sub
```

Code snippet from DynamicallyLoadingWorkflow

The preceding code expects three XAML files in the same directory as the executable. It randomly selects one of the three, loads it using `ActivityXamlServices.Load`, and executes it. You can run this multiple times to confirm that it selects the different workflows.

While this is a simple example of loading the workflows dynamically, the method can be quite useful when building workflow applications. For example, you may have separate workflows based on customer type or product. You can use this method to load the correct workflow from a library of workflows as needed. In addition, as your needs change, you can update the XAML files, without having to update your application to reflect the changes.

REHOSTING THE WORKFLOW DESIGNER

One common request when working with workflows is to enable users to create and edit their own workflows. In the past, this has been problematic because you'd then have to either recreate the functionality yourself using WPF or figure out the interfaces required to get it to work. With this version of WF, however, it has become much easier.

You can host the workflow designer surface in any WPF application by creating a new instance of the `WorkflowDesigner` class and inserting the `View` property into the location of the host. The `WorkflowDesigner` class also makes the standard property grid available to your application using the `PropertyInspectorView` property.

Create a new WPF application to host the workflow designer. The main window of the application will host a collection of available controls, as well as the workflow designer and property window. The following code shows the XAML for the application:

```xml
<Window x:Class="MainWindow"
        xmlns="http://schemas.microsoft.com/winfx/2006/xaml/presentation"
        xmlns:x="http://schemas.microsoft.com/winfx/2006/xaml"
        xmlns:sys="clr-namespace:System;assembly=mscorlib"
        xmlns:tool="clr-namespace:System.Activities.Presentation.Toolbox;
            assembly=System.Activities.Presentation"
        Title="Rehosting Workflow Designer" Height="500" Width="700" >
    <Window.Resources>
```

```xml
        <sys:String x:Key="AssemblyName">System.Activities, Version=4.0.0.0,
    Culture=neutral, PublicKeyToken=31bf3856ad364e35</sys:String>
        <sys:String x:Key="CustomActivityAssembly">CustomActivities</sys:String>
    </Window.Resources>
    <Grid x:Name="DesignerGrid">
        <Grid.ColumnDefinitions>
            <ColumnDefinition Width="200" />
            <ColumnDefinition Width="*" />
        </Grid.ColumnDefinitions>
        <Grid.RowDefinitions>
            <RowDefinition Height="1*" />
            <RowDefinition Height="1*" />
        </Grid.RowDefinitions>
        <Border>
            <tool:ToolboxControl>
                <tool:ToolboxControl.Categories>
                    <tool:ToolboxCategory CategoryName="Basic">
                        <tool:ToolboxItemWrapper
                          AssemblyName="{StaticResource AssemblyName}" >
                            <tool:ToolboxItemWrapper.ToolName>
                                System.Activities.Statements.Sequence
                            </tool:ToolboxItemWrapper.ToolName>
                        </tool:ToolboxItemWrapper>
                        <tool:ToolboxItemWrapper
                          AssemblyName="{StaticResource AssemblyName}">
                            <tool:ToolboxItemWrapper.ToolName>
                                System.Activities.Statements.WriteLine
                            </tool:ToolboxItemWrapper.ToolName>
                        </tool:ToolboxItemWrapper>
                        <tool:ToolboxItemWrapper
                          AssemblyName="{StaticResource CustomActivityAssembly}">
                            <tool:ToolboxItemWrapper.ToolName>
                                CustomActivities.EncryptActivity
                            </tool:ToolboxItemWrapper.ToolName>
                        </tool:ToolboxItemWrapper>
                        <tool:ToolboxItemWrapper
                          AssemblyName="{StaticResource CustomActivityAssembly}">
                            <tool:ToolboxItemWrapper.ToolName>
                                CustomActivities.DecryptActivity
                            </tool:ToolboxItemWrapper.ToolName>
                        </tool:ToolboxItemWrapper>
                    </tool:ToolboxCategory>
                </tool:ToolboxControl.Categories>
            </tool:ToolboxControl>
        </Border>
        <Border Name="DesignerBorder" Grid.Column="1" Grid.RowSpan="2"  />
        <Border Grid.Row="2" Grid.Column="0" Name="PropertyGridBorder" />
    </Grid>
</Window>
```

The application's main window uses a grid to lay out the "Toolbox" of available activities added above and a property view on the left, and the bulk of the window hosting the designer. The designer and property grid will be added in code later, but `Border` controls have been added at the appropriate locations in the XAML where they will appear. Figure 26-21 shows the resulting window in the designer.

Notice that a custom namespace has been added to the XAML for the `System.Activities.Presentation` namespace. This includes the classes that will be used to insert the Toolbox items. You need to add each of the desired activities individually. This gives you the flexibility to customize the controls you present to end users.

FIGURE 26-21

In addition to the standard controls, you can also include custom controls. I created a new Activity Library project (CustomActivities) and added the EncryptActivity and DecryptActivity activities to that project. I then referenced that project from this one. If you look at the preceding XAML, you will see a new resource created pointing at that assembly. The activities are then loaded just as you load the standard activities.

All that remains is to create the new instance of the WorkflowDesigner, and insert it into the application:

```vb
Imports System.Activities
Imports System.Activities.Core.Presentation
Imports System.Activities.Presentation

Class MainWindow
    Public Sub New()
        InitializeComponent()

        'load the standard control metadata (for the "toolbox")
        Dim designerMeta As New DesignerMetadata
        designerMeta.Register()

        'create the new design surface
        Dim designer As New WorkflowDesigner()
        'adding a sequence as a default activity
        designer.Load(New System.Activities.Statements.Sequence())

        'add the designer into the app
        DesignerBorder.Child = designer.View
        'add the default property grid to the app
        PropertyGridBorder.Child = designer.PropertyInspectorView
    End Sub
End Sub
```

Code snippet from RehostingDesigner

The DesignerMetadata class provides the information used by the designer to display the controls on the design surface. If you fail to register this class first, the designer won't be able to draw the appropriate designers for each control.

You can customize the `WorkflowDesigner` before adding it to the application. In this case, a default `Sequence` activity is added.

Finally, the designer and property window are inserted into the main window. The final result (see Figure 26-22) allows the end user to create or edit workflows. Saving the workflow is left as an exercise for you (but the `WorkflowDesigner.Save` and `WorkflowDesigner.Load` methods would likely come in handy).

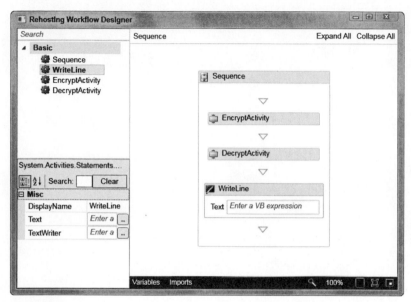

FIGURE 26-22

SUMMARY

While Windows Workflow Foundation does not have the visual glitz of WPF or the broad reach of WCF, it is a highly useful addition to the .NET Framework. Most business applications have some need for workflows, and having a standard means of creating a workflow ensures that the workflow is fully featured and accurately reflects business needs. As WF is readily available with the .NET Framework, you no longer need to create your own workflow capabilities for each application. Moreover, WF is extensible, so you can take advantage of it in your applications without being limited to the included features.

As with the other components of the .NET Framework, WF integrates well into other applications, including Windows Forms and ASP.NET applications. It provides the means to extract the frequently complex workflow from those applications and to graphically design it. This graphical representation can be used to communicate the process to business users, increasing the chance that the workflow is represented correctly. Finally, as business needs change, it is a simple process to update the workflow, without requiring changes to the core application.

27

Localization

WHAT YOU WILL LEARN IN THIS CHAPTER

➤ Understanding culture types

➤ Getting culture settings from a thread

➤ Declaring culture in ASP.NET

➤ Understanding differences in dates

➤ Understanding differences in currency & numbers

➤ Understanding differences in sorting

➤ Using culture specific resource files

As the audience for an application expands, businesses often realize they need to globalize the application. Of course, the ideal is to build the application to handle an international audience right from the start, but in most cases this may not be feasible because building for localized versions requires extra work and cost.

The core of any localization effort is the translation of resources, and user interface changes. Such changes are application specific and therefore not really open to generic implementation across the multitude of potential cultures for which you might choose to target an application. However, some common elements of localization such as date support or numeric and currency formats can be implemented by .NET Framework classes.

The .NET Framework has made a considerable effort to support the internationalization of .NET applications. API support, server controls, and even Visual Studio itself equip you to do the extra work required to bring your application to an international audience. This chapter looks at some of the important items to consider when building your applications for the world.

CULTURES AND REGIONS

As an example, the ASP.NET page that is pulled up in an end user's browser runs under a specific culture and region setting. When building an ASP.NET application or page, the defined culture in which it runs is dependent upon a culture and region setting specified either in the server in which the application is run or in a setting applied by the client (the end user). By default, ASP.NET runs under a culture setting defined by the server. Stated simply, unless you specifically look for a client's requested culture, your application will run based on the server's culture settings.

The world is made up of a multitude of cultures, each of which has a language and a set of defined ways in which it views and consumes numbers, uses currencies, sorts alphabetically, and so on. The .NET Framework defines languages and regions using the *Request for Comments 1766* standard definition (tags for identification of languages — www.ietf.org/rfc/rfc1766.txt), which specifies a language and region using two-letter codes separated by a dash. The following table provides examples of some culture definitions:

CULTURE CODE	DESCRIPTION
en-US	English language; United States
en-GB	English language; United Kingdom (Great Britain)
en-AU	English language; Australia
en-CA	English language; Canada
fr-CA	French language; Canada

The examples in this table define five distinct cultures. These five cultures have some similarities and some differences. Four of the cultures speak the same language (English), so the language code of "en" is used in these culture settings. Following the language setting is the region setting. Even though most of these cultures speak the same language, it is important to distinguish them further by setting their region (such as US for the United States, GB for the United Kingdom, AU for Australia, and CA for Canada). These settings reflect the fact that the English used in the United States is slightly different from the English used in the United Kingdom, and so forth. Beyond language, differences exist in how dates and numerical values are represented. This is why a culture's language and region are presented together.

The differences between the cultures in the table do not break down by region only. Many countries contain more than a single language, and each may have its own preference for notation of dates and other items. For example, en-CA specifies English speakers in Canada. Because Canada is not only an English-speaking country, it also includes the culture setting of fr-CA for French-speaking Canadians.

Understanding Culture Types

The culture definition just given is called a *specific culture* definition. This definition is as detailed as you can possibly get, defining both the language and the region. The other type of culture definition is a *neutral culture* definition. Each specific culture has a specified neutral culture with which it is associated. For instance, the English language cultures shown in the previous table are separate, but they also belong to one neutral culture: EN (English). The diagram presented in Figure 27-1 illustrates how these culture types relate to one another.

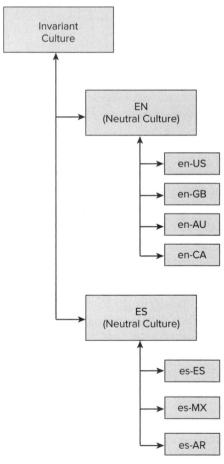

FIGURE 27-1

From this diagram, you can see that many specific cultures belong to a neutral culture. Higher in the hierarchy than the neutral culture is an *invariant culture*, which is an agnostic culture setting that should be utilized when passing items (such as dates and numbers) around a network. When performing these kinds of operations, you should make your back-end data flows devoid of user-specific culture settings. Instead, apply these settings in the business and presentation layers of your applications.

In addition, pay attention to neutral culture when working with your applications. In most cases, you are going to build applications with views that are more dependent on a neutral culture than on a specific culture. For instance, if you have a Spanish version of your application, you'll probably make this version available to all Spanish speakers regardless of where they live. In many applications, it won't matter whether the Spanish speaker is from Spain, Mexico, or Argentina. In cases where it does make a difference, use the specific culture settings.

Looking at Your Thread

When the end user requests an ASP.NET page or runs a Windows Forms dialog, the item is executed on a thread from the thread pool. That thread has a culture associated with it. You can get information about the culture of the thread programmatically and then check for particular details about that culture.

To see an example of working with a thread and reading the culture information of that thread, start with the basic Windows Forms application created in Chapter 1. To reproduce this create a new project called ProVB2010_Localization, and add the appropriate button and text box controls. A copy of the code in this chapter is part of the code download with the name ProVB2010_Localization.

Add a new `Sub DisplayCultureInfo` and have it called by the Click event handler for the test button on the form. When the `TestButton_Click` event is fired, the user's culture information is retrieved and displayed in the `TextBox` control. The code for the new `Sub` is presented here:

```vb
Private Sub DisplayCultureInfo()
    Dim ci As New System.Globalization.CultureInfo(
        System.Threading.Thread.CurrentThread.CurrentCulture.ToString())
    TextBox1.Text = "CURRENT CULTURE'S INFO" & Environment.NewLine
    TextBox1.Text += "Name: " & ci.Name & Environment.NewLine
    TextBox1.Text += "Parent Name: " & ci.Parent.Name & Environment.NewLine
    TextBox1.Text += "Display Name: " & ci.DisplayName & Environment.NewLine
    TextBox1.Text += "English Name: " & ci.EnglishName & Environment.NewLine
    TextBox1.Text += "Native Name: " & ci.NativeName & Environment.NewLine
    TextBox1.Text += "Three Letter ISO Name: " &
        ci.ThreeLetterISOLanguageName & Environment.NewLine
    TextBox1.Text += "Calendar Type: " & ci.Calendar.ToString() & Environment.NewLine
End Sub
```

Code snippet from Form1.vb

This simple form creates a `CultureInfo` object from the `System.Globalization` namespace and assigns the culture from the current thread that is running using the `System.Threading` `.Thread.CurrentThread.CurrentCulture` `.ToString` call. Once the `CultureInfo` object is populated with the end user's culture, details about that culture can be retrieved using a number of available properties that the `CultureInfo` object offers. Example results of running the form are shown in Figure 27-2.

Note that in the code download there is an additional button on the form based on additional changes that are made to this sample project.

The `CultureInfo` object contains a number of properties that provide you with specific culture

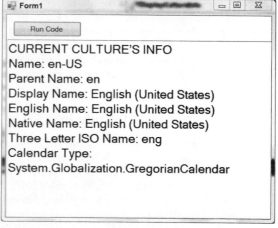

FIGURE 27-2

information. The items displayed are only a small sampling of what is available from this object. From this figure, you can see that the en-US culture is the default setting in which the thread executes. In addition to this, you can use the `CultureInfo` object to get at a lot of other descriptive information about the culture. You can always change a thread's culture on the overloads provided via a new instantiation of the `CultureInfo` object, as shown here:

Available for download on Wrox.com

```vb
Private Sub DisplayCultureInfo()
    System.Threading.Thread.CurrentThread.CurrentCulture =
        New Globalization.CultureInfo("th-TH")
    Dim ci As Globalization.CultureInfo =
        System.Threading.Thread.CurrentThread.CurrentCulture

    ' Dim ci As New System.Globalization.CultureInfo(
    '    System.Threading.Thread.CurrentThread.CurrentCulture.ToString())
    TextBox1.Text = "CURRENT CULTURE'S INFO" & Environment.NewLine
    TextBox1.Text += "Name: " & ci.Name & Environment.NewLine
    TextBox1.Text += "Parent Name: " & ci.Parent.Name & Environment.NewLine
    TextBox1.Text += "Display Name: " & ci.DisplayName & Environment.NewLine
    TextBox1.Text += "English Name: " & ci.EnglishName & Environment.NewLine
    TextBox1.Text += "Native Name: " & ci.NativeName & Environment.NewLine
    TextBox1.Text += "Three Letter ISO Name: " &
        ci.ThreeLetterISOLanguageName & Environment.NewLine
    TextBox1.Text += "Calendar Type: " & ci.Calendar.ToString() & Environment.NewLine
End Sub
```

Code snippet from Form1.vb

In this example, only a couple of lines of code are changed to assign a new instance of the `CultureInfo` object to the `CurrentCulture` property of the thread being executed by the application. The culture setting enables the `CultureInfo` object to define the culture you want to utilize. In this case, the Thai language of Thailand is assigned. The results produced in the `TextBox` control are illustrated in Figure 27-3.

From this figure, you can see that the .NET Framework provides the native name of the language used even if it is not a Latin-based letter style. In this case, the results are presented for the Thai language in Thailand, including some of the properties associated with this culture (such as an entirely different calendar than the one used in Western Europe and the United States).

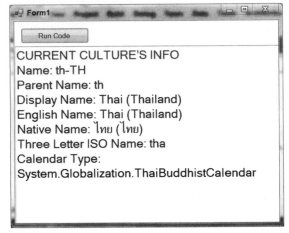

FIGURE 27-3

Declaring Culture Globally in ASP.NET

ASP.NET enables you to easily define the culture that is used either by your entire ASP.NET application or by a specific page within your Web application, using what are termed *server-side culture declarations*. You can specify the culture for any of your ASP.NET applications by means of the appropriate configuration files. To demonstrate this, close the ProVB2010_Localization application you started with and create a new ASP.NET website called ProVB_Russian. Alternatively, you can open this download folder as a website in Visual Studio 2010. On the default.aspx page add a new Calendar control from the toolbox, following the text: Welcome to ASP.NET!

To change the default language used by this control you can specify culture settings in the `web.config` file of the application itself, as illustrated here:

Available for download on Wrox.com

```
<configuration>
  <system.web>
    <globalization culture="ru-RU" uiCulture="ru-RU" />
  </system.web>
</configuration>
```

Code snippet from ProVB_Russian\web.config

Only the `<globalization>` line will need to be added to your default `web.config` file; it should also be noted that based on the page specific settings described below, this line has been commented out in the code download.

Note the two attributes represented: `culture` and `uiCulture`. The `culture` attribute enables you to define the culture to use for processing incoming requests, whereas the `uiCulture` attribute enables you to define the default culture needed to process any resource files in the application (use of these attributes is covered later in the chapter).

Note that one additional option you have when specifying a culture on the server is to define this culture in the root `web.config` file for the server. Thus, if you are setting up a web server that will be used with only a single culture, you can specify that culture at the server level, instead of needing to specify it as part of the settings for each application running on the server. This can be useful if you are installing Web applications created outside of your native culture, but where you want date, currency, sorting, and similar formats to default appropriately.

In the preceding snippet, the culture established for this ASP.NET application is the Russian language in the country of Russia. In addition to setting the culture at either the server-wide or the application-wide level, another option is to set the culture at the page level, as shown here:

Available for download on Wrox.com

```
<%@ Page Title="Home Page" Language="VB" MasterPageFile="~/Site.Master"
    AutoEventWireup="false"
    CodeFile="Default.aspx.vb" Inherits="_Default"
    UICulture="ru-RU" Culture="ru-RU"%>
%>
```

Code snippet from ProVB_Russian\default.aspx

This example specifies that the Russian language and culture settings are used for everything on the page. You can see this in action by using this @Page directive and a simple calendar control on the page. Figure 27-4 shows the output. Notice that marking the page as using Russian settings does not automatically translate text within the page; it only updates the embedded control added to the page.

Adopting Culture Settings in ASP.NET

In addition to using server-side settings to define the culture for your ASP.NET pages, you also have the option to define the culture according to what the client has set as his or her preference in a browser instance.

When end users install Microsoft's Internet Explorer or some other browser, they have the option to select their preferred cultures in a particular order (if they have selected more than a single culture preference). To see this in action in IE, select Tools ➪ Internet Options

WELCOME TO ASP.NET!

To learn more about ASP.NET visit www.asp.net.

<		Ноябрь 2009				>
Пн	Вт	Ср	Чт	Пт	Сб	Вс
26	27	28	29	30	31	1
2	3	4	5	6	7	8
9	10	11	12	13	14	15
16	17	18	19	20	21	22
23	24	25	26	27	28	29
30	1	2	3	4	5	6

You can also find documentation on ASP.NET at MSDN.

FIGURE 27-4

from the IE menu. On the first tab provided (General) is a Languages button at the bottom of the dialog. Select this button and you are provided with the Language Preference dialog shown in Figure 27-5.

To add any additional cultures to the list, click the Add button and select the appropriate culture from the list. After you have selected any cultures present in the list, you can select the order in which you prefer to use them. Thus, a user with multiple settings in this list will have a version of the application with their first language choice before anything else; if a version that supports that language is not available, their second and then consecutive versions are checked. The first available language matching one of their preferences will be presented.

Making language selections, the end user can leverage the automatic culture recognition feature provided in ASP.NET. Instead of specifying a distinct culture in any of the configuration files or from the @Page directive, you can also state that ASP.NET should automatically select the culture provided by the end user requesting the page. This is done using the auto keyword, as illustrated here:

```
<%@ Page UICulture="auto" Culture="auto" %>
```

With this construction in your page, the dates, calendars, and numbers appear in the preferred culture of the requester. What happens if you have translated resources

FIGURE 27-5

in resource files (shown later in the chapter) that depend on a culture specification? Or what if you have only specific translations and therefore can't handle every possible culture that might be returned to your ASP.NET page? In this case, you can specify the auto option with an additional fallback option if ASP .NET cannot find any of the culture settings of the user (such as culture-specific resource files). This usage is illustrated in the following code:

```
<%@ Page UICulture="auto:en-US" Culture="auto:en-US" %>
```

In this case, the automatic detection is utilized; but if the culture preferred by the end user is not present, then en-US is used.

TRANSLATING VALUES AND BEHAVIORS

In the process of globalizing your .NET application, you may notice a number of aspects that are handled differently compared to building an application that is devoid of globalization, including how dates are represented and how currencies are shown. This section looks at some of these issues.

Understanding Differences in Dates

Different cultures specify dates and time very differently. For instance, take the following date as an example:

```
08/11/2008
```

Is this date August 11, 2008 or is it November 8, 2008? It should be the job of the business logic layer or the presentation layer to convert all date and times for use by the end user. To avoid interpretation errors, always use the same culture (or invariant culture) when storing values, such as dates and times, in a database or other data store.

Setting the culture at the server level in ASP.NET or within a Windows Forms application, as shown in the earlier examples, enables your .NET application to make these conversions for you. You can also simply assign a new culture to the thread in which the code is running. For instance, consider the following sub, which can be called from the `ButtonTest Click` event handler (note that this `Sub` is dependent on these `Imports` statements):

Available for
download on
Wrox.com

```
Imports System.Globalization
Imports System.Threading

Private Sub DisplayCalendarByCulture()
    Dim dt As DateTime = New DateTime(2010, 3, 2, 13, 5, 1, 10)

    Thread.CurrentThread.CurrentCulture = New CultureInfo("pt-br")
    TextBox1.Text +=
      Thread.CurrentThread.CurrentCulture.EnglishName & " : " & _
      dt.ToString() & Environment.NewLine

    Thread.CurrentThread.CurrentCulture = New CultureInfo("en-US")
    TextBox1.Text +=
      Thread.CurrentThread.CurrentCulture.EnglishName & " : " & _
      dt.ToString() & Environment.NewLine

    Thread.CurrentThread.CurrentCulture = New CultureInfo("es-mx")
    TextBox1.Text +=
      Thread.CurrentThread.CurrentCulture.EnglishName & " : " & _
      dt.ToString() & Environment.NewLine

    Thread.CurrentThread.CurrentCulture = New CultureInfo("es-es")
    TextBox1.Text +=
      Thread.CurrentThread.CurrentCulture.EnglishName & " : " & _
      dt.ToString() & Environment.NewLine

    Thread.CurrentThread.CurrentCulture = New CultureInfo("ru-RU")
    TextBox1.Text +=
      Thread.CurrentThread.CurrentCulture.EnglishName & " : " & _
      dt.ToString() & Environment.NewLine

    Thread.CurrentThread.CurrentCulture = New CultureInfo("fi-FI")
    TextBox1.Text +=
      Thread.CurrentThread.CurrentCulture.EnglishName & " : " & _
      dt.ToString() & Environment.NewLine

    Thread.CurrentThread.CurrentCulture = New CultureInfo("ar-SA")
    TextBox1.Text +=
      Thread.CurrentThread.CurrentCulture.EnglishName & " : " & _
      dt.ToString() & Environment.NewLine

    Thread.CurrentThread.CurrentCulture = New CultureInfo("am-ET")
    TextBox1.Text +=
      Thread.CurrentThread.CurrentCulture.EnglishName & " : " & _
      dt.ToString() & Environment.NewLine

    Thread.CurrentThread.CurrentCulture = New CultureInfo("as-IN")
    TextBox1.Text +=
      Thread.CurrentThread.CurrentCulture.EnglishName & " : " & _
      dt.ToString() & Environment.NewLine

    Thread.CurrentThread.CurrentCulture = New CultureInfo("th-TH")
    TextBox1.Text +=
      Thread.CurrentThread.CurrentCulture.EnglishName & " : " & _
```

```
                 dt.ToString() & Environment.NewLine

        Thread.CurrentThread.CurrentCulture = New CultureInfo("zh-cn")
        TextBox1.Text +=
            Thread.CurrentThread.CurrentCulture.EnglishName & " : " & _
            dt.ToString() & Environment.NewLine

        Thread.CurrentThread.CurrentCulture = New CultureInfo("zh-tw")
        TextBox1.Text +=
            Thread.CurrentThread.CurrentCulture.EnglishName & " : " & _
            dt.ToString() & Environment.NewLine

        Thread.CurrentThread.CurrentCulture = New CultureInfo("ko-kr")
        TextBox1.Text +=
            Thread.CurrentThread.CurrentCulture.EnglishName & " : " & _
            dt.ToString() & Environment.NewLine

        Thread.CurrentThread.CurrentCulture = New CultureInfo("zh-hk")
        TextBox1.Text +=
            Thread.CurrentThread.CurrentCulture.EnglishName & " : " & _
            dt.ToString() & Environment.NewLine
    End Sub
```

Code snippet from Form1.vb

Using the ProVB2010_Localization test form again, you can test this code. The code snippet captures the
current date time for output, but does so while referencing a dozen or more different cultures, one for
each copy output to the screen. The date/time construction used by the defined culture is written to the
`TextBox` control. The result from this code operation is presented in Figure 27-6.

FIGURE 27-6

Clearly, the formats used to represent a date/time value can be dramatically different between cultures —
some, such as Saudi Arabia (ar-SA) and Thailand, (th-TH) use entirely different calendar baselines.

Differences in Numbers and Currencies

In addition to date/time values, numbers are displayed quite differently from one culture to the next. How can a number be represented differently in different cultures? Well, it has less to do with the actual number (although certain cultures use different number symbols) and more to do with how the number separators are used for decimals or for showing amounts such as thousands, millions, and more. For instance, in the English culture of the United States (en-US), numbers are represented in the following fashion:

```
5,123,456.00
```

From this example, you can see that the en-US culture uses a comma as a separator for thousands and a period for signifying the start of any decimals that might appear after the number is presented. It is quite different when working with other cultures. The following code block shows an example of representing numbers in other cultures:

```
Private Sub Numbers()
    Dim myNumber As Double = 5123456.0

    Thread.CurrentThread.CurrentCulture = New CultureInfo("en-US")
    TextBox1.Text += Thread.CurrentThread.CurrentCulture.EnglishName &
        " : " & myNumber.ToString("n") & Environment.NewLine

    Thread.CurrentThread.CurrentCulture = New CultureInfo("vi-VN")
    TextBox1.Text += Thread.CurrentThread.CurrentCulture.EnglishName &
        " : " & myNumber.ToString("n") & Environment.NewLine

    Thread.CurrentThread.CurrentCulture = New CultureInfo("fi-FI")
    TextBox1.Text += Thread.CurrentThread.CurrentCulture.EnglishName &
        " : " & myNumber.ToString("n") & Environment.NewLine

    Thread.CurrentThread.CurrentCulture = New CultureInfo("fr-CH")
    TextBox1.Text += Thread.CurrentThread.CurrentCulture.EnglishName &
        " : " & myNumber.ToString("n") & Environment.NewLine

End Sub
```

Code snippet from Form1.vb

Adding this code to your project and running it from the click event produces the results shown in Figure 27-7.

As you can see, cultures show numbers in numerous different formats. The second culture listed in the figure, vi-VN (Vietnamese in Vietnam), constructs a number exactly the opposite from the way it is constructed in en-US. The Vietnamese culture uses periods for the thousand separators and a comma for signifying decimals, a somewhat common format around the world. Finnish uses spaces for the thousand separators and a comma for the decimal separator, whereas the French-speaking Swiss use an apostrophe for separating thousands, and a period for the decimal separator. This demonstrates that not only do you need to consider dates and language constructs, but that it is also important to "translate" numbers to the proper format so that users of your application can properly understand the numbers represented.

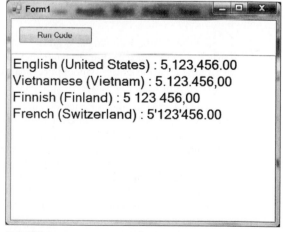

FIGURE 27-7

Another scenario in which you represent numbers is when working with currencies. It is one thing to *convert* currencies so that end users understand the proper value of an item; it is another to translate the construction of the currency just as you would a basic number.

Each culture has a distinct currency symbol used to signify that a number represented is an actual currency value. For instance, the en-US culture represents currency in the following format:

```
$5,123,456.00
```

The en-US culture uses a U.S. dollar symbol ($), and the location of this symbol is just as important as the symbol itself. For en-US, the $ symbol directly precedes the currency value (with no space in between the symbol and the first character of the number). Other cultures use different symbols to represent currency and often place those currency symbols in different locations.

Create another Sub that can be called from the button's click event handler, and this time format the same numbers using the built-in .NET currency formatting, as shown in the following code:

```vb
Private Sub Currency()
    Dim myNumber As Double = 5123456.0

    Thread.CurrentThread.CurrentCulture = New CultureInfo("en-US")
    TextBox1.Text += Thread.CurrentThread.CurrentCulture.EnglishName & _
        " : " & myNumber.ToString("c") & Environment.NewLine

    Thread.CurrentThread.CurrentCulture = New CultureInfo("vi-VN")
    TextBox1.Text += Thread.CurrentThread.CurrentCulture.EnglishName & _
        " : " & myNumber.ToString("c") & Environment.NewLine

    Thread.CurrentThread.CurrentCulture = New CultureInfo("fi-FI")
    TextBox1.Text += Thread.CurrentThread.CurrentCulture.EnglishName & _
        " : " & myNumber.ToString("c") & Environment.NewLine

    Thread.CurrentThread.CurrentCulture = New CultureInfo("fr-CH")
    TextBox1.Text += Thread.CurrentThread.CurrentCulture.EnglishName & _
        " : " & myNumber.ToString("c") & Environment.NewLine
End Sub
```

Code snippet from Form1.vb

Executing the preceding Sub displays the output shown in Figure 27-8.

Not only are the numbers constructed quite differently from one another, but the currency symbol and the location of the symbol in regard to the number are quite different as well.

Note that when you are using currencies on an ASP.NET page and you have provided an automatic culture setting for the page as a whole (such as setting the culture in the @Page directive), you need to specify a specific culture for the currency that is the same in all cases. Unlike dates, for which the differences are primarily display oriented, with a currency there is an expectation of value conversion. Thus, reformatting a currency can cause expensive errors unless you are actually doing a currency conversion.

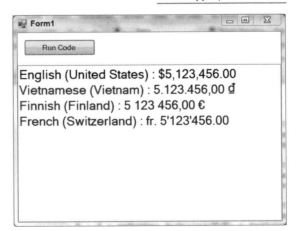

FIGURE 27-8

For instance, if you are specifying a U.S. dollar currency value in your data, , you do not want your ASP .NET page to display that value as something else (for example, the euro) based on translating the remainder of the page information to another language. Of course, if you actually performed a currency conversion and showed the appropriate euro value along with the culture specification of the currency, that makes sense and is the best solution.

Therefore, if you are using an automatic culture setting on your ASP.NET page and you are *not* converting the currency, you should perform something similar to the following code for currency values:

```
Dim myNumber As Double = 5123456.00
Dim usCurr As CultureInfo = New CultureInfo("en-US")
Response.Write(myNumber.ToString("c", usCurr))
```

Understanding Differences in Sorting

You have learned to translate textual values and alter the construction of the numbers, date/time values, currencies, and more when you are globalizing an application. You should also take care when applying culture settings to some of the programmatic behaviors that you establish for values in your applications. One operation that can change based upon the culture setting applied is how .NET sorts strings. You might think that all cultures sort strings in the same way (and generally they do), but sometimes differences exist. For example, the following shows a sorting operation occurring in the en-US culture:

Available for download on Wrox.com

```
Imports System.Collections.Generic

Private Sub Sorting()
    Thread.CurrentThread.CurrentCulture = New CultureInfo("en-US")
    'Thread.CurrentThread.CurrentCulture = New CultureInfo("fi-FI")

    Dim myList As List(Of String) = New List(Of String)

    myList.Add("Washington D.C.")
    myList.Add("Helsinki")
    myList.Add("Moscow")
    myList.Add("Warsaw")
    myList.Add("Vienna")
    myList.Add("Tokyo")

    myList.Sort()

    For Each item As String In myList
        TextBox1.Text += item.ToString() & Environment.NewLine
    Next
End Sub
```

Code snippet from Form1.vb

For this example to work, you have to reference the `System.Collections` and the `System.Collections.Generic` namespaces because this example makes use of the `List(Of String)` object.

In this example, a generic list of capitals from various countries of the world is created in random order. Then the `Sort` method of the generic `List(Of String)` object is invoked. This sorting operation sorts the strings according to how sorting is done for the defined culture in which the application thread is running. The preceding code shows the sorting as it is done for the en-US culture. The result of this operation when used within the ProVB2010_Localization form is shown in Figure 27-9.

This is pretty much what you would expect. Now, however, change the previous example so that the culture is set to the Finnish culture. Do this by uncommenting the second line of the Sub Sorting and commenting out the first line of the Sub Sorting which sets the "en-US" culture settings, in the preceding snippet.

If you run the same bit of code under the Finnish culture setting, you get the results presented in Figure 27-10.

FIGURE 27-9

FIGURE 27-10

Comparing the Finnish culture sorting shown in Figure 27-10 and the U.S. English culture sorting done in Figure 27-9, you can see that the city of Vienna is in a different place in the Finnish version. This is because in the Finnish language, there is no difference between the letter V and the letter W. Therefore, if you are sorting using the Finnish culture setting, Vi comes after Wa, and thus, Vienna appears last in the list of strings in the sorting operation.

ASP.NET RESOURCE FILES

When you work with ASP.NET, resources are handled by resource files. A resource file is an XML-based file that has a .resx extension. You can have Visual Studio help you construct this file. Resource files provide a set of items that are utilized by a specified culture. In your ASP.NET applications, you store resource files as either *local resources* or *global resources*. The following sections describe how to use each type of resource.

Making Use of Local Resources

You might be surprised how easily you can build an ASP.NET page so that it can be *localized* into other languages. In fact, the only thing you need to do is build the ASP.NET page as you normally would and then use some built-in capabilities from Visual Studio to convert the page to a format that enables you to plug in other languages easily.

To see this in action, build a simple ASP.NET website called ProVB_Localization and open the `Default` `.aspx` page as presented here. Note that we have added a few simple controls to replace the default labels generated with a new page. This page will be referred to later in the chapter as the "ASP.NET page code block." Keep in mind that the downloaded code will not match this initial code snippet as this chapter modifies this code to support multiple languages.

```
<%@ Page Title="Home Page" Language="VB" MasterPageFile="~/Site.Master" AutoEventWireup="false"
    CodeFile="Default.aspx.vb" Inherits="_Default" %>

<asp:Content ID="HeaderContent" runat="server" ContentPlaceHolderID="HeadContent">
</asp:Content>
<asp:Content ID="BodyContent" runat="server" ContentPlaceHolderID="MainContent">

    <div>
        <asp:Label ID="Label1" runat="server"
         Text="What is your name?"></asp:Label><br />
        <br />
        <asp:TextBox ID="TextBox1" runat="server"></asp:TextBox> 
        <asp:Button ID="Button1" runat="server" Text="Submit Name" /><br />
        <br />
        <asp:Label ID="Label2" runat="server"></asp:Label>
    </div>

</asp:Content>
```

Code snippet from ProVB_Localization\Default.aspx

As you can see, there is not much to this page. It is composed of a couple of `Label` controls, as well as `TextBox` and `Button` controls. Update the click event handler for `Button1` to set the `Label2.Text` property text to the `TextBox1.Text` property value. This way, when users enter their name into the text box, the `Label2` server control is populated with the inputted name.

The next step is what makes Visual Studio so great. To change the construction of this page so that it can be localized easily from resource files, open the page in Visual Studio and ensure that you are in Design view. Next, using the Visual Studio menu, select Tools ⇨ Generate Local Resource. Note that you can select this tool only when you are in the Design view of your page.

Selecting Generate Local Resource from the Tools menu causes Visual Studio to create an `App_LocalResources` folder in your project if you don't have one already. A `.resx` file based upon this ASP.NET page is then placed in the folder. For instance, if you are working with the `Default.aspx` page, then the resource file is named `Default.aspx.resx` (see Figure 27-11).

FIGURE 27-11

Right-click on the `.resx` file, select `View Code`. If `View Code` isn't present on your default menu, select `Open With`; you'll get a dialog with a list of editor options. From the Open With dialog, select the `XML (Text) Editor` as the program to open this file using the OK button. After doing this, you should find the `View Code` option on the context menu for this file. When the `.resx` file opens, you'll notice that the `.resx` file is nothing more than an XML file with an associated schema at the beginning of the document. The resource file that is generated for you takes every possible property of every translatable control on the page and gives each item a key value that can be referenced in your ASP.NET page. Looking at the page's code, note that all the text values you placed in the page have been retained, but they have also been placed inside the resource file. Visual Studio changed the code of the `Default.aspx` page as shown in the following code block:

```
<%@ Page Title="Home Page" Language="VB" MasterPageFile="~/Site.Master"
    AutoEventWireup="false" CodeFile="Default.aspx.vb" Inherits="_Default"
    culture="auto" meta:resourcekey="PageResource1" uiculture="auto" %>

<asp:Content ID="HeaderContent" runat="server" ContentPlaceHolderID="HeadContent">
</asp:Content>
<asp:Content ID="BodyContent" runat="server" ContentPlaceHolderID="MainContent">
    <div>
        <asp:Label ID="Label1" runat="server"
            Text="What is your name?" meta:resourcekey="Label1Resource1"></asp:Label>
        <br /> <br />
        <asp:TextBox ID="TextBox1" runat="server"
          meta:resourcekey="TextBox1Resource1"></asp:TextBox> 
        <asp:Button ID="Button1" runat="server" Text="Submit Name"
            meta:resourcekey="Button1Resource1" /><br />
        <br />
        <asp:Label ID="Label2" runat="server" meta:resourcekey="Label2Resource1"></asp:Label>
    </div>

</asp:Content>
```

Code snippet from ProVB_Localization\Default.aspx

From this bit of code, you can see that the `Culture` and `UICulture` attributes have been added to the `@Page` directive with a value of `auto`, thus, enabling this application to be localized. In addition, the attribute `meta:resourcekey` has been added to each of the controls, along with an associated value. This is the key from the `.resx` file that was created on your behalf. Double-clicking on the `Default.aspx.resx` file opens the resource file in the Resource Editor, shown in Figure 27-12, built into Visual Studio. Keep in mind the code download will have additional settings not shown if you are working along with the chapter.

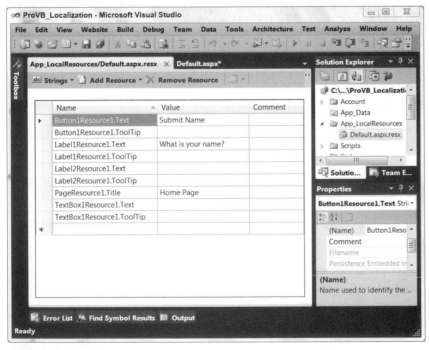

FIGURE 27-12

Note that a few properties from each of the server controls have been defined in the resource file. For instance, the `Button` server control has its `Text` and `ToolTip` properties exposed in this resource file, and the Visual Studio localization tool has pulled the default `Text` property value from the control based on what you placed there. Looking more closely at the `Button` server control constructions in this file, you can see that both the `Text` and `ToolTip` properties have a defining `Button1Resource1` value preceding the property name. This is the key that is used in the `Button` server control shown earlier.

In the following aspx source, a `meta:resourcekey` attribute has been added to a button control. In this case it references `Button1Resource1`. All the properties using this key in the resource file (for example, the `Text` and `ToolTip` properties) are applied to this `Button` server control at runtime.

Available for
download on
Wrox.com

```
<asp:Button ID="Button1" runat="server" Text="Submit Name"
 meta:resourcekey="Button1Resource1" />
```

Code snippet from ProVB_Localization\Default.aspx

Adding Another Language Resource File

The `Default.aspx.resx` file created in the last section is used by the application as the default or invariant culture. No specific culture is assigned to this resource file. If for a given request no culture can be determined, then this is the resource file that is utilized. To add another resource file for the `Default.aspx` page that handles another language altogether, copy and paste the `Default.aspx.resx` file into the same `App_LocalResources` folder and rename the newly copied file. If you use `Default.aspx.fi-FI.resx`, give the following keys the values shown to make a Finnish-language resource file:

```
Button1Resource1.Text    Lähetä Nimi
Label1Resource1.Text     Mikä sinun nimi on?
PageResource1.Title      Näytesivu
```

Once you have created this file, take an additional step and create a custom resource in both resource files using the key `Label2Answer`. The `Default.aspx.resx` file should have the following new key:

```
Label2Answer             Hello
```

Now you can add the key `Label2Answer` to the `Default.aspx.fi-FI.resx` file as shown here:

```
Label2Answer             Hei
```

You now have resources for specific controls, and a resource that you can access later programmatically.

Finalizing the Building of the Default.aspx Page

Finalizing the `Default.aspx` page, you want to add a `Button1_Click` event so that when the end user enters a name into the text box and clicks the Submit button, the `Label2` server control provides a greeting pulled from the local resource files. When all is said and done, your default page should have a code-behind element that matches the following code:

Available for
download on
Wrox.com

```vb
Partial Class _Default
    Inherits System.Web.UI.Page

    Protected Sub Button1_Click(ByVal sender As Object,
            ByVal e As System.EventArgs) Handles Button1.Click
        Label2.Text = GetLocalResourceObject("Label2Answer") &
            " " & TextBox1.Text
    End Sub
End Class
```

Code snippet from ProVB_Localization\Default.aspx.vb

In addition to pulling local resources using the `meta:resourcekey` attribute in the server controls on the page to access the exposed attributes, you can also access any property value contained in the local resource file by using the `GetLocalResourceObject`. When using `GetLocalResourceObject`, you simply use the name of the key as a parameter, as shown here:

```
GetLocalResourceObject("Label2Answer")
```

With the code from the `Default.aspx` page in place and the resource files completed, you can run the page, entering a name in the text box and then clicking the Submit Name button to get a response, as shown in Figure 27-13.

What happened behind the scenes that caused this page to be constructed in this manner? First, only two resource files — `Default.aspx.resx` and `Default.aspx.fi-FI.resx` — are available. The `Default.aspx.resx` resource file is the invariant culture resource file, whereas the `Default.aspx.fi-FI.resx` resource file is for a specific culture (fi-FI). Because the browser requesting the `Default.aspx` page was set to en-US as the preferred culture, ASP.NET found the local resources for the `Default.aspx` page. From there, ASP.NET checked for an en-US-specific version of the `Default.aspx` page. Because there isn't a specific page for the en-US culture, ASP.NET checked for an EN-(neutral culture)-specific page. Not finding a page for the EN neutral culture, ASP.NET was then forced to use the invariant culture resource file of `Default.aspx.resx`, producing the page shown in Figure 27-13.

If you now set your IE language preference as fi-FI and rerun the `Default.aspx` page, you'll see a Finnish version of the page, as shown in Figure 27-14.

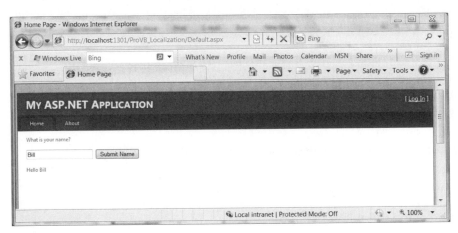

FIGURE 27-13

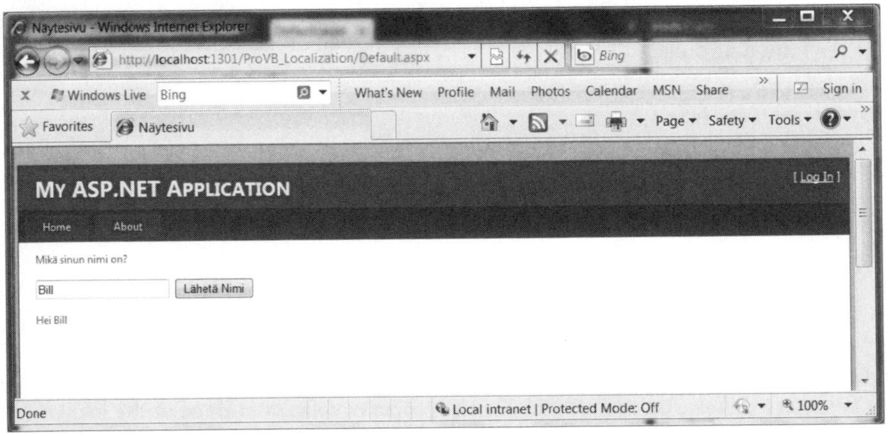

FIGURE 27-14

In this case, having set the IE language preference to fi-FI, you are presented with this culture's page instead of the invariant culture page presented earlier. ASP.NET found this specific culture through use of the `Default.aspx.fi-FI.resx` resource file.

You can see that all the control properties that were translated and placed within the resource file are utilized automatically by ASP.NET, including the page title presented in the title bar of IE.

Neutral Cultures Are Generally Preferred

When you are working with the resource files from this example, note that one of the resources is for a *specific culture*. The `Default.aspx.fi-FI.resx` file is for a specific culture — the Finnish language as spoken in Finland. Another option would be to make this file work not for a specific culture, but instead for a neutral culture. To do so, simply name the file `Default.aspx.FI.resx`. In this case, it doesn't make any difference because no other countries speak Finnish; but it would make sense for languages such as German, Spanish, or French, which are spoken in multiple countries.

For instance, if you are going to have a Spanish version of the `Default.aspx` page, you could definitely build it for a specific culture, such as `Default.aspx.es-MX.resx`. This construction is for the Spanish language as spoken in Mexico. With this in place, if someone requests the `Default.aspx` page with the language setting of es-MX, that user is provided with the contents of this resource file. If the requester has a setting of es-ES, he or she will not get the `Default.aspx.es-MX.resx` resource file, but the invariant culture resource file of `Default.aspx.resx`. If you are going to make only a single translation for your site or any of your pages, construct the resource files to be for neutral cultures, not specific cultures.

If you have the resource file `Default.aspx.ES.resx`, then it won't matter if the end user's preferred setting is set to es-MX, es-ES, or even es-AR — that user gets the appropriate ES neutral-culture version of the page.

Global Resources

Besides using only local resources that specifically deal with a particular page in your ASP.NET application, you also have the option to create *global* resources that can be used across multiple pages. To create a resource file that can be utilized across the entire application, right-click on the solution in the Solution Explorer of Visual Studio and select Add New Item. From the Add New Item dialog, select Resource File. Visual Studio prompts you to place this file in a new folder called App_GlobalResources. You'll see that this file already exists in the sample code download. Once again, your first resource file is the invariant culture resource file. Add a single string resource with the key `LabelText` and assign a long string value to this key. The string "Non-Variant Format Label Text" was used in the code download. Next, add a third `Label` control, `Label3` to the bottom of your existing page.

Now that you have the invariant culture resource file completed, the next step is to add another resource file, but this time name it `Resource.es.resx`. Again, for this resource file, use a string key of `LabelText` and paste in the Spanish translation of the preceding text.

The point of a global resource file is to have access to these resources across the entire application. You can access the values that you place in these files in several ways. One way is to work the value directly into any of your server control declarations. For instance, you can place the following privacy statement in a `Label` server control as shown here:

Available for download on Wrox.com

```
<asp:Label ID="Label3" runat="server"
  Text='<%$ Resources: Resource, LabelText %>'></asp:Label>
```

Code snippet from ProVB_Localization\Default.aspx.vb

With this construction in place, you can now grab the appropriate value of the `LabelText` global resource, depending on the language preference of the end user requesting the page. To make this work, you use the keyword `Resources` followed by a colon. Next, you specify the name of the resource file. In this case, the name of the resource file is `Resource`, because this statement goes to the `Resource.resx` and `Resource.es.resx` files in order to find what it needs. After specifying the particular resource file to use, the next item in the statement is the key — in this case, `LabelText`.

Another way to achieve the same result is to use some built-in dialogs within Visual Studio. Highlight the server control you want in Visual Studio from Design view so that the control appears within the Properties window. For my example, I highlighted a `Label` server control. From the Properties window, click the button within the `Expressions` property. This launches the Expressions dialog, where you can bind the `LabelText` value to the `Text` property of the control, as shown in Figure 27-15.

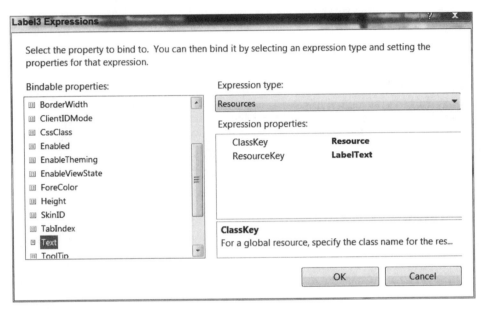

FIGURE 27-15

To make this work, highlight the `Text` property in the Bindable properties list. Then select an expression type from the drop-down list on the right-hand side of the dialog. Your options include AppSettings, ConnectionStrings, and Resources. Select Resources. You are then asked for the `ClassKey` and `ResourceKey` property values. The `ClassKey` is the name of the file that should be utilized. In this example, the name of the file is `Resource.resx`, so use the `Resources` keyword as a value. You are provided with a drop-down list in the `ResourceKey` property section, with all the keys available in this file. Because only a single key exists at this point, only the `LabelText` key appears in this list. Make this selection and click OK. The `Label` server control changes and now appears as it was presented earlier in the two-line code block.

Note that the resources provided via global resources are available in a strongly typed manner. For instance, you can programmatically get at a global resource value by using the construction presented in the following example:

```
Label3.Text = Resources.Resource.LabelText.ToString()
```

Figure 27-16 shows that you have full IntelliSense for these resource values.

However in the case of the sample download the changes shown for the `.aspx` file were maintained (although commented out). Enabling this line in the sample application, combined with a request that specifies a Spanish language culture, results in a page with the Spanish text for Label3.

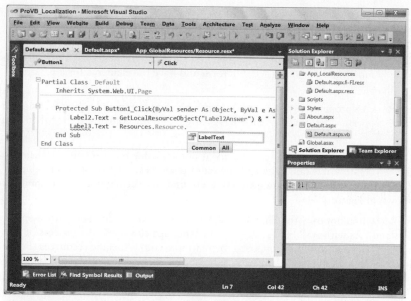

FIGURE 27-16

RESOURCE FILES IN WINDOWS FORMS

Just as with ASP.NET, you can also work with resource files (.resx) for Windows applications using Visual Studio. To see how to localize a Windows Forms application, you will want to reopen the ProVB_2010Localization project introduced earlier in this chapter. In this case you are going to add a new form to your Localization project called UsingResx.vb.

Like the ASP.NET form described earlier in this chapter (and identified as "ASP.NET page code block"), this Windows Forms dialog should contain a couple of Label controls, a Button, and a TextBox control. Initially, your form (with its controls) should look like the one shown in Figure 27-17.

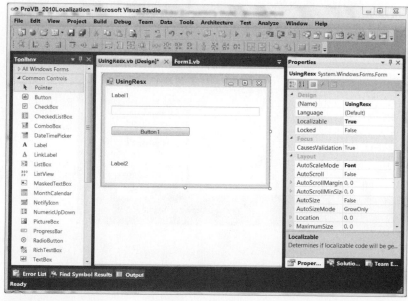

FIGURE 27-17

Before you get started, turn on localization features for the form. Keep in mind that the following steps can also be used for a form that already exists if you are converting an existing form to deal with more than one language.

Selecting the form in the designer, go to the Properties window and change the `Localizable` property to `True`. This enables you to apply more than one language to a form and have the elements for a particular culture stored in a resource file.

After you have set the `Localizable` property to `True`, you can then provide alternate language values for the controls on the form. The properties that you currently have assigned to the controls are for the Default language setting.

As with ASP.NET, if a culture is undetermined or a resource file is not available for this culture, then the Default settings are utilized. To create a new language-specific set of resources, the first step is to change the `Language` property of the form to the desired language. You will find this setting within the `Language` property of the form, as shown in Figure 27-18.

Notice that the property window lists not only the Finnish language as an option, but also culture-specific options such as Finnish (Finland). As with ASP.NET, selecting the language can speed the process of creating localized version(s) of your application, as opposed to creating country-specific resources. From the language property window shown in Figure 27-18, select Finnish as the language and then change the values of the three controls as follows:

```
Button1.Text    Lähetä Nimi
Label1.Text     Mikä sinun nimi on?
Label2.Text     Hei
```

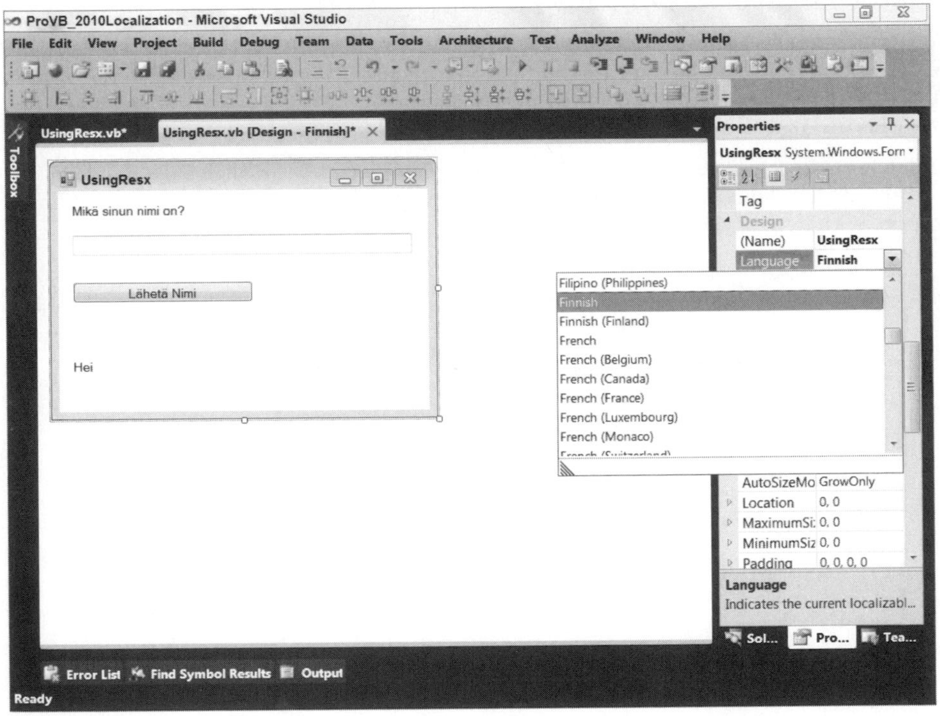

FIGURE 27-18

Note that once you change the value of the Language property, the title of the design window in Visual Studio is also updated to reflect that you are looking at the design for the Finnish view.

Next you are going to set up a couple of methods for your form. First, by double-clicking on the form's button, you will create a Button1_Click event. Within this event you'll add code to assign the value of the TextBox1.Text property to Label2. Additionally, you will add a constructor to the form so that you can specify the current culture info for the thread on which the form is being created. The code-behind for this form is as follows:

```vb
Imports System.Threading
Imports System.Globalization

Public Class UsingResx
    Sub New()
        'Thread.CurrentThread.CurrentCulture = New CultureInfo("fi-FI")
        'Thread.CurrentThread.CurrentUICulture = New CultureInfo("fi-FI")

        ' This call is required by the designer.
        InitializeComponent()

        ' Add any initialization after the InitializeComponent() call.

    End Sub
    Private Sub Button1_Click(ByVal sender As System.Object,
                ByVal e As System.EventArgs) Handles Button1.Click
        Label2.Text += TextBox1.Text
    End Sub
End Class
```

Code snippet from UsingResx.vb

The preceding code shows that you have added two lines that will specify the culture info on the current thread prior to processing the form. Leaving these two lines commented out, running the application, and using the Open UsingResx button to open the UsingResx form produces the output shown in Figure 27-19. After doing this, uncomment the two lines, which will simulate a user whose system settings are defined as Finnish. Again, accessing the UsingResx form, the display automatically changes to the one shown in Figure 27-20.

FIGURE 27-19

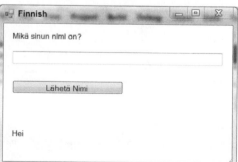

FIGURE 27-20

Where are all the translations stored? Just as with ASP.NET, they are stored in the resource file for this form. Using the Solution Explorer to show all the files in your solution, you will now find a `UsingResx.resx` file and a `UsingResx.fi.resx` file, as shown in Figure 27-21.

Opening the `UsingResx.resx` file will cause Visual Studio to open the file in a manner that enables you to directly edit the values it stores. The default resource file stores some type references as well as other properties of the controls on the form, as shown in Figure 27-22.

Opening the `UsingResx.fi.resx` file instead shows only the three changed properties and the updated page title. The rest of the properties are read from the default resource file. The contents of the Finnish resource file are presented in Figure 27-23.

FIGURE 27-21

Name	Value	Comment
$this.Text	UsingResx	
>>$this.Name	UsingResx	
>>$this.Type	System.Windows.Forms.Form,	
>>Button1.Name	Button1	
>>Button1.Parent	$this	
>>Button1.Type	System.Windows.Forms.Button,	
>>Button1.ZOrder	1	
>>Label1.Name	Label1	
>>Label1.Parent	$this	
>>Label1.Type	System.Windows.Forms.Label,	
>>Label1.ZOrder	3	
>>Label2.Name	Label2	
>>Label2.Parent	$this	
>>Label2.Type	System.Windows.Forms.Label,	
>>Label2.ZOrder	0	
>>TextBox1.Name	TextBox1	
>>TextBox1.Parent	$this	
>>TextBox1.Type	System.Windows.Forms.TextBox,	
>>TextBox1.ZOrder	2	
Button1.Text	Button1	
Label1.Text	Label1	
Label2.Text	Label2	

FIGURE 27-22

Name	Value	Comment
Button1.Text	Lähetä Nimi	
Label1.Text	Mikä sinun nimi on?	
Label2.Text	Hei	

FIGURE 27-23

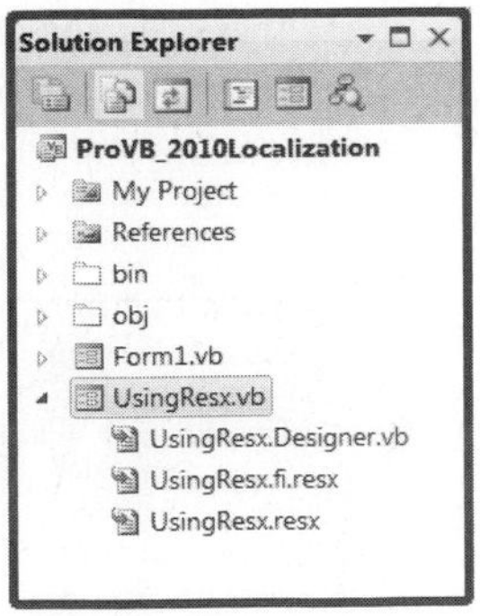

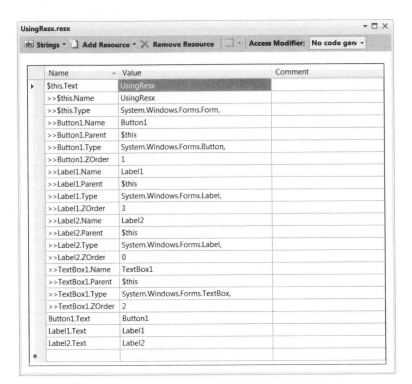

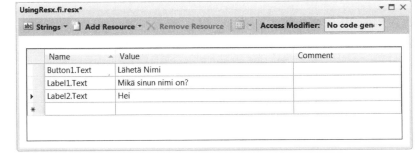

Visual Studio 2010 provides an editor for working with resource files. You have already seen some of the views available from the Resource Editor. Resources are categorized visually according to the data type of the resource. This chapter has covered only the handling of strings, but other categories exist (such as images, icons, audio files, miscellaneous files, and other items). These options are shown in Figure 27-24.

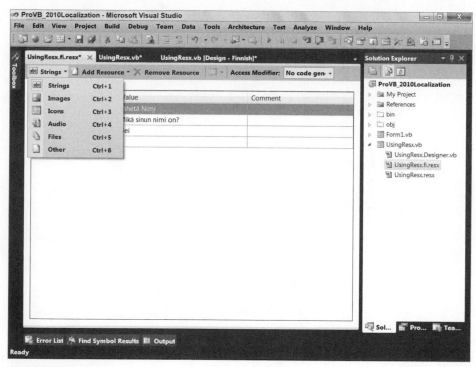

FIGURE 27-24

SUMMARY

This chapter has looked at some of the localization tools available to you. It started with a review of the Culture types and how to determine the preferred culture for either a thread or Web request. It looked at understanding how different cultures may treat the same date or number differently for display and just as importantly how .NET can automate this handling for you. It also examined differences with currency with a warning about the need to convert a value and not just swap the display formatting when dealing with currency. The chapter then looked at how .NET supports both Windows Forms and ASP.NET use of multiple resource files to provide support for different languages and cultures.

While .NET has provided many tools to help you with this process, you should keep in mind that these tools only make the process easier when looking; when you want to localize an application, you need to plan to work with someone familiar with the language, and ideally the culture, you will target.

In addition to making many of the changes described in this chapter, localization is a process that requires consideration of multiple different time zones, consideration for information that reads Left to Right vs cultures which expect information to flow Right to Left, and other issues that are outside the scope of the tools you use. While that seems like a lot, you'll note that the same concepts for using resource files exist between Windows Forms and ASP.NET.

28

COM-Interop

WHAT YOU WILL LEARN IN THIS CHAPTER

- ➤ Review of COM
- ➤ Calling COM from .NET
- ➤ Interop with ActiveX controls
- ➤ Configuring .NET assemblies to be called from COM
- ➤ Introduction to P/Invoke

A vast body of technology surrounds Microsoft's Component Object Model (COM). Over the years, this model has been the cornerstone of so much Microsoft-related development that we have to take a long, hard look at how to integrate all that technology into the world of .NET.

This chapter begins by taking a brief backward glance at COM, and then compares it with the way that components interact in .NET. It also takes a look at the tools Microsoft provides to help link the two together. Having looked at the theory, you then try it out by building a few example applications. First you take a legacy basic COM object and run it from a Visual Basic 2010 program. Then you repeat the trick with a full-blown ActiveX control. Next, you run some Visual Basic code in the guise of a COM object. Finally, this chapter takes a look at some tools associated with going below the COM layer and into the P/Invoke layer of the operating system.

 The COM-related examples in this chapter are exclusive to a 32-bit environment. Attempting to run these examples on a 64-bit environment will result in runtime errors unless you reset the project settings to specifically target a 32-bit (x86) operating system.

When considering the differences between COM and .NET, keep in mind one thing: COM is, to a large extent, where .NET came from. In addition, with all the time and resources that have been invested in this technology, it is important to consider the best ways to both maintain these investments and integrate them into new investments you make, and over time migrate your components to .NET-based implementations for the transition to 64-bit computing.

UNDERSTANDING COM

Before looking into the COM-.NET interoperability story, it is important to understand COM's main concepts. This section does not attempt to do more than skim the surface of COM. While the basic concepts are fundamentally simple, the underlying technology is anything but simple. Some of the most impenetrable books on software ever written have COM as their subject, and we have no wish to add to these.

COM was Microsoft's first full-blown attempt to create a language-independent standard for programming. The idea was that interfaces between components would be defined according to a binary standard. This means that you could, for the first time, invoke a VB component from a VC++ application, and vice versa. It would also be possible to invoke a component in another process or even on another machine, via Distributed COM (DCOM). You will not be looking at out-of-process servers here, however, because the vast majority of components developed were in process.

A COM component implements one or more *interfaces*, a few of which are standards provided by the system. In addition to the required interfaces, a COM component adds custom interfaces defined by the component developer. An interface defines the various methods that an application may invoke. Once specified, an interface definition is supposed to be inviolate, so that even when the underlying code changes, applications that use the interface do not need to be rebuilt. If the component developers find that they have left something out, then they should define a new interface containing the extra functionality in addition to what remains in the original interface. This has, in fact, happened with a number of standard Microsoft interfaces. For example, the `IClassFactory2` interface extends the `IClassFactory` interface by adding features for managing the creation of licensed objects.

The key to getting applications and components to work together is *binding*. COM offers two forms of binding, early and late:

➤ In *early binding*, the application uses a *type library* at compile time to determine how to link in to the methods in the component's interfaces. A type library can exist as a separate file, with the extension `.tlb`, or as part of the DLL containing the component code.

➤ In *late binding*, no connection is made between the application and its components at compile time. Instead, the COM runtime searches through the component for the location of the required member when the application is actually run. This advantage is offset by two main disadvantages: It is slower and potentially unreliable. If a programming error is made (e.g., the wrong method is called or the right method is called but with the wrong number of arguments), it is not caught at compile time and instead creates a runtime error for the end user.

When a type library is not explicitly referred to, there are two ways to identify a COM component: by *class ID* (`CLSID`), which is actually a GUID, and by *ProgID*, which is a string and looks something like "`MyProject .MyComponent`." These are all cross-referenced in the registry. In fact, COM makes extensive use of the registry to maintain links between applications, their components, and their interfaces. Experienced COM programmers know their way around the registry blindfolded.

VB6 has encapsulated many of COM's implementation details, to the extent that many VB6 programmers were unaware that they were developing COM components. For instance, if you create a DLL containing an instance of a VB6 class, then you have in fact created a COM object without even asking for one. The relative ease of this process is demonstrated in this chapter.

There are clearly similarities between COM and .NET; in fact, you can see the evolution from a two-tier `ProgID` to the .NET namespace model. However, .NET obviously came about after COM's binary protocols were defined, so to a large extent, all you have to do to make them work together is put a wrapper around a COM object to turn it into a .NET assembly, and vice versa.

COM AND .NET IN PRACTICE

To see how all this seamless integration works we have to simulate a legacy situation. Suppose your enterprise depends on a particular COM object that was written for you a long time ago by staff who are no longer in the organization. All you know about the component is that the code within it works and you need to employ it for your .NET application.

You have one, possibly two, options in this case. If you have the source code of the COM component (which is not always the case) and you have sufficient time (budget), then you can upgrade the object to .NET and continue to maintain it as a .NET assembly. For the purist, or for someone looking at migrating to a 64-bit solution, this is the ideal solution. Visual Studio does offer an upgrade for VB-6 based on COM objects, but it does not cope well with COM objects using interfaces specified as abstract classes. Nor does it handle COM objects written in C++, so if you are considering an upgrade you need to factor in time to manually recreate the core logic provided by the object using .NET.

If upgrading the object to a .NET component is not an option for you, then all you really can do is include the DLL as it stands as a COM object, register it on the server containing the .NET Framework, and use the .NET interoperability tools to integrate the two technologies. Moving forward, because COM is a 32-bit protocol, either you will need to consider rewriting the component from scratch or you will have a permanent dependency on the 32-bit compatibility layer within your 64-bit environment. Since this is the option which requires interoperating with the existing component, it is the option that this chapter implements.

Therefore, what you need for this example is a genuine legacy COM object. This chapter uses a VB6 component to integrate within a .NET application. For the next section, this chapter steps back in time and uses VB6 for the classic component required. If you are not very interested in VB6, then feel free to skip this section. In any case, the DLL created is available as part of the code download for this book.

A Legacy Component

For the legacy component, imagine that you have an analytics engine that requires a number of calculations. Because of the highly complex nature of these calculations, their development was given to specialists, while the user interface for the application was given to some UI specialists. A COM interface was specified to which all calculations must conform. This interface is given the name `IMegaCalc` and has the following methods:

METHOD	DESCRIPTION
`Sub AddInput(InputValue as Double)`	Adds the input value to the calculation
`Sub DoCalculation( )`	Performs the calculation
`Function GetOutput( ) as Double`	Gets the output from the calculation
`Sub Reset( )`	Resets the calculation for the next time

The following steps use VB6 to create an ActiveX DLL which can be referenced from .NET. If you aren't interested in working with VB6 you can use the copy of this DLL which is part of the code download. The VB6 folder for this chapter has all of the VB6 projects precompiled for registration and use. You can jump ahead to Registering the component.

Implementing the Component

For the purposes of this example, the actual calculation that you are going to perform is fairly mundane: The component will calculate the mean of a series of numbers. Create an ActiveX DLL project called MeanCalculator2. Add a reference to the type library for the interface that you are going to implement by selecting the MegaCalculator2 DLL via the References dialog box that opens when you select Project ⇨ References.

Having done that, go ahead and write the code for the mean calculation. You do that in a class called
`MeanCalc`:

```
Option Explicit
Dim mintValue As Integer
Dim mdblValues() As Double
Dim mdblMean As Double
Private Sub Class_Initialize()
  Reset
End Sub
Private Sub IMegaCalc_AddInput(InputValue As Double)
  mintValue = mintValue + 1
  ReDim Preserve mdblValues(mintValue)
  mdblValues(mintValue) = InputValue
End Sub
Private Sub IMegaCalc_DoCalculation()
  Dim iValue As Integer
  mdblMean = 0#
  If (mintValue = 0) Then Exit Sub
  For iValue = 1 To mintValue
    mdblMean = mdblMean + mdblValues(iValue)
  Next iValue
  mdblMean = mdblMean / mintValue
End Sub
Private Function IMegaCalc_GetOutput() As Double
  IMegaCalc_GetOutput = mdblMean
End Function
Private Sub IMegaCalc_Reset()
  mintValue = 0
End Sub
```

Code snippet from MeanCalc

Step 2: Registering the Legacy Component

If you have made it this far, then you should now have
your legacy component. When developing your new
.NET application on the same machine, you do not
need to do anything more because your component is
already registered by the build process. However, if
you are working on an entirely new machine, then you
must register it there. To do that, open a command
window (on Windows Vista and Windows 7, ensure
that you start the command window with administrator permissions) and register it with the following
command using `regsvr32.exe` found at `C:\Windows\system32`:

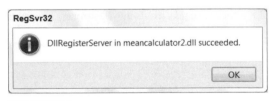

FIGURE 28-1

```
regsvr32 MeanCalculator2.dll
```

You should then see the result shown in Figure 28-1.

The .NET Application

For the .NET application used in this chapter, you only need to instantiate an instance of the `MeanCalc` object
and get it to figure out a mean calculation for you. In order to accomplish that, create a .NET Windows
Forms Application project in Visual Basic called CalcApp. Laid out, the form looks like what is shown in
Figure 28-2.

The two text boxes are called `txtInput` and `txtOutput`, respectively; the second one is not enabled for user
input. The three command buttons are `btnAdd`, `btnCalculate`, and `btnReset`, respectively.

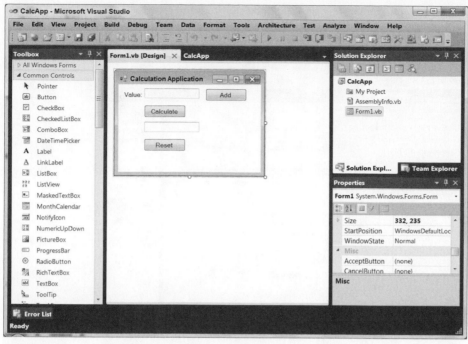

FIGURE 28-2

Referencing the Legacy COM Component from .NET

Before you dive into writing the code behind the buttons on the form, you first need to make your new application aware of the `MeanCalculator2` component. Add a reference to the component via the Project Properties. From the References tab select the "Add.." button to open the Add Reference dialog box. This dialog contains five tabs: .NET, COM, Projects, Browse, and Recent. From the COM tab, select Interop .MeanCalculator2 (see Figure 28-3).

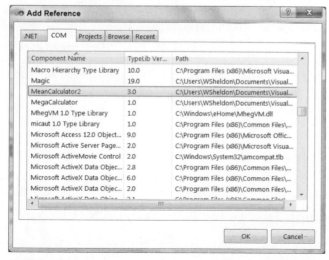

FIGURE 28-3

Note that in the list of references shown in the References tab, you can now see the `MeanCalculator` component. This view is presented in Figure 28-4.

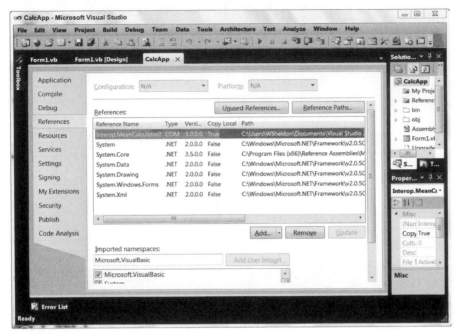

FIGURE 28-4

Inside the .NET Application

Now that you have successfully referenced the components in the .NET application, you can finish coding the application, using the functionality provided via the COM components. To start making use of the new capabilities provided by the COM component, add to the code a global variable (`mobjMean`) that will hold a reference to an instance of the mean calculation component, as shown here:

Available for download on Wrox.com

```
Public Class Form1
    Dim mobjMean As MeanCalculator2.MeanCalc = New MeanCalculator2.MeanCalc()
```

Code snippet from Form1

Next, add the code behind the form's buttons. First, working with the Add button, add the following code that calls the COM component:

Available for download on Wrox.com

```
Private Sub btnAdd_Click(ByVal sender As System.Object, _
                         ByVal e As System.EventArgs) _
                         Handles btnAdd.Click
    mobjMean.AddInput(CDbl(txtInput.Text))
    txtInput.Text = ""
End Sub
```

Code snippet from Form1

This adds whatever is in the input text box into the list of numbers for the calculation. Next, here's the code-behind for the Calculate button:

Available for download on Wrox.com

```
Private Sub btnCalculate_Click(ByVal sender As System.Object, _
                               ByVal e As System.EventArgs) _
                               Handles btnCalculate.Click
    mobjMean.DoCalculation()
```

```
        txtOutput.Text = CStr(mobjMean.GetOutput())
    End Sub
```

This performs the calculation, retrieves the answer, and puts it into the output text box — all of this from the COM component. Finally, the code behind the Reset button simply resets the calculation:

```
    Private Sub btnReset_Click(ByVal sender As System.Object, _
            ByVal e As System.EventArgs) Handles btnReset.Click
        mobjMean.Reset()
        txtInput.Text = ""
        txtOutput.Text = ""
    End Sub
```

Trying It All Out

As noted at the start of this chapter you need to ensure that your application targets an x86 environment. To do this go to Build Menu and select Build Configuration. From the Configuration Manager dialog select the Active Solution Platform and select <New…> to open the New Project Platform dialog. Within this dialog change the setting for the value "New platform" from Any CPU to x86 as shown in Figure 28-5.

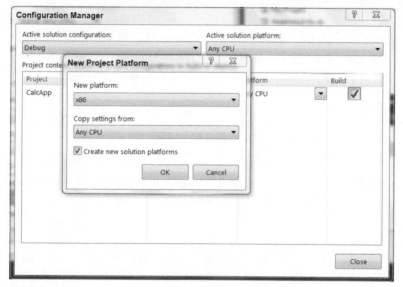

FIGURE 28-5

Compile and run the application and place a value in the first text box — for example, 2 — and click the Add button on the form. Next, enter another value — for example, 3 — and click the Add button again. When you click Calculate, you'll get the mean of the two values (2.5 in this case), as shown in Figure 28-6.

Using TlbImp Directly

In the preceding example, there is actually quite a lot going on under the hood. Every time you import a COM DLL into Visual Studio, it creates a *default interop assembly*, which is basically a

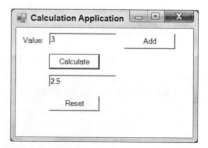

FIGURE 28-6

.NET assembly (DLL) that acts as a wrapper for the COM object. If you are doing this a lot, then it might be better to do the wrapping once and for all, and then let your application developers import the resulting .NET assembly instead. Let's see how you might accomplish this task.

The process that creates the default interop assembly on behalf of Visual Studio is called `TlbImp.exe`. The name stands for *Type Library Import*, and that's pretty much what the process does. It is included in the .NET Framework SDK, and you might find it convenient to extend the PATH environment variable on your machine to include the \bin directory of the .NET Framework SDK.

`TlbImp` takes a COM DLL as its input and generates a .NET assembly DLL as its output. By default, the .NET assembly has the same name as the type library, which will — in the case of VB6 components — always be the same as the COM DLL. This means you have to explicitly specify a different output file. You do this by using the `/out:` switch. If you want to see what's going on at each step in the process, then you should also specify the `/verbose` flag:

```
tlbimp MeanCalculator2.dll /out:MeanCalculatorNet2.dll
```

Having converted your COM DLLs into .NET assemblies, you can now reference them in an application as you would any other .NET DLL.

Late Binding

You've seen that you can successfully do early binding on COM components within a .NET application, but what if you want to do late binding instead? Suppose you don't have access to a type library at application development time. Can you still make use of the COM component? Does the .NET equivalent of late binding even exist?

The answer is yes, it does, but it is not as transparent as it is with VB6. Let's take a look at what occurred in VB6. If you wanted to do early binding, you would do this:

```
Dim myObj As MyObj
Set myObj = New MyObj
MyObj.MyMethod (…)
```

For late binding, it would look like this instead:

```
Dim myObj As Object
Set myObj = CreateObject ("MyLibrary.MyObject")
MyObj.MyMethod (…)
```

There is actually an enormous amount of activity going on under the hood here but most of that is beyond the concern of a .NET developer.

An Example for Late Binding

For the sample being built in this chapter, let's extend the calculator to a more generic framework that can feed inputs into a number of different calculation modules, rather than just the fixed one it currently implements. For this example, you'll keep a table in memory of calculation ProgIDs and present the user with a combo box to select the correct one.

The Sample COM Object

The first item to note with late binding is that you can only late bind to the default interface, which in this case is `MeanCalculator2.MeanCalc`. Fortunately, this component was developed as a standalone library, with no references to other interfaces.

The Calculation Framework

For your generic calculation framework, you'll create a new application in Visual Basic 2010 called CalcFrame. You will basically use the same dialog box as before, but with an extra combo box at the top of the form. This new layout is illustrated in Figure 28-7.

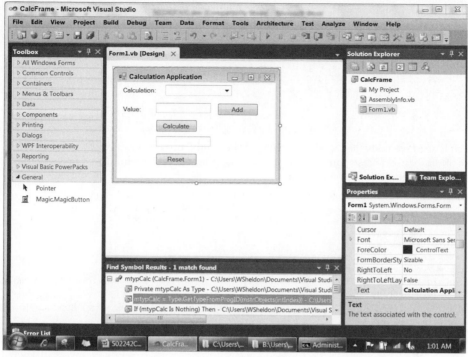

FIGURE 28-7

The new combo box is called `cmbCalculation`. For this to work, you also need to disable the controls `txtInput`, `btnAdd`, `btnCalculate`, and `btnReset` until you know whether the selected calculation is valid. You'll want to access the properties of the new drop down and add two. Begin your application by importing the `Reflection` namespace, which you need for handling the application's late binding:

```
Imports System.Reflection
```

Once the form is in place, add a few member variables to the code of your application:

Available for download on Wrox.com

```
Public Class Form1
    Inherits System.Windows.Forms.Form
    Private mstrObjects() As String
    Private mnObject As Integer
    Private mtypCalc As Type
    Private mobjcalc As Object
```

Code snippet from Form1

From there, add a few new lines to `Form1_Load`:

Available for download on Wrox.com

```
Private Sub Form1_Load(ByVal sender As System.Object, _
    ByVal e As System.EventArgs) Handles MyBase.Load
    mnObject = 0
    AddObject("Mean", "MeanCalculator2.MeanCalc")
    AddObject("StdDev", "StddevCalculator.StddevCalc")
    If (mnObject > 0) Then
        cmbCalculation.SelectedIndex = 0
    End If
End Sub
```

Code snippet from Form1

What you are doing here is building a list of calculations. When you're finished, you select the first one in the list. Let's take a look at that subroutine `AddObject`:

```
Private Sub AddObject(ByVal strName As String, ByVal strObject As String)
    cmbCalculation.Items.Add(strName)
    mnObject = mnObject + 1
    ReDim Preserve mstrObjects(mnObject)
    mstrObjects(mnObject - 1) = strObject
End Sub
```

Code snippet from Form1

The preceding code segment adds the calculation name to the combo box, and its ProgID to an array of strings. Neither of these is sorted, so you get a one-to-one mapping between them. Check out what happens when you select a calculation via the combo box:

```
Private Sub cmbCalculation_SelectedIndexChanged(ByVal sender As System.Object,
                                    ByVal e As System.EventArgs) _
                    Handles cmbCalculation.SelectedIndexChanged
    Dim intIndex As Integer
    Dim bEnabled As Boolean
    intIndex = cmbCalculation.SelectedIndex
    mtypCalc = Type.GetTypeFromProgID(mstrObjects(intIndex))
    If (mtypCalc Is Nothing) Then
        mobjcalc = Nothing
        bEnabled = False
    Else
        mobjcalc = Activator.CreateInstance(mtypCalc)
        bEnabled = True
    End If
    txtInput.Enabled = bEnabled
    btnAdd.Enabled = bEnabled
    btnCalculate.Enabled = bEnabled
    btnReset.Enabled = bEnabled
End Sub
```

Code snippet from Form1

There are two key calls in this example. The first is to `Type.GetTypeFromProgID`. This takes the incoming `ProgID` string and converts it to a `Type` object. This process either succeeds or fails; if it fails, then you disable all the controls and let the user try again. If it succeeds, however, then you create an instance of the object described by the type. You do this in the call to the static method `Activator.CreateInstance()`.

For this example, assume that the user has selected a calculation that you can successfully instantiate. What next? The user enters a number and clicks the Add button on the form:

```
Private Sub btnAdd_Click(ByVal sender As System.Object, _
    ByVal e As System.EventArgs) Handles btnAdd.Click
    Dim objArgs() As Object
    objArgs = New Object(0) {CDbl(TxtInput.Text)}
    mtypCalc.InvokeMember("AddInput", BindingFlags.InvokeMethod, _
        Nothing, mobjCalc, objArgs)
    txtInput.Text = ""
End Sub
```

Code snippet from Form1

The important call here is to the `InvokeMember()` method. Let's take a closer look at what is going on. Five parameters are passed into the `InvokeMember()` method:

➤ The first parameter is the name of the method that you want to call: `AddInput` in this case. Therefore, instead of going directly to the location of the routine in memory, you ask the .NET runtime to find it for you.

➤ The value from the `BindingFlags` enumeration tells it to invoke a method.

➤ The next parameter provides language-specific binding information, which is not needed in this case.

➤ The fourth parameter is a reference to the COM object itself (the one you instantiated using `Activator.CreateInstance`).

➤ Finally, the fifth parameter is an array of objects representing the arguments for the method. In this case, there is only one argument, the input value.

Something very similar to this is going on underneath VB6 late binding, except that here it is exposed in all its horror. In some ways, that's not a bad thing, because it should highlight the point that late binding is something to avoid if possible. Anyway, let's carry on and complete the program. Here are the remaining event handlers for the other buttons:

Available for download on Wrox.com

```vb
Private Sub btnCalculate_Click(ByVal sender As System.Object, _
            ByVal e As System.EventArgs) Handles btnCalculate.Click
    Dim objResult As Object
    mtypCalc.InvokeMember("DoCalculation", BindingFlags.InvokeMethod, _
                        Nothing, mobjCalc, Nothing)
    objResult = mtypCalc.InvokeMember("GetOutput", _
                    BindingFlags.InvokeMethod, Nothing, mobjCalc, Nothing)
    txtOutput.Text = Cstr(objResult)
End Sub
Private Sub btnReset_Click(ByVal sender As System.Object, _
            ByVal e As System.EventArgs) Handles btnReset.Click
    mtypCalc.InvokeMember("Reset", BindingFlags.InvokeMethod, _
        Nothing, mobjCalc, Nothing)
    txtInput.Text = ""
    txtOutput.Text = ""
End Sub
```

Code snippet from Form1

Running the Calculation Framework

Let's quickly complete the job by running the application. Figure 28-8 shows what happens when you select the nonexistent calculation StdDev.

As shown in the screenshot, the input fields have been disabled, as desired. Figure 28-9 shows what happens when you select Mean. You can then enter a couple of numeric values and retest the Mean calculation. This time, the input fields are enabled, and the calculation can be carried out as before.

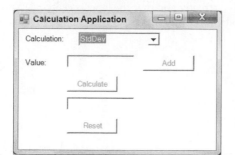

FIGURE 28-8

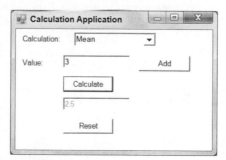

FIGURE 28-9

One final word about late binding: This sample took care to ensure that you checked whether the object was successfully instantiated. In a real-life application, you also need to ensure that the method invocations are successful and that all exceptions are caught — you do not have the luxury of having the compiler find all your bugs for you.

ACTIVEX CONTROLS

Let's move on from basic COM objects to ActiveX controls. You are going to do much the same thing you did with the basic COM component (apart from late binding, which has no relevance to ActiveX controls): Build a legacy control using VB6 and then import it into your .NET Visual Basic project.

The Legacy ActiveX Control

For your legacy ActiveX control, you are going to build a simple button-like object that is capable of interpreting a mouse click and can be one of two colors according to its state. To accomplish this task, you will take a second foray into VB6, so if you don't have VB6 handy, feel free to skip the next section, download the OCX file (it's Magic.ocx under the VB6\Magic\ directory in the sample code), and pick it up when you start developing your .NET application.

Step 1: Creating the Control

This time, within the VB6 IDE, you need to create an ActiveX Control project. For this example, call the project Magic, and the control class `MagicButton`, to reflect its remarkable powers. From the Toolbox, select a `Shape` control and place it on the `UserControl` form that VB6 provides for you. Rename the shape provided on the form to `shpButton`, and change its properties as follows:

PROPERTY	VALUE
FillStyle	0 'Solid
Shape	4 'Rounded Rectangle
FillColor	&H008F8F8F&

The fill color hex value represents the color Gray. Next add a label on top of the `Shape` control and rename it to `lblText`. Change this control's properties to the following:

PROPERTY	VALUE
BackStyle	0 'Transparent
Alignment	2 'Center

Switch to the code view of the `MagicButton` component. Within the code presented, add two properties called `Caption` and `State`, and an event called `Click()`, as well as code to handle the initialization of the properties and persisting them, to ensure that the shape resizes correctly and that the label is centered. You also need to handle mouse clicks within the code. The final code of the `MagicButton` class should look as follows:

```
Option Explicit
Public Event Click()
Dim mintState As Integer
Public Property Get Caption() As String
    Caption = lblText.Caption
End Property
Public Property Let Caption(ByVal vNewValue As String)
    lblText.Caption = vNewValue
    PropertyChanged ("Caption")
End Property
Public Property Get State() As Integer
    State = mintState
End Property
Public Property Let State(ByVal vNewValue As Integer)
```

```
        mintState = vNewValue
        PropertyChanged ("State")
        If (State = 0) Then
          shpButton.FillColor = &HFFFFFF&
        Else
          shpButton.FillColor = &H8F8F8F&
        End If
      End Property
      Private Sub UserControl_InitProperties()
        Caption = Extender.Name
        State = 1
      End Sub
      Private Sub UserControl_ReadProperties(PropBag As PropertyBag)
        Caption = PropBag.ReadProperty("Caption", Extender.Name)
        State = PropBag.ReadProperty("State", 1)
      End Sub
      Private Sub UserControl_WriteProperties(PropBag As PropertyBag)
        PropBag.WriteProperty "Caption", lblText.Caption
        PropBag.WriteProperty "State", mintState
      End Sub
      Private Sub UserControl_Resize()
        shpButton.Move 0, 0, ScaleWidth, ScaleHeight
        lblText.Move 0, (ScaleHeight - lblText.Height) / 2, ScaleWidth
      End Sub
      Private Sub lblText_Click()
        RaiseEvent Click
      End Sub
      Private Sub UserControl_MouseUp(Button As Integer, Shift As Integer, _
                            X As Single, Y As Single)
        RaiseEvent Click
      End Sub
```

Code snippet from MagicButton

If you build this, you'll get an ActiveX control called `Magic.ocx`.

Step 2: Registering Your Legacy Control

You now have your legacy control. As before, if you are developing your new .NET application on the same machine, then you don't need to do anything else because your control is registered by the build process. However, if you are working on an entirely new machine or if you didn't build the control in Visual Basic 6, then you need to register it there. As before, open a command window and register it as follows:

```
regsvr32 Magic.ocx
```

You should again see the dialog shown in Figure 28-1, this time indicating that your Magic.ocx component has been successfully registered. Having done that, you are ready to build your .NET application.

A .NET Application, Again

This .NET application is even more straightforward than the last one. All you are going to do this time is display a button that changes color whenever the user clicks it. To begin, create a .NET Windows Application project in Visual Basic called ButtonApp. Before you start to develop it, however, extend the Toolbox to incorporate your new control by right-clicking within the General section of the Toolbox and selecting Choose Items. Figure 28-10 shows the context menu. Once you select Choose Items, you'll see the window shown in Figure 28-11.

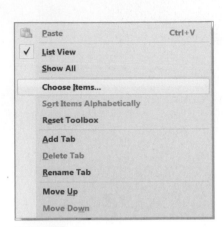

FIGURE 28-10

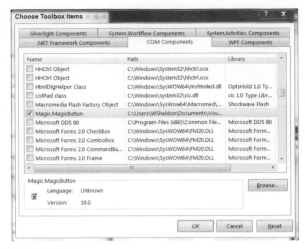

FIGURE 28-11

When you click the OK button, your `MagicButton` class is now available to you in the Toolbox (see Figure 28-12). Add the `Magic.MagicButton` control to your form, as shown in Figure 28-13, by dragging the control onto the form. Note that references to AxMagic and Magic are automatically added to the project in the Solution Explorer window within the References folder, as shown in Figure 28-14.

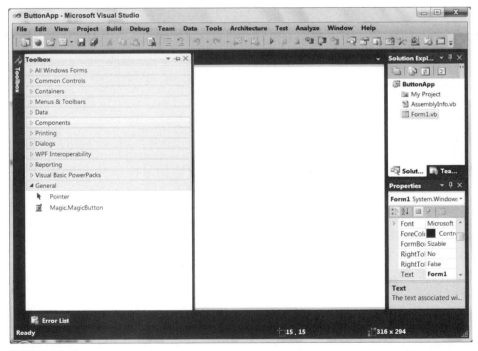

FIGURE 28-12

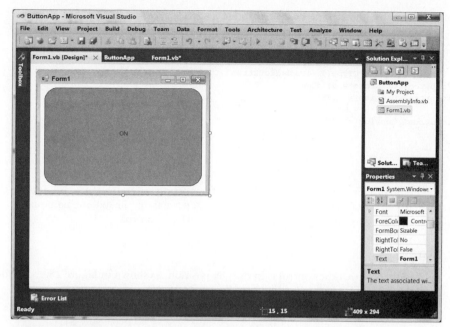

FIGURE 28-13

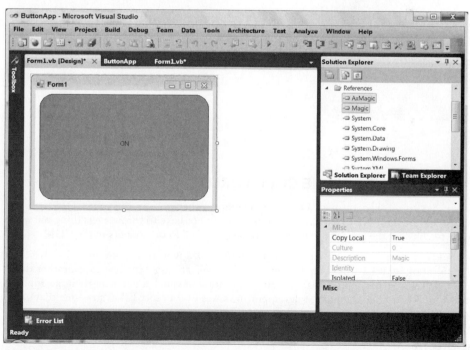

FIGURE 28-14

All you need to do now is initialize the Caption property to ON, and code up a handler for the mouse Click event:

```
Private Sub AxMagicButton1_ClickEvent(ByVal sender As System.Object, _
           ByVal e As System.EventArgs) Handles AxMagicButton1.ClickEvent
    AxMagicButton1.CtlState = CType(1 - AxMagicButton1.CtlState, Short)
    If (AxMagicButton1.CtlState = 0) Then
        AxMagicButton1.Caption = "OFF"
    Else
        AxMagicButton1.Caption = "ON"
    End If
End Sub
```

Code snippet from Form1

Note something slightly peculiar happening here. In the course of importing the control into .NET, the variable State mutated into CtlState. This is because there is already a class in the AxHost namespace called State, which is used to encapsulate the persisted state of an ActiveX control.

Trying It All Out, Again

When you run this application, note that the control is in the ON position, as shown in Figure 28-15. If you click the control, it changes to the OFF position, as shown in Figure 28-16.

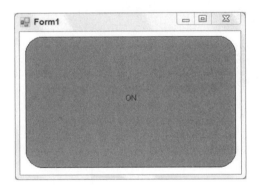

FIGURE 28-15

FIGURE 28-16

USING .NET COMPONENTS IN THE COM WORLD

So far, this chapter has established, through a couple of examples, that you can use your COM legacy components within any of your .NET-based applications. You do not have to throw everything out *quite* yet. Now it's time to consider the opposite question: Can you run .NET components in the COM world?

Why on earth would you want to run .NET components in the COM world? It is not immediately obvious, in fact, because migration to .NET would almost certainly be application-led in most cases, rather than component-led. However, it is possible (just) to imagine a situation in which a particularly large application remains not based on .NET, while component development moves over to .NET. Let's assume that's the case for the next section. The technology is quite cool, anyway.

A .NET Component

Let's take a look at the .NET component. Here, you will implement an exact copy of the functionality created earlier with the MegaCalculator and MeanCalculator components, except you will use Visual Basic 2010, rather than VB6.

Begin by creating a Class Library project called MegaCalculator2. Here is the entire code of the interface for the Class Library:

```
Public Interface IMegaCalc
    Sub AddInput(ByVal InputValue As Double)
    Sub DoCalculation()
    Function GetResult() As Double
    Sub Reset()
End Interface
```

Code snippet from IMegaCalc

Now create another Class Library project called MeanCalculator3. This will contain a class called MeanCalc that is going to implement the interface IMegaCalc, as a mirror of the MeanCalc in your original VB6 MeanCalculator2 project. As before, you need to add a reference to MegaCalculator2 first, although, to make this easier, go to the File menu and choose to add an existing project to this solution and import the MegaCalculator2 project into the current solution. Now add a reference to this project that is part of the solution.

Once that reference exists you can add the following class definition for MeanCalc:

```
Public Class MeanCalc
    Implements MegaCalculator2.IMegaCalc
    Dim mintValue As Integer
    Dim mdblValues() As Double
    Dim mdblMean As Double
    Public Sub AddInput(ByVal InputValue As Double) _
        Implements MegaCalculator2.IMegaCalc.AddInput
        mintValue = mintValue + 1
        ReDim Preserve mdblValues(mintValue)
        mdblValues(mintValue - 1) = InputValue
    End Sub
    Public Sub DoCalculation() _
        Implements MegaCalculator2.IMegaCalc.DoCalculation
        Dim iValue As Integer
        mdblMean = 0
        If (mintValue = 0) Then Exit Sub
        For iValue = 0 To mintValue - 1 Step 1
            mdblMean = mdblMean + mdblValues(iValue)
        Next iValue
        mdblMean = mdblMean / iValue
    End Sub
    Public Function GetResult() As Double Implements _
                    MegaCalculator2.IMegaCalc.GetResult
        GetResult = mdblMean
    End Function
    Public Sub Reset() Implements MegaCalculator2.IMegaCalc.Reset
        mintValue = 0
    End Sub
    Public Sub New()
        Reset()
    End Sub
End Class
```

Code snippet from MeanCalc

Before compiling this application, make sure the component that you are building is COM-visible. To do this, right-click on the MeanCalculator3 solution within Visual Studio 2010 Solution Explorer and select Properties from the context menu.

From the Properties window, select the Application tab, and then select the Assembly Information button to open the Assembly Information dialog. At the bottom of this dialog you will find a check box called Make assembly COM-Visible (see Figure 28-17). Make sure that this is checked and then compile the application.

This component is quite similar to the VB6 version, apart from the way in which `Implements` is used. After this is all in place, build the assembly. If you have security issues with this compilation, then you need to ensure that you are running Visual Studio as an administrator. Now we come to the interesting part: How do you register the resulting assembly so that a COM-enabled application can make use of it?

RegAsm

The tool provided with the .NET Framework SDK to register assemblies for use by COM is called `RegAsm`. This tool is very simple to use. If all you are interested in is late binding, then you simply run it as presented in Figure 28-18. Make sure you've started the Command window as administrator.

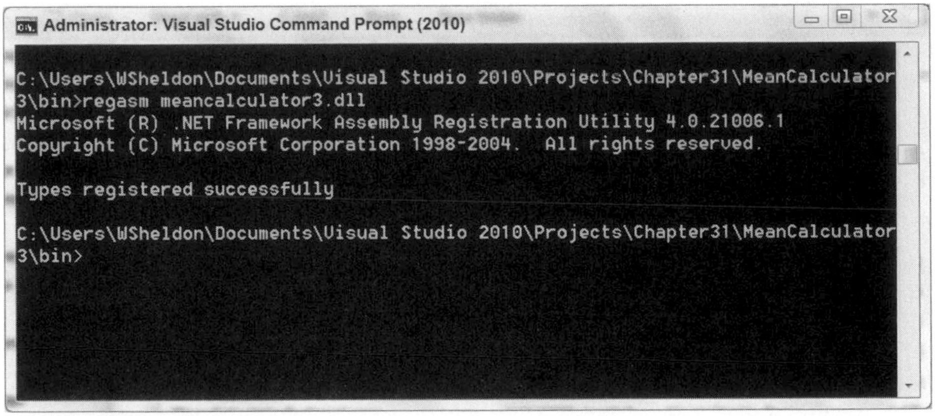

FIGURE 28-17

FIGURE 28-18

The only challenge with `RegAsm` is finding the thing. It is usually found lurking in %SystemRoot%\Microsoft.NET\Framework\<version> where version is the current .NET Framework version number. You might find it useful to add this to your path in the system environment. You can also use the Visual Studio command prompt (found in the Microsoft Visual Studio menu under Visual Studio Tools) to directly access this tool.

However, there is probably even less reason for late binding to an exported .NET component than there is for early binding, so we'll move on to look at early binding. For this, you need a type library, so add another parameter, `/tlb` as shown on the following line and in Figure 28-19:

```
C:\Users\[user name]\Documents\Visual Studio 2010\Projects\[Project Hierarchy]
\bin: regasm meancalculator3.dll /tlb:meancalculator3.tlb
```

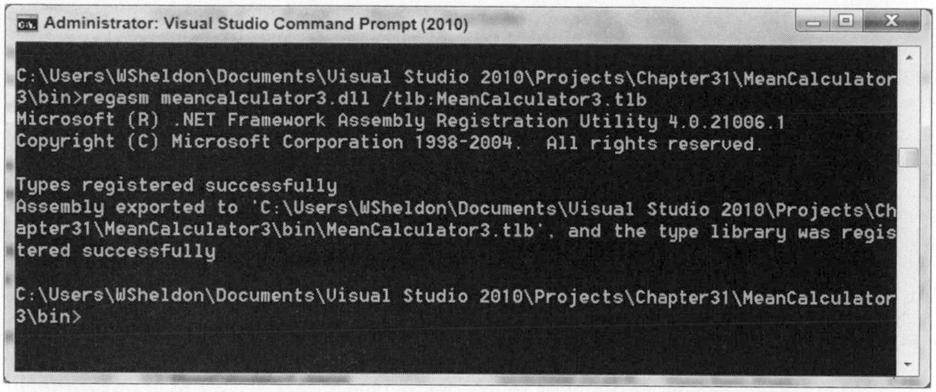

FIGURE 28-19

Now, when you look in the target directory, not only do you have the original MeanCalculator3.dll, you've also acquired a copy of the MegaCalculator2.dll and two type libraries: MeanCalculator3 .tlb and MegaCalculator2.tlb. You may need both of these if you need to register your new libraries on a machine not running .NET (for example a machine with only VB6 installed), so it was good of RegAsm to provide them for you. You need the MegaCalculator2 type library for the same reason that .NET needed the MegaCalculator assembly: because it contains the definition of the IMegaCalc interface that MeanCalculator is using, in this case in a format familiar to Regsvr32. Of course without .NET you still can't run your components on that machine, but you could have them in place for build purposes.

At that point it is simply a matter of creating a reference to your components in VB6 and running your application. Appendix B talks about the Interop libraries which were provided by the Visual Basic team to simplify this process even further, and if you are working to incorporate .NET capabilities with an existing COM based application it is suggested you refer to this section.

TlbExp

In fact, Microsoft provides you with not one, but *two* tools for registering .NET apps as COM objects. The other one is TlbExp, which, as its name suggests, is the counterpart of TlbImp. You can use TlbExp to achieve the same result as RegAsm in the previous section.

P/INVOKE

While up until now we've focused on interfacing with COM, it bears noting that .NET can also interoperate below the COM layer with traditional C/C++ DLLs. Since even with Windows 7 the core interfaces for Windows are provided outside of .NET and often unrelated to COM, you may find yourself wanting to implement a call to get at some operating system level feature. The P/Invoke interface allows .NET developers to make calls to existing or custom methods implemented in a traditional language. However, it is, to say the least, difficult.

I worked on a P/Invoke project for which we manually created each of the necessary interface definitions in order to support calls to external methods. To say that this was a painful process I would prefer to never repeat is an understatement. However, it was an effective way to access capabilities not provided by .NET.

Fortunately, Jarod Parsons, who was working with the Visual Basic team, has helped simplify this process for us. As part of the Visual Basic Team blog on MSDN, Jarod posted an excellent entry that refers to a tool that he helped create which will automatically find and generate P/Invoke proxies for you. You can find his blog post at http://blogs.msdn.com/vbteam/archive/2008/03/14/making-pinvoke-easy.aspx.

In addition to the blog post, Jarod introduces a tool for generating the P/Invoke signatures. The P/Invoke Interop Assistant enables you to find existing P/Invoke interfaces and automatically generate the necessary Visual Basic code to call these interfaces from your .NET application. The P/Invoke Interop Assistant is available as a free download from MSDN at http://code.msdn.microsoft.com/WindowsAPICodePack.

Windows API Code Pack

One more tool that is available to Visual Basic developers is the Windows API Code Pack for Microsoft .NET Framework. This is another free download from MSDN targeting operating system APIs, which aren't directly available from within the .NET Framework. In this case the authors have chosen to create a library which provides .NET classes to wrap the associated P/Invoke calls.

The code pack provides a C# library which you can reference from your Visual Basic project. You can then make calls to take advantage of things like the Windows 7 taskbar via this library. The library ships with several additional examples demonstrating how to use the various library classes to access different capabilities with the OS. You can download the files from MSDN at http://code.msdn.microsoft .com/WindowsAPICodePack

SUMMARY

Even with the migration to 64-bit environments, COM is not going to go away for quite some time, so .NET applications have to interoperate with COM, and they have to do it well. By the end of this chapter, you have achieved several things:

➤ You made a .NET application early bind to a COM component, using the import features available in Visual Basic.

➤ You looked at the underlying tool, TlbImp.

➤ You managed to make the application late bind as well, although it wasn't a pleasant experience.

➤ You incorporated an ActiveX control into a .NET user interface, again using the features of Visual Basic.

➤ You looked at using RegAsm and TlbExp to export type libraries from .NET assemblies in order to enable VB6 applications to use .NET assemblies as if they were COM components.

➤ Additional interop capabilities provided by P/Invoke were introduced along with two freely available tools which allow you to leverage these capabilities.

29

Network Programming

WHAT YOU WILL LEARN IN THIS CHAPTER

➤ Basic network programming topics

➤ Communicating with network servers using the classes of the System.Net namespace

➤ Creating sockets to create servers and clients

➤ Using Internet Explorer in your applications

Just as it is difficult to live your life without talking with people, your applications also need to communicate, perhaps with other programs or perhaps with hardware devices. As you have seen throughout this book, you can use a variety of techniques to have your program communicate, including Windows Communication Foundation (WCF), .NET Remoting, Web Services, and Enterprise Services. This chapter looks at yet another way to communicate: using the basic protocols on which the Internet and many networks have been built. You will learn how the classes in the System.Net namespace can provide a variety of techniques for communicating with existing applications such as Web or FTP servers, and how you can use them to create your own network applications.

Before starting to write applications using these classes, however, it would be good to get some background on how networks are bolted together, and how machines and applications are identified.

PROTOCOLS, ADDRESSES, AND PORTS

No discussion of a network is complete without a huge number of acronyms, seemingly random numbers, and the idea of a protocol. For example, the World Wide Web runs using a protocol called Hypertext Transfer Protocol (HTTP). Similarly, there is the File Transfer Protocol (FTP), the Network News Transfer Protocol (NNTP), and Gopher, among many others. Each application you run on a network communicates with another program using a defined protocol. The protocol is simply the expected messages each program will send the other, in the order they should be sent. For a real-world example, consider a scenario in which you want to go see a movie with a friend. A simplified conversation could look like this:

```
You: Dials phone
Friend: Hears phone ringing, answers phone. "Hello?"
You: "Hello. Want to go see 'Freddie and Jason Escape from New York, Part 6'?"
Friend: "No, I saw that one already. What about 'Star Warthogs'?"
```

```
You: "OK, 9:30 showing downtown?"
Friend: "Yes."
You: "Later."
Friend: "See you." Hangs up
```

Apart from a bad taste in movies, you can see a basic protocol here. Someone initiates a communication channel. The recipient accepts the channel and signals the start of the communication. The initial caller then sends a series of messages to which the recipient replies, either to signify they have been received or to indicate a positive or a negative response. Finally, one of the messages indicates the end of the communication channel, and the two disconnect.

Similarly, network applications have their own protocols; for example, sending an e-mail using SMTP (Simple Mail Transfer Protocol) could look like this:

```
220 schroedinger Microsoft ESMTP MAIL Service, Version: 6.0.2600.2180 ready at Wed,
6 Oct 2004 15:58:28 -0700
HELLO
250 schroedinger Hello [127.0.0.1]
FOO
500 5.3.3 Unrecognized command
MAIL FROM: me
250 2.1.0 me@schroedinger....Sender OK
RCPT TO: him
250 2.1.5 him@schroedinger
DATA
354 Start mail input; end with <CRLF>.<CRLF>
subject: Testing SMTP
Hello World, via mail.
.
250 2.6.0 <SCHROEDINGERKaq65r500000001@schroedinger> Queued mail for delivery
QUIT
221 2.0.0 schroedinger Service closing transmission channel
Connection to host lost.
```

In this case, lines beginning with numbers are coming from the server, while the items in uppercase (and the message itself) were sent from the client. If the client sends an invalid message (such as the FOO message in the preceding example), then it receives a gentle rebuff from the server, while correct messages receive the equivalent of an "OK" or "Go on" reply. Traditionally, for SMTP and many other protocols (including HTTP), the reply is a three-digit number (see Table 29-1) identifying the result of the request. The text after the number, such as 2.1.0 me@schroedinger . . . Sender OK, isn't really needed, and many servers attempt to be overly cute or clever here, so it isn't a good idea to assume anything about this text. The return values for the services generally fall into one of the five ranges shown in Table 29-1. Each range identifies a certain family of responses.

TABLE 29-1: Standard Response Ranges

RANGE	DESCRIPTION
100–199	Message is good, but the server is still working on the request.
200–299	Message is good, and the server has completed acting on the request.
300–399	Message is good, but the server needs more information to work on the request.
400–499	Message is good, but the server could not act on the request. You may try the request again to see whether it works in the future.
500–599	The server could not act on the request. Either the message was bad or an error occurred. It likely won't work next time.

Other protocols use these response ranges as well (leading to the infamous HTTP 404 error for "Page not found"), but they don't have to. Having a good reference is key to your success, and the best reference for existing protocols is the Request for Comments (RFC) for the protocol. These documents outline the definitions that are used by protocol authors to create their implementation of the standard. Many of these RFCs are available on the IETF (`www.ietf.org`) and the World Wide Web Consortium (`www.w3.org`) websites.

Addresses and Names

The next important topic necessary to a thorough understanding of network programming is the relationship between the names and addresses of each of the computers involved. Each form of network communication (such as TCP/IP networks like the Internet) has its own way of mapping the name of a computer (or host) to an address. The reason for this is simple: Computers deal with numbers better than text, and humans can remember text better than numbers (generally). Therefore, while you may have named your computer something clever like "l33t_#4x0R," applications and other computers know it by its IP (Internet Protocol) address.

The IP address is a 32-bit value, usually written in four parts (each one a byte that is a number from 0 to 255), such as 192.168.1.39. This is the standard on which the Internet has operated for many years. However, as only about four billion unique addresses are possible using this method, another standard, IPv6, has been proposed. It is called IPv6 because it is the sixth recommendation in the series (the older 32-bit addresses are often called IPv4 to differentiate them from this new standard). With IPv6, a 128-bit address is used, leading to a maximum number of about 3×10^{28} unique addresses, which should be more than enough for every Internet-enabled toaster.

This IP address (whether IPv4 or IPv6) must uniquely identify each host on a network (actually subnetwork, but we'll get to that). If not, messages will not be routed to their destination properly, and chaos will ensue. The matter gets more complicated when another 32-bit number, the subnet mask, enters the picture. This is a value that is masked (using a Boolean AND operation) over the address to identify the subnetwork of the network on which the computer resides. All addresses on the same subnetwork must be unique. Two subnetworks may have the same address, however, as long as their subnet masks are different.

Many common subnetworks use the value 255.255.255.0 for the subnet mask. When this is applied to the network address, as shown in the following example, only the last address is considered significant. Therefore, the subnetwork can include only 254 unique addresses (0 and 255 are used for other purposes).

```
Network address:     192.168. 1.107
Subnet Mask:         255.255.255. 0
Result:              192.168. 1. 0
```

Because computers and humans use two different means of identifying computers, there must be some way to relate the two. The term for this process is *name resolution*. In the case of the Internet, a common means of name resolution is yet another protocol, the Domain Naming System (DNS). A computer, when faced with an unknown text-based name, will send a message to the closest DNS server. It then determines whether it knows the IP address of that host. If it does, it passes this back to the requester. If not, it asks another DNS server it knows. This process continues until either the IP address is found or you run out of DNS servers. After the IP address is found, all of the servers (and the original computer) store that number for a while in case they are asked again.

Keeping in mind the problems that can ensue during name resolution can often solve many development problems. For example, if you are having difficulty communicating with a computer that should be responding, then it may be that your computer simply can't resolve the name of the remote computer. Try using the IP address instead. This removes any name-resolution problems from the equation, and may allow you to continue developing while someone else fixes the name-resolution problem.

Ports: They're Not Just for Ships

As described earlier, each computer or host on a network is uniquely identified by an address. How does your computer realize which of possibly many applications running are meant to receive a given message arriving on the network? This is determined by the port at which the message is targeted. The port is another number, in this case an integer value from 1 to 32,767. The unique combination of address and port identifies the target application.

For example, assume you currently have a Web server (IIS) running, as well as an SMTP server, and a few browser windows open. When a network message comes in, how does the operating system "know" which of these applications should receive the packet? Each of the applications (either client or server) that may receive a message is assigned a unique port number. In the case of servers, this is typically a fixed number, whereas client applications, such as your Web browser, are assigned a random available port.

To make communication with servers easier, they typically use a well-known assigned port. In the case of Web servers, this is port 80, while SMTP servers use port 25. You can see a list of common servers and their ports in the file `%windir%sudhasystem32sudhadriverssudhaetcsudhaservices`.

A small segment of this file appears as below:

```
smtp           25/tcp    mail                #Simple Mail Transfer Protocol
time           37/tcp    timserver
time           37/udp    timserver
rlp            39/udp    resource            #Resource Location Protocol
nameserver     42/tcp    name                #Host Name Server
nameserver     42/udp    name                #Host Name Server
nicname        43/tcp    whois
domain         53/tcp                        #Domain Name Server
domain         53/udp                        #Domain Name Server
bootps         67/udp    dhcps               #Bootstrap Protocol Server
bootpc         68/udp    dhcpc               #Bootstrap Protocol Client
tftp           69/udp                        #Trivial File Transfer
gopher         70/tcp
finger         79/tcp
http           80/tcp    www www-http        #World Wide Web
```

If you're writing a server application, then you can either use these common port numbers (and you should if you're attempting to write a common type of server) or choose your own. If you're writing a new type of server, then you should choose a port that has not been assigned to another server; choosing a port higher than 1024 should prevent any conflicts, as these are not assigned. When writing a client application, there is typically no need to assign a port, as a dynamic port is assigned to the client for communication with a server.

 Ports below 1024 should be considered secure ports, and applications that use them should have administrative access.

Firewalls: Can't Live with Them, Can't Live without Them

Many people have a love-hate relationship with firewalls. While they are invaluable in today's network, sometimes it would be nice if they got out of the way. A firewall is a piece of hardware or software that monitors network traffic, either incoming, outgoing, or both. It can be configured to allow only particular ports or applications to transmit information beyond it. Firewalls protect against hackers or viruses that may attempt to connect to open ports, leveraging them to their own ends. They protect against spyware applications that may attempt to communicate out from your machine. As a means of protecting the network, your computer(s) and your data, they are invaluable. However, they also "protect" against any network programming you may attempt to do. You must invariably cooperate with your network administrators, working within their guidelines for network access. If they make only certain ports available, then your applications should use only those ports. Alternately, you may be able to get them to configure the firewalls involved to permit the ports needed by your applications. Thankfully, creating network messages is a bit easier with Visual Basic 2010. The following sections demonstrate how.

THE SYSTEM.NET NAMESPACE

Most of the functionality used when writing network applications is contained within the `System.Net` and `System.Net.Sockets` namespaces. This chapter covers the following main classes in these namespaces:

➤   `WebRequest` and `WebResponse`, and their subclasses, including `FtpWebRequest`

➤   `WebClient`, the simplified `WebRequest` for common scenarios

➤   `HttpListener`, which enables you to create your own Web server

> *There are many more classes, methods, properties, and events included in the* `System .Net` *and* `System.Net.Sockets` *namespaces. You can locate the current reference for these namespaces at* `http://msdn.microsoft.com/library/system.net.aspx` *as of this writing.*

Web Requests (and Responses)

When most people think of network programming these days, they're really thinking of communication via a Web server or client. Therefore, it shouldn't be surprising that there is a set of classes for this communication need. In this case, it is the abstract `WebRequest` class and the associated `WebResponse`. These two classes represent the concept of a request/response communication with a Web server, or similar server. As these are abstract classes — that is, `MustInherit` classes — they cannot be created by themselves. Instead, you create the subclasses of `WebRequest` that are optimized for specific types of communication.

The most important properties and methods of the `WebRequest` class are shown in Table 29-2.

TABLE 29-2: Significant Properties and Methods of WebRequest

MEMBER	DESCRIPTION
Create	Method used to create a specific type of `WebRequest`. This method uses the URL (either as a string or as an Uri class) passed to identify and create a subclass of `WebRequest`.
GetRequestStream	Method that allows access to the outgoing request. This enables you to add additional information, such as `POST` data, to the request before sending.
GetResponse	Method used to perform the request and retrieve the corresponding `WebResponse` class.
Credentials	Property that enables you to set the user ID and password for the request if they are needed to perform it.
Headers	Property that enables you to change or add to the headers for the request.
Method	Property used to identify the action for the request, such as `GET` or `POST`. The list of available methods is specific to each type of server.
Proxy	Property that enables you to identify a proxy server for the communication if needed. You generally don't need to set this property, as Visual Basic 2010 detects the settings for Internet Explorer and uses them by default.
Timeout	Property that enables you to define the duration of the request before you "give up" on the server.

Each subclass of WebRequest supports these methods, providing a very consistent programming model for communication with a variety of server types. The basic model for working with any of the subclasses of WebRequest can be written in the following pseudo-code:

```
Declare variables as either WebRequest and WebResponse, or the specific child classes
Create the variable based on the URL
Make any changes to the Request object you may need
Use the GetResponse method to retrieve the response from the server
Get the Stream from the WebResponse
Do something with the Stream
```

If you decide to change the protocol (e.g., from HTTP to a file-based protocol), then you may only need to change the URL used to retrieve the object.

WebRequest Child Classes

Three of the commonly used types of WebRequest in the .NET Framework are FileWebRequest, FtpWebRequest, and HttpWebRequest. FileWebRequest is used infrequently; it represents a request to a local file, using the "file://" URL format. You have likely seen this type of request if you attempted to open a local file using your Web browser. FtpWebRequest is used to work with FTP servers. As such, it supports a number of methods for querying the FTP server to locate and create files and directories. Generally, however, the subclass most developers will use is HttpWebRequest. This class enables you to make HTTP requests to a Web server without requiring a browser. This could enable you to communicate with a Web server, or, using the time-honored tradition of "screen scraping," to retrieve data available on the Web.

One hurdle many developers encounter when first working with HttpWebRequest is that there is no available constructor. Instead, you must use the WebRequest.Create method (or the Create method of your desired subclass) to create new instances of any of the subclasses. This method uses the URL requested to create the appropriate subtype of WebRequest. For example, this would create a new HttpWebRequest:

```
Imports System.Net //earlier in the class/module
Dim req As HttpWebRequest = WebRequest.Create("http://msdn.microsoft.com")
```

Note that if you have Option Strict turned on (and you should), the preceding code will produce an error. Instead, you should explicitly cast the return value of Create to the desired type:

```
Dim req As HttpWebRequest =
  DirectCast(WebRequest.Create("http://msdn.microsoft.com"),
  System.Net.HttpWebRequest)
```

Putting It Together

In order to demonstrate how to use WebRequest/WebResponse, the following example (DefinePad in the download) shows how to wrap a Web call into a Visual Basic class. In this case, we'll wrap Google's define: keyword, which enables you to retrieve a set of definitions for a word (e.g., www.google.com/search?q = define%3A + protocol), and then use that in a sample application.

When creating a Windows Forms application with Visual Studio 2010, it sets the Target Framework for the application to the .NET Framework 4 Client Profile. In order to add a reference to System.Web, you need to change this to the .NET Framework 4 profile. You set this by selecting the Advanced Compile Options (see Figure 29-1) on the Compile tab of the project's properties.

1. Create a new Windows Forms Application project named "DefinePad."

2. Add a new class to the project by right-clicking the project and selecting Add > Class. This will hold the actual WebRequest code. Call it GoogleClient.

3. Add a reference to the System.Web DLL, as you will need access to some of its functionality later.

4. In the GoogleClient.vb file, add Imports statements to make the coding a little briefer:

   ```
   Imports System.IO
   Imports System.Net
   Imports System.Web
   Imports System.Collections.Generic
   ```

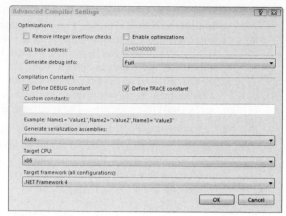

FIGURE 29-1

Available for download on Wrox.com

5. The main function in GoogleClient will be a Define function that returns an array of strings. Each string will be one definition returned by Google:

```vb
Public Function Define(ByVal word As String) As String()
    Dim req As HttpWebRequest = Nothing
    Dim resp As HttpWebResponse
    Dim query As String
    Dim result As New List(Of String)
    query = "http://www.google.com/search?q=define%3A" & _
        HttpUtility.UrlEncode(word)
    Try
        req = DirectCast(WebRequest.Create(query), HttpWebRequest)
        With req
            .Method = "GET"
            resp = req.GetResponse
            If resp.StatusCode = HttpStatusCode.OK Then
                ParseResponse(resp.GetResponseStream, result)
            Else
                MessageBox.Show("Error calling definition service")
            End If
        End With
    Catch ex As Exception
    End Try
    Return result.ToArray()
End Function
```

Code snippet from DefinePad

The first task is to guarantee that no invalid characters appear in the query string when you send the request, such as a space, an accented character, or other non-ASCII characters. The System.Web.HttpUtility class has a number of handy shared methods for encoding strings, including the UrlEncode method. This replaces characters with a safe representation of the character that looks like %value, where the value is the Unicode code for the character. For example, in the definition of the query variable above, the %3A is actually the colon character (":"), which has been encoded. Anytime you retrieve a URL based on user input, encode it because there is no guarantee the resulting URL is safe to send.

Once the query is ready, you create the WebRequest. As the URL is for an HTTP resource, an HttpWebRequest is created. While the default method for WebRequest is a GET, it's still good practice to set it. You'll create the ParseResponse method shortly to process the stream returned from the server.

One other piece of code worth mentioning is the return value for this method, and how it is created. In order to return arrays of a specific type (rather than return actual collections from a method), you must either know the actual size to initialize the array or use the `List` generic type or the older `ArrayList`. These classes behave like the Visual Basic 6.0 `Collection` class, which enables you to add items, and grows as needed. They also have a handy method that enables you to convert the array into an array of any type; you can see this in the return statement. The `ArrayList` requires you to do a bit more work. If you want to use an `ArrayList` for this method, then you must identify the type of array you'd like to return. The resulting return statement would look like this using an `ArrayList`:

```
Return result.ToArray(GetType(String))
```

6. The `ProcessRequest` method parses the stream returned from the server and converts it into an array of items. Note that this is slightly simplified; in a real application, you would likely want to return an array of objects, where each object provides access to the definition and the URL of the site providing it:

```
Private Sub ParseResponse (ByVal input As System.IO.Stream, _
  ByRef output As List(Of String))
        'definitions are in a block beginning with <p>Definitions for...
        'then are marked with <li> tags

Dim reader As New StreamReader(input)
        Dim work As String = reader.ReadToEnd
        Dim blockStart As String = "<p>Definitions of"
        Dim pos As Integer = work.IndexOf(blockStart)
        Dim posEnd As Integer
        Dim temp As String
    Do
        pos = work.IndexOf("<li>", pos + 1)
        If pos > 0 Then
            posEnd = work.IndexOf("<br>", pos)
            temp = work.Substring(pos + 4, posEnd - pos - 4)
            output.Add(ParseDefinition(temp))
            pos = posEnd + 1
        End If
    Loop While pos > 0
End Sub
```

Code snippet from DefinePad

The code is fairly simple, using the time-honored tradition of *screen scraping* — processing the HTML of a page to find the section you need and then removing the HTML to produce the result.

7. The last part of the `GoogleClient` class is the `ParseDefinition` method that cleans up the definition, removing the link and other HTML tags:

```
Private Function ParseDefinition(ByVal input As String) As String
    Dim result As String = ""
        Dim lineBreak As Integer
        lineBreak = input.IndexOf("<br>")
        If lineBreak > 0 Then
            result = input.Substring(0, input.IndexOf("<br>"))
        Else
            result = input
        End If
        Return result.Trim
    End Function
```

Code snippet from DefinePad

8. Now, with the class in hand, you can create a client to use it. In this case, you'll create a simple text editor that adds the capability to retrieve definitions for words. Go back to the form created for the application and add controls as shown in Figure 29-2.

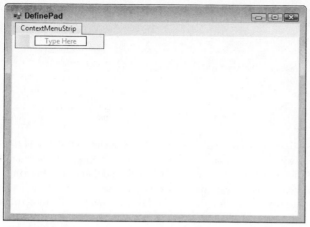

FIGURE 29-2

9. The user interface for DefinePad is simple: a `TextBox` and a `ContextMenuStrip`. Set the properties as shown in the following table:

CONTROL	PROPERTY	VALUE
TextBox	Name	TextField
	Multiline	True
	Dock	Fill
	ContextMenuStrip	DefinitionMenu
ContextMenuStrip	Name	DefinitionMenu

10. The only code in the form is for the `Opening` event of the `ContextMenuStrip`. Here, you add the definitions to the menu. Add the following code to the handler for the `Opening` event:

```vb
Private Sub DefinitionMenu_Opening(ByVal sender As Object, _
  ByVal e As System.ComponentModel.CancelEventArgs) _
  Handles DefinitionMenu.Opening
    Dim svc As New GoogleClient
    Dim definitions() As String
    Dim definitionCount As Integer
    DefinitionMenu.Items.Clear()
    Try
        'define the currently selected word
        If TextField.SelectionLength > 0 Then
            definitions = svc.Define(TextField.SelectedText)
            'build context menu of returned definitions
            definitionCount = definitions.Length
            If definitionCount > 6 Then
                definitionCount = 6
            ElseIf definitionCount = 0 Then
                'we can't do any more, so exit
                Dim item As New ToolStripButton
                item.Text = "Sorry, no definitions available"
                DefinitionMenu.Items.Add(item)
                Exit Sub
            End If
            For i As Integer = 1 To definitionCount
                Dim item As New ToolStripButton
```

```
                    item.Text = definitions(i-1)
                    DefinitionMenu.Items.Add(item)
                Next
            End If
        Catch ex As Exception
            MessageBox.Show(ex.Message, "Error getting definitions",
                MessageBoxButtons.OK, MessageBoxIcon.Error)
        End Try
    End Sub
```

Code snippet from DefinePad

The bulk of the code in this event is to limit the number of items displayed in the menu. The actual functional part of the routine is the call to the `Define` method of the `GoogleClient`. If you trace through the code as it runs, you'll see the `WebRequest` generated, the call made, and the resulting response stream parsed into the individual items as desired. Finally, you can use the returned list to create a set of menu items (that don't actually do anything), and display the "menu." Clicking on any definition closes the menu.

11. To test the application, run it. Type or copy some text into the text box, select a word, and right-click on it. After a brief pause, you should see the definitions for the word (Figure 29-3 shows definitions of "protocol").

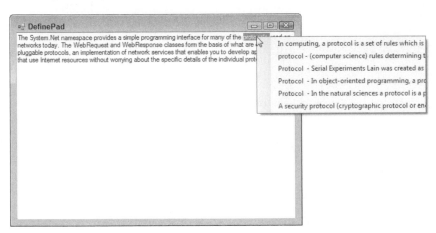

FIGURE 29-3

While it isn't as sexy as Web services, using this technique (`WebRequest`, screen scraping of the resulting HTML) can provide access to a great deal of the Internet's functionality for your applications.

Simplifying Common Web Requests with WebClient

When I first saw a demo of `WebRequest` class in early 2000, I was delighted. Here was the capability to easily access Internet resources. However, one of the other attendees of the demo asked, "Why is that so difficult? You need to do so much to get it to work." The next time I saw the same `WebRequest` demo, the presenter concluded with, "For those of you doing the common scenarios, we have an even easier way." He then went on to show us how to use `System.Net.WebClient`.

For those times when you just want to send a GET or POST request and download a file or the resulting data, you can forget about `WebRequest`/`WebResponse`. `WebClient` abstracts away all of the little details of making Web requests, and makes it amazingly easy to grab data from the Web. It does this by abstracting out the most commonly used tasks people perform with `WebRequest`/`WebResponse`. The `WebClient` class includes methods for uploading and downloading data, strings, and files.

All of the `DownloadX` and `UploadX` methods also support an asynchronous version of the method, called `DownloadXAsync`, such as `DownloadFileAsync` or `UploadValuesAsync`. These methods perform the actual request on a background thread, and fire an event when the task is completed. If your application has some form of user interface, such as a form, then you should generally use these methods to keep your application responsive.

As the `WebClient` class uses the `WebRequest` classes to actually perform its magic, it can greatly simplify network coding. For example, just replace the code used in the `WebRequest` sample created earlier.

Before:

```
Public Function Define(ByVal word As String) As String()
    Dim req As HttpWebRequest = Nothing
    Dim resp As HttpWebResponse
    Dim query As String
    Dim result As New List(Of String)
    query = "http://www.google.com/search?q=define%3A" &
      HttpUtility.UrlEncode(word)
    Try
        req = DirectCast(WebRequest.Create(query), HttpWebRequest)
        With req
            .Method = "GET"
            resp = req.GetResponse
            If resp.StatusCode = HttpStatusCode.OK Then
                ParseResponse(resp.GetResponseStream, result)
            Else
                MessageBox.Show("Error calling definition service")
            End If
        End With
    Catch ex As Exception
    End Try
    Return result.ToArray()
End Function
```

Code snippet from DefinePad

After:

```
Public Function Define(ByVal word As String) As String()
    Dim client As New WebClient
    Dim query As String
    Dim result As New List(Of String)
    query = "http://www.google.com/search?q=define%3A" &
      HttpUtility.UrlEncode(word)
    Try
        result = ParseResponse(client.DownloadString(query))
    Catch ex As Exception
    End Try
    Return result.ToArray()
End Function
Private Function ParseResponse(ByVal data As String) As List(Of String)
    Dim result As New List(Of String)

    Dim blockStart As String = "<p>Definitions of"
    Dim pos As Integer = data.IndexOf(blockStart)
    Dim posEnd As Integer
    Dim temp As String
    Do
        pos = data.IndexOf("<li>", pos + 1)
        If pos > 0 Then
            posEnd = data.IndexOf("<br>", pos)
            temp = data.Substring(pos + 4, posEnd - pos - 4)
            result.Add(ParseDefinition(temp))
```

```
                    pos = posEnd + 1
            End If
        Loop While pos > 0

        Return result
    End Function
```

Code snippet from DefinePad

`WebClient` avoids all of the stream handling required for `WebRequest`. However, you should still know how `WebRequest` operates, as this knowledge is directly relatable to `WebClient`.

SOCKETS

There may be times when you need to transfer data across a network (either a private network or the Internet) but the existing techniques and protocols do not exactly suit your needs. For example, you cannot download resources using the techniques discussed earlier in this chapter, and you cannot use Windows Communication Foundation, Web services, or remoting. In these cases, the best course of action is to roll your own protocol using *sockets*.

TCP/IP and, therefore, the Internet itself are based on sockets. The principle is simple: Establish a port at one end and allow clients to "plug in" to that port from the other end. Once the connection is made, applications can send and receive data through a stream. For example, HTTP nearly always operates on port 80, so a Web server opens a socket on port 80 and waits for incoming connections (Web browsers, unless told otherwise, attempt to connect to port 80 in order to make a request of that Web server).

In .NET, sockets are implemented in the `System.Net.Sockets` namespace and use classes from `System.Net` and `System.IO` to get the stream classes. Although working with sockets can be a little tricky outside of .NET, the framework includes classes that enable you to open a socket for inbound connections (`System.Net` `.TcpListener`) and for communication between two open sockets (`System.Net.TcpClient`). These two classes, in combination with some threading shenanigans, enable you to build your own protocol through which you can send any data you like. With your own protocol, you have ultimate control over the communication.

To demonstrate these techniques, you are going to build Wrox Messenger, a very basic instant messenger application similar to MSN Messenger.

Building the Application

You will wrap all the functionality of your application into a single Windows application, which will act as both a server that waits for inbound connections and a client that has established outbound connections.

Create a new Windows Forms Application project called "WroxMessenger." Change the title of `Form1` to Wrox Messenger and add a `TextBox` control called `ConnectToField` and a `Button` control called `ConnectButton`. Set the name of the form to `ConnectForm`. The form should appear as shown in Figure 29-4.

FIGURE 29-4

You will learn more about this in greater detail later, but for now it is very important that all of your UI code runs in the same thread, and that the thread is actually the main application that creates and runs your form.

To keep track of what is happening, you will add a field to the form that enables you to store the ID of the startup thread and report that ID on the caption. This helps provide a context for the thread/UI issues discussed later. You also need some namespace imports and a constant specifying the ID of the default port. Add the following code to your form:

```
Imports System.Net
Imports System.Net.Sockets
Imports System.Threading
Public Class ConnectForm
```

```
Private Shared _mainThreadId As Integer
Public Const ServicePort As Integer = 10101
```

Code snippet from WroxMessenger

Next, create a New method for the form and add this code to the constructor that populates the field and changes the caption:

Available for
download on
Wrox.com

```
Public Sub New()
    ' This call is required by the Windows Form Designer.
    InitializeComponent()
    ' Add any initialization after the InitializeComponent() call.
    _mainThreadId = System.Threading.Thread.CurrentThread.GetHashCode()
    Text &= "-" & _mainThreadId.ToString()
End Sub
```

Code snippet from WroxMessenger

To listen for incoming connections, you will create a separate class called Listener. This class uses an instance of System.Net.Sockets.TcpListener to wait for incoming connections. Specifically, it opens a TCP port that *any* client can connect to — sockets are not platform-specific. Although connections are always made on a specific, known port, the actual communication takes place on a port of the TCP/IP subsystem's choosing, which means you can support many inbound connections at once, despite the fact that each of them connects to the same port. Sockets are an open standard available on pretty much any platform. For example, if you publish the specification for your protocol, then developers working on Linux can connect to your Wrox Messenger service.

When you detect an inbound connection, you are given a System.Net.Sockets.TcpClient object. This is your gateway to the remote client. To send and receive data, you need to obtain a System.Net.NetworkStream object (returned through a call to GetStream on TcpClient), which returns a stream that you can use.

Create a new class called Listener. This thread needs members to hold an instance of a System.Threading .Thread object, and a reference back to the ConnectForm class that is the main form in the application. Not covered here is how to spin up and down threads, or synchronization. (Refer to Chapter 33 if you need more information about that.)

Here is the basic code for the Listener class:

Available for
download on
Wrox.com

```
Imports System.Net.Sockets
Imports System.Threading
Imports System.Net

Public Class Listener
    Implements IDisposable

    Private main As ConnectForm
    Private listener As TcpListener
    Private thread As Thread
    Public Sub New(ByVal main As ConnectForm)
        main = main
    End Sub
    Public Sub SpinUp()
        ' create and start the new thread...
        thread = New Thread(AddressOf ThreadEntryPoint)
        thread.Start()
    End Sub End Class
```

Code snippet from WroxMessenger

The obvious missing method here is ThreadEntryPoint. This is where you need to create the socket and wait for inbound connections. When you get them, you are given a TcpClient object, which you pass back to your form, where the conversation window can be created. You create this method in the Listener.vb class file.

To create the socket, create an instance of TcpListener and give it a port. In your application, the port you are going to use is 10101. This port should be free on your computer, but if the debugger breaks on an exception when you instantiate TcpListener or call Start, then try another port. Once you have done that and called Start to configure the object to listen for connections, you drop into an infinite loop and call AcceptTcpClient. This method blocks until the socket is closed or a connection becomes available. If you get Nothing back, then either the socket is closed or there is a problem, so you drop out of the thread. If you get something back, then you pass the TcpClient over to your form through a call to the (not yet built) ReceiveInboundConnection method. Add this new method to the Listener class you created earlier:

```
' ThreadEntryPoint...
Protected Sub ThreadEntryPoint()
    ' Create a socket...
    listener = New TcpListener(IPAddress.Loopback, ConnectForm.ServicePort)
    listener.Start()
    ' Loop infinitely, waiting for connections.
    Try
        Do While True
            ' Get a connection...
            Dim client As TcpClient = listener.AcceptTcpClient()
            If client Is Nothing Then
                Exit Do
            End If
            ' Process it...
            main.ReceiveInboundConnection(client)
        Loop
    Catch
        'eat any exceptions
    End Try
End Sub
```

Code snippet from WroxMessenger

It is in the ReceiveInboundConnection method that you create the Conversation form that the user can use to send messages. You'll add this method to the form shortly.

Creating Conversation Windows

When building Windows Forms applications that support threading, there is always the possibility of running into a problem with the Windows messaging subsystem. This is a very old part of Windows that powers the Windows user interface (the idea has been around since version 1.0 of the platform, although the implementation on modern Windows versions is far removed from the original).

Even those who are not familiar with old-school Windows programming, such as MFC, Win32, or even Win16 development, should be familiar with events. When you move a mouse over a form, you get MouseMove events. When you close a form, you get a Closed event. There is a mapping between these events and the messages that Windows passes around to support the actual display of the windows. For example, whenever you receive a MouseMove event, a message called WM_MOUSEMOVE is sent to the window by Windows, in response to the mouse driver. In .NET and other rapid application development (RAD) environments such as Visual Basic and Delphi, this message is converted into an event that you can write code against.

Although this is getting way off the topic — you know how to build Windows Forms applications by now and don't need the details of messages such as WM_NCHITTEST or WM_PAINT — it has an important implication. In effect, Windows creates a message queue for each thread into which it posts the messages that the thread's windows have to work with. This queue is looped on a virtually constant basis, and the messages are distributed to the appropriate window (remember that small controls such as buttons and text boxes are also windows). In .NET, these messages are turned into events, but unless the message queue is looped, the messages do not get through.

Suppose Windows needs to paint a window. It posts a `WM_PAINT` message to the queue. A message loop implemented on the main thread of the process containing the window detects the message and dispatches it on to the appropriate window, where it is processed. Now suppose that the queue is not looped. The message is never picked up and the window is never painted.

In a Windows application, a single thread is usually responsible for message dispatch. This thread is typically (but not necessarily) the main application thread — the one that is created when the process is first created. If you create windows in a different thread, then that new thread has to support the message dispatch loop so that messages destined for the windows get through. However, with `Listener`, you have no code for processing the message loop, and there is little point in writing any because the next time you call `AcceptTcpClient`, you are going to block, and everything will stop working.

The trick, therefore, is to create the windows only in the main application thread, which is the thread that created `ConnectForm` and is processing the messages for all the windows created in this thread. You can pass calls from one thread to the other by calling the `Invoke` method of `ConnectForm`.

This is where things start to get complicated. There is a very lot of code to write to get to a point where you can see that the socket connection has been established and get conversation windows to appear. Here is what you need to do:

- ➤ Create a new Conversation form. This form needs controls for displaying the total content of the conversation, plus a `TextBox` control for adding new messages.
- ➤ The Conversation window needs to be able to send and receive messages through its own thread.
- ➤ `ConnectForm` needs to be able to initiate new connections. This will be done in a separate thread that is managed by the thread pool. When the connection has been established, a new Conversation window needs to be created and configured.
- ➤ `ConnectForm` also needs to receive inbound connections. When it gets one of these, a new conversation must be created and configured.

Let's look at each of these challenges.

Creating the Conversation Form

The simplest place to start is to build the new conversation form (creatively named `ConversationForm`), which needs three `TextBox` controls (`UsernameField`, `AllMessagesField`, and `MessageField` in order on the form) and a `Button` control (`SendButton`), as shown in Figure 29-5. The `AllMessagesField` and `MessageField` are both configured with `Multiline=True`.

This class requires a number of fields and an enumeration. It needs fields to hold the username of the user (which you will default to `Foo`), the underlying `TcpClient`, and the `NetworkStream` returned by that client. The enumeration indicates the direction of the connection (which will help you when debugging):

FIGURE 29-5

Available for download on Wrox.com

```
Imports System.Net
Imports System.Net.Sockets
Imports System.Text
Imports System.Threading
Imports System.Runtime.Serialization.Formatters.Binary
Public Class ConversationForm
    Private _username As String = "Foo"
    Private _client As TcpClient
    Private _stream As NetworkStream
    Private _direction As ConversationDirection
```

```
Public Enum ConversationDirection As Integer
    Inbound = 0
    Outbound = 1
End Enum
```

At this point, we won't look into the issues surrounding establishing a thread for exchanging messages, but we will look at implementing the ConfigureClient method. This method eventually does more work than this, but for now it sets a couple of fields and calls UpdateCaption:

```
Public Sub ConfigureClient(ByVal client As TcpClient, _
            ByVal direction As ConversationDirection)
    ' Set it up...
    _client = client
    _direction = direction
    ' Update the window...
    UpdateCaption()
End Sub
Protected Sub UpdateCaption()
    ' Set the text.
    Dim builder As New StringBuilder(_username)
    builder.Append(" - ")
    builder.Append(_direction.ToString())
    builder.Append(" - ")
    builder.Append(Thread.CurrentThread.GetHashCode())
    builder.Append(" - ")
    If Not _client Is Nothing Then
        builder.Append("Connected")
    Else
        builder.Append("Not connected")
    End If
    Text = builder.ToString()
End Sub
```

Note a debugging issue to deal with: If you are connecting to a conversation on the same machine, then you need a way to change the name of the user sending each message; otherwise, things get confusing. That is what the topmost TextBox control is for. In the constructor, set the text for the UsernameField.Text property:

```
Public Sub New()
    ' This call is required by the Windows Form Designer.
    InitializeComponent()
    ' Add any initialization after the InitializeComponent() call.
    UsernameField.Text = _username
End Sub
```

On the TextChanged event for this control, update the caption and the internal _username field:

```
Private Sub UsernameField_TextChanged(ByVal sender As System.Object,
                ByVal e As System.EventArgs) _
                Handles UsernameField.TextChanged
    _username = UsernameField.Text
    UpdateCaption()
End Sub
```

Initiating Connections

The `ConnectForm` needs to be able to both initiate connections and receive inbound connections — the application is both a client and a server. You have already created some of the server portion by creating `Listener`; now you will look at the client side.

The general rule when working with sockets is that anytime you send anything over the wire, you must perform the actual communication in a separate thread. Virtually all calls to send and receive do so in a blocking manner; that is, they block until data is received, block until all data is sent, and so on.

If threads are used well, then the UI will keep running as normal, irrespective of the problems that may occur during transmitting and receiving. This is why in the `InitiateConnection` method on the `ConnectForm`, you defer processing to another method called `InitiateConnectionThreadEntryPoint`, which is called from a new thread:. Add this method to the code for the `ConnectForm`:

Available for
download on
Wrox.com

```vbnet
Private Sub InitiateConnectionThreadEntryPoint(ByVal state As Object)
    Try
        ' Get the host name...
        Dim hostName As String = CStr(state)
        ' Resolve...
        Dim hostEntry As IPHostEntry = Dns.GetHostEntry(hostName)
        If Not hostEntry Is Nothing Then
            ' Create an end point for the first address.
            Dim endPoint As New IPEndPoint(hostEntry.AddressList(0), ServicePort)
            ' Create a TCP client...
            Dim client As New TcpClient()
            client.Connect(endPoint)
            ' Create the connection window...
            ProcessOutboundConnection(client)
        Else
            Throw New ApplicationException("Host '" & hostName & _
                "' could not be resolved.")
        End If
    Catch ex As Exception
        HandleInitiateConnectionException(ex)
    End Try
End Sub
```

Code snippet from WroxMessenger

Inside the thread, you try to convert the hostname that you are given into an IP address (localhost is used as the hostname in the demonstration, but it could be the name of a machine on the local network or a hostname on the Internet). This is done through the shared `GetHostEntry` method on `System.Net.Dns`, and returns a `System.Net.IPHostEntry` object. Because a hostname can point to multiple IP addresses, you will just use the first one that you are given. You take this address expressed as an IP (for example, 192.168.0.4) and combine it with the port number to get a new `System.Net.IPEndPoint`. Then you create a new `TcpClient` from this `IPEndPoint` and try to connect.

If at any time an exception is thrown (which can happen because the name could not be resolved or the connection could not be established), you pass the exception to `HandleInitiateConnectionException`. If it succeeds, then you pass it to `ProcessOutboundConnection`. Both of these methods will be implemented shortly:

Available for
download on
Wrox.com

```vbnet
Private Sub InitiateConnectionThreadEntryPoint(ByVal state As Object)
    Try
        ' Get the host name...
        Dim hostName As String = CStr(state)
        ' Resolve...
        Dim hostEntry As IPHostEntry = Dns.GetHostEntry(hostName)
        If Not hostEntry Is Nothing Then
            ' Create an end point for the first address.
```

```
            Dim endPoint As New IPEndPoint(hostEntry.AddressList(0), ServicePort)
            ' Create a TCP client...
            Dim client As New TcpClient()
            client.Connect(endPoint)
            ' Create the connection window...
            ProcessOutboundConnection(client)
        Else
            Throw New ApplicationException("Host '" & hostName & _
                "' could not be resolved.")
        End If
    Catch ex As Exception
        HandleInitiateConnectionException(ex)
    End Try
End Sub
```

Code snippet from WroxMessenger

When it comes to `HandleInitiateConnectionException`, you start to see the inter-thread UI problems that were mentioned earlier. When there is a problem with the exception, you need to tell the user, which means you need to move the exception from the thread-pool-managed thread into the main application thread. The principle for this is the same; you need to create a delegate and call that delegate through the form's `Invoke` method. This method does all the hard work in marshaling the call across to the other thread.

Here is what the delegates look like. They have the same parameters as the calls themselves. As a naming convention, it is a good idea to use the same name as the method and tack the word "Delegate" on the end:

Available for download on Wrox.com

```
Public Class ConnectForm
    Private Shared _mainThreadId As Integer
    ' delegates...
    Protected Delegate Sub HandleInitiateConnectionExceptionDelegate( _
                                        ByVal ex As Exception)
```

Code snippet from WroxMessenger

In the constructor for `ConnectForm`, you capture the thread caller's thread ID and store it in `_mainThreadId`. Here is a method that compares the captured ID with the ID of the current thread:

Available for download on Wrox.com

```
Public Shared Function IsMainThread() As Boolean
    If Thread.CurrentThread.GetHashCode() = _mainThreadId Then
        Return True
    Else
        Return False
    End If
End Function
```

Code snippet from WroxMessenger

The first thing you do at the top of `HandleInitiateConnectionException` is check the thread ID. If it does not match, then you create the delegate and call it. Notice that you set the delegate to call back into the same method because the second time it is called, you would have moved to the main thread; therefore, `IsMainThread` returns `True`, and you can process the exception properly:

Available for download on Wrox.com

```
Protected Sub HandleInitiateConnectionException(ByVal ex As Exception)
    ' main thread?
    If IsMainThread() = False Then
        ' Create and call...
        Dim args(0) As Object
        args(0) = ex
        Invoke(New HandleInitiateConnectionExceptionDelegate(AddressOf _
            HandleInitiateConnectionException), args)

        ' return
```

```
        Return
    End If
    ' Show it.
    MessageBox.Show(ex.GetType().ToString() & ":" & ex.Message)
End Sub
```

The result is that when the call comes in from the thread-pool-managed thread, `IsMainThread` returns `False`, and the delegate is created and called. When the method is entered again as a result of the delegate call, `IsMainThread` returns `True`, and you see the message box.

When it comes to `ProcessOutboundConnection`, you have to again jump into the main UI thread. However, the magic behind this method is implemented in a separate method called `Process-Connection`, which can handle either inbound or outbound connections. Here is the delegate:

```
Public Class ConnectForm
    Private Shared _mainThreadId As Integer
    Private _listener As Listener
    Protected Delegate Sub ProcessConnectionDelegate(ByVal client As _
        TcpClient, ByVal direction As ConversationForm.ConversationDirection)
    Protected Delegate Sub HandleInitiateConnectionExceptionDelegate(ByVal _
        ex As Exception)
```

Here is the method itself, which creates the new conversation form and calls the `ConfigureClient` method:

```
Protected Sub ProcessConnection(ByVal client As TcpClient, _
    ByVal direction As ConversationForm.ConversationDirection)
    ' Do you have to move to another thread?
    If IsMainThread() = False Then
        ' Create and call...
        Dim args(1) As Object
        args(0) = client
        args(1) = direction
        Invoke(New ProcessConnectionDelegate(AddressOf ProcessConnection), args)
        Return
    End If

    ' Create the conversation window...
    Dim conversation As New ConversationForm()
    conversation.Show()
    conversation.ConfigureClient(client, direction)
End Sub
```

Of course, `ProcessOutboundConnection` needs to defer to `ProcessConnection`:

```
Public Sub ProcessOutboundConnection(ByVal client As TcpClient)
    ProcessConnection(client, ConversationForm.ConversationDirection.Outbound)
End Sub
```

Now that you can connect to something on the client side, let's look at how to receive connections (on the server side).

Receiving Inbound Connections

You have already built `Listener`, but you have not created an instance of it or spun up its thread to wait for incoming connections. To do that, you need a field in `ConnectForm` to hold an instance of the object. You also need to tweak the constructor. Here is the field:

```
Public Class ConnectForm
    Private _mainThreadId As Integer
    Private _listener As Listener
```

Here is the new code that needs to be added to the constructor:

```
Public Sub New()
    ' This call is required by the Windows Form Designer.
    InitializeComponent()
    ' Add any initialization after the InitializeComponent() call.
    _mainThreadId = System.Threading.Thread.CurrentThread.GetHashCode()
    Text &= "-" & _mainThreadId.ToString()
    ' listener...
    _listener = New Listener(Me)
    _listener.SpinUp()
End Sub
```

Code snippet from WroxMessenger

When inbound connections are received, you get a new `TcpClient` object. This is passed back to `ConnectForm` through the `ReceiveInboundConnection` method. This method, like `ProcessOutboundConnection`, defers to `ProcessConnection`. Because `ProcessConnection` already handles the issue of moving the call to the main application thread, `ReceiveInboundConnection` looks like this:

```
Public Sub ReceiveInboundConnection(ByVal client As TcpClient)
    ProcessConnection(client, ConversationForm.ConversationDirection.Inbound)
End Sub
```

Code snippet from WroxMessenger

If you run the project now, you should be able to click the Connect button and see two windows — Inbound and Outbound (see Figure 29-6).

If you close all three windows, the application keeps running because you have not written code to close down the listener thread, and having an open thread like this keeps the application open. Select Debug ⇨ Stop Debugging in Visual Studio to close the application down by killing all running threads.

By clicking the Connect button, you are calling `InitiateConnection`. This spins up a new thread in the pool that resolves the given hostname (localhost) into an IP address. This IP address, in combination with a port number, is then used in the creation of a `TcpClient` object. If the connection can be made, then `ProcessOutboundConnection` is called, which results in the first of the conversation windows being created and marked as "outbound."

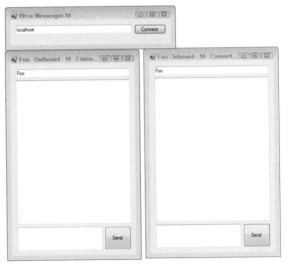

FIGURE 29-6

This example is somewhat artificial, as the two instances of Wrox Messenger should be running on separate computers. On the remote computer (if you are connecting to localhost, this will be the same computer), a connection is received through the `AcceptTcpClient` method of `TcpListener`. This results in a call to `ReceiveInboundConnection`, which in turn results in the creation of the second conversation window, this time marked as "inbound."

Sending Messages

The next step is to determine how to exchange messages between the two conversation windows. You already have a `TcpClient` in each case, so all you have to do is send binary data down the wire on one side and pick it up at the other end. The two conversation windows act as both client and server, so both need to be able to send and receive.

You have three challenges to meet:

➤ You need to establish one thread to send data and another thread to receive data.

➤ Data sent and received needs to be reported back to the user so that he or she can follow the conversation.

➤ The data that you want to send has to be converted into a wire-ready format, which in .NET terms usually means serialization.

The power of sockets enables you to define whatever protocol you like for data transmission. If you wanted to build your own SMTP server, you could implement the (publicly available) specifications, set up a listener to wait for connections on port 25 (the standard port for SMTP), wait for data to come in, process it, and return responses as appropriate.

It is best to work in this way when building protocols. Unless there are very strong reasons for not doing so, make your server as open as possible; don't tie it to a specific platform. This is how things are done on the Internet. To an extent, things like Web services should negate the need to build your own protocols; as you go forward, you will rely instead on the "remote object available to local client" paradigm.

Now it is time to consider the idea of using the serialization features of .NET to transmit data across the network. After all, you have already seen this in action in previous chapters with WCF, Web services, and remoting. You can take an object in .NET, use serialization to convert it to a string of bytes, and expose that string to a Web service consumer, to a remoting client, or even to a file.

The `System.Runtime.Serialization.Formatters` namespace includes a number of classes you can use to format your messages, including the `BinaryFormatter` and `SoapFormatter` classes. You could use either of those classes, or create your own custom formatter, to convert data for transmission and reception. In this case, you are going to create a new class called `Message` and use the `BinaryFormatter` class to crunch it down into a wire-ready format and convert it back again for processing.

This approach is not ideal from the perspective of interoperability, because the actual protocol used is lost in the implementation of the .NET Framework, rather than being under your absolute control.

If you want to build an open protocol, this is *not* the best way to do it. Unfortunately, an explanation of the best way is beyond the scope of this book, but a good place to start is to look at existing protocols and standards and model any protocol on their approach. `BinaryFormatter` provides a quick-and-dirty approach, which is why you are going to use it here.

The Message Class

Add a new class to the project, named `Message`. The `Message` class contains two fields, `username` and `message`, which form the entirety of the data that you want to transmit. The code for this class follows; note how the `Serializable` attribute is applied to it so that `BinaryFormatter` can change it into a wire-ready form. You are also providing a new implementation of `ToString`:

```
Imports System.Text
<Serializable()> Public Class Message
    Private username As String
    Private message As String
    Public Sub New(ByVal name As String)
        username = name
    End Sub
```

```
Public Sub New(ByVal name As String, ByVal message As String)
    username = name
    message = message
End Sub
Public Overrides Function ToString() As String
    Dim builder As New StringBuilder(username)
    builder.Append(" says:")
    builder.Append(ControlChars.CrLf)
    builder.Append(message)
    builder.Append(ControlChars.CrLf)
    Return builder.ToString()
End Function
End Class
```

Code snippet from WroxMessenger

Now all you have to do is spin up two threads: one for transmission and one for reception, updating the display. You need two threads *per conversation*, so if you have 10 conversations open, you need 20 threads plus the main UI thread, plus the thread running `TcpListener`.

Receiving messages is easy. When calling `Deserialize` on `BinaryFormatter`, you give it the stream returned to you from `TcpClient`. If there is no data, then this blocks. If there is data, then it is decoded into a `Message` object that you can display. If you have multiple messages coming down the pipe, then `BinaryFormatter` keeps processing them until the pipe is empty. Here is the method for this, which should be added to `ConversationForm`. Remember that you haven't implemented `ShowMessage` yet:

Available for download on Wrox.com

```
Protected Sub ReceiveThreadEntryPoint()
    ' Create a formatter...
    Dim formatter As New BinaryFormatter()
    ' Loop
    Do While True
        ' Receive...
        Dim message As Message = formatter.Deserialize(_stream)

        If message Is Nothing Then
            Exit Do
        End If
        ' Show it...
        ShowMessage(message)
    Loop
End Sub
```

Code snippet from WroxMessenger

Transmitting messages is a bit more complex. You want a queue (managed by a `System.Collections.Queue`) of outgoing messages. Every second, you will examine the state of the queue. If you find any messages, then you use `BinaryFormatter` to transmit them. Because you will be accessing this queue from multiple threads, you use a `System.Threading.ReaderWriterLock` to control access. To minimize the amount of time you spend inside locked code, you quickly transfer the contents of the shared queue into a private queue that you can process at your leisure. This enables the client to continue to add messages to the queue through the UI, even though existing messages are being sent by the transmit thread.

First, add the following members to `ConversationForm`:

Available for download on Wrox.com

```
Public Class ConversationForm
    Private _username As String = "Foo"
    Private _client As TcpClient
    Private _stream As NetworkStream
    Private _direction As ConversationDirection
    Private _receiveThread As Thread
    Private _transmitThread As Thread
```

```
Private _transmitQueue As New Queue()
Private _transmitLock As New ReaderWriterLock()
```

Now, add this method (again to `ConversationForm`):

```
Protected Sub TransmitThreadEntryPoint()
    ' Create a formatter...
    Dim formatter As New BinaryFormatter()
    Dim workQueue As New Queue()
    ' Loop
    Do While True
        ' Wait for the signal...
        Thread.Sleep(1000)
        ' Go through the queue...
        _transmitLock.AcquireWriterLock(-1)
        Dim message As Message
        workQueue.Clear()
        For Each message In _transmitQueue
            workQueue.Enqueue(message)
        Next
        _transmitQueue.Clear()
        _transmitLock.ReleaseWriterLock()
        ' Loop the outbound messages...
        For Each message In workQueue
            ' Send it...
            formatter.Serialize(_stream, message)
        Next
    Loop
End Sub
```

When you want to send a message, you call one version of the `SendMessage` method. Here are all of the implementations, and the `Click` handler for `buttonSend`:

```
Private Sub SendButton_Click(ByVal sender As System.Object, _
    ByVal e As System.EventArgs) Handles SendButton.Click
    SendMessage(MessageField.Text)
End Sub
Public Sub SendMessage(ByVal message As String)
    SendMessage(_username, message)
End Sub
Public Sub SendMessage(ByVal username As String, ByVal message As String)
    SendMessage(New Message(username, message))
End Sub
Public Sub SendMessage(ByVal message As Message)
    ' Queue it
    _transmitLock.AcquireWriterLock(-1)
    _transmitQueue.Enqueue(message)
    _transmitLock.ReleaseWriterLock()
    ' Show it...
    ShowMessage(message)
End Sub
```

`ShowMessage` is responsible for updating `AllMessagesField` so that the conversation remains up to date (notice how you add the message both when you send it and when you receive it so that both parties have an up-to-date thread). This is a UI feature, so it is good practice to pass it over to the main application thread for processing. Although the call in response to the button click comes off the main application thread, the one from inside `ReceiveThreadEntryPoint` does not. Here is what the delegate looks like:

```vb
Public Class ConversationForm
    ' members...
    Private _username As String = "Foo"
    Private _client As TcpClient
    Private _stream As NetworkStream
    Private _direction As ConversationDirection
    Private _receiveThread As Thread
    Private _transmitThread As Thread
    Private _transmitQueue As New Queue()
    Private _transmitLock As New ReaderWriterLock()
    Public Delegate Sub ShowMessageDelegate(ByVal message As Message)
```

Code snippet from WroxMessenger

Here is the method implementation:

```vb
Public Sub ShowMessage(ByVal message As Message)
    ' Thread?
    If ConnectForm.IsMainThread() = False Then
        ' Run...
        Dim args(0) As Object
        args(0) = message
        Invoke(New ShowMessageDelegate(AddressOf ShowMessage), args)
        ' Return...
        Return
    End If
    ' Show it...
    AllMessagesField.Text &= message.ToString()
End Sub
```

Code snippet from WroxMessenger

All that remains now is to spin up the threads. This should be done from within `ConfigureClient`. Before the threads are spun up, you need to obtain the stream and store it in the `private _stream field`. After that, you create new `Thread` objects as normal:

```vb
Public Sub ConfigureClient(ByVal client As TcpClient, _
        ByVal direction As ConversationDirection)
    ' Set it up...
    _client = client
    _direction = direction
    ' Update the window...
    UpdateCaption()
    ' Get the stream...
    _stream = _client.GetStream()
    ' Spin up the threads...
    _transmitThread = New Thread(AddressOf TransmitThreadEntryPoint)
    _transmitThread.Start()
    _receiveThread = New Thread(AddressOf ReceiveThreadEntryPoint)
    _receiveThread.Start()
End Sub
```

Code snippet from WroxMessenger

At this point, you should be able to connect and exchange messages, as shown in Figure 29-7.

Note that the screenshots show the username of the inbound connection as Bar. This was done with the `UsernameField` text box so that you can follow which half of the conversation comes from where.

Shutting Down the Application

You have yet to solve the problem of neatly closing the application, or, in fact, dealing with one person in the conversation closing down his or her window, indicating a wish to end the conversation. When the process ends (whether neatly or forcefully), Windows automatically mops up any open connections and frees up the port for other processes.

Suppose you have two computers, one window per computer, as you would in a production environment. When you close your window, you are indicating that you want to end the conversation. You need to close the socket and spin down the transmission and reception threads. At the other end, you should be able to detect that the socket has been closed, spin down the threads, and tell the user that the other user has terminated the conversation.

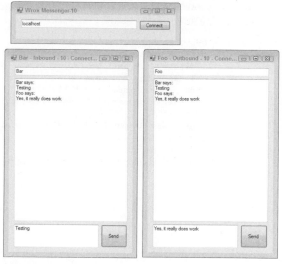

FIGURE 29-7

This all hinges on being able to detect when the socket has been closed. Unfortunately, Microsoft has made this very hard due to the design of the `TcpClient` class. `TcpClient` effectively encapsulates a `System.Net.Sockets.Socket` class, providing methods for helping to manage the connection lifetime and communication streams. However, `TcpClient` does not have a method or property that answers the question "Am I still connected?" Therefore, you need to get the `Socket` object that `TcpClient` is wrapping, and then you can use its `Connected` property to determine whether the connection has been closed.

`TcpClient` does support a property called `Client` that returns a `Socket`, but this property is protected, meaning you can only access it by inheriting a new class from `TcpClient`. There is another way, though: You can use *reflection* to get at the property and call it without having to inherit a new class.

Microsoft claims that this is a legitimate technique, even though it appears to violate every rule in the book about encapsulation. Reflection is designed not only for finding out which types are available, and learning which methods and properties each type supports, but also for invoking those methods and properties whether they're protected or public. Therefore, in `ConversationForm`, you need to store the socket:

```
Public Class ConversationForm
    Private _username As String = "Foo"
    Private _client As TcpClient
    Private _socket As Socket
```

Code snippet from WroxMessenger

In `ConfigureClient`, you use reflection to peek into the `Type` object for `TcpClient` and dig out the `Client` property. Once you have a `System.Reflection.PropertyInfo` for this property, you can retrieve its value by using the `GetValue` method. Don't forget to import the `System.Reflection` namespace:

```
Public Sub ConfigureClient(ByVal client As TcpClient, _
            ByVal direction As ConversationDirection)
    ' Set it up...
    _client = client
    _direction = direction
    ' Update the window...
```

```
    UpdateCaption()
    ' Get the stream...
    _stream = _client.GetStream()
    ' Get the socket through reflection...
    Dim propertyInfo As PropertyInfo = _
        _client.GetType().GetProperty("Client", _
        BindingFlags.Instance Or BindingFlags.Public)
    If Not propertyInfo Is Nothing Then
        _socket = propertyInfo.GetValue(_client, Nothing)
    Else
        Throw New Exception("Could not retrieve Client property from TcpClient")
    End If
    ' Spin up the threads...
    _transmitThread = New Thread(AddressOf TransmitThreadEntryPoint)
    _transmitThread.Start()
    _receiveThread = New Thread(AddressOf ReceiveThreadEntryPoint)
    _receiveThread.Start()
End Sub
```

Code snippet from WroxMessenger

Applications are able to check the state of the socket either by detecting when an error occurs because you have tried to send data over a closed socket or by actually checking whether the socket is connected. If the `Socket` has not been initialized (that is, it is `Nothing`) or the `Socket` has not been connected, then you give the user some feedback and exit the loop. By exiting the loop, you effectively exit the thread, which is a neat way of quitting the thread. Notice as well that you might not have a window at this point (you might be the one who closed the conversation by closing the window), so you wrap the UI call in a `Try Catch` (the other side will see a `<disconnect>` message):

Available for
download on
Wrox.com

```
Protected Sub TransmitThreadEntryPoint()
    ' Create a formatter...
    Dim formatter As New BinaryFormatter()
    Dim workQueue As New Queue()
    ' name...
    Thread.CurrentThread.Name = "Tx-" & _direction.ToString()
    ' Loop...
    Do While True
        ' Wait for the signal...
        Thread.Sleep(1000)
        ' Disconnected?
        If _socket Is Nothing OrElse _socket.Connected = False Then
            Try
                ShowMessage(New Message("Debug", "<disconnect>"))
            Catch
            End Try
            Exit Do
        End If
        ' Go through the queue...
```

Code snippet from WroxMessenger

`ReceiveThreadEntryPoint` also needs some massaging. When the socket is closed, the stream is no longer valid and so `BinaryFormatter.Deserialize` throws an exception. Likewise, you quit the loop and therefore neatly quit the thread:

```
Protected Sub ReceiveThreadEntryPoint()
    ' Create a formatter...
    Dim formatter As New BinaryFormatter()
    ' Loop...
    Do While True
        ' Receive...
```

```
            Dim message As Message = Nothing
            Try
                message = formatter.Deserialize(_stream)
            Catch
            End Try

            If message Is Nothing Then
                Exit Do
            End If
            ' Show it...
            ShowMessage(message)
        Loop
    End Sub
```

How do you deal with actually closing the socket? You tweak the `Dispose` method of the form itself (you can find this method in the Windows-generated code section of the file), and if you have a `_socket` object, you close it:

```
<System.Diagnostics.DebuggerNonUserCode()> _
Protected Overrides Sub Dispose(ByVal disposing As Boolean)
    Try
        If disposing AndAlso components IsNot Nothing Then
            components.Dispose()
        End If
        ' Close the socket...
        If Not _socket Is Nothing Then
            _socket.Close()
            _socket = Nothing
        End If
    Finally
        MyBase.Dispose(disposing)
    End Try
End Sub
```

Code snippet from WroxMessenger

Now you will be able to start a conversation; and if one of the windows is closed, then `<disconnect>` will appear in the other, as shown in Figure 29-8. In the background, the four threads (one transmit and one receive per window) will spin down properly.

The application itself still will not close properly, even if you close all the windows, because you need to stop the `Listener` when `ConnectForm` closes. To do so, make `Listener` implement `IDisposable`:

```
Public Class Listener
    Implements IDisposable
    Public Sub Dispose() Implements System.IDisposable.Dispose
        ' Stop it...
        Finalize()
        GC.SuppressFinalize(Me)
    End Sub
    Protected Overrides Sub Finalize()
        ' Stop the listener...
        If Not _listener Is Nothing Then
            _listener.Stop()
            _listener = Nothing
        End If
        ' Stop the thread...
        If Not _thread Is Nothing Then
```

FIGURE 29-8

```
            _thread.Join()
            _thread = Nothing
        End If
        ' Call up...
        MyBase.Finalize()
    End Sub
```

Code snippet from WroxMessenger

Now all that remains is to call `Dispose` from within the `ConnectForm`. A good place to do this is in the `Closed` event handler:

Available for download on Wrox.com

```
Private Sub ConnectForm_FormClosed(ByVal sender As Object,
        ByVal e As System.Windows.Forms.FormClosedEventArgs) _
                        Handles Me.FormClosed
    If Not _listener Is Nothing Then
        _listener.Dispose()
        _listener = Nothing
    End If
End Sub
```

Code snippet from WroxMessenger

After the code is compiled again, the application can be closed.

USING INTERNET EXPLORER IN YOUR APPLICATIONS

A common requirement of modern applications is to display HTML files and other files commonly used with Internet applications. Although the .NET Framework has considerable support for common image formats (such as GIF, JPEG, and PNG), working with HTML used to be a touch trickier in versions 1.0 and 1.1 of the .NET Framework. Life was made considerably easier with the inclusion of the `WebBrowser` control in the .NET Framework 2.0.

You don't want to have to write your own HTML parser, so using this control to display HTML pages is, in most cases, your only option. Microsoft's Internet Explorer was implemented as a standalone component comprising a parser and a renderer, all packaged up in a neat COM object. The `WebBrowser` control "simply" wraps this COM object. There is nothing to stop you from using this COM object directly in your own applications, but it is considerably easier to use the newer control for hosting Web pages in your applications.

Yes, a COM object. Considering that writing an HTML parser is extremely hard, and writing a renderer is extremely hard, it is easy to conclude that it's much easier to use interop to get to Internet Explorer in .NET applications than to have Microsoft try to rewrite a managed version of it just for .NET. Maybe we will see "Internet Explorer .NET" eventually, but for now you have to use interop.

Windows Forms and HTML — No Problem!

These sections demonstrate how to build a mini-browser application. Sometimes you might want to display HTML pages without giving users UI widgets, such as a toolbar or the capability to enter their own URLs. You might also want to use the control in a nonvisual manner. For example, using the `WebBrowser` control, you can retrieve Web pages and then print the results without ever needing to display the contents.

Allowing Simple Web Browsing in Your Windows Application

The first step is to create a new Windows Forms Application project called `MyBrowser`. On the default form, change the name to `MainForm`, place a single `TextBox` control (named `AddressField`) and the `WebBrowser` control (named `TheBrowser`), as shown in Figure 29-9.

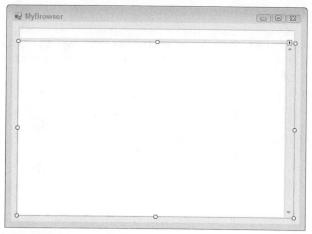

FIGURE 29-9

The idea is that when the end user presses the Enter (or Return) key, the URL entered in the text box will be the HTML page that is retrieved and displayed in the WebBrowser control. To accomplish this task, use the following code for your form:

```
Public Class MainForm
    Private Sub AddressField_KeyPress(ByVal sender As Object,
        ByVal e As System.Windows.Forms.KeyPressEventArgs) Handles AddressField.KeyPress
        If e.KeyChar = Chr(13) Then
            TheBrowser.Navigate(AddressField.Text)
        End If
    End Sub
End Class
```

Code snippet from MyBrowser

For this simple example, you check the key presses that are made in the AddressField TextBox control, and if the key press is a specific one — the Enter key — then you use the WebBrowser control's Navigate method to navigate to the requested page. The Navigate method can take a single String value, which represents the location of the Web page to retrieve. The example shown in Figure 29-10 shows the Wrox website.

FIGURE 29-10

Launching Internet Explorer from Your Windows Application

Sometimes, the goal is not to host a browser inside the application but to allow users to find the website in a typical Web browser. For an example of this task, add a `LinkLabel` control (named JumpLink) to the MyBrowser form. For instance, you can have a form that has a `LinkLabel` control on it that simply states "Visit your company website!"

Once this control is in place, use the following code to launch the company's website in an independent browser, as opposed to directly in the form of your application:

```
Public Class MainForm
    Private Sub JumpLink_LinkClicked(ByVal sender As System.Object, _
        ByVal e As System.Windows.Forms.LinkLabelLinkClickedEventArgs) Handles _
        LinkLabel1.LinkClicked
        Dim wb As New WebBrowser
        wb.Navigate("http://www.wrox.com", True)
    End Sub
End Class
```

Code snippet from MyBrowser

In this example, when the `LinkLabel` control is clicked by the user, a new instance of the `WebBrowser` class is created. Then, using the `WebBrowser` control's `Navigate` method, the code specifies the location of the Web page, as well as a Boolean value that specifies whether this endpoint should be opened within the Windows Form application (a `False` value) or from within an independent browser (a `True` value). By default, this is set to `False`. With the preceding construct, when the user clicks the link found in the Windows application, a browser instance is instantiated and the Wrox website is immediately launched.

Updating URLs and Page Titles

Note that when working with the MyBrowser example in which the `WebBrowser` control is directly in the form, when you click the links, the text in the `AddressField` control is not updated. You can fix this by listening for events coming off the `WebBrowser` control and adding handlers to the control.

It is easy to update the form's title with the HTML page's title. Create a `DocumentTitleChanged` event and update the form's `Text` property:

```
Private Sub TheBrowser_DocumentTitleChanged(ByVal sender As Object, _
    ByVal e As System.EventArgs) Handles TheBrowser.DocumentTitleChanged
    Me.Text = TheBrowser.DocumentTitle.ToString()
End Sub
```

Code snippet from MyBrowser

In this case, when the `WebBrowser` control notices that the page title has changed (due to changing the page viewed), the `DocumentTitleChanged` event will fire. In this case, you change the form's `Text` property (its title) to the title of the page being viewed using the `DocumentTitle` property of the `WebBrowser` control.

Next, update the text string that appears in the form's text box, based on the complete URL of the page being viewed. To do this, you can use the `WebBrowser` control's `Navigated` event:

```
Private Sub TheBrowser_Navigated(ByVal sender As Object, _
    ByVal e As System.Windows.Forms.WebBrowserNavigatedEventArgs) Handles _
    TheBrowser.Navigated
    AddressField.Text = TheBrowser.Url.ToString()
End Sub
```

Code snippet from MyBrowser

In this case, when the requested page is finished being downloaded in the `WebBrowser` control, the `Navigated` event is fired. You simply update the `Text` value of the `AddressField` control to be the URL of the page. This means that once a page is loaded in the `WebBrowser` control's HTML container, if the URL changes in this process, then the new URL will be shown in the text box. For example, if you employ these steps and navigate to the Wrox website (`www.wrox.com`), the page's URL will immediately change to `http://www.wrox.com/WileyCDA/`. This process also means that if the end user clicks one of the links contained within the HTML view, then the URL of the newly requested page will also be shown in the text box.

Now if you run the application with the preceding changes put into place, the form's title and address bar will work as they do in Microsoft's Internet Explorer, as demonstrated in Figure 29-11.

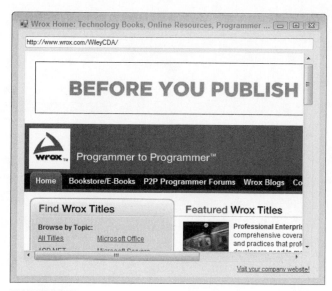

FIGURE 29-11

SUMMARY

Programming directly to the network provides a great deal of power and flexibility. Of course, all of that power and flexibility comes at a cost. Many of the services that are built into higher-level technologies, such as Web services or remoting, aren't built into the `WebRequest` or `Socket` classes, and must often be recreated. However, in those situations where you must communicate with an existing application, or when you need the ultimate in control and speed, using the classes in the `System.Net` namespace makes life easier than it would be otherwise.

This chapter looked at many of the classes that expose network programming. You've learned how to make Web requests without a browser so you could use the data on the Internet in your applications; you've seen how you can leverage the bare sockets layer to write your own communication protocols, and you've been introduced to some of the classes in Visual Basic 2010 for creating FTP clients and Web servers.

30

Application Services

WHAT YOU WILL LEARN IN THIS CHAPTER

➤ Choices for implementing application services

➤ Characteristics of one of the most common technologies for application services, namely Windows Services

➤ How to interact with a Windows Service using Visual Studio 2010 and the management applets in the Windows Control Panel

➤ How to create, install, and communicate with a Windows Service using Visual Basic

➤ How to debug a Windows Service from within Visual Studio 2010

Modern, multitasking operating systems often need to run applications that operate in the background and that are independent of the user who is logged in. For example, an application that provides a service interface to obtain data needs to service external requests for data regardless of whether there is a current user.

Over time, the number of choices to implement application services has increased. Originally, the main choice was Windows Services, but other choices have been added as .NET and Windows have evolved.

USING IIS FOR APPLICATION SERVICES

Depending on the version of Windows in use and the Windows options that have been installed, there are multiple ways to host .NET programs in the background. Chapter 14 covered Web Services and Windows Communication Foundation (WCF) services, both of which are examples of technologies that can use Internet Information Services (IIS) to load programs and run them independent of the user.

If you are using IIS 7.0 or above, you also have the option to run WCF services using the Windows Process Activation Service (normally called WAS). This allows hosting of WCF services using non-HTTP protocols such as TCP. As with IIS, no code needs to be written; only the proper configuration is necessary.

Another option that offers more control over when and how background programs are loaded is called Windows Services. The basic concept goes back to Windows NT, when this capability was called NT Services, but the name was changed for Windows 2000 and later versions.

WINDOWS SERVICES

The tasks carried out by Windows Services are typically long-running tasks and have little or no direct interaction with a user. Many of the constituent parts of Windows and other products use Windows Services to carry out their functions. For example, some versions of Windows install an indexing service to enable searching of the file system. IIS and SQL Server both use Windows Services for important functionality. Such applications may be started when the computer is booted and often continue to run until the computer is shut down.

Example scenarios for creating your own Windows Services would include programs such as the following:

➤ **A file watcher** — Suppose you are running an FTP server that enables users to place files in a particular directory. You could use a Windows Service to monitor and process files within that directory as they arrive. The service runs in the background and detects when files are changed or added within the directory, and then extracts information from these files in order to process orders, or update address and billing information. You will see an example of such a Windows Service later in this chapter.

➤ **An automated stock price reporter** — You could build a system that extracts stock prices from a Web service or website and then e-mails the information to users. You could set thresholds such that an e-mail is sent only when the stock price reaches a certain price. This Windows Service can be automated to extract the information every 10 minutes, every 10 seconds, or whatever time interval you choose. Because a Windows Service can contain any logic that does not require a user interface, you have a lot of flexibility in constructing such applications.

➤ **A system activity logger** — You might want to have a service that monitors a TCP channel and accepts activity log entries. The service could then place the log entries in an appropriate location, such as a database. Having a single service would relieve your application of the responsibility for knowing how activity is logged. They would only need to know how to send an entry to your service.

CHARACTERISTICS OF A WINDOWS SERVICE

To properly design and develop a Windows Service, it is important to understand how it differs from a typical Windows program. Here are the most important characteristics of a Windows Service:

➤ It can start before a user logs on. The system maintains a list of Windows Services, which can be set to start at boot time. Services can also be installed such that they require a manual startup and will not start at bootup.

➤ It can run under a different account from that of the current user. Most Windows Services provide functionality that needs to be running all the time, and some load before a user logs on, so they cannot depend on a user being logged on to run.

➤ It has its own process. It does not run in the process of a program communicating with it.

➤ It typically has no built-in user interface. This is because the service may be running under a different account from that of the current user, or the service may start at bootup, which means that calls to put up a user interface might fail because they are out of context.

➤ Under certain operating systems, activities permitted in normal programs are not allowed in Windows Services. For example, you can play a sound from a Windows Service in Windows XP, but you cannot do so in Windows Vista, Windows Server 2008, or Windows 7.

➤ User interaction with the service is accomplished either via a built-in Windows program, the *Service Control Manager,* or using a special external program you develop. Creation of such an external program is covered in this chapter. The Service Control Manager can be accessed through the Computer Management section of the Control Panel.

➤ It requires a special installation procedure; just clicking on a compiled Windows service EXE will not run it. The program must run in a special context in the operating system, and a specific installation process is required to do the configuration necessary for a Windows Service to be run in this special context.

INTERACTING WITH WINDOWS SERVICES

You can view the services that are used on your computer by opening the Service Control Manager user interface. To do so in Windows 2000, select Administrative Tools ➪ Services in the Control Panel. In Windows XP Professional, select Start ➪ All Programs ➪ Administrative Tools ➪ Services. In Windows Vista, select Start ➪ Control Panel ➪ System and Maintenance ➪ Administrative Tools. In Windows 7, select Start ➪ Control Panel ➪ Administrative Tools ➪ Services.

Using the Service Control Manager, a service can be set to automatically start when the system is booted, or it can be started manually. Services can also be stopped or paused. The list of services contained in the Service Control Manager includes the current state for each service. Figure 30-1 shows the Service Control Manager in Windows Vista.

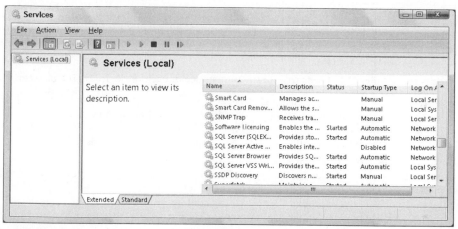

FIGURE 30-1

The Status column indicates the current state of the service. If this column is blank, then the service has not been started since the last time the computer was booted. Other possible values for Status are Started, Stopped, and Paused. You can access additional settings and details concerning a service by double-clicking it.

When a service is started, it automatically logs into the system using one of the following accounts:

➤ **User account** — A regular Windows account that allows the program to interact with the system; in essence, the service impersonates a user.

➤ **LocalSystem account** — Not associated with a particular user. This built-in account has a lot of privileges, and can roughly be thought of as the equivalent of an administrator account for services.

➤ **LocalService account** — Not associated with a particular user. This built-in account has a more limited set of privileges, and is commonly used for routine services.

➤ **NetworkService account** — Not associated with a particular user. This built-in account is similar to LocalService, but is designed for services that communicate across the local network rather than working only on the local system.

The Service Control Manager shown in Figure 30-1 is part of the operating system (OS), which is what supports Windows Services; it is not a part of the .NET Framework. Any service run by the OS is exposed through the Service Control Manager, regardless of how the service was created or installed. You can also examine the installed Windows Services via the Server Explorer in Visual Studio 2010.

CREATING A WINDOWS SERVICE

Creating a Windows Service in .NET requires using several .NET classes, which provide the necessary interface to the operating system required by a Windows Service.

The .NET Framework Classes for Windows Services

Several base classes are needed to create a Windows Service:

➤ System.ServiceProcess.ServiceBase — Provides the base class for the Windows Service. The class containing the logic that will run in the service inherits from ServiceBase. A single executable can contain more than one service, but each service in the executable is a separate class that inherits from ServiceBase.

➤ System.Configuration.Install.Installer — This is a generic class that performs the installation chores for a variety of components. One class in a Windows Service process must inherit and extend Installer in order to provide the interface necessary to install the service under the various Windows operating systems.

Each class that inherits from Installer needs to contain an instance of each of the following classes:

➤ System.ServiceProcess.ServiceProcessInstaller — This class contains the information needed to install a .NET executable that contains Windows Services (that is, an executable that contains classes that inherit from ServiceBase). The .NET installation utility for Windows Services (InstallUtil.exe, discussed later) calls this class to get the information it needs to perform the installation.

➤ System.ServiceProcess.ServiceInstaller — This class also interacts with the InstallUtil .exe installation program. Whereas ServiceProcessInstaller contains information needed to install the executable as a whole, ServiceInstaller contains information about a specific service in the executable. If an executable contains more than one service, then an instance of ServiceInstaller is needed for each one.

For most Windows Services you develop, you can let Visual Studio 2010 take care of Installer, ServiceProcessInstaller, and ServiceInstaller. You just need to set a few properties. The class you should thoroughly understand is ServiceBase, as this is the class that contains the essential functionality of a Windows Service.

The ServiceBase Class

The ServiceBase class contains several useful properties and methods, but initially it is more important to understand the methods that are fired by the Service Control Manager when the state of the service is changed. Table 30-1 describes the most important of these methods.

TABLE 30-1: Important ServiceBase Events

EVENT	DESCRIPTION
OnStart	Occurs when the service is started. This is where the initialization logic for a service is usually placed.
OnStop	Occurs when the service is stopped. Cleanup and shutdown logic are generally placed here.

EVENT	DESCRIPTION
OnPause	Occurs when the service is paused. Any logic required to suspend operations during a pause goes here.
OnContinue	Occurs when a service continues after being paused.
OnShutdown	Occurs when the operating system is being shut down.
OnSessionChange	Occurs when a change event is received from a Terminal Session service. This method was new in .NET Framework 2.0.
OnPowerEvent	Occurs when the system's power management software causes a change in the power status of the system. This is typically used to change the behavior of a service when a system is entering or leaving a "suspended" power mode. This is more frequent with end users who are working on laptops.
OnCustomCommand	Occurs when an external program has told the Service Control Manager that it wants to send a command to the service. The operation of this event is covered in "Communicating with the Service."

The events used most frequently are OnStart, OnStop, and OnCustomCommand. The OnStart and OnStop events are used in almost every Windows service written in Visual Basic, and the OnCustomCommand is used when any special configuration of the service is needed while the service is running.

All of these are Protected events, so they are only available to classes that inherit from the ServiceBase class. Because of the restricted context in which it runs, a Windows Service component that inherits from ServiceBase often lacks a public interface. While you can add public properties and methods to such a component, they are of limited use because programs running in a normal user context cannot obtain an object reference to running a Windows Service component, which is running in a special system context created by the System Control Manager.

To be active as a Windows Service, an instance of the ServiceBase class must be started via the shared Run method of the ServiceBase class. However, normally you don't have to write code to do this because the template code generated by a Visual Studio 2010 Windows Service project places the correct code in the Main subroutine of the project for you.

The most commonly used property of the ServiceBase class is the AutoLog property. This Boolean property is set to True by default. If True, then the Windows service automatically logs the Start, Stop, Pause, and Continue events to an event log. The event log used is the Application Event Log and the Source in the log entries is taken from the name of the Windows service. This automatic event logging is stopped by setting the AutoLog property to False.

The following File Watcher example goes into more detail about the automatic logging capabilities in a Windows service, and about event logs in general.

Installation-Oriented Classes

The Installer, ServiceProcessInstaller, and ServiceInstaller classes are quite simple to build and use if you are employing Visual Studio 2010. After you create your Windows Service project, Visual Studio 2010 will create a class file called Service1.vb for you. To add the Installer, ServiceProcessInstaller, and ServiceInstaller classes to your project, simply right-click the design surface of this ServiceBase class, Service1.vb, and select Add Installer. This creates the code framework necessary to use them.

The Installer class (named ProjectInstaller.vb by default in a Windows Service project) generally needs no interaction at all — it is ready to use when created by Visual Studio 2010. However, it may be appropriate to change some properties of the ServiceProcessInstaller and ServiceInstaller classes. You can do this by simply highlighting these objects on the design surface and changing their properties directly in the Properties window of Visual Studio 2010. The properties that are typically modified for `ServiceProcessInstaller` include the following:

➤ `Account` — This specifies the type of account under which the entire service application will run. Different settings give the services in the application different levels of privilege on the local system. For simplicity, this chapter uses the highest level of privilege, LocalSystem, for most of the examples. If this property is set to `User` (which is the default), then you must supply a username and password when the service is installed. (You'll see more about that when `InstallUtil.exe` is discussed later in the chapter.) That user's account is used to determine privileges for the service. If there is any possibility that a service could access system resources that should be "out of bounds," then using the User setting to restrict privileges is a good idea. Besides LocalSystem and User, other possible settings for the `Account` property include NetworkService and LocalService.

➤ `HelpText` — This specifies information about the service that will be displayed in certain installation options.

If the `Account` property is set to User, then it is good practice to set up a special user account for the service, rather than rely on some existing account intended for a live user. The special account can be set up with exactly the appropriate privileges for the service. This way, it is not as vulnerable to having its password or its privileges inadvertently changed in a way that would cause problems in running the service.

For the `ServiceInstaller` class, the properties you might change include the following:

➤ `DisplayName` — The name of the service displayed in the Service Manager or the Server Explorer can be different from the class name and the executable name if desired, though it is better to make this name the same as the class name for the service.

➤ `StartType` — This specifies how the service is started. The default is Manual, which means you must start the service yourself, as it will not start automatically after the system boots. If you want the service to always start when the system starts, then change this property to Automatic. The Service Manager can be used to override the `StartType` setting.

➤ `ServiceName` — The name of the service that this `ServiceInstaller` handles during installation. If you changed the class name of the service after using the Add Installer option, then you would need to change this property to correspond to the new name for the service.

`ServiceProcessInstaller` and `ServiceInstaller` are used as necessary during the installation process, so there is no need to understand or manipulate the methods of these.

Multiple Services within One Executable

It is possible to place more than one class that inherits from the `ServiceBase` class in a single Windows Service executable. Each such class then allows for a separate service that can be started, stopped, and so on, independently of the other services in the executable.

If a Windows Service executable contains more than one service, then it must contain one `ServiceInstaller` for each service. Each `ServiceInstaller` is configured with the information used for its associated service, such as the displayed name and the start type (automatic or manual). However, the executable still needs only one `ServiceProcessInstaller`, which works for all the services in the executable. It is configured with the account information that is used for all the services in the executable.

The ServiceController Class

Another important .NET Framework class used with Windows Services is `System.ServiceProcess.ServiceController`. This class is not used when constructing a service; it is used by external applications to communicate with a running service, enabling operations such as starting and stopping the service. The `ServiceController` class is described in detail in the section "Communicating with the Service."

Other Types of Windows Services

The `ServiceBase` and `ServiceController` classes can be used to create typical Windows Services that work with high-level system resources such as the file system or performance counters. However, some Windows Services need to interact at a deeper level. For example, a service may work at the kernel level, fulfilling functions such as that of a device driver.

Presently, the .NET Framework classes for Windows Services cannot be used to create such lower-level services, which rules out both Visual Basic and C# as tools to create them. C++ is typically the tool of choice for these types of services. If the C++ is used, the code for such services would typically run in unmanaged mode.

Another type of service that cannot be created with the .NET Framework classes is one that interacts with the Windows desktop. Again, C++ is the preferred tool for such services.

You'll look at the types of services that *are* possible during the discussion of the `ServiceType` property of the `ServiceController` class, in "Communicating with the Service."

CREATING A WINDOWS SERVICE IN VISUAL BASIC

Here is a high-level description of the necessary tasks to create a Windows Service. These tasks are demonstrated later in a detailed example:

1. Create a new project of the type Windows Service. By default, the service will be in a module named `Service1.vb`, but it can be renamed, like any other .NET module. The class automatically placed in `Service1.vb` is named `Service1` by default, and it inherits from the `ServiceBase` class.

2. Place any logic that needs to run when the service is started in the `OnStart` event of the service class. You can find the code listing for the `Service1.vb` file by double-clicking this file's design surface.

3. Add any additional logic that the service needs to carry out its operation. Logic can be placed in the class for the service, or in any other class module in the project. Such logic is typically called via some event that is generated by the operating system and passed to the service, such as a file changing in a directory, or a timer tick.

4. Add an installer to the project. This module provides the interface to the Windows operating system to install the module as a Windows Service. The installer is a class that inherits from `System.Configuration.Install.Installer`, and it contains instances of the `ServiceProcessInstaller` and `ServiceInstaller` classes.

5. Set the properties of the installer modules as necessary. The most common settings needed are the account under which the service will run and the name the service will display in the Service Control Manager.

6. Build the project. This results in an EXE file. For example, if the service were named `WindowsService1`, then the executable file would be named `WindowsService1.exe`.

7. Install the Windows Service with a command-line utility named `InstallUtil.exe`. (As previously mentioned, a service cannot be started by just running the EXE file.)

8. Start the Windows Service with the Service Control Manager or with the Server Explorer in Visual Studio 2010.

You can also start a service from the command console if the proper paths to .NET are set. The command is as follows:

```
NET START <servicename>
```

Note that the `<servicename>` used in this command is the name of the service, not the name of the executable in which the service resides.

Depending on the configuration of your system, a service started with any of the aforementioned methods will sometimes fail, resulting in an error message indicating that the service did not start in a timely fashion. This may be because the .NET libraries and other initialization tasks did not finish fast enough to suit the Service Control Manager. If this happens, attempt to start the service again; if it has no actual defects, it usually succeeds the second time.

> Steps 2 through 5 can be done in a different order. It doesn't matter whether the installer is added and configured before or after the logic that does the processing for the service is added.

At this point, a service is installed and running. The Service Control Manager can stop the service, or it will be automatically stopped when the system is shut down. The command to stop the service in a command console is as follows:

```
NET STOP <servicename>
```

The service does not automatically start the next time the system is booted unless it is configured for that. This can be done by setting the StartType property for the service to Automatic when developing the service, or it can be done in the Service Manager. Right-clicking the service in the Service Manager provides access to this capability.

Developing a Windows Service project is similar to most other Visual Basic projects. There are a few important differences, however:

➤ You cannot debug the project in the environment as you normally would with any other Visual Basic program. The service must be installed and started before it can be debugged. It is also necessary to attach to the process for the service to do debugging. Details about this are included in the section "Debugging the Service."

➤ Even though the result of the development is an EXE, you should not include any message boxes or other visual elements in the code. The Windows Service executable is more like a component library in that sense, and should not have a visual interface. If you include visual elements such as message boxes, the results can vary. In some cases, the UI code will have no effect. In other cases, the service may hang when attempting to write to the user interface.

➤ Finally, be especially careful to handle all errors within the program. The program is not running in a user context, so a runtime error has no place to report itself visually. Handle all errors with structured exception handling, and use an Event Log or other offline means to record and communicate runtime errors.

CREATING A FILE WATCHER SERVICE

To illustrate the outlined steps, the following example monitors a particular directory and reacts when a new or changed file is placed in the directory. The example Windows Service application waits for those files, extracts information from them, and then logs an event to a system log to record the file change.

Creating a Solution for the Windows Service

First, you need an appropriate solution in place to hold the Windows Service. To do so, follow these steps:

1. Create a new Windows Service project using Visual Studio 2010. Name the project **FileWatcherService**.
2. In the Solution Explorer, rename Service1.vb to FileWatcherService.vb.
3. Click the design surface for FileWatcherService.vb. In the Properties window, change the ServiceName property from Service1 to FileWatcherService. The earlier rename in step 2 changes the name of the

class on which the service is based, while the `ServiceName` property changes the name of the service as known to the Service Control Manager.

4. Add an installer to the project. Go back to the design surface for FileWatcherService and right-click it. Select Add Installer. A new file called `ProjectInstaller1.vb` is created and added to the project. The `ProjectInstaller1.vb` file has two components added to its design surface: `ServiceProcessInstaller1` and `ServiceInstaller1`.

5. On the `ProjectInstaller.vb` design surface, highlight the `ServiceProcessInstaller1` control. In its Properties window, change the `Account` property to LocalSystem.

6. Highlight the `ServiceInstaller1` control. In its Properties window, type in **FileWatcherService** as the value of the `DisplayName` property. (The `ServiceName` property will already have this value.)

7. Build the project by right-clicking on the solution and selecting Build from the menu. An EXE named `FileWatcherService.exe` will be created for the service.

At this point, you have a Windows Service that is compiled and ready to be installed, but it doesn't do anything yet. The preceding steps are very similar for every Windows Service you would create; the main points that vary are the name and the type of account you choose to use. The next part, however, is specific to a particular Windows Service: creating the application logic to support the functionality you need in the Windows Service.

Adding .NET Components to the Service

This example service will have the capability to watch a directory for file changes and log events to report its activity. Two .NET components will facilitate these capabilities: the `FileSystemWatcher` component and the `EventLog` component.

The FileSystemWatcher Component

The `FileSystemWatcher` component is used to monitor a particular directory. The component implements `Created`, `Changed`, `Deleted`, and `Renamed` events, which are fired when files are placed in the directory, changed, deleted, or renamed, respectively.

The operation that takes place when one of these events is fired is determined by the application developer. Most often, logic is included to read and process the new or changed files. However, you are just going to write a message to a log file.

To implement the component in the project, drag and drop a `FileSystemWatcher` control from the Components tab of the Toolbox onto the design surface of `FileWatcherService.vb`. (Be sure not to drag the component onto `ProjectInstaller.vb`. If `ProjectInstaller.vb` is still the displayed design surface, you'll need to click on the tab for the `FileWatcherService.vb` design surface.) This control is automatically called `FileSystemWatcher1`.

The EnableRaisingEvents Property

The `FileSystemWatcher` component should not generate any events until the service is initialized and ready to handle them. To prevent this, set the `EnableRaisingEvents` property of `FileSystemWatcher1` to False. This prevents the component from firing any events. You will enable it during the `OnStart` event in the service. These events fired by the `FileSystemWatcher` component are controlled using the `NotifyFilter` property, discussed later.

The Path Property

The path that you want to monitor is the TEMP directory on the C: drive, so set the `Path` property to `C:\TEMP` (be sure to confirm that there is a TEMP directory on your C: drive). Of course, this path can be changed to monitor any directory depending on your system, including any network or removable drives.

The NotifyFilter Property

For this example, you only want to monitor when a file is freshly created or the last modified value of a file has changed. To do this, set the `NotifyFilter` property to `FileName, LastWrite`. Note that you can specify multiple changes to monitor by including a comma-separated list. Even though the property has a drop-down, you'll need to type in the value to get both parts of it.

You could also watch for other changes such as attributes, security, size, and directory name changes as well, just by including those options as part of the `NotifyFilter` property.

The Filter Property

The types of files that you will look for are text files, so set the `Filter` property to `*.txt`. Note that if you were going to watch for all file types, then the value of the `Filter` property would be set to `*.*` (which is the default).

The IncludeSubdirectories Property

If you wanted to watch subdirectories, you would set the `IncludeSubdirectories` property to `True`. This example leaves it as `False`, which is the default value. Figure 30-2 shows how the properties should be set.

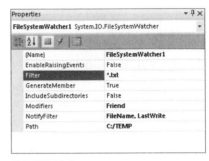

FIGURE 30-2

Adding FileSystemWatcher Code to OnStart and OnStop

Now that some properties are set, let's add some code to the `OnStart` event for `FileWatcherService.vb`. You want to start the `FileSystemWatcher1` component so it will start triggering events when files are created or copied into the directory you are monitoring, so set the `EnableRaisingEvents` property to `True`:

```
Protected Overrides Sub OnStart(ByVal args() As String)
    ' Add code here to start your service. This method should set things
    ' in motion so your service can do its work.
    ' Start monitoring for files
    FileSystemWatcher1.EnableRaisingEvents = True
End Sub
```

Code snippet from FileWatcherService

After the file monitoring properties are initialized, you are ready to start the monitoring. When the service stops, you need to stop the file monitoring process. Add the following code to the `OnStop` event:

```
Protected Overrides Sub OnStop()
    ' Add code here to perform any tear-down necessary to stop your service.
    ' Stop monitoring for files
    FileSystemWatcher1.EnableRaisingEvents = False
End Sub
```

Code snippet from FileWatcherService

The EventLog Component

Now you are ready to place an `EventLog` component in the service to facilitate the logging of events. Event logs are available under the Windows operating system, and were discussed in Chapter 6. As with many other system-level features, the use of Event Logs is simplified in .NET because a .NET Framework base class does most of the work for you.

Depending on your system's configuration and installed software, there should be several Event Logs on the system. Normally, your applications should only write to the Application Log. A property of a log entry called Source identifies the application writing the message. This property does not have to share the same name as the executable of the application, but it is often given that name to make it easy to identify the source of the message.

You can look at the events in the Event Log by using the Event Viewer. Select Control Panel ⇨ Administrative Tools ⇨ Event Viewer on Windows 2000; Start ⇨ All Programs ⇨ Administrative Tools ⇨ Event Viewer on Windows XP; and Start ⇨ Control Panel ⇨ System and Maintenance ⇨ Administrative Tools ⇨ Event Viewer on Windows Vista and Windows 7. The example uses the Event Viewer to ensure that the service is generating events.

It was mentioned earlier in the chapter that the AutoLog property of the ServiceBase class determines whether the service automatically writes events to the Application Log. The AutoLog property instructs the service to use the Application event log to report command failures, as well as information for OnStart, OnStop, OnPause, and OnContinue events on the service. What is actually logged to the event log is an entry indicating whether the service started successfully and stopped successfully, and any errors that might have occurred.

You can turn off event log reporting by setting the AutoLog property to False in the Properties window for the service, but leave it set to True for this example. That means some events will be logged automatically (without you including any code for them). If desired, you can add some code to the service to log additional events not covered by the AutoLog property.

Drag and drop an EventLog control from the Components tab of the Toolbox onto the designer surface of FileWatcherService.vb. This control is automatically called EventLog1.

Set the Log property for Eventlog1 to Application, and set the Source property to FileWatcherService.

The Created Event

Next, you will place some logic in the Created event of the FileSystemWatcher component to log when a file has been created. This event fires when a file has been placed or created in the directory that you are monitoring. It fires because the information last modified on the file has changed.

Bring up FileSystemWatcher1.vb in the code editor. Select FileSystemWatcher1 from the left hand drop-down list and then select Created from the right hand drop-down list. The Created event will be added to your code. Add code to the Created event as follows:

Available for download on Wrox.com

```
Public Sub FileSystemWatcher1_Created(ByVal sender As Object, _
        ByVal e As System.IO.FileSystemEventArgs) _
        Handles FileSystemWatcher1.Created
    Dim sMessage As String
    sMessage = "File created in directory - file name is " + e.Name
    EventLog1.WriteEntry(sMessage)
End Sub
```

Code snippet from FileWatcherService

Notice that the event argument's object (the object named "e" in the event parameters) includes a property called Name. This property holds the name of the file that generated the event.

At this point, you could add the other events for FileSystemWatcher (Changed, Deleted, Renamed) in a similar way and create corresponding log messages for those events. To keep the example simple, you will just use the Created event in this service.

Build the service again to compile the new functionality. You are now ready to install the service and test it.

Installing the Service

The utility for installing the service, `InstallUtil.exe`, must be run from a command line. `InstallUtil.exe` is located in the .NET utilities directory, found at `C:\WINNT\Microsoft.NET\Framework\v4.0.xxxxx` on Windows 2000 and NT systems, or `C:\Windows\Microsoft.NET\Framework\v4.0.xxxxx` on Windows XP, Windows Vista, Windows 7, Windows Server 2003, and Windows Server 2008 ("xxxxx" is a placeholder for the version number of the .NET Framework you have installed).

You'll need a command window to access this utility. It is available by choosing Microsoft Visual Studio 2010 ⇨ Visual Studio Tools ⇨ Visual Studio Command Prompt (2010). Depending on your security settings, you may wish to right-click on the link for the command window, and select Run as Administrator.

In the command window, change to the directory that contains `FileWatcherService.exe`. By default, when using Visual Studio 2010, you'll find this executable at `C:\Users\[ user ]\ Documents\Visual Studio 2010\\Projects\FileWatcherService\ FileWatcherService\obj\Debug` if you are currently using a Debug configuration in Visual Studio, or in `C:\Users\[ user ]\ Documents\Visual Studio 2010\\Projects\FileWatcherService\ FileWatcherService\obj\Release` if you are currently using the Release configuration. Once found, run the following command:

```
InstallUtil FileWatcherService.exe
```

Check the messages generated by `InstallUtil.exe` to ensure that installation of the service was successful. The utility generates several lines of information; if successful, the last two lines are as follows:

```
The Commit phase completed successfully.
The transacted install has completed.
```

If the preceding two lines do not appear, then you need to read all the information generated by the utility to find out why the install didn't work. Reasons might include a bad pathname for the executable, or trying to install the service when it is already installed (it must be uninstalled before it can be reinstalled; the uninstall process is described later). Also, if you did not select Run as Administrator for the command window, you may get an error relating to insufficient security privileges.

If your service has the Account property of the `ServiceProcessInstaller` *set to* User, *you will need to arrange for a user name and password during installation. The user name and password to use are passed as parameters in the InstallUtil command. The* `InstallContext` *class is then used in code inside your* `ServiceProcessInstaller` *to set the* UserName *and* Password *properties. The documentation for the* `InstallContext` *class includes an example.*

Starting the Service

Later in this chapter, you will create your own "control panel" screen to start and stop the service. For now, to test the new Windows service, you will use the Service Control Manager built into Windows to start the FileWatcherService service. It was shown previously in Figure 30-1. Open the Service Control Manager and locate the FileWatcherService service. If you already had the Service Control Manager open, you'll need to refresh it after installing the FileWatcherService.

If the FileWatcherService service does not appear in the list, then the installation failed. Try the installation again and check the error messages. Right-click the FileWatcherService service and select the Start menu option.

To test the service, copy or create a `.TXT` file in the `C:/TEMP` directory (or any other directory you decided to use). You should be able to see a corresponding event in the event log for your machine, using the Event Viewer as described earlier.

Figure 30-3 shows the Event Viewer with several example messages created by the service. If you right-click one of the events for FileWatcherService, you will see a detail screen. Notice that the message corresponds to the event log message you constructed in the `Created` event of the `FileSystemWatcher` control in the service, as shown in Figure 30-4.

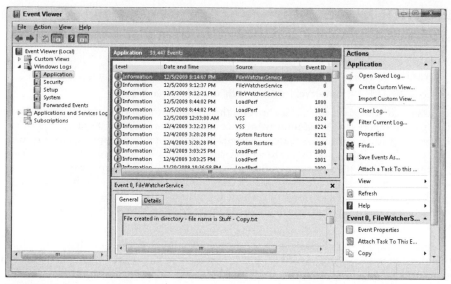

FIGURE 30-3

Uninstalling the Service

Uninstalling the service is very similar to installing it. The service must be in a stopped state before it can be uninstalled, but the uninstall operation will attempt to stop the service if it is running. The uninstall operation is done in the same command window as the install operation, and the command used is the same as the one for installation, except that the option /u is included just before the name of the service. Remember that you need to navigate to C:\Users\[user]\Documents\Visual Studio 2010\Projects\ FileWatcherService\ FileWatcherService\obj\Debug (or the equivalent Release directory, depending on your current configuration) to run this command:

```
InstallUtil.exe /u FileWatcherService.exe
```

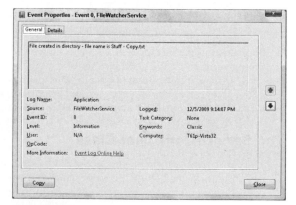

FIGURE 30-4

You can tell that the uninstall was successful if the information displayed by the utility contains the following line:

```
Service FileWatcherService was successfully removed from the system.
```

If the uninstall is not successful, then read the rest of the information to determine why. Besides typing in the wrong pathname, another common reason for failure is trying to uninstall a service that is in a running state and could not be stopped in a timely fashion.

Once you have uninstalled FileWatcherService, it will no longer show up in the list of available services to start and stop (at least, after a refresh it won't).

 A Windows Service must be uninstalled and reinstalled every time you make changes to it.

COMMUNICATING WITH THE SERVICE

Up to this point, you have learned how to do the following:

➤ Create a Windows service using Visual Basic

➤ Start and stop a service with the Service Control Manager from the Control Panel

➤ Make a service work with a system-level function such as a FileSystemWatcher

If these procedures are sufficient to start, stop, and check on the service through the Server Explorer or the Service Control Manager, and there is no need for any other communication with the service, then this is all you have to do. However, it is often helpful to create a specialized application to manipulate your service. This application will typically be able to start and stop a service, and check on its status. The application may also need to communicate with the service to change its configuration. Such an application is often referred to as a *control panel* for the service, even though it does not necessarily reside in the operating system's Control Panel. A commonly used example of such an application is the SQL Server Service Manager, whose icon appears in the tray on the taskbar (normally in the lower-right section of the screen) if you have SQL Server installed.

Such an application needs a way to communicate with the service. The .NET Framework base class that is used for such communication is ServiceController. It is in the System.ServiceProcess namespace. You need to add a reference to System.ServiceProcess.dll (which contains this namespace) before a project can use the ServiceController class.

The ServiceController class provides an interface to the Service Control Manager, which coordinates all communication with Windows Services. However, you do not have to know anything about the Service Control Manager to use the ServiceController class. You just manipulate the properties and methods of the ServiceController class, and any necessary communication with the Service Control Manager is accomplished on your behalf behind the scenes.

Because multiple instances of ServiceController that are communicating with the same service can have timing conflicts, it is a good idea to use exactly *one* instance of the ServiceController class for each service you are controlling. Typically, that means using a module-level object variable to hold the reference to the active ServiceController, and instantiating the ServiceController during the initialization logic for the application. The following example uses this technique.

The ServiceController Class

The constructor for the ServiceController requires the name of the Windows Service with which it will be communicating. This is the same name that was placed in the ServiceName property of the class that defined the service. You will see how to instantiate the ServiceController class shortly.

The ServiceController class has several members that are useful in manipulating services. Table 30-2 describes the most important methods, followed by the most important properties in Table 30-3.

TABLE 30-2: Important ServiceController Methods

METHOD	DESCRIPTION
Start	A method to start the service
Stop	A method to stop the service
Refresh	A method to ensure that the ServiceController object contains the latest state of the service (needed because the service might be manipulated from another program)
ExecuteCommand	A method used to send a custom command to the service. This method is covered later in the section "Custom Commands."

TABLE 30-3: Important ServiceController Properties

PROPERTY	DESCRIPTION
CanStop	A property indicating whether the service can be stopped
ServiceName	A property containing the name of the associated service
Status	An enumerated property that indicates whether a service is stopped, started, in the process of being started, and so on. The ToString method on this property is useful for getting the status in a string form for text messages. The possible values of the enumeration are as follows:
	ContinuePending — The service is attempting to continue.
	Paused — The service is paused.
	PausePending — The service is attempting to go into a paused state.
	Running — The service is running.
	StartPending — The service is starting.
	Stopped — The service is not running.
	StopPending — The service is stopping.
ServiceType	A property that indicates the type of service. The result is an enumerated value. The enumerations are as follows:
	Win32OwnProcess — The service uses its own process (this is the default for a service created in .NET).
	Win32ShareProcess — The service shares a process with another service (this advanced capability is not covered here).
	Adapter, FileSystemDriver, InteractiveProcess, KernelDriver, RecognizerDriver — These are low-level service types that cannot be created with Visual Basic because the ServiceBase class does not support them. However, the value of the ServiceType property may still have these values for services created with other tools.

Integrating a ServiceController into the Example

To manipulate the service, you need to create a program with an appropriate user interface. For simplicity, the example presented will use Windows Forms. Here are step-by-step instructions to create the example:

1. Create a new Windows Forms Application program and name it **FileWatcherPanel**.

2. Add three new buttons to the blank Form1 form, with the following names and text labels:

NAME	TEXT
BtnCheckStatus	Check Status
BtnStartService	Start Service
BtnStopService	Stop Service

3. Add a reference to the DLL that contains the ServiceController class: Select Project ➪ Add Reference. On the .NET tab, highlight the System.ServiceProcess option and click OK.

4. Add this line at the top of the code for Form1:

```
Imports System.ServiceProcess
```

5. As discussed, the project needs only one instance of the ServiceController class. Create a module-level object reference to a ServiceController class by adding the following line of code within the Form1 class:

```
Private myController As ServiceController
```

6. Create a Form Load event in Form1, and place the following line of code in it to instantiate the ServiceController class:

```
myController = New ServiceController("FileWatcherService")
```

You now have a ServiceController class named myController that you can use to manipulate the FileWatcherService Windows service. In the click event for btnCheckStatus, place the following code:

```
Dim sStatus As String
myController.Refresh()
sStatus = myController.Status.ToString
MsgBox(myController.ServiceName & " is in state: " & sStatus)
```

Available for download on Wrox.com

Code snippet from FileWatcherPanel

In the click event for btnStartService, place this code:

```
Try
    myController.Start()
Catch exp As Exception
    MsgBox("Could not start service or the service is already running")
End Try
```

Available for download on Wrox.com

Code snippet from FileWatcherPanel

In the click event for btnStopService, place this code:

```
If myController.CanStop Then
    myController.Stop()
Else
    MsgBox("Service cannot be stopped or the service is already stopped")
End If
```

Available for download on Wrox.com

Code snippet from FileWatcherPanel

Run and test the program. The service may already be running because of one of your previous tests. You may need to copy or create some text files in your watched directory to see if the service is running. If your program cannot stop or start the service, your user account may not have sufficient security privileges, so you may need to start Visual Studio 2010 with Run as Administrator.

More about ServiceController

ServiceController classes can be created for *any* Windows service, not just those created in .NET. For example, you could instantiate a ServiceController class that was associated with the Windows Service for Internet Information Services (IIS) and use it to start, pause, and stop IIS. The code would look just like the code used earlier for the application that controlled the FileWatcherService service. The only difference is that the name of the service would need to be changed in the line that instantiates the ServiceController (step 6).

Keep in mind that the ServiceController is not communicating directly with the service. It is working through the Service Control Manager. That means the requests from the ServiceController to start, stop, or pause a service do not behave synchronously. As soon as the ServiceController has passed the request to the Services Control Manager, it continues to execute its own code without waiting for the Service Control Manager to pass on the request, or for the service to act on the request.

CUSTOM COMMANDS

Some services need additional operations besides starting and stopping. For example, for the FileWatcherService, you might want to support multiple file extensions, using a different `FileSystemWatcher` component for each.

With most components, you would implement such functionality through a public interface. That is, you would put public properties and methods on the component. However, you cannot do this with a Windows Service because it has no public interface that you can access from outside the service.

To deal with this need, the interface for a Windows Service contains a special event called `OnCustomCommand`. The event arguments include a numeric code that can serve as a command sent to the Windows Service. The code can be any number in the range 128 to 255. (The numbers under 128 are reserved for use by the operating system.)

To fire the event and send a custom command to a service, the `ExecuteCommand` method of the `ServiceController` is used. The `ExecuteCommand` method takes the numeric code that needs to be sent to the service as a parameter. When this method is accessed, the `ServiceController` class tells the Service Control Manager to fire the `OnCustomCommand` event in the service, and to pass it the numeric code.

The next example demonstrates this process in action. Suppose you want to be able to change the file filter being used for the FileWatcherService service. You cannot directly send the filter that you want, but you can pick various values of the filter, and associate a custom command numeric code with each.

For example, assume you want to be able to set filters of *.txt, *.dat, or *.docx. You could set up the following correspondence:

CUSTOM COMMAND NUMERIC CODE	FILTER FOR FILESYSTEMWATCHER
201	*.txt
203	*.docx
210	*.dat

The correspondences in the table are completely arbitrary. You could use any codes between 128 and 255 to associate with the filters. These were chosen because they are easy to remember.

First, you need to change the FileWatcherService service so that it is able to accept the custom commands for the beep interval. To do that, first make sure the FileWatcherService service is uninstalled from any previous installs. Then open the Visual Studio 2010 project for the FileWatcherService service.

Create an `OnCustomCommand` event in the service: Open the code window for `FileWatcherService.vb` and type **Protected Overrides OnCustomCommand**. By this point, IntelliSense will kick in and you can press the Tab key to autocomplete the shell event. Notice how it only accepts a single `Integer` as a parameter:

```
Protected Overrides Sub OnCustomCommand(ByVal command As Integer)
    MyBase.OnCustomCommand(command)
End Sub
```

In the `OnCustomCommand` event handler, replace the single line that was generated automatically (the one beginning with `MyBase`) with the following code:

```
Select Case command
    Case 201
        FileSystemWatcher1.Filter = "*.txt"
    Case 203
        FileSystemWatcher1.Filter = "*.docx"
    Case 210
        FileSystemWatcher1.Filter = "*.dat"
End Select
```

Code snippet from FileWatcherService

Build the FileWatcherService service, reinstall it, and start it.

Now you can enhance the FileWatcherPanel application created earlier to set the filter. To enable users to select the file filter, you will use radio buttons. On the FileWatcherPanel program `Form1` (which currently contains three buttons), place three radio buttons. Set their text labels as follows:

```
RadioButton1 - TXT files
RadioButton2 - DOCX files
RadioButton3 - DAT files
```

Place a button directly under these option buttons. Name it `btnSetFilter` and set its text to Set Filter. In the click event for this button, place the following code:

```
Dim nFilterCommand As Integer = 201
If RadioButton1.Checked Then
    nFilterCommand = 201
End If
If RadioButton2.Checked Then
    nFilterCommand = 203
End If
If RadioButton3.Checked Then
    nFilterCommand = 210
End If
myController.ExecuteCommand(nFilterCommand)
```

Code snippet from FileWatcherPanel

At this point, `Form1` should look something like the screen shown in Figure 30-5.

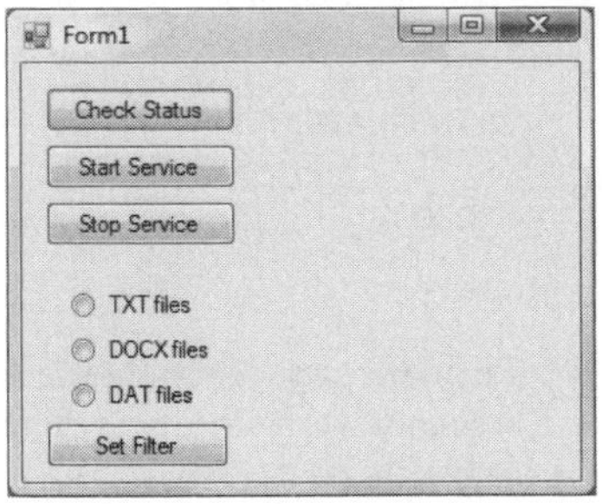

Start the FileWatcherPanel control program and test the capability to change the filter by adding different file types with each filter setting and examining the resulting logged events.

PASSING STRINGS TO A SERVICE

Because the `OnCustomCommand` event only takes numeric codes as input parameters, you cannot directly pass strings to the service. For example, if you wanted to reconfigure a directory name for a service, you could not just send the directory name over. Instead, it would be necessary to

FIGURE 30-5

place the information to be passed to the service in a file in some known location on disk. Then a custom command for the service could instruct it to look at the standard file location and read the information in the file. What the service did with the contents of the file would, of course, be customized for the service.

DEBUGGING THE SERVICE

Because a service must be run from within the context of the Service Control Manager, rather than from within Visual Studio 2010, debugging a service is not as straightforward as debugging other Visual Studio 2010 application types. To debug a service, you must start the service and then attach a debugger to the process in which it is running. You can then debug the application using all of the standard debugging functionality of Visual Studio 2010.

 Don't attach to a process unless you know what the process is and understand the consequences of attaching to and possibly killing that process.

To avoid going through this extra effort, you may want to test most of the code in your service in a standard Windows Forms application. This test-bed application can have the same components (FileSystemWatchers, EventLogs, Timers, and so on) as the Windows Service, and thus will be able to run the same logic in events. Once you have checked out the logic in this context, you can just copy and paste it into a Windows Service application.

However, sometimes the service itself needs to be debugged directly, so it is important to understand how to attach to the service's process and do direct debugging. You can only debug a service when it is running. When you attach the debugger to the service, you are interrupting it. The service is suspended for a short period while you attach to it. It is also interrupted when you place breakpoints and step through your code.

Attaching to the service's process enables you to debug most, but not all, of the service's code. For instance, because the service has already been started, you cannot debug the code in the service's `OnStart` method this way, or the code in the `Main` method that is used to load the service. To debug the `OnStart` event or any of the Visual Studio 2010 designer code, you have to add a dummy service and start that service first. In the dummy service, you would create an instance of the service that you want to debug. You can place some code in a `Timer` object and create the new instance of the object that you want to debug after 30 seconds or so. Allow enough time to attach to the debugger before the new instance is created. Meanwhile, place breakpoints in your startup code to debug those events, if desired.

Follow these steps to debug a service:

1. Install the service.
2. Start the service, either from the Service Control Manager or from code.
3. In Visual Studio 2010, load the solution for the service. Then select Attach to Process from the Debug menu. The Attach to Process dialog appears (see Figure 30-6).

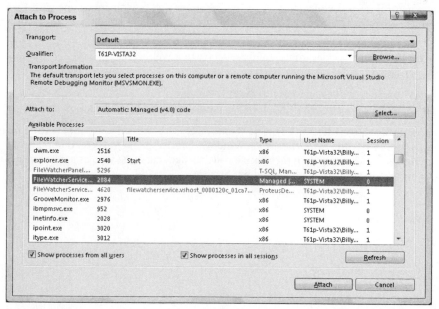

FIGURE 30-6

4. For a Windows Service, the desired process to attach to is not a foreground process; be sure to enable the check boxes next to the "Show processes from all users" and "Show processes in all sessions" options.

5. In the Available Processes section, click the process indicated by the executable name for the service, and then click Attach.

6. You can now debug your process. Place a breakpoint in the code for the service at the place you want to debug. Cause the code in the service to execute (by placing a file in a monitored directory, for example).

7. When finished, select Stop Debugging from the Debug menu.

Let's go through an actual scenario, using your earlier FileWatcherService example. Bring up both the FileWatcherService project and the FileWatcherPanel project in separate instances of the Visual Studio 2010 IDE. Make sure that the FileWatcherService service has been started.

In the FileWatcherService project, select Debug ⇨ Attach to Processes; you will get a dialog similar to the one shown in Figure 30-6. Check the boxes for "Show processes from all users" and "Show processes in all sessions." This will expand the list of processes, and one of the processes in the list will be `FileWatcherService.exe`. Highlight it and click Attach. You are now attached to the process running FileWatcherService in the background.

Place a breakpoint on the first line of the `OnCustomCommand` event:

```
Select Case command
```

Now you are ready to check debugging. Bring up the FileWatcherPanel program and start it. Press one of the radio buttons to change the watched file extension. Switch back to the FileWatcherService project. The cursor will be on the breakpoint line in `OnCustomCommand`. You can use the normal commands at this point to step through the code.

SUMMARY

This chapter presented a general overview of what a Windows Service is and how to create one with Visual Basic. The techniques in this chapter can be used for many different types of background service, including the following:

➤ Automatically moving statistical files from a database server to a Web server

➤ Pushing general files across computers and platforms

➤ A watchdog timer to ensure that a connection is always available

➤ An application to move and process FTP files, or indeed files received from any source

While Visual Basic cannot be used to create every type of Windows Service, it is effective for creating many of the most useful ones. The .NET Framework classes for Windows Services make this creation relatively straightforward. The designers generate much of the routine code needed, enabling you, as a developer, to concentrate on the code specific to your particular Windows Service.

31

Assemblies and Reflection

WHAT YOU WILL LEARN IN THIS CHAPTER

➤ What assemblies are and how they are used

➤ The general structure of an assembly

➤ How assemblies can be versioned

➤ The global assembly cache (GAC), including how and when to use it

➤ How assemblies are located and loaded by the CLR

➤ Using reflection to inspect assemblies in order to determine the types they contain and the interfaces of those types

➤ Dynamic loading of assemblies, allowing your application to inject functionality that was not available at compile time

By now, you've probably developed some programs in .NET, so you've seen the modules produced by the .NET compilers, which have file extensions of `.dll` or `.exe`. Most .NET modules are DLLs, including class libraries and those that serve as code-behind for ASP.NET. Windows applications, console applications, and Windows Services are examples of .NET modules that are executables and thus have an extension of `.exe`.

These .NET-compiled modules, both DLLs and EXEs, are referred to as *assemblies*. Assemblies are the unit of deployment in .NET, containing both compiled code and metadata that is needed by the .NET common language runtime (CLR) to run the code. Metadata includes information such as the code's identity and version, dependencies on other assemblies, and a list of types and resources exposed by the assembly.

Basic development in .NET doesn't require you to know any more than that. However, as your applications become more complex, and as you begin considering such issues as deployment and maintenance of your code, you need to understand more about assemblies. For advanced scenarios, you'll also need to know how to inspect assemblies to find out the types they contain and the interfaces of those types. This inspection capability is known as *reflection*.

After you are familiar with these essentials, Chapter 34 uses this information to discuss deployment in depth.

ASSEMBLIES

The assembly is used by the CLR as the smallest unit for the following:

➤ Deployment

➤ Version control

➤ Security

➤ Type grouping

➤ Code reuse

An assembly must contain a *manifest*, which tells the CLR what else is in the assembly. The other elements can be any of the following three categories:

➤ Type metadata

➤ Microsoft Intermediate Language (MSIL) code

➤ Resources

An assembly can be just one file. Figure 31-1 details the contents of a single-file assembly.

Alternatively, the structure can be split across multiple files, as shown in Figure 31-2. This is just one example of a multiple-file assembly configuration.

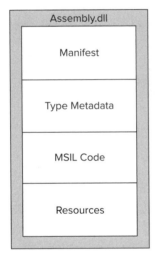

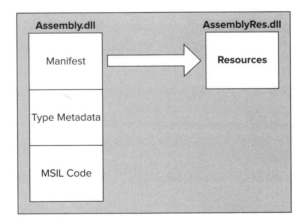

FIGURE 31-1   **FIGURE 31-2**

An assembly can only have one manifest section across all the files that make up the assembly. There is nothing stopping you, however, from having a resource section (or any of the other available section types, such as Metadata and MSIL code) in each of the files that make up an assembly.

THE MANIFEST

The manifest is the part of the assembly that contains a list of the other elements contained in the assembly and basic identification information for the assembly. The manifest contains the largest part of the information that enables the assembly to be self-describing. Elements listed in the manifest are placed in appropriate sections. The manifest includes the sections displayed in Figure 31-3. These sections are covered later in the chapter.

To look at the manifest for a particular assembly, you can use the IL Disassembler (Ildasm.exe), which is included with the Windows SDK installed with Visual Studio 2010. The version of Ildasm.exe in the SDK for .NET Framework 4 can examine assemblies created with earlier versions of the .NET Framework. A shortcut to ildasm.exe is included on the Start menu in All Programs ⇨ Microsoft Visual Studio 2010 ⇨ Microsoft Windows SDK Tools, and it is named IL Disassembler.

When Ildasm.exe loads, you can browse for an assembly to view by selecting File ⇨ Open. Once an assembly has been loaded into Ildasm.exe, it disassembles the metadata contained within the assembly and presents you with a tree-view layout of the data. Initially, the tree view shows only top-level elements, as illustrated in Figure 31-4. This example has only one namespace element in the tree, but if an assembly contains classes in more than one namespace, then additional elements will be shown.

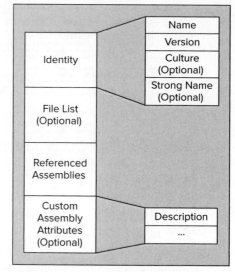

FIGURE 31-3

The full path of the assembly you are viewing represents the root node. The first node below the root is called MANIFEST; and as you've probably guessed, it contains all the information about the assembly's manifest. If you double-click this node, a new window is displayed with the information contained within the manifest. The manifest for a complex assembly can be rather long. For our example, three sections of a manifest are shown in Figures 31-5, 31-6, and 31-7. Figure 31-5 shows the top of the manifest, which contains the external references needed by this assembly, such as other .NET assemblies on which this assembly depends. If the assembly depends on COM libraries, those will be shown as external modules and listed before the external assemblies.

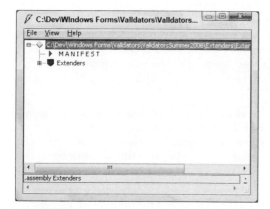

FIGURE 31-4

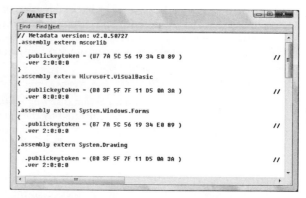

FIGURE 31-5

Figure 31-6 shows a portion of the manifest further down, containing the beginning of the section for the actual assembly. The first items listed in the manifest for the assembly itself are the attributes that apply to the assembly.

Further down are items such as resources that reside in the assembly. Figure 31-7 shows a bitmap named checkmark8.bmp that is used by this particular assembly.

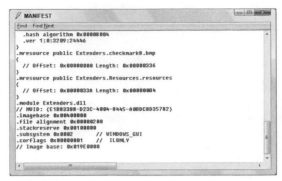

FIGURE 31-6   **FIGURE 31-7**

Assembly Identity

The manifest for an assembly also contains information used to uniquely identify the assembly. This section contains some standard information, such as the version number, and may also contain some optional elements, such as a strong name for the assembly. Assemblies come in two types: *application-private* and *shared* (differences between the two types are covered shortly), and they have slightly different identity information.

The Version Number

The manifest for an assembly contains a version number, which is indicated by the `.ver` directive in `Ildasm.exe`. Figure 31-7, shown earlier, includes a `.ver` directive on the following line in the `.assembly` section:

```
.ver 1.0.2473.30111
```

A version number contains four parts:

```
Major : Minor : Build : Revision
```

Assemblies that have the same name but different version numbers are treated as completely different assemblies. If you have an assembly on your machine that has a version number of 1.5.2.3 and another version of the same assembly with a version number of 1.6.0.1, then the CLR treats them as different assemblies. The version number of an assembly is part of what is used to define dependencies between assemblies.

Strong Names

The manifest can also contain an optional *strong name* for an assembly. The strong name is not a name per se, but a public key that has been generated by the author of the assembly to uniquely identify it. A strong name is used to ensure that your assembly has a unique signature compared to other assemblies that may have the same name. Strong names were introduced to combat DLL hell by providing an unambiguous way to differentiate among assemblies.

A strong name is based on public-private key encryption and creates a unique identity for your assembly. The public key is stored in the identity section of the manifest. A signature of the file containing the assembly's manifest is created and stored in the resulting EXE or DLL file. The .NET Framework uses these two signatures when resolving type references to ensure that the correct assembly is loaded at runtime. A strong name is indicated in the manifest by the `.publickey` directive in the `.assembly` section.

Signing an Assembly with a Strong Name

As mentioned above, applying a strong name to an assembly is based on public-private key encryption. The public and private keys are related, and a set is called a public-private *key pair*. Applying a strong name to an assembly is usually called *signing* the assembly with the strong name.

Visual Studio 2010 gives you a straightforward way to sign an assembly. The project's Properties page (accessed by right-clicking on a project and choosing Properties) contains a Signing tab. You simply check the CheckBox labeled "Sign the assembly" and then specify a key pair file. The drop down for the strong name key file allows you to browse for a key pair file, or create a new one.

You can also control the signing process manually. You can create a key pair with the `sn.exe` utility, which is also in the Windows SDK installed with Visual Studio 2010. Here's the syntax for using `sn.exe` to create a key pair:

```
sn -k pairname.snk
```

You should replace *pairname* with an appropriate name, often the name of your product or system. The same key pair can be used to apply a strong name to all the assemblies in your system.

Once you have a key pair, you need to add it to any projects in Visual Studio that need to generate a strongly named assembly. To do that, just select Project ⇨ Add Existing Item, and browse to the key pair.

The final step is to change the module `AssemblyInfo.vb` to apply the strong name. `AssemblyInfo.vb` was automatically created when your project was created, and is under the My Project area in the Solution Explorer. If you can't see a plus sign to expand My Project, press the Show All Files button at the top of the Solution Explorer.

In `AssemblyInfo.vb`, insert a line that looks like this:

```
<Assembly: AssemblyKeyFile("pairname.snk")>
```

Again, you should replace *pairname* with the name you actually used for the key pair file earlier. The next time your project is built, the resulting assembly will have a strong name, generated by using the key pair you have indicated.

You can also sign an assembly with a strong name by compiling at the command line. This might be the case if you want to sign the assembly outside of Visual Studio. A typical command line to compile and sign a Visual Basic assembly looks like this:

```
vbc /reference:Microsoft.VisualBasic.dll /reference:System.Windows.Forms.dll
/target:library /keyfile:c:\mykeys\keypair.snk /out:MyAssembly.dll
/rootnamespace:MyAssembly *.vb
```

The separate elements of the command line have been placed on different lines for ease of reading, but they should all be on the same line in actual use. The preceding is just a template. You would need to change the `/reference` options to include any references needed by your assembly. You would also need to specify the correct file path for your own key pair file (`.snk` file) and apply your assembly and root namespace names.

Finally, strong names can be applied with a technique called *delay signing*. That's a topic beyond the scope of this chapter, but the Visual Studio help files include step-by-step instructions. Delayed signing is helpful when assemblies need to be properly strongly named during development (so that any problems with strong names are detected at that point), but it is undesirable for all the developers to have a copy of the key pair that will be used for signing the final compiled version of the assembly.

The Culture

The final part of an assembly's identity is its *culture*, which is optional. Cultures are used to define the country/language for which the assembly is targeted.

The combination of name, strong name, version number, and culture is used by the CLR to enforce version dependencies. For example, you could create one version of your assembly targeted at English users, another for German users, another for Finnish users, and so on.

Cultures can be general, as in the case of English, or more specific, as in the case of US-English. Cultures are represented by a string that can contain two parts: primary and secondary (optional). The culture for English is "en," and the culture for US-English is "en-us." See Chapter 27 for more about cultures in .NET.

If a culture is not indicated in the assembly, then it is assumed that the assembly can be used for any culture. Such an assembly is said to be *culture neutral*. You can assign a culture to an assembly by including the attribute AssemblyCulture from the System.Reflection namespace in your assembly's code (usually within the AssemblyInfo.vb file):

```
<Assembly: AssemblyCulture("en")>
```

The culture of an assembly is represented in the manifest by the .locale directive in the .assembly section.

Referenced Assemblies

It was mentioned earlier that the first section of the manifest contains referenced assemblies. An assembly reference is indicated in the manifest with the .assembly extern directive (refer to Figure 31-5).

The first piece of information included is the name of the referenced assembly. Figure 31-5 shows a reference to the mscorlib assembly. This name is used to determine the name of the file that contains the actual assembly. The CLR takes the name of the assembly reference and appends .dll. For instance, in the last example, the CLR will look for a file called mscorlib.dll. The assembly mscorlib is a special assembly in .NET that contains all the definitions of the base types used in .NET, and is referenced by all assemblies.

The .publickeytoken Directive

If the assembly being referenced contains a strong name, then a hash of the public key of the referenced assembly is stored as part of the record to the external reference. This hash is stored in the manifest using the .publickeytoken directive as part of the .assembly extern section. The assembly reference shown in Figure 31-5 contains a hash of the strong name of the mscorlib assembly. The stored hash of the strong name is compared at runtime to a hash of the strong name (.publickey) contained within the referenced assembly to help ensure that the correct assembly is loaded. The value of the .publickeytoken is computed by taking the lower 8 bytes of a hash (SHA1) of the strong name of the referenced assemblies.

The .ver Directive

The version of the assembly being referenced is also stored in the manifest. This version information is used with the rest of the information stored about a reference to ensure that the correct assembly is loaded (this is discussed later). If an application references version 1.1.0.0 of an assembly, it will not load version 2.1.0.0 of the assembly unless a version policy (also discussed later) exists to indicate otherwise. The version of the referenced assembly is stored in the manifest using the .ver directive as part of an .assembly extern section.

The .locale Directive

If an assembly that is being referenced has a culture, then the culture information is also stored in the external assembly reference section, using the .locale directive. The combination of name, strong name (if it exists), version number, and culture are what constitute a unique version of an assembly.

ASSEMBLIES AND DEPLOYMENT

The information in the manifest enables the reliable determination of the identity and version of an assembly. This is the basis for the deployment options available in .NET, and for the side-by-side execution of assemblies that helps .NET overcome DLL hell. This section looks at these issues in detail.

Application-Private Assemblies

It was mentioned earlier that assemblies can be of two types. The first is an application-private assembly. As the name implies, this type of assembly is used by one application only and is not shared. This is the default style of assembly in .NET and is the main mechanism by which an application can be independent of changes to the system.

Application-private assemblies are deployed into the application's own directory. Because application-private assemblies are not shared, they do not need a strong name. This means that, at a minimum, they only need to have a name and version number in the identity section of the manifest. Because the assemblies are private to the application, the application does not perform version checks on the assemblies, as the application developer has control over the assemblies that are deployed to the application directory. If strong names exist, however, the CLR will verify that they match.

If all the assemblies that an application uses are application-private and the CLR is already installed on the target machine, then deployment is quite simple. Chapter 23 discusses this implication in more detail.

Shared Assemblies

The second type of assembly is the shared assembly. As the name suggests, this type of assembly can be shared among several different applications that reside on the same server. This type of assembly should only be used when it is important to share assemblies among many applications. For example, if a Windows Forms control purchased as part of a package is used in many of your applications, then it is better to install a shared version of the assembly, rather than copies of it, for each application. The .NET Framework assemblies themselves are also examples of shared assemblies.

Certain requirements are placed upon shared assemblies. The assembly needs to have a globally unique name, which is not a requirement of application-private assemblies. As mentioned earlier, a strong name is used to create a globally unique name for an assembly. As the assembly is shared, all references to the shared assembly are checked to ensure that the correct version is being used by an application.

Shared assemblies are stored in the global assembly cache (GAC), which is usually located in the assembly folder in the Windows directory (in a typical Windows XP or Vista installation, `C:\Windows\assembly`). However, it's not enough to just copy an assembly into that directory. In fact, if you browse to that directory using Windows Explorer, you'll find that you can't just drag files in and out of it. The process for placing an assembly in the GAC is similar in concept to registering a COM DLL, a process discussed in detail later in this chapter.

No other changes to the code of the assembly are necessary to differentiate it from that of an application-private assembly. In fact, just because an assembly has a strong name does not mean that it has to be deployed as a shared assembly; it could just as easily be deployed in the application directory as an application-private assembly.

Installing a shared assembly into the GAC requires administrator rights on the machine. This is another factor complicating deployment of shared assemblies. Because of the extra effort involved in the creation and deployment of shared assemblies, you should avoid this type of assembly unless you really need it.

The Global Assembly Cache

Each computer that has the .NET runtime installed has a global assembly cache. However, assemblies in the GAC are always stored in the same folder, no matter which version of .NET you have. The folder is a subfolder of your main Windows folder, and it is named Assembly. If you have multiple versions of the .NET Framework, assemblies in the GAC for all of them are stored in this directory.

As previously noted, a strong name is required for an assembly placed in that GAC. That strong name is used to identify a particular assembly. However, another piece of metadata is also used for verification of an assembly. When an assembly is created, a hash of the assembly is placed in the metadata. If an assembly is changed (with a binary editor, for example), the hash of the assembly will no longer match the hash in the metadata. The metadata hash is checked against the actual hash when an assembly is placed in the GAC with the `gacutil.exe` utility (described later). If the two hash codes do not match, the installation cannot be completed.

The strong name is also used when an application resolves a reference to an external assembly. It checks whether the public key stored in the assembly is equal to the hash of the public key stored as part of the reference in the application. If the two do not match, then the application knows that the external assembly has not been created by the original author of the assembly.

You can view the assemblies contained within the GAC by navigating to the directory using the Windows Explorer.

The gacutil.exe utility that ships with .NET is used to add and remove assemblies from the GAC. To add an assembly into the GAC with the gacutil.exe tool, use the following command line:

```
gacutil.exe /i myassembly.dll
```

Recall that the assembly being loaded must have a strong name.

To remove an assembly, use the /u option, like this:

```
gacutil.exe /u myassembly.dll
```

gacutil.exe has a number of other options. You can examine them and see examples of their usage by typing in the following command:

```
gacutil.exe /?
```

VERSIONING ISSUES

In COM, the versioning of DLLs had some significant limitations. For example, a different DLL with the same nominal version number could be indistinguishable from the one desired.

.NET's versioning scheme was specifically designed to alleviate the problems of COM. The major capabilities of .NET that solve versioning issues are as follows:

➤ Application isolation

➤ Side-by-side execution

➤ Self-describing components

Application Isolation

For an application to be isolated, it should be self-contained and independent. This means that the application should rely on its own dependencies for ActiveX controls, components, or files, and not share those files with other applications. The option of having application isolation is essential for a good solution to versioning problems.

If an application is isolated, components are owned, managed, and used by the parent application alone. If a component is used by another application, even if it is the same version, the other application must have its own copy. This ensures that each application can install and uninstall dependencies and not interfere with other applications.

 Does this sound familiar? This is what most early Windows and DOS applications did until COM required registration of DLLs in the registry and placement of shared DLLs in the system directory. The wheel surely does turn!

The .NET Framework enables application isolation by allowing developers to create application-private assemblies. These are in the application's own directory; and if another application needs the same assembly, it can be duplicated in that application's directory.

This means that each application is independent from the others. This isolation works best for many scenarios. It is sometimes referred to as a *zero-impact deployment* because when you either install or uninstall such an application, you are in no danger of causing problems for any other application.

Side-By-Side Execution

Side-by-side execution occurs when multiple versions of the same assembly can run at the same time. Side-by-side execution is performed by the CLR. Components that are to execute side by side must be installed within the application directory or a subdirectory of it.

With application assemblies, versioning is not much of an issue. The interfaces are dynamically resolved by the CLR. If you replace an application assembly with a different version, the CLR will load it and make it work with the other assemblies in the application, as long as the new version doesn't have any interface incompatibilities. The new version may even have interface elements that are new and therefore don't exist in the old version (new properties or methods). As long as the existing class interface elements used by the other application assemblies are unchanged, the new version will work fine. In the following discussion of exactly how the CLR locates a referenced assembly, you'll learn more about how this works.

Self-Describing Components

In the earlier section on the manifest, the self-describing nature of .NET assemblies was mentioned. The term "self-describing" means that all the information the CLR needs to know to load and execute an assembly is inside the assembly itself.

Self-describing components are essential to .NET's side-by-side execution. Once the CLR knows that the extra version is needed, everything else about the assembly needed to run side by side is in the assembly itself. Each application can get its own version of an assembly, and all the work to coordinate the versions in memory is performed transparently by the CLR.

Versioning becomes more important with shared assemblies. Without good coordination of versions, .NET applications with shared assemblies are subject to some of the same problems as COM applications. In particular, if a new version of a shared assembly is placed in the GAC, then there must be a means to control which applications get which version of a shared assembly. This is accomplished with a *versioning policy*.

Version Policies

As discussed earlier, a version number includes four parts: major, minor, build, and revision. The version number is part of the identity of the assembly. When a new version of a shared assembly is created and placed in the GAC, any of these parts can change. Which ones change affects how the CLR views compatibility for the new assembly.

When the version number of a component only changes according to its build and revision parts, it is compatible. This is often referred to as *Quick Fix Engineering (QFE)*. It's only necessary to place the new assembly in the GAC, and it will automatically be considered compatible with applications that were created to use the folder version even though those applications are expecting a different build number and revision.

If either the major or minor build number changes, however, compatibility is not assumed by the CLR. In that case, there are manual ways to indicate compatibility if necessary, and these are covered later in this section.

When an application comes across a type that is implemented in an external reference, the CLR has to determine what version of the referenced assembly to load. What steps does the CLR go through to ensure that the correct version of an assembly is loaded? To answer this question, you need to understand version policies and how they affect which version of an assembly is loaded.

The Default Versioning Policy

Let's start by looking at the default versioning policy. This policy is followed in the absence of any configuration files that would modify the versioning policy. The runtime default behavior is to consult the manifest for the name of the referenced assembly and the version of the assembly to use.

If the referenced assembly does not contain a strong name, then it is assumed that the referenced assembly is application-private and is located in the application's directory. The CLR takes the name of the referenced assembly and appends .dll to create the filename that contains the referenced assembly's manifest. The CLR then searches in the application's directory for the filename. If it's found, then it uses the version indicated, even if the version number is different from the one specified in the manifest. Therefore, the version numbers of application-private assemblies are not checked, because the application developer, in theory, has control over which assemblies are deployed to the application's directory. If the file cannot be found, the CLR raises a System.IO.FileNotFoundException.

Automatic Quick Fix Engineering Policy

If the referenced assembly contains a strong name, then the process by which an assembly is loaded is different:

1. The three different types of assembly configuration files (discussed later) are consulted, if they exist, to see whether they contain any settings that will modify which version of the assembly the CLR should load.

2. The CLR then checks whether the assembly has been requested and loaded in a previous call. If it has, it uses the loaded assembly.

3. If the assembly is not already loaded, then the GAC is queried for a match. If a match is found, it is used by the application.

4. If any of the configuration files contains a codebase (discussed later) entry for the assembly, then the assembly is looked for in the location specified. If the assembly cannot be found in the location specified in the codebase, then a TypeLoadException is raised to the application.

5. If there are no configuration files or no codebase entries for the assembly, then the CLR probes for the assembly starting in the application's base directory.

6. If the assembly still isn't found, then the CLR asks the Windows Installer service if it has the assembly in question. If it does, then the assembly is installed and the application uses it. This is a feature called *on-demand installation.*

If the assembly hasn't been found by the end of this entire process, then a TypeLoadException is raised.

Although a referenced assembly contains a strong name, this does not mean that it has to be deployed into the GAC. This enables application developers to install a version with the application that is known to work. The GAC is consulted to see whether it contains a version of an assembly with a higher build revision number to enable administrators to deploy an updated assembly without having to reinstall or rebuild the application. This is known as the *Automatic Quick Fix Engineering Policy.*

Configuration Files

The default versioning policy described earlier may not be the most appropriate policy for your requirements. Fortunately, you can modify this policy through the use of XML configuration files to meet your specific needs. Two types of configuration files can hold versioning information:

➤ The first is an *application configuration file*, and it is created in the application directory. As the name implies, this configuration file applies to a single application only. You need to create the application configuration file in the application directory with the same name as the application filename and append .config. For example, if you have a Windows Forms application called HelloWorld .exe installed in the C:\HelloWorld directory, then the application configuration file would be C:\HelloWorld\HelloWorld.exe.config. Note that if your project contains an app.config file, that file is copied to the application configuration file during a build of your project.

➤ The second type of configuration file is called the *machine configuration file*. It is named machine .config and can be found in the C:\Windows\Microsoft.NET\Framework\v4.0.xxxx\ CONFIG directory. The machine.config file overrides any other configuration files on a machine and can be thought of as containing global settings.

The main purpose of the configuration file is to provide binding-related information to the developer or administrator who wishes to override the default policy handling of the CLR.

Specifically, the configuration file, as it's written in XML, has a root node named `<configuration>`, and it must have the end node of `</configuration>` present to be syntactically correct. The configuration file is divided into specific types of nodes that represent different areas of control. These areas are as follows:

➤ Startup

➤ Runtime

➤ Remoting

➤ Crypto

➤ Class API

➤ Security

Although all of these areas are important, this chapter covers only the first two. All of the settings discussed can be added to the application configuration file. Some of the settings (these are pointed out) can also be added to the machine configuration file. If a setting in the application configuration file conflicts with one in the machine configuration file, then the setting in the machine configuration file is used. When we talk about assembly references in the following discussion of configuration settings, we are talking exclusively about *shared assemblies* (which implies that the assemblies have a strong name, as required by assemblies in the GAC).

Startup Settings

The `<startup>` node of the application and machine configuration files has a `<requiredRuntime>` node that specifies the runtime version required by the application. This is because different versions of the CLR can run on a machine side by side. The following example shows how you would specify the version of the .NET runtime inside the configuration file:

```
<configuration>
  <startup>
    <requiredRuntime version ="4.0.xxxx" safemode ="true"/>
  </startup>
</configuration>
```

Runtime Settings

The runtime node, which is written as `<runtime>` (not to be confused with `<requiredRuntime>`), specifies the settings that manage how the CLR handles garbage collection and versions of assemblies. With these settings, you can specify which version of an assembly the application requires, or redirect it to another version entirely.

Loading a Particular Version of an Assembly

The application and machine configuration files can be used to ensure that a particular version of an assembly is loaded. You can indicate whether this version should be loaded all the time or should only replace a specific version of the assembly. This functionality is supported through the use of the `<assemblyIdentity>` and `<bindingRedirect>` elements in the configuration file, as shown in the following example:

Available for download on Wrox.com

```
<configuration>
  <runtime>
    <assemblyBinding xmlns="urn:schemas-microsoft-com:asm.v1">
      <dependentAssembly>
        <assemblyIdentity name="AssemblyName"
                          publickeytoken="b77a5c561934e089"
                          culture="en-us"/>
          <bindingRedirect oldVersion="*"
                          newVersion="2.0.50.0"/>
```

```
          </dependentAssembly>
        </assemblyBindings>
      </runtime>
    </configuration>
```

The `<assemblyBinding>` node is used to declare settings for the locations of assemblies and redirections via the `<dependentAssembly>` node and the `<probing>` node (which you will look at shortly).

In the last example, when the CLR resolves the reference to the assembly named `AssemblyName`, it loads version 2.0.50.0 instead of the version that appears in the manifest. If you want to load only version 2.0.50.0 of the assembly when a specific version is referenced, then you can replace the value of the `oldVersion` attribute with the version number that you would like to replace (for example, 1.5.0.0). The `publickeytoken` attribute is used to store the hash of the strong name of the assembly to replace. This ensures that the correct assembly is identified. The same is true of the `culture` attribute.

Defining the Location of an Assembly

The location of an assembly can also be defined in both the application and machine configuration files. You can use the `<codeBase>` element to inform the CLR of the location of an assembly. This enables you to distribute an application and have the externally referenced assemblies downloaded the first time they are used (on-demand downloading):

```
<configuration>
  <runtime>
    <assemblyBinding xmlns="urn:schemas-microsoft-com:asm.v1">
      <dependentAssembly>
        <assemblyIdentity name="AssemblyName"
                          publickeytoken="b77a5c561934e089"
                          culture="en-us"/>
        <codeBase version="2.0.50.0"
                  href="http://www.wrox.com/AssemblyName.dll/>
      </dependentAssembly>
    </assemblyBindings>
  </runtime>
</configuration>
```

You can see from this example that whenever a reference to version 2.0.50.0 of the assembly `AssemblyName` is resolved (and the assembly isn't already on the user's computer), the CLR will try to load the assembly from the location defined in the `href` attribute. The location defined in the `href` attribute is a standard URL and can be used to locate a file across the Internet or locally.

If the assembly cannot be found or the details in the manifest of the assembly defined in the `href` attribute do not match those defined in the configuration file, then the loading of the assembly will fail and you will receive a `TypeLoadException`. If the version of the assembly in the preceding example were actually 2.0.60.0, then the assembly would load because the version number is only different by build and revision number.

Providing the Search Path

The final use of configuration files to consider is that of providing the search path to use when locating assemblies in the application's directory. This setting applies only to the application configuration file (`AppName.exe.config`, for example). By default, the CLR searches for an assembly only in the application's base directory — it will not look in any subdirectories. You can modify this behavior by using the `<probing>` element in an application configuration file, as shown in the following example:

```
<configuration>
  <runtime>
    <assemblyBinding xmlns="urn:schemas-microsoft-com:asm.v1">
      <probing privatePath="regional"/>
    </assemblyBinding>
  </runtime>
</configuration>
```

Code snippet from CodeSnippetsChapter31

The `privatePath` attribute can contain a list of directories relative to the application's directory (separated by a semicolon) that you would like the CLR to search when trying to locate an assembly. The `privatePath` attribute cannot contain an absolute pathname.

As part of resolving an assembly reference, the CLR checks in the application's base directory for it. If it cannot find it, then it looks through, in order, all the subdirectories specified in the `privatePath` variable, as well as looking for a subdirectory with the same name as the assembly. If the assembly being resolved is called `AssemblyName`, then the CLR also checks for the assembly in a subdirectory called `AssemblyName`, if it exists.

This isn't the end of the story, though. If the referenced assembly being resolved contains a culture setting, then the CLR also checks for culture-specific subdirectories in each of the directories it searches in. For example, if the CLR is trying to resolve a reference to an assembly named `AssemblyName` with a culture of en and a `privatePath` equal to that in the last example, and the application being run has a home directory of `C:\ExampleApp`, then the CLR will look in the following directories (in the order shown):

- ➤ C:\ExampleApp
- ➤ C:\ExampleApp\en
- ➤ C:\ExampleApp\en\AssemblyName
- ➤ C:\ExampleApp\regional\en
- ➤ C:\ExampleApp\regional\en\AssemblyName

As you can see, the CLR can probe quite a number of directories to locate an assembly. When an external assembly is resolved by the CLR, it consults the configuration files first to determine whether it needs to modify the process by which it resolves an assembly. As discussed, you can modify the resolution process to suit your needs.

BASICS OF REFLECTION

As mentioned in Chapter 4, you can explore the internals of a given assembly using a process called *reflection*. You can find out what assemblies are loaded into your current application domain. You can discover what types reside in each assembly, and for any given type, the methods and properties exposed by the type. You can even execute a method or change a property value via reflection, even though you might not know the name of the method or property at compile time.

In this section, you'll see the basic code required for each of these operations. The code uses classes in the `System.Reflection` namespace, most notably the `Assembly` class, and each example assumes that the code module has an `Imports` statement to import `System.Reflection`.

Major classes needed to use reflection capabilities include the following:

- ➤ `Assembly` — Contains members to examine an assembly's metadata and even manipulate the assembly
- ➤ `AppDomain` — Contains information about the currently running application domain
- ➤ `Type` — Gives access to information about a .NET type

After this section, you will also see an additional capability provided through reflection: dynamic loading. You'll see how to gain a reference to an assembly on-the-fly and generate an instance of a type within the assembly.

> *While the process of reflection is powerful and enables you to perform operations that would otherwise be impossible, you should be aware of the performance implications of using reflection heavily. Some reflection operations are rather slow; code that contains many such operations, as in a loop, can cause your program to experience noticeable delays.*

The Assembly Class

Almost all work with reflection will require you to work with the `Assembly` class. An instance of this class is associated with a .NET assembly.

There are several ways to get a reference to an instance of an `Assembly` class. Several shared methods of the `Assembly` class can return such an instance. The ones most commonly used are as follows:

➤ `GetAssembly` — Takes a Type instance and returns a reference to the assembly containing that Type. The assembly must already be available in the current application domain.

➤ `GetExecutingAssembly` — Returns the assembly that contains the code currently being executed.

➤ `LoadFile` — Loads an assembly using a string containing the filename in which the assembly resides.

➤ `LoadFrom` — Loads an assembly from a string containing a filename or URL.

Here is a code example that gets an assembly reference using each of the first three of these methods. The fourth method is covered in the section on dynamic loading later in the chapter.

Available for download on Wrox.com

```
Dim Assembly1 As [Assembly]
Assembly1 = [Assembly].GetAssembly(GetType(System.Boolean))
' This would return a reference to mscorlib

Dim Assembly2 As [Assembly]
Assembly2 = [Assembly].GetExecutingAssembly
' This would return a reference to the assembly
' containing this code.

Dim Assembly3 As [Assembly]
Dim sFileName As String
sFileName = "C:\Dev\MyProject\bin\Release\MyLibrary.dll"
Assembly3 = [Assembly].LoadFile(sFileName)
```

Code snippet from CodeSnippetsChapter31

You can also get a reference to an assembly by first getting a list of the assemblies loaded into an application and then choosing an assembly from that list.

Getting Currently Loaded Assemblies

The application domain is the context for your current running application. You can work with an application domain using the `AppDomain` class in the `System` namespace. `AppDomain` has a shared property called `CurrentDomain` that will return the application domain in which you are currently running.

An application domain instance has a `GetAssemblies` method to obtain the assemblies currently loaded in the application domain. `GetAssemblies` returns an array of type `Assembly`.

Putting these capabilities together, you can print out the long name of each assembly in the current application domain using the following code:

```
Dim LoadedAssemblies As Assembly()
'Get the list of loaded assemblies from the current AppDomain.
LoadedAssemblies = AppDomain.CurrentDomain.GetAssemblies()

For Each LoadedAssembly In LoadedAssemblies
    ' There are many operations available on
    ' each assembly. This code simply lists the
    ' assembly's full name.
    Console.WriteLine(LoadedAssembly.FullName)
Next
```

Code snippet from CodeSnippetsChapter31

The Type Class

Chapter 4 discussed types in .NET. To recap, a type is a class, structure, or native value type such as a `Double` or `Boolean`.

A type is represented during reflection by an instance of the `Type` class. As Chapter 4 explained, you can get a reference to a type by using the `GetType` method of the type. However, you can also get a reference to a type via a method on an instance of the `Assembly` class that is associated with the assembly containing the type.

Finding the Types in an Assembly

The `GetTypes` method of an `Assembly` class instance returns an array containing all the types in the assembly. You can also get a reference to a single type in an assembly with the `GetType` method, which takes a string with the fully qualified namespace path name of the type.

For example, the following code will print out the names of all the types in the assembly containing the currently executing code:

```
Dim CurrentAssembly As [Assembly]
CurrentAssembly = [Assembly].GetExecutingAssembly
For Each IndividualType In CurrentAssembly.GetTypes
    Console.WriteLine(IndividualType.Name)
Next
```

Code snippet from CodeSnippetsChapter31

Finding the Members of a Type

Reflection also allows you to explore a type and discover the members (properties and methods) of the type. The `GetProperties` method of a type will return an array of property descriptor objects, and the `GetMethods` method will return an array of method descriptors in the form of `MethodInfo` instances. The more general `GetMembers` method will return all the members of a `Type`, including properties, methods, events, and so forth. The following code, when placed inside a class, will print out all the properties, events, and public methods for the class:

```
For Each Member In Me.GetType.GetMembers
    Console.WriteLine(Member.Name)
Next

For Each IndividualProperty In Me.GetType.GetProperties
    Console.WriteLine(IndividualProperty.Name)
Next
```

Code snippet from CodeSnippetsChapter31

There is some redundancy between these two methods. At a binary level, properties are actually pairs of get and set methods. That means you will see the get and set methods for a type's properties when you list out the methods.

Visual Basic Sub and Function routines are both considered methods in reflection. The only difference is that a Sub has no return value. If a method is a Function, and thus does have a return value, reflection allows you to discover the type of that return value.

Methods may have calling parameters. Reflection allows you to discover the calling parameters of a method, if there are any, using the GetParameters method of the MethodInfo instance for the method. The GetParameters method returns an array of ParameterInfo objects.

Using parameters, if any, a method can be invoked with the Invoke method of the MethodInfo instance. Suppose, for example, that the current class has a function named CalculateFee that takes an integer for customer ID and returns a decimal value.

Here is sample code to print the parameters for the method:

Available for download on Wrox.com

```
Dim MyMethodInfo As MethodInfo = Me.GetType.GetMember("CalculateFee")(0)
For Each ParamInfo In MyMethodInfo.GetParameters
    Console.WriteLine("Parameter name:" & ParamInfo.Name)
    Console.WriteLine("Parameter type:" & ParamInfo.ParameterType.Name)
Next
```

Code snippet from CodeSnippetsChapter31

To set up the parameter values and invoke the method, the code would look like this:

Available for download on Wrox.com

```
Dim MyMethodInfo2 As MethodInfo = _ Me.GetType.GetMember("CalculateFee")(0)

'Create array of objects to serve as parameters.
'In this case, only one integer is needed.
Dim MyParameters() As Object = {4321}
Dim oReturn As Object
oReturn = MyMethodInfo2.Invoke(Me, MyParameters)
' Now cast oReturn to Decimal
```

Code snippet from CodeSnippetsChapter31

The code download for this chapter includes a WPF program that enables you to locate an assembly on disk and load the types from that assembly. For any type available in the assembly, you can then load all the methods of the type.

DYNAMIC LOADING OF ASSEMBLIES

The preceding discussion about locating and loading assemblies refers to assemblies that are known at compile time through the application's references. There is an alternative method of locating and loading an assembly that is useful for certain scenarios.

In this technique, the location of the assembly is supplied by the application, using a URL or filename. The normal rules for locating the assembly do not apply — only the location specified by the application is used.

The location is just a string variable, so it may come from a configuration file or a database. In fact, the assembly to be loaded may be newly created, and perhaps did not even exist when the original application was compiled. Because the information to load the assembly can be passed into the application on-the-fly at runtime, this type of assembly loading is called *dynamic loading*.

The LoadFrom Method of the Assembly Class

The Assembly class has a shared method called LoadFrom that takes a URL or filename and returns a reference to the assembly at that location. Here's a code example of LoadFrom in action, getting an assembly reference from a URL:

```
Dim asmDynamic As [Assembly]
asmDynamic = [Assembly].LoadFrom("http://www.dotnetmasters.com/loancalc2.dll")
```

As previously discussed, the brackets around `Assembly` are needed because it is a reserved keyword in Visual Basic. The brackets indicate that the word applies to the `Assembly` class, and the keyword is not being used.

After these lines are executed, the code contains a reference to the assembly at the given location. That enables the reflection operations discussed earlier for finding types in the assembly. Recall that one such operation is getting a reference to a particular type (which could be a class, structure, or enumeration) in the assembly.

For dynamic loading, normally the `GetType` method of the `Assembly` class is used to get the reference, using a string that represents the identification of the type. The identification consists of the full namespace path that uniquely identifies the type within the current application. Once a reference to a type is obtained, an instance of the type can be created, even though the assembly was loaded dynamically.

For example, suppose that you wanted to get an instance of a certain form in the assembly, with a namespace path of `MyProject.Form1`. The following line of code would get a reference to the type for that form:

```
Dim typMyForm As Type = formAsm.GetType("MyProject.Form1")
```

The type reference can then be used to generate an instance of the type. To do this, you need another class in the `System` namespace called the `Activator` class. This class has a shared method called `CreateInstance`, which takes a type reference and returns an instance of that type. You could, therefore, get an instance of the form with these lines:

```
Dim objForm As Object
objForm = Activator.CreateInstance(typMyForm)
```

`CreateInstance` always returns a generic object. That means it may be necessary to coerce the returned reference to a particular type to gain access to the type's interface. For example, assuming that you knew the object was actually a Windows form, you could cast the preceding instance into the type of `System.Windows.Forms.Form` and then do normal operations that are available on a form:

```
Dim FormToShow As Form = CType(objForm, System.Windows.Forms.Form)
FormToShow.MdiParent = Me
FormToShow.Show()
```

At this point, the form will operate normally. It will behave no differently from a form that was in a referenced assembly (except for potential code access security limitations, as discussed in Chapter 32).

If the newly loaded form needs to load other classes in the dynamic assembly, nothing special needs to be done. For example, suppose that the form just shown needs to load an instance of another form, named `Form2`, that resides in the same dynamically loaded assembly. The standard code to instantiate a form will work fine. The CLR will automatically load the `Form2` type because it already has a reference to the assembly containing `Form2`.

Furthermore, suppose that the dynamically loaded form needs to instantiate a class from another DLL that is not referenced by the application. For example, suppose that the form needs to create an instance of a `Customer` object, and the `Customer` class is in a different DLL. As long as that DLL is in the same folder as the dynamically loaded DLL, the CLR will automatically locate and load the second DLL.

Dynamic Loading Example

To see dynamic loading in action, try the following step-by-step example:

1. Create a new Windows Forms Application project in Visual Studio and name it **DynamicLoading**. On the blank `Form1` that appears, drag a `Button` control from the Toolbox, and set its `Text` property to `Load`.

2. Double-click the Load button to get to its Click event in the Code Editor. Then go to the top of the code module and insert the following `Imports` statement:

```
Imports System.Reflection
```

Available for download on Wrox.com

3. Insert the following code into the button's Click event:

```
Dim sLocation As String = "C:\Deploy\DynamicForms.dll"
If My.Computer.FileSystem.FileExists(sLocation) Then
    Dim sType As String = "DynamicForms.Form1"
    Dim DynamicAssembly As [Assembly] = _
              [Assembly].LoadFrom(sLocation)
    Dim DynamicType As Type = DynamicAssembly.GetType(sType)
    Dim DynamicObject As Object
    DynamicObject = Activator.CreateInstance(DynamicType)
    ' We know it's a form - cast to form type
    Dim FormToShow As Form = CType(DynamicObject, Form)
    FormToShow.Show()
Else
    MsgBox("Unable to load assembly " & sLocation & _
            " because the file does not exist")
End If
```

Code snippet from Form1.vb in project DynamicLoading

4. Run the program and click the Load button. You should get a message box with the message "Unable to load assembly C:\Deploy\DynamicForms.dll because the form does not exist." Leave this program running while you carry out the next few steps.

5. Start another separate Visual Studio instance, and create a new Windows Forms Application project named **DynamicForms**. On the blank Form1 that appears, drag over a few controls. It doesn't really matter what controls you drag onto Form1. The version that can be downloaded for the book includes some labels, buttons, and text boxes.

6. In the properties for DynamicForms, change the application type to Class Library.

7. Build the DynamicForms project by selecting Build ➪ Build DynamicForms from the Visual Studio menu. This will place a file named DynamicForms.dll in the project's \bin\Debug directory (or the \bin\Release directory if you happen to have the Release configuration set in Visual Studio).

8. Create a directory named C:\Deploy and copy the DynamicForms.dll file to that directory.

9. Return to the running program DynamicLoading. Click the Load button again. This time, it should load the assembly from the DLL you just copied and launch an instance of Form1 from the DynamicForms project.

Notice that the DynamicForms.dll was created and compiled after the DynamicLoading.exe project that loaded it. It is not necessary to recompile or even restart DynamicLoading.exe to load a new assembly dynamically, as long as DynamicLoading.exe knows the location of the assembly and the type to be loaded from it.

Putting Assemblies to Work

The previous code examples include hard-coded strings for the location of the assembly and the identification of the type. There are uses for such a technique, such as certain types of Internet deployment of an application. However, when using dynamic loading, it is common for these values to be obtained from outside the code. For example, a database table or an XML-based configuration file can be used to store the information.

This enables you to add new capabilities to an application on-the-fly. A new assembly with new functionality can be written, and then the location of the assembly and the identity of the type to load from the assembly can be added to the configuration file or database table.

Unlike application assemblies automatically located by the CLR, which must be in the application's directory or a subdirectory of it, dynamically loaded assemblies can be anywhere the application knows how to access. Possibilities include the following:

> ➤ A website
> ➤ A directory on the local machine
> ➤ A directory on a shared network machine

The security privileges available to code vary, depending on where the assembly was loaded from. Code loaded from a URL via HTTP, as shown earlier, has a very restricted set of privileges by default compared to code loaded from a local directory. Chapter 32 has details on code access security, default security policies, and how default policies can be changed.

SUMMARY

Assemblies are the basic unit of deployment and versioning in .NET. You can write and install simple applications without knowing much about assemblies. More complex applications require an in-depth understanding of the structure of assemblies, the metadata they contain, and how assemblies are located and loaded by the CLR.

You have learned how the identity of an assembly is used to allow multiple versions of an assembly to be installed on a machine and run side by side. This chapter explained how an assembly is versioned, the process by which the CLR resolves an external assembly reference, and how you can modify this process through the use of configuration files.

You also learned about how an assembly stores information, such as version number, strong name, and culture, about any external assemblies that it references, and information checked at runtime to ensure that the correct version of the assembly is referenced. You saw how you can use versioning policies to override this in the case of a buggy assembly. The assembly is the single biggest aid in reducing the errors that can occur due to DLL hell, and in helping with deployment.

You've also seen how to examine assemblies to discover the types they contain, and the members of those types. You can even invoke a method on a type using the capabilities of reflection.

The chapter also discussed the capability to load an assembly dynamically, based on a location that is derived at runtime. This capability is useful for some special deployment scenarios, such as simple Internet deployment. Understanding all these elements helps you understand how to structure an application, when and how to use shared assemblies, and the deployment implications of your choices for assemblies.

Simple applications are usually created with no strong names or shared assemblies, and all assemblies for the application are deployed to the application directory. Versioning issues are rare as long as class interfaces are consistent.

Complex applications may require shared assemblies to be placed in the GAC, which means that those assemblies must have strong names, and you must control your version numbers. You also need to understand your options for allowing an application to load a version of an assembly other than the one it would load by default, or for loading assemblies dynamically using an application-specific technique to determine the assembly's location. This chapter has covered the basics for all of these needs.

32

Security in the .NET Framework

WHAT YOU WILL LEARN IN THIS CHAPTER

- ➤ Concepts and definitions
- ➤ Permissions
- ➤ Roles
- ➤ Principals
- ➤ Code access permissions
- ➤ Role-based permissions
- ➤ Identity permissions
- ➤ User Access Control (UAC)
- ➤ Encryption
- ➤ Hashing
- ➤ Symmetric Key Encryption
- ➤ Asymmetric Key Encryption
- ➤ Digital Signatures
- ➤ X.509 Certificates
- ➤ SSL

This chapter covers the basics of security and cryptography. It begins with a brief discussion of the .NET Framework's security architecture, because this affects all the solutions you may choose to implement.

The .NET Framework provides you with best practices, tools, and core functionality with regard to security. You have the System.Security.Permissions namespace, which enables you to control code access permissions along with role-based and identity permissions. Through your code, you can control access to objects programmatically, as well as receive information on the current permissions of objects. This security framework will assist you in determining whether you have permissions to run your code, instead of getting halfway through execution and having to deal with permission-based exceptions.

Cryptography is the cornerstone of the .NET Web Services security model, so the second half of this chapter discusses the basis of cryptography and how to implement it. Specifically, it covers the following:

➤ Hash algorithms

➤ SHA

➤ MD5

➤ Secret key encryption

➤ Public key cryptography standard

➤ Digital signatures

➤ Certification

➤ Secure Sockets Layer communications

Let's begin by looking at some security concepts and definitions.

 As always, the code for this chapter is available for download from www.wrox.com, *which you may want in order to follow along.*

SECURITY CONCEPTS AND DEFINITIONS

Table 32-1 describes the different types of security presented in this chapter and how they relate to real-world scenarios.

TABLE 32-1: Types of Security

SECURITY TYPE	RELATED CONCEPT IN SECURITY .PERMISSIONS NAMESPACE	PURPOSE
NTFS	None	Allows for detailed file system rights, e.g., locking down of specific files
Cryptographic	Strong name and assembly, generation, SignCode.exe utility	Use of public key infrastructure and certificates
Programmatic	Groups and permission sets	For use in pieces of code that are being called into. Provides extra security to prevent users of calling code from violating security measures implemented by the programs that are not provided for on a machine level.
User Access Control	Users run without administrative permission	Provided by the operating system to help users protect their system from unexpected changes that might occur when logged in using the machine's administrator account.

There are many approaches to providing security on the machines where your shared code is hosted. If multiple shared code applications are on one machine, each piece of shared code can be called from many front-end applications. Each piece of shared code will have its own security requirements for accessing environment variables — such as the registry, the file system, and other items — on the machine that it is running on. From an NTFS perspective, the administrator of your server can only lock down those items on the machine that are not required to be accessed from any piece of shared code running on it. Therefore, some applications need additional security built-in to prevent any calling code from doing things it is not supposed to do.

One of the more significant changes to security in .NET 4 is the removal of Code Access Security policies. Similar to the old Permview.exe, CasPol.exe is now an obsolete utility, and as such coverage of this topic has been omitted. Additionally, the PermCalc.exe tool has also been made obsolete with .NET 4.

To limit your Internet applications' access to the local file system, you create a permission set that limits that access and associates the Internet application group with this permission set. By default, the .NET environment provides one code group named All Code that is associated with the FullTrust permission set.

A permission set is a combination of security configurations. This set defines what each authorized user has access to and what that user can do on that machine — for instance, whether the user can read environment variables or the file system, or execute other code.

Security that is used within the programming environment also makes use of permission sets. Through code you can control access to files in a file system, environment variables, file dialogs, isolated storage, reflections, registry, sockets, and UI. Isolated storage and virtual file systems are new operating system–level storage locations that can be used by programs and are governed by the machine security policies. These file systems keep a machine safe from file system intrusion by designating a regulated area for file storage. The main access to these items is controlled through code access permissions.

Although many methods that we use in Visual Basic provide an identifiable return value, the only time we get a return value from security methods is when the method fails. When a security method succeeds, it does not provide a return value. If it fails, then it returns an exception object reflecting the specific error that occurred.

PERMISSIONS IN THE SYSTEM.SECURITY.PERMISSIONS NAMESPACE

The `System.Security.Permissions` namespace is the namespace used in code to establish and use permissions associated with objects, including the file system, environment variables, and the registry. The namespace controls access to both operating system–level objects as well as code objects. In order to use this namespace in your project, you need to import it. Using this namespace gives you access to the `CodeAccessPermission` and `PrincipalPermission` classes for using role-based permissions and information supplied by identity permissions. `CodeAccessPermission` controls access to the operating system–level objects. Role-based permissions and identity permissions grant access to objects based on the identity of the user of the program that is running (the user context).

Table 32-2 lists the members of the `System.Security.Permissions` namespace that apply to Windows application programming. While there is a description accompanying each member, those classes that end with `Attribute`, such as `EnvironmentPermissionAttribute`, are classes that enable you to modify the security level at which your code is allowed to interact with each respective object. These objects create a declarative model for setting security that can be leveraged across multiple different implementation models.

The default environment will provide a given level of access. It is not possible to grant access beyond this level via code access security; however, when working with these classes you can specify exactly what should or should not be available in a given situation. Additionally, these classes have been marked to prevent inheritance. It really wouldn't be a very secure system if you could inherit from one of these classes. Code could be written to override the associated security methods and grant unlimited permissions.

Table 32-2 also deals with security in regard to software publishers. A *software publisher* is a specific entity that is using a digital signature to identify itself in a Web-based scenario.

TABLE 32-2: Members of System.Security.Permissions

CLASS	DESCRIPTION
CodeAccessSecurityAttribute	Base class for code access security attribute classes
DataProtectionPermission	Controls access to the data protection APIs , T
DataProtectionPermissionAttribute	Allows declarative control of DataProtectionPermssion via code
EnvironmentPermission	Controls the capability to see and modify system and user environment variables

continues

TABLE 32-2 *(continued)*

CLASS	DESCRIPTION
EnvironmentPermissionAttribute	Allows security actions for environment variables to be added via code
FileDialogPermission	Controls the capability to open files via a file dialog
FileDialogPermissionAttribute	Allows security actions to be added for file dialogs via code
FileIOPermission	Controls the capability to read and write files in the file system
FileIOPermissionAttribute	Allows security actions to be added for file access attempts via code
GacIdentityPermission	Defines the identity permissions for files that come from the global assembly cache (GAC)
GacIdentityPermissionAttribute	Allows security actions to be added for files that originate from the GAC
HostProtectionAttribute	Allows for the use of security actions to determine host protection requirements
IsolatedStorageFilePermission	Controls access to a private virtual file system within the isolated storage area of an application
IsolatedStorageFilePermissionAttribute	Allows security actions to be added for private virtual file systems via code
IsolatedStoragePermission	Controls access to the isolated storage area of an application
IsolatedStoragePermissionAttribute	Allows security actions to be added for the isolated storage area of an application
KeyContainerPermission	Controls access to key containers
KeyContainerPermissionAccessEntry	Defines the access rights for particular key containers
KeyContainerPermissionAccess EntryCollection	Represents a collection of KeyContainerPermission-AccessEntry objects
KeyContainerPermissionAccess EntryEnumerator	Represents the enumerators for the objects contained in the KeyContainerPermissionAccessEntryCollection object
KeyContainerPermissionAttribute	Allows security actions to be added for key containers
MediaPermission	The permission set associated with the capability to access audio, video, and images. WPF leverages this capability.
MediaPermissionAttribute	Allows code to set permissions related to the MediaPermission set
PermissionSetAttribute	Allows security actions to be added for a permission set
PrincipalPermission	Controls the capability to verify the active principal
PrincipalPermissionAttribute	Allows verification of a specific user. Security principals are a user and role combination used to establish security identity.
PublisherIdentityPermission	Allows access based on the identity of a software publisher
PublisherIdentityPermissionAttribute	Allows security to be defined for a software publisher

CLASS	DESCRIPTION
ReflectionPermission	Controls access to nonpublic members of a given type
ReflectionPermissionAttribute	Allows security to be defined for public and nonpublic members of a given type
RegistryPermission	Controls access to registry keys and values
RegistryPermissionAttribute	Allows security to be defined for the registry
ResourcePermissionBase	Controls the capability to work with the code access security permissions
ResourcePermissionBaseEntry	Allows you to define the smallest part of a code access security permission set
SecurityAttribute	Controls which security attributes are representing code; used to control security when creating an assembly
SecurityPermission	This collection is used in code to specify a set of permissions for which access will be defined.
SecurityPermissionAttribute	Allows security actions for the security permission flags
StorePermission	Controls access to stores that contain X.509 certificates
StorePermissionAttribute	Allows security actions to be added for access stores that contain X.509 certificates
StrongNameIdentityPermission	Defines the permission level for creating strong names
StrongNameIdentityPermissionAttribute	Allows security to be defined on the StrongNameIdentityPermission set
StrongNamePublicKeyBlob	The public key information associated with a strong name
TypeDescriptorPermission	Permission set that controls partial-trust access to the TypeDescriptor class
TypeDescriptorPermissionAttribute	Allows security to be defined on the TypeDescriptorPermission set
UIPermission	Controls access to user interfaces and use of the Windows clipboard
UIPermissionAttribute	Allows security actions to be added for UI interfaces and the use of the clipboard
UrlIdentityPermission	Permission set associated with the identity and related permissions for the URL from which code originates
UrlIdentityPermissionAttribute	Allows security to be defined on the UrlIdentityPermission set
WebBrowserPermission	Controls the capability to create the WebBrowser control
WebBrowserPermissionAttribute	Allows security to be defined on the WebBrowser Permission set
ZoneIdentityPermission	Defines the identity permission for the zone from which code originates
ZoneIdentityPermissionAttribute	Allows security to be defined on the ZoneIdentity Permission set

Code Access Permissions

Code access permissions are controlled through the `CodeAccessPermission` class within the `System.Security` namespace The code access permissions are used extensively by the common language runtime (CLR) to manage and secure the operating environment.

The code access permissions grant and deny access to portions of the operating system such as the file system, but although your code can request permission changes, there is a key limit. Code using this API can request to reduce the rights of the user currently executing the code, but the API will not grant rights that a user does not have within his or her current context or based on those available from the CLR.

When code is downloaded from a website,and the user then attempts to run the code; the CLR can choose to limit the rights of that code given that it shouldn't by default be trusted. For example, requesting access to the system registry will be denied if the operating system does not trust that code. Thus, the primary use of code access security by application developers is to limit the permissions already available to a user given the current context of what the user is doing. Code access security leverages many of the same core security methods used across the various security categories, many of which are described in Table 32-3.

TABLE 32-3: Methods of CodeAccessPermission

METHOD	DESCRIPTION
Assert	Sets the permission to full access so that the specific resource can be accessed even if the caller hasn't been granted permission to access the resource
Copy	Copies a permission object
Demand	Returns an exception unless all callers in the call chain have been granted the permission to access the resource in a given manner
Deny	In prior versions of .NET you would use this to explicitly deny access. This will still work, but it's becoming obsolete and should be avoided.
Equals	Determines whether a given object is the same instance of the current object
FromXml	Establishes a permission set given a specific XML encoding. This parameter that this method takes is an XML encoding.
Intersect	Returns the permissions that two permission objects have in common
IsSubsetOf	Returns a result indicating whether the current permission object is a subset of a specified permission
PermitOnly	Specifies that only those rights within this permission set can be accessed even if the user of the assembly has been granted additional permission to the underlying objects. This is one of the more common permission levels when working with custom permission sets.
RevertAll	Reverses all previous assert, deny, or permit-only methods
RevertAssert	Reverses all previous assert methods
RevertDeny	Reverses all previous deny methods
RevertPermitOnly	Reverses all previous permit-only methods
Union	Creates a permission that is the union of two permission objects

Identity Permissions

Identity permissions are pieces of information, also called *evidence*, by which an assembly can be identified. Examples of the evidence would be the strong name of the assembly or the digital signature associated with the assembly.

> *A strong name is a combination of the name of a program, its version number, and its associated cryptographic key and digital signature files.*

Identity permissions are granted by the runtime based on information received from the trusted host, or the operating system's loader. Therefore, they are permissions that you don't specifically request. Identity permissions provide additional information to be used by the runtime. The identity information can take the form of a trusted host's URL or can be supplied via a digital signature, the application directory, or the strong name of the assembly. Identity permissions are similar to code access permissions discussed in the preceding section. They derive from the same base class as the code access permissions.

Role-Based Permissions

Role-based permissions are permissions granted based on the user and the role that code is being called with. Users are authenticated within the operating system platform and hold a Security Identifier (SID) that is associated within a security context. The SID is associated with one or more roles or group memberships that are established within a security context. .NET supports those users and roles associated within a security context and has support for generic and custom users and roles through the concept of principals.

A *principal* is an object that holds the current caller's credentials. This includes the identity of the user. Principals come in two types: Windows principals and non-Windows principals. Windows-based principal objects are objects that store the Windows SID information regarding the current user context associated with the code that is calling into the module role-based permissions that are being used. Non-Windows principals are principal objects that are created programmatically via a custom login methodology and which are made available to the current thread.

Role-based permissions are not set against objects within your environment like code access permissions. They are checked within the context of the current user and user's role. The concepts of principals and the PrincipalPermission class are used to establish and check permissions. If a programmer passes the user and role information during a call as captured from a custom login, then the PrincipalPermission class can be used to verify this information as well.

The PrincipalPermission class does not grant access to objects, but has methods that determine whether a caller has been given permissions according to the current permission object through the Demand method. If a security exception is generated, then the user does not have sufficient permission. As an example of how you might use these methods, the following code snippet captures the current Windows principal information and displays it on the screen in a text box. It is included as part of the ProVB_Security project, which has the same basic structure as the ProVB_VS2010 project introduced in Chapter 1. Each element of the principal information could be used in a program to validate against, and thus restrict, code execution based on the values in the principal information. This example inserts an Imports System.Security.Principal line at the top of Form1.vb so you can directly reference identity and principal objects without full namespace qualifiers:

```
Imports System.Security.Principal

'<PrincipalPermissionAttribute(SecurityAction.Demand, Name:="WSheldon", Role:="Users")> _
Private Sub DisplayPrincipalIdentity()
    ' The attribute above can be used to check security declaratively
    ' similar to how you would check using WPF or Silverlight.
    ' The code below uses imperative commands to get security information.
    Dim objIdentity As WindowsIdentity = WindowsIdentity.GetCurrent()
    TextBox1.Text = "User Name: " & objIdentity.Name & Environment.NewLine
    TextBox1.Text &= "Is Guest: " & objIdentity.IsGuest.ToString()
        & Environment.NewLine
```

```
TextBox1.Text &= "Is Authenticated: " & objIdentity.IsAuthenticated.ToString()
    & Environment.NewLine
Dim objPrincipal As New Security.Principal.WindowsPrincipal(objIdentity)
' Determine if the user is part of an authorized group.
TextBox1.Text &= "Is in Role Users? " & objPrincipal.IsInRole("Users")
    & Environment.NewLine
TextBox1.Text &= "Is in Role Administrators? "
    & objPrincipal.IsInRole("Administrators")
End Sub
```

Code snippet from Form1.vb

This code illustrates a few of the properties that could be used to validate against when a caller wants to run your code. The attribute at the top of this is commented out at this point by design. It represents a declarative security check similar to what you would use from the XAML in a WPF or Silverlight project. First, however, lets examine this code being run, as shown in Figure 32-1.

It starts by retrieving the user name of the currently authenticated Windows principal. Pay attention to the fact that this is a fully qualified username with the machine name included. It then uses the identity checks to see if the current identity is the Guest account, and ensures that the user was authenticated.

At this point the snippet creates a new `WindowsPrincipal` based on the current user's identity. This object allows you to query to see if the current user is in a role. In this case, my account is in the role of a user as a member of the Users security group, but is not in the role of an administrator even though it is part of the Administrators group.

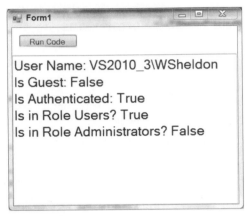

FIGURE 32-1

Roles are typically defined via security groups, but I was careful to not say that this method allowed you to determine if a user were in a given group. That's because under Windows Vista and Windows 7, the operating system keeps a user from running in the Administrator role even if they are part of the Administrators group. Thus, the check for whether the code is running in the role Administrators returns false — even though my WSheldon account is in fact a member of the Administrators group on this machine. Only if the user chooses to have their permission elevated will this query return true.

 The issue of permission elevation in relation to User Access Control (UAC) and the fact that the WSheldon account is in fact an Administrator on the system is discussed later in this chapter.

However, now uncomment the attribute line that precedes this method. Notice that it is making a Demand security query and passing a user name, and a role name as part of this name. Because these are named optional parameters, the code could in theory only check for a role, which is a much more usable check in a real-world application. However, in this case only use a name and do not include the machine as part of the full user name. As a result, when `ButtonTest` is clicked this declarative check fails and the error shown in Figure 32-2 is displayed.

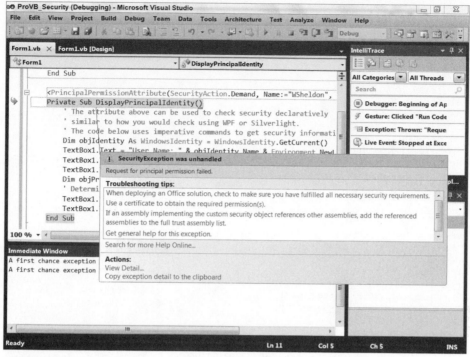

FIGURE 32-2

This illustrates how the same objects that have been available since the early versions of .NET are still used within XAML to enable the same level of security to declarative applications. The principal and identity objects are used in verifying the identity or aspects of the identity of the caller attempting to execute your code. Based on this information, your application can either lock down system resources or adjust the options available to users within your custom application. The `Identity` and `Principal` objects make it possible to have your application respond as changes to user roles occur within Active Directory.

MANAGING CODE ACCESS PERMISSION SETS

This section looks at programmatic access to permissions. The example extends the ProVB_Security project discussed earlier. This example illustrates how when a method fails, an exception object containing the result is generated. Note that in the case of a real-world example, you would be setting up permissions for a calling application. In many instances, you don't want a calling application to be able to access the registry, or you want a calling application to be able to read memory variables but not change them. Keep in mind that you can only limit those permissions which are already available to a user based on their identity. You can't grant access to a portion of the operating system via code that the user doesn't have access to based on their identity.

The example first sets up the permission that is wanted and then grants the code the appropriate access level. Then code that accesses this security object illustrates the effect of these new permissions on the code:

```
Private Sub TestFileIOPermission()
    Dim oFp = New FileIOPermission(
```

```vb
                        FileIOPermissionAccess.AllAccess,
                        "C:\Test")
        oFp.PermitOnly()
        'Try
        Dim strmWrite As New IO.StreamWriter(
            File.Open("C:\Test\Permission.txt",
            IO.FileMode.Open))
        strmWrite.WriteLine("Hi there!")
        strmWrite.Flush()
        strmWrite.Close()
        Dim objWriter As New IO.StreamWriter(
            File.Open("C:\Test\NoPermission.txt",
            IO.FileMode.Open))
        objWriter.WriteLine("Hi there!")
        objWriter.Flush()
        objWriter.Close()

        'Uncomment the lines below (comment those above) to reverse the test.

        'Dim oFp = New FileIOPermission(FileIOPermissionAccess.Read, "C:\")
        'oFp.PermitOnly()
        'Dim temp = oFp.AllFiles.ToString()
        'Dim strmWrite = New IO.StreamWriter(
        '                File.Open("C:\Test\Permission.txt",
        '                IO.FileMode.Open))
        'strmWrite.WriteLine("Hi there!")
        'strmWrite.Flush()
        'strmWrite.Close()
        'Dim objWriter = New IO.StreamWriter(
        '                File.Open("C:\Test\NoPermission.txt",
        '                IO.FileMode.Open))
        'objWriter.WriteLine("Hi there!")
        'objWriter.Flush()
        'objWriter.Close()
        ''Catch objA As System.Exception
        ''MessageBox.Show(objA.Message)
        ''End Try
    End Sub
```

Code snippet from Form1.vb

The first example attempts to access a file in the file system. This illustrates the use of the `FileIOPermission` class. Create a new folder on your `C:\` drive called Test. Within this folder create two new files, the first file `C:\Test\Permission.txt` will use the default permissions assigned when you created the account. The second file `C:\Test\NoPermission.txt` (these files are not part of the download) has its permissions modified.

To do this, access the file's properties by right-clicking on the file and choosing Properties. On the Properties dialog select the Security tab and then use the Advanced button. Within the Advanced Security Settings dialog use the Change Permission button to open the Advanced Security Settings dialog. Next go to the bottom of this dialog and unclick the check box "Include inheritable permissions from this object's parent" check box. You will need to verify that you want to add the security settings for this file to the file itself. After returning to the original Properties dialog by clicking the OK buttons you will want to remove the settings for Authorized Users. To do this you will need to use the Edit button to access the Permission dialog where you can use the Remove button. After having done this you will have removed the default modify permission for authenticated users to this file. The result should be the permission level that is depicted in Figure 32-3. Note that there are only three Group or usernames assigned permissions.

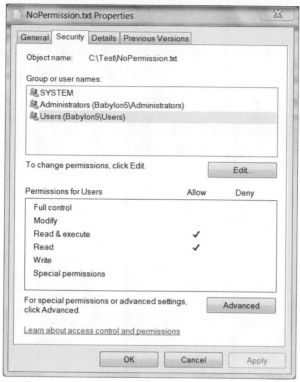

FIGURE 32-3

Looking at the previous code snippet notice that the Sub TestFileIOPermission first grants FileIO write permissions to the current user and attempts to access both files. This will fail for the `NoPermissions.txt` file because code access security can't grant additional access to a user at runtime. You can see this result in the error shown in Figure 32-4.

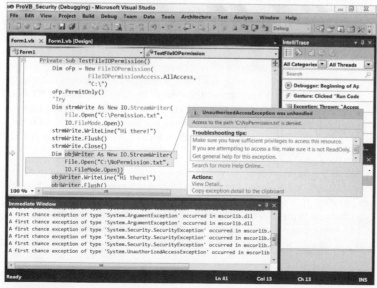

FIGURE 32-4

Now to test the reverse, comment out the top half of the preceding method and uncomment the bottom half. Now the method uses the `PermitOnly` assignment to limit the user to ReadOnly permissions for the FileIO permission set. In this case the code will fail when attempting to write to the `Permission.txt` file because of the stricter limits of this setting as opposed to what the operating system would allow. You can see this result in the error shown in Figure 32-5.

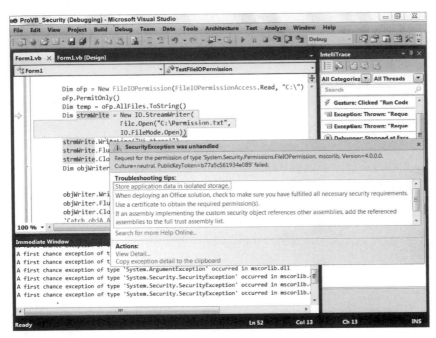

FIGURE 32-5

USER ACCESS CONTROL

With the introduction of Windows Vista and continuing with Windows 7, developers became aware of a new security model: User Access Control (UAC). The core premise of UAC is that even a user with administrative rights should normally run in the context of a reduced privilege user account. The concept is quite simply a best practice. Unfortunately, as with any situation where rights are reduced, application developers and users have spent so much time running with elevated permissions that any time the system interrupts what they want they become upset. But for security to work, sometimes its best to keep access limited and force you to recognize when you are granting access. This is what the UAC system does: it locks the access; you still have the ability to grant that access, but the system makes you pause and evaluate if that access should be granted. If you get a UAC prompt when you aren't expecting it, or realize that software you don't fully trust is attempting privileged access that you may not expect or want it to have, you are far better off than had the system not prompted you to grant that access. All for the price of a click of your mouse.

UAC gets a bit of a bad rap in part because it was introduced to end users as part of Vista before custom application developers, or even Microsoft developers, could get out in front of the required code changes. Thus, user's were asking, "Why am I getting this prompt?" Developers, having no real good answers then, had to answer, "Because Vista changed things." The unfortunate result is that many people and organizations have turned off UAC. However, as a developer you should now have it reenabled on your desktop and should begin to understand how to work both within its default constraints and beyond them.

DEFINING YOUR APPLICATION UAC SETTINGS

By default in Visual Studio 2010, your application settings include information related to UAC. It is possible to create your application so that it ships with certain permissions. Within your application manifest you'll find the section `requestedPrivileges`. This section is where the requested UAC execution level for your application is defined.

To get to your application manifest, right-click on your project in Solution Explorer and select Properties. In the Properties pane, select the Application tab and there you'll find a button labeled View Windows Settings. Selecting this button will open your application manifest (`app.manifest`) XML file in the editor window. Within the XML, you'll find the `requestedPrivileges` node, a copy of which is shown in the following code block:

Available for download on Wrox.com

```xml
<requestedPrivileges xmlns="urn:schemas-microsoft-com:asm.v3">
  <!-- UAC Manifest Options
      If you want to change the Windows User Account Control level replace the
      requestedExecutionLevel node with one of the following.

  <requestedExecutionLevel  level="asInvoker" uiAccess="false" />
  <requestedExecutionLevel  level="requireAdministrator" uiAccess="false" />
  <requestedExecutionLevel  level="highestAvailable" uiAccess="false" />

      Specifying requestedExecutionLevel node will disable file and registry
      virtualization. If you want to utilize File and Registry Virtualization
      for backward compatibility then delete the requestedExecutionLevel node.-->
  <requestedExecutionLevel level="asInvoker" uiAccess="false" />
</requestedPrivileges>
```

Code snippet from app.manifest

The beauty of this XML is that Microsoft took the time to include meaningful XML comments about the `requestedExecutionLevel` setting. By default, as shown in the preceding snippet, your application requests to run `asInvoker`. Thus, as discussed earlier when looking at which group you are running as, this means you are running as a user, not an administrator.

As the comments make clear, it is possible to change this to `requireAdministrator`, so make this change. Next ensure that you have both the Sub `DisplayPrincipalIdentity()` and the Sub `TestFileIOPermission()` uncommented in the `ButtonTest` click event handler within the ProVB_Security project. Finally, within the Sub `TestFileIOPermission()`, ensure that you have restored which block is commented out; the code should look like the previous listing where the bottom half of the method is commented and the top half is uncommented. Now that you have indicated that this application requires administrator privileges, you can repeat the first test where the user account didn't have permission to write to `NoPermission.txt`, but where the code attempted to grant permission. Note, this test depends on the Administrator having permission to access the file `C:\Test\NoPermission.txt`. Save your change to the app.manifest and attempt to run the application. If you are running on Windows 7 and didn't start Visual Studio 2010 using Run as Administrator you should get the error shown in Figure 32-6.

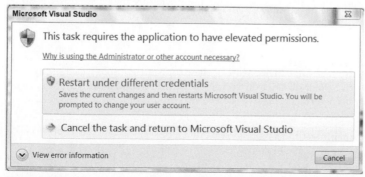

FIGURE 32-6

What happened? As noted above, the error message in Figure 32-6 is dependent on having not started Visual Studio with the Run as Administrator option from the right-click context menu. Since Visual Studio is running under your downgraded rights at the level of user, when it attempts to create a new process with the rights for administrator, the system refuses.

Just as you can't use code access security to grant the running account additional rights, you can't use the application manifest for the same purpose. The operating system knows that the current process has only user rights, so when you attempt to have that process spawn a new debugging process with administrator rights, the operating system throws an error.

You can get around this in one of two ways. The first, obviously, is to start or restart Visual Studio running as Administrator. Alternatively, you can go to the bin/debug folder and manually start the ProVB_Security.exe executable outside of the debugger. In either case you should now be prompted to grant administrator rights to this assembly, because the current code does not sign the assembly. Accepting this grant of elevated privileges, the results should be similar to what is shown in Figure 32-7.

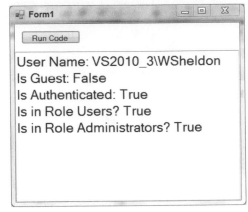

The successful completion of the Run Code button highlights two important points. First, as shown in Figure 32-7, the fact that the WSheldon account is in fact an administrator is now reflected in the onscreen permission display. Second, no error was thrown in the attempt to write the NoPermission.txt because the application is now running with the rights of an Administrator.

FIGURE 32-7

Regarding the uiAccess setting within the application manifest, this Boolean value defaults to false, and in most cases this is the correct setting. Changing this value to true will allow your code to update the user interface that is part of another assembly. However, setting this to true means that the application must be signed and that it must run from a trusted location.

As noted, signing your application will make the elevated privileges warning more meaningful and user friendly. Application signing is typically done during deployment, which is covered in detail in Chapter 34. It is not suggested that you just go in and start marking all of your applications with the requireAdministrator flag. Instead, you should elevate a user's rights when those rights are needed. Unfortunately, this option is only available at the time your application starts, but there is an important capability involved. In short, if you mark your application as essentially requiring Administrator rights, only administrators will be able to run the application.

Thus, the third application activation alternative is to use the highestAvailable setting. This setting allows both users and administrators to run your application. Within your application code, you'll need to check what privileges are available to the current user. As demonstrated earlier in this chapter, this will allow you to enable or disable application features depending upon whether the current user is an administrator.

Security Tools

Microsoft provides many security tools in its .NET SDK. Most of these tools are console-based utility applications. These tools can be used to help implement the security processes outlined earlier. They are not described in great detail, though they do deserve a review. Basically, two groups of tools are provided with the SDK:

➤ Permissions and assembly management tools

➤ Certificate management tools

Table 32-4 describes the permissions and assembly management tools. Table 32-5 describes the certificate management tools.

TABLE 32-4: Permissions and Assembly Management Tools

PROGRAM NAME	DESCRIPTION
Storeadm.exe	An administrative tool for isolated storage management. It restricts code access to the file system.
Peverify.exe	Checks whether the executable file will pass the runtime test for type-safe coding
Sn.exe	Creates assemblies with strong names — that is, a digitally signed namespace and version information

TABLE 32-5: Certificate Management Tools

PROGRAM NAME	DESCRIPTION
Makecert.exe	Creates an X.509 certificate for testing purposes
Certmgr.exe	Assembles certificates into a CTL (Certificate Trust List). It can also be used for revoking certificates.
Cert2spc.exe	Creates an SPC (Software Publisher Certificate) from an X.509 certificate

Exceptions Using the SecurityException Class

Originally, using the .NET Framework versions 1.0/1.1, the SecurityException class provided very little information in terms of actually telling you what was wrong and why an exception was thrown. Due to this limitation, the .NET Framework 2.0 added a number of new properties to the SecurityException class. Table 32-6 details some of these properties.

TABLE 32-6: Common SecurityException Properties

PROPERTY	DESCRIPTION
Action	Retrieves the security action that caused the exception to occur
Data	Gets a collection of key/value pairs that provide user-defined information about an exception
Demanded	Returns the permissions, permission sets, or permission set collections that caused the error to occur
DenySetInstance	Returns the denied permissions, permission sets, or permission set collections that caused the security actions to fail
FailedAssemblyInfo	Returns information about the failed assembly
FirstPermissionThatFailed	Returns the first permission contained in the permission set or permission set collection that failed
GrantedSet	Returns the set of permissions that caused the security actions to fail
HelpLink	Gets or sets a link to a help file associated with this error
InnerException	A reference to an earlier exception that triggered the current exception
Method	Returns information about the method connected to the exception
PermissionState	Returns the state of the permission that threw the exception
PermissionType	Returns the type of the permission that threw the exception

continues

TABLE 32-6 *(continued)*

PROPERTY	DESCRIPTION
PermitOnlySetInstance	Returns a permission set or permission set collection that is part of the permit-only stack frame if a security action has failed
RefusedSet	Returns the permissions that were refused by the assembly
Source	Gets or sets the name of the application or object that triggered the error
Url	Returns the URL of the assembly that caused the exception
Zone	Returns the zone of the assembly that caused the exception

Clearly, you can get your hands on a lot of information if a security exception is thrown in your application. For instance, you can use something similar to the following Catch section of code to check for security errors:

```
Dim myFile as FileInfo

Try
    myFile = _
        My.Computer.FileSystem.GetFileInfo("C:\Test\NoPermission.txt")
Catch ex As Security.SecurityException
    MessageBox.Show(ex.Method.Name.ToString())
End Try
```

ENCRYPTION BASICS

Rather than present an exposition of cryptography, this section is meant to familiarize you with basic techniques required to deal with .NET security and protect your Web services through encryption. There are four different categories of cryptography: encoding, hashing, and symmetric and asymmetric encryption.

First let's review each of these four different cryptographic categories. The first is encoding, which, as you may already know, if you are at all familiar with encryption, doesn't actually protect information. The most common encodings are things like UTF8, UTF7, and Base64 encoding. These encodings are typically used to take information that might interact with a container and hide the special characters. Thus, if you want to embed binary data within an XML file and want to ensure that the binary data won't interfere with the XML, you can Base64 the data, and it can safely be placed within an XML file.

Encoding is quite common for passing hidden or state data in Web pages, MIME, and XML file formats. For example, in ASP.NET, ViewState is an encoded block of information about the state of an ASP.NET page. However, keep in mind that encoded data, while not immediately humanly readable, uses a public algorithm to create its string. Encoding algorithms are designed to be quickly and easily reversed, and without any form of implied privacy. This means that anyone can reverse the encoded data, so for ASP.NET, ViewState does not protect the data which has been encoded, it just allows for transport of that data. To reiterate, encoding does not protect information.

The next item in the list of cryptography categories is hashing. Hashing algorithms digest sequences of data, creating a "random" output for the input string. A hash has a private key that can be varied by each application using the hash. Using a different key ensures you get different random string representations. While changing a single character will result in an entirely different result, the key to a hash is that there is no way to decrypt the original string from that result. In fact, hashing algorithms are specifically designed to not support the decryption of data once it has been hashed. At the same time, a hash always produces the same result for a given input string.

In terms of degree of security, hash keys are generally judged by the size of the encryption key, with larger keys (512-bit) providing greater security than shorter (128-bit) keys. Two popular hashing algorithms are SHA (Secure Hash Algorithm) and MD5 (Message-Digest algorithm 5). These hash keys are used for everything from saving passwords to signing digital documents; in other words, the hash is generated and encrypted using a private key.

Hashing works for passwords and pass phrases (longer authentication strings, which are far more difficult to guess) by never actually decrypting the password value. In order to validate your protected data, you reenter that data, which is then hashed, and the original hash is compared to the hashing of the newly entered text. If these two hashed values match, then the same text was entered. If the hashed values don't match, it means that the correct password or other information was not entered. In this way the original password can be protected not only from outsiders, but also from insiders who might want to impersonate another user.

Hashing algorithms, unlike other forms of encryption, are meant to be nonreversible. This is an important part of the security they provide. Note that in most cases, complex algorithms can be developed to reverse a hash, the most common being the creation of a dictionary of hashed values. However, the point of a hash is to create a "random" string based on input and ensure that the "random" element is repeatable for the same string. Thus, each password attempt is hashed, and the result is compared to the stored hash value for that user's password or pass phrase; matches mean success, and there is no relationship to 'how close' the entered text is to the correct text, because the hashed value is "random" for any given set of characters.

Symmetric encryption is commonly used to protect data such as private messages or data that will be retrieved. Symmetric key encryption is suitable for situations where the encrypted data needs to be accessed by someone in the same organization as the one who protected it. In this scenario, a key might be embedded within an application or stored as part of some device that the organization members control. It is important to keep the key private, as the same key is used to both encrypt and decrypt the data. Private keys work well as long as only those people who are authorized to view the protected data have them. It breaks down when attempting to interchange private data with the world at large. For that you need one key used by outsiders and a different key used by insiders.

Asymmetric public key encryption is most widely used in protecting the data that may be shared with an outside group. It is also used for digital signatures. Public key encryption is based on asymmetric keys, which means you always have a pair of keys. One key is known to all and is called the *public key*. The other key of the pair is kept secret and is known only to the owner. This is called the *private key*. If you use the public key to encrypt data, it can only be decrypted using the corresponding private key of the key pair, and vice versa.

Because the public key is known to all, anyone can decrypt information protected by the private key. However, the private key is known only to the owner, so this process acts as a digital signature. In other words, if the public key decrypts the message, then you know that the sender was the owner of the private key. It is important to remember that when data is protected using the public key, only the holder of the private key can decrypt it; another holder of the public key will be unable to decrypt the protected information.

In some cases an entire set of data is encrypted — for example, HTTPS does this. Similarly, asymmetric encryption is also used for digital signatures. Rather than encrypt the whole document using the private key, a public key and an agreed upon hash algorithm describing the data is used to "sign" the document. The signature is attached to the document, and the receiver then decrypts it using the private key. The result of the decryption is compared with rerunning the same hash on the key document characteristics that were agreed upon for the hash; if the results match, then the document is considered authentic. The result of this process is a *digital signature* associated with the digital document. This process works bi-directionally, so a document can be signed with the private key and the signature can be checked with the public key.

Because the holder of the private key will be able to read the data, it is very important that when you create a key pair, the private key must be protected and never shared.

Hash Algorithms

Hash algorithms are also called *one-way functions* because of their mathematical property of nonreversibility. The hash algorithms reduce large strings into a fixed-length binary byte array.

To verify a piece of information, the hash is recomputed and compared against a previously computed hash value. If both values match, then the newly provided data is correct. Cryptographic hashing algorithms map strings of data to a fixed-length result. Thus, two strings of different length will have a hash of the same size.

Although it is theoretically possible for two documents to have the same MD5 hash result, it is computationally impossible to create a meaningful forged document having the same hash key as the original hash value.

Cryptographic Hash Algorithms

The abstract class `System.Security.Cryptography.HashAlgorithm` represents the concept of cryptographic hash algorithms within the .NET Framework. The framework provides eight classes that extend the `HashAlgorithm` abstract class:

➤ `MD5CryptoServiceProvider` (extends abstract class `MD5`)

➤ `RIPEMD160Managed` (extends abstract class `RIPEMD160`)

➤ `SHA1CryptoServiceProvider` (extends abstract class `SHA1`)

➤ `SHA256Managed` (extends abstract class `SHA256`)

➤ `SHA384Managed` (extends abstract class `SHA384`)

➤ `SHA512Managed` (extends abstract class `SHA512`)

➤ `HMACSHA1` (extends abstract class `KeyedHashAlgorithm`)

➤ `MACTripleDES` (extends abstract class `KeyedHashAlgorithm`)

The last two classes belong to a class of algorithm called *keyed hash algorithms*. The keyed hashes extend the concept of the cryptographic hash with the use of a shared secret key. This is used for computing the hash of data transported over an unsecured channel.

To demonstrate this, a hashing example is available as part of the code download. The `TestHashKey.vb` file is part of the ProVB_Security solution. This class can be called using the following line of code:

```
TextBox1.Text = TestHashKey.Main("..\..\TestHashKey.vb")
```

Code snippet from TestHashKey.vb

Calling the shared method `Main` using the line of code above from the `ButtonTest_Click` event handler will run the following example code telling it to encrypt a copy of the source file TestHashKey.vb:

```vbnet
'TestHashKey.vb
Imports System
Imports System.IO
Imports System.Security.Cryptography
Imports System.Text

Public Class TestHashKey
    Public Shared Function Main(ByVal pathToFileToProtect As String) As String
        Dim key() As Byte = Encoding.ASCII.GetBytes("My Secret Key".ToCharArray())
        Dim hmac As HMACSHA1 = New HMACSHA1(key)
        Dim fs As FileStream = File.OpenRead(pathToFileToProtect)
        Dim hash() As Byte = hmac.ComputeHash(fs)
        Dim b64 As String = Convert.ToBase64String(hash)
        fs.Close()
        Return b64
    End Function
End Class
```

Code snippet from TestHashKey.vb

The preceding snippet creates the object instance of the .NET SDK Framework class with a *salt* (a random secret to confuse a snooper). The next four lines compute the hash, encode the binary hash into a printable Base64 format, close the file, and then return the Base64 encoded string. Running this will result in the hashed output shown in Figure 32-8.

FIGURE 32-8

The previous example uses an instance of the HMACSHA1 class. The output displayed is a Base64 encoding of the binary hash result value. As noted earlier, Base64 encoding is widely used in MIME and XML file formats to represent binary data. To recover the binary data from a Base64-encoded string, you could use the following code fragment:

```
Dim orig() As Byte = Convert.FromBase64String(b64)
```

The XML parser, however, does this automatically, as shown in later examples.

SHA

Secure Hash Algorithm (SHA) is a block cipher that operates on a block size of 64 bits. However, subsequent enhancements of this algorithm have bigger key values, thus, increasing the value range and therefore enhancing the cryptographic utility. Note that the bigger the key value sizes, the longer it takes to compute the hash. Moreover, for relatively smaller data files, smaller hash values are more secure. To put it another way, the hash algorithm's block size should be less than or equal to the size of the data itself.

The hash size for the SHA1 algorithm is 160 bits. Similar to the HMACSHA1 code discussed previously, the following code shows an example of using this algorithm:

```vb
'TestSHA1.vb
Imports System
Imports System.IO
Imports System.Security.Cryptography
Imports System.Text

Public Class TestSHA1
    Public Shared Function Main(ByVal pathToFileToProtect As String) As String

        Dim fs As FileStream = File.OpenRead(pathToFileToProtect)
        Dim sha As SHA1 = New SHA1CryptoServiceProvider
        Dim hash() As Byte = sha.ComputeHash(fs)
        Dim b64 As String = Convert.ToBase64String(hash)
        fs.Close()
        Return b64
    End Function
End Class
```

Code snippet from TestSHA1.vb

The .NET Framework provides larger key size algorithms as well — namely, SHA256, SHA384, and SHA512. The numbers at the end of the name indicate the block size.

The class SHA256Managed extends the abstract class SHA256, which in turn extends the abstract class HashAlgorithm. The forms authentication module of ASP.NET security (System.Web.Security .Forms AuthenticationModule) uses SHA1 as one of its valid formats to store and compare user passwords.

MD5

Message-Digest algorithm 5 (MD5) is a cryptographic, one-way hash algorithm. The MD5 algorithm competes well with SHA. MD5 is an improved version of MD4, devised by Ronald Rivest of Rivest, Shamir and Adleman (RSA) fame. In fact, FIPS PUB 180-1 states that SHA-1 is based on principles similar to MD4. The salient features of this class of algorithms are as follows:

➤   It is computationally unfeasible to forge an MD5 hash digest.

➤   MD5 is not based on any mathematical assumption such as the difficulty of factoring large binary integers.

➤   MD5 is computationally cheap, and therefore suitable for low-latency requirements.

➤   It is relatively simple to implement.

MD5 was the de facto standard for hash digest computation, due to the popularity of RSA. The .NET Framework provides an implementation of this algorithm through the class MD5CryptoServiceProvider in the System .Security.Cryptography namespace. This class extends the MD5 abstract class, which in turn extends the abstract class HashAlgorithm. This class shares a common base class with SHA1, so the examples previously discussed can be easily replicated by updating the SHA1 source to reference the MD5CryptoServiceProvider instead of the SHA1 provider.

```
Dim md5 As MD5 = New MD5CryptoServiceProvider()
Dim hash() As Byte = md5.ComputeHash(fs)
```

RIPEMD-160

Based on MD5, RIPEMD-160 started as a project in Europe called the RIPE (RACE Integrity Primitives Evaluation) project Message Digest in 1996. By 1997, the design of RIPEMD-160 was finalized. RIPEMD-160 is a 160-bit hash algorithm that is meant to be a replacement for MD4 and MD5.

The .NET Framework 2.0 introduced the RIPEMD160 class to work with this iteration of encryption techniques. As you should recognize from the preceding MD5 example, switching to this provider is also easily accomplished:

```
Dim myRIPEMD As New RIPEMD160Managed()
Dim hash() As Byte = myRIPEMD.ComputeHash(fs)
```

Symmetric Key Encryption

Symmetric key encryption is widely used to encrypt data files using passwords. The simplest technique is to seed a random number using a password, and then encrypt the files with an XOR operation using this random number generator.

The .NET Framework provides an abstract base class SymmetricAlgorithm. Five concrete implementations of different symmetric key algorithms are provided by default:

➤ AesCryptoServiceProvider (extends abstract class Aes)

➤ DESCryptoServiceProvider (extends abstract class DES)

➤ RC2CryptoServiceProvider (extends abstract class RC2)

➤ RijndaelManaged (extends abstract class Rijndael)

➤ TripleDESCryptoServiceProvider (extends abstract class TripleDES)

Let's explore the SymmetricAlgorithm design. As indicated by the following example code, two separate methods are provided to access encryption and decryption. You can run a copy of symmetric encryption using the sample code. Uncomment the following line of code in the ButtonTest_Click event handler in Form1.vb. An example of this call is shown below:

Available for download on Wrox.com

```
SymEnc.Main(TextBox1, 0, "..\..\SymEnc.vb", "DESencrypted.txt", True)
```

Code snippet from Form1.vb

Here is code that encrypts and decrypts a file, given a secret key:

Available for download on Wrox.com

```
'SymEnc.vb
Imports System.Security.Cryptography
Imports System.IO
Imports System.Text
Imports System

Public Class SymEnc
    Private Shared algo() As String = {"DES", "RC2", "Rijndael", "TripleDES"}
    Private Shared b64Keys() As String = {"YE32PGCJ/g0=", _
    "vct+rJ09WuUcR61yfxniTQ==", _
    "PHDPqfwE3z25f2UYjwwfwg4XSqxvl8WYmy+2h8t6AUg=", _
```

```
"Q1/lWoraddTH3IXAQUJGDSYDQcYYuOpm"}
Private Shared b64IVs() As String = {"onQX8hdHeWQ=", _
"jgetiyz+pIc=", _
"pd5mgMMfDI2Gxm/SK15I8A==", _
"6jpFrUh8FF4="}

Public Shared Sub Main(ByVal textBox As TextBox, ByVal algoIndex As Integer,
                ByVal inputFile As String, ByVal outputFile As String,
                ByVal encryptFile As Boolean)

    Dim fin As FileStream = File.OpenRead(inputFile)
    Dim fout As FileStream = File.OpenWrite(outputFile)
    Dim sa As SymmetricAlgorithm = SymmetricAlgorithm.Create(algo(algoIndex))
    sa.IV = Convert.FromBase64String(b64IVs(algoIndex))
    sa.Key = Convert.FromBase64String(b64Keys(algoIndex))
    textBox.Text = "Key length: " & CType(sa.Key.Length, String) & Environment.NewLine
    textBox.Text &= "Initial Vector length: " & CType(sa.IV.Length, String) &
    Environment.NewLine
    textBox.Text &= "KeySize: " & CType(sa.KeySize, String) & Environment.NewLine
    textBox.Text &= "BlockSize: " & CType(sa.BlockSize, String) & Environment.NewLine
    textBox.Text &= "Padding: " & CType(sa.Padding, String) & Environment.NewLine
    If (encryptFile) Then
        Encrypt(sa, fin, fout)
    Else
        Decrypt(sa, fin, fout)
    End If
End Sub
```

Code snippet from SyncEnc.vb

The parameters to `Main` provide the `Textbox` where the output will be displayed and the index from the array `algo`, which is the name of the algorithm to be used. It then looks for the input and output files, and finally a `Boolean` indicating whether the input should be encrypted or decrypted.

Within the code, first the action is to open the input and output files. The code then creates an instance of the selected algorithm and converts the initial vector and key strings for use by the algorithm. Symmetric algorithms essentially rely on two secret values: one called the key; the other, the initial vector, both of which are used to encrypt and decrypt the data. Both private values are required for either encryption or decryption.

The code then outputs some generic information related to the encryption being used and then checks which operation is required, executing the appropriate static method to encrypt or decrypt the file.

To encrypt, the code gets an instance of the `ICryptoTransform` interface by calling the `CreateEncryptor` method of the `SymmetricAlgorithm` class extender. The encryption itself is done in the following method:

Available for download on Wrox.com

```
Private Shared Sub Encrypt(ByVal sa As SymmetricAlgorithm, _
ByVal fin As Stream, _
ByVal fout As Stream)
    Dim trans As ICryptoTransform = sa.CreateEncryptor()
    Dim buf() As Byte = New Byte(fin.Length) {}
    Dim cs As CryptoStream = _
    New CryptoStream(fout, trans, CryptoStreamMode.Write)
    Dim Len As Integer
    fin.Position = 0
    Len = fin.Read(buf, 0, buf.Length)
    While (Len > 0)
        cs.Write(buf, 0, Len)
        Len = fin.Read(buf, 0, buf.Length)
    End While
    cs.Close()
```

```
        fin.Close()
    End Sub
```

Code snippet from SymEnc.vb

For decryption, the code gets an instance of the `ICryptoTransform` interface by calling the `CreateDecryptor` method of the `SymmetricAlgorithm` class instance. To test this you can uncomment the line of code which follows the call to encrypt and matches the line below:

```
SymEnc.Main(TextBox1, 0, "DESencrypted.txt", "DESdecrypted.txt", False)
```

Code snippet from Form1.vb

The following code provides the decryption method:

```
Private Shared Sub Decrypt(ByVal sa As SymmetricAlgorithm, _
ByVal fin As Stream, _
ByVal fout As Stream)
    Dim trans As ICryptoTransform = sa.CreateDecryptor()
    Dim buf() As Byte = New Byte(fin.Length) {}
    Dim cs As CryptoStream = _
    New CryptoStream(fin, trans, CryptoStreamMode.Read)
    Dim Len As Integer
    Len = cs.Read(buf, 0, buf.Length - 1)
    While (Len > 0)
        fout.Write(buf, 0, Len)
        Len = cs.Read(buf, 0, buf.Length)
    End While
    fin.Close()
    fout.Close()
End Sub
```

Code snippet from SymEnc.vb

The class `CryptoStream` is used for both encryption and decryption. You'll find it listed both in the Decrypt method shown in the preceding code snippet and also in the earlier code snippet that showed the Encrypt method. Notice however, that depending on if you are encrypting or decrypting, the parameters to the constructor for the `CryptoStream` differ.

You'll also notice if you review the code in SymEnc.vb, that this code supports testing of encryption and decryption using any of the four symmetric key implementations provided by the .NET Framework. The second parameter to `Sub Main` is an index indicating which algorithm to use. The secret keys and associated initialization vectors (IVs) were generated by a simple source code generator, examined shortly.

If you haven't done so yet, you should run the application and verify the contents of the `DESencrypted.txt` and `DESdecrypted.txt` files. If the new methods run to completion, the screen display should look similar to what is shown in Figure 32-9.

To generate the keys, a simple code generator is available in the file `SymKey.vb`. It can be extracted and compiled as a command-line executable to generate your own keys. The code used is shown in the following snippet:

```
'SymKey.vb
Imports System.Security.Cryptography
Imports System.Text
Imports System.IO
Imports System
Imports Microsoft.VisualBasic.ControlChars

Public Class SymKey
```

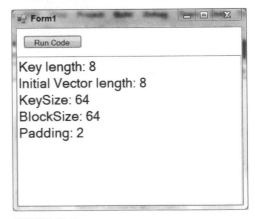

FIGURE 32-9

```
Public Sub Main(ByVal CmdArgs() As String)
    Dim keyz As StringBuilder = New StringBuilder
    Dim ivz As StringBuilder = New StringBuilder
    keyz.Append("Dim b64Keys() As String = { _" + VbCrLf)
    ivz.Append(vbCrLf + "Dim b64IVs() As String = { _" + vbCrLf)
    Dim comma As String = ", _" + vbCrLf
    Dim algo() As String = {"DES", "RC2", "Rijndael", "TripleDES"}
    For i As Integer = 0 To 3
        Dim sa As SymmetricAlgorithm = SymmetricAlgorithm.Create(algo(i))
        sa.GenerateIV()
        sa.GenerateKey()
        Dim Key As String
        Dim IV As String
        Key = Convert.ToBase64String(sa.Key)
        IV = Convert.ToBase64String(sa.IV)
        keyz.AppendFormat(vbTab + """" + Key + """" + comma)
        ivz.AppendFormat(vbTab + """" + IV + """" + comma)
        If i = 2 Then comma = " "
    Next i
    keyz.Append("}")
    ivz.Append("}")
    Console.WriteLine(keyz.ToString())
    Console.WriteLine(ivz.ToString())
End Sub
End Class
```

Code snippet from SymEnc.vb

The preceding program creates a random key and an initializing vector for each algorithm. The output from this can be copied into the SymEnc.vb program.

PKCS

The Public Key Cryptographic System (PKCS) is a type of asymmetric key encryption. This system uses two keys, one private and the other public. The public key is widely distributed, whereas the private key is kept secret. One cannot derive or deduce the private key by knowing the public key, so the public key can be safely distributed.

The keys are different, yet complementary. That is, if you encrypt data using the public key, then only the owner of the private key can decipher it, and vice versa. This forms the basis of PKCS encryption.

If the private key holder encrypts a piece of data using his or her private key, any person with access to the public key can decrypt it. The public key, as the name suggests, is available publicly. This property of the PKCS is exploited along with a hashing algorithm, such as SHA or MD5, to provide a verifiable digital signature process.

The abstract class System.Security.Cryptography.AsymmetricAlgorithm represents this concept in the .NET Framework. Four concrete implementations of this class are provided by default:

➤ DSACryptoServiceProvider, which extends the abstract class DSA

➤ ECDiffieHellmanCngCryptoServiceProvider, which extends the ECDiffieHellmanCng abstract class

➤ ECDsaCngCryptoServiceProvider, which extends the abstract class ECDsaCng

➤ RSACryptoServiceProvider, which extends the abstract class RSA

The Digital Signature Algorithm (DSA) was specified by the National Institute of Standards and Technology (NIST) in January 2000. The original DSA standard, however, was issued by NIST much earlier, in August 1991. DSA cannot be used for encryption and is good only for digital signature. Digital signature is discussed in more detail in the next section.

Similarly, the ECDsa algorithm is also an elliptic curve algorithm, in this case combined with the Digital Signature Algorithm. This is then enhanced with a Cryptographic Next Generation algorithm.

RSA algorithms can also be used for encryption as well as digital signatures. RSA is the de facto standard and has much wider acceptance than DSA. RSA is a tiny bit faster than DSA as well.

RSA can be used for both digital signature and data encryption. It is based on the assumption that large numbers are extremely difficult to factor. The use of RSA for digital signatures is approved within the FIPS PUB 186-2 and is defined in the ANSI X9.31 standard document.

Digital Signature Example

Digital signature is the encryption of a hash digest (for example, MD5 or SHA-1) of data using a public key. The digital signature can be verified by decrypting the hash digest and comparing it against a hash digest computed from the data by the verifier.

As noted earlier, the private key is known only to the owner, so the owner can sign a digital document by encrypting the hash computed from the document. The public key is known to all, so anyone can verify the signature by recomputing the hash and comparing it against the decrypted value, using the public key of the signer.

The .NET Framework provides DSA and RSA digital signature implementations by default. This section considers only DSA, as both implementations extend the same base class, so all programs for DSA discussed here work for RSA as well.

First, you need to produce a key pair. To do this, you'll need the following method, which has been added to the ProVB_Security main form. It can be called once from the ButtonTest click event to generate the necessary files in your application's folder:

Available for
download on
Wrox.com

```vb
Private Sub GenDSAKeys()
    Dim dsa As DSACryptoServiceProvider = New DSACryptoServiceProvider
    Dim prv As String = dsa.ToXmlString(True)
    Dim pub As String = dsa.ToXmlString(False)
    Dim fileutil As FileUtil = New FileUtil
    fileutil.SaveString("dsa-key.xml", prv)
    fileutil.SaveString("dsa-pub.xml", pub)
End Sub
```

Code snippet from Form1.vb

This method generates two XML-formatted files, dsa-key.xml and dsa-pub.xml, containing private and public keys, respectively. This code is dependent on an additional class, FileUtil that is available in the project to wrap some of the common file I/O operations. This file is shown in the following code snippet:

Available for
download on
Wrox.com

```vb
'FileUtil.vb
Imports System.IO
Imports System.Text
Public Class FileUtil
    Public Sub SaveString(ByVal fname As String, ByVal data As String)
        SaveBytes(fname, (New ASCIIEncoding).GetBytes(data))
    End Sub
    Public Function LoadString(ByVal fname As String)
        Dim buf() As Byte = LoadBytes(fname)
        Return (New ASCIIEncoding).GetString(buf)
    End Function
    Public Function LoadBytes(ByVal fname As String)
        Dim finfo As FileInfo = New FileInfo(fname)
        Dim length As String = CType(finfo.Length, String)
        Dim buf() As Byte = New Byte(length) {}
        Dim fs As FileStream = File.OpenRead(fname)
        fs.Read(buf, 0, buf.Length)
        fs.Close()
```

```
            Return buf
        End Function
        Public Sub SaveBytes(ByVal fname As String, ByVal data() As Byte)
            Dim fs As FileStream = File.OpenWrite(fname)
            fs.SetLength(0)
            fs.Write(data, 0, data.Length)
            fs.Close()
        End Sub
        Public Function LoadSig(ByVal fname As String)
            Dim fs As FileStream = File.OpenRead(fname)
            ' Need to omit the trailing null from the end of the 0 based buffer.
            Dim buf() As Byte = New Byte(39) {}
            fs.Read(buf, 0, buf.Length)
            fs.Close()
            Return buf
        End Function
    End Class
```

Code snippet from FileUtil.vb

To create the signature for a data file, reference the `DSASign` class from the `ButtonTest` click event handler. The following code signs the data:

```
'DSASign.vb
Imports System
Imports System.IO
Imports System.Security.Cryptography
Imports System.Text

Public Class DSASign
    Public Shared Sub Main()

        Dim fileutil As FileUtil = New FileUtil
        Dim xkey As String = fileutil.LoadString("dsa-key.xml")
        Dim fs As FileStream = File.OpenRead("..\..\FileUtil.vb")
        Dim data(fs.Length) As Byte
        fs.Read(data, 0, fs.Length)
        Dim dsa As DSACryptoServiceProvider = New DSACryptoServiceProvider
        dsa.FromXmlString(xkey)
        Dim sig() As Byte = dsa.SignData(data)
        fs.Close()
        fileutil.SaveBytes("FileUtilSignature.txt", sig)
    End Sub
End Class
```

Code snippet from DSASign.vb

The two lines of code that reference the `DSACryptoServiceProvider` and `dsa.FromXmlString` method actually create the DSA provider instance and reconstruct the private key from the XML format. Next, the file is signed using the call to `dsa.SignData` while passing the file stream to be signed to this method. The `FileStream` is then cleaned up and the resulting signature is saved into the output file.

Now that you have a data file and a signature, the next step is to verify the signature. The class `DSAVerify` can be leveraged to verify that the signature file created is in fact valid:

```
'DSAVerify.vb
Imports System
Imports System.IO
Imports System.Security.Cryptography
Imports System.Text

Public Class DSAVerify
```

```vb
Public Shared Function Main() As String

    Dim fileutil As FileUtil = New FileUtil
    Dim xkey As String = fileutil.LoadString("dsa-key.xml")
    Dim fs As FileStream = File.OpenRead("..\..\FileUtil.vb")
    Dim data(fs.Length) As Byte
    fs.Read(data, 0, fs.Length)
    Dim xsig() As Byte = fileutil.LoadSig("FileUtilSignature.txt")
    Dim dsa As DSACryptoServiceProvider = New DSACryptoServiceProvider
    dsa.FromXmlString(xkey)
    Dim verify As Boolean = dsa.VerifyData(data, xsig)
    Return String.Format("Signature Verification is {0}", verify)
    End Function
End Class
```

Code snippet from DSAVerfiry.vb

During testing you may want to ensure that both of these methods are enabled at the same time. This will ensure that you are encrypting and decrypting with the same keys. When working correctly, your display should look similar to what is shown in Figure 32-10.

There are many helper classes in the `System.Security` `.Cryptography` and `System.Security.Cryptography` `.Xml` namespaces. These classes provide numerous features to help deal with digital signatures and encryption. They also provide overlapping functionality, so there is more than one way of doing the same thing.

FIGURE 32-10

X.509 Certificates

X.509 is a public key certificate exchange framework. A public key certificate is a digitally signed statement by the owner of a private key, trusted by the verifier (usually a certifying authority), that certifies the validity of the public key of another entity. This creates a trust relationship between two unknown entities. X.509 is an ISO standard specified by the document ISO/IEC 9594-8. X.509 certificates are also used in SSL (Secure Sockets Layer), which is covered in the next section.

Many certifying authority services are available over the Internet. VeriSign (www.verisign.com) is one of the most popular, and was founded by the RSA trio themselves. Other providers may cost less but if you intend to make your certificate public, you'll want to investigate if they are default providers within the Windows operating system. Alternatively, at the low-cost end, and during development, you can run your own Certificate Authority (CA) service over an intranet using Microsoft Certificate Services.

The Microsoft .NET Framework SDK also provides tools for generating certificates for testing purposes. The following command generates a test certificate:

```
makecert -n CN=ProVB test.cer
```

The certificate is with the code at the solution directory level.

Three classes dealing with X.509 certificates are provided in the .NET Framework in the namespace `System.Security.Cryptography.X509Certificates`. The following program loads and manipulates the certificate created earlier:

```vb
' CertLoad.vb
Imports System
Imports System.Security.Cryptography.X509Certificates

Public Class CertLoad
    Public Shared Sub Main(ByVal certFilePath As String, ByVal textbox As TextBox)

        Dim cert As X509Certificate = _
```

```
    X509Certificate.CreateFromCertFile(certFilePath)
    textbox.Text = "Hash = " & cert.GetCertHashString() & Environment.NewLine
    textbox.Text &= "Effective Date = " &
        cert.GetEffectiveDateString() & Environment.NewLine
    textbox.Text &= "Expire Date = " &
        cert.GetExpirationDateString() & Environment.NewLine
    textbox.Text &= "Issued By = " & cert.Issuer & Environment.NewLine
    textbox.Text &= "Issued To = " & cert.Subject & Environment.NewLine
    textbox.Text &= "Algorithm = " & cert.GetKeyAlgorithm() & Environment.NewLine
    textbox.Text &= "Pub Key = " & cert.GetPublicKeyString() & Environment.NewLine
  End Sub
End Class
```

Code snippet from CertLoad.vb

The static method loads `CreateFromCertFile` (the certificate file) and creates a new instance of the class `X509Certificate`. When working correctly, the results are displayed in ProVB_Security as shown in Figure 32-11. The next section deals with Secure Sockets Layer (SSL), which uses X.509 certificates to establish the trust relationship.

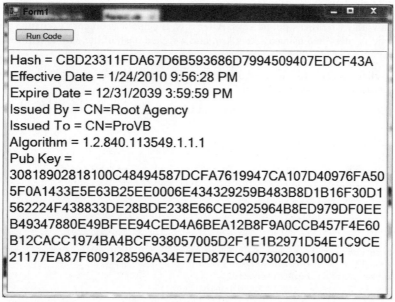

FIGURE 32-11

Secure Sockets Layer

The Secure Sockets Layer (SSL) protocol provides privacy and reliability between two communicating applications over the Internet. SSL is built over the TCP layer. In January 1999, the Internet Engineering Task Force (IETF) adopted an enhanced version of SSL 3.0 called *Transport Layer Security (TLS)*. TLS is backwardly compatible with SSL, and is defined in RFC 2246. However, the name SSL was retained due to wide acceptance of this Netscape protocol name. This section provides a simplified overview of the SSL algorithm sequence. SSL provides connection-oriented security via the following four properties:

➤   Connection is private and encryption is valid for the current session only.

➤   Symmetric key cryptography, like DES, is used for encryption. However, the session symmetric key is exchanged using public key encryption.

➤ Digital certificates are used to verify the identities of the communicating entities.

➤ Secure hash functions, such as SHA and MD5, are used for message authentication code (MAC).

The SSL protocol provides the following features:

➤ **Cryptographic security** — Using a symmetric key for session data-encryption, and a public key for authentication

➤ **Interoperability** — Interpolates OS and programming languages

➤ **Extensibility** — Adds new data-encryption protocols that are allowed within the SSL framework

➤ **Relative efficiency** — Reduces computation and network activity by using caching techniques

Two entities communicating using SSL protocols must have a public-private key pair, optionally with digital certificates validating their respective public keys.

At the beginning of a session, the client and server exchange information to authenticate each other. This ritual of authentication is called the *handshake protocol*. During this handshake, a session ID, the compression method, and the cipher suite to be used are negotiated. If the certificates exist, then they are exchanged. Although certificates are optional, either the client or the server may refuse to continue with the connection and end the session in the absence of a certificate.

After receiving each other's public keys, a set of secret keys based on a randomly generated number is exchanged by encrypting them with each other's public keys. After this, the application data exchange can commence. The application data is encrypted using a secret key, and a signed hash of the data is sent to verify data integrity.

Microsoft implements the SSL client in the .NET Framework classes. However, the server-side SSL can be used by deploying your service through the IIS Web server.

The following code demonstrates a method for accessing a secured URL. It takes care of minor details, such as encoding:

```vb
' Cryptography/GetWeb.vb
Imports System
Imports System.IO
Imports System.Net
Imports System.Text

Public Class GetWeb
    Dim MaxContentLength As Integer = 16384 ' 16k

    Public Shared Function QueryURL(ByVal url As String) As String
        Dim req As WebRequest = WebRequest.Create(url)
        Dim result As WebResponse = req.GetResponse()
        Dim ReceiveStream As Stream = result.GetResponseStream()
        Dim enc As Encoding = System.Text.Encoding.GetEncoding("utf-8")
        Dim sr As StreamReader = New StreamReader(ReceiveStream, enc)
        Dim response As String = sr.ReadToEnd()
        Return response
    End Function

End Class
```

Code snippet from Cryptography/GetWeb.vb

Using this method from the ProVB_Security application allows you to retrieve the information associated with the selected Web page. In this case, you can pass the URL www.amazon.com to the method from the ButtonTest click event handler. The resulting display should be similar to what is shown in Figure 32-12.

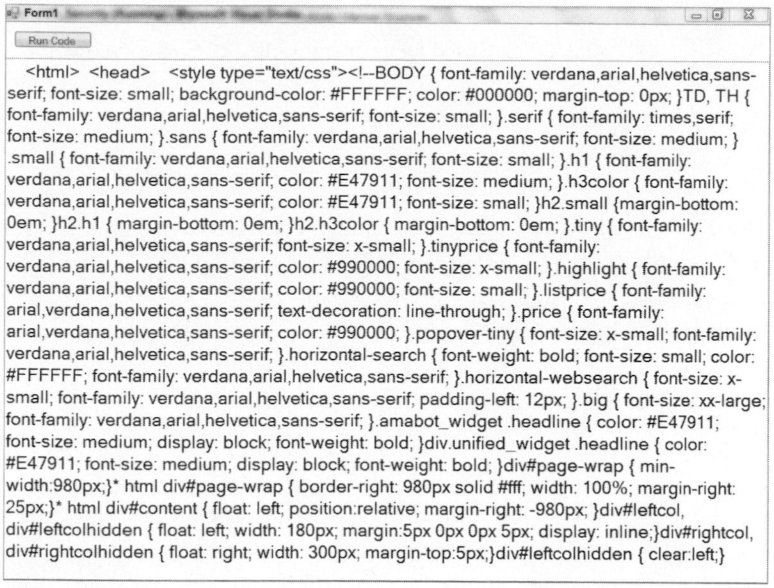

FIGURE 32-12

SUMMARY

This chapter covered the basics of security and cryptography. It began with an overview of the security architecture of the .NET Framework. The chapter introduced the four types of security within Windows and .NET: NTFS, User Access Control (UAC), cryptographic, and programmatic.

It then examined the security tools and functionality that the .NET Framework provides. You looked at the `System.Security.Permissions` namespace and learned how you can control code access permissions, role-based permissions, and identity permissions. You also learned how to manage code access permissions and UAC for your assembly.

The second half of the chapter looked at cryptography, both the underlying theory and how it can be applied within your applications. You looked at the different types of cryptographic hash algorithms, including SHA, MD5, symmetric key encryption, and PKCS. You should also understand how you can use digital certificates, such as X.509 and Secure Socket Layer (SSL) certificates.

33

Parallel Programming Using Tasks and Threads

WHAT YOU WILL LEARN IN THIS CHAPTER

➤ Understanding the new task-based programming model and the Task Parallel Library

➤ Launching, controlling, managing, and synchronizing parallel tasks

➤ Refactoring loops to run them in parallel using Parallel.For and Parallel.ForEach

➤ Transforming existing sequential code into parallelized code

➤ Measuring the speed gain and the scalability offered by parallelized code

➤ Working with different degrees of parallelism

➤ Understanding the advantages of working with concurrent collections

➤ Implementing a parallel producer-consumer pattern

➤ Parallelizing LINQ queries using PLINQ

In the last few years, multicore technology has become the mainstream in CPU designs, and microprocessor manufacturers continue to improve their processing power. However, the shift to multicore is an inflexion point for software design philosophy.

This chapter is about the new lightweight concurrency model offered by Visual Basic 2010 with .NET Framework 4 and its related hardware technologies. A comprehensive treatment of the challenges offered by the new multicore designs could easily fill 600 pages or more, so this chapter attempts to strike a reasonable balance between detail and succinctness.

LAUNCHING PARALLEL TASKS

It was really difficult to develop applications capable of taking full advantage of multicore microprocessors working with previous .NET Framework versions. It was necessary to launch, control, manage, and synchronize multiple threads using complex structures prepared for some concurrency but not tuned for the modern multicore age.

.NET Framework 4 introduces the new *Task Parallel Library (TPL)*, born in the multicore age and prepared to work with a new lightweight concurrency model. The TPL provides a lightweight framework that enables developers to work with the following parallelism scenarios, implementing task-based designs instead of working with heavyweight and complex threads:

➤ **Data parallelism** — There is a lot of data and it is necessary to perform the same operations for each piece — for example, encrypting 100 Unicode strings using the Advanced Encryption Standard *(AES)* algorithm with a 256-bits key.

➤ **Task parallelism** — There are many different operations that can run concurrently, taking advantage of parallelism — for example, generating hash codes for files, encrypting Unicode strings, and creating thumbnail representations of images.

➤ **Pipelining** — A mix of task and data parallelism. It is the most complex scenario because it always requires the coordination between multiple concurrent specialized tasks — for example, encrypting 100 Unicode strings using the AES algorithm with a 256-bits key and then generating a hash code for each encrypted string. This pipeline could be implemented running two concurrent tasks: the encryption and the hash code generation. Each encrypted Unicode string would enter into a queue in order to be processed by the hash code generation algorithm.

The easiest way to understand how to work with parallel tasks is by using them. Thus, you can take your first step toward creating parallelized code with the methods offered by the `System.Threading.Tasks.Parallel` static class.

System.Threading.Tasks.Parallel Class

The most important namespace for TPL is the new `System.Threading.Tasks`. It offers access to classes, structures, and enumerations introduced in .NET Framework 4, including the new `System.Threading.Tasks.Parallel` static class. Therefore, it is a good idea to import this namespace whenever you want to work with TPL:

```
Imports System.Threading.Tasks
```

This way, you will avoid large references. For example, instead of writing `System.Threading.Tasks.Parallel.Invoke`, you will be able to write `Parallel.Invoke`. In order to simplify the code, I will assume the aforementioned import is used in all the code snippets. However, remember that you can download the sample code for each code snippet and listing.

The main class is `Task`, representing an asynchronous and potentially concurrent operation. However, it is not necessary to work directly with instances of `Task` in order to create parallel code. Sometimes, the best option is to create parallel loops or regions, especially when the code seems to be appropriate for a sequential loop. In these cases, instead of working with the lower-level `Task` instances, it is possible to work with the methods offered by the `Parallel` static class (`System.Threading.Tasks.Parallel`):

➤ `Parallel.For` — Offers a load-balanced, potentially parallel execution of a fixed number of independent `For` loop iterations

➤ `Parallel.ForEach` — Offers a load-balanced, potentially parallel execution of a fixed number of independent `ForEach` loop iterations

➤ `Parallel.Invoke` — Offers the potentially parallel execution of the provided independent actions

These methods are very useful when you are refactoring existing code to take advantage of potential parallelism. However, it is very important to understand that it is not as simple as replacing a `For` statement with `Parallel.For`. Many techniques for refactoring existing loops are covered in detail later in this chapter.

Parallel.Invoke

The easiest way to try to run many methods in parallel is by using the new `Invoke` method provided by the `Parallel` class. For example, suppose that you have the following four independent subroutines that perform a format conversion, and you are sure it is safe to run them concurrently:

- ➤ ConvertEllipses
- ➤ ConvertRectangles
- ➤ ConvertLines
- ➤ ConvertText

You can use the following line in order to launch these subroutines, taking advantage of potential parallelism:

```
Parallel.Invoke(AddressOf ConvertEllipses, AddressOf ConvertRectangles,
AddressOf ConvertLines, AddressOf ConvertText)
```

In this case, each `AddressOf` operator creates a function delegate that points to each subroutine. The definition of the `Invoke` method receives an array of `Action` (`System.Action()`) to execute in parallel.

The following code produces the same results using single-line lambda expression syntax for the subroutines to run. Instead of using the aforementioned `AddressOf` operator, it adds `Sub()` before each method name.

```
Parallel.Invoke(Sub() ConvertEllipses(), Sub() ConvertRectangles(), Sub()
ConvertLines(), Sub() ConvertText())
```

New to Visual Basic 2010 is the following multi-line lambda expression syntax to run the subroutines. The following code uses them to produce the same result:

Available for
download on
Wrox.com

```
Parallel.Invoke(Sub()
                ConvertEllipses()
                ' Do something else adding more lines
            End Sub,
            Sub()
                ConvertRectangles()
                ' Do something else adding more lines
            End Sub,
            Sub()
                ConvertLines()
                ' Do something else adding more lines
            End Sub,
            Sub()
                ConvertText()
                ' Do something else adding more lines
            End Sub)
```

Code snippet from Snippet01

 One of the great advantages of using the new multi-line lambda expression syntax is that it enables you to define and run in parallel more complex multi-line subroutines without needing to create additional methods. When working with parallel programming using TPL, it is very important to master delegates and lambda expressions.

Lack of Execution Order

The following explanations apply to any of the previously shown code examples. The `Parallel.Invoke` method will not return until each of the four subroutines shown earlier has completed. However, completion could occur even with exceptions.

The method will try to start the four subroutines concurrently, taking advantage of the multiple *logical cores*, also known as *hardware threads*, offered by one or more physical microprocessors. However, their actual parallel execution depends on many factors. In this case, there are four subroutines. This means that `Parallel.Invoke` needs at least four logical cores available to be able to run the four methods concurrently.

In addition, having four logical cores doesn't guarantee that the four subroutines are going to start at the same time. The underlying scheduling logic could delay the initial execution of some of the provided subroutines because one or more cores could be too busy. It is indeed very difficult to make accurate predictions about the execution order because the underlying logic will try to create the most appropriate execution plan according to the available resources at runtime.

Figure 33-1 shows three of the possible concurrent execution scenarios that could take place according to different hardware configurations or diverse workloads. It is very important to keep in mind that the same code doesn't require a fixed time to run. Therefore, sometimes, the ConvertText method could take more time than the ConvertLines method, even using the same hardware configuration and input data stream.

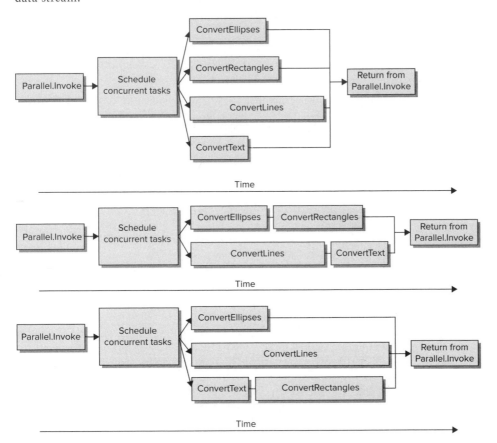

FIGURE 33-1

The top diagram represents an almost ideal situation, the four subroutines running in parallel. It is very important to consider the necessary time to schedule the concurrent tasks, which adds an initial overhead to the overall time.

The middle diagram shows a scenario with just two concurrent lanes and four subroutines to run. On one lane, once ConvertEllipses finishes, ConvertRectangles starts. On the other lane, once ConvertLines finishes, ConvertText starts. Parallel.Invoke takes more time than the previous scenario to run all the subroutines.

The bottom diagram shows another scenario with three concurrent lanes. However, it takes almost the same amount of time as the middle scenario, because in this case the `ConvertLines` subroutine takes more time to run. Thus, `Parallel.Invoke` takes almost the same amount of time as the previous scenario to run all the subroutines, even using one additional parallel lane.

> *The code written to run concurrently using* `Parallel.Invoke` *doesn't have to rely on a specific execution order. If you have concurrent code that needs a specific execution order, you can work with other mechanisms provided by the TPL. These are covered in detail later in this chapter.*

Advantages and Disadvantages

The key advantage of using `Parallel.Invoke` is its simplicity; you can run many subroutines in parallel without having to worry about tasks or threads. However, it isn't suitable for all the situations in which it is possible to take advantage of parallel execution. `Parallel.Invoke` has many trade-offs, including the following:

➤ If you use it to launch subroutines that need very different times to run, it will need the longest time to return control. This could mean that many logical cores stay idle for long periods of time. Therefore, it is very important to measure the results of using this method — that is, the speed gain achieved and the logical core usage.

➤ If you use it to launch delegates with different running times, it will need the longest time to return.

➤ It imposes a limit on the parallel scalability because it calls a fixed number of delegates. In the previous example, if you run it in a computer with 16 logical cores, it will launch only four subroutines in parallel. Therefore, 12 logical cores could remain idle.

➤ Each call to this method adds an overhead before running the potentially parallel subroutines.

➤ Like any parallelized code, the existence of interdependencies or uncontrolled interaction between the different subroutines could lead to concurrency bugs that are difficult to detect, and unexpected side effects. However, this trade-off applies to any concurrent code; it isn't a problem limited to using `Parallel.Invoke`.

➤ As there are no guarantees made about the order in which the subroutines are executed, it isn't suitable for running complex algorithms that require a specific execution plan of concurrent methods.

➤ Because exceptions could be thrown by any of the delegates launched with different parallel execution plans, the code to catch and handle these exceptions is more complex than the traditional sequential exception handling code.

> *The aforementioned trade-offs apply to the use of* `Parallel.Invoke` *as explained in the examples. However, it is possible to combine various different techniques to solve many of these trade-offs. You will learn about many of these mechanisms in this chapter.* `Parallel.Invoke` *is ideal to begin working with parallelism and to measure potential speed gains running CPU-intensive methods in parallel. You can improve the code later using the other parallelization methods provided by TPL.*

Parallelism and Concurrency

The previously explained example provides a good transition to the differences between *parallelism* and *concurrency*, because they aren't the same thing, as shown in Figure 33-2.

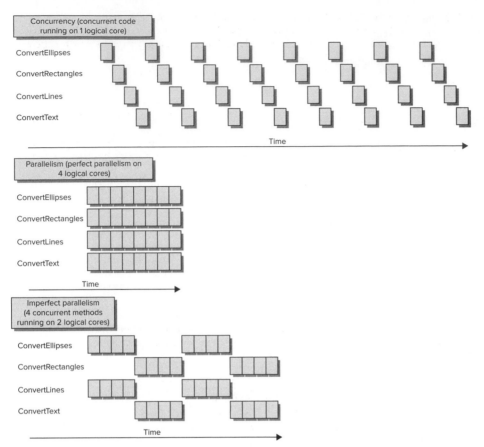

FIGURE 33-2

Concurrency means that different parts of code can start, run, and complete in overlapping time periods. Concurrency can happen even on computers with a single logical core. When many parts of code run concurrently on a computer with a single logical core, time-slicing mechanisms and fast context switches can offer the impression of parallel execution. However, on this hardware, it requires more time to run many parts of code concurrently than to run a single part of code alone, because the concurrent code is competing for hardware resources (refer to Figure 33-2). You can think of concurrency as many cars sharing a single lane. This is why concurrency is also defined as a form of virtual parallelism but it isn't real parallelism.

Parallelism means that different parts of code can actually run simultaneously, i.e., at the same time, taking advantage of real parallel processing capabilities found in the underlying hardware. Parallelism isn't possible on computers with a single logical core. You need at least two logical cores in order to run parallel code. When many parts of code run in parallel on a computer with multiple logical cores, time-slicing mechanisms and context switches also occur, because typically many other parts of code are trying to use processor time. However, when real parallelism occurs, you can achieve speed gains because many parts of code running in parallel can reduce the overall necessary time to complete certain algorithms. The diagram shown in Figure 33-2 offers two possible parallelism scenarios:

➤ An ideal situation: perfect parallelism on four logical cores (four lanes). The instructions for each of the four methods run in a different logical core.

➤ A combination of concurrency and parallelism, imperfect parallelism, whereby four methods take advantage of just two logical cores (two lanes). Sometimes the instructions for each of the four methods run in a different logical core, in parallel, and sometimes they have to wait for their time-slice. Therefore, in this case, there is concurrency combined with parallelism. This is the most common situation, because it is indeed very difficult to achieve a perfect parallelism even on real-time operating systems (RTOS).

When parts of code run in parallel with other parts, sometimes new bugs are introduced because of parallelism — that is, they appear only when certain parts of code run exactly at the same time. These bugs can be difficult to locate, making parallel programming even more complex than concurrent programming. Luckily, TPL offers many structures and new debugging features that can help to avoid many parallelism nightmares.

TRANSFORMING SEQUENTIAL CODE TO PARALLEL CODE

Until recently, most Visual Basic code was written with a sequential and synchronous execution approach. Therefore, a lot of algorithms have been designed with neither concurrency nor parallelism in mind. Typically, you won't find algorithms that can be completely converted to fully parallelized and perfectly scalable code. It could happen, but it represents an ideal situation and it isn't the most common scenario.

When you have sequential code and you want to take advantage of potential parallelism to achieve better performance, you have to find *hotspots*. Then you can convert them to parallel code, measure speedups, identify potential scalability, and ensure that you haven't introduced new bugs while transforming the existing sequential code to parallel code.

A hotspot is a part of the code that takes significant time to run. You can achieve speedups if it is split into two or more pieces running in parallel. If part of the code doesn't take significant time to run, the overhead introduced by TPL could reduce the performance improvement to worthless or even make the parallelized code run slower than the sequential version. Once you begin working with the different options offered by TPL, it is going to be easier for you to detect the hotspots in sequential code.

Detecting Hotspots

Listing 33-1 shows an example of a very simple console application that runs two sequential subroutines:

➤ GenerateAESKeys — This runs a For loop to generate the number of AES keys specified by the NUM_AES_KEYS constant. It uses the GenerateKey method provided by the System.Security .Cryptography.AesManaged class. Once the key is generated, it stores the results of converting the Byte array into a hexadecimal string representation (ConvertToHexString) in the hexString local variable.

➤ GenerateMD5Hashes — This runs a For loop to compute a number of hashes, using the Message-Digest algorithm 5 (MD5 algorithm), specified by the NUM_MD5_HASHES constant. It uses the user name to call the ComputeHash method provided by the System.Security.Cryptography.MD5 class. Once the hash is generated, it stores the results of converting the Byte array into a hexadecimal string representation (ConvertToHexString) in the hexString local variable.

The highlighted lines of code in Listing 33-1 are the ones added to measure the time it takes to run each subroutine, and the total elapsed time. It starts a new Stopwatch, calling its StartNew method at the beginning of each method, and then it writes the elapsed time to the Debug output.

LISTING 33-1: Simple serial AES keys and MD5 hash generators

```vb
Imports System
Imports System.Text
Imports System.Security.Cryptography
' This import will be used later to run code in parallel
Imports System.Threading.Tasks

Module Module1

    Private Const NUM_AES_KEYS As Integer = 800000
    Private Const NUM_MD5_HASHES As Integer = 100000

    Function ConvertToHexString(ByRef byteArray() As Byte)
        ' Convert the byte array to hexadecimal string
        Dim sb As New StringBuilder()

        For i As Integer = 0 To (byteArray.Length() - 1)
            sb.Append(byteArray(i).ToString("X2"))
        Next

        Return sb.ToString()
    End Function

    Sub GenerateAESKeys()
        Dim sw = Stopwatch.StartNew()
        Dim aesM As New AesManaged()
        Dim result() As Byte
        Dim hexString As String
        For i As Integer = 1 To NUM_AES_KEYS
            aesM.GenerateKey()
            result = aesM.Key
            hexString = ConvertToHexString(result)
            ' Console.WriteLine(hexString)
        Next
        Debug.WriteLine("AES: " + sw.Elapsed.ToString())
    End Sub

    Sub GenerateMD5Hashes()
        Dim sw = Stopwatch.StartNew()
        Dim md5M As MD5 = MD5.Create()
        Dim result() As Byte
        Dim data() As Byte
        Dim hexString As String
        For i As Integer = 1 To NUM_MD5_HASHES
            data = Encoding.Unicode.GetBytes(Environment.UserName + i.ToString())
            result = md5M.ComputeHash(data)
            hexString = ConvertToHexString(result)
            ' Console.WriteLine(hexString)
        Next
        Debug.WriteLine("MD5: " + sw.Elapsed.ToString())
    End Sub

    Sub Main()
        Dim sw = Stopwatch.StartNew()
        GenerateAESKeys()
        GenerateMD5Hashes()
        Debug.WriteLine(sw.Elapsed.ToString())
        ' Display the results and wait for the user to press a key
```

```
        Console.ReadLine()
    End Sub
End Module
```

Code snippet from Listing01

The For loop in the GenerateAESKeys subroutine doesn't use its controlled variable (i) in its code because it just controls the number of times it generates a random AES key. However, the For loop in the GenerateMD5Hashes subroutine uses its controlled variable (i) to add a number to the computer's user name. Then, it uses this string as the input data to call the method that computes its hash, as shown here:

```
For i As Integer = 1 To NUM_MD5_HASHES
    data = Encoding.Unicode.GetBytes(Environment.UserName + i.ToString())
    result = md5M.ComputeHash(data)
    hexString = ConvertToHexString(result)
    ' Console.WriteLine(hexString)
Next
```

Code snippet from Listing01

The lines of code that write the generated keys and hashes to the default console output appear commented in Listing 33-1 because these operations would generate a bottleneck that would distort the accuracy of the time measurement.

Figure 33-3 shows the sequential execution flow for this application and the time it takes to run each of the two aforementioned subroutines in a specific computer with a dual-core microprocessor.

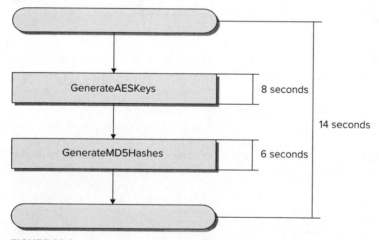

FIGURE 33-3

GenerateAESKeys and GenerateMD5Hashes need approximately 14 seconds to run. The first one takes 8 seconds and the latter 6 seconds. Of course, these times will vary considerably according to the underlying hardware configuration.

There is no interaction between these two subroutines. Thus, they are completely independent from each other. As the subroutines run one after the other, in a sequential way, they aren't taking advantage of the parallel processing capabilities offered by the additional core(s). Therefore, these two subroutines represent a clear hotspot where parallelism could help to achieve a significant speedup over sequential execution. For example, it is possible to run both subroutines in parallel using Parallel.Invoke.

Measuring Speedups Achieved by Parallel Execution

Replace the `Main` subroutine shown in the simple console application with the following new version, launching both `GenerateAESKeys` and `GenerateMD5Hashes` in parallel, using `Parallel.Invoke`:

```
Sub Main()
    Dim sw = Stopwatch.StartNew()
    Parallel.Invoke(Sub() GenerateAESKeys(), Sub() GenerateMD5Hashes())
    Debug.WriteLine(sw.Elapsed.ToString())
End Sub
```

Code snippet from Snippet02

Figure 33-4 shows the parallel execution flow for the new version of this application and the time it takes to run each of the two subroutines in a specific computer with a dual-core microprocessor.

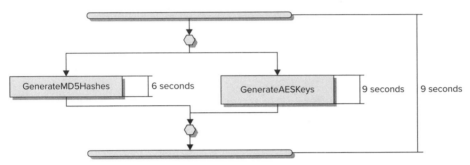

FIGURE 33-4

Now, `GenerateAESKeys` and `GenerateMD5Hashes` need approximately nine seconds to run because they take advantage of both cores offered by the microprocessor. Thus, it is possible to calculate the speedup achieved using the following formula:

Speedup = (Serial execution time) / (Parallel execution time)

In the preceding example, 14 / 9 = 1.56 times faster, usually expressed as a 1.56x speedup over the sequential version. `GenerateAESKeys` takes more time than `GenerateMD5Hashes` to run, nine seconds versus six seconds. However, `Parallel.Invoke` doesn't continue with the next line until all the delegates finish their execution. Therefore, during three seconds, the application is not taking advantage of one of the cores, as shown in Figure 33-5.

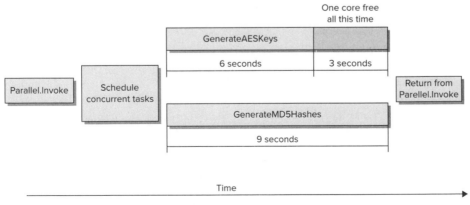

FIGURE 33-5

In addition, if this application runs on a computer with a quad-core microprocessor, its speedup over the sequential version would be nearly the same, as it won't scale to take advantage of the two additional cores found in the underlying hardware.

In this section, you saw how it is possible to detect hotspots by adding some code to measure the elapsed time to run certain methods. By changing just a few lines of code, a noticeable improvement in speed was achieved. Now it is time to learn other TPL structures that can help to achieve better results and offer improved scalability when the number of available cores increases.

 There is no need to initialize TPL in order to begin working with its classes and methods. TPL does a lot of work under the hood and does its best to optimize its scheduling mechanisms to take advantage of the underlying hardware at runtime. However, choosing the right structure to parallelize a hotspot is a very important task.

Understanding Parallel and Concurrent Execution

Now, uncomment the lines that send output to the console in both `GenerateAESKeys` and `GenerateMD5Hashes`:

```
Console.WriteLine(hexString)
```

Writing to the console will generate a bottleneck for the parallel execution. However, this time, there is no need to measure accurate times. Instead, you can view the output to determine that both methods are running in parallel. Listing 33-2 shows a sample console output generated by this application. The highlighted lines, the shorter hexadecimal strings, correspond to the MD5 hashes. The others represent AES keys. Each AES key takes less time to generate than each MD5 hash. Remember that the code creates 800,000 AES keys (`NUM_AES_KEYS`) and 100,000 MD5 hashes (`NUM_MD5_HASHES`).

LISTING 33-2: Example output generated by AES keys and MD5 hash generators running in parallel

```
0364DBC9A8FA3EAC793FC53AAE6D0193484087634C3033C470D96C72F89D7254
E410BCB82B36729CB7CCCCDFE30746F2DF141CC8275790360E2ED731F8C7113D
66CF85EA8FC77746A7C4A116F68D802D7167AE9E7C5FB0B6B85D44B8929386DE
0421897DCF492380BADF872205AE32D94632C60022A4E965652524D7023C59AD
C3BEF1DFFF5A9CAB11BFF8EA3F7DEFC97D91562A358DB56477AD445ACB4F1DE3
AF521D65489CA5C69517E32F652D464676E5F2487E438124DBF9ACF4157301AA
A641EB67C88A29985CFB0B2097B12CFB9296B4659E0949F20271984A3868E0B3
D7A05587DFDFD0C49BEF613F2EB78A43
90BF115C60B2DECA60C237F3D06E42EE
B3519CBA0137FD814C09371836F90322
1415C19F7F93306D35186721AF6B8DDE56427BB9AF29D22E37B34CB49E96BB49
208B73D3E6468F48B950E5F5006DDF30FE7A1B3BCC46489F7722BD98D54079D7
ACD0312DFF1BF29ECA2721DAFA9B20AB5FBDBD20E76C150C5CCE4026990C9D26
EB68C902145439F2A66514B9D89E9A958F18EE15D491014D3DCB312781F277D1
9DB8ABF087C78091F1E77AC769FF175A
F3EFB2804A969D890AFABCE17E84B26E
B342A8A253003754B752B85C67DA1560F30CD36A1AA759A0010E1F8E5045CBB5
9681656DC08F29AB1911A1CCCFBE6B468D1DF7B9D8722324E5E2BB4A314EC649
7DE56E111213655F54D6F8656238CA5E
196D194BA2B786EADD1B6852645C67C5
BA7AC6B878064E98D98336CA5DE45DEC
875DAB451CCE3B5FBD8E5091BAD1A8ED7DB2FF8C9E3EEA834C6DEA7C2467F27E
C1AA2CB88AB669317CB90CD842BF01DB26C6A655D10660AF01C37ECC7AEDA267
66E1F4F56E04FC9BFF225F68008A129D93F9B277ADAB43FF764FB87FFD098B78
```

Now, comment the lines that send output to the console in both `GenerateAESKeys` and `GenerateMD5Hashes` again.

PARALLELIZING LOOPS

Both `GenerateAESKeys` and `GenerateMD5Hashes` represent an opportunity to run iterations in parallel. They generate the input data to simplify the example and perform the same operation for each piece. Thus, it represents a data parallelism scenario. It is possible to refactor the loops to run the operations in parallel. This way, instead of running both subroutines in parallel, each one can take full advantage of parallelism and automatically scale according to the number of existing logical cores.

Parallel.For

You can think of refactoring an existing `For` loop to take advantage of parallelism as a simple replacement of `For` with `Parallel.For`. Unfortunately, it isn't as simple as that.

Listings 33-3 and 33-4 refactor the subroutines shown in the preceding section, showing the code for both the original loops and the new code with the refactored loops using the imperative syntax to implement the data parallelism offered by `Parallel.For`. The new methods, `ParallelGenerateAESKeys` and `ParallelGenerateMD5Hashes`, try to take advantage of all the cores available, relying on the work done under the hood by `Parallel.For` to optimize its behavior according to the existing hardware at runtime.

LISTING 33-3: The original GenerateAESKeys subroutine with the sequential For loop, and its parallelized version

Original sequential For version

```
Sub GenerateAESKeys()
    Dim sw = Stopwatch.StartNew()
    Dim aesM As New AesManaged()
    Dim result() As Byte
    Dim hexString As String
    For i As Integer = 1 To NUM_AES_KEYS
        aesM.GenerateKey()
        result = aesM.Key
        hexString = ConvertToHexString(result)
        ' Console.WriteLine(hexString)
    Next
    Debug.WriteLine("AES: " + sw.Elapsed.ToString())
End Sub
```

Code snippet from Listing02

Parallelized version using Parallel.For

```
Sub ParallelGenerateAESKeys()
    Dim sw = Stopwatch.StartNew()
    Parallel.For(1, NUM_AES_KEYS + 1, Sub(i As Integer)
                        Dim result() As Byte
                        Dim hexString As String

                        Dim aesM As New AesManaged()
                        aesM.GenerateKey()
                        result = aesM.Key
                        hexString = ConvertToHexString(result)
```

```
                                      ' Console.WriteLine(hexString)
                              End Sub)
              Debug.WriteLine("AES: " + sw.Elapsed.ToString())
       End Sub
```

LISTING 33-4: The original GenerateMD5Hashes subroutine with the sequential For loop, and its parallelized version

Original sequential For version

```
Sub GenerateMD5Hashes()
       Dim sw = Stopwatch.StartNew()
       Dim md5M As MD5 = MD5.Create()
       Dim result() As Byte
       Dim data() As Byte
       Dim hexString As String
       For i As Integer = 1 To NUM_MD5_HASHES
              data = Encoding.Unicode.GetBytes(Environment.UserName + i.ToString())
              result = md5M.ComputeHash(data)
              hexString = ConvertToHexString(result)
              ' Console.WriteLine(hexString)
       Next
       Debug.WriteLine("MD5: " + sw.Elapsed.ToString())
End Sub
```

Parallelized version using Parallel.For

```
Sub ParallelGenerateMD5Hashes()
       Dim sw = Stopwatch.StartNew()
       Parallel.For(1, NUM_MD5_HASHES + 1, Sub(i As Integer)
                            Dim md5M As MD5 = MD5.Create()
                            Dim result() As Byte
                            Dim data() As Byte
                            Dim hexString As String
                            data = Encoding.Unicode.GetBytes(Environment.UserName + i.ToString())
                            result = md5M.ComputeHash(data)
                            hexString = ConvertToHexString(result)
                            ' Console.WriteLine(hexString)
                      End Sub)
       Debug.WriteLine("MD5: " + sw.Elapsed.ToString())
End Sub
```

The most basic version of the class function Parallel.For has the following parameters:

➤ fromInclusive — The first number for the iteration range (Integer or Long).

➤ toExclusive — The number before which the iteration will stop, this number is an exclusive upper bound (Integer or Long). The iteration range will be from fromInclusive up to toExlusive − 1. It is very important to pay attention to this parameter because the classic For loop defines the iteration range using an inclusive upper bound. Thus, when converting a For loop to a Parallel.For loop, the original upper bound has to be converted to an upper bound minus 1.

➤ body — The delegate to be invoked, once per iteration, and without a predefined execution plan. It can be of the type Action(Of Integer) or Action (Of Long) depending on the type used in the iteration range definition.

> *Parallel.For* *supports neither floating-point values nor steps. It works with* Integer *and* Long *values and it runs adding 1 in each iteration. In addition, it partitions the iteration range according to the available hardware resources at runtime and runs the body in parallel tasks. Thus, there are no guarantees made about the order in which the iterations are executed. For example, in an iteration from 1 to 101 - 1 (100 inclusive), the iteration number 50 could begin running before the iteration number 2, which could also be executing in parallel, because the time it takes to run each iteration is unknown and variable. Because the loop could be split into many parallel iterations, it's impossible to predict the execution order. The code has to be prepared for parallel execution and it must avoid undesired side effects generated by parallel and concurrent executions.*

In addition, `Parallel.For` can return a `ParallelLoopResult` value because parallelized loops, like any parallelized code, are more complex than sequential loops. Because execution is not sequential, you cannot access a variable to determine where the loop stopped its execution. In fact, many chunks are running in parallel.

Refactoring an Existing Sequential Loop

Listing 33-3 showed the original `GenerateAESKey` subroutine with the sequential `For` loop. It is a good practice to create a new subroutine, function, or method with a different name when refactoring sequential code to create a parallelized version. In this case, `ParallelGenerateAESKeys` is the new subroutine.

The original `For` loop's iteration range definition is as follows:

```
For i As Integer = 1 To NUM_AES_KEYS
```

This means that it will run the loop body `NUM_AES_KEYS` times, from 1 (inclusive) to `NUM_AES_KEYS` (inclusive).

It is necessary to translate this definition to a `Parallel.For`, adding 1 to `NUM_AES_KEYS` because it is an exclusive upper bound:

```
Parallel.For(1, NUM_AES_KEYS + 1,
```

The third parameter is the delegate. In this case, this loop doesn't use the iteration variable. However, the code uses multi-line lambda expression syntax to define a subroutine with an `Integer` parameter (`i`) that is going to work as the iteration variable, holding the current number:

```
Parallel.For(1, NUM_AES_KEYS + 1, Sub(i As Integer)
```

An `End Sub)` replaces the previous `Next` statement.

The preceding code was prepared to run alone, or perhaps with other methods running in parallel. However, each iteration was not designed to run in parallel with other iterations of the same loop body. Using `Parallel.For` changes the rules. The code has some problems that need to be solved. The sequential iterations shared the following three local variables:

- ➤ `aesM`
- ➤ `result()`
- ➤ `hexString`

The loop body has code that changes the values of these variables in each iteration — for example, the following lines:

```
aesM.GenerateKey()
result = aesM.Key
hexString = ConvertToHexString(result)
```

First, the key generated by calling the GenerateKey method of the AesManaged instance, stored in aesM, is held in the Key property. Then, the code assigns the value stored in this property to the result variable. Finally, the last line assigns the product of converting it to a hexadecimal string to hexString, the third local variable. It is really difficult to imagine the results of running this code in parallel or concurrently, because it could result in a very large mess. For example, one part of the code could generate a new key, which would be stored in the aesM.Key property that was going to be read in another part of the code running in parallel. Therefore, the value read from the aesM.Key property is corrupted.

One possible solution could be using synchronization structures to protect each value and state that is changing. However, that's not appropriate in this case because it would add more code and more synchronization overhead. There is another solution that is more scalable: refactoring the loop body, transferring these local variables as local variables inside the subroutine acting as a delegate. In order to do this, it is also necessary to create an instance of AesManaged inside the loop body. This way, it is not going to be shared by all the parallel iterations. This change adds more instructions to run for each iteration, but it removes the undesirable side effects and creates safe and stateless parallel code. The following lines show the new body. The highlighted lines of code are the variables moved inside the delegate:

```
Sub(i As Integer)
    Dim result() As Byte
    Dim hexString As String
    Dim aesM As New AesManaged()

    aesM.GenerateKey()
    result = aesM.Key
    hexString = ConvertToHexString(result)
    ' Console.WriteLine(hexString)
End Sub)
```

Code snippet from Listing03

A very similar problem has to be solved in order to transform the original loop body found in GenerateMD5Hashes. Listing 33-4 showed the original subroutine with the sequential For loop. In this case, ParallelGenerateMD5Hashes is the new subroutine. It was necessary to use the same aforementioned refactoring technique because we don't know whether the MD5 instance holds internal states that could generate problems. It is safer to create a new independent instance for each iteration. The following lines show the new body. The highlighted lines of code are the variables moved inside the delegate:

```
Sub(i As Integer)
    Dim md5M As MD5 = MD5.Create()
    Dim result() As Byte
    Dim data() As Byte
    Dim hexString As String
    data = Encoding.Unicode.GetBytes(Environment.UserName + i.ToString())
    result = md5M.ComputeHash(data)
    hexString = ConvertToHexString(result)
    ' Console.WriteLine(hexString)
End Sub)
```

Code snippet from Listing03

Measuring Scalability

Replace the Main subroutine with the following new version, launching first ParallelGenerateAESKeys and then ParallelGenerateMD5Hashes:

```
Sub Main()
    Dim sw = Stopwatch.StartNew()
    ParallelGenerateAESKeys()
```

```
ParallelGenerateMD5Hashes()
Debug.WriteLine(sw.Elapsed.ToString())
End Sub
```

Code snippet from Listing03

Now, `ParallelGenerateAESKeys` and `ParallelGenerateMD5Hashes` need approximately 7.5 seconds to run, because each one takes full advantage of both cores offered by the microprocessor. Thus, the speedup achieved is 14 / 7.5 = 1.87x over the sequential version. It is better than the previous performance gain achieved using `Parallel.Invoke` (1.56x) because the time wasted in that version is now used to run the loops, using parallel chunks in an attempt to load-balance the work done by each core. `ParallelGenerateAESKeys` takes 4.2 seconds and `ParallelGenerateMD5Hashes` takes 3.3 seconds.

Using `Parallel.For` to parallelize this code has another advantage: The same code can scale when executed with more than two cores. The sequential version of this application running on a computer with a specific quad-core microprocessor needs approximately 11 seconds to run. It is necessary to measure the time needed to run the sequential version again because each hardware configuration will provide different results with both sequential and parallel code.

In order to measure the achieved speedup, you will always need a baseline calculated on the same hardware configuration. The version optimized using `Parallel.For` needs approximately 4.1 seconds to run. Each subroutine takes full advantage of the four cores offered by the microprocessor. Thus, the speedup achieved is 11 / 4.1 = 2.68x over the sequential version. `ParallelGenerateAESKeys` takes 2.12 seconds and `ParallelGenerateMD5Hashes` takes 1.98 seconds.

The parallelized code is capable of scaling as the number of cores increases. That didn't happen with the `Parallel.Invoke` version. However, it doesn't mean that the parallelized code will offer a linear speedup. In fact, most of the time, there is a limit to the scalability — that is, once it reaches a certain number of cores, the parallelized algorithms won't achieve additional speedup.

In this case, it was necessary to change the code for the loop's body used in each iteration. Thus, there is an additional overhead in each iteration that wasn't part of each sequential iteration, and calling delegates is more expensive than calling direct methods. In addition, `Parallel.For` and its underlying work adds additional overhead to distribute and coordinate the execution of different chunks with parallel iterations. This is why the speedup is not near 4x and is approximately 2.68x when running with four cores. Typically, the parallelized algorithms won't offer a linear speedup. Furthermore, serial and hardware architecture-related bottlenecks can make it very difficult to scale beyond a certain number of cores.

It is very important to measure speedup in order to determine whether the overhead added to parallelize the code brings present and potentially future (further scalability) performance benefits.

The diagram shown in Figure 33-6 represents one of the possible execution flows, taking advantage of the four cores. Each box shown inside a method represents a chunk that is automatically created by `Parallel.For` at runtime.

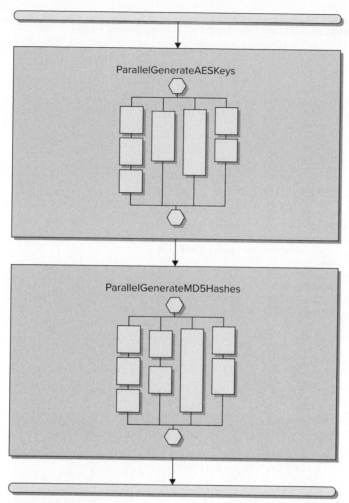

FIGURE 33-6

Parallel.ForEach

Sometimes, refactoring an existing For loop as previously explained can be a very complex task, and the changes to the code could generate too much overhead for each iteration, reducing the overall performance. Another useful alternative is to partition all the data to be processed into parts that can be run as smaller loops in parallel, defining a custom partitioner, a mechanism tailored to split the input data into specific pieces that overrides the default partitioning mechanism. It is possible to use a Parallel.ForEach loop with a override partitioner in order to create new versions of the sequential loops with a simpler refactoring process.

Listing 33-5 shows the new code with the refactored loops using the imperative syntax to implement data parallelism offered by Parallel.ForEach, combined with a sequential For loop and a custom partitioner created with System.Collections.Concurrent.Partitioner. The new methods, ParallelPartitionGenerateAESKeys and ParallelPartitionGenerateMD5Hashes, also try to take advantage of all the cores available, relying on the work done under the hood by Parallel.ForEach and the range partitioning performed to distribute smaller sequential loops inside as many parallel loops as available cores. The code also optimizes its behavior according to the existing hardware at runtime.

The code uses another important namespace for TPL, the new `System.Collections.Concurrent` namespace. This namespace offers access to useful collections prepared for concurrency and custom partitioners introduced in .NET Framework 4. Therefore, it is a good idea to import this namespace to work with the new examples:

```
Imports System.Collections.Concurrent
```

Available for download on Wrox.com

LISTING 33-5: Another parallellized version of the original sequential loops using Parallel .ForEach with a custom partitioner

```vb
Sub ParallelPartitionGenerateAESKeys()
    Dim sw = Stopwatch.StartNew()
    Parallel.ForEach(Partitioner.Create(1, NUM_AES_KEYS + 1),
            Sub(range)
                Dim aesM As New AesManaged()
                Dim result() As Byte
                Dim hexString As String
                Debug.WriteLine("Range ({0}, {1}. Time: {2})",
                range.Item1, range.Item2, Now().TimeOfDay)
                For i As Integer = range.Item1 To range.Item2 - 1
                    aesM.GenerateKey()
                    result = aesM.Key
                    hexString = ConvertToHexString(result)
                    ' Console.WriteLine("AES: " + hexString)
                Next
            End Sub)
    Debug.WriteLine("AES: " + sw.Elapsed.ToString())
End Sub

Sub ParallelPartitionGenerateMD5Hashes()
    Dim sw = Stopwatch.StartNew()
    Parallel.ForEach(Partitioner.Create(1, NUM_MD5_HASHES + 1),
            Sub(range)
                Dim md5M As MD5 = MD5.Create()
                Dim result() As Byte
                Dim data() As Byte
                Dim hexString As String
                For i As Integer = range.Item1 To range.Item2 - 1
                    data = Encoding.Unicode.GetBytes(
                            Environment.UserName + i.ToString())
                    result = md5M.ComputeHash(data)
                    hexString = ConvertToHexString(result)
                    ' Console.WriteLine("MD5:" + hexString)
                Next
            End Sub)
    Debug.WriteLine("MD5: " + sw.Elapsed.ToString())
End Sub
```

Code snippet from Listing05

The class function `Parallel.ForEach` offers 20 overrides. The definition used in Listing 33-5 has the following parameters:

➤ source — The partitioner that provides the data source split into multiple partitions

➤ body — The delegate to be invoked, once per iteration, and without a predefined execution plan. It receives each defined partition as a parameter — in this case, `Tuple(Of Integer, Integer)`.

In addition, `Parallel.ForEach` can return a `ParallelLoopResult` value. The information offered in this structure is covered in detail later in this chapter.

Working with Partitions in a Parallel Loop

Listing 33-3 showed the original `GenerateAESKey` subroutine with the sequential `For` loop. The highlighted lines of code shown in Listing 33-5 represent the same sequential `For` loop. The only line that changes is the `For` definition, which takes into account the lower bound and the upper bound of the partition assigned by `range.Item1` and `range.Item2`:

```
For i As Integer = range.Item1 To range.Item2 - 1
```

In this case, it is easier to refactor the sequential loop because there is no need to move local variables. The only difference is that instead of working with the entire source data, it splits it into many independent and potentially parallel partitions. Each one works with a sequential inner loop.

The following call to the `Partitioner.Create` method defines the partitions as the first parameter for `Parallel.ForEach`:

```
Partitioner.Create(1, NUM_AES_KEYS + 1)
```

This line splits the range from 1 to `NUM_AES_KEYS` into many partitions with an upper bound and a lower bound, creating a `Tuple(Of Integer, Integer)`. However, it doesn't specify the number of partitions to create. `ParallelPartitionGenerateAESKeys` includes a line to write the lower and upper bounds of each generated partition and the actual time when it starts to run the sequential loop for this range.

```
Debug.WriteLine("Range ({0}, {1}. Time: {2})",
                range.Item1, range.Item2, Now().TimeOfDay)
```

Replace the `Main` subroutine with the following new version, launching first `ParallelPartitionGenerateAESKeys` and then `ParallelParallelGenerateMD5Hashes`:

```
Sub Main()
    Dim sw = Stopwatch.StartNew()
    ParallelPartitionGenerateAESKeys()
    ParallelPartitionGenerateMD5Hashes()
    Debug.WriteLine(sw.Elapsed.ToString())
End Sub
```

Code snippet from Listing05

As shown in Listing 33-6, the partitioner creates 13 ranges. Thus, the `Parallel.ForEach` will run 13 sequential inner `For` loops with ranges. However, they don't start at the same time, because that wouldn't be a good idea with four cores available. The parallelized loop tries to load-balance the execution, taking into account the available hardware resources. The highlighted line shows the complexity added by both parallelism and concurrency. If you take into account the time, the first partition that reaches the sequential inner `For` loop is (66667, 133333) and not (1, 66667). Remember that the upper bound values shown in Listing 33-6 are exclusive.

LISTING 33-6: Debug output example generated running ParallelPartitionGenerateAESKeys with a quad-core microprocessor

```
Range (133333, 199999. Time: 15:45:38.2205775)
Range (66667, 133333. Time: 15:45:38.2049775)
Range (266665, 333331. Time: 15:45:38.2361775)
Range (199999, 266665. Time: 15:45:38.2205775)
Range (1, 66667. Time: 15:45:38.2205775)
Range (333331, 399997. Time: 15:45:39.0317789)
Range (399997, 466663. Time: 15:45:39.0317789)
Range (466663, 533329. Time: 15:45:39.1097790)
Range (533329, 599995. Time: 15:45:39.2345793)
Range (599995, 666661. Time: 15:45:39.3281794)
Range (666661, 733327. Time: 15:45:39.9365805)
Range (733327, 799993. Time: 15:45:40.0145806)
Range (799993, 800001. Time: 15:45:40.1705809)
```

In addition, the order in which the data appears in the debug output is different because there are many concurrent calls to the `WriteLine`. In fact, when measuring speedups, it is very important to comment these lines before the loop begins because they have affect the overall time by generating a bottleneck.

This new version using `Parallel.ForEach` with custom partitions needs approximately the same time as the previous `Parallel.For` version to run.

Optimizing Partitions According to Number of Cores

It is possible to tune the generated partitions in order to match them with the number of logical cores found at runtime. `System.Environment.ProcessorCount` offers the number of logical cores or logical processors detected by the operating system. Hence, it is possible to use this value to calculate the desired range size for each partition and use it as a third parameter for the call to `Partitioner.Create`, using the following formula:

$$((numberOfElements / numberOfLogicalCores) + 1) \text{ As Integer or As Long}$$

`ParallelPartitionGenerateAESKeys` can use the following code to create the partitions:

```
Partitioner.Create(0, NUM_AES_KEYS, (CInt(NUM_AES_KEYS / Environment.ProcessorCount) + 1))
```

A very similar line can also help to improve `ParallelPartitionGenerateMD5Hashes`:

```
Partitioner.Create(1, NUM_MD5_HASHES, (CInt(NUM_MD5_HASHES / Environment.ProcessorCount) + 1))
```

As shown in Listing 33-7, now the partitioner creates four ranges because the desired range size is CInt((800000 / 4) + 1) = 200001. Thus, the `Parallel.ForEach` will run four sequential inner `For` loops with ranges, according to the number of available logical cores.

> **LISTING 33-7:** Debug output example generated running the optimized partitions version of **ParallelPartitionGenerateAESKeys with a quad-core microprocessor**
>
> ```
> Range (1, 200002. Time: 16:32:51.3754528)
> Range (600004, 800000. Time: 16:32:51.3754528)
> Range (400003, 600004. Time: 16:32:51.3754528)
> Range (200002, 400003. Time: 16:32:51.3754528)
> ```

Now, `ParallelPartitionGenerateAESKeys` and `ParallelPartitionGenerateMD5Hashes` need approximately 3.40 seconds to run because each one generates as many partitions as cores available and uses a sequential loop in each delegate; therefore, it reduces the previously added overhead. Thus, the speedup achieved is 11 / 3.4 = 3.23x over the sequential version. The reduced overhead makes it possible to reduce the time from 4.1 seconds to 3.4 seconds.

 Most of the time, the load-balancing schemes used by TPL under the hood are very efficient. However, you know your designs, code, and algorithms better than TPL at runtime. Therefore, considering the capabilities offered by modern hardware architectures and using many of the features included in TPL, you can improve overall performance, reducing unnecessary overhead introduced by the first loop parallelization without the custom partitioner.

The diagram shown in Figure 33-7 represents one of the possible execution flows with the numbers for the lower and upper bounds for each partition, taking advantage of the four cores with the optimized partitioning scheme.

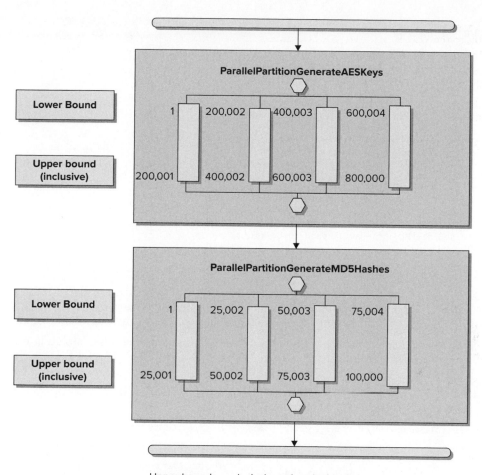

Upper bounds are inclusive values in this diagram.

FIGURE 33-7

Working with IEnumerable Sources of Data

`Parallel.ForEach` is also useful to refactor existing `ForEach` loops that iterate over a collection that exposes an `IEnumerable` interface.

The simplest definition of the class function `Parallel.ForEach`, used in Listing 33-8 to generate a new version of the MD5 hashes generation subroutine, `ParallelForEachGenerateMD5Hashes`, has the following parameters:

➤ `source` — The collection that exposes an IEnumerable interface and provides the data source.

➤ `body` — The delegate to be invoked, once per iteration, and without a predefined execution plan. It receives each element of the `source` collection — in this case, an `Integer`.

LISTING 33-8: A parallelized version of the GenerateMD5Hashes subroutine using Parallel .ForEach with an IEnumerable source

```
Private Function GenerateMD5InputData() As IEnumerable(Of Integer)
    Return Enumerable.Range(1, NUM_AES_KEYS)
End Function
```

continues

LISTING 33-8 *(continued)*

```
Sub ParallelForEachGenerateMD5Hashes()
    Dim sw = Stopwatch.StartNew()
    Dim inputData = GenerateMD5InputData()

    Parallel.ForEach(inputData, Sub(number As Integer)
                Dim md5M As MD5 = MD5.Create()
                Dim result() As Byte
                Dim data() As Byte
                Dim hexString As String
                data = Encoding.Unicode.GetBytes(
                    Environment.UserName + number.ToString())
                result = md5M.ComputeHash(data)
                hexString = ConvertToHexString(result)
                ' Console.WriteLine("MD5:" + hexString)
            End Sub)
    Debug.WriteLine("MD5: " + sw.Elapsed.ToString())
End Sub
```

Code snippet from Listing08

The `GenerateMD5InputData` function returns a sequence of `Integer` numbers from 1 to `NUM_AES_KEYS` (inclusive). Instead of using the loop to control the numbers for the iteration, the code in the `ParallelForEachGenerateMD5Hashes` subroutine saves this sequence in the `inputData` local variable.

The following line calls `Parallel.ForEach` with the source (`inputData`) and a multi-line lambda delegate subroutine, receiving the `number` for each iteration:

```
Parallel.ForEach(inputData, Sub(number As Integer)
```

The line that prepares the input data for the hash computing method also changes to use the value found in `number`:

```
data = Encoding.Unicode.GetBytes(Environment.UserName + number.ToString())
```

 In this case, performance isn't really good compared with the other versions. However, when each iteration performs time-consuming operations, it would improve performance with an `IEnumerable` collection. The subroutine needs almost 16 seconds to run in the same hardware configuration used for the last examples. However, it should be obvious that this isn't an optimal implementation because the code has to iterate the 100,000 items of a sequence. It does it in parallel but it takes more time than running loops with less overhead. It also consumes more memory. The example isn't intended to be a best practice for this case. The idea is to understand the different opportunities offered by the `Parallel` class methods and to be able to evaluate them.

Exiting from Parallel Loops

If you want to interrupt a sequential loop, you can use `Exit For` or `Exit For Each`. When working with parallel loops, it requires more complex code because exiting the delegate body sub or function doesn't have any effect on the parallel loop's execution, as it is the one that's being called on each new iteration. In addition, because it is a delegate, it is disconnected from the traditional loop structure.

Listing 33-9 shows a new version of the `ParallelForEachGenerateMD5Hashes` subroutine, called `ParallelForEachGenerateMD5HashesBreak`. Now, the `loopResult` local variable saves the result of calling the `Parallel.ForEach` class function. Moreover, the delegate body subroutine receives a second parameter — a `ParallelLoopState` instance:

```
Dim loopResult = Parallel.ForEach(inputData, Sub(number As Integer, loopState As
ParallelLoopState)
```

LISTING 33-9: A new version of the ParallelForEachGenerateMD5Hashes subroutine that
enables exiting from the loop

```
Private Sub DisplayParallelLoopResult(ByVal loopResult As ParallelLoopResult)
    Dim text As String
    If loopResult.IsCompleted Then
        text = "The loop ran to completion."
    Else
        If loopResult.LowestBreakIteration.HasValue = False Then
            text = "The loop ended prematurely with a Stop statement."
        Else
            text = "The loop ended by calling the Break statement."
        End If
    End If
    Console.WriteLine(text)
End Sub


Sub ParallelForEachGenerateMD5HashesBreak()
    Dim sw = Stopwatch.StartNew()
    Dim inputData = GenerateMD5InputData()

    Dim loopResult = Parallel.ForEach(inputData, Sub(number As Integer, loopState As
    ParallelLoopState)
            'If loopState.ShouldExitCurrentIteration Then
            '    Exit Sub
            'End If
            Dim md5M As MD5 = MD5.Create()
            Dim result() As Byte
            Dim data() As Byte
            Dim hexString As String
            data = Encoding.Unicode.GetBytes(Environment.UserName + number.ToString())
            result = md5M.ComputeHash(data)
            hexString = ConvertToHexString(result)
            If (sw.Elapsed.Seconds > 3) Then
                loopState.Break()
                Exit Sub
            End If
            ' Console.WriteLine("MD5:" + hexString)
        End Sub)
    DisplayParallelLoopResult(loopResult)
    Debug.WriteLine("MD5: " + sw.Elapsed.ToString())
End Sub


Private Function GenerateMD5InputData() As IEnumerable(Of Integer)
    Return Enumerable.Range(1, NUM_AES_KEYS)
End Function
```

Code snippet from Listing09

Understanding ParallelLoopState

The instance of ParallelLoopState (*loopState*) offers two methods to cease the execution of a
Parallel.For or Parallel.ForEach:

➤ Break — Communicates that the parallel loop should cease the execution beyond the current
iteration, as soon as possible

➤ Stop — Communicates that the parallel loop should cease the execution as soon as possible

Using these methods doesn't guarantee that the execution will stop as soon as possible, because parallel loops are complex and sometimes it is difficult to cease the execution of all the parallel and concurrent iterations. The difference between Break and Stop is that the former tries to cease execution once the current iteration is finished, whereas the latter tries to cease it immediately.

The code shown in Listing 33-9 calls the Break method if the elapsed time is more than 3 seconds:

```
If (sw.Elapsed.Seconds > 3) Then
    loopState.Break()
    Exit Sub
End If
```

It is very important to note that the code in the multi-line lambda is accessing the sw variable that is defined in ParallelForEachGenerateMD5HashesBreak. It reads the value of the Seconds read-only property.

It is also possible to check the value of the ShouldExitCurrentIteration read-only property in order to make decisions when the current or other concurrent iterations make requests to stop the parallel loop execution. Listing 33-9 shows a few commented lines that check whether ShouldExitConcurrentIteration is True:

```
If loopState.ShouldExitCurrentIteration Then
    Exit Sub
End If
```

If the property is true, then it exits the subroutine, avoiding the execution of unnecessary iterations. The lines are commented because in this case an additional iteration isn't a problem; therefore, it isn't necessary to add this additional instruction to each iteration.

Analyzing the Results of a Parallel Loop Execution

Once the Parallel.ForEach finishes its execution, loopResult has information about the results, in a ParallelLoopResult structure.

The DisplayParallelLoopResult subroutine shown in Listing 33-9 receives a ParallelLoopResult structure, evaluates its read-only properties, and outputs the results of executing the Parallel.ForEach loop to the console. Table 33-1 explains the three possible results of in this example.

TABLE 33-1: ParallelLoopResult Read-only Properties

CONDITION	DESCRIPTION
IsCompleted = True	The loop ran to completion.
IsCompleted = False And LowestBreakIteration.HasValue = False	The loop ended prematurely with a Stop statement.
IsCompleted = False And LowestBreakIteration.HasValue = True	The loop ended by calling the Break statement. The LowestBreakIteration property holds the value of the lowest iteration that called the Break statement.

It is very important to analyze the results of a parallel loop execution because continuation with the next statement doesn't mean that it completed all the iterations. Thus, it is necessary to check the values of the ParallelLoopResult properties or to include customized control mechanisms inside the loop bodies. Again, converting sequential code to parallel and concurrent code isn't just replacing a few loops. It is necessary to understand a very different programming paradigm and new structures prepared for this new scenario.

Catching Parallel Loop Exceptions

As many iterations run in parallel, many exceptions can occur in parallel. The classic exception management techniques used in sequential code aren't useful with parallel loops.

When the code inside the delegate that is being called in each parallelized iteration throws an exception that isn't captured inside the delegate, it becomes part of a set of exceptions, handled by the new `System.AggregateException` class.

You have already learned how to handle exceptions in your sequential code in Chapter 6. You can apply almost the same techniques. The only difference is when an exception is thrown inside the loop body, which is a delegate. Listing 33-10 shows a new version of the `ParallelForEachGenerateMD5Hashes` subroutine, called `ParallelForEachGenerateMD5HashesException`. Now, the body throws a `TimeOutException` if the elapsed time is more than three seconds:

```
If (sw.Elapsed.Seconds > 3) Then
    Throw New TimeoutException("Parallel.ForEach is taking more than 3 seconds to complete.")
End If
```

Available for
download on
Wrox.com

LISTING 33-10: A new version of the ParallelForEachGenerateMD5Hashes subroutine, throwing and handling exceptions

```
Sub ParallelForEachGenerateMD5HashesExceptions()
    Dim sw = Stopwatch.StartNew()
    Dim inputData = GenerateMD5InputData()
    Dim loopResult As ParallelLoopResult

    Try
        loopResult = Parallel.ForEach(inputData,
            Sub(number As Integer, loopState As ParallelLoopState)
                'If loopState.ShouldExitCurrentIteration Then
                '    Exit Sub
                'End If
                Dim md5M As MD5 = MD5.Create()
                Dim result() As Byte
                Dim data() As Byte
                Dim hexString As String
                data = Encoding.Unicode.GetBytes(Environment.UserName + number.ToString())
                result = md5M.ComputeHash(data)
                hexString = ConvertToHexString(result)
                If (sw.Elapsed.Seconds > 3) Then
                    Throw New TimeoutException("Parallel.ForEach is taking
more than 3 seconds to complete.")
                End If
                ' Console.WriteLine("MD5:" + hexString)
            End Sub)
    Catch ex As AggregateException
        For Each innerEx As Exception In ex.InnerExceptions
            Debug.WriteLine(innerEx.ToString())
            ' Do something considering the innerEx Exception
        Next
    End Try
    DisplayParallelLoopResult(loopResult)
    Debug.WriteLine("MD5: " + sw.Elapsed.ToString())
End Sub
```

Code snippet from Listing10

A `Try...Catch...End Try` block encloses the call to `Parallel.ForEach`. Nevertheless, the line that catches the exceptions is

```
Catch ex As AggregateException
```

instead of the classic

```
Catch ex As Exception
```

An `AggregateException` contains one or more exceptions that occurred during the execution of parallel and concurrent code. However, this class isn't specifically for parallel computing, it can be used to represent one or more errors that occur during application execution. Therefore, once it is captured, it is possible to iterate through each individual exception contained in the `InnerExceptions` read-only collection of `Exception`. In this case, the `Parallel.ForEach` without the custom partitioner will display the contents of many exceptions. The loop result will look like it was stopped using the `Stop` keyword. However, as it is possible to catch the `AggregateException`, you can make decisions based on the problems that made it impossible to complete all the iterations. In this case, a sequential `For Each` loop retrieves all the information about each `Exception` in `InnerExceptions`. Listing 33-11 shows the information about the first two exceptions converted to a string and sent to the Debug output.

```
Catch ex As AggregateException
    For Each innerEx As Exception In ex.InnerExceptions
        Debug.WriteLine(innerEx.ToString())
        ' Do something considering the innerEx Exception
    Next
End Try
```

LISTING 33-11: Debug output, with two exceptions found in the InnerExceptions collection

```
System.TimeoutException: Parallel.ForEach is taking more than 3 seconds to complete.
    at ConsoleApplication3.Module1._Closure$__2._Lambda$__9(Int32 number,
    ParallelLoopState loopState) in
    C:\Users\Public\Documents\ConsoleApplication3\ConsoleApplication3\Module1.vb:line 255
    at System.Threading.Tasks.Parallel.<>c__DisplayClass32`2.<PartitionerForEachWorker>b__30()
    at System.Threading.Tasks.Task.InnerInvoke()
    at System.Threading.Tasks.Task.InnerInvokeWithArg(Task childTask)
    at System.Threading.Tasks.Task.<>c__DisplayClass7.<ExecuteSelfReplicating>b__6(Object )
System.TimeoutException: Parallel.ForEach is taking more than 3 seconds to complete.
    at ConsoleApplication3.Module1._Closure$__2._Lambda$__9(Int32 number,
    ParallelLoopState loopState) in
    C:\Users\Public\Documents\ConsoleApplication3\ConsoleApplication3\Module1.vb:line 255
    at System.Threading.Tasks.Parallel.<>c__DisplayClass32`2.<PartitionerForEachWorker>b__30()
    at System.Threading.Tasks.Task.InnerInvoke()
    at System.Threading.Tasks.Task.InnerInvokeWithArg(Task childTask)
    at System.Threading.Tasks.Task.<>c__DisplayClass7.<ExecuteSelfReplicating>b__6(Object )
```

 As you can see in Listing 33-11, the two exceptions display the same information to the Debug output. However, most of the time you will use a more sophisticated exception management technique, and you will provide more information about the iteration that is generating the problem. This example focuses on the differences between an `AggregateException` *and the traditional* `Exception`. *It doesn't promote the practice of writing information about errors to the Debug output as a complete exception management technique.*

SPECIFYING THE DESIRED DEGREE OF PARALLELISM

TPL methods always try to achieve the best results using all the available logical cores. Sometimes, however, you don't want to use all the available cores in a parallel loop, either because you have specific needs, and therefore better plans for the remaining available cores, or you want to leave one core free to create a responsive application and the remaining core can help you run another part of code in parallel. In these cases, you want to specify the *maximum degree of parallelism* for a parallel loop.

ParallelOptions

TPL enables you to specify a different maximum desired degree of parallelism by creating an instance of the new ParallelOptions class and changing the value of its MaxDegreeOfParallelism property. Listing 33-12 shows a new version of the two well-known subroutines that use Parallel.For, ParallelGenerateAESKeysMaxDegree and ParallelGenerateMD5HashesMaxDegree.

Now, they receive an Integer with the maximum desired degree of parallelism, maxDegree. Each subroutine creates a local instance of ParallelOptions and assigns the value received as a parameter to its MaxDegreeOfParallelism property, which is a new parameter for each parallel loop before the body. This way, the loop won't be optimized to take advantage of all the available cores (MaxDegreeOfParallelism = -1). Instead, it will be optimized as if the total number of available cores were equal to the maximum degree of parallelism specified in the property:

```
Dim parallelOptions As New ParallelOptions()
parallelOptions.MaxDegreeOfParallelism = maxDegree
```

Available for download on Wrox.com

LISTING 33-12: Specifying maximum desired degree of parallelism for Parallel.For loops

```
Sub ParallelGenerateAESKeysMaxDegree(ByVal maxDegree As Integer)
    Dim parallelOptions As New ParallelOptions()
    parallelOptions.MaxDegreeOfParallelism = maxDegree
    Dim sw = Stopwatch.StartNew()
    Parallel.For(1, NUM_AES_KEYS + 1, parallelOptions,
        Sub(i As Integer)
                Dim result() As Byte
                Dim hexString As String

                Dim aesM As New AesManaged()
                aesM.GenerateKey()
                result = aesM.Key
                hexString = ConvertToHexString(result)
                ' Console.WriteLine("AES:" + hexString)
            End Sub)
    Debug.WriteLine("AES: " + sw.Elapsed.ToString())
End Sub

Sub ParallelGenerateMD5HashesMaxDegree(ByVal maxDegree As Integer)
    Dim parallelOptions As New ParallelOptions
    parallelOptions.MaxDegreeOfParallelism = maxDegree
    Dim sw = Stopwatch.StartNew()
    Parallel.For(1, NUM_MD5_HASHES + 1, parallelOptions,
        Sub(i As Integer)
                Dim md5M As MD5 = MD5.Create()
                Dim result() As Byte
                Dim data() As Byte
                Dim hexString As String
                data = Encoding.Unicode.GetBytes(Environment.UserName + i.ToString())
                result = md5M.ComputeHash(data)
                hexString = ConvertToHexString(result)
                ' Console.WriteLine("MD5:" + hexString)
            End Sub)
    Debug.WriteLine("MD5: " + sw.Elapsed.ToString())
End Sub
```

Code snippet from Listing12

> *It is not convenient to work with static values for the desired degree of parallelism, because it can limit scalability when more cores are available. These options should be used carefully; it is best to work with relative values according to the number of available logical cores, or consider this number in order to prepare the code for further scalability.*

This way, it is possible to call both subroutines with a dynamic value, considering the number of logical cores at runtime:

```
ParallelGenerateAESKeysMaxDegree(Environment.ProcessorCount - 1)
ParallelGenerateMD5HashesMaxDegree(Environment.ProcessorCount - 1)
```

Both `Parallel.For` loops are going to try to work with the number of logical cores minus 1. If the code runs with a quad-core microprocessor, then it will use just three cores.

The following is *not* a best practice for final code. However, sometimes you want to know whether two parallelized subroutines offer better performance if they are executed at the same time, limiting the number of cores for each one. You can test this situation using the following line:

Available for download on Wrox.com

```
Parallel.Invoke(Sub() ParallelGenerateAESKeysMaxDegree(2), Sub()
ParallelGenerateAESKeysMaxDegree(2))
```

Code snippet from Listing12

The two subroutines will be launched in parallel and each will try to optimize its execution to use two of the four cores of a quad-core microprocessor. The obvious drawback of the previous line is that it uses a static number of cores. Nonetheless, this is just for performance testing purposes.

`ParallelOptions` also offers two additional properties to control more advanced options:

➤ `CancellationToken` — Allows assigning a new `System.Threading.CancellationToken` instance in order to propagate notification that parallel operations should be cancelled. The usage of this property is covered in detail later in this chapter.

➤ `TaskScheduler` — Allows assigning a customized `System.Threading.Tasks.TaskScheduler` instance. It is usually not necessary to define a customized task scheduler to schedule parallel tasks unless you are working with very specific algorithms.

Understanding Hardware Threads and Logical Cores

The `Environment.ProcessorCount` property provides the number of logical cores. However, sometimes the number of *logical* cores, also known as *hardware threads*, is different from the number of *physical* cores.

For example, an Intel Core i7 microprocessor with four physical cores offering hyperthreading technology doubles the number to eight logical cores. Therefore, in this case, `Environment.ProcessorCount` is eight, not four. The operating system also works with eight logical processors.

All the code created using TPL runs using multiple software *threads*. Threads are the low-level lanes to run many parts of code in parallel, taking advantage of the presence of multiple cores in the underlying hardware. However, most of the time, the code running in these lanes has some imperfections. It waits for I/O data or other threads to finish, or it causes latency as it waits for data to be fetched from the different caches available in the microprocessor or the system memory. This means that there are idle execution units.

HyperThreading technology offers an increased degree of instruction-level parallelism, by duplicating the architectural states for each physical core in order to mitigate the imperfections of the parallel code running code from a second thread when the first one is waiting. This way, it appears to be a microprocessor with two times the real number of physical cores.

Logical cores are not the same as real physical cores. Although this technique sometimes improves performance through increased instruction-level parallelism when each physical core has two threads with independent instruction streams, if the software threads don't have many data dependencies, the performance improvements could be less than expected. It depends on the application.

As TPL uses the number of hardware threads, or logical cores, to optimize its execution, sometimes certain algorithms won't offer the expected scalability as more cores appear because they aren't real physical cores.

For example, if an algorithm offered a 6.5x speedup when executed with eight physical cores, it would offer a more reticent 4.5x speedup with a microprocessor with four physical cores and eight logical cores with hyperthreading technology.

CREATING AND MANAGING TASKS

TPL introduced the new task-based programming model to translate multicore power into application performance without having to work with low-level, more complex and heavyweight, threads. It is very important to understand that *tasks* aren't threads. Tasks run using threads. However, it doesn't mean they replace threads. In fact, all the parallel loops used in the previous examples run by creating tasks, and their parallel and concurrent execution is supported by underlying threads, as shown in Figure 33-8.

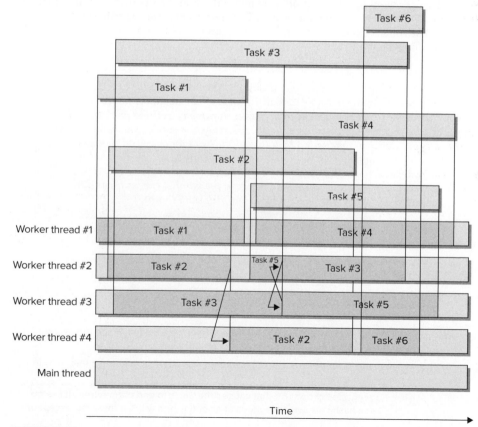

FIGURE 33-8

When you work with tasks, they run their code using underlying threads (software threads, scheduled on certain hardware threads, or logical cores). However, there isn't a one-to-one relationship between tasks and threads. This means you aren't creating a new thread each time you create a new task. The CLR creates the necessary threads to support the tasks' execution needs. Of course, this is a simplified view of what goes on when creating tasks.

Synchronizing code running in multiple threads is indeed complex. Thus, a task-based alternative offers an excellent opportunity to leave some synchronization problems behind, especially those regarding work scheduling mechanisms. The CLR uses *work-stealing queues* to reduce the locks and to schedule small work chunks without adding a significant overhead. Creating a new thread introduces a big overhead, but creating a new task "steals" work from an existing thread. Therefore, tasks offer a new lightweight mechanism for parts of code capable of taking advantage of multiple cores.

The default task scheduler relies on an underlying thread pool engine. Thus, when you create a new task, it will use the steal-working queues to find the most appropriate thread to enqueue it. It steals work from an existing thread or creates a new one when necessary. The code included in tasks will run in one thread, but this happens under the hood, and the overhead is smaller than manually creating a new thread.

System.Threading.Tasks.Task

So far, TPL has been creating instances of `System.Threading.Tasks.Task` under the hood in order to support the parallel execution of the iterations. In addition, calling `Parallel.Invoke` also creates as many instances of `Task` as delegates are called.

A `Task` represents an asynchronous operation. It offers many methods and properties that enable you to control its execution and get information about its status. The creation of a `Task` is independent of its execution. This means that you have complete control over the execution of the associated operation. The `Task` class provides the following properties:

> *When you launch many asynchronous operations as* `Task` *instances, the task scheduler will try to run them in parallel in order to load-balance all the available logical cores at runtime. However, it isn't convenient to use tasks to run any existing piece of code because tasks add an overhead. Sometimes it doesn't make sense to use tasks. Although this overhead is smaller than that added by a thread, it is still an overhead that has to be considered. For example, it doesn't make sense to create tasks to run two lines of code as two independent asynchronous tasks that solve very simple calculations. Remember to measure the speedups achieved between the parallel execution and the sequential version to decide whether parallelism is appropriate or not.*

Table 33-2 explains the three possible situations considered in this example.

TABLE 33-2: Task Read-only Properties

PROPERTY	DESCRIPTION
AsyncState	A state `Object` supplied when you created the `Task` instance
CreationOptions	The `TaskCreationOptions` enum value used to provide hints to the task scheduler in order to help it make the best scheduling decisions
CurrentId	The unique ID for the `Task` being executed. It is not equivalent to a thread ID in unmanaged code.
Exception	The `AggregateException` that caused the `Task` to end prematurely. It is a null value if the `Task` hasn't thrown exceptions at all or finished without throwing exceptions.

PROPERTY	DESCRIPTION
Factory	Provides access to the factory methods that allow the creation of Task instances with and without results
Id	The unique ID for the Task instance
IsCanceled	A Boolean value indicating whether the Task instance was canceled
IsCompleted	A Boolean value indicating whether the Task has completed its execution
IsFaulted	A Boolean value indicating whether the Task has aborted its execution due to an unhandled exception
Status	The TaskStatus value indicating the current stage in the life cycle of a Task instance

Understanding a Task's Life Cycle

It is very important to understand that each Task instance has a life cycle. However, it represents concurrent code potentially running in parallel according to the possibilities offered by the underlying hardware and the availability of resources at runtime. Therefore, any information about the Task instance could change as soon as you retrieve it, because its states are changing concurrently.

A Task instance completes its life cycle just once. After it reaches one of its three possible final states, it doesn't go back to any previous state, as shown in the state diagram in Figure 33-9.

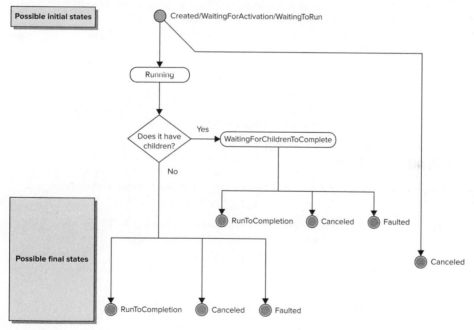

FIGURE 33-9

A Task instance has three possible initial states, depending on how it was created, as described in Table 33-3.

TABLE 33-3: Initial States for a Task Instance

VALUE	DESCRIPTION
TaskStatus.Created	A Task instance created using the Task constructor has this initial state. It will change once there is a call to either Start or RunSynchronously, or if the task is canceled.
TaskStatus.WaitingForActivation	This is the initial state for tasks created through methods that allow the definition of continuations — that is, tasks that aren't scheduled until other dependent tasks finish their execution.
TaskStatus.WaitingToRun	This is the initial state for a task created through TaskFactory. StartNew. It is waiting for the specified scheduler to pick it up and run it.

Next, the task status can transition to the TaskStatus.Running state, and finally move to a final state. If it has attached children, it isn't considered complete and will transition to the TaskStatus. WaitingForChildrenToComplete state. Once its children tasks complete, the task moves to one of the three possible final states shown in Table 33-4.

TABLE 33-4: Final States for a Task Instance

VALUE	DESCRIPTION
TaskStatus.Canceled	A cancellation request arrived before the task started its execution or during it. The IsCanceled property will be True.
TaskStatus.Faulted	An unhandled exception in its body or the bodies of its children made the task end. The IsFaulted property will be True and the Exception property will be non-null and will hold the AggregateException that caused the task or its children to end prematurely.
TaskStatus.RanToCompletion	The task completed its execution. It ran to the end of its body without being canceled or throwing an unhandled exception. The IsCompleted property will be True. In addition, IsCanceled and IsFaulted will be both False.

Using Tasks to Parallelize Code

In a previous example, you used Parallel.Invoke to launch two subroutines in parallel:

```
Parallel.Invoke(Sub() GenerateAESKeys(), Sub() GenerateMD5Hashes())
```

It is possible to do the same job using two instances of Task, as shown in Listing 33-13. Working with instances of Tasks offers more flexibility to schedule and start independent and chained tasks that can take advantage of multiple cores.

LISTING 33-13: Working with tasks

```
' Create the tasks
Dim t1 = New Task(Sub() GenerateAESKeys())
Dim t2 = New Task(Sub() GenerateMD5Hashes())
' Start the tasks
t1.Start()
t2.Start()
' Wait for all the tasks to finish
Task.WaitAll(t1, t2)
```

Code snippet from Listing13

The first two lines create two instances of `Task` with a lambda expression to create a delegate for `GenerateAESKeys` and `GenerateMD5Hashes`. `t1` is associated with the first subroutine, and `t2` with the second. It is also possible to use multi-line lambda expression syntax to define the action that the `Task` constructor receives as a parameter. At this point, the `Status` for both `Task` instances is `TaskStatus.Created`. The subroutines aren't running yet, but the code continues with the next line.

Starting Tasks

Then, the following line starts the *asynchronous execution* of `t1`:

```
t1.Start()
```

The `Start` method initiates the execution of the delegate in an independent way, and the program flow continues with the instruction after this method, even though the delegate has not finished its execution. The code in the delegate associated with the task runs concurrently and potentially in parallel with the main program flow, the *main thread*. This means that at this point, there is a main thread and another thread or threads supporting the execution of this new task.

The execution of the main program flow, the main thread, is synchronous. This means that it will continue with the next instruction, the line that starts the *asynchronous execution* of `t2`:

```
t2.Start()
```

Now the `Start` method initiates the execution of the delegate in another independent way and the program flow continues with the instruction after this method, even though this other delegate has not finished its execution. The code in the delegate associated with the task runs concurrently and potentially in parallel with the main thread and the code inside `GenerateAESKeys` that is already running. This means that at this point, there is a main thread and other threads supporting the execution of the two tasks.

 It is indeed easy to run asynchronous code using `Task` instances and the latest language improvements added to Visual Basic. With just a few lines, you can create code that runs asynchronously, control its execution flow, and take advantage of multicore microprocessors or multiple processors.

The sequence diagram in Figure 33-10 shows the parallel and asynchronous execution flow for the main thread and the two tasks.

Visualizing Tasks Using Parallel Tasks and Parallel Stacks

The Visual Basic 2010 IDE offers two new debugging windows: Parallel Tasks and Parallel Stacks. They offer information about the tasks that are running, including their status and their relationship with the underlying threads. These new debugging windows allow you to monitor what is going on under the hood with tasks and threads in .NET Framework 4 but they also let you see the Visual Basic code that is running in each task and thread. By running the code, step by step, you can see the differences between synchronous and asynchronous execution.

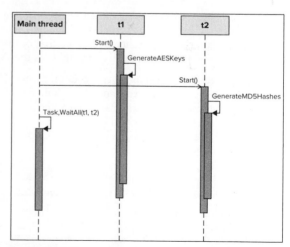

FIGURE 33-10

For example, if you insert a breakpoint on the line `Task.WaitAll(t1, t2)` and your microprocessor has at least two cores, you will be able to see two tasks running in parallel. To do so, select Debug ➪ Windows ➪ Parallel Tasks (Ctrl + Shift + D, K). The IDE will display the Parallel Tasks dialog shown in Figure 33-11, which includes a list of all the tasks and their status (scheduled, running, waiting, waiting-deadlocked, etc.).

	ID	Status	Location	Task	Thread Assignment	AppDomain
▽	1	▶ Running	ConsoleApplication3.Module1.ConvertToHexString	<lambda12>()	384 (Worker Thread)	1 (ConsoleApplication3.vshost.exe)
▽	2	▶ Running	ConsoleApplication3.Module1.GenerateMD5Hashes	<lambda13>()	1020 (Worker Thread)	1 (ConsoleApplication3.vshost.exe)

FIGURE 33-11

There are two tasks:

➤   Task ID 1: `<lambda12>()` — Assigned to Worker thread ID 384

➤   Task ID 2: `<lambda13>()` — Assigned to Worker thread ID 1020

Therefore, in this case, each of the two tasks is assigned to a different thread. The status for both tasks is Running, and they are identified by an auto-generated lambda name and number, `<lambda12>()` and `<lambda13>()`. This happens because the code uses lambda expressions to generate the delegates associated with each task.

If you double-click on a task name, the IDE will display the next statement that is going to run for the selected task. Remember that the threads assigned to these tasks and the main thread are running concurrently and potentially in parallel, according to the available hardware resources and the decisions taken by the schedulers.

> *The CLR task scheduler tries to steal work from the most appropriate underlying thread, by consuming time from an idle one. It can also decide to create a new thread to support the task's execution. However, this procedure doesn't guarantee that the underlying threads are going to run in parallel, even when the necessary number of logical cores is available. The operating system scheduler distributes the cores between the dozens or hundreds of threads scheduled to receive processor time from the available cores. This is why the same concurrent code can run with different parallelism levels and different concurrent times on the same hardware configuration.*

You can check what is going on with each different concurrent or parallel task. You have similar options to those offered by previous Visual Basic versions with threads, but the information is better because you can check whether a task is scheduled or waiting-deadlocked. You can also order and group the information shown in the windows, as you can with any other Visual Basic IDE feature.

The Parallel Tasks grid includes a column named Thread Assignment. This number is the ID shown in the Threads window. Thus, you know which managed thread is supporting the execution of a certain task. You can also check the next statement and additional detailed information for each different thread. To do so, select Debug ➪ Windows ➪ Threads (Ctrl + Alt + H). The IDE will display the Threads dialog shown in Figure 33-12, which includes a list of all the threads, their category, and their locations.

	ID	Managed ID	Category	Name	Location	Priority
∧ ConsoleApplication3.vshost.exe (id = 3504) : C:\Users\Public\Documents\ConsoleApplication3\ConsoleApplication3\bin\Debug\ConsoleApplication3.vshost.exe						
▽	3644	0	Worker Thread	<Thread Ended>	<not available>	Normal
▽	5532	0	Worker Thread	<No Name>	<not available>	Highest
▽	2476	7	Worker Thread	vshost.RunParkingWindow	✓ [Managed to Native Transition]	Normal
▽	5156	6	Worker Thread	<No Name>	<not available>	Normal
▽	5968	10	Main Thread	Main Thread	✓ ConsoleApplication3.Module1.Main	Normal
▽	4340	9	Worker Thread	.NET SystemEvents	✓ [Managed to Native Transition]	Normal
⇨	1020	11	Worker Thread	Worker Thread	✓ ConsoleApplication3.Module1.GenerateMD5Hashes	Normal
▽	384	12	Worker Thread	Worker Thread	✓ ConsoleApplication3.Module1.ConvertToHexString	Normal
▽	5044	0	Worker Thread	<No Name>	<not available>	Normal

FIGURE 33-12

Although it isn't visible in the black-and-white screenshot, the Threads dialog uses a different color and name to distinguish the main thread, the one that is usually running the UI code or supporting the Main subroutine (Main thread, green square), and the others (Worker thread, yellow square). The running tasks steal work from worker threads, not the main thread. Therefore, the tasks must use delegates to update the UI in order to run code in the main thread for this purpose.

There is a simpler way to visualize the relationship between tasks and threads. You can select Debug ⇨ Windows ⇨ Parallel Stacks (Ctrl + Shift + D, S). The IDE will display the Parallel Stacks window shown in Figure 33-13, which includes a diagram with all the tasks or threads, their status, and their relationships. The default view is Threads.

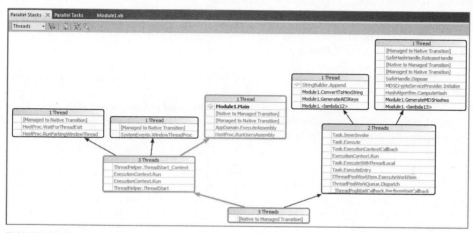

FIGURE 33-13

The two threads on the right side of the diagram are running the code scheduled by the two tasks. Each thread shows its call stack. The thread that supports `Module1.<lambda12>` is running the `GenerateAESKeys` subroutine — specifically, code inside the call to the `ConvertToHexString` subroutine. The thread that supports `Module1.<lambda13>` is running the `GenerateMD5Hashes` subroutine and it shows many native-to-managed-code transitions and vice versa. This diagram indicates what each thread is doing with a great level of detail.

You can change the value for the combo box in the upper-left corner from Threads to Tasks, and the IDE will display a diagram with all the tasks, including their status, relationships, and the call stack, as shown in Figure 33-14.

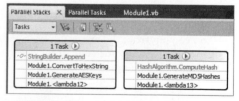

FIGURE 33-14

Waiting for Tasks to Finish

At some point, you need to wait for certain tasks, started with an asynchronous execution, to finish. The following line calls the `Task.WaitAll` method, which will wait for the `Task` instances received as a `ParamArray`, separated by commas. This method has a synchronous execution, which means that the main thread won't continue with the next statement until the `Task` instances received as parameters finish their execution.

```
Task.WaitAll(t1, t2)
```

Here, t1 and t2 have to finish their execution. The current thread — in this case, the main thread — will wait until both tasks finish their execution. However, it is very important that this time waiting for the tasks to finish is not a loop continuously checking a status and consuming a lot of CPU cycles. The `WaitAll` method uses a lightweight mechanism to reduce the need for CPU cycles as much as possible. This way, once these tasks finish their execution, the next statement will run.

Because the `WaitAll` method uses a synchronous execution, if the tasks take one minute to run, then the thread where this method was called (in this case, the main thread) will be waiting for this amount of time. Therefore, sometimes you want to limit the number of milliseconds to wait for the tasks to finish. You can use another definition for the `Task.WaitAll` method that accepts an array of `Task` instances and the number of milliseconds to wait. The method returns a `Boolean` value indicating whether the tasks where able to finish within the specified timeout. The following code waits for t1 and t2 to finish their execution with a three-second timeout:

Available for
download on
Wrox.com

```
If Task.WaitAll(New Task() {t1, t2}, 3000) = False Then
    Console.WriteLine("GenerateAESKeys and GenerateMD5Hashes are taking more than 3
seconds to complete.")
    Console.WriteLine(t1.Status.ToString())
    Console.WriteLine(t2.Status.ToString())
End If
```

Code snippet from Snippet03

If t1 and t2 don't finish in three seconds, the code displays a message and the status for both tasks. If no exceptions occurred in the code for these tasks, they could be still running. The `Task.WaitAll` method with a specific timeout doesn't cancel the tasks if they take more time to run; it just returns from its synchronous execution with the `Boolean` result.

It is also possible to call the `Wait` method for a `Task` instance. In this case, the current thread will wait until that task finishes its execution. Of course, there is no need to send the task instance as a parameter because the `Wait` method is an instance method. The `Task.Wait` method also supports a timeout in one of its definitions. The following code waits for t1 to finish and if it doesn't complete its work in three seconds, it displays a message and its status:

Available for
download on
Wrox.com

```
If t1.Wait (3000) = False Then
    Console.WriteLine("GenerateAESKeys is taking more than 3 seconds to complete.")
    Console.WriteLine(t1.Status.ToString())
End If
```

Code snippet from Snippet04

Canceling Tasks Using Tokens

You can interrupt the execution of `Task` instances through the use of *cancellation tokens*. To do so, it is necessary to add some code in the delegate, in order to create an cancelable operation that is capable of terminating in a timely manner.

Listing 33-14 shows two new versions of the AES keys and MD5 hash generators. The changes made in order to support cancellation appear in bold. The new `GenerateAESKeysCancel`, replacing the old `GenerateAESKeys`, receives a `System.Threading.CancellationToken` instance and throws an `OperationCanceledException` calling the `ThrowIfCancellationRequested` method. This way, the `Task` instance transitions to the `TaskStatus.Canceled` state and the `IsCanceled` property will be `True`.

Available for
download on
Wrox.com

LISTING 33-14: Canceling tasks using tokens with the changes in the AES keys and MD5 hash generators

```
Sub GenerateAESKeysCancel(ByVal ct As System.Threading.CancellationToken)
    ct.ThrowIfCancellationRequested()
    Dim sw = Stopwatch.StartNew()
    Dim aesM As New AesManaged()
```

```vb
        Dim result() As Byte
        Dim hexString As String
        For i As Integer = 1 To NUM_AES_KEYS
            aesM.GenerateKey()
            result = aesM.Key
            hexString = ConvertToHexString(result)
            ' Console.WriteLine("AES: " + hexString)
            If ct.IsCancellationRequested Then
                ct.ThrowIfCancellationRequested()
            End If
        Next
        Debug.WriteLine("AES: " + sw.Elapsed.ToString())
    End Sub

    Sub GenerateMD5HashesCancel(ByVal ct As System.Threading.CancellationToken)
        ct.ThrowIfCancellationRequested()
        Dim sw = Stopwatch.StartNew()
        Dim md5M As MD5 = MD5.Create()
        Dim result() As Byte
        Dim data() As Byte
        Dim hexString As String
        For i As Integer = 1 To NUM_MD5_HASHES
            data = Encoding.Unicode.GetBytes(Environment.UserName + i.ToString())
            result = md5M.ComputeHash(data)
            hexString = ConvertToHexString(result)
            ' Console.WriteLine("MD5:" + hexString)
            If ct.IsCancellationRequested Then
                ct.ThrowIfCancellationRequested()
            End If
        Next
        Debug.WriteLine("MD5: " + sw.Elapsed.ToString())
    End Sub

Sub Main()
    Dim cts As New System.Threading.CancellationTokenSource()
    Dim ct As System.Threading.CancellationToken = cts.Token

    Dim t1 = Task.Factory.StartNew(Sub() GenerateAESKeysCancel(ct), ct)
    Dim t2 = Task.Factory.StartNew(Sub() GenerateMD5HashesCancel(ct), ct)

    ' Sleep the main thread for 1 second
    Threading.Thread.Sleep(1000)

    cts.Cancel()

    Try
        If Task.WaitAll(New Task() {t1, t2}, 1000) = False Then
            Console.WriteLine("GenerateAESKeys and GenerateMD5Hashes are taking more
than 1 second to complete.")
            Console.WriteLine(t1.Status.ToString())
            Console.WriteLine(t2.Status.ToString())
        End If
    Catch ex As AggregateException
        For Each innerEx As Exception In ex.InnerExceptions
            Debug.WriteLine(innerEx.ToString())
            ' Do something else considering the innerEx Exception
        Next
    End Try
    If t1.IsCanceled Then
        Console.WriteLine("The task running GenerateAESKeysCancel was cancelled.")
    End If
```

continues

LISTING 33-14 *(continued)*

```
    If t2.IsCanceled Then
        Console.WriteLine("The task running GenerateMD5HashesCancel was cancelled.")
    End If
        ' Display the results and wait for the user to press a key
        Console.ReadLine()
End Sub
```

Code snippet from Listing14

The first line of GenerateAESKeysCancel will throw the aforementioned exception if its cancellation was already requested at that time. This way, it won't start the loop if unnecessary at that point.

```
ct.ThrowIfCancellationRequested()
```

In addition, after each iteration of the loop, new code checks the token's IsCancellationRequested. If it is True, it calls the ThrowIfCancellationRequested method. Before calling this method, when IsCancellationRequested is True, it is possible to add clean-up code when necessary:

```
If ct.IsCancellationRequested Then
    ' It is important to add clean up code here when necessary
    ct.ThrowIfCancellationRequested()
End If
```

This extra code adds a small amount of overhead to each iteration of the loop. However, it adds the capability of observing the OperationCanceledException and comparing its token to the one associated to the Task instance. If they are the same and its IsCancelledProperty is True, the Task instance understands that there is a request for cancellation and makes the transition to the Canceled state, interrupting its execution. When there is code waiting for the cancelled Task instance, this also generates an automatic TaskCanceledException, which is wrapped in an AggregateException.

In this case, the main subroutine creates a CancellationTokenSource, *cts*, and a Cancellation Token, *ct*:

```
    Dim cts As New System.Threading.CancellationTokenSource()
    Dim ct As System.Threading.CancellationToken = cts.Token
```

CancellationTokenSource is capable of initiating cancellation requests, and CancellationToken communicates it to asynchronous operations.

It is necessary to send a CancellationToken as a parameter to each task delegate; therefore, the code uses one of the definitions of the TaskFactory.StartNew method. The following lines create and start two Task instances with associated actions and the same CancellationToken instance (ct) as parameters:

```
    Dim t1 = Task.Factory.StartNew(Sub() GenerateAESKeysCancel(ct), ct)
    Dim t2 = Task.Factory.StartNew(Sub() GenerateMD5HashesCancel(ct), ct)
```

The preceding lines use the Task class Factory property to retrieve a TaskFactory instance that can be used to create tasks with more options than those offered by direct instantiation of the Task class. In this case, it uses the StartNew method, which is functionally equivalent to creating a Task using one of its constructors and then calling Start to schedule it for execution.

Then, the code calls the Sleep method to make the main thread sleep for one second. This method suspends the current thread for the indicated time — in this case, specified as an Integer in milliseconds:

```
    Threading.Thread.Sleep(1000)
```

The main thread remains suspended for one second, but the threads that are supporting the tasks' execution won't be suspended. Therefore, the tasks will be scheduled to begin their execution.

One second later, the main thread communicates a request for cancellation for both tasks through the `CancellationTokenSource` instance's `Cancel` method:

```
cts.Cancel()
```

The cancellation token is evaluated in the two delegates launched by the `Task` instances, as previously explained.

Adding a few lines, it is indeed easy to cancel asynchronous actions. However, it is very important to add the necessary clean-up code.

A `Try...Catch...End Try` block encloses the call to `Task.WaitAll`. Because there was a request for cancellation for both tasks, there will be two benign exceptions of type `OperationCanceledException`.

The `IsCanceled` property for both tasks is going to be `True`. Checking this property, you can add code whenever a task was cancelled.

Handling Exceptions Thrown by Tasks

As many tasks run in parallel, many exceptions can occur in parallel. Task instances also work with a set of exceptions, handled by the previously explained `System.AggregateException` class.

Listing 33-15 shows the highlighted lines that add an unhandled exception in the `GenerateAESKeysCancel` subroutine.

Comment the code that requested cancellation for both tasks:

```
' cts.Cancel()
```

Available for
download on
Wrox.com

LISTING 33-15: An unhandled exception in the subroutine called by an asynchronous delegate

```vbnet
Sub GenerateAESKeysCancel(ByVal ct As System.Threading.CancellationToken)
    ct.ThrowIfCancellationRequested()
    Dim sw = Stopwatch.StartNew()
    Dim aesM As New AesManaged()
    Dim result() As Byte
    Dim hexString As String
    For i As Integer = 1 To NUM_AES_KEYS
        aesM.GenerateKey()
        result = aesM.Key
        hexString = ConvertToHexString(result)
        ' Console.WriteLine("AES: " + hexString)
        If (sw.Elapsed.Seconds > 0.5) Then
            Throw New TimeoutException("GenerateAESKeysCancel is taking more than 0.5
seconds to complete.")
        End If
        If ct.IsCancellationRequested Then
            ct.ThrowIfCancellationRequested()
        End If
    Next
    Debug.WriteLine("AES: " + sw.Elapsed.ToString())
End Sub
```

Code snippet from Listing15

Add the following lines to the `Main` subroutine:

Available for
download on
Wrox.com

```vbnet
If t1.IsFaulted Then
    For Each innerEx As Exception In t1.Exception.InnerExceptions
        Debug.WriteLine(innerEx.ToString())
        ' Do something else considering the innerEx Exception
    Next
End If
```

Code snippet from Listing15

Because there is an unhandled exception in t1, its IsFaulted property is True. Therefore, t1.Exception, an AggregateException, contains one or more exceptions that occurred during the execution of its associated delegate. After checking the IsFaulted property, it is possible to iterate through each individual exception contained in the InnerExceptions read-only collection of Exception. You can make decisions according to the problems that made it impossible to complete the task. Listing 33-16 shows the information about the unhandled exception converted to a string and sent to the Debug output.

LISTING 33-16: Debug output with the exceptions found in the InnerExceptions collection

```
System.TimeoutException: GenerateAESKeysCancel is taking more than 0.5 seconds to complete.
    at ConsoleApplication3.Module1.GenerateAESKeysCancel(CancellationToken ct) in
C:\Wrox\Professional_VB_2010\ConsoleApplication3\ConsoleApplication3\Module1.vb:line 427
    at ConsoleApplication3.Module1._Closure$__3._Lambda$__12() in
C:\Wrox\Professional_VB_2010\ConsoleApplication3\ConsoleApplication3\Module1.vb:line 337
    at System.Threading.Tasks.Task.InnerInvoke()
    at System.Threading.Tasks.Task.Execute()
```

Unhandled exceptions inside asynchronous operations are usually complex problems because sometimes you need to perform important clean-up operations. For example, when an exception occurs, you can have partial results and you could have to remove these values if the job doesn't complete because of an exception. Thus, you have to consider clean-up operations when working with tasks.

Returning Values from Tasks

So far, task instances did not return values; they were delegates running subroutines. However, it is also possible to return values from tasks, invoking functions and using Task(Of *TResult*) instances, where *TResult* has to be replaced by the returned type.

Listing 33-17 shows the code for a new function that generates the well-known AES keys and then returns a list of the ones that begin with the character prefix received as one of the parameters (*prefix*). GenerateAESKeysWithCharPrefix returns a List of String.

The Main subroutine uses the definition of the TaskFactory.StartNew method, but this time it calls it from a Task(Of TResult) instance and not a Task instance. Specifically, it creates a Task(Of List(Of String)) instance, sending it a CancellationToken as a parameter to the task delegate:

```
Dim t1 = Task(Of List(Of String)).Factory.StartNew(Function()
GenerateAESKeysWithCharPrefix(ct, "A"), ct)
```

The delegate is a function that returns a List(Of String), which is going to be available in the Task(Of Result) instance (t1) through its Result property, after the associated delegate completes its execution and the function returns a value.

The main thread waits for t1 to finish and then checks whether it completed its execution, checking the previously explained Task instance properties.

Then, it iterates through each string in the list, returned by the function called in the previous task, and displays the results on the console. It does this job running a new asynchronous task, t2.

LISTING 33-17: Returning a list of String instances from a task

```
Function GenerateAESKeysWithCharPrefix(ByVal ct As
System.Threading.CancellationToken, ByVal prefix As Char) As List(Of String)
    ct.ThrowIfCancellationRequested()
    Dim sw = Stopwatch.StartNew()
```

```vbnet
        Dim aesM As New AesManaged()
        Dim result() As Byte
        Dim hexString As String
        Dim keysList As New List(Of String)
        For i As Integer = 1 To NUM_AES_KEYS
            aesM.GenerateKey()
            result = aesM.Key
            hexString = ConvertToHexString(result)
            If Left(hexString, 1) = prefix Then
                keysList.Add(hexString)
            End If
            If ct.IsCancellationRequested Then
                ' It is important to add clean up code here
                ct.ThrowIfCancellationRequested()
            End If
        Next
        Return keysList
        Debug.WriteLine("AES: " + sw.Elapsed.ToString())
    End Function

    Sub Main()
        Dim sw = Stopwatch.StartNew()
        Dim cts As New System.Threading.CancellationTokenSource()
        Dim ct As System.Threading.CancellationToken = cts.Token

        Dim t1 = Task(Of List(Of String)).Factory.StartNew(
            Function() GenerateAESKeysWithCharPrefix(ct, "A"), ct)

        Try
            t1.Wait()
        Catch ex As AggregateException
            For Each innerEx As Exception In ex.InnerExceptions
                Debug.WriteLine(innerEx.ToString())
                ' Do something else considering the innerEx Exception
            Next
        End Try
        If t1.IsCanceled Then
            Console.WriteLine("The task running GenerateAESKeysWithCharPrefix was cancelled.")
            Exit Sub
        End If
        If t1.IsFaulted Then
            For Each innerEx As Exception In t1.Exception.InnerExceptions
                Debug.WriteLine(innerEx.ToString())
                ' Do something else considering the innerEx Exception
            Next
            Exit Sub
        End If

        Dim t2 = Task.Factory.StartNew(Sub()
            ' Do something with the result returned by the task's delegate
            For i As Integer = 0 To t1.Result.Count - 1
                Console.WriteLine(t1.Result(i))
            Next
        End Sub, TaskCreationOptions.LongRunning)

        Debug.WriteLine(sw.Elapsed.ToString())
        ' Display the results and wait for the user to press a key
        Console.ReadLine()
    End Sub
```

Code snippet from Listing17

TaskCreationOptions

The code creates and starts the second task, `t2`, using the StartNew method and multi-line lambda expression syntax. However, in this case, it uses a different definition that receives a `TaskCreationOptions` parameter that specifies flags to control optional behavior for the creation, scheduling, and execution of tasks.

The `TaskCreationOptions` enumeration has the four members described in Table 33-5.

TABLE 33-5: Optional Behaviors for Tasks

VALUE	DESCRIPTION
`TaskCreationOptions.AttachedToParent`	The task is attached to a parent task. You can create tasks inside other tasks.
`TaskCreationOptions.None`	The task can use the default behavior.
`TaskCreationOptions.LongRunning`	The task will take a long time to run. Therefore, the scheduler can work with it as a coarse-grained operation. You can use this option if the task is likely to take many seconds to run. It is not advisable to use this option when a task takes less than one second to run.
`TaskCreationOptions.PreferFairness`	This option tells the scheduler that tasks scheduled sooner should be run sooner and tasks scheduled later should be run later.

> It is possible to combine multiple `TaskCreationOptions` *enum values using bitwise operations.*

Chaining Two Tasks Using Continuations

Clearly, the previous case shows an example of chained tasks. Task `t1` produces a result and `t2` needs it as an input in order to start processing it. In these cases, instead of adding many lines that check for the successful completion of a precedent task and then schedule a new task, TPL enables you to chain tasks using continuations.

You can call the `ContinueWith` method for any task instance and create a continuation that executes when this task successfully completes its execution. It has many definitions, the simplest of which defines an action as done when creating `Task` instances.

The following lines show a simplified version of the code used in the previous example to display the results generated by `t1`:

```
Dim t1 = Task(Of List(Of String)).Factory.StartNew(Function()
GenerateAESKeysWithCharPrefix(ct, "A"), ct)

Dim t2 = t1.ContinueWith(Sub(t)
                            ' Do something with the result returned by the task's delegate
                            For i As Integer = 0 To t.Result.Count - 1
                                Console.WriteLine(t.Result(i))
                            Next
                        End Sub)
```

Code snippet from Snippet05

It is possible to chain many tasks and then wait for the last task to be executed. However, you have to be careful with the continuous changes in the states when checking their values for all these asynchronous operations. In addition, it is very important to consider all the potential exceptions that could be thrown.

Preparing the Code for Concurrency and Parallelism

Parallel and concurrent programming applied to certain complex algorithms is not as simple as shown in the previously explained examples. Sometimes, the differences between a reliable and bug-free parallelized version and its sequential counterpart could reveal an initially unexpected complexity. The code can become too complex, even when taking advantage of the new features offered by TPL. In fact, a complex sequential algorithm is probably going to be a more complex parallel algorithm. Therefore, TPL offers many new data structures for parallel programming that simplify many complex synchronization problems:

➤ Concurrent collection classes

➤ Lightweight synchronization primitives

➤ Types for lazy initialization

The aforementioned data structures were designed to avoid *locks* wherever possible, and use fine-grained locking when they are necessary on their different shared resources. Locks generate many potential bugs and can significantly reduce scalability. However, sometimes they are necessary because writing lock-free code isn't always possible.

These new data structures enable you to forget about complex lock mechanisms in certain situations, because they already include all the necessary lightweight synchronization under the hood. Therefore, it is a good idea to use these data structures whenever possible.

Synchronization Primitives

Furthermore, .NET Framework 4 offers synchronization primitives for managing and controlling the interactions between different tasks and their underlying threads, including the following operations:

➤ **Locking** — As with relational databases, sometimes you need to ensure that only one piece of code is working with a variable at that time. Unfortunately, the same problems that appear when working with concurrent access in a relational database are also present in concurrent and parallel code.

➤ **Signaling** — It provides a waiting and signaling mechanism to simplify the communication between different tasks and their underlying threads. The previously explained cancellation token is a clear example of signaling among many tasks. The mechanisms to wait for certain tasks to complete and the continuations are also examples of signaling implementations.

➤ **Lock constructors (interlocked operations)** — These provide a mechanism to perform *atomic operations*, such as addition, increment, decrement, exchange, or conditional exchange, depending on the results of a comparison and read operations.

Synchronization Problems

The aforementioned synchronization primitives are advanced topics that require an in-depth analysis in order to determine the most convenient primitive to apply in a given situation. Nowadays, it is important to use the right synchronization primitive in order to avoid potential pitfalls, explained in the following list, while still keeping the code scalable.

Many techniques and new debugging tools can simplify the most complex problems, such as the following:

➤ **Deadlock** — At least two tasks are waiting for each other, but the wait never ends because they won't continue with other instructions until the other task releases the protection held over certain resources. The other task is also waiting for resources held by its counterpart to resume its execution. As no task is willing to release its protection, none of them make any progress, and the tasks continue to wait for each other forever. Consider the following situation, task $t1$ holds a protection over resource A and is waiting to gain exclusive access over resource B. However, at the same time, task $t2$ holds a protection over resource B and is waiting to gain exclusive access over resource A. This is one of the most horrible bugs.

➤ **Race conditions** — Many tasks read from and write to the same variable without the appropriate synchronization mechanism. It is a correctness problem. Erroneous parallelized code could generate wrong results under certain concurrency or parallel execution scenarios. However, when executed in some circumstances, it could generate the expected results because the race may finish correctly. Consider the following situation: task *t1* writes a value to public variable A. Then, task *t2* writes another value to public variable A. When task *t1* reads the value for the public variable A, it will hold a different value than the one that it had originally written to it.

Understanding Concurrent Collection Features

Lists, collections, and arrays are excellent examples of when complex synchronization management is needed to access them concurrently and in parallel. If you have to write a parallel loop that adds elements in an unordered way into a shared collection, you have to add a synchronization mechanism to generate a *thread-safe* collection. The classic lists, collections, and arrays are not thread-safe because they aren't prepared to receive concurrent instructions to add or remove elements. Therefore, creating a thread-safe collection is indeed a very complex job.

Systems.Collections.Concurrent

Luckily, TPL offers a new namespace, System.Collections.Concurrent, for dealing with thread-safe issues. As previously explained, this namespace provides access to the custom partitioners for parallelized loops. However, it also offers access to the following collections prepared for concurrency:

➤ BlockingCollection(Of T) — Similar to the classic blocking queue data structure — in this case, prepared for producer-consumer scenarios in which many tasks add and remove data. It is a wrapper of an IProducerConsumer(Of T) instance, providing blocking and bounding capabilities.

➤ ConcurrentBag(Of T) — Offers an unordered collection of objects. It is useful when ordering doesn't matter.

➤ ConcurrentDictionary(Of TKey, TValue) — Similar to a classic dictionary, with key-value pairs that can be accessed concurrently

➤ ConcurrentQueue(Of T) — A FIFO (First In, First Out) collection whereby many tasks can enqueue and dequeue elements concurrently

➤ ConcurrentStack(Of T) — A LIFO (Last In, First Out) collection whereby many tasks can push and pop elements concurrently

 You don't have to worry about locks and synchronization primitives while using the aforementioned collections in many tasks, because they are already prepared to receive concurrent and parallel methods calls. They solve potential deadlocks and race conditions and they make it easier to work with parallelized code in many advanced scenarios.

ConcurrentQueue

It would be difficult to use a classic shared list to add elements from many independent tasks created by the Parallel.ForEach method. You would need to add synchronization code, which would be a great challenge without restricting the overall scalability. However, it is possible to add strings to a queue (enqueue strings) in a shared ConcurrentCollection inside the parallelized code, because it is prepared for adding elements concurrently.

Listing 33-18 uses a shared ConcurrentQueue(Of String), *Keys*, in order to hold the strings that contain the AES keys that begin with a certain prefix, generated in a parallelized loop with the custom partitioner.

All the tasks created automatically by `Parallel.ForEach` are going to call the `Enqueue` method to add the elements that comply with the condition.

```
Keys.Enqueue(hexString)
```

It is indeed simple to work with a `ConcurrentQueue`. There is no need to worry about synchronization problems because everything is controlled under the hood.

Available for download on Wrox.com

LISTING 33-18: Enqueueing the generated keys in a ConcurrentCollection

```vb
Private Keys As Concurrent.ConcurrentQueue(Of String)

Sub ParallelPartitionGenerateAESKeysWCP(ByVal ct As
System.Threading.CancellationToken, ByVal prefix As Char)
    ct.ThrowIfCancellationRequested()
    Dim sw = Stopwatch.StartNew()
    Dim parallelOptions As New ParallelOptions()
    ' Set the CancellationToken for the ParallelOptions instance
    parallelOptions.CancellationToken = ct
    Parallel.ForEach(Partitioner.Create(1, NUM_AES_KEYS + 1), parallelOptions,
        Sub(range)
            Dim aesM As New AesManaged()
            Dim result() As Byte
            Dim hexString As String
            'Debug.WriteLine("Range ({0}, {1}. Time: {2})",
            '                range.Item1, range.Item2, Now().TimeOfDay)
            For i As Integer = range.Item1 To range.Item2 - 1
                aesM.GenerateKey()
                result = aesM.Key
                hexString = ConvertToHexString(result)
                ' Console.WriteLine("AES: " + hexString)
                If Left(hexString, 1) = prefix Then
                    Keys.Enqueue(hexString)
                End If
                parallelOptions.CancellationToken.ThrowIfCancellationRequested()
            Next
        End Sub)
    Debug.WriteLine("AES: " + sw.Elapsed.ToString())
End Sub

Sub Main()
    Dim cts As New System.Threading.CancellationTokenSource()
    Dim ct As System.Threading.CancellationToken = cts.Token
    Keys = New ConcurrentQueue(Of String)

    Dim tAsync = New Task(Sub() ParallelPartitionGenerateAESKeysWCP(ct, "A"))
    tAsync.Start()

    ' Do something else
    ' Wait for tAsync to finish
    tAsync.Wait()

    Console.ReadLine()
End Sub
```

Code snippet from Listing18

For example, it is possible to run many LINQ queries to display partial statistics while running the task that is adding elements to the `ConcurrentQueue` (`Keys`). Listing 33-19 shows a new `Main` subroutine that checks whether the task (`tAsync`) is running or waiting to run, and while this happens it runs a LINQ query to show the number of keys that contain an `F` in the shared `ConcurrentQueue` (`Keys`).

LISTING 33-19: Reporting partial progress querying a ConcurrentQueue being updated by an asynchronous task

```vb
Sub Main()
    Dim cts As New System.Threading.CancellationTokenSource()
    Dim ct As System.Threading.CancellationToken = cts.Token

    Keys = New ConcurrentQueue(Of String)
    Dim tAsync = Task.Factory.StartNew(Sub() ParallelPartitionGenerateAESKeysWCP(ct, "A"))

    Do While (tAsync.Status = TaskStatus.Running) Or (tAsync.Status = TaskStatus.WaitingToRun)
        ' Display partial results
        Dim countQuery = Aggregate key In Keys
                         Where key.Contains("F")
                         Into Count()

        Console.WriteLine("So far, the number of keys that contain an F is: {0}", countQuery)
        ' Sleep the main thread for 0.5 seconds
        Threading.Thread.Sleep(500)
    Loop

    tAsync.Wait()

    ' Do something else

    Console.ReadLine()
End Sub
```

Code snippet from Listing19

Another useful feature is the capability to remove an element at the beginning of the queue in a safe way using its `TryDequeue` method:

```vb
Dim firstKey As String
If Keys.TryDequeue(firstKey) Then
    ' firstKey has the first key added to the ConcurrentQueue
Else
    ' It wasn't possible to remove an element from the ConcurrentQueue
End If
```

`TryDequeue` returns a `Boolean` value indicating whether the operation was successful. It returns the element using an output attribute — in this case, a `String` received by reference (`firstKey`).

It is possible to add and remove elements in different tasks.

ConcurrentStack

`ConcurrentStack` is very similar to the previously explained `ConcurrentQueue`, but it uses different method names to better represent a stack (a LIFO collection). Its most important methods are `Push` and `TryPop`.

`Push` inserts an element at the top of the `ConcurrentStack`. If `Keys` were a `ConcurrentStack(Of String)`, the following lines would add *hexString* at the top of the stack:

```vb
If Left(hexString, 1) = prefix Then
    Keys.Push(hexString)
End If
```

You can remove an element at the top of the stack in a safe way using its `TryPop` method. However, in this case, the method will return the last element added because it is a stack and not a queue:

```vb
Dim firstKey As String
If Keys.TryPop(firstKey) Then
```

```
          ' firstKey has the last key added to the ConcurrentStack
      Else
          ' It wasn't possible to remove an element from the ConcurrentStack
      End If
```

`TryPop` also returns a `Boolean` value indicating whether the operation was successful.

Transforming LINQ into PLINQ

You already learned that LINQ is very useful to query and process different data sources. If you are using LINQ to Objects, now it is possible to take advantage of parallelism using its parallel implementation, *Parallel LINQ (PLINQ)*.

> *PLINQ implements the full set of LINQ query operators and adds new additional operators for parallel execution. PLINQ can achieve significant speedups over its LINQ counterpart, but it depends on the scenario, as always with parallelism. If the query involves an appreciable number of calculations and memory-intensive operations and ordering doesn't matter, the speedups could be significant. However, when ordering matters, the speedups could be reduced.*

As you might have expected, LINQ and PLINQ can work with the previously explained concurrent collections. The following code defines a simple but intensive function to count and return the number of letters in a string received as a parameter:

Available for download on Wrox.com

```
Function CountLetters(ByVal key As String) As Integer
    Dim letters As Integer = 0
    For i As Integer = 0 To key.Length() - 1
        If Char.IsLetter(key, i) Then letters += 1
    Next
    Return letters
End Function
```

Code snippet from Snippet06

A simple LINQ expression to return all the AES keys with at least 10 letters containing an A, an F, a 9, and not a B, would look like the following:

```
Dim keysWith10Letters = From key In Keys
                        Where CountLetters(key) >= 10 And key.Contains("A")
                        And key.Contains("F") And key.Contains("9") And Not
                        key.Contains("B")
```

In order to transform the aforementioned LINQ expression into a PLINQ expression that can take advantage of parallelism, it is necessary to use the `AsParallel` method, as shown here:

```
Dim keysWith10Letters = From key In Keys.AsParallel()
                        Where CountLetters(key) >= 10 And key.Contains("A")
                        And key.Contains("F") And key.Contains("9") And Not
                        key.Contains("B")
```

This way, the query will try to take advantage of all the available logical cores at runtime in order to run faster than its sequential version.

It is possible to add code at the end of the `Main` subroutine to return some results according to the PLINQ query:

Available for download on Wrox.com

```
Dim sw = Stopwatch.StartNew()

Dim keysWith10Letters = From key In Keys.AsParallel()
                        Where CountLetters(key) >= 10 And key.Contains("A")
```

```
                          And key.Contains("F") And key.Contains("9") And Not
                          key.Contains("B")

    Console.WriteLine("The code generated {0} keys with at least ten letters, A,
    F and 9 but no B in the hexadecimal code.", keysWith10Letters.Count())
    Console.WriteLine("First key {0}: ", keysWith10Letters(0))
    Console.WriteLine("Last key {0}: ", keysWith10Letters(keysWith10Letters.Count() - 1))
    Debug.WriteLine(sw.Elapsed.ToString())

    Console.ReadLine()
```

Code snippet from Snippet06

This code shows the number of keys that comply with the conditions, the first one and the last one, stored in the results of the PLINQ query that worked against the `ConcurrentQueue(Of String)`.

ParallelEnumerable and Its AsParallel Method

The `System.Linq.ParallelEnumerable` class is responsible for exposing most of PLINQ's additional functionality, including its most important one: the `AsParallel` method. Table 33-6 summarizes the PLINQ-specific methods.

TABLE 33-6: PLINQ Operators Exposed by ParallelEnumerable

VALUE	DESCRIPTION
AsOrdered()	PLINQ must preserve the ordering of the source sequence for the rest of the query or until it changes using an `Order By` clause.
AsParallel()	The rest of the query should be parallelized, whenever possible.
AsSequential()	The rest of the query should run sequentially, as traditional LINQ.
AsUnordered()	PLINQ doesn't have to preserve the ordering of the source sequence.
ForAll()	An enumeration method that enables the results to be processed in parallel, using multiple tasks
WithCancellation	Enables working with a cancellation token to permit cancelation of the query execution as previously explained with tasks
WithDegreeOfParallelism	PLINQ will be optimized as if the total number of available cores were equal to the degree of parallelism specified as a parameter for this method.
WithExecutionMode	This can force parallel execution when the default behavior would be to run it sequentially as traditional LINQ.
WithMergeOptions	This can provide hints about the way PLINQ should merge the parallel pieces of the result on the thread that is consuming the query.

In addition, `AsParallel` offers an `Aggregate` overload that enables the implementation of parallel reduction algorithms. It enables intermediate aggregation on each parallelized part of the query and a final aggregation function that is capable of providing the logic to combine the results of all the generated partitions.

Sometimes is useful to run a PLINQ query with many different degrees of parallelism in order to measure its scalability. For example, the following line runs the previously shown PLINQ query to take advantage of no more than three cores:

```
    Dim keysWith10Letters = From key In Keys.AsParallel().WithDegreeOfParallelism(3)
                        Where CountLetters(key) >= 10 And key.Contains("A") And
```

AsOrdered and Order By

Because using `AsOrdered` and the `Order By` clause in PLINQ queries can reduce any speed gains, it is very important to compare the speedup achieved against the sequential version before requesting ordered results.

If a PLINQ query doesn't achieve significant performance improvements, you have another interesting option to take advantage of parallelism: running many LINQ queries in independent tasks or using `Parallel.Invoke`.

Working with ForAll and a ConcurrentBag

The `ForAll` extension method is very useful to process the results of a query in parallel without having to write a parallel loop. It receives an action as a parameter, offering the same possibilities that the same parameter received by the Task constructors. Therefore, using lambda expressions, you can combine parallelized processing actions from the results of a PLINQ query. The following lines add elements in parallel to a new `ConcurrentBag` (*keysBag*), an unordered collection of `Integer`, counting the letters for each of the keys in the results of the previous PLINQ query:

```
Dim keysWith10Letters = From key In Keys.AsParallel()
                        Where CountLetters(key) >= 10 And key.Contains("A")
                        And key.Contains("F") And key.Contains("9") And Not
                        key.Contains("B")

Dim keysBag As New ConcurrentBag(Of Integer)
keysWith10Letters.ForAll(Sub(i) keysBag.Add(CountLetters(i)))
```

Code snippet from Snippet07

This parallel processing is possible because `ConcurrentBag` *is one of the concurrent collections that allows many elements to be added by multiple tasks running in parallel.*

SUMMARY

This chapter provided an overview of the new task-based programming model introduced with .NET Framework 4 by introducing some of its classes, structures, and enumerations. In order to help you tackle the multicore revolution, it also explained several related concepts used in basic concurrent and parallel programming designs, including the following key points:

➤ You have to plan and design with concurrency and parallelism in mind. TPL offers structures that simplify the process of creating code that takes advantage of multicore architectures.

➤ You don't need to recompile your code in order to take advantage of additional cores. TPL optimizes the parallel loops and the distributions of tasks in underlying threads using load-balancing scheduling according to the available hardware resources at runtime.

➤ You can parallelize existing loops and measure the achieved performance gains.

➤ You can launch tasks and combine everything you learned so far about lists and arrays to work with multiple tasks and manage their execution.

➤ Concurrent collections provide a way to update collections in parallel and concurrent tasks without worrying about complex synchronization mechanisms.

➤ You can transform a LINQ query into PLINQ in order to test the speedup achieved with multicore architectures.

➤ Backward compatibility is possible with threaded code written in previous versions of Visual Basic and .NET Framework.

34

Deployment

WHAT YOU WILL LEARN IN THIS CHAPTER

➤ The major built-in options for deploying .NET applications

➤ How to create deployment projects within Visual Studio

➤ How to use ClickOnce to deploy Windows applications such as those based on Windows Forms or WPF

➤ How to access the IIS Web Deployment Tool for deployment of Web projects

Applications developed with the .NET Framework have a host of deployment options that were not available for older, COM-based software. These options completely change the economics of deployment. The changes are so important that they can even alter the preferred architecture for a system written in .NET.

Deployment encompasses many activities required to place an application into a production environment, including setting up databases, placing software in appropriate directories on servers, and configuring options for a particular installation. Deployment also includes handling changes and upgrades to the application.

This chapter covers the major deployment options for .NET applications. Chapter 31 on assemblies should be considered a prerequisite for this chapter, as assemblies are the basic unit of deployment.

First, you'll look at some of the problems that can occur when you deploy applications, along with a number of terms that are used when talking about application deployment. Then you'll learn how .NET addresses many of these deployment issues. The remainder of the chapter covers the following:

➤ Creating deployment projects in Visual Studio 2010 that enable initial installation of applications

➤ Deployment of the .NET Framework itself on systems where it does not already reside

➤ Updating applications on servers, including components and ASP.NET applications

➤ Installing and updating Windows Forms applications on client machines with ClickOnce

 Deployment in .NET is a huge topic that can't be covered completely within one chapter. This chapter should provide you with a basic understanding of the options available, and a desire to learn more about them.

APPLICATION DEPLOYMENT

In the context of this chapter, *application deployment* includes two principal functions:

➤ The process of taking an application, packaging it up, and installing it on another machine

➤ The process of updating an already installed application with new or changed functionality

Deployment can, in some cases, also include placing the .NET Framework itself on a particular machine. This chapter assumes that the .NET Framework is installed on any machines in question. During the discussion of creating deployment projects, you will learn what to do if the .NET Framework is not available on a system.

Why Deployment Is Straightforward in .NET

As covered in the Chapter 31, assemblies in .NET are self-describing. All the information needed to execute an assembly is normally contained in the assembly itself. There is no need to place any information in the Windows registry. If the CLR can find an assembly needed by an application (the process of location was discussed in the previous chapter), then the assembly can be run.

The previous chapter also discussed side-by-side execution of .NET assemblies. Multiple versions of an assembly can be executed by .NET, even if they have exactly the same interface and nominal version number. The implication for deployment is that each application can deploy the assemblies it needs and be assured that there will be no conflict with assemblies needed by other applications.

These .NET capabilities provide a range of deployment possibilities, from simple to complex. The following section looks at the simplest method of deployment, which harkens back to the days of DOS XCOPY deployment.

XCOPY Deployment

The term *XCOPY deployment* was coined to describe an ideal deployment scenario. Its name derives from the DOS xcopy command. XCOPY deployment means that the only thing you need to do in order to deploy an application is copy the directory (including all child directories) to the computer on which you want to run the program.

XCOPY deployment is fine for very simple applications, but most business applications require other dependencies (such as databases and message queues) to be created on the new computer. .NET cannot help with those, so applications that have them need more sophisticated deployment.

Using the Windows Installer

All the operations systems that support .NET Framework 4 also have the *Windows Installer* service available. It was specifically created for installing applications onto a Windows system.

The Windows Installer service uses a file, called a *Windows Installer package file*, to install an application. Such files have an extension of .msi, an abbreviation derived from "Microsoft Installer." The files that make up a product can be packaged inside the .msi file, or externally in a number of cabinet files.

When the user requests that a particular application be installed, he or she can just double-click the .msi file. The Windows Installer service reads the file and determines what needs to be done to install the application (such as which files need to be copied and where). All the installation rules are implemented centrally by the service and do not need to be distributed as part of a setup executable. The Windows Installer package file contains a list of actions (such as *copy file mfc40.dll to the Windows system folder*) and what rules need to be applied to these actions.

The Windows Installer service also has a rollback method to handle failed installations. If the installation fails for some reason, the Windows Installer service will roll back the computer to its original state.

You can manually create a Windows Installer package file using the Windows Installer SDK tools, but it's much easier to use Visual Studio. Several templates in VS 2010 create projects that output .msi files, as discussed in detail in the section "Visual Studio Deployment Projects," later in this chapter.

ClickOnce Deployment

An alternative to Windows Installer for Windows Forms and WPF applications is *ClickOnce*. This deployment technology was first included in Visual Studio 2005. Creating ClickOnce deployments is simpler than creating .msi files, but the most important ClickOnce advantage is that it is designed to deploy over the Internet. ClickOnce is discussed later in the chapter in the section "Internet Deployment of Windows Applications."

CHOOSING A FRAMEWORK VERSION

Visual Studio 2010 enables you to target a particular version of the framework. You can choose to base your application on version 2.0, 3.0, 3.5, or 4 of the framework by selecting it from the Advanced Compiler Settings dialog, which is available by selecting the properties for a project, navigating to the Compile page, and clicking the Advanced Compile Options button. The Advanced Compiler Settings dialog is shown in Figure 34-1, and the last option in the dialog is a drop-down list for the version of the .NET Framework you want to target.

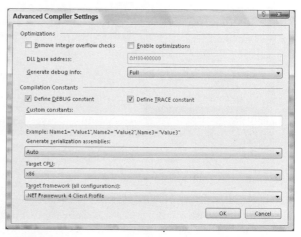

The capability to choose a version of the framework was introduced in Visual Studio 2008. When .NET Framework 3.5 Service Pack 1 was released, a new option was added for choosing a "Client Profile" version of the framework.

FIGURE 34-1

A Client Profile is a subset of the .NET Framework intended for client-based programs, which typically means user programs based on Windows Forms or WPF. The Client Profile leaves out a lot of framework functionality that is only applicable to a server. When targeting the Client Profile, deployment to a machine that does not have the necessary version of the .NET Framework is significantly faster.

Visual Studio 2010 retains the capability to use a Client Profile, though the way to choose a Client Profile on the Advanced Compiler Settings dialog is different. In Visual Studio 2008 with the service pack, a check box is used to select the Client Profile, whereas the drop-down in Visual Studio 2010 includes options for .NET Framework versions with and without the Client Profile.

VISUAL STUDIO DEPLOYMENT PROJECTS

Visual Studio 2010 provides two main options for creating a deployment project in a Visual Studio solution. The first option is a limited edition of InstallShield 2010. This chapter does not cover using the limited edition of this third-party product.

The second option is a set of project templates that can be used to help package your application and deploy it. Most of these templates use Windows Installer technology. Before looking at the project templates, however, it is important to understand the difference between setup and deployment. *Setup* is the process that you use to package your application. *Deployment* is the process of installing an application on another machine, usually through a setup application/process.

Project Templates

The deployment project templates available within Visual Studio 2010 can be created by the same means as any other project type, by using the New Project dialog, shown in Figure 34-2.

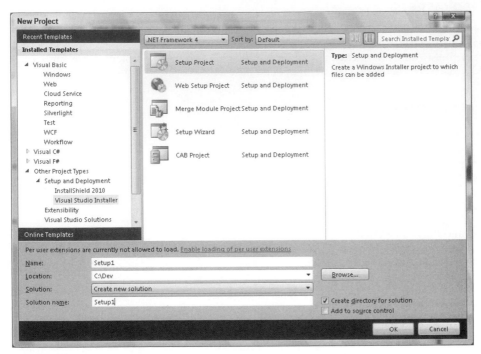

FIGURE 34-2

As shown in the figure, you first select the Other Project Types node, then the Setup and Deployment node, and finally the Visual Studio Installer node from the tree view of project types on the left side of the dialog. Of the five available project templates, four are actual project templates:

➤ CAB Project
➤ Merge Module Project
➤ Setup Project
➤ Web Setup Project

The fifth is a wizard (called the Setup Wizard) that can be used to help create any of the project templates listed.

The CAB Project Template

The CAB Project template is used to create a *cabinet file*. A cabinet file (.cab) can contain any number of files. It is often used to package a set of related components in an application.

Controls hosted within Internet Explorer are often packaged into a cabinet file, with a reference added to the file in the Web page that uses the control. When Internet Explorer encounters this reference, it confirms that the control isn't already installed on the user's computer, at which point it downloads the cabinet file, extracts the control, and installs it to a protected part of the user's computer.

You can compress cabinet files to reduce their size and consequently the amount of time it takes to download them.

The Merge Module Project Template

The Merge Module Project template is used to create a *merge module*, which is similar to a cabinet file in that it can be used to package a group of files. The difference is that a merge module file (.msm) cannot be used by itself to install the files that it contains. The merge module file created by this project template can only be used within another setup project.

Merge modules were introduced as part of the Microsoft Windows Installer technology to enable a set of files to be packaged into an easy-to-use file that could be reused and shared between Windows Installer–based setup programs. The idea is to package all the files and any other resources (e.g., registry entries, bitmaps, and so on) that are dependent on each other into the merge module.

This type of project can be very useful for packaging a component and all its dependencies. The resulting merge file can then be used in the setup program of each application that uses the component. This enables applications, such as Crystal Reports, to have a prepackaged deployment set that can be integrated into the deployment of other applications.

The Setup Project Template

The Setup Project template is used to create a standard Windows Installer setup for an application, which is normally installed in the Program Files directory of a user's computer.

The Web Setup Project Template

The Web Setup Project template is used to create a Windows Installer setup program that can be used to install a project into a virtual directory of a Web server. Its intended use is to create a setup program for a Web application, which may contain ASP.NET Web Forms or Web services.

To a large degree, the functionality in this template has been superceded by a new tool, the IIS Web Deployment Tool, also known as `MSDeploy.exe`. A brief introduction to this tool is included in the section below entitled The IIS Web Deployment Tool.

The Setup Wizard

You can use the Setup Wizard to help guide you through the creation of any of the previous setup and deployment project templates.

Creating a Deployment Project

A deployment project can be created in exactly the same way as any other project in Visual Studio 2010. It can be standalone, or it can be part of a solution that contains other projects.

To illustrate a typical deployment project, the following section contains a simple walk-through of one of the most commonly used templates for a deployment project — the Setup Project, which is used to deploy a Windows application. The walk-through will assume a Windows Forms application, though the process is almost identical for a WPF application.

Walk-through

First, create an application that will serve as the desktop application you want to deploy. Create a new project and choose Windows Forms Application from the list of available Visual Basic project templates. Name the project **SampleForDeployment** and don't add any code to it yet.

Next, add a new project to the solution and choose Setup Project from the list of available Setup and Deployment templates. You now have a Visual Studio solution containing two projects.

When created, the deployment project does not contain any files. It has a folder called Detected Dependencies, which is discussed later. You will need to add the executable file from your Windows application SampleForDeployment to the deployment project.

You add files to a setup deployment project using the Add function, which is available in two places: You can select the deployment project in the Solution Explorer and use the Add option from the Project menu, or you can right-click the setup project file in the Solution Explorer and choose Add from the pop-up menu. Both methods enable you to choose from one of four options:

➤ If you select File from the submenu, you are presented with a dialog that enables you to browse for and select a particular file to add to the setup project. This method is suitable if a file needed by the application is not the output from another project within the solution.

➤ The Merge Module option enables you to include a merge module in the deployment project. Third-party vendors can supply merge modules or you can create your own with Visual Studio.

➤ The Assembly option can be used to select a .NET component (assembly) to be included in the deployment project.

➤ If the deployment project is part of a solution (as in this walk-through), you can use the Project ➪ Add ➪ Project Output submenu item. This enables you to add the output from any of the projects in the solution to the setup project.

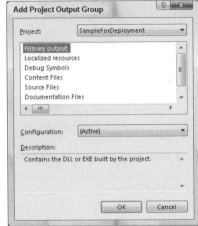

Add the output of the Windows Forms Application project to the setup project. Select the Project Output menu item to bring up the dialog shown in Figure 34-3.

FIGURE 34-3

The Add Project Output Group dialog is divided into several parts:

➤ The combo box at the top contains a list of names of all the nondeployment projects in the current solution. In your case, there is only one project: SampleForDeployment.

➤ Below the combo box is a list box containing all the possible outputs from the selected project. You are interested in the Primary output, so make sure that this is selected. (Other options for output are described in the MSDN for Visual Studio help files.)

➤ Below the list of possible outputs is a combo box from which you can select the configuration to use for the selected project. You will use the (Active) option here, because this uses whatever configuration is in effect when the project is built.

Click OK to return to the solution.

At this point, not only has the output from the Windows application been added to the Setup project, but the Detected Dependencies folder also contains an entry.

Whenever you add a .NET component to this deployment project, its dependencies are added to this folder. Any dependencies of the dependencies are also added, and so on until all the required files have been added. The files listed in the Detected Dependencies folder are included in the resulting setup and, by default, are installed into the application's directory as application-private assemblies. This default behavior helps reduce the possible effects of DLL hell by making the application use its own copies of dependent files.

If you don't want a particular dependency file to be included in the resulting setup, you can exclude it by right-clicking the file entry under Detected Dependencies and selecting Exclude from the pop-up menu. For example, you may decide that you want to exclude a detected dependency from the setup of an application because you know that the dependency is already installed on the target computer. The dependency will then have a small "circle and slash" icon before its name to indicate that it has been excluded.

Dependencies can also be excluded by selecting the particular dependency and using the Properties window to set the Exclude *property to* True*. The listed dependencies are refreshed whenever a .NET file is added to or removed from the setup project, taking into account any files that have already been excluded.*

You can select an item in the setup project in the Solution Explorer and that particular item's properties will be displayed in the Properties window. Because there are too many properties to discuss them all, we will take a look at the properties from the root setup node and each of the two different project items. First, however, ensure that the root setup node is selected, and take some time to browse the list of available properties.

The root setup node represents the output from this deployment project type: a Windows Installer package (.msi). Therefore, the Properties window contains properties that affect the resulting .msi that is produced.

Important Properties of the Root Setup Node

The ProductName property is used to set the text name of the product that this Windows Installer package is installing. By default, it is set to the name of the setup project (in this case, Setup1). The value of this property is used throughout the steps of the resulting setup. For instance, it is used for the text of the title bar when the resulting .msi file is run. The property is used along with the Manufacturer property to construct the default installation directory: C:\ProgramFiles\ < Manufacturer > \ < ProductName > . The ProductName property is also used within the Control Panel by the Add/Remove Programs applet to show that the application is installed.

The AddRemoveProgramsIcon property enables you to set the icon that appears in the applet of the Control Panel that is used to add and remove programs to a system. (The applet is named Add/Remove Programs in Windows XP and Programs and Features in Window Vista and Windows 7.) The default of (None) means that the default icon will be used. You can select an icon with the (Browse) option. The icon can be a standalone icon file or you can select an executable or DLL that contains an icon you want to use.

The Title property is used to set the textual title of the application that is installed. By default, this property has the same name as the setup project.

In addition, you may need to set several additional properties of the root node. The remaining properties for the root setup node are for various advanced options and are not discussed in this walk-through.

Properties of the Primary Output Project Item

Previously, you added the primary output from the SampleForDeployment Windows Forms project to your deployment project. It should now appear as an item in that project. Primary Output project items also have several important properties that you should know about, including the ones shown in Table 34-1.

TABLE 34-1: Primary Output Project Item Properties

PROPERTY	DESCRIPTION
Condition	This enables you to enter a condition that will be evaluated when the installation is run. If the condition evaluates to True, then the file is installed; if the condition evaluates to False, then the file is not installed. If you only want a particular file to be installed and the installation is being run on Microsoft Windows Vista or later, you could enter the following for the condition: VersionNT >= 600
Dependencies	Selecting this property displays a window showing all the dependencies of the selected project output.
Exclude	You can use this property to indicate whether you want the project output to be excluded from the resulting Windows Installer package.

continues

TABLE 34-1 *(continued)*

PROPERTY	DESCRIPTION
Folder	This property enables you to select the target folder for the project outputs.
KeyOutput	This property expands to provide information about the main file that makes up the project output. In your case, it will show information for the `SampleForDeployment.exe` file.
Outputs	Selecting this property displays a window listing all the files that are part of the project output, and indicates where these files are located on the development machine.
Permanent	This property is used to indicate whether the files that make up the project output should be removed when the application is uninstalled (`False`) or left behind (`True`). It is advisable to remove all the files installed by an application when the application is uninstalled. Therefore, this property should be set to `False`, which is the default.
ReadOnly	This property is used to set the read-only file attribute of all the files that make up the project output. As the name suggests, this makes the file read-only on the target machine.
Register	This property enables you to instruct the Windows Installer to register the files contained within the project output as COM objects. This only applies to projects (e.g., the Class Library project template) that have been compiled with the Register for COM interop project property set.
Vital	This property is used to indicate that the files contained within the project output are vital to the installation — if the installation of these files fails, then the installation as a whole should fail. The default value is `True`.

Properties of the Detected Dependency Items

Items that reside in the DetectedDependencies folder have some of the preceding properties, and they also have some read-only properties that provide you with detailed information about the item. This chapter does not include a detailed discussion of those informational properties.

This has been only a brief look at the Setup Project template. It uses all the project defaults and provides a standard set of steps to users when they run the Windows Installer package. Of course, a real application needs more than a single application file and its dependencies. You can customize the setup project extensively to meet those additional needs.

Besides adding more files to the deployment project, you may need to create shortcuts, directories, registry entries, and so on. These customizations and more can be accomplished using the set of built-in editors, which are covered in the section "Modifying the Deployment Project."

Creating a Deployment Project for an ASP.NET Web Application

You can also create a deployment project for an ASP.NET Web application. Such a deployment project can then publish a web site, including such tasks as creating a virtual directory. However, Web deployment projects are less commonly used in Visual Studio 2010 than in earlier versions. As mentioned earlier in the chapter, a newer option is available in Visual Studio 2010 for deployment of web projects called the IIS Web Deployment Tool. It's also sometimes referred to as one-click deployment.

This new deployment option is preferred in most cases because it relieves you of the need to create a separate deployment project. The section below, entitled IIS Web Deployment Tool, covers the basics of using this option for web application deployment.

However, you still have the option of creating a setup and deployment project for Web applications. You might choose to do that if you need certain advanced options of a dedicated deployment project, such as putting up dialogs to guide the user through deployment.

In that case, the template to use is the Web Setup Project template. There is one major difference between this template and the previously described Setup Project template: The Web Setup Project will, by default, deploy the application to a virtual directory of the Web server on which the setup is run, whereas a Setup Project deploys the application to the Program Files folder on the target machine by default.

There are substantial similarities between producing a deployment project for this scenario and producing a Windows Application deployment project as shown in the walk-through. They both produce a Windows Installer package and have the same set of project properties discussed earlier.

As in the previous walk-through, you need to add the output of the Web application to the deployment project. This is accomplished in much the same way as earlier, by right-clicking on a Web Setup project and selecting Add ⇨ Project Output. There is one key difference: When you add the project representing the website, the only option you have for the type of files to add is Content Files, which encompasses the files that make up the website.

As before, if you build such a project, the result is an `.msi` file, which can be used in this case to deploy a website.

MODIFYING THE DEPLOYMENT PROJECT

In the walk-through, you created a default Windows Installer package for a particular project template. You didn't customize the steps or actions that were performed when the package was run. What if you want to add a step to the installation process in order to display a ReadMe file to the user? Or what if you need to create registry entries on the installation computer?

This section focuses on additional capabilities for deployment projects. Most of these capabilities are accessed by using a series of "editors" to change parts of the deployment project. You can use six editors to customize a Windows Installer–based deployment project:

- ➤ File System Editor
- ➤ Registry Editor
- ➤ File Types Editor
- ➤ User Interface Editor
- ➤ Custom Actions Editor
- ➤ Launch Conditions Editor

The editors are accessible through the View ⇨ Editor menu option or by using the corresponding buttons at the top of the Solution Explorer.

You can also modify the resulting Windows Installer package through the project's Properties window. This section takes a brief look at each of the six editors and the project properties, and describes how you can use them to modify the resulting Windows Installer package. You will use the project previously created in the Windows application walk-through.

Project Properties

The first step to take in customizing the Windows Installer package is to use the project's property pages. The Property Pages dialog is accessed by right-clicking the root of the setup project in the Solution Explorer and selecting Properties from the pop-up menu. You can also select the Properties item from the Project menu when the setup project is the active project. Both of these methods will bring up the dialog shown in Figure 34-4.

The Build Page

The only page available from the Property Pages dialog is the Build page. The options on this page can be used to affect the way that the resulting Windows Installer package is built.

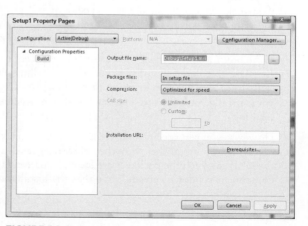

FIGURE 34-4

As with most other projects in VS 2010, you can create different build configurations. Use the Configuration combo box to select the build configuration for which you want to alter properties. In Figure 34-4, notice that you are modifying the properties for the currently active build configuration: Debug. The button labeled Configuration Manager enables you to add, remove, and edit the build configurations for this project.

The Output File Name setting can be used to modify where the resulting Windows Installer package (.msi) file is created. You can modify the filename and path directly, or you can click the Browse button.

Package Files

The next setting, Package Files, enables you to specify how the files that make up the installation are packaged. The possible options are:

➤ **As loose uncompressed files-**When you build the project, the files that are to be included as part of the installation are copied to the same directory as the resulting Windows Installer package (.msi) file. As mentioned earlier, this directory can be set using the Output file name setting.

➤ **In a setup file-**When the project is built, the files that are to be included as part of the installation are packaged in the resulting Windows Installer package file. When you use this method, you have only one file to distribute. This is the default setting.

➤ **In cabinet file(s)-**With this option, when the project is built, the files that are to be included as part of the installation are packaged into a number of cabinet files.

Prerequisites

Prerequisites are standard components that may be needed to install or run the application but are not a part of it. There are several of these, as shown in Figure 34-5, which shows the dialog that is displayed when the Prerequisites button is clicked.

The .NET Framework is checked by default, and so is the Windows Installer. You should only uncheck these if you are sure that all the machines on which your application will be installed already have the correct versions of these prerequisites installed. As mentioned earlier in this chapter, Visual Studio 2010 allows targeting of the .NET Framework version you would like to use, so the targeted version of the framework needs to be coordinated with the prerequisites.

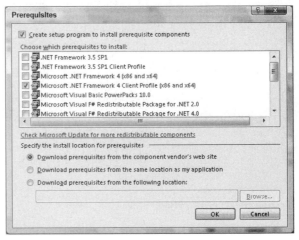

FIGURE 34-5

If the box for any of these prerequisites is checked, then the resulting installation package will automatically check for the presence of that prerequisite, installing it if required. If you are installing from a CD or network share, then it is common for the packages that install these prerequisites to be placed in the same location as your installation package. The default settings assume that this is true and install the prerequisites from that location.

However, you can specify a different location for packages that install prerequisites. You can select the "Download prerequisites from the following location:" option at the bottom of the dialog and then specify the URL at which the packages are located. Alternately, you can select "Download prerequisites from the component vendor's web site," and then the Installation URL on the previous dialog will be used (refer to Figure 34-5).

Compression

You also have the option to modify the compression used when packaging the files that are to be contained within the installation program. The three options (Optimized for speed, Optimized for size, and None) are self-explanatory and therefore not covered. The default is Optimized for Speed.

Setting the Cabinet File Size

If you want to package the files in cabinet files, then you have the option to specify the size of those resulting cabinet file(s):

➤ The first option is to let the resulting cabinet file be of an unlimited size. What this effectively means is that all the files are packaged into one big cabinet file. The resulting size of the cabinet file depends on the compression method selected.

➤ If you are installing from floppy disks or CDs, then creating one large cabinet file may not be wise. In this case, you can use the second option to specify the maximum size of the resulting cabinet file(s). If you select this option, then you need to specify the maximum allowed size for a cabinet file (this figure is in KB). If all the files that need to be contained within this installation exceed this size, then multiple cabinet files are created.

The File System Editor

The File System Editor is automatically displayed for you in VS 2010's document window when you first create the Setup project. You can also access this editor (and the other editors that are available) via the View ➪ Editor menu option in the Visual Studio 2010 IDE. The File System Editor is used to manage all the file system aspects of the installation, including the following:

➤ Creating folders on the user's machine

➤ Adding files to the folders defined

➤ Creating shortcuts

Basically, this is the editor that you use to define what files need to be installed and where they should be installed on the user's machine. The File System Editor is divided into two main panes in the document window (see Figure 34-6).

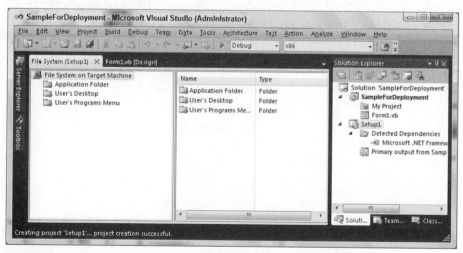

FIGURE 34-6

The left pane shows a list of the folders that have been created automatically for the project. When you select a folder in the left pane, two things happen: first, the right pane of the editor displays a list of the files to be installed into the selected folder, and second, the Properties window will change to show you the properties of the currently selected folder. Depending on the size of the Visual Studio 2010 window, you might not see the right-hand pane unless you widen the screen.

Adding Items to a Folder

To add an item that needs to be installed to a folder, you can either right-click the folder in the left pane and choose Add from the pop-up menu or you can select the required folder, right-click in the right pane, and again choose Add from the pop-up menu. You will be presented with four options, three of which were discussed earlier in the walk-through:

- ➤ Project output
- ➤ File
- ➤ Assembly

The fourth option (Folder) enables you to add a subfolder to the currently selected folder. This subfolder then becomes a standard folder that can be used to add files. If you add any .NET components or executables, the dependencies of these components are also added to the installation automatically.

Adding Special Folders

When you create a new deployment project, a set of standard folders is created for you (listed in the desktop application section). If the folders created do not match your requirements, you can also use the File System Editor to add special folders. To add a special folder, right-click anywhere in the left pane (other than on a folder), and you will be presented with a pop-up menu containing one item: Add Special Folder. This menu item expands to show you a list of folders that you can add to the installation (folders already added to the project are grayed out).

You can choose from several system folders, which are summarized in Table 34-2.

TABLE 34-2: Add Special Folder Options

NAME	DESCRIPTION	WINDOWS INSTALLER PROPERTY
Common Files Folder	Files (nonsystem) that are shared by multiple applications are usually installed to this folder.	[CommonFilesFolder]
Common Files (64-bit) Folder	Same as Common Files Folder, but for 64-bit systems	[CommonFiles64Folder]
Fonts Folder	Used to contain all the fonts installed on the computer. If your application uses a specific font, then you should install it in this folder.	[FontsFolder]
Program Files Folder	Most applications are installed in a directory below the Program Files Folder. This acts as the root directory for installed applications.	[ProgramFilesFolder]
Program Files (64-bit) Folder	Same as Program Files Folder, but for 64-bit systems	[ProgramFiles64Folder]
System Folder	This folder is used to store shared system files. The folder typically holds files that are part of the OS.	[SystemFolder]

NAME	DESCRIPTION	WINDOWS INSTALLER PROPERTY
System (64-bit) Folder	Same as System Folder, but for 64-bit systems	[System64Folder]
User's Application Data Folder	This folder is used to store data on a per-application basis, specific to a user.	[CommonAppDataFolder]
User's Desktop	This folder represents the user's desktop. It can be used to create and display a shortcut that can be used to start your application.	[DesktopFolder]
User's Favorites Folder	Used as a central place to store links to the user's favorite websites, documents, folders, and so on	[FavoritesFolder]
User's Personal Data Folder	This folder is where a user stores important files. It is normally referred to as My Documents.	[PersonalFolder]
User's Programs Menu	This folder is where shortcuts are created to applications that appear on the user's Program menu. This is an ideal place to create a shortcut to your application.	[ProgramMenuFolder]
User's Send To Menu	Stores all the user's send-to shortcuts. A send-to shortcut is displayed when you right-click a file in the Windows Explorer and choose Send To. The send-to shortcut usually invokes an application, passing in the pathname of the file it was invoked from.	[SendToFolder]
User's Start Menu	This folder can be used to add items to the user's Start menu. This is not often used.	[StartMenuFolder]
User's Startup Folder	Used to start applications whenever the user logs in to the computer. If you want your application to start every time the user logs in, then you can add a shortcut to your application in this folder.	[StartupFolder]
User's Template Folder	This folder contains templates specific to the logged-in user. Templates are usually used by applications such as Microsoft Office 2000.	[TemplateFolder]
Windows Folder	The Windows root folder. This is where the OS is installed.	[WindowsFolder]
Global Assembly Cache Folder	Used to store all shared assemblies on the user's computer	

If none of the built-in folders match your requirements, you can create your own custom folder. Right-click in the left pane of the File Editor and choose Custom Folder from the pop-up menu.

The new folder is created in the left pane of the editor. The folder name appears in Edit mode, so enter the name of the folder and press Enter. The folder will now be selected, and the Properties window will change to show the properties of the new folder. The properties of a folder are summarized in Table 34-3.

TABLE 34-3: Custom Folder Options

PROPERTY	DESCRIPTION
(Name)	The name of the selected folder. The `Name` property is used within the setup project as the means by which you select a folder.
AlwaysCreate	Indicates whether this folder should be created on installation even if it's empty (`True`). If the value is `False` and no files are to be installed into the folder, then the folder isn't created. The default is `False`.
Condition	This enables you to enter a condition that will be evaluated when the installation is run. If the condition evaluates to `True`, then the folder is created; if the condition evaluates to `False`, then the folder won't be created. For example, you might only want to create a folder if you are on a certain version of an operating system, or only if the user has selected a particular option on one of your install dialogs. See the section on the Launch Conditions Editor below for discussion on creating conditions in your deployment project. Note that a custom folder must be empty for it to be created based on a condition.
DefaultLocation	This is where you define where the folder is going to be created on the target machine. You can enter a literal folder name (such as `C:\Temp`), or you can use a Windows Installer property, or a combination of the two. A Windows Installer property contains information that is filled in when the installer is run. The preceding table of special folders contains a column called Windows Installer property. The property defined in this table is filled in with the actual location of the special folder at runtime. Therefore, if you enter [WindowsFolder] as the text for this property, the folder created represents the Windows special folder.
Property	Defines a Windows Installer property that can be used to override the `DefaultLocation` property of the folder when the installation is run
Transitive	Indicates whether the condition specified in the condition property is reevaluated on subsequent (re)installs. If the value is `True`, then the condition is checked on each additional run of the installation. A value of `False` causes the condition to be run only the first time the installation is run on the computer. The default value is `False`.

Suppose you name your folder "Wrox Press" and you set the `DefaultLocation` property for your folder to [FavoritesFolder]\Wrox Press. You could add some shortcuts to this folder using the technique described in the following section. When the installation is run, a new folder is added to the user's Favorites folder called Wrox Press, and those shortcuts are placed in it.

Creating Shortcuts

The first step in creating a shortcut is to locate the file that is the target of the shortcut. In the File System editor, first select the folder the file resides in, and then select the target file and right-click it. The pop-up menu that appears includes an option to create a shortcut to the selected file, which is created in the same folder. Select this option.

To add the shortcut to the user's desktop, you need to move this shortcut to the folder that represents the user's desktop. Likewise, you could move this shortcut to the folder that represents the user's Programs menu. Cut and paste the new shortcut to the User's Desktop folder in the left pane of the editor. The shortcut will be added to the user's desktop when the installation is run. You should probably rename the shortcut, which is easily accomplished via the Rename option of the pop-up menu.

This has been only a brief tour of the File System Editor. There are many additional capabilities that you can explore.

The Registry Editor

You can use the Registry Editor to do the following:

➤ Create registry keys

➤ Create values for registry keys

➤ Import a registry file

Like the File System Editor, the Registry Editor is divided into two panes, as illustrated in Figure 34-7.

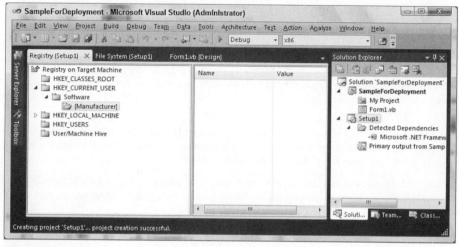

FIGURE 34-7

The left pane of the editor represents the registry keys on the target computer. When you select a registry key, two things happen. One, the right pane of the editor is updated to show the values that are to be created under the selected registry key. Two, if the registry key selected is not a root key in the left pane, then the Properties window is updated with a set of properties for this registry key.

When you create a new deployment project, a set of registry keys is created for you that correspond to the standard base registry keys of Windows. Notice in Figure 34-7 that there is a key defined with a name of [Manufacturer]. When the installation is run, this will be replaced with the value of the Manufacturer property described earlier in the chapter. [Manufacturer] is a property of the installation and can be used elsewhere within it. Several of these properties are defined, and they can be used in much the same way (consult the "Deployment Properties" topic in the MSDN documentation for a full list).

Adding a Value to a Registry Key

Before adding a value, you must select (or create) the registry key that will hold the value. There are several ways to add the registry value:

➤ Right-click the registry key and use the resulting pop-up menu.

➤ Right-click in the right pane and use the resulting pop-up menu.

➤ Use the Action menu.

For illustrational purposes here, select one of the Software registry keys. The Action menu contains one item, New, which contains a number of submenu items:

➤ Key

➤ String Value

- ➤ Environment String Value
- ➤ Binary Value
- ➤ DWORD Value

Using this menu, you can create a new registry key below the currently selected key (via Key), or you can create a value for the currently selected registry key using one of the four Value types: String, Environment String, Binary, and DWORD.

For example, suppose you need to create a registry entry that informs the application whether or not to run in Debug mode. The registry value must be applicable to a particular user, must be called Debug, and must contain the text True or False.

The first step is to select the following registry key in the left pane of the editor:

> HKEY_CURRENT_USER\Software [Manufacturer].

The registry key HKEY_CURRENT_USER is used to store registry settings that apply to the currently logged-in user.

Now you want to create a value that it is applicable to only this application, not all applications created by you. You need to create a new registry key below the HKEY_CURRENT_USER ⇨ Software ⇨ [Manufacturer] key that is specific to this product, so select Action ⇨ New ⇨ Key.

When the key is created, the key name is editable, so give it a name of [ProductName] and press Enter. This creates a key that is given the name of the product contained within this Windows Installer package. The ProductName property of the setup was discussed earlier in this chapter.

Now that you have created the correct registry key, the next step is to create the actual registry value. Make sure that your new registry key is selected, choose String Value from the Action ⇨ New menu, and give the new value a name of "Debug."

Once the value has been created, you can set a default value for it in its Properties window; in this case False. When the Windows Installer package is run, the value will be created and given a name of Debug and a value of False. If a value already exists in the registry, then the Windows Installer package will overwrite the existing value with what is defined in the Registry Editor.

You can move around most keys and values in the Registry Editor by using cut and paste or simply by dragging and dropping the required item.

The alternative to creating registry entries during installation is to have your application create registry entries the first time they are needed. However, this has one significant difference from registry keys created with a Windows Installer package. The uninstall corresponding to a Windows Installer installation automatically removes any registry keys created during the install. If the registry entries are created by the application instead, then the uninstall has no way of knowing that these registry entries should be removed.

Importing Registry Files

If you already have a registry file (a .reg file) containing the registry settings that you would like to be created, you can import the file into the Registry Editor. To import a registry file, you need to ensure that the root node ("Registry on Target Machine") is selected in the left pane of the editor. You can then use the Import item of the Action menu to select the registry file to import.

 Registry manipulation should be used with extreme caution. Windows relies heavily on the registry, so you can cause yourself a great number of problems if you delete, overwrite, or change registry values and keys without knowing the full consequences of the action.

If you want to create the registry entries that are required to create file associations, then use the editor covered next.

The File Types Editor

The File Types Editor can be used to create the required registry entries to establish a *file association* for the application being installed. A file association is simply a link between a particular file extension and a particular application. For example, the file extension .docx is normally associated with Microsoft WordPad or Microsoft Word.

When you create a file association, not only do you create a link between the file extension and the application, you also define a set of actions that can be performed from the context menu of the file with the associated extension. For example, when you right-click a document with an extension of .docx, you get a context menu that can contain any number of actions, such as Open and Print. The action in bold (Open, by default) is the default action to be called when you double-click the file, so in the example, double-clicking a Word document starts Microsoft Word and loads the selected document.

Let's walk through the creation of a file extension for the application. Suppose that the application uses a file extension of .set and that the file is to be opened in the application when it is double-clicked. Start the File Types Editor, which contains a single pane. In a new deployment project, this pane will only contain a root node called "File Types on Target Machine."

To add a new file type, make sure the root element is selected in the editor. You can then choose Add File Type from the Action menu, or right-click on the root node and select Add File Type. Give the new file type the name "Example File Type."

Next, you must set the extension and application for this file type. Use the Properties window (shown in Figure 34-8). Enter **.set** as the value for the Extensions property.

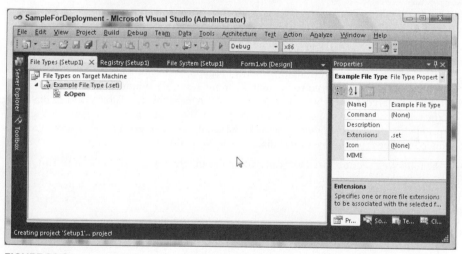

FIGURE 34-8

To associate an application with this file type, use the Command property. The ellipses button for this property presents you with a dialog from which you can select an executable file contained within any of the folders defined in the File System Editor. In this case, you'll select Primary Output from WindowsApplication (active) from the Application Folder as the value for Command.

When this new file type was first created, a default action was added for you called &Open — select it. Now take a look at the Properties window again. Notice the Arguments property: You can use this to add command-line arguments to the application defined in the last step. In the case of the default action that has been added for you, the arguments are "%1", where the value "%1" will be replaced by the filename that invoked the action. You can add your own hard-coded arguments (such as /d). You can set an action to be the default by right-clicking it and selecting Set as Default from the pop-up menu.

The User Interface Editor

The User Interface Editor is used to manage the interface that is shown during installation of the application. This editor enables you to define the dialogs that are displayed to the user and in what order they are shown. The User Interface Editor is shown in Figure 34-9.

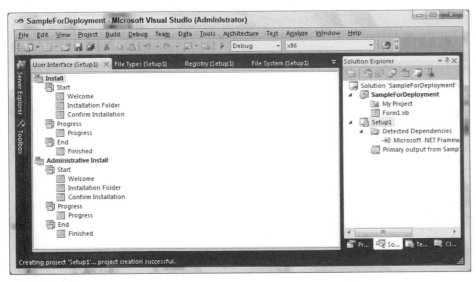

FIGURE 34-9

The editor uses a tree view with two root nodes: Install and Administrative Install. Below each of these nodes are three nodes that represent the stages of installation: Start, Progress, and End. Each of the three stages can contain a number of dialogs that are displayed to the user when the resulting Windows Installer package is run. A default set of dialogs is predefined when you create the deployment project. Which default dialogs are present depends on the type of deployment project: Setup Project or Web Setup Project. Figure 34-9 shows the dialogs that were added by default to a Setup Project. However, if you are creating a Web Setup Project, the Installation Folder dialog will be replaced by an Installation Address dialog.

Using Figure 34-9, the following section discusses the two modes in which the installer can be run, and explains the three stages of the installation.

Installation Modes

The installation can run in two modes, which correspond to the two root nodes of the editor: Install and Administrative Install. These distinguish between an end user installing the application and a system administrator performing a network setup.

 To use the Administrative Install mode of the resulting Windows Installer package, you can use `msiexec.exe` *with the* `/a` *command-line parameter:* `msiexec.exe /a < PACKAGE > .msi`.

The Install mode is most frequently used and is what you will use in this exercise. As mentioned earlier, the installation steps are divided into three stages, represented as subnodes of the parent installation mode.

The Start Stage

The Start stage is the first stage of the installation. It contains the dialogs that need to be displayed to the user before the actual installation of the files begins. The Start stage should be used to gather any information from the user that may affect what is installed and where it is installed.

This stage is commonly used to ask the user to select the base installation folder for the application and which parts of the system should be installed. Another common task at this stage is asking users for their name and organization. At the end of this stage, the Windows Installer service determines how much disk space is required on the target machine and checks whether this amount of space is available. If the space is not available, then the user receives an error and the installation will not continue.

The Progress Stage

The Progress stage is the second stage of the installer. This is where the actual installation of the files occurs. There isn't usually any user interaction during this stage, and typically one dialog indicates the current progress of the install, which is calculated automatically.

The End Stage

Once the actual installation of the files has finished, the installer moves into the End stage. The most common use of this stage is to inform the user that the installation has been completed successfully. It is also often used to provide the option to run the application immediately or to view any release notes.

Customizing the Order of Dialogs

The order in which the dialogs appear within the tree view determines the order in which they are presented to the user during an installation. Dialogs cannot be moved between different stages at runtime.

The order of the dialogs can be changed by dragging the respective dialogs to the position in which you want them to appear. You can also move a particular dialog up or down in the order by right-clicking it and selecting either Move Up or Move Down.

Adding Dialogs

A set of predefined dialogs has been added to the project for you, enabling actions such as prompting a user for a registration code. If these do not match your requirements, you can add or remove dialogs in any of the stages.

When adding a dialog, you have the choice of using a built-in dialog or importing one. To illustrate how to add a dialog, consider an example of adding a dialog to display a ReadMe file to the user of a Windows Installer package. The ReadMe file needs to be displayed before the actual installation of the files occurs.

The first step is to choose the mode in which the dialog is to be shown: Install or Administrative Install. In this example, you will use the Install mode. Next, you need to determine the stage at which the dialog is shown. In the example, you want to display the ReadMe file to the user before the actual installation of the files occurs, which means you have to show the ReadMe file in the Start stage. Make sure the Start node is selected below the Install parent node.

You are now ready to add the dialog. Using the Action menu again, select the Add Dialog menu item, which will display the dialog shown in Figure 34-10, from which you can choose the desired dialog.

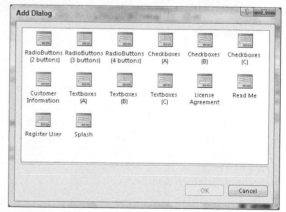

FIGURE 34-10

As you can see, several built-in dialogs are available. Each dialog includes a short description that appears at the bottom of the window to inform you of its intended function. In this case, you want to use the Read Me dialog, so select it and click OK.

New dialogs are always added as the last dialog in the stage that they are added to, so now you need to move it into the correct position. In this case, you want the Read Me dialog to be shown immediately after the Welcome dialog, so drag and drop it into position.

Properties of the Dialogs

Like most other project items in Visual Studio, dialog boxes have a set of properties that you can change to suit your needs using the Properties window. If you make sure a dialog is selected, you will notice that the Properties window changes to show its properties. The properties that appear vary according to the dialog selected. Details of all the properties of the built-in dialog boxes can be found by looking at the "Properties for the User Interface Editor" topic in the MSDN documentation.

The Custom Actions Editor

The Custom Actions Editor (see Figure 34-11) is used for fairly advanced installations. It enables you to define actions that are to be performed due to one of the following installation events: Install, Commit, Rollback, and Uninstall. For example, you can use this editor to define an action that creates a new database when the installation is committed.

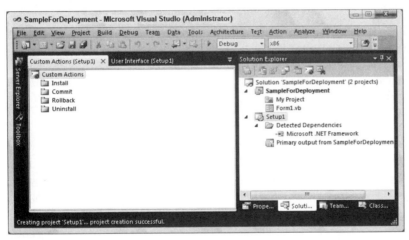

FIGURE 34-11

The custom actions that are added using this editor can be Windows script-based, compiled executables, or DLLs. Load the editor by right-clicking on the Setup1 project and selecting View ⇨ Custom Actions. The editor uses a tree view to represent the information. The four nodes in the tree view represent each of the four installation events to which you can add custom actions.

As with the User Interface Editor, the order in which the actions appear determines the order in which they are run, but you can modify this by dragging and dropping the actions or using the context menus of the actions to move them up or down.

Adding a Custom Action

To add a custom action, you must select the node of the event into which you want to install the action. You can then use the Action menu to select the executable, DLL, or script that implements the custom action. The four actions defined in the editor are described in Table 34-4.

TABLE 34-4: Custom Action Event Nodes

EVENT	DESCRIPTION
Install	The actions defined for this event will be run when the installation of the files has finished, but before the installation has been committed.
Commit	The actions defined for this event will be run when the installation has been committed and has therefore been successful.
Rollback	The actions defined for this event will be run when the installation fails or is cancelled and rolls back the machine to the state it was in before the install was started.
Uninstall	The actions defined for this event will be run when the application is being uninstalled from the machine.

Suppose that you want to start your application as soon as the installation is completed successfully. Use the following process to accomplish this.

First, decide when the action must occur. Using the preceding table, you can see that the Commit event will be run when the installation has been successful. Ensure that this node is selected in the editor. You are now ready to add the actual action you want to occur when the Commit event is called. Using the Action menu again, select the Add Custom Action menu item, which will display a dialog that you can use to navigate to and select a file (.exe, .dll, or Windows script) from any that are included in the File System Editor. For this example, navigate into the Application Folder by double-clicking it and then select Primary output from SampleForDeployement (Active), which is contained within the Application Folder.

As with most items in the editors, the new custom action has a number of properties. Table 34-5 describes some of the properties you are most likely to need.

TABLE 34-5: Typical Custom Action Properties

PROPERTY	DESCRIPTION
(Name)	This is the name given to the selected custom action.
Arguments	This property enables you to pass command-line arguments into the executable that makes up the custom action. This only applies to custom actions that are implemented in executable files (.exe). By default, the first argument passed in indicates what event caused the action to run. It can have the following values: /Install, /Commit, /Rollback, /Uninstall.
Condition	This enables you to enter a condition that will be evaluated before the custom action is run. If the condition evaluates to True, then the custom action will run; if the condition evaluates to False, then the custom action will not run.
CustomActionData	This property enables you to pass additional information to the custom action.
InstallerClass	If the custom action is implemented by an Installer class in the selected component, then this property must be set to True. If not, it must be set to False (consult the MSDN documentation for more information on the Installer class, which is used to create special installers for such .NET applications as Windows Services. The Installer class is located in the System.Configuration.Install namespace).

Set the InstallClass property to equal False because your application does not contain an Installer class.

That's it. When you run the Windows Installer package and the installation is successful, the application will automatically start. The custom action that you implemented earlier is very simple, but custom actions can be used to accomplish any customized installation actions that you could want. Take some time to play around with what can be accomplished using custom actions. For instance, try creating a custom action that writes a short file into the Application directory.

The Launch Conditions Editor

The Launch Conditions Editor can be used to define a number of conditions for the target machine that must be met before the installation will run. For example, if your application relies on the fact that users must have Microsoft Word installed on their machine, you can define a launch condition that will check this.

You can define a number of searches that can be performed to help create launch conditions:

➤ File search

➤ Registry search

➤ Windows Installer search

As with the Custom Actions Editor, the Launch Conditions Editor (shown in Figure 34-12) uses a tree view to display the information contained within it. The example shows a Launch Conditions Editor that has had an item added. The steps for adding that item are covered later.

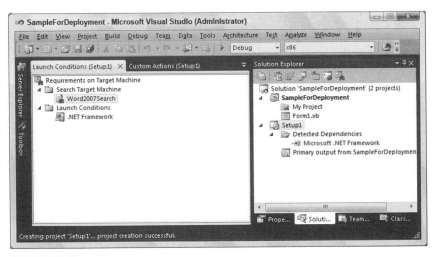

FIGURE 34-12

There are two root nodes. The first (Search Target Machine) is used to display the searches that have been defined. The second (Launch Conditions) contains a list of the conditions that will be evaluated when the Windows Installer package is run on the target machine.

As with many of the other editors, the order in which the items appear below these two nodes determines the order in which the searches are run and the order in which the conditions are evaluated. If you wish, you can modify the order of the items in the same way that you did with the previous editors.

 The searches are run and then the conditions are evaluated as soon as the Windows Installer package is run, before any dialogs are shown to the user.

We are now going to look at an example of adding a file search and launch condition to a setup project. For this exercise, suppose that you want to make sure that your users have Microsoft Word 2007 installed on their machine before they are allowed to run the installation for your application.

Adding a File Search

To add a file search, you begin by searching for the Microsoft Word 2007 executable. After ensuring that the Search Target Machine node is currently selected in the editor, add a new file search by selecting the

Add File Search item from the Action menu. The new item should be given a meaningful name, so enter **Word2007Search** (refer to Figure 34-12).

Modifying the File Search Properties

Like most items contained within the editors mentioned in this chapter, the new file search item has a set of properties that you can modify using the Properties window. The properties of the file search item determine the criteria that will be used when searching for the file. Most of the properties are self-explanatory and have been covered in previous sections, so they are not covered here.

In this example, you need to search for the Microsoft Word 2007 executable, which means that a number of these properties need to be modified to match your own search criteria.

The first property that requires modification is `FileName`. In this case, you are searching for the Microsoft Word 2007 executable, so enter `winword.exe` as the value for this property. Previous versions of Microsoft Word used the same filename.

There is no need to search for the file from the root of the hard drive. The `Folder` property can be used to define the starting folder for the search. By default, the value is `[SystemFolder]`, which indicates that the search will start from the Windows system folder. There are several of these built-in values; if you are interested, you can see what these folders correspond to in the section "Adding Special Folders."

In this example, you do not want to search the Windows system folder because Microsoft Word is usually installed in the Program Files folder. Set the value of the `Folder` property to `[ProgramFilesFolder]` to indicate that this should be your starting folder.

When the search begins, it will search only the folder specified in the `Folder` property, as indicated by the default value (0) of the `Depth` property. The `Depth` property is used to specify how many levels of subfolders are searched for the file in question, beginning from the starting folder specified. Note that there are performance issues associated with the `Depth` property. When a search is performed for a file that is very deep in the file system hierarchy, it can take a long time to find the file. Therefore, wherever possible, use a combination of the `Folder` and `Depth` properties to decrease the possible search range. The file that you are searching for in your example will probably be at a depth of greater than 1, so change the value to 3.

There may be different versions of the file that you are searching for on a user's machine. You can use the remaining properties to specify a set of requirements for the file that must be met in order for it to be found, such as minimum version number or minimum file size.

You are searching for the existence of Microsoft Word 2007, which means you need to define the minimum version of the file that you want to find. To search for the correct version of `winword.exe`, you need to enter `12.0.0.0` as the value for the `MinVersion` property. This ensures that the user has Microsoft Word 2007 or later installed and not an earlier version.

To use the results of the file search, there must be a name for the results. This name is assigned to a Windows Installer property and is normally used to create a launch condition later. The `Property` property is where this name is specified.

For our example, enter `WORDEXISTS` as the value for the `Property` property. If the file search is successful, then the full path to the found file will be assigned to this Windows Installer property; otherwise, it will be left blank. At this point, the Properties window should look like the window shown in Figure 34-13.

FIGURE 34-13

Creating a Launch Condition

A file search alone is pretty useless. The second step of the process of ensuring that the user has Microsoft Word 2007 installed is creating a launch condition that uses the results of the file search.

Make sure that the Launch Conditions node is selected in the editor, and add a new launch condition to the project by selecting Add Launch Condition from the Action menu. You need to give this new item a meaningful name; in this case, give it a name of **Word2007Exists** (see Figure 34-14).

This new item has a number of properties that you need to modify. The first property to change is called `Message`, and it is used to set the text of the message box that appears if this condition is not met. Enter any meaningful description that explains why the installation cannot continue.

The next property that you need to change is called `Condition`. It is used to define a valid deployment condition that is evaluated when the installation runs. The deployment condition entered must evaluate to `True` or `False`. When

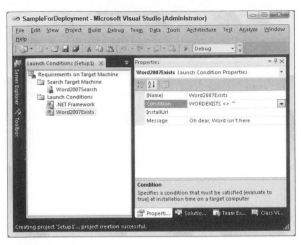

FIGURE 34-14

the installer is run, the condition is evaluated; if the result of the condition is `False`, then the message defined is displayed to the user and the installation stops.

For this example, you need to enter a condition that takes into account whether the `winword.exe` file was found. You can use the Windows Installer property defined earlier (`WORDEXISTS`) as part of the condition. Because the property is empty if the file was not found, and non-empty if the file was found, you can perform a simple test to determine whether the property is empty to create the condition. Enter `WORDEXISTS <> ""` as the value for the `Condition` property. At this point, the editor will look like Figure 34-14.

It is hoped that based on the preceding discussion of this search, you will be able to use the other searches and create your own launch conditions. That completes our brief tour of the editors that you can use to modify the resulting Windows Installer package to suit your needs. Although you have looked only briefly at the functionality of the editors, it should be clear that they are extremely powerful, and worth investment of your time for further investigation.

Building

The final step is to build the deployment or setup project you have created. There is no difference between how you build a Visual Basic .NET application and a deployment/setup project. If the project is the only project contained within the solution, then you can just use the Build item from the Build menu, which will cause the project to be built. As with the other projects, you are informed of what is happening during the build through the Output window.

The deployment/setup project can also be built as part of a multiproject solution. If the Build Solution item is chosen from the Build menu, then all the projects in the solution will be built. Any deployment or setup projects are built last. This ensures that if they contain the output from another project in the solution, they pick up the latest build of that project.

INTERNET DEPLOYMENT OF WINDOWS APPLICATIONS

The earlier discussions of creating an installation package for your application assumed that you were able to transfer the MSI file to each machine that needed installation, either electronically or via some storage medium such as a CD-ROM. This works well for installations within an organization and can work acceptably for initial installation from CD-ROMs on distributed systems.

However, the availability of the Internet has raised the bar for acceptable deployment of Windows-based client applications. Perhaps the most important advantage of browser-based applications has been their ease of deployment for the user. For Windows Forms applications to be cost-competitive with browser-based applications, low-cost deployment over the Internet is needed.

Fortunately, there are several ways you can achieve low-cost deployment over the Internet, including two that are supported by default with .NET and Visual Studio 2010:

➤ "No-touch" deployment

➤ ClickOnce deployment

No-Touch Deployment

Built into all versions of the .NET Framework is the capability to run applications from a Web server instead of from the local machine. There are two ways to do this, depending on how the application is launched.

First, an application EXE that exists on a Web server can be launched via a standard HTML hyperlink. For example, an application named MyApp.exe that is located at www.mycompany.com/apps can be launched with the following HTML in a Web page:

```
<a href="http://www.mycompany.com/apps/MyApp.exe">Launch MyApp</a>
```

When the hyperlink is clicked on a system with the .NET Framework installed, Internet Explorer transfers control to the .NET Framework to launch the program. The Framework then tries to load the EXE assembly, which does not yet exist on the client. At that point, the assembly is automatically fetched from the deployment Web server and placed on the local client machine. It resides on the client machine in an area called the *application download cache*, which is a special directory on the system managed by the .NET. Framework.

If the EXE tries to load a class from another application assembly (typically, a DLL), then that assembly is assumed to be in the same directory on the Web server as the EXE. The application assembly is also transferred to the application download cache and loaded for use. This process continues for any other application assemblies needed. The application is said to *trickle-feed* to the client system.

Automatic Updating

Whenever an assembly in the application download cache is needed, the .NET Framework automatically checks for a new version in the appropriate directory on the Web server. Thus, the application can be updated for all client machines by simply placing an assembly on the Web server.

Using a Launch Application

One drawback of this technique for deploying the application is that it can be launched only from a Web page or some other means of accessing a URL (such as a shortcut or the Start ➪ Run dialog).

To get around this limitation, you can get a similar deployment capability by using a small launching application that uses dynamic loading to start the main application. Dynamic loading was discussed in Chapter 31. In this case, the location for the assembly used in dynamic loading will be the URL of the assembly on the Web server. An application that uses this technique still gets all the trickle-feeding and auto-update features of an application launched straight from a URL.

Limitations of No-Touch Deployment

No-touch deployment is useful for simple applications, but it has some serious drawbacks for more complex applications:

➤ An active Internet connection is required to run the application — no offline capability is available.

➤ Only assemblies can be deployed via no-touch deployment — application files such as configuration files cannot be included.

➤ Applications deployed via no-touch deployment are subject to code-access security limitations, as discussed in Chapter 32.

➤ No-touch deployment has no capability to deploy any prerequisites for the application or any COM components that it may need.

Given these limitations of no-touch deployment, starting with the 2.0 version of the .NET Framework, Microsoft added an alternative called *ClickOnce*. It is essentially a complete replacement for no-touch deployment. Thus, while no-touch deployment is still supported in .NET Framework 2.0 and higher, it is no longer recommended and is not covered in further detail in this chapter.

ClickOnce Deployment

ClickOnce has several advantages over alternatives such as no-touch deployment, including the following:

➤ **Updating from a web server** — No-touch deployment allows only completely automatic updating from the Web server, whereas ClickOnce can also be set up to allow more control by the user regarding when the application is installed and uninstalled.

➤ **Offline access** — Applications deployed with ClickOnce can be configured to run in an offline condition also. Applications that can be run offline have a shortcut installed on the Start menu.

ClickOnce also has advantages over applications installed with Windows Installer. These include auto-updating of the application from the deployment server, and installation of the application by users who are not administrators. (Windows Installer applications require the active user to be an administrator of the local machine. ClickOnce applications can be installed by users with fewer permissions.)

ClickOnce deployment can be done from a Web server, a network share, or read-only media such as a CD-ROM or DVD-ROM. The following discussion assumes you are using a Web server for deployment, but you can substitute a network share if you do not have access to a Web server.

> *ClickOnce does not require any version of the .NET Framework to be installed on the Web server you use for ClickOnce deployment. However, it does require that the Web server understand how to handle files with extensions* `.application` *and* `.manifest`. *The configuration for these extensions is done automatically if the Framework is installed on the Web server. On servers that don't contain the .NET Framework, you will probably have to do the configuration manually.*
>
> *Each extension that a Web server can handle must be associated with an option called a MIME type that tells the Web server how to handle that file extension when serving a file. The MIME type for each extension used by ClickOnce should be set to "application/ x-ms-application." If you don't know how to configure MIME types for your Web server, ask a network administrator or other professional who can do so.*

Configuring an Application for ClickOnce

For a simple case, no special work is needed to prepare a typical Windows application to be deployed via ClickOnce. Unlike the deployment options discussed earlier, it is not necessary to add additional projects to the solution. If you use standard options in ClickOnce, then it is also unnecessary to add any custom logic to your application. All of the work to enable ClickOnce deployment for an application can be performed by selecting options in the IDE.

Although it is possible to control the ClickOnce deployment by writing your own custom logic controlling the ClickOnce deployment processes, that capability is beyond the scope of this book and is not covered here. Instead, this chapter explains the basic configuration of ClickOnce and common options that don't require you to write any code.

Online versus Locally Installed Applications

Applications installed via ClickOnce are one of two types:

➤ Online applications, which can be accessed by the user only when the system has a connection to the website used to deploy the application

➤ Offline applications, which can be used when no connection is available

Online applications must be launched with a URL (Uniform Resource Locator), a standard filename, or a UNC (Universal Naming Convention) filename. This may be done in various ways, such as clicking a link in a Web page, typing a URL into the Address text box of a browser, typing a filename into the Address text box of Windows Explorer, or selecting a shortcut on the local machine that contains the URL or filename. However, ClickOnce does not automatically add any such mechanisms to a user's machine to access the application. That is up to you.

Offline applications can also be launched with a URL or UNC, and are always launched that way the first time. The differences are as follows:

➤ When ClickOnce performs the initial install of the application on the user's machine, by default it places a shortcut to the application on the user's Start ➪ Programs menu.

➤ The application can be started from the shortcut, and will run with no connection to the original location used for installation. Of course, any functionality of the application that depends on a network or Internet connection will be affected if the system is not online. It is your responsibility to build the application in such a way that it functions properly when offline.

Deploying an Online Application

A deployment walk-through for a simple Windows application will demonstrate the basics of ClickOnce. This first walk-through deploys an online application to a Web server, which is one of the simpler user scenarios for ClickOnce.

First, create a simple Windows Forms Application in Visual Studio, and name it **SimpleApp**. On the blank `Form1` that is created as part of the application, place a single button.

To enable ClickOnce deployment, access the Build menu and select the Publish SimpleApp option. The ClickOnce Publish Wizard will appear. The first screen of the wizard is shown in Figure 34-15.

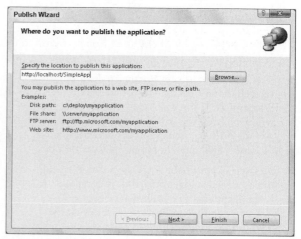

FIGURE 34-15

The location defaults to a local Web server if you have one; but as discussed earlier, deployment can be done on a remote website, a network share, or even a local directory. You should change the location if the default is not appropriate for your circumstances. Once you've verified the publish location, click Next.

Select one of the two types of ClickOnce applications discussed earlier. Because this example is for an online application, click the second option to make the application available online only, as shown in Figure 34-16.

Click Next to see a summary of your selections, and then click Finish. The ClickOnce deployment process will begin. A new item will be added to your project called "SimpleApp_ TemporaryKey.pfx," a complete build will be done, a new virtual directory will be created for the application on the Web server, and the files needed to deploy the application will be copied to that virtual directory. (The new item is discussed later in the section "Signing the Manifest.")

FIGURE 34-16

 If your publish operation fails, look in the Output window for Visual Studio to determine the reason. Usually, either Internet Information Server (IIS) is not running or you don't have the appropriate permissions to publish to a website.

IIS is not installed by default on recent versions of Windows. Under Vista and Windows 7, you need to ensure that the account in which you are developing with Visual Studio has appropriate security permissions to create new websites under IIS.

When the process is complete, a Web page will be generated that contains the link needed to deploy the application. The Web page has a Run button that activates the link. If you click this button, the application will be deployed by ClickOnce. (You may wish to view the source for this Web page to obtain the HTML needed to launch the application from your own Web pages.)

First, the prerequisites for the application are verified. In this case, that just means the .NET Framework. If the website is remote, then you will see a Security Warning dialog much like you would get if you attempted to download a file, and you'll need to select the Run option.

Next, an Application Run - Security Warning dialog is displayed, asking if it is acceptable to run the application, as shown in Figure 34-17. You can run the application by selecting the Run button, or select Don't Run, which aborts the process. For now, select Run, and after a short delay you will see the application's form appear.

FIGURE 34-17

If you now make any changes to the SimpleApp application, you must publish the application again to make the changes available via ClickOnce. You can do that by stepping through the Publish Wizard again. More details about automatic updating of ClickOnce applications are provided later in this chapter in the section "The Update Process."

Deploying an Application That Is Available Offline

In the second screen of the Publish Wizard, if you select the first option, then the installation process has some differences:

➤ The Web page that ClickOnce generates to test the deployment has an Install button instead of a Run button.

➤ When the button is pressed, a shortcut to the application is added to the user's Start ➪ Programs menu. The shortcut is in the program folder named for the company name that was entered when Visual Studio was installed.

➤ The application is launched at the end of the install process, as it was with an online application, but subsequent launches can be accomplished with the same URL or via the shortcut in the Start menu.

Files and Directories Produced by ClickOnce

The virtual directory used by ClickOnce to deploy your application contains a number of files for different aspects of the deployment. Figure 34-18 shows what the directory for SimpleApp looks like after ClickOnce has finished copying all the necessary files.

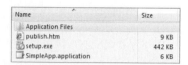

FIGURE 34-18

The virtual directory contains a folder for the first version of SimpleApp, which by default is version 1.0.0.0. It also contains the Web page that was displayed after ClickOnce finished, which is named `publish.htm`.

The next file is `Setup.exe`. This is an executable that does not need the .NET Framework to run. It is used during the ClickOnce process for all the activities that must take place before the application is launched. This includes activities such as checking for the presence of the .NET Framework. It is discussed further later in the chapter in the section "The Bootstrapper."

The next file is `SimpleApp.application`. The ".application" extension is specific to ClickOnce, and indicates the special file called a manifest, introduced in Chapter 31. This is an XML-based file that contains all the information needed to deploy the application, such as what files are needed and what options have been chosen. There is also a file named `SimpleApp_1_0_0_0.application`, which is the manifest specifically associated with version 1.0.0.0.

Each version of the application has its own manifest, and the one named `SimpleApp.application` (with no embedded version number) is typically the currently active one. (Thus, the link to the application does not need to change when the version number changes.)

Other files associated with a version are in the folder for that version.

Signing the Manifest

Because the manifest controls the update process, it is essential that ClickOnce be assured that the manifest is valid. This is done by signing the manifest, using a public-private key pair. As long as a third party does not have the key pair, that party cannot "spoof" a manifest, preventing any malicious interference in the ClickOnce deployment process.

A key pair is automatically generated when you publish with ClickOnce. However, you can supply your own key pair if you like. Options for signing the application are discussed later in the section "ClickOnce Configuration Options."

Note that your application assemblies do not need to be signed in order for them to be used in a ClickOnce deployment. Only the manifest must be signed. The manifest contains hash codes of all the assemblies involved, and those hash codes are checked before assemblies are used. This prevents malicious third parties from inserting their own versions of your assemblies.

The Update Process

By default, all ClickOnce applications check for updates each time the application is launched. This is done by getting the current version of the manifest and checking whether any changes were made since the last time the application was launched. This process is automatic, so there's nothing you need to do to make it happen, but it's helpful for you to understand the steps that are taken.

For an online application, if a change is detected, then it is immediately applied by downloading any changed files. Then the application is launched. This is conceptually similar to a browser-based application because the user has no option to use an older version.

For an application available offline, if changes are detected, then the user is asked whether the update should be made. The user can choose to decline the update. A configuration option enables you to specify a minimum version number, which forces a user to accept an update. You will look at ClickOnce configuration options later.

If an update is made for an offline application, then the previous version is kept. The user can then roll back to that version using the Add/Remove Programs option in the Control Panel. A user can also uninstall the ClickOnce-deployed application from that same location.

Only one previous version is kept. Older versions are removed when a new version is installed, so the only versions available at any point in time are the current version and the one immediately before it. A rollback can be made to the immediately preceding version, but not to any earlier versions.

You can control the update process by including code in your application that detects when changes have been made and applies the changes as necessary. As previously mentioned, this chapter does not cover writing such logic. You can find samples in the MSDN documentation for this capability.

ClickOnce Configuration Options

In Visual Studio 2010, the properties for a Windows Application project include several pages that affect ClickOnce. (You can access the properties for a project by right-clicking on it in the Solution Explorer and selecting Properties.)

The Signing tab includes options for signing the ClickOnce manifest. There are buttons to select a particular certificate from a store or a file, or to generate a new test certification for signing. This page also contains an option to sign the assembly that is compiled from the project, but as mentioned previously, this is not necessary for ClickOnce to operate.

The Security tab provides settings related to the code access security permissions needed by the application to run. Because the application is being deployed from a source other than the local machine, if you use ClickOnce, code access security limitations are in effect, as described in Chapter 32. A typical example of the Security tab is shown in Figure 34-19.

Using the options on the Security tab, you can arrange to test your application against a particular set of permissions. To do that, change from the default option "This is a full trust application" to the option immediately below it, "This is a partial trust application." Then select the zone from which the application will be installed. When the application is run by Visual Studio, permission for that zone will be enforced.

All of the other ClickOnce configuration options are on the Publish tab, shown in Figure 34-20.

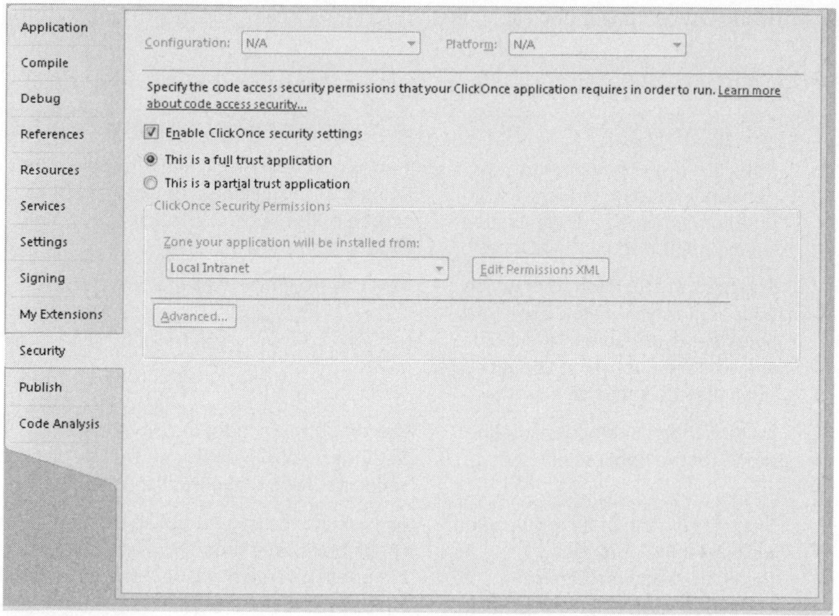

Application	Configuration: N/A ▼ Platform: N/A ▼
Compile	
Debug	Specify the code access security permissions that your ClickOnce application requires in order to run. Learn more about code access security...
References	☑ Enable ClickOnce security settings
Resources	● This is a full trust application
Services	○ This is a partial trust application
Settings	ClickOnce Security Permissions
Signing	Zone your application will be installed from:
My Extensions	Local Intranet ▼ Edit Permissions XML
Security	Advanced...
Publish	
Code Analysis	

FIGURE 34-19

Application	Configuration: N/A ▼ Platform: N/A ▼
Compile	
Debug	Publish Location
References	Publishing Folder Location (web site, ftp server, or file path):
	http://localhost/SimpleApp/
Resources	Installation Folder URL (if different than above):
Services	
Settings	Install Mode and Settings
Signing	● The application is available online only Application Files...
My Extensions	○ The application is available offline as well (launchable from Start menu) Prerequisites...
Security	Updates...
Publish	Options...
Code Analysis	Publish Version
	Major: Minor: Build: Revision:
	1 0 0 1
	☑ Automatically increment revision with each publish
	Publish Wizard... Publish Now

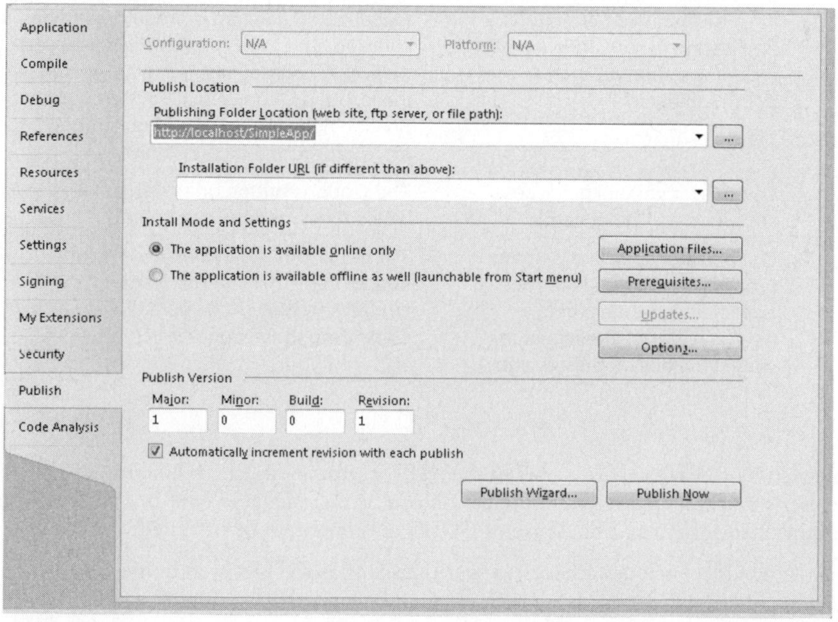

FIGURE 34-20

You can set many options with the Publish page, but Table 34-6 describes some of the most important ones.

TABLE 34-6: Important Publish Page Options

PROPERTY/OPTION	DESCRIPTION	WHERE TO SET IT ON THE PAGE
Publishing Location	Specifies the virtual directory, network directory, or local directory to which the application will be published by ClickOnce	Text box labeled Publishing Folder Location. (Note that this can also be set in the first screen of the Publish Wizard.)
Installation URL	Specifies the location from which your application will be deployed by users. By default, this is the same as the Publishing Location, but it may be set to be elsewhere.	Text box labeled Installation Folder URL
Install Mode	Selects the online only vs. offline mode for the application	Option buttons under Install Mode and Settings. (Note that this can also be set in the second screen of the Publish Wizard.)
Publish Version	Sets the version of the application for publishing purposes. ClickOnce requires version changes to properly auto-update the application.	The text boxes under Publish Version. If the check box under those boxes is checked, the publish version will be automatically incremented each time the application is published.
Prerequisites	Specifies the software that must be installed before your application can itself be installed, including elements such as the .NET Framework	The Prerequisites button brings up a dialog that enables standard prerequisites to be checked. The .NET Framework is checked by default. This dialog also enables you to specify the location for downloading prerequisites. See the next section, "The Bootstrapper," for more information on prerequisites.
Miscellaneous options	Options for various purposes, such as the product name	The Options button brings up a dialog in which these options can be set.
Update options	Options that control the update process, including when the application updates (before or after it starts), the minimum version number required, etc.	These options are available only for applications that can run offline. The Updates button brings up a dialog controlling these options.

The Bootstrapper

Because applications deployed by ClickOnce are a part of the .NET Framework, the .NET Framework must be available on the user's machine before your application can be installed and run. In addition, your application may require other items, such as a database or COM component, to be installed.

To provide for such needs, ClickOnce includes a *bootstrapper* that runs as the first step in the ClickOnce process. The bootstrapper is not a .NET program, so it can run on systems that do not yet have the .NET Framework installed. The bootstrapper is contained in a program called Setup.exe, which is included by ClickOnce as part of the publishing process.

When setup.exe runs, it checks for the prerequisites needed by the application, as specified in the Prerequisites options discussed previously. If needed, these options are then downloaded and installed. Only if the user's system contains installed prerequisites does ClickOnce attempt to install and run your Windows application.

The MSDN documentation includes more details on configuring and using the ClickOnce bootstrapper.

Manual Editing of ClickOnce Manifests

Sometimes an application manifest created by ClickOnce needs to be manually changed. For example, if the application contains dynamically loaded .NET DLLs (as discussed in Chapter 31), then such DLLs are not automatically included in a ClickOnce manifest.

In creating a manifest for an installation, ClickOnce relies on the compile-time references for the application being deployed. It will place any application assemblies that have compile-time references into the manifest.

However, dynamically loaded assemblies do not have a compile-time reference, which means ClickOnce can't put them in the manifest automatically. If you have dynamically loaded assemblies in your Windows Forms application, then you must add them to the manifest manually.

ClickOnce includes a tool for manually editing the manifest. Named MAGE.exe, it can be started by selecting Microsoft Visual Studio 2010 ⇨ Microsoft Windows SDK Tools ⇨ Manifest Generation and Editing Tool. It offers a UI to open a manifest and perform various manual operations on it. MAGE.exe can also be used from the command line, so you can create batch files or PowerShell scripts to automate insertion of files in a ClickOnce manifest.

How to use MAGE.exe is beyond the scope of this chapter, but the help files for MAGE.exe are extensive, and you can find MSDN samples that demonstrate how to use it.

Rolling Back or Uninstalling ClickOnce Applications

In addition to deploying an application for use, ClickOnce also provides the capability to uninstall or roll back applications that are deployed with the offline option. Such applications will have an entry in the section of the Control Panel for adding and removing programs (called Add/Remove Programs in Windows XP and Programs and Features in Windows Vista and Windows 7). That entry will offer an uninstall option — and if a rollback version is present, an option to roll back the last update.

Only one level of rollback is available. If multiple updates have occurred, then the user can only roll back to the most recent one. Once a rollback is done, no further rollback is possible until another update has been deployed.

ClickOnce versus Other Deployment Technologies

ClickOnce is a complete replacement for no-touch deployment. However, in some deployment scenarios ClickOnce may not be the ideal solution. For example, ClickOnce can deploy only a per-user installation. It cannot install an application once to be used by all users on the system.

ClickOnce may be used in combination with technologies such as the Windows Installer. If you create .msi files, as discussed earlier in the chapter, you may include them as part of ClickOnce's bootstrapper process. This is an advanced technique not discussed in this book, but you can learn more about this capability in the MSDN documentation.

For scenarios in which ClickOnce is not appropriate, you may wish to use more customized deployment technologies, including commercial products such as InstallShield.

IIS WEB DEPLOYMENT TOOL

As a part of the development of Internet Information Server 7 (IIS7), Microsoft developed a tool named MSDeploy.exe to assist in moving projects from previous versions of IIS into IIS7. If you are using IIS as your web server technology, you can use this tool to deploy your Visual Studio 2010 web applications.

Visual Studio 2010 integrates with the IIS Web Deployment Tool through a special tab on the Properties page for a web project. The tab is labeled Package/Publish Web. Figure 34-21 shows the tab.

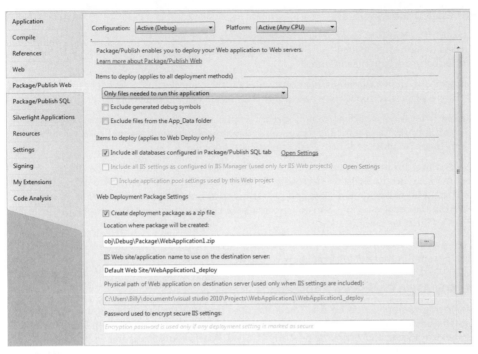

FIGURE 34-21

The end product of the IIS Web Deployment Tool is a zip file containing all the files relevant to publishing your web site. The options shown in Figure 34-21 allow control over how this file is created.

The output of the IIS Web Deployment Tool is then automatically created and used when the Build ⇨ Publish option is selected from Visual Studio. Figure 34-22 shows the Publish dialog, and you'll note that the default Publish method is Web Deploy, which uses the IIS Web Deployment Tool. The process of using this dialog is sometimes called a one-click deployment.

The IIS Web Deployment Tool includes many advanced capabilities, such as deployment of databases and the ability to transform Web.config settings during a publish/deployment of a web site. These advanced capabilities are beyond the scope of this chapter. The help files for the Package/Publish Web Tab and the Publish dialog contain information on those additional capabilities.

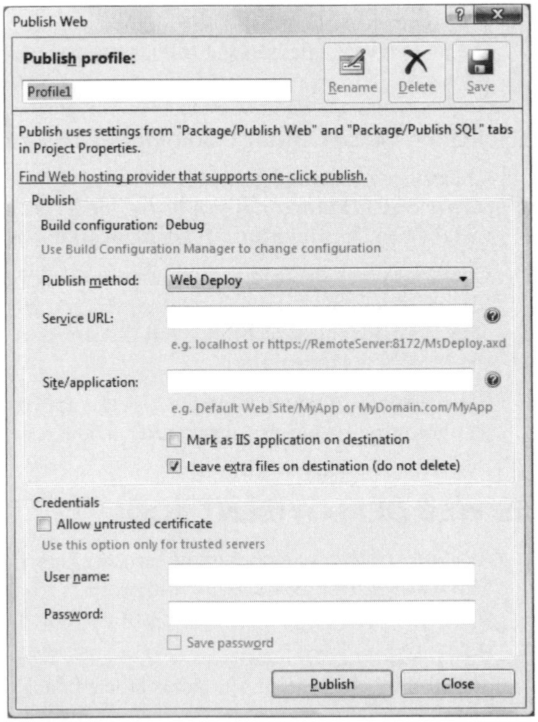

FIGURE 34-22

SUMMARY

An application must be deployed to be useful. How an individual application should be deployed depends heavily on circumstances. Factors such as the geographic distribution of the application, its complexity, and how often it will be updated must all be considered when choosing an appropriate strategy.

The main possibilities for deployment are as follows:

➤ XCOPY deployment

➤ Installation via the Windows Installer

➤ No-touch deployment

➤ ClickOnce deployment

➤ The IIS Web Deployment Tool (sometimes called one-click deployment)

➤ Deployment with other technologies, such as InstallShield or your own custom-written deployment programs

This chapter has covered the first five of these, with some discussion of their applicability. It will be helpful for you to understand all of these options to make appropriate decisions for the deployment of individual applications.

On the one hand, if you are deploying a simple utility, for example, you might want to install it by simply copying files. On the other hand, complex standalone applications that have many dependencies on COM-based components will more often use Windows Installer technology. Applications that depend on Web services for data will often be best deployed with ClickOnce. Corporate applications with special needs for security during installation, or that need to install an application once for multiple users, may be better off using custom deployment technology. Many Web applications can often be installed by publishing with the IIS Web Deployment Tool, but complex ones might require a Web deployment project.

You should also be aware that these options are not mutually exclusive. You might have an application with COM dependencies that needs to use an `.msi` file for an initial install, but gets the rest of the application and future updates via ClickOnce. Whatever your application, the plethora of application deployment technologies available for .NET-based applications means you should be able to find an option or combination that suits your needs.

The Visual Basic Compiler

When the .NET Framework was first introduced, one nice addition for the Visual Basic developer was the inclusion of a standalone language compiler. This meant you were not required to have the Visual Studio .NET 2002 IDE in order to build Visual Basic applications. In fact, you could take the .NET Framework from the Microsoft website (free of charge) and build Web applications, classes, modules, and more very simply, using a text editor such as Notepad. You could then take the completed files and compile them using the Visual Basic compiler.

The Visual Basic compiler is included along with the default .NET Framework install. Each version of the framework has a new compiler. In fact, note that while the core of the .NET 3.5 release is still running on the .NET Framework 2.0, the .NET Framework 3.5 release includes new compilers for both the Visual Basic and C# languages. Similarly, version 4 of the .NET Framework also ships with a new compiler. The compiler for the .NET Framework 2.0 is vbc.exe, and it can be found at C:\WINDOWS\Microsoft.NET\Framework\v2.0.50727\vbc.exe

The compiler for the .NET Framework 4 is also called vbc.exe, and it can be found at C:\WINDOWS\Microsoft.NET\Framework\v4.0\vbc.exe

Note that on a 64-bit system you will actually find a folder for the framework under C:\Windows\Microsoft.NET\Framework64\V4.0. This version of the compiler runs within the 64-bit memory space, but keep in mind that Visual Studio 2010 is still a 32-bit application. This mismatch is part of the reason why you need to target the x86 version of the compiler if you want to enable Edit and Continue debugging in Visual Studio 2010.

As for the future, it was announced at the 2008 Professional Developers Conference (PDC) that Microsoft was rewriting the language compilers using .NET. The goal is that with the release of V.Next (a version beyond 2010), the language compilers will have a 64-bit version. In the case of Visual Basic, the next version of the compiler will be written primarily in Visual Basic.

THE VBC.EXE.CONFIG FILE

In addition to the vbc.exe file, there is a vbc.exe.config file in the directory as well. This XML file is used to specify the versions of the .NET Framework for which the compiler should build applications. Now that there are three versions of the .NET Framework available for our applications to work with, it is important to understand how this configuration file actually works.

With the .NET Framework 3.5 installed, you will find the `vbc.exe.config` file with the following construction:

```
<?xml version ="1.0"?>
<configuration>
    <startup>
        <supportedRuntime version="v2.0.50727" safemode="true"/>
        <requiredRuntime version="v2.0.50727" safemode="true"/>
    </startup>
</configuration>
```

Even though you are dealing with the .NET Framework 3.5, you can see that the compiler compiles the code to run off of the 2.0 version of the framework. This was true for both .NET Framework 3.0 and .NET Framework 3.5. Both of these releases leveraged the .NET Framework 2.0 core libraries. However, with .NET Framework 4 this config file is updated to reference `version="v4.0"`, and modified by default to show only the supported runtime. Note that since this appendix is being completed prior to the final RTM release, the final build number that will appear has been replaced with an *.

```
<?xml version ="1.0"?>
<configuration>
    <startup>
        <supportedRuntime version="v4.0.*" />
    </startup>
</configuration>
```

This `.config` file, `vbc.exe.config`, is basically a typical .NET Framework configuration file with the default `<configuration>` root element included. Nested within the `<configuration>` element, you need to place a `<startup>` element. This is the only child element that is possible in the configuration file of `vbc.exe`.

Nested within the `<startup>` element, you can use two possible elements: `<supportedRuntime>` and `<requiredRuntime>`.

The `<requiredRuntime>` element is actually needed only if your application is going to run on the .NET Framework 1.0 (the very first iteration of the .NET Framework). If your application is going to run from this version, then you build the `vbc.exe.config` file as follows:

```
<?xml version ="1.0"?>
<configuration>
    <startup>
        <requiredRuntime version="v1.0.3705" safemode="true"/>
    </startup>
</configuration>
```

Currently, working with three different versions of the .NET Framework, you may wish to compile your applications using the Visual Basic compiler so that they target multiple versions of the framework explicitly. To do this, you could use the `<supportedRuntime>` element:

```
<?xml version ="1.0"?>
<configuration>
    <startup>
        <supportedRuntime version="v2.0.50727" safemode="true"/>
        <supportedRuntime version="v1.1.4322" safemode="true"/>
    </startup>
</configuration>
```

This construction states that the application should first try to run on version 2.0.50727 of the .NET Framework; and that if this version of the .NET Framework isn't found, then the next preferred version of the framework that the compiled object should work with is version 1.1.4322.

When working in this kind of construction, you need to order the framework versions in the XML file so that the most preferred version of the framework you want to utilize is the uppermost element, and the least preferred version of the framework appears last in the node list.

Keep in mind that this is similar to what Visual Studio will automatically do for you when you choose to target a version of the .NET Framework. As noted in Chapter 1, you can choose to target .NET 2.0,

.NET 3.0, .NET 3.5 or .NET 4 with your application. In order to leverage this targeting at the compiler, you want to ensure that your library references match the framework target you intend to support. Attempting to support .NET 2.0 while referencing something like the WPF libraries isn't going to work.

The `<supportedRuntime>` element is meant for .NET Framework versions 1.1 and later. If you are going to utilize the .NET Framework version 1.0, then you should use the `<requiredRuntime>` element.

The `<supportedRuntime>` element contains two possible attributes: `version` and `safemode`. Both attributes are optional. The attribute `version` enables you to specify the specific version you want your application to run against, whereas `safemode` specifies whether the registry should be searched for the particular framework version. The `safemode` attribute takes a Boolean value, and the default value is `false`, meaning the framework version is not checked.

Finally, note that in order to leverage this setting, you'll need to test your application against these various .NET versions.

SIMPLE STEPS TO COMPILATION

To show how the Visual Basic compiler works in the simplest manner, we can begin by looking at how to compile a single-class file:

1. Create a module file called `MyModule.vb`. We will keep the module simple, as this example is meant to show you how to compile the items using the `vbc.exe` compiler:

```
Module Module1
    Sub Main()
        Console.WriteLine("Howdy there")
        Console.ReadLine()
    End Sub
End Module
```

2. Once your file is in place, it is time to use the Visual Basic compiler. If you have Visual Studio on the computer, then you can open the Visual Studio command prompt (found at Start ➪ All Programs ➪ Microsoft Visual Studio 2010 ➪ Visual Studio Tools ➪ Visual Studio Command Prompt (2010). Once open, just navigate to the location of the file and then run the compiler against the file (shown shortly).

3. In most cases, you are probably going to be using the Visual Basic compiler on computers that do not have Visual Studio on them. In those cases, one option is to copy and paste the `vbc.exe`, `vbc.exe .config`, and `vbc.rsp` files to the folder where the class file you wish to compile is located. Then you can open a command prompt by selecting Run from the Start menu and typing **cmd** in the text box.

Another option is to add the compiler to the path itself. This is done by typing the following at the command prompt:

```
path %path%;C:\WINDOWS\Microsoft.NET\Framework\v4.0.*
Now you can work with the compilation normally, and the vbc.exe compiler will
be found upon compilation. Yet another option is to work from the Windows
folder, using an explicit reference to the file to be compiled. However, this
option is frowned upon, as you are likely to start creating project-specific
files within your .NET Framework folder hierarchy.
```

4. Once the command prompt is open, navigate to the folder that contains the class file that needs compiling. From this location, type the following command at the command prompt:

```
vbc.exe MyModule.vb
```

Items can be compiled in many ways using the Visual Basic compiler, but this is the simplest way to compile this module. This command compiles the `.vb` file so that it can be utilized by your applications. Running the preceding command produces the following:

```
C:\CoolStuff>vbc.exe MyModule.vb
Microsoft (R) Visual Basic Compiler version 10.0.*
Copyright (c) Microsoft Corporation.  All rights reserved.
```

What does this operation actually do? Well, in this case, it has created an `.exe` file for you in the same directory as the `MyModule.vb` file. Looking there, you will find `MyModule.exe` ready to run.

The Visual Basic compiler has a number of options that enable you to dictate what sorts of actions the compiler will take with the compilation process. These flags will be defined soon, but you can specify additional settings by using a forward slash followed by the name of the option and the setting assigned to the option. For instance, if you were going to add a reference to `Microsoft.VisualBasic.dll` along with the compilation, you would construct your compiler command as follows:

```
vbc.exe MyModule.vb /reference:Microsoft.VisualBasic.dll
```

Some of the options listed in this appendix have a plus sign (+) or a minus sign (-) next to them. A plus sign signifies that the option should be enabled, whereas the minus sign signifies that the option should not be enabled. For instance, the following signifies that documentation should be enabled:

```
vbc.exe MyModule.vb /reference:Microsoft.VisualBasic.dll /doc+
```

The following, however, signifies that documentation should not be enabled:

```
vbc.exe MyModule.vb /reference:Microsoft.VisualBasic.dll /doc-
```

COMPILER OPTIONS

This section takes a comprehensive look at options available for the Visual Basic compiler. To see the full list, type the following command:

```
vbc.exe /?
```

Output Files

The following sections explain the output files.

/doc[+:-]

By default, the compiler does not produce the XML documentation file upon compilation. This feature of Visual Basic enables developers to put structured comments in their code that can then be turned into an XML document for easy viewing (along with a style sheet). Including the `/doc` option causes the compiler to create this documentation. Structure your command as follows if you want to produce this XML documentation file:

```
vbc.exe MyModule.vb /doc
```

You can also specify the name of the XML file as follows:

```
vbc.exe MyModule.vb /doc:MyModuleXmlFile.xml
```

/out

Using the `/out` option enables you to change the name and extension of the file that was produced from the compilation. By default, it is the name of the file that contains the `Main` procedure or the first source code file in a DLL. To modify this yourself instead of using the defaults, you could use something similar to the following:

```
vbc.exe MyModule.vb /out:MyReallyCoolModule.exe
```

/target

This setting enables you to specify what exactly is output from the compilation process. There are four options: an EXE, a DLL, a module, or a Windows program:

➤ **/target:exe** — Produces an executable console application. This is the default if no `/target` option is specified.

➤ **/target:library** — Produces a dynamic link library (also known as a DLL)

> ➤ **/target:module** — Produces a module

> ➤ **/target:winexe** — Produces a Windows program

You can also use a short form of this by just using `/t:exe`, `/t:library`, `/t:module,` or `/t:winexe`.

Input Files

The following sections explain the input files.

/addmodule

This option is not available to Visual Studio, but is possible when using the Visual Basic compiler. Using `/addmodule` enables you to add a `.netmodule` file to the resulting output of the compiler. In the following example the MyOtherModule.netmodule is a filename. You can append one or more module files. Module files aren't quite the same as an assembly, in that they are specifically compiled using the /target:module option which creates a netmodule file appropriate for inclusion as part of other compilations. An example of using /addmodule would look something similar to the following construction:

```
vbc.exe MyModule.vb /addmodule:MyOtherModule.netmodule
```

/link

This enables you to reference metadata from the specified interop assembly. Since .NET 4 supports the no Primary Interop Assembly (PIA) feature, you need to link in the appropriate interop assemblies at compilation time. Use this option to link the PIA metadata into the assembly during compilation so that the associated Interop Assembly isn't required at deployment. It can be abbreviated as /l.

```
vbc.exe MyModule.vb /l:COMponent.dll
```

/recurse

The `/recurse` option tells the compiler to compile all the specified files within a specified directory. Also included will be all child directories of the directory specified. Here is one example of using `/recurse`:

```
vbc.exe /target:library /out:MyComponent.dll /recurse:MyApplication\Classes\*.vb
```

This command takes all of the `.vb` files from the `MyApplication/Classes` directory and its subdirectories and creates a DLL called `MyComponent.dll`.

/reference

The `/reference` option enables you to make references to other assemblies in the compilation process. Use it as follows:

```
vbc.exe MyModule.vb /reference:MyAssembly.dll
```

You can also shorten the command option by using just `/r`:

```
vbc.exe MyModule.vb /r:MyAssembly.dll
```

You can make a reference to multiple assemblies by separating them with a comma:

```
vbc.exe MyModule.vb /reference:MyAssembly.dll, MyOtherAssembly.dll
```

Resources

The following sections elaborate on the resources in the compiler.

/linkresource

Instead of embedding resources directly in the generated output file (such as with the `/resource` option), the `/linkresource` option enables you to create the connection between your output file and the resources that they require. You would use this option in the following manner:

```
vbc.exe MyModule.vb /linkresource:MyResourceFile.res
```

You can specify whether the resource file is supposed to be public or private in the assembly manifest. By default, the resource file is referenced as public. Here is an example of its use:

```
vbc.exe MyModule.vb /linkresource:MyResourceFile.res,private
```

You can shorten the `/linkresource` option to just `/linkres`.

/resource

The `/resource` option enables you to reference managed resource objects. The referenced resource is then embedded in the assembly. You would do this in the following manner:

```
vbc.exe MyModule.vb /resource:MyResourceFile.res
```

Like the `/linkresource` option, you can specify whether the reference to the resource should be made either public or private. This is done as follows (the default is public):

```
vbc.exe MyModule.vb /resource:MyResourceFile.res,private
```

You can shorten the `/resource` option to just `/res`.

/win32icon

Use this option to embed an `.ico` file (an image that is actually the application's icon) in the produced file, as shown in the following example:

```
vbc.exe MyModule.vb /win32icon:MyIcon.ico
```

/win32resource

This option enables you to embed a Win32 resource file into the produced file. Use as shown in the following example:

```
vbc.exe MyModule.vb /win32resource:MyResourceFile.res
```

Code Generation

The following sections address options available for code generation.

/debug[+:-]

By default, the Visual Basic compiler will not build objects with attached debugging information included in the generated object. Using the `/debug` option causes the compiler to place this information in the created output file. In addition, you can choose to debug full, which is the default, or to emit a PDB file only. The use of this option is shown here:

```
vbc.exe MyModule.vb /debug
vbc.exe MyModule.vb /debug:full
vbc.exe MyModule.vb /debug:pdbonly
```

/optimize[+:−]

If you go to your project's property page (found by right-clicking on the project in the Visual Studio Solution Explorer), you will see a page for compilation settings. From this page, you can make all sorts of compilation optimizations. To keep your command-line compiler from ignoring these instructions, set the `/optimize` flag in your compilation instructions:

```
vbc.exe MyModule.vb /optimize
```

By default, optimizations are turned off.

/removeintchecks[+:-]

By default, the Visual Basic compiler checks all your integer calculations for any possible errors. Possible errors include division by zero or overflow situations. Using the `/removeintchecks` option causes the compiler to not look for these kinds of errors in the code of the files being compiled. You would use this option as follows:

```
vbc.exe MyModule.vb /removeintchecks
```

Errors and Warnings

/nowarn

The `/nowarn` option actually suppresses the compiler from throwing any warnings. There are a couple of ways to use this option. The first option is to simply use `/nowarn` without any associated values:

```
vbc.exe MyModule.vb /nowarn
```

Instead of suppressing all the warnings that the compiler can issue, the other option at your disposal is to specify the exact warnings you wish the compiler to suppress, as shown here:

```
vbc.exe MyModule.vb /nowarn:42016
```

In this case, you are telling the compiler not to throw any warnings when it encounters a 42016 error (an implicit conversion warning error). To interject more than one warning code, separate the warning codes with a comma as illustrated here:

```
vbc.exe MyModule.vb /nowarn:42016, 42024
```

You can find a list of available warnings by searching for "Configuring Warnings in Visual Basic" in the MSDN documentation.

/warnaserror[+:-]

In addition to finding and reporting errors, the compiler can also encounter situations that are only considered warnings. Even though warnings are encountered, the compilation process continues. Using the `/warnaserror` option in the compilation process causes the compiler to treat all warnings as errors. Use this option as shown here:

```
vbc.exe MyModule.vb /warnaserror
```

You might not want each warning to cause an error to be thrown, but instead only specific warnings. For these occasions, you can state the warning ID number that you want to look out for, as shown here:

```
vbc.exe MyModule.vb /warnaserror:42016
```

You can also check for multiple warnings by separating the warning ID numbers with commas:

```
vbc.exe MyModule.vb /warnaserror:42016, 42024
```

Language

The following sections detail Visual Basic language-specific options.

/define

The `/define` option enables you to define conditional compiler constants for the compilation process. This is quite similar to using the `#Const` directive in your code. Here is an example:

```
vbc.exe MyModule.vb /define:Version="4.11"
```

This option can be shortened to `/d`. You can also place definitions for multiple constants, as shown here:

```
vbc.exe MyModule.vb /d:Version="4.11",DebugMode=False
```

For multiple constants, just separate the constants with commas.

/imports

A commonly used compiler option, the `/imports` option enables you to import namespaces into the compilation process:

```
vbc.exe MyModule.vb /imports:System
```

Add multiple namespaces by separating them with a comma:

```
vbc.exe MyModule.vb /imports:System, System.Data
```

/langversion

This option enables you to specify a language version. This version is based on the Visual Basic version not the .NET version. For example, .NET 4 ships with Visual Basic 10.

```
vbc.exe MyModule.vb /langversion:10
```

/optionexplicit[+:-]

Always a good idea, using /optionexplicit causes the compiler to check whether any variables in the code are used before they are even declared (yes, this is possible and very bad practice). Using this setting, when variables are found before they are even declared, the compiler throws an error. By default, the compiler does not check the code using the /optionexplicit option. Use this option as shown in the following example:

```
vbc.exe MyModule.vb /optionexplicit
```

/optionstrict[+:-]

It's also a good idea to use the /optionstrict option in the compilation process. Using this option causes the compiler to check whether you are making any improper type conversions in your code. Widening type conversions are allowed, but when you start performing narrowing type conversions, using this option will cause an error to be thrown by the compiler. By default, the compiler does not look for these types of errors with your type conversions. Use this option as follows:

```
vbc.exe MyModule.vb /optionstrict
```

/optioncompare

By default, the Visual Basic compiler compares strings using a binary comparison. If you want the string comparisons to use a text comparison, then use the following construction:

```
vbc.exe MyModule.vb /optioncompare:text
```

/optioninfer[+:-]

New to the .NET Framework 3.5 version of the compiler, this option specifies that you want to allow type inference of variables. Use this option as illustrated in the following example:

```
vbc.exe MyModule.vb /optioninfer
```

/rootnamespace

Use this option to specify the namespace to use for compilation:

```
vbc.exe MyClass.vb /rootnamespace:Reuters
```

Miscellaneous Features

The rest of this appendix covers some of the other very useful features in the compiler

/?

When you don't have this book for reference, you can use the Visual Basic compiler for a list of options by using the /? option, as shown here:

```
vbc.exe /?
```

This causes the entire list of options and their definitions to be displayed in the command window.

/help

The /help option is the same as the /? option. Both of these options produce the same result: a list of options that can be used with the compiler.

/noconfig

By default, the Visual Basic compiler uses the vbc.rsp resource file in the compilation process. Using the /noconfig option tells the compiler not to use this file in the compilation process, as shown here:

```
vbc.exe MyClass.vb /noconfig
```

/nologo

This option causes the compiler to perform its compilation without producing the compiler information set shown in previous examples. This is really only useful if you are invoking the compiler in your application, showing the results it produces to the end users, and you have no desire to show this information to users in the result set.

/quiet

Like some of the other compiler options, the /quiet option is available only to the command-line compiler; it is not available when compiling your applications using Visual Studio. The /quiet option removes some of the error notifications from the error text output that is typically generated. Normally, when the compiler encounters an error that disallows further compilation, the error notification includes the line of code in the file where the error occurred. The line that is presented has a squiggly line underneath the exact bit of code where the error occurred. Using the /quiet option causes the compiler to show only the notification line, leaving the code line out of the output. This might be desirable in some situations.

/verbose

Adding this command causes the compiler to output a complete list of what it is doing, including the assemblies that are being loaded and the errors that it receives in the compilation process. Use it as follows:

```
vbc.exe MyModule.vb /reference:Microsoft.VisualBasic.dll /verbose
```

This would produce results such as the following (abbreviated because the result output is rather lengthy):

```
Adding assembly reference 'C:\WINDOWS\Microsoft.NET\Framework\v4.0.*\System.
Data.dll'
```

In addition:

```
Adding import 'System'
Adding import 'Microsoft.VisualBasic'
Adding file 'C:\MyModule.vb'
Adding assembly reference 'C:\WINDOWS\Microsoft.NET\Framework\v4.0.*\Microso
ft.VisualBasic.dll'
Compiling...
```

Then the compiler starts loading assemblies . . .

```
Loading C:\WINDOWS\Microsoft.NET\Framework\v4.0.*\mscorlib.dll.
Loading C:\WINDOWS\Microsoft.NET\Framework\v4.0.*\Microsoft.VisualBasic.dll.
```

. . . until it finishes:

```
Building 17d14f5c-a337-4978-8281-53493378c1071.vb.
Building C:\CoolStuff\MyModule.vb.
Compilation successful
```

Advanced Features

The following sections discuss optimization and other advanced features that are available.

/baseaddress

When creating a DLL using the `/target:library` option, you can assign the base address of the DLL. By default, this is done for you by the compiler, but if you wish to make this assignment yourself, you can. To accomplish this, you would use something similar to the following:

```
vbc.exe MyClass.vb /target:library /baseaddress:0x11110000
```

All base addresses are specified as hexadecimal numbers.

/bugreport

The `/bugreport` option creates a file that is a full report of the compilation process. This file contains your code and version information on the computer's operating system and the compiler itself. Use this option in the following manner:

```
vbc.exe MyModule.vb /bugreport:bugsy.txt
```

/codepage

By default, the compiler expects all files to be using an ANSI, Unicode, or UTF-8 code page. Using the compiler's `/codepage` option, you can specify the code page that the compiler should actually be using. Setting it to one of the defaults is shown here:

```
vbc.exe MyClass.vb /codepage:1252
```

1252 is used for American English and most European languages, although setting it to Japanese Kanji would be just as simple:

```
vbc.exe MyClass.vb /codepage:932
```

/delaysign[+:-]

This compiler option needs to be used in conjunction with the `/key` or `/keycontainer` option, which deals with the signing of your assembly. When used with the `/delaysign` option, the compiler will create a space for the digital signature that is later used to sign the assembly, rather than actually signing the assembly at that point. You would use this option in the following manner:

```
vbc.exe MyModule.vb /key:myKey1.sn /delaysign
```

/errorreport

This option defines how to handle internal compiler errors. The possible settings are `prompt`, `send`, `none`, or the `default` queue. Prompt will prompt the user for permission to send the error to Microsoft. `Send` will automatically send the error to Microsoft, and `None` reports errors in a text file only.

/filealign

Not typically used by most developers, the `/filealign` setting enables you to specify the alignment of sections, or blocks of contiguous memory, in your output file. It uses the following construction:

```
vbc.exe MyModule.vb /filealign:2048
```

The number assigned is the byte size of the file produced, and valid values include 512, 1024, 2048, 4096, 8192, and 16384.

/keycontainer

This command causes the compiler to create a sharable component and places a public key into the component's assembly manifest while signing the assembly with a private key. Use this option as follows:

```
vbc.exe MyModule.vb /keycontainer:myKey1
```

If your key container has a name that includes a space, then you have to place quotes around the value as shown here:

```
vbc.exe MyModule.vb /keycontainer:"my Key1"
```

/keyfile

Similar to the `/keycontainer` option, the /key option causes the compiler to place a public key into the component's assembly manifest while signing the assembly with a private key. Use this as follows:

```
vbc.exe MyModule.vb /key:myKey1.sn
```

If your key has a name that includes a space, then you must place quotes around the value as shown here:

```
vbc.exe MyModule.vb /key:"my Key1.sn"
```

/libpath

When making references to other assemblies while using the `/reference` compiler option (described earlier), you will not always have these referenced assemblies in the same location as the object being compiled. You can use the `/libpath` option to specify the location of the referenced assemblies, as illustrated here:

```
vbc.exe MyModule.vb /reference:MyAssembly.dll /libpath:c:\Reuters\bin
```

If you want the compiler to search for the referenced DLLs in more than one location, then specify multiple locations using the `/libpath` option by separating the locations with a semi-colon:

```
vbc.exe MyModule.vb /reference:MyAssembly.dll /libpath:c:\Reuters\bin, c:\
```

This command means that the compiler will look for the `MyAssembly.dll` in both the `C:\Reuters\bin` directory and the root directory found at `C:\`.

/main

Using the `/main` or `/m` option, you can point the compiler to the class or module that contains the `Sub Main` procedure. Use it as follows:

```
vbc.exe MyClass.vb /main:MyClass.vb
```

/moduleassemblyname

This option specifies the name of the assembly the module will be a part of.

/netcf

This option cannot be executed from Visual Studio itself, but you can use this flag from the Visual Basic command-line compiler. Using `/netcf` causes the compiler to build your application so that the result is targeted for the .NET Compact Framework, not the full .NET Framework itself. To accomplish this, use the following construct:

```
vbc.exe MyModule.vb /netcf
```

/nostdlib

By default, the Visual Basic compiler uses standard libraries (`System.dll`) and the `vbc.rsp` resource file in the compilation process. Using the `/nostdlib` option tells the compiler not to use this file in the compilation process, as shown here:

```
vbc.exe MyClass.vb /nostdlib
```

/platform

The `/platform` option enables you to specify the platform the compilation should be geared for. Possible options include the following:

➤ **/platform:x86** — Compiles the program for an x86 system

➤ **/platform:x64** — Compiles the program for a 64-bit system

➤ **/platform:Itanium** — Compiles the program for an Itanium system

➤ **/platform:anycpu** — Compiles the program so that it can be run on any CPU system. This is the default setting.

/sdkpath

This option enables you to specify the location of `mscorlib.dll` and `Microsoft.VisualBasic.dll` if they are located somewhere other than the default location. This setting is really meant to be used with the `/netcf` option, described earlier, and is used as follows:

```
vbc.exe /sdkpath:"C:\Program Files\Microsoft Visual Studio 8
    \CompactFrameworkSDK\v1.0.5000\Windows CE" MyModule.vb
```

/utf8output[+:−]

By default, when you use the Visual Basic command-line compiler, it provide console output during the compilation process. However, in some international configurations, the console is expecting UTF-8 character encoding, and as a result no output is displayed. If your system is configured such that you need UTF-8 output, you'll want to include this flag with your compilation so that the compiler's console output is visible. The Visual Studio IDE does not use this since it controls it's internal console display.

@<file>

This option allows you to embed the command-line settings into a text file which will be processed. If you have a compilation that you frequently perform, or one that is rather lengthy, you can instead create a `.rsp` file, a simple text file containing all the compilation instructions needed for the compilation process. Of course you can use an extension other than `.rsp`. Historically `.rsp` files were associated with response files used by linkers. Here is an example `.rsp` file:

```
# This is a comment
/target:exe
/out:MyCoolModule.exe
/linkresource=MyResourceFile.res
MyModule.vb
SomeOtherClassFile.vb
```

If you save this as `MySettingsFile.rsp`, then you can use it as shown in the following example:

```
vbc.exe @MySettingsFile.rsp
```

You can also specify multiple settings files:

```
vbc.exe @MySettingsFile.rsp @MyOtherResponseFile.rsp
```

/vbruntime[+:-]

The `/vbruntime` option enables you compile the program with the Visual Basic runtime. Use it as follows:

```
vbc.exe MyModule.vb /vbruntime
```

You can also specify which runtime to use, as shown here:

```
vbc.exe MyModule.vb /vbruntime:Microsoft.VisualBasic.dll
```

LOOKING AT THE VBC.RSP FILE

As stated earlier, the `vbc.rsp` file is used by default to indicate a set of standard libraries available to the compiler. When a compilation is being done, the Visual Basic compiler uses the `vbc.rsp` file for each compilation (unless you specify the `/noconfig` option). Inside this `.rsp` file is a list of compiler commands:

```
# This file contains command-line options that the VB
# command-line compiler (VBC) will process as part
# of every compilation, unless the "/noconfig" option
```

```
# is specified.
# Reference the common Framework libraries
/r:Accessibility.dll
/r:Microsoft.Vsa.dll
/r:System.Configuration.Install.dll
/r:System.Data.dll
/r:System.Design.dll
/r:System.DirectoryServices.dll
/r:System.dll
/r:System.Drawing.Design.dll
/r:System.Drawing.dll
/r:System.EnterpriseServices.dll
/r:System.Management.dll
/r:System.Messaging.dll
/r:System.Runtime.Remoting.dll
/r:System.Runtime.Serialization.Formatters.Soap.dll
/r:System.Security.dll
/r:System.ServiceProcess.dll
/r:System.Web.dll
/r:System.Web.Mobile.dll
/r:System.Web.RegularExpressions.dll
/r:System.Web.Services.dll
/r:System.Windows.Forms.Dll
/r:System.XML.dll

/r:System.Workflow.Activities.dll
/r:System.Workflow.ComponentModel.dll
/r:System.Workflow.Runtime.dll
/r:System.Runtime.Serialization.dll
/r:System.ServiceModel.dll

/r:System.Core.dll
/r:System.Xml.Linq.dll
/r:System.Data.Linq.dll
/r:System.Data.DataSetExtensions.dll
/r:System.Web.Extensions.dll
/r:System.Web.Extensions.Design.dll
/r:System.ServiceModel.Web.dll

# Import System and Microsoft.VisualBasic
/imports:System
/imports:Microsoft.VisualBasic
/imports:System.Linq
/imports:System.Xml.Linq
```

These commands reflect the references and imports that are done for each item that you compile using this command-line compiler. Feel free to play with this file as you choose. If you want to add your own references, then add them to the list and save the file. From then on, every compilation that you make will include the new reference(s). If you become more familiar with using the Visual Basic command-line compiler, you will see a lot of power in using .rsp files — even the default Visual Basic one.

B

Visual Basic Power Packs Tools

This appendix takes a look at the Visual Basic Power Packs Tools. These tools started as a set of off-cycle release packages that focused on helping developers, who are maintaining traditional VB6 applications, begin the process of transitioning to Visual Basic .NET. Key portions of the original Power Packs have been incorporated as features within Visual Studio. In addition to the Power Packs this chapter looks at a second tool for those working with VB6, the VB6 Interop Toolkit. These tools contain a set of features intended for developers with years of Visual Basic experience to replicate tasks and behaviors that were easy in VB6 in Visual Basic .NET.

This appendix briefly examines the two installation packages that are currently available. These packages were released targeting Visual Studio 2005, and have been updated for Visual Studio 2010. Additionally, elements of the Visual Basic Power Packs 3.0 package for printing were fully integrated with Visual Studio 2008 SP1 and continue to ship with Visual Studio 2010.

This appendix focuses on three areas:

➤ Power Packs background, including goals and installation
➤ The Interop Forms Toolkit 2.1
➤ The Visual Basic Power Packs 3.0

These tools are available as free downloads; however, due to licensing restrictions on the Express Editions, Visual Basic Express and the other Express Editions do not support any add-ins. Thus, to leverage the Interop Forms Toolkit, you need a licensed version of Visual Studio Standard or above. Why you would want to leverage the Power Packs is a question best answered by understanding the issues that the Power Packs address. These aren't just technology for technology's sake: They address very real issues that traditional VB developers are facing today.

VISUAL BASIC POWER PACKS

The Visual Basic Power Packs were introduced by Microsoft's Visual Basic Development team to introduce new features and capabilities needed by Visual Basic developers between major releases of Visual Studio. The main focus has been on helping Visual Basic 6.0 developers who have implemented solutions that aren't easily migrated in one fell swoop to .NET. There are two problems:

➤ Like it or not, the migration wizard that originally shipped with .NET 1.0 doesn't meet the requirements of a developer migrating a real-world application.
➤ Once they are working in .NET, typical developers face challenges with certain tasks that under Visual Basic 6.0 were easy but in Visual Basic .NET are not.

Each of these two issues is currently addressed by a different package.

In a perfect world, when Visual Basic .NET 1.0 came out, the transition from Visual Basic 6.0 to .NET would have felt seamless. The migration wizard that was introduced would have looked through your project files, found all of the custom COM components for which you had source available, and then been able to convert every line of VB 6.0 source code to VB.NET without any problem.

Unfortunately, we don't live in that world, and, in fact, the migration wizard left several gaps in coverage. These gaps in code migration didn't affect a demonstration, but were of significant concern if you were trying to update an application to .NET. This meant that your primary tool for migration forced you into an all-or-nothing decision with regard to moving your application, but at the same time couldn't fully complete the process. As a result, you faced a scenario in which you couldn't really add new capabilities to your application without converting it, and converting a decent-sized application with all of the associated manual migration elements could take months — time you didn't have.

Recently, the same scenario again appeared with the anticipated end of the Windows Forms user interface. However, in this case, as discussed in Chapter 15, Microsoft found a better way to handle the migration. Instead of including a wizard that tried to manage the entire application at once, they created a set of components that enabled you to interoperate between your existing code and the new feature set. The most exciting part about this is that when .NET 1.0 shipped, it actually included this same capability for COM. In theory, there was also support for calling .NET components from COM, but, in reality, that interface was difficult, so the Visual Basic team stepped up to the plate and created a package that would solve that problem.

The Visual Basic Interop Forms Toolkit 2.1 does this. It was designed to enable you to create and implement a form in .NET, after which the toolkit makes it easy for you to wrapper this form so that it can function as a working component within your existing VB6 application. The wrapper handles integrating the .NET form with your application, enabling you to maintain a common environment for the data, context, and even messaging. Events can be passed between your new .NET form and your existing Visual Basic application. The result is that now you can extend your existing VB6 application with new .NET features without the cost and risk associated with attempting to migrate your entire application in one fell swoop.

Of course, this was only one aspect of the migration challenge for VB6 developers. The second key aspect was that under Visual Basic 6.0, it was easy for developers to carry out tasks such as printing. .NET follows a paradigm that is much closer to the C++ model. It provides a great deal of control and is fully customizable. However, the ability to control and customize your output also introduces a layer of complexity for managing those capabilities. VB6 developers often just wanted to output a display or add a geometric shape to the form. As a result of the added complexity of these tasks, developers were often unsure how to implement the same capabilities they had under VB6.

Again the Visual Basic team stepped up and created the Visual Basic Power Packs 3.0. This is a separate installation package from the Interop Forms Toolkit; and instead of targeting code that can be integrated with traditional COM applications, it focuses on making it just as easy to do things, like printing, as they were in Visual Basic 6.0.

In addition, instead of waiting for the next release of Visual Studio, the Visual Basic team scheduled these Power Packs as standalone deliverables so that users could take advantage of them much sooner.

Although originally released outside the Visual Studio release cycle, more of these tools get incorporated with the Visual Studio baseline with each release. The printing capabilities introduced in the Power Packs were included within Visual Studio 2008. Next, Service Pack 1 for Visual Studio 2008 incorporated the full 3.0 package. As of Visual Studio 2010, the Data Repeater control was added within Visual Studio, which continues to support all of the previous Power Packs 3.0 tools.

Getting the Visual Basic Power Packs

The Power Packs are available as free downloads, although as a Visual Studio 2010 user you don't need to download the Power Packs. However, if you are looking to extend existing VB6 applications with .NET you will need the Interop Forms Toolkit 2.1. The download for the Interop Forms Toolkit 2.0 can be found at `www.microsoft.com/downloads/details` `.aspx?familyid=934de3c5-dc85-4065-9327-96801e57b81d&displaylang=en`. As this book went to press, the Interop Forms Toolkit 2.1 was still in beta, so you'll have to Bing its download location or go through one of the Visual Basic forums to get the most recent release. The 2.1 release of the Interop Forms Toolkit is a maintenance release to ensure installation compatibility with Visual Studio 2010. Version 2.0 does not install with Visual Studio 2010.

The download for the Visual Basic Power Packs 3.0 can be found at `www.microsoft.com/downloads/` `details.aspx?FamilyID=371368A8-7FDC-441F-8E7D-FE78D96D4063&displaylang=en`.

Keep in mind that the two separate download packages are different tools available to Visual Basic developers.

Additional forums are available to discuss issues or ask questions regarding use of the tools. The Interop Forms Toolkit forum is at `http://forums.microsoft.com/MSDN/ShowForum` `.aspx?ForumID=879&SiteID=1`.

The forum for the Power Packs is at `http://forums.microsoft.com/MSDN/ShowForum` `.aspx?ForumID=903&SiteID=1`.

USING THE INTEROP FORMS TOOLKIT 2.1

To begin working with the Interop Forms Toolkit, download the packages. The default download page includes three files for download, as shown in Figure B-1.

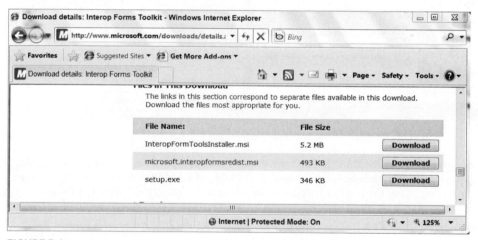

FIGURE B-1

Download all three of these files to a local directory of your choice:

➤ `InteropFormToolsInstaller.msi` — This file, which is also the largest, contains the actual application files that need to be installed.

➤ `microsoft.interopformsredist.msi` — This file, as its name implies, is a redistributable version of the Interop Forms Toolkit of tools.

➤ `setup.exe` — As you can tell by its size, the third file relies on the `installation.msi` file, but if you are running on Vista then you'll need this file.

Once you have downloaded all three files, run the setup file to install the tool. Aside from selecting the installation directory and similar standard setup screens, there are no special steps related to installing this package. One thing to note, regardless of whether you are running Visual Studio 2005, Visual Studio 2008, Visual Studio 2010 or some combination of all three, is that the installation package updates your Visual Studio environment.

> *Because Visual Basic Express Edition does not support add-ins, this application will not be updated when you install the software.*

To validate your installation, there are three easy items you can check. First, once the installation is complete, the help topic associated with the Interop Forms Toolkit 2.1 should open. Second, when you access the Tools menu, the first item in the menu should be the option to Generate Interop Form Wrapper Classes. This menu item should be located above the standard option to Attach Process. Third, and probably most important, when you access the File menu and select the New Project dialog, you should see two new project types within the Visual Basic section, as shown in Figure B-2.

FIGURE B-2

The first custom project type is the VB6 Interop User Control project type. This type of project enables you to create user controls that can then be used to populate the body of an MDI window. This project type was introduced with version 2.0 of the Interop Forms Toolkit and is the solution the Visual Basic team developed to support interoperation within an MDI environment.

The second project type is the VB6 InteropForm Library project. As the original project type, it was designed to enable you to create a DLL that defines a .NET form.

After you have validated that your installation is working, the next step is to create a simple Interop Form.

Creating a Simple Interop Form

Select the project type shown in Figure B-2 and rename the solution **ProVB_AppB_InteropForm**. Click OK to generate your source project files. The resulting project opens, and you can open and edit your new Windows Form. However, note that what you are creating, while it supports the Form Designer, isn't a standalone executable. If you open your project properties, you'll find that your project will build as a DLL, not a standalone executable.

Another thing to note is that as part of the generation of your project, a file named `InteropInfo.vb` is created. This file takes settings that might otherwise exist in your `AssemblyInfo.vb` file and places them here so they are a bit more apparent. The first line references the standard COM Interop classes and turns these settings off. This is important because you won't be using traditional COM Interop; you've added a new Interop class specifically for this purpose. By moving this setting into a separate file, if you do accidentally cause the AssemblyInfo.vb file to be regenerated by Visual Studio, you'll get a compile error. This is good because you can quickly and easily delete the newly duplicated line from AssemblyInfo.vb and not wonder why your project suddenly isn't working correctly. Compile errors are always better than runtime errors. The other item in this file is a declaration that extends the My namespace to include the Interop Toolbox. In general, you shouldn't make any changes to this file, but now you know what it's doing.

Opening InteropForm1.vb in the designer, you have a typical design surface for a form, on which you can add controls. Behind the scenes is the code that contains the following:

```
Imports Microsoft.InteropFormTools
<InteropForm()> _
Public Class InteropForm1
End Class
```

Code snippet from InteropForm1

As you can see, the default class definition has been decorated with an attribute indicating that this class should be considered an InteropForm. This enables the postprocessor that is used to generate your COM wrappings to recognize which type of wrapping should be applied to this class.

For now, however, go to the Form Designer, and, because this is a truly simple demo, drag a label and a TextBox control onto the display. Within the code, create the four other types of interface members you'll want in your production code: an initializer, a property, a method, and an event (in that order). The following code is placed within your class definition:

```
Public Sub New()
    ' This call is required by the Windows Form Designer.
    InitializeComponent()
    ' Add any initialization after the InitializeComponent() call.
End Sub
<InteropFormInitializer()> _
Public Sub New(ByVal label As String)
    Me.New()
    Label1.Text = label
End Sub
<InteropFormProperty()> _
Public Property TextBoxText() As String
    Get
        Return TextBox1.Text
    End Get
    Set(ByVal value As String)
        TextBox1.Text = value
    End Set
End Property
<InteropFormMethod()> _
Public Sub ChangeLabel(ByVal lbl As String)
    Label1.Text = lbl
    RaiseEvent CustomEvent(lbl)
End Sub
<InteropFormEvent()> _
Public Event CustomEvent As CustomEventSig
'Declare handler signature…
Public Delegate Sub CustomEventSig(ByVal lblText As String)
```

Code snippet from InteropForm1

For the initialization code, you'll note that first a default New constructor is created. When you define the default New constructor, it adds the call to InitializeComponent, which handles the creation of your controls within the form. Thus, when the object is initialized, you will be able to reference the controls you have placed on the form.

The next step is to create a parameterized constructor so that you can quite literally pass a parameter as part of the initialization process. Note that similar to the class itself, the exposed initialization method has an attribute as part of its declaration. Each type of class member that is to be exposed gets an attribute matching the type of that method. Thus, for the New method, the type of the attribute is InteropFormInitializer. For this simple example, the parameterized New(ByVal label As String) simply changes the text associated with the label. Finally, although this class is defined in .NET syntax, COM and VB6 don't allow parameterized New statements. Thus, when you reference this parameterized initializer, you'll find that the method name is in fact Initialize.

Next, the code defines and exposes a public property. In this case, to help simplify the code, there isn't a private member variable to hold the value; this provides an easy way for the code that creates this form to set and retrieve the value of the text box. Similarly, there is a method to allow the calling code to update the label shown on the form. Note that it has also been attributed; and after you update the label for demonstration purposes, it raises the custom event that is defined next.

That event, called CustomEvent, is defined with an attribute, but the event that is defined must also define the signature or definition of its handlers. In this case, the Delegate CustomEventSig handles a single parameter. This .NET code, as noted, provides a basic example of each of the primary types of Interop you'll want to carry out. The next step is to generate your Interop methods.

One of the key differences between an InteropForms project and an Interop User Control project is this step. Only the InteropForms project requires the generation of custom COM wrappers. To do this, access the Tools menu and select Generate InteropForm Wrapper Classes. There is no user interface; instead, the generation process will create a new directory in your project containing the InteropForm1.wrapper.vb class, as shown in Figure B-3.

 For readers developing on Vista and Windows 7: Keep in mind that registry access requires elevated permissions. You need to start Visual Studio with the Run as Administrator option on your right-click context menu. If you don't, then when you attempt to automatically register your newly built DLL as a COM component, you'll get an error, which Visual Studio reflects as a Build Error.

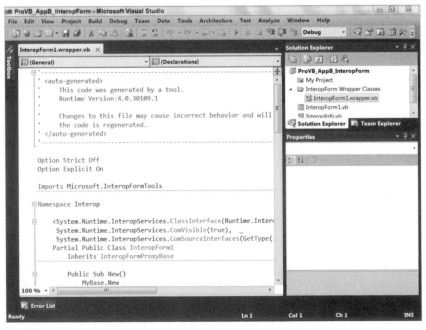

FIGURE B-3

At this point, your application is ready to be called from VB6. If you follow best practices, you'll have the VB6 integrated development environment (IDE) installed on the machine with Visual Studio 2010. In that scenario, you can immediately go to your VB6 project and reference the necessary DLLs, both the Interop Forms Toolkit DLL and your custom DLL. Otherwise, you'll need to get ready for deployment now instead of later.

Deployment

To deploy your Interop Forms project, you need a traditional MSI installation. Creating a setup project is covered in Chapter 34, so the details of creating your setup project aren't repeated here. However, note a couple of special steps. In order for your new Interop Forms project to work on the client, the client needs both the .NET Framework 2.0 redistributable and the second MSI you downloaded earlier in this chapter, microsoft.interopformsredist.msi (refer to Figure B-1). If you are using Visual Studio to create your installation package, then you can add these items as prerequisites for installing your DLL via the user interface.

The recommendation is to create a simple setup project in Visual Studio for installing your Interop Forms project and the associated prerequisites and have this run in advance of whatever legacy installation project you have. To extend an existing MSI, you need to carry out the appropriate steps for the tool generating your MSI, a subject beyond the scope of this appendix.

Debugging

When you first start planning to work with the toolkit, you might try to keep the VB6 IDE on a separate machine from your primary development machine. However, this leads to two issues. First, in order to work with the Interop Forms tools on your VB6 machine, you need to install the tools package a second time. That's a minor issue. Second, because VB6 doesn't know how to step into .NET applications, if you want to debug the Interop Form you created in .NET, you have a problem. The solution to this, of course, is to run both development environments on the same machine.

Alternatively, you can try to create a simple Windows Forms EXE that will call and initiate your Interop Forms project from within .NET. The debugging isn't perfect, of course, because you aren't actually calling your code across the correct interface, but it should enable you to find most pure .NET coding issues. You can also leverage the Debug and Trace classes, but you won't have any interactive breakpoints in that scenario.

This still leaves unresolved the issue that you can't just open Visual Studio and expect the VB6 IDE to call it when you are in Debug mode. Therefore, this section briefly discusses debugging Interop Forms Toolkit projects when you are running your VB6 application.

Once you have compiled your .NET application, you have a DLL. This DLL is then exposed to your VB6 development environment and added as another COM component in your VB6 application. However, when you debug, you can't step into this DLL from Visual Basic. Presuming you have started your Visual Basic 6.0 project so that its process is now running, your next step is to open Visual Studio and your Interop Forms project. It is hoped that you have set typical breakpoints in your source code and you might even add new breakpoints.

Next, go to the Tools menu in Visual Studio and select the Attach to Process menu item. At this point, you get a dialog containing a list of running processes. Locate the "Visual Basic 6.0.exe" process. Once you have found this process, which represents the running application in VB6, attach to this process.

At this point, you can work with your running application; and when the call is made into your .NET code, Visual Studio detects the call into the DLL and stops you on your breakpoint. In order for Visual Studio to detect the DLL call, you must be calling the same copy of your DLL that your Interop Forms project references. In other words, you can't just copy it off to some other location on your local machine for installation.

If you stop and restart your VB6 application, Visual Studio will maintain the attachment, but if you close the VB6 IDE, then you'll need to reattach the debugger in Visual Studio.

VB6 Development

Overall, the development process in VB6 is simple. Once you have either built your project or deployed it to the machine on which you have the VB IDE, you'll need to add references to both the Microsoft Interop Form Toolkit library and your custom DLL. Keep in mind that both of the DLLs must be registered on your VB6 IDE machine in order for them to be visible. If you are building on the same machine, then they are automatically visible. Once you have added references for these libraries, you can create a new instance of your Interop Form's `Form` class and call the standard methods and any custom methods you've exposed on that form.

The one key point to remember, which was mentioned earlier but bears repeating, is that if you have created a custom constructor, in order to use it, you will call an `Initialize` method on your Interop Form's `Form` class.

Final Interop Tips

As noted earlier in the book during the discussion of the WPF Interop controls, the Interop control packages aren't perfect. Each has certain limitations that reduces its desirability for the long term. To resolve this, keep track of how much of various branches you have already converted. There will be a point where it is time to convert a larger section so that you can reduce the number of different Interop DLLs that you are using.

Along these lines, note that you can't put an Interop Form and an Interop user control into the same project. Each of these items needs its own DLL; and, in fact, you should consider it a best practice to only expose the DLL for a single form or control. Similarly, don't plan on calling a VB6 form from within your Interop Form. The Interop logic was written to enable you to call .NET from VB6.

In terms of interfaces, the Interop layer was designed to support only a minimum number of interface types. In particular, the `String`, `Integer`, and `Boolean` types should be at the core of what you expect to pass in terms of data. In theory, the `Object` type is supported, which enables you to pass custom data, so you could pass a `Recordset` from .NET to VB6 or vice versa; of course, VB6 doesn't know about a `Dataset` object, so you need to reference VB6 types as the generic object. In general, the best practice is to keep your interfaces as simple as possible.

When you start the VB6 IDE with your project, it attaches to your DLL. Normally this isn't an issue until you first run your VB6 application. At this point, you can't rebuild your Interop project. The Interop project is, in fact, referenced and therefore locked by VB6. If you need to rebuild your Interop project, you need to first shut down the VB6 development environment so that your code will correctly reference your latest build. As noted previously, debugging your Interop project from VB6 isn't the most productive set of steps.

If you change any of the method attributes, you need to regenerate the Interop wrapper classes that you generated in the last step of creating your Interop Forms project. Moreover, although it wasn't covered, you can raise errors from .NET into VB6. To do this, you want to leverage the following method call on the custom `My` namespace that was defined as part of your Interop Form:

```
My.InteropToolbox.EventMessenger.RaiseApplicationEvent("CRITICAL_ERROR", _ "Error
Detail.")
```

The other runtime issue that you may encounter is that certain internal events to your .NET application will not be triggered in the same fashion that they were in VB6. Under VB6, for example, when you referenced a property on a `Form` class, this triggered the `Load` event on that class. Under .NET, the `Load` event is not fired until the form is being displayed, so you need to recognize the impact on any code that you previously set to run on the `Load` event.

The remaining issue is related to the VB6 IDE. The IDE and VB6 don't really recognize that if you have started a .NET DLL, there are other in-memory classes to release. For a deployed application, this isn't an issue because when the application is closed, all of the memory associated with the process is automatically released. When you are debugging in VB6, however, the core process is associated with the IDE, not your application. As a result, the resources are not released between debugging cycles. To ensure that they are released, you can explicitly instantiate a series of code modifications contained in the Interop help files and release the .NET resources associated with your application. The recommendation is to implement these calls only after your references with the Interop tools are functioning correctly.

USING THE POWER PACKS 3.0 TOOLS

Unlike the Interop Forms Toolkit, the Power Packs extensions are intended to facilitate some of the same development simplicity that existed in VB6 for tasks such as printing. These classes aren't meant to support Interop, they are meant to support migration in the sense that the code for creating simple geometric shapes or using the VB style of form printing could be implemented using syntax similar to that of VB6. After these Power Packs were released, the printing syntax was so popular that the Visual Basic team migrated those classes into the core features of Visual Studio 2008. The continued success of the 3.0 features led to the inclusion of the most of the 3.0 Power Packs classes in Service Pack 1 for Visual Studio 2008. These components, along with the repeater control continue to ship with Visual Studio 2010.

Similar to the Interop Forms Toolkit, the Power PacksTools are already installed for Visual Studio 2010. For previous versions of Visual Studio then can be downloaded and installed from the Microsoft downloads. If you review a typical Windows Forms project in Visual Studio 2010, you'll see the display shown in Figure B-4, which already includes the controls as part of your default Toolbox.

Unlike the Interop Forms Toolkit, there is no need to begin with a special project template. There is no COM Interop involved because the Power Packs don't target VB6. They target experienced VB developers who want to be able to continue to implement certain tasks in the same way they could in VB6.

When your application ships, you still need to ensure that you create a dependency for the Power Packs library if you aren't using the DLLs that are included with Visual Studio, but that's it. Additionally, because the Power Packs are just another set of .NET libraries, there aren't any issues related to debugging.

For the sample project shown in Figure B-4, you can create a new Windows Forms application and add the `PrintForm` control to it. Visual Studio 2010 has a Toolbox section for the Visual Basic Power Packs, showing the `OvalShape` and `RectangleShape` shape controls along with the `LineShape`, `Data Repeater` and `PrintForm` controls, as shown in Figure B-4.

Add a `RectangleShape` to the upper section of the display and an `OvalShape` to the center of the display. Without getting into pages of details here, using the Visual Studio designer, you should customize the look and feel of the display by adding a variety of controls. Take some time to color and fill the shape controls with a solid color. The gradient colors are defined by selecting a fill color (Coral), a FillGradientColor (Navy), a FillGradientStyle (Horizontal), and a FillStyle (Solid). All of this can and should be done within the Visual Studio designer to achieve a display similar to what is shown in Figure B-5.

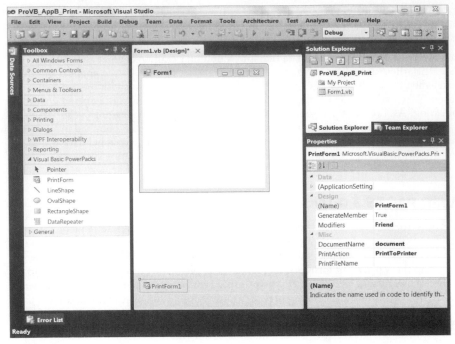

FIGURE B-4

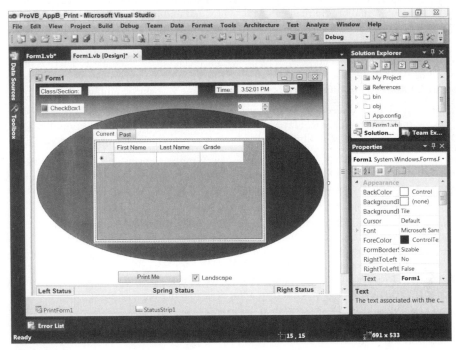

FIGURE B-5

The application should build. The next step is to ensure that the check box in the lower-right center, labeled "Landscape" in the figure, is checked. Having done this, label the button in the bottom center of the display "Print Me" and double-click it in the Design view to trigger the automatic event handler generation.

The only code needed for this printing demonstration is placed within the handler for this button. The code hides the button, determines whether or not the Landscape check box is checked, and uses the Power Packs `PrintForm` control to Print Preview the document. Once this is completed, the Print Me button is made visible again:

```vb
Private Sub ButtonPrintForm_Click(ByVal sender As System.Object,
                ByVal e As System.EventArgs) Handles ButtonPrintForm.Click
    ' Hide the print button since you don't want to see it in the output.
    ButtonPrintForm.Visible = False
    ' Set the printing to landscape mode by default
    PrintForm1.PrinterSettings.DefaultPageSettings.Landscape =
                                            CheckBox2.Checked
    ' Update the print action to PrintPreview so instead of wasting paper
    ' we see what the output would look like if sent to a printer.
    PrintForm1.PrintAction = Printing.PrintAction.PrintToPreview
    ' Execute the print logic.
    PrintForm1.Print(Me,
            PowerPacks.Printing.PrintForm.PrintOption.ClientAreaOnly)
    'PrintForm1.Print()
    ' Restore the print button
    ButtonPrintForm.Visible = True
End Sub
```

Code snippet from Form1

The code shows how you can reference the `PrinterSettings` property, which contains the page settings to change details regarding how the page is printed. The `PrintAction` defines what the control should do. There are three options: print to the default/selected printer, print to a file, or use the Print Preview window. In this case, displaying the results (print preview) is the most useful option.

The next line is all you need by default to print the current window. Note that this control doesn't call the form to determine what is visible on the form. Instead, it essentially captures the current screenshot of the form for printing.

The current code uses the `ClientAreaOnly` option, which you are encouraged to test. If you open and resize this project so that it is fairly wide, and print in profile mode, you'll see how the control truncates the printed image (see Figure B-6).

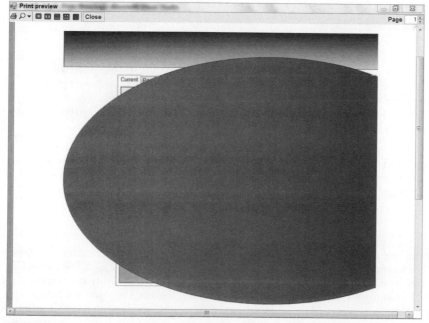

FIGURE B-6

As shown in Figure B-6, the default behavior is to show the contents of the screen without the border displayed. Unfortunately, in this case the printout shows less than the full window contents. However, don't stop at this option; try out other options. The various display options do not always capture the screen accurately, so test. In some cases the only things visible in the Print Preview window are the shape controls.

However, before you print again, go to the print event handler and comment out the parameterized print line and uncomment the default print line. In this case, specify the window, which is Me, and then add one of the print options. The results, which are now correct, are shown in Figure B-7.

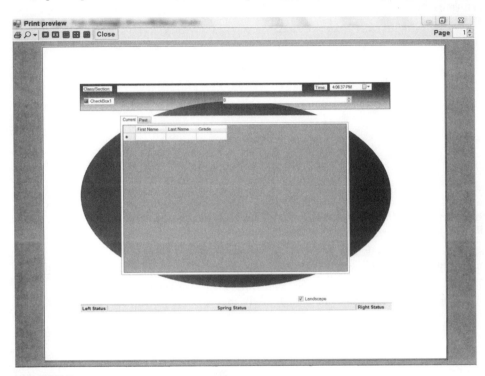

FIGURE B-7

Overall, the Power Packs shape controls enable you to easily add a custom look to your otherwise gray forms. The controls are somewhat limited, but if you want a quick and easy way to add some graphics, they do the trick. Similarly, the Print control is a quick and easy way to create a hard copy of what your application is displaying. However, keep in mind that the Print control sacrifices capabilities and customizations in order to provide a simple interface.

The Power Packs 3.0 provide tools that VB6 developers can leverage for migrating an application; and for a rapid application design (RAD) prototype, they provide a dynamic and visually interesting display. Just keep in mind that when it comes to the shape controls, if you need any sort of fancy graphics, then it is recommended that you leverage the graphical capabilities provided as part of WPF.

SUMMARY

This appendix covered the Visual Basic Power Packs. This set of off-cycle release tools enables experienced Visual Basic developers to leverage their knowledge and existing code with the new capabilities of .NET. The Visual Basic team has created two downloadable packages that improve your ability to manage COM to .NET Interop migration and to continue to print and create graphics the same way you did before. As with all Interop-focused solutions, there are key limitations in working with the Interop Forms Toolkit, but in general it provides classes that will help you if you need to migrate an existing application in a controlled and cost-effective manner. In particular, this appendix highlighted the following:

- The focus of the Visual Basic Power Packs
- How to integrate Visual Basic 2010 forms with Visual Basic 6.0 applications
- Leveraging printing and drawing controls that behave similarly to those in Visual Basic 6.0

Although there are currently only two Power Packs, you can keep track of what is occurring in the Visual Basic Developer Center at http://msdn.microsoft.com/en-us/vbasic/default.aspx.

Workflow 2008 Specifics

As discussed in Chapter 26, Windows Workflow Foundation (WF) has changed substantially in the .NET Framework 4. The models used to organize your workflows have changed, and many of the older activities do not have counterparts in the new version. This appendix discusses the version of WF supported by the .NET Framework versions 3.0 and 3.5 (i.e., Visual Basic 2005 with .NET Framework 3.0 and Visual Basic 2008). This information is retained in this edition for those users who still need to maintain existing WF solutions using these older versions. For new applications, the new model is highly recommended. Here, the older style of building workflows is called Windows Workflow Foundation 3.x (or just WF 3.x).

BUILDING WORKFLOWS

The actual workflow files in WF 3.x are XML files written in a version of XAML. This is the same XAML used to describe Windows Presentation Foundation (WPF) files. (See Chapter 17 for more details on WPF.) They describe the actions to perform within the workflow, and the relationship between those actions. You can create a workflow using only a text editor, but Visual Studio makes creating these workflows much easier. It provides a graphical designer that enables developers to visually design the workflow, creating the XAML in the background. The following code shows a section of the XAML for a workflow:

```
<RuleDefinitions xmlns="http://schemas.microsoft.com/winfx/2006/xaml/workflow">
  <RuleDefinitions.Conditions>
    <RuleExpressionCondition Name="TranslationCallWorked">
      <RuleExpressionCondition.Expression>
        <ns0:CodeBinaryOperatorExpression Operator="ValueEquality"
         xmlns:ns0="clr-namespace:System.CodeDom;Assembly=System, Version=2.0.0.0,
         Culture=neutral, PublicKeyToken=b77a5c561934e089">
          <ns0:CodeBinaryOperatorExpression.Left>
            <ns0:CodeBinaryOperatorExpression Operator="ValueEquality">
              <ns0:CodeBinaryOperatorExpression.Left>
                <ns0:CodeMethodInvokeExpression>
                  <ns0:CodeMethodInvokeExpression.Parameters>
                    <ns0:CodeFieldReferenceExpression
                      FieldName="OutputTextProperty">
                      <ns0:CodeFieldReferenceExpression.TargetObject>
                        <ns0:CodeTypeReferenceExpression
                          Type="TranslateActivity.TranslateActivity" />
                      </ns0:CodeFieldReferenceExpression.TargetObject>
```

```
              </ns0:CodeFieldReferenceExpression>
           </ns0:CodeMethodInvokeExpression.Parameters>
           <ns0:CodeMethodInvokeExpression.Method>
              <ns0:CodeMethodReferenceExpression MethodName="GetValue">
                 <ns0:CodeMethodReferenceExpression.TargetObject>
                    <ns0:CodeThisReferenceExpression />
                 </ns0:CodeMethodReferenceExpression.TargetObject>
              </ns0:CodeMethodReferenceExpression>
           </ns0:CodeMethodInvokeExpression.Method>
        </ns0:CodeMethodInvokeExpression>
     </ns0:CodeBinaryOperatorExpression.Left>
     <ns0:CodeBinaryOperatorExpression.Right>
        <ns0:CodePrimitiveExpression />
     </ns0:CodeBinaryOperatorExpression.Right>
  </ns0:CodeBinaryOperatorExpression>
</ns0:CodeBinaryOperatorExpression.Left>
<ns0:CodeBinaryOperatorExpression.Right>
  <ns0:CodePrimitiveExpression>
     <ns0:CodePrimitiveExpression.Value>
        <ns1:Boolean xmlns:ns1="clr-namespace:System;Assembly=mscorlib,
           Version=2.0.0.0, Culture=neutral,
           PublicKeyToken=b77a5c561934e089">false</ns1:Boolean>
     </ns0:CodePrimitiveExpression.Value>
  </ns0:CodePrimitiveExpression>
</ns0:CodeBinaryOperatorExpression.Right>
  </ns0:CodeBinaryOperatorExpression>
     </RuleExpressionCondition.Expression>
  </RuleExpressionCondition>
     </RuleDefinitions.Conditions>
  </RuleDefinitions>
```

The workflow comprises a number of rule definitions. Each definition includes activities, conditions, and expressions. Activities are the steps involved in the workflow. They are executed based on the workflow's design and the conditions included. Conditions control the behavior of the workflow; they are evaluated and may result in code running. Finally, expressions describe the individual tests used as part of the conditions. For example, each side of an equality condition would be expressions. When building the workflow by hand, you are responsible for creating the markup. Fortunately, Visual Studio writes it as you design your workflow.

Windows Workflow Foundation 3.x supports two main styles of creating workflows: *sequential* and *state machine*. Sequential workflows (see Figure C-1) are the classic flowchart style of process. They begin when some action initiates the workflow, such as the submission of an expense report or a user decision to check out a shopping cart. The workflow then continues stepwise through the activities until it reaches the end. There may be branching or looping, but generally the flow moves down the workflow. Sequential workflows are best when a set series of steps is needed for the workflow.

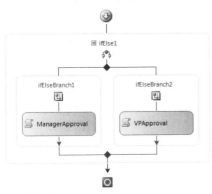

FIGURE C-1

State machine workflows (see Figure C-2) are less linear than sequential workflows. They are typically used when the data moves through a series of steps toward completion. At each step, the state of the application has a particular value. Transitions move the state between steps. This style of workflow is common in hardware systems. One example of a state machine workflow that most people are familiar with (unfortunately) is voice mail. Most voice-mail systems are collections of states, represented by a menu. You move between the states by pressing the keys of your phone. State machine workflows can be useful when the process you are modeling is not necessarily linear. There may still be some required steps, but generally the flow may iterate between the steps for some time before completion.

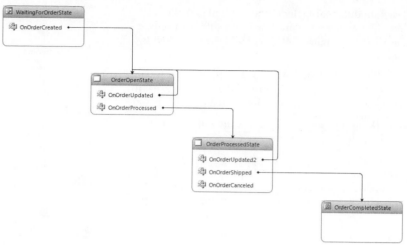

FIGURE C-2

A good way to identify a candidate for a state machine workflow is determining whether the process is better defined in terms of modes, rather than a linear series of steps. For example, a shopping site is a classic example of a state machine. The user is either in browse mode or cart view mode. Selecting checkout would likely initiate a sequential workflow, as the steps in that process are more easily described in a linear fashion.

A Simple Workflow

As with any other programming endeavor, the best way to understand WF is to create a simple workflow and extend it incrementally. Start Visual Studio and create a new Sequential Workflow Console application (see Figure C-3) called HelloWorkflow. Note that you will need to target the .NET Framework 3.5 (or 3.0) in order to see this project type when you are creating the new project. The dropdown list at the top of the New Project dialog (highlighted in Figure C-3) allows you to select the version of the .NET Framework used by the project. Select .NET Framework 3.5 from the list.

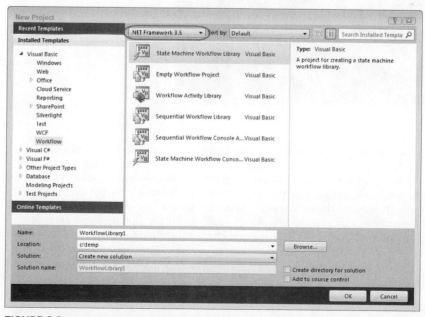

FIGURE C-3

This project creates two files: a module that includes the Main file for the application and the workflow. The sequential workflow begins life with only two steps: start and finish, as shown in Figure C-4. You build the workflow by adding steps between these two.

To begin, drag a Code activity between the start and finish markers. Note that even if you are targeting the .NET Framework 3.5, most of the controls are still located within the Windows Workflow 3.0 section of the Toolbox.

Notice the red exclamation mark on the new activity in the diagram (shown in grayscale in Figure C-5). WF makes heavy use of these tips to help you set required properties.

Click the code tip and select the menu item "Property 'ExecuteCode' is not set." This will bring up the Properties window for the Code activity. Enter **SayGreetings** and press Enter. This brings up the code window for the activity. Add the following code:

Available for
download on
Wrox.com

```vb
Private Sub SayGreetings(ByVal sender As System.Object, _
   ByVal e As System.EventArgs)
      Console.WriteLine("Hello world, from workflow")
      Console.WriteLine("Press enter to continue")
      Console.ReadLine()
End Sub
```

FIGURE C-4

FIGURE C-5

Code snippet from HelloWorld

Notice that coding the action for the activity is the same as any other event. Run the project to see the console window (see Figure C-6), along with the message you should be expecting.

FIGURE C-6

While trivial, the project makes a useful test bed for experimenting with the various activities. Add an `IfElse` activity before the `Code` activity. `IfElse` activities are one of the main ways to add logic and control of flow to your workflows. They have a condition property that determines when each half of the flow will be executed. The condition may be code that executes or a declarative rule. For this example, declarative rules are enough. You create these rules in the Select Condition Editor (see Figure C-7). To display the Select Condition Editor, select Declarative Rule Condition for the Condition property of the first `ifElseBranchActivity` component. Once you have selected Declarative Rule Condition, you can click the ellipsis on the `ConditionName` property to display the dialog.

Clicking New brings up the Rule Condition Editor (see Figure C-8). This enables you to create simple expressions that will be used by the `IfElse` activity to determine flow.

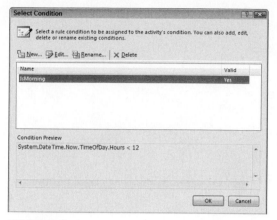

FIGURE C-7

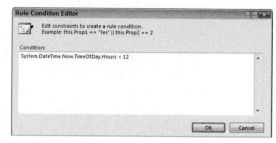

FIGURE C-8

Click the New button on the Select Condition Editor to add a new rule to the `If` half of the `IfElse` activity to determine whether the current time is before noon:

```
System.DateTime.Now.TimeOfDay.Hours < 12
```

Right-click on the activity and select Add Branch to create a third branch to the `IfElse` activity. Set the condition for this one as you did for the first activity, but use 18 for the value.

Add a Code activity to each of the three sections of the diagram (see Figure C-9). You will use these activities to affect the message that is displayed. Assign the properties as follows:

ACTIVITY	PROPERTY	VALUE
codeActivity2	ExecuteCode	SetMessageMorning
codeActivity3	ExecuteCode	SetMessageAfternoon
codeActivity4	ExecuteCode	SetMessageEvening

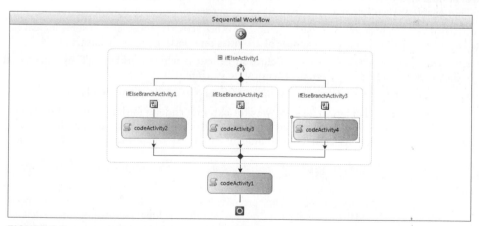

FIGURE C-9

Finally, update the code for the SayGreetings method created earlier to include the new `Message` variable, and the methods used to set the value.

```
Public class Workflow1
    Inherits SequentialWorkflowActivity
    Private Message As String
```

```
      Private Sub SayGreetings(ByVal sender As System.Object, _
          ByVal e As System.EventArgs)
          Console.WriteLine(Message & ", from workflow")
          Console.WriteLine("Press enter to continue")
          Console.ReadLine()
      End Sub
      Private Sub SetMessageMorning(ByVal sender As System.Object, _
        ByVal e As System.EventArgs)
          Message = "Good morning"
      End Sub
      Private Sub SetMessageAfternoon(ByVal sender As System.Object, _
        ByVal e As System.EventArgs)
          Message = "Good afternoon"
      End Sub
      Private Sub SetMessageEvening(ByVal sender As System.Object, _
        ByVal e As System.EventArgs)
          Message = "Good night"
      End Sub
  End Class
```

Each of the three `SetMessage` methods changes the greeting as appropriate. The final greeting is displayed in the `SayGreetings` method. Run the project again. You should be greeted appropriately for the time of day.

While this workflow is probably overkill to generate a simple message, the example does show many of the common steps used in defining a workflow. Workflows are composed of multiple activities. Many activities can in turn be composed of other activities. Activities may use declarative properties, or code may be executed as needed.

Standard Activities

The standard activities for WF 3.x are defined within the `System.Workflow.Activities` namespace. These activities can be divided into five major categories:

➤ **Activities that communicate with external code** — These activities are either called by external code to initiate a workflow or used to call to external code as part of a workflow.

➤ **Control of flow activities** — These activities are the equivalent of Visual Basic's `If` statement or `While` loop. They enable the workflow to branch or repeat as needed to carry out a step.

➤ **Scope activities** — These activities group a number of other activities together into some logical element. This is usually done to mark a number of activities that participate in a transaction.

➤ **State activities** — These activities are used exclusively in state machine workflows. They represent the state of the process involved as part of the overall state machine.

➤ **Action activities** — These activities perform some action as part of the overall workflow.

In order for a workflow to begin, there must be some way for external code to initiate it. In addition, a workflow would be limited if there were no way for the workflow to execute external code and/or Web services. The standard activities that are used to communicate with external code include the following:

ACTIVITY	DESCRIPTION
CallExternalMethod	As the name implies, this activity calls an external method. The activity requires two properties. The first property identifies an interface shared by the workflow and the external code. The second property identifies the method on that interface that will be called. If the method requires additional parameters, they appear on the property grid after setting the other two properties. This activity is frequently used in combination with the `HandleExternalEvent` activity. This activity executes the external method synchronously, so be cautious when calling external methods that take a long time to execute.

ACTIVITY	DESCRIPTION
HandleExternalEvent	Receives a trigger from an external block of code. This is a commonly used activity to initiate a workflow when the workflow is running in the context of a Windows Forms or ASP.NET application. As with the `CallExternalMethod` activity, it requires at least two properties. The first property identifies a shared interface and the second property identifies the event on that interface that will be received.
InvokeWebService	Calls an external Web service. You assign a WSDL file to the activity and it generates a proxy class for the Web service. You must also identify the method on the class that will be called. The `SessionId` property is used to identify the session that will be used for the requests. All requests with the same `SessionId` value share the session. If the `SessionId` is blank, then this activity creates a new session per request.
InvokeWorkflow	Calls another workflow. This is a useful activity for chaining multiple workflows together, reducing the complexity of each workflow. Keep in mind that this external workflow is called synchronously, so the original workflow will not be processed until the called workflow completes.
WebServiceInput	Receives an incoming Web service request. You must publish the workflow containing this activity for it to work. You publish the workflow by selecting Publish as Web Service from the Project menu. This generates a new Web Service project that includes the output from the workflow project as well as an ASMX file that serves as the address for the workflow.
WebServiceOutput	Produces the output for a Web service request. This activity is used in partnership with the `WebServiceInput` activity.
WebServiceFault	Triggers a Web service error. This is used in partnership with the `WebServiceInput` activity to signal an error with the Web service call.

All programming languages need some form of flow control to regulate the applications. Visual Basic includes language elements such as `If..Else`, `Do..While`, `For..Next`, and `Select Case` to perform these actions. WF includes a number of activities to perform similar actions, although the options are more limited:

ACTIVITY	DESCRIPTION
IfElse	Provides for executing two or more different workflow paths based on the status of a condition. The condition may be code or an expression. This is a commonly used activity to branch a workflow.
Listen	Provides for executing two or more different workflow paths based on an event. The path chosen is selected by the first event that occurs. This is a useful activity for monitoring a class that could generate multiple events (such as a class that could either approve or reject a request).
Policy	Provides for executing multiple rules. Each rule is a condition with some resulting action. This activity provides a way to group multiple related rules into a single activity.
Replicator	Enables the workflow to create multiple instances of an activity for processing. The resulting child activities may run serially or in parallel. This is an excellent way to divide a large task: For example, you could have the `Replicator` activity create multiple child activities that are responsible for mailing a newsletter to a large list. The child activities could run in parallel, dividing the list into smaller groups for faster processing.
While	Loops the workflow until a condition has been met. The condition may be the result of code or an expression. This is typically used to receive multiple input values or to process multiple requests, such as a batch job.

Several composite activities may cooperate to complete a single logical action by grouping other activities:

ACTIVITY	DESCRIPTION
CompensatableSequence	Similar to the Sequence activity (see below), this activity differs in that it supports "undoing" the child activities. You can think of this in terms of a transaction: If one child activity fails, then the completed activities must be undone. The CompensatableSequence activity includes handles that enable the developer to perform this correction.
ConditionedActivityGroup	Includes a number of child activities that are run based on a condition. All child activities will execute until some defined condition occurs. This provides a means of grouping a number of related activities into a single activity.
EventDriven	Responds to an external event to initiate a set of activities. This is similar to the HandleExternalEvent activity, but the events are internal to the workflow. This activity is commonly used in a state machine workflow to move between the states.
FaultHandler	Enables handling an error within a workflow. You use the FaultHandler activity to either correct or report the error gracefully. For example, a timeout may occur, triggering a fault condition in the workflow. This handler would contain other activities that are responsible for an alternate method of processing the item.
Parallel	Contains a series of child activities that run concurrently. You should only use this if either the child activities do not affect the data or the order of change is not important.
Sequence	Contains a series of child activities that run in order. This is the default model for a workflow. Each child activity must complete before the next one begins.

State activities represent the current state of the data and process for the workflow. They are only used within state machine workflows:

ACTIVITY	DESCRIPTION
State	Represents the current state of the workflow. For example, in a workflow driving a voice-mail system, the state would represent the current menu item selected by the client.
StateFinalization	Provides an activity to handle the actions needed as a given state is completed. This would provide a place to record the user's selection or to free up resources used by the state.
StateInitialization	Provides an activity to handle the actions needed before the given state is entered. This would enable the creation of any data or code needed to prepare for the state functioning.

The final group of activities are those that perform some action. You already saw this activity type in the form of the CodeActivity. These activities are the cornerstone of any workflow. The standard activities in this group include the following:

ACTIVITY	DESCRIPTION
Code	Enables custom Visual Basic code to be performed at a stage in the workflow. You can use these wherever you need to perform some action not done by another activity. Whenever you use one of these — especially if you use the same type of code frequently — you should consider moving the code into a custom activity.
Compensate	Enables custom code to undo a previous action. This is typically done if an error occurs within the workflow.

ACTIVITY	DESCRIPTION
Delay	Pauses the flow of the workflow. This is typically used to schedule some event. For example, you might have a workflow that is responsible for printing a daily report. The Delay activity could be used to schedule this printout so that it is ready as the workers come in to read it. You can either set the delay explicitly by setting the TimeoutDuration property or set it via code using the event identified in the InitializeTimeoutDuration property.
Suspend	Temporarily stops the workflow. This is usually due to some extraordinary event that you would want an administrator or developer to correct. The workflow will continue to receive requests, but not complete them past the Suspend activity. The administrator may then resume the workflow to complete processing.
Terminate	Ends the workflow immediately. This should only be done in extreme situations such as when the workflow is not capable of any further processing (e.g., it has lost the connection to a database or other needed resource).
Throw	Creates an exception that can be caught by the code hosting the workflow. This provides a means of propagating an error from the workflow to the containing code.

Building Custom Activities

In addition to the standard activity library, WF supports extensibility through the creation of custom activities. Creating custom activities is a matter of creating a new class that inherits from Activity (or one of the existing child classes). Several available attributes enable customization of the activity and how it appears when you use it in your workflows.

Creating custom activities is the primary means of extending WF. You might use custom activities to simplify a complex workflow, grouping a number of common activities into a single new activity. Alternatively, custom activities can create a workflow that is easier to understand, using terms that are more familiar to the developers and business experts. Finally, custom activities can be used to support software used within the business, such as activities to communicate with a existing system.

So you can see the steps required for creating a custom activity, the next exercise creates a simple activity that wraps the Google translation service. Create a new project using the Workflow Activity Library template, called TranslationActivity. Again, you will have to target the .NET Framework 3.5 to view the correct template. This project will create a DLL that contains the activities you create. It will include a single custom activity initially. This activity inherits from SequenceActivity, so it might include multiple child activities. You can change this as needed, but it's a good enough default for most activities. Drag a Code activity onto the designer. This activity does the actual translation work.

Because the new activity will be used to convert between a number of set language pairs, create an enumeration containing the valid options. This enumeration can be expanded as new options become available:

Available for download on Wrox.com

```
Public Enum TranslationOptions As Integer
    EnglishToFrench
    EnglishToSpanish
    EnglishToGerman
    EnglishToItalian
    EnglishToRussian
    EnglishToChinese
    FrenchToEnglish
    SpanishToEnglish
    GermanToEnglish
    ItalianToEnglish
    RussianToEnglish
    ChineseToEnglish
End Enum
```

Code snippet from TranslateActivity

The new activity has three properties: the input text, a language pair that defines the source and target languages, and the output text (the latter being a read-only property). You can create properties normally in an activity, but it is beneficial to create them so that they participate in the workflow and are available to other activities. In order to do this, use the following pattern to describe your properties:

```
Public Shared SomeProperty As DependencyProperty = _
    DependencyProperty.Register("PropertyName", _
    GetType(ReturnType), _
    GetType(ClassName))
    Public Property PropertyName () As ReturnType
    Get
        Return CType(MyBase.GetValue(SomeProperty), _
            ReturnType)
    End Get
    Set(ByVal value As ReturnType)
        MyBase.SetValue(SomeProperty, value)
    End Set
End Property
```

Code snippet from TranslateActivity

The initial shared field of type `DependencyProperty` identifies the field that will be used to communicate with other activities. `DependencyProperty` is a common type used in WF programming, enabling easier communication between nested types. The `Public` property enables the more common use of the property. Notice that it stores the data in the shared property between all instances of the type.

As described, there are three properties in the translate activity:

```
Public Shared InputTextProperty As DependencyProperty = _
    DependencyProperty.Register("InputText", _
    GetType(System.String), _
    GetType(TranslateActivity))
Public Shared TranslationTypeProperty As DependencyProperty = _
    DependencyProperty.Register("TranslationType", _
    GetType(TranslationOptions), _
    GetType(TranslateActivity))
Public Shared OutputTextProperty As DependencyProperty = _
    DependencyProperty.Register("OutputText", _
    GetType(System.String), _
    GetType(TranslateActivity))
<DesignerSerializationVisibility(DesignerSerializationVisibility.Visible)> _
    <BrowsableAttribute(True)> _
    <DescriptionAttribute("Text to be translated")> _
    Public Property InputText() As String
    Get
        Return CStr(MyBase.GetValue(InputTextProperty))
    End Get
    Set(ByVal value As String)
        MyBase.SetValue(InputTextProperty, value)
    End Set
End Property
<DesignerSerializationVisibility(DesignerSerializationVisibility.Visible)> _
<BrowsableAttribute(False)> _
<DescriptionAttribute("Translated text")> _
Public ReadOnly Property OutputText() As String
    Get
        Return CStr(MyBase.GetValue(OutputTextProperty))
    End Get
End Property
<DesignerSerializationVisibility(DesignerSerializationVisibility.Visible)> _
<BrowsableAttribute(True)> _
<DescriptionAttribute("Language pair to use for the translation")> _
```

```
      Public Property TranslationType() As TranslationOptions
          Get
              Return CType(MyBase.GetValue(TranslationTypeProperty), TranslationOptions)
          End Get
          Set(ByVal value As TranslationOptions)
              MyBase.SetValue(TranslationTypeProperty, value)
          End Set
      End Property
```

Code snippet from TranslateActivity

While you may be tempted to not include the line continuation characters on some of these long lines, remember that you are targeting .NET Framework 3.5, so you will need to continue to use line continuation characters here.

Attributes are added to the properties to enable communication with the designer. The core translation method is assigned to the ExecuteCode property of the Code activity. It calls the Google AJAX translation service:

Available for
download on
Wrox.com

```
      Private Const SERVICE_URL As String = _
      "http://ajax.googleapis.com/ajax/services/language/translate"
      Private Sub Translate(ByVal sender As System.Object, _
          ByVal e As System.EventArgs)
          Dim reqString As String = _
            String.Format("{0}?v=1.0&q={1}&langpair={2}", _
            SERVICE_URL, _
            Encode(Me.InputText), _
            BuildLanguageClause(Me.TranslationType))
          Dim respString As String
          Dim req As HttpWebRequest
          Try
              req = CType(WebRequest.Create(reqString), HttpWebRequest)
              req.ProtocolVersion = HttpVersion.Version10
              Using resp As HttpWebResponse = CType(req.GetResponse(), _
                HttpWebResponse)
                  If resp.StatusCode = HttpStatusCode.OK Then
                      respString = ExtractText(resp.GetResponseStream)
                  Else
                      respString = "Error translating text"
                  End If
              End Using
              If Not String.IsNullOrEmpty(respString) Then
                  MyBase.SetValue(OutputTextProperty, _
                    Decode(respString))
              End If
          Catch ex As Exception
              Console.WriteLine("Error translating text: " & ex.Message)
          End Try
      End Sub
```

Code snippet from TranslateActivity

A typical request to the Google AJAX translation service is performed using the service URL, available at http://ajax.googleapis.com/ajax/services/language/translate. You can get more information on this API at http://code.google.com/apis/ajaxlanguage/documentation. The service then returns a JSON (JavaScript Object Notation) response. A typical response looks like

```
{"responseData": {
 "translatedText":"Ciao mondo"
},
"responseDetails": null, "responseStatus": 200}
```

where the result is the text after the "translatedText" label. You could use normal string handling to find the resulting text. Instead, I've used the JSON handling code from the System.ServiceModel.Web.dll. To use these classes, you need to include references to the .NET assemblies System.ServiceModel.Web.dll, and System.Runtime.Serialization.dll.

The routines used by the Translate method are as follows:

```vb
Private _langOptions As New List(Of String)()
Public Sub New()
    ' This call is required by the Windows Form Designer.
    InitializeComponent()
    ' Add any initialization after the InitializeComponent() call.
    _langOptions.Add("en|fr")
    _langOptions.Add("en|es")
    _langOptions.Add("en|de")
    _langOptions.Add("en|it")
    _langOptions.Add("en|zn-CH")
    _langOptions.Add("en|ru")
    _langOptions.Add("fr|en")
    _langOptions.Add("es|en")
    _langOptions.Add("de|en")
    _langOptions.Add("it|en")
    _langOptions.Add("ru|en")
    _langOptions.Add("zn-CH|en")
End Sub
    Private Function Encode(ByVal value As String) As String
        Return Web.HttpUtility.UrlEncode(value)
    End Function
    Private Function Decode(ByVal value As String) As String
        Return Web.HttpUtility.HtmlDecode(value)
    End Function
    Private Function BuildLanguageClause( _
        ByVal languages As TranslationOptions) As String
        Dim result As String = String.Empty
        result = Encode(_langOptions.Item(languages))
        Return result
    End Function
    Private Function ExtractText(ByVal data As Stream) As String
        Dim result As String = String.Empty
        Dim reader As XmlDictionaryReader = _
            JsonReaderWriterFactory.CreateJsonReader(data, _
            XmlDictionaryReaderQuotas.Max)

        While reader.Read
            If reader.Name = "translatedText" Then
                result = reader.ReadElementString()
            End If
        End While
        Return result
    End Function
```

Code snippet from TranslateActivity

The _langOptions list is used to track the strings needed by the various language pairs. This is used by the BuildLanguageClause method to write the appropriate pair to the posted data. The order of the items in the TranslationOptions enumeration matches the order in which items are added to the list, so the BuildLanguageOptions method simply does a lookup into the list.

The ExtractText function uses a XmlDictionaryReader to extract the translated text. This is created using the JsonReaderWriterFactory class. To use these classes, you also need to add a couple of imports to the Translate.vb file:

```
Imports System.Net
Imports System.Runtime.Serialization.Json
Imports System.Xml
Imports System.IO
```

Code snippet from TranslateActivity

The resulting activity can now be compiled and included in other workflows. Just as with custom controls, you can add this DLL to the Toolbox using the Choose Toolbox Items dialog after it has been compiled. If the Workflow Activity project is in the same solution as the workflow, it will be automatically added to the Toolbox after it has been compiled. Figure C-10 shows the `Translate` activity added to the earlier example.

Recall that the Message field was used to store the message you wanted the workflow to generate. This is the text you want to translate. Select the `TranslateActivity` and click the ellipses button on the `InputText` property in the property grid to bring up the `Bind` property dialog (see Figure C-11). This enables you to visually connect the Message field to the input of the `TranslateActivity`.

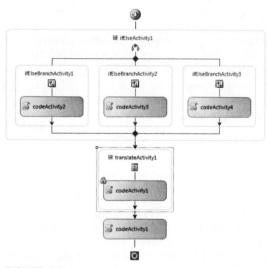

FIGURE C-10

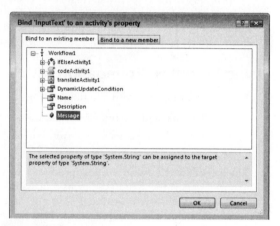

FIGURE C-11

The last change to the workflow is to update the text you output. Change the code for the `SayGreetings` method to display the `OutputText` of the `TranslateActivity`, as shown here:

```
Private Sub SayGreetings(ByVal sender As System.Object, _
    ByVal e As System.EventArgs)
    Console.WriteLine(translateActivity1.OutputText & ", from workflow")
    Console.WriteLine("Press enter to continue")
    Console.ReadLine()
End Sub
```

Code snippet from HelloWorkflowTranslate

Select the `TranslationType` and run the test project. Depending on the time of day and the language selected, you should see something similar to what is shown in Figure C-12.

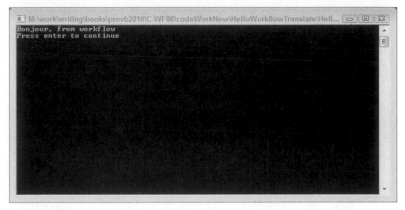

FIGURE C-12

USING WORKFLOWS WITH OTHER APPLICATIONS

Workflows are not typically standalone applications, or run as part of a console application, although this is an excellent way to develop them initially. Usually workflows are created to work within some larger application, so you need to integrate your workflow with the rest of your application, whether it is a Windows Forms application or ASP.NET.

Using Workflow Foundation with Windows Forms

When combining WF with Windows Forms, there are three main points of contact:

➤   hosting (and starting) the workflow

➤   setting parameters for the workflow

➤   getting data out of the workflow.

The workflow runs within a host process. This process may be the Windows Forms process itself or an external one. If the Windows Forms process is hosting the workflow, then the workflow only exists as long as the application is running. The alternative is a workflow hosted within a Windows Service or another Windows Forms application. In this case, your application needs to use some form of interprocess communication to communicate with the workflow. Typically, communication between the two applications would take the form of sockets; remoting; or the application that hosts the workflow needs to initialize the WF runtime, load the workflow, and start it. In addition, the workflow host may initialize event handlers for the events that the WF runtime will throw. The following code shows an example of hosting the WF runtime and loading a workflow:

```
Imports System.Workflow.Activities
Imports System.Workflow.ComponentModel
Imports System.Workflow.Runtime
Public Class MainForm
    Private WithEvents wr As WorkflowRuntime
    Private wf As WorkflowInstance
    Private Sub TranslateButton_Click(ByVal sender As System.Object, _
        ByVal e As System.EventArgs) _
        Handles TranslateButton.Click
        If wr Is Nothing Then
            wr = New WorkflowRuntime
            wr.StartRuntime()
        End If
        'load a new instance of the workflow
        Me.EventList.Items.Add("Translating: " & Me.MessageField.Text)
        Dim parms As New Dictionary(Of String, Object)
        parms.Add("Message", Me.MessageField.Text)
```

```
            wf = wr.CreateWorkflow(GetType(TranslateWorkflow.SimpleWorkflow), parms)
            'start the workflow
            wf.Start()
        End Sub
        Private Sub MainForm_FormClosing(ByVal sender As Object, _
            ByVal e As System.Windows.Forms.FormClosingEventArgs) _
            Handles Me.FormClosing
            If wr IsNot Nothing Then
                If wr.IsStarted Then
                    wr.StopRuntime()
                End If
            End If
        End Sub
```

Code snippet from HelloWorldWinForms

In addition, you have to load references to the three workflow DLLs, and to the assembly that holds the workflow you want to create. Notice that you must create and start the WF runtime before you can load and start workflows. While the preceding code creates only a single instance of a workflow, you can create multiple instances from a single application. Stopping the runtime is not absolutely necessary but gives you better control when the resources used by the WF runtime are freed.

The second step in working with WF and Windows Forms is providing parameters to the workflow. This is done by supplying a `Dictionary` when you create the workflow. The items in the `Dictionary` should match the public properties of the workflow. This changes the code used to create the workflow in the preceding sample as follows:

Available for download on Wrox.com

```
'load a new instance of the workflow
Dim parms As New Dictionary(Of String, Object)
parms.Add("Message", Me.MessageField.Text)
wf = wr.CreateWorkflow(GetType(TranslateWorkflow.SimpleWorkflow), parms)
```

Code snippet from HelloWorldWinForms

By using a `Dictionary` with an `Object` value, any type of data can be supplied to the workflow. This provides flexibility in terms of the number and type of parameters you supply to the workflow, including changing the parameters over time.

The final step when working with WF and Windows Forms is retrieving data from the workflow. This is slightly more difficult than it may first seem because the workflow runs on a separate thread from the Windows Forms code. Therefore, the workflow can't directly access the controls on a form, and vice versa. The communication between the two is best performed by having the workflow generate events. The following code receives the `WorkflowCompleted` event and updates the `ListBox` control on the form:

Available for download on Wrox.com

```
        Private Sub wr_WorkflowCompleted(ByVal sender As Object, _
            ByVal e As System.Workflow.Runtime.WorkflowCompletedEventArgs) _
            Handles wr.WorkflowCompleted
            If Me. EventList.InvokeRequired Then
                Me. EventList.Invoke(New EventHandler(Of WorkflowCompletedEventArgs)( _
                        AddressOf Me.wr_WorkflowCompleted), _
                        New Object() {sender, e})
            Else
                Me.EventList.Items.Add("Translation: " & _
                    e.OutputParameters("Message").ToString())
            End If
        End Sub
```

Code snippet from HelloWorldWinForms

Recall that the workflow runtime is actually running on a separate thread. Therefore, any attempts to access the `EventList` directly throw an exception. The first time through this code, the `InvokeRequired` property of the `EventList` is `true`. This means that the running code is executing on a separate thread. In this case, the code invokes a new instance of the event, passing in copies of the sender and `EventArgs`. This has the side effect of marshaling the data across to the thread containing the form. In this case, `InvokeRequired` is `false`, and you can retrieve the data from the workflow. Figure C-13 shows the result.

Combining ASP.NET with Windows Workflow Foundation raises many of the same issues involved in using WF with other technologies. That is, you still need to host the services and the runtime of WF within the host process under which ASP.NET runs — within IIS. However, developing solutions using ASP.NET offers more features and requires more decisions than other solutions. In particular, it is possible to publish workflows

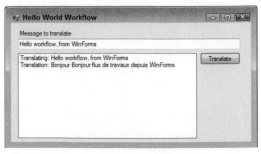

FIGURE C-13

as ASP.NET Web services. Hosting workflows within ASP.NET solutions is similar to hosting workflows with Windows Forms, but an ASP.NET solution might actually be supporting multiple concurrent users. This means that you must be more aware of where the runtime is created and how instances are created and freed.

You can host a workflow as a Web service if it has one or more `WebServiceInput` activities. This activity represents a SOAP endpoint. The `WebServiceInput` activity needs two properties set: `InterfaceType` and `MethodName`. Communication between the client code and the Web service is achieved via a shared interface. This interface is the value needed for the `InterfaceType` property. It represents the contract between the client code and the `WebServiceInput` activity. The `MethodName` identifies the method on the interface that will initiate the Web service call. The first `WebServiceInput` activity should have the `IsActivating` property set to `true`. In addition to the `WebServiceInput` activity, the workflow should also include a `WebServiceOutput` activity if the method includes a return value. Including a `WebServiceFault` activity is also useful if you need to return an error to the client code. If the Web service has parameters or return values, these may be mapped to the properties of the workflow using the Bind property dialog (see Figure C-14). Open this dialog by clicking the ellipsis next to the property in the Properties window.

Once you have built the workflow, including the `WebServiceInput` and `WebServiceOutput` activities (see Figure C-15), you then publish it as a Web service. This adds an additional ASP.NET Web Service project to the solution. The wizard creates the ASMX file that wraps the workflow and adds the required settings to the `web.config` file. The ASMX wrapper does nothing but delegate to the workflow class.

```
<%@WebService Class="TranslateService.TranslateWorkflow_WebService" %>
```

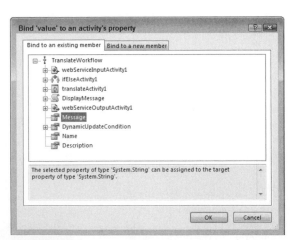

FIGURE C-14

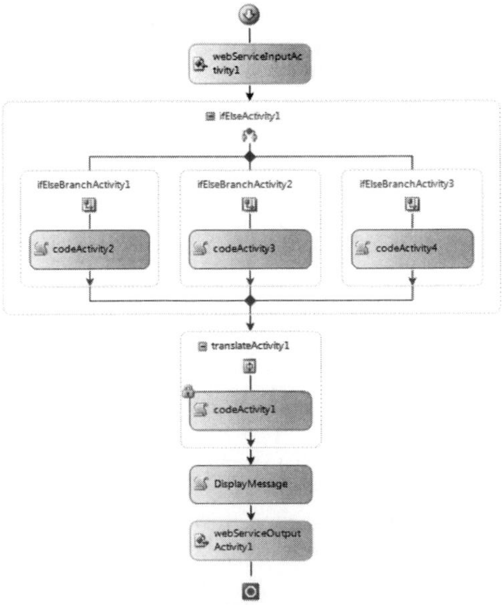

FIGURE C-15

The additional settings in the configuration file add a new section for configuring the workflow runtime and load the workflow HTTP handler that translates the incoming request:

```xml
<?xml version="1.0"?>
<configuration>
  <configSections>
    <section name="WorkflowRuntime"
      type="System.Workflow.Runtime.Configuration.WorkflowRuntimeSection,
      System.Workflow.Runtime, Version=3.0.00000.0, Culture=neutral,
      PublicKeyToken=31bf3856ad364e35"/>
  </configSections>
  <WorkflowRuntime Name="WorkflowServiceContainer">
    <Services>
    <add type="System.Workflow.Runtime.Hosting.ManualWorkflowSchedulerService,
        System.Workflow.Runtime, Version=3.0.0.0, Culture=neutral,
        PublicKeyToken=31bf3856ad364e35"/>
    <add
      type="System.Workflow.Runtime.Hosting.DefaultWorkflowCommitWorkBatchService,
        System.Workflow.Runtime, Version=3.0.0.0, Culture=neutral,
        PublicKeyToken=31bf3856ad364e35"/>
    </Services>
  </WorkflowRuntime>
  <appSettings/>
  <connectionStrings/>
  <system.web>
    <httpModules>
      <add type="System.Workflow.Runtime.Hosting.WorkflowWebHostingModule,
        System.Workflow.Runtime, Version=3.0.0.0, Culture=neutral,
        PublicKeyToken=31bf3856ad364e35" name="WorkflowHost"/>
    </httpModules>
  </system.web>
</configuration>
```

The resulting Web service works just like any other created by Visual Studio: You can access it in a browser to receive a test form (see Figure C-16), request the WSDL, and access it using Web service clients.

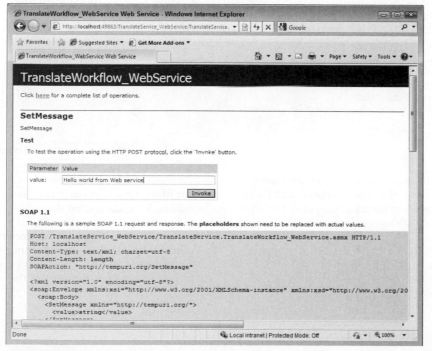

FIGURE C-16

Beyond Web services, ASP.NET applications can also host and access regular workflows. When hosting workflows in ASP.NET, keep in mind that your application may be accessed by many concurrent users, so you must be aware of when you create the runtime instance. In addition, remember that each workflow instance can use a good deal of memory. Therefore, limit the creation of workflows to when they are needed and free them quickly when they are no longer needed.

As you will probably want a single workflow runtime instance supporting all of your workflows, the best place to create the workflow runtime is when the application first starts. You can do this in the application's `Start` event in the `global.asax` file:

```
Sub Application_Start(ByVal sender As Object, ByVal e As EventArgs)
    Dim wfRun As New System.Workflow.Runtime.WorkflowRuntime
    Dim wfSked As _
        New System.Workflow.Runtime.Hosting.ManualWorkflowSchedulerService
    wfRun.AddService(wfSked)
    wfRun.StartRuntime()
    Application.Item("WorkflowRuntime") = wfRun
End Sub
```

Code snippet from TranslateService

This ensures that the same runtime is available to all sessions. Next, free up the resources used by the runtime when the application ends:

```
Sub Application_End(ByVal sender As Object, ByVal e As EventArgs)
    Dim wfRun As System.Workflow.Runtime.WorkflowRuntime
    wfRun = CType(Application.Item("WorkflowRuntime"), _
        System.Workflow.Runtime.WorkflowRuntime)
    wfRun.StopRuntime()
End Sub
```

Code snippet from TranslateService

Running a workflow instance is now a matter of retrieving the runtime instance and using it to execute the workflow. This leads to another issue related to the way Web pages are handled. Recall that the workflow typically runs asynchronously. This could mean that the workflow instance continues to run in the background after the Web page has returned. Therefore, you must run the workflow instance synchronously, so that it completes before returning data to the Web page:

```
Dim wfRun As WorkflowRuntime
wfRun = CType(Application.Item("WorkflowRuntime"), WorkflowRuntime)
Dim wfSked As ManualWorkflowSchedulerService
wfSked = wfRun.GetService(GetType(ManualWorkflowSchedulerService))
Dim wfInst As WorkflowInstance
wfInst = wfRun.CreateWorkflow(GetType(SimpleWorkflow))
wfInst.Start()
wfSked.RunWorkflow(wfInst.InstanceId)
```

Code snippet from TranslateService

The preceding code extracts the workflow runtime from the `Application` storage. It then retrieves the workflow scheduling service that was associated with the runtime as part of the `Application_Start` event handler. This scheduling service executes the workflows synchronously. This ensures that the entire workflow runs before the Web page is returned. The runtime is also used to create a new instance of the workflow desired, which is then started and associated with the scheduler. You could provide parameters to the workflow just as you did with the Windows Forms sample, by creating a Dictionary and populating it with the properties. This Dictionary would then be provided as a second parameter on the `CreateWorkflow` call. Similarly, you could retrieve the result of the workflow using the `OutputParameters` property in the `Completed` event handler for the workflow, just as you did with Windows Forms.

SUMMARY

While Windows Workflow Foundation does not have the visual glitz of WPF or the broad reach of WCF, it is a highly useful addition to the .NET Framework. Most business applications have some need for workflows, and having a standard means of creating this workflow ensures that the workflow is fully featured and accurately reflects business needs. As WF is readily available with the .NET Framework, developers no longer need to recreate a core business rules engine with each application. WF is extensible, so developers can take advantage of it in their applications, without being limited to the designed features.

As with the other components of the .NET Framework, WF integrates well into other applications, including Windows Forms and ASP.NET applications. It provides the means to extract the frequently complex workflow from those applications and to graphically design it. This graphical representation can be used to communicate the process to business users, increasing the chance that the workflow is represented correctly. Finally, as business needs change, it is a simple process to update the workflow, without requiring changes to the core application.

Enterprise Services

Chapter 28 explored the vast hinterland of legacy software known as COM. This appendix looks at "what COM did next" and how it fits into the world of .NET, in the form of *.NET Enterprise Services*.

To understand Enterprise Services, you must go back in time (all the way to the last century!) when a number of technologies began to emerge from Microsoft, including *Microsoft Transaction Server (MTS)*, *Microsoft Message Queuing (MSMQ)*, and *Microsoft Clustering Services*. The aim of these developments was to increase the scalability, performance, and reliability of applications.

Handling transactions involved a considerable extension to the NT/COM runtime. It also involved the introduction of several new standard COM interfaces, some to be used or implemented by transactional components and some to be used or implemented by the underlying resource managers, such as SQL Server. These additions, along with some other innovations relating to areas such as asynchronous COM, came to be known as *COM+*.

This appendix explores the .NET Enterprise Services. In particular, it looks at transaction processing and queued components using the classes of the System.EnterpriseServicesnamespace. The System.EnterpriseServices provides a number of classes that wrap the technologies that composed COM+. These include the classes that represent the ObjectContext, and the component interfaces that assist the system in transactions and queuing.

This is an enormous subject that could easily fill a whole book by itself, so this appendix only scratches the surface of it. However, by the end of the appendix, you will understand how all the pieces fit together. Let's begin by looking at what transactions are, and how they fit into Visual Basic.

TRANSACTIONS

A *transaction* is one or more linked units of processing placed together as a single unit of work, which either succeeds or fails. If the unit of work succeeds, then all the work is committed. If the unit fails, then every item of processing is rolled back and the process is returned to its original state.

The standard transaction example involves transferring money from account A to account B. The money must either end up in account B (and nowhere else), or—if something goes wrong—stay in account A (and go nowhere else). This avoids the very undesirable case in which you have taken money from account A but haven't put it in account B.

The ACID Test

Transaction theory starts with *ACID*, an acronym describing the following properties that all transactions should have:

➤ **Atomicity**—A transaction is *atomic*; that is, everything is treated as one unit. However many different components the transaction involves, and however many different method calls are made on those components, the system treats it as a single operation that either entirely succeeds or entirely fails. If it fails, then the system is left in the state it was in before the transaction was attempted.

➤ **Consistency**—All changes are done in a consistent manner. The system goes from one valid state to another.

➤ **Isolation**—Transactions that are going on at the same time are isolated from each other. If transaction A changes the system from state 1 to state 2, transaction B will see the system in either state 1 or 2, but not some half-baked state in between the two.

➤ **Durability**—If a transaction has been committed, the effect is permanent, even if the system fails.

Let's illustrate this with a concrete example. Imagine that after spending a happy afternoon browsing in your favorite bookstore, you decide to shell out some of your hard-earned dollars for a copy of, yes, *Professional Visual Basic 2010* (a wise choice). You take the copy to the checkout and exchange a bit of cash for the book. A transaction is going on here: You pay money and the store provides you with a book.

The important aspect of this transaction isn't the exchange of money, but that only two reasonable outcomes are possible—either you get the book and the store gets its money or you don't get the book and the store doesn't get its money. If, for example, there is insufficient credit on your credit card, then you'll leave the shop without the book. In that case, the transaction doesn't happen. The only way for the transaction to complete is both for you to get the book and for the store to get its money. This is the principle of *atomicity*.

If the store provides you with a copy of some other book instead, then you would reasonably feel that you ended up with an outcome that was neither anticipated nor desirable. This would be a violation of the principle of *consistency*.

Now imagine that there is one copy of the book in the store, and another potential buyer of that book has gone up to the cashier next to you. As far as the person at the other checkout is concerned, your respective transactions are *isolated* from each other (even though you are competing for the same resource). Either your transaction succeeds or the other person's does. What definitely *doesn't* happen is that the bookstore decides to exert the wisdom of Solomon and give you half each.

Now suppose you take the book home and the bookstore calls you to ask if they can have the book back. Apparently, an important customer (well, far more important than you, anyway) needs a copy. You would find this a tad unreasonable, and a violation of the principle of *durability*.

At this point, it's worth considering what implications all this is likely to have on the underlying components. How can you ensure that all of the changes in the system can be unwound if the transaction is aborted at some point? Perhaps you're in the middle of updating dozens of database files and something goes wrong.

There are three aspects to rescuing this situation with transactions:

➤ Knowledge that something has gone wrong

➤ Knowledge to perform the recovery

➤ Coordination of the recovery process

The middle part of the process is handled by the resource managers themselves. The likes of SQL Server and Oracle are fully equipped to deal with transactions and rollback (even if the resource manager in question is restarted partway through a transaction), so you don't need to worry about any of that. The last part of the process, coordination, is handled by the .NET runtime (or at least the Enterprise Services part of it). The first part, knowing that something is wrong, is shared between the components themselves and the .NET runtime.

This isn't at all unusual: Sometimes a component can detect that something has gone wrong itself and signal that recovery is necessary, while on other occasions it may not be able to do so, because it has crashed.

Later, you will see how all this works as you build a transactional application.

TRANSACTIONAL COMPONENTS

To understand what components are actually managed by Enterprise Services and what purpose they serve, you need to consider what a typical real-world *n*-tier application looks like. The bottom tier is the persistent data store, typically a database such as SQL Server or Oracle. However, there are other possible data stores, including the file system (on Windows NT and above). These are termed *resource managers* because they manage resources. The software here is concerned with maintaining the integrity of the application's data and providing rapid and efficient access to it.

The top tier is the user interface. This is a completely different specialization, and the software here is concerned with presenting a smooth, easy-to-follow front end to the end user. This layer shouldn't actually do any data manipulation at all, apart from whatever formatting is necessary to meet each user's presentational needs. The interesting stuff is in the tiers in between—in particular, the business logic. In the .NET/COM+ transactional model, the software elements that implement this are components running under the control of the Enterprise Services runtime.

Typically, these components are called into being to perform some sort of transaction and then, to all intents and purposes, disappear again. For example, a component might be called into play to transfer information from one database to another in such a way that the information is either in one database or the other, but not both. This component might have a number of different methods, each of which does a different kind of transfer. However, each method call would carry out a complete transfer:

```
Public Sub TransferSomething()
   TakeSomethingFromA
   AddSomethingToB
End Sub
```

Crucially, this means that most transaction components have no concept of *state*; there are no properties that hold values between method calls. You can see the reason for this if you imagine what would happen if you had a number of instances of the preceding components all vying for the attention of the database. If instance one of the control started the transfer, remembering the state or current values of A and B just after instance two had done the same, you could end up with the state being different between the two instances. This would violate the isolation of the transaction. Persistence is left to the outside data stores in this model.

The business logic is the area of the system that requires all the transactional management. Anything that happens here needs to be monitored and controlled to ensure that all the ACID requirements are met. The neatest way to do this in a component-oriented framework is to develop the business logic as components that are required to implement a standard interface. The transaction management framework can then use this interface to monitor and control how the logic is implemented from a transactional point of view. The transaction interface is a means for the business logic elements to talk to the transaction framework and for the transaction framework to reply to the logic elements.

So what's all this about not having state? Well, if you maintain state inside your components, then you immediately have a scaling problem. The middle tiers of your application are now seriously resource hungry. If you want an analogy from another area of software, consider why the Internet scales so well: because HTTP is a stateless protocol. Every HTTP request stands in isolation, so no resources are tied up in maintaining any form of session. It's the same with transactional components.

This is not to say that you can never maintain state inside your transactional components. You can, but it's not recommended, and the examples in this appendix don't illustrate it.

An Example of Transactions

For the transaction example, you'll build a simple business-logic component that transfers data from one bank account to another account. The current balance in the first bank account will be represented by a row in one database, while the other will be represented by a row in another database.

Before beginning, note one important point: You can't have transactions without any resource managers. It's very tempting to assume that you can experiment with transactional component services without actually involving, say, a database, because (as you shall see) none of the methods in the transactional classes make any explicit references to one. However, if you do try to do this, then you will find that your transactions don't actually trouble the system's statistics. Fortunately, you don't need to lay out your hard-earned cash for a copy of SQL Server (nice though that is), because a lightweight (but fully functional) version of SQL Server is available: *SQL Server 2008 Express Edition*, or more simply *SQL Server Express*. In addition, SQL Express is available separately, so you can even work with databases if you use Visual Basic Express.

Creating the Databases

First, set up the databases. Check whether the Server Explorer tab is visible in Visual Studio (see Figure D-1). If not, then open it by selecting View ➤ Server Explorer. Create a new database in the Data Connections tree.

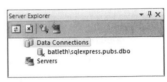

Right-click Data Connections and select Create New SQL Server Database from the menu. The Create New SQL Server Database dialog appears (see Figure D-2).

FIGURE D-1

Enter the database name (**BankOfWrox**) and select Use Windows Authentication. After clicking OK, you are prompted to create the database if it doesn't exist. You should now see BankOfWrox in the list of data connections (see Figure D-3).

FIGURE D-2

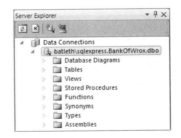

FIGURE D-3

Set up the database. If you open the new node, you will see several other nodes, including Tables. Right-click this and then select Add New Table from the menu. Another dialog should appear (see Figure D-4). Create two columns, Name and Amount, as shown. Make sure that Name is set up to be the primary key. When you click Close, you'll be asked whether you want to save the changes to Table1. Select Yes, and the Choose Name dialog will appear (see Figure D-5).

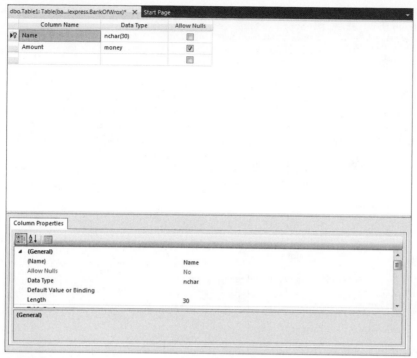

FIGURE D-4

Use the name **Accounts** for the table. You should now see a child node called Accounts below Tables in the tree. That completes the creation of BankOfWrox. Repeat the process for the BankOfMe database. The structure is exactly the same (although it doesn't need to be for the purposes of this example). Don't forget to set Name as the primary key. You could have created these two as separate rows in the same database, but it doesn't really simulate the scenario for which Enterprise Services is intended (inter-application communication).

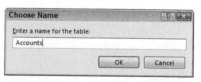

FIGURE D-5

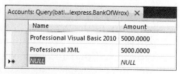

FIGURE D-6

Populating Your Databases

The next thing to do is populate the databases. If you right-click over Accounts for either database and select Show Table Data from Table from the menu, you will see a grid that enables you to add rows and initialize the values of their columns (see Figure D-6).

Enter two accounts in BankOfWrox—Professional Visual Basic 2010 and Professional XML—and allocate $5,000 to each. Now repeat the process for BankOfMe, setting up one account, Me, with $0 in it.

The Business Logic

The next step is to create the transactional component to support the business logic. Create a new Class Library project called Transactions. Then, add a reference to `System.EnterpriseServices` (see Figure D-7).

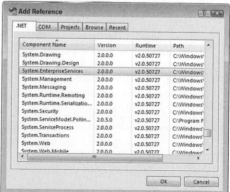

FIGURE D-7

This reference is needed because in order to come under the control of the Enterprise Services runtime, the component must inherit from the `System.EnterpriseServices.ServicedComponent` class:

Available for download on Wrox.com

```
Imports System.EnterpriseServices
Imports System.Configuration
Imports System.Data.SqlClient
<Assembly: ApplicationName("WroxTransactions")>
<Assembly: ApplicationAccessControl(True)>
Public Class BankTransactions
    Inherits ServicedComponent
```

Code snippet from Transactions

Here's the main function in the component, `TransferMoney`:

Available for download on Wrox.com

```
Public Sub TransferMoney(ByVal amount As Decimal, _
  ByVal sourceBank As String, _
  ByVal sourceAccount As String, _
  ByVal destinationBank As String, _
  ByVal destinationAccount As String)
    Try
        Withdraw(sourceBank, sourceAccount, amount)
        Try
            Deposit(destinationBank, destinationAccount, amount)
        Catch ex As Exception
            'deposit failed
            Throw New _
            ApplicationException("Error transfering money, deposit failed.", _
              ex)
        End Try
        'both operations succeeded
        ContextUtil.SetComplete()
    Catch ex As Exception
        'withdraw failed
        Throw New _
        ApplicationException("Error transfering money, withdrawal failed.", _
          ex)
    End Try
End Sub
```

Code snippet from Transactions

Ignoring for the moment the references to `ContextUtil`, you have effectively divided the logic into two halves: the half that takes money from the Wrox account (represented by the private function `Withdraw`), and the half that adds it to your account (represented by the private function `Deposit`). In order for the function to complete successfully, each of the two halves must complete successfully.

The `ContextUtil` class represents the context of the transaction. Within that context are basically two bits that control the behavior of the transaction from the point of view of each participant: the *consistent* bit and the *done* bit. The done bit determines whether or not the transaction is finished, so that resources can be reused. The consistent bit determines whether or not the transaction was successful from the point of view of the participant. This is established during the first phase of the two-phase commit process. In complex distributed transactions involving more than one participant, the overall consistency and completeness are voted on, such that a transaction is only consistent or done when everyone agrees that it is. If a transaction completes in an inconsistent state, then it is not allowed to proceed to the second phase of the commit.

In this case, there is only a single participant, but the principle remains the same. You can determine the overall outcome by setting these two bits, which is done via `SetComplete` and `SetAbort`, which are static methods in the `ContextUtil` class. Both of these set the done bit to `True`. `SetComplete` also sets the consistent bit to `True`, whereas `SetAbort` sets the consistent bit to `False`. In this example, `SetComplete` is set only if both halves of the transaction are successful.

The First Half of the Transaction

Now it's time to see what's going on in the two halves of the transaction itself. The component is responsible for reading from and writing to the two databases, so it needs two connection strings. You could hard-code these into the component, but a better solution is to use the project settings feature to include them. Double-click My Project in the Solution Explorer and navigate to the Settings tab. Add the two connection strings using the names BankOfWrox and BankOfMe, as shown in Figure D-8.

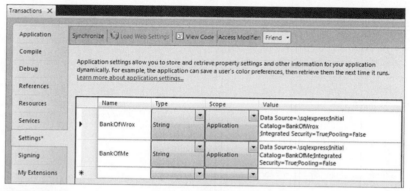

FIGURE D-8

1. Here's the function that removes money from the Wrox account:

```
Private Sub Withdraw(ByVal bank As String, _
    ByVal account As String, _
    ByVal amount As Decimal)
```

Code snippet from Transactions

2. Establish a connection to the database and retrieve the current account balance from it:

```
Dim ConnectionString As String
Dim SQL As String
Dim conn As SqlConnection = Nothing
Dim cmdCurrent As SqlCommand
Dim currentValue As Decimal
Dim cmdUpdate As SqlCommand
ConnectionString = My.Settings.Item(bank).ToString
SQL = String.Format("SELECT Amount FROM Accounts WHERE Name = '{0}'", _
    account)
```

Code snippet from Transactions

3. The call to ExecuteScalar retrieves a single value from the database —in this case, the amount for the requested account. Note that there is an exception handler started with the Try keyword. You'll finish the Try block in a moment:

```
Try
    conn = New SqlConnection(ConnectionString)
    conn.Open()
    cmdCurrent = New SqlCommand(SQL, conn)
    currentValue = CDec(cmdCurrent.ExecuteScalar())
```

Code snippet from Transactions

4. Note the current balance and determine whether you can afford to transfer the amount asked for. If not, raise an exception:

```
'check for overdrafts
        If amount > currentValue Then
            Throw New ArgumentException("Attempt to overdraft account")
        End If
```

Code snippet from Transactions

5. Otherwise, subtract the amount and update the table accordingly:

```
'otherwise, we're good to withdraw
SQL = _
        String.Format("UPDATE Accounts SET Amount = {0} WHERE Name = '{1}'", _
        currentValue - amount, account)
cmdUpdate = New SqlCommand(SQL, conn)
cmdUpdate.ExecuteNonQuery()
```

Code snippet from Transactions

6. Close the exception handler and the database:

```
Catch ex As Exception
        Throw New DataException("Error withdrawing", ex)
    Finally
        If Not conn Is Nothing Then
            conn.Close()
        End If
    End Try
End Sub
```

Code snippet from Transactions

The Second Half of the Transaction

The second half of the transaction is similar, except that the failure conditions are slightly different. First, the code stipulates that you can't transfer less than $50. Second, a bug has been included such that an attempt to transfer a negative amount will cause a divide by zero. (You'll see why this was added in a moment.) Here's the code:

```
Private Sub Deposit(ByVal bank As String, _
    ByVal account As String, _
    ByVal amount As Decimal)
    Dim ConnectionString As String
    Dim SQL As String
    Dim conn As SqlConnection = Nothing
    Dim cmdCurrent As SqlCommand
    Dim currentValue As Decimal
    Dim cmdUpdate As SqlCommand
    ConnectionString = My.Settings.Item(bank).ToString
    SQL = String.Format("SELECT Amount FROM Accounts WHERE Name = '{0}'", _
        account)
    If amount < 0 Then
        amount = amount / 0
    ElseIf amount < 50 Then
        Throw New ArgumentException("Value of deposit must be greater than $50")
    Else
        Try
            conn = New SqlConnection(ConnectionString)
            conn.Open()
            'get the current value
            cmdCurrent = New SqlCommand(SQL, conn)
            currentValue = CDec(cmdCurrent.ExecuteScalar())
```

```
        SQL = _
         String.Format("UPDATE Accounts SET Amount = {0} WHERE Name = '{1}'", _
          currentValue + amount, account)
        cmdUpdate = New SqlCommand(SQL, conn)
        cmdUpdate.ExecuteNonQuery()
      Finally
        If Not conn Is Nothing Then
            conn.Close()
        End If
      End Try
    End If
End Sub
```

Code snippet from Transactions

The business logic component is complete. Let's see how you can bring it under the control of Enterprise Services. First, of course, you need to build your DLL. Select Build Transactions from the Build menu.

Why was the divide by zero error included? This gives you a chance to see what happens to the transaction when an exception occurs in your code. The transaction will automatically fail and roll back, which means that your data will still be in a good state at the end.

Registering Your Component

Because the Enterprise Services infrastructure is COM-oriented, you need to expose the .NET component as a COM component, and register it with Component Services. Component Services handles all transaction coordination; that is, Component Services tracks any changes and restores the data should the transaction fail. First, some changes to the component are needed to enable this COM interaction. Prepare to take a trip down memory lane.

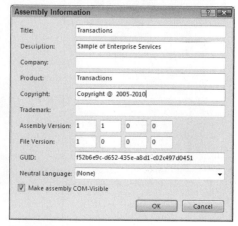

All COM components must have a GUID (globally unique identifier) that uniquely identifies it to the COM infrastructure. This was done for you in Visual Basic 6.0, but .NET requires you to add a value. In addition, your component needs an attribute to make it visible to COM. You can set both of these in the Assembly Information dialog. Double-click My Project in the Solution Explorer. On the Application page, click Assembly Information. There should already be a GUID assigned to your component. Check the option Make Assembly COM-Visible, as shown in Figure D-9. This makes all of the Public types accessible to COM.

You should also update the Assembly Version fields as you make changes to the component.

FIGURE D-9

 Chapter 28 contains more information about strong names and assemblies.

The problem is that the assembly is a private assembly. In order to make it available to the transaction framework, it needs to be a shared assembly. To do this, give the assembly a *cryptographically strong name*, generally referred to as its *strong name*.

Cryptographically strong means that the name has been signed with the private key of a dual key pair. This isn't the place to go into a long discussion about dual-key cryptography, but essentially a pair of keys is generated, one public and one private. If something is encrypted using the private key, it can only be decrypted using the public key from that pair, and vice versa. It is therefore an excellent tool for preventing tampering with information. If, for example, the name of an assembly were to be encrypted using the private key of a pair, then the recipient of a new version of that assembly could verify the origin of that new version, and be confident that it was not a rogue version from some other source. This is because only the original creator of the assembly retains access to its private key.

Giving the Assembly a Strong Name

You now need to ensure that your assembly uses the strong name. You can create a new strong name file, or assign an existing strong name file on the Signing tab of the Project Properties (see Figure D-10).

Registering with Component Services

Once you've built the DLL again, you can run RegSvcs to register the DLL with Component

FIGURE D-10

Services (see Figure D-11). RegSvcs is a command-line tool, so start a Windows Command Prompt. You will find the RegSvc.exe tool in the directory `%Windir%\Microsoft.NET\Framework\v4.0.21006` directory. To register a DLL, simply pass the full path of the DLL on the command-line:

```
regsvcs.exe {path to DLL}\transactions.dll
```

To unregister a DLL, include the `/u` parameter on the command-line.

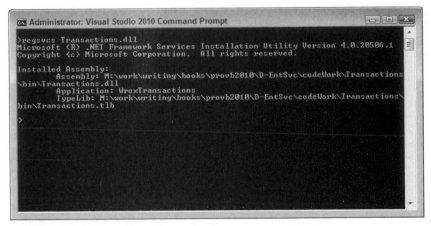

FIGURE D-11

 Running RegSvcs.exe requires administrative permissions. Therefore, when running under Windows Vista or Windows 7, you should start the command prompt by selecting "Run As Administrator." Otherwise, RegSvcs will fail when run.

RegSvcs does a few things at this point. It creates a COM type library for the DLL, which enables it to communicate with COM, and it creates a COM+ application for the component.

The Component Services Console

The *Component Services Console* is the control interface for Component Services. This is an MMC snap-in, which you can find by selecting Control Panel ➤ Administrative Tools ➤ Component Services (see Figure D-12). If the Component Services tool is not available, you can also run it by selecting Run from the start menu/orb and running `c:\windows\system32\comexp.msc`.

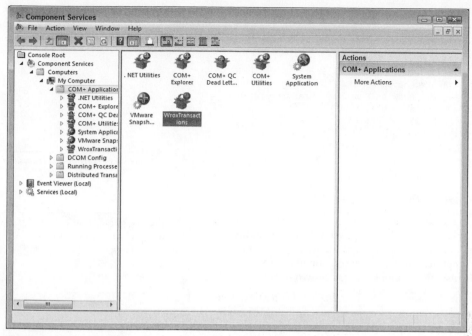

FIGURE D-12

You should be able to find the sample under COM+ Applications. A COM+ application is a set of related COM+ components that have been packaged together. RegSvcs creates a new application for every component that it registers. If you want to bundle together a series of components from separate DLLs, you can do so, but only by creating a new application via the Component Services Console (right-click COM+ Applications and then select New). You'll explore the console a little more as you go on.

Now you need a test application. More important, you need to tell Component Services that you're interested in transactions.

Test Application

Create a Windows Application project called TestTransactions and a very simple form (see Figure D-13).

FIGURE D-13

The text field is called TransferField and the command button is called TransferButton. In order to access the transactional component, add references to a couple of DLLs. First, add a reference to the transactional component DLL itself. You'll need to browse for this, as it isn't currently in the global assembly cache. Second, in order to access the objects in this DLL, you also need to make the application aware of the `System.EnterpriseServices` assembly, so add a reference to that as well. Having done that, it's time to import Transactions into the application:

```
Imports Transactions
```

Here's the code behind the TransferButton button:

Available for
download on
Wrox.com

```
Private Sub TransferButton_Click(ByVal sender As System.Object, _
    ByVal e As System.EventArgs) Handles TransferButton.Click
    Dim txn As New BankTransactions
    Try
        txn.TransferMoney(CDec(Me.TransferField.Text),
          "BankOfWrox", "Professional Visual Basic 2010",
```

```
        "BankOfMe", "Me")
      MessageBox.Show(String.Format("{0:C} transfered from {1} to {2}",
          CDec(Me.TransferField.Text), "BankOfWrox", "BankOfMe"),
          "Transfer Succeeded",
          MessageBoxButtons.OK,
          MessageBoxIcon.Information)
    Catch ex As Exception
      MessageBox.Show(ex.Message, "Transfer failed",
          MessageBoxButtons.OK,
          MessageBoxIcon.Error)
    End Try
  End Sub
```

Code snippet from TestTramsactions

The Transaction Attribute

Now it's time to tell Component Services how the component should enter a transaction. There are two ways of doing this: via the Component Services Console or via an attribute in code. To do it via the Component Services Console, open the Explorer tree to locate the Transactions component (as shown in Figure D-14).

Right-click on the Transactions.DLL and select Properties. You can view the available options for the transactions for this class by going to the Transactions tab. Select one of the available options; you'll learn what these all mean in a moment. It's a little tiresome to require the system manager to do this every time, especially if you already know that your component is always going to have the same transaction characteristics. An alternative mechanism is available: You can explicitly set up an attribute in the code for your component.

Attributes are items of declarative information that can be attached to the elements of code, such as classes, methods, data members, and properties. Any code that accesses classes that include attributes can query the values assigned at runtime. One such attribute is called `TransactionAttribute`, which,

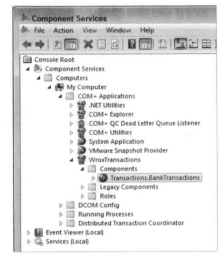

FIGURE D-14

unsurprisingly, is used for specifying the transaction characteristics of a component class. The value of this attribute is taken from an enumeration called `TransactionOption`. Both `TransactionAttribute` and `TransactionOption` are found within the `System.EnterpriseServices` namespace. The enumeration can take the following values:

VALUE	DESCRIPTION
Disabled	Ignores any transaction in the current context. This is the default.
NotSupported	Creates the component in a context with no governing transaction.
Required	Shares a transaction if one exists. Creates a new transaction if necessary.
RequiresNew	Creates the component with a new transaction, regardless of the state of the current context.
Supported	Shares a transaction if one exists. If it doesn't, then it creates the component.

The available values are exactly the same as the ones shown in the Transaction tab. This case is a standalone transaction, so either `RequiresNew` or `Required` are equally valid. However, you would most commonly select `RequiresNew` to create a component that will participate in an existing transaction or create a new transaction if needed.

Before changing the component, unregister the current version to avoid any confusion. As described above, this is done by running the RegSvcs tool on the DLL, including the /u command-line parameter. Now return to the Transactions project and make the change:

```
<Assembly: ApplicationName("WroxTransactions")>
<Assembly: ApplicationAccessControl(True)>
<Transaction(TransactionOption.RequiresNew)> _

Public Class BankTransactions
    Inherits ServicedComponent
```

Code snippet from Transactions

Having made the change, rebuild the Transactions project and then register it as before. Now run the test application and start the Component Services Console application. Enter 1000 and click the Execute button. You might be able to see the number of current active transactions briefly go from none to one (depending on your computer, this may be too fast to see), followed by the number of committed transactions and the total both increasing by one. That's it. You've implemented your first transaction. If you check the two databases, the amount in the BankOfWrox Professional Visual Basic account has been reduced to $4,000, whereas the account in BankOfMe has been increased by $1,000.

Invalid Data

What happens if you enter a value that you know is invalid? There are two options here: either try to transfer more money than there is in the Professional Visual Basic account, or try to transfer more than the "approved limit." Run the application again and try to transfer $10. As expected, the transaction will fail, and no changes will be made to the accounts. Professional Visual Basic still has $4,000, and your account still has $1,000. This isn't too much of a big deal, because the invalid condition is spotted before any database manipulation is carried out. If you check the transaction statistics, the number of *aborted* transactions has been incremented this time. You can find these statistics in the Component Services console under Distributed Transaction Coordinator ➤ Local DTC ➤ Transaction Statistics.

Now try to transfer $10,000. This time, the first part of the transaction is successful, but the *second* part fails. Again the number of aborted transactions is incremented, but what's happened to the database? Well, fortunately for everyone concerned, there is still $4,000 in the Professional Visual Basic account, and still $1,000 in your account. The *entire* transaction has failed.

When Something Goes Wrong

Recall that bit of mindless vandalism that was added to the Deposit function so that it would divide by zero if the user entered a negative value? Here's where you get to try it out. Run the application again and try to transfer $-1. You should receive an error message. It was halfway through a transaction, but when you look at the transaction statistics, the aborted count has increased by one. More important, if you check the databases, the Pro VB account *still* has $4,000, and the other account still has $1,000, so you're protected against software failures as well.

OTHER ASPECTS OF TRANSACTIONS

Dealing with transactions involves several other topics as well, including just-in-time (JIT) activation and object pooling.

Just-in-Time

Creating and deleting components takes time. Instead of discarding the component when finished with it, why not keep it around in case it's needed again? The mechanism by which this is done is called *just-in-time (JIT) activation*, and it's set by default for all automatic transactional components (it's unset by default for all other COM+ components, however). This is another reason why holding state is undesirable within components—it limits the ability to share them.

All good transactional components are entirely stateless, but real life dictates differently. For example, you might want to maintain a link to your database, one that would be expensive to set up every time. The JIT mechanism provides a couple of methods that you can override in the `ServicedComponent` class in this case.

The method that is invoked when a JIT component is activated is called `Activate`, and the component that is invoked when it is deactivated is called, unsurprisingly, `Deactivate`. In `Activate` and `Deactivate` you put the things that you would normally put in your constructor and deconstructor. JIT can also be activated by adding the `JustInTimeActivation` attribute to any class within the `ServicedComponent` class.

Object Pooling

You can, if you want, take this a step further and maintain a pool of objects already constructed and prepared to be activated whenever required. When an object is no longer required (i.e., it's deactivated), it is returned to the pool until the next time it is needed. By retaining objects, you don't have to continually create them anew, which reduces your application's performance costs. You can use the `ObjectPooling` attribute within your class to determine how the pool operates:

```
<Transaction(TransactionOption.RequiresNew), _
ObjectPooling(MinPoolSize:=5, MaxPoolSize:=20, _
                    CreationTimeOut:=30)> _
Public Class BankTransactions
```

QUEUED COMPONENTS

The traditional component programming model is very much a *synchronous* one. Put simply, you invoke a method and you wait until you get a result back. Unfortunately, many real-world problems are inherently *asynchronous*. You can't always wait for a response to your request before moving on to the next task. A real-world analogy is the difference between phoning someone and sending an e-mail. Phoning is a synchronous process; either the phone is answered (a successful transaction) or it isn't (or you've called a wrong number, another form of unsuccessful transaction). E-mailing someone is asynchronous; you have no control over how long the e-mail takes to arrive, or when the person will actually look at it. Therefore, in order to tackle everything that the real world throws at us, you need an asynchronous component model for those scenarios where it is appropriate.

Why only some scenarios? The synchronous model is quite simple to manage, because the three possible outcomes of a request are quite straightforward to handle. First, the request can be successful. Second, the request can fail. Finally, the target of the request can simply not respond at all, in which case it times out. However, when dealing with asynchronous requests, expect all manner of unusual conditions. For example, the target system may not currently be operational, so you have to make a decision regarding how long to wait before it comes back up again. Each outstanding request takes up system resources, so they need to be managed carefully. You need to be able to determine when the response comes back; you need to make certain that the recipient only receives a given message once, and so on. You are, in fact, dealing with a different infrastructure than MTS here, an infrastructure to handle reliable messaging. Microsoft's product to tackle this type of problem is Microsoft Message Queuing (MSMQ).

The idea behind reliable messaging is that once you have asked the system to send a message to a given target, you can effectively stop worrying about it. The system handles the storing and forwarding of messages to their target. It also handles retries and timeouts, ensuring a message is received only once, and returning a message to the dead letter queue if all else fails. MSMQ is, in fact, a whole technology in itself, and can seem quite complex. However, Enterprise Services provides a handy, simple abstraction called *queued components*.

Queued components take the sometimes gnarly aspects of working with MSMQ and make them easier to deal with than the raw queue handling. Instead, you have the concepts of *recorders*, *listeners*, and *players*.

Recorders create messages that are put on a queue. Eventually, a listener receives the message. This could happen immediately or it could take weeks if the two components are disconnected. Finally, the player does whatever the message requests. Naturally, this places some restrictions on the kind of component that can be used. For example, you can't have any output arguments or return values. If you have either of these, the values can't be set until the action is complete, removing the benefit of the asynchronous aspects of the call. However, there are some cool things that you can do, explored in the next section.

> *In order to run the queued components examples, you need MSMQ, which comes with Windows 2000, XP, Vista, and Windows 7. However, you need to install it separately using the Add Windows Components dialog. (On Windows Vista and Windows 7, this is the "Turn Windows Features on or off" link from the Programs and Features item in the Control Panel.)*

An Example of Queued Components

This example creates a very simple logging component that takes a string as its input and writes it out to a sequential file, as well as outputs it in a message box. To keep the example simple, the client and the server are on the same machine; in a production scenario they would be separate. The benefit of using queued components here is that the logging doesn't slow down the main process.

Create a Class Library project called Queues and add a reference to the `System.EnterpriseServices` namespace. You can delete the default Class added to the project. Next, define an interface:

Available for download on Wrox.com

```
Public Interface IReporter
    Sub Log(ByVal message As String)
End Interface
```

Code snippet from Queues

Notice that the `Log` method follows the requirements listed earlier. There is no return value, and all parameters are input only. You need to separate the interface from the implementation because the implementation, residing on the server, is going to be sitting on another machine somewhere. The client isn't the slightest bit interested in the details of this; it only needs to know how to interface to it.

Add a new class, called Reporter, that will implement this interface. As with the transactional component, you inherit from `ServicedComponent`, and implement the interface just defined. However, notice the `<InterfaceQueuing()>` attribute that indicates to the Component Services runtime that the interface can be queued (this is the same for the interface):

Available for download on Wrox.com

```
<InterfaceQueuing(Interface:="IReporter")> Public Class Reporter
    Inherits ServicedComponent
    Implements IReporter
```

Code snippet from Queues

In the logging method, simply output a message box, open a `StreamWriter` component to append to the log file, and then close it:

Available for download on Wrox.com

```
Sub Log(ByVal message As String) Implements IReporter.Log
    MsgBox(strText)
    Using writer As _
        New StreamWriter("c:\account.log", True)
        writer.WriteLine(String.Format("{0}: {1}", _
            DateTime.Now, message))
        writer.Close()
    End Using
End Sub
End Class
```

Code snippet from Queues

That's it for the component's code. To enable queuing, click Show All Files on the Solution Explorer to see the hidden files for the project. Expand the My Project item and then open the `AssemblyInfo.vb` file. Ensure that it has these attributes:

```
'Enterprise Services attributes
<Assembly: EnterpriseServices.ApplicationAccessControl(False,
    Authentication:=EnterpriseServices.AuthenticationOption.None)>
<Assembly: EnterpriseServices.ApplicationQueuing(Enabled:=True,
    QueueListenerEnabled:=True)>
<Assembly: EnterpriseServices.ApplicationName("WroxQueue")>
```

Code snippet from Queues

Next, ensure that queuing is correctly enabled for this component. The next line is a special line to enable message queuing to work correctly in a workgroup environment, by switching off authentication. If you didn't do this, you would need to set up an entire domain structure and create specific users for the queues. (In a production scenario, that's exactly what you would use, so you would need to remove this line.) Finally, ensure that the component runs as a server, rather than a library. This was optional for transactional components, but it's mandatory for queued components. You'll soon see why. In addition, add a strong name file to your project, as you did with the `Transactions` component.

Consoles Again

It's time to build your Queues component. Once built, register it using RegSvcs just as you did with the `Transactions` component. Take a look at the Component Services Console to see how it's going. Also, look closely at Figure D-15. It looks fine, but there's one other console to check out: the *Computer Management Console*. Access this either from the system console or by right-clicking the My Computer icon and selecting Manage from the menu. Tucked away at the bottom is the relevant part. Open Services and Applications to find it. Component Services has set up some queues for us. There are five queues feeding into the main one, so the infrastructure is ready. Keep in mind that all this would be running on the server machine in a production scenario, not the client.

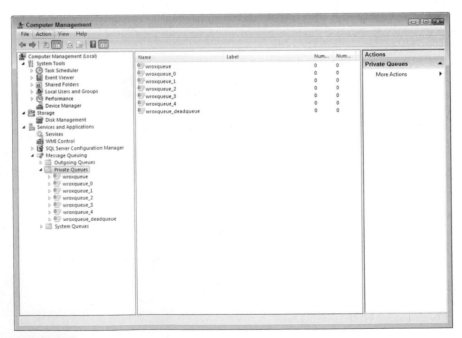

FIGURE D-15

Building the Client

The problem is that all the code you've written in this project is built on top of the MSMQ infrastructure, which is, inevitably, a COM infrastructure. Worse, the current tasks involve *marshaling* COM objects into a stream suitable for inserting into a queued message. For the purposes of this discussion, think of marshaling as intelligently serializing the contents of a method invocation on an interface. You do this in such a way that they can then be deserialized at the other end and turned into a successful invocation of the same method in a remote implementation of the interface. You get COM to do this for us by constructing a *moniker*, which is basically an intelligent name.

Begin by creating a Windows Application project called TestReporter. Add a reference to the `Reporter` component in the usual manner. Figure D-16 shows the form.

FIGURE D-16

The text box is called MessageField, and the button is called SendButton. Here's the code:

Available for download on Wrox.com

```vb
Imports System.Runtime.InteropServices
Public Class MainForm
    Inherits System.Windows.Forms.Form
    Private Sub SendButton_Click(ByVal sender As System.Object, _
                        ByVal e As System.EventArgs) _
                        Handles SendButton.Click
```

Code snippet from TestReporter

Here's the crucial section. Note the references to the interface and how the object is instantiated:

Available for download on Wrox.com

```vb
Dim logger As Queues.IReporter
Try
    logger = _
        CType(Marshal.BindToMoniker("queue:/new:Queues.Reporter"), _
        Queues.IReporter)
```

Code snippet from TestReporter

Once the object is created, you can make the queued call:

```vb
logger.Log(Me.MessageField.Text)
```

Finally, release the reference to the underlying COM object:

Available for download on Wrox.com

```vb
    Marshal.ReleaseComObject(logger)
    MessageBox.Show("Message sent")
Catch ex As Exception
    MessageBox.Show(ex.Message, "Error sending message")
End Try
```

Code snippet from TestReporter

It's not pretty, but you only have to do it once to use it repeatedly.

Queuing Invocations

Now try using this application to put a message onto the queue (see Figure D-17). Run the client application and enter a suitable message, such as "Hello everyone."

FIGURE D-17

You've created a message, so that represents the invocation. If you were able to read the message, you would see the message, typed in earlier, embedded somewhere in it. (Unfortunately, the console only allows you to inspect the start of the message, but you should be able to see the name of the component in there.) Why hasn't anything happened? You haven't actually started your server. Recall that the component has to run as a server; this is why. The server has to sit there all the time, serving the incoming queue. Therefore, return to the Component Services Console, right-click WroxQueue, select Start from the menu, and you're off. Lo and behold, there's the message box (see Figure D-18).

Now that the message has been delivered, return to the Component Services Console. Right-clicking over the message queue and selecting Refresh confirms that the message has indeed been removed from the queue. Look in `account.log` and notice that it has been updated as well. Running the application results in the message boxes popping up right away, as the server is now running and responding to the messages entering the queue.

FIGURE D-18

Transactions with Queued Components

Why were you instructed to call that file `account.log`? MSMQ, like SQL Server, is a resource manager, and it can take part in transactions. This may seem a little counterintuitive at first because how on earth can anything as asynchronous as MSMQ have anything to do with transactions? The key is that it is *reliable*. Anything you put into a queue is guaranteed to come out the other end. If you take a transaction to the point at which a message is securely in the queue, you definitely have something that can participate. What happens at the other end of the queue is an entirely separate transaction. Of course, if something goes wrong there, you may need to look at setting up a compensating transaction coming back the other way to trigger some kind of rollback.

For the final example, then, you can take the original transactional component and add in a queued element, so that not only does the transfer of money take place, but that fact is also logged to a remote file. Use exactly the same queued component as last time.

Begin by making a clone of TestTransactions called TestQueuedTransactions. Add a reference to Queues and an `Imports` statement:

```
Imports System.Runtime.InteropServices
```

You also need a new private subroutine:

Available for
download on
Wrox.com

```
Private Shared Sub LogTransaction(ByVal amount As Decimal, _
    ByVal sourceBank As String, ByVal sourceAccount As String, _
    ByVal destinationBank As String, ByVal destinationAccount As String)
    Dim logger As Queues.IReporter
    Try
        logger =
            CType(Marshal.BindToMoniker("queue:/new:Queues.Reporter"),
            Queues.IReporter)
        logger.Log(String.Format("{0:c} transfered from {1}:{2} to {3}:{4}",
            amount,
            sourceBank, sourceAccount,
            destinationBank, destinationAccount))
        Marshal.ReleaseComObject(logger)
        MessageBox.Show("Message sent")
    Catch ex As Exception
        MessageBox.Show(ex.Message, "Error sending message")
    End Try
End Sub
```

Code snippet from TestQueuedTransactions

This may look similar to the previous queued component example application. Finally, add a call to this subroutine in the `Button_Click` event handler:

Available for
download on
Wrox.com

```
Private Sub TransferButton_Click(ByVal sender As System.Object,
    ByVal e As System.EventArgs) Handles TransferButton.Click
    Dim txn As New Transactions.BankTransactions
    Try
        txn.TransferMoney(CDec(Me.TransferField.Text),
            "BankOfWrox", "Professional VB",
            "BankOfMe", "Me")
        LogTransaction(CDec(Me.TransferField.Text),
            "BankOfWrox", "Professional VB",
            "BankOfMe", "Me")
        MessageBox.Show(String.Format("{0:C} transfered from {1} to {2}",
            CDec(Me.TransferField.Text), "BankOfWrox", "BankOfMe"),
            "Transfer Succeeded",
            MessageBoxButtons.OK,
            MessageBoxIcon.Information)
    Catch ex As Exception
        MessageBox.Show(ex.Message, "Transfer failed",
            MessageBoxButtons.OK,
            MessageBoxIcon.Error)
    End Try
End Sub
```

Code snippet from TestQueuedTransactions

Here, you've included a queued component in the transaction. It's been deliberately placed at the beginning to determine whether it genuinely takes part in the two-phase committal. If the transaction fails, then you shouldn't see any messages come through the queue.

You also need to make a small change to the `Reporter` component, but you must shut it down via the Component Services Console first. The change is very simple. To ensure that the queued component takes part in the transaction, it must be marked with the `Transaction` attribute:

```
<InterfaceQueuing(Interface:="Reporter.IReporter"),
Transaction(TransactionOption.Required)>
Public Class Reporter
```

Code snippet from Queues

If you now transfer $500, you'll see the usual "Transfer complete" message box; and if you start up the `WroxQueue` component, you also see the message box from the queued component (see Figure D-19).

If you try it again, you see the queued message coming through first, so you know it's OK for valid transfers. What happens if you try to transfer $100? As you know from the earlier example, this will fail, and indeed, you'll see the "Transfer failed" message box from the main component, but not a peep out of the queued component.

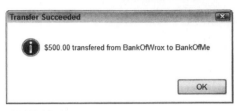

FIGURE D-19

SUMMARY

This appendix looked at creating applications using the classes of `System.EnterpriseServices`. You first examined transactions and their importance in maintaining data integrity when multiple simultaneous changes may affect your data. Properly applied, transactions can ensure that even with multiple users editing data, your database always reflects the correct data. You also looked at asynchronous processing using MSMQ and queued components. Many scenarios, such as logging or other "background" processes, are better handled using asynchronous code. Queued components make building these asynchronous handlers much easier. Many other aspects of Enterprise Services were beyond the scope of this appendix, including role-based security, object constructors, and more.

Programming for the Cloud

Can you hear it? Those drums beating in the programming jungle: They're getting louder and louder. All of the major vendors have begun to offer some sort of "cloud computing" services, and Microsoft is no exception.

This appendix looks at Windows Azure, a new set of tools from Microsoft for creating applications that run within their cloud. This includes the capability to create highly scalable websites, massively parallel computation tools, or some combination of the two. It looks at how creating these applications differs from the way you normally work, and some of the benefits of creating applications that run in the cloud.

THE RISE OF THE CLOUD

Cloud computing is very much the latest buzzword in computing, but just about every vendor means something slightly different when they use it, and they're all basically right. However, a few consistent concepts emerge when discussing cloud computing:

➤ The services are provided by one or more computers in a data center.

➤ You can easily add new servers, typically with either a Web interface or a configuration option. These new servers are available within a few minutes of the request.

➤ Any given server might be servicing requests from multiple cloud applications, without any interaction between these applications.

➤ The developer creating the cloud application is usually constrained, especially in matters of reading and writing data. For example, you cannot directly read and write to the file system, and the choice in databases is limited, as you will see later in this appendix.

➤ The cost of using the cloud is typically billed based on actual usage, rather than a set rate per server. This is one of the main points that distinguishes cloud computing from a simple data-center-hosted application.

In the case of Windows Azure, your applications run within a virtual machine on a server running within one of Microsoft's data centers. These virtual machines provide all the services you need to run your application. Adding new "servers" is simply a matter of creating a new copy of your virtual machine. This means that a new server can run your application in a matter of minutes, not days or weeks.

Cloud Scenarios

There are a number of scenarios in which making use of cloud computing can be highly useful, including the following:

➤ Websites that have highly variable scaling needs

➤ As a means of reducing the maintenance cost of a server farm

➤ Providing a highly scalable parallel processing environment

Scalability

Some websites have highly variable traffic patterns. For example, a site that sells a product might have higher traffic during peak gift-giving seasons (see Figure E-1).

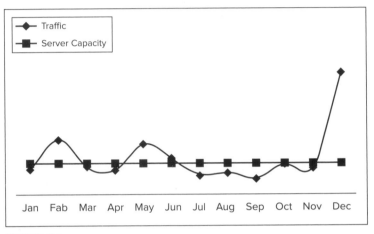

FIGURE E-1

One line represents the capacity of a single Web server, in terms of the number of requests it can respond to. The other line represents incoming traffic. From the graph, you can see that the site will have difficulty maintaining good server loads at least three times during the year: in February, May, and December. During these times, the number of people attempting to access the site exceeds the available server capacity. This would lead to slower response times from the site, which would likely lead to visitors going elsewhere.

At this point, you have a few alternatives. You could increase the available server capacity by using more servers. However, this means that you now have the cost of acquiring and maintaining those servers, even though they will remain idle most of the year. In this case, that would mean you would need four times the number of servers to meet the December traffic requirements.

As an alternative, you could use Windows Azure to host your Web application. This enables you to easily add new servers only when they are needed, shutting them down again when they are not. As shown in Figure E-2, this option gives you a closer fit between your needs and the capacity of the servers.

This is one of the main benefits of using a cloud computing service like Azure — you can easily scale your application by adding new servers when needed. You only pay for the computer access you use at any given time.

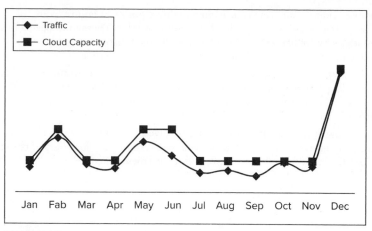

FIGURE E-2

Cost Savings

While computers have become relatively inexpensive commodity items for most companies, they still have a cost. The first major decision you face when buying a new computer is whether to buy it for your current needs and capacity or target some future anticipated capacity. In addition to the capital outlay required to buy the computer, it also has costs associated with maintenance: Someone needs to set up software on the machine, install patches as necessary, and, most important, back up the computer and restore data as needed. In a small company, this might all be done by a single individual; in a larger company, by entire departments. Either way, the initial cost of the computer is not the only cost involved. In addition to these ongoing expenses, you also will likely need to upgrade the computer(s), adding more expense.

The argument here for cloud computing is that someone else is managing the actual computer(s), and you simply provide the software. If you need more capacity, you turn on new servers as needed. These changes are transparent to users, and can be done rapidly in the case of highly variable needs. Compare that to getting a new physical computer ready and able to receive requests. Even if you overnight the computer from your supplier, you still need to configure it, load software, and add it to your network or data center. With cloud computing, you have a system that is backed up regularly, fully patched, and will likely be upgraded regularly.

Parallel Processing

While most applications that have a user interface spend a lot of time just waiting for input, some applications do a large amount of processing — for example, an application that accesses a data warehouse to determine customer shopping trends, or an application that processes video. These applications typically don't have sexy UIs, and just spend their time crunching away at numbers.

The traditional solution in this scenario is to have multiple computers process the data. Speeding up the calculations is a matter of adding a new server to the set. However, as mentioned earlier, this is not just a simple matter of buying a new server. A number of ongoing costs are involved.

Here, the argument for cloud computing is quite strong. By leveraging the cloud, you gain the benefits of flexible control over the available computing power, and the costs become more predictable.

The Case against Cloud Computing

While the above cases show scenarios where cloud computing can be useful, there are also arguments against putting your applications and data into the cloud:

➤ Your data is no longer under your control. With all of your data in the cloud, you are now relying on the cloud provider to maintain, backup and (at least partly) secure your data. In addition, you must trust them to not access or share your data.

➤ While one of the key benefits of cloud computing is providing multiple points of failure, your application can still be taken down by failure of the cloud computing vendor. There have been a few very visible (and lengthy) outages by Amazon, Google and others. Some of these outages have been caused by relatively trivial factors, such as a technician altering the network routing.

➤ Some developers feel that the development model and constraints that the cloud environment imposes is too big a change. For example, while working with SQL Azure is mostly like working with SQL Server, there are some missing features. If your application depends on these features, then obviously cloud computing is not for you.

➤ While the cost of cloud computing is variable, it may not actually save you money in the long run. As with many decisions regarding long term costs, you would need to determine this for yourself based on your required server capacities, the available hardware, and replacement schedules.

AZURE

Windows Azure is Microsoft's cloud platform. It consists of a number of servers located within Microsoft data centers (see Figure E-3). The Azure platform consists of three main components:

➤ The Fabric (also known as the AppFabric, short for application fabric), which integrates the servers and creates the base cloud services

➤ The Storage services, which store the data to be used by the various parts of the cloud

➤ The Compute service, which represents the developer-centric part of the cloud, hosting the Web and worker roles of their applications

The following sections look at these three components in more detail.

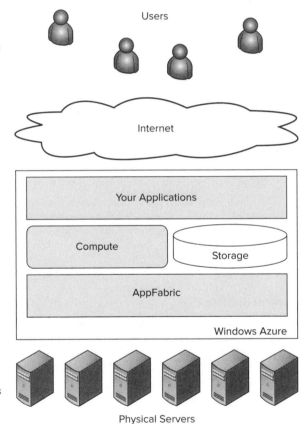

FIGURE E-3

The Fabric

The servers that represent Azure run software that creates a consistent environment, called the Azure Fabric (or AppFabric if you don't like typing). This fabric is what turns a normal data center into a cloud center, and it consists of fabric agents running on each of the servers in the data center, as well as multiple controllers that manage the agents (see Figure E-4). The fabric controllers manage the virtual machines running on the servers, so if one of the virtual machines crashes, the fabric controller starts a new virtual machine to carry on. In addition, the fabric controller provides load balancing between the various Web roles that might be running a website.

The fabric also includes a number of servers providing data storage. When a request is made to save data, it is actually written to multiple locations simultaneously. This ensures that the failure of a single component does not affect the operation of the whole.

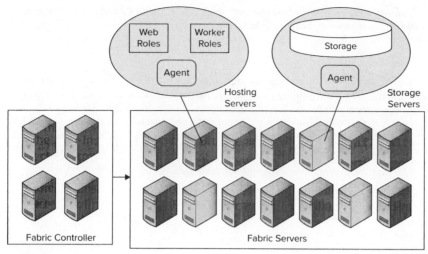

FIGURE E-4

As you likely don't have your very own AppFabric for testing purposes, you might worry about developing Azure applications. However, a development environment is installed with the Azure Tools for Visual Studio. This enables you to create and test your applications within a simulated Azure environment that behaves like the live AppFabric.

FIGURE E-5

You can access this development by clicking the icon in the notification area of the task bar (see Figure E-5).

From the icon, you can stop the development Fabric and Storage services. In addition, you can view the root URLs used by the three Storage services (see Figure E-6), as well as the current applications loaded in the Fabric (see Figure E-7).

FIGURE E-6

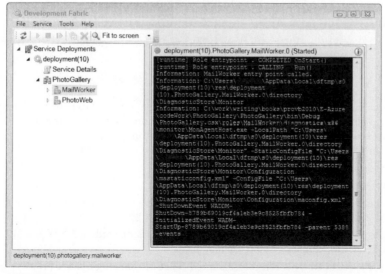

FIGURE E-7

The Development Fabric window enables you to view the trace logs of the various running Web and worker roles, as well as view the current settings for these running services.

Storage Services

The Storage services provide the means of saving data for your cloud applications. Why not just let you use existing data storage mechanisms? The main problem with allowing you to just write as needed is that your code is running within multiple virtual machines. If you were allowed to use file I/O and write to the hard drive, Azure would have to ensure that this data was written consistently across all of the virtual machines running your application. In addition, it would have to duplicate this data in any new virtual machines that might start after the data was written. As you can imagine, these would be very difficult problems to solve.

Instead, Windows Azure provides four storage mechanisms for saving data:

➤   Blob storage

➤   Table storage

➤   Queues

➤   SQL Azure

These are actually provided by separate instances within the cloud, and not dependant on your applications. All of your data is stored multiple times throughout the cloud — for redundancy and reliability — as well as backed up and maintained.

Blob Storage

The simplest form of storage available within Azure is blob storage. As the name implies, blob (Binary Large Object) storage simply gives you a set of space to store binary information. Blobs are created within containers, and can be quite large (they have a maximum individual size of 50GB). Each container may hold multiple blobs, but there is no real hierarchy such as you have on your disk drive.

Blobs are excellent storage when you have video or audio data, or when you want to create your own storage mechanism (maybe you want to keep a 50GB XML file in the cloud for some reason). You access these blobs using a REST interface, and with a URL like one of the following:

```
http://{your account}.blob.core.windows.net/{container}/{blob}
http://127.0.0.1:10000/devstoreaccount1/{container}/{blob}
```

The first URL scheme is used when accessing the live servers, while the second is used when accessing storage in the development environment.

WCF Data Services (see Chapter 12) makes working with these URLs (and blob storage) fairly transparent to the developer.

Table Storage

The next form of storage available with Azure is table storage. While the name implies database access, it is actually much simpler than that. Table storage enables you to create one or more tables for your application. Each table consists of one or more entities; and each entity has one or more properties, each with a name, a value, and a type. All of that sounds like a normal database, but the difference is in the details. The primary differences between a storage table and a database table are as follows:

➤   A storage table is not stored within a relational database.

➤   You cannot use SQL to query a storage table, nor do you use ADO.NET to access it. Instead, you use WCF Data Services to access them.

➤   Each entity within a table might have different sets of properties. That is, the individual "rows" of data within a table do not have to match a specific schema.

➤   When you edit an entity, the entire entity is considered altered. That is, changing a single property of the entity means that the entire entity is considered changed.

Table storage represents a very flexible data storage mechanism, and it should be considered your first option for record-like data. It does have some limitations, however. The maximum size of an entity is 1MB; the maximum number of properties on an entity is 252 (three system properties are added to all entities); and property names are case sensitive. The available property types are as follows:

➤ `Binary`

➤ `Boolean`

➤ `DateTime`

➤ `Double`

➤ `Guid`

➤ `Int32`

➤ `Int64`

➤ `String`

As mentioned above, three system properties are added to each entity:

➤ `PartitionKey` — This is a key value used to group entities within a table. You could almost view it as a subcollection within the table or as a sort, as the entities with the same `PartitionKey` are grouped logically together within the table. This is a string value, up to 1KB. The developer is responsible for creating and maintaining these key values.

➤ `RowKey` — Another key value used to uniquely identify an entity within a partition. The developer is responsible for creating and maintaining these key values. As with `PartitionKey`, this is a string value, with a maximum size of 1KB.

➤ `Timestamp` — This is updated whenever the entity is altered.

As with the Blob storage, you can use the ADO.NET Data Services client to access your tables. The URL to access a given entity would look similar to the following:

```
http://{your account}.table.core.windows.net/{your table}(PartitionKey='{value}',
RowKey='{value}')
http://127.0.0.1:10002/devstoreaccount1/{your table}(PartitionKey='{value}',
RowKey='{value}')
```

Again, the first URL scheme is used for the live environment, the second for the development environment. If your storage needs require more space or you prefer a SQL interface, you should look at SQL Azure for data storage (see the following section on SQL Azure).

Queues

Unlike blobs and tables, the queue service for Azure is not used to store items directly. Instead, they are used as a communication mechanism, typically between a Web role and one or more worker roles, or between two worker roles. Queues work very much like Microsoft Message Queuing (MSMQ), in that you submit a message at one end, and it is guaranteed to come out the other. However, unlike MSMQ, the messages are not guaranteed to come out in the same order submitted. Nor are they guaranteed to only be processed once. Therefore, your processing code should be fairly defensive about making changes multiple times.

The actual message submitted to the queue has very few limitations. It might be a string, a block of data, or a URL to an item stored in blob or table storage. The only major limitation is that its size must be less than 8KB.

If you have multiple worker roles (or even multiple instances of worker roles) processing the same queue, you are probably worried about having a message read by multiple instances. Fortunately, Azure queues provide a very simple mechanism for preventing this. Once a worker has read a message from the queue, that message becomes invisible to all other worker roles for 30 seconds. During that time, the worker can do whatever processing is necessary to use the message. As part of that processing, the worker should delete the message from the queue to prevent other workers from reading the message after 30 seconds.

Just as with blob and table storage, you use the WCF Data Services client to create and access the queues. The URL schemes used by the queue storage look like the following:

```
http://{your account}.queue.core.windows.net/{queue}/messages
http://127.0.0.1:10001/devstoreaccount1/{queue}/messages
```

SQL Azure

During the initial few preview releases of Windows Azure, the preceding three storage mechanisms were the only ones available. However, many developers prefer to use SQL databases, so the Azure developers created SQL Azure. This gives you the familiar programming model, enabling the use of ADO.NET and LINQ to access your database, while still enabling the scalability of the cloud. Basically, the only disadvantage of using SQL Azure over the other storage services is that it is an additional cost over just Windows Azure.

There are a few significant differences between a local SQL Server and SQL Azure, however:

➤ You do not have access to the physical configuration of the database. That is, you cannot set where the files are stored or configured. In addition, T-SQL commands that take a file as a parameter (such as sp_attach_db) are not available.

➤ You cannot access backup or restore commands for the databases.

➤ The SQL Server Profiler cannot be used with SQL Azure databases.

➤ SQL Azure does not support CLR user-defined types.

➤ You cannot use text, ntext or image data types.

You work with the SQL Azure database just as you would with other SQL Server databases. You can manipulate your databases using the command-line tool sqlcmd, or with SQL Server Management Studio if you prefer a graphical user interface.

 In order to use SQL Server Management Studio to access your databases, you must be running the SQL Server 2008 R2 November 2009 CTP (or later) version of the tools.

In addition, developers have created a number of tools to make working with SQL Azure easier. One of the most useful is the Microsoft Sync Framework Power Pack for SQL Azure, which (besides having one of those horridly long names that Microsoft is becoming known for) allows you to synchronize a database on your network to one running within SQL Azure. This uses the same Sync Framework you saw when working with SQL Server Compact (see Chapter 12), and enables you to select the tables you want to synchronize (see Figure E-8).

While SQL Azure provides a familiar — and powerful — alternative to the other storage mechanisms, keep in mind that it is billed in addition to the existing services. In addition, you need to register to request a SQL Azure application key separately from the Windows Azure account key.

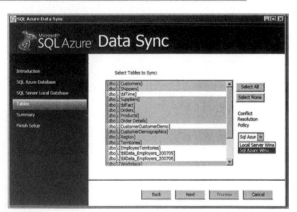

FIGURE E-8

Compute Services

In addition to a public interface and data storage, most applications also require some processing. Of course, this processing can be included in the other two components. However, there are times when you need longer-running or asynchronous processing in your application. For example, you might need to perform some analysis of a large block of data, such as sales analysis on a data warehouse, or convert videos into alternative formats.

Alternately, your application might need to poll an external data source at regular intervals. In these cases, it's not a good idea to include this functionality within your user interface. Instead, you can use the Azure Compute services to perform these operations. This provides highly scalable processing, billed at a rate based on actual usage (that is, per CPU-hour). It's like having a highly scalable supercomputer available to your application.

As described earlier in the Queues section, you communicate with the worker roles via queues. As Compute services consist entirely of worker roles, you therefore use queues to communicate with your Compute services. You send the data necessary for computation by adding a message to a queue. The worker role running within the Compute services retrieves the first available message from a queue and performs whatever processing is required, then deletes the message to prevent other workers from retrieving it. The worker role can then use the other storage services to save data as needed.

Windows Azure Tools for Visual Studio

Before you can create solutions using Windows Azure, you must first install the Windows Azure Tools for Visual Studio. You can access this install by clicking File ➪ New Project (see Figure E-9). Selecting the Enable Windows Azure Tools option will send you to the Microsoft Download Center to download the current version of these tools.

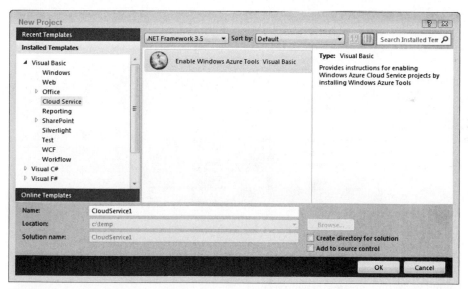

FIGURE E-9

In order to run the development environment for Windows Azure, you need to run Visual Studio 2010 as an administrator. Otherwise, you will see the error message shown in Figure E-10 when you attempt to run your application. To run Visual Studio as an administrator in Windows Vista or Windows 7, right-click the icon and select Run as Administrator. You may be required to enter your user ID and password at this point.

In addition, in order to deploy your applications to the cloud, you need to obtain a developer key. This key is also used for all requests for data. Currently, you get a key by making a request at `http://go.microsoft.com/fwlink/?LinkID=129453`. However, developing using the Windows Azure Tools for Visual Studio does not require this key, only when you are deploying your application to the live servers.

FIGURE E-10

You need to exit Visual Studio to install the tools. After you run the installer, you will see the option enabling you to create an Azure service (see Figure E-11).

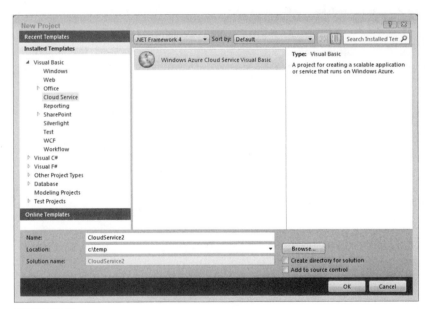

FIGURE E-11

Creating a Windows Azure Project

To explore the features available when creating applications with Windows Azure, create a new project called **CloudToDo**.

Selecting that option brings you to the New Cloud Service Project dialog (see Figure E-12). This dialog enables you to select the initial types of service you will be creating. Of course, you can add others to your project later.

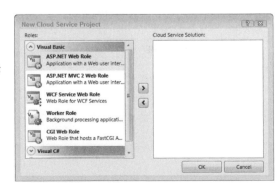

FIGURE E-12

Currently, you can create five types of service:

➤ **ASP.NET Web role** — This is a standard Web service that will host an ASP.NET application in the cloud. You would include one of these to provide a visible user interface to your cloud.

➤ **MVC 2 Web role** — This is a Web service that will host an application built using the ASP.NET MVC Framework.

➤ **WCF Web role** — This is a Web service that includes one or more WCF services. You would include one of these to provide Web Services in your application.

➤ **Worker role** — This is a nonvisible application that will run within your cloud. Typically, these are background tasks needed by your Web application, or calculation services. For example, you might have a worker role to transfer orders to a fulfillment service, or a worker role that processes data to determine trends.

➤ **CGI Web role** — This is a Web service that is designed to run Web applications written in PHP, Python, Ruby, or other non-ASP.NET languages.

For now, add a single Web role to the application, called `ToDoWeb`. After adding the Web role, set the name by clicking the pencil icon. This will be the user interface for the application.

The Web role looks and works exactly like an ASP.NET application: You get an initial `default.aspx` page, and it includes a `web.config` file and the jQuery script libraries. The one difference is the addition of a `WebRole.vb` file. This file contains two methods:

➤ `OnStart` — This method overrides the method in the base class `RoleEntryPoint`. This is called when the role is initialized within the Azure fabric, and could be thought of as analogous to a constructor. You can perform any initialization required at this point. The method should return true if the role is ready to participate in the Azure environment, or false if something prevents it from doing so. For example, you could connect to your data sources here. If they were not available for some reason, you could set `OnStart` to false to prevent the Web role from initializing.

➤ `RoleEnvironmentChanging` — This is an event the Azure environment may call when some change has been made to the configuration of a running instance. This enables your application to reload the configuration settings and act accordingly.

After a brief grind or two of your hard drive, you should see something like Figure E-13 in the Solution Explorer. In addition to the ASP.NET application, you have the Windows Azure project that consists of the single Web role you added, and two configuration files.

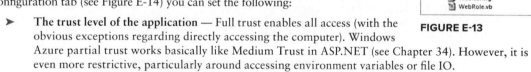

FIGURE E-13

The two configuration files identify the port that the Web role will listen on, as well as the size and number of instances that will run. You can edit these files by hand, but it is much easier to use Visual Studio to edit them. Right-click on ToDoWeb in the Roles folder and select Properties to configure your Web application. From the Configuration tab (see Figure E-14) you can set the following:

➤ **The trust level of the application** — Full trust enables all access (with the obvious exceptions regarding directly accessing the computer). Windows Azure partial trust works basically like Medium Trust in ASP.NET (see Chapter 34). However, it is even more restrictive, particularly around accessing environment variables or file IO.

➤ **The number of instances your application will run** — This can be changed later from the Windows Azure management screens.

➤ **The "size" of the virtual machine that will run your application** — These are basic combinations of number of CPUs, memory size, and disk space. While they will change as the underlying computers become more powerful, as of this writing the available sizes map to the following capacities:

VM SIZE	CPU CORES	MEMORY	DISK SPACE
Small	1	1.7 GB	250 GB
Medium	2	3.5 GB	500 GB
Large	4	7 GB	1 TB
ExtraLarge	8	15 GB	2 TB

➤ **Whether the Web role works using HTTP, HTTPS, or a combination of the two** — If your application receives any secure information from the user, you should use HTTPS. Otherwise, HTTP should be good enough for most uses.

In addition, you configure the endpoints using the Endpoints tab of the configuration (see Figure E-15). This tab enables you to define the ports used by the Web role, as well as the certificate to use for HTTPS.

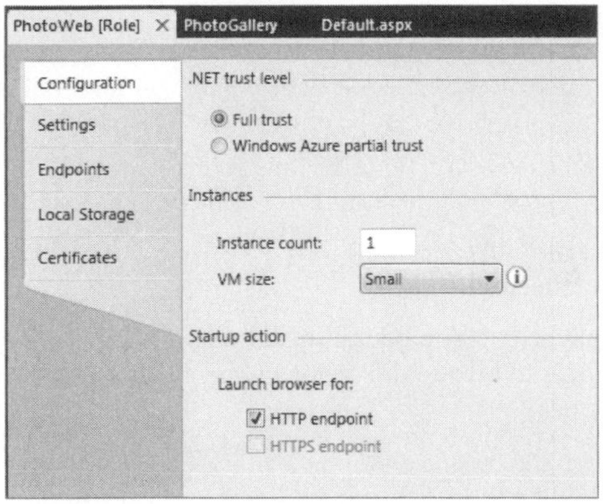

FIGURE E-14

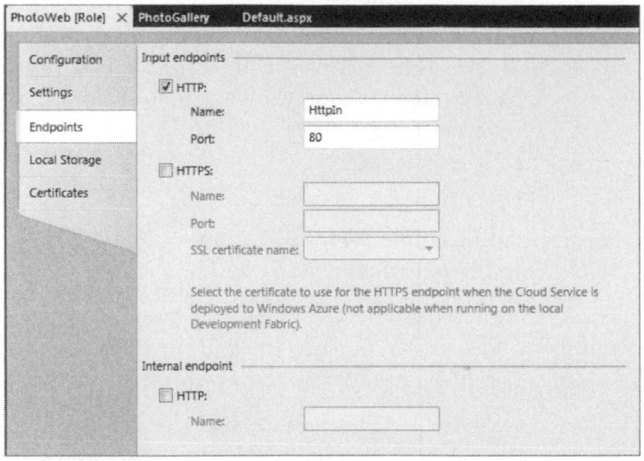

FIGURE E-15

You use the Settings tab to define any additional settings for your project, just as you do for other projects. However, while you're working in the development environment, it is a good idea to set the application to use the connection strings appropriate to the development environment, rather than attempt to access the services deployed to the cloud. Click the Add Setting button, and name the new setting **DataConnectionString**, and the type **ConnectionString**. Click the ellipses on the value property to display the Storage Connection String dialog (see Figure E-16).

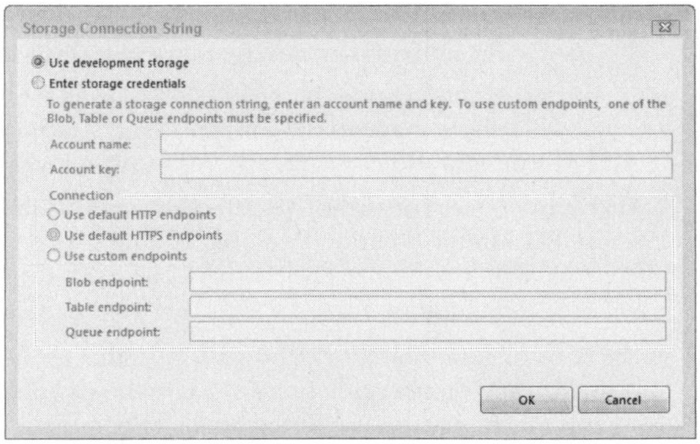

For now, select the first option, "Use development storage." As you can probably guess, when it comes time to deploy this application to the

FIGURE E-16

cloud, you will need to enter your credentials in order to access the services. Once you have saved the setting, the Settings tab should look like Figure E-17.

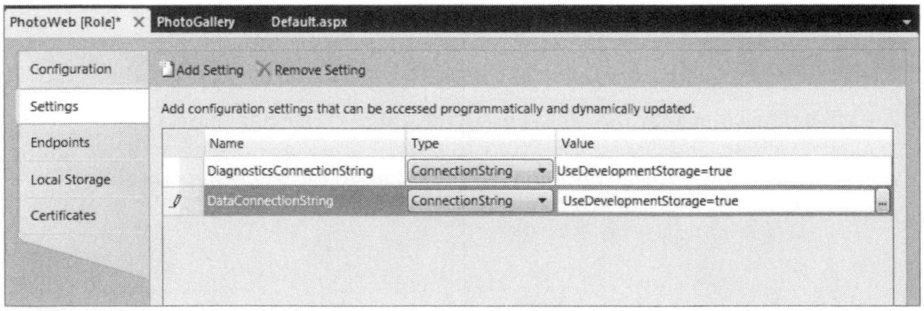

FIGURE E-17

You work with the Web role just as you would any other ASP.NET site. In this case, the application will be a simple to-do list.

Using Table Storage

The application must save the to-do items, along with whether they are completed. Normally, this would be in a SQL Server database, but here we'll use the Azure table storage to save that information.

To use table storage, you need to define a class that represents the data to be saved. This class needs to provide properties for the attributes of your data, along with TimeStamp, PartitionKey, and RowKey properties. The PartitionKey and RowKey properties are used to uniquely identify each item in the storage, and the TimeStamp property identifies when the item was last changed. In addition, you need to add a <DataServiceKey("PartitionKey", "RowKey")> attribute to your class. This is used to identify the key fields to the Data Services infrastructure.

To avoid all that effort, you can instead simply inherit your class from the provided TableServiceEntity class. This provides all the changes listed above. The Task class used by the project is kept intentionally simple:

Available for
download on
Wrox.com

```vbnet
Imports Microsoft.WindowsAzure.StorageClient

Public Class Task
    Inherits TableServiceEntity

    Public Property Name As String
    Public Property IsComplete As Boolean

    Public Sub New()
        'need to set the PartitionKey and RowKey
        'for each instance
        'normally, you would want to have multiple partitions
        'to spread the data out across servers
        PartitionKey = DateTime.Now.ToString("u")
        'rowkey must be unique within each partition
        'data is sorted based on RowKey
        RowKey = String.Format("{0}-{1}",
                               DateTime.Now.Ticks,
                               Guid.NewGuid.ToString)

    End Sub

End Class
```

Code snippet from CloudToDo

As you can see, the Task class will track the name of the task, and a Boolean flag marks whether the task has been completed. The PartitionKey and RowKey properties are assigned in the constructor for the class. Here, all the tasks are assigned a partition based on the date they are created. You should select a PartitionKey so that your entries are distributed across multiple storage nodes. For example, you might assign the PartitionKey based on the date of entry (as done here), the first letters of the filename, or an album organizing a collection of photos.

The RowKey acts like the unique index for each partition, so you should select a value that is guaranteed to be unique. In addition, items are sorted within each partition based on the RowKey. In the preceding example, the RowKey is assigned based on the system time when the object is created (in ticks), with a GUID added at the end to ensure uniqueness, even if multiple entries are added simultaneously.

The client code will use the Data Services library to access table storage, so you need to add a reference to the `System.Data.Services.Client.dll`. This will be used by the data context class to query the table storage:

```vb
Imports Microsoft.WindowsAzure.StorageClient
Imports Microsoft.WindowsAzure

Public Class TaskContext
    Inherits TableServiceContext

    Public Sub New(ByVal baseAddress As String,
                   ByVal credentials As StorageCredentials)
        MyBase.New(baseAddress, credentials)
    End Sub
    Public Function Tasks() As IQueryable(Of Task)
        Return MyBase.CreateQuery(Of Task)("Tasks")
    End Function
    Public Sub AddTask(ByVal name As String,
            ByVal isComplete As Boolean)
        Dim t As New Task
        With t
            .Name = name
            .IsComplete = isComplete
        End With

        MyBase.AddObject("Tasks", t)
        Try
            MyBase.SaveChanges()
        Catch ex As Exception
            Trace.WriteLine(ex.Message, "Error")
        End Try
    End Sub
End Class
```

Code snippet from CloudToDo

The `TaskContext` class is used to access the table storage. It inherits from `TableServiceContext`, which in turn inherits from `DataServiceContext`, adding support for connecting to Azure tables.

When you create a new `TableServiceContext` class, you must override the constructor to provide an implementation that takes the URL to the service, and the credentials to use. This information will be provided when you call the data service. In addition to the constructor, you can provide any data access methods to be used by your application. Here, there are two methods: one to return all the photos and another to add a new photo.

Next, you must initialize the table storage for your application. Open the `WebRole.vb` class in your project and update the OnStart method as shown below:

```vb
Imports Microsoft.WindowsAzure.Diagnostics
Imports Microsoft.WindowsAzure.ServiceRuntime
Imports Microsoft.WindowsAzure
Imports Microsoft.WindowsAzure.StorageClient

Public Class WebRole
    Inherits RoleEntryPoint
        Private _configName As String
        Private _configSetter As Func(Of String, Boolean)

    Public Overrides Function OnStart() As Boolean

        DiagnosticMonitor.Start("DiagnosticsConnectionString")


AddHandler RoleEnvironment.Changing, AddressOf RoleEnvironmentChanging
```

```vbnet
CloudStorageAccount.SetConfigurationSettingPublisher(
    AddressOf ConfigurationSettingPublisher)

        'loads the account from settings
        Dim account As CloudStorageAccount =
            CloudStorageAccount.FromConfigurationSetting("DataConnectionString")
        'creates the tables in table storage
        CloudTableClient.CreateTablesFromModel(GetType(TaskContext),
                                        account.TableEndpoint.AbsoluteUri,
                                        account.Credentials)

        Return MyBase.OnStart()

    End Function

    Private Sub ConfigurationSettingPublisher(ByVal configName As String,
            ByVal configSetter As Func(Of String, Boolean))

        ' We have to store these to be used in the RoleEnvironment Changed handler
        _configName = configName
        _configSetter = configSetter

        ' Provide the configSetter with the initial value
        configSetter(RoleEnvironment.GetConfigurationSettingValue(configName))

        AddHandler RoleEnvironment.Changed, AddressOf RoleEnvironmentChanged

    End Sub

    Private Sub RoleEnvironmentChanging(ByVal sender As Object,
            ByVal e As RoleEnvironmentChangingEventArgs)

        ' If a configuration setting is changing
        If (e.Changes.Any(Function(change) TypeOf _
                        change Is RoleEnvironmentConfigurationSettingChange)) Then
            ' Set e.Cancel to true to restart this role instance
            e.Cancel = True
        End If

    End Sub

    Private Sub RoleEnvironmentChanged(ByVal anotherSender As Object,
            ByVal arg As RoleEnvironmentChangedEventArgs)

        If (arg.Changes.OfType(Of RoleEnvironmentConfigurationSettingChange)().Any( _
            Function(change As RoleEnvironmentConfigurationSettingChange) _
                change.ConfigurationSettingName = _configName)) Then

            If (_configSetter(
                RoleEnvironment.GetConfigurationSettingValue(_configName))) Then

                RoleEnvironment.RequestRecycle()
            End If
        End If

    End Sub
End Class
```

Code snippet from CloudToDo

The account is loaded from the DataConnectionString setting you created earlier. At the moment, this would return UseDevelopmentStorage=true, but once you deploy the application it will include your application key and account name.

The `CreateTablesFromModel` method creates the tables based on the class you created. It requires that you pass the type of the data context class you created, along with the target URL, to the table storage service and your credentials.

At this point, you're ready to add an interface to the application. In this case, it's a simple `DataGrid`, with a couple of fields to add new tasks:

Available for download on Wrox.com

```
<%@ Page Language="vb" AutoEventWireup="false" CodeBehind="Default.aspx.vb"
Inherits="ToDoWeb._Default" %>

<!DOCTYPE html PUBLIC "-//W3C//DTD XHTML 1.0 Transitional//EN"
    "http://www.w3.org/TR/xhtml1/DTD/xhtml1-transitional.dtd">

<html xmlns="http://www.w3.org/1999/xhtml">
<head runat="server">
    <title>Cloud To-Do</title>
    <link href="Site.css" rel="stylesheet" type="text/css" />

</head>
<body>
    <form id="form1" runat="server">
    <div id="page">
    <h1>Cloud To-Do</h1>
    <div id="taskList">
            <asp:GridView ID="TaskGrid" runat="server"
                    AutoGenerateColumns="False"
                    GridLines="None">
        <Columns>
          <asp:BoundField DataField="Name" HeaderText="Name"  />
          <asp:CheckBoxField DataField="IsComplete" HeaderText="Is Complete"  />
         </Columns>
        </asp:GridView></div>

        <div id="taskEntry">
            <p>New task: <asp:TextBox runat="server" id="TaskField" /></p>
            <p><asp:CheckBox runat="server" ID="CompleteField"
            Text="Is complete?" TextAlign="Left" /></p>
            <p style="text-align:right"><asp:LinkButton runat="server"
            ID="SaveButton" Text="Insert" /></p>
        </div>
        <hr />
        <div id="status">
        <asp:Label runat="server" ID="Message" CssClass="message" /></div>
    </div>
    </form>
</body>
</html>
```

Code snippet from CloudToDo

The `TaskGrid` will display the current list of tasks, and the bottom portion of the screen has a `TextBox`, `CheckBox` and `LinkButton` that will be used to define new tasks.

Finally, it's time to add the code that will bolt the user interface to the functionality of the application. Right-click on the `Default.aspx` page in the Solution Explorer, and select View Code to add the `Imports` statements and page-level variables to the class:

Available for download on Wrox.com

```
Imports Microsoft.WindowsAzure.ServiceRuntime
Imports Microsoft.WindowsAzure.StorageClient
Imports Microsoft.WindowsAzure
Imports System.Data.Services.Client

Public Class _Default
```

```
        Inherits System.Web.UI.Page

    Dim account As CloudStorageAccount
    Dim ctx As TaskContext
    Dim statusMessage As String = String.Empty
End Class
```

Next, add code to the `Page Load` event handler that will initialize the `TaskContext` class:

```
Private Sub Page_Load(ByVal sender As Object, _
        ByVal e As System.EventArgs) Handles Me.Load

    account = CloudStorageAccount.FromConfigurationSetting("DataConnectionString")
    ctx = New TaskContext(account.TableEndpoint.ToString, _
                            account.Credentials)
    BindGrid()

End Sub
```

The `CloudStorageAccount` class has a static method that reads the setting you defined earlier to read the information about accessing your Web and worker roles. This provides all the base credentials and URLs that the constructor of the `TaskContext` class uses to communicate with the table storage. In this case, as the `DataConnectionString` is set to use the development environment, the `TaskContext` will access the local environment.

The `BindGrid` method retrieves the current tasks and binds them to the `DataGrid`:

```
Private Sub BindGrid()
    Try
        Me.TaskGrid.DataSource = ctx.Tasks
        Me.TaskGrid.DataBind()
    Catch ex As DataServiceRequestException
        statusMessage = ("Unable to connect to the table storage server." & _
            ex.Message)
    End Try
    Me.Message.Text = statusMessage
End Sub
```

This code is fairly simple, but it is put here in a separate method to be reused throughout the application.

The code to save the new tasks is as follows:

```
Protected Sub SaveButton_Click(ByVal sender As Object, _
        ByVal e As EventArgs) Handles SaveButton.Click

    Try
        ctx.AddTask(TaskField.Text, CompleteField.Checked)
        BindGrid()

    Catch ex As DataServiceRequestException
        statusMessage = ("Unable to connect to the table storage server." & _
            ex.Message)
    End Try
    Me.Message.Text = statusMessage
End Sub
```

The context has already been instantiated, so all that needs to be done is to call the `AddTask` method, passing in the two values. This then calls the Table storage (via Data Services) to insert the new entry. To confirm, the `DataGrid` is rebound to retrieve the newly added entry.

Build your application, and after a bit of a pause to start up the website and the development environment, you should be able to add a few tasks (see Figure E-18). Note: I added a bit of CSS to jazz things up a little (see site.css in the sample project).

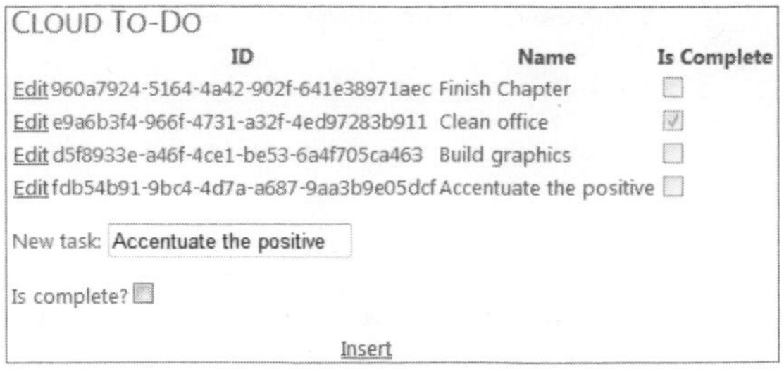

FIGURE E-18

Working with Table storage is not very different from using Data Services to communicate with other databases. The basic process is as follows:

1. Define your entity type. This has to inherit from `TableServiceEntity` to pick up the needed properties and attributes (or you can do it yourself).

2. Create a data context class to communicate with Table storage to save that entity. This class inherits from `TableServiceContext` (which extends the standard `DataServiceContext` class of Data Services).

3. Create the tables within Table storage (obviously, this only needs to be done once).

4. Use your data context class to create and edit your data.

Using Blob Storage

If you were working with a normal ASP.NET page, you would save the data to the local file system on the Web server (or possibly within your database). As that option is not available with Windows Azure applications, you will use blob storage to save the files. The mechanics for setting up blob storage are simpler than the steps you went through to connect to the table storage. You do not need to create an entity class. You only need to ensure that you have created the blob container, and that you assign a unique ID to each blob. In addition to saving the blob itself, you can attach metadata to the blob. This can provide a place to store additional properties about it.

Create a new Windows Azure application, called **CloudContacts**. This application will enable you to enter some contact information, along with a photo of the contact. The photo will be saved to blob storage, and the additional properties added to the metadata for the photo. Include a single Web role in the project, called `ContactWeb`.

As you did with the Web role in the CloudToDo application, you should add a setting for the `DataConnectionString` to the `ContactWeb` role in the CloudContacts project. Right-click on the project in the Solution Explorer and select Properties to open the project's property dialog; on the Settings tab, click `Add` to add a new setting named `DataConnectionString`. Set the type of this property to `ConnectionString`, and set the value as `Use Development Storage=True`. In addition, create a new string setting called `Container`, and set the value to the container name you would like (perhaps something like `Contacts`).

The user interface for the application consists of a set of controls for adding new contacts, and a `ListView` control to display the entries (see Figure E-19):

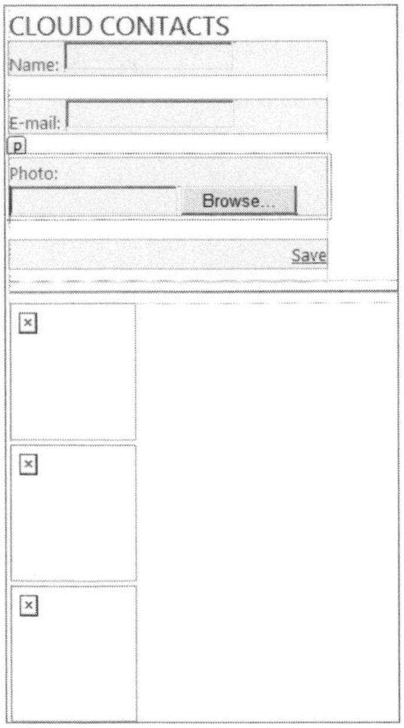

FIGURE E-19

```
Imports Microsoft.WindowsAzure.StorageClient

Public Class _Default
    Inherits System.Web.UI.Page

    Private store As New BlobStore

    Protected Sub Page_Load(ByVal sender As Object,
                            ByVal e As System.EventArgs) Handles Me.Load
        store.EnsureContainerExists()
        If Not IsPostBack Then
            BindGrid()
        End If
    End Sub

    Private Sub BindGrid()
        ContactList.DataSource = store.GetData()
        ContactList.DataBind()
    End Sub

    Protected Sub SubmitButton_Click(ByVal sender As Object,
                             ByVal e As EventArgs) Handles SubmitButton.Click
        If PhotoFile.HasFile Then
            store.SaveContact(Guid.NewGuid().ToString(),
                        NameField.Text,
                        EmailField.Text,
                        PhotoFile.PostedFile.ContentType,
                        PhotoFile.FileBytes)

            BindGrid()
        Else
            Message.Text = "No image file"
        End If

    End Sub
End Class
```

Code snippet from CloudContacts

The code for working with the blob storage will be within the BlobStore class. As shown, this class will have at least three methods:

➤   EnsureContainerExists — Creates the container if it doesn't already exist, or returns the already created container

➤   GetData — Returns the entries currently stored in the blob container

➤   SaveContact — Adds a new entry into the blob container

Here is the code for the BlobStore class:

```
Imports Microsoft.WindowsAzure
Imports Microsoft.WindowsAzure.StorageClient
Imports Microsoft.WindowsAzure.ServiceRuntime

Public Class BlobStore
    Public Function GetContainer() As CloudBlobContainer
        CloudStorageAccount.SetConfigurationSettingPublisher(
            Function(configName, configSetter) _
                configSetter(RoleEnvironment.GetConfigurationSettingValue(configName)))

        Dim account =
          CloudStorageAccount.FromConfigurationSetting("DataConnectionString")
```

```vb
        Dim client = account.CreateCloudBlobClient()

        Return client.GetContainerReference(
            RoleEnvironment.GetConfigurationSettingValue("ContainerName"))
    End Function

    Public Sub EnsureContainerExists()
        Dim container = GetContainer()
        container.CreateIfNotExist()

        Dim permissions = container.GetPermissions()
        permissions.PublicAccess = BlobContainerPublicAccessType.Container
        container.SetPermissions(permissions)
    End Sub

    Public Function GetData() As IEnumerable(Of IListBlobItem)
        Dim options As BlobRequestOptions = New BlobRequestOptions()
        options.BlobListingDetails = BlobListingDetails.All
        options.UseFlatBlobListing = True

        Return GetContainer().ListBlobs(options)
    End Function

    Public Sub SaveContact(ByVal id As String,
                           ByVal name As String,
                           ByVal email As String,
                           ByVal mimeType As String,
                           ByVal buffer As Byte())
        ' Create a blob in container and upload image bytes to it
        Dim blob = Me.GetContainer().GetBlobReference(id)

        blob.Properties.ContentType = mimeType

        ' Create some metadata for this image
        Dim metadata = New NameValueCollection()
        metadata("ContactID") = id
        metadata("Name") = name
        metadata("Email") = If([String].IsNullOrEmpty(email), "unknown", email)

        ' Add and commit metadata to blob
        blob.Metadata.Add(metadata)
        blob.UploadByteArray(buffer)
    End Sub
End Class
```

Code snippet from CloudContacts

The GetContainer method connects to the assigned AppFabric the service is running under. It loads the account as you did when working with table storage. It then uses that account to create a new CloudBlobClient. This is the class you use to communicate with blob storage. In this case, you use it to return the name of the container you configured earlier.

The EnsureContainerExists method uses that GetContainer method to create or return the container. Permissions are added to allow anyone access to the container. Alternately, you could have restricted access to just an individual blob, turned security off completely, or assigned shared access permissions to the container.

The GetData method simply returns an IEnumerable of all the blobs stored in the container. This enables you to iterate over the contents later.

Finally, the SaveContact method creates a new blob, using a Guid (assigned when you call SaveContact) as the ID value for the new entry. As shown earlier, additional metadata is created as a simple NameValueCollection and attached to the new blob entry before saving.

That is all that is required to communicate with blob storage. You should be able to run the class now and add a few new contacts (see Figure E-20).

Working with blob storage is definitely different from working with a database or even table storage. However, the process is relatively straightforward:

➤ Create a blob container.

➤ Create new blobs within that container using `GetBlobReference`. You can also use this method to retrieve individual blobs, using the ID you assigned to them.

➤ You can also load (and read) blobs from a stream if it is more convenient (look for the `UploadFromStream` and `DownloadToStream` methods).

FIGURE E-20

Using a Worker Role

So far, you have only been using Web roles in your applications. These are the roles you will use to create user interfaces for your cloud applications. However, you likely also need your application to perform some processing that doesn't fit into the Web model. It may be some asynchronous processing your website needs to perform in the background, or it may be only some completely user interface–free number-crunching that needs to execute. Either way, you add this functionality to your applications using worker roles. They are the equivalent of code libraries for your cloud applications.

You use queues to communicate with worker roles. The worker role is responsible for periodically polling the queue for new jobs. Once it has processed a message, it must also delete the message, to prevent other workers from retrieving it.

To explore the use of queues, you will extend the CloudToDo application to add a worker role to send out an e-mail when a task has been marked complete.

First, you need to add edit functionality to the application, to enable users to mark a task as complete. Set the `AutoGenerateEditButton` property of the `GridView` to true. In addition, add three methods to the code-behind page for adding the update functionality:

Available for
download on
Wrox.com

```vbnet
Private Sub TaskGrid_RowCancelingEdit(ByVal sender As Object, _
        ByVal e As System.Web.UI.WebControls.GridViewCancelEditEventArgs) _
        Handles TaskGrid.RowCancelingEdit
    TaskGrid.EditIndex = -1
    BindGrid()
End Sub

Private Sub TaskGrid_RowEditing(ByVal sender As Object, _
        ByVal e As System.Web.UI.WebControls.GridViewEditEventArgs) _
        Handles TaskGrid.RowEditing
    TaskGrid.EditIndex = e.NewEditIndex
    BindGrid()
End Sub

Private Sub TaskGrid_RowUpdating(ByVal sender As Object, _
        ByVal e As System.Web.UI.WebControls.GridViewUpdateEventArgs) _
        Handles TaskGrid.RowUpdating
    Try
        Dim id As String
        Dim task As TextBox
        Dim complete As CheckBox

        With TaskGrid.Rows(e.RowIndex)
```

```
                    id = .Cells(1).Text
                    task = CType(.Cells(2).Controls(0), TextBox)
                    complete = CType(.Cells(3).Controls(0), CheckBox)
                End With

                ctx.UpdateTask(id, task.Text, complete.Checked)
                'turn off edit
                TaskGrid.EditIndex = -1
                BindGrid()

            Catch ex As DataServiceRequestException
                statusMessage = ("Unable to connect to the table storage server." &
                    ex.Message)
            End Try
            Me.Message.Text = statusMessage
        End Sub
```

Code snippet from CloudToDoWithQueue

The `RowCancelingEdit` and `RowEditing` methods are relatively simple methods used to switch the desired row of the `GridView` into or out of edit mode. The bulk of the update is in the `RowUpdating` method. This is called when the user clicks the Update link on the row while editing. In this method, the code reads the new values from the edit controls on the `GridView` and submits them to a new `UpdateTask` method that will be created in a moment. It then sets the `GridView` not to display the edit functionality and redisplays the current data.

The next step is to add the method to update the data in the table storage:

```
        Public Sub UpdateTask(ByVal id As String,
                              ByVal name As String,
                              ByVal isComplete As Boolean)

            Try
                'get existing task by name
                Dim t As Task = (From f In Me.Tasks
                                 Where f.TaskID = id
                                 Select f).FirstOrDefault
                'update properties
                With t
                    .Name = name
                    .IsComplete = isComplete
                End With
                If isComplete Then
                    'send to the Worker role
                    ProcessTask(t)
                End If

                'save
                MyBase.UpdateObject(t)
                MyBase.SaveChanges()
            Catch ex As Exception
                Trace.WriteLine(ex.Message, "Error")
            End Try
        End Sub
```

Code snippet from CloudToDoWithQueue

As this code will update an existing task, the first step is to retrieve the current values. This uses LINQ to query the underlying data service to retrieve the item by ID. You then set the new values and call `UpdateObject` to mark it for submission when `SaveChanges` is called.

The `ProcessTask` method will add the task to the queue if the task is being marked complete:

```
Private Sub ProcessTask(ByVal t As Task)
    'submits task to the queue for email
    Dim account =
        CloudStorageAccount.FromConfigurationSetting("DataConnectionString")
    Dim client = account.CreateCloudQueueClient()

    'create or get queue
    Dim queue As CloudQueue = client.GetQueueReference("emailqueue")
    queue.CreateIfNotExist()

    'create message
    Dim msg As New CloudQueueMessage(DumpTask(t))
    queue.AddMessage(msg)

End Sub
```

Code snippet from CloudToDoWithQueue

The code for communicating with queue storage is similar to that used for blob storage. You get a reference to the queue, create a new message, and add it to the queue.

> *One of the most likely (and perplexing) errors that occurs when using queues in Windows Azure is related to case: The name of the queue must be all lowercase. If the name of the queue includes uppercase characters, the code will fail on the call to* `CreateIfNotExist`*. Fortunately, there is a simple solution: Keep away from the Shift key.*

The `DumpTask` method simply converts the updated task into a string to be added to the queue:

```
Private Function DumpTask(ByVal t As Task) As String
    Dim result As New StringBuilder
    result.AppendLine("Task completion notification")
    result.AppendFormat("Task: {0} completed at {1}",
                        t.Name,
                        DateTime.Now.ToString("r"))

    Return result.ToString
End Function
```

Code snippet from CloudToDoWithQueue

Now you can turn your attention to the actual worker role. Right-click on the Roles folder in the Solution Explorer. Select Add ➪ New Worker Role Project and add a new worker role, named `EmailWorker`. Visual Studio will add a new project to the solution, and the new role will appear in the folder. Add the `sDataConnectionString` property to this new role as you did for the Web roles you created earlier: right-click on the project and select properties to open the properties dialog. Add a new item (named `DataConnectionString`) on the Settings tab. Set the type of the item to `ConnectionString`, and the value set to use the development storage.

The main part of the code required for the worker role is in the `Run` method. This is called by the AppFabric after the role has been initialized. Typically, you will either perform some long task here or periodically poll a queue to find something to process. Here, you poll the queue for new messages to e-mail:

```
Public Overrides Sub Run()

    ' This is a sample implementation for EmailWorker. Replace with your logic.
    Trace.WriteLine("EmailWorker entry point called.", "Information")

    ' initialize the account information
```

```
Dim account =
  CloudStorageAccount.FromConfigurationSetting("DataConnectionString")

' retrieve a reference to the messages queue
Dim client As CloudQueueClient = account.CreateCloudQueueClient()
Dim queue = client.GetQueueReference("emailqueue")

While (True)
    Thread.Sleep(10000)
    If queue.Exists() Then
        Dim msg = queue.GetMessage()
        If (msg IsNot Nothing) Then
            EmailMessage(msg)
            Trace.TraceInformation(String.Format("Message '{0}' processed.",
                msg.AsString))
            queue.DeleteMessage(msg)
        End If
    End If

End While

End Sub
```

Code snippet from CloudToDoWithQueue

Just as you did on the client side, the first steps are to retrieve the account, and then retrieve an instance of CloudQueueClient and use that to open the queue. You call GetMessage to retrieve any message added, process the message, and call DeleteMessage to prevent it from being processed again. Recall that after you call GetMessage, the message will be invisible to other workers for 30 seconds, so your processing should take less than this amount of time or you might end up with multiple results.

You can hard-code your settings for the actual e-mail but a better solution is to load them from a secure location, such as the project's settings. Right-click the EmailWorker project and open the Properties dialog. On the Settings tab, add the following properties:

PROPERTY	TYPE	DESCRIPTION
SmtpServer	String	The IP address or hostname of your SMTP server. You should be able to get this from your e-mail administrator or service.
SmtpPort	Integer	The port on the SMTP server that provides SMTP access. This may be 25 if the server is not set to use security, or another port if secure. Again, contact your administrator if you have questions.
UserID	String	The user account on the SMTP server (if you need to log in)
Password	String	The password for the user account on the SMTP server (if you need to log in)
Recipient	String	The e-mail address that will receive the message. Set this to your e-mail account to receive the notification message.

The EmailMessage method uses these settings to send the message using the SmtpClient class in the System.Net.Mail namespace:

Available for download on Wrox.com

```
Private Sub EmailMessage(ByVal message As CloudQueueMessage)
    'create message
    Dim msg As New Mail.MailMessage
    With msg
        .Subject = "Task completion notification"
        .To.Add(My.Settings("Recipient").ToString)
        .Body = message.AsString
        .BodyEncoding = Text.Encoding.ASCII
        .From = New Mail.MailAddress(My.Settings("UserID").ToString)
    End With
    Dim userid As String = My.Settings("UserID").ToString
    Dim pwd As String = My.Settings("Password").ToString
```

```
    Dim host As String = My.Settings("SmtpServer").ToString
    Dim port As Integer = CInt(My.Settings("SmtpPort"))
    Dim smtp As New Mail.SmtpClient(host, port)
    With smtp
        .EnableSsl = True
        .Credentials = New NetworkCredential(userid, pwd)
        Try
            .Send(msg)
        Catch ex As Exception
            Trace.WriteLine(ex.Message, "Error")
        End Try

    End With
End Sub
```

Code snippet from CloudToDoWithQueue

The AsString method of the CloudQueueMessage class returns the contents of the message. There is also an AsBytes method if you need to process the message bytes themselves. The remainder of the code creates a new MailMessage using the settings you created earlier, and sends the message on to the assigned SMTP server.

You should now be able to run the application and edit an entry. Mark an entry as complete and save the entry. If the network guardians are in your favor, you should soon see the e-mail in your inbox (see Figure E-21).

FIGURE E-21

Working with queue storage is perhaps the simplest solution of the three storage models. Of course, the items you write to the queue have less permanence than items in the other two storage mechanisms. Queue storage really only needs to be used as a communication mechanism, so the messages are more transient. The process of using queue storage is as follows:

1. Open the account as you did for the other two storage types.
2. Use the account to create an instance of CloudQueueClient.
3. Use that client to create a new queue.
4. Write messages to the queue.
5. On the other side, use the client to read the queue.
6. Process the messages.
7. Remember to delete the message after processing it.

Deploying the Service

Once you've completed your application, you're ready to leave the comfortable surroundings of Visual Studio and the development environment and move your application to the live servers.

Right-click on your project in Visual Studio, and select Publish. This will start your web browser and send you to the Windows Azure site (http://windows.azure.com). Here you can sign up for the live Windows Azure services. You will need to sign in with your Live ID to access the site. If this is your first time creating a project, you need to agree to the terms and set up payments (have a credit card or purchase order handy).

Once you have entered in all the information, you can then return to the Windows Azure page to add your service(s) to your cloud. During the Publish process, Visual Studio created two files. The first, with a .cspkg extension, is the Service Package file containing all the DLLs and other components of your Windows Azure solution. The second, with a .cscfg extension, is the configuration file that describes to Windows Azure how to deploy your application. This is the file that contains the number of instances to run and their size, among other settings.

On the Windows Azure website, you can select one of your projects (see Figure E-22) to begin the wizard that steps you through the process of deploying your application. You define the name of the service (e.g., CloudToDo), and select the URL that will be the new home for your shiny new cloud application. The most important step is to load the two created files (see Figure E-22), and then start the application (see Figure E-23).

FIGURE E-22

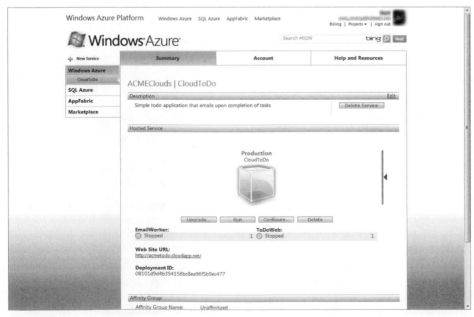

FIGURE E-23

As your application needs grow, you can configure the application to add more instances. At the moment, the user interface for this is a little Spartan (see Figure E-24). Alternately, you can edit the configuration file using Visual Studio and upload a new copy to affect the deployment.

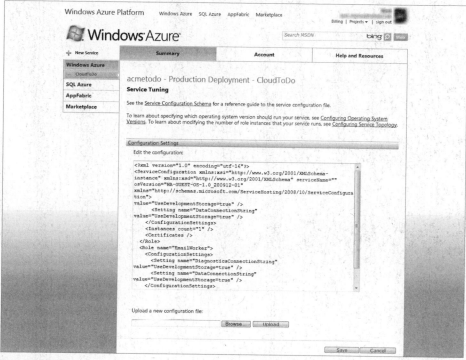

FIGURE E-24

SUMMARY

Not every application is well suited to running in a cloud environment. The additional complexity and constraints these environments add to your application can make them restrictive and limited. However, some applications really do benefit from running in a cloud. Applications that involve highly variable server demands, long-running calculations, or processing all benefit from running within a cloud. In addition, scenarios with limited IT support will benefit, as you can now rely upon the cloud providers themselves to set up and maintain your computers. As always, the only way to truly decide whether Windows Azure is a good solution for your application is to weigh the factors of cost, scalability (and availability), and development time.

INDEX

H

O